A SENSE OF HISTORY

A SENSE OF HISTORY

THE BEST WRITING FROM PAGES OF
AMERICAN HERITAGE

ibooks
new york
www.ibooks.net

DISTRIBUTED BY SIMON & SCHUSTER, INC.

ibooks, inc.
24 West 25th Street
New York, NY 10010

Distributed by Simon & Schuster, Inc., 1230 Avenue of the Americas, New York,
NY 10020

The ibooks World Wide Web Site address is: http://www.ibooks.net

ISBN: 0-7434-7454-6

First ibooks printing September 2003

10 9 8 7 6 5 4 3 2

Share your thoughts about *A Sense of History* and other ibooks titles in the new
ibooks virtual reading group at www.ibooks.net

CONTENTS

FOREWORD

Professional historians periodically lament their seeming inability to reach beyond a readership of fellow specialists and graduate students. From the 1930s to his death in 1970, Allan Nevins was the foremost proponent of a greater effort by academic historians to write for that large audience of educated laypeople who hunger for readable history and need to know it if they are to be informed citizens.

Nevins was ideally qualified to crusade for this cause. With a background in journalism, where he had learned to write lucid, sprightly prose, Nevins joined the faculty of Columbia University in 1931. He produced respected works of history and biography that combined thorough scholarship with lively writing. To provide an outlet for other historians to do the same, Nevins hoped to establish a popular magazine of history sponsored by the American Historical Association. Dominated by academic historians, the AHA at its annual meeting in 1938 voted by a narrow margin to reject Nevins's proposal for such a magazine.

Angry and embittered, Nevins wrote an article for the *Saturday Review of Literature* in which he expressed contempt for "Professor Dryasdust" who "destroys the public for historical work by convincing it that history is synonymous with heavy, stolid prosing."

World War II and the postwar years intervened to delay the plans of Nevins and others to found a popular history magazine on their own. Finally in 1954 they succeeded, and *American Heritage* was born. Immediately successful, this magazine mushroomed to a circulation of more than 300,000. Some academics wrote for *American Heritage*, but most of the contributors were journalists, freelance writers, and independent historians. Their research was thorough, their writing spirited, and the articles were generously illustrated—three hallmarks of the magazine from the beginning to the present. The articles ranged over the whole of American history, written in a narrative rather than statistical or analytical style with an emphasis on human-interest subjects.

On the thirtieth anniversary of its founding, *American Heritage* culled from more than two thousand articles thus far published the best fifty-one. A great success even though these articles were unaccompanied by illustrations, *A Sense of History* was reprinted in 1995 with three additional titles. That volume also included reflections by fifty-two writers and public figures on how America had changed—for better or worse—over the forty years from 1954 to 1994.

This new printing of the 1995 edition brings those reflections as well as the fifty-four articles to a new generation of readers. The articles cover the sweep of American history from the Indian mound builders to the 1990s. The nineteenth century is the favorite period, however, with twenty-three articles compared with thirteen for the twentieth century. Five pieces are concerned with the period before 1800, while a dozen are timeless or range over more than a century and deal with broad themes like the writing of history and immigration. The largest single thematic category of the essays might be described as social/cultural history with a strong human interest component—baseball, the story of Johnny Appleseed, famous trials, Nathaniel Hawthorne's love of Sophia Peabody, life on the overland trails, and many other fascinating subjects. Wars are the subject of nine articles, politics of seven, the West of four, business and finance of three, slavery and antislavery of three, technology and foreign policy of two each. In all of these stories, human beings rather than abstractions hold center stage. Varying in length from six to forty-nine pages, each of the essays can be read in one sitting—but they are so engaging that most readers will devour several before putting down the book. *A Sense of History* is indeed a movable feast. Enjoy.

James M. McPherson
February 2003

INTRODUCTION

It turns out that even having the privilege of spending your entire working life at a magazine of history cannot inoculate you against melancholy surprise at how quickly history rips along. I see from looking at the copyright page of *A Sense of History* that it's been more than a decade since I began helping assemble the book. Two Presidents, the Cadillac STS, the Gulf War, *The Bridges of Madison County,* a stock market crash—all have dashed past since I last read through, say, John Lukacs's tribute to the great historian George Bancroft or Gene Smith's tour of the Western Front and said to myself: Hey, this is *good.*

But time's scary tempo does trail its solaces, and among them is the fact that during the decade that seems to have slipped by while I was arguing with the dry cleaner this book became something of a classic. Reading through it again, I'm glad to see that it deserves to be.

A Sense of History is the essence of the outcome of an experiment initiated more than forty years ago by three young men—Oliver Jensen, Joseph Thorndike, and James Parton—who were all working for the most successful magazine in the history of civilization, *Life.* Of course, *Life*'s fame rested largely on its superb pictures: *Life* photographers would take the reader to a glamorous party at the St. Regis Hotel and in with the first wave to Omaha Beach. Such a richly varied visual brew percolated through the imaginations of Jensen, Thorndike, and Parton, and in time they determined to strike out on their own and found a magazine that would blend the techniques of journalism with the discipline of history and thus give American history (already being barricaded by the academy) back to the people who had made it.

Americans responded, and *American Heritage* was a success from the start (it's touching to me that the older subscribers invariably refer to it as "*The American Heritage*"). People made a fuss about the pictures—and they were glorious; indeed, the outriders of all the pictorial histories that are a staple in today's publishing—but the editors took care to ensure that the writing was at a level to match the finest of the illustrations.

A Sense of History is proof of that. No pictures; just stories. But what good stories! They reflect an inaugural premise of the magazine. Its first editor, Bruce Catton, wrote on page 8 of the December 1954 issue: ". . . History after all is the story of people: a statement that might seem too obvious to be worth making if it were not for the fact that history so often is presented in terms of vast incomprehensible forces moving far under the surface, carrying human beings along, helpless, and making them conform to a pattern whose true shape they never see. The pattern does exist, often enough, and it is important to trace it. Yet it is good to remember that it is the people who make the pattern, and not the other way around."

Like any living thing, the magazine has gone through many changes over the years—it originally had hard covers, for instance, and carried no advertising—but also like any other living thing, it remains fundamentally the same creature. As you'll see, the mainspring that drives the stories in this book is the doings of people—people long dead, people who wore clothes of astonishing ugliness and inutility, people who found dialect humor funny and who thought it was a big deal to travel forty miles from the town where they'd been born; but people who, just like you, took delight in gossip, adored their children (when they weren't busy being enraged by them), and on the whole were eager to dodge the imperatives of history. Perhaps the most serious pleasure this book has to offer is the record of what these people did when they found that history wasn't letting them off the hook—how they discovered that their institutions or their parents or their popular songs had given them something they could draw on while they met challenges as hard as human beings ever faced.

Of course, not all of them faced those challenges well. There are plenty of cowards in this compendium, and cutthroats and forgers and bigots and fakes. There have to be, because the editors tried to stuff a nation's worth of people into some nine hundred pages.

This anthology began in the early 1980s as a thirtieth anniversary project for *American Heritage*. Byron Dobell was editor then and thus in charge of the job (which I like to think makes the inclusion of a story of mine seem a little less blatant), and we stared by asking Geoffrey C.

Ward, a former editor then busy at work on what would become a fine two-volume biography of Franklin Roosevelt's early years, to read thoroughly the 180-odd issues—more than two thousand articles!—that had then appeared and recommend an initial selection of stories. Geoff's list evolved into this book.

I read the pieces weighing one against another and trying to make sure that various eras were represented, for it early became clear that this could and should be an informal history of the United States. And that happened: the book begins with an inquiry into the prehistoric mound builders, goes forward through Revolution and Civil War, and the rise of the great industrial fortunes, to the struggle against Hitler and on up to our own time. It is history seen from a hundred intimate angles: the industrial revolution encapsulated by George Eastman and his Kodak; the conestoga wagon incarnating the entire Westward migration; World War II in Europe watched from above by a young artillery spotter in his "Maytag Messerschmitt," an airplane that actually cost less than the crate it came in. Here are those two very different titans, Carnegie and Rockefeller, and their colleague J. P. Morgan bailing out the federal government during a fiscal pinch; here is David McCullough's splendid profile of Harriet Beecher Stowe and Malcolm Cowley on Nathaniel Hawthorne in love; here is Johnny Appleseed, the man himself pulled back out of the mist, a most appealing alternative to the standard braggarts of our Western folklore.

When *A Sense of History* first appeared, it enjoyed an immediate strong success. In fact, it was a main selection of the Book of the Month Club—the only time *American Heritage* has been thus favored, and one of the very, very few times BOMC chose an anthology. The book remains so fresh that although eighty more issues of *American Heritage* have appeared since its publication, some of them really quite fine, we are adding to this new edition only three stories that seem especially timely: John Lukacs's look at historical revisionism, which is being practiced with a vengeance just now, Bernard Weisberger's magisterial survey of the history of immigration, valuable in a time when the Golden Door seems again to be swinging shut and, bracketing the volume with surveys, a poll sent out on the fortieth anniversary of *American Heritage* in 1994 seeking to determine what had most changed in the past four decades. The wide variety of provocative answers looked both back and forward, and thus, in performing history's most valuable function—as both compass and memory—seemed an especially suitable way to close the book.

Reading this anthology on the eve of its reissuing, I found myself thinking more and more about my earliest days at *American Heritage*, in

1965, when it was a company of many divisions and scores of employees, large and generous-spirited enough to tolerate the fumblings of an amateur mailboy during the summer of his senior year of high school. Looking back on those days across three decades I realize that I was on the fringes of a publishing world now as thoroughly vanished as the side-wheelers of the Fall River Line that my sometime boss Oliver Jensen describes herein. The magazine was printed with honest-to-god type cast from molten lead, reconfigured by printers in accordance with notations made by the proofreaders on long, thin galley sheets. There was a Xerox machine in the office, but carbon paper did the real copying work. Everybody smoked; everybody drank—Gibsons, sidecars—and we in the mailroom ate lunch at the automat while the editors went to restaurants with burgundy banquettes and lamps on the tables where tough old waiters in nacreous tuxedos moved through the comforting gloom.

All this seems incredibly remote—and indeed that world is exactly as far away from me now as was the New York of F. Scott Fitzgerald when I first started pushing my mailcart—but the stories in this book, reprinted just as they first ran, have aged not at all. If these various tales have one thing in common, it is a freshness, a vigor in the telling, that can make, say, the supple negotiations that brought our bruised young republic an incredibly favorable peace with Britain in 1815 a good deal closer to us than is John Lindsay's Manhattan.

That, in the end, is the legacy of the broad vision and rigorous standards the founders brought to their new magazine forty years ago. They wanted to present history in such a way that reading it was not a sort of dutiful civic corollary to a trip to the dentist but an enthralling experience that could rekindle in us the conviction that our lives are shaped and informed every day by the ghosts that stand at our shoulder. *A Sense of History* is testament to how well they succeeded.

Richard F. Snow

A SENSE OF HISTORY

I WISH I'D BEEN THERE

To mark the thirtieth anniversary of *American Heritage* in December of 1984, the editors asked a number of public figures, authors, and scholars, including members of the Society of American Historians, to consider this question:

> *What is the one scene or incident in American history you would like to have witnessed—and why?*

Taken together, the answers turn out to be an amusing, moving, and surprisingly coherent narrative history of the nation from the Age of the Dinosaur to the Age of Watergate.

STAR-STRUCK BEGINNING

The great event that made all of human history possible occurred some sixty-five million years ago. Its primary evidence lies in America.

Few people know that mammals evolved at the same time as dinosaurs, more than two hundred million years ago. They did not arise later and drive dinosaurs to extinction by their superiority. They lived, rather, for one hundred million years as small, rat-sized creatures in the interstices of an ecological world ruled by dinosaurs. In no way did they challenge or displace dinosaurs. Then, some sixty-five million years ago, dinosaurs were wiped out (along with many other forms of life) in one of the great episodes of mass extinction that have punctuated the history of life. The small mammals survived and took over a world emptied of its former rulers. We evolved much later as a result of this good fortune (we are a cosmic accident, not the result of a predictable process). If the extinction had not occurred, dinosaurs would probably still dominate the earth, and conscious creatures would not have evolved.

But what wiped out the dinosaurs? We now have good evidence that a large extraterrestrial body—an asteroid or comet—struck the earth at this time, perhaps sending aloft a cloud of dust making the earth too cold and dark for large reptiles (the "nuclear winter" scenario is based on the same argument). I would like to have seen the explosion and its aftermath; I only hope I would have known when to duck.

Stephen Jay Gould, *Professor of Geology and Alexander Agassiz Professor of Biology, Harvard University.*

1

WHO CAME FIRST?

I would like to have had an extra long life, and to have sat on a pier between 1200 and 1500, to see who besides Columbus and Sebastian Cabot showed up.

Noel Perrin, *Professor of English, Dartmouth College.*

ADMIRAL OF THE OCEAN SEA

I would like to have been among that small company of sailors in the moonlit, predawn moment, October 12, 1492, when a lookout aboard a small vessel hailed the sand cliffs of an island never before seen by the eyes of Europeans.

Had I rushed to the ship's rail with Christopher Columbus, I would have witnessed his triumph and shared in the joy and amazement of his companions. Although I would not have known it at the time, I would have been present at the instant that began the European colonization of America.

Virginia V. Hamilton, *Professor and University Scholar in History, University of Alabama, Birmingham.*

FIRST TASTE OF AMERICA

Nothing so attracts and holds my imagination as the fact of the virgin North American continent as the amazed Europeans first saw it. Here was "a plaine wildernes as God first made it," in the words of John Smith. It bespoke Eden itself, a beautiful land already planted, in which all possibilities might be realized.

Most tantalizing was the thought of it all, the very scent of it, from over the horizon at sea. For three centuries, European explorers plying uncertainly in Atlantic waters far from the sight of land repeated a certain moment: they smelled on the west wind the distant flowering forest.

Columbus wrote of his 1492 exploration, "There came so fair and sweet a smell of flowers or trees from the land." Europe had nothing like it: richly mixed hardwoods all in flower, from the salt coast to the distant interior plains. John Cabot smelled it, too, from the sea off Newfoundland. Giovanni da Verrazano was a hundred leagues off the North Carolina shore when he smelled the great woods—"the sweetest odors." Raleigh's settlers, approaching the continent on which they would plant the first English colony, smelled the blossoming land off the southern coast: they "felt a most dilicate sweete smell, though they saw no land."

The first permanent colonists found that the New World not only smelled good, it was, for the most part, edible. Those early years in Jamestown were rough, and many people starved. Still, they found the energy to pass down to us what might be called "First Bite Narratives." (I have all these accounts from John Bakeless's wonderful book *The Eyes of Discovery.*)

The Virginia colonists described with wild enthusiasm the enormous strawberries they found—"foure times bigger and better"—and the grapes, and the beach plums. They heartily approved the grand edible nuts of the hardwood forest, the chestnut, walnut, and hickory. But these were mostly old bites. Their first bites were apt to be less enthusiastic.

Wild cranberries they dismissed: "they differ not much from poyson."

Jimson weed they should have dismissed. Later colonists tried a salad of boiled Jimson weed, which reportedly made them insane for eleven days.

William Strachey was apparently the first colonial wretch to hazard a summer persimmon. He received what John Bakeless described as a "botanical shock." "They are harsh and choakie," Strachey wrote, "and furre in a man's mouth." Another bold persimmon-biter wrote, "It will draw a man's mouth awry with much torment."

The best of bites, and the worst of bites, was attempted much later, in 1638. One John Josselyn, Englishman, walking near Scarborough, Maine, tried to bite into a hornet's nest. He thought it was a pineapple. By the time the hornets got through with him, his friends found him unrecognizable.

Poor John Josselyn. He had a much better time in this peculiar new world when he first saw lightning bugs: "I thought the whole Heavens had been on fire seeing so many sparkles flying in the air."

Annie Dillard, *Adjunct Professor of English, Wesleyan University.*

ANNE HUTCHINSON ON TRIAL

The amazingly scrupulous records we have of Anne Hutchinson's trial in early November of 1637 tantalize me into wishing I could have been there. Hers was a religious culture and ours is pluralist and secular, but the troubling issues from back then have analogies now. In facing state (John Winthrop) and church (John Cotton), she represented dissent against establishment. As so often since, neither side looked good, and, from other angles, both sides made a case. They fought over the covenant of grace and the covenant of works, ideas almost incomprehensible to many today. Yet they are signal issues about liberty and license versus law and responsibility, and remain alive.

Why go to Europe for Joan of Arc when in America someone on trial also claimed to have heard voices? That is, instead of sticking to the letter of the text, she claimed the spirit spoke directly. What are claims of authority even now? How much do we, must we, live by the book? And there are classic woman-man issues here. Without question, her accusers-prosecutors-judges-sentencers, who were one and the same persons, and who banished her, were harder on her because she was a woman, not a mere dissenter or heretic.

The personalities draw me: Anne Hutchinson—gifted, charismatic, often wild, destined to be killed in an Indian massacre. John Winthrop—judgmental and yet enthralled. John Cotton—half leaning toward Hutchinson but not daring to be caught there. Here was a combat of minds and spirits more interesting than massacres or wars; it still haunts.

Martin E. Marty, *Fairfax M. Cone Distinguished Service Professor, University of Chicago.*

MUCH WELCOME, ENGLISHMEN

Three centuries ago Pemaquid was a vast, vaguely bounded expanse of Indian tribal lands centering around what is now the town of Bristol, Maine. It fronted on no fewer than fifty miles of Atlantic littoral and incorporated scores of offshore islands such as Georges, Monhegan, and Damariscove.

It was—and is—permeated with unrecorded, unrecognized, unsubstantiated, forgotten history. Unquestionably it was the real birthplace of New England and the northeast U.S.A. Fishermen from England had at least summer settlements there decades before the Pilgrims landed on Cape Cod; in fact their handouts saved the Pilgrims from starvation, but the Pemaquidians seemed to prefer anonymity to avoid attracting competitors to their locale.

Take me back to the Pemaquid of about 1650. I'd like to have a long chat with honest old Samoset, "Lord of Pemaquid," "Lord of Monhegan" —the Indian who brought his friend Massasoit to Plymouth Colony in 1621 and immortalized himself by greeting the Pilgrims in passable English: "Much welcome, Englishmen. Much welcome, Englishmen." He had picked up his English accent in exchanges with countless British fishermen, captains, and explorers on his home ground at Pemaquid. His life spanned the whole era of the exploration and settlement of Maine.

As one of the few recognized on-the-spot participants in and observers of New England events, he would be capable of putting into perspective and giving a vivid review of what actually transpired in his province; he might give the earliest New England history an entirely new slant, even though he entertained a conviction that the white man, with his insatiable appetite for dried codfish, was a little eccentric. He alone could reconstruct the authentic Pemaquid scene covering a period that I, as a longtime summer resident, would like to have witnessed.

W. Storrs Lee, *retired, former Dean, Middlebury College.*

THE DEATH OF MARQUETTE

On May 18, 1675, a handbell rang from the east shore of Lake Michigan. It was the only sound that afternoon in all the vast wilderness of lake and hills and forest, and it marked the passing of a Jesuit Father, Jacques Marquette. His great and stirring mission among the Illinois Indians had come to an end on Easter morning when he celebrated mass before five thousand of them. They had stood in rings around him in an open field —old men, chiefs, and warriors, with women and children on the outer fringe. No Indian had ever experienced anything like that service: if not all of them were converted, all were deeply moved. The young men escorted Marquette and his two French companions from their town to the head of Lake Michigan to say farewell. They did not try to keep him with them but begged him to come back when he was able. They knew that he was very ill, and had been desperately so when he had returned the fall before to winter with them according to his promise.

His canoe, paddled by Pierre Porteret and a *voyageur*, Jacques Largillier, followed the eastern shore. When, days later, they came to a stream beside a small hill, Marquette told them to stop there so he could end his life on land. All winter, besides other ailments, he had suffered from dysentery; now it was a raging, bloody flux.

When he died, one of the men whispered the names of Mary and Jesus in his ear as he had asked. The other rang the bell.

I wish I might have been there to hear those small and lonely notes. They marked the end of the most spiritual and also down-to-earth of all the Jesuit missionaries, and also the end of a simplicity and faith that were not to be reborn in America.

Walter D. Edmonds, *author.*

WITCH TRIAL

Maybe it's my Quaker ancestry (on the paternal side) that has me choosing personally to witness a small jewel of a thing that happened in nascent Pennsylvania on February 27, 1684. Back then, it seems, Quakers were not altogether immune to the witch-mindedness of their day; and here was an elderly woman, doubtless psychotic, on trial for witchcraft. William Penn, creator of the colony and temporarily a resident there, lent his proprietary presence and took part in examining the accused.

"Art thou a witch?" he asked her. "Hast thou ever ridden through the air on a broomstick?" The poor old thing insisted that indeed she had. Penn told her in effect that he knew of no law against it and recommended that the jury dismiss her. So they found her guilty not of witchcraft but merely of having the "common fame of being a witch" and set her free.

To have been there would have shown one what must have been the most benevolent poker face ever seen. Further, this was probably the most civilized thing to have occurred on the North American continent since Columbus's landing—a spontaneous leap ahead of the terms of the time. And for relish, I don't doubt the old lady hobbled away pretty huffy about not having been taken seriously.

J. C. Furnas, *author.*

THE END OF THE FRENCH EMPIRE

I would like to have been in the British ranks on the Plains of Abraham on the morning of September 13, 1759, at the moment when Wolfe's British army defeated Montcalm's French forces. Rarely have single battles proved decisive to history, but those that have so proved were usually enormously decisive. Wolfe's victory was one such engagement.

Although more war would follow, that battle essentially ended the French empire in North America, an empire that had contended with the English colonies over the course of one hundred and fifty years for the culture, the economy, the native inhabitants, the soil, and the soul of North America. Wolfe's victory ensured that North America would be mostly English-speaking, but it also, because of British imperial policy, ensured that a French culture would survive in a British Canada.

British Canada was one of the many causes of the American Revolution that resulted in an independent United States. American opposition to, and then friendship with, British Canada figured in many major events in American history, from the westward movement to the Civil War, to the titanic struggles against Germany in the twentieth century.

The language we speak, the culture we embrace, the American history we study, and the policies our government follows today, we owe in part to that fateful engagement west of Quebec city.

Franklin B. Wickwire, *Professor of History, University of Massachusetts at Amherst.*

EIGHT DEAD, TEN WOUNDED AT LEXINGTON

Like most people, I am variously impelled by greed, curiosity, and other ignoble motives—mixed in, of course, with Higher Things. Consequently, I would like to have been there when Kidd buried his treasure, when HMS *Vulture* docked in New York and the fleeing Benedict Arnold had his interview with Sir Henry Clinton, and when Jack Kennedy had his date (if he did) with Marilyn Monroe. I would be rather gripped by watching Squanto brief the Pilgrims on how to cope with the New England winter; and seeing John Adams, as our first ambassador to our ex-king, try to make conversation with that d-d-d-difficult old m-m-m-monarch; and Peter Cooper nursing his little teakettle, the Tom Thumb, in the race with the horse. Or Lincoln wisecracking at a cabinet meeting.

But most of all, I would like to have been at Lexington Green on the morning of the nineteenth of April, 1775. It might be possible to discern who actually fired first, a question argued ever since, but what interests me much more is the spirit of the moment, the attitude of the British officer, Major Pitcairn; of John Parker, the militia captain; of the disciplined but ignorant Redcoats, of the farmers, and of onlookers. It's one thing to be part of history, but rather different, ordinary, horrible to be there and be hit. All over quickly, they say, whereupon the drums pick up the beat and the fifes play and the files parade off to Concord and the rude bridge of Emerson's hymn. Even so, long ago, in the Roman Empire; on the Belgian border when the Uhlans heaved up the gates of a village and paraded in; all over the world since time began. Tum-ta-ta-tum, and we march. Maybe the drums are a bigger menace than the weapons.

Oliver Jensen, *one of the founders of* American Heritage *magazine*.

WE DECLARE INDEPENDENCE

July 8, 1776, was a warm, sunny day in Philadelphia, and as the hour of noon approached, people began to gather in the statehouse yard. Residents mingled with others who had traveled from the surrounding countryside. Although one observer commented, "There were few respectable people among them," those present included Mayor Samuel Powel, other city officials, and some members of the Continental Congress. As the yard began to fill, the people waited patiently, their eyes occasionally seeking the platform of the crudely constructed structure erected in 1769 for observing the transit of Venus.

The crowd had become restless when, shortly after twelve, Philadelphia's sheriff, William Dewees, arrived and climbed the observatory stairs followed by his acting deputy, Col. John Nixon. As Dewees approached the railing and prepared to speak, the people quieted. "Under the authority of the Continental Congress and by order of the Committee of Safety," he began, "I proclaim a declaration of independence." Colonel Nixon then stepped forward and proceeded to read the document.

The people listened attentively as he read, and when he had finished, they demonstrated their approbation with three hearty huzzahs. There was little comment as the crowd dispersed. Some followed the speakers to the courthouse, where the document was again read, and then observed as the king's arms were removed first from the courthouse and then from the statehouse. Others made their way to Armitage's tavern to while away a few hours. For most of them the Declaration was not new, for it had been published in the Philadelphia newspapers two days earlier and again that morning.

It was not until evening that the city properly celebrated the momentous decision that had been announced that day. It was a pleasant night, the sky filled with stars, and great bonfires were lighted throughout the city. The arms of King George III were taken out to the commons, placed on a pile of casks, and burned as the crowd watched and cheered. All through the night the bells of the churches tolled, reminding the people that they had been witnesses to the beginning of a new era in American history.

Silvio A. Bedini, *Keeper of the Rare Books of the Smithsonian Institution.*

WASHINGTON STEMS DISASTER

I would most like to have been once in the presence of George Washington. In that rich lifetime were many revealing moments, but my choice would be March 15, 1783. Britain had conceded the military triumph of the American colonies. Fighting had ceased. But despite the promise of impending peace, a binding treaty was not in place. Washington held warily to "an old and true maxim that to make a good peace, you ought to be prepared to carry on the war." Yet to his dismay, throughout his officer corps, the indispensable backbone of the army he must hold intact, raged such anger against the indifference of Congress to their needs that an ugly proposal of mutiny had won support. Washington called a meeting and addressed his malcontents in person. He asked for their continued patience with Congress, implored them not to sully their glorious achievement by a disgraceful act, and promised his intervention on their behalf. As he read his remarks, he paused. He took out his spectacles and begged his audience's indulgence while putting them on, observing that he had grown old in their service and now found himself growing blind. That gesture, an officer remembered later, "forced its way into the heart." And Washington prevailed. It was a quintessential Washingtonian gesture, genuine but also studied, for he had mastered the histrionics as well as the dynamics of leadership. It was one of his great moments, and to have been there would have been one of mine.

George F. Scheer, *historian, editor, and author.*

SECRETS OF THE CONSTITUTIONAL CONVENTION

There is one supreme event that I'd like to have witnessed: the Constitutional Convention, and more specifically the unrecorded deliberations of the Committee of Detail and especially the Committee of Eleven that submitted its report on August 24, 1787. The central issue, which would be resolved only by force of arms in the Civil War, was defined by George Mason of Virginia: it was whether the general government would have the power to "prevent the increase of slavery." In August it appeared that the convention faced a nonnegotiable conflict over the future of American slavery. We know the bare details about the adoption of the three-fifths compromise, the slave-trade extension clause, and the fugitive-slave clause. But we know very little about the actual deals made or the meanings attached to such crucial words as *migration, commerce, importation,* and *such persons.*

As an inside witness at Philadelphia I could easily test Staughton Lynd's hypothesis that a secret bargain was struck by the two deliberative bodies: the North winning the exclusion of slavery from the Northwest in exchange for the three-fifths representation of slaves. Despite all that has been written on the subject, these agreements, which ran counter to so many vital regional interests, are still the greatest mystery in American history. They go far beyond the somewhat limited issue of black slavery. An understanding of what really went on in Philadelphia (and possibly New York) would enrich our understanding of negotiated compromise between irreconcilable forces—clearly an issue of continuing importance. It would also tell us much about the nature of the federal Union and the validity of conflicting interpretations that led to America's greatest internal crisis.

David Brion Davis, *Sterling Professor of History, Yale University.*

THE BILL OF RIGHTS

I would like to have witnessed the decisive moment when the amendments of the Bill of Rights were adopted, when freedom of the press, of speech, of religion, of assembly and all the other citizen rights were set into the Constitution.

Without this affirmation of the rights of individuals as against the power of the state, our country might have taken a far different course. The twentieth century has shown that although literacy has increased in most of the countries of the world, as in our own, even the educated citizen is helpless if there are no established and widely accepted curbs on the power of the state.

Millicent Fenwick, *Ambassador to the United States Mission to the United Nations Agencies for Food and Agriculture and former U.S. Congresswoman.*

JEFFERSON'S COMEUPPANCE

My wish would put me in Thomas Jefferson's study when he got his comeuppance as a bird watcher. The President, a dedicated naturalist, was a subscriber to *The American Ornithology,* a pioneer work by Alexander Wilson (often called the father of American ornithology), and he had asked Wilson to identify a rare species that had mystified him for years. It was, he wrote, "heard... but scarcely ever to be seen but on the top of tallest trees from which it perpetually serenades us with the sweetest notes... clear as those of a nightingale. I have followed it for years without ever but once getting a good view of it."

Flattered at being appointed presidential adviser on birds, Wilson tried to track down the elusive singer and came to a disappointing conclusion. To avoid a kind of ornithological *lèse majesté*, however, he never informed Jefferson directly but noted in a volume of his *Ornithology* that he had been asked about a puzzling bird by a "distinguished gentleman whose name, were I at liberty to give it, would do honor to my humble performance." And he identified the bird as a wood thrush, which, though a very sweet singer, is anything but rare or even uncommon.

Most bird watchers keep life lists of birds they have seen. I keep one of watchers. So I would like to have been with Jefferson as he read this and to have seen his chagrin at realizing he had succumbed to the watcher's perennial weakness—an eagerness to puff up his list by making a rarity out of a familiar species. I've seen it happen with many birders, but a *rara avis* like Jefferson would be a notable addition to my list.

Joseph Kastner, *editor and author.*

10

WITH LEWIS AND CLARK

To have been a member of the Lewis and Clark expedition has long been one of my historical fantasies. To have traversed that vast and silent wilderness, filled with mystery, danger, and beauty, would have been—as Thomas Jefferson once figured it—equivalent to traveling backward in time, beyond the dawn of civilization, to confront unspoiled nature in a way that will never again be possible on this planet.

David M. Kennedy, *Professor of History, Stanford University.*

REACHING SHERMAN PEAK

Ten years ago I stood on a remote, nondescript rock outcropping in northern Idaho, and in my mind's eye I conjured up a vision of some men who had preceded me there by more than a century and a half. They were Meriwether Lewis, William Clark, and the Corps of Discovery; their arrival at Sherman Peak was the climax of their crossing of the Lolo Trail, the Indians' old buffalo road through the northern Rockies—and in some ways it was the climax of their transcontinental journey.

Lewis and Clark were such extraordinary leaders that much of their great exploration seemed remarkably uneventful. The outcome was in doubt only during those excruciating days on the Lolo. Winter was coming on, game was scarce, the terrain almost impassable to man or beast; the men were exhausted, their feet were freezing, they were on starving times. They ate their horses, a raven, a coyote.

It was a near thing, but when they stumbled up onto Sherman Peak, they could see open prairie to the west, and they knew that their ordeal was over. Soon after, they met a band of Nez Perce Indians. It was the first contact between white men and that estimable tribe, and the amicable Nez Perce received the explorers warmly, provided them with buffalo meat, salmon and camas root, and then guided them down the Snake and the Columbia to the Pacific, thus making possible the completion of a journey that would irrevocably shape the future. Although Lewis and Clark didn't find the Northwest Passage they were looking for, they would draw the nation west, and nothing would ever be the same again.

Don Moser, *editor of* Smithsonian *magazine.*

FIRST GLIMPSE OF THE PACIFIC

I wish I had been with Lewis and Clark in November 1805 when they first glimpsed the object of all their labors, the reward of all their anxie-

11

ties—the Pacific Ocean—and to have looked over William Clark's shoulder as he scribbled in his logbook: "Ocean in view! O! the joy."

They had explored a region more unknown to them than the moon is to us, and accomplished the feat without machines or electronics, but solely by the wills and sinews and spirits of mortal men.

Dee Brown, *retired Professor of Library Administration, University of Illinois, Urbana.*

HOMECOMING

I would like to have been in St. Louis toward noon on September 23, 1806, when Lewis and Clark and their men returned from the Pacific. Word had preceded them, and a mixed crowd of French, Spanish, blacks, Indians, Canadians, and Americans, some in broadcloth and some in buckskin, were waiting when they pulled into the boat landing at the levee. Gunfire, cheers, excitement.

We in St. Louis knew by then that our country had increased its size majestically by purchasing the Louisiana Territory. We knew—some of us at least—that beyond the Rockies was a river called variously the Oregon and the Columbia, to which the otter trader Robert Gray had established a claim for the United States—a claim Great Britain disputed.

But what did it all *mean*? Well, we'd know now. We'd hear it from those burned and bearded homecomers who'd crossed endless plains black with buffalo and had gaped at great, grizzled bears they could hardly believe in; who'd followed the trails of unnamed tribes through deep forests of evergreens, past snowy peaks incalculably high, on and on into what became the American dream of the West. For the first time we could feel it in our bones: our only bound was the western sea. We were truly a continental nation.

David Lavender, *author.*

THE ERIE CANAL

I would like to have witnessed the opening of the Erie Canal late in October 1825 —the grand procession that started in Buffalo, where the canalboat *Seneca Chief* moved slowly into the canal carrying two kegs of pure Lake Erie water and a huge portrait of Governor Clinton in a Roman toga. I wish I had been in the procession, preferably riding on the canalboat carrying two Indian youths, two bears, two fawns, et cetera, and of course named *Noah's Ark.* Then, after traveling a week on the canal through Rochester, Syracuse, Utica, Schenectady, and Albany, I wish I had been in

New York City for the final "Grand Aquatic Display" as Clinton poured that Erie water into the Atlantic, and for the mile-and-a-half parade in Manhattan, as throngs—including me—gaped.

Then I would have wanted to take a canalboat west so that I could more closely study the canal walls and bottoms that had to be sealed against boat wash and muskrats; the locks with their stone-lined channels and big wooden gates; the bridges and aqueducts built high over rivers and ravines, strong enough to support boat, crew, and cargo. Sitting back on my "settle" on top of a canalboat, I would contemplate a kind of caste system on the canal: my own long and lean canal packet, the "grandee of the Erie," carrying only passengers and serving them fine meals; the emigrants' "line boat," carrying families and their stoves and furniture and chickens; the freighters carrying owners, horses, and cargo; the shantyboat, a one-room hovel on a flatboat, which moved by hitching a ride on another craft; and—at the bottom of the caste—the timber raft, mere piles of logs lashed together and topped by a shanty for the crew.

James MacGregor Burns, *Woodrow Wilson Professor of Government, Williams College.*

JACKSON TOASTS THE UNION

I'd like to have been a waiter at Brown's Indian Queen Hotel in the City of Washington in the year 1830. While I would like to confine my duties to a single evening, April 13, it would be worth a year carrying dishes just to be there that evening. The dinner menu doesn't matter—no one now remembers. It was the toasts that counted. And not the twenty-four regular ones (real drinkers there were in those days) but the volunteers. The President of the United States had decided to use the occasion. He was ready for his many enemies in rebellious South Carolina, where the wretched word *nullification* had been heard again in regard to a federal tariff. Hayne had opposed Webster in the Senate, and the President had had enough of it. In the days before the dinner he had scribbled out several possible toasts and pitched them into the fire until he got the right one. Holding up his glass that evening, white hair shining, everyone on his feet, Martin Van Buren on a chair so he could see, Old Hickory fixed his glance on John C. Calhoun: "Our Union: It must be preserved." Calhoun had risen with the rest, and his hand trembled so that a little yellow wine trickled down the side of his glass.

Robert H. Ferrell, *Distinguished Professor of History, Indiana University, Bloomington.*

INVENTING THE TELEGRAPH

Incidents in history are usually significant only in combination with a succession of other incidents. Isolated incidents can assume importance only when they summarize an epoch in one dramatic moment or when fuller knowledge of the event might alter interpretations.

The moment of Samuel F. B. Morse's proclaimed "flash of genius," during which he believed that he invented the telegraph, retains critical uncertainties. Morse was returning to the United States on the S.S. *Sully* in 1832 when he engaged in spirited conversations on Ampère's recent electromagnetic experiments. The Boston chemist Dr. Charles T. Jackson told him that the length of wire did not retard the speed of electricity. Morse declared, euphorically, "I see no reason why intelligence might not be instantaneously transmitted by electricity to any distance." He always believed this idea was the true invention, and it was wholly his own.

Others denied it, including those already experimenting in the field. Jackson believed that he and Morse had cooperated in reaching Morse's declaration and that they had agreed to cooperate in developing the telegraph. Lawsuits collected conflicting remembrances, and our present understanding of all invention has become complex. Yet whatever the whole truth, Morse's "moment" was a key point in setting the course toward "instantaneous" electrical communication—toward the telegraph, the telephone, radio, radar, television, and the computer.

Brooke Hindle, *Senior Historian, the National Museum of American History of the Smithsonian Institution.*

DANIEL WEBSTER, THE MAGNIFICENT

Ralph Waldo Emerson's Scottish friend Thomas Carlyle said of Daniel Webster: "No man can be as great as that man looks." Looked and *sounded.* I elect to have heard and seen him; but I don't choose one of the famous set-piece occasions (in the Supreme Court, or the Senate, or at Bunker Hill, where an attentive multitude listened for hours in the hot sun). Instead I go for a more relaxed, almost neighborly set of vignettes, spread out over several days in August 1843.

Webster had come to Concord, Massachusetts, to argue a case before the Suffolk County bar. Emerson went along to observe and was enchanted. Even among prominent attorneys Webster was, said Emerson, "a schoolmaster among his boys." His rhetoric was "perfect, so homely, so fit, so strong." He dominated the scene, even to adjourning the court, "which he did by rising, & taking his hat & looking the Judge coolly in the face."

In the evenings I would with Daniel be entertained in local parlors, where Emerson found him irresistibly "goodnatured" and "nonchalant." A glowing Concord lady said Webster was "magnificent," as prodigious as Niagara Falls.

What a President Webster might have been! But history is full of *if* and *alas*. In a few years New Englanders—and Emerson—were denouncing him as a compromiser over slavery. In that heady week of 1843, though, they (and I) would have been content merely to appreciate the magic of "godlike Daniel."

Marcus Cunliffe, *University Professor, The George Washington University.*

THOREAU'S WALDEN

I would have liked to visit Thoreau's hut: nothing in our past interests me more. The Gettysburg address perhaps, but it was a big crowd and I would get tired waiting. The tea party in Boston sounds like an escapade that became big news; but the hut—that I would like to have seen, with a tape measure to verify the figures in *Walden*, and check up on other details —not to put down Henry David but simply to see what the distance was between the facts and his fancy. He had such a large fancy.

Leon Edel, *Emeritus Citizen Professor of English, University of Hawaii.*

CROSSING THE MISSISSIPPI

The one event I would most like to have participated in was hardly recorded—the first vision of that endless sea of grass, when the first explorers crossed the Mississippi and headed west across those plains the like of which no other world boasted, the plains that extended to the horizon, deep with grass to a man's armpits. There buffalo lazily wandered, heedless and secure, feeding on this natural abundance, fearless of man, be he white or red. That ocean of land would vanish as men cut it, plowed it, burned it, ravaged it, killed the buffalo, killed the Indians, turned it into a network of steel, concrete, and plowed furrows, and exterminated one of the wonders of the world. I cannot get the sight of it out of my eyes, and it brings me close to tears.

Harrison Salisbury, *journalist and author.*

PROLOGUE TO THE CIVIL WAR

For me the moments of highest drama in our history are the congressional debates preceding the monumental tragedy that was our Civil War. Like the chorus in a Greek drama, the players had their say and moved offstage within two years' time.

In the Senate were not only Clay, Calhoun, and Webster but Benton and Sam Houston, who refused to secede when Texas did. They were all there. Clay had already spoken, in all his golden eloquence; Calhoun, sitting by like a ghost, had had his last warning read for him on March 4, 1850, which, according to the press, might have forced the Northern senators to bow to the will of the South, "had it not been for Mr. Webster's masterly playing." The day was March 7, when Webster delivered his magnificent oration in defense of the Union he so loved, Calhoun creeping into the chamber to hear his great antagonist once more.

Within a month, Calhoun was gone, murmuring that he would die happy if the Union could be preserved. Two years later, Henry Clay died in Washington; Webster died in Massachusetts that same year, his last gaze fixed on the flag of the Union, "not a stripe obscured." None of the three lived to see the curtain rise on the great tragedy, which John Calhoun had foreseen. I would like to have been there with the press that March, but with the insights of my present incarnation, knowing that in the end, the Union would be preserved.

Margaret Coit Elwell, *biographer and retired Professor of Social Science, Fairleigh Dickinson University.*

LINCOLN'S FAREWELL

I wish I could have witnessed that intimate moment when Lincoln, as President-elect, said farewell to his neighbors at Springfield. I grew up in a county-seat town in central Illinois and as a boy I heard how Lincoln, the lawyer, traveled the eighth judicial circuit, put up at the West Side House on the courthouse square, and joked and jousted with the local wits under the locust trees. I remember descendants of those trees. Here is the scene on the morning of February 11, 1861, at the little brick station of the Great Western Railway in Springfield:

Clouds hung low. A cold drizzle set the mood. When the engineer sounded his whistle, the people made way as Lincoln walked onto the car and stepped out onto its platform. And he said to them, in part: "To this place, and the kindness of these people I owe everything ... I now leave, not knowing when, or whether ever, I may return, with a task before me greater than that which rested upon Washington." Need I go on? The words are famous, down to the closing "I bid you an affectionate farewell." For years I had an old photograph of the West Side House and a copy of Lincoln's remarks tacked on my study door. In central Illinois, he was one of ours.

Gerald Carson, *author.*

INSIDE LEE'S MIND

This is an invitation to fantasy—to see the unseeable, to witness the unwitnessable, to summon the past into the present. Since we are entering an imaginary world through the looking glass, why not go for broke? Why not choose to recover what no one has ever seen, not even the participants, not even the protagonist? Many of the most important events of history never had any witnesses, were in fact invisible. Yet they happened, and historians are always writing about them. They were the decisions, the fateful commitments, and they took place entirely within the mind and heart. If we may enter the mind as we enter the looking glass, many temptations present themselves. No accounting for choices in such matters. Forced to pick one, I would look in on the mind of Col. Robert E. Lee on being offered the command of Union forces in 1861.

C. Vann Woodward, *Sterling Professor of History Emeritus, Yale University.*

EMANCIPATION

The incident that I would like to have witnessed is that described in Thomas Wentworth Higginson's *Army Life in a Black Regiment.* He writes of a ceremony in South Carolina on January 1, 1863, celebrating the coming into effect of the Emancipation Proclamation. The ceremony was conventional and simple until Higginson got up to speak and waved the American flag before the audience of black soldiers, white civilians and officers, and a large number of slaves, who at that moment were legally receiving their freedom for the first time. As the flag was being waved, Higginson tells us, "there suddenly arose... a strong male voice (but rather cracked and elderly), into which two women's voices instantly blended, singing, as if by an impulse that could no more be repressed than the morning note of the song-sparrow—

" 'My Country, 'tis of thee, Sweet Land of Liberty, of thee I sing!' "

The ceremony ended as the former slaves sang on, irrepressibly, through verse after verse. Higginson motioned the few whites who began to join in to be silent. The moment, as he said, was electric. "Nothing could be more wonderfully unconscious; art could not have dreamt of a tribute to the day of jubilee that should be so affecting; history will not believe it...."

This incident epitomizes the most profound moment in America's social history: that point when millions of people ceased to be slaves in the home of the free and set in motion the historic challenge that white America make real its own vision.

Carl N. Degler, *Margaret Byrne Professor of American History, Stanford.*

PICKETT'S CHARGE

And so, the last great old-style infantry charge in history begins. With the sun flashing off their muskets, fifteen thousand men—a phalanx of men a mile across and half a mile deep—begins to move silently, slowly, in parade fashion, out of the shadows of the trees and into the open, sun-baked fields...this antique military creature, a giant throwback to how men fought in the Middle Ages, has just made it to within two hundred yards of the Union guns when the Federals open up with canister...

This moment fills me with awe. Somehow I would have liked to be present during the ominous march of George Pickett and his men on the third day of fighting at Gettysburg in 1863. Not only to see this deadly spectacle but to know at the same time the outcome was ensuring that our great and noble experiment in government was going to last.

Philip Kunhardt, Jr., *author and editor.*

THE ASSAULT ON FORT WAGNER

I would like to have witnessed the attack on Fort Wagner, South Carolina, by Federal troops on the evening of July 18, 1863. The fort—a massive affair made of logs, earth, and sand—stood at the northern tip of an island that curved around into Charleston Harbor. Its capture was to be preliminary to taking the city.

The assault was led by the 54th Massachusetts, the first black regiment recruited in a free state. In command was Col. Robert Gould Shaw, of Boston blue blood and of true heroic character. At starlight, the regiment—600 troops and 22 officers—made for the earthwork at the double-quick, with orders to seize it by bayonet assault. The Confederate forces within opened up a devastating fire from cannons, naval guns, and mortars. Men were falling on all sides; every flash of fire, a survivor would say, showed the ground dotted with the wounded or killed. Colonel Shaw gained the rampart before he was shot through the heart.

Among the 158 wounded from the 54th was Wilky James, 1st lieutenant and adjutant to Colonel Shaw; the eighteen-year-old younger brother of William and Henry James. There were 12 known dead, but there were 100 missing, some dead, some captured. Half of the 54th Massachusetts was wiped out; successive attacks by other units during the night ended with 1,515 casualties (the Confederates suffered 174).

It was a complete disaster. But something about the "brave black regiment," as it came to be called, so gallantly leading the way in this venture (at this moment in a war that many believed to be about slavery and freedom) ignited the Northern imagination. It was celebrated over the years in poems by Emerson, James Russell Lowell, Paul Lawrence Dunbar, Robert Lowell, and many others, and in essays by Frederick Douglass, Justice Holmes, and others. When the memorial frieze to Colonel Shaw and the 54th by Augustus Saint-Gaudens was inaugurated in Boston in 1897, the chief speaker was William James.

R.W.B. Lewis, *Neil Gray Professor of Rhetoric, Yale University.*

COMING TO TERMS

I wish most of all that I could have been a listener aboard the steamer transport *River Queen*, just off Hampton Roads, on February 3, 1865.

This, of course, was the conference between Abraham Lincoln, who was accompanied by Secretary of State William H. Seward, and Vice-President Alexander H. Stephens, who represented the Confederate States of America, and was accompanied by Sen. R. M. T. Hunter and former Supreme Court Justice John A. Campbell. They were trying to work out some way to quickly end the Civil War and to restore the Union.

I wish I could have been there, first, simply to see these leaders of the Union and the Confederacy. Think what a contrast they made! There was the gigantically tall Abraham Lincoln and the minute, wizened Alexander Stephens. Apart from that, I would have been a witness to the one and only time when true leaders of the North and the South sat down seriously to talk about terms of reconciliation and peace. Finally, from witnessing this encounter, I would know what Abraham Lincoln's real policy of Reconstruction was, and could better judge what he might have accomplished had he not been assassinated. I know of no other single episode in the history of the Civil War that is so significant, and I wish I could have been there.

David Herbert Donald, *Charles Warren Professor of American History, Harvard University.*

THE LINCOLN CABINET

I would choose to be at one of the cabinet meetings of early 1865, as the Civil War was ending, when Abraham Lincoln, out of all the strange and glorious forces within him, had totally matured as a statesman-saint. An especially revealing meeting must have been the one at which Lincoln talked of an appropriation of four hundred million dollars, an immense sum for the time, to help the South recover. Though Lincoln had assumed virtually dictatorial authority over the conduct of the war, he did listen to his cabinet, even invited them to vote, and then from time to time outvoted them. "Seven no and one aye, the ayes have it," was his legendary summation of the powers of the President vis-à-vis his cabinet. But the Lincoln cabinet meetings were far from the perfunctory sessions of the recent Presidencies. (I worked in the Carter White House for a year; there were four cabinet meetings while I was there, meaningless gatherings of forty to fifty people.) Lincoln's cabinet dissuaded him from proposing his magnanimous Reconstruction grant. They felt the Congress wasn't ready. Lincoln made it clear he would set aside the idea only temporarily. The dialogue must have illuminated the ways in which Lincoln, at the height of his powers, could strike the balance between "practical politics" and longer-range purpose and vision. I would like to have listened.

Hedley Donovan, *Fellow of the Faculty of Government, Harvard University.*

SURRENDER AT APPOMATTOX

Lee's surrender to Grant at Appomattox on April 9, 1865—not the meeting between Lee and Grant at which the terms were discussed, which has become almost legendary and hackneyed, but rather the hours that followed: Lee riding among the remnants of his army, comforting, reassuring, speaking to the men from horseback, and the formal surrender ceremony later, heavy with emotion, when the colors were furled and the arms were stacked. The scene, laden with significance, was one of the truly momentous events in American history for what it symbolized. Men wept, not, I suspect, because of the failure of their cause—for long before that day the cause, if it was understood at all, had ceased to evoke the dedication it once inspired. Rather I think it was because the hardship and sacrifice was suddenly over, because the shedding of blood had ended, and because the memories of all those thousands who didn't make it to the final day came rushing to the fore. They might also have wept, if they knew what we know, for a world and a time that was now lost forever.

Things would never be the same again. The America of the early nineteenth century had passed; the nation left its formative period and entered into a maturity in which the romantic ideals, aspirations, and yearnings of that earlier time would no longer have any place. It was this moment that symbolized, perhaps more than any other, the Americans' loss of innocence. It was all put together by Lee in his farewell to his troops, full of pathos and sincerity and imparting as few other documents have the meaning of those mid-April days. Lee's farewell address must be read aloud to capture its real impact; it never fails to touch the heart.

Robert W. Johannsen, *James G. Randall Distinguished Professor of History, University of Illinois, Urbana-Champaign.*

ALL QUIET IN SPRINGFIELD

If wishes were horses, beggars would ride. I would ride with a young carpenter, Ed Beall of Alton, Illinois, in the last week of April 1865, on assignment for the Chicago & Alton Railroad. In Springfield the Lincoln house at Eighth and Jackson streets was to be draped in mourning. Ed was a rangy youth with a long reach. While comrades on the roof paid out a rope, he slid down, headfirst, to the eaves, where black "droopers" were set in place. Then the crew moved on to the Illinois statehouse to build a catafalque in the assembly hall.

On a railroad siding in Chicago lay a special train, twelve days' slow journey from Washington. Its black-draped coaches carried a military company in dress uniforms. In the next car were Gen. "Fighting Joe" Hooker, Secretary Edwin M. Stanton, Gov. Richard Yates, and Lincoln's old friend Chief Justice David Davis. Inside the last car, bearing the President's seal, a large coffin rested beside a small one. The small casket contained the body of twelve-year-old Willie Lincoln, who had died three years before in Washington. Now he was to be buried beside his father in Springfield.

At midnight the train began to move. It crept through Joliet, Wilmington, and Bloomington, where acres of people waited in silence. The last downgrade carried it into Springfield. There, on the crest of Oak Ridge Cemetery, Ed Beall and his mates were building a platform. At sunrise their work was done.

On an empty lumber wagon Ed jolted through streets thronged with carts, traps, carriages, and folk on foot—all pressing toward the C & A Depot. When the funeral train halted, the multitude engulfed it. From the rear coach strode General Hooker. He broke stride at a man reaching for a spectator's wallet. One of his brisk feet sent the pickpocket sprawling. Drums throbbed and bells tolled as thousands moved to the statehouse

21

where Ed Beall in his overalls divided the lines filing past a draped coffin. At noon a final procession marched to Oak Ridge, where the two coffins were placed in a hillside tomb. It smelled of evergreens on the dim stone floor.

Slowly the crowd dispersed, and Springfield grew as quiet as the country town where Lincoln had come in 1837. From his assignment with history, Ed Beall caught a freight train and returned to repairing boxcars on the Chicago & Alton run.

Walter Havighurst, *Research Professor of English, Miami University, Ohio.*

"TO SHOW WHERE THEIR FLAG HAD BEEN . . ."

The triumphal victory parade of the Union Armies in Washington, May 23 *and* May 24, 1865, is the scene that would have given me the most pleasure. There is an unforgettable description in *The Letters of Mrs. Henry Adams*: "A lovely summer afternoon—blue sky overhead—roses everywhere all over the houses—regiment after regiment came marching past, bands playing—squads of contrabands looking on. We sang out as each regiment passed, 'What regiment are you?' 'Michigan!' 'Wisconsin!' 'Iowa!'

". . . We were early and got nice seats . . . and eighty feet from us across the street sat the President, Generals Grant, Sherman, Howard, Hancock, Meade . . .

"About nine-thirty the band struck up 'John Brown,' and by came Meade with his staff, splendidly mounted. Almost all the officers in the army had their hands filled with roses. . . . And so it came, this glorious old Army of the Potomac, for six hours marching past, eighteen or twenty miles long, their colours telling their sad history. Some regiments with nothing but a bare pole, a little bit of rag only, hanging a few inches, to show where their flag had been. Others that had been Stars and Stripes, with one or two stripes hanging, all the rest shot away. . . .

"Wednesday, another glorious day—bright and cool, and we sit in the same place as before and see Sherman ride by at the head of 70,000 men, who, in physique and marching, surpass decidedly the Potomac Army. . . ."

Alfred Kazin, *Distinguished Professor of English, City University of New York Graduate Center.*

FIRST FLIGHT

I would like to have witnessed Jacob Brodbeck's first manned aircraft flight over Luckenback, Texas, in 1865. Newspaper clippings attest to the fact that there were witnesses, but they do not describe what the craft looked like, except to say that it was powered by a large clock spring. Brodbeck decided to call his machine an "airship."

William Goetzmann, *Stiles Professor of American Studies and History, University of Texas, Austin.*

GRANT PUTS THE ARMY IN ITS PLACE

Washington, D.C., January–February 1868: The War Department office of Ulysses S. Grant, who then wore two hats, one as interim secretary of war and the other as the commanding general of the United States Army. Grant, the most popular living American by far, at least outside the ex-Rebel states, had a visitor, his most popular contemporary, Gen. William Tecumseh Sherman. Grant had learned that President Andrew Johnson was trying to entice Sherman into cooperating in a scheme by which Johnson apparently hoped to create, without constitutional or legislative sanction, a new army department under Sherman's command. It was to number perhaps ten thousand men, be directly linked to the White House, and would be stationed near Baltimore. Evidently Johnson envisaged this new military department as being wholly under his own authority and outside the chain of command going through the War Department, as statutes pursuant to the Constitution required. Johnson apprehended impeachment. His efforts to deflect the Army in the South away from obedienc to statutes favoring racial equality had become increasingly frantic. Now Johnson was willing to risk Balkanizing the regular army into a President's force and a congressional one. And Sherman, deeply conservative on matters of race equality, was willing at least to entertain the notion of cooperating with the President in this risky enterprise.

Sherman and Grant were old friends and combat comrades. Grant invited Sherman, recently in from the field, to his War Department office for what became an hours-long, closed-door, off-the-record session. The usual rumor experts of army headquarters and the War Department were frustrated as, at times, the voices of the two generals penetrated the heavy doors to Grant's rooms, but so dimly that the most acute ears bent that way could make out few words. Finally Sherman emerged. He looked shaken. Soon after this meeting he took the train out of Washington to St. Louis and, except for brief ceremonial occasions, did not return to Washington's dangers for almost twenty years.

What, I dearly want to know, did Grant tell Sherman? How did the latter respond? Sherman's decision not to play the President's hazardous game and to listen to his immediate superior officer—who was soon to be his commander in chief—helped to keep the American army subservient to all its constitutional masters, not to one alone.

Harold M. Hyman, *William Pettus Hobby Professor of History, Rice University.*

THE GOLDEN SPIKE

In these dark days of rampant terrorism, toxic waste, acid rain, and statesmen playing games of nuclear "chicken," I'd like to have been present at some incident that might cheer me up. The scene that comes instantly to mind is the Golden Spike ceremony at Promontory Point, Utah, on May 10, 1869, when the nation was at long last linked by rail "from sea to shining sea." Specifically, I'd like to have been present at the exact second when A. J. Russell took his famous picture of the two locomotives coming together.

No moment in American history could be more exhilarating, more joyful, more full of promise. I want to drink it all in. I want to mix with that boisterous crowd of tracklayers, soldiers, dishwashers, gamblers, and strumpets. I want to listen to the 21st Infantry band thumping away. I want to watch the cowcatchers touch. I want to sample the bottle of champagne held out by the man standing on the Central Pacific's locomotive Jupiter. I want to know who the lady is in the exact center of the preliminary photograph, but who vanishes in the final, climactic shot. I want to know the identity of the one man in the picture who turned his back to the camera. Was he just inattentive, or was his likeness perhaps posted as "WANTED" in every post office in the West? I want to watch Leland Stanford swing his hammer—and miss the golden spike.

Above all, I want to feel—even for a moment—the pride of achievement and bright hopes for the future that thrilled this crowd and the nation itself.

Walter Lord, *narrative historian.*

RAILS WEST

My choice would be that cool and bright Monday out in Promontory, Utah, when top rail officials, their guests, and dozens of track workmen watched as token touches were made on a $400 golden spike by a silver sledge.

The flamboyant, nationwide celebration marked an event as important to Americans as the opening of the Suez Canal —also in 1869—was to western Europeans. The antebellum generation of railroad development saw an iron network connect eastern seaports with established towns and cities, and by 1860 reach the edge of the frontier from Wisconsin to Texas. In the 1870s and 1880s the westward-reaching trans-Mississippi rail lines moved well ahead of the frontier, created new communities, and pulled millions of settlers into the West. In the last decades of the nineteenth century these new rail lines were taking the Texas longhorn from the Kansas cow town to Chicago, were serving the gold and silver miners of Leadville and Virginia City, and were moving to eastern markets the crops of the prairie homesteader and farmer. Well before 1900 these Western railroads had helped close the last American frontier.

John F. Stover, *Professor of History, Purdue University.*

STEALING THE PRESIDENCY

I would like to have witnessed the dawn meeting that took place in the Fifth Avenue Hotel on November 8, 1876. Present were John C. Reid, the managing editor of *The New York Times*, Zachariah Chandler, chairman of the Republican National Committee, and one or two other politicians. The subject: How to steal the Presidency of the United States.

During the preceding night it had become apparent that Samuel J. Tilden, the Democratic candidate, was ahead by some two hundred and fifty thousand in the popular vote. Almost every newspaper in New York, including the Republican *Tribune*, had conceded victory to the Democrats. But John Reid discovered that not even the Democrats knew who had carried Florida, South Carolina, and Louisiana, three states the Republicans theoretically controlled, thanks to the federal troops still stationed on their soil. If the Republicans could hold these states, their candidate, Rutherford B. Hayes, would win by one electoral vote.

As a lifelong student of American politics, I would love to know what they said—and thought—as they went about perpetrating the most terrific act of corruption in our history. Reid soon persuaded Chandler to send telegrams to Republican leaders of the disputed states, containing such pointed suggestions as "Don't be defrauded." Within hours, emissaries with bags full of money were riding south to make sure that the officials counting the votes were properly motivated.

Each state had a "canvassing board," which was empowered to throw out the vote of a county if it was tainted by fraud or violence. Enough counties were disqualified to provide Republican majorities—in Florida's case a breathless forty-five votes. A few years later, copies of telegrams found in the files of Western Union and leaked to the press revealed that the Democrats had also tried to buy up the canvassing boards on November 8, 1876, but thanks to John Reid and Zachariah Chandler, the Republicans got there firstest with the mostest cash.

All in all, it makes Watergate look like tiddlywinks.

Thomas Fleming, *novelist and historian.*

THE BLIZZARD OF '88

I'd want to be in New York City with my maternal grandfather during the Blizzard of 1888. He told me of it one day—I must have been four or five—as we walked across the frozen part of the Central Park lake. Even now, the memory of the skaters and a small bonfire on the other shore blends both with his account of the East River freezing over and with skaters in subsequently seen Currier and Ives prints of Central Park as it was in his youth. Scraps of his observations—the motionless city, the El trains stalled for hours —blend today with facts from published history —the thirty-foot drifts in Herald Square, the necessity of communicating with Boston via transatlantic cable through London, the food shortages. At four I couldn't know to ask what I would today, and so I want to be walking beside him on Monday, March 12, 1888. An ambitious young man of nineteen, just starting to work for an engineering journal, he was unable to get to work. But what did he do that day? What did he see? A lover of theater, was he one of the handful of people who managed to watch Ellen Terry and Henry Irving in *Faust*? Did he watch one of the multitude of fires that burned themselves out because no fire engines could reach them? I'd want answers to questions that, even now, I hardly know enough to ask.

John Hollander, *poet and Professor of English, Yale University.*

AN EVENING AT HULL HOUSE

Hull House was a pioneering social settlement, established in Chicago in 1889 by twenty-nine-year-old Jane Addams. It was the model for settlement houses in cities all across America, staffed by people who shared Addams's vision of political reform and the need to develop the new field of professional social service.

The Hull House community included the most imaginative and energetic reformers and social activists of their generation: Alice Hamilton, who would be a pioneer in industrial disease and the first woman member of the faculty of Harvard Medical School; Florence Kelly, translator of Friedrich Engels, first factory inspector in Illinois and tireless investigator of industrial conditions; Julia Lathrop, first head of the federal Children's Bureau. They were joined by dozens of younger women, representatives of the first large generation of college-educated women, driven by their conviction that they should use their education to improve society. They helped organize trade-union women, walked picket lines, established residences for single working women, ran a day nursery for working mothers, devised and lobbied for progressive legislation. Hull House offered an array of evening classes, concerts, and dramatic readings to nurture the minds of those it served.

Those who lived in Hull House apartments could order food from a central kitchen, but most came each night to the main dining room, where idealism ran high and the activities of the day and plans for the future could be discussed over dinner with guests like Charlotte Perkins Gilman, Sidney and Beatrice Webb, and Gov. John P. Altgeld.

The Hull House community was perhaps the most formidable group of intellectuals and social activists gathered in this country since Jefferson's dinners at the White House. I would love to have observed a Hull House dinner—even if I couldn't eat more than would a fly on the wall.

Linda K. Kerber, *Professor of History, University of Iowa.*

FALL RIVER LEGEND

I would be invisible but nonetheless present in a certain house at 92 Second Street in Fall River, Massachusetts, on the sweltering hot morning of August 4, 1892. At breakfast I would join elderly, tightfisted Andrew Borden, his second wife, Abby, rather stout at two hundred pounds and five feet tall, and Lizzie, the thirty-two-year-old unmarried daughter of Andrew and his first wife. The necessity of my invisibility would become only too apparent later in the morning, but at this point I would be rather thankful to be under no obligation to partake of the cold mutton, bananas, and black coffee.

Following this meal, the last for Andrew and Abby, I would observe Andrew leaving the house for a walk, after meticulously locking the door, as was his habit. I wouldn't have long to wait—perhaps an hour at most— before learning the secret that has mystified generations of Americans, and put the name Lizzie Borden forever into the annals of American legend.

In the second-floor guest bedroom around ten o'clock I would see the hand that held the hatchet and the nineteen blows that rained down on Abby's head and shoulders. I would hear Lizzie laughing as the Borden maid, Bridget, struggled with the locked door to let Andrew back in the house about an hour later. I would observe him lying down on the sitting-room couch for a nap and then, within a few minutes, I would be a witness to the third horror of the morning (if you count the breakfast as the first). It wouldn't be easy to stand by as Andrew's brains were splattered over the nearby wall in a shower of blood. But I'd know whether the brutal perpetrator was Bridget, Emma (Lizzie's sister who was supposedly out of town but who conceivably could have returned), John Morse (a houseguest the night before and brother of the first Mrs. Borden), an intruder, or, indeed, Lizzie, who was found innocent of the crimes by a jury ten months later.

I would know, but I'd never tell.

Judson D. Hale, Sr., *editor of* Yankee *magazine and* The Old Farmer's Almanac.

DARROW FOR THE DEFENSE

My one scene occurred in the Municipal Court of Oshkosh, Wisconsin, over three weeks ending November 2, 1898. It was the jury trial of Thomas I. Kidd, George Zentner, and Michael Troiber, all of the Woodworkers' Union, on a charge of conspiracy to injure the business of the Paine Lumber Company. The trial helped to establish a union's right to strike free of conspiracy charges. Counsel for the men was Clarence Darrow, then forty-one and starting to be known as the "Attorney for the Damned" after his defense of Eugene V. Debs in the Pullman Strike of 1894.

Kidd and his associates had been arrested in a strike for a wage increase and union recognition. In the trial, George M. Paine, proprietor of the company, was called as a witness, giving Darrow an opportunity to cross-examine with singular effectiveness. His questions exposed the "infamy of Paine's business methods—the inhumanity and contempt he displayed toward the men who worked in his factory, his hypocrisy and rapaciousness in dealing with his workers," as Kevin Tierney phrased it in Darrow's biography.

Darrow's speech to the jury took two days and was delivered without notes. "While you have been occupied for the last two weeks in listening to the evidence in this case, and while the court will instruct you as to the technical rules of law under which this evidence is to be applied, still it is impossible to present the case to you without a broad survey of the great questions that are agitating the world today," he began. "For whatever its form, this is not really a criminal case. It is but an episode in the great battle for human liberty, a battle which was commenced when the tyranny and oppression of man first caused him to impose upon his fellows and which will not end so long as the children of one father shall be compelled to toil to support the children of another in luxury and ease."

Darrow's peroration was a classic. "Gentlemen," he said, "I leave this case with you. Here is Thomas I. Kidd. It is a matter of the smallest consequence to him or to me what you do; and I say it as sincerely as I ever spoke a word . . . I do not appeal for him. That cause is too narrow for me, much as I love him. . . . I appeal to you, gentlemen, not for Thomas I. Kidd, but I appeal to you for the long line—the long, long line reaching back through the ages, and forward to the years to come—the long line of despoiled and downtrodden people of the earth."

The jury was out for fifty minutes. Returning, it announced that it had voted acquittals for all three men. For his work in the Kidd case Darrow received a fee of two hundred and fifty dollars.

Alden Whitman, *book critic and historian.*

A PLEA FOR CIVIL RIGHTS

Coatesville, Pennsylvania, August 18, 1912: In a rented room of the Nagel Building, opposite the church, John Jay Chapman, aged fifty, the literary critic from Boston who had in his younger days fought for reform with Theodore Roosevelt in New York, is holding a prayer meeting in memory of "the Negro Zacharia Walker," lynched in Coatesville on August 13 of the previous year.

Renting the room, advertising the meeting in the paper, and answering the suspicious questions of Coatesville citizens had been trying. Chapman was acting alone, but nobody believed this. *Civil rights* were words not yet thought of, but here surely was their first self-appointed champion, performing a symbolic act.

Chapman read his text, which begins: "We are met to commemorate the anniversary of one of the most dreadful crimes in history—not for the purpose of condemning it, but to repent of our share in it." Those listening were: Miss Edith Martin, a friend of the Chapmans, from New York; "an anti-slavery old Negress who lives in Boston and was staying in Coatesville"; and "a man who was . . . an 'outpost' finding out what was up."

I wish I had been a fourth member of that audience.

Jacques Barzun, *past president of the National Institute of Arts and Letters.*

TR'S BITE

I would like to have seen someone I've always distrusted a bit but fear I might have admired a good deal. I'd like to have seen Theodore Roosevelt.

Not at San Juan Hill, not shooting wild animals, setting up the National Park Service, entertaining Booker T. Washington at the White House, or getting the Russians and Japanese to sign a peace treaty.

I would like to have seen him at Madison Square Garden in the fall of 1912 when he was running for President on his own Bull Moose ticket against both Woodrow Wilson and William Howard Taft. There he was, rejected by politicians of the Republican party he had served, but determined to regain the Presidency after stepping aside for Taft four years earlier.

Both major parties feared him, but the Progressives of the day—Felix Frankfurter, Walter Lippmann, Learned Hand—thought he was a demigod. "TR bit me and I went mad," William Allen White said, speaking for a generation of intellectuals.

That night at Madison Square Garden was TR's first public appearance after having been wounded in an assassination attempt. Everyone went mad. It was one of his greatest moments. Politics never seemed quite so innocent after that. I'd like to know if I would have gone a little mad too.

Ronald Steel, *author.*

THE WAR TO END WARS

The incident that I should most like to have witnessed was in a small way one that I actually took part in—the Armistice Day celebrations of November 11, 1918. I wish I might have seen the surging crowds in the great cities, but I did live through that evening as an eight-year-old boy in a small Boston suburb, parading up and down the street with my friends in a kind of delirium, shouting, singing, waving whatever flags we could lay hands on. I remember I had a red British merchant marine flag. The Hun had been defeated, evil ground into the dust. Keep the World Safe for Democracy! The War to End Wars! Those were the slogans even children mouthed and believed in. There was a spontaneity to that first Armistice celebration that the twin victories of World War II lacked. I saw both the V-E and V-J celebrations in London and found them flaccid, contained, artificial. For one thing, we had to wait three days until officially allowed to celebrate. Nothing like the spontaneity of 1918. Yes, I wish I might have seen the great cities on the first Armistice night. Never again such confident belief.

Francis Russell, *author.*

RHAPSODY IN BLUE

I would like to have been present at Aeolian Hall, February 12, 1924.

That was the evening when Gershwin's *Rhapsody in Blue* was first performed.

I like Gershwin, but I also know that *Rhapsody in Blue* (the very title is a maudlin one, with the touch of a cliché) is not the best of his compositions: it is a period piece. But what a period! That night in 1924 represented the coming of age of American genius. In one polyphonic and saxophonic swoop the creative talent of America swept ahead of Europe, of all the modernisms of Europe. That odd young man, the son of uneducated Jewish immigrants, brought up in the near-slums of New York, created something that was, and remained, quintessentially American, strident at times but suffused with a melancholy elegance of harmonies beyond the imagination and sensitivity of almost anything that the Old World could have produced at that time. It was modern, in a way in which no other achievement had been modern: not Whitman's poetry, not Berlin's ragtime, not the Brooklyn Bridge, not the Woolworth Building, all of which still bore traces of the sentiments of an American Victorianism.

I would have wanted to sense the reactions of that audience: the quality of the applause, and perhaps a moment of silence before the nervous chatter began in the steam-heated foyer, outside of which the high-wheeled large cars were hooting and the electricity glittered in the winter evening of New York. The sour vulgarities of the reign of Coolidge notwithstanding, it was then that America sparkled at the top of the world.

John Lukacs, *Professor of History, Chestnut Hill College.*

THE DEPRESSION

What I'd like is twenty-four hours in New York City in the depths of the Depression. Say my birthday on May 9, 1932. I'd like to see the city with the brownstones before the glass towers came, the speakeasies, the multitude of newspapers, the smell of a nation in trouble beyond what we can imagine. I'd pop down to Whitehall Street to see recruiting officers in Sam Browne belts, I'd walk along East Side tenement streets thinking about what this real estate would be worth, one day. I'd listen to what they were saying about Hoover when he was President Hoover, not an evil spirit dragged up for political condemnation. I'm sure the food in most restaurants would be awful—at least that has improved in this half-century—but I'd like to be among people who dressed right, kept their dignity and their class—or so I imagine—and knew who they were and what they were. Give me that! Twenty-four hours only, though, please.

Gene Smith, *author.*

THE 1932 WORLD SERIES

Among the thousands of baseball games I would give an eyetooth to have seen was the third game of the 1932 World Series.

Little rode on the game itself: the New York Yankees, nearing the end of the Ruth-Gehrig era, would take four straight games from the Cubs, outscoring the Northenders 37 to 19. The august New Yorkers, winners of seven pennants in twelve years, disliked the Cubs for their tightfisted treatment of an ex-teammate, Mark Koenig; they hoped to humiliate them.

This was the setting for Babe Ruth's appearance at the plate in the fifth inning. The Wrigley Field faithful cheered encouragement to Cub pitcher Charlie Root. Ruth, belly advancing in front of his dainty feet, walked to the plate and dug into the lefthanders' batter's box. (I have a seat behind the third-base dugout with an unimpeded view of Ruth's round face.) One strike; then another.

Suddenly, according to popular account, Ruth pointed to the stands, predicting with his gesture a home run on the next pitch. Root's right-hand delivery met the thirty-seven-year-old Bambino's bat head on; the ball arced into the stands for a home run; Ruth had "called his shot"!

Is this true? Eyewitness accounts differ. Maybe Ruth had nothing so specific in mind. But what if he did? It would be a stunning achievement. As others have written, even *hitting* a major leaguer's pitched ball may be the single most difficult of all athletic feats. Home runs are another matter altogether. A fairly typical home-run champion of our own day might hit a home run every thirteen or fourteen official at bats—every fifteen plate appearances including bases on balls. In his entire career, Ruth averaged one home run every 14.6 plate appearances, in the 1932 season one every 14.3. So the odds against even the mighty Babe smacking one over the fence were too long for most betting men. What humiliation if he had struck out!

But did Babe Ruth worry about odds? If so, what bold defiance of the averages! My mind's eye sees an unmistakable, if casual, gesture, as though to say, "seven ball in the side pocket." Only those who have held both a pool cue and a Louisville Slugger in their hands can realize the monumental gap between calling for the one and calling for the other.

One of the greatest moments of bravado in our history, and I would have wanted to judge for myself what happened.

Robert L. Beisner, *Chairman, Department of History, American University.*

FDR THUNDERS

In 1936 I was a fourteen-year-old volunteer working at the Massachu-setts Democratic campaign headquarters in Springfield's Kimball Hotel; my immediate superior was nineteen-year-old Lawrence F. O'Brien. On the last day of October I wanted to hitchhike to New York and hear the President speak in Madison Square Garden, but Larry couldn't spare me, so I missed FDR's greatest political philippic. He had put up with a lot from the Republicans during that campaign. The voters had been told that he was a diseased tyrant out to destroy private property, the Constitution, even civilization itself; the chairman of the Republican Na-tional Committee had gone on the air to charge that under Social Secu-rity every American would be required to wear round his neck a steel dog tag ("like the one I'm now holding") stamped with his Social Security number. Until October 31 either Ray Moley or Louis Howe had been on hand to discourage or soften wrathful presidential replies, but they were elsewhere that Saturday evening, and if I could be passed back through a kind of time warp, I would like to be right by the platform as FDR entered the Garden.

Nearly fifteen minutes passed before he could say a word. The band was playing "Happy Days Are Here Again," and the sound of the audience—packed to the roof of the huge hall—was earsplitting. Roosevelt finally raised his arms, like a biblical patriarch, and a hush fell. He turned up that great organ of a voice, identifying his "old enemies": "Business and finan-cial monopoly, speculation, reckless banking, class antagonism," and "or-ganized money," adding "Government by organized money is just as dan-gerous as Government by organized mob." The crowd, on its feet through-out, ringing cowbells, howled its approval. In an edged voice he said: "Never before in all our history have these forces been so united against one candidate as they stand today. They are unanimous in their hate for me—and I welcome their hatred." *The New York Times* compared the ap-plause to "roars which rose and fell like the sound of waves pounding in the surf." The President declared: "I should like to have it said of my first Administration that in it the forces of selfishness met their match." Now his voice swelled: "I should like to have it said—." He had to pause, the ova-tion had begun; he raised his arms again and the din abated: "I should like to have it said of my second Administration that *in it these forces met their master*." The cheering surged and continued long after his departure.

Demagoguery? Of course. So were Tom Paine's pamphlets. So were Churchill's speeches in 1940. But imagine a President of the United States, who presided in our times, fighting the right adversaries on the right issues, using powerful language as a weapon to drive them into eternal

33

obscurity! Even the recollection of it makes you proud.
William Manchester, *Adjunct Professor of History and Writer-in-Residence, Wesleyan University.*

FDR AND LBJ

I would have enjoyed witnessing the private conversations between President Franklin D. Roosevelt and the young congressman from Texas, Lyndon Johnson.

There were a considerable number of these informal talks, and not merely because Roosevelt was fond of Johnson. In explaining the frequency with which the President would invite Johnson for breakfast chats (with the President sitting up in bed with a blue Navy cape around his shoulders) and to the Oval Office (Johnson had already set his sights on the White House, and one can only imagine his feelings during those conversations in that bright, sunny room in which he longed to sit in his own right), Roosevelt's aide James H. Rowe said: "You've got to remember that these were two great political geniuses," and that FDR could talk to LBJ on a level on which he could talk to few men. "A most remarkable young man," the President said shortly after he first met the twenty-eight-year-old congressman from the remote Texas hill country, and familiarity reinforced that opinion. Roosevelt not only told Harold Ickes that Johnson was "the kind of uninhibited young pro he would have liked to have been as a young man" (and might have been "if he hadn't gone to Harvard"), but added that "this boy could well be the first Southern President." To anyone interested as I am in the inner workings of politics, these talks between the President who was already such a master of the subject and the young man who was already known as "the wonder kid of politics" would have been fascinating. Lady Bird Johnson says that "every time" her husband came back from the White House, "he was on a sort of high." Listening to those conversations would have given me a high, too.

Robert A. Caro, *author.*

PEARL HARBOR

To witness Franklin D. Roosevelt—on the night of December 7, 1941, as the news came in. Who brought him the dispatches? How did he react? Whom did he turn to? Whom did he call? When did he begin to word his "day of infamy" speech? When did he find time to be alone, and think before they carried him up to bed?

Theodore H. White, *reporter, correspondent, and historian.*

THE NEWS REACHES CHURCHILL

The scene is not America, it is London. It is late evening of December 7, 1941, and Winston Churchill has just heard the news of Pearl Harbor. "So we had won after all," he said, "England would live, Britain would live; the Commonwealth and the Empire would live.... Once again in our long Island history we should emerge, however mauled or mutilated, safe and victorious we should not be wiped out. Our history would not come to an end. Hitler's fate was sealed, Mussolini's fate was sealed." The next day he went to the House of Commons to make the announcement. That is the scene I should most like to have been a part of, the address I should most like to have heard.

Listen to Churchill, and recall, as you do, that sonorous voice, the veritable voice of History and, as it turned out, the voice of Doom: "The enemy has attacked with an audacity which may spring from recklessness, but which may also spring from a conviction of strength. The ordeal to which the English-speaking world and our heroic Russian Allies are being exposed will certainly be hard.... Yet when we look around us over the sombre panorama of the world, we have no reason to doubt the justice of our cause or that our strength and will-power will be sufficient to sustain it. We have at least four fifths of the population of the globe upon our side. We are responsible for their safety and their future. In the past we have had a light which flickered, in the present we have a light which flames, and in the future there will be a light which shines over all the land and sea."

Henry Steele Commager, *Professor Emeritus and John W. Simpson Lecturer, Amherst College.*

THE BOMB

I would like to have witnessed the explosion at Alamogordo, on July 16, 1945, for at that moment the history of the past met the history of the future as the two had never met before. Science had then achieved its most visible and awful triumph. On that account, a knowledge of history became indispensable as the surest way in which men and women might learn to understand their limitations—though they have yet to do so —and might thereby prevent the extermination of life on this earth.

John Morton Blum, *Sterling Professor of History, Yale University.*

TRUMAN DEFEATS DEWEY

I would like to have been present on that post-election morning in 1948 when Harry S. Truman heard that he had won over the invincible Thomas Dewey.

I would love to have seen his face and heard his feisty remarks. His victory was so personal and so double-edged it proved how wrong we all were about the man. In the campaign he was underestimated and demeaned. We were oblivious to his nature, his strong characteristics. He refused to accept defeat, he came out fighting. He had faith in himself and his purpose, he ran a remarkable underdog campaign. He captured the imagination of America and pulled off one of the most amazing campaign upsets in American history. We should have learned from this victory never to underestimate this man again, this haberdasher from Independence, Missouri, who grew in the job and made the tough decisions at a time when our nation needed tough decisions.

Time is giving us a more constructive historical perspective of Harry Truman. Many of us are now cognizant of how wrong we were about him. I would love to have seen his face on the morning that was the beginning of his triumph and our future understanding of him.

Victor Gotbaum, *Executive Director, District Council 37, American Federation of State, County and Municipal Employees, AFL-CIO.*

RIDGWAY IN KOREA

On the Korean battlefield in the closing days of December 1950, there occurred the most remarkable display of leadership in the history of American arms—the resurrection of the 8th United States Army by its new commander, Lt. Gen. Matthew B. Ridgway.

It was an army defeated and demoralized by the unexpected intervention of Chinese Communist Forces that had sent it reeling back hundreds of miles in confusion and disarray. The situation was precarious, and the total evacuation of the Korean Peninsula was being seriously considered. But if the 8th Army was defeated, its new commander was not. Dismissing plans for further retreat, General Ridgway ordered the 8th Army to prepare the attack. Within days he had seized the moral initiative and begun to dominate the battlefield. Three months later, Seoul had been recaptured, and the Chinese and North Koreans pushed back across the South Korean frontier.

Fascinated with technology and with the weapons of war, we are liable to forget that at its most fundamental level, war is a contest of wills. A century and a half ago, that master military theoretician, Karl von Clausewitz, observed that in the face of battlefield disaster, "[all] gradually comes to rest on the commander's will alone. The ardor of his spirit must rekindle the flame of purpose in all others; his inward fire must revive their hope." General Ridgway did precisely that. In so doing, he serves as a constant reminder that human spirit, not weaponry, is the true foundation of our national security.

Col. Harry G. Summers, Jr., *author, faculty member of the Army War College.*

THE CIVIL RIGHTS ACT OF 1964

I would like to have watched Lyndon B. Johnson sign the Civil Rights Act of 1964. I make this choice because I was there—in spirit, at least. I have always been somewhat split between North and South, by parentage if not conviction. It happens that I was visiting Louisiana relatives that weekend, or whatever it was, that included July 4, 1964—the act was passed in June, but the actual signing took place July 2. On that day some of the relatives had taken me out yachting, and we were anchored at Pass Christian. Some people were talking about the civil rights workers who had disappeared. Somebody said they were probably buried a long way down in Mississippi soil. I was not sure if the speaker thought that good or bad: I was busy trying to make out the strange flags that were being flown by a lot of our neighbors.

"What's that?" I asked at last. "What's that funny flag on that launch over there?"

They scoffed at me. "It's the Confederate flag," they explained at last.

Then word came through on the radio about the signing.

Emily Hahn, *free-lance writer.*

NIXON'S LAST DAYS

My taste as to scenes which I would like to have witnessed varies from the morbid to the wonderful. Years ago I thought I would like to have been a fly on a wall of the bunker watching the last days and hours of the Third Reich, a terrible but engrossing sight. But no longer. For the last decade I have yielded entirely to the wish that I could have been there in the White House on that day when Richard Nixon decided to resign his Presidency and knelt with my old friend Henry Kissinger to pray. And how God, too, must have wondered!

John Kenneth Galbraith, *Powell M. Warburg Professor of Economics Emeritus, Harvard University.*

HOW TO WRITE HISTORY

By DIXON WECTER

When it's done properly, nothing *is better*

A chimpanzee with a stack of empty boxes and a banana hanging out of reach soon learns by his own experience. But man alone learns from the experience of others. History makes this possible. In the broadest sense all that we know is history. More strictly, it is the road map of the past. True, the terrain never repeats itself to the last detail, any more than does the ribbon of highway sweeping past a motorist. But the contours, with all their variations, give the alert observer knowledge about safe driving and, often, clues about what lies ahead, since resemblances of a general sort occur endlessly. The past is also a fascinating story for its own sake, shedding light upon the eternal behavior of human beings, singly and in the mass, adding richly to any reader's knowledge about himself and the world he lives in.

Some think of history as the process of accumulating bundles of facts, dates, statistics, for storage in some antiquarian's bin or scholar's cupboard. But it is a great deal more, namely, a review of the success and failure of man's life on this planet. History examines the rise and fall of nations and cultures, with their heroes and political leaders, and the often ragged record of mankind's experiments in living together through war and peace, its struggles for bread and leisure and faith, its germinal ideas and collective symbols.

History was once written and taught mainly as a tale of intrigue and bloodshed. In those days arose the old French proverb that "happy is a nation which has no history." By the light of a better definition this saying seems foolish. A cultural group, and indeed the whole human race, keeps its character precisely because it cherishes some remembrance of things past. Whether this memory is an ennobling one, say, the influence of the Lincoln tradition in American life, or a corrupting one such as the effect wrought by Bismarck upon the behavior of modern Germany, is another matter. At all events, the remembered past is a present and powerful thing for good or evil. Croce spoke truly when he said that all living history is contemporaneous.

What is "the past"? One of the most elastic ideas ever conceived by mind, it ranges from the remotest records left on earth down to the wake of the second hand as it sweeps around the dial. People who urge us to "live in the present" rarely weigh the literal meaning of their advice. "The present," that infinitesimal spark gone before we can photograph it on our brain, comes close to being an illusion. "The future" is still more impalpable since its content and impact upon us have not yet been registered. Beside these two concepts, "the past" seems curiously solid and real. It represents time and events met, realized, and built into the fabric of understood experience. Man is not only the sole creature able to learn from what happened to others, miles and centuries away, but also the only one capable of stretching the so-called present to its maximum. We do this unconsciously when talking about "the present day" or "the present generation." By just such an extension in time, all history that interests us and has something to tell us is living history.

Like other good things, history can be abused and misused. A dull narrator can make even its most meaningful chapters seem drab and unimaginative—an act of exhumation, followed by a grim inventory of the bones. Mr. Dooley once observed that "history is a post-mortem examination. It tells ye what a country died iv." Condescension toward the past is a graver mistake. For example, the darkness of what used to be termed the Dark Ages existed chiefly in the minds of the analysts.

History can also be abused by carelessness in handling the facts or a desire merely to make them sensational and shocking. Still worse, the muse called Clio can be sold down the river to become the handmaid of propaganda, brazenly perverting the truth. In a mood of cynicism Mark Twain once declared, "The very ink with which all history is written is merely fluid prejudice." To a history student forced to read between the party lines—the schoolchildren of Hitler's Reich or those under the Soviet Politburo—freedom to learn and reach one's own conclusions becomes just as impossible as to the student of sciences similarly debauched.

Yet history, along with kindred social studies like ethnology, anthropology, and sociology when honestly used helps enormously to splinter those barriers of prejudice and explode those lies which create hatred between races, sections, and national groups. Few indeed are the bigots and reactionaries found among true historians. Anybody setting out sympathetically to re-create the past can hardly help becoming less of a provincial himself, in both time and space. Among history's inescapable lessons, for example, are the folly of aggressive war, the stupidity of persecuting others because of their race or opinions, and the futility of trying to destroy the freedom of the mind.

The American record is not flawless, as we all know. The nation whose literature and history lack vigorous self-criticism is more apt to illustrate the suppression of free speech than the attainment of alleged perfection. But on the whole, from the Founding Fathers on, the American panorama is one we need not blush to own, one in which we may often take hearty pride. This is a history good citizens need to know, to understand their world and to be able to improve it. With our faith in majority government we see the importance of clearer self-knowledge for those expected to do the thinking and voting.

This need applies not only to the nation, but to each region and state with its especial traditions and interests. Yet masses of local records, letters, diaries, private papers, business archives, and old-timers' recollections are being lost year after year, by decay, fire, and death, all through simple ignorance. A friend of mine remembers an intelligent young woman in St. Joseph, Missouri, who after hearing a talk a couple of years ago on the centennial of the Hannibal & St. Joe Railroad—in which the speaker described its background of courage and hope as it battled great odds to become an important feeder into the frontier West—came up and told him, "I didn't know that was history. I didn't know the Midwest had a history. I thought history was Plymouth Rock and Bunker Hill."

Ignorance about what happened in our town, state, region, and country, as well as to our neighbors—in this age when all nations are neighbors—is bad citizenship in any policy-making democracy. So it has always been. But today, when we find ourselves the foremost champion of democracy in times of unprecedented physical power, such ignorance is not only shameful but dangerous.

And yet a century ago the reading of history was much more popular among educated people than it seems today. The school and college student used to get at least a smattering of Xenophon, Thucydides, Caesar, Livy, Plutarch, Tacitus, and then in his adult years, for pleasure, read not only Gibbon and Macaulay and Carlyle but our home-grown historians like Washington Irving, Prescott, Parkman—best sellers all. If the decline of Latin and Greek is responsible for ground lost on the former front, the blame for our retreat on the second sector lies gravely with those now writing American history.

For all its huge, able, often highly original output, the last half century of American research has yielded almost no great books worthy to stand as literature beside the classics of our first hundred years. Industry minus art, accumulation lacking charm, data without digestion—such shortcomings explain this popular allergy against American history as written. A great many school texts are pretty repulsive, while history for the adult seems hardly more inviting. After diligently harvesting the grain of fact, too few investigators seem to have time left for threshing out the chaff or milling the flour. Their energy is exhausted long before the job is done—so that readers have to choose between the pedant's dry straw and the half-baked loaf turned out by historical romancers.

How *not* to write history is the first question. Surely it need not be penned in the grand manner once the vogue. The Duc de Sully always put on court dress before sitting down to work on his memoirs, just as French surgeons in the day of Lisfranc used to garb themselves for a major operation in white tie and tails as befitted the august encounter between life and death. Edward Gibbon, though among the greatest of historians, often wearies modern readers with his massive style. The so-called father of American history, George Bancroft, had a hankering for resonant periods like "The pusillanimous man assents from cowardice, and recovers boldness with the assurance of impunity." The stilted-heroic in writing is now as much out of fashion as the equestrian statue.

Then came the scientific approach to history, which tightened up research methods, fostered thoroughness, and pruned away some of the flowers of rhetoric. Under the guidance of many German and a few British and American scholars who gloried in the epithet "colorless," historians began to think themselves successful when their writing grew chilly and impersonal. But it is well to remember that the pioneer of that tribe, the Prussian von Ranke, called history both a science and an art.

The writing of good history is just that. As a science it can make no compromise with the slipshod and false; as an art it must seize upon the durable and significant, firmly rejecting the rest. The doting antiquary, like the untaught Mohammedan, saves every scrap of paper blown his way by the wind because it might contain the sacred name of Allah. But the scholar of broad vision cannot shirk his job of selection. Horse sense, independence, and strict integrity are vital to the good writing of good history. Neither Chesterton and Belloc, on the extreme Catholic right, nor Bukharin and Tarle, on the Marxist left, are trustworthy guides through the mazes of the past. If the historian warps his evidence to fit some prejudice or preconceived pattern, he has failed us. The late Charles Beard came more and more to advocate the deliberate cultivation of "assumptions" by the historian, but applying his own counsels of defeat Beard declined steadily from front rank into the role of propagandist and ax-grinder. Trends in whitewashing or debunking come and go, but history written with a steady hand will outlast them all.

This doesn't mean that a good historian must be drained of individuality—a research automaton for dredging up facts and offering them to the public in a mechanical scoop. Nor does it require him to lack personal stability or a core of conviction about principles, like those whom Shaw has described as having minds so open there is nothing left but a draft.

If the author's saturation in his subject is so real that he develops affections and dislikes, his writing is sure to be more warm and vigorous than if he strikes the attitude of a biologist dissecting a frog. On a basis of sound inquiry and reasoned belief he should form those value judgments from which no historian worth his salt must flinch. We simply demand that he treat the material fairly, give an accounting for the generalizations he draws, and, while playing his thesis to win, never stack the cards. He cannot fabricate evidence—whether documents, conversations, or incidents. At this fork he parts company with the romancer. What the storied and spacious past needs is not invention but insight and interpretation.

Yet the field of current literature is thickly populated with burrowing scholars too indifferent to write well and with slick fictioneers too lazy to dig for themselves. Public taste naturally favors the latter, and so the historical romance stays entrenched atop the best-seller list year after year. The quality of such books is as variable as the barometer, usually rising in direct relation to their fidelity to sources. Thus, while Kenneth Roberts and Margaret Mitchell have mixed sound history and original research with their dramatic gifts, Heaven help those whose knowledge of the past depends upon Howard Fast or Taylor Caldwell.

If the professional historians see the flag of popular following wrenched from their grasp by the romancers, as I have said, they have largely themselves to blame. A great deal of the fault lies with the bloodlessness of so much academic writing—the traditions of dull competence that have grown up about the Ph.D. dissertation and the learned monograph. Instead of "wearing all that weight of learning lightly like a flower," in Tennyson's phrase, these savants wear it not a little pridefully like a ball and chain. This is not to disparage solid scholarship or belittle necessary toil over government documents, statistics, diaries, and all manner of dusty archives. Parkman and Prescott drudged too, before achieving a distillate of crystal clarity and palatable flavor.

Some years ago, before the illustrious heyday of Winston Churchill, George M. Trevelyan grumbled that history was no longer read widely because it had ceased to be written by "persons moving at large in the world of letters or politics" like his great-uncle Macaulay. It is perhaps too much to require the average historian to sit in Parliament or Congress or Cabinet, to plunge up to the neck in the civic activities of his time, travel all over the globe, steep himself in a dozen languages and cultures, or even write poetry and fiction as aids to his craftsmanship in the manner of Carl Sandburg. Any of these experiences, however, will enrich him. Think of those lively annalists of early Virginia, for instance, like Robert Beverley, William Byrd, and Thomas Jefferson—planters and men of affairs, business, and politics, who wrote all the better for the versatility of their lives. Or of the later historian-statesmen like Theodore Roosevelt, Albert J. Beveridge, and Woodrow Wilson.

Some of our best professionals have been the least sedentary. A zest for field work adds freshness, originality, and vigor to the sinews of writing—as instanced by Francis Parkman's journey over the Oregon Trail and sojourn among the Sioux; Douglas S. Freeman's patient exploration of every crater in the battlefields of northern Virginia; Samuel Eliot Morison's sailing with the Navy in the Second World War. Before writing *Admiral of the Ocean Sea* Morison navigated the Atlantic in a sailing boat comparable to the *Santa Maria*—in fact doing almost everything Columbus did except discover America. The feel of an ax or a rifle butt or fishing rod in the hand, a pack at the back, wind upon the face, salt air in the nostrils, are all good disciplines for the writing of history. An apt historian learns of the past through all his senses. I once met an eccentric spinster archaeologist who claimed that she could date any Roman aqueduct by the flavor on her tongue of its crumbling masonry—she had tasted them all.

Too often the savor of drama, the sense of reliving the past, the communicable thrill of a story to tell, is buried under the accretion of data. Yet history is inevitably dramatic. The very word comes from the same root as "story"; narration is of the essence. A sense of comedy has its place at the historian's elbow no less than tragedy. The re-creation of a dominant personality, or daily life of an era, or the power generated by its ideas, calls for exact knowledge fired by historical imagination. To say also that the chronicle of great events calls for a touch of poetry is not to call down upon us showers of cadenced prose and purple passages, beloved of the swashbucklers and patrioteers. It means that powers of symmetry, proportion, aesthetic design, controlled emotion, even a knack of playfulness, and at high moments a certain unforced eloquence can be summoned into the service of truth.

The artist's structural gift—not merely the lumping together of details to be hurled at the reader like a soggy snowball—yields writing that can be read with pleasure. The structure ought to be clean and firm, yet not obtruding the bones of its skeleton. Topic sentences should marshal the squadrons of argument along without seeming to be drillmasters. Passages spongy with the deadwood of jargon or encrusted with the barnacles of cliché, or ranging from the highbrow-recondite to the insultingly obvious, quotations herded in such droves as to suggest that the writer is too timid to speak for himself—these vices have no place on the pages of good history.

The best writing has been defined as the richest thoughts put into the simplest language. As applied to history, such discourse should resemble the easy, informal, but never careless talk of a well-educated man speaking to friends. To bore, to shout, to preach, to patronize, to grow flabbily garrulous, are all bad manners in society, that is, among intelligent readers who happen to be nonspecialists. A classroom full of students cannot choose but hear, but professors should never forget that the common reader finds it all too easy to shut his book or chuck the magazine into the wastebasket. The pretentious, the sentimental, and the flippant are prone to invite such treatment.

A good writer varies his pace to suit the mood and his reader's comfort. The crisp, clear statement is his staple. The staccato sentence belongs to the pulse of modern living, to journalism as well as the age of planes and high explosives, but it can be exaggerated just as surely as Clarendon and Hume and Montesquieu overworked the compound-complex sentence, geared to the era of Augustan Latinity, of oxcarts and sailing ships. Nevertheless, the best English and French historians of modern times give us models in writing that many an American might well imitate. These scholars overseas skillfully conceal the grubbing that laid their foundations, the scaffolding that made possible the walls—just as the bright Oxford undergraduate of my day "swotted" furiously over his books during the long vacation with no observers at hand, and returned in term-time to the unhurried career of a gentleman and sportsman. The one thing that a writer need *not* communicate is all the pain and toil that went into his finished product.

Nothing said here is meant to give aid and comfort to the elegant trifler with the Horace Walpole touch in historiography. His species has never rooted deeply in American soil. As a people we have always put such stress upon factual content, specialization, and accomplishment, as to turn the old Greek maxim "Know thyself" into the American vulgate as "Know thy stuff." Dilettantism has never been our besetting sin and needs no encouragement now.

But the historian who joins ripe learning to skill and charm in the telling commands the ear not only of the American public but also of the world—whose hunger for clarification among the welter of ideas in which we live made Spengler and H. G. Wells such phenomenal successes after the First World War, and Arnold Toynbee after the Second.

The historian who can write has a sobering responsibility. He is not only promised a wide and interested audience reading over his shoulder, but also assured that posterity will borrow many of its ideas from him, whether true or false. The reputation of Tiberius has been blackened for all time by the brilliant calumnies of Tacitus. Cromwell will always be a hero in shining armor to the devotees of Carlyle, and Warren Hastings a double-dyed villain to the thousands who still cherish their Macaulay. Two such diverse Presidents of the United States as Herbert Hoover and Franklin D. Roosevelt have been deeply concerned about the verdict of posterity—as evidenced, among other signs, by great libraries of their personal papers which they endowed supposedly to the end of time.

A readable historian of his own times will be accepted as the foremost witness par excellence, generation after generation. But by way of compensation, the historian who arrives on the scene long afterwards enjoys advantages too. Though a million details, important and unimportant, will be lost for lack of recording or proper preservation, the disclosure of diaries and secret archives, the fitting together of broken pieces from the mosaic, the settling of controversial dust and cooling of old feuds, and the broad perspective down the avenues of time, all make it possible for him to know an era in its grand design better than most men who lived through it.

To remind ourselves again of Croce's saying that all living history is contemporaneous, the recorders of that history—the writers who make it real for the largest number of people—are those who lend it the gift of immortality and the power to affect thoughts, emotions, and deeds centuries after the event.

—August 1957

"... AND THE MOUND BUILDERS VANISHED FROM THE EARTH"

By ROBERT SILVERBERG

What became of the prehistoric race that built such elaborate ceremonial mounds?
Nineteenth-century America had a romantic but self-serving answer.

To the early European settlers of North America, this land had one serious shortcoming: it lacked visible signs of a past. Egypt had her pyramids, England her Stonehenge, Greece her Acropolis; but those who came to this green New World failed to find those traces of awesome antiquity on which romantic myths could be founded. It was not cheering to feel that one was entering an empty land peopled only by naked, wandering savages. Mexico and South America had yielded stone temples and golden cities, but here in the north was, seemingly, a continent only of wood and plains, inhabited by simple huntsmen and equally simple sedentary farmers. Were there no grand, imagination-stirring symbols of vanished greatness? In all this mighty domain, was there nothing to compare with the antiquities of the Old World?

Men in search of a myth will usually find one, if they work at it. In the Thirteen Colonies the mythmakers had little raw material for their fantasies; but as the colonists gradually spread westward and southward they came upon mysterious and tantalizing earthen mounds. It was obvious that they were manmade relics of an earlier time. How were they to be interpreted?

The mounds lacked beauty and elegance, perhaps. They were mere heaps of earth. Some were of colossal size, like the Cahokia mound in Illinois, standing one hundred feet high and covering sixteen acres; others were mere blisters rising from the ground. Some stood in solitary grandeur above broad plains, while others sprouted in thick groups. All were overgrown with trees and shrubs, so that their outlines could barely be distinguished. Once cleared, the mounds revealed a regularity and symmetry of form. Within them were found evidences of former civilization: human bones, weapons, tools, jewelry.

The greatest concentration of mounds lay in the heart of the continent —in Ohio, Illinois, Indiana, and Missouri. There were subsidiary mound areas in western Tennessee and Kentucky, and nearly every major waterway of the Midwest was rimmed by clusters of them; there were also outlying mound zones from western New York to Nebraska. In the South, mounds lined the Gulf of Mexico from Florida to eastern Texas, and reached up through the Carolinas and across to Oklahoma. There were so many of them—ten thousand in the valley of the Ohio River alone— that they seemed surely to be the work of a vanished race which with incredible persistence had erected them in the course of hundreds or perhaps thousands of years, and then had disappeared from our land.

Why a vanished race?

Because the Indians of the Midwest, as the settlers found them, were sparse in number and limited in ambition; they were seminomadic savages who seemed incapable of the sustained effort needed to quarry and shape tons of earth. Nor did they have any traditions about the mounds; when questioned, they shrugged and spoke vaguely about ancient tribes.

The mounds naturally came under close scrutiny. By the early nineteenth century hundreds if not thousands of them had been examined, measured, and partly excavated. These early studies revealed a great variety of shape. Near the Great Lakes they tended to be gigantic effigies, in low relief, of birds, reptiles, beasts, or men—apparently of some sacred significance. These effigy mounds are most common in Wisconsin, although the best known is the Great Serpent mound in Ohio, an earthen snake twenty feet wide and a yard high that wriggles along for some 1,330 feet. In the Ohio Valley, the customary shape of a mound was conical, up to eighty or ninety feet in height; these usually contained tombs. Elsewhere, notably in the South, there were immense flat-topped mounds, truncated pyramids of earth, some terraced or having graded roadways leading to their summits. Mounds of this sort appeared to have been platforms for temples.

In addition to effigy mounds, burial mounds, and temple mounds, two types of embankments were seen, mainly in the Ohio-Indiana-Illinois-Missouri zone. On hilltops, huge "forts" covering many acres had been erected with formidable dirt walls. In lowland sites were found striking geometrical enclosures—octagons, circles, squares, ellipses—with walls five to thirty feet high surrounding plots of as much as two hundred acres. Running out from the enclosures often were parallel walls many miles long, forming great avenues.

From the beginning, antiquarians worked hard to explain the mounds.

Scholars ransacked history for evidence of ancient mound-building cultures and found it in Herodotus, in Homer, in the annals of Rome, in the Viking sagas; even in the Old Testament, which described how the Canaanites and Israelites had worshipped their deities in "high places"—surely, said the scholars, artificial mounds. The discovery of the American mounds opened the floodgates of speculation. If the Israelites had built mounds in the Holy Land, why not in Ohio? Learned men suggested that our land had been visited in antiquity by Hebrews, Greeks, Persians, Romans, Vikings, Hindus, Phoenicians—anyone, in short, who had ever built a mound in the Old World.

In this way was born a legend that dominated the American imagination throughout the nineteenth century. It was the myth of the Mound Builders, a lost race of diligent and gifted artisans who had passed across the scene in shadowed prehistory, ultimately to be exterminated by the treacherous, ignorant red-skinned savages who even now were causing so much trouble for the Christian settlers of the New World. The myth took root, flourished, grew mightily; men spun tales of lost kings and demolished cities; a new religion even sprang from the legends. What was the truth behind all this supposition?

Deserted and overgrown earthworks were found by the settlers who began to enter the Ohio Valley in the 1750s, and within two decades sporadic and tentative descriptions of them were appearing. In 1787 a contingent of New Englanders arrived in Ohio and founded a village they called Marietta. Shortly, accounts of the extensive Marietta earthworks were exciting eastern scholars. Ezra Stiles, the president of Yale, argued that they proved the descent of the Indians from Canaanites expelled from Palestine by Joshua. Benjamin Franklin, however, asserted that the Ohio mounds might have been constructed by Hernando de Soto in his wanderings. This contention was echoed by Noah Webster, although the lexicographer later abandoned the idea and credited the mounds to aborigines.

General Rufus Putnam, one of Marietta's founders, made a careful map of the earthworks there. One feature was an irregular square enclosure covering about forty acres and containing four truncated pyramids, the largest of them 188 feet by 132 feet at the base, and ten feet high. Other mounds lay nearby, and at right angles to the enclosure was an avenue 680 feet long, 150 feet wide, bordered by embankments eight to ten feet high. "This passage," wrote the archaeologist Ephraim George Squier in 1847, "may have been the grand avenue leading to the sacred plain above, through which assemblies and processions passed, in the solemn observances of a mysterious worship."

The founding fathers of Marietta ordered the most impressive of these mounds preserved as public parks, and they remain to this day. A clever Mariettan, the Reverend Manasseh Cutler, attempted in 1788 to compute the age of the mounds by counting the growth rings in the stumps of trees found on them; he calculated that the mounds had been erected no more recently than the early fourteenth century, and might well be over a thousand years old.

As the westward migration accelerated, interest in the mounds and their builders became intense—and theories of their origin multiplied. Benjamin Smith Barton, a Philadelphia naturalist, suggested in 1787 that they were Viking tombs; for it had been noticed that Norsemen had interred their lords in burial mounds not much different from those in Ohio. Barton went on to suggest that after their sojourn in Ohio the Vikings had moved along to Mexico, whose stone pyramids seemed to many like improved versions of the earthworks in the United States. Barton's fanciful notions contrasted with the more conservative ideas of another Philadelphian, the famed botanist William Bartram, who had taken a solitary jaunt through the mound country of the Southeast in 1773–77. Bartram examined dozens of mounds, such as the Ocmulgee group opposite the present city of Macon, Georgia, and Mount Royal on the St. Johns River in Florida. It seemed to him likely that some of the mounds were the work of the Creek and Cherokee Indians who still occupied the regions, and that others, the grandest, had been constructed by unknown predecessors. Yet when he queried the Cherokees he reported that they "are as ignorant as we are, by what people or for what purpose those artificial hills were raised." Still, at no point did Bartram postulate Vikings or other non-Indian transients as their builders; to his sober way of thinking, the mounds were probably the relics of some vanished Indian civilization. Thomas Jefferson, who not surprisingly was intensely interested in the mounds, was even more open-minded. "It is too early to form theories on those antiquities," he wrote in 1787. "We must wait with patience till more facts are collected."

Jefferson himself, a lifelong student of Indian lore, excavated a Virginia mound sometime prior to 1781 and published an account of his findings in his monograph *Notes on the State of Virginia* (1785). His archaeological technique was strikingly modern, giving careful attention to stratification and the position of artifacts; but he offered no imaginative explanations of the mound's purpose or origin.

Others were less hesitant, especially after the founding of such towns as Cincinnati, Manchester, Chillicothe, and Portsmouth brought a deluge of new data about the Ohio mounds. The English astronomer Francis Baily, accompanying a party of settlers down the Ohio in 1796, stopped to examine a group of mounds on what is today the West Virginia side of the river, and made the first recorded notice of the striking Grave Creek tumulus, which unknown pioneers had already discovered and partly excavated. The mounds, Baily wrote, must have been "built by a race of people more enlightened than the present Indians, and at some period of time very far distant." This viewpoint was to be prevalent in the controversy that raged over the mounds for the next hundred years.

Identifying the vanished race became a popular scholarly pastime. The Ten Lost Tribes of Israel, of whom nothing had been heard since the conquest of Jerusalem by the Assyrians in 722 B.C., were a favorite choice. Many accounts appeared of the Hebrew migration to the Americas, listing dates of arrival, routes taken by specific tribes, and the mounds erected by each. There was no shortage of other ideas, however. Caleb Atwater, an Ohio postmaster who was the first to carry out an extensive archaeological study of the mounds, cited the presence of Old World mounds from Wales to Russia, and brought the Mound Builders to America via Asia, the Bering Strait, and Alaska. Writing in 1820, Atwater provided parallels between the cultures of India and ancient Ohio to prove his point: "The temples, altars, and sacred places of the Hindoos were always situated on the bank of some stream of water. The same observation applies to the temples, altars, and sacred places of those who erected our tumuli." The migration had occurred long ago, he says—"as early as the days of Abraham and Lot," maybe—judging by "the rude state of many of the arts among them." After building the humble earthen heaps in Ohio, though, the Mound Builders had begun gradually to move south, gaining in skill all the while, until they reached Mexico. This can be seen in the line of mounds that, Atwater says, "continue all the way into Mexico, increasing indeed in size, number, and grandeur, but preserving the same forms."

In comparison with some of his contemporaries, Atwater was a model of controlled, judicious thought. Among the fantasists was William Henry Harrison, who had first seen the mound country as a young officer fighting against the Ohio Indians in 1791. Some thirty years later, as a retired United States senator not yet thinking of the White House, Harrison produced a romantic analysis of the Mound Builders, imagining stirring battles, sweeping migrations of tribes, mighty hosts of enlightened beings streaming through the heartland of what one day would be the United States. He wrote: "We learn first, from the extensive country covered by their remains, that they were a numerous people. Secondly, that they were congregated in considerable cities. . . . Thirdly, that they were essentially an agricultural people; because, collected as they were in great numbers, they could have depended on the chase but for a small portion of their subsistence."

He imagined "that they were compelled to fly from a more numerous or a more gallant people," abandoning their great settlements. As for the hilltop fortifications, "it was here that a feeble band was collected . . . to make a last effort for the country of their birth, the ashes of their ancestors, and the altars of their gods. . . ."

Such vivid depictions caught the public fancy, and other "historians" were soon profiting from the fad. In 1833 a journalist named Josiah Priest published an elaborate explanation of the mounds in a jumbled volume, *American Antiquities*. It was a best seller: some 22,000 copies were bought in thirty months.

The speculative ferment over the mounds naturally had its impact on the imaginations of poets and novelists. The first domestic treatment of the subject in verse seems to have been "The Genius of Oblivion," published in 1823 by the New Hampshire poet Sarah J. Hale. Her thesis was that the Mound Builders were refugees from the Phoenician city of Tyre, who fled to America. In "Thanatopsis," the poem that established his reputation in 1817 when he was only twenty-three, William Cullen Bryant spoke of the ancient race of men interred in "one mighty sepulchre" among "the hills rock-ribbed and ancient as the sun." Fifteen years later, in "The Prairies," he was moved by a visit to the mound country to evoke "the dead of other days" and "the mighty mounds that overlook the river."

>   . . . A race, that long has passed away,
> Built them;—a disciplined and populous race
> Heaped, with long toil, the earth. . . .
>   . . . The red men came—
> The roaming hunter tribes, warlike and fierce,
> And the mound-builders vanished from the earth. . . .
>   . . . The gopher mines the ground
> Where stood the swarming cities. All is gone;
> All—save the piles of earth that hold their bones,
> The platforms where they worshipped unknown gods. . . .

Novelists, too, heeded the appeal of the mounds, and for a while the genre of Mound Builder fiction was an active subbranch of American popular literature. A typical specimen is Cornelius Matthews's *Behemoth: A Legend of the Mound-Builder* (1839), which described the efforts of the Mound Builders to cope with a mammoth of supernatural size and strength that rampaged through their cities until slain by a hero named Bokulla.

Such fictions were avidly consumed by a New York farm boy named Joseph Smith, who was to found a major religion with tenets based on the Mound Builder tales. Born in 1805, Smith as a boy was given to experiencing religious visions, and also to speculating on the origin of the mounds. His mother later recalled: "He would describe the ancient inhabitants of this continent, their dress, mode of travelling, and the animals upon which they rode; their cities, their buildings, with every particular; their mode of warfare; and also their religious worship. This he would do with as much ease, seemingly, as if he had spent his whole life with them."

In 1823, Smith declared, an angel named Moroni came to him at night and showed him a book written on golden plates, which he could find buried in a hillside near Palmyra, New York. Four years later he began, with divine aid, to translate the plates, and by 1830 he produced the 588-page Book of Mormon.

The Book of Mormon, which inspired a religious movement that endured vicious persecution, the martyrdom of its leaders, and the official opposition of the United States government, reveals that Joseph Smith had carefully studied the Mound Builder legends. Owing much in style to the King James Bible, and deriving many of its themes from the Old Testament, it tells how, about 600 B.C., a party of Israelites escapes from Jerusalem just prior to its destruction by Nebuchadnezzar. Through God's guidance they cross the ocean to America, where they prosper and multiply, building mighty cities and great mounds and surrounding them with huge fortifications. But they split into two factions, the Nephites and the Lamanites. The Nephites till the land and become rich, but the Lamanites are ungodly, and sink into savagery. To punish them, God turns their skins red. They are, in fact, the ancestors of the American Indians. The Nephites, too, grow corrupt, backsliding into idolatry, and God, angered by their sins, sends the Lamanites to destroy them. In a climactic battle in A.D. 401 the last of the Nephites are engulfed by the red-skinned barbarians; one priest survives to compile the record on golden plates, which he buries and which remain hidden until discovered and translated by Smith.

By some two million Americans today The Book of Mormon is regarded in the same light as the Gospels or the Five Books of Moses. To their critics, however, Mormon beliefs are merely amusing fantasies, and the sacred Book of Mormon itself is just another literary expression of the Mound Builder mythology.

In the middle years of the nineteenth century came a reaction against the more extravagant expressions of the lost-race myth. New archaeological research helped to foster this cooler attitude. Abelard Tomlinson, a member of the family that owned the property on which the vast Grave Creek mound stands in what is now West Virginia, excavated it in 1838. Sinking a seventy-seven-foot shaft, he found a stone-covered log-walled chamber that enclosed a skeleton decorated with a profusion of copper rings, shell beads, and mica plates. The Grave Creek artifacts were examined by Henry Rowe Schoolcraft, one of the great early figures of American anthropology, who pondered the problem of the mounds and in 1851 concluded: "There is little to sustain a belief that these ancient works are due to tribes of more fixed and exalted traits of civilization, far less to a people of an expatriated type of civilization, of either an ASIATIC OR EUROPEAN origin, as several popular writers very vaguely, and with little severity of investigation, imagined. . . . There is nothing, indeed, in the magnitude and structure of our western mounds which a semi-hunter and semi-agricultural population, like that which may be ascribed to the ancestors of Indian predecessors of the existing race, could not have executed."

Schoolcraft was a generation ahead of his time. Americans, scholarly and otherwise, ignored his strictures and continued to relish the fantasies of a departed civilization.

Ephraim Squier produced his era's definitive study of the Mound Builders in 1847: *Ancient Monuments of the Mississippi Valley*, a ponderous folio written in collaboration with an Ohio physician, Edwin H. Davis, and published by the newly founded Smithsonian Institution. Their book instantly established itself as a work of commanding importance in American archaeology. As a summary of the knowledge of its particular field at that time, it was remarkable; as a model for later workers, it was invaluable; as a detailed record of the Ohio mounds as they appeared about 1847, it was unique. Squier and Davis described, classified, and analyzed hundreds of mounds, suggested varying purposes for them, and provided detailed charts so accurate and attractive that blowups of them are posted today at many of the surviving Ohio earthworks. Yet Squier and Davis adhered to the lost-race theory. Any visitor to the mounds, they wrote, must surely come away impressed by the "judgment, skill, and industry of their builders. . . . a degree of knowledge much superior to that known to have been possessed by the hunter tribes of North America previous to their discovery by Columbus, or indeed subsequent to that event." The handsome tools, weapons, and pottery excavated from mounds, the vigorous pipes carved in animal forms, and other finely wrought Mound Builder relics called forth from them the judgment that "as works of art they are immeasurably beyond anything which the North American Indians are known to produce, even at this day, with all the suggestions of European art and the advantages afforded by steel instruments." It was an accurate observation, but it led the scholars to mistaken inferences.

The modern era in archaeology was now beginning. The cities of Egypt and Assyria were being exhumed; the Neanderthal skull had been found, transforming man's view of his past; Heinrich Schliemann was planning his excavation of Troy. In the United States some archaeologists continued to revolve the Israelite, Viking, and Mexican theories of the Mound Builders' origin; others introduced the exciting theory that they were survivors of the lost island Atlantis; and still others began to search for a more rational explanation of the earthen monuments. To most, the existence of the Mound Builders as a distinct, ancient, and vanished race still looked like the most probable alternative, especially after certain pipes in the form of elephant effigies turned up near Davenport, Iowa. It was generally agreed that the mammoths and other American elephants had died out thousands of years ago; and if elephant effigies were being uncovered in mounds, did that not prove the great antiquity of the Mound Builders? The voices of those who ascribed the mounds to the ancestors of recent Indian tribesmen were drowned out.

But then a new voice was heard through the land: that of John Wesley Powell, the one-armed Civil War veteran best known for his 1869 journey down the turbulent Colorado River. He had become, ten years later, the founder of the Smithsonian Institution's Bureau of Ethnology. With great eloquence and passion Powell had called for such a department to study the North American Indians. He did not at first intend that his department should do any archaeological work; he planned only to survey the languages, arts, institutions, and mythologies of extant tribes. But in 1881 a group of archaeologists quietly lobbied behind Powell's back and got Congress to tack an extra five thousand dollars to the Bureau of Ethnology's budget for "continuing archaeological investigation relating to moundbuilders and prehistoric mounds."

Powell was not pleased, for he did not have funds enough even to do the ethnological work as he thought proper; but he obeyed Congress's behest, and set up a division within the bureau to investigate the mounds. He himself had done some mound digging in the Midwest from 1858 to 1860, and had found glass, iron, and copper artifacts in them that seemed plainly to have been acquired from white men. This led him to the conclusion that some of the mounds "were constructed subsequent to the advent of the white man on this continent." Since Congress had mandated a mound examination, Powell decided to use the opportunity to check his own theories. Late in 1881 he picked Cyrus Thomas, an Illinois-born entomologist, botanist, and archaeologist, to take charge of the bureau's mound explorations. When Thomas came to the Bureau of Ethnology he was, he said, a "pronounced believer in the existence of a race of Mound Builders, distinct from the American Indians." Powell gave him one clerical assistant and three field assistants and told them to draw up a plan for a mound survey. The slayer of the myth was at hand, whether he himself knew it or not.

As Thomas laid his plans, another Bureau of Ethnology staff member,

Henry W. Henshaw, fired the opening salvo of the campaign in the bureau's second annual report, published in 1883. Henshaw took out after Squier and Davis, though paying homage to their "skill and zeal" and to "the ability and fidelity which mark the presentation of their results to the public." He punctured certain erroneous zoological conclusions that they had drawn from animal-effigy pipes, which to them seemed to indicate Mound Builder commerce with South America and Africa. Then he turned on the famous elephant effigies "found" in Iowa, pronouncing them clumsy fakes. This drew outraged cries from the Davenport Academy of Natural Sciences in Iowa, which had sponsored the discovery of the elephant pipes and resented the "intemperate zeal" of the Bureau of Ethnology, which from its "commanding position . . . in the world of science" had chosen to deliver "an attack of no ordinary severity . . . upon the Davenport Academy of Natural Sciences."

While Henshaw battled with the Iowans over the authenticity of the elephant pipes, Thomas and his assistants roamed the Midwest and Southeast, collecting thousands of artifacts from mounds, including a good many of European manufacture, such as silver bracelets and crosses and specimens of machine-worked copper. All this served to reinforce Powell's original conviction that " . . . a few, at least, of the important mounds of the valley of the Mississippi had been constructed and used subsequent to the occupation of the continent by Europeans, and that some, at least, of the mound builders were therefore none other than known Indian tribes."

Thomas's first formal theoretical statement on the mounds occupied more than a hundred pages of the Bureau of Ethnology's fifth annual report, released in 1887. Though he stated again and again that his conclusions were preliminary, Thomas's agreement with the Powell position was evident on every page. He opposed the "lost race" theory, and said: " . . . whether the 'Indian theory' proves to be correct or not, I wish to obtain for it at least a fair consideration. I believe the latter theory to be the correct one, as the facts so far ascertained appear to point in that direction, but I am not wedded to it; on the contrary, I am willing to follow the facts wherever they lead."

Thomas conceded that the picture of a mighty nation occupying the great valley of the Mississippi, with a chief ruler, a system of government, a vast central city, was "fascinating and attractive." He saw the romance in the image of the disappearance of this nation "before the inroads of savage hordes, leaving behind it no evidence of its existence, its glory, power, and extent save these silent forest-covered remains." But he warned that this theory, when once it has taken possession of the mind, "warps and biases all its conclusions."

After publishing several subsequent shorter reports, Thomas settled down to the production of his magnum opus: the massive essay, covering 730 quarto pages of small type, that fills the whole of the Bureau of Ethnology's twelfth annual report (1894). Here the Mound Builder myth was interred at last beneath a monument of facts. The heart of the report, covering nearly 500 pages, was simply a digest of field research, interspersed only occasionally with quotations from early explorers or with Thomas's interpretative conjectures. This was followed by an essay of some eighty pages on the types and distribution of mounds, showing with considerable force and skill the implausibility of assigning all the earthworks to a single "race." Lastly, Thomas reviewed the entire mound problem as it had unfolded since the eighteenth century, dealing in turn with each of the theories he was overthrowing. He deflated the lost-race fantasy with vigor and conviction. His basic conclusion, vital to any comprehension of American prehistory, was cool and rational: "The moundbuilders were divided into different tribes and peoples, which, though occupying much the same position in the culture scale, and hence resembling each other in many of their habits, customs, and modes of life, were as widely separated in regard to their ethnic relations and languages as the Indian tribes when first encountered by the white race."

That statement needed refining—for actually the various mound-building groups did not occupy "much the same position in the culture scale." But it went to the essential truth of the situation: the archaeologists, as they sought to unravel the mystery of the mounds, had to be prepared to deal with diversity, not unity. Thomas's great report marked the end of an era. No longer could one speak of "the Mound Builders" in quite the same way, with the old implications of a single empire. But Thomas had raised as many questions as he had answered. It remained for archaeologists to examine the contents of the mounds more closely, to analyze the cultural traits of their builders, to study relationships—in short, to develop a coherent picture of the ancient American past.

That picture has largely come clear today, though all the problems are far from solved. In place of a monolithic race of Mound Builders, archaeologists have identified a succession of mound-building cultures spanning several thousand years. Careful excavation, comparison of artifacts and structural techniques, and use of such modern archaeological methods as carbon-14 dating have served to replace the old myth with reasonably certain scientific conclusions. Skeletal and cultural evidence shows clear kinship between the builders of the mounds and their less advanced neighbors and successors.

The pioneers of the earthworks were the Adena people, named from the estate near Chillicothe, Ohio, where their characteristic artifacts were first identified. The Adena culture, it appears, took form about 1000 B.C., and was typified by the burial of the dead in log-walled tombs beneath conical earthen mounds. One archaeological faction holds that the Adenas were migrants from Mexico, carrying with them cultural traits superior to those of the Ohio valley where they settled; a more recent thesis makes them indigenous to the Northeast and the lower Great Lakes area. The Grave Creek mound in West Virginia, the largest conical mound in the United States, is Adena work, as is Ohio's Great Serpent mound.

About 400 B.C., apparently, a new group of Indians entered Adena territory: the Hopewells, named for a site in Ross County, Ohio, considered typical of their culture. These people were long-headed, unlike the round-headed Adenas, and they brought with them to Ohio an elaborate way of life that flowered wonderfully after the collision, peaceful or otherwise, with the Adenas. The Hopewell folk were, in effect, the Mound Builders of whom the nineteenth-century mythmakers dreamed. Although neither Phoenician nor Hindu nor Viking but merely American Indians out of the eastern woodlands, they did fill many of the qualifications of that phantom race of superior beings to whom the Ohio mounds had so often been attributed. They extended their influence out of southern Ohio into Indiana and Illinois and southeastern Iowa, northward to Wisconsin and Michigan, southward down the Mississippi past St. Louis. They evolved a complex funereal ritual including the erection of groups of conical mounds to house their dead notables; and they buried in the mounds a wealth of fine goods manufactured from exotic raw materials obtained through trade from such distant points as the Gulf coast and the Southwest.

Most of the mounds and earthworks that can be seen in Ohio today were made by the Hopewells. The most awesome, perhaps, is the great enclosure at Newark, which once covered four square miles. Only fragments remain: a joined circle and octagon, another circular enclosure, and some parallel walls. Though these structures are in part incorporated in a municipal golf course, they retain their majesty and splendor. From Hopewell mounds have come jewelry of bone, shell, and stone, breastplates and headdresses of copper, and ornaments cut from sheets of glittering mica. The abundance and high artistic quality of these burial goods mark the vitality and imagination of this remarkable culture. A strong Mexican influence is present in much Hopewell art, leading even the most conservative archaeologists to trace a flow of ideas out of Mexico and up the Mississippi to Ohio.

The end of the Hopewells came about A.D. 550, perhaps even earlier. They ceased to build their great ceremonial centers, and in another two centuries their distinctive way of life had disappeared, their territory was depopulated, and the people themselves had been absorbed into humbler tribes. We do not know why. "Cultural fatigue" has been suggested; a change of climate, perhaps; civil war; even that old standby, invasion by savages. There are indeed indications that toward the end the Hopewells took to the hills and tried to hold out behind high earthen walls. It was in vain; the forest closed over their mounds, and simpler folk took possession of their domain. Within a few generations, the newcomers had forgotten whatever they knew about the Hopewells. So mythical Mound Builders of non-Indian blood had to be invented by the white man, and fabulous tales woven about them, while outraged Hopewell spectres glowered in silent fury.

Long after the Hopewell collapse, the mound idea burst forth again in the Southeast, in a quite different form. Once again great ceremonial centers were erected; once more an elaborate social system came into being; there were developments in art and technology that rivaled and often exceeded Hopewell at its finest. The new mounds, however, were flat-topped platforms on which wooden temples, not burial structures, rose. These earthen pyramids, eighty to one hundred feet high and covering acres of ground, appeared first in Alabama, Georgia, and the rest of the Gulf coast states, and spread as far west as Texas and as far north as Illinois. By A.D. 900 most Indian tribes living along the Mississippi and its major tributaries knew something about the gospel of the platform-mound religion, and within another three centuries a chain of major ceremonial centers stretched across the continent from Oklahoma to Alabama. The Temple Mound people were agriculturalists, apparently far more skillful farmers than the Hopewells; we have found their hoes, made of stone, shell, or the shoulder blades of animals, and even the traces of their fields. They made excellent jewelry and pottery which shows obvious influence from the arts and crafts of Mexico, and their giant mounds, too, seem earthen imitations of Mexico's truncated pyramids.

Their culture flourished and expanded for hundreds of years, reaching a strange climax about 1500 with the development of the so-called Southern Cult, a religious movement typified by grotesque decorative styles employing figures of buzzards and snakes, flying horned serpents, weeping eyes, skulls, and eerie faces. The appearance of this cult has been explained as a shock reaction springing from the bloody and disastrous invasion of de Soto and his Spaniards in 1539–43, but recent research has shown that it antedates de Soto, and may have been an expression of vitality rather than terror, its symbols representing harvest and renewal rather than death and nightmare.

But by the end of the sixteenth century the Temple Mound culture was in decay, and its important centers—Cahokia in Illinois, Etowah in Georgia, Spiro in Oklahoma, Moundville in Alabama, and others—were abandoned.

They were already in decline when the white man appeared, and they withered at his touch. The ancient customs lingered, reduced and diluted; about the huge mounds of revered ancestors the familiar rituals and festivals continued, but in a mechanical, ever less meaningful way, until their inner nature was forgotten and their practitioners could no longer remember that it was their own great-great-grandfathers who had built the mounds. The Creek, Chickasaw, and Choctaw Indians who occupied the Southeast when the Europeans came were in all likelihood the unknowing descendants of the Temple Mound folk. But only the Natchez Indians maintained their old ways into the eighteenth century, when the French destroyed their culture.

Archaeologists today, having disposed of the Mound Builder legend, busily search for detailed knowledge of the development, decline, and possible relationships of the Adena, Hopewell, and Temple Mound people, reducing romance to a complex series of phases, aspects, and cultural traditions. They smile at the fancies of yesteryear. Some of the mounds remain, celebrated locally as tourist attractions; and it is difficult now to comprehend the intensity of interest they provoked a century and more ago, or to grasp the deeper motives that led so many to believe that they were the work of superior beings hidden in the mists of time. Yet there is magic in the mounds now, despite the labors of those who have shown us why we must not talk of a nation of Mound Builders. Looking at these mysterious grassy monuments, one succumbs easily to fantasy, and feels the presence of the ghosts of departed grandeur; and then, in warm understanding, one reaches out across the decades to the makers of the Mound Builder myth.

—June 1969

THE HUNT FOR THE REGICIDES

By ALEXANDER WINSTON

They had sent King Charles to the scaffold, but the Commonwealth they proclaimed had failed. Now they were fugitives in New England with a big price on their heads.

The death warrant was signed on Monday, and the business was then pushed with all haste. At ten o'clock on Tuesday morning—it was January 30, 1649—Captain Hacker brought King Charles out of St. James' Palace. The air was still and very cold—ice was piled up under the Thames bridges. Charles walked briskly, urging his guard to be quick: "March apace!" To the solemn muted roll of drums he crossed the park between lines of soldiers and entered Whitehall. The crowd that had streamed in from all over London shivered in the streets, packed tight as pebbles on a beach. About two o'clock Hacker, who was observed to have been seized with trembling, escorted the King along the corridors of Whitehall Palace and through a dismantled window of the banqueting hall directly onto the broad, black-draped scaffold. There, at last, Charles saw the block with its iron staples and tackle, the close ranks of soldiery, the masked headsmen grotesque in false grizzled beards and wigs. With composure, the King made a short speech, and then, handing his "George" (a jeweled collar from which hung a pendant of St. George slaying the dragon) to Bishop William Juxon with the one word, "Remember!" he pushed his hair up under a white satin cap and lay down to the block. The axe glinted: a shudder ran through the crowd and a vast groan echoed up the streets. In that instant the fifty-nine signers of the death warrant became regicides.

Their lives would never be the same again. For the next decade they struggled to make a success of the Commonwealth government and, failing, watched in despair the Stuart Restoration of 1660. At the return of Charles II, regicides who had had the good fortune to die in peace during the Commonwealth were condemned posthumously, their bodies exhumed and abused, and their heirs' property confiscated. Of the living, twenty-four vanished into royal dungeons or were executed with the cruelty reserved for traitors; a mere dozen escaped abroad. The three who fled to the American colonies have written a dramatic page in our history.

Among those who dared to kill a king on that fateful day in 1649 were Edward Whalley, William Goffe, and John Dixwell. In the gray, strenuous world of the Puritan revolt they were mighty men, deeply committed to an astringent and demanding faith, and strong in the conviction that the political cause for which they fought was just. As they saw it, Charles Stuart had threatened their political and religious liberties from the moment that he ascended the throne in 1625. Dissolving stubborn Parliaments, ruling by council and decree, levying new taxes to pay for his disastrous misadventures on the Continent, Charles had alienated all defenders of parliamentary rights. Further, his attempt to force the Prayer Book on the churches had raised cries of popery from Puritans. The Calvinistic Scots revolted. With King, nobles, and church leagued against Parliament and people, the issue was joined beyond conciliation; only arms would settle it. Charles had raised his standard at Nottingham in August of 1642.

Whalley, Oliver Cromwell's cousin, had thrown himself into the civil war at the first rattle of sabers. With the zealot's eye he saw the King as a traducer of liberties, and the established church as Roman Catholicism in disguise. Essentially he was a soldier, but like many men in an era when the rawest recruit argued theology and politics over the campfire, he was up to his elbows in affairs of state; and he was appointed one of the 135 members of the special High Court of Justice that tried the King. About half of those appointed never attended, but Whalley missed only one session of the Court and stood up to vote for the execution. He was among the fifty-nine signers of the death warrant, writing his name in fourth place, immediately after the bold, fierce signature of Oliver Cromwell.

William Goffe had married Whalley's only daughter, Frances. His career paralleled that of his father-in-law, and their lives were knit to the end. An able soldier, a frequent "prayer-maker, preacher and presser for righteousness and freedom," he attended a meeting of officers gathered for mutual counsel on the fate of the King and spoke with such fervor, and invoked God's wrath on Charles with such eloquence, that tears flowed. Goffe voted for the execution and signed the warrant in fourteenth place.

Compared to Whalley and Goffe, Dixwell was a quiet one. His ability to vanish into the wainscoting was to serve him well in his later years as a fugitive. He sat in three Parliaments and was twice a member of the

Council of State, a position that he held at the time of the King's trial. Never distinguished as a soldier, he was commissioned as colonel of a Kentish troop after the fighting was over. There is evidence, taken from the trials of the regicides in 1660, that Dixwell was less than enthusiastic about the condemnation of Charles. However, he attended the sessions regularly and signed the warrant thirty-eighth, in a precise, clerical hand.

Cromwell's Commonwealth gained for English power abroad a prestige unknown since Elizabeth, but at home it was less successful. Cromwell found it necessary to dismiss the House of Commons as willfully as Charles had done. After 1655 he governed through major generals (among them Whalley and Goffe), each commanding a district. They quelled sporadic Royalist uprisings, raised money from reluctant lords, and imposed their Puritan habits on the whole population. England sickened of drab morality and army rule. The dissident factions held together by Cromwell's strong mixture of God and gunpowder split apart at his death in 1658, and his son, the amiable Richard, had neither the wit nor the will to control them. During the spring of 1660 the Great Experiment staggered to its ruin.

In that year General George Monk, who had been Oliver Cromwell's trusted lieutenant in Scotland, marched his troops into London, declaring for a free Parliament. From his listening post in the Dutch fortress-city of Breda, wily Charles Stuart, son of the dead king, issued an intention of general amnesty (except for those whom the new Parliament might choose to single out) should he return to the throne. In early May the new Parliament proclaimed Charles king and immediately buckled down to the vengeful business of making exceptions to those covered by the general amnesty. It was a time to flee.

Dixwell waited until Parliament named him specifically as unpardonable. Then, sending word that he was ill and could not surrender until he recovered, he slipped across the Channel and eventually found his way to the prosperous town of Hanau in Prussia. No further word is heard of him until his appearance in the New England colonies five years later. Whalley and Goffe risked no such delay. On May 4, 1660, a few days before Charles was formally proclaimed king, they kissed their families good-bye and took horse for Gravesend, where passage awaited them on the *Prudent Mary*, bound for Boston. In the streets of Gravesend, they watched with bitterness the proclamation of the restored monarchy. Goffe wrote in his journal that "there was much rejoicing among the people, but God's people lamented over the great profaneness with which that joy was expressed." He added darkly, "It was observed that many dogs did that day run mad: and died suddenly in the town."

On boarding the ship, Whalley and Goffe assumed the names of Edward Richardson and William Stephenson. But they were unused to slinking in a corner and had no regrets for their part in the King's death. They did little to conceal their identity from such sympathetic fellow passengers as Captain Daniel Gookin, a prominent member of the Massachusetts Bay Colony, and William Jones of the New Haven Colony, whose wife was the daughter of one of the colony's leading citizens. On the morning of July 27 they looked confidently upon the scattered roofs of Boston beside the sunlit channel of the Charles.

The fugitives had some reason for their confidence. Most of the New England colonists had felt, in one way or another, the heel of bishop and king. On this far continent, an ocean away from England, they were continuing the Puritan theocracy which had collapsed at home. England might persuade them but in the end could not coerce them. They were already masters of evasion and delay when orders from the mother country were not to their liking; if Charles was on the throne, let him say so; until then they would follow their natural sympathies. It was no wonder that Governor John Endecott warmly embraced the newcomers, expressing hope that more men of their distinction would lend strength to the colonies.

On the day of their arrival Whalley and Goffe went four miles upriver to Cambridge as guests of Captain Gookin. There they lived openly, their identities well known. "Colonels Whalley and Goffe were entertained by the magistrates with great solemnity, and feasted in every place, after they were told that they were traitors, and ought to be apprehended," grumbled a Royalist report to England. John Crowne, a Royalist (he later returned to England and became a famous Restoration playwright), said that the regicides "were treated like men dropped down from heaven."

They may have felt that way. At the Cambridge church Goffe handed to the minister a piece of paper extolling God's mercy to them in their many dangers (including the voyage over "the great deeps") and asking him to offer praise to God in their behalf during prayers.

In the tranquil New England summer, they supped with the Reverend Charles Chauncy, president of Harvard College, and made calls in some of the surrounding towns. The general opinion was that they were sober, righteous, and godly men. (Present-day America offers no parallel to this reception: but imagine, by way of very rough analogy, that John Wilkes Booth escaped safely to Virginia, to be warmly greeted by Jefferson Davis, prayed over in Richmond churches, and sumptuously dined by the president of William and Mary College.)

It was too idyllic to last. While Whalley and Goffe were in Boston to attend a lecture, a newcomer off a Scottish ship insulted them in the streets (the authorities told him to mind his manners or get out of town), and the same ship brought news that all former members of the High Court that had condemned King Charles I were liable to arrest and confiscation of property. It is a measure of colonial opinion that, even then, no one moved to seize Whalley and Goffe; to the contrary, when a violent Royalist named Thomas Breedon complained that the colony was housing traitors, Endecott replied firmly that he would not "meddle with them" without an executive order; and the marshal general, whose duty it was to arrest them, grinned in Breedon's face and taunted him to "speak against Whalley and Goffe if you dare, if you dare!"

This was bold talk for English subjects on English soil. Toward the end of November a ship brought the final Act of Pardon and Oblivion. Whalley and Goffe were among thirty (along with Dixwell) "absolutely excepted" from pardon. This was followed by a specific order to seize the two regicides, who were known to be in the colony. A reward of £100, a lordly sum in those days, was offered for their capture, dead or alive. The last grisly bit of news was that some of the regicides had already been hung—briefly, to get the feel of it—then drawn and quartered while still alive.

The colony's response to this royal edict was so slow as to amount to connivance. Not until February 22 of the year 1661 did increasing apprehension force steps to be taken. On that day the Court of Assistants—the Massachusetts upper chamber, of which Captain Daniel Gookin was a member—met to debate what should be done about the embarrassing guests. Opinion in the council was so divided that no decision was reached, but it had become plain that for their own safety Whalley and Goffe should go to some more remote parts.

On February 26, with an Indian for guide, they set out for New Haven, 160 snowy miles away. On March 8, being assured that the two were safely out of the Massachusetts jurisdiction, Endecott put on a fine show of action. He handed a warrant to the same marshal general who had sneered in Captain Breedon's face. That gentleman searched diligently as far as Springfield, but had to report, with a smile of satisfaction, that the fugitives were nowhere to be found.

In New Haven, the travelers had a friend in William Jones, whom they had met on the *Prudent Mary*, and found a new supporter in John Davenport, pastor of the New Haven church. Mr. Davenport knew the terrors of flight at first hand. While he had been rector of St. Stephen's Church in London his Puritan leanings had aroused the suspicion of his bishop, William Laud (later Archbishop of Canterbury), relentless advocate of episcopacy and throne. Davenport had fled to Holland "disguised in a gray suit and overgrown beard." Later he and other members of his church had chartered a ship in order to seek religious freedom in an isolated corner of New England. One of his first sermons in New Haven prepared his flock for the arrival of political and religious refugees: "Hide the outcasts, betray not him that wandereth," was the text, from the book of Isaiah.

Two weeks after the *Prudent Mary* dropped anchor Davenport wrote to Governor John Winthrop, in Hartford, telling him about the distinguished passengers, and wafered this addition to the side of the letter: "It is Commissary-General Whalley, sister Hooke's brother, and his son-in-law who is with him is Col. Goffe: both godly men and escaped pursuit in England narrowly. I hope to see them here." "Sister Hooke's" husband, the Reverend William Hooke, had earlier been Davenport's assistant in the New Haven church.

On March 7, nine days from Cambridge, the travelers lodged in the comfort of Mr. Davenport's house, and the town buzzed with the news of their arrival.

Now the chase began in earnest. A pair of young Englishmen—Thomas Kellond, a merchant, and Thomas Kirke, a sea captain—at the moment in Boston with time on their hands, swore to dig the regicides out of hiding. When they offered to make a personal search south of Massachusetts, Governor Endecott could hardly refuse.

Armed with the King's proclamation and letters from Endecott to the various governors, the two left Boston hot after the fugitives. Pushing at the rate of forty miles a day, they reached Governor Winthrop, of the Connecticut Colony, in Hartford on May 10 and Deputy Governor William Leete, of the New Haven Colony, in Guilford on Saturday, May 11. Leete, in the presence of several local citizens, opened the credentials that Kellond and Kirke handed him and began to read the King's proclamation aloud. The two Royalists protested that it were better "to be more private in such concernments," but the damage was done. Everyone within hearing knew their mission.

Leete adopted the Fabian tactics of delay and evasion. He told Kellond and Kirke that he could not permit a search in New Haven without consulting the magistrates of the colony. Fuming, the pursuers demanded fresh horses, in order to press on to New Haven immediately. Leete smoothly agreed, but somehow found unusual difficulty in producing the mounts. As the afternoon waned, Kellond and Kirke saw that they could not reach New Haven, eighteen miles away, before the Sabbath began at sundown and all official business ceased.

But in Guilford, fretting away the Sabbath, the pursuers seem to have found citizens ready to betray the fugitives. One, a disgruntled fellow whom Leete had once ordered whipped for a misdemeanor, reported that Whalley and Goffe were not only in New Haven but that Leete knew it full well. Others said that Mr. Davenport had taken in a supply of food greatly excessive for his family; that Whalley and Goffe, watching a militia drill, had told the troops that if they had two hundred friends in arms they would snap their fingers at England; and that an Indian runner had already left Guilford to warn Mr. Davenport of the pursuit.

Monday at dawn Kellond and Kirke saddled up for New Haven, "but to our certain knowledge," they later told Endecott, "one John Meggs was sent on horseback before us." Governor Leete followed in the course of the morning, and the magistrates, slowly rounded up, argued the matter for six hours, finally deciding that nothing so delicate could be done without a full meeting of the freemen. This would take four more days.

We can imagine that Kellond and Kirke were fit to explode. They warned the stubborn New Haveners that "for theire respect to two Traitors they would do themselves injury and possibly ruine themselves and the whole Colony of New-Haven," and shaking its rebellious dust from their shoes they went on to search for the regicides in the Dutch settlement at New Amsterdam.

They might have saved their rage. At the news from Guilford, Whalley and Goffe had left town on Saturday and taken refuge in a cave on a rocky bluff nearby, which they called Providence Hill. There, among cyclopean boulders deposited by glaciers of the Ice Age, they found safety, if not comfort. Every day, a farmer left basins of food for them on a stump at the foot of the hill. When the farmer's small sons, who carried them there, wondered that the basins always vanished and then reappeared empty, the farmer said that someone was working in the woods.

In England, under the royal thumb, sympathizers expressed awe at New Haven's bravado. The Reverend William Hooke wrote to Davenport: "I am almost amazed sometimes to see what crosse-capers some of you do make. I should breake my shinnes should I do the like."

Those who harbored Whalley and Goffe were in danger of more than broken shins. By law they were under the same condemnation as traitors —subject to being hung, drawn, and quartered alive, although in the case of ladies the sentence was moderated to burning at the stake. The fugitives offered to surrender rather than bring tragedy upon their protectors.

Persuaded against it, they went to Milford, about nine miles southwest of New Haven, where they lived for three years with one Micah Tompkins, the first two years in utter seclusion "without so much as going into the orchard." John Davenport knew where they were; so, most certainly, did Benjamin Fenn, the Milford magistrate. Fenn showed the most brazen courage of all. He was one of two New Haven commissioners to the United Colonies, a small advisory body representing Massachusetts, Connecticut, and New Haven. The commissioners met in Plymouth on

September 5, 1661, and voted a general order to arrest the regicides. Fenn simply refused to sign it. At the moment Whalley and Goffe were living within a mile of his house.

In the spring of 1664 Charles sent to Boston what amounted to an expeditionary force. Royal agents commanding four ships and 450 troops dropped anchor on April 23 with three grand designs in view: to take possession of New Amsterdam for England, to investigate thoroughly the general condition of the colonies, and to bring Whalley and Goffe home either in chains or in coffins.

The pack was again on the scent; the quarry must run for cover. Whalley and Goffe returned to their cave on Providence Hill. This time Indians chanced upon their hiding place, and, one dark night, a panther screamed noisily before the smoke-blackened entrance. These hazards, together with the onset of winter, decided them to move to Hadley, Massachusetts, a settlement about eighty miles north on the remote frontier of the Connecticut Valley. They traveled only at night. By prearrangement with Mr. Davenport they were received in Hadley by the Reverend John Russell. In one of the sunny upstairs chambers of Mr. Russell's house, which had a convenient hideaway under the floor by the chimney, the hunted men lived for ten years undisturbed.

We shall never know how many hardy souls in Hadley defied royal authority to protect the outcasts. Few secrets can be kept in a frontier community of fifty families where news consists mostly of gossip. With children (including John Russell's) chattering, and servant girls trading tidbits over the back fence, it seems incredible that all Hadley would not know, and that some wretch, itching for the tantalizing £100, would not have written a letter—one small letter, a few scratches of the pen—to Boston. Yet the fact remains: Whalley and Goffe were never betrayed during their decade in Hadley.

By way of sickening contrast, see what a turncoat New Englander, George Downing, did to three regicides in Holland. Downing came of good colonial stock (his uncle had been Governor John Winthrop of Massachusetts), but after graduating from Harvard in 1642 (with the first class), he went to England, where, no doubt, opportunities were greater. There Colonel John Okey, a leader of the Puritan revolt, befriended him and made him chaplain of his regiment. As Cromwell's agent in Holland, Downing spied very efficiently on Charles and his meager court at Breda. Then, when he saw that the Restoration was inevitable, Downing went over secretly to the Stuart cause, feeding official information to Charles, for which he was rewarded by remaining as Charles's minister to Holland after 1660. His friend and mentor, Colonel Okey, together with another escaped regicide, John Barkestead, applied for permission to come into Holland from Hanau. Colonel Okey wrote to inquire of his trusted comrade-in-arms if he would be safe in Holland. Downing replied that he had no order to molest them, "and they might be as free and safe there as himself." As soon as they arrived, he arranged their arrest and also picked up Miles Corbet, another regicide, who had come to welcome them. All three went back to England in chains, to a brutal death. Even Samuel Pepys, stout Royalist that he was, scorned Downing as "a perfidious rogue." Fortunately for Whalley and Goffe, Hadley had no George Downing.

John Dixwell, the quiet one, had not joined Okey and Barkestead on their fatal venture into Holland. With his genius for survival, he had stayed in Hanau, where he had become a burgess. On February 10, 1665 traveling under the name of James Davids, he appeared in Hadley, visited his old comrades for a time, and vanished as silently as he had come. It will be eight years before we see him again.

After 1667 Goffe gave up keeping a ciphered diary (it was destroyed when a mob sacked Governor Thomas Hutchinson's Boston house in 1765) but continued a steady correspondence. The Reverend Increase Mather of Boston sent Goffe's letters to England under cover of his own. Goffe wrote to his wife, pretending that he was Walter Goldsmith, and that she was his mother, Frances Goldsmith. The Reverend William Hooke he addressed as "D.G.," and his sister, Mrs. Hooke, was "Aunt Jane." All of his letters were from "Ebenezer," the biblical place where Samuel set up a stone to commemorate a victory of God's people over the Philistines. He and Whalley relished news from England, especially when it concerned conjectures about their own whereabouts. Rumour had them in Brussels, Holland, Switzerland; when one of the regicides, John Lisle, was shot to death in Lausanne they took wry comfort in the report that they had been murdered at the same time.

In August of 1674 Goffe wrote that Whalley, now about sixty, was in poor health. He had evidently had a stroke. "He complains of no pain, and hath a good stomache, for the most part, to eat thrise in the day, sleepes well the latter part of the night and morning, and troubles not himself much with one thing or another that I can discern, but quietly waites to see what the Lord will do with him." In one of Goffe's next letters (according to Hutchinson) Goffe speaks of his friend as "now with God." Whalley probably died in the latter part of 1674; no one knows where he was buried.

The next year Goffe's refuge was shaken by the outbreak of King Philip's War. Indians attacked all through the Connecticut Valley. Deerfield and

Springfield went up in flames; at Bloody Brook, seventy-one soldiers and teamsters died in an ambush. On June 12, 1676, Indian raiders attacked both north and south gates of the Hadley stockade, but were driven off. And therein lies the famous legend of "the Angel of Hadley."

Governor Hutchinson gave credence to this legend with this note in his *History of the Massachusetts Bay Colony*, published in 1764: "I am loth to omit an anecdote handed down through Governor Leveret's family. . . . It appears that the town people [of Hadley] were at church when an alarm sounded of an Indian attack and suddenly came from nowhere a man who organized them for defence and won the day, then disappeared."

Nineteenth-century fiction writers made the most of it. The mysterious stranger is a pivotal figure of James Fenimore Cooper's *Wept of Wish-ton-Wish*. Brandishing "a shining broadsword such as were then used by the cavaliers of England," he rallies the panicked congregation: "Arm, men of the Wish-ton-Wish! arm, and to your defences!" The stranger was unknown to the end. His rough gravestone bore the one word: "Submission." He left only "an orderly book of a troop of horse, which tradition says had some connection with his fortunes. Affixed to this defaced and imperfect document is a fragment of some diary or journal, which has reference to the condemnation of Charles I to the scaffold."

Sir Walter Scott read a newspaper article about the finding of human bones in the cellar of John Russell's house and concluded that this was "the obscure grave to which the remains of Whalley were committed." Upon this fragile basis he inserted the legend into a novel, *Peveril of the Peak*, and cast Whalley as the nameless champion. He was tall, august, dressed in elk skin, sword and gun in hand. His voice had the roll of thunder in the Berkshires: "Follow me and you shall see this day that there is a Captain in Israel!" He quickly divided the settlers into two forces, surprised the Indians' rear, and routed them with such bloody slaughter that the tribe "never recovered."

Was the mysterious old warrior actually William Goffe? It may not be all legend. Hadley was now a garrison town where some of the officers were men vowed to bag the regicides; if Goffe had really showed himself at the attack, Hadley would soon have become too hot for him. Sure enough, the old Cromwellian was soon on the run.

He was in Hartford by early September of 1676. The loneliness, the loss of human society, the long separation from his family weighed upon him heavily. The last known letter from his pen—dated April 2, 1679—is a pitiable plea to Increase Mather for news of his wife and daughter. A year later a contemptible no-good named John London reported to Hartford authorities that Goffe was living in town with a Captain Bull. For his trouble, London was hauled out of bed on the Sabbath and brought before the appropriate Hartford officials, who gave him a cold reception. They forbade him to leave the county without permission. This order London promptly violated, making his way to New York (now British) and telling his story to Governor Edmund Andros. On order from Andros a sixth and final search was made throughout the colonies. No sign of Goffe was found. We hear no more of him; he may have been already beyond the reach of kings.

John Dixwell, after his brief visit with Whalley and Goffe in Hadley in 1665, had vanished like smoke in a gale. But in 1673 we find him comfortably settled in New Haven, still using the name James Davids, retired merchant aged sixty-six, a dignified, sober, and God-fearing man whose acquaintance with British government policy and European history impressed his few confidants.

In that year he married a Mrs. Benjamin Ling, a widow who died within a month, and four years later he took a younger bride of thirty-one with the evocative name of Bathsheba How, by whom he had three children.

The last stroke of danger was not past. Sir Edmund Andros, the King's man if there ever was one, attended a New Haven church service. He stared at the cultivated old gentleman in the pew, remarking that he surely was not the retired merchant that he professed to be. At afternoon worship Dixwell was absent—a rarity with him—and the psalm scored an obvious point:

Why dost thou tyrant boast abroad
Thy wicked works to praise?
Dost thou not know there is a God
Whose mercies last always?

Sir Edmund did not like the choice and said so. The deacon explained that they took the psalms in order, and this one had come in its turn. Andros huffed but said no more.

Through the years others recognized him, but Dixwell continued to live in relative peace. After 1685, when he dared to join the New Haven church as "James Davids, alias Jn° Dixwell," the Reverend James Pierpont was certain of his illustrious parishioner. The two of them beat a private pathway between their adjoining houses, and Mr. Pierpont told his wife that Mr. Davids knew more about religion than anyone else in town.

On March 18, 1688, the last of the New England fugitives rested from the chase. Dixwell was buried on the New Haven green between the church and the future site of Yale College. At his request the stone bore only the initials "J.D.," with age (eighty-one) and date, "lest his enemies might dishonour his ashes." This precaution did not suffice. Yale President Ezra Stiles wrote in 1794: "Often have we heard the Crown Officers aspersing and vilifying them [the regicides]; and some so late as 1775 visited and treated the grave with marks of indignity too indecent to mention."

The bitterness hung on because the Puritan fight for freedom hung on. The regicides were not men to repent acts of conscience. "If it had to be done," Whalley once said, "I would do it again." While the redcoats spat on Dixwell's stone in 1775, the American colonists were finishing what the short and tumultuous Commonwealth had fitfully begun. In their graves the regicides must have stirred. If, now, they ever gather for a shadowy rendezvous on Providence Hill to remember older battles and the sad years of their exile, they can look proudly at the bronze plaque set by the city of New Haven upon the stone of Judges' Cave. The inscription ends: OPPOSITION TO TYRANTS IS OBEDIENCE TO GOD.

—December 1964

"THEN AND THERE THE CHILD INDEPENDENCE WAS BORN"

By RICHARD B. MORRIS

Long before Lexington, James Otis's fight for civil liberties gave heart to the rebel cause. But why did he behave so strangely as the Revolution neared?

ew freedoms are more fundamental to our way of life—and few so clearly differentiate our democracy from the rival system which seeks to bury it—than the freedom from the midnight knock on the door, from the arbitrary invasion of a man's home by soldiery or police. Enshrined in the Fourth Amendment to the Constitution, the right is nevertheless still a matter of contention: almost every year that passes sees cases based upon it coming before the United States Supreme Court. Given the almost inevitable conflict between the legitimate demands of civil authority and the equally legitimate demands of individual freedom, it is likely that the controversy will be always with us.

What one famous Supreme Court justice called "the right most valued by civilized man," the right to be let alone, is a venerable one in America: long before the Revolution, violation of it by representatives of the king rankled deeply in the hearts of his American subjects; it was, indeed, one of the major reasons they eventually decided they could no longer serve him.

The issue was first expounded in the course of an extraordinary forensic argument made in the year 1761 before five scarlet-robed judges in the council chamber of the Town-house in Boston. The speaker was James Otis, Jr., then thirty-six years old, born in nearby West Barnstable and considered the ablest young lawyer at the Boston bar.

His plea for the right of privacy was at once significant and poignant. It was significant because without the burning moral issue thus precipitated, it might have been possible for the cynical to dismiss the forthcoming Revolution as a mere squabble between colonies and mother country over taxation. The poignancy of Otis's plea derives from the brilliant young lawyer's subsequent curious conduct: while many of his friends became leaders in the fight for independence, he followed a mysterious zigzag course that unfortunately, in the eyes of some of his contemporaries, cast doubt upon his loyalty to the cause of freedom.

The specific occasion of Otis's appearance was an application to the Superior Court of Massachusetts Bay by Charles Paxton, Surveyor of Customs for the Port of Boston, for writs of assistance. These were general warrants which, as they were commonly interpreted, empowered customs officers under police protection arbitrarily to enter—if necessary, to break into—warehouses, stores, or homes to search for smuggled goods. The intruders were not even required to present any grounds for suspecting the presence of the illicit items. Such writs had been authorized in England—where they were issued by the Court of Exchequer—since the time of Charles II, but nothing like them had been used in the colonies prior to the French and Indian War. The only writs theretofore procurable had been specific search warrants issued by the regular common-law courts; but these had authorized search only in places specified in the warrants and only upon specific information, supported by oath, that smuggled goods were hidden there. True, an act of King William III regulating colonial trade had given the customs officers in America the same rights of search as their opposite numbers in England enjoyed. But it was a new question whether the royal order extended to colonial courts the same authority to issue the writs that the Court of Exchequer exercised in the mother country.

During the final phase of the Second Hundred Years' War between Britain and France, however, writs of assistance had been issued in Massachusetts to facilitate the feverish if futile efforts of customs officers to stamp out illegal trade between the colonists and the enemy—in Canada and the French West Indies. These writs had been issued in the name of King George II, but that monarch died in October, 1760, and his grandson succeeded to the throne as George III. According to law, the old writs expired six months after the death of a sovereign, and new ones had to be issued in the name of his successor. Now, in February of 1761, while the issue hung in the balance—George III would not be crowned until September—Surveyor Paxton's case came to trial.

Sixty-three prominent Boston merchants joined to oppose him, retaining the brilliant, impassioned, unstable Otis—and his amiable and temperate associate, Oxenbridge Thacher—to represent them. In order to take their case, Otis resigned his office as Advocate General of the Vice-Admiralty Court, in which capacity he would have been expected to represent the Crown and present the other side of the argument. That task was now assigned to Jeremiah Gridley, a leader of the Boston bar, who appeared as counsel for the customs officers.

Behind Otis's resignation lay deep personal animosities that added drama to the legal battle. Not long before, the chief justiceship of the Superior Court—which would hear the arguments on the writs of assistance and render a decision—had fallen vacant. William Shirley, then governor of the colony, had promised the post to Otis's father, but Shirley's successor, Francis Bernard, had ignored the commitment and instead named his lieutenant governor, Thomas Hutchinson. Already the target of colonists who resented his nepotistic use of the lieutenant governorship, Hutchinson now earned additional criticism for holding two offices at the same time. And his appointment of course precipitated a feud with the influential Otises; young James, according to rumor, declared "he would set the province in flames, if he perished by the fire."

Nevertheless Hutchinson, attired in his new judicial robes, took his seat in the great Town-house council chamber as the trial opened on February 24. With him on the bench were Justices Lynde, Cushing, Oliver, and Russell. Gridley opened for the Crown. He argued that such general writs were being issued in England by the Court of Exchequer, which had the statutory authority to issue them; the province law of 1699, he continued, had granted the Superior Court jurisdiction in Massachusetts "generally" over matters which the courts of King's Bench, Common Pleas, and Exchequer "have or ought to have."

Thacher replied first. Addressing himself largely to technical issues, he denied that the Superior Court could exercise the right of the Court of Exchequer in England to issue such writs. Then Otis arose to speak. One contemporary critic described him as "a plump, round-faced, smoothed skinned, short-necked, eagle-eyed politician," but to John Adams—who attended the trial, reported it in his diary, and was to write an account of it more than fifty years later—"Otis was a flame of fire."

He had prepared his argument with care. Although his oration covered some four or five hours and was not taken down stenographically, it left on Adams an indelible impression. With a "profusion of legal authorities," Adams tells us, "a prophetic glance of his eye into futurity, and a torrent of impetuous eloquence, he hurried away everything before him." Adams continued: "Every man of a crowded audience appeared to me to go away, as I did, ready to take arms against writs of assistance." And he concluded: "Then and there the child Independence was born."

More important than the electrifying effect of Otis's argument upon his auditors was its revolutionary tenor. Anticipating ideas that would be set forth in the Declaration of Independence fifteen years later, Otis argued that the rights to life, liberty, and property were derived from nature and implied the guarantee of privacy, without which individual liberty could not survive. (Venturing beyond the immediate issue, Otis declared that liberty should be granted to all men regardless of color—an abolitionist note that startled even the sympathetic Adams.)

Relying on English lawbooks to prove that only special warrants were legal, Otis attacked the writs as "instruments of slavery," which he swore to oppose to his dying day with all the powers and faculties God had given him. Defending the right of privacy, he pointed out that the power to issue general search warrants placed "the liberty of every man in the hands of every petty officer." The freedom of one's house, he contended, was "one of the most essential branches of English liberty." In perhaps his most moving passage he was reported to have declared: "A man's house is his castle, and whilst he is quiet he is as well guarded as a prince in his castle. This writ, if it should be declared legal, would totally annihilate this privilege. Custom-house officers may enter our houses when they please; we are commanded to permit their entry. Their menial servants may enter, may break locks, bars, and everything in their way; and whether they break through malice or revenge, no man, no court, can inquire. Bare suspicion without oath is sufficient. This wanton exercise of this power is not a chimerical suggestion of a heated brain. . . . What a scene does this open! Every man, prompted by revenge, ill humor, or wantonness to inspect the inside of his neighbor's house, may get a writ of assistance. Others will ask it from self-defense; one arbitrary exertion will provoke another, until society be involved in tumult and blood." With remarkable prescience Otis's words captured the mood of the midnight visitation by totalitarian police which would terrify a later era less sensitive to individual freedom.

Otis then proceeded to denounce the Navigation Acts, which had regulated the trade of the empire since the time of Cromwell, exposing their nuisance aspects with great wit. By implication he acknowledged the widespread existence of smuggling, and went so far as to contend that "if the King of Great Britain in person were encamped on Boston Common, at the head of twenty thousand men, with all his navy on our coast, he would not be able to execute these laws. They would be resisted or eluded." Turning to the similarly unenforceable Molasses Act, passed by Parliament in 1733 to protect the British West Indies planters from the competition of the foreign West Indies, he charged that the law was enacted "by a foreign legislature, without our consent, and by a legislature who had no feeling for us, and whose interest prompted them to tax us to the quick."

The nub of Otis's argument was that, even if the writs of assistance had been authorized by an Act of Parliament, "an act against the Constitution is void. An act against natural equity is void; and if an act of Parliament should be made, in the very words of this petition, it would be void. The executive courts[1] must pass such acts into disuse." This contention—that Parliament was not omnipotent and could be restrained by the unwritten Constitution and a higher law—was a notion soon to be pushed further by John Adams and other members of the Massachusetts bar; the argument became familiar in the colonies well before the Declaration of Independence was adopted.

Measured by its effect on its auditors and its immediate impact on the majority of the court, Otis's speech ranks among the most memorable in American history, alongside Patrick Henry's fiery oration protesting the Stamp Act, Fisher Ames's memorable defense of Jay's Treaty in the House of Representatives, and Daniel Webster's classic reply to Hayne. Had a decision been rendered on the spot, Otis and Thacher would have won, for all the judges save Thomas Hutchinson were against the writs; even from *his* opinion, carefully worded, opponents of the writs could take comfort: "The Court has considered the subject of writs of assistance," the chief justice announced, "and can see no foundation for such a writ; but as the practice in England is not known [owing to the interregnum], it has been thought best to continue the question to the next term, and that in the meantime opportunity may be given to know the result." But the crafty chief justice, aware that he stood alone among his colleagues, was merely buying precious time.

Another hearing was held in November, 1761. This time Robert Auchmuty joined Gridley in defense of the writs. The arguments lasted "the whole day and evening," covering much the same ground as the previous hearing. But the court had now before it information that under the new monarch, George III, writs of assistance were being issued in the mother country by the Court of Exchequer; the Massachusetts judges accordingly felt that they could no longer refuse to issue them too. Writing years later, John Adams recounted that "the Court clandestinely granted them."

Thomas Hutchinson had won a pyrrhic victory. It was he who had talked the rest of the court into agreeing to a delay to learn what the English practice was and he who was chiefly responsible for granting the

---

[1] By "executive courts" he meant the regular courts of law as distinguished from the Massachusetts legislature, known as the General Court. Otis's argument presaged a special and unique role for the United States Supreme Court, the exercise of the power to declare laws unconstitutional.

writs. He was to pay dearly in personal popularity. Moreover, at the younger Otis's prompting, the legislature manifested its displeasure with the decision not only by reducing the salary of the judges of the Superior Court, but by cutting out entirely Hutchinson's allowance as chief justice. And that was only the beginning. During the riots in Boston in 1765 over the passage of the Stamp Act, Hutchinson's mansion was sacked and his library and papers scattered—out of revenge, Governor Bernard claimed, for his connection with the writs. Henceforward, Hutchinson was to be the leader of the Court party and a frank advocate of coercion to secure colonial obedience to Parliament.

As for James Otis, his initial attack upon the writs had made him the darling of the populace of Boston and the leader of the radical party. Taking the issue to the people at once—in May of 1761—he won election to the Massachusetts General Court. When the news of it reached Worcester, Brigadier Timothy Ruggles, then chief justice of the common pleas court and later a Tory exile, declared at a dinner party in John Adams's presence, "Out of this election will arise a damned faction, which will shake this province to its foundation."

Ruggles's gloomy forebodings proved even more accurate than he could have expected, for the year 1761 triggered the Revolutionary movement, and the Otises, father and son, set off the chain reaction. That same year the father was reelected Speaker of the House. Together they succeeded in pushing through an act forbidding the courts to issue any writ that did not specify under oath the person and place to be searched. On the advice of the justices of the Superior Court, Governor Bernard refused to approve the legislation; overoptimistically he stigmatized it as a "last effort of the confederacy against the customhouse and laws of trade."

The constitutional views which Otis first expounded in the writs of assistance case were given more elaborate formulation in a forceful political tract, "A Vindication of the Conduct of the House of Representatives," which he published in 1762. Therein he enunciated the Whig view that all men are naturally equal, and that kings are made to serve the people, not people the ends of kings.

It would be gratifying to report that the man who had made a political career out of his opposition to the writs was in the forefront of the Revolution when the fighting actually got under way. Regrettably, he was not. Quick-tempered and tense, increasingly eccentric and even abusive, Otis simply was not cast in the heroic mold. Whether from self-interest, fear, expediency, irresponsibility, or family friction (his wife was a high Tory and a shrew), or from a combination of all five, Otis now followed a vacillating course that branded him a recreant to his own principles, loathed by his foes, deserted by his followers.

It all started with what looked suspiciously like a deal. In 1764 Governor Bernard appointed Otis Senior chief justice of the Court of Common Pleas and judge of probate in Barnstable County. In that same year the son issued his "Rights of the British Colonies Asserted and Proved," the most influential American pamphlet published prior to John Dickinson's "Letters from a Farmer in Pennsylvania." Written in opposition to the Sugar Act, Otis's tract took the position that Parliament had no right to tax the colonies and that taxation was "absolutely irreconcilable" with the rights of the colonists as British subjects—indeed, as human beings. Nevertheless, it gave comfort to the Court party by affirming the subordination of the colonies to Great Britain and the right of Parliament to legislate for them in matters other than taxation. Hailed by the Whigs in England, the pamphlet elicited a grudging compliment from Lord Mansfield, who quickly pounced on Otis's concession of the supremacy of the Crown. When someone said that Otis was mad, Mansfield rejoiced that in all popular assemblies "madness is catching." The evidence that the younger Otis's more conciliatory tone was the *quid pro quo* for his father's appointment is at best circumstantial, but informed people felt that the connection was obvious.

Otis pursued his irresolute, even self-contradictory course during the Stamp Act controversy. In his "Vindication of the British Colonies" he reversed his earlier position: Parliament *did* have the authority to impose taxes, he said, though he questioned whether the taxes imposed were fair. In two subsequent tracts he again shifted his ground. Arguing against the writs of assistance, he had decried laws enacted "by a foreign legislature, without our consent." Now he even accepted the theory of "virtual representation"—the fiction that the colonies were virtually represented in Parliament, in the sense that the interests of all Englishmen were theoretically represented by the whole body of Parliament—though propertyless subjects could not vote, though many Members represented "rotten boroughs," and though many English cities had no Member at all. "Representation," Otis conceded, "is now no longer a matter of right but of indulgence only." But in the second tract he swung completely around again, denied the right of taxation without representation, and demanded actual representation in Parliament.

Considering his erratic and equivocal wanderings, it is little wonder that when Otis ran again for the House he was attacked in a bit of doggerel appearing in the Boston *Evening Post* and attributed to a customs official not noted for his sobriety:

So Jemmy rail'd at upper folks *while Jemmy's Dad was out,*
But Jemmy's Dad has now a place, *so Jemmy's turn'd about.* . . .

And Jemmy is a silly dog, and Jemmy is a tool,
And Jemmy is a stupid cur, and Jemmy is a fool. . . .

The attack outraged the voters' sense of decency and "Jemmy" was elected to the House by a small majority. When he had thought himself ruined, Otis ruefully admitted, "the song of a drunkard saved me."

Sent as a Massachusetts delegate to the Stamp Act Congress in New York in 1765, Otis had the satisfaction of seeing his constitutional doctrine of no taxation without representation embodied in the Resolves adopted by that body. But the radical leaders refused to incorporate his demand for actual representation of the colonies in the House of Commons. Most of them were wary of a trap, for a grant of token representation to the colonies could not have checked the anticolonial course of the majority in Parliament.

Although far more moderate on the Stamp Act issue than either Patrick Henry or Daniel Dulany, Otis plucked up his courage and under the pseudonym "John Hampden" published in the Boston press a sweeping denial of Parliament's right to tax the colonies. But by now his waverings had placed him under suspicion. Forced to defend himself at a Boston town meeting held in the spring of 1776, and to deny charges that his behavior was the result of "weak nerves" or "cowardice," he offered to meet George Grenville in single combat on the floor of Faneuil Hall to settle the whole issue. Again returned to the House with his popularity temporarily restored, Jemmy was humiliated when Governor Bernard vetoed his selection by his colleagues as Speaker as simply "impossible." Thenceforward for several years he collaborated with Sam Adams in directing the radical party in the House.

In February, 1768, Sam Adams drew up a circular letter denouncing Lord Townshend's external tax measures—import duties on such items as glass, lead, paper and tea—enacted by Parliament. Lord Hillsborough, Secretary of State for the colonies, promptly denounced Adams's letter, ordered the Massachusetts legislature to rescind it and instructed the colonial governors that the assemblies of other colonies be prevented, by dissolution if necessary, from endorsing it. Otis launched into an abusive two-hour tirade against Hillsborough, ridiculing king's ministers who, like Hillsborough, had been educated by travel on the European continent as "the very frippery and foppery of France, the mere outside of monkeys." Although he withheld criticism of George III, he delivered an encomium on Oliver Cromwell and defended the execution of Charles I. That same year, following the arrival in Boston of two regiments of redcoats, Otis wrote to an English correspondent: "You may ruin yourselves, but you cannot in the end ruin the colonies. Our fathers were a good people.

We have been a free people, and if you will not let us remain so any longer, we shall be a great people, and the present measures can have no tendency but to hasten [with] great rapidity, events which every good and honest man would wish delayed for ages, if possible, prevented forever."

Unfortunately for his continued effectiveness as a political leader, no checkrein could be placed on Otis's abusive conduct toward others. "If Bedlamism is a talent, he has it in perfection," commented Tory Judge Peter Oliver, and even friendly critics agreed that Otis was unbalanced. The dispatch of troops to Boston heightened tempers. In 1769 Otis got into a coffeehouse brawl with John Robinson, a customs official. It is charitable to conclude that the caning he received accelerated his mental disintegration. In any event, two years later his family and friends requested he be examined by a sanity commission; as judge of probate, his old foe, Hutchinson, had the satisfaction of appointing its members, who found Otis to be a lunatic. Although he had intermittent lucid spells thereafter, he played no role at all during the Revolution. Instead, it was his brother Joseph who fought at Bunker Hill. James's death was appropriately dramatic. On May 23, 1783, he was standing in the doorway of a farmhouse in Andover when he was struck down by lightning. "He has been good as his word," commented Hutchinson. "Set the province in a flame and perished in the attempt."

A whole generation passed before John Adams, in a series of letters to the newspapers in 1818, established the legend of James Otis's heroic role. Even Virginians came to speak reverently of the "god-like Otis," and perhaps it is only fitting that he should be judged by his most brilliant and seminal achievement rather than by the sadder years when darkness fell upon him. It is only proper, too, that we recognize the writs of assistance case for what it was in fact—first of a series of crises which culminated at Lexington and Concord.

The attack against the writs, initiated by Otis, developed into a notable series of legal battles, fought not only in Massachusetts but throughout the colonies. Local justices of the peace in the Bay Colony refused in 1765 to grant them on the ground that they were repugnant to the common law. They continued to be issued by that province's Superior Court, but individuals sometimes managed to defy them: in 1766 a merchant named Daniel Malcolm, presumably on the advice if not at the instigation of Otis, refused to admit the customs officials into part of his cellar, even though they were armed with writs of assistance, and warned them that he would take legal action against them if they entered. The customs men backed down.

Meantime opposition to the writs was spreading to other colonies. In 1766 the customs collector of New London, Connecticut, sought legal advice as to his power of search and seizure, but the judges at New Haven felt that in the absence of a colonial statute they could make no determination. The collector referred the matter to the Commissioner of Customs in England, who in turn asked the advice of Attorney General William de Grey. His opinion came as a shock to the customs officials, for he found that the Courts of Exchequer in England "do not send their Processes into the Plantations, nor is there any Process in the plantations that corresponds with the description in the act of K[ing] W[illiam]."

Aware that the ground was now cut from under them, the Lords of Treasury saw to it that the Townshend Acts passed in 1767 contained a clause specifically authorizing superior or supreme courts in the colonies to grant writs of assistance. Significantly, the American Board of Commissioners of Customs set up under the act sought between 1767 and 1773 to obtain writs in each of the thirteen colonies, but succeeded fully only in Massachusetts and New Hampshire. But as late as 1772 charges were made in Boston that "our houses and even our bed chambers are exposed to be ransacked, our boxes, chests, and trunks broke open, ravaged and plundered by wretches, whom no prudent man would venture to employ even as menial servants."

In other colonies the issue was stubbornly fought out in the courts. New York's Supreme Court granted the writs when the customs officers first applied for them in 1768, though not in the form the applications demanded; finally, the court flatly refused to issue the writs at all. In Pennsylvania the Tory Chief Justice, William Allen, refused also on the ground that it would be "of dangerous consequence and was not warranted by law." The writs were denied, too, in every southern colony save South Carolina, which finally capitulated and issued them in 1773. Significantly, the courts, though often manned by royal appointees, based their denials on the grounds advanced by Otis in the original Paxton case, going so far as to stigmatize the writs as unconstitutional.

What is important to remember throughout the controversy in which Otis played so large a part is that the colonists were seeking to define personal liberties—freedom of speech, the press, and religion—which even in England, right up to the eve of the American Revolution, were not firmly enshrined in law. Indeed, the issues of whether a person could be arrested under a general warrant or committed to prison on any charge by a privy councillor were not settled until the 1760s. Then Lord Camden took a strong stand for freedom from police intrusion. Less dramatically perhaps than in the colonies, similar issues of civil liberties were being thrashed out in the mother country, but in the colonies this struggle laid the groundwork upon which the new Revolutionary states, and later the federal government, built their safeguards for civil liberties.

In Virginia, where the issue was contested most bitterly, writs of assistance were condemned in the Bill of Rights of June 12, 1776, as "grievous and oppressive." Condemnation was also reflected in the clauses in the Declaration of Independence denouncing the King because he had made judges dependent for their tenure and their salaries upon his will alone. Five other states soon followed Virginia in outlawing the writs. Of these, Massachusetts in her constitution of 1780 provided the most explicit safeguards. The relevant section of the state constitution, notable because it served as the basis for Madison's later incorporation of such a guarantee in the federal Bill of Rights, reads as follows: "XIV. Every subject has a right to be secure from all unreasonable searches and seizures of his person, his houses, his papers and all his possessions. All warrants, therefore, are contrary to this right, if the cause or foundation of them be not previously supported by oath or affirmation; and if the order in the warrant to a civil officer, to make search in suspected places, or to arrest one or more suspected persons, or to seize their property, be not accompanied with a special designation of the persons or objects of search, arrest, or seizure; and no warrant ought to be issued but in cases, and with the formalities prescribed by the laws." John Adams, who wrote that constitution, had remembered his lessons very well indeed.

More succinctly than the guarantee in the Massachusetts constitution, the Fourth Amendment to the federal Constitution affirmed "the right of the people to be secure in their persons, houses, papers, and effects, against unreasonable searches and seizures," and declared that "no warrants shall issue, but upon probable cause, supported by oath or affirmation, and particularly describing the place to be searched, and the persons or things to be seized."

In our own day, several members of a Supreme Court heavily preoccupied with safeguarding personal liberty have conspicuously defended the guarantees in the Fourth Amendment. It was the late Justice Louis Brandeis who, in his dissenting opinion in a wiretapping decision of 1928 (*Olmstead v. U.S.*) opposing police intrusion without a search warrant, championed "the right to be let alone—the most comprehensive of rights and the right most valued by civilized man. . . . To protect that right," he asserted, "every unjustifiable intrusion by the Government upon the privacy of the individual, whatever the means employed, must be deemed a violation of the Fourth Amendment."

More recently Justice Felix Frankfurter has opposed searches conducted as an incident to a warrant of arrest. In a notable dissent (*Harris v. U.S.*, 1946) he pointed out that the decision turned "on whether one gives the [Fourth] Amendment a place second to none in the Bill of Rights, or considers it on the whole a kind of nuisance, a serious impediment in the war against crime. . . . How can there be freedom of thought or freedom of speech or freedom of religion," he asked, "if the police can, without warrant, search your house and mine from garret to cellar merely because they are executing a warrant of arrest?" He went on to warn: "Yesterday the justifying document was an illicit ration book, tomorrow it may be some suspect piece of literature." Again, in a more recent case (*United States v. Rabinowitz*, 1950), Justice Frankfurter dissented from a decision authorizing federal officers to seize forged postage stamps without search warrant but as an incident to arrest. He said pointedly: "It makes all the difference in the world whether one recognizes the central fact about the Fourth Amendment, namely, that it was a safeguard against recurrence of abuses so deeply felt by the Colonies as to be one of the potent causes of the Revolution, or whether one thinks of it as merely a requirement for a piece of paper."[2]

Once it was a powerful monarch concerned about securing every shilling of customs revenue. Today it is a great republic legitimately concerned about the nation's security. Once it was the knock on the door. Today it is wiretapping or other electronic devices. The circumstances and techniques may differ. As the tragic James Otis would have realized, the issue remains the same.

—February 1962

---

[2]In 1957 Mrs. Dollree Mapp of Cleveland, Ohio, was arrested for possessing obscene literature seized in her home by police, apparently without a warrant. Her subsequent conviction was upheld by two state appeal courts, but on June 19, 1961, the Supreme Court reversed the conviction, declaring that evidence obtained by search and seizure in violation of the Fourth Amendment is inadmissible in a state court, as it is in a Federal court. On the other hand, in the case of Burton N. Pugach of New York City, accused of conspiring to maim the girl who had rejected him, the Supreme Court on February 27, 1961, had upheld the right of state officials and state courts to use evidence obtained by wiretapping, a modern method of gathering evidence which many feel also violates a citizen's privacy. So the historic conflict between private right and the public good goes on.

"IN THE NAME OF THE GREAT JEHOVAH AND THE CONTINENTAL CONGRESS!"

By KENNETH S. DAVIS

So thundered Ethan Allen as he seized Fort Ticonderoga. The declamation has a legendary ring to it—but Allen had the rare ability to live up to legend.

He was such a man as legend is made of—and when first we see him, in Bennington's Catamount Tavern on the evening of May 1, 1775, his gaudy legend is already so thick and close around him that we can only imperfectly distinguish it from the man himself. Must we do so in order to know him as he "really" was? After all, his legend was no imposed creation of professional image-makers. It emanated from him directly, naturally, for the most part spontaneously—though he was not above adding to it now and then by playing a quite conscious role. In all probability, the legend illuminates more of his essential character than it distorts.

For instance, as he sits now in Landlord Stephen Fay's taproom he is tossing down his huge gullet a concoction known as a "Stonewall." It consists of the hardest possible cider liberally laced with rum—a liquid hellfire of a drink—and has derived its name from the fact that it facilitates the building of those hundreds of miles of wall which every year are extended across the settled areas of New England. Not a man on the New Hampshire Grants can down more Stonewalls at a sitting than Ethan Allen.

On one occasion in this very taproom—so the story went—he drank a number unusual even for him before beginning a long journey afoot through the wilderness with his great friend and cousin, Remember Baker. When the drinks began to wear off, the two lay down beside a sun-warmed rock and fell into deep sleep. Some time later, Baker was awakened by an ominous, dry, hissing sound. Turning his head, he saw to his horror a huge rattlesnake coiled on Allen's chest, striking again and again at the arms, the shoulders, and the neck of the still sleeping giant. Springing to his feet and grabbing his gun, Baker moved cautiously to prod the snake away. Before he could do so, however, the snake slithered onto the grass, its lifted head weaving, its body fantastically writhing. Utterly astounded, Baker saw that the snake was looking at him cross-eyed! Then, incredibly, it emitted a mighty hiccup and hiccuped again as it disappeared into a blueberry thicket. Baker was still staring in frozen astonishment when Ethan Allen awoke and began to curse the "damnable blood-sucking mosquitoes" that had bitten him in his sleep. . . .

Witness, too, the sign under which Allen drinks on this May evening. It is no ordinary tavern sign. Mounted on a twenty-five-foot pole in the yard, it consists of a huge stuffed catamount with bared fangs snarling toward New York, symbolizing the "war" that has been waged by the Green Mountain Boys against the hated Yorkers these five years past. It may also remind onlookers of another often-repeated story. As Allen strode along a mountain path one day, he was attacked by the largest catamount imaginable. The great cat leaped without warning upon his back, whereupon Ethan calmly reached up over his head, grabbed his attacker by the throat, threw it on the ground before him, and strangled it to death without once relaxing his grip! When he arrived at his destination that evening he complained that the "goddamn Yorkers" had "trained . . . varmints" to claw him down. On yet another occasion, attacked by a wounded bear, he is reputed to have killed it by ramming his powder horn down its throat.

No doubt about it, this Ethan Allen is the original rough, tough, ringtailed terror of the mountains, a giant in stature (he stands six and a half feet tall), beautifully proportioned, and immensely strong. He chews up nails and spits them out as buckshot. He seizes bushel bags of salt with his teeth and throws them over his head as fast as two men can bring them to him. Alone in the woods, he encounters two surveyors for New York land claimants; lifting one in each hand, he beats them together until they yell for mercy and promise never again to set foot on the New Hampshire Grants. Alone again, he encounters a New York sheriff with no fewer than six armed deputies, all sent from Albany for the express purpose of arresting him; he lays them all senseless and bleeding on the ground without even getting his wind up.

Nor is his fighting prowess limited to physical encounters. In the war of words he is, if anything, even more effective. Take, for example, his extended comments on the Act of Outlawry passed in 1774 by the legislative assembly of New York. Governor William Tryon in Albany has been empowered to issue a proclamation commanding Ethan Allen and seven others, all named in the act, to surrender to New York authorities within seventy days or be judged "attainted of felony" and, upon capture, to suffer death without trial or benefit of clergy. This law, cries Ethan in print, is "replete with malicious turpitude!" He goes on: "And inasmuch as the malignity of their disposition towards us, hath flamed to an immeasurable and murderous degree, they have, in their new fangled laws, . . . so calculated them, as to correspond with the depravedness of their minds and morals;—in them laws, they have exhibited their genuine pictures. The emblems of their insatiable, avaricious, overbearing, inhuman, barbarous and blood guiltiness of disposition and intention is therein pourtrayed in that transparent immagery of themselves, which cannot fail to be a blot, and an infamous reproach to them, to posterity."

And what is this quarrel with New York in which Ethan Allen has made his fame? It is a complex and involved dispute over real estate. New Hampshire, once a part of the Massachusetts Bay Colony, assumed that its western boundary was a northward extension of Massachusetts's western line—a line running some twenty miles east of the Hudson and through Lake Champlain into Canada. Its Royal governor, Benning Wentworth, felt he was sustained in this view by the fact that the first land grants in this area had been made by the provincial government of Massachusetts. He therefore ordered surveys and by 1762 had granted some sixty townships, including Bennington, which was named for him, receiving for each of them £20 in cash plus five hundred of the choicest acres reserved as his personal property. Onto these New Hampshire Grants, as the territory came to be called, settlers began to move in significant numbers after the French and Indian War. They had paid for their land; they had secured titles to it under the Crown.

The validity of these titles, however, was challenged by the provincial government of New York. The Royal governor in Albany claimed that on the basis of the original charter granted by Charles II to the Duke of York in in 1664 his province extended eastward to the Connecticut River. Moreover, he managed to obtain a ruling to that effect from the Crown. He then divided the disputed territory, or the map of it, into four counties, established (on paper) a court of justice in each, and ordered the settlers to surrender their land titles and repurchase them under grants from New York. If they failed to do so their grants would be sold to New York landlords at prices of from £200 to £250 per township; the money would go into his own pocket, of course.

Naturally those who held New Hampshire titles were outraged. Very few of them complied with the Albany order. The rest promptly found themselves faced with writs of ejection issued in favor of New York landlords and backed by New York courts. They organized. They sent an emissary to the King, who, sympathizing with settlers who had already paid once for land that had since been improved by their labor, ordered New York to make no more grants pending a further study of the matter—an order New York failed to heed. Thus, as Ethan Allen explained: "[T]he inhabitants . . . [were] drove to the extremity of either quitting their possessions or resisting the Sheriff and his posse. In this state of desperacy, they put on fortitude and chose the latter expedient." Thus the legal dispute became a violent quarrel, exacerbated by the great differences in historical background and social organization between New York and New England: New York with its system of vast landholdings, its rigid class distinctions, its Tory politics; New England with its Puritan tradition, its predominance of small farmers and entrepreneurs, its relatively democratic society and growing passion for independence from George III's England.

In Bennington and Rutland counties a convention was formed whose elected delegates ruled that no person in the district could take grants or have them confirmed under the government of New York, forbade inhabitants to hold any office or accept any honor or profit from New York, and required all military and civil officers who acted under the authority of New York to suspend their functions. To enforce these rules and to defend the settlers, a military association was formed, the Green Mountain Boys, a "regiment" of some five "companies" whose colonel commandant was—and on this May evening in 1775 still is—Ethan Allen.

He it is who, with his Boys, has "seized their [*i.e.*, the New York] magistrates and emissaries, and in fine, all those their abettors who dared to venture upon the contested lands, and chastised them with the whips of the wilderness, the growth of the land they coveted." (One Benjamin Hough, who had accepted a New York commission as justice of the peace, received two hundred lashes across his naked back before being banished.) He it is who locked two captured Yorker sheriffs in separate rooms on the same side of a house one night, strung up a realistically stuffed straw man from a tree where both could see it in the morning, and then told each that the other had been hanged and that the same fate awaited him if ever he returned. (They were released to flee in separate terror to Albany, where, with an astonished mingling of relief and humiliation, they met each other on the street.)

But it is a larger quarrel than the one with New York that agitates Ethan Allen's mind as he sits this night in Catamount's dimly lit taproom. . . .

Just twelve days have passed since the bloody events of April 19, 1775, on Lexington Common and at Concord Bridge—and Ethan has assessed their significance. Years later, describing the feelings which now animate him, he would write: "Ever since I arrived to a state of manhood, I have felt a sincere passion for liberty. The history of nations doomed to perpetual slavery, in consequence of yielding up to tyrants their natural born liberties, I read with a sort of philosophical horror; so that the first systematical and bloody attempt at Lexington, to enslave America, thoroughly electrified my mind, and fully determined me to take part with my country."

And indeed the part he has already determined to take at the earliest possible moment is as dangerously dramatic as it is politically and militarily important. What he contemplates amidst the cheerful fumes and potent furies of the guzzled Stonewalls is nothing less than the capture with his Green Mountain Boys of the most famous British strongpoint in North America—Fort Ticonderoga, situated on the western shore of Lake Champlain at a point commanding the short portage between Champlain and Lake George. Originally a French fort called Carillon, it was completed in 1755, its basic design being that originated by the brilliant French military engineer, the Marquis de Vauban. Built of stone, it has a star-shaped outer wall whose approaches were originally ingeniously prepared for defense and, within the wall, numerous bombproof shelters and firing points so arranged as to be mutually reinforcing. It gained world fame during the French and Indian War when Montcalm held it with 3,600 troops against a well-equipped but poorly led attacking force of 15,000 British and Americans; Montcalm on that occasion inflicted 2,000 casualties while suffering only 300 of his own. Even though Ticonderoga was later captured by Lord Jeffery Amherst, it is still widely regarded as impregnable—the "Gibraltar of America," as some have called it.

Ethan Allen knows better, for the British, who obtained permanent possession of the fort at the Peace of Paris in 1763, have permitted it to fall into disrepair; it is now occupied by no more than a token force. But he also knows that Ticonderoga and its neighboring fort at Crown Point may well become impregnable when they are repaired and fully manned, as they will surely be very soon. Ticonderoga can then become a springboard for British attacks southward into the very heart of the colonies, aimed at splitting them apart.

Thus Allen has resolved to capture these forts—and for the last two months plans have been pressed forward. The venture can succeed, however, only if complete tactical surprise is achieved. Secrecy must enshroud the fact that an attack is so much as contemplated, and this secrecy must extend not only to the British but also to many leading Americans who continue to hope that ultimately, in spite of everything, a nonviolent solution of the crisis will be reached. Once Allen's plan is carried out, their hope will be destroyed completely. A politically decisive act—for even in Boston no direct attack on Crown property has yet been made by the Americans—it will make the Revolution irrevocable. It may also be an act of decisive military importance: if it succeeds, it will not only deprive the British of an immense strategic advantage in a crucial area during the crucial opening months of conflict, but may also supply the rebels with war matériel they desperately need—matériel in the absence of which they cannot possibly win the battles that must be fought around and in and for the key city of Boston.

The vital path that has led Ethan Allen to the Catamount Tavern, on the eve of his rendezvous with destiny, began in Litchfield, Connecticut, where he was born on January 21, 1738, the first child of Joseph and Mary Baker Allen. A few months later his parents moved with him from Litchfield to nearby Cornwall, on the banks of the Housatonic—a raw new community hewn out of hilly, rocky, wooded wilderness, isolated, lacking even a mill. The move was natural for the family: the Allens had been a pioneering race—restless, boldly adventurous, physically and mentally independent, seeking the farthest frontier as if by instinct—ever since the first of them landed in Massachusetts in 1632. This first Allen had shortly thereafter removed with the radical Reverend Thomas Hooker, pastor of the Dorchester Company, into the wild lower valley of the Connecticut River, away from the rigorously enforced pieties of the Massachusetts theocracy. In the century since, four generations of Allens (averaging ten children per generation) had lived in eight different localities, each more newly settled than the last.

On the produce and terrific labor of a pioneer farm—carving fields out of dense woods and clearing glacial rock from them—the boy Ethan grew remarkably big and strong, wise in the ways of the woods, skilled in the handling of tools and weapons, able to follow a faint trail through the wilderness and live off the land through which he passed. He was also intellectually precocious. He had little opportunity for formal schooling. He was, as he later confessed, "deficient in education and had to acquire the knowledge of grammar and language, as well as the art of reasoning, principally from a studious application to it, which after all, I am sensible, lays me under disadvantages, particularly in matters of composition. . . ." But he was driven by a rare hunger to know and understand the things expressed in language, by a passion for speculative thought about origins and meanings, and by a poetic need to speak his piece, not just in ways understandable but in ways eloquent, moving, memorable.

Books were not easily come by in Cornwall. The Bible was the only one readily available, and he learned it well—especially the Old Testament, whose people and stories harmonized better with his immediate environment than did those of the New. He read everything else he could get his hands on, too, and asked eager questions of the best educated and most mentally alert of all those he met. Further, as he later said, he formed the habit of committing "to manuscript such sentiments or arguments as appeared most consonant to reason, lest through the debility of memory, my improvement should have been less gradual." He practiced this "method of scribbling ... for many years, from which I experienced great advantages in the progression of learning and knowledge."

Two men chiefly stimulated and guided the growth of his mind and character. One was Joseph Allen, his father, an honorable and hardworking man who thought for himself in religious and political matters and loved to argue; despite his espousal of religious views that in the opinion of most of his neighbors were dangerously heretical, he was elected a selectman and moderator of the town meeting. Joseph Allen instilled into his eldest son's character, by precept and example, the strength of his own moral principle, but at the same time he kept the boy's mind open and flexible. He obviously recognized, too, Ethan's intellectual superiority, for he sent him to study, in preparation for entrance into Yale, under the Reverend Jonathan Lee in nearby Salisbury.

Unfortunately, the arrangement had barely begun to work when Joseph Allen suddenly died, and Ethan found himself the responsible head of a large and far from affluent family. Yale was, thereafter, an impossibility for him.

He farmed for a time. In the summer of 1757 he enlisted with other men from Cornwall in a company that marched north to Lake George, intending to help defend Fort William Henry, at the head of the Hudson River valley, from the French and their Indian allies; but the fort had been taken before the lake was reached and so the men marched back home again. These two bloodless weeks were Ethan's sole service in the French and Indian War.

During the next four years, in ways doubtless honorable but unrecorded in history, he managed to accumulate a little capital with which he and one of his cousins purchased the fifty-acre Cream Hill farm in Cornwall. He also invested in a low-grade iron ore operation near Salisbury and in a blast furnace for smelting, enterprises in which he himself both labored and supervised the labor of others. In June of 1762 he married Mary Bronson, daughter of a miller who had ground his grain from the Cornwall farm. She is a woman of whom almost nothing is now known save that she was sickly and pious and illiterate; that she was shamefully neglected by her husband though she bore him several children, three of whom (all daughters) survived him; that she nagged him unmercifully when he was at home (he seldom was); and that she died of consumption before she was fifty.

Ethan brought his bride to Salisbury, to live near his smelting enterprise. And it was in that village and at about this time that he became intimately acquainted with the second of the two men who chiefly influenced him—Dr. Thomas Young, only five years older than he, a graduate of Yale who practiced medicine in and around Salisbury. Doctor Young was a man of advanced ideas on all matters, including medicine. He once "ingrafted" (inoculated) Ethan with smallpox pus, at Ethan's request but in violation of a local ordinance against such interference with the ways of a wrathful God. Though Ethan escaped smallpox, he was threatened with prosecution; he promptly flew into so profane a rage against the two selectmen who accused him (one was his former tutor, Jonathan Lee) that he was brought into court on a charge of blasphemy and disturbance of the peace. Smallpox virus was, however, the least important of the doctor's inoculations of the young giant who became, very soon, his disciple as well as his friend.

For Doctor Young was a deist in religion, a skeptical materialist in philosophy, and a champion of the most extreme forms of natural-rights doctrine in political theory. He lent Ethan his books and his notes on books he had read, and he explored with the younger man the evident absurdities and self-contradictions of the orthodox Calvinist religion. One result was a release from all inhibitions of Ethan's natural propensity and talent for violent, picturesque profanity. Another was his ambition to write a philosophical work that would free the world of the stultifying myths of Christianity and substitute for them a "System of Natural Religion" based on scientific observation and the strictest logical reasoning. As a matter of fact, he and Young arranged to collaborate on this project, the survivor to publish it if the other died before the treatise was completed; both of them would work at it off and on for years.

Yet another effect of Young on Ethan was to introduce the latter to the legalistic and intellectual aspects of the then-rising conflict between New York and New Hampshire—a controversy of vital concern to the people of Salisbury, many of whom held New Hampshire land titles. Young wrote a pamphlet on the subject wherein, to Ethan's great edification, "Liberty and Property" were deemed the twin "household gods of Englishmen," so closely joined as to be inseparable.

Ethan felt himself increasingly cramped in Connecticut. For one thing, he was in rather frequent trouble with the law as a result of his swearing, drinking, and brawling. In the spring of 1765, having sold his interest in the blast furnace to one George Caldwell, he celebrated the deal by getting drunk with Caldwell and ended by fighting with him. Allen was brought before the justice of the peace on the charge that he "did in a tumultuous and offensive manner with threatening words and angry looks strip himself even to his naked body and with force and arms without law or right did assault and actually strike the person of George Caldwell of

Salisbury in the presence and to the disturbance of many of His Majesty's good subjects." He was fined ten shillings.

A little later he had another violent row with Caldwell and the latter's friend Robert Branthwaite, during which he struck Branthwaite and then "in an angry and violent manner stripped off his cloaths to his naked body and with a club struck . . . Caldwell on the head," according to the official charge made by the constable who arrested all three. Hours later he again "stripped off his cloaths to his naked body and in a threatening manner with his fist lifted up repeated . . . three times [to Caldwell]: 'You lie you dog' and also did with a loud voice say that he would spill the blood of any that opposed him."

All this happened on the day before his departure for Northampton, Massachusetts, to oversee a lead mine in which he was financially interested. He moved his family with him, but his stay in Northampton was brief. The selectmen ordered him to leave after the local minister had complained of his loud, persistent, fearsome profanity.

He returned to Salisbury in disgust, and there he was soon actively enlisted in the dispute centered on the New Hampshire Grants—enlisted on the side of the Connecticut men whose titles had been first granted by Benning Wentworth. Salisbury may have become too civilized by then for Ethan's taste, but it was still a new and raw pioneering community which attached to his drunken brawling no such opprobrium as had been his lot in staid and settled Northampton. Indeed, this propensity of his may actually have recommended him, in a way, to the holders of contested titles. He was rough and tough; but such a man was needed to serve their interests in the north. He was also, they clearly realized, highly intelligent and essentially trustworthy, else they would not have entrusted him with the management of their defense in an Albany law court in the summer of 1770. The test case involved one John Small, who had received a New York grant to land in the town of Shaftsbury, and Josiah Carpenter, who had a New Hampshire title to the same land. Carpenter lost, of course (the presiding judge, Robert Livingston, was himself one of the largest holders of New York titles to the disputed land). "War" was then begun. . . .

The land grants issue gave Ethan Allen his opportunity. Here was space enough, freedom enough for a giant's full self-expression.

With three of his brothers—Ira, Herman, and Zimri—and his cousin Remember Baker, he became a partner in the so-called Onion River Company, a loosely organized speculative enterprise which purchased some 77,000 acres along Lake Champlain north and south of the mouth of the Onion River (later renamed the Winooski). Ira operated as the principal business manager, stationed at Onion River; Herman as the Connecticut representative, in Salisbury; and Ethan as salesman, promotion man, and political lobbyist (the cost of printing his political pamphlets was charged to the company).

Ethan was also the company's chief armed guard, having built two forts on Onion River land and several times driven off "trespassers"—New York titleholders—with parties of Green Mountain Boys. Thus no one on the Grants had now a greater material interest in the defeat of New York's claims—for none stood to make a greater money profit from it— than Ethan Allen.

But the essential motivation for his public activities was not economic, and no one who knew him really well ever assumed that it was. Indeed the Onion River Company had been Ira's idea originally; he had had to talk his oldest brother into it. In essence, Ethan was the very opposite of acquisitive. He may consciously have longed for a kind of mystically undefined Glory and perhaps, though this is less certain, for a coercive Power over other men; but he was no coldly calculating machine that must run wholly on energies supplied from the outside. On the contrary, he was himself an energy that must spend itself—an electric energy that radiated an aura felt by all those around him on the Grants; it entered into them, inspired them, became a means of communication between them—became, so to speak, the vital substance and texture of human community.

His sense of justice was acute. Once he visited with his Boys the town of Durham, whose residents held their titles from New York. With a little violence and many threats, he forced them to give up the New York titles and agree to buy New Hampshire ones. But when he found out a little later that the sellers of the New Hampshire titles were asking outrageous prices—as outrageous as those of the "thieving Yorker land-jobbers"—he was furious. In an open letter he told the Durham men that they "in justice ought to have [the titles] at a reasonable rate, as new lands were valued at the time you purchased them." If the New Hampshire title-holders demanded "an exorbitant price . . . , we scorn it, and will assist you in mobbing such avaricious persons, for we mean to use force against oppression, and that only."

He had a distaste amounting to loathing for all that was devious, dishonest, and underhanded in personal relationships. On one occasion a note for $150 which he had signed fell due at a time when he could not conveniently pay it. He asked for an extension, but was refused. The matter was taken into court, where Allen's lawyer sought to gain the needed time by denying that the signature on the note was genuine. Allen, sitting in a far corner of the room, listened in astonishment, then sprang to his feet and cried to his lawyer: "I didn't hire you to come here and lie! That's a true note. I signed it. I'll pay it. . . . What I employed you for was to get this business put over to the next court—not come here and lie and juggle about it!" The postponement was granted. . . .

And indeed as he slept into the dark morning hours of May 2, 1775, he had just given a further proof that selfish economic motives were subordinate in him to other, disinterested ones. When the news from Lexington and Concord first reached the Grants, many who lived there were in a quandary. They had by that time reason to believe that the Crown was on their side in the quarrel with New York and would ultimately uphold their land claims if the colonies remained colonial. The Crown would certainly do so if, at this critical juncture, they declared their loyalty to it. On the other hand, if they declared for independence and Britain won the war that must follow, New York's claims would as certainly be upheld.

Hence there was at once an anxious policy meeting at Bennington—first gathered in Landlord Fay's Catamount taproom, no doubt, but soon adjourned to the meetinghouse—attended by the leaders of the Green Mountain Boys, the Council of Safety, and other principal inhabitants. At this meeting, some urged the economic advantages of adhering to the Crown. Others counseled a policy of wait-and-see. Both of these groups had in mind and doubtless stressed, some of them on the basis of bitter experience, the vulnerability of the Grants to attacks by British troops with Indian allies coming down Lake Champlain from Canada.

But Ethan Allen scorned such prudent considerations. Since "futurity," as he called it, was "unfathomable," such decisions as faced them now must be made in terms of right versus wrong, of freedom versus tyranny. He called for bold, forthright action on the side of colonial independence —and the majority was with him. . . .

Soon after daylight on May 2, 1775, Herman Allen dismounted from a winded horse in the yard of the Catamount, having ridden hard through the night from Pittsfield. He brought exciting news, and just the news that brother Ethan wanted most to hear.

The Revolutionary Committee of Correspondence in Hartford, which Allen had asked for help, wanted Ticonderoga taken *at once*. To finance the expedition, £300 had been drawn from the Connecticut Colony treasury; Noah Phelps and Bernard Romans were on their way with it, using part of it to obtain men and supplies as they proceeded. Connecticut men had been and were being recruited, and so were men from Massachusetts; they would arrive in Bennington within a day or two to join with the Green Mountain Boys. A couple of representatives were being dispatched to Albany to consult with the leading independence man there, Dr. Joseph Young, and "ascertain" from him "the temper of the people." It was assumed that Ethan Allen, colonel commandant of the Green Mountain Boys, would lead the expedition.

Fourteen Connecticut men, including Phelps and Romans with the money, and Ethan's brother Levi, arrived in Bennington on Wednesday, May 3; they were led by Captain Edward Mott of Hartford. On the following day Colonel James Easton of Pittsfield arrived with thirty-nine men he had raised. Meanwhile Ethan had sent out calls to his Boys, asking them to assemble at Shoreham, near the southeastern end of Champlain and almost directly opposite Ticonderoga; they were to take all necessary precautions on the way to ensure that word of the impending action did not reach the enemy. Anyone found on the road leading from Ticonderoga was to be seized and interrogated by Green Mountain Boys; anyone found moving toward Ticonderoga was to be forced to turn back.

On Monday morning, May 8, Ethan and the others arrived at Castleton, some twenty miles south of the final rendezvous point, Hand's Cove in Shoreham. The nerve center for the enterprise became, for the moment, Richard Bentley's house, where the leaders met to give the expedition, for the first time, a definite if loose organization. A war committee was established for overall planning and direction of the enterprise. Captain Mott was elected chairman. Ethan Allen was named to command the actual assault. This was in accordance with the promise to the Mountain Boys that they would serve under officers of their choice; Ethan was always their unanimous choice. Seth Warner, habitually Ethan's second-in-command, was continued in that post.

From Castleton, Ethan dispatched a messenger to tell all the Boys he could find in the countryside to assemble at the Cove at the earliest possible moment for an impending great "wolf hunt." This messenger was one Gershom Beach, a blacksmith whose name might now eclipse Paul Revere's if Longfellow had been a Vermonter—for Beach, according to the generally accepted story, travelled *on foot* from Castleton through Rutland, Pittsford, Brandon, Leicester, Salisbury, Middlebury, and Whitting to Shoreham, a total of some sixty miles, in just twenty-four hours!

At Castleton, Ethan also made arrangements for military intelligence. Noah Phelps was to enter the fort as a spy: he went in the guise of a farmer seeking a barber and actually did obtain a haircut. Phelps returned on the eve of the attack to tell Allen that no more than fifty troops were in the place, that they were entirely without suspicion of the impending attack, and that there was a gap in the fort's south wall. There was every chance, said Phelps, that a surprise attack would succeed.

Meanwhile the war committee had taken steps to solve the most pressing immediate problem, that of obtaining boats in which to transport the attacking force across the lake. A fifteen-year-old Castleton boy named Noah Lee had come forward with a suggestion. There were boats and even a schooner at the landing of Tory Philip Skene's nearby baronial estate, Skenesboro. Why not capture them, along with Skene and his retainers and family? Thirty men under Captain Sam Herrick were sent to do so, young Lee among them. Simultaneously, for double insurance, Asa Douglas was sent north on a boat-stealing expedition.

As things turned out, Douglas's activities were crucially important. He stopped sometime after nightfall on May 9 at the home of Mr. Stone of Bridport. Two teen-aged boys, Joseph Tyler and James Wilcox, were asleep in Stone's house when Douglas's knock and talk of boats awakened them. They knew where a boat was. One of Skene's large scows was tied up at a Bridport landing that very moment, watched over by a Negro of Skene's whose love for liquor was notorious. The boys armed themselves with a jug of rum and a plausible tale about wanting the boat to take them to join a hunting party at Shoreham, went down to the landing, and were soon on their way to Hand's Cove. Douglas, a little later, managed to steal another boat for himself, a large one, and head for the Cove with it. Both boats arrived in the early morning darkness of May 10. By that time, however, the situation at Hand's Cove had grown unexpectedly tense.

The rendezvous point was a deep hollow, a quarter of a mile wide in places, between heavily wooded hills. A considerable body of men could gather there without being observed from the opposite shore, and by midnight a considerable number—some 150—had done so. Huddled against the night's chill around shielded fires, they talked and laughed rather nervously together, checked and rechecked their firearms, and watched the dark, huge, striding figure of Ethan Allen. He was not a notably patient man; he sent again and again to the sentinels he had posted on shore to watch for the boats; and one may imagine the fearful oaths which poured from him as hours passed beyond the time he had set for the embarkation of his increasingly restless "army."

Nor was he in the slightest soothed when, around two o'clock in the morning, there appeared in his camp a very splendid martial figure, mounted and accompanied by a *valet de chambre* (the first ever seen, probably, in all the Grants). The stranger announced that he was Colonel Benedict Arnold and had come to take command of the assault! He had a handsome uniform, with scarlet coat and gold epaulettes that glinted in the light of a quarter moon. He had a document, a commission from the Committee of Safety in Cambridge, Massachusetts. He had, too, an imperious manner, the kind of egotistic effrontery that is sometimes characterized as the "habit of command"—and there is some evidence that, surprisingly, he was able to overawe Ethan Allen in that moment of acute anxiety.

But if Ethan wavered for a moment, his Boys did not, and they promptly made him realize that any yielding on his part would mean the end in failure of the whole enterprise. They would take their guns and go home if they were not permitted to serve, as they had been promised, under officers of their choice.

In the end, a compromise was reached. Quite possibly it was at this moment that one of the sentinels posted on the lakeshore rushed up to tell Ethan that, at long last, a boat was approaching, whereupon Ethan, anxious to avoid any further waste of time, permitted an ambiguous solution that would save Arnold's face and keep him quiet until the task was done. Arnold, he said, could march at his side as the assault was made. Arnold himself later claimed that he had agreed to share the command equally with Allen—an unlikely arrangement which was certainly not accepted by the Boys at the time.

The boat whose prow now nosed into the shore was the large scow stolen by Joe Tyler and Jim Wilcox at Bridport, and scarcely had it been beached when the second boat appeared, the one Asa Douglas had commandeered. Ethan Allen made a swift decision. He had 150 men, two boats, and two miles of open water to cross in a darkness that would be yielding to the gray light of dawn within an hour or so. By loading the boats to absolute capacity, he could get little more than half his men across in one trip; there was not sufficient time for two. Accordingly, he divided his forces. He left Seth Warner in command at Hand's Cove, to cross when the two boats returned, or immediately if Herrick's men should happen to show up with the boats from Skenesboro. He himself led the assault force—85 men, including Benedict Arnold—loading the boats so heavily their gunwales were awash.

The landing was made just north of a projection into the lake known as Willow Point. At once Allen lined up his men in three ranks, seeing them in silhouette against a horizon that was just beginning to pale with dawn, and made a little speech. According to his own account, he reminded them that they had been for years "a scourge and terror to arbitrary power," whose "valour has been famed abroad," but that "we must this morning either quit our pretensions to valour, or possess ourselves of this fortress in a few minutes." He urged none of his men to go contrary to their will and asked those who would go voluntarily to "poise your firelocks." Every gun was lifted.

The column, headed by Allen with Arnold beside him, moved swiftly and silently into a road that led past a charcoal oven, a redoubt, a well, and around the eastern outer wall of the fort to the broken gate in the southern face. Through this sprang Ethan Allen, waving his sword. A

British sentry, posted inside, sprang up, aimed his cocked musket pointblank at the charging giant, and pulled the trigger. There was a flash in the pan; the gun had misfired. The sentry then very sensibly fled, yelling at the top of his lungs to rouse his comrades, though this seemed unnecessary since Ethan and his men, pursuing him through an archway into the center of the fort, now emitted terrifying Indian war whoops. The sentry took refuge in a bombproof across the way while Ethan, briefly, formed his men in a hollow square.

Then, abruptly, all pretense of military discipline gave way, to the shocked outrage of Benedict Arnold. The men rushed with fearsome yells of "No Quarter" toward the barracks whence emerged at that moment a soldier with fixed bayonet. He made a thrust toward the nearest man, but Ethan rushed him from the side and knocked him down with the flat of his sword, sparing his life on condition he point out the commandant's room. Toward this, up a stairway, rushed Ethan, yelling "Come out of there, you damned old rat!" and demanding with a string of oaths the fort's immediate surrender.

A bewildered half-naked officer (he was a lieutenant, the second-in-command) appeared at the head of the stairs, trousers in hand. What was this all about? he wanted to know. In whose name was this "surrender" demanded?

"In the name of the Great Jehovah and the Continental Congress!" cried Ethan Allen. He also roared that he would kill every man, woman, and child in the place if he did not obtain "immediate possession of the Fort and all the effects of George the Third."

Then the door of the commandant's room opened, and Captain William Delaplace, who had had time to don his full uniform, appeared. There being nothing else he could do, he surrendered his sword to Ethan Allen and ordered his men paraded without arms.

And then, for the conquerors of Ticonderoga, including Seth Warner's rear guard which soon arrived, there followed one of the gayest, most riotous binges in all American history. For "the Refreshment of the Fatigued Soldiary," Ethan appropriated some ninety gallons of rum from Delaplace's private stock (he gave the Captain a receipt for it, later paid by Connecticut), and soon all the Americans save the highly disapproving, very military Benedict Arnold were glowingly alcoholic. Arnold, indeed, provided the only discordant note in the otherwise joyous harmony of the occasion by reasserting his claim to command on the grounds that he had an official written commission whereas Ethan Allen did not. This caused Chairman Mott of the war committee to give Ethan a written commission. It also placed Arnold in considerably more personal danger than he had been in during the assault, for the drunken Green Mountain Boys derided him, threatened him, even took pot shots at him. His scarlet coat was such a splendid target.

Ethan himself stayed sober enough to write and dispatch several letters to official bodies announcing his triumph, but their language testifies to an uncommon exhilaration, even for him. Here, for instance, is his message to the "Massachusetts Provential Congress": "I have to inform You with Pleasure Unfelt Before that on breake of Day on the 10th of may 1775, by the Order of the General Assembly of the Colony of Connecticut took the Fortress of Ticonderoga by Storm the soldiary was Composed of about one Hundred Green Mountain Boys and Near Fifty Veteran Soldiers from the Province of Massachusetts Bay the Latter was under the Command of Col. James Easton who behaved with Great Zeal and fortitude. Not only in Council but in the Assault the Soldiary behaved with such resisless fury that they so terrified the Kings Troops that They Durst not Fire on their Assailants and our Soldiary was Agreeably Disappointed the Soldiary behaved with uncommon ranker when they leaped into the fourt."

Two days later, Seth Warner took Crown Point without firing a shot (his captives were a sergeant, eight privates, ten women and children). A few days after that, Benedict Arnold was given command of the schooner that Herrick had captured at Skenesboro. He rechristened it the *Liberty* and set out for the northern end of the lake, where, without bloodshed, he captured a British sloop, the only warship on Champlain.

Thus, without the loss of a single life, with a casual and even comic air wholly incommensurate with the importance of the event, Ethan Allen's expedition reduced three key British strongpoints—Ticonderoga, Crown Point, and St. John's in the north (for the latter was impotent so long as the Americans controlled the lake)—and obtained for the American cause what was, for its time and place, an immense booty: upward of a hundred cannon (the figure is uncertain), several huge mortars and two or three howitzers, 100 stands of small arms, ten tons of musket and cannon balls, three cartloads of flints, a warehouse full of boat-building materials, thirty new carriages, and sundry other war supplies. Next winter, in one of the logistical triumphs of the Revolution, General Henry Knox, on orders from Washington, transported much of the Ticonderoga matériel by sled across the snows to Cambridge; Ticonderoga cannon, at once set up on Dorchester Heights, may well have decided the battle for Boston in favor of the Americans.

Of at least equal and more immediate importance was the effect of Allen's feat on American morale. The British were not invincible! Plain Americans were more than a match for them. A thrill of pride, an increased self-confidence spread throughout the colonies, overcoming the vacillating timidity which at first prevented the Continental Congress from operating at all effectively as the ruling body of a country at war.

Witness the first communication Ethan Allen received from the Congress after the news of his conquest had reached it. He was ordered to remove the captured war matériel to the south end of Lake George for safekeeping until such time as it could be "returned to His Majesty" when the "former Harmony" between Great Britain and the Colonies, "so ardently wished for by the latter," was reestablished! Ethan's response was explosive. He was "God damned" if he would obey such an order. "It is bad policy to fear the resentment of an enemy," he wrote back, obviously contemptuous, in a letter recommending an immediate attack on Montreal, it being his "humble [sic] opinion, that the more vigorous the Colonies push the war against the King's troops in Canada the more friends we shall find in that Country."

Subsequently he decided to go personally before the Congress in an effort to inject into this apparently flabby body some rigidity of courage and initiative. Accompanied by Seth Warner, he headed for Philadelphia by way of Bennington, arriving in the latter place (according to plausible legend) on a Sunday when the Reverend Jedediah Dewey preached a sermon of thanksgiving to God on the capture of Ticonderoga. Ethan, having been told what the sermon subject would be, attended, but grew increasingly restive as the minister in an interminable prayer thanked God over and over again, in the most abject humility, for the great fort's downfall. At last Ethan could contain himself no longer. He rose in his place, to the astonishment of the congregation, and reminded Parson Dewey in a loud voice that God had not reduced the fort without assistance. "Aren't you going to mention the fact that I was there?" he demanded. To which Parson Dewey is said to have replied: "Ethan Allen, thou great infidel, sit down and be quiet!"

In Philadelphia, Allen, as the hero of Ticonderoga, managed to inspire the Congress with some of his own optimistic courage. The raising of a regiment from the Grants, to serve under officers of its own choosing, was authorized. A proposed attempt upon Montreal was approved. But so far as his influence upon our national destiny is concerned this was perhaps the high point of Ethan Allen's career.

There followed for him a period of grave personal misfortune. To the surprise of almost everyone and to his own deep hurt, he was not chosen to command the Grants regiment, nor was he even made a subordinate officer of it. The voting was done not by active Green Mountain Boys but by a meeting of various town committees—older men who had long frowned upon Ethan's heretical views and riotous ways and who feared his impetuosity. Their choice for colonel of the regiment was the relatively staid, sober-minded Seth Warner. It is a measure of Ethan's bigness of character that in his disappointment he did not attempt to sabotage the regiment: he did all he could to ensure its and Warner's success. However, there seems no doubt that the rebuffs he had received made him over-eager to perform great deeds. He was used as an advance scout and recruiting agent by General Philip Schuyler and General Richard Montgomery, who were mounting the expedition to take Canada, of which Warner and the Green Mountain Boys were also a part. He was without commission or authority when, one day in that autumn of 1775, he rashly attempted to take Montreal with a bare handful of men and was himself captured instead, with such of his men as had not deserted him, after a noisy if remarkably unsanguinary gun fight. His capture was the forerunner of a greater misfortune for the Americans. Though a force commanded by Montgomery managed to take Montreal, it was defeated and Montgomery killed at Quebec that December.

Allen spent the next two and a half years as a British prisoner of war—a year in England, the rest aboard ships at sea and in British-held New York City.

Upon his release in an exchange in May of 1778, he visited General Washington at Valley Forge. The latter immediately wrote to the President of the Congress about him, praising his "fortitude and firmness" which seemed "to have placed him out of the reach of misfortune." Washington went on: "There is an original something in him that commands admiration; and his long captivity and sufferings have only served to increase if possible, his enthusiastic zeal. He appears very desirous of rendering his services to the States, and of being employed; and at the same time he does not discover any ambition for high rank. Congress will herewith receive a letter from him; and I doubt not they will make such provision for him, as they may think proper and suitable."

But Ethan never actively served under the commission which the Congress gave him. His personal fame was augmented and the national interest served by his publication, in the spring of '79, of a personal narrative wherein he told of taking Ticonderoga and of his "Captivity and Treatment by the British." It was an exciting adventure story which went through eight editions in two years, and its account of his mistreatment by his captors (he had indeed been cruelly handled) was effective in fanning popular hatred of the enemy. His subsequent career, however, was identified not with the emergent United States but with the emergent state of Vermont, to whose interests, as a matter of fact, he soon sacrificed much of his reputation as national patriot.

As early as March 1, 1775, Ethan in a letter to Oliver Wolcott had boldly proposed that the Grants be transformed into a distinct and independent state—a state free alike of New York and New Hampshire. When he returned as a hero from his long captivity he found his dream becoming a reality. Shortly after Ethan's capture, General Montgomery had been killed, and the Canadian expedition had been abandoned, leaving the Grants' frontier to the north and northwest unprotected against the enemy. Rather than call for protection from the New York militia, thus tacitly admitting Yorker sovereignty over them and endangering their land titles, the men of the Grants determined to defend themselves. Early in 1777, in a convention assembled at Westminster, they declared the Grants to be a free and independent state—at first called New Connecticut—petitioning the Congress for admission to what was then known as the Association of States. (It was Ethan's old friend and mentor of Salisbury, Dr. Thomas Young, who first suggested the name Vermont—French for Green Mountain—a suggestion that had happily been accepted.) Since the Congress had thus far refused to recognize the new state's existence, even though it had established a constitution (the first in America specifically to prohibit slavery) and had elected a governor, a legislature, and other officers, Vermont considered itself to be, and Ethan certainly considered it to be, an independent republic. To it he now gave his whole allegiance; of it he promptly became, as he had been on the Grants of old, the leading man.

It was in this role that he entered upon the most dubious phase of his career. During the closing years of the Revolutionary War he secretly intrigued with the British in Canada in order to prevent an invasion of his republic from the north, at the same time roaring his defiance of every order of the Congress which did not recognize Vermont's independence or which seemed to threaten the legal title of Vermonters to the land they occupied. Such military activity as he engaged in during this period was aimed not at the British but at the suppression of "treason" within his republic and at Yorker (and congressional) threats from without. When the actual fighting of the Revolution had ended, Vermont was still an independent republic. She remained so until March 4, 1791, when, in the third session of the Congress, under the Constitution of the United States, she was admitted to the Union as the fourteenth state—an event for which Ethan Allen was more responsible than any other man.

But by the time it occurred he had been dead more than two years, and even in the state he had done so much to create, his name was under something of a cloud.

In part this was due to his British intrigues: there were many even in Vermont who looked upon these mysterious activities as treasonable. But mostly it was due to his publication in 1784 of the philosophical and religious work which he and Dr. Thomas Young, who died in 1777, had projected when they were young men together in Salisbury long before. The work's full title indicates its scope and nature: *Reason, The Only Oracle of Man; Or, A Compenduous System of Natural Religion, to which is Added Critical Remarks on the Truth and Harmony of the Four Cospels with Observations on the Instructions Given by Jesus Christ and on the Doctrines of Christianity.*

It is a work of some importance in American intellectual history, though now almost forgotten, for it helped to relax the strong hold of orthodox Calvinism on the New England mind and conscience. "As far as we understand nature, we are become acquainted with the character of God," wrote Ethan, "for the knowledge of nature is the revelation of God." He attacked the central dogma of Calvinism by arguing that "Human liberty, agency and accountability, cannot be attended with eternal consequences, either good or evil." The book was denounced and its author abused in print and from a hundred pulpits; even to own a copy was to be suspected, by the pious, of infidelism.

Consistent with the view of Ethan as an "awful Infidel, one of ye wickedest men yt ever walked this guilty globe" (so said one Reverend Nathan Perkins, who looked upon Allen's grave with "pious horror"), was the widely told and evidently true story of Ethan's second marriage. His first wife having died in Sunderland in 1783 while Ethan, typically, was not at home, he was available and vulnerable to the very real charms of a young widow named Fanny Montresor Buchanan, whom he met early in 1784. She was the stepdaughter of a notorious Tory named Crean Bush, who had committed suicide in disgrace in 1778, and the widow of a British officer killed in an early action of the Revolution. She was as widely different in all respects from poor Mary Allen as one woman may be from another.

She was beautiful, imperious, vivacious, and impious. When Allen first met her and promptly let it be known that he desired her, she was told by someone that if she married him she would "be queen of a new state." "Yes," she replied, "and if I married the Devil I would be queen of hell." But marry him she did, after a scandalously brief courtship. The ceremony was performed by Judge Moses Robinson, chief justice of the Republic of Vermont, and was shockingly interrupted by Ethan when the Judge asked him if he promised "to live with Fanny Buchanan agreeable to the laws of God." Allen refused to answer until the Judge agreed that the God referred to was the God of Nature, and the laws those "written in the great book of Nature." He then made the necessary promise and left for Sunderland with his bride a few minutes later.

A daughter and son were soon born to them, the latter in 1787 shortly after they had moved (retired, as Ethan put it) to a farm near Burlington.

It was on this farm, two years later, during one of the hardest winters in all Vermont history, that he died. The manner of his departure was of a piece with the manner of his living. He had driven with his Negro hired hand across the thick ice of Lake Champlain to South Hero Island, to borrow a load of hay from his cousin Ebenezer Allen. Ebenezer had sent out word that Ethan was coming, so there was soon assembled a large party abundantly supplied with Stonewalls and punch and flip—many of them old Green Mountain Boys—for a carouse that lasted most of the night. Shortly after daylight—and after a final stiff drink—Ethan was deposited atop the sled-load of hay and there he lay in seeming peace as the Negro drove the team homeward. On the way he suffered what the newspapers of the time called an "epileptic fit." A few hours later, on February 12, 1789, he was dead.

When news of the event reached New Haven, the Reverend Doctor Ezra Stiles, president of Yale, known as an "inveterate chronicler" of things which might interest posterity, noted in his diary: "General Ethan Allen of Vermont died and went to Hell this day."

Ethan himself, without undue seriousness, had anticipated a different otherworldly fate. He was fond of telling about a dream he had had in which he was among several men standing in line at heaven's gate. One by one the men were questioned by the gatekeeper; then each of those admitted was asked to sit in a specifically designated seat inside, there to await further disposition. Not so Ethan Allen. The gatekeeper looked at him sharply when he gave his name.

"You're the man who took Ticonderoga?" the gatekeeper asked.

"The very same."

The gatekeeper's stern visage broke into a warm smile.

"Come in," said he. "Come in, Ethan! Sit down wherever you please!"

—October 1963

OUR TWO GREATEST PRESIDENTS

By CLINTON ROSSITER

Everyone knows who they were. This shrewd and witty assessment reminds us why they were.

The myth and the reality of American history seldom come within shouting distance of one another. What the average American believes and what the historians would like him to believe about, let us say, the first winter in Plymouth, or the Boston Massacre, or Mrs. Bixby's five sons, are two quite different things.

Occasionally, however, happy legend and hard fact match up almost exactly. An example is the judgment, shared alike by tenth-graders in Topeka and professors of history at Harvard, that the two best Presidents we have ever had—best in character, best in performance, best in influence—were George Washington and Abraham Lincoln.

I have no argument with either the tenth-graders or the historians. With the former, I agree that Washington and Lincoln used the powers of the Presidency for high and patriotic ends; with the latter, I agree that they, along with Andrew Jackson, Woodrow Wilson, and Franklin D. Roosevelt, were the chief architects of the imposing office now at 1600 Pennsylvania Avenue. My purpose is simply to assemble the unimpeachable facts and common opinions about the presidential careers of these two great men, and thus to bring reality to the support of myth. In the course of this pleasant exercise there may also emerge certain interesting comparisons between Washington and Lincoln.

George Washington's influence was felt upon the Presidency even before there was a Presidency. The temper of the years immediately after the Revolution was hostile to the claims of executive power, and Article II of the Constitution, which established an Executive both strong and independent, must have come as something of a surprise even to those men who favored the creation of a new national government. No single fact had more to do with the shaping of this splendid office in the Convention of 1787 than the universal assumption that Washington would be chosen as its first occupant—and chosen and chosen and chosen again until claimed by the grave. As Pierce Butler wrote a relative in England, "*Entre nous*, I do [not] believe they [the executive powers] would have been so great, had not many of the members cast their eyes toward General Washington as President; and shaped their ideas of the Powers to be given the President, by their opinions of his Virtue."

The well-known fact of the General's "Virtue" was also an influential force in the ratifying conventions throughout the new states. Many men who agreed with Patrick Henry's warning that Article II was an "awful squint toward monarchy" were lulled into acquiescence by the comforting thought that the Cincinnatus of the West, no candidate for kingship, would be the man to put it into commission. Who else but his old commander could Alexander Hamilton have had in mind when he insisted in *The Federalist* upon the essential republicanism of the Presidency? Who else could be counted on so confidently to display "a due dependence on the people" and "a due responsibility" in this new and untried office?

The most meaningful judgment one can make of Washington's eight years in the Presidency is that he fulfilled the hopes of the friends of the Constitution and spiked the fears of its critics.

The hopes of its friends were that the creation of an energetic Executive, independent of the legislature yet integrated into the constitutional structure, would introduce the one factor most sorrowfully missing from the equation of government under the Articles of Confederation: authority to execute the laws of the United States with dispatch and vigor. The government of the new republic was in desperate need of power, power to make policy and power to carry it through. Article I of the Constitution as interpreted by Madison, Ellsworth, and the other gentlemen of Congress proved to be the answer to the first half of this need. Article II as interpreted by Washington proved to be the answer to the second half.

He was certainly not a President in the image of the Roosevelts or Truman. When a situation called for decisive action, he took a painful amount of time making up his mind. For example, he sought the advice of both Hamilton and Jefferson even when he knew that they would only confuse and delay him with their antithetical counsels. He recognized that his decisions might set precedents, and this recognition gave an extra measure of gravity to his conduct of the office.

When Washington was ready, however, he acted confidently and with courage. The remarkable thing is how consistently he chose to act strongly rather than to abstain huffily, to advance rather than to retreat in his skirmishes with Congress over the uncharted territory left between them by the Constitution.

His major contributions to government under the leadership of a vigorous Executive were recorded in the field of foreign relations. The recognition of republican France, the proclamation of neutrality, the reception and dismissal of the French minister Genêt, the negotiation of Jay's treaty, the use of personal agents, and the refusal to lay diplomatic correspondence before the House of Representatives were just a few of his actions that set precedents for all future Presidents to follow.

Critics of the Constitution had feared that the Executive outlined in Article II would prove too rich a blend of strength and independence, and that the government of the United States would go the way of most other popular governments—straight into tyranny. That it did not take this well-traveled road was the result of many factors: the political maturity of the people, the widespread spirit of liberty, the vigilance of the opposition, the excellence of the Constitution, and, not least important, the single-minded devotion of Washington to the principles of "republican government." Two or three arbitrary acts could easily have aroused a demand for an amendment designed to cut the Presidency down to size. But Washington was simply not a man given to arbitrary action. His conduct was always eminently constitutional, and he repeatedly proved the point that Hamilton had labored in *The Federalist*: that executive power was wholly consistent "with the genius of republican government" and even essential to sound conduct of such government.

It is not easy or indeed pleasant to imagine the fate of this great gamble in constitutional government if Washington had refused to accept his election to the Presidency. If he had stayed at Mount Vernon, as he wanted desperately to do, another man—probably John Adams or John Rutledge or John Jay or George Clinton—would have been the first President of the United States, and that could easily have meant the undoing of the Constitution. The plain fact is that we can go right down the list of all those who ever held high office in the United States and not discover a man so perfectly suited for the delicate task of finding the right balance of authority and restraint in the executive branch. Washington did the new republic a mighty service by fitting the Presidency carefully into the emerging pattern of American constitutionalism.

He did a great deal more than this, of course, for he put his own enormous prestige behind the new Constitution and thus made it acceptable to the American people. Men like Senator Maclay of Pennsylvania poked fun at the pomp and circumstance of "the Washington court," but they could hardly deny that his grand tours through the states—for example, through New England in 1789 and the South in 1791—reinforced popular trust in the Constitution and stirred popular interest in the Presidency. On the first of these trips he fought a polite but dogged battle with vain Governor John Hancock of Massachusetts over one of the most ancient questions of applied political science: Who should call first on whom? The battle was fierce, and consumed most of his first two days in Boston; but a stubborn Washington, who insisted icily that Hancock make the first call, finally won a victory of profound symbolic importance for the authority of the new national government and, more to the point, for the prestige of its chief of state. The humbling of a governor in 1789 and the enforcement of the Federal laws in the Whiskey Rebellion of 1793 are two precedents that stood Dwight D. Eisenhower in good stead in the Little Rock crisis of 1957.

Washington's great gifts to the Presidency and to the republic were dignity, power, and constitutionalism, and the greatest of these, surely, was constitutionalism. It has been said of Washington that he could have been a king but chose to be something more exalted: the first elected head of the first truly free government. In his inaugural address he made clear the solemnity of his mandate: "The preservation of the sacred fire of liberty and the destiny of the republican model of government are justly considered, perhaps, as *deeply*, as *finally*, staked on the experiment intrusted to the hands of the American people."

It was Washington's glory as President that he never broke faith with this solemn vision of the American mission. Well could Jefferson write in gratitude that he had conducted the councils of the new nation "through the birth of a government, new in its form and principles, until it had settled down into a quiet and orderly train," chiefly by "scrupulously obeying the laws through the whole of his career, civil and military, of which the history of the world furnishes no other example."

In the years between Washington's departure in 1797 and Lincoln's arrival in 1861, the Presidency became a subject of hot political and constitutional controversy. In one camp stood those who, following Andrew Jackson at a respectful distance, insisted upon a strong and independent Presidency as the steady focus of our constitutional system. In the other stood those who, falling back on the old Whig tradition, insisted upon a weak and dependent Presidency as the willing junior partner of a powerful Congress.

Lincoln came to the office with very few advance thoughts about the authority it embodied. He had never put himself publicly in either camp, and many of his critics were certain that his administration would prove too feeble for the awesome task at hand. Lincoln soon proved them grossly wrong in their judgments of his character and their fears for the Presidency.

In sharp contrast to the vacillating Buchanan, who had denied his own authority to coerce a state to remain in the Union, Lincoln turned to military force as the final answer to secession. He was never greatly concerned about the forms his actions might take. It was enough for him to act—as Commander-in-Chief, supervisor of the faithful execution of the laws, and sole legatee of the unbounded grant of power we can read for ourselves in the first few words of Article II of the Constitution: "It became necessary for me to choose whether, using only the existing means, agencies, and processes which Congress had provided, I should let the Government fall at once into ruin or whether, availing myself of the broader powers conferred by the Constitution in cases of insurrection, I would make an effort to save it, with all its blessings, for the present age and for posterity."

The way in which Lincoln moved step by step to sweeping authority can be read in the timetable of his actions in the eleven weeks of mingled despair and hope between the fall of Fort Sumter and the meeting of a special session of Congress on July 4, 1861.

April 15: He calls out "the militia of the several states of the Union, to the aggregate number of seventy-five thousand," in order to suppress the rebellion and enforce the laws. At the same time, he summons the two houses of Congress to convene in special session on July 4, thus giving himself a free hand to crush the rebellion swiftly without the vexatious presence of an unpredictable legislature.

April 19: He clamps a blockade on the ports of seven seceded states, a course of action hitherto regarded as contrary to both the Constitution and the law of nations except when the government is embroiled in a declared, foreign war. A week later the blockage is made complete.

April 20: He orders a total of nineteen vessels to be added immediately to the Navy "for purposes of public defense."

April 20: He proceeds quietly, almost offhandedly, to take a number of extraordinary actions. He pledges the credit of the United States for a temporary loan of a quarter of a billion dollars; closes the Post Office to "treasonable correspondence"; authorizes persons "represented to him as being or about to engage in disloyal and treasonable practices to be arrested by special civil as well as military agencies and detained in military custody"; and directs Secretary of the Treasury Chase to advance $2,000,000 of unappropriated funds to three private citizens of New York who are absolutely unauthorized to receive them, "to be used by them in meeting such requisitions as should be directly consequent upon the military and naval measures necessary for the defense and support of the government."

April 27: He empowers the commanding general of the United States

Army to suspend the writ of habeas corpus along the line of communication between Philadelphia and Washington, this in the face of almost unanimous opinion that the constitutional clause regulating the writ is directed to Congress alone, and that the President has no share in this power of suspension.

May 3: He boldly invades the reserved area of congressional power by appealing for "42,034 volunteers to serve for the period of three years," and by enlarging the Regular Army by 22,714 and Navy by 18,000.

July 2: He extends from Philadelphia to New York the line along which the writ of habeas corpus may be suspended.

These actions add up to the so-called "Lincoln dictatorship," a pattern of presidential activity unparalleled in the history of the United States. By the time Congress had come together on July 4, Lincoln had set on foot a complete program—military, executive, legislative, and even judicial—to suppress the insurrection. When one thinks of the governments that have operated under the label of "dictatorship" in recent years, any such description of Lincoln's weeks of unchecked power rings like blatant hyperbole. Yet it cannot be denied that he took many steps of an unprecedented, radical, and constitutionally questionable character.

Lincoln greeted the session of July 4 with a special message, a remarkable state paper in which he described most of the actions he had taken, rationalized the more doubtful of these by referring to "the war power of the government" (his phrase and evidently his idea), and invited congressional ratification. Lincoln himself apparently entertained no doubts about the legality of his calling out the militia and establishing the blockade, nor did he find it necessary to explain why he had chosen to postpone the emergency meeting of Congress to July 4. For his actions of a more legislative and therefore constitutionally more doubtful character, he gave a different justification: "These measures, whether strictly legal or not, were ventured upon, under what appeared to be a popular demand, and a public necessity; trusting then, as now, that Congress would readily ratify them. It is believed that nothing has been done beyond the Constitutional competency of Congress."

He asserted that the power to suspend the writ of habeas corpus could belong to him as well as to Congress, but he tactfully left the subsequent disposal of this matter to the legislators. The whole tenor of his message implied that the government of the United States, like all governments, possessed a final power of self-preservation, a power to be wielded primarily by the President of the United States. And this power extended even to the breaking of fundamental laws of the nation—if such a step were unavoidable. "Are all the laws, *but one* to go unexecuted, and the government itself go to pieces lest that one be violated? Even in such a case, would not the official oath be broken if the government should be overthrown, when it was believed that disregarding the single law would tend to preserve it?"

In other words, in an instance of urgent necessity, an official of a constitutional state may act more faithfully to his oath of office if he breaks one law in order that the rest may endure. This was a powerful and unique plea for the doctrine of paramount necessity. It established no definite rule for the use of emergency power in this country, but it does stand as a fateful example of how a true democrat in power is likely to act if there is no other way for him to preserve the constitutional system he has sworn to defend.

Once Congress had reassembled in answer to the President's call, it did what it could to cut him down from an Andrew Jackson to, at the very most, a James K. Polk. Lincoln, however, although always respectful of Congress, went forward resolutely on his power-directed course, taking one extraordinary action after another on the basis of the "war power." He had brought the office of the Presidency to a new plateau of power and prestige, and he kept it there to the end. His interpretation of his powers was stabilized at an exalted level, and it appears that he considered himself constitutionally empowered to do just about anything that the military situation demanded. "As Commander-in-Chief in time of war," he told some visitors from Chicago, "I suppose I have a right to take any measure which may best subdue the enemy." We need not look beyond the Emancipation Proclamation and the declaration of martial law in Indiana to learn what he meant by "any measure."

On July 4, 1861, Lincoln had put the searching question, "Is there, in all republics, this inherent, and fatal weakness? Must a government, of necessity, be too *strong* for the liberties of its own people, or too *weak* to maintain its own existence?" By April 15, 1865, he had given, once and for all, the great answer of constitutionalism: It need not be either—not if conducted by a man who, paradoxically, can venerate the Constitution even as he dips into it deeply for extraordinary power.

To set up a comparison of two great Presidents like Washington and Lincoln is at best a rather futile business. There are, to be sure, a number of minor points one can make with conviction and some little profit. For example, no two men could have been more different in their methods of day-to-day administration, and no two men could have been more alike in the reliance they placed in trusted subordinates. It is certainly worth noting that the Cabinet of each of these outstanding Presidents ranks among the best three or four ever assembled. If Washington had his Hamilton, Jefferson, Knox, and Randolph, Lincoln had his Seward, Chase, Stanton, and Welles. Each of these skillful groups of lieutenants is a standing reproach to the popular assumption that strong Presidents have surrounded themselves with weak men and weak Presidents with strong men.

In the end, I think, there was one profound similarity, and likewise one profound dissimilarity, between the Presidencies of Washington and Lincoln. The similarity was essentially a question of *style*, for each was, in his own way, a pragmatic statesman who had little use for doctrine and much for the process of trial and error, and who was most successful in the Presidency when he played by ear. In this sense, both Washington and Lincoln were "characteristically American." Each had principles in which he believed with something akin to childlike faith, but the principles were never permitted to harden into dogmas that might obstruct the hard choices that had to be made. Each accepted happily the ground rules of American constitutionalism, but within these rules he played the game with an eye for practical success rather than for doctrinal consistency. Each had virtually no precedents on which to fall back for aid and comfort —Lincoln because he was the first President to face decisions in a genuine crisis, Washington because he was the first President to face any decisions at all—and each set a whole array for later Presidents to follow gratefully. And both of them did this most effectively, I repeat, when they hardly knew what they were doing—except that in their respective circumstances they were doing what any sensible man could see just had to be done.

The most important dissimilarity between Washington and Lincoln was in the *roles* they played. Each was called upon by history to meet the crisis of his own age, and the crisis of 1789–97 was not at all like the crisis of 1861–65. Both proved themselves devoted friends of constitutional government, but they were forced to prove their friendship in different ways. We are grateful to Washington because, in a time of *construction*, he was scrupulous in honoring the letter and spirit of the Constitution. We are grateful to Lincoln because, in a time of *dissolution*, he honored the spirit of the Constitution by stretching the letter almost to its limits.

If Lincoln had been in Washington's position, would he have been equally scrupulous? If Washington had been in Lincoln's, would he have been equally bold? The answer to that double-barreled question lies in the healthily pragmatic attitude toward the responsibilities of the presidential office that these uncommon men held in common, and the answer, surely, is a resounding "yes." Each man met resolutely the challenge that history flung in his face, and each would have met the other's no less resolutely. What more could we care to claim for our two greatest men, who were also, more than coincidentally, our two greatest Presidents?

—February 1959

THE GARDEN OF EDEN AND THE DEACON'S MEADOW

By PERRY MILLER

The single greatest difference between us and our early nineteenth-century counterparts has nothing to do with social or sexual mores; it is the astonishing total command they had of the Old Testament. Why did it mean so much to them? And why did we lose it?

Polly certainly missed her vocation when she was trained for a servant," says Miss Mehitable in Harriet Beecher Stowe's *Oldtown Folks*. "She is a born professor of theology. She is so circumstantial about all that took place at the time the angels fell, and when the covenant was made with Adam in the Garden of Eden, that I sometimes question whether she really might not have been there personally."

Mrs. Stowe published this delicious piece of cultural history in 1869, purporting to describe a New England of about 1790; actually, she was pushing back into an eighteenth-century setting everything she remembered (and she remembered everything) about the world of her childhood, in Litchfield, Connecticut, around 1820. In New England, but also in every intensely Protestant community within the United States—which is to say, as of that date, virtually all American communities—there were innumerable Pollys. They did not all have to be females or servants; almost any adult could be as circumstantial about the Garden of Eden or the pit into which Joseph was thrust as about Deacon Badger's meadow— probably more circumstantial. When primitive painters like Edward Hicks and Erastus Salisbury Field turned their talents to picturing Eden they were hardly drawing on their creative imaginations. Field's painting of the Garden was a scene that thousands of his contemporaries could recognize as readily as we do a photograph of the Eiffel Tower.

The remarkable aspect about this sort of painting, and of such daily conversation as we find reliably recorded, is that the biblical vision out of which these particular examples come was so predominantly, almost exclusively, confined to the Old Testament. There are hundreds of Edens,

Josephs, Elijahs for every rare Crucifixion or still more rare re-creation of the Manger, while Madonnas are, of course, nonexistent. Scenes and themes from Hebrew history are so pervasive in the literature—from Captain Ahab down to Mrs. Lydia Sigourney's *Aaron on Mount Hor*—that one can only stand today in speechless amazement at what a large intimacy with the Old Testament writers could assume as a matter of course among their readers:

> *But then, as Moses raised*
> *The mystic breastplate, and that dying eye*
> *Caught the last radiance of those precious stones,*
> *By whose oracular and fearful light*
> *Jehovah had so oft his will reveal'd*
> *Unto the chosen tribes, whom Aaron loved,*
> *In all their wanderings—but whose promised land*
> *He might not look upon—he sadly laid*
> *His head upon the mountain's turfy breast,*
> *And with one prayer, half wrapp'd in stifled groans,*
> *Gave up the ghost.*

One might well suppose that Lydia Sigourney also had been there personally! Her myriad admirers had no difficulty accepting on her say-so the botanical fact that Mount Hor was "turfy."

The Old Testament is truly so omnipresent in the American culture of 1800 or 1820 that historians have as much difficulty taking cognizance of it as of the air the people breathed. But as soon as you pause to ask the reason for this preoccupation with the Old Testament by a people intensely concerned about securing for themselves the salvation promised in the New, you find yourself in the realm of those intangibles which are the warp and woof of history, upon which politics and even economics are comparatively surface embellishments. But the deeper irony of the situation is the fact that in these very decades which produced in folk art and in popular literature the greatest efflorescence of the Hebraic imagination, Protestant piety was turning steadily away from the Old Testament toward an ecstatic rediscovery of the New. Such poems as Mrs. Sigourney's or such panels as Mary Ann Willson's *Prodigal Son* are not harbingers of the nineteenth century: they are the last lingering rays from a sun that set with the eighteenth century. If these creations are to be properly characterized, they should be called not "primitives" but the end products of a sophisticated culture that was receding before the onslaught of a new primitivism, that of the camp meeting.

It was this revolution in Protestant piety, with its communal shouting to the Lord for a mass salvation, that gradually shifted attention away from the Old Testament. However, in a curious way, the political Revolution of 1776 delayed the change. The Great Awakening of 1740, that which George Whitefield ignited, pointed the way to a surging emotionalism that might have washed out the traditional churchly standards of doctrine and practice, but as it subsided the "Old Lights" regained so much ground that their Biblicism was still vivid enough to provide symbolic parallels to the cause of the patriots. Though we think of the Revolution as led by rationalists like Jefferson or Franklin, who based the cause on scientific nature and common sense rather than on the example of Israel, still among the masses the Hebraic analogy was at least as powerful an incentive as the declaration of inalienable rights. "My dear countrymen," begins a typical communication in the Boston *Gazette* for May 6, 1782, "my sincere wish and prayer to God is, that our Israel may be saved from the rapacious jaws of a tyrant." After the victory, in 1785, Timothy Dwight published what he conceived to be a native American epic, *The Conquest of Canaan*. This is as full of gore and battle and savage exultation as the most inveterate student of the Old Testament could desire; the hero, the "Leader," is Joshua, but the book is dedicated to "George Washington, Esquire," thus tactfully but emphatically making the point that a colossal retelling of the Jewish conquest of Canaan was in fact a narrative of Washington's conquest of America.

The fixation of colonial Protestantism upon the Old Testament—a phenomenon to be noted in every settlement—has one obvious explanation: bands of European immigrants seemed, to themselves at least, the modern equivalents of a chosen people taking possession of the promised land. It was natural, indeed inevitable, for William Bradford, looking back to the landing at Plymouth in the harsh December of 1620 and reviewing the desperate predicament, to cry out, even in his old age, "What could now sustain them but the Spirit of God and His Grace?" and then to answer his rhetorical question by quotations not from the Sermon on the Mount but by quotations from Deuteronomy and the Psalms. In 1648 Thomas Shepard had to defend the Bay Colony against the charge then being made in England by the Puritans who had stayed home and fought the Cavaliers, that the New Englanders had fled from the post of danger. Shepard went immediately to Hebrew precedent: "What shall we say of the singular providence of God bringing so many shiploads of His people, through so many dangers, as upon eagles' wings, with so much safety from year to year?" Thereupon he bolstered his thesis with attestations from Exodus and Micah.

Furthermore, the Calvinist elements among the settlers—this applies to Presbyterians in the middle colonies and even to the original pioneers of Virginia as well as to the Puritans of New England—had still a further reason to think of themselves as Israel: even before they reached these shores, their theology had been considerably recast into the terminology of the covenant. To secure a perspective on themselves and their place in universal history, they had elaborated the "federal" doctrine that the covenant made with Abraham was that covenant of Grace which replaced the Covenant of Works that God made with Adam—that first covenant on which Miss Mehitable's Polly was so circumstantial. The covenant of Abraham had, according to this theology, extended unbroken from the children of Abraham to the present church, and was most binding on those churches that were then reforming the abuses of Antichrist. The effect was to give the migrants a deep sense of their being directly connected with the histories of Jacob, Noah and Moses.

"Thus stands the cause between God and us," Governor John Winthrop preached to the Great Migration in 1630, even before it reached the coast of Massachusetts. "We are entered into a covenant with Him for this work, we have taken out a commission; the Lord hath given us leave to draw our own articles, we have professed to enterprise these actions upon these and these ends." To make clear his meaning, the Governor invoked three passages from the Old Testament—Leviticus, I. Samuel, and Micah—and only one from Ephesians. The great crime of Roger Williams, in the eyes of the orthodox, was not so much that he advocated religious liberty but that he came to this heresy out of a previous and more shocking heresy; he denied that the covenant made with Abraham had continued unbroken down to the covenant of God with the Commonwealth of Massachusetts Bay. He repudiated the hold of the Old Testament upon the churches of Christ, with the result that the orthodox the more vigorously reaffirmed their allegiance to it. Thus from Rhode Island in 1676 could come the jibe of Benjamin Franklin's grandfather, Peter Folger: "New England they are like the Jews, as like as like can be."

The dreadful experience of English Calvinism with the "sectaries" of the English civil wars has always to be kept in mind as the factor which sealed its Hebraism, a state of mind that would persist for another century and a half. Long after the Levellers and Anabaptists had gone, long after Roger Williams's "typology" was forgotten, the churches shuddered at the memory of these radicals. Far from London, on the frontier outpost of Concord in Massachusetts, Peter Bulkeley preached upon *The Gospel-Covenant*, his manuscript being sent home for publication in 1651, so that Englishmen could heed this American warning: "And yet now some are risen up, renewing again that vile doctrine in these days of grace, teaching us to cast aside the scriptures of the Old Testament, as if they were like a bond cancelled and out of date. O Lord, whither will our deluded hearts carry us, if thou, Lord, keepest us not in the way of thy truth!"

By keeping resolutely in the way of the Lord's truth as set forth in both Testaments, but by reading the New always in the light of the more dramatic Old, American Protestants grew to regard themselves as so like the Jews that every anecdote in the tribal history seemed a part of their own recollection. They proclaimed, says Harriet Beecher Stowe, a religion of asceticism, but they would never have achieved the tremendous success of pushing the frontier steadily back or of sailing and trafficking in the seven seas had they not added to this asceticism "the spirit of the Old Testament, in which material prosperity is always spoken of as the lawful reward of piety, in which marriage is an honor, and a numerous posterity a thing to be desired." By its isolation and its homogeneity New England seemed most close to the pattern of Israel, but the archetype was almost as present to the imagination of Kentucky pioneers. Describing the migration in 1780 of his parents, James B. Finley could remark: "Like ancient Israel, who, while reviling the temple in troublous times, had to bear about them the weapons of war, so the ministers of the Gospel at that day were obliged to carry carnal as well as spiritual weapons." Thus they felt a kinship with Joshua and Hiram, closer than any relationship to their cousins in Europe, and accordingly named their numerous posterity Samuel, Benjamin and Eli, Mehitable and Judith, Abraham, and even Peleg.

Consequently, by the time of the Revolution a mentality had long been sustained and perfected that made easy an identification of the new nation with the children of Abraham. This secularizing of the covenant, as it might be called, was so natural and so unconscious a maneuver that it was enacted without anyone's being particularly aware that it had happened, let alone appreciating its implications. It became, as is obvious, one of the sources, perhaps the principal one, for American exceptionalism. For a long time, well into the nineteenth century, the image could be constantly invoked by nationalistic writers. Thus Herman Melville, arguing in 1850 that this nation should give up the barbarous custom of flogging in its navy whether or not Britain retained it, exhorted: "Escaped from the house of bondage, Israel of old did not follow after the ways of the Egyptians." Exulting in all the proverbial intoxication of the metaphor, Melville could shamelessly assert: "We Americans are the peculiar, chosen people—the Israel of our time; we bear the ark of the liberties of the world."

Yet all during these decades from 1800 to 1850 the continuous, self-renewing revival that historians call the Second Great Awakening—the one that commenced at Cain Ridge in Kentucky, that burned over and over the farms of upstate New York and rolled over the plains of Illinois, and finally was carried by evangelists like Charles Grandison Finney and Lyman Beecher into the burgeoning cities, there to blaze fitfully as fanned by Dwight Moody and Billy Sunday—this Awakening was exciting a new sort of piety which put aside the legalistic covenant and focused the Christian life entirely on the orgy of conversion. The orthodoxy of the seventeenth and eighteenth centuries was theological, logical, metaphysical; therefore it could devise and elaborate such a complex conception as the covenant. The new revival was everywhere anti-intellectual. Whether they were Methodists or Baptists or Campbellites, the motto of all these exhorters was in effect Wesley's "I know, because I feel." As one convert said of Parson John Ingersoll, "He made salvation seem so plain, so easy, I wanted to take it to my heart without delays." Few may have gone to quite such extremes as Alexander Campbell, but he was representative in so stressing the New Testament that the remaining adherents of the older Protestantism could accuse him of "throwing away the Old Testament." To generalize—not too sweepingly—one may say that by the end of the century the most popular presentations of Protestantism in this country dwelt comparatively little on the stories of Noah or the Prodigal Son, while lithographs of the Resurrection or the Supper at Emmaus drove from the walls of ordinary families and into their attics the embarrassing paintings they may have inherited from their colonial forebears.

Therefore the survival into the early nineteenth century of such a recalcitrant Hebraism as these "primitives" exhibit is to be found mainly in older settlements where pastoral conditions still reinforced the analogy with Israel, or where the more complex (and conservative) theology of pristine Calvinism resisted the emotionalism of the frontier and the city. Mrs. Stowe was herself one who moved with the century further and further from the intellectuality of her heritage. *Uncle Tom's Cabin* was effective because it spoke the language of revived pietism, and Uncle Tom was made a sentimentalized Christ-figure, not an Israelite in bondage. *Oldtown Folks* is in part a bitter attack upon what she called the "tragedy" of New England life: this, she says, consisted of a "constant wrestling of thought with infinite problems which could not be avoided, and which saddened the days of almost every one who grew up under it." Yet at the same time she looked back with an irresistible nostalgia to a grandeur that had, with the softening of doctrine, been lost. And the heart of this magnificence, she explicitly realized, had been that people then lived in constant face-to-face intimacy with Hebrew literature. The dramas of the Old Testament were their own dramas, the ordeals were theirs and the triumphs.

Just as a child brought up under the shadow of a cathedral, Mrs. Stowe mused, would have his mind stocked with legends of saints and angels which he could not understand, "so this wonderful old cathedral book insensibly wrought a sort of mystical poetry into the otherwise hard and sterile life of New England." She was undoubtedly speaking out of her own experience when she had her hero remark that, "although in details relating to human crime and vice, the Old Bible is the most plain-spoken book conceivable, it never violated the chastity of a child's mind, or stimulated an improper curiosity." To her dismay, she says through her alias, she was in later years astonished to learn the real meaning of passages she had formerly listened to "with innocent gravity." (Innocent gravity may well stand as expressing the essential charm of the illustrations for this article.) Harriet thus reveals, as no social historian can, why the colonial acceptance of the Old Testament gave way, however reluctantly, to the pragmatic pietism of the revival: she and her generation could no longer stand up to the violence in the Old Testament which their grandparents had taken in stride, not as pertaining to the record of a distant and exotic people in Palestine, but as the axiomatic premise of their own existence.

Indeed, as Harriet continues, she casts more and more light onto the world out of which these paintings came, a civilization that was steadily being transformed during her lifetime and that she could describe in 1869 as utterly vanished. The hero remarks that his grandfather's prayers were completely Hebraistic: "They spoke of Zion and Jerusalem, of the God of Israel, the God of Jacob, as much as if my grandfather had been a veritable Jew; and except for the closing phrase, 'for the sake of thy Son, our Saviour,' might all have been uttered in Palestine by a well-trained Jew in the time of David."

Henry Adams, searching at the beginning of *The Education* to indicate how remote the time in which he wrote was from the world into which, in 1838, he had been born, instinctively compared his status as an Adams to that of one "born in Jerusalem under the shadow of the Temple and circumcised in the Synagogue by his uncle the high priest, under the name of Israel Cohen." Just that real, just that tangible, just that comprehensible had the Old Testament been to the primitive American mind. Though the mood of the culture had undergone many changes since then, and no doubt will move even further from the original, still the stamp of this long period of Hebraistic imagination will always be impressed upon it. This is part of our submerged memory; from day to day we ignore it, until suddenly we are confronted with such crude but eloquent tableaux as are here reproduced, and before them, to our astonishment, we recognize our own forgotten selves.

—December 1955

THE BATTLE OF LAKE ERIE

By RICHARD F. SNOW

With the Old Northwest hanging in the balance, a British commodore who had served with Nelson at Trafalgar sailed out to meet a twenty-seven-year-old American captain whose jerry-built fleet had half the crew it needed, and whose second-in-command evidently wanted him to lose.

In the late summer of 1812 a Great Lakes merchant captain named Daniel Dobbins arrived in Washington. He had had a dreadful time getting there, and his journey could not have been made more pleasant by the fact that he was bringing some very bad news with him.

On July 12, a month after President Madison announced a state of war between the United States and Great Britain, General William Hull had invaded Canada with twenty-two hundred men. Hull issued a number of sententious proclamations about the liberty and prosperity that would follow in the wake of his invasion, and then almost immediately quailed before minor British resistance and false reports of large numbers of the enemy nearby. By August 8 Hull was back in Detroit, where, a week later, he surrendered all his troops and his well-supplied garrison to a force half the size of his, composed mainly of militia and Indians. Whatever the reason for Hull's extraordinary performance—it was variously ascribed to cowardice, senility, and treason—his capitulation left the American Northwest in the control of the British and Daniel Dobbins a prisoner.

This was particularly bad luck for Dobbins, for he was believed by his captors to have violated an earlier parole. He was told that he was to be executed but escaped from the British camp in a thunderstorm. A reward was offered for his scalp, and so, having anticipated this, he hid in a wrecked boat on the shore of the Detroit River. At length he made for the river's mouth, where he found an abandoned Indian dugout. He paddled across Lake Erie to Sandusky and there got hold of a horse, which he rode to Cleveland. Then, again in a canoe, he pressed on to the harbor of Presque Isle—which was beginning to be known as the town of Erie—where the officer in command of a small blockhouse told him to carry his doleful news to Washington. So Dobbins traveled the long, dangerous forest road to Pittsburgh and then headed east.

Soon after he finally reached the capital, he was taken before President Madison, who immediately summoned a cabinet meeting to discuss Dobbins's news. At the very beginning of the war Madison had hoped to take Canada by invasion, thereby obviating the need for a costly American fleet on the Lakes. Now Hull's defeat had shown him that such a fleet was indispensable. Dobbins must have given a good account of himself, since Madison turned to him for advice. What did the lake captain think was the best place for building a fleet on Lake Erie? Dobbins recommended Presque Isle and was promptly given the service rank of sailing master and orders to proceed to Erie and build a flotilla.

However well Dobbins may have impressed the rattled Madison, it is unlikely that he would have been given his post had not Lake Erie seemed something of a side show. The President, quite reasonably, expected the real contest to take place on Lake Ontario, for Ontario dominated all the supply routes from the St. Lawrence to the upper Lakes. Although there was no American navy at all on Erie, there was already one of sorts on Ontario, its mainstay a sixteen-gun brig. Across the lake, operating out of Kingston Harbor, was a British fleet mounting upward of seventy guns. It was clear then that a first-rate commander was needed to seize the advantage on Lake Ontario. So the Navy Department gave the crucial command of the naval forces on Lakes Ontario and Erie to Isaac Chauncey.

Chauncey was an irritable, vigorous, corpulent man who had commanded his first ship when he was just nineteen. Now he was forty years old, a well-respected veteran of the Tripolitan war, where his courage under fire had drawn a special commendation from the exacting Commodore Preble. After the war he spent a year's furlough from the Navy as captain of a ship belonging to John Jacob Astor and then returned to the service to take command of the Brooklyn Navy Yard. On September 3 of 1812 he was called from this last duty to go to the Lakes; and by the end of the month, when he embarked on an antediluvian steamboat for the twenty-one-hour trip to Albany, he had already sent north scores of soldiers, sailors, and ship carpenters. He seemed to be the perfect man for the job.

Dobbins was also heading north late in September. His destination, Presque Isle, was a narrow finger of land six miles long, hooked out into Lake Erie and enclosing a superb natural harbor three miles long and more than a mile wide. A sandbar across the entrance to the bay presented some difficulties, but once inside, a ship was safe from any storm that might blow up. Aside from this harbor and the fine timber that grew all about it, there was nothing there to encourage the construction of a fleet. There were forty-seven houses in the bleak little community, one blacksmith shop, and a few men who knew how to use whipsaws. There was no metal to speak of within a hundred miles, nor was there any rope or sailcloth to be had. The only cannon in the place was a small iron boat howitzer; it had been found on the beach years before, and the villagers liked to shoot it off on the Fourth of July.

When Dobbins got to Presque Isle on September 24, he had two thousand dollars and a few carpenters with which to build a navy. Two thousand dollars wasn't very much money for the task, but Dobbins, acting on the assumption that there would be more coming, spent with a free hand. He set the price of timber at a dollar a tree. He sent to Meadville, some thirty miles away, for some steel and paid the blacksmith $2.00 a day to forge the steel into axes. Sawyers were to earn $1.25 a day and axemen 62½ cents. Hauling was worth $4.00 a day to those who had horses or oxen.

A few days after his arrival Dobbins wrote a letter to "Commodore Chauncey or the commanding officer of the lake at Buffaloe": "SIR: I have the honor to transmit to you . . . a copy of my instructions from the Secretary of the Navy and assure you, Sir, that I stand ready to execute any orders you may be pleased to issue. . . ."

Dobbins must have been infuriated by the reply that he received a few days later: "It appears to me utterly impossible to build Gun Boats at Presqu'ile; there is not a sufficient depth of water on the bar to get them into the Lake. Should there be water, the place is at all times open to the attacks of the Enemy. . . . From a slight acquaintance I have with our side of Lake Erie . . . I am under the impression [it] has not a single Harbor calculated to fit out a Naval expedition, and the only one convenient I am at present at. . . . I have no further communication to make on the subject."

This frustrating message was not signed by Chauncey but by Lieutenant Jesse Duncan Elliott. Elliot, who had just turned thirty, had been sent by Chauncey to take command of operations on Lake Erie. He was a vain man, and he was a troublemaker.

Elliott's rank was superior to the one hastily conferred on Dobbins. But Dobbins knew Lake Erie; he had been sailing the Lakes for more than a decade. He was sure that he had picked the right spot in Presque Isle, and he was still very much a civilian, with a good republican mistrust of military wisdom.

He wrote Elliott a testy letter explaining he had "as perfect a knowledge of this lake as any other man on it" and went ahead with his work.

It was well that he did, for Elliott had lit on a curious spot for his operations. He was at Black Rock, near Buffalo, in a harbor so close to the British base across Niagara at Fort Erie that soldiers frequently exchanged shots across the river. Moreover, vessels seeking the open lake would have to work their way through three miles of channels against a four-knot current right under the guns of the enemy. In this cul-de-sac Elliott had assembled a fleet of small schooners, bought up and down the lake.

Despite his dubious anchorage, however, Elliott did lead a spirited cutting-out operation a few days after he wrote his highhanded letter to Dobbins. Along with fifty sailors and fifty soldiers under Army Captain Nathan Towson, he put out from the American shore in darkness and moved against two British vessels that were riding at anchor in front of the fort. His barges were spotted from the deck of the brig *Caledonia*, but Towson scrambled aboard despite heavy musketry and managed to bring the brig—and its welcome cargo of $150,000 worth of pelts—back to Black Rock. Elliott secured the brig *Detroit* (which had been captured from Hull at Detroit) but ran her aground and, under heavy artillery fire, ordered her burned. Long afterward Towson, rankling over the scant credit that the Army received in Elliott's official report, would try to provoke him into a duel; but for the moment the country was happy with this small success, and Elliott was a hero. Congress voted him a sword, and the next summer he was promoted to master commandant, over the heads of thirty of his senior lieutenants.

Elliott had added another ship to his squadron, but bottled up as it was in Black Rock, neither the *Caledonia* nor any other of his ships was of any immediate use to him.

Meanwhile, as autumn burned itself out in the forests around him, Dobbins worked to get ships by less spectacular means than splashy nighttime raids. He laid down the keels for two brigs and three gunboats. Supplies trickled in from Philadelphia, and from Pittsburgh by way of the Allegheny and French rivers. Dobbins paid one J. McDonald $200 for four foremasts, four mainmasts, four main booms, and four bowsprits. John Greenwood turned out sixty sweeps and fifty 14-foot oars for $92.25, and N. Richardson attempted to sell him the products of a "very extensive rope-walk in Kentucky." Winter blew down from the north, and one of his workers died; others began to desert. Dobbins did all he could to keep them there and all the while wrote increasingly desperate letters to Chauncey and then to the Secretary of the Navy begging for instructions: "The boats that I have laid down are 50 feet keel 17 feet beams 5 feet hold and from appearances will be fast sailors if you wish me to go on with the work you will Pleas give me orders to draw I have expended a considerable sum more than the two thousand dollars . . . I have brot the iron from Pittsburgh which comes high the Roads have been so bad if I am directed to go on with the work Pleas let me hear as soon as Posible."

Chauncey maintained a monumental silence, and it seems that the Secretary of the Navy did as well. But at last, in late December, Chauncey left his base on Lake Ontario to pay a visit to Lake Erie. There he found that the carpenters who had been converting the schooners at Black Rock to naval vessels had finally been discouraged by the combination of winter and enemy musketry and had returned to New York, leaving the ships in a dismal state of disrepair. Chauncey journeyed on to Presque Isle, where he studied the harbor and decided that Dobbins had been right; it was the best place for the American navy.

Dobbins soon received assistance more material than Chauncey's approval. In January of 1813 the Navy Department sent Noah Brown, a superb New York shipbuilder, up to Lake Erie to build two large brigs. And at about the same time Oliver Hazard Perry petitioned Chauncey for a command on the Lakes.

Perry had been born twenty-seven years before in Rhode Island. Despite his family's Quaker wellsprings, his father, Christopher, had fought in the Revolution, and Oliver was wild to get to sea by the time he was thirteen. The next year his father took him in as a midshipman on his frigate, and the boy saw action in the Caribbean at the time of the Tripolitan war and was made an acting lieutenant in 1803 and a permanent one four years later. He spent the first two years of his lieutenancy employed in the frustrating task of building gunboats; these balky craft were part of an illusory scheme to keep the British navy from violating Jefferson's embargo. At last, in 1809, he was given command of the schooner *Revenge*. He got some creditable attention when he captured an American ship whose skipper had, in effect, stolen her from her owners and sailed her under English colors. For the most part, however, his duty was unspeakably tedious; he was to cruise up and down the Atlantic coast on the lookout for seizures of American ships by British men-of-war—which in any event the fourteen small guns of the *Revenge* would have been powerless to forestall. Even so, it was better than gunboat service. Then in January of 1811 the *Revenge*, making for New London in a thick fog, ran aground and sank. The pilot was in charge at the time, and Perry was completely exonerated at the court of inquiry that followed. Nevertheless he was dismayed to find himself back on gunboat duty, operating out of Newport. Fretful and restless, he wrote everyone he could think of, begging for a different service; and at last, a little more than a year after the loss of the *Revenge*, Chauncey petitioned Perry to serve under him, saying that the young captain could "be employed to great advantage, particularly on Lake Erie, where I shall not be able to go so early as I expected, owing to the increasing force of the enemy on this lake."

Chauncey had made a brilliant choice, but in his petition can be read a clue to the shortcomings that would hamstring the man in his own operations on Lake Ontario. He was always haunted by the "increasing force of the enemy," and it is fortunate indeed that his English counterpart across the lake, Sir James Lucas Yeo, harbored the same fears. Yeo turned up available for duty when he lost his ship on an uncharted reef in the West Indies. The court-martial took a lenient view of his mishap and acquitted Yeo; then, for little better reason than the fact that he had lost his ship and needed a job, he was given command of the British naval forces on the Lakes.

He immediately began to build ships on Lake Ontario, and Chauncey did the same. All through the spring and summer of 1813 the balance of naval power seesawed back and forth as Yeo and Chauncey launched ever larger ships. Chauncey was a magnificent organizer; he produced a strong fleet out of raw timber in the wilderness but was always scared to fight it. And so with Yeo; he built the ships but lacked the determination to use them as they should be used. The two growing navies sparred timidly at each other and then retired to equip themselves better for the decisive action that would someday come. This shipbuilding race was carried to extremes; by the end of the war Chauncey had nearly finished building a 130-gun ship of the line, a vessel three times larger than anything America had on salt water. But by that time Perry's operations on Lake Erie had made the command of Lake Ontario seem little more than a tactical exercise.

As soon as Perry got his transfer order from the Navy Department, he sent fifty carpenters and sailors north to Erie, and he himself set out by sleigh. He arrived at Presque Isle at dusk on March 27. Noah Brown, the New York shipbuilder, had arrived two weeks before and was there with Dobbins to greet Perry when he arrived in the haggard town. The winter had slowed construction down, but Perry found the two brigs well under way as he first examined them in the fading light.

Perry took command vigorously and at once. He sent parties out into the wilderness to scare up a detachment of carpenters that had left Philadelphia for Erie weeks before, and put pressure on the carpenters who were already there. As more straggled in the pace of work increased, although Perry never had more than two hundred men building his fleet. He was in a hurry—he wanted to get out on the lake as soon as possible —and he rushed his men. As the ships took shape it became obvious that they would bear some of the marks of hasty construction. They were made of green timber; trees that were standing in the forest at daybreak would often be part of a hull by dusk. It is said that Brown, coming upon a carpenter who was taking too much time with a particular task, said to the man: "We want no extras; plain work, plain work, is all we want. They are only required for battle; if we win, that is all that will be wanted of them. If the enemy are victorious, the work is good enough to be captured." Wooden-peg construction was used largely in all sailing ships of the era, but the scarcity of metal forced the Erie builders to use pegs in places where nails were considered vital. There was nothing to be done about it; Perry had all he could do to scare up enough iron to make mounts for the guns.

The guns themselves were coming in now. The first to arrive, four twelve-pounders, were brought from Black Rock by Dobbins early in April. The breezy pragmatism of the shipbuilding was less evident in the selection of the ordnance. Perry himself often left Erie to visit foundries where he supervised the casting of round shot and inspected artillery.

On the fifteenth of April two gunboats, each mounting a 32-pounder cannon, waddled off the stays into the water, and two weeks after that another gunboat was launched. Then, toward the end of May, Perry traveled up to Lake Ontario, joined Chauncey, and played a major role in the American attack on the British garrison at Fort George, at the mouth of the Niagara River. The British spiked their guns, withdrew from the fort, and decided that Fort Erie, at the other end of the river, was now also untenable. The troops were pulled out of Fort Erie, thereby making it possible for the Americans to move the small fleet that had long been stuck tight across the river at Black Rock.

There were no British guns banging away at Perry while he got the ships out of Jesse Elliott's favorite harbor, but it was still a frightful task. The vessels had to edge along the shore, towed by oxen against the strong current. All the ships made Presque Isle in safety, but the strain was beginning to tell on Perry. He was a hardy-looking type, tall and burly, but his healthy appearance was deceptive. He had not been strong as a child, and as an adult he was prey to what was then known as bilious fever. Since that convenient diagnosis was used to identify almost any intestinal disorder, it is impossible to say what his ailment really was. It is perhaps significant that it seemed to strike him after periods of prolonged stress.

In any event, Perry was sick by the time he returned to Presque Isle, and there he found most of his work force to be sick as well. Those who could work stayed at their jobs in double shifts, sawing and hammering long into the night. Sail, shot, and anchors came in from Pittsburgh, and the rest of the guns arrived.

By mid-July the job was done; the fleet was afloat in Presque Isle Bay. The two brigs, which represented about two-thirds of Perry's strength

—they were each a hundred and ten feet long and mounted twenty guns —were rigged and armed. Word had come through of the death of Captain James Lawrence of the frigate *Chesapeake* in his brief, luckless fight with the *Shannon*. Perry immediately named one of his brigs the *Lawrence*; the other he called the *Niagara*. Noah Brown, his work done, returned to New York. He would not be paid for his labors until March, 1814.

Perry had his fleet, but his greatest frustrations and anxieties were still ahead of him. He had no sailors to man his ships, and Chauncey, whose job it was to see that he got them, did not want to send him any. After the attack on Fort George, Chauncey had written warmly of Perry: "He was present at every point where he could be useful, under showers of musketry, but fortunately escaped unhurt." As Perry began to badger him for men, however, Chauncey soured and finally became hostile.

Yet Perry was under constant pressure to go out and fight. The Secretary of the Navy, ignorant of the situation on Lake Erie, wrote Perry demanding that he cooperate with General William Henry Harrison. After Hull had been annihilated at Detroit, Harrison raised a force that was known by the somewhat pathetic name of "the second Northwestern Army." Now Harrison had his troops in northern Ohio, facing the army of British General Henry Procter. Neither general could move without being assured of friendly control on Lake Erie; so in order to cooperate with Harrison, Perry had to secure the lake for the Americans. There was nothing that Perry wished to do more, but neither Harrison nor the Navy Department knew that he was for the moment powerless to move. The Department had been sending men to Chauncey right along. These men were designated for service on Lake Erie as well as Lake Ontario, the Department's optimistic theory being that Chauncey would wisely select the number of men needed by Perry and then dispatch them to Presque Isle. Chauncey, on the other hand, felt that he needed the men on Lake Ontario and kept them there.

Perry, by now frantic, wrote strong letters to Chauncey. He sent Dobbins out to try to drum up recruits and promised ten dollars a month to anybody who would serve for four months or until a decisive battle was fought. His recruiting drew a meager responsive; not more than sixty men volunteered. Then in mid-July he received an urgent order from the Navy Department and a letter from Harrison, both demanding that he sail. And on the same day the topsails of a British fleet poked up over the horizon off Presque Isle.

In an ecstasy of frustration Perry wrote a strained, grandiloquent letter to Chauncey: "The enemy's fleet of six sail are now off the bar of this harbour. What a golden opportunity if we had men. . . . I am constantly looking to the eastward; every mail and every traveller from that quarter is looked to as the harbinger of the glad tidings of our men being on their way. . . . Give me men, sir, and I will acquire both for you and myself honour and glory on this lake, or perish in the attempt. . . . Think of my situation; the enemy in sight, the vessels under my command more than sufficient, and ready to make sail, and yet obliged to bite my fingers with vexation for want of men."

Perry did not worry about the British sailing in and sinking his ships; the sandbar would prevent that. But on any dark night they might land a force in boats and attack the garrison and burn his flotilla. He had some rudimentary fortifications, but they were weak and manned by a ludicrous regiment of Pennsylvania militia who, apparently afraid of the dark, would not stand watch at night. When Perry questioned their captain about this peculiar shortcoming, he received the reasonable reply, "I told the boys to go, Captain, but the boys won't go."

Three days after his last letter Perry wrote Chauncey another: "For God's sake and yours, and mine, send me men and officers, and I will have them all in a day or two." But no men came, and the British fleet rode easily in the calm weather, always in view, mocking Perry's impotence.

It might have given Perry some scant solace to know that the commander of the British fleet was harassed by exactly the same difficulties that were dogging him. Robert Heriot Barclay was the sort of officer who made possible Britain's long maritime supremacy. The same age as Perry, he had spent more than half his life at sea. He had lost an arm serving with Nelson at Trafalgar, and after the great three-deckers he was used to, the scrabbly little collection of craft on Lake Erie must have seemed very modest to him. Still it represented a command, although one officer had already refused it on the grounds that the squadron was undermanned and in poor shape. Barclay reached his fleet at Amherstburg, where the Detroit River spills into the western end of Lake Erie, in the spring of 1813 and immediately went to work with the same energy Perry had shown. His first request was for men, but Yeo, who was cut from the same cloth as Chauncey, wanted to keep his sailors on Lake Ontario. Barclay complained that virtually every man Yeo did send his way was "a poor devil not worth his salt." Nevertheless Barclay managed to win the loyalty of such men as he had and worked them into an effective fighting force. It was obvious that he was in better shape than Perry when he brought his fleet out to blockade Presque Isle.

At last Chauncey doled out a few men, though they were not much to Perry's liking. "The men that came . . . ," Perry complained, "are a motley set, blacks, soldiers, and boys. . . ." Chauncey sent him an exasperated reply, saying: "I regret that you are not pleased with the men sent you . . . for, to my knowledge, a part of them are not surpassed by any seamen we have in the fleet; and I have yet to learn that the color of the skin, or the cut and trimmings of the coat, can affect a man's qualifications or usefulness." As it turned out, perhaps a quarter of Perry's crew were blacks, and they fought superbly when the time came.

Perry had men now—not many, but enough to sail his ships. His immediate problem was the sandbar. Though it had long protected his fleet, it was now a hindrance, for it would be a simple matter for Barclay to sweep down and shoot apart Perry's squadron while the ships were being worked across the bar into the open lake. Barclay's fleet kept watch over Perry until the end of July, and then, unaccountably, it vanished. It has been said the British captain was called away to go to a banquet across the lake; whatever the reason, his departure would prove to be a costly mistake.

Perry, rejoicing in his opponent's absence, went to work. Getting the ships out of the harbor turned out to be a nightmarish job. Before he left, Noah Brown had built some "camels"—scows with no draft to speak of that could be flooded and then pumped out. As they were pumped dry they rose, lifting a ship braced between them enough so that she could negotiate the bar. But the bar was shallower than anyone had thought, and both the *Lawrence* and the *Niagara* got hung up on it. This meant four days of the worst kind of work: taking off all the guns and fittings, rowing them ashore, and then bringing them back again. And all the time this was going on, there was the chance that Barclay would reappear and finish things for good. He did finally reappear, but by then the *Lawrence* was out in open water, and Barclay declined to fight.

With his whole fleet across the bar Perry was joined by Jesse Duncan Elliott, who had brought down two more schooners from Buffalo, as well as two lieutenants, eight midshipmen, and eighty-nine seamen. Chauncey and Perry had long before agreed that the latter would need at least seven hundred and forty men to man his ships, but he was putting to sea with fewer than four hundred—less than a quarter of them part of the regular Navy. Nevertheless Perry was out of the harbor, with his squadron complete and ready to fight. Then, soon after his ships had cleared the bar, he wrote to the Secretary of the Navy resigning his command.

Perry must have been half mad with fatigue and strain. He was sick again, and his acrimonious exchange with Chauncey was rankling him. "I cannot serve longer," he wrote, "under an officer who has been so totally regardless of my feelings." Perry had a quick temper, and he most likely regretted the letter after he sent it; in any event, the request—no doubt to Perry's great relief—was not taken seriously. The Secretary replied in a temperate letter, saying: "A change of commander, under existing circumstances, is equally inadmissible as it respects the interest of the service and your own reputation. It is right that you should reap the harvest which you have sown."

It was weeks before Perry could reap his harvest, but they were valuable weeks. He cruised around the lake, exercising his crews and getting the feel of his squadron. He met with General Harrison, who, on September 1, sent him a hundred Kentucky soldiers with their fabulous long rifles; the lanky, skeptical men poked around the ships and made a general nuisance of themselves. They brought Perry's complement up to four hundred and ninety. Still weak from his sickness yet anxious for action, Perry based his squadron in Put-in Bay, a fine harbor in the Bass Islands, some thirty miles southeast of Amherstburg.

Barclay knew Perry was nearby, but he was loath to fight him, for his own ships were desperately undermanned. He had a fine new brig, the *Detroit*, built at Amherstburg. Yeo was no more anxious to give over guns than he was men, and so the ship had been constructed without her builders having any idea of what sort of armament she was to carry. Eventually Barclay armed her with field guns borrowed from General Procter. There were six different types of cannon among her nineteen guns, which would mean inconceivable difficulties with ammunition supply once the fighting started. By now Procter was desperate; thousands of his Indian allies were consuming rations, and until the Americans were dislodged from the lake, no more food could come in. Barclay was faced with the choice of abandoning the fleet or going out to fight. For a British naval officer that was no choice at all. When Barclay reluctantly weighed anchor late in the day on September 9, there was one day's supply of flour left at Amherstburg.

On that night Perry called his officers aboard his ship and discussed the battle he knew was imminent. Barclay's strongest ships were the *Detroit* and the *Queen Charlotte*, which mounted seventeen guns. These would be engaged by the *Lawrence*, Perry's flagship, and her sister ship, the *Niagara*, which Perry had placed under the command of Jesse Elliott. Perry drew up a line of battle and then, paraphrasing Nelson's great dictum, said: "If you lay your enemy alongside, you cannot be out of place." The officers returned to their ships, and a full autumn moon came out and rolled across the sky. Living things chittered and peeped on the shore of the harbor, and the ships lay motionless on the water in the bright, still night.

The next morning at sunup the lookouts sighted the British fleet, and Perry stood out for open water. It was a fine, cloudless day, with fluky breezes that eventually steadied and swung around to the southeast, giving the American ships the weather gauge—the important ability to force or decline battle as they chose. The schooner *Chippewa* led the enemy line, followed by Barclay's flagship, the *Detroit*, the brig *Queen Charlotte*, the brig *Hunter* of ten guns, the schooner *Lady Prevost*, and the sloop *Little Belt*. Perry accordingly arranged his line so that the *Lawrence* was in the van, with the schooners *Ariel* and *Scorpion* standing by her weather bow, the *Caledonia* next, to fight the *Hunter*, and then the *Niagara*, with which Elliott was to engage the *Queen Charlotte*. The gunboat schooners *Somers*, *Porcupine*, and *Tigress* and the sloop *Trippe* would take on the *Lady Prevost* and the *Little Belt*. Dobbins should have been there in the schooner *Ohio*, but he had been sent to Erie to pick up supplies.

The American ships cleared for action; stands of cutlasses were set up on deck, shot was placed near the guns, and the hatches were closed save for a ten-inch-square aperture through which the powder charges would be passed. Sand was sprinkled on the decks so that the sailors could keep their footing when the blood began to flow. Perry brought the ship's papers, wrapped in lead, to the ship's surgeon and told him to throw them overboard should the *Lawrence* be forced to strike. Sometime during the morning he hoisted his battle flag, a blue banner bearing the dying words attributed to Captain Lawrence: "Don't Give up the Ship." It was a curious slogan, in a way, filled as it was with negative implications —the ship, after all, had been given up—but the crew cheered when they saw it unfurl in the light breeze.

Then there was nothing more to be done. Perry turned to one of his officers. "This is the most important day of my life," he said.

The British fleet had been freshly painted, and the ships looked clean and formidable, bearing toward the Americans in the sunny morning. At about a quarter to twelve the sailors on *Lawrence* heard a band playing what sounded like "Rule Britannia," the music faint across the water. There was an enormous weight of reputation riding with those English men-of-war on a lake in the middle of North America. When the band was finished, the *Detroit* fired a ranging shot. A few minutes later she fired another, which hit the *Lawrence*. The two ships were still a mile apart, and Perry realized that Barclay had the edge on him. All but two of Perry's guns were 32-pounder carronades, short-barreled pieces that were deadly at short range but not good for much beyond 250 yards. Barclay, on the other hand, was well supplied with long guns. Perry's only hope was to engage Barclay closely, so he held his fire while the two ships closed, and the Briton picked his ship apart in a ghastly sort of target practice.

After a half hour the *Lawrence's* rigging was almost useless, but Perry was close enough for his guns to take effect. The *Lawrence* opened fire, but she was virtually unsupported; she had sailed into action accompanied only by two small schooners. Far away through the smoke could be seen the *Niagara*, an idle spectator to the savage fight that was taking shape. Jesse Duncan Elliott had not yet begun to fight. Nor did he intend to, it seemed to the sailors on the *Lawrence*. The *Queen Charlotte*, finding that the *Niagara* would not come within range, now ran down on the *Lawrence*, and Perry found himself being fired on by some forty guns.

The destruction on the decks of the *Lawrence* was appalling. The air was filled with iron and great jagged splinters of wood, and the wounded tottered below faster than Usher Parsons, the surgeon, could treat them. "It seemed," he said, "as though heaven and earth were at loggerheads." John Brooks, the affable and popular lieutenant of marines and the handsomest man in the fleet, had his hip carried away by a cannonball and lay on the deck in agony, begging for a pistol with which to kill himself. Lying next to him, Samuel Hambleton, the purser, who was also wounded, took a verbal disposition of his will before the lieutenant died. The wounded crawled away to hide, but there was no safe, stout corner in the hastily built brig. Parsons was helping a midshipman to his feet after dressing a wound in his arm when the boy was torn out of his hands by a shot that smashed through the hull. Five cannonballs passed through the cabin where he was working. Blood spilled on the deck faster than men could throw sand on it, and sailors slipped and fell as they strained at the guns. The hammocks were shot apart, and the scraps of cloth that filled them danced in the smoky air like snowflakes. They settled on the bloody head of Lieutenant John Yarnall, Perry's second-in-command, and gave him the appearance of a huge owl as he kept the guns manned and working. Spars and rigging tumbled down from aloft, round shot hulled the ship again and again, men fell dead and were clawed apart by canister; and through it all the ship's dog, a small black spaniel, wailed and keened.

Courage takes strange forms. It is said that Perry suffered a psychopathic fear of cows and would splash across a muddy road to avoid going near one of the innocuous beasts; but here he was, in the center of and bearing full responsibility for what was undoubtedly the worst place on earth at the moment, and he was utterly composed. An hour and a half into the chaotic afternoon he appeared at the skylight over the sickbay and calmly asked Parsons to spare him one of his assistants. He returned six times and finally, with all the assistants gone, asked if there were any wounded who could pull a rope. A few men actually dragged themselves back to the deck. But it was no use. By 2:30 P.M., after an almost unbelievable defense, there was not a gun working on the *Lawrence*, and 89 percent of her crew was down. And off out of range the *Niagara* still stood undamaged; Parsons says that many of the wounded cursed her in their last words.

Nobody will ever know what was going through Jesse Duncan Elliott's mind as he watched his sister ship get hammered into a listing ruin. He was some years older than Perry and felt that he should have had command of the squadron, and his jealousy may have been such that, like John Paul Jones's mad ally Captain Landais, he stood back waiting for his superior to be killed so that he could come in at the end of the fight and claim the victory. Much later his apologists would give the insufficient explanation that he was simply obeying orders by keeping the line of battle intact. The *Caledonia* was a slow sailor, and he was stuck behind her, reluctant to leave his station. Whatever the reason, as the *Lawrence*'s last gun stopped firing Elliott did leave the line and pass to windward of the ruined flagship. He was sure that Perry was dead, and it is a pity that there is no clear record of his reactions when Perry clambered up over the side of the *Niagara* and stood facing him.

On board the *Lawrence* Perry, miraculously unhurt, had determined that there still was a ship's boat, also miraculously unhurt. He had hauled down the "Don't Give up the Ship" battle flag—but not the American flag—and took it with him as he climbed into the boat, leaving Yarnall in command of the ship and the nine men still fit for duty. Thickly banked powder smoke covered him for part of the way as he made for the *Niagara*, but for most of the fifteen-minute journey the water around him was roiled with musketry and round shot. But Perry made it through unhurt.

As he climbed aboard Elliott's ship he saw, with "unspeakable pain," Yarnall lower the flag of the *Lawrence* in surrender. But it did not stay lowered for long, and the British never had a chance to take possession of the ship. Perry exchanged a word or two with Elliott, sent him back in the *Lawrence*'s dinghy to bring up the gunboats, and then, taking command of the *Niagara*, steered her toward the *Detroit*.

The British had taken quite a mauling before they finally silenced the *Lawrence*. A Canadian prisoner who visited the *Detroit* a month after the battle wrote that "it would be impossible to place a hand upon that broadside which had been exposed to the enemy's fire without covering some portion of a wound, either from grape, round, canister, or chain shot." Barclay was down—his remaining arm had been disabled and he had other wounds as well—and many of his officers were dead. The *Detroit* had gotten tangled up with the *Queen Charlotte* and could not get clear. The British were expecting the American fleet to sail away, leaving them their hard-won prize of the derelict *Lawrence*. Most of them, then, must have known that the game was up when they saw the *Niagara* with all sail set and hardly a scratch on her bearing down upon them. The American ship passed between the *Detroit* and the *Hunter*, her guns double-shotted, both broadsides booming out. It was enough. The gunboats were coming up, the *Niagara* had every gun in action, and the day was lost. At about three o'clock Barclay struck his colors.

Perry—hatless, filthy, his breeches black with smoke and blood—thought of General Harrison waiting on his word. He found an old envelope and wrote on the back of it: "DEAR GENL: We have met the enemy, and they are ours—two ships, two brigs, one schooner, and one sloop. Yours with great respect and esteem, O. H. PERRY."

Perry returned to the *Lawrence* that afternoon to receive the surrender of the British officers. As he climbed aboard a very few unwounded men, the surgeon among them, came forward to greet him. He stared speechlessly at the survivors and the carnage around him. When the British came aboard, he quietly refused their swords and inquired after Captain Barclay. Forty-one British had been killed and ninety-four wounded. The Americans had suffered twenty-seven killed and ninety-six wounded, most of them on the terribly ravaged *Lawrence*. Four men had died on Elliott's ship.

Soon after Harrison got word of Perry's triumph, he started out after Procter. Perry ferried his men across the now friendly lake. When Procter got news of the outcome of the battle, he realized that his situation was hopeless. He retreated, but not fast enough, and Harrison caught up with him and beat him decisively at the Battle of the Thames. Detroit and the Northwest were regained for good. As Washington Irving said in a biography of Perry that he whipped out a few weeks after the victory: "The last roar of cannon that died along the shores of Lake Erie was the expiring note of British domination."

There was no question of the decisive results of the battle, but controversy over Elliott's role in it arose almost immediately and did not subside for thirty years. Perry, perhaps simply relieved and ebullient over the victory, mentioned Elliott favorably in his official report to the Secretary of the Navy. There were mutterings from Perry's subordinates when the two captains each got an equal share out of the $225,000 prize money for the capture of Barclay's fleet, and later an enraged Perry retracted his initial statement when it became evident that Elliott felt he had not received enough credit.

Barclay returned to London and faced a court-martial, which acquitted him with honor, although his only subsequent command was a brief one on a tiny bomb vessel. A London magazine, reporting the incident, indicated that shortly before Perry left the *Lawrence*, Elliott was making away from the battle. When this report reached the States, it meant a court of inquiry for Elliott—a hasty affair in which nothing was really decided.

Storm clouds always gathered thickest around Elliott's head. In 1818 he challenged Perry to a duel. Perry in turn filed charges against Elliott and demanded his court-martial, but President Monroe pigeonholed the matter; and the next year Perry died, killed by a fever he had contracted while on duty along the South American coast. Elliott continued to court controversy, and in 1839 the whole thing blew up again when James Fenimore Cooper published a history of the Navy in which he sought to justify Elliott's behavior. It never was conclusively settled, though Elliott struck off a medal for Cooper. The rest of his career was an amalgam of duels and challenges and courts-martial. He flickered in and out of favor with successive administrations and was in command of the Philadelphia Navy Yard when he died in 1845.

But despite all the creaky rationale formulated by Elliott's friends, the day was Perry's and Perry's alone. Through his own desperate initiative he had, at the very last moment, come through the smoke to win a lost battle. Henry Adams summed it up at the end of his description of the action: "No process of argument . . . could deprive Perry of the fame justly given him by the public, or detract from the splendor of his reputation as the hero of the war. More than any other battle of the time, the victory on Lake Erie was won by the courage and obstinacy of a single man."

As for Daniel Dobbins, he spent the rest of his life on the Lakes, navigating them for forty years and never, he liked to boast, losing so much as a spar. When the President awarded a sword to each midshipman and sailing master who served well on Lake Erie, Dobbins wrote saying that he would like one too. But he was told that since he had not been in the battle, he was not eligible, and he never got his sword.

—February 1976

THE PEACE OF CHRISTMAS EVE

By FRED L. ENGELMAN

The American ministers gathered in Belgium in the summer of 1814 to seek a cessation of hostilities with Great Britain. It was a particularly tricky business, since the United States certainly wasn't winning the two-year-old war. On the other hand, we could field a negotiating team that included Albert Gallatin, Henry Clay, and John Quincy Adams.

It was St. John's Day, a gentle introduction to summer, and the road, bowered by leafing elms and poplars and oaks, carved through lush grain fields and meticulous flower gardens. The two reluctant traveling companions had set out from Antwerp at nine that morning. For more than an hour they had been delayed at the River Scheldt, a crowded anchorage for British men-of-war, while petty officials bickered over their tolls, but by early afternoon they were halfway to Ghent, the old Flemish capital, where they were to seek peace with the British.

The older, squatter "Minister Plenipotentiary and Extraordinary of the United States" was John Quincy Adams—minister to Russia, son of his nation's second President, and a righteous pedant who was humorless to the point of exasperation. The younger commissioner possessed more humor but infinitely less virtue. He was Jonathan Russell, United States minister to Sweden, and he barely had been able to present his credentials in Stockholm before departing on the three-week journey. For Adams the trip was an unexpected delight, and now that he was back among the scenes of his early manhood he was moved almost to tears. At four o'clock on this June 24, 1814, their carriage came to a halt in Ghent's Place d'Armes before the Hotel des Pays-Bas. Adams was gratified to find that they were the first commissioners to arrive.

In less than two weeks, three other United States ministers joined them. Three days after Adams and Russell had established themselves came James Asheton Bayard, a patrician senator from Delaware and the only Federalist on the commission. He was homesick and in chronic ill health, and he was provincially unable to accept European customs. In little more than a year he would die, just six days after reaching his home in Wilmington.

The day after Bayard's arrival brought rain: it also brought Henry Clay, wearied by an "excessively unpleasant" trip from Gothenburg, Sweden. Not yet the Henry Clay who engineered great sectional compromises and aspired endlessly to the Presidency, this lanky, carelessly dressed, lean-faced, bushy-haired young man of thirty-seven had been a United States senator from Kentucky, and a former Speaker of the House. He championed the interests of the trans-Appalachian West with the devotion of a guardian who well understood the potential of his ward. A prime instigator of the War of 1812, he was now in Ghent to aid in effecting a happy conclusion to this great crusade, which had an unfortunate tendency to resemble comic opera, deadly and expensive though it was.

For as Clay sought the warmth and dryness of the Hotel des Pays-Bas, British troop transports nosed toward the mouth of the St. Lawrence. Their burden, four brigades strong, would, in little more than two months, be camped on the western shore of Lake Champlain in the sleepy New York State village of Plattsburgh. Here they would be but hours from almost certain victory and the probable dissolution of the United States.

But to Clay, as he watched the shadows of evening reflected in the puddles of the Place d'Armes, British military intentions were but a suspicion. It was enough to question British intentions for peace and to wait impatiently for the coming of their commissioners.

John Quincy Adams, the first man named to the American commission and consequently its titular head, had already instituted regular seminars for his charges when Albert Gallatin, the most astute member of the group, arrived from Paris. This scion of wealthy Swiss gentry had established and celebrated his maturity by emigrating to the American colonies, then in revolt against England. Continental manners and speech notwithstanding, he gained recognition in the bear pit of western Pennsylvania politics and soon rose to national eminence, serving for twelve years as Secretary of the Treasury under Jefferson and Madison. He was probably the most illustrious and dependable servant of the often-feeble Madison administration and, fortunately for his adopted country, he was to exert his tact, patience, humor, and brilliance throughout the trying months in Ghent.

Partly from inclination, but mostly because of British evasion, Gallatin and the other American commissioners had been meandering through northern Europe, like so many disgruntled and separated patrons of a misguided tour. More than a year before, Gallatin and Bayard had sailed from New Castle, Delaware, for St. Petersburg, Russia. There they intended, with Adams's assistance, to treat with England under the benevolent mediation of Czar Alexander I. They arrived in St. Petersburg only to discover that Lord Liverpool's government, on the grounds that the war was an internal affair, had rejected the Czar's thoughtful but meddlesome overture, and that the Czar himself was somewhere in the wake of Napoleon's retreat across Europe. Gallatin and Bayard spent six dreary and confining months in the frigid Russian capital before pushing on through Berlin and Amsterdam for London.

But before arriving there, Gallatin and Bayard received confirmation that President Madison had accepted the British proposal for direct negotiations in Gothenburg, Sweden, and that Henry Clay and Jonathan Russell were sailing from New York to join the original commission of three. Clay and Russell had scarcely unpacked their bags in Sweden—and Adams, a dour and self-pursuing Eliza, was still battling Baltic ice floes —when Gallatin and Bayard assented to, and to some extent encouraged, a British proposal to make Ghent, not Gothenburg, the scene of their discussions. Ghent was a mere Channel crossing from London, and Gallatin and Bayard hoped that this proximity would enable the British commission to act with greater dispatch.

By July 6, 1814, the entire American mission was assembled. They were to wait a month for their British counterparts to arrive, and this added delay did little to invigorate their waning faith in the success of their enterprise. Adams, true to his nature, was especially gloomy, but the others disagreed with his prediction that the negotiations for peace would be of short duration and that their sojourn in Ghent would be brief. To occupy their time they held preparatory meetings, wrote letters to all who might provide news or influence, recalled their young messengers and secretaries from the dubious pleasures of Paris, witnessed the mass marriage of twenty-six "ugly" brides to their younger-looking grooms, and went house-hunting. Lacking their real enemy to squabble with, they disputed with their perspective landlord. A shaky compromise was eventually reached, and the Americans moved into their own house on the Rue des Champs, reluctantly agreeing to pay their host, in addition to room and board, one franc each time he popped the cork from a bottle of wine.

Not until late evening of the first Saturday in August did the British mission arrive in Ghent. Two days later, after fifteen months of fruitless inquiries and travel, the Americans for the first time met their adversaries—Lord Gambier, a churchgoing, armchair admiral who was approaching senescence; Henry Goulburn, the thirty-year-old Under Secretary for War and the Colonies, who in time was to be Chancellor of the Exchequer; and Dr. William Adams, an obscure Admiralty lawyer who was destined to justify his obscurity.

It was symptomatic of London's attitude toward the United States that the government had briefly considered naming Lord Bathurst, Colonial Secretary, head of the commission to Ghent but decided that the settlement of this contemptible uprising did not rate a ranking cabinet minister. They sent instead a commission whose members were unknown even to the populace of Great Britain and at its head placed a man who had gained his peerage for participating, on one of his infrequent seagoing excursions, in the bombardment of defenseless Copenhagen. At Ghent, Lord Gambier was never more than a polite, impressive-looking, usually silent figurehead. Dr. William Adams did his best to make up for Gambier's taciturnity, but he was no Demosthenes. In his most uncontrollable moments he was a sputtering old fool who talked himself and the British cause into impossible corners. His family, he told the American Adams, was on the downgrade, and John Quincy, quite willing to agree, was much relieved to discover that they probably were not cousins.

Early in the afternoon on the eighth day of August, Lord Gambier, after he and Adams had exchanged pious hopes for peace, turned the meeting over to Goulburn, who promptly rattled off the British terms. If the Americans insisted, the British would discuss the impressment of American seamen—one of the major published reasons the United States had gone to war—but Goulburn suggested that this was about all they would do about the problem. The British would require some revisions along the Canadian boundary. They would not renew the privilege —written into the Treaty of Paris in 1783—that allowed the Americans to dry fish on Canadian coasts. And most important, as an indispensable condition to be accepted before any other matters could be discussed, the treaty must embrace terms of peace and suitable boundaries for Britain's "Indian allies." In later verbal and written communications, the English commissioners were to admit that this would mean a buffer state between the United States and Canada, which in extent would swallow most of the present states of Ohio, Indiana, Illinois, Wisconsin, and Michigan —more, when the boundary "revisions" were added, than the land mass of the British Isles. Another stipulation, prohibiting American arms on or near the Great Lakes, was added less than two weeks later, along with British reaffirmation of their right to sail the Mississippi.

The Americans were stunned. Bayard called the terms those of a conqueror to the conquered. Posterity might raise questions, but in that summer of 1814 the government of Lord Liverpool saw no reason to doubt the wisdom or justice of its demands. For most of Henry Goulburn's lifetime his nation had been locked in a sometimes lonely world struggle with France. The British could not countenance the claims and complaints of a semicolonial neutral when their fate was in the grasping hands of Napoleon. In 1812, he had already penetrated Russia when the English Cabinet received the bitter news that the Americans had treacherously declared war on them. For a year and a half the British were much too busy in Europe to worry about proper punishment for the transatlantic upstarts, but at Fontainebleau, in April of 1814, a forlorn ex-emperor of France waved farewell to his troops and commenced his humiliating journey to Elba. Now it was possible to deal with the would-be invaders of Canada, the distant cousins who brazenly embarrassed the world's greatest naval power, those noisy colonials who kept insisting they were independent and equal. For the first time in twenty years, all Europe was at peace, and the British lion roared in triumph. "There is no public feeling in the country stronger than that of indignation against the Americans," said the *London Times* of April 15, and on English and continental docksides ominous lines of Wellington's seasoned veterans, the potent symbols of this indignation, waited to board their America-bound transports.

The five highly independent Americans who composed the uneasy family of "Bachelors' Hall" on the Rue des Champs were stung but not altogether taken unaware by the severity of the British demands. Yet even the shrewd and usually imperturbable Gallatin was upset by the apparent evidence that the British government was entranced by its own propaganda. He had anticipated lip service to popular demands, but Lords Liverpool, Castlereagh, and Bathurst, the real English negotiators, seemed to be in earnest. And Gallatin's discomfiture increased when he considered the now seemingly absurd terms so fervently expressed in the instructions to the American commission.

A sorely tried, peaceable James Madison had signed the declaration of war on June 18, 1812, because he sincerely believed that this was the only way to gain respect for neutral rights and to teach the English that they could not with impunity whisk English-speaking mariners, many of them American citizens, off American ships—on the often debatable grounds that they were deserters from His Majesty's Navy. Ostensibly, Americans had taken up arms for freedom of the seas.

Not all their aspirations, though, had been maritime. The largely Federalist coastal states, willing for the sake of profit to suffer restrictions on their commerce and to swallow insults to national pride, were almost unanimously opposed to an open rupture with Great Britain. It was this attitude that lay behind New England's refusal to cooperate in the war. The narrow margin of votes in favor of war came from the West and the South, states that for the most part had neither ships to sail nor oceans to sail upon. One had to be deaf to miss the westerners in Congress, Henry

Clay very notable among them, who clearly spelled out the West's reason for going to war: greedy appreciation of Canadian real estate. The motto of the day became "On to Canada!" and the march had begun even before the care-worn James Madison could put his pen to the war document. Sadly, however, the invasion of Canada became a sort of Gilbert and Sullivan fiasco, and as Adams and his colleagues faced their adversaries at Ghent in the summer of 1814, the military initiative had passed to the British. Yet hope lingered painfully in the battered American breast: the hunger for Canada and the sincere but impracticable desire for a guarantee of the rights of neutrals.

The delay in the start of the negotiations, and the great time lag in communications, made most of the instructions to the American peace mission irrelevant by the time the commissioners received them. The basis for a sizable portion of the American neutral rights objective was removed less than a week after the American declaration of war, when Lord Liverpool's government revoked the Orders in Council—its legal justification for interference with American ships on the high seas. This left impressment the sole ostensible reason for prosecuting the war, for only incompetent generals and uninhibited politicians could publicly avow American designs on Canada.

In some of his instructions (which, for good reason, were never published) James Monroe, Secretary of State and sometime gratuitous adviser to the War Department, did go so far as to include the desirability of the cession of Canada. He suffered from the delusion that Canada, like an overripe fruit, would drop into the American basket anyway; so England might as well face facts and get it over with. Monroe also wrote to his ministers of the necessity for getting some meaningful definition of a blockade and of neutral rights in general. In addition, he covered other, less significant points, but the bulk of his prose was lavished on impressment.

For assurances that this evil alone would cease, the American commissioners were authorized to sign a peace treaty, but if they failed on this point "all further negotiations will cease, and you will return home without delay."

With the end of hostilities in Europe, the British no longer found it necessary to recruit their Navy by wholesale kidnapping, but they would sooner have given London to the Turks than surrender their "right" to impressment. The Americans in Ghent were keenly aware of this. None of them seriously nourished the hope that the British could be convinced of the pernicious and unlawful effects of impressment, and Gallatin had written as much to Monroe several times over. But as a hot August sun warmed the Flemish canals, the abolition of impressment was still the

141

primary goal the five Americans were expected to achieve. Regarding the proposed cession of Canada as patently insupportable, they had quietly put it to rest before the peace talks began, although Adams, in a moment of madness, would later try but fail to revive the subject.

Jonathan Russell, the weakest link in the American peace chain, was off visiting Dunkirk at the time his colleagues were absorbing the harsh British terms of the first conference on August 8. That evening after dinner, Adams, Bayard, Clay, and Gallatin were discussing their brief for the morrow when a messenger arrived from Paris with more recent instructions from Monroe. By one o'clock the next morning they had deciphered the code and were able to read, much to their relief, "you may omit any stipulation on the subject of impressment, if found indispensably necessary. . . ." The four men needed little more to convince them of the indispensable necessity. One of the principal causes of the war was now an all-but-forgotten resolution, and Adams had a rather trivial case to present to the British later that day.

He carefully explained to them that he and his colleagues were not instructed on Indians or fisheries, but that they would like to reach some definition of the respective rights of neutrals and belligerents, and that they intended to put forward claims of indemnity for British seizure of United States shipping before and during the first six months of the war. These American terms, however, were dwarfed by the enormity of the British ultimatum.

Actually, it made scant difference what case the Americans presented. The triumphant British held the initiative, and far from pressing for Canada, the American commissioners would need all their wits to preserve the United States.

Wit, skill, and determination they had. However dissonant their private councils might be, they wrote firm, trenchant notes, the propaganda value of which was to influence the British government in a way it did not anticipate. In conference they were admirable courtroom lawyers who bettered the third-rate British commission at almost every stop. To the horror of their superiors in London, the three Englishmen virtually admitted that the Indian buffer state and the propositions for Canadian boundary rectifications were ill-disguised efforts to chew off hunks of American territory. Gallatin, at one point, asked what would happen to the thousands of American citizens who lived in the projected Indian utopia that the British demanded, and William Adams brusquely answered that they would have to shift for themselves. His careless words were to gain notoriety in the United States.

Whatever the personal advantages the American commission held over their immediate adversaries, however, there was no escaping the fact that the British government held the high military cards. Their crack European veterans were already ravaging the American coast, and Sir George Prevost was coming down the western shore of Lake Champlain at the head of an imposing army that was to be used, in the words of a British colonel, " to give Jonathan a good drubbing." The British in Ghent happily informed their American opposites of British doings across the Atlantic, and a successful peace seemed hopelessly elusive when on August 21, after several inconclusive British-American meetings, John Adams sat down at his desk to draft the first written American answer to all the British demands so far. His despair was not lifted when his companions examined his efforts. Gallatin thought some of his expressions were "offensive"; Clay was sarcastic about his "figurative" eighteenth-century language; Russell, who had returned from Dunkirk, set about improving John Quincy's grammar; and Bayard thought everything should be stated somewhat differently. For four days they dismembered each other's offerings, and at 11:00 P.M. on August 24 they had combined the remnants into a note that none of them really liked. It would, Adams predicted, "bring the negotiations very shortly to a close."

When they broke up their meeting to retire it was still early evening in Washington. The five Americans in Ghent had no way of knowing that Dolley Madison would spend the night in a tent; that her husband, leader of the American people, would ignominiously ride through most of the darkness along a Virginia road choked with refugees; that when dawn came to Washington, the Capitol, symbol of American majesty and dreams, would be hardly more than smoldering ruins at the feet of the enemy.

Gallatin, Adams, and company were not to hear of the shame of Washington until October 1. But the negotiations did not come to an untimely end for the simple reason that the British did not want them to end. In early September there was another exchange of notes between the two commissions, and then for ten days there was silence while the Americans awaited the next British move. It was the morning of September 20 when the third British note was delivered to John Quincy Adams. The Americans answered it a week later and once again settled back impatiently to bide their time. They were at dinner when the fourth British note arrived on October 8; coming two months after the negotiations commenced, it represented the first dramatic break in the British demands.

The British had, in fact, been softening their diplomatic blows for a month, but the Americans were so accustomed to saying "no" with vehemence and frequency that their vision was blurred when they read prose that had originated in Whitehall, and they failed fully to perceive the changes. Even Goulburn and his companions were not certain of their government's intentions.

The true spokesman of the British commission and the one who handled the correspondence with the ruling triumvirate of Prime Minister Liverpool, Foreign Minister Castlereagh, and Colonial Secretary Bathurst was Henry Goulburn. He was an honest, devoted, undiplomatic diplomat who smarted from surplus zeal. He was convinced, not without reason, that his mission was to rub Yankee noses in the dirt. Not that he had anything against the American commissioners, but they would give in or Goulburn would send them packing. He heaped unwanted advice and mistaken notions on his superiors, and, to their chagrin, he gleefully wrote to them when he thought the Americans were about to go home. He ached to apply the *coup de grâce*. He was to ache unrelievedly.

To some extent, Goulburn and his companions can be forgiven for mistaking their government's somewhat uncertain aims. Neglectfully, but sometimes intentionally, the British Cabinet largely failed to correct their messenger boys' illusions. Both Liverpool and Castlereagh complained that the three lonely gentlemen had "taken an erroneous view of the line to be adopted," but as late as September 16 Goulburn wrote a sarcastic letter to Bathurst, saying that he could not thank him enough "for so clearly explaining what are the views and objects of the government."

In fact, the most important of these objects was delay. Lord Liverpool and his advisers were not altruistically devoted to the interests of the North American Indians, but they did mean to put up a geographical barrier between Canada and the obstreperous American filibusters; what they failed to accomplish by diplomacy they serenely expected to gain on the bloody field of glory—after which they could dictate a peace. You cannot skin a cat, however, once he has fled captivity, and Goulburn's diligent reports that the Americans, despairing of any real progress, were about to go home finally caused concern in London.

In truth, the British government had been sorely vexed by the unyielding stand of the American commission. The nearly bankrupt American government was disintegrating under the dual pressures of English arms and New England's tendencies toward disunion, and yet the men at Ghent would not budge. Furthermore, although the ordinary Englishman wanted to wallop the American, he would not much longer be disposed to pay for the pleasure.

And all was not well in Europe. The mad Bonaparte appeared to be safely tucked away on Elba, but Paris was chafing under the yoke of fat Louis, and Alexander of Russia was casting covetous glances toward Poland's territory. Liverpool, who though the Czar was "half an American" and therefore not altogether rational, hastened Castlereagh to the Congress of Vienna to see what could be done about the mystical despot's ambitions, but for a time the British were to have visions of a Slavic Napoleon.

With pressures mounting, the British government slightly reduced its demands in its notes of September 4 and 19, but the notes were ambiguously worded, and after the British commissioners got through with them they were contradictory as well, in tenor if not in fact. London had sternly advised its representatives in Ghent to constrain their editing so that it did not alter intent, but neither they nor the Americans fully understood what the intent really was, and Goulburn did not mean to lose face even if his government did. To both notes, the Americans returned their usual exasperating retorts. These upset and infuriated the British Cabinet, but the annoyance of the transatlantic war itself was becoming politically unbearable and economically prohibitive. On October 1, Liverpool wrote to Castlereagh in Vienna of the Cabinet's "anxious desire to put an end to the war. . . . I feel too strongly," he continued, "the inconvenience of a continuance of the war not to make me desirous of concluding it at the expense of some popularity." To accomplish this, the ultimatum with regard to the Indians was scaled down. The note delivered to the American dinner table just a week later no longer demanded an Indian state in the American backyard; it was simply necessary that peace with the Indians be part of the British-American peace treaty. The British also had omitted entirely any pretension of maintaining unilateral armaments on the shores and waters of the Great Lakes, a claim which they had already begun to soft-pedal in a previous note.

Thus the two insurmountable barriers to serious discussions had been removed. Of course the British Privy Council, with a bombastic assist from the eager Goulburn, could not refrain from stating their much-diminished Indian ultimatum in abrupt and menacing tones: the Americans would accept this milder cathartic or negotiations would close. And, significantly, the note laid claim to a small helping of Maine. With confidence the British waited for the next mail pouch from their commanders in America; the news, they were sure, would justify making the peace treaty a real estate deed — a touch of Maine, a bit of New York, an island, a fort, a port here and there.

The British note was delivered to a house whose occupants were getting on one another's nerves. The confined living quarters and the frustrating pursuit of peace were taking their toll. None of the other American commissioners was long at ease with the querulous John Quincy. Bayard, who for six months had endured Adams's company in Russia, thought the man "singularly cold and repulsive"; it is tragic when one reflects that

145

Bayard was the closest thing to a friend Adams had in Ghent. And Clay, who by a mocking quirk of fate had rooms adjoining those of the commissioner from Massachusetts, grew even further apart from him. Not only were there extensive political differences, but Clay gambled, enjoyed foul cigars, did much to increase the landlord's corkage profits, and reputedly gave vain chase to a resisting chambermaid. He emptied his room of card players and went to bed at five in the morning, just as John Quincy Adams was rising with the sun to begin his daily study of the Bible. When the day's meetings and miscellaneous occupations were over, Adams joined the others at a four o'clock dinner and suffered through two more hours of cigar stink, bad wine, and desultory conversation. Most evenings he took a walk about the city—alone, he wrote his wife, because no one would go with him. He was in bed by nine.

By late September the three-storied house on the Rue des Champs resembled an isolated boarding school during winter term. Its occupants were tired of one another's company, depressed by the plight of their country, and numb from British diplomatic attacks. They wrangled over trifles. For days they passionately disputed over which of their messengers and secretaries would carry which dispatch—and ended by not sending the dispatches at all. Gallatin and Bayard began to show signs of "despondency." Momentarily they talked of complying with some of the terms in the British note of September 19, but Adams and Clay, acting in concert for a change, stiffened their resolution. It was well they did; for otherwise the British might never have had to give way in the note which now arrived on October 8.

The first American reaction to the note was circumspect but optimistic. For five days Adams and his companions drafted, edited, and debated their answer. Adams raged. He was violently opposed to accepting the Privy Council's ultimatum on the Indians, softened though it was when stripped of its rhetoric. He wanted to match the "arrogance" of the fifteen-page British note word for word, insult for insult. He even exhumed Monroe's instructions and decided that he and his colleagues should, after all, advise the British that it was to their own advantage to give up Canada. Gallatin and Clay tried to reason with him, but it was Bayard, being "perfectly friendly and confidential," who calmed him down—by producing a bottle of Chambertin and dispensing solace and prudence along with the wine. Two days later, at noon on October 14, Adams joined the others in Clay's room and grudgingly signed his name to their answer.

That answer spewed forth a torrent of words on the subject of Indians, but the British mandate on Indian pacification was accepted, however ungraciously. It was, said the American commissioners, similar to their own suggestions on the matter (suggestions which had been made, strangely enough, in September by the same John Quincy Adams who went livid when he saw the words in British handwriting). In conclusion, the Americans asked for a complete treaty project from the British, to which they would respond with one of their own. "May it please God," intoned Adams, after the note had been sent, "to forgive our enemies, and to turn their hearts!"

What the Lord did to British hearts will remain a celestial mystery. In any event, on October 17, while the British commissioners were considering their rejoinder, it was their turn to receive bad news from America. On September 11, Thomas Macdonough, working his ships as if they were water-borne carrousels, had outlasted a superior British naval force in Plattsburgh Bay, and Sir George Prevost, who was to have severed New England from the not-so-United States, had sunk in spirit as his naval brothers were sinking in fact and promptly marched his intimidating horde back to Canada. A few days later, Robert Ross, the general who had put the torch to Washington, lay dying near unconquered Baltimore, listening to the same bomb bursts that provoked patriotic verse in Francis Scott Key.

The discouraging news did not, however, noticeably temper the next British note to the American commission. It insisted that the Americans accede to the principle of hold-what-you-have, specifying that a good part of Maine and some forts and islands should be given to Canada, and repeating the prohibition against the drying of fish on Canadian shores. On the matter of a treaty project, the British demurred. Their terms were clear, they said; it was up to the Americans to produce a plan. The American answer was prompt and negative, and it gave Lord Liverpool the queasy sensation of balancing on a seesaw that could not touch ground at either end. He wanted to break off the negotiations and fight, but he thought of the Czar, of Talleyrand, of the British budget, and wept. On the last day of October Anthony St. John Baker, secretary to the British mission at Ghent, trotted across town with a note that was brief, terse, and only too familiar. The British *had* given their terms. They had nothing more to say. They awaited the American project. They were, they neglected to say, stalling.

The American commissioners had in fact been discussing and composing a treaty project for two days when Baker surrendered his blunt message and a packet of London newspapers to four sober men, three of them the restless audience for an Adams monologue. Only Jonathan Russell was missing; it may well have been one of his greatest contributions to the progress of peace.

An occasional merchant, lawyer, and unlikely diplomat from Rhode Island, Jonathan Russell was a perverse and bristling mixture of acute self-adoration and gelatinous principle. Like a sulky little boy, he fumed when Gallatin forgot to tell him of a Ghent social invitation, and at the end of September he moved away from his condescending peers and back to the more appreciative companionship of the secretaries and messengers at the Hotel des Pays-Bas. Adams he hated. Gallatin he suspected. Bayard he dismissed. Clay, the man in whom "all the nobler passions have found their home," was his idol and, Russell hoped, his viaduct to a political future. In Ghent Russell's course was that of a wayward carriage, but in November he latched on to Clay and, usually, whenever the latter raised his hand two votes were counted.

Clay would have snickered had he known of Russell's praise. Clay was the epitome of crude, calculating, dice-throwing western ambition, and in him lay the source of the overstatement of the American attitudes at Ghent. The British, he maintained, were nothing more than card players, faking a flush when they held a pair of deuces. At a time when his companions floundered in a vale of pessimism and made sounds like departing tourists, Clay blandly asked the British for his passport and sent Goulburn's spirits surging. But Clay was playing "brag." He later asked Adams if he knew how to play. John Quincy most surely did not. It is, said Adams, the art of "holding your hand, with a solemn and confident phiz. . . ." Adams, however, could not put on such a "phiz."

When the British temporized and insisted on an American draft of a treaty, the United States commission was not surprised, but after months of total, unstinting defense they were flustered by the necessity for assuming the initiative. Clay, whose card-playing simile appeared to have been justified, was more depressed than elated. His 1812 speeches echoed in his ears, and he felt the demanding hands of his constituents on his shoulders. From his seldom-used pen came an article specifically calling for the temporary abandonment of impressment. Russell, of course, concurred, and Adams, after arguing both sides of the case, added his own vote and gave the Clay forces a three-to-two victory. Clay was loath to match the gesture, however, when Adams proposed *status quo ante bellum*—no boundary changes, no articles prohibiting impressment or clarifying neutral rights—as an alternative to be presented with the project. You could not, Clay pointed out, play "brag" after showing your hand.

Clay, of course, was yearning to try a little American finesse on the British, but he also quavered when he realized that 1815 might be nothing more than 1812 three years later—no American territory in Canada, no guarantee of neutral rights, just two or more years of running in place. One thing he would not do. He would not let the Mississippi become a British canal, as the British seemed to desire, simply to allow New England fishermen the privilege of "drying fish on a desert." But it was Adams's neighbors who did the fishing and Adams's father who in 1783 had ensured the right; the name of Adams would not appear on a treaty that surrendered it. Clay's name would not be signed to a note that mentioned the Mississippi.

Adams sat tight. Clay scowled and paced the floor. The benign Gallatin quietly spoke to both of them. On the night of November 9, with Russell absent in pursuit of more pleasurable activities and with most of Ghent in bed, Gallatin, with Bayard's judicious assistance, preached compromise. The next day, Adams and Clay, still grumbling, brought a precarious unanimity to the American treaty draft and an accompanying note that offered restoration of the *status quo*, said nothing of the Mississippi, and assumed openly that the fisheries right could not have been abrogated by the war.

The American project crossed the Channel to a Cabinet still not sure of what it wanted. On Sunday, the thirteenth of November, Lord Liverpool sat brooding in Fife House—the American treaty draft and two letters from Wellington before him. The draft from Ghent, he reflected, was a studied insult, the product of beggars who did not know their own poverty. Yet from Paris—where Wellington, saviour of England, was now minister to France—came an icy gust of candor. "You can get no territory," he wrote, "indeed the state of your military operations, however creditable, does not entitle you to demand any; and you only afford the Americans a popular and creditable ground, which I believe their government are looking for, not to break off the negotiations, but to avoid to make peace." If the Cabinet insisted, the Duke would, next year, go to America, where "I shall do you but little good"; for British claims rested with British sailors on the bottom of Plattsburgh Bay.

October and November were months of misery for Liverpool. The budget watchers in Parliament were after his scalp, and taxes could go no higher. In Vienna, Castlereagh beseeched and threatened; Alexander smiled, and continued to ogle Poland; and all Europe, snickering at British reverses, softly applauded the Americans. Talleyrand wooed the Czar and glimpsed opportunity in Allied dissension. The Parisians spat at Louis, yearned for the return of Bonaparte, and cheered the American victory at Plattsburgh and Prevost's retreat into Canada.

Lord Liverpool was digesting Wellington's report of the cheering when the British press published the first month of the Ghent negotiations —information that the American Congress had thoughtfully provided. Englishmen were appalled and secretly admired the American resistance, and in Parliament the Opposition sharpened its knives and asked who would pay for this nonsense.

At Ghent a mortified Henry Goulburn slumped wearily into his desk chair and began his reply to Bathurst's most recent instructions. "You know," he wrote, bitterly, "that I was never much inclined to give way to the Americans: I am still less inclined to do so after the statement of our demands with which the negotiation opened, and which has in every point of view proved most unfortunate." Nevertheless, he followed Bathurst's orders directing him to oppose most of the American project, to press for navigation rights on the Mississippi, and to stay silent on the fisheries. But the hand that had reached out for American territory had been withdrawn, and Goulburn had a foreboding that another hand might appear to accept the offer of *status quo ante bellum*. On Sunday, November 27, Baker carried the news to the Americans.

When they finished reading the British reaction to their project, even Adams, the eternal pessimist, thought peace was "probable." The others were sure of it, and Clay wagered his life that the British earnestly desired a speedy conclusion. A ban on impressment and the article on indemnities for maritime spoilage were dead matters, but it is questionable that they ever really lived. There was still unfinished business, however, which, in the absence of any real obstacles, loomed large. The Americans answered on the thirtieth. On December 1, the two commissions met in their first conference since August 10. Two more meetings followed—on the tenth of December and on the twelfth.

The five Americans, more than ever, became unrelenting lawyers. They drove Goulburn and Dr. Adams, already wretched with their country's shame, into whorls of rage. They demanded explanations which the three embarrassed Britishers were unable to provide, and messengers shuttled back and forth across the Channel. But by the beginning of the third week in December most of the points had been settled. Only three remained. The British held, claimed, and intended to keep Moose Island, a speck off the Massachusetts coast. Both sides denied the other's rights set forth in the treaty of 1783 but demanded their own—the British their privilege of navigating the Mississippi, the Americans their fish-drying franchise. The latter two were connected in thought if not in fact, and both the fisheries and Moose Island were particular problems of Massachusetts, the home of John Quincy Adams. As Adams fought and pleaded for the rights of his neighbors, his neighbors were trudging to Hartford, where they intended to reform the American government or perhaps leave it.

In those first weeks of December Adams was alone to a degree that was intense even for his lifetime. He admitted that he contended for objects "so trifling and insignificant that neither of the two nations would tolerate a war for them," but he could not go home without them. Clay, on the other hand, gagged at the thought of British ships on the Mississippi. He and Adams shouted at one another. They would not listen to compromise. They would not sign the treaty.

Bayard joined Adams in his nocturnal walks about Ghent and talked to him like a kindly Dutch uncle. Gallatin, who in every respect was now the American leader, reasoned with both Adams and Clay. He offered suggestions; he teased Adams out of some of his obstinacy; he told Clay to stop acting like a little boy; he turned their acid to humor; in despair, he shouted back at them. By December 14 Adams stood alone. His colleagues would make one more attempt, but whatever its success they would sign a treaty with or without him. Finally, at 3:30 that afternoon, they sent their note, which all had signed. Moose Island could be excepted from the article on territorial restoration—today it is part of Eastport, Maine—but the conflicting claims must be settled soon after the war ended. Mention of the Mississippi and the fisheries was to be omitted from the treaty. These claims, too, would be decided after the war.

A week and a day later, Bayard hurried through the streets of Ghent in search of the perambulating Adams. The British had accepted. Peace was but a detail.

The details were composed the next day, Friday, December 23, at the American house. The two commissions met at noon and arranged the procedure for the following day. At three o'clock they separated to draw up copies for signing. The Americans were not sure what to think. Clay was sullen. Gallatin said that all treaty commissions were unpopular. Adams was sure that they would be "censured and reproached" at home. Yet the five of them felt relief.

A nd in a few months they would be heroes. The treaty would reach Washington on February 14; two days later the Senate would vote unanimously for ratification; and on the eighteenth, President Madison would call it "highly honorable to the nation," as, with thanks and joy, he read his proclamation. Post riders, who had already carried the news of Andrew Jackson's glorious victory at New Orleans, would ride night and day throughout the country. They would gallop into Philadelphia on a Sunday morning as congregations streamed from their churches and steeple bells made a New Year's Eve of the Sabbath. In rebellious Boston, school children would delight in an unexpected holiday from classes. New York would be ablaze with torchlight parades and nearly deafened by a barrage of cannon fired in gleeful celebration.

For a document that was little more than an armistice, the Treaty of Ghent had far-reaching influence. It said nothing about impressment, which was already an archaic practice, and nothing about neutrals' rights, which would never be respected to anyone's satisfaction. Boundary problems, territorial claims—in fact, all other disputes—were to be settled later by joint commissions. The treaty was no more than an instrument that restored the *status quo*, but it raised the silly little American democracy to a new level of respect in European eyes, and it brought a delicate peace between Great Britain and the United States—a peace that would eventually become a firm partnership. Fenians, explorers, Confederates, Maine potato farmers, New Brunswick roughnecks, rumrunners, tourists—all of these would, from time to time, disturb the tranquility of the U.S.-Canadian border, but that boundary would become the longest unguarded frontier in the world. And the two belligerents of 1812 would learn, through their joint commissions, an adult way of reconciling at least some of their differences. This would be the legacy of the document that was signed at Ghent on that December 24, 1814.

At four in the afternoon of that Christmas eve the American commission arrived at the British Chartreux, a former monastery where Napoleon had spent one of his honeymoons. In the courtyard, Baker's carriage stood ready for the dash to Ostend, where he would take ship for London. The British greeting was almost warm, and for two hours the three Englishmen and the five Americans pored over the treaty copies and made corrections. At six, with darkness spreading over Ghent and the carillon of St. Bavon pealing its Christmas message, the eight gentlemen gathered about the long table and officially attested to a "Treaty of Peace and Amity Between His Britannic Majesty and the United States of America." When all had signed, Lord Gambier presented the British copies to the Americans and said that he hoped the treaty would be permanent. Adams, in turn, handed over the American copies and replied that his government, too, wished that this would be the last Anglo-American treaty of peace. And at six-thirty the Americans disappeared into the solemn night with peace in their pockets.

—December 1960

PRIMER FROM A GREEN WORLD

By WALTER HAVIGHURST

William McGuffey's First Reader *taught millions of Americans how to read.*
His Second Reader *taught them how to live.*

L ate in the year 1825 two riders jogged into Oxford, Ohio, from the
Cincinnati road and pulled up at the old college building. Down
from the saddles slipped a man and a boy, William Holmes McGuffey and
his nine-year-old brother Alexander H. The unknown new professor carried a bag of books and a roll of clothing to a room on the second floor
of the old wing. He was 25 years old, about to be graduated *in absentia*
from Washington College in Pennsylvania, and ready to begin his career.
Forty years later his name would be as familiar as the alphabet.

Six months before, President Bishop of Miami University, on a speaking tour in the valley, had heard of a zealous young teacher in a country
school outside of Paris, Kentucky. The school, it was said, was in a
smokehouse, but the scholars came early and stayed late. Bishop was interested in such a teacher. He found a serious young man with a high broad
forehead, a big homely nose, and deeply lighted eyes. He was teaching
reading, writing, and figuring, but on his plank desk were texts in Latin,
Greek, and Hebrew. Bishop offered him the chair of ancient languages at
Miami University at a salary of $600.

One of eleven children of a Scotch-Irish farmer who had settled in
New Connecticut (northeastern Ohio) and chopped out his own road to
the village of Youngstown, McGuffey had struggled for an education. It
was hit or miss, at home or brief periods in rural schools, until his formal
education began when he was eighteen. But by that time his hungry
mind had stored away whole chapters, verbatim, from the Bible. He got
to college at twenty and between terms he taught school in the frontier
settlements. Now with news of appointment to a college faculty he rode

153

home. A few weeks later, with his young brother beside him, he clattered off for Oxford, 300 miles across the state of Ohio. Miami had a grammar school where Aleck could prepare for the course in college.

At Miami brother Alexander, promptly named "Red," became a great tree-climber and broad-jumper in the college yard and a notorious swimmer, splasher, and ducker in the deep hole in Four Mile Creek; a few years later he was a leading declaimer and debater in the literary halls. Meanwhile Professor McGuffey was married to the niece of an Oxford merchant and ordained into the Presbyterian ministry. He preached on Sundays, alternating between the college chapel and rural congregations within horseback range of Oxford. In 1833 he moved his wife and two small daughters into their new brick house across from the south gate of the campus.

Every morning Professor McGuffey walked the path where the library now stands to the old college and climbed to his classroom in the southwest corner on the second floor. There was a determined elegance in his garb: a silk stovepipe hat and a suit of glossy black bombazine, a shiny celluloid collar and a black bow tie. Long-necked, intent, and humorless, with a leathery skin and a farm boy's big hands, he did not look easy in that dress. But he was at home in the classroom. His mind was clear, orderly, exact; his language ready and precise. He treated abstract and complex ideas in concrete and simple terms. One of his literary masters was the succinct Alexander Pope.

McGuffey was zealous, ambitious, and resourceful. Before breakfast he met students in his study for practice in elocution and forensics. Between classes he gathered neighborhood children to test the appeal of simple poems and stories. In his study stood a revolving eight-sided desk, made by himself in his own woodshed, with eight pie-shaped drawers—just right for filing word lists, spelling rules, reading exercises and selections. The young professor was compiling a series of schoolbooks.

From his terms of teaching McGuffey knew the somber lessons which introduced children to the wonder of the printed page. The famed *New England Primer* (five million copies printed since 1690) began with the bedrock of Calvinistic theology—"In Adam's Fall, we sinnéd all." McGuffey was sufficiently old school in the pulpit, but like the children in his schoolrooms he had grown up in a new green world—a world of creeks and woods and meadows, of dogs and horses, sheep and cattle, orchards, pastures and farmyards. Already he had published a "Treatise on Methods of Reading." As he walked the campus path he pondered the teaching of children in the new West.

In the strenuous Revolutionary period the leading American textbook was *Webster's Elementary Speller*. It contained a lengthy moral catechism, a series of moral fables, a collection of readings in prose and verse, and word lists ranging from "bag" to "equiponderant." Thousands of these "Blue-Back Spellers" came over the mountains, packed with the pots, pans, and pails in the movers' wagons. The one notable schoolbook between the *New England Primer* and McGuffey's Readers, it was also the family anthology and encyclopedia.

By 1830 Lexington, Louisville, and Cincinnati were centers of a new western book trade. Printers had brought movable presses over the mountains and down the river; publishers saw bright prospects in a bookless country. Soon Cincinnati took the lead, with a stream of almanacs, farm manuals, spelling books (including a new edition of Webster), school readers, testaments, and hymn books pouring from the presses. It was a new business; it existed not only because of the high cost of freighting books across the mountains but also because of the growing sectional consciousness of the new country. "Western books for western people" was a persuasive slogan.

A second-floor room on lower Main Street in Cincinnati housed the small firm of Truman and Smith, publishers of *Ray's Arithmetic* and a few other elementary schoolbooks. Winthrop B. Smith had an idea for a series of Eclectic Readers, and he looked for an educator to compile them. In 1833 he proposed the series to Catharine Beecher, daughter of the president of Lane Seminary and sister of the future author of *Uncle Tom's Cabin*. Miss Beecher was preoccupied with higher education for women —she opened in Cincinnati the Western Female Institute—and declined the task. Probably it was she who suggested a professor at Miami University; through the activities of a pioneer teachers' association, the Western Teachers' College Institute, McGuffey was acquainted with the Beechers. Smith soon made a contract with McGuffey for the publication of six books—a Primer, a Speller, and four Readers—for which the compiler would receive royalty payments of $1,000. No one could foresee that the series would make the fortune of Winthrop Smith and of a whole series of publishers who followed him.

Before the first meeting with Truman and Smith, McGuffey had filed in his octagonal desk a sheaf of pages beginning "A is for Ax." Now he took the manuscript to one of his students, Welsh-born Benjamin Chidlaw, asking him to make a careful copy for publication. Chidlaw was living on 32 cents a week, cooking porridge and potatoes on his stove in the old North Hall.

The *First* and *Second* Readers were published in 1836; the *Primer* and the *Third* and *Fourth* Readers followed in 1837. To the selections were added questions, rules of pronunciation, and exercises in spelling—an apparatus in which Catharine Beecher collaborated. By 1843 the series was selling a million copies a year.

In 1844 appeared McGuffey's Rhetorical Guide, an anthology of English and American literature, compiled for a fee of $500 by his brother Alexander. The former tree-climber was then a leading Cincinnati lawyer, the son-in-law of Dr. Daniel Drake, and a warm friend of the Beecher family. The Rhetorical Guide bore the name "A. H. McGuffey," which was close enough, especially in English script, to "W. H. McGuffey" to be accepted as coming from the same hand. A revision of the series in 1853 added the Rhetorical Guide to the set as the *Fifth Reader*. With selections from the great historians, orators, novelists, essayists, and poets, it became the most famous Reader of all. More than a schoolbook, it was a literary storehouse for family reading and a portable library for ambitious youths in a nearly bookless country.

The enlarged series swept southward and westward into thousands of new school districts as settlements spread. By 1860 sales of the Readers passed two million copies a year. When Cincinnati could not fill the orders, other publishers were licensed to produce the McGuffey series: Clark, Austin, Maynard and Company in New York; Lippincott Company in Philadelphia; Cobb, Pritchard and Company in Chicago. After the Civil War the Methodist Book Concern in Nashville published huge editions for distribution in the South. In the second half of the nineteenth century the proprietors became successively W. B. Smith and Company; Sargent, Wilson & Hinkle; Wilson, Hinkle & Company; Van Antwerp, Bragg & Company; and finally the American Book Company.

The Gilded Age was a golden age for the McGuffey publishers, who rode the wave of American expansion. The Readers went west in freight wagons and with emigrant caravans; traders packed them into Indian reservations; they turned up in sod schoolhouses on the prairie, in cow towns on the plains, and in mining camps in the Rockies and the Sierras. Between 1870 and 1890 the series sold sixty million copies. They were the basic schoolbooks in 37 states. Except for New England, where they never got started, the McGuffey Readers blanketed the nation.

In the 1890s the texts were translated into Spanish, and American imperialism carried them into the thatch-roof schools of Puerto Rico and the Philippines. A Tokyo edition, with alternate pages in English and Japanese, was used in schoolrooms under the shadow of Fujiyama.

After 1900 the business dwindled, and by 1920 the time of the Readers was past. But a new phenomenon was beginning. Change comes swiftly in America, but memory lingers. In the headlong twentieth century people recalled the old district school and the dog-eared Readers. From West Virginia to California McGuffey clubs sprang up. Groups of old residents held McGuffey reunions and retired schoolmasters formed McGuffey societies. A national federation of McGuffey societies met annually on the Miami campus, a congress of piety and remembrance. They recalled the lessons of long ago—The Boy Who Cried Wolf! Wolf!; Mr. Toil and Hugh Idle; Try, Try Again; Harry and the Guide Post; the Honest Boy and the Thief. They told and retold how young William Holmes McGuffey walked six miles to recite Latin to his tutor, how he memorized poems, orations, and whole books of the Bible. They wrote odes to the great educator "whose classroom was a nation" and sang hymns to his memory.

In 1932 Henry Ford, the man who had done most to change McGuffey's America past recognition, issued a facsimile edition of the 1857 series and moved McGuffey's log cabin birthplace to his museum at Dearborn, Michigan, beside the Ford laboratories. Collectors were bidding up the prices of the earliest McGuffey's—one hundred, two hundred, three hundred dollars for a tattered *Primer* or *First Reader*. By that time McGuffey meant the horse and buggy days, the Saturday night bath, the creak of the kitchen pump and the wood box behind the stove, the lost American innocence and piety. He had become a myth as American as Uncle Sam and as homespun as linsey-woolsey.

Fifteen sets of school readers were published in America between 1820 and 1841, but for some reason the McGuffey series ran away with the race.

Perhaps the clue is in the first lesson—A is for Ax. While children learned those letters the ax was ringing in every clearing, it was hewing logs for cabins and schoolhouses, it was changing the mid-continent. Thud, thud, thud—in the sound of the ax the future of America was beating like a pulse. The picture showed a boy not as tall as the ax helve leaning against a stump. It was a real ax, from the child's real world, the roughhewn, hopeful, equalitarian world of the Jacksonian West. After ax came box, cat, and dog; nut, ox, and pig; vine, wren, and yoke—all homely and familiar things. The lessons were alive with children at work, at play, at school: boys with hoops, kites, skates; girls with dolls, sleds, and jumping ropes. Reading could be fun.

It was also morality. The selections were shrewdly eclectic moral lessons attuned to the mixed people of the Ohio Valley and the expanding nation. They contained enough Puritanism to satisfy transplanted Yankees, enough Cavalier manner to fit the attitudes of the South, enough practical optimism to appeal to ambitious Scotch, German, and Irish settlers, and enough assurance of the material rewards of virtue to gratify all. Reading itself was described as a means to morality.

The books were vigorously western, but that has always been a relative term and it did not limit their market. The life they pictured and the ethic they advanced had an almost nationwide appeal. Yet in certain ways they were keyed to the newer country beyond the Appalachians. In the *Fourth Reader* an essay by Daniel Drake stated a belief which the books themselves were serving: "Measures should be taken to mould a unified system of manners out of the diversified elements which are scattered over the West. We should foster western genius, encourage western writers, patronize western publishers, augment the number of western readers, and create a western heart." McGuffey's texts were an immeasurable influence in creating a common mind and heart among the mingled strains that peopled the Ohio Valley and surged on to the farther West.

The Readers pictured a land where opportunity is open to all—all who will soberly and steadily pursue it. Scores of lessons repeated the gospel of success; each new Reader put it in stronger terms.

Here was the spreading myth of democratic, practical, middle-class America: work, strive, persevere, and success will follow. Virtue is its own reward, more precious than riches, but the virtuous become rich also. George, in the *Second Reader*, having confessed to breaking a merchant's window with a snowball, felt happy for doing what was right. But the story is not over. The merchant took honest George into his employ, with the happy outcome that "George became the merchant's partner and is now rich."

Industry is the watchword in the McGuffey books. "The idle boy is almost invariably poor and miserable," said the *Third Reader*; "the industrious boy is happy and prosperous." Lazy Ned, who wouldn't pull his sled uphill, died a dunce. Mr. Toil "had done more good than anybody else in the World." The lessons contained no wonderers or wanderers, no pilgrims or seekers, no rebels, reformers, or dissenters, but endless examples of practical ambition and prosaic success.

Yet along with this dutiful morality, the Readers contained selections of simple charm and of lasting literary worth. Once past the two-syllable limits of the *Second Reader*, the scholar met Hawthorne, Irving, Bryant, Longfellow, Whittier, Dickens, Lamb, Goldsmith, Milton, Shakespeare. The *Fourth Reader*, on a present junior high school level, had color and vitality; few of its selections have gone bad. The *Fifth* and *Sixth* Readers were mature, varied, and discriminating anthologies of poetry and prose. These volumes were read in the family circle, at church socials and grange suppers, as well as in the schoolroom. They were cherished by scholars long after school days were past. Hamlin Garland, who read them on the prairies of Iowa and South Dakota, wrote in *A Son of the Middle Border*: "I wish to acknowledge my deep obligation to Professor McGuffey, whoever he may have been, for the dignity and grace of his selections. From the pages of his Readers I learned to know and love the poems of Scott,

Byron, Southey, Wordsworth, and a long line of English masters. I got my first taste of Shakespeare from the selections which I read in those books." Many other nineteenth-century Americans have expressed the same gratitude.

While his name and a kind of fame went across the country, McGuffey kept on with his academic labors. After seven strenuous years as a college president, first at Cincinnati College and then at Ohio University, he began in 1845 a long term of teaching at the University of Virginia. Declining the presidency of Miami in 1854, he stayed there till his death in 1873. To the undergraduates he was "Old Guff," teaching moral philosophy and living quietly in Pavilion 9, while his textbooks made ten millionaires. Unlike the diligent lads in the Readers he did not get rich. A story says that each year at Christmastime the publishers sent him a barrel of hams.

—August 1957

CHILDREN OF DARKNESS

By *STEPHEN B. OATES*

Nat Turner's bloody slave rebellion made real the constant nightmare of the antebellum South

U ntil August 1831, most Americans had never heard of Virginia's Southampton County, an isolated, impoverished neighborhood located along the border in the southeastern part of the state. It was mostly a small farming area, with cotton fields and apple orchards dotting the flat, wooden landscape. The farmers were singularly fond of their apple crops: from them they made potent apple brandy, one of the major sources of pleasure in this hardscrabble region. The county seat, or "county town," was Jerusalem, a lethargic little community where pigs rooted in the streets and old-timers spat tobacco juice in the shade of the courthouse. Jerusalem lay on the bank of Nottoway River some seventy miles south of Richmond. There had never been any large plantations in Southampton County, for the soil had always been too poor for extensive tobacco or cotton cultivation. Although one gentleman did own eighty slaves in 1830, the average was around three or four per family. A number of whites had moved on to new cotton lands in Georgia and Alabama, so that Southampton now had a population that was nearly 60 percent black. While most of the blacks were still enslaved, an unusual number—some seventeen hundred, in fact—were "free persons of color."

By southern white standards, enlightened benevolence did exist in Southampton County—and it existed in the rest of the state, too. Virginia whites allowed a few slave schools to operate—then a crime by state law—and almost without complaint permitted slaves to hold illegal religious meetings. Indeed, Virginians liked to boast that slavery was not so harsh in their "enlightened" state as it was in the brutal cotton plantations in the Deep South. Still, this was a dark time for southern whites—a time of sporadic insurrection panics, especially in South Carolina, and of rising abolitionist militancy in the North—and Virginians were taking no chances. Even though their slaves, they contended, were too happy and too submissive to strike back, Virginia was nevertheless almost a military garrison, with a militia force of some hundred thousand men to guard against insurrection.

Southampton whites, of course, were caught in the same paradox: most of the white males over twenty-one voluntarily belonged to the militia and turned out for the annual drills, yet none of them thought a slave revolt would happen here. *Their* blacks, they told themselves, had never been more content, more docile. True, they did get a bit carried away in their religious meetings these days, with much too much singing and clapping. And true, there were white preachers who punctuated their sermons with what a local observer called "ranting cant about equality" and who might inspire black exhorters to retail that doctrine to their congregations. But generally things were quiet and unchanged in this remote tidewater county, where time seemed to stand as still as a windless summer day.

It happened with shattering suddenness, an explosion of black rage that rocked Southampton County to its foundations. On August 22, 1831, a band of insurgent slaves, led by a black mystic called Nat Turner, rose up with axes and plunged southeastern Virginia—and much of the rest of the South—into convulsions of fear and racial violence. It turned out to be the bloodiest slave insurrection in southern history, one that was to have a profound and irrevocable impact on the destinies of southern whites and blacks alike.

Afterward, white authorities described him as a small man with "distinct African features." Though his shoulders were broad from work in the fields, he was short, slender, and a little knock-kneed, with thin hair, a complexion like black pearl, and large, deep-set eyes. He wore a mustache and cultivated a tuft of whiskers under his lower lip. Before that fateful August day whites who knew Nat Turner thought him harmless, even though he was intelligent and did gabble on about strange religious powers. Among the slaves, though, he enjoyed a powerful influence as an exhorter and self-proclaimed prophet.

He was born in 1800, the property of Benjamin Turner of Southampton County and the son of two strong-minded parents. Tradition has it that his African-born mother threatened to kill him rather than see him grow up in bondage. His father eventually escaped to the North, but not before he had helped inculcate an enormous sense of self-importance in his son. Both parents praised Nat for his brilliance and extraordinary imagination; his mother even claimed that he could recall episodes that happened before his birth—a power that others insisted only the Almighty could have given him. His mother and father both told him that he was intended for some great purpose, that he would surely become a prophet. Nat was also influenced by his grandmother, who along with his white masters taught him to pray and to take pride in his superior intelligence. He learned to read and write with great ease, prompting those who knew him to remark that he had too much sense to be raised in bondage—he "would never be of any service to any one as a slave," one of them said.

In 1810 Benjamin Turner died, and Nat became the property of Turner's oldest son Samuel. Under Samuel Turner's permissive supervision Nat exploited every opportunity to improve his knowledge: he studied white children's school books and experimented in making paper and gunpowder. But it was religion that interested him the most. He attended Negro religious meetings, where the slaves cried out in ecstasy and sang hymns that expressed their longing for a better life. He listened transfixed as black exhorters preached from the Bible with stabbing gestures, singing out in a rhythmic language that was charged with emotion and vivid imagery. He studied the Bible, too, practically memorizing the books of the Old Testament, and grew to manhood with the words of the prophets roaring in his ears.

Evidently Nat came of age a bit confused if not resentful. Both whites and blacks had said he was too intelligent to be raised a slave; yet here he was, fully grown and still in bondage. Obviously he felt betrayed by false hopes. Obviously he thought he should be liberated like the large number of free blacks who lived in Southampton County and who were not nearly so gifted as he. Still enslaved as a man, he zealously cultivated his image as a prophet, aloof, austere, and mystical. As he said later in an oral autobiographical sketch, "Having soon discovered to be great, I must appear so, and therefore studiously avoided mixing in society, and wrapped myself in mystery, devoting myself to fasting and prayer."

Remote, introspective, Turner had religious fantasies in which the Holy Spirit seemed to speak to him as it had to the prophets of old. "Seek ye the kingdom of Heaven," the Spirit told him, "and all things shall be added unto you." Convinced that he "was ordained for some great purpose in the hands of the Almighty," Turner told his fellow slaves about his communion with the Spirit. "And they believed," Turner recalled, "and said my wisdom came from God." Pleased with their response, he began to prepare them for some unnamed mission. He also started preaching at black religious gatherings and soon rose to prominence as a leading exhorter in the slave church. Although never ordained and never officially a member of any church, he was accepted as a Baptist preacher in the slave community, and once he even baptized a white man in a swampy pond. There can be little doubt that the slave church nourished Turner's self-esteem and his desire for independence, for it was not only a center for underground slave plottings against the master class, but a focal point for an entire alternate culture—a subterranean culture that the slaves sought to construct beyond the white man's control. Moreover, Turner's status as a slave preacher gave him considerable freedom of movement, so that he came to know most of Southampton County intimately.

Sometime around 1821 Turner disappeared. His master had put him under an overseer, who may have whipped him, and he fled for his freedom as his father had done. But thirty days later he voluntarily returned. The other slaves were astonished. No fugitive ever came back on his own. "And the negroes found fault, and murmured against me," Turner recounted later, "saying that if they had my sense they would not serve any master in the world." But in his mind Turner did not serve any earthly master. His master was Jehovah—the angry and vengeful God of ancient Israel—and it was Jehovah, he insisted, who had chastened him and brought him back to bondage.

At about this time Nat married. Evidently his wife was a young slave named Cherry who lived on Samuel Turner's place. But in 1822 Samuel Turner died, and they were sold to different masters—Cherry to Giles Reese and Nat to Thomas Moore. Although they were not far apart and still saw each other from time to time, their separation was nevertheless a painful example of the wretched privations that slavery placed on black people, even here in mellowed Southampton County.

As a perceptive man with a prodigious knowledge of the Bible, Turner was more than aware of the hypocrisies and contradictions loose in this Christian area, where whites gloried in the teachings of Jesus and yet discriminated against the "free coloreds" and kept the other blacks in chains. Here slave owners bragged about their benevolence (in Virginia they took care of their "niggers") and yet broke up families, sold Negroes off to whip-happy slave traders when money was scarce, and denied intelligent and skilled blacks something even the most debauched and useless poor whites enjoyed: freedom. Increasingly embittered about his condition and that of his people, his imagination fired to incandescence by prolonged fasting and Old Testament prayers, Turner began to have apocalyptic visions and bloody fantasies in the fields and woods southwest of Jerusalem. "I saw white spirits and black spirits engaged in battle," he declared later, "and the sun was darkened—the thunder rolled in the heavens, and blood flowed in streams—and I heard a voice saying, 'Such is your luck, such you are called to see, and let it come rough or smooth,

163

you must surely bare it.' " He was awestruck, he recalled, but what did the voice mean? What must he bare? He withdrew from his fellow slaves and prayed for a revelation; and one day when he was plowing in the field, he thought the Spirit called out, "Behold me as I stand in the Heavens," and Turner looked up and saw forms of men there in a variety of attitudes, "and there were lights in the sky to which the children of darkness gave other names than what they really were—for they were the lights of the Saviour's hands, stretched forth from east to west, even as they extended on the cross on Calvary for the redemption of sinners."

Certain that Judgment Day was fast approaching, Turner strove to attain "true holiness" and "the true knowledge of faith." And once he had them, once he was "made perfect," then the Spirit showed him other miracles. While working in the field, he said, he discovered drops of blood on the corn. In the woods he found leaves with hieroglyphic characters and numbers etched on them; other leaves contained forms of men—some drawn in blood—like the figures in the sky. He told his fellow slaves about these signs—they were simply astonished—and claimed that the Spirit had endowed him with special knowledge of the seasons, the rotation of the planets, and the operation of the tides. He acquired an even greater reputation among the county's slaves, many of whom thought he could control the weather and heal disease. He told his followers that clearly something large was about to happen, that he was soon to fulfill "the great promise that had been made to me."

But he still did not know what his mission was. Then on May 12, 1828, "I heard a loud noise in the heavens," Turner remembered, "and the Spirit instantly appeared to me and said the Serpent was loosened, and Christ had laid down the yoke he had borne for the sins of men, and that I should take it on and fight against the Serpent." Now at last it was clear. By signs in the heavens Jehovah would show him when to commence the great work, whereupon "I should arise and prepare myself, and slay my enemies with their own weapons." Until then he should keep his lips sealed.

But his work was too momentous for him to remain entirely silent. He announced to Thomas Moore that the slaves ought to be free and would be "one day or other." Moore, of course, regarded this as dangerous talk from a slave and gave Turner a thrashing.

In 1829 a convention met in Virginia to draft a new state constitution, and there was talk among the slaves—who communicated along a slave grapevine—that they might be liberated. Their hopes were crushed, though, when the convention emphatically rejected emancipation and restricted suffrage to whites only. There was also a strong backlash against antislavery publications thought to be infiltrating from the North, one of which—David Walker's *Appeal*—actually called on the slaves to revolt. In reaction the Virginia legislature enacted a law against teaching slaves to read and write. True, it was not yet rigorously enforced, but from the blacks' viewpoint slavery seemed more entrenched in "enlightened" Virginia than ever.

There is no evidence that Turner ever read antislavery publications, but he was certainly sensitive to the despair of his people. Still, Jehovah gave him no further signs, and he was carried along in the ebb and flow of ordinary life. Moore had died in 1828, and Turner had become the legal property of Moore's nine-year-old son—something that must have humiliated him. In 1829 a local wheelwright, Joseph Travis, married Moore's widow and soon moved into her house near the Cross Keys, a village located southwest of Jerusalem. Still known as Nat Turner even though he had changed owners several times, Nat considered Travis "a kind master" and later said that Travis "placed the greatest confidence in me."

In February 1831, there was an eclipse of the sun. The sign Turner had been waiting for—could there be any doubt? Removing the seal from his lips, he gathered around him four slaves in whom he had complete trust —Hark, Henry, Nelson, and Sam—and confided what he was called to do. They would commence "the work of death" on July 4, whose connotation Turner clearly understood. But they formed and rejected so many plans that his mind was affected. He was seized with dread. He fell sick, and Independence Day came and passed.

On August 13 there was another sign. Because of some atmospheric disturbance the sun grew so dim that it could be looked at directly. Then it seemed to change colors—now pale green, now blue, now white—and there was much excitement and consternation in many parts of the eastern United States. By afternoon the sun was like an immense ball of polished silver, and the air was moist and hazy. Then a black spot could be seen, apparently on the sun's surface—a phenomenon that greatly aroused the slaves in southeastern Virginia. For Turner the black spot was unmistakable proof that God wanted him to move. With awakened resolution he told his men that "as the black spot passed over the sun, so shall the blacks pass over the earth."

It was Sunday, August 21, deep in the woods near the Travis house at a place called Cabin Pond. Around a crackling fire Turner's confederates feasted on roast pig and apple brandy. With them were two new recruits—Jack, one of Hark's cronies, and Will, a powerful man who intended to gain his freedom or die in the attempt. Around midafternoon Turner himself made a dramatic appearance, and in the glare of pine-knot torches they finally made their plans. They would rise that night and "kill all the white people." It was a propitious time to begin, because many whites of the militia were away at a camp meeting. The revolt would be so swift and so terrible that the whites would be too panic-stricken to fight back. Until they had sufficient recruits and equipment, the insurgents would annihilate everybody in their path—women and children included. When one of the slaves complained about their small number (there were only seven of them, after all), Turner was quick to reassure him. He had deliberately avoided an extensive plot involving a lot of slaves. He knew that blacks had "frequently attempted similar things," but their plans had "leaked out." Turner intended for his revolt to happen completely without warning. The "march of destruction," he explained, "should be the first news of the insurrection," whereupon slaves and free blacks alike would rise up and join him. He did not say what their ultimate objective was, but possibly he wanted to fight his way into the Great Dismal Swamp some twenty miles to the east. This immense, snake-filled quagmire had long been a haven for fugitives, and Turner may have planned to establish a slave stronghold there from which to launch punitive raids against Virginia and North Carolina. On the other hand, he may well have had nothing in mind beyond the extermination of every white on the ten-mile route to Jerusalem. There are indications that he thought God would guide him after the revolt began, just as He had directed Gideon against the Midianites. Certainly Turner's command of unremitting carnage was that of the Almighty, who had said through his prophet Ezekiel: "Slay utterly old and young, both maids and little children, and women. . . ."

The slaves talked and schemed through the evening. Night came on. Around two in the morning of August 22 they left the woods, bypassed Giles Reese's farm, where Cherry lived, and headed for the Travis homestead, the first target in their crusade.

All was still at the Travis house. In the darkness the insurgents gathered about the cider press, and all drank except Turner, who never touched liquor. Then they moved across the yard with their axes. Hark placed a ladder against the house, and Turner, armed with a hatchet, climbed up and disappeared through a second-story window. In a moment he un-barred the door, and the slaves spread through the house without a sound. The others wanted Turner the prophet, Turner the black messiah, to strike the first blow and kill Joseph Travis. With Will close behind, Turner en-tered Travis's bedroom and made his way to the white man's bed. Turner swung his hatchet—a wild blow that glanced off Travis's head and brought him out of bed yelling for his wife. But with a sure killer's instinct Will moved in and hacked Travis to death with his axe. In minutes Will and the others had slaughtered the four whites they found in the house, including Mrs. Travis and young Putnam Moore, Turner's legal owner. With Putnam's death Turner felt that at last, after thirty years in bondage, he was free.

The rebels gathered up a handful of old muskets and followed "General Nat" out to the barn. There Turner paraded his men about, leading them through every military maneuver he knew. Not all of them, however, were proud of their work. Jack sank to his knees with his head in his hands and said he was sick. But Hark made him get up and forced him along as they set out across the field to the next farm. Along the way somebody remembered the Travis baby. Will and Henry returned and killed it in its cradle.

And so it went throughout that malignant night, as the rebels took farm after farm by surprise. They used no firearms, in order not to arouse the countryside, instead stabbing and decapitating their victims. Although they confiscated horses, weapons, and brandy, they took only what was necessary to continue the struggle, and they committed no rapes. They even spared a few homesteads, one because Turner believed the poor white inhabitants "thought no better of themselves than they did of negroes." By dawn on Monday there were fifteen insurgents—nine on horses—and they were armed with a motley assortment of guns, clubs, swords, and axes. Turner himself now carried a light dress sword, but for some mysterious reason (a fatal irresolution? the dread again?) he had killed nobody yet.

At Elizabeth Turner's place, which the slaves stormed at sunrise, the prophet tried once again to kill. They broke into the house, and there, in the middle of the room, too frightened to move or cry out, stood Mrs. Turner and a neighbor named Mrs. Newsome. Nat knew Elizabeth Turner very well, for she was the widow of his second master, Samuel Turner. While Will attacked her with his axe the prophet took Mrs. Newsome's hand and hit her over the head with his sword. But evidently he could not bring himself to kill her. Finally Will moved him aside and chopped her to death as methodically as though he were cutting wood.

With the sun low in the east, Turner sent a group on foot to another farm while he and Will led the horsemen at a gallop to Caty Whitehead's place. They surrounded the house in a rush, but not before several people fled into the garden. Turner chased after somebody, but it turned out to be a slave girl, as terrified as the whites, and he let her go. All around him, all over the Whitehead farm, there were scenes of unspeakable violence. He saw Will drag Mrs. Whitehead kicking and screaming out of the house and almost sever her head from her body. Running around the house, Turner came upon young Margaret Whitehead hiding under a cellar cap between two chimneys. She ran crying for her life, and Turner set out after her—a wild chase against the hot August sun. He overtook the girl in a field and hit her again and again with his sword, but she would not die. In desperation he picked up a fence rail and beat her to death. Finally he had killed someone. He was to kill no one else.

After the Whitehead massacre the insurgents united briefly and then divided again, those on foot moving in one direction and Turner and the mounted slaves in another. The riders moved across the fields, kicking their horses and mules faster and faster, until at last they raced down the land to Richard Porter's house, scattering dogs and chickens as they went. But the Porters had fled—forewarned by their own slaves that a revolt was under way. Turner knew that the alarm was spreading now, knew that the militia would soon be mobilizing, so he set out alone to retrieve the other column. While he was gone Will took the cavalry and raided Nathaniel Francis's homestead. Young Francis was Will's owner, but he could not have been a harsh master: several free blacks voluntarily lived on his farm. Francis was not home, and his pregnant young wife survived Will's onslaught only because a slave concealed her in the attic. After killing the overseer and Francis's two nephews, Will and his men raced on to another farm, and another, and then overran John Barrow's place on the Barrow Road. Old man Barrow fought back manfully while his wife escaped in the woods, but the insurgents overwhelmed him and slit his throat. As a tribute to his courage they wrapped his body in a quilt and left a plug of tobacco on his chest.

Meanwhile Turner rode chaotically around the countryside, chasing after one column and then the other, almost always reaching the farms after his scattered troops had done the killing and gone. Eventually he found both columns waiting for him at another pillaged homestead, took charge again, and sent them down the Barrow Road, which intersected the main highway to Jerusalem. They were forty strong now and all mounted. Many of the new recruits had joined up eager "to kill all the white people." But others had been forced to come along as though they were hostages. A Negro later testified that several slaves—among them three teen-age boys—"were constantly guarded by negroes with guns who were ordered to shoot them if they attempted to escape."

On the Barrow Road, Turner's strategy was to put his twenty most dependable men in front and send them galloping down on the homesteads before anybody could escape. But the cry of insurrection had preceded them, and many families had already escaped to nearby Jerusalem, throwing the village into pandemonium. By midmorning church bells were tolling the terrible news—*insurrection, insurrection*—and shouting men were riding through the countryside in a desperate effort to get the militia together before the slaves overran Jerusalem itself.

As Turner's column moved relentlessly toward Jerusalem, one Levi Waller, having heard that the blacks had risen, summoned his children from a nearby schoolhouse (some of the other children came running too) and tried to load his guns. But before he could do so, Turner's advance horsemen swept into his yard, a whirlwind of axes and swords, and chased Waller into some weeds. Waller managed to escape, but not before he saw the blacks cut down his wife and children. One small girl also escaped by crawling up a dirt chimney, scarcely daring to breathe as the insurgents decapitated the other children—ten in all.

Turner had stationed himself at the rear of his little army and did not participate in these or any other killings along the Barrow Road. He never explained why. He had been fasting for several days and may well have been too weak to try any more killing himself. Or maybe as God's prophet he preferred to let Will and the eight or nine other lieutenants do the slaughtering. All he said about it afterward was that he "sometimes got in sight in time to see the work of death completed" and that he paused to view the bodies "in silent satisfaction" before riding on.

Around noon on Monday the insurgents reached the Jerusalem highway, and Turner soon joined them. Behind them lay a zigzag path of unredeemable destruction: some fifteen homesteads sacked and approximately sixty whites slain. By now the rebels amounted to fifty or sixty—including three or four free blacks. But even at its zenith Turner's army showed signs of disintegration. A few reluctant slaves had already escaped or deserted. And many others were roaring drunk, so drunk they could scarcely ride their horses, let alone do any fighting. To make matters worse, many of the confiscated muskets were broken or too rusty to fire.

Turner resolved to march on Jerusalem at once and seize all the guns and powder he could find there. But a half mile up the road he stopped at the Parker farm, because some of his men had relatives and friends there. When the insurgents did not return, Turner went after them—and found his men not in the slave quarters but down in Parker's brandy cellar. He ordered them back to the highway at once.

On the way back they met a party of armed men—whites. There were about eighteen of them, as far as Turner could make out. They had already routed his small guard at the gate and were now advancing toward the Parker house. With renewed zeal Turner rallied his remaining troops and ordered an attack. Yelling at the top of their lungs, wielding axes, clubs, and gun butts, the Negroes drove the whites back into Parker's cornfield. But their advantage was short-lived. White reinforcements arrived, and more were on the way from nearby Jerusalem. Regrouping in the cornfield, the whites counterattacked, throwing the rebels back in

169

confusion. In the fighting some of Turner's best men fell wounded, though none of them died. Several insurgents, too drunk to fight any more, fled pell-mell into the woods.

If Turner had often seemed irresolute earlier in the revolt, he was now undaunted. Even though his force was considerably reduced, he still wanted to storm Jerusalem. He led his men away from the main highway, which was blocked with militia, and took them along a back road, planning to cross the Cypress Bridge and strike the village from the rear. But the bridge was crawling with armed whites. In desperation the blacks set out to find reinforcements: they fell back to the south and then veered north again, picking up new recruits as they moved. They raided a few more farms, too, only to find them deserted, and finally encamped for the night near the slave quarters on Ridley's plantation.

All Monday night news of the revolt spread beyond Southampton County as express riders carried the alarm up to Petersburg and from there to the capitol in Richmond. Governor John Floyd, fearing a state-wide uprising, alerted the militia and sent cavalry, infantry, and artillery units to the stricken county. Federal troops from Fortress Monroe were on the way, too, and other volunteers and militia outfits were marching from contiguous counties in Virginia and North Carolina. Soon over three thousand armed whites were in Southampton County, and hundreds more were mobilizing.

With whites swarming the countryside, Turner did not know what to do. During the night an alarm had stampeded their new recruits, so that by Tuesday morning they had only twenty men left. Frantically they set out for Dr. Simon Blunt's farm to get volunteers —and rode straight into an ambush. Whites barricaded in the house opened fire on them at pointblank range, killing one or more insurgents and capturing several others—among them Hark Travis. Blunt's own slaves, armed with farm tools, helped in the defense and captured a few rebels themselves.

Repulsed at Blunt's farm, Turner led a handful of the faithful back toward the Cross Keys, hoping to gather reinforcements. But the signs were truly ominous, for armed whites were everywhere. At last the militia overtook Turner's little band and in a final, desperate skirmish killed Will and scattered the rest. Turner, alone and in deep anguish, escaped to the vicinity of the Travis farm and hid in a hole under some fence rails.

By Tuesday evening a full-scale manhunt was under way in southeastern Virginia and North Carolina as armed whites prowled the woods and swamps in search of fugitive rebels and alleged collaborators. They chased the blacks down with howling dogs, killing those who resisted —and many of them resisted zealously—and dragging others back to

Jerusalem to stand trial in the county court. One free black insurgent committed suicide rather than be taken by white men. Within a week nearly all the bona fide rebels except Turner had either been executed or imprisoned, but not before white vigilantes—and some militiamen—had perpetrated barbarities on more than a score of innocent blacks. Outraged by the atrocities committed on whites, vigilantes rounded up Negroes in the Cross Keys and decapitated them. Another vigilante gang in North Carolina not only beheaded several blacks but placed their skulls on poles, where they remained for days. In all directions whites took Negroes from their shacks and tortured, shot, and burned them to death and then mutilated their corpses in ways that witnesses refused to describe. No one knows how many innocent Negroes died in this reign of terror—at least a hundred and twenty, probably more. Finally the militia commander of Southampton County issued a proclamation that any further outrages would be dealt with according to the articles of war. Many whites publicly regretted these atrocities but argued that they were the inevitable results of slave insurrection. Another revolt, they said, would end with the extermination of every black in the region.

Although Turner's uprising ended on Tuesday, August 24, reports of additional insurrections swept over the South long afterward, and dozens of communities from Virginia to Alabama were seized with hysteria. In North Carolina rumors flew that slave armies had been seen on the highways, that one—maybe led by Turner himself—had burned Wilmington, butchered all the inhabitants, and was now marching on the state capital. The hysteria was even worse in Virginia, where reports of concerted slave rebellions and demands for men and guns swamped the governor's office. For a time it seemed that thousands of slaves had risen, that Virginia and perhaps the entire South would soon be ablaze. But Governor Floyd kept his head, examined the reports carefully, and concluded that no such widespread insurrection had taken place. Actually no additional uprisings had happened anywhere. Out of blind panic whites in many parts of the South had mobilized the militia, chased after imaginary insurgents, and jailed or executed still more innocent blacks. Working in cooperation with other political and military authorities in Virginia and North Carolina, Floyd did all he could to quell the excitement, to reassure the public that the slaves were quiet now. Still, the governor did not think the Turner revolt was the work of a solitary fanatic. Behind it, he believed, was a conspiracy of Yankee agitators and black preachers —especially black preachers. "The whole of that massacre in Southampton is the work of these Preachers," he declared, and demanded that they be suppressed.

Meanwhile the "great bandit chieftain," as the newspapers called him, was still at large. For more than two months Turner managed to elude white patrols, hiding out most of the time near Cabin Pond where the revolt had begun. Hunted by a host of aroused whites (there were various rewards totaling eleven hundred dollars on his head), Turner considered giving himself up and once got within two miles of Jerusalem before turning back. Finally on Sunday, October 30, a white named Benjamin Phipps accidentally discovered him in another hideout near Cabin Pond. Since the man had a loaded shotgun, Turner had no choice but to throw down his sword.

The next day, with lynch mobs crying for his head, a white guard hurried Turner up to Jerusalem to stand trial. By now he was resigned to his fate as the will of Almighty God and was entirely fearless and unrepentant. When a couple of court justices examined him that day, he stated emphatically that *he* had conceived and directed the slaughter of all those white people (even though he had killed only Margaret Whitehead) and announced that God had endowed him with extraordinary powers. The justices ordered this "fanatic" locked up in the same small wooden jail where the other captured rebels had been incarcerated.

On November 1 one Thomas Gray, an elderly Jerusalem lawyer and slaveholder, came to interrogate Turner as he lay in his cell "clothed with rags and covered with chains." In Gray's opinion the public was anxious to learn the facts about the insurrection—for whites in Southampton could not fathom why their slaves would revolt. What Gray wanted was to take down and publish a confession from Turner that would tell the public the truth about why the rebellion had happened. It appears that Gray had already gathered a wealth of information about the outbreak from other prisoners, some of whom he had defended as a court-appointed counsel. Evidently he had also written unsigned newspaper accounts of the affair, reporting in one that whites had located Turner's wife and lashed her until she surrendered his papers (remarkable papers, papers with hieroglyphics on them and sketches of the Crucifixion and the sun). According to Gray and to other sources as well, Turner over a period of three days gave him a voluntary and authentic confession about the genesis and execution of the revolt, recounting his religious visions in graphic detail and contending again that he was a prophet of Almighty God. "Do you not find yourself mistaken now?" Gray asked. Turner replied testily, "Was not Christ crucified?" Turner insisted that the uprising was local in origin but warned that other slaves might see signs and act as he had done. By the end of the confession Turner was in high spirits, perfectly "willing to suffer the fate that awaits me." Although Gray considered him "a gloomy fanatic," he thought Turner was one of the most articulate men he had ever met. And Turner could be frightening. When, in a burst of enthusiasm, he spoke of the killings and raised his manacled hands toward heaven, "I looked on him," Gray said, "and my blood curdled in my veins."

On November 5, with William C. Parker acting as his counsel, Turner came to trial in Jerusalem. The court, of course, found him guilty of committing insurrection and sentenced him to hang. Turner, though, insisted that he was not guilty because he did not feel so. On November 11 he went to his death in resolute silence. In addition to Turner, the county court tried some forty-eight other Negroes on various charges of conspiracy, insurrection, and treason. In all, eighteen blacks—including one woman—were convicted and hanged. Ten others were convicted and "transported"—presumably out of the United States.

But the consequences of the Turner revolt did not end with public hangings in Jerusalem. For southern whites the uprising seemed a monstrous climax to a whole decade of ominous events, a decade of abominable tariffs and economic panics, of obstreperous antislavery activities, and of growing slave unrest and insurrection plots, beginning with the Denmark Vesey conspiracy in Charleston in 1822 and culminating now in the worst insurrection Southerners had ever known. Desperately needing to blame somebody besides themselves for Nat Turner, Southerners linked the revolt to some sinister Yankee-abolitionist plot to destroy their cherished way of life. Southern zealots declared that the antislavery movement, gathering momentum in the North throughout the 1820s, had now burst into a full-blown crusade against the South. In January 1831, William Lloyd Garrison had started publishing *The Liberator* in Boston, demanding in bold, strident language that the slaves be immediately and unconditionally emancipated. If Garrison's rhetoric shocked Southerners, even more disturbing was the fact that about eight months after the appearance of *The Liberator* Nat Turner embarked on his bloody crusade —something southern politicians and newspapers refused to accept as mere coincidence. They charged that Garrison was behind the insurrection, that it was his "bloodthirsty" invective that had incited Turner to violence. Never mind that there was no evidence that Turner had ever heard of *The Liberator*; never mind that Garrison categorically denied any connection with the revolt, saying that he and his abolitionist followers were Christian pacifists who wanted to free the slaves through moral suasion. From 1831 on, northern abolitionism and slave rebellion were inextricably associated in the southern mind.

But if Virginians blamed the insurrection on northern abolitionism, many of them defended emancipation itself as the only way to prevent further violence. In fact, for several months in late 1831 and early 1832 Virginians engaged in a momentous public debate over the feasibility of manumission. Out of the western part of the state, where antislavery and anti-Negro sentiment had long been smoldering, came petitions demanding that Virginia eradicate the "accursed," "evil" slave system and colonize all blacks at state expense. Only by removing the entire black population, the petitions argued, could future revolts be avoided. Newspapers also discussed the idea of emancipation and colonization, prompting one to announce that "Nat Turner and the blood of his innocent victims have conquered the silence of fifty years." The debate moved into the Virginia legislature, too, and early in 1832 proslavery and antislavery orators harangued one another in an unprecedented legislative struggle over emancipation. In the end most delegates concluded that colonization was too costly and too complicated to carry out. And since they were not about to manumit the blacks and leave them as free men in a white man's country, they rejected emancipation. Indeed, they went on to revise and implement the slave codes in order to restrict blacks so stringently that they could never mount another revolt. The modified codes not only strengthened the patrol and militia systems, but sharply curtailed the rights of free blacks and all but eliminated slave schools, slave religious meetings, and slave preachers. For Turner had taught white Virginians a hard lesson about what might happen if they gave slaves enough education and religion to think for themselves.

In the wake of the Turner revolt, the rise of the abolitionists, and the Virginia debates over slavery, the other southern states also expanded their patrol and militia systems and increased the severity of their slave codes. What followed was the Great Reaction of the 1830s and 1840s, during which the South, threatened it seemed by internal and external enemies, became a closed, martial society determined to preserve its slave-based civilization at whatever cost. If Southerners had once apologized for slavery as a necessary evil, they now trumpeted that institution as a positive good—"the greatest of all the great blessings," as James H. Hammond phrased it, "which a kind providence has bestowed." Southern postmasters set about confiscating abolitionist literature, lest these "incendiary" tracts invite the slaves to violence. Some states actually passed sedition laws and other restrictive measures that prohibited Negroes and whites alike from criticizing slavery. And slave owners all across the South tightened up slave discipline, refusing to let blacks visit other plantations and threatening to hang any slave who even looked rebellious. By the 1840s the Old South had devised such an oppressive slave system that organized insurrection was all but impossible.

Even so, southern whites in the antebellum period never escaped the haunting fear that somewhere, maybe even in their own slave quarters, another Nat Turner was plotting to rise up and slit their throats. They never forgot him. His name became for them a symbol of terror and violent retribution.

But for antebellum blacks—and for their descendants—the name of Nat Turner took on a profoundly different connotation. He became a legendary black hero who broke his chains and murdered white people because slavery had murdered Negroes. Turner, said an elderly black man in Southampton County only a few years ago, was "God's man. He was a man for war, and for legal rights, and for freedom."

Nat Turner remains an enigmatic and controversial figure in our own time, thanks largely to the furor generated by William Styron's novel The Confessions of Nat Turner *(Random House, 1967). Although principally based on Turner's* Confessions *as given to Thomas Gray, the novel portrayed Turner as a celibate bachelor afflicted with masturbation fantasies about Margaret Whitehead—a psychosexual supposition unsupported by any known evidence. Styron also violated the historical record in many other details, so that from the point of view of historical scholarship his novel must be regarded as an inaccurate and unacceptable recreation of Turner and his insurrection.*

These shortcomings were emphatically brought to public attention in a volume called William Styron's Nat Turner: Ten Black Writers Respond *(Beacon Press, 1968). Unfortunately, although the book included trenchant essays by Mike Thelwell and Vincent Harding that subjected Styron's novel to valid historical criticism, most of the other selections were mere diatribes, filled with their own inaccuracies and attempting to enshrine the figure of Nat Turner as a flawless black god—a military genius and inflexible white-hater with whom today's blacks ought to identify.*

In reconstructing the Nat Turner story for my own narrative, I made extensive use of Henry Irving Tragel's The Southampton Slave Revolt of 1831 *(Random House, 1973), a valuable collection of documents about virtually all aspects of the rebellion. It includes a detailed, annotated chronology of Turner's life and the revolt itself, numerous contemporary newspaper reports, a verbatim record of the slave trials, Governor Floyd's diary and correspondence, and most of the previously published accounts, including the original* Confessions *to Thomas Gray as published in Baltimore in 1831. I am also indebted to Eric Foner, whose* Nat Turner *(Prentice-Hall, 1971), another compilation of source materials, includes a great deal about the role of the slave church in the genesis of the Turner insurrection.*   —S.B.O.

—October 1973

JACKSON'S FIGHT WITH THE 'MONSTER'

By BRAY HAMMOND

Andrew Jackson battled the Bank of the United States with all his furious confidence. Was his victory the nation's loss?

R elief, sir!" interrupted the President. "Come not to me, sir! Go to the monster. It is folly, sir, to talk to Andrew Jackson. The government will not bow to the monster. . . . Andrew Jackson yet lives to put his foot upon the head of the monster and crush him to the dust."

The monster, "a hydra of corruption," was known also as the Second Bank of the United States, chartered by Congress in 1816 as depository of the federal government, which was its principal stockholder and customer. The words were reported by a committee which called on President Jackson in the spring of 1834 to complain because he and Secretary of the Treasury Roger Taney had removed the federal deposits from the federal depository into what the Jacksonians called "selected banks" and others called "pet banks." The President was disgusted with the committee.

"Andrew Jackson," he exclaimed in the third person as before, "would never recharter that monster of corruption. Sooner than live in a country where such a power prevailed, he would seek an asylum in the wilds of Arabia."

In effect, he had already put his foot on the monster and crushed him in the dust. He had done so by vetoing a new charter for the Bank and removing the federal accounts from its books. So long as the federal Bank had the federal accounts, it had been regulator of the currency and of credit in general. Its power to regulate had derived from the fact that the federal Treasury was the largest single transactor in the economy and the largest bank depositor. Receiving the checks and notes of local banks deposited with it by government collectors of revenue, it had had constantly to come back on the local banks for settlements of the amounts which the checks and notes called for. It had had to do so because it made those amounts immediately available to the Treasury, wherever desired. Since settlement by the local banks was in specie, i.e., silver and gold coin, the pressure for settlement automatically regulated local bank lending; for the more the local banks lent, the larger the amount of their notes and checks in use and the larger the sums they had to settle in specie. This loss of specie reduced their power to lend.

All this had made the federal Bank the regulator not alone of the currency but of bank lending in general, the restraint it had exerted being fully as effective as that of the twelve Federal Reserve Banks at present, though by a different process. With its life now limited to two more years and the government accounts removed from its books, it was already crushed but still writhing.

The Jacksonian attack on the Bank is an affair respecting which posterity seems to have come to an opinion that is half hero worship and half discernment. In the words of Professor William G. Sumner, the affair was a struggle "between the democracy and the money power." Viewed in that light, Jackson's victory was a grand thing. But Sumner also observed —this was three-quarters of a century ago—that since Jackson's victory the currency, which previously had owned no superior in the world, had never again been so good. More recently Professor Lester V. Chandler, granting the Bank's imperfections, has said that its abolition without replacement by something to take over its functions was a "major blunder" which "ushered in a generation of banking anarchy and monetary disorder." So the affair stands, a triumph and a blunder.

During Andrew Jackson's lifetime three things had begun to alter prodigiously the economic life of Americans. These were steam, credit, and natural resources.

Steam had been lifting the lids of pots for thousands of years, and for a century or so it had been lifting water from coal mines. But only in recent years had it been turning spindles, propelling ships, drawing trains of cars, and multiplying incredibly the productive powers of man. For thousands of years money had been lent, but in most people's minds debt had signified distress—as it still did in Andrew Jackson's. Only now was its productive power, long known to merchants as a means of making one sum of money do the work of several, becoming popularly recognized by enterprising men for projects which required larger sums than could be assembled in coin. For three centuries or more America's resources had been crudely surmised, but only now were their variety, abundance, and accessibility becoming practical realities. And it was the union of these three, steam, credit, and natural resources, that was now turning Anglo-Saxon America from the modest agrarian interests that had preoccupied her for two centuries of European settlement to the dazzling possibilities of industrial exploitation.

In the presence of these possibilities, the democracy was becoming transformed from one that was Jeffersonian and agrarian to one that was financial and industrial. But it was still a democracy: its recruits were still men born and reared on farms, its vocabulary was still Jeffersonian, and its basic conceptions changed insensibly from the libertarianism of agrarians to that of *laissez faire*. When Andrew Jackson became President in 1829, boys born in log cabins were already becoming businessmen but with no notion of surrendering as bankers and manufacturers the freedom they might have enjoyed as farmers.

There followed a century of exploitation from which America emerged with the most wealthy and powerful economy there is, with her people the best fed, the best housed, the best clothed, and the best equipped on earth. But the loss and waste have long been apparent. The battle was only for the strong, and millions who lived in the midst of wealth never got to touch it. The age of the Robber Barons was scarcely a golden age. It was scarcely what Thomas Jefferson desired.

It could scarcely have been what Andrew Jackson desired either, for his ideals were more or less Jeffersonian by common inheritance, and the abuse of credit was one of the things he abominated. Yet no man ever did more to encourage the abuse of credit than he. For the one agency able to exert some restraint on credit was the federal Bank. In destroying it, he let speculation loose. Though a hard-money devotee who hated banks and wanted no money but coin, he fostered the formation of swarms of banks and endowed the country with a filthy and depreciated paper currency which he believed to be unsound and unconstitutional and from which the Civil War delivered it in the administration of Abraham Lincoln thirty years later.

This, of course, was not Andrew Jackson's fault, unless one believes he would have done what he did had his advisers been different. Though a resolute and decisive person, he also relied on his friends. He had his official cabinet, largely selected for political expediency, and he had his "kitchen cabinet" for informal counsel. Of those advisers most influential with him, all but two were either businessmen or closely associated with the business world. The two exceptions were Major William B. Lewis, a planter and neighbor from Tennessee who came to live with him in the White House, and James K. Polk, also of Tennessee, later President of the United States. These two, with Jackson himself, constituted the agrarian element in the Jacksonian adminstration. Several of the others, however, were agrarian in the sense that they had started as poor farm boys.

Martin Van Buren, probably the ablest of Jackson's political associates, was a lawyer whose investments had made him rich. Amos Kendall, the ablest in a business and administrative sense, later made the telegraph one of the greatest of American business enterprises and himself a man of wealth. He provided the Jacksonians their watchword, "The world is governed too much." He said "our countrymen are beginning to demand" that the government be content with "protecting their persons and property, leaving them to direct their labor and capital as they please, within the moral law: getting rich or remaining poor as may result from their own management or fortune." Kendall's views may be sound, but they are not what one expects to hear from the democracy when struggling with the money power.

Roger Taney, later Chief Justice, never got rich, but he liked banks and was a modest investor in bank stock. "There is perhaps no business," he said as Jackson's secretary of the treasury, "which yields a profit so certain and liberal as the business of banking and exchange; and it is proper that it should be open as far as practicable to the most free competition and its advantages shared by all classes of society." His own bank in Baltimore was one of the first of the pets in which he deposited government money.

David Henshaw, Jacksonian boss of Massachusetts, was a banker and industrialist whose advice in practical matters had direct influence in Washington. Henshaw projected a Jacksonian bank to take the place of the existing institution but to be bigger. (A similar project was got up by friends of Van Buren in New York and one of the two was mentioned favorably by Jackson in his veto message as a possible alternative to the existing United States Bank.) Samuel Ingham, Jackson's first secretary of the treasury, was a paper manufacturer in Pennsylvania and later a banker in New Jersey. Churchill C. Cambreleng, congressional leader of the attack on the Bank, was a New York businessman and former agent of John Jacob Astor. These are not all of the Jacksonians who were intent on the federal Bank's destruction, but they are typical.

There was a very cogent reason why these businessmen and their class generally wanted to kill the Bank of the United States. It interfered with easy money; it kept the state banks from lending as freely as they might otherwise and businessmen from borrowing.

New York, for example, was now the financial and commercial center of the country and its largest city, which Philadelphia formerly had been. The customs duties collected at its wharves and paid by its businessmen were by far the largest of any American port, and customs duties were then the principal source of federal income. These duties were paid by New York businessmen with checks on New York banks. These checks were deposited by the federal collectors in the New York office of the Bank of the United States, whose headquarters were in Philadelphia and a majority of whose directors were Philadelphia businessmen. This, Amos Kendall observed, was a "wrong done to New York in depriving her of her natural advantages."

It was not merely a matter of prestige. As already noted, the United States Bank, receiving the checks of the New York businessmen, made the funds at once available to the secretary of the treasury. The Bank had therefore to call on the New York banks for the funds the checks represented. This meant that the New York banks, in order to pay the federal Bank, had to draw down their reserves; which meant that they had less money to lend; which meant that the New York businessmen could not borrow as freely and cheaply as they might otherwise. All this because their money had gone to Philadelphia.

Actually the situation was not so bad as my simplified account makes it appear. For one thing, the goods imported at New York were sold else-where in the country, and more money came to New York in payment for them than went out of the city in duties paid the government. But I have described it in the bald, one-sided terms that appealed to the local politi-cians and to the businessmen prone to grumbling because money was not so easy as they would like. There was truth in what they said, but it amounted to less than they made out.

New York's grievance was special because her customs receipts were so large and went to a vanquished rival. Otherwise the federal Bank's pres-sure on the local banks—all of which were state banks—was felt in some degree through the country at large. Wherever money was paid to a fed-eral agency—for postage, for fines, for lands, for excise, for import duties —money was drawn from the local banks into the federal Bank. The flow of funds did not drain the local banks empty and leave them nothing to do, though they and the states' rights politicians talked as if that were the case. The federal Bank was simply their principal single creditor.

And though private business brought more money to New York and other commercial centers than it took away, the federal government took more away than it brought. For its largest payments were made elsewhere —to naval stations, army posts, Indian agents, owners of the public debt, largely foreign, and civilians in the government service throughout the country. In the normal flow of money payments from hand to hand in the economy, those to the federal government and consequently to the federal Bank were so large and conspicuous that the state banks involved in making them were disagreeably conscious of their size and frequency.

These banks, of course, were mostly eastern and urban rather than western and rural, because it was in eastern cities that the federal govern-ment received most of its income. Accordingly, it was in the eastern busi-ness centers, Boston, New York, Baltimore, and Charleston, that re-sentiment against Philadelphia and the federal Bank was strongest. This resentment was intensified by the fact that the federal Bank's branch offices were also competitors for private business in these and other cities, which the present Federal Reserve Banks, very wisely, are not.

General Jackson's accession to the presidency afforded an opportunity to put an end to the federal Bank. Its charter would expire in seven years. The question of renewal was to be settled in that interval. Jackson was popular and politically powerful. His background and principles were agrarian. An attack on the Bank by him would be an attack "by the democracy on the money power." It would have, therefore, every political advantage.

The realities behind these words, however, were not what the words implied. The democracy till very recently had been agrarian because most of the population was agricultural. But the promoters of the assault on the Bank were neither agrarian in their current interests nor representative of what democracy implied.

In the western and rural regions, which were the most democratic in a traditional sense, dislike of the federal Bank persisted, though by 1829 it had less to feed on than formerly. Years before, under incompetent managers, the Bank had lent unwisely in the West, had been forced to harsh measures of self-preservation, and had made itself hated, with the help, as usual, of the state banks and states' rights politicians. But the West needed money, and though the Bank never provided enough it did provide some, and in the absence of new offenses disfavor had palpably subsided by the time Jackson became President.

There were also, in the same regions, vestiges or more of the traditional agrarian conviction that all banks were evil. This principle was still staunchly held by Andrew Jackson. He hated all banks, did so through a long life, and said so time after time. He thought they all violated the Constitution. But he was led by the men around him to focus his aversion on the federal Bank, which being the biggest must be the worst and whose regulatory pressure on the state banks must obviously be the oppression to be expected from a great, soulless corporation.

However, not all agrarian leaders went along with him. For many years the more intelligent had discriminated in favor of the federal Bank, recognizing that its operations reduced the tendency to inflation which, as a hard-money party, the agrarians deplored. Altogether, it was no longer to be expected that the agrarian democracy would initiate a vigorous attack on the federal Bank, though it was certainly to be expected that such an attack would receive very general agrarian support.

It was in cities and within the business world that both the attack on the Bank and its defense would be principally conducted. For there the

Bank had its strongest enemies and its strongest friends. Its friends were the more conservative houses that had dominated the old business world but had only a minor part in the new. It was a distinguished part, however, and influential. This influence, which arose from prestige and substantial wealth, combined with the strength which the federal Bank derived from the federal accounts to constitute what may tritely be called a "money power." But it was a disciplined, conservative money power and just what the economy needed.

But it was no longer *the* money power. It was rivaled, as Philadelphia was by New York, by the newer, more vigorous, more aggressive, and more democratic part of the business world.

The businessmen comprising the latter were a quite different lot from the old. The Industrial Revolution required more men to finance, to man, and manage its railways, factories, and other enterprises than the old business world, comprising a few rich merchants, could possibly provide. The Industrial Revolution was set to absorb the greater part of the population.

Yet when the new recruits, who yesterday were mechanics and farmers, offered themselves not only as laborers but as managers, owners, and entrepreneurs requiring capital, they met a response that was not always respectful. There was still the smell of the barnyard on their boots, and their hands were better adapted to hammer and nails than to quills and ink. The aristocrats were amused. They were also chary of lending to such borrowers; whereupon farmers' and mechanics' banks began to be set up. These banks found themselves hindered by the older banks and by the federal Bank. They and their borrowers were furious. They resisted the federal Bank in suits, encouraged by sympathetic states' rights politicians, and found themselves blocked by the federal courts.

Nor were their grievances merely material. They disliked being snubbed. Even when they became wealthy themselves, they still railed at "the capitalists" and "the aristocrats," as David Henshaw of Massachusetts did, meaning the old families, the Appletons and Lawrences whom he named, the business counterparts of the political figures that the Jacksonian revolution had replaced. Henshaw and his fellow Jacksonian leaders were full of virtue, rancor, and democracy. Their struggle was not merely to make money but to demonstrate what they already asserted, that they were as good as anyone, or more so. In their denunciation of the federal Bank, one finds them calling it again and again "an aristocracy" and its proprietors, other than the federal government, "aristocrats."

The Jacksonians, as distinct from Jackson himself, wanted a world where *laissez faire* prevailed; where, as Amos Kendall said, everyone would be free to get rich; where, as Roger Taney said, the benefits of banks would be open to all classes; where, as the enterprising exploiters of the land unanimously demanded, credit would be easy. To be sure, relatively few would be rich, and a good many already settling into an urban industrial class were beginning to realize it. But that consideration did not count with the Jacksonian leaders. They wanted a new order. But what they achieved was the age of the Robber Barons.

The attack on the old order took the form of an attack on the federal Bank for a number of reasons which may be summed up in political expediency. A factor in the success of the attack was that the president of the Bank, Nicholas Biddle, was the pampered scion of capitalists and aristocrats. He was born to wealth and prominence. He was elegant, literary, intellectual, witty, and conscious of his own merits. When at the age of 37 he became head of the largest moneyed corporation in the world he was wholly without practical experience. In his new duties he had to rely on brains, self-confidence, and hard work.

With these he did extraordinarily well. He had a remarkable grasp of productive and financial interrelations in the economy. The policies he formulated were sound. His management of the Bank, despite his inexperience, was efficient. His great weakness was naïveté, born of his ignorance of strife.

This characterization, I know, is quite contrary to the conventional one, which makes Biddle out a master of intrigue and craft such as only the purity of Andrew Jackson could overcome. But the evidence of his being Machiavelli is wholly the assertion of his opponents, whose victory over him was enhanced by a magnification of his prowess. One of these, however, the suave Martin Van Buren, who knew him well and was a judge of such matters, ascribed no such qualities to him but instead spoke of the frankness and openness of his nature; it was in Daniel Webster that Van Buren saw wiliness.

Nicholas Biddle's response to the Jacksonian attack was inept. He was slow in recognizing that an attack was being made and ignored the warnings of his more astute friends. He expected the public to be moved by careful and learned explanations of what the Bank did. He broadcast copies of Jackson's veto message, one of the most popular and effective documents in American political history, with the expectation that people in general would agree with him that it was a piece of hollow demagogy. He entered a match for which he had no aptitude, impelled by a quixotic sense of duty and an inability to let his work be derogated. He engaged in a knock-down-drag-out fight with a group of experts as relentless as any American politics has ever known. The picture he presents is that of Little Lord Fauntleroy, lace on his shirt and good in his heart, running into those rough boys down the alley.

In his proper technical responsibilities Nicholas Biddle was a competent central banker performing a highly useful and beneficial task. It is a pity he had to be interrupted, both for him and for the economy. For him it meant demoralization. He lost track of what was going on in the Bank, he made blundering mistakes, he talked big. These things his opponents used tellingly against him. He turned from able direction of the central banking process to the hazardous business of making money, of which he knew nothing and for which his only knack lay in an enthusiastic appraisal of America's great economic future. In the end his Bank of the United States broke, he lost his fortune, he was tried on criminal charges (but released on a technicality), and he died a broken man.

This was personal misfortune, undeserved and severe. The more important victim was the American people. For with destruction of the United States Bank there was removed from an overexcitable economy the influence most effective in moderating its booms and depressions.

Andrew Jackson had vetoed recharter in 1832 and transferred the federal accounts to the pet banks in 1833 and 1834. The Bank's federal charter expired in 1836, though Nicholas Biddle obtained a charter from Pennsylvania and continued the organization as a state bank. The period was one of boom. Then in 1837 there was panic, all the banks in the country suspended, prices fell, and business collapsed. It was all Andrew Jackson's fault, his opponents declared, for killing the federal Bank. This was too generous. Jackson was not to blame for everything. The crisis was worldwide and induced by many forces. It would have happened anyway. Yet certainly Jackson's destruction of the Bank did not help. Instead it worsened the collapse. Had the Bank been allowed to continue the salutary performance of the years immediately preceding the attack upon it, and had it been supported rather than undermined by the administration, the wild inflation which culminated in the collapse would have been curbed and the disaster diminished. Such a course would have been consistent with Jackson's convictions and professions. Instead he smote the Bank fatally at the moment of its best performance and in the course of trends against which it was needed most. Thereby he gave unhindered play to the speculation and inflation that he was always denouncing.

To a susceptible people the prospect was intoxicating. A continent abounding in varied resources and favorable to the maintenance of an immense population in the utmost comfort spread before the gaze of an energetic, ambitious, and clever race of men, who to exploit its wealth had two new instruments of miraculous potency: steam and credit. They rushed forward into the bright prospect, trampling, suffering, succeeding, failing. There was nothing to restrain them. For about a century the big rush lasted. Now it is over. And in a more critical mood we note that a number of things are missing or have gone wrong. To be sure, we are on top of the world still, but it is not very good bookkeeping to omit one's losses and count only one's gains.

That critical mood was known to others than Jackson. Emerson, Hawthorne, and Thoreau felt it. So did an older and more experienced contemporary of theirs, Albert Gallatin, friend and aide in the past to Thomas Jefferson, and now president of a New York bank but loyal to Jeffersonian ideals. "The energy of this nation," he wrote to an old friend toward the end of Andrew Jackson's administration, "is not to be controlled; it is at present exclusively applied to the acquisition of wealth and to improvements of stupendous magnitude. Whatever has that tendency, and of course an immoderate expansion of credit, receives favor. The apparent prosperity and the progress of cultivation, population, commerce, and improvement are beyond expectation. But it seems to me as if general demoralization was the consequence; I doubt whether general happiness is increased; and I would have preferred a gradual, slower, and more secure progress. I am, however, an old man, and the young generation has a right to govern itself. . . ." In these last words, Mr. Gallatin was echoing the remark of Thomas Jefferson that "the world belongs to the living." Neither Gallatin nor Jefferson, however, thought it should be stripped by the living. Yet nothing but the inadequacy of their powers seems to have kept those nineteenth-century generations from stripping it. And perhaps nothing else could.

But to the extent that credit multiplies man's economic powers, curbs upon credit extension are a means of conservation, and an important means. The Bank of the United States was such a means. Its career was short and it had imperfections. Nevertheless it worked. The evidence is in the protest of the bankers and entrepreneurs, the lenders and the borrowers, against its restraints. Their outcry against the oppressor was heard, and Andrew Jackson hurried to their rescue. Had he not, some other way of stopping its conservative and steadying influence could doubtless have been found. The appetite for credit is avid, as Andrew Jackson knew in his day and might have foretold for ours. But because he never meant to serve it, the credit for what happened goes rather to the clever advisers who led the old hero to the monster's lair and dutifully held his hat while he stamped on its head and crushed it in the dust.

Meanwhile, the new money power had curled up securely in Wall Street, where it has been at home ever since.

—June 1956

JOHNNY APPLESEED

By EDWARD HOAGLAND

John Chapman was very different from the frontiersman of legend—a vegetarian who didn't believe in horseback riding, would not wear furs, and went his quiet way for half a century. But in the end he did as much to subdue the American wilderness as any of the famous trailblazers and hellroarers.

There is in the western country a very extraordinary missionary of the New Jerusalem. A man has appeared who seems to be almost independent of corporal wants and sufferings. He goes barefooted, can sleep anywhere, in house or out of house, and live upon the coarsest and most scanty fare. He has actually thawed the ice with his bare feet.

"He procures what books he can of the New Church; travels into the remote settlements, and lends them wherever he can find readers, and sometimes divides a book into two or three parts for more extensive distribution and usefulness. This man for years past has been in the employment of bringing into cultivation, in numberless places in the wilderness, small patches (two or three acres) of ground, and then sowing apple seeds and rearing nurseries. . . ."—From a report of the *Society for Printing, Publishing and Circulating the Writings of Emanuel Swedenborg,* Manchester, England, January 1817.

" . . . he ran with the rabbit and slept with the stream."—Vachel Lindsay, *In Praise of Johnny Appleseed.*

Of Jonathan Chapman
Two things are known,
That he loved apples,
That he walked Alone. . . .

The Stalking Indian,
The beast in its lair
Did no hurt
While he was there.

For they could tell,
As wild things can,
That Jonathan Chapman
Was God's own man.
—From *A Book of Americans* by Rosemary and Stephen Vincent Benét.

He was real flesh and blood, not a folk construction like Paul Bunyan —and he plied the trade of an appleman for almost fifty years with inspired generosity, not ascending solely to a single day's public drama, like the steel-driving hero of Big Bend Tunnel in West Virginia, John Henry. Yet Johnny Appleseed, too, has survived simply as a folk figure of whom little is known, as a memory fuzzy in outline, mainly inscribed in children's literature and turn-of-the-century romances and poetry or Louis Bromfield novels.

Born John Chapman (1774–1845) in Leominster, Massachusetts, he proved to be a man with a mission along the frontier, which in those days included western Pennsylvania, Ohio, Indiana, Illinois, and Iowa. If he had kept a diary, he might be compared to John James Audubon and George Catlin, who come down to us through their own words and pictures, although—more of a frontiersman then they were—he worked humbly and busily to facilitate that frontier's passing. In a way, his name is as durable as Andrew Jackson's, who died in the same year, but he has been remarkably neglected by the historians, probably because he conforms to none of the national stereotypes and illustrates nobody's theories.

We think of the swaggering, unscrupulous prototype frontiersman who bushwhacked Indians and scouted for the Long Knives, the mountainmen who went into the bush with two horses and a squaw, and in order to live, ate his pack horse in January, his saddle horse in February, and his sad squaw in March. In the gaudy parade of liars, killers, pranksters, boasters and boosters that fill up B. A. Botkin's *A Treasury of American Folklore*, Johnny Appleseed, along with Abe Lincoln and George Washington, occupies a tiny section entitled "Patron Saints." (John Henry and Paul Bunyan are "Miracle Men.") But, legendary walker that he was, he is fabled as much for abusing his feet as for sporting tin pots on his head or cardboard headgear. In icy weather, at best he wore castoffs given to him —sometimes one shoe and one broken boot, tied on with varicolored string wound around his ankle, sometimes only one shoe, with which he broke trail through the snow for his bare foot. He preferred, if possible, nothing at all. There is the story of Johnny quietly confronting a pharisaical camp-meeting preacher who had demanded of the congregation, "Where now is the man like the primitive Christian who is traveling to Heaven barefooted and clad in coarse raiment?" Johnny of course walked forward in the upside-down coffee sack with holes for his head and arms that was his usual garb, and lifted his bruised bare feet, one by one, putting them right on the pulpit stump.

Nowadays we like heroes in *boots*, however. Saxophone players, clerical workers, hair stylists, "anti-heroes," ladies dressed for the office, partially disrobed ladies, vacationers fussily dashing into an airport taxi, all are likely to wear cowboy boots, jack boots, ski boots, sandhog boots, desert boots, with kinky belt buckles that broadcast a physical vigor and spiritual sadism the wearer doesn't really even aspire to feel. Our great West, our old westering impulse, has become a costume jewel.

Anomalous, unassimilable, Johnny Appleseed was a frontiersman who would not eat meat, who wished not to kill so much as a rattlesnake, who pitied the very mosquitoes that flew into the smoke of his campfire. He liked to hear the wolves howl around him at night and was unafraid of bears, yet reportedly slept without shelter one snowy night, rather than roust out of hibernation a mother bear and her cubs who had crept into a hollow tree that he had intended using. Although he would sometimes buy a worn-out horse to save it from mistreatment, boarding it with one of his friends for the winter—and though he scoured the woods in the fall for lame horses that the pioneers, packing their way through the country, had abandoned—apparently he believed that riding the beasts was discourteous to them, and he only employed a horse to carry his bags of seeds or, late in his life, to drag an old wagon.

Though in a sense he was the nation's paramount orchardist of the nineteenth century, Johnny Appleseed denounced as wickedness the practices of grafting and pruning, by which all commercial fruit is produced, because of the torture he thought such a knifing must inflict on the tree. He was shy in a crowd but a regular sermonizer among people he felt at home with—probably a bit of a bore at times, but no simpleton. In Steubenville, Cincinnati, and Urbana, Ohio, he knew the leading New Church Swedenborgians, and between his arrival in central and northern Ohio and the time of his death, Swedenborgian societies sprang up in at least twelve of the counties there, many individuals testifying that it was Chapman, the colporteur of Christian literature, who had first "planted the seed."

As a religious enthusiast, he was more on the Franciscan model than the harsh zealots, from the Puritan to Mormon, whom American social historians are accustomed to writing about. And as an entrepreneur with considerable foresight about the eventual patterns of settlement, he allowed himself to be utterly clipped and gypped in matters of real estate through much of his life. When somebody jumped one of his land claims, his main concern seemed to be whether they would still let him take care of his apple trees. When he sold apple seedlings, he like to be paid with an IOU, scarcely having any use for money except to give it away to needy families, and left to God and the debtor's own conscience the question of whether he was finally paid. Instead, he bartered for potatoes, corn meal, salt and flour, and peddled cranberries—a fruit that the pioneers combined into stews or dried with suet for a midwinter treat. Often he shucked corn, split rails, and girdled trees for his keep. He ate nuts and wild plums in the woods on his trips, and cooked his corn mush, roasted his potatoes, and probably carried Indian-style "journey bread," which was made by boiling green corn till it was half done, drying it again in the sun, then browning it in hot ashes when ready to eat, pounding it fine, and possibly stirring in birch or maple syrup or summer berries or honey (though Johnny always left enough of that in the comb for the bees to live on). If many people never paid him for the seedlings he distributed so diligently, others returned his kindness by their hospitality to him as he passed back and forth. The belt of territory he worked in shifted gradually westward during the course of his life, but he wintered in the easternmost towns —after his strenuous summers at the borders of settlement—and so would migrate between several homesites, several circles of friends.

He gave little gifts of tea when he had money, but probably didn't drink it himself, preferring a biblical drink of milk or milk and honey. He did use snuff, however, and would sip a dram of hard liquor to warm up in cold weather—if one can generalize fairly about his conduct from isolated instances of testimony about five decades of such intense and fervent activity. He was wiry in build, short by our standards but average for then, with peculiarly piercing blue eyes, good teeth, a scanty dark beard that later turned gray, and uncut dark hair, parted down the middle and tucked behind his ears. When not in a coffee sack, he dressed in a collarless tow-linen smock or straight-sleeved coat that hung down to his heels, over a shirt and burr-studded pants that had been traded to him for his apple seeds.

He was quick-talking and restlessly energetic as a visitor, but windbeaten, hollow-cheeked, and gaunt-looking from eating so little and walking so far. Yet somehow, despite his eccentric demeanor, he was remarkably effective in the impression he made, "some rare force of gentle goodness dwelling in his looks and breathing in his words," as W. D. Haley wrote in *Harper's New Monthly Magazine* for November 1871, in the first biographical sketch which brought Johnny Appleseed to national attention. Not even small boys made fun of him, knowing his boldness at bearing pain—besides walking barefoot in the snow, he would poke needles into himself without flinching, for the children's edification. He had a string of good stories of Indians and wolves for them, and presents of ribbon and whatnot that he carried with him to give to their sisters.

He felt comfortable with children, and probably wistful, particularly with girls. Holding a six-year-old child on his lap, he would speak of some day having a "pure wife in heaven." He seems to have imagined that it might be possible to adopt an orphan of about that age and raise her up to be just such a wife, even on earth. There are indications that at least once he tried, but that in adolescence the girl, like other girls, began to flirt with other men. Another time he announced that two female spirits had shown themselves to him and told him they would be his wives in the afterlife, bidding him abstain until then. He took an untheatrical view of the hereafter, however—a place he didn't think would be all that different in geography or its earthly occupations from the world he lived in. Resurrection was the simple continuation of the spiritual being without its corporeal or "natural" adjuncts, and the indifference to physical discomfort which he cultivated can no doubt be partly ascribed to his impatience to see that process speeded says Robert Price, his principal biographer. But he liked to joke that Hades at its worst wouldn't be worse than "smoky houses and scolding women" or "Newark," a raunchy Ohio border settlement.

Despite his small roach of a beard, unkemptly clipped, and his dark horny feet and deliberately apostolic costume, he kept himself clean, and "in his most desolate rags" was "never repulsive," his acquaintances reported. Arriving at a house where he was known, he happily stretched out on his back on the floor near the door, with his head on his knapsack and his feet tilted up against the log wall. Removing his discolored Bible and Swedenborgian tracts from the pouch he created for them inside his smock by tying his belt tightly, he would ask with exuberance, "Will you have some fresh news right from Heaven?" While the men smoked or fleshed a fox skin and the women cooked or quilted, he read and extemporized, his voice now roaring scriptural denunciations of evil, now soft and soothing. By middle age, he didn't hesitate to introduce himself to strangers as "Johnny Appleseed," enjoying his notoriety, but before accepting hospitality he would make sure there was plenty of food in the house for the children.

In good weather he slept outside; otherwise he would lie down on the floor close to the door of the cabin, as he "did not expect to sleep in a bed in the next world." But one can picture the suppers of applesauce, apple pie, apple strudel, apple dumplings, apple turnover, apple cider, apple butter, and apple brown betty he was served by farm wives who had settled in the vicinity of his nurseries. One also can imagine the kidding he endured for bringing hard cider and applejack into the country (which already had "white lightning"—corn liquor). After the article in *Harper's* by W. D. Haley twenty-six years after his death, there was a sudden revival of interest in Johnny Appleseed, with people writing their recollections or hearsay memories of him to small-town newspapers throughout the Midwest. He was compared to John the Baptist, a voice in the wilderness heralding a new religion, and professors said he had personified the spirit of democracy—one for all—in the New World. In more saccharin accounts, professional romancers reported that apple blossoms tapped at his window when he was born and strewed themselves over his grave when he died. "His mush-pan slapped on his windy head, his torn shirt flapping, his eyes alight, an American ghost," wrote Frances Frost.

In his earthly life, Ophia D. Smith noted in a centennial tribute by Swedenborgians in 1945, "Johnny Appleseed was a one-man circulating library, a one-man humane society, a one-man [medical] clinic, a one-man missionary band, and a one-man emigrant-aid society." But because of the distance that separates us, and as a result of the void in scholarship until Robert Price's biography in 1954—the fact that for many years historians simply ignored him as a character fit only for children's stories—we can't make a good estimate of the quality of his mind. We do know he corresponded with a distinguished co-religionist in Philadelphia, William Schlatter, who was also his supplier of evangelical tracts, though unfortunately none of Chapman's letters have survived. We know, too, that he planted medicinal herbs wherever he went, plants such as mullein, pennyroyal, catnip, horehound, rattlesnake root, wintergreen, and dandelion (a native of Europe), instructing the settlers in their use. His favorite was the two-foot-high, bad-smelling mayweed, or "dogfennel," another alien, which spoiled the taste of milk when cows ate it and for a while was called "Johnnyweed," with the idea that he might have been planting it everywhere as a practical joke. On the contrary, he seems to have really believed that its noxious smell in every Ohio dooryard would ward off outbreaks of malaria.

We know that he stayed out of fights in the rowdiest communities, even when provoked, according to his adage of living by the law of love although fearing no man. But we don't know how consistently he refused to eat animal flesh, or how constantly cheerful he was, or whether his habits of self-punishment—which might smack of the perverse to our modern temperament—discomposed his neighbors, who were an infinitely hardier lot and more inclined to defer to the example of the self-mortifying earlier Christian martyrs. Though he must have brewed gentler poultices for other people's wounds, his method of healing his own was to sear the offending location with a piece of iron—as the Indians did—and then treat the burn. Such fortitude won the Indians' respect, and he planted some trees in the Indian villages as well as in white towns. For his stoicism, his knowledge of herbal medicine, and his selflessness, which they recognized as a manifestation of godliness, they seem to have revered him. More important, he respected and sympathized with them at a time when many white woodsmen shot them on sight like vermin, to clear the woods, or else humiliated them by catching their horses and tying sticks in their mouths and clapboards to their tails and letting the horses run home with the clapboards on fire. Swedenborg himself had said, "All things in the world exist from Divine Origin . . . clothed with such forms in nature as enable them to exist there and perform their use and thus correspond to higher things." So the Swedenborgian spirit-world of souls and angels coexistent with a natural world, in which the true order of Creation had been diverted by man's misapplication of his free will from the love of God to his own ego, quite corresponded, as far as it went, with the Indians' view. To his credit, Chapman, who seems to have been friendly with the Quakers of Ohio, too, was able to recognize this.

He was born—John Chapman—in poor circumstances in Leominster, in a cabin overlooking the Nashua River. His father, Nathaniel, was a farmer, carpenter, and wheelwright descended from Edward Chapman, who had arrived in Boston from Shropshire in 1639. Scarcely a year after the birth of John, his second child, the father left to fight in the Revolution as one of the original Minutemen, first at Bunker Hill in 1775, then with General Washington's army in New York the next year, wintering at Valley Forge in 1777–78. John's mother had died meanwhile. In 1780, following his discharge as a captain, Nathaniel Chapman married again, a Miss Lucy Cooley of Longmeadow, near Springfield, Massachusetts, and fathered ten more children by her. Though we have no proof that "Johnny Appleseed" was brought from his grandparents' house in Leominster to grow up here, he probably did spend his later boyhood on the Connecticut River, learning to handle a raft and pirogue, learning about wildlife, with this new brood.

Longmeadow was on the Connecticut Path, walked by settlers going west toward the upper Susquehanna River, two hundred miles away. It's thought that John Chapman, around 1792, at the age of eighteen, set out with his half-brother Nathaniel, who was seven years younger, for this frontier. They paused in the Wilkes-Barre region for a year or two, then may have ventured south to the Potomac in eastern Virginia and dawdled along from there toward Fort Cumberland, then, via Braddock's Road, to the Monongahela, and on by 1797 to Pittsburgh, during what was now John Adams's presidency. According to one story, they traveled up the Allegheny that fall to Olean, New York, in search of an uncle who was supposed to have built a cabin there, only to discover that he had pushed on west. With scant provisions, they took over his abandoned home, and nearly starved. What saved them, it's said, is that while John hiked out to earn money for food, some passing Indians luckily dropped in on his brother and provisioned him and taught him to hunt. (We don't know if John was already a vegetarian—which would have been a terrible disadvantage for both in enduring such a winter.)

In any case, the experience may have estranged the two. With the warm weather, they separated, Nathaniel, in his late teens, being old enough to strike off independently and to settle eventually on Duck Creek near Marietta in southern Ohio on the Ohio River, where by 1805 Nathaniel senior, the former Minuteman, also moved with his family. The older Chapman, though a captain in time of war, had been an indifferent provider, and died in 1807. One of his daughters, named Persis, and nineteen years younger than "Johnny Appleseed," later was to play an important and softening role in Johnny's life; but there is little evidence that John and Nathaniel ever troubled to see much of each other again, until 1842. That was fifty years after they had sauntered out from Longmeadow together, and John, famous and cranky and old, with a "thick bark of queerness on him," as Robert Price expresses it, and only three years short of his death, trudged east from Fort Wayne, Indiana, where he was living with Persis and her family, to Marietta, for a final reunion.

Mr. Price—who devoted, he says, the better part of twenty-five years to sifting the provable from unprovable legends about Johnny Appleseed —does not believe the Chapman boys ever went from Wilkes-Barre to Virginia. Indeed, with the affectionate overfamiliarity of an expert who has perhaps overmastered a subject, he slightly belittles the legends he does not believe. But he ascribes adventures aplenty to them in the area of the upper Allegheny near Warren, in northwestern Pennsylvania, where he has found evidence they had moved by 1797. In the spring of 1798, along Big Brokenstraw Creek, Johnny may have planted his first apple seeds. Only four other settlers were in residence on the creek, but they were busy fellows who within ten years would be rafting pine logs clear to New Orleans. Johnny probably lost his patches of orchard land to a more aggressive citizen. The next season—his brother gone by now—he had moved fifty miles, to French Creek, another tributary of the Allegheny. He was an exceedingly vigorous soul, doubtless a whiz at wielding an axe (one posthumous legend has him competing with Paul Bunyan). This was a time of wrestling great oaks and stupendous pines, of big snowstorms, when reportedly he toughed out one winter holed up on an island on French Creek subsisting on butternuts alone. That spring, or another, he was so impatient to get an early start downriver that he set his canoe on a block of ice on the Allegheny, where it would not be crushed in the jams, and fell asleep and floated a hundred miles or so before he bothered to wake up.

It was an element in the myth of Johnny Appleseed that he could doze off in the most dangerous circumstances—so calm he was. Once, in Seneca territory, he was being chased by a war party, before he had made his name favorably known to them, and as the story goes, he slipped into a swampy reedbed and lay with just his mouth above water, napping until the warriors gave up hunting him. In Ohio the Indians he knew were Delawares, Mohicans, and Wyandots, who were soon driven out of the state in the aftermath of the attacks they mounted (or allegedly hoped to mount) with British encouragement during the War of 1812. That summer and fall, with his woodcraft and marathon-endurance, John Chapman fulfilled a hero's role, once racing thirty miles from Mansfield to Mount Vernon, Ohio, to summon reinforcements and arouse the white settlers to the peril posed by General William Hull's surrender to British forces at Detroit. He spouted biblical language, according to at least one witness, though inevitably there were some false alarms: "The spirit of the Lord is upon me, and he hath anointed me to blow the trumpet in the wilderness, and sound an alarm in the forest; for behold, the tribes of the heathen are round about your doors, and a devouring flame followeth after them." This is the self-dramatist in him that made Casey Jones, John Henry, and Davy Crockett heroes also.

Casey Jones died from driving his locomotive faster than he ought to have. But Mr. Price reminds us that Chapman lived out his three score and ten years, and that the error of folklore is to simplify. The young buck strenuously logging, snowshoeing, existing on butternuts in the French Creek period, must have been quite a different figure from "Johnny Appleseed" practicing his kindnesses and charities during the two and a half decades he lived in Ohio and brought apples to Ashland, Bucyrus, Cohocton, Findlay, New Haven, Van Wert, and many another town on giveaway terms. Odd as he was—with the gossip that trailed him hinting that earlier in life he may have been kicked in the head by a horse—he seems almost to have passed for a solid citizen here. People didn't mind him dandling their babies on his lap. He even suffered (we may infer) the very insignia of solid citizenship, a "midlife crisis," somewhere during the years from 1809 to 1824, when he would have been between thirty-five and fifty years old.

That is, he had been a mystic before, and he ended his days in Indiana as a kind of landmark, with the "thick bark of queerness" still on him, thoroughly a mystic again. But for a few years in central Ohio apparently he tried to become a practical man. He speculated in a couple of town lots in Mount Vernon, one of which he sold after nineteen years for a profit of five dollars. By 1815 he had leased four quarter-sections of land of a hundred and sixty acres each for ninety-nine years at nineteen dollars a year apiece—a Mrs. Jane Cunningham his partner. But a recession occurred in 1819, tightening the money supply miserably. As a man accustomed to selling his goods for IOUs, he saw his principal holdings forfeited for want of money. His biographer makes the point that toward the close of his life, perhaps under Persis's influence, he bought another two hundred acres, around Fort Wayne. Altogether, a documented total of twenty-two properties, amounting to twelve hundred acres, can be totted up that he leased or owned for a time. But it would be a good guess to say that he accepted the 1819 recession as a lesson that he was intended to be an appleman, not a speculator, and an instrument of the bounty of God.

He had arrived on the Licking River in Ohio from the Allegheny in 1801, aged twenty-six. Only three families lived in what has become Licking County, but Ohio was only two years short of statehood by then. Ebenezer Zane was blazing Zane's Trace from Wheeling, on the Ohio River, through Zanesville and Chillicothe, capital of the Northwest Territory, toward Maysville, Kentucky. Farther north, there was an access path from Pittsburgh for a hundred and sixty miles to the Black Fork of the Mohican River, and from Pittsburgh by an old Indian trail to Fort Sandusky and on toward Detroit. He seems to have come this first time on foot with a horseload of seeds. More than three hundred thousand apple seeds will fit in a single bushel, so he had his work cut out for him. He may have been wearing his fabled mush pan on his head (if he ever did), with plenty of plantings in Pennsylvania behind him and his vision of the figure he wanted to cut for the rest of his life in front of him.

But we don't know if Johnny preferred winter to summer apples, or sharp flavors to sweet. We don't really know how hard he worked, because, set against this picture of a religious zealot for whom apple trees in their flowering were a living sermon from God, is the carefree master of woodcraft who supposedly strung his hammock between treetops and lazed away the pleasant days. He came back in succeeding summers to his nurseries to tend them—back to these patent and bounty lands "homesteaded," in a later phrase, or deeded to Revolutionary soldiers, or to the Refugee Tract, reserved for Canadians who had been persecuted by the British, and the Firelands, granted to Connecticut citizens in recompense for damage inflicted during the war. Straight land sales on settled portions of the Ohio River at this time involved terms of two dollars an acre, with fifty cents down.

In 1806—and perhaps the prettiest of all of the memories of John Chapman that have survived—he was noticed by a settler in Jefferson County, on the Ohio, drifting past in two canoes lashed together and heaped with cider-press seeds, both craft being daubed with mud and draped with moss to keep the load moist. He stopped to establish a planting a couple of miles below town, and probably another at the mouth of the Muskingum, at Marietta, near where his father had settled the year before. Ascending the Muskingum, past Zanesville, to a tributary called Walhonding, or White Woman's Creek, where the Licking River comes in, he poled up to the Mohican River and finally to the Black Fork of the Mohican, where he already may have had a nursery growing, because central Ohio by now was not unfamiliar country to him. His earlier seedlings would have been ready to sell if five years had passed.

With this canoe trip, his fame began. He had been a local character, but there were other applemen who made a business of selling trees, mostly as a sideline to farming. (Five pennies per sapling was the price at the time.) Furthermore, a hundred years before John Chapman ever arrived, the French had brought apple seeds to the Great Lakes and Mississippi, so that some of the Indian towns along the old trails already had orchards, from which the settlers could trade or pilfer as the Indians gradually were driven away. But where Johnny differed was that he alone had set himself the task of anticipating the patterns of settlement, as a public mission, across what had become by 1803 the state of Ohio. He moved along coincident with or a step ahead of the first flying parties of settlers, to have apple trees of transplantable age ready for them when they got their land cleared. Apple vinegar was the basic preservative for pickling vegetables such as beans, cucumbers, and beets; apple butter was a principal pleasure of winter meals; and apple brandy was one of the first cash exports that could be floated downriver to New Orleans. So he began to be recognized as something of a public servant as he went about.

He planted on a loamy, grassy ground, usually at riverside. He would clear a patch and plant and fence it, sometimes sleeping in his hammock, looking startlingly serene, swinging there, to travelers who were full of frightening tales of the woods. Or he might strip slabs of bark from a giant elm and lay them against it for a lean-to, or toss together a quick Indian hut of poles and bark, stretching out on a bed of leaves inside. And then he drifted on, grubbed more ground clear, constructed another barrier fence. Some of these little gardens he never bothered to hunt up again, confident that the settlers would discover them. Others he hurried back to, hearing that a herd of cattle had broken in. Through these oak, hickory, and beech forests hogs ranged, as well as cattle, and there were great flocks of passenger pigeons, and wolves, which the more brutal pioneers skinned alive and turned loose to scare the rest of the pack. On the Whetstone River, near the Clear Fork of the Mohican, the Vandorn boys helped him build a fourteen-by-sixteen-foot cabin for wintering over, impressed at how fearlessly he slept on top of a windfall as the wolves and owls howled.

He liked to plant on quarter-sections set aside for the support of the first schools, or might do so on an existing farm if the owner agreed to share what grew. Once a few years had passed, he didn't need to make such long trips for seeds and, if he were working thirty miles away, might deputize a farmer who lived close to an orchard to honor the notes he wrote out for people who wished to purchase trees.

By 1816 Persis had moved with her family from Marietta to Perrysville, on the Mohican's Black Fork. So, with some of his kin in the area (his brother-in-law worked for him), and with the good will which his exploits in the War of 1812 had engendered and the investments in land that he was attempting to pay for, the region around Perrysville became his home. During his late forties he traveled less, but even after he had lost most of his land and had renewed his vows of poverty—moving west again with horseloads of apple seeds to the Miami and Tiffin rivers—he came back to Perrysville to winter with family and friends.

His fifties seem to have been severely austere, like his twenties and thirties. He planted on the Sandusky; had fifteen thousand trees at Milan on the Huron; started a nursery in Defiance in northwest Ohio when that village was six years old, and other nurseries along the proposed route of the Miami and Erie Canal. From Toledo he traveled west up the Maumee River toward Indiana, working the banks of its tributaries—the Blanchard, the Auglaize, the St. Mary's—the population of Ohio, meanwhile, having vaulted from 45,000 in 1800 to 580,000 in 1820.

In 1822 he may have gone to Detroit to sightsee, and, around 1826, to Urbana and Cincinnati. In 1830, just after the future city of Fort Wayne had been plotted, he is said to have landed on the waterside from the Maumee in a hollow log filled with seeds. Thereafter he labored in Indiana, boarding with Allen County families like the Hills and Worths for a dollar or two per week, but still going back to Perrysville to spend each winter, until 1834, when Persis and her husband moved out to join him.

Various myths have him continuing on to the Ozarks, to Minnesota, to the foothills of the Rockies. He did not, but undoubtedly he gave seeds to pioneers who ventured much farther west. He may have seen Illinois and the Mississippi River and crossed into Iowa. But Allen County lies at the watershed separating the Wabash, flowing to the Mississippi, from the Maumee, flowing toward Lake Erie and eventually the St. Lawrence, so it is appropriate that Johnny stopped here. Like the plainsmen and mountainmen, he was a man still "with the bark on," but apples were his particular witness to God, and apples do not grow well on the Great Plains. "I, John Chapman (by occupation a gatherer and planter of apple seeds)," begins a deed from the Fort Wayne days. He was an appleman first of all. Maybe he didn't even long to participate in the drama of the Great West ahead.

He was a legend by now—a bluebird, to the bluejay figure of the raftsman Mike Fink, who had poled the Ohio River nearby at about the same time. Mike Fink, a very rough guy who died twenty years earlier than Johnny on a trip to the Rockies, once set his common-law wife on fire in a pyre of leaves when she winked at another man. He is more typical of the frontiersmen we remember. What would a conventional movie-maker do with a vegetarian frontiersman who did not believe in horseback riding and wore no furs; who planted fruit trees in praise of a Protestant God, and gave much of his money away to impoverished families he met; who would "punish" one foot that had stepped on an angleworm by walking with it bare over stony ground and regretted for years killing a rattlesnake that had bitten him in the grass; who would douse his campfire when mosquitoes fell into it?

Near Persis's home in Fort Wayne, he had a log cabin and eleven cleared acres and timber cut for a barn, when he died in 1845. He didn't die there, but at the home of the Worth family on the St. Joseph River not far off, presumably of pneumonia contracted during a fifteen-mile trudge in mid-March, leading his black ox to repair an orchard fence that cattle had trampled down.

At his death—so the Worths said—he had on a coffee sack, as well as the waist sections of four pairs of old pants cut off and slit so that they lapped "like shingles" around his hips, under an antiquated pair of pantaloons.

His life extended from the battle of Bunker Hill to the inauguration of James K. Polk as president; and the last person who claimed to have seen Johnny Appleseed with his own eyes didn't die until just before World War II. He was a frontier hero "of endurance that was voluntary, and of action that was creative and not sanguinary," as that 1871 issue of *Harper's* put it. Historians, by neglecting individuals of such munificent spirit as Johnny, and leaving us with only the braggarts and killers, underestimate the breadth of frontier experience, and leave us the poorer.

—*December 1979*

THE MINISTER AND THE MILL GIRL

By GEORGE HOWE

Pregnant Maria Cornell had been found hanging from a loop of three-strand hemp, and it looked as though Parson Avery had done it. An absorbing reconstruction of a classic nineteenth-century murder case.

About nine on the morning of Friday, December 21, 1832, John Durfee, a farmer of Tiverton, Rhode Island, was driving his team through his stackyard when he noticed something inside swaying against one of the five-foot stakes. Leaping forward, he saw the body of a woman. Her knees hung six inches above the ground; her legs were bent backward, the toes balancing on the grass: her head lolled forward from a cord attached six inches below the top of the stake. Durfee tried to lift her with one hand, while loosing the cord with the other, but small as she was, her weight was too great for him. He shouted for help. In a moment his father, with Bill Allen and Ben Negus, the farm hands, ran up from the darkness. Allen cut the cord with his knife, and they laid the body on the ground.

The dead woman's black hair cascaded from the pleats of her calash —the "bashful bonnet," it was often called. Her cheeks were frostbitten, and her tongue was caught between her teeth. Her brown cloak was hooked up the front, except at the very top. Beneath it, one arm hung straight, and one was bent up to her breast, as if to ease the cord at her throat. There were gloves on her hands, and half a comb in her hair; the other half they found outside the stackyard. Her shoes lay together a few inches to her right, with a red bandanna beside them. On the "fog"—last year's dead grass—there were no footprints, for the ground was frozen. The noose by which she hung was not the slipknot, but what farmers call a double hitch and sailors, a clove hitch. The cord was three-strand hemp, no thicker than a goose quill. It cut into her neck just below the right ear, and her right cheek rested against the stake.

Tiverton is one of the townships in Newport County. Durfee's farm lay half a mile below the Massachusetts line at Fall River. Someone ran into the village for Elihu Hicks, the coroner, and someone else to Fall River for a doctor. Hicks arrived within an hour. Picking a jury from the gathering crowd, he swore them in inside the stackyard. Then the body was carried to Durfee's house under a horse blanket, with straw beneath the broken neck.

By this time there were two Fall River men who could identify the body: Dr. Thomas Wilbur and the Reverend Mr. Bidwell of the Methodist Church. Dr. Wilbur examined it with the help of the female bystanders. Beneath the petticoat was the imprint of two hands. When Aunt Hannah Wrightington asked Dorcas Ford what she thought they proved, Dorcas whispered, "Rash violence!"

The girl was Maria Cornell—her full name was Sarah Maria Cornell—of Mr. Bidwell's own congregation. The minister sent Durfee to Mrs. Hathaway's in Fall River, where Maria had boarded, to fetch her effects. Durfee soon returned with a trunk and a bandbox, and with Mrs. Hathaway herself. In the bandbox Hicks found a letter, undated and unmailed, addressed to Bidwell. He made the minister read it aloud: "Sir: I take this opportunity to inform you that for reasons known to God and my own soul I wish no longer to be connected with the Methodist Society. When I came to this place I thought I should enjoy myself among them but as I do not enjoy any Religion at all, I have not seen a well nor a happy day since I left Thompson campground. You will therefore please to drop my name from [the Bible Class], and I will try to gain all the instruction I can from your public labours. I hope I shall feel different some time or other. The Methodists are my people when I enjoy any Religion. To them I was Indebted under God for my spiritual birth. I once knew what it was to love God with all my heart once felt God was my father, Jesus my friend and Heaven my home but have awfully departed and sometimes feel I shall lose my soul forever. I desire your prayer that God would help me from this. Yours respectfully, Sarah M. Cornell."

Beside it, under her trinkets and ribbons, lay three letters addressed to her—one yellow, one pink, and one white—and a soiled scrap of paper, dated the very day before. Hicks read it aloud: "If I should be missing, enquire of the Rev. Mr. Avery in Bristol. He will know where I have gone. Dec. 20. S.M. Cornell."

Bristol, Rhode Island, lies across Mount Hope Bay in full sight of Fall River and Tiverton. The Reverend Ephraim K. Avery, a friend and fellow laborer of Bidwell's, was the minister of the Methodist Church there. On hearing Avery's name, Bidwell took horse through Fall River, round the head of the bay, and down through Warren to Bristol. It was seven o'clock when he reached the town. He whispered the news of the suicide to his friend, outdoors in the dark, on the narrow dog-leg of Wardwell Street, where Avery lived. Avery did not ask him to spend the night, and we can guess he would have declined. Bidwell rode home.

The deputy sheriff for Fall River was a young sleuth named Harvey Harnden. Hicks and Harnden spent Saturday morning over the three remaining letters found in the bandbox, which led them to suspect Avery of murder.

However, the coroner's jury, when it returned its verdict, was more cautious: "On viewing the body of said Sarah Maria Cornell, here lying dead, upon their oaths [they] do say that they believe the said Cornell committed suicide by hanging herself upon a stake in said yard, and was influenced to commit said crime by the wicked conduct of a married man, which we gather from Dr. Wilbur, together with the contents of three letters found in the trunk of said Cornell. And we the jurors aforesaid, upon their oaths aforesaid do say the aforesaid Sarah Maria Cornell in manner aforesaid came to her death by the causes aforesaid."

Not content with this, Harnden, with Hicks, Durfee, and another man, crossed on Sunday by bridge to Aquidneck Island and by horse ferry to Bristol. The four called on Squire John Howe, justice of the peace for Bristol, and asked him to hold Elder Avery on suspicion of murder. Durfee swore out the complaint. Reluctantly, the Squire promised to send the constable that evening to arrest the suspect, and set a hearing for the next Wednesday, the day after Christmas, with his colleague Levi Haile from the neighboring town of Warren.

On Monday, back in Durfee's barn, Dr. Wilbur performed a post-mortem on Maria's body, exhumed for the purpose. If she had lived, he told Harnden, she would have borne a daughter in five months. A second jury then returned a verdict, accusing Avery of being the "principal or accessory" in her death.

Maria was then buried against a stone wall in the very field where she had been found, with prayer read by Elder Bidwell to a tearful, angry crowd. That evening—December 24, 1832—Harnden, amid cheers and groans, presented the new verdict to a meeting in the Lyceum Hall at Fall River, promising that it should reach the two justices when their hearing opened two days later in Bristol. The citizens appointed him to head a "committee to aid the inhabitants of Tiverton."

Pending the hearing, Squire Howe had released Avery in his own recognizance. The Parson, a self-confident man of thirty-seven, engaged three lawyers, to whom he admitted easily that he had known Maria Cornell in meeting at Lowell, Massachusetts, before being stationed in Bristol;

that he had seen her once since then, at Elder Bidwell's revival meeting in Fall River on October 19; that on December 20, the day before her body was found, he had crossed the ferry from Bristol to Aquidneck Island for a stroll, as the ferry master could testify; that he had returned to the ferry at nine o'clock, too late to cross, and had slept at the ferryhouse; that the Fall River men might claim to have seen him in their village, but that Mrs. Jones, who lived on the west side of the Island, could testify to seeing him cross her field in the afternoon, much too late for him to reach Fall River and return to the ferry by nine.

"Sister Jones," he told her solemnly, "my life is worth thousands of worlds. Can you not recall that you saw me in the afternoon?"

But Mrs. Jones shook her head. She had seen a stranger in the *morning*, and could not even be sure whether what he carried on his shoulder was a walking stick or a clam hoe.

On Christmas Day, in those still-Puritan times a holiday of no importance, a hundred men of Fall River chartered the steamer *King Philip* for an invasion of Bristol. They swarmed up from the dock and surrounded the parsonage, even forcing their way into the sinkroom. Avery, who had performed a marriage that very morning, listened upstairs with his family. While William Paull, the Bristol sheriff, stood helpless on the outskirts, one stouthearted Bristolian faced the mob.

"What do you want?" he asked them.

"We've come for Elder Avery and will have him dead or alive," said Harnden.

"That you shall not," answered the Bristol man, and shoved him outdoors. There might have been a lynching if the bell of the *King Philip* had not rung just then. The crowd trooped down, empty-handed, for the return trip to Fall River.

Next morning the hearing opened in the courthouse on the Bristol Common, just beside Avery's white-pillared chapel. Luke Drury, Collector of the Port, acted as clerk. The room was filled from morning to night. The squires were strict. They refused to examine Harnden's three letters, and when he asked Dr. Wilbur to describe Maria's condition, they refused to accept an answer. On January 7, they discharged Avery on the grounds that the complaint was signed by a private citizen (Durfee) instead of by the coroner, and that there was not much evidence against Avery anyway. That very evening Harnden read their verdict to an ugly crowd which overflowed the Congregational Church in Fall River. If the Bristol court would not bring Avery to justice, he promised them, he would do so by himself.

Avery, whose life was in danger from the Fall River mob, sought advice from the Reverend John Bristed, the Episcopalian rector of Bristol. He might not expect comradeship from his colleague, but he could expect wisdom, for Bristed had been a lawyer in New York before taking orders. He advised Avery to leave town till the excitement died down.

A very got out of Bristol just in time. Harnden had persuaded Judge Randall of the Rhode Island superior court to issue a warrant against Avery for suspicion of murder, with a request for extradition in case he had fled to another state. Now Harnden, arriving an hour after Avery left, was told by a neighbor that a carriage drawn by two white horses had picked Avery up outside the feed mill and headed northward. Above tiny Rhode Island lay the breadth of Massachusetts, and beyond it, like fingers spreading from a palm, the upper states of New England, and beyond them, Canada, where the fugitive would be safe.

The sleuth did not give up the chase. He hired a horse and sulky, disguised himself in a fur cap and pea jacket, and set out in pursuit. In turn he visited Providence, Pawtucket, Attleboro, Wrentham, Dedham, Boston, and finally Lowell, suspecting that his quarry had hidden there among his—and Maria's—former congregation. But nobody in Lowell had seen Avery. It was January 18 by now, and at night in the American House, the sheriff oiled a sheet of paper, laid it over the innkeeper's gazetteer, and traced on it the roads of southern New England. They all led to Boston; he should have searched there more thoroughly.

"I then left Lowell [he writes] stopping but seldom for the reason that at most of the public houses through that part of the country, including the whole distance to Boston . . . a man must be proof against most gasses and obnoxious exhalations in order to withstand the effluvia of new rum. Yet there are several houses in the [district] that are cleanly and well-kept, and in which a man can sit down and feel himself at home, and be well entertained. But in some others, on going into the barroom, the first question put to you will be, 'Mister, how fur are you going this way? What may I call your name, Sir, if I may be so bold? 'Taint any of my business, sir, but what's your business up this way. What's the news down to General Court?' "

Arriving in Boston, he picked up the trail of the two white horses. The landlord of the Bromfield House had seen a certain Elder Gifford drive in behind them on January 10. Harnden remembered Elder Gifford as an observer sent down to the hearing by the New England Methodist Conference. Gifford was cornered by Harnden's knowledge of his journey from Bristol. After they had exchanged promises—that Gifford would not warn Avery if Harnden did not betray Gifford—he weakly suggested that the sheriff try Rindge, New Hampshire.

Next day [i.e., on Sunday, January 20], having crossed the state line,

Harnden picked up a New Hampshire deputy sheriff named Edwards. There were not many Methodists in Rindge, said he, and those few all lived close together on a country lane just off the northbound pike.

Harnden appealed for reinforcement to Edwards; he called in a young man who drove a bread cart, and so knew the Methodist road. He eagerly promised to "keep dark."

The three men bedded down at Colonel French's tavern in Fitzwilliam, north of the Methodist road. After a few hours' sleep, Harnden dispatched the other two southward, with orders to reconnoiter the road en route. He promised to meet them at noon in the public house at Rindge.

But when the posse gathered, he found that Edwards had learned nothing; it was clear that he had spent the morning in the bar. The baker, however, traveling the road in his sleigh, had heard there would be a Methodist prayer meeting that evening at a certain Captain Mayo's, three miles north of the village. Harnden ordered him to attend it in the guise of a repentant sinner and to stay through it to the end.

The baker started off without supper, only to return before Harnden and Edwards had finished their pie and ask for some himself. He had been unable to survive the prayer meeting. Accompanied by his aides, Harnden then drove the baker's sleigh to Captain Mayo's. He opened the door without knocking. Two men and a woman sat in the keeping room with a single candle before them. He asked for Captain Mayo. A stocky man with a pipe in his hand allowed he was the Captain.

"I am here after *Ephraim K. Avery*," Harnden announced.

"Ephraim K. Avery?" the Captain repeated slowly.

"Yes sir," said Harnden.

"*Ephraim K*. Avery!" Mayo repeated, as if there were more than one. "I never knew such a man as Ephraim K. Avery."

"*I* know such a man," said Harnden grimly. "I have come a great way after him; I came on *purpose* after him, and I *must* have him; and Capt. Mayo, the better way is for you to go to the room where Mr. Avery is, tell him a Mr. Harnden is here and wishes to see him, and let him come forward; for he is in your house, and if he comes not forward I shall search your house, for I *must* have him."

At this point Mrs. Mayo slipped into another room, closing the door behind her. Getting no help from the Captain, Harnden started the search alone, taking a single candle. While his posse guarded the doors, he explored both floors and even lifted the trap door to the attic. On the way down he met Mrs. Mayo, who whispered to him from the dark, "You seek innocent blood."

He threw open the door of a second-floor room, where a low fire burned in the fireplace. A candle before it was extinguished, but the wick still smouldered. Finding the room empty, he went downstairs, where his eye fell on a closed door that had been open when he passed it before.

"I thought to look behind the door [he writes] and should have done so earlier, if the object of my search had been so large about the breast as most men. I must give the gentleman credit for requiring less room than I thought possible for any man to do."

Avery had been hiding behind the door, and now he was taken at last. He had grown a beard and wore green spectacles. Harnden took him by the hand.

"Do endeavor to overcome this agitation," Harnden said; "you need fear no personal violence, you shall be kindly treated."

Then for the first time he heard Avery speak.

"I suppose you cannot legally take me from this state, without a warrant from the Governor," he said weakly. "Have you such a warrant?"

Harnden showed him Judge Randall's warrant, and after Avery had packed, Harnden drove him back to Rindge in the baker's sleigh.

Next morning the posse disbanded. Harnden carried his prisoner by stage to Boston. Back at the Bromfield House, he found Colonel Bradford Durfee of the Vigilance Committee waiting with money and congratulations. The next day he pushed on toward Rhode Island. The citizenry waited at the crossroads. During the chase excitement had been intense through the countryside, for it was not only Avery, but Harnden, also, who had disappeared. Rumor had spread that the minister had escaped to Canada or to Cuba—even that he had been a pirate in the West Indies for ten years, before taking the cloth. It was reported that Harnden had chained him in irons and was exhibiting him for a fee on the return from Rindge—a charge Harnden denied.

Late in the afternoon of January 23, the coach reached Fall River, and on the twenty-fifth Harnden handed his prisoner over to the sheriff of Newport County, Rhode Island, at the state line, not far above Maria's hastily dug grave. The grand jury for the 1833 term of the Supreme Court of the state of Rhode Island and Providence Plantations then indicted the Reverend Ephraim K. Avery for murder in the first degree.

His trial opened on May 6, in the lower hall of the eighteenth-century Colony House (then known as the State House) on the Newport Parade. It took 101 talesmen to produce a jury of twelve.

Five hundred spectators crowded into the pillared courtroom. Reporters came from as far away as Philadelphia, but the law forbade them to publish their stories while the trial was still in progress.

Avery pleaded not guilty. He spoke in a firm voice, holding his right hand in his breast pocket. Thereafter he sat silent, for the law did not allow the defendant in a capital case to testify. He was clad in a brown surtout; in place of a collar he wore a white handkerchief knotted at his neck, and he hid his eyes behind the green spectacles.

The prosecution was led by Albert C. Greene, the state's attorney general, whose high stock, in his portrait, seems to lengthen the disdainful egg-shaped face above it. To defend Avery, the Methodist Conference hired a team of lawyers headed by Jeremiah Mason of Boston, after Daniel Webster the smartest and dearest advocate in New England. Like Webster, he had been a senator of the United States. He stood six foot three, with one shoulder higher than the other, but the voice that issued from his enormous frame was a falsetto squeak. The whole courtroom leaned forward as the two lawyers unfolded the story of Ephraim Avery and Maria Cornell.

Lowell, Massachusetts, at the falls of the Merrimack River, was the industrial showplace of America. In 1820 it had been a barren waste. Ten years later it had fifteen thousand inhabitants and seven newspapers. Brick cotton mills, up to seven stories high, lined the watercourses, each capped with a belfry and surrounded by snug green-shuttered boardinghouses. Most of the workers were farm girls, who looked to a short experience in the mills as an introduction to life, much as their brothers looked to a few years at sea.

Among the factory hands was a little black-eyed sparrow of a girl named Maria Cornell, who stood only five feet tall. Born at Rupert, Vermont, in 1802, she had been apprenticed at twelve as a seamstress in Norwich, Connecticut, by her widowed mother. Mason showed that she had been discharged from Norwich for breaking the heddles on her loom; that she had lost other jobs—at Jewett City, Connecticut, for promiscuous behavior, and at Dorchester, Massachusetts, for calling the Methodist elders "a pack of damned fools." She had also been dismissed from the Methodist congregation at Slatersville, Rhode Island, for lewdness. Who, asked Greene, could blame them for reading her out of meeting? She did not blame them herself, Mason answered.

In 1828, repentant, she had moved to Lowell to work as a weaver in Appleton Mill Number 1. Her wages were $4 for a six-day week, of which $1.25 was withheld by the company for lodging and meals at her boardinghouse. In 1830 the Conference stationed the Reverend Mr. Avery in the growing mill town. He was thirty-three then, and must have looked as he did now in the box: a good six feet tall, with dark hair brushed up in front and curling long behind. He had a round chin, lank cheeks, and full lips. He had come first from "York State," where he had tended store for his father, a wounded veteran of the Revolution. He had studied medicine before divinity and was something of a naturalist as well.

With his invalid wife, Sophia, his five-year-old boy Edwin and his infant daughter Catherine, he took lodgings at the house of a Mr. Abbott. There was a study for him on the ground floor—the devout called it the Prophet's Chamber—with shelves for his collection of minerals, a couch of his own, and a separate door to the street. While Sophia spent her days upstairs with the children, he would take his tall cane after breakfast and tramp the countryside—no one knew where—till it was time for tea and evening prayer at home.

Maria was one of his flock. His rectitude, perhaps, served to reawaken the Devil within her. He had not been in Lowell a month before she stole a piece of muslin from a store; it was retrieved from within her shawl. She even rode out with a young man to the nearby village of Belvidere, where, says the State's testimony, "They called for a chamber and he treated her with wine."

When Avery heard this story, he threatened to expel her from meeting. She promised to reform again; she offered to work without pay as his servant if he would relent. But young Edwin, Mason proved, had once told his mother, as if it were a trifle, "Pa kissed Maria in the road." Then the neglected lady forgot her meekness and, when Avery wanted to hire Maria to do housework, refused to have her in the house. Pious and penitent though she might be, the minister could not keep such a magdalen in the church. In October of 1830, five months after reaching Lowell, he read her out for theft and lewdness. She took the road again, this time to Somersworth, across the New Hampshire line.

Though she could not live with the Methodist Church, she could not live without it either. Avery had warned the Reverend Mr. Storrs of Somersworth. Storrs testified that when, as gently as he could, he had excluded her from a "Love-Feast" (a religious service for those who profess to have experienced a "second blessing"), she had cried to him, standing tiptoe with her arm across her breast, "You think to triumph over me now. But what care I for Mr. Avery and the Methodist Church? I will have my revenge, though it cost me my life."

She struggled through a year at Somersworth. Then on June 1, 1832, she fled with her loneliness to Woodstock, in the northeast corner of Connecticut, to join her sister Lucretia, who was married to the tailor Grindell Rawson. He made her his bookkeeper, and she wrote out his bills in a bold, clear hand.

Although the doors of Woodstock meeting closed against her, she managed to join a Bible class at a hamlet called Muddy Brook. And no one could bar her from the camp meetings which abounded in the countryside.

Their whole purpose was to save lost sheep. Card sharps, horsejockeys, liquor peddlers, and fallen women, among the hundreds who truly sought redemption, flocked to the great circles cleared among the pines. The crowd would sway on the narrow benches set up before the preachers' stand. Delegations from neighboring villages pitched white tents at the edge of the woods and laid their provisions on the center table, where they were shared by all.

The camp meeting at Thompson, Connecticut, only a few miles from Woodstock, opened on Monday, August 27, 1832. On Tuesday John Paine, the Woodstock expressman, dressed in a dark coat, light pantaloons, and a green-lined palm-leaf hat, drove Maria to Thompson and dropped her, with bandbox and hamper, at the Muddy Brook tent. By this time Avery had been rotated from Lowell to Bristol, Rhode Island, which lies sixty miles southeast of Thompson—a long trip by chaise, even for a man in good health—and Avery, four days before, had broken his ankle on a stone wall and fainted from the pain. Though he limped as he walked, and was not even on the list of preachers, he drove to the meeting. At Thompson he boarded in the Plainfield tent. Between meals he sat with the preachers in the stand or rested in the official tent behind it.

The prosecution did not claim that he knew Maria would be there and admitted that he did not meet her till Thursday, the last day of camp. That morning at six o'clock the horn blew for sunrise prayer. As the echo of Amen died away, the Reverend Elias Scott warned his colleague that there were bad characters on the ground. Avery nodded; he had seen Maria gazing up at the stand, and when he caught her eye, she turned her back on him. He agreed with Scott that it was their duty to warn the Muddy Brook tent master of her character and took the stern assignment on himself. He listened to the preaching from ten o'clock till noon. He took dinner with Plainfield, and tea with Weston. At 7:25 P.M. the horn sounded for the last service. Half an hour later, after the prayer of dismissal, the Thompson meeting was over for another year.

Of the next hour the only word is Maria's own, written to her sister in a letter submitted by the State: "I went up and asked to talk with him. 'There is no room for us at the tents,' he said. 'Go along further and I will overtake you.' He did overtake me, outside the fence, and we passed on, arm in arm, into the woods. When in the woods some distance, he asked me to sit down, and I did. I asked him if he had burned my letters, the ones I wrote him from Somersworth, asking to be retained in meeting. 'No, but there is one condition on which I will settle the difficulty.' About this time he took one of my hands and put one of his own into my bosom. I tried to get away from him, but could not. Afterwards he promised to burn the letters when he returned to Bristol."

A month later she discovered her plight. Her only salvation, she wrote to her sister on November 18, was to hide again. This time she chose Fall River, a bustling village of five thousand. Next to Lowell, it was New England's fastest-growing mill village, and as the fish hawk flies it is only four miles from Bristol. Three times a week the *King Philip* plied between the two, on her way to and from Providence; and the stage, through Warren, ran twice a day. On October 3, Maria set down her trunk at a boardinghouse and started work the next Monday in the weave-shed of the Anawan Mill. She tended four looms. In the twelve-hour workday she could run off 130 yards of cloth, for which she was paid a half cent a yard. In good health, she could make sixty-five cents, or four shillings —for some people, fifty years after the Revolution, still reckoned in shillings and pence.

On Friday, October 19, Avery, as Parson Bidwell's guest, preached at the evening service in Fall River, as he had told Squire Howe. The night was not so dark but that a passerby saw a short woman, at the edge of the emerging crowd, pluck at the sleeve of Avery's cloak. The evidence of what they said is again from Bidwell's testimony.

"Mr. Avery," Maria whispered, "I want to speak with you."

He turned to look down at her. "Maria, I do not wish to have anything to say with you."

"You must. I want you to say you will not hurt me here. You have ruined me at Somersworth and Lowell."

"Say rather that you have ruined yourself. I have never wanted nor tried to hurt you, Maria, but I can give no such promise. It is only just that Elder Bidwell should be warned."

"Nobody knows me here," she insisted, "and will not unless you tell them. Don't tell them, will you? I mean to behave myself well."

"That will be seen," he answered, pushing on after the Bidwells, "I shall talk with you tomorrow."

He came to see her the next evening, Maria wrote her sister, and she spent an hour with him. "He said . . . that if that was my case [the unborn child] was not his, and said I must go to a doctor immediately; said he had burned my letters—if he had have known what would have happened he would have kept them—said I must never swear it, for if that was my case he would take care of me—spoke very feeling of his wife and children—said I must say it belonged to a man that was dead, for, said he, I am dead to you—that is, I cannot marry you. He owned and denied [his guilt] two or three times. . . . I pledged him my word and honor I would not expose him if he would settle it. Therefore you must not mention his name to anyone . . .

"What the result will be I know not. . . . I do not, however, wish you to do anything for me till I send you word. . . . The girls make from 3 to 4 dollars per week in the summer, but the days are short now and the water is low now. We can't do very much . . . I do not want for anything at present. I have kept at home except on the Sabbath, but the methodists begin to know me and say good morning Sister, as I go to the factory. I am glad that you have plenty of work. I hope you will get along for help. . . . You must not forget you have a sister in Fall River. My love to Mother. You must burn this letter. Farewell. Your sister, Sarah M. Cornell."

The folded yellow letter in her bandbox, unsigned, bore the Bristol postmark and the date November 13, 1832: "Miss Cornell— . . . I will do all you ask, only keep it secret. I wish you to write me as soon as you get this, naming a time and place where I can see you, and wait for my answer before I come . . . I will keep your letter till I see you, and wish you to keep mine, and have them when I see you. Write soon—Say nothing to no one. Yours in haste."

On Monday, the twenty-fifth, Avery set off from Bristol by Chadwick's stage for a four-day prayer meeting in Providence. On Tuesday morning, dressed in the black goat-hair cloak called a camlet, he stepped aboard the *King Philip* at her dock. He handed a pink letter to Orswell, her engineer, with a tip of ninepence, and asked him to leave it for Miss Cornell at Mrs. Hathaway's in Fall River. (At the trial, Orswell identified the letter, which was the second found in the bandbox, but could not positively identify Avery because of his green spectacles.) That evening Maria received it:

Providence, Nov. 26, 1832

Dear Sister:
As I told you I am willing to help you and do for you. As circumstances are, I should rather you would come to Bristol in the stage the 18th of December and stop at the Hotell and stay till six in the evening and then go up directly across the main street to a brick building neare to the stone meeting house where I will meet you and talk with you. When you stop at the tavern either inquire for work or go out on to the street in pretense of looking for some or something else and I may see you. Say nothing about me or my family. Should it storm on the 18th come the 20th. If you cannot come and it will be more convenient to meet me at the methodist meeting house in summerset just over the ferry on either of the above *eve'g* I will meet you there at the same hour or if you cannot do either, I will come to fall river on one of the above evenings when there will be the least passing, I should think before the mills stop work. . . . When you write, direct your letter to *Betsy Hills* and not as you have to me. *Remember this*. Your last letter I am afraid was broken open. Wear

your calash not your plain bonnet. You can send your letter by mail.

Yours &c,

B.H.

Betsy Hills was the crippled niece of Mrs. Avery who helped with the housework. Inside the flap was a postscript: "—Let me still enjoin the secret. Keep the letters in your bosom or burn them up."

But he did not wait for her to come to Bristol. On the eighth, ten days before the assignation, he walked the fourteen roundabout miles to Fall River. He bought a half-sheet of white paper—the third found in the bandbox—scribbled a note on it, sealed it with a purple wafer, and dropped it at the post office in the penny box for local delivery: "—I will be her on the 20th if pleasant at the place named, at six o'clock. If not pleasant, the next Monday evening. Say nothing, etc."

The twentieth was the day before John Durfee had found Maria's body in the stackyard.

After noonday dinner, Avery started out from his house in Bristol. He wore his peaked walking hat and the same brown surtout he wore later in the courtroom. He carried a red bandanna under his arm with a package in it. He eased his limp on a walking stick. There were no spectacles on his nose. At the foot of Ferry Hill in Bristol, two miles from home, he shouted across to George Pearse, the ferryman, who was tied up on the Island side. Pearse brought the horse scow over, apologizing that he must charge sixteen cents instead of eight, since he had to cross twice. He ported the sweep and clucked to the pair in the deck stalls; they plodded the disk of the treadmill; the paddles began to turn, and the scow edged into the channel.

Waving his cane toward the west side of the Island, Avery told Pearse he was out for a ramble, in spite of his still-lame ankle. He aimed to call on Brother Cook, four miles down-island. On the way, he thought to look at the Butt's Hill Fort, where his father had fought in the Revolution, and perhaps at the coal deposits on the western shore. Pearse saw him limp up the hill to the windmill on the crest, and then out of sight, with his cane to help him.

Eastward in Fall River, at four that afternoon, Maria asked her overseer to excuse her for the rest of the day. Lucy Hathaway promised to watch her looms—one was broken anyway—for the half hour that remained till dark. Maria walked home to her lodging, changed to her brown cloak and calash, and went out, telling Mrs. Hathaway she would be home early. At the same time, a little beyond the Tiverton bridge connecting the

211

Island to the mainland, Annis Norton saw a dark-spectacled six-footer, in a snug snuff-colored surtout and tapered beaver, striding uphill toward Fall River.

"At that rate," laughed Annis, "he'll reach Ohio by sunrise."

The sun set at half past four; the moon would not rise till ten. In the dusk, on the hill just short of Fall River, Benjamin Manchester and Abner Davis were blasting rock. Having kindled their shavings, they ran to the shelter of a stone wall. At that moment a stranger, taller than common height, climbed the same wall farther down. "Look out," they shouted to him. He halted till the rock had stopped falling, then started across the field. He climbed the opposite wall into John Durfee's pasture. Durfee saw him too, dark as it was. The stranger gazed at Durfee's stackyard, then squared his shoulders, and passed into the dusk, toward Fall River.

There, in Lawton's Hotel, a clock peddler was eating supper. At quarter of six a long-legged stranger with dark glasses on his nose walked into the sitting room and ordered supper too. He wore a fur cap and had no cane. While waiting for his food he walked into the bar and returned with half a tumbler of brandy, which he drank neat at the trestle table, without speaking to the peddler. Having eaten, he paid Margaret Hambly, the waitress, and walked out into the dark.

At seven o'clock, Zeruiah Hambly, Margaret's mother, happening to open the door with a lantern in her hand, saw a tall man and a short woman, arm in arm, walk down the lane in the direction of Durfee's farm. At half past seven, Eleanor Owen heard shrieks from the same direction. She was washing the tea dishes in the sinkroom, but kept on washing them.

Everyone went to bed early, to save candles. But at 9:10 P.M. John Borden, on the Tiverton side of the bridge, passed a stranger striding from the direction of Fall River; and a few minutes later William Anthony, on the Island side, foddering his cattle late, saw a figure come from the same direction and disappear toward the ferry. The moon was not yet up.

Whoever the stranger was—if indeed there was not more than one of him—the Reverend Ephraim K. Avery soon afterward awakened Jeremiah Gifford, who tended the wharf on the Island side of the ferry. Gifford resented being roused from his four-poster. He peered at the wooden clock on his mantel; the hands just lacked quarter of ten. The minister asked to be ferried to Bristol.

Gifford grumbled that it would be inconvenient. The wind was high, and it was very cold.

Avery persisted, saying his family was unwell and needed him at home.

The ferryman still refused. He did, however, give Avery a room for the night. The minister was up at five for an impatient breakfast. He crossed as the sunrise bell sounded from the Congregational Church in Bristol and trudged up Ferry Hill, reaching home in time for a second meal. In the afternoon he, Mrs. Avery, and their son walked downtown for tea with Mrs. Nancy Gladding, who testified that he was cheerful and affable; his demeanor was that of a Christian and a gentleman. Soon afterward, as we have seen, Elder Bidwell brought him the news of Maria Cornell's death.

The State had a hard time drawing a description of the corpus delicti from the ladies who had laid it out, and one of them snapped, "I never heard such questions asked of *nobody*."

Attorney General Greene described it anyway, to the courtroom's horror, while Avery sat impassive behind his spectacles. The crowd's hatred for him spread to encompass the black-robed elders who attended him. When the gentle Bidwell entered the courtroom, someone called out, "Here comes another of the damned murderers."

Mason, on the other hand, was waked up one night by a man who said an angel had appeared at his bedpost to tell him, "Mr. Avery is innocent of this crime," and immediately vanished. He begged to take the stand with this evidence, and Mason said he might do so, provided he brought the angel with him.

No one had seen Avery at the places where the defense claimed he had spent the afternoon—not at the Fort, nor at the mine, nor at Brother Cook's. The only people he had met on the Island—a boy driving sheep and a man with a torn hat—could not be found, nor had anyone else seen them. Mrs. Jones, being a Quaker, would not take the oath but despite the minister's solemn admonition that she had seen him *after* noon, affirmed that her stranger had passed in the morning. Jane Gifford, the ferry master's daughter, swore that Avery had told her he "had business with Brother Cook"; Cook swore he was away from home all day. Mason countered that Avery had not told Jane he had actually *seen* Cook; and besides, Jane had been read out of meeting just as Maria had.

On the other hand, none of the witnesses who claimed that Avery had gone to Fall River could surely identify him. The red bandanna at Maria's feet looked like the one that Pearse had seen him carry, but could not be proved to be the same. Harnden hired two boys to walk from Lawton's Tavern to the ferryhouse, to show there was time for a murder on the way. It took them an hour and a quarter, but they admitted on cross-examination that they might have trotted a little going downhill. He bought a forty-dollar patent lever watch to prove that the Bristol bell was half an hour slow; but this evidence must have been prompted by civic jealously, for it did not affect the final outcome of the case.

Greene called 78 prosecution witnesses. Mason, for the defense, called

160, mostly clergymen to prove that Avery's character was good and women to prove that Maria's was bad. He produced an expert on penmanship who deposed that the three letters were forged and a cordwainer who swore that a stranger—not Avery—had given him a letter to deliver to Orswell at the *King Philip* on the very morning the state claimed Avery had delivered his. By a miracle of coincidence both letters were pink and both were addressed to Miss Cornell in Fall River. Brother Jillson of Providence testified that Brother Avery could not possibly have reached the *King Philip* between the services at sunrise and at nine, as he had shaved and eaten breakfast in between.

Mason implied that Maria had forged the three letters and then hanged herself to incriminate Avery. To support this, Miss Louisa Whitney, for the defense, stated that the clove hitch was used by weavers like Maria and herself to repair the harness of their looms. On the stand she tied one and drew it taut at her own neck, amid the gasps of the courtroom. Another weaver, for the State, denied that she had ever used a clove hitch.

Mason saved his heaviest artillery for the end. He called Dr. Walter Channing, professor of midwifery and medical jurisprudence at Harvard, who declared it was impossible to tighten a clove hitch on anyone who resisted. Using the report of Dr. Wilbur's post-mortem, he proved by a dozen authorities that Maria's unborn child could have been conceived *before* the Thompson camp meeting.

Greene summed up for seven hours, and Mason for eight. Justice Eddy then charged the exhausted jurymen, who retired with a hand bell at seven o'clock on Saturday evening, June 1. The case had lasted four weeks —longer, Mason told the jury in his closing arguments, than any previous trial in the history of the republic's jurisprudence.

On Sunday morning the jury was still locked up. Most of the spectators went to church. At noon, after a hearty dinner, courtesy of the State, Foreman Trevett rang the hand bell. The sheriff called the jurymen to their box and tolled the bell in the tower of Colony House. At this signal the men instantly left church, leaving their wives behind. In five minutes the courtroom was full again.

For a breathless quarter hour the sheriff had to hunt for Jeremiah Mason, while jury and prisoner stared at each other in profound silence. At last he lumbered in. The trial ended thus:

CLERK: Gentlemen of the Jury, have you agreed upon your verdict?
JURY: We have.
CLERK: Who shall speak for you?
JURY: Our foreman.

CLERK: Mr. Foreman, what say you? Is the prisoner at the bar guilty or not guilty?

FOREMAN TREVETT: Not guilty.

For the first time Avery showed emotion. He passed his hand under his glasses and held it to his eyelids for a moment. Then he took off the glasses for good. The clergy crowded up to shake his hand; the rest of the audience filed out to the Parade, muttering its disgust. Avery was discharged. In half an hour his friends had him aboard a sloop which wafted him in three hours, with the wind behind her, to Bristol. The village had not expected a verdict on the Sabbath, but the word soon spread. A crowd followed him from the wharf to Wardwell Street but let him enter the house alone.

"Sophia," they heard him say, "I am freed from the thrall."

She toppled forward in her chair.

The news of his acquittal appeared in newspapers all over the country. He preached in his own meetinghouse on Sunday and in Boston the next Sunday. In the week between, the Methodist Conference, which had charged him with adultery, absolved him and voted that "in view of brother Avery's confinement and afflictions, and the influence they have had upon his health and constitution, the Bishop is hereby respectfully requested to give him such an appointment and relation to the church, as will afford him the most favorable opportunity of recovering his health."

Bishop Henning reappointed him to Bristol, with an assistant. But the notorious preacher could not face the crowds who flocked to hear him. He had been acquitted, but the trials had ruined him. Mason's fee of $6,000 had almost ruined the Methodist Conference.

Leaving his family at home, Avery began a speaking tour of vindication. But he was hissed at Hartford when he rose to preach on Ephesians 2:8 ("For by grace are ye saved, through faith, and not of yourselves"). At his benefit sermon in Richmond, Massachusetts, the collection was hardly enough for his horse's oats. In Boston, when he was recognized in the street, a mob of five hundred threatened to hang him. A straw effigy of him, kneeling in prayer with a rope at his neck, was set up outside Durfee's stackyard, and so frightened a young sinner of Tiverton that he put one around his own neck and hanged himself.

Avery's letters to Maria were hawked in colored facsimile at the news parlors. Drury wrote an account of the hearing, and Hallett, clerk of the court, one of the trial. Harnden's story of the capture at Rindge sold thirteen thousand copies. In New York the Richmond-Hill Theatre presented a melodrama called *The Factory Girl, or the Fall River Tragedy.* Lurid accounts of the case, with woodcuts, appeared throughout the country. And though Avery published his version of the facts in a so-called *Statement*, it convinced nobody.*

Before the end of the year he fled to his wife's family in Connecticut, but suspicion and mockery pursued him. Finally he resigned from the ministry to move out west. He bought a fifty-acre farm in Lorain County, Ohio. In the quiet reaches of the Western Reserve he lived out the blameless life of a farmer with Sophia and the children until he died, with suspicion outrun, in 1869.

His estate amounted to $111. Sophia sold his buffalo robe and sleigh to pay for his gravestone. The Lorain *Constitutionalist* gave him this farewell:

> *Servant of God, well done;*
> *Thy glorious warfare is past;*
> *The battle is fought, the victory won,*
> *And thou art crowned at last.*

Whether Maria or he had tightened the clove hitch, she had had her revenge.

—October 1961

---

* Among the published curiosities of the Avery case is a sixteen-page purported confession—to adultery but not "wilful murder"—entitled "Explanation of the Circumstances Connected with the Death of Sarah Maria Cornell, by Ephraim K. Avery." It bears the legend: Providence;/ William S. Clark, Printer/1834/Price 12½ cents. It turns out, however, that there was no printer named Clark in Providence around that time, and that this document was a deception, published in New York and sold for a quick profit before the fraud could be detected.

THE HAWTHORNES IN PARADISE

By MALCOLM COWLEY

Nathaniel was poor, glum, and sunk in his solitude. Then an invalid named Sophia Peabody transformed his life. "How strange," he wrote, "that such a flower as our affection should have blossomed amid snow and wintry winds."

There are only a few great love stories in American fiction, and there are fewer still in the lives of famous American writers. Nathaniel Hawthorne wrote one of the greatest, *The Scarlet Letter*. He also lived a story that deserves to be retold—with all the new knowledge we can bring to bear on it—as long as there are lovers in New England; it was his courtship and conquest of Sophia Peabody. Unlike his first novel, the lived story was neither sinful nor tragic. Everything in the foreground was as softly glowing as a June morning in Salem, but there were shadows in the background and obstacles to be surmounted; among them were poverty, seemingly hopeless invalidism, conniving sisters, political intrigues, a silken temptress, a duel that might have been fought to the death, and inner problems more threatening than any of these. It was as if Hawthorne had needed to cut his way through a forest of thorns —some planted by himself—in order to reach the castle of Sleeping Beauty and waken her with a kiss, while, in the same moment, he wakened himself from a daylong nightmare.

When he first met Sophia, Hawthorne was thirty-three years old, and he had spent twelve of those years in a dreamlike seclusion. Day after day he sat alone in his room, writing or reading or merely watching a sunbeam as it bored through the blind and slowly traveled across the opposite wall. "For months together," he said long afterward, in a letter to the poet R. H. Stoddard, "I scarcely held human intercourse outside of my own family; seldom going out except at twilight, or only to take the nearest way to the most convenient solitude." He doubted whether twenty people in Salem even knew of his existence.

217

In remembering those years, Hawthorne sometimes pictured his solitude as being more nearly absolute than it had been. There were social moments even then. Every summer he took a long trip on his Manning uncles' stagecoach lines and "enjoyed as much of life," he said, "as other people do in the whole year's round." In Salem he made some whist-playing acquaintances and learned a little about the intricacies of Democratic party politics. He had a college friend, Horatio Bridge, of Augusta, Maine, to whom he wrote intimate letters, and Bridge was closely connected with two rising political figures, also Democrats and college friends of Hawthorne's, Congressman Jonathan Cilley of Maine, and Franklin Pierce, the junior senator from New Hampshire. All three were trying to advance Hawthorne's career, and Bridge had rescued him from complete obscurity by guaranteeing a publisher against loss and thereby inducing him to issue the first book with Hawthorne's name on it, *Twice-Told Tales*.

After the book appeared in the early spring of 1837, its author made some mild efforts to emerge into Salem society, where the young ladies admired him for his courtesy, his deep-set eyes—so blue they were almost black—and his air of having a secret life. He thought of marriage and even fancied himself in love that spring, as Romeo did before meeting Juliet, but his courtship of a still-unidentified woman was soon broken off. Hawthorne was beginning to fear that he would never be able to rejoin the world of living creatures. His true solitude was inward, not outward, and he had formed the habit of holding long conversations with himself, like a lonely child. His daylong nightmare was of falling into a morbid state of self-absorption that would make everything unreal in his eyes, even himself. "None have understood it," says one of his heroes, Gervayse Hastings of "The Christmas Banquet," who might be speaking for the author, "—not even those who experience the like. It is a chilliness—a want of earnestness—a feeling as if what should be my heart were a thing of vapor—a haunting perception of unreality! . . . All things, all persons . . . have been like shadows flickering on the wall." Then putting his hand on his heart, he says, "Mine—mine is the wretchedness! This cold heart . . ."

Sophia Amelia Peabody, five years younger than Hawthorne, never suffered from self-absorption or an icy heart, but she had a serious trouble of her own. A pretty rather than a beautiful woman, with innocent gray eyes set wide apart, a tiptilted nose, and a mischievous smile, she had beaux attending her whenever she appeared in society; the trouble was that she could seldom appear. When Sophia was fifteen, she had begun to suffer from violent headaches. Her possessive mother explained to her that suffering was woman's peculiar lot, having something to do with the sin of Eve. Her ineffectual father had her treated by half the doctors in Boston, who prescribed, among other remedies, laudanum, mercury, arsenic, hyoscyamus, homeopathy, and hypnotism, but still the headaches continued. Once as a desperate expedient she was sent to Cuba, where she spent two happy years on a plantation while her quiet sister Mary tutored the planter's children. Now, back in Salem with the family—where her headaches were always worse—she was spending half of each day in bed. Like all the Peabody women, she had a New England conscience and a firm belief in the True, the Beautiful, and the Transcendental. She also had a limited but genuine talent for painting. When she was strong enough, she worked hard at copying pictures—and the copies sold—or at painting romantic landscapes of her own.

Sophia had been cast by her family in a role from which it seemed unlikely that she would ever escape. Just as Elizabeth Peabody was the intellectual sister, already famous as an educational reformer, and Mary was the quiet sister who did most of the household chores, Sophia was the invalid sister, petted like a child and kept in an upstairs room. There were also three brothers, one of them married, but the Peabodys were a matriarchy and a sorority; nobody paid much attention to the Peabody men. It was written that when the mother died, Sophia would become the invalid aunt of her brother's children; she would support herself by painting lampshades and firescreens, while enduring her headaches with a brave smile. As for Hawthorne, his fate was written too; he would become the cranky New England bachelor, living in solitude and writing more and more nebulous stories about other lonely souls. But they saved each other, those two unhappy children. Each was the other's refuge, and they groped their way into each other's arms, where both found strength to face the world.

It was Elizabeth, the intellectual sister, who first brought them together, unthinkingly, in a moment of triumph for herself. She had long admired a group of stories, obviously by one author, that had been appearing anonymously in the annual editions of a gift book, *The Token*, and in the *New England Magazine*. Now she learned that the author was a Salem neighbor. Always eager to inspire a new genius, she made patient efforts to inveigle him into the Peabody house on Charter Street, with its square windows looking over an old burying ground where Peabodys and Hathornes—as the name used to be spelled—were sleeping almost side by side. She even took the bold step of paying several visits to the Hawthorne house on Herbert Street, known as "Castle Dismal," where nobody outside the family had dared to come for years.

Usually she was received by Hawthorne's younger sister, Louisa, who, Miss Peabody said disappointedly, was "quite like everybody else." The older sister, Elizabeth—usually called Ebe—was known with good reason as "the hermitess," but she finally consented to take a walk with her enterprising neighbor. Madam Hawthorne, the mother, stayed in her room as always, and Nathaniel was nowhere to be seen. He did, however, send Miss Peabody a presentation copy of his book, and she replied by suggesting some journalistic work that he had no intention of doing. Then, on the evening of November 11, 1837, came her moment of triumph. Elizabeth was sitting in the parlor, looking at a five-volume set of Flaxman's classical engravings that she had just been given by Professor Felton of Harvard, when she heard a great ring at the front door.

"There stood your father," she said half a century later in a letter to her nephew Julian Hawthorne, "in all the splendor of his young beauty, and a hooded figure hanging on each arm." The figures were Louisa and Ebe. Miss Peabody bustled them into the parlor and set them to looking at Flaxman's illustrations for *The Iliad*. Then she ran upstairs to the invalid's room and said, "Oh, Sophia, Mr. Hawthorne and his sisters have come, and you never saw anything so splendid—he is handsomer then Lord Byron! You must get up and dress and come down. We have Flaxman too."

Sophia laughed and said, "I think it would be rather ridiculous to get up. If he has come once he will come again."

A few days later he came again, this time in the afternoon. "I summoned your mother," Miss Peabody said in the same letter, "and she came down in her simple white wrapper, and glided in at the back door and sat down on the sofa. As I said, 'My sister, Sophia—Mr. Hawthorne,' he rose and looked at her—he did not realize how intently, and afterwards, as we went on talking, she would interpose frequently a remark in her low sweet voice. Every time she did so, he looked at her with the same intentness of interest. I was struck with it, and painfully. I thought, what if he should fall in love with her. . . ." Miss Peabody explained why that was a painful thought; it was because "I had heard her so often say, nothing would ever tempt her to marry, and inflict upon a husband the care of such a sufferer." But there was an unspoken reason too, for it is clear from other letters that Elizabeth Peabody wanted Nathaniel Hawthorne for herself. Whether she hoped to marry him we cannot be sure, but there is no question that she planned to become his spiritual guide, his literary counselor, his muse and Egeria.

Sophia had no such intentions. She told her children long afterward that Hawthorne's presence exerted a magnetic attraction on her from the beginning, and that she instinctively drew back in self-defense. The power she felt in him alarmed her; she did not understand what it meant. By degrees her resistance was overcome, and she came to realize that they had loved each other at first sight. . . . That was Sophia's story, and Hawthorne did not contradict her. There is some doubt, however, whether he told her about everything that happened during the early months of their acquaintance.

What followed their first meeting was a comedy of misunderstandings with undertones of tragedy. Hawthorne was supposed to be courting Elizabeth—Miss Peabody, as she was called outside the household; *the* Miss Peabody, as if she had no sisters. There was a correspondence between them. In one of her missives—and that is the proper word for them—she warned Hawthorne that her invalid sister would never marry. His answer has been lost, but Miss Peabody quoted him as saying, "Sophia is a rose to be worn in no man's bosom." Satisfied on this point, she advised him to study German, write books for children, and have no truck with Democratic politicians. She liked to think of him as an otherworldly genius who might save the soul of America, if only he would read the German philosophers in the original. Hawthorne obediently studied German, but he did not take kindly to advice about his personal affairs, and Miss Peabody went off to West Newton to live with her married brother. While she was there, Sophia wrote her a series of letters. Most of them mentioned Mr. Hawthorne, more and more warmly, but Sophia maintained the pretense that her interest in him was intellectual, or at most sisterly, and that he was still Elizabeth's suitor. Meanwhile Hawthorne himself was secretly involved with a Salem heiress.

The story of his involvement, and of the duel to which it nearly led, was told in some detail by Julian Hawthorne in his biography of his parents. Unfortunately Julian did not give names (except "Mary" and "Louis") or offer supporting evidence. Poor Julian, who was sometimes irresponsible, has never been trusted by scholars, and the result is that later biographers of Hawthorne either questioned the story or flatly rejected it. Quite recently Norman Holmes Pearson of Yale, who is preparing the definitive edition of Hawthorne's letters, discovered an interesting document in the Morgan Library. He wrote an article about it for the *Essex Institute*'s quarterly, one for which other scholars stand in his debt. The article was a memorandum by Julian on a conversation with Miss Peabody, one in which she described the whole affair, giving names and circumstances and supporting Julian's story at almost every point. She even explained by implication why the principal figures in the story had to be anonymous. Two of them were still living in 1884, when Julian's book was published, and one of them was the widow of a president of Harvard.

Her name when Hawthorne knew her was Mary Crowninshield Silsbee, and she was the daughter of a former United States Senator Nathaniel

Silsbee, a great man in New England banking and shipping. Julian says that she was completely unscrupulous, but admits that she had "a certain kind of glancing beauty, slender, piquant, ophidian, Armida-like." Armida—in Tasso's *Jerusalem Delivered*—was a heathen sorceress, daughter of the king of Damascus, who lured the boldest of the Crusaders into her enchanted garden. Mary Silsbee exercised her lures on the brilliant young men she met in her travels between Salem and Washington. One of them was John Louis O'Sullivan of Washington, who was laying ambitious plans for a new magazine to be called the *Democratic Review*.

The young editor was a friend of Hawthorne's classmate Jonathan Cilley, the rising congressman from Maine. Cilley had given him a copy of *Twice-Told Tales* as soon as the book appeared. O'Sullivan was impressed by it and wrote to the author soliciting contributions at the generous rate, for the time, of five dollars a page. He also told Miss Silsbee about Hawthorne. Fascinated by O'Sullivan's picture of a mysterious Salem genius, Armida at once determined, Julian says, "to add him to her museum of victims."

Her method of operation was to cast herself on Hawthorne's mercy by revealing what she told him were the secrets of her innermost soul. She read him long and extremely private passages from her diary—"all of which," Julian says, "were either entirely fictitious, or such bounteous embroideries on the bare basis of reality, as to give what was mean and sordid an appearance of beauty and a winning charm." Hawthorne, who had never considered the possibility that a Salem young lady might be a gratuitous liar, began to regard himself as Miss Silsbee's protector and champion. But he disappointed her by offering none of his own confidences in return.

She tried a new stratagem. Early in February, 1838, she summoned Hawthorne to a private and mysterious interview. With a great deal of calculated reluctance she told him that his friend O'Sullivan, "presuming upon her innocence and guilelessness"—as Julian tells the story—"had been guilty of an attempt to practise the basest treachery upon her; and she passionately adjured Hawthorne, as her only confidential and trusted friend and protector, to champion her cause." Hawthorne promptly wrote a letter to O'Sullivan, then in Washington, and challenged him to a duel. The letter has disappeared, but there is another to Horatio Bridge written on February 8—possibly the same day—in which he speaks darkly of a rash step he has just taken.

O'Sullivan must have discussed the challenge with their friend Jonathan Cilley; then he wrote a candid and friendly letter to Hawthorne refusing the challenge. But he did more than that; he made a hurried trip to Salem and completely established his innocence of the charge against him. Although Hawthorne could scarcely bring himself to believe that Miss Silsbee had made an utter fool of him, he had to accept the evidence. In Miss Peabody's words, he called on Armida and "crushed her."

To this point the story had been a comedy, or even a farce, but it soon had a tragic sequel on the national scene. In 1838 the House of Representatives was equally divided between conservatives and radicals, not to mention the other division between southerners and northern antislavery men. Jonathan Cilley was a rising leader among the radical free-soil Democrats, and there are some indications that his political enemies had decided to get rid of him. On a flimsy pretext, he was challenged to a duel by a fire-eating southern congressman, William J. Graves of Kentucky. He was still hesitating whether to accept the challenge when somebody said to him—according to Julian's story—"If Hawthorne was so ready to fight a duel without stopping to ask questions, you certainly need not hesitate." Horatio Bridge denied this part of the story, but there is no doubt that Hawthorne considered himself partly responsible for what followed. The duel, fought with rifles at ninety yards, took place on the afternoon of February 24. After the first exchange of shots, and again after the second, Cilley's second tried to effect a reconciliation, but Graves and his second both declined. Cilley said, "They thirst for my blood." On the third exchange, he was hit in the body and fell dying.

Hawthorne brooded over the duel for a long time. His memorial of Cilley, which was among the first of his many contributions to the *Democratic Review*, reads as if he were making atonement to the shade of his friend. In a somewhat later story, "The Christmas Banquet," from which I have quoted already, he describes a collection of the world's most miserable persons. One of them is "a man of nice conscience, who bore a blood stain in his heart—the death of a fellow-creature—which, for his more exquisite torture, had chanced with such a peculiarity of circumstances, that he could not absolutely determine whether his will had entered into the deed or not. Therefore, his whole life was spent in the agony of an inward trial for murder."

Julian's story would lead us to believe that Hawthorne, once again, was thinking of himself.

There were other causes for worry in those early months of 1838, when Hawthorne was still supposed to be courting Sophia's intellectual sister. One of the chief causes was Mary Silsbee, who refused to let him go. Miss Peabody's memorandum says that Mary somehow "managed to renew relations with him," and that she then offered to marry him as soon as he was earning $3,000 a year, a large income for the time. Hawthorne answered that he never expected to have so much. When his sister Ebe heard the story, she remarked—according to Miss Peabody—"that he would never marry at all, and that he would never *do* anything; that he was an ideal person." But Hawthorne did something to end the affair; he disappeared from Salem.

Before leaving town on July 23, he paid what was known as a take-leave call on Sophia. "He said he was not going to tell any one where he should be for the next three months," she told Elizabeth in a letter; "that he thought he should change his name, so that if he died no one would be able to find his gravestone. . . . I feel as if he were a born brother. I never, hardly, knew a person for whom I had such a full and at the same time perfectly quiet admiration." Then, suspecting that she had gone too far, she added, "I do not care about seeing him often; but I delight to remember that *he is*." It was as near as she could come to telling Elizabeth that she was already in love.

At the end of September when Hawthorne came back to Salem—from North Adams, his mysterious hiding place—Miss Silsbee had disappeared from his life. She had renewed her acquaintance with another suitor, now a widower of forty-nine with an income well beyond her minimum requirement; he was Jared Sparks, the editor of George Washington's papers, who would become president of Harvard. Hawthorne now had more time to spend at the house on Charter Street. He was entertained by whichever sister happened to be present, or by all three together, but it began to be noticed that his visits were longer if he found Sophia alone. One day she showed him an illustration she had drawn, in the Flaxman manner, for his story "The Gentle Boy." It showed the boy asleep under the tree from which his Quaker father had been hanged.

"I want to know if this looks like your Ilbrahim," she said.

Hawthorne said, meaning every word, "He will never look otherwise to me."

Under the Peabody influence, he was becoming almost a social creature. There was a sort of literary club that met every week in one of the finest houses on Chestnut Street, where the Salem merchants lived. The house belonged to Miss Susan Burley, a wealthy spinster who liked to patronize the arts. Hawthorne was persuaded to attend some of Miss Burley's Saturday evenings—usually as an escort for Mary or Elizabeth, since the invalid sister was seldom allowed to venture into the night air. There was one particularly cold evening when Sophia insisted that she was going to Miss Burley's whether or not she was wanted. Hawthorne laughed and said she was not wanted; the cold would make her ill. "Meanwhile," Sophia reported in a letter, "I put on an incalculable quantity of clothes. Father kept remonstrating, but not violently, and I gently imploring. When I was ready, Mr. Hawthorne said he was glad I was going. . . . We walked quite fast, for I seemed stepping on air."

The evening at Miss Burley's marked a change in their relations. From that time Sophia began taking long walks with Mr. Hawthorne in spite of the winter gales. Elizabeth was busy with her affairs in Boston, and Mary, the quiet sister, looked on benevolently. Sophia never felt tired so long as she could hold Mr. Hawthorne's arm. It was during one of their walks, on a snowy day just before or after New Year's, 1839, that they confessed their love for each other. Clinging together like happy children frightened of being so happy, they exchanged promises that neither of them would break. They were married now "in the sight of God," as old-fashioned people used to say, and as Hawthorne soon told Sophia in slightly different words, but that was a secret they would keep to themselves for a long time to come.

In the middle of January Hawthorne went to work as a weigher and gauger for the Boston Custom House. It was a political appointment made by the collector of the port, who was George Bancroft, the historian. Hawthorne had been recommended to him by several influential persons, including Miss Peabody, who may have hoped to get him out of Salem. Bancroft justified the appointment to Washington by writing that Hawthorne was the "biographer of Cilley," and thus a deserving Democrat. Cilley again. . . . It was as if the college friend for whose death Hawthorne felt responsible had reached out of the grave to help him. Many other deserving Democrats had sought for the post, but it was not a sinecure, and he worked as hard as Jacob did for Rachel, while saving half his salary of $1,500 a year. Every other Saturday he took the cars to Salem and spent an evening with Sophia. On the Saturdays in Boston he sent her a long letter, sometimes written in daily installments.

"What a year the last has been!" he wrote on January 1, 1840. " . . . It has been the year of years—the year in which the flower of our life has bloomed out—the flower of our life and of our love, which we are to wear in our bosoms forever." Three days later he added, "Dearest, I hope you have not found it impracticable to walk, though the atmosphere be so wintry. Did we walk together in any such weather, last winter? I believe we did. How strange, that such a flower as our affection should have blossomed amid snow and wintry winds—accompaniments which no poet or novelist, that I know of, has ever introduced into a love-tale. Nothing like our story was ever written—or ever will be—for we shall not feel inclined to make the public our confidant; but if it could be told, methinks it would be such as the angels might delight to hear."

As a matter of fact, Hawthorne wrote the story from day to day, in that series of heartfelt letters to Sophia, and the New England angels would delight to read them. It is true that the tone of them is sometimes too reverent for the worldly taste of our century. "I always feel," Hawthorne says in July, 1839, "as if your letters were too sacred to be read in the midst of people, and (you will smile) I never read them without first washing my hands." We also smile, but in a different spirit from Sophia's. We feel a little uncomfortable on hearing the pet names with which he addresses her, almost all superlatives: "Dearissima," "mine ownest love," "Blessedest," "ownest Dove," "best, beautifullest, belovedest, blessingest of wives." It is confusing to find that he calls her "mine own wife," and himself "your husband" or "thy husband," for three years before the actual marriage. His use of "thee" and "thou" in all the letters written after March, 1840, though it reveals his need for deeper intimacy of expression, still gives an archaic look to the writing. But the feelings expressed are not in the least archaic; they are those of a restrained but passionate man, truly in love for the first and last time, and gifted with an extraordinary talent for self-awareness.

Long afterward Sophia, then a widow, tried to delete the passion before she permitted the letters to be read by others. She scissored out some of the dangerous passages, and these are gone forever. Others she inked out carefully, and most of these have been restored by the efforts of Randall Stewart—the most trustworthy biographer of Hawthorne—and the staff of the Huntington Library. They show that Hawthorne was less of an otherworldly creature than Miss Peabody pictured him as being. "Mine own wife," he says in one of the inked-out passages (November, 1839), "what a cold night this is going to be! How I am to keep warm, unless you nestle close, close into my bosom, I do not by any means understand —not but what I have clothes enough on my mattress—but a husband cannot be comfortably warm without his wife." There is so much talk of beds and bosoms that some have inferred, after reading the restored text, that Hawthorne and Sophia were lovers for a long time before their marriage—and most of these readers thought no worse of them. But the records show that this romantic notion has to be dismissed. Much as Hawthorne wanted Sophia, he also wanted to observe the scriptural laws of love. "Mr. Hawthorne's passions were under his feet," Miss Peabody quoted Sophia as saying. If he had made Sophia his mistress, he would have revered her less, and he would have despised himself.

"I have an awe of you," he wrote her, "that I never felt for anybody else. Awe is not the word, either, because it might imply something stern in you; whereas—but you must make out for yourself. . . . I suppose I should have pretty much the same feeling if an angel were to come from Heaven and be my dearest friend. . . . And then it is singular, too," he added with his Salem obduracy, "that this awe (or whatever it is) does not prevent me from feeling that it is I who have charge of you, and that my Dove is to follow my guidance and do my bidding." He had no intention of submitting to the Peabody matriarchs. "And will not you rebel?" he asked. "Oh, no; because I possess the power to guide you only so far as I love you. My love gives me the right, and your love consents to it."

Sophia did not rebel, but the Peabodys were confirmed idealists where Hawthorne was a realist, and sometimes she tried gently to bring him round to their higher way of feeling. Once she refused to kiss him good night because she had smelled a cigar on his breath. Another time she made the mistake of urging him to hear the famous Father Taylor, who preached to the sailors.

"Dearest," he said, "I feel somewhat afraid to hear this divine Father Taylor, lest my sympathy with thy admiration of him should be colder and feebler than thou lookest for. Belovedest wife, our souls are in happiest unison; but we must not disquiet ourselves if every tone be not re-echoed from one to the other—if every slightest shade be not reflected in the alternate mirror. . . . I forewarn thee, sweetest Dove, that thy husband is a most unmalleable man; thou are not to suppose, because his spirit answers to every touch of thine, that therefore every breeze, or even every whirlwind, can upturn him from his depths."

But this conflict of wills is a minor note of comedy in the letters. In time Sophia learned to yield almost joyfully, not so much to Hawthorne's unmalleable nature as to his love. It is love that is the central theme of the letters—unquestioning love, and beneath it the sense of almost delirious gratitude that both of them felt for having been rescued from death-in-life. Sophia refused to worry about her health. "If God intends us to marry," she said to Hawthorne, "He will let me be cured; if not, it will be a sign that it is not best." She depended on love as her physician, and imperceptibly, year by year, the headaches faded away. As for Hawthorne, he felt an even deeper gratitude for having been rescued from the unreal world of self-absorption in which he had feared to be imprisoned forever. "Indeed, we are but shadow," he wrote to Sophia, "—we are not endowed with real life, and all that seems most real about us is but the thinnest substance of a dream—till the heart is touched. That touch creates us—then we begin to be. . . ." In the same letter he said: "Thou only hast taught me that I have a heart—thou only hast thrown a deep light downward, and upward, into my soul. Thou only hast revealed me to myself; for without thy aid, my best knowledge of myself would have been merely to know my own shadow—to watch it flickering on the wall, and mistake its fantasies for my own real actions. . . . Now, dearest, dost thou comprehend what thou has done for me?"

His four novels, beginning with *The Scarlet Letter*, were written after his marriage and written because Sophia was there to read them. Not only Nathaniel Hawthorne but the world at large owes the gentle Sophia more than can be expressed.

When Miss Peabody was told of the engagement, after more than a year, she took the news bravely. Her consolation was that having Hawthorne as a brother-in-law might be almost as rewarding as having him for a husband; she could still be his Egeria. Not yet knowing how unmalleable he was, she still thought of forging him into the shape of her dream. Meanwhile she offered to serve as a secret courier and forward his letters to Salem. With Sophia's health improving, it was Hawthorne's inability to support a wife—especially a delicate wife who needed a servant in the household—that now seemed to be the chief remaining obstacle to the marriage.

The post in the Boston Custom House did not solve the problem. It left him with little time alone or energy for writing, and he could not be sure of keeping it after the next election. Hawthorne resigned at the end of 1840, a few months before he would have been dismissed—as were almost all of his colleagues—by the victorious Whigs. After some hesitation he took a rash step, partly at the urging of Miss Peabody. He invested his Custom House savings in George Ripley's new community for intellectual farmers: Brook Farm. It was the last time he would accept her high-minded advice.

The dream was that Hawthorne would support himself by working in the field only a few hours each day, and only in the summer; then he could spend the winter writing stories. He and Sophia would live in a cottage to be built on some secluded spot. Having bought two shares of stock in the community at $500 each—later he would lend Ripley $400 more—he arrived at Brook Farm in an April snowstorm. Sophia paid him a visit at the end of May. "My life—how beautiful is Brook Farm!" she wrote him on her return. ". . . I do not desire to conceive of a greater felicity than living in a cottage, built on one of those lovely sites, with thee." But Hawthorne, after working for six weeks on the manure pile—or gold mine, as the Brook Farmers called it—was already disillusioned. "It is my opinion, dearest," he wrote on almost the same day, "that a man's soul may be buried and perish under a dungheap or in a furrow of the field, just as well as under a pile of money." By the middle of August, he had decided to leave Brook Farm. "Thou and I must form other plans for ourselves," he told Sophia; "for I can see few or no signs that Providence purposes to give us a home here. I am weary . . . of waiting so many ages. Yet what can be done? Whatever may be thy husband's gifts, he has not hitherto shown a single one that may avail to gather gold."

"Thy husband" and "mine own wife" were drawing closer to marriage, simply because they had exhausted their vast New England patience. "Words cannot tell," Sophia had written, "how immensely my spirit demands thee. Sometimes I almost lose my breath in a vast heaving toward thy heart." Hawthorne, now vegetating in Salem—while the Peabodys were in Boston, where Elizabeth had opened a bookshop—was looking desperately for any sort of literary work. In March, 1842, he went to Albany to see John Louis O'Sullivan, who was again editing the *Democratic Review*. On the strength of the promises that O'Sullivan was always ready to make, Hawthorne decided to wait no longer; he would try to support a wife on what he could earn as a writer. It was a bold decision for an age when American writers were miserably paid and when Poe, his principal rival, had never earned as much as $1,000 in one year.

The wedding was set for the last day of June. During a visit to the Emersons, Miss Peabody found a home for the young couple; it was the Ripley house in Concord, where the parson used to live. Hawthorne could no longer defer telling his family about the engagement, after keeping it secret for three years.

Now at last it became evident that there was and had always been another obstacle to his marriage.

The final obstacle was his older sister, Ebe the hermitess. She adored her handsome brother and clung to him as her only link with the world. The stratagem she found for keeping him was to insist that their mother would die of shock if she learned that he was marrying an invalid. Hawthorne loved his mother, though he had never been able to confide in her. This time he finally took the risk. "What you tell me is not a surprise to me," Madam Hawthorne said, " . . . and Sophia Peabody is the wife of all others whom I would have chosen for you." When Ebe had recovered from her fury at hearing the news, she wrote Sophia a frigid letter of congratulation. "Your approaching union with my brother makes it incumbent upon me to offer you the assurances of my sincere desire for your mutual happiness. With regard to my sister and myself, I hope nothing will ever occur to render your future intercourse with us other than agreeable, particularly as it need not be so frequent or so close as to require more than reciprocal good will."

There would be, in fact, no intercourse with Ebe. She retired to a farmhouse in Beverly, where she spent the rest of her long life reading in her room and walking on the shore.

Three weeks before the date set for the wedding, Sophia terrified everyone by taking to her bed. There was talk of an indefinite postponement. Fortunately a new doctor explained that it was nothing unusual for a bride to run a fever, and so another date was chosen: Saturday morning, July 9. It was a few days after Hawthorne's thirty-eighth birthday, while

Sophia was almost thirty-three. At the wedding in the parlor behind Miss Peabody's bookshop, there were only two guests outside the immediate family. It started to rain as the bride came down the stairs, but then the sun broke through the clouds and shone directly into the parlor. Hawthorne and Sophia stepped into a carriage and were driven across the Charles River, along the old road through Cambridge and Lexington, into the Land of Eden.

And so they lived happily ever after? They lived happily for a time, but as always it came to an end, and the lovers too. For Hawthorne after twenty years of marriage, the end was near when he went feebly pacing up and down the path his feet had worn along the hillside behind his Concord house, while he tried to plan a novel that refused to be written. For Sophia the end was a desolate widowhood without the man who, she never ceased to feel, "is my world and all the business of it." But the marriage was happy to the end, and at the beginning of it, during their stay at the Old Manse, they enjoyed something far beyond the capacity of most lovers to experience: three years of almost unalloyed delight.

On the morning after their first night in the Old Manse, Hawthorne wrote to his younger sister, Louisa, the one who was quite like everybody else. "Dear Louse," he said affectionately, "the execution took place yesterday. We made a christian end, and came straight to Paradise, where we abide at the present writing." Sophia had the same message for her mother, although she expressed it more ecstatically. "It is a perfect Eden round us," she said. "Everything is as fresh as in first June. We are Adam and Eve and see no persons round! The birds saluted us this morning with such gushes of rapture, that I thought they must know us and our happiness."

The Hawthornes at thirty-eight and thirty-three were like children again—like children exploring a desert island that every day revealed new marvels. Their only fear was that a ship might come to rescue them. Once the great Margaret Fuller wrote them and suggested that another newly married couple, her sister Ellen and Ellery Channing, might board with them at the Manse. Hawthorne sent her a tactful letter of refusal. "Had it been proposed to Adam and Eve," he said, "to receive two angels into their Paradise, *as boarders*, I doubt whether they would have been altogether pleased to consent." The Hawthornes were left happily alone with Sarah the maid and Pigwiggin the kitten.

They were exercising a talent that most New Englanders never acquire, that of living not in the past or in dreams of the future, but in the moment itself, as if they were already in heaven. Sophia wrote letters each morning or painted in her studio, while Hawthorne worked meditatively in the garden that Henry Thoreau had planted for them. In the afternoon they explored the countryside together or rowed on the quiet river, picking waterlilies. Hawthorne wrote in his journal: "My life, at this time, is more like that of a boy, externally, than it has been since I was really a boy. It is usually supposed that the cares of life come with matrimony; but I seem to have cast off all care, and live with as much easy trust in Providence, as Adam could possibly have felt, before he had learned that there was a world beyond his Paradise."

Sometimes they ran footraces down the lane, which Sophia grandly called "the avenue." Sometimes in the evening she wound the music box and, forgetting her Puritan training, danced wildly for her lover. "You deserve John the Baptist's head," he teased her. In the records of that time—there are many of them, all a delight to read—there is only one hint of anything like a quarrel. It arose when one of their walks led them to an unmown hayfield. Hawthorne, who had learned about haying at Brook Farm, told Sophia not to cross it and trample the grass. "This I did not like very well and I climbed the hill alone," Sophia wrote in the journal they were keeping together. "We penetrated the pleasant gloom and sat down upon a carpet of dried pine leaves. Then I clasped him in my arms in the lovely shade, and we laid down a few moments on the bosom of dear Mother Earth. Oh, how sweet it was! And I told him I would not be so naughty again, and there was a very slight diamond shower without any thunder or lightning and we were happiest."

There was some thunder and lightning even during those three sunny years at the Old Manse. Sophia's mother and her sister Elizabeth had insisted that she must never bear children, but she longed for them ardently. One day in the first February she fell on the ice—where she had been sliding while Hawthorne skated round her in flashing circles—and suffered a miscarriage. When her first baby was born in March, 1844, it lingered, as Hawthorne said, "ten dreadful hours on the threshold of life." It lived and the parents rejoiced, but now they had financial worries: O'Sullivan took years to pay for the stories he printed, and Ripley hadn't returned the money advanced to Brook Farm. There were weeks when Hawthorne was afraid to walk into Concord for the mail, lest he meet too many of his creditors. Sophia's love did not waver, then or for the rest of her life, nor did her trust in the wisdom and mercy of Providence. It had snatched her from invalidism and spinsterhood and transported her to Paradise. It had made her "as strong as a lion," she wrote to her sister Mary, "as elastic as India rubber, light as a bird, as happy as a queen might be," and it had given her a husband whose ardent love was as unwavering as her own. She was expressing in five words all her faith in Providence, and indeed all her experience of life, when she stood at the window in

Hawthorne's study one April evening at sunset and wrote with her diamond ring on one of the tiny panes—for him to see, for the world to
remember:

> *Man's accidents are God's purposes.*
> *Sophia A. Hawthorne 1843*

—December 1958

THE TAMMANY PIONEERS

By RICHARD REINHARDT

In 1846 Colonel Jonathan Drake Stevenson headed west around the Horn with a scapegrace rabble recruited from New York's political wards, oyster cellars, and gin mills—the future leaders of California

The lumpy peninsula now called San Francisco was humanized at some unrecorded moment of prehistory by brown-skinned Californians of the Costanoan strain. It was Europeanized in the eighteenth century by a small delegation of Spanish cavaliers, camp followers, and missionary priests; and it was Americanized seventy years later by a succession of commodores and company commanders, among whom was a mercenary swaggerstick named Jonathan Drake Stevenson, who propelled himself into the westward course of empire in the spring of 1846, the year the United States went to war with Mexico.

Then, as now, many Americans regarded the Mexican War as an expansionist adventure, and nothing gave more substance to this opinion than the official participation of Colonel J. D. Stevenson, the living personification of Manifest Destiny. Seen in the meanest light, the colonel was a bottom-rank New York City politician—a minor functionary of Tammany Hall with a demonstrated skill in advancing his own political fortunes and a manifest sense of his personal destiny. He had a vulturous nose and a hawkish brow, a hyperventilated chest and a gusseted waistline. Despite his ripe age (forty-six), he always held himself guts-up, like a musketeer at present arms, and his words rolled out in magnificently cadenced phrases, punctuated with exclamations of "My good man!" and "You, sir!" Had he stayed in Manhattan, he undoubtedly would have wound up a high sachem in the wigwam of Fernando Wood or Bill Tweed, dispensing street-repair contracts and saloon permits with winsome partiality. Instead, he made his way to Washington, D.C., on a crucial spring day in 1846 and succeeded in having himself appointed commander in chief of a seventeen-thousand-mile expedition to carry Anglo-Saxon civilization to the far Pacific coast.

The point of the expedition, as president James Knox Polk saw it, was to recruit a regiment of volunteers—skilled artisans, sturdy young farmers, wheelwrights, blacksmiths, and others—and send them by ship around Cape Horn to California. Enlisted in the East under the militia statutes of New York, trained and disciplined by a respected army officer, the men would be mustered out on the Pacific coast as colonists of a new American province. Admittedly, California was an uninviting place—a desert shore, visited a few times each year by Yankee trading ships that unloaded cheap mirrors, combs, and leather shoes and came back with cattle hides and tallow; but a well-selected group of young Americans, nurtured in the traditions of the Republic, soon would transform this wilderness into a thriving commonwealth.

The President never explained why he chose Stevenson, a civilian, to command the regiment. Stevenson liked to think it was because he personally had secured the Democratic nomination for Polk. Since nobody else, including Polk, ever gave him credit for that accomplishment, the real explanation probably was less flattering to the colonel. Perhaps it was because he had called that day at the home of Postmaster General Amos Kendall, the Man to See in Washington, and had reminded Kendall of various services that he, Stevenson, discreetly had performed among the contentious Democrats of Manhattan. Perhaps it was because Stevenson knew Polk's Secretary of War, William L. Marcy—and Marcy, who is remembered for his succinct enunciation of the guiding principle of nineteenth-century American politics, "To the victors belong the spoils," was a man who never slighted his friends. Or perhaps it was because the President's brother-in-law, who was commandant of cadets at West Point, had turned down the assignment.

In any case, Polk wanted a commander and Stevenson wanted a job. The result was a colonial enterprise that left a deeper mark on California than had any Costanoan tribe or Spanish fort or covered-wagon cavalcade. The men of Stevenson's regiment became the mayors, legislators, congressmen, judges, sheriffs, tax collectors, and county clerks of the new state. Seven of the regimental officers were among the forty-eight delegates who drafted the first California constitution. The first millionaire in San Francisco was from the regiment. So were the first sheriff, the first port collector, the first published author, and the first editor of the first important newspaper. The colonel himself found a niche in history as the first grand master of the Masonic Lodge in California; one of his subordinates made it as the first authentic English-speaking highwayman. Names from the roster adorn the lesser streets and alleys of San Francisco—Folsom,

Stevenson, Leavenworth, Rausch, Green, Naglee, Gilbert, Hardie, Shannon, Russ—and the regiment abundantly supplied the underpopulated territory with gunfighters, knife throwers, ballot-box stuffers, and disturbers of the peace.

In short, Colonel Stevenson and his New York volunteers were the founding fathers of American California, although they were not at all the type of colonists the President had in mind.

Earlier in 1846 Polk had dispatched several smaller forces to California. A squadron of one hundred dragoons from the Army of the West was marching overland by way of New Mexico. A battalion of Mormon volunteers was en route from Fort Leavenworth to San Diego. An artillery company was rounding the Horn by ship. Already on the Pacific coast were several naval vessels and an armed survey party headed by the quarrelsome gadabout of the Western frontier, Captain John C. Frémont. Stevenson's volunteers, getting a late start, obviously could serve no useful purpose except as an army of occupation; but Polk was eager to conceal his territorial ambitions. To this end, he asked Secretary Marcy to send a confidential letter to General Thomas Sidney Jessup, letting him in on the plans and cautioning him to be quiet in handling the logistics so that news of the expedition would not trickle out.

Colonel Stevenson, however, was giddy at the prospect of leading bayonet charges and liberating mission Indians. He rushed back to New York, full of winks and nudges. On the Fourth of July, at a get-together of militia officers of New York City at City Hall, he elbowed up to the speaker's platform and blurted out the happy news that he had been called "to a distant and perilous service" on the northwest coast of Mexico, where his regiment of volunteers would be discharged at the end of the war.

To the Free Soilers in Congress, who had been saying all along that the war was only an excuse to annex four or five new slave states carved out of former Mexican territory, this announcement sounded like an official admission of guilt. Representative George Ashmun, a Whig from Massachusetts, flushed out Marcy's correspondence about the regiment and indignantly read it to the House.

"It is no longer pretended that our purpose is to repel invasion," Ashmun said. "The mask is off; the veil is lifted; and we see in the clearest characters invasion, conquest, and colonization emblazoned on our banners. . . . We behold an expedition about to sail from New York to a distant region of the globe, which it cannot possibly reach in less than four to six months, commanded by a mere political fortune-hunter of not the highest character, and destined to accomplish the conquest and dismemberment of a sister republic whose weakness seems to make her a ready prey to men whose purposes are those of plunder!"

Colonel Stevenson did not reply to this gratuitous slur on his character, made in the privileged sanctuary of the Congress. He was fully occupied trying to enlist, equip, and train more than seven hundred men in one month for a strategic expedition that would have done credit to Hannibal —for, of course, the regiment was by no means "about to sail." It existed only in Colonel Stevenson's patriotic dreams. The day after his announcement, the colonel placed a notice in the New York papers, inviting volunteers to come down to the state arsenal on White Street and sign up; and, on the sixth, a militia captain named Seymour Steele set up a recruiting desk at Stonewall's Hotel, a favorite meeting place for Democratic ward heelers. Governor Silas Wright, although he disliked Stevenson almost as much as he did Polk and Marcy, agreed to assign to the regiment several volunteer companies that had been forming upstate.

But recruiting was slow, the weather was stifling, and to make things worse, Marcy kept sending reminders that this was supposed to be an elite corps: "The President expects, and indeed requires, that great care should be taken to have it composed of suitable persons—I mean persons of good habits—as far as practicable of various pursuits. . . ."

The colonel did succeed in corralling an entire family of such "suitable persons" as a result of stopping to have his watch repaired by a German jewelry maker named Emanuel Charles Christian Russ, who was nursing a grievance against New York. A year and a half earlier, while Russ and his family had been out watching a memorial parade in honor of President Jackson, burglars had broken into his shop and stolen Russ's life's savings, twenty thousand dollars. Since that time, Russ had repeatedly declared that he would rather live in the wilderness than remain in this urban jungle, and Colonel Stevenson's crusade sounded like an ideal opportunity to emigrate to the end of the earth. In return for free passage to California, Russ volunteered his own services and those of his oldest son, Adolph, as a private soldier; his two younger sons, Charles and Augustus, as fifer and drummer, respectively, of the regimental band; and his wife, Christiana, and six younger children, as laundresses, cooks, and scullery moppets.

The Russes were hard-working, frugal Lutherans from Saxony, accustomed to breakfasting on a quart apiece of home-brewed lager and making do on a family income of three dollars a day. If the colonel had been able to find more like them, it is possible that San Francisco would have turned out quite differently—more like Cleveland, say, or Minneapolis. Instead, in his desperate haste, Stevenson was compelled to accept virtually any man who wanted to make the trip. His volunteer officers included bankrupt lawyers from small towns in upstate New York, unemployed cadets from Philadelphia, newspaper editors, job printers, and doctors without formal education; and entirely too many of the men in the ranks were restless young bucks from the bloody sixth ward, sprung from the oyster cellars of Howard Street, the minstrel theaters of Chatham Street, and the gin mills of lower Broadway. Soon everyone was calling the regiment "Stevenson's Lambs" or "Stevenson's California B'hoys," which was not at all the effect Polk wanted; and the colonel had to make a hasty tour of the city, giving propitiatory speeches about the splendid character and moral purposes of the volunteers, none of which mitigated the incessant sneering of Horace Greeley's *Tribune* and other papers of Whig inclination.

On mustering day, August 1, only a few companies were filled. One or two were wafting downriver on the night steamer from Albany; another was trudging over from the seventh-ward Democratic headquarters on the East River. Seymour Steele's A Company lined up on Nassau Street in the muggy morning haze, a rabble with the smell of whiskey on them, and trailed off, single file, through Fulton Street and Broadway to the Battery. It was a Saturday, and nobody came outside to cheer.

How the colonel hated this! Unkempt men, straggling through town, drifting out to Governors Island, setting up their brand new white canvas tents every which way on the lawns of Fort Columbus, wolfing sweet crackers and warm beer, complaining about the heat, the sunburn, the half-cooked pork, the brackish coffee. What was needed was discipline! A firm, military schedule, clearly set forth in the order book. Rise to drumbeats at 4:30 A.M. and drill from five to seven. Breakfast and cleanup, then drill again from ten to twelve. Dinner at two, drills five to seven, then supper. Final roll call at nine, with every private soldier to enter his tent, douse the lights, and keep quiet.

First thing Monday, the colonel called together the full regiment, such as it was—two long lines of men in motley, facing the choppy harbor in a pearl-pink summer dawn, mouths crumpled shut in sleepy discontent, stretching, hands clasped on buttocks, eyes roving back to the beloved city. The colonel spoke with eloquence about the friendly, gentlemanly attitudes that would prevail, the bounteous new home awaiting them, the courage and sacrifice of battle. California was in a state of "armed insurrection." They must be prepared to fight and die. An impressionable corporal caught the gist of it in his diary: "Roast beef and two dollars a day, plenty of whiskey, golden Jesuses, pretty Mexican girls, safe investments, quick returns."

Muskets were issued, bayonets passed out. The daily drills began, and the hectic purchase of supplies: 1,606 barrels of salt pork, pickles, sugar, vinegar, pickled onions and sauerkraut; tons of coffee; bushels of beans; thousands of pounds of soap and candles; hundreds of crates of muskets, rifles, cartridges, primers, fuses, quick matches, slow matches, cannon balls, canisters, shells. There were four 6-pound field guns, two 12-pound howitzers, four 10-inch mortars, twenty 32-pound iron guns, and all the wagons, tools, and portable forges that Captain Joseph Folsom, the assistant quartermaster, could lay his hands on.

A regimental uniform was designed: light trousers with scarlet piping along the outer seam; a dark blue, single-breasted frock coat with a stand-up collar and scarlet cuffs; and a conical blue cloth cap with a black patent-leather visor in the newest French army style—"very becoming," said the New York *Herald*, which approved of everything about the war. At $9.50, however, it struck the volunteers as an extravagant fancy: they got only $12.00 a year for clothing, and $12.00 a month in pay.

As for the officers, they were expected to put together their own kit. One young lieutenant, rushing around Manhattan on a sultry afternoon, ran up a frightful bill at the outfitting shops: one pair of gold lace shoulder straps, $2.00; mattress and pillow, $9.50; four pairs of white drill pants, $21.00; two white marshal's vests, $8.00; one India rubber cloak, $16.00; one silk vest, $2.50; one double percussion gun, $39.38; one pair of gilt epaulets, $10.00; one silk sash, $12.00; two and one-third dozen pairs of white gloves, $21.00; one glove box, $4.00. Add to this a copy of Scott's *Tactics* and a copy of Cooper's *Tactics*, pillow sheeting, cotton sheeting, cold counterpanes, buckshot, powder, several dozen pairs of black prunella stockings, plus four or five bottles of Monongahela (rye) whisky, a dozen bottles of old brandy, and a ten-gallon keg of sherry (a sensible contribution to the officer's mess), and you reached a level of military procurement that significantly enhanced the popularity of Mr. Polk's War with the merchant class.

Meantime, on Governors Island the enthusiasm of the volunteers melted in the August sun. Most of the men were afflicted with what they called "summer complaint," a form of galloping diarrhea attributed to New York water; and others turned up with more serious complaints attributed to New York women. Captain Kimball Dimmick, lately of Chenango County, New York, often felt so puny in the morning, what with the megrims and the cholera morbus, the whining of the men, and the carping of the *Tribune*, that he had to fortify himself with brandy and sugar before he could face the 5:00 A.M. drill, and then he would venture out to find the island seething with mischief and disaffection. First one company, then another, refused to buy the very becoming uniforms. The colonel reacted by locking several-score troublemakers in the guardhouse; and *that* caused so much grumbling that he had to bring in a company of army regulars to restore respect for authority. "If we sail for California, I have no doubt that Stevenson would die at the first opportunity," Captain Dimmick wrote to his wife. "I would not dare to go in his shoes. . . ."

Almost every day the parents or friends of some recruit would appear at the colonel's tent to serve him a writ of habeas corpus for the release of a disgruntled volunteer who had decided he was too young, too old, or too frail to go to California. One ill-fated company lost thirty men in a day and was left with only twenty-two of its original seventy-seven recruits. Another, commanded by the former superintendent of a starchy military school in Vermont, lost four by desertion, eight by medical discharge, and one to a constable who arrived with a warrant and handcuffs.

To seal off some of the leaks, the colonel posted a cordon around the island and ordered that any soldier moving about the grounds must pass a guard tent and give a secret password. Defectors continued to scamper past the sentry post, however, cheered on by crowds of admiring volunteers. It was reported that a startled picket, hearing footsteps and a splash, rushed out and shouted: "Say *Newport* or I'll shoot!" The story was untrue, of course, like most of the trash in the opposition press; but the security system obviously did not work. During the eight weeks from muster day to sailing day, Colonel Stevenson had to replace close to five hundred recruits, almost a 100 percent turnover, and the screening became increasingly haphazard.

To add to his anxiety, the colonel was being subjected to various means of legal harassment. Certain putative creditors, apprised of his imminent departure, haled him into court, where an unfriendly judge forced him to post a bond to guarantee that he would stay within the jurisdiction of the courts of New York, an obvious impossibility for a military officer en route to distant and perilous service. Next, a group of volunteers, disqualified because of physical disabilities, brought suit, charging Stevenson with illegally detaining them for twenty days before giving them a medical examination. This malicious litigation apparently had been instigated by a mercenary soldier and free-lance revolutionary by the name of Thomas Jefferson Sutherland—a would-be officer and tactical advisor to the expedition, whom the colonel had rejected with characteristic vigor. ("I am quite capable, sir, of directing this expedition as the President has entrusted me to do, sir, without the advice of consultants. . . . Good day, sir!")

Sutherland was a filibuster with an appetite for Mexican girls and golden Jesuses, and he craved a tour of California. He sent a petition directly to Secretary Marcy through some friends in the capital, warning that legal entanglements would prevent Stevenson from leaving New York and suggesting that an acquaintance of Sutherland's from Philadelphia—one Captain Henry M. Naglee of Company D—be appointed commander, instead. Marcy forwarded the letter to Colonel Stevenson, who answered by setting a sailing date—Friday, September 25. Sutherland's intrigue was precisely the sort of challenge the colonel relished: covert, political, and dastardly. A few years earlier, during a presidential election, Stevenson had served his party and himself by playing double-agent in a plot the Whigs had concocted to import dozens of unemployed pipelayers from Philadelphia to New York to vote as repeaters in the precincts of lower Manhattan. Stevenson was therefore wise to all the dirty tricks of wicked statesmen and adept in all the classic postures of defense. He at once doubled the guard on Governors Island and gave instructions not to allow any unidentified persons to land. Leaving camp, he would draw his cloak up to his earlobes and surround himself with bodyguards. At midnight on September 23, accompanied by six men armed with cutlasses and pistols, he crossed the channel to Brooklyn in a rowboat with muffled oars and said a furtive farewell to his three daughters in the house of a friend.

The government had chartered three vessels, each with a capacity of seven hundred tons, to transport the volunteers. The *Susan Drew*, commanded by the mild-mannered West Pointer Lieutenant Colonel Henry S. Burton, was distinguished by her figurehead—a blowsy blonde (presumably Susan) with an upturned backside of transcendent grandeur. The *Loo Choo*, under Major Hardie, was graced by most of the literary and forensic talent in the group; and the *Thomas Perkins* was honored by the personal presence of Colonel Stevenson, who chose her, after careful reflection, as his flagship.

On Wednesday afternoon, September 23, steamers towed the transports down from the Brooklyn Naval Yard and warped them against the quay at Governors Island. All sails drooped. The decks were strewn with crates and boxes; hawsers dangled from the railings; and the sailors were grousing about having to sail on Friday. As for the regiment, every company was under strength, and one had dried up completely. The colonel, out of respect for maritime superstition, agreed to hold off the day of departure until Saturday; but he ordered the volunteers to board the ships immediately. He had received word from a friend in the sheriff's office that process servers were on their way.

Last letters must now be sealed and mailed, last gifts dispatched: a pair of gloves, a smelling bag, a needle case. Captain Dimmick, braced with sugared brandy, wrote his wife: "Cheer up—be courageous for days of

Joy are yet to come. The God of Battles will Shield me and nerve my arm in the hour of danger against my country's foes and protect and console you in your lonely hours. . . ."

Last orders: Colonel Stevenson to company commanders—"All clothing and other articles refused to be paid for must be delivered to the Quarter Master at the Store Tent of the Regiment within four hours. . . ."

Last visitors: Lieutenant John Hollingsworth's Uncle Chase drew Captain Naglee aside and muttered in his ear, as old men do: "Naglee, if anything happens to him [Hollingsworth], say he died a clever fellow and bury him with the honors of war."

Naglee assured him the regiment would never come within a hundred miles of an armed Mexican.

"Yes," said Uncle Chase, "but you may fall out among yourselves. . . ."

Last souvenirs: a lithographer on Nassau Street turned out a satirical engraving of a volunteer in uniform, embracing a sorrowful doxy two feet taller than himself.

"Goodbye, Liz! Here's my daggero type likeness! I'd stand treat but I haint got the ghost of a red cent left, our uniforms is so very expensive."

And Liz, tearful but game: "Well Jake as you'r goin away, I've got three shillin so let's go down to George Brown's in Pearl Street and get two stews and a couple of horns!"

Last parade: the chaplain of the island, the Reverend Dr. John McVickar, a teacher of moral and intellectual philosophy at Columbia University, came down to hand out Bibles. The men stood glassy eyed and dripping, while Dr. McVickar read a sermon on the heavy task of colonizing a "new, distant and dubious settlement." As the chaplain saw it, squinting in the bleaching light, this expedition was a "living scion cut off the Parent American Stock, destined to engraft the Institutions of the East on the wild plants of the West." It was a burden, he admitted, to carry civilization to the wilderness; but that was the price one paid for belonging to the Anglo-Saxon race, "a race that has never yet turned back, whose course has ever been onward and upward, and over whose destined empire there would seem to hang no other cloud than that which may arise from their possible unworthiness, should they be found to turn into base gain, or a lust of dominion, a trust of power committed to their hands for the Civilizing and Christianizing of the earth."

During the sermon Colonel Stevenson peered across the harbor toward the Battery and saw a clot of agitated figures getting into boats. He held his ground with difficulty while the Reverend Chaplain was handing him a Bible and a Book of Common Prayer inscribed: "To the Leader of the Expedition and Probable Ruler of the New Colony." Defensive tactics swamped his mind. He would station men along the gunwales of his flagship, each with a thirty-two-pound cannon ball in hand and orders to let fall on any boat that tried to fasten to the side. His own boat would guard the bottom of the ladder, with four armed men aboard to challenge process servers. He would have a marksman at the ready to drive off marauders, and the ship's cannon loaded with grapeshot and canister.

There followed a nervous day aboard the *Thomas Perkins*. Peeking from his cabin, the colonel spied a little steamer wallowing purposefully down the East River. At once he summoned a musketeer and had him take aim at the pilot in the wheelhouse. Meanwhile, the deck officer of the *Perkins* shouted a warning to stand off or die. The steamer quickly drew away, confirming Colonel Stevenson's suspicions that it was filled with deputies. He went below and dashed off letters to the President, the Secretary of War, the commander of the naval escort, the captains of the towing ships —even the sheriff of New York—notifying one and all that he intended to leave port at dawn Saturday at the head of his command—"peaceably if I can, forcibly if I must." In later years it gave him satisfaction to remember this fine moment of ferocity.

At sunrise on the crucial day, training his spyglass on the nether tip of Manhattan Island, the colonel descried (or thought he did) a column of men piling into a harbor boat. An excruciating moment: the regimental band was bravely trumpeting "The Girl I Left Behind Me"; Fort Columbus fired its guns; two swift steamers took the *Thomas Perkins* in tow; and still they did not move, waiting for the ebb tide. A reporter came aboard with a flag from the benevolent *Herald*. A messenger arrived with a parting editorial from the malign *Tribune*: "As a specimen of utter, hopeless failure, this California expedition will stand without a superior, perhaps without an equal, in the annals of any nation." Still, the ships did not move. At last the colonel heard a boatswain pass the order to cast off. The tow ships had a head of steam. By the time the harbor steamer carrying the sheriff's posse (if, indeed, it *was* a sheriff's posse) had reached Governors Island, the New York regiment of volunteers was slipping through the Narrows.

Sighing, Colonel Stevenson put down his glasses and commanded the flotilla to heave to while he made a final round of salutes and handshakes. It turned out that one captain, two lieutenants, four sergeants, and thirty soldiers had been left behind in the excitement. The regiment numbered fewer than six hundred men. Secretary Marcy would have to send another transport in a month or two to reinforce the scion of civilization.

Past Sandy Hook, the expedition met the open sea. Guns and boxes slithered to and fro. Barrels rumbled fore and aft. Every timber creaked and popped, and the bellying sails snapped full of blue-green spray. Colonel Stevenson, feeling a sudden surge beneath his tongue, scratched out a full week's orders and made a rapid inspection of the billets. At the galley hatch, indignity overcame him. He tottered to his bunk and did not rise for days. When he ventured out again, it was October: the *Perkins* had found the southwest trades and was plowing the mid-Atlantic stream at eight to ten knots, through myriads of jellyfish, rising and floating up like blobs of opalescent butter. The air was soft; the laundrywomen shyly came up from below, and the colonel took a turn around the deck.

His rough recruits were lounging at the rail, quarreling, puking, goosing one another, pining already for the joys of New York, sweet home of chicken fricassees, clam pots, chunk apple pies, egg flips, spruce beer, and gingerbread. Not even James Knox Polk could have mistaken these for country squires. Theirs was a bristling urban world of Irish saloons and German groceries, ward bosses, volunteer fire brigades, and rifle guards that marched with fife and drum on Sunday afternoons, led by mascots in tall fur shakos and black porters with a bull's-eye target. It was a world of accessible comforts and easy companionship in which a man could pause on almost any street to wet the whistle at a tavern of the proper stripe. It was a world of Barn-Burners and Hunkers, Soft-Shells and Hard-Shells, Loco-Focos and Anti-Renters, Native Americans and National Reformers, factions and rivalries and splinters of Byzantine complexity, which dealt with one another with all manner of bizarre and slanderous propaganda, stuffed ballot boxes, graveyard voting rosters, dark-lantern marches, kidnapings, arson, riots, slungshot, and brass knuckles.

These, presumably, were the Institutions of the East that certain of the New York volunteers intended to engraft upon the wild root stock of the Pacific coast. As a first step, they set about establishing them on the colonel's transport ships. Almost every day Stevenson was compelled to promulgate new rules, and almost every day the men devised new antics not yet categorically proscribed: diving overboard for an unauthorized swim, climbing the rigging for an unsanctioned view, refusing to fall in line until one had finished shaving, eating in the bunkroom. . . .

To remind the regiment of their historic mission, the colonel would order the drummers to beat the long, insistent roll "To Quarters! All hands on deck to repel boarders!" Then, with everyone rolled out, he would deliver a fine, brisk, soul-inflating speech, afire with the enthusiasm of those rousing songs they used to sing at Niblo's Gardens—"Success to California . . . likewise to Oregon . . . and the rooster that crows there . . . must be Uncle Sam . . . "

But the boys were too far from the pain and glory of war. Their pranks began to smack of revolution. An impudent corporal in Company F called Sergeant Webster a son of a bitch. A frisky recruit in Company B poured flour and molasses over the sleeping person of Private John B. Brady; and *every single man* in the supposedly well-behaved company of Captain Francis Lippitt (he was the military academy martinet from Vermont) contrived to "lose" his very becoming French hat. The colonel sensed that he would have to rise to the occasion. He read aloud the articles of war, adding reminders: sleeping on duty will get you twenty days in the guardhouse, with two hours of each day trussed to the rigging by both hands; insubordination—leg irons and a ball and chain. Hereafter, all soldiers of the regiment shall go to bed at 9:00 P.M. to the sound of a drum.

The bedtime regulation caused an ominous rumble of discontent. It was as hot as Hades below deck, and you could not eat or smoke or sing. One of the sergeants, passing the order along, told his platoon he didn't give a damn whether they obeyed it or not. The colonel, fortuitously, overheard. Hastily convening a court-martial, he broke the sergeant to the ranks and sentenced him to holystone the deck. The sergeant glared at him defiantly.

"Have him trussed up by the thumbs until he apologizes," said Colonel Stevenson. "Maintain discipline, sir."

Next day, Captain Folsom, the staff quartermaster, came in to report that the sergeant's punishment was upsetting the men.

"Did you know they're planning a mutiny this afternoon?"

The colonel inflated his chest and examined Folsom, a West Pointer and no slouch, but not as spunky as he might have been.

"No, sir," the colonel said. "But I *do* know that there will be no mutiny aboard this ship this afternoon. And further, Captain Folsom—you are well aware that I sleep over nine hundred pounds of gunpowder; but do you not know, sir, that I have a train from that powder to my berth? I do, sir, and you can rest assured that before I will suffer the command of this vessel to pass from me, there will not be a plank left for a soul aboard to cling to. And now, Captain Folsom, let the mutiny proceed!"

The captain presumably spread word that Colonel Stevenson had come unglued and was threatening to blow up the ship, for the mutiny did not proceed.

The arrival in Rio de Janeiro, the expedition's first stop, was something less than a triumph. To the colonel's annoyance, his flagship came in last. The Brazilians failed to fire a welcoming salute; and the men of Captain Lippitt's rowdy company, on sighting the rest of the flotilla in the harbor, gave three cheers and threw their newly reissued French hats over the side. When the colonel went around to inspect the other ships, he learned that discipline aboard the *Susan Drew* had broken down even more disastrously than it had done aboard the *Perkins*. An entire company had rebelled against bathing in a vat of seawater on the deck; and then, after Captain Naglee had put them in confinement, they had torn down the walls of the guardhouse, laughing and singing rudely, and had dumped the wreckage overboard. It was only after Lieutenant Colonel Burton had clamped the ringleaders into double irons that any sort of order was restored, and baths apparently were out of the question for the rest of the voyage.

Colonel Stevenson went ashore in a belligerent mood, and he found nothing there to improve his temper. The Brazilians were flagrantly cheating his soldiers, and his soldiers were acting like Vikings on a raid. One of the boys was in jail for stealing a valuable dog from the Hotel Pharoux; another had drawn a pistol on a member of the Imperial Guard; and countless others were so drunk they had to be hog-tied and hauled back to the ships like carcasses of beef. It was distressing but not surprising to learn that the court of Brazil had filed a formal protest with the minister of the United States and had suspended diplomatic relations between the two countries.

The dramatic implications of the situation struck the colonel immediately. His patriotic spirit soared. He fired off a letter to the Brazilian government, pledging his full support to the American minister, the Honorable Mr. Henry Wise, and canceling plans for a ritual exchange of cannon fire with the shore batteries the next day. Then, with Mr. Wise at his side, he rushed back to the *Thomas Perkins*, climbed to the poop deck, and, in ringing tones, told such men as could be assembled to prepare for war. Within twenty-four hours he would be leading an armed expedition through the streets of this impertinent capital.

The effect of this speech, as Stevenson remembered it, was "electrical." An explosion of hysterical cheering spread from vessel to vessel, despite the fact that the men on the other ships had no idea what the fuss was all about. Twenty thousand bewildered Brazilians came down to the quay to find out what was going on. All in all, it was a "a great splutter," as one of the officers said.

That a war did not ensue was due as much to the forbearance of the Brazilians as to the obvious impossibility of mustering a sober landing force. Shore leave was suspended for a day or two, and the Brazilians settled for the recall of the American minister.

When things had quieted down, Colonel Stevenson got off an official letter to Secretary Marcy, reporting events to date and emphasizing the pleasant news that discipline had been "as good as could be expected of volunteers," considering that most of them were under inexperienced officers. Twenty-two recruits, having achieved their apparent object of escaping from New York, elected to remain without permission in Rio; and the first night out of port the dissidents of the *Susan Drew* again tore down the reconstructed brig.

The balance of the trip to California was uneventful, save for the washing overboard of several men (one of whom drowned) off Tierra del Fuego. A newspaper called the *Fish Market Reporter*, edited by Obadiah Dolphin, Zachariah Flounder, Sephomiah Blackfish, and Ezekiel Sheepshead, appeared on the *Susan Drew*; amateur actors in grotesque robes played Shakespearean tragedies on the *Loo Choo*, and motion sickness again assaulted the commander in chief aboard the *Thomas Perkins*. Around Cape Horn the weather was properly foul, although it was midsummer in that latitude. Snow fell on Christmas Day. Seals and penguins sported near the ships. The men stayed below, chewing and spitting, drinking hot punch, and eating a holiday portion of plum duff.

The colonel, determined to beat the rest of the fleet to San Francisco, decided to bypass Valparaiso, Chile, while the *Loo Choo* and the *Susan Drew* put in for water. He did not regret his decision. On the ships that made port at that hard-bitten Chilean town, the boys smuggled themselves into water barrels, slipped through portholes, and stowed away in bumboats of fruits and vegetables. Twenty-nine escaped, but the *Perkins* sailed on, its cargo of Anglo-Saxon manhood more or less intact, and came through the Golden Gate at noon on March 5, 1847. Colonel Stevenson, standing on the deck with Captain Arthur, breathed for the first time the strange aroma of the California land, a distillate of chaparral and oaks and lupine from the grassy hills around San Francisco Bay.

Upon entering the straits, the colonel thought at first that the great expanse of the bay was as empty as the moon. Flocks of seabirds floated on the water, and the island of Alcatraz was white with gulls. He issued a call to arms and buckled on his sword. Then they sighted two American men-of-war and a little hide drogher from Boston, taking on water at the port of Sausalito. As they lowered the topgallant sail and came around the Yerba Buena Cove, the colonel could see the flag of the United States flying over the adobe buildings of the Mexican *cuartel*. He was too late to conquer California. It had been conquered months before, and Colonel Jonathan Drake Stevenson would never be the Ruler of the New Colony.

Gazing up at the scattering of wretched sheds and shacks above the cove, the colonel tasted the gall of disappointment. There were no golden Jesuses here for him. San Francisco was only an isolated army post on the outer limits of a fallen empire, a minor harbor in the hide-and-tallow trade: three or four frame buildings, put up by renegade Americans, a billiard room, a bar or two, a blacksmith's shop, a trading post, a few corrals, a couple of adobe warehouses for storing salted rawhides. Some dark-haired women were washing underwear in a stream that trickled down among the windblown hills.

But a Spanish-speaking Californian named Mariano Vallejo and a Frenchman named Victor Prudhom rowed out to the ship to deliver a formal little speech of welcome; and the colonel, drawn up stiff and pigeon-chested, responded on behalf of the regiment, the President, and the state of New York. Afterward, feeling somewhat bouncier, he sent a courier to General Stephen Watts Kearny, down at the provincial capital in Monterey, announcing that the army of occupation had arrived. Excepting a few men with colds, all were healthy and "able to perform any duty you may require of them."

Next day, the colonel landed his troops by boat at Clark's Point, a spit at the foot of Telegraph Hill, and on the following day marched them out to the Presidio, a deserted Spanish barracks on a slope above the straits. Blackbirds were so thick underfoot they had to be kicked aside as the troops walked. The boys swept out the buildings, posted a guard, and began the occupation of California.

On March 12 the *Susan Drew* came in; ten days after that, the *Loo Choo*; and at the end of April the transport *Brutus* with the stragglers and the late recruits. By then San Francisco Bay was cluttered with Yankee vessels —sloops of war, transports, storeships, and frigates. General Kearny's dragoons had come in, overland, and soldiers and sailors outnumbered all the previous American settlers in California by more than two-to-one. They ran the territory as a military camp, with a governor-general in Monterey and a magistrate in San Francisco to keep track of five or six hundred whites and a couple of hundred Indians, mestizos, blacks, and Polynesians.

The volunteers spread up and down the coast. The colonel took three companies to Monterey, where they dug redoubts and sulked. Three under Burton went to Santa Barbara, occupied a homey Spanish barracks, and amused themselves for a year or so shooting doves and putting on minstrel shows with banjos made of sheepskin stretched on flour sieves. Three under Major Hardie stayed at the Presidio of San Francisco; and a single company went up to Sonoma, the northern edge of European influence.

Ultimately, Colonel Stevenson wound up with the command of the Pueblo of Los Angeles, a quiet village in the center of a dusty plain. The Spanish-speaking Californians received him gently: they were accustomed to blue-eyed gringos from Boston and figured he was another of the same. It was a decorous, benign regime. The colonel kept the articles of war and the army regulations constantly at hand. On holidays he read the Declaration of Independence in English and Spanish and ate courtly suppers in the company of Abel Stearns, a storekeeper from New England, and his Spanish wife.

A single incident aggrieved the colonel's pastoral reign. A young lieutenant, after nipping *aguardiente* in the duty shack, tried to storm Abel Stearns's liquor store and was heard to call the respected proprietor, his wife, and her sister "a bunch of pimps." Stevenson sent apologies and cashiered the lieutenant.

On the eve of the New Year, 1848, the colonel and his boys were hosts to the gentry of Los Angeles at a grand ball and supper. Stevenson raised a dozen toasts—to the president, to the Nation, to the ladies, to old friends in the States ("God grant that we may spend our next New Year among them"), and bashfully accepted a toast to himself. If anyone toasted the future, the sentiment was not recorded. The future was beyond belief, beyond imagination.

Three weeks later, in a millrace on the American River in northern California, John Marshall spotted the flicker of gold. By the end of summer, 1849, the Los Angeles garrison, like every other encampment of the New York volunteers, was abandoned, the harbinger of Anglo-Saxon civilization scattered to the hills, the coastal towns and villages of California half-deserted. The little port of San Francisco had become the focus of world migration. Captain Folsom, the staff quartermaster, having secured appointment as collector of the port, was on his way to becoming a millionaire. The Russ family, purveyors of Moroccan leather and holiday fireworks, had opened a jewelry shop and begun assembling an empire of hotels, beer gardens, office buildings, and residential blocks. Sergeant John C. Pulis, late of Lippitt's monstrous Company F, had become the first sheriff of San Francisco. Lieutenant Edward Gilbert was editing the *Alta California*, the leading newspaper in the territory; Captain Naglee (he of the bathtime rebellion) had founded the territory's first bank; Lieutenant Hewlett had opened a boardinghouse; Captain Frisbee had started a commission agency and was in prospect of marrying the eldest daughter of General Vallejo; Lieutenant Vermeule, the plague of Abel Stearns, had set himself up as a lawyer and would soon be elected a delegate to the California constitutional convention and a member of the state legislature; and the Reverend Mr. Thaddeus M. Leavenworth, chaplain to the regiment, had attained the quasi-judicial position of alcalde of San Francisco and was granting homesteads and auctioning public lands with a Christian generosity that scandalized even his former associates.

As for the colonel, he was well on his way to a second career (and a second marriage and a second family) as a legal counselor, politician, and founder of a grandiose ghost city called New-York-of-the-Pacific, which endures today only in the name of a slough on the edge of San Francisco Bay.

The former New York boys were scattered by then throughout California, styling themselves doctors, lawyers, judges, or capitalists. A few in San Francisco called themselves the "Hounds"—or, on formal occasions, the "Regulators." They were the first recognizable New York-style drinking-and-marching society in the Far West, and their raucous behavior soon aroused the more orderly citizens of the town to form the prototype of San Francisco's several committees of vigilance.

For better or worse, the Americanization of California had begun.

—*June 1979*

THE FARTHER CONTINENT OF JAMES CLYMAN

By RICHARD RHODES

Surveyor, mountain man, soldier, businessman, wanderer, captain of immigrants—no one man more thoroughly embodied the Westward-moving frontier

In medias res: Fort Laramie on the Oregon-California Trail, June 27, 1846, a day of reckoning. Francis Parkman was there, beginning the tour that he would chronicle in *The California and Oregon Trail*, the Harvard man come out West for health and curiosity, patronizing, disdaining the common emigrants who halted at the fort to tighten their iron tires and recruit their oxen, effusively admiring the stylish Sioux. The Sioux were there in the thousands, camped round Laramie at the invitation of the American Fur Company to trade, at truce with the emigrants, preparing war against the Crows. Lillburn Boggs was there, former governor of Missouri who had driven the Mormons from his state and thus indirectly set them on their exodus to Utah. Boggs had just been elected captain of a large party of emigrants. William H. "Owl" Russell, Kentucky colonel, had resigned the post the week before in a dispute over campsites, and drunk now, he cornered fastidious Parkman and belched indignation. The Boggs or Russell Party included businessmen and farmers from Illinois, emigrants from Germany and Ireland: George and Jacob Donner, James Frazier Reed, Lewis Keseberg, Patrick Breen. Soon George Donner would captain it. The Donner Party, it would come to be called.

Another traveler was there as well. He had just returned from California. For convenience he had accompanied a promoter and erstwhile author named Lansford W. Hastings along the way. Hastings had published a book popular among the emigrants—one of the Donners had a copy in his saddlebags—*The Emigrants' Guide to Oregon and California*. The traveler knew the quality of the book and the quality of the man, and meant to condemn them both. He passed Francis Parkman, this traveler, at Fort Bernard, some six miles beyond Laramie, but laconically chose not to record the event in his journal. Parkman made the note, not much impressed: another greasy, trail-worn mountain man.

The traveler, James Clyman, camped among friends at Laramie. He enjoyed "a cup of excellent coffee . . . the first I had tasted since the early part of last winter." He talked with his friends "until a late hour." Near the end of his life he reported the substance of that conversation. One of his friends at Laramie was James Frazier Reed. Reed and Clyman and Abraham Lincoln had been together in Jacob Early's company in the Black Hawk War. Now Reed and the Donners were hot for California, Clyman cold. Reed at least was hot for Hastings's new cutoff, which the promoter had grandly sketched in *The Emigrants' Guide*: "The most direct route for the California emigrants, would be to leave the Oregon route, about two hundred miles east from Fort Hall; thence bearing west southwest, to the Salt Lake; and thence continuing down to the bay of St. Francisco." But Clyman had just endured that route in reverse, and so had Hastings, for the first time. So Reed and Clyman argued. "Mr. Reed, while we were encamped at Laramie, was enquiring about the route. I told him to 'take the regular wagon track, and never leave it—it is barely possible to get through if you follow it—and it may be impossible if you don't.' Reed replied, ' There is a nigher route, and it is of no use to take so much of a roundabout course.' I admitted the fact, but told him about the great desert and the roughness of the Sierras, and that a straight route might turn out to be impracticable." It did, as we know, and led the Donner Party to disaster. To twenty days wasted cutting forty miles through the untracked Wasatch Mountains. To five days and four nights crossing the Great Salt Desert without water, the oxen scattered, the wagons abandoned, the cattle lost. To early Sierra snow, and snow burial, and poor beef and boiled hides, and finally, in extremity, the flesh of the dead. If Reed and the Donners had listened to Clyman they would have achieved California in mid-September, as most of the other emigrants did, roundabout course or not. Governor Boggs listened, and left the party for Oregon the next day.

James Clyman has not been given his due. He was farmer's son, surveyor, mountain man, soldier, businessman, wanderer, captain of emigrants, and finally farmer again; he saw much of the opening of the West, and contributed his considerable skills to it; he was present at the inception of more than one great event; but he was not celebrated nationally in his own lifetime, as Daniel Boone and Jim Bridger were, nor has he been accorded much more than passing references and footnotes since. He deserves better. His life was varied and dramatic: he was himself the westward-moving frontier. His journals are important historical documents. Most of all, Clyman's quality as a human being—his exceptional character—can enlarge our understanding of the intellectual and emotional range of the American pioneer. A nation at its best is at least a composite of its best men. Clyman was one of them.

James Clyman was born in Fauquier County, Virginia, on a farm his father leased from George Washington, in 1792. The retired first President often rode the boundaries of his lands, and Clyman may have met him on one of those rides. Clyman's father wanted more than a life lease, even on Washington land. He wanted land of his own. He moved the family to Pennsylvania and then to Ohio when Clyman was fifteen. Clyman himself struck out early. After a young manhood spent wandering the Midwest as a farm hand, woodchopper, and provisioner, he hired on with a government surveyor in Indiana. In 1822, having learned the trade, he contracted with William S. Hamilton, Alexander Hamilton's son, to finish a course of surveying Hamilton had begun along the Vermilion River in Illinois. More surveying, along the Sangamon, led him to St. Louis, early in 1823, to collect his pay. "My curiosity now being satisfied St Louis being a fine place for Spending money I did not leave immediately not having spent all my funds I loitered about without employment." That is a foretaste of Clyman's humor, dry and ironic. He would need it in years to come.

In St. Louis he caught the eye of Lieutenant Governor William H. Ashley, who was preparing to make his fortune in the fur trade and "was engaging men for a Trip to the mouth of the Yellow Stone river." Ashley hired Clyman to help in recruiting, scouring out likely candidates "in grog Shops and other sinks of degredation." When the keelboats sailed from St. Louis up the Missouri, the Ashley Expedition was ninety strong. Jedediah Smith, the calm devout mountain man, would meet it along the way. "A description of our crew I cannt give," Clyman wrote later, "but Fallstafs Battallion was genteel in comparison." I am looking for mind here: Clyman had only "a smattering" of education, but its texts were the best of the day. His journals allude to Byron, Milton, Shakespeare, and to the Bible; the wryness was his own.

The expedition met a setback up the Missouri, fighting off two villages of Arikaras—eleven wounded, fifteen dead. "The worst disaster in the history of the Western fur trade," Dale L. Morgan calls it in his book *Jedediah Smith and the Opening of the West.* "Fallstafs Battallion" hastily retreated from the sand bar below the villages under the withering fire from the Arikara fusils, but Smith held his ground, Clyman fighting beside him. Forced at last to swim the river to escape, Clyman let go the rifle and pistols that weighed him down. Three Arikaras swam after him and chased him for more than an hour across the prairie beyond the river before he found a hole to hide in on the other side of the hill. He made his way back to a point of land below the battle site and the boats, retreating downriver, luckily picked him up.

Ashley then sent a party of men westward on horseback, Clyman among them and William Sublette, captained by Jedediah Smith. In the Black Hills they surprised a grizzly, and Clyman learned another trade. The grizzly attacked Smith, badly chewing his head and almost tearing off one ear. "None of us having any sugical Knowledge what was to be done one Said come tak hold and he wuld say why not you so it went around I asked the Capt what was best he said . . . if you have a needle and thread git it out and sew up my wounds . . . I got a pair of scissors and cut off his hair and then began my first Job of dressing wounds . . . after stitching all the other wounds in the best way I was capbl and according to the captains directions the ear being the last I told him I could do nothing for his Eare O you must try to stich up some way or other said he then I put in my needle stiching it through and over and over laying the lacerated parts togather as nice as I could with my hands . . . this gave us a lisson on the character of the grissly Baare which we did not forget." Smith survived the ordeal and the men rode on west, through "a grove of Petrifid timber," across shale and waste and prairie to the Powder River, among the Crows to trade horses, to the Wind River Valley to winter in. Their rations were short. When they could find them they shot mountain sheep and antelope and buffalo. Caught out one night in a blizzard, Clyman and Sublette nearly froze. Clyman saved them; Sublette was too stiff with cold to move.

The party went without meat for four hungry days before the provisioning team of Clyman and Sublette tracked a buffalo and brought it down, "many of the men eating large slices raw." Their bellies full, they rode west for water across a high, cold plain at the southern terminus of the Wind River chain. The water they found flowed west. It was Pacific water: they had crossed the Continental Divide and rediscovered the South Pass (first discovered by Robert Stuart in 1812), the broad road through the Rockies that would open the western continent to wagons, and thus to family emigration, and thus eventually to annexation to the United States.

He trapped beaver on the Green River that winter and spring, detached from Smith, and the next June, waiting at the Sweetwater to rendezvous, had to hide out from Indians for eleven days and lost contact with the other men and lost his horses too. He "began to get lonesome." With "plenty of Powder but only eleven bullets" he struck out for civilization—on foot, a distance of six hundred miles over landscape he'd never seen before and which he walked in eighty days. He lost most of his powder and bullets in another encounter with Indians. Down to one bullet, he retrieved the ball from the occasional buffalo he shot and chewed it round again. "I could not sleep and it got so damp I could not obtain fire and I had to swim several rivers." He realized he was wandering in circles and jerked himself straight. "I went on for some time with my head down when raising my eyes with great surprise I saw the stars & stripes waving over Fort [Atkinson] I swoned emmediately . . . certainly no man ever enjoyed the sight of our flag better than I did. . . ." Thus Clyman's wilderness initiation. He would never again find himself at so great a loss.

When he recovered, he turned around with Ashley and headed back west. His story for the next three years is a story of trapping and hunting and exploring, living for the most part out on his own a thousand miles from store and home. The year 1826 was a high point. Smith was looking for new beaver country, breaking trail on the north shore of the Great Salt Lake. The party could go no farther on horseback—there was nothing for the horses to eat. Clyman, Moses "Black" Harris, and probably Louis Vasquez and a man named Henry G. Fraeb, built bullboats, hide canoes, and paddled south along the lake shore, riding high in that dead, bitter water. Its circumnavigation took them twenty-four days. They knew thirst and probably hunger. They might have seen dead trout and catfish floating, washed in from mountain streams. They may have seined for the brine shrimp that even today are harvested from the lake. Significantly, they found no outlet. Fanciful geographers had imagined that the salt lake was an arm of the Pacific—they consistently had underestimated the continent since Columbus's day—Clyman's circumnavigation proved that it was not. "This wide spread Sterility," Clyman called the lake and the land beyond it when he saw it again in a later year. He did not return to St. Louis until the fall of 1827, and not all was sterile on his four-year tour. He sold his last year's catch of beaver skins for $1,251, wealth enough to buy a substantial farm.

He bought the farm, in Illinois, and set up his two brothers to manage it. Farming was not yet to his taste. He participated in the Black Hawk War. He went into partnership with a man named Hiram Ross and laid claim to government land in wilderness Wisconsin, land on which Milwaukee was later founded. Too many people came on; he moved out. In November, 1835, traveling with a man named Burdett, looking for wilder land, he bought a canoe from an Indian woman whose son and husband weren't at home, intending to float a river. A mile-and-a-half float brought him to sundown, and he and Burdett stopped at a deserted cabin to camp. Clyman went out to collect wood while Burdett started a fire. The

Indians, father and son, trailed them to retrieve the canoe and, says an old chronicle, "to avenge the death of a brother of the squaw, who was killed by a soldier at Fort Winnebago, two years before."

The son shot Burdett; Clyman came running back; the father raised his gun; Clyman took off, dodging through the woods. Not all his luck was with him: one bullet broke his left arm below the elbow, and the son, taking up Clyman's own shotgun, managed to hit him in the thigh. "This last shot was not very effective," the chronicle goes on, "on account of the distance Clyman was from them by that time, for he could run like a deer; and the principal effect was to make him, as he expressed it, 'as mad as hell' to be peppered in that way with his own gun, and he would have liked to return the compliment very much, but as *sauve-qui-peut* was the order of the day just then, he kept on, until the voices of his pursuers . . . were lost in the distance, when he hid under a fallen tree." At one point the Indians actually stood on the tree wondering where Clyman had gone.

He made his way at night, then, carrying his broken left arm in his right, on foot, through rain and unbroken wilderness, and continued the next day and the next night and part of one day more, to Milwaukee, a distance of fifty miles. For a time, in and around Milwaukee, no Indian felt safe in Clyman's presence. The chronicler: "And it might truthfully be said that the fear of him was upon every Indian then here, for not one of them would remain in the town twenty minutes after they got sight of him. A whole regiment of soldiers could not have inspired them with a greater desire for the solitude of the wilderness, than did the presence of this one man."

An interlude then to wandering: Clyman settled down. He built a saw-mill in Wisconsin in 1836 with Hiram Ross, near what is now Wauwatosa, and he remained in business until at least 1841. This is the man at forty-eight, in 1840: look at him now: he has yet to make, twice more, the great emigration: "He was nearly or quite six feet tall," remembered an acquaintance, "erect and straight of rather sparse build though well formed and firm in person with a firm and elastic tread, deliberate in all his movements of a sandy complexion high and very slightly receding forehead neither very broad nor very narrow rather a thin elongated face, rather a small mouth slightly inclined to pucker good teeth but like his persona rather long and narrow." Another acquaintance thought he looked like Washington, the Washington of "Lot Trumbull's portrait . . . at Yale College."

"A hoosier gentleman," another said. And another—men didn't forget him—"His manner very quiet, modest, voice pleasant and low very amiable and agreeable person." Hiram Ross, his sawmill partner: "Clyman was over six feet high rather slender his personal appearance was very pleasant his trait of character was good he was a straight forward and up right man." In 1835, when his old friend Dan Beckwith died, Clyman "armed with pick and shovel, wended down to the Old Williams Burying Ground and dug a grave in the frozen soil. There were other willing hands to help, but Jim, with the Soul of a Poet, wanted . . . to pay last tribute to his Friend."

He had endurance, and patience, and a mind. Running the sawmill, whiling away his time, Ross outside on a cold winter afternoon building a sleigh, he filled a ledger with philosophical musings and wry observations: "Two things Infinite Time and space Two things more appear to be attached to the above infinity (viz) Matter and number Matter appears to pervade the infinity of space and number attempts to define quantity of matter as well as to give bounds to space—which . . . Expands before matter and number—and all human speculation is here bounden in matter and number leaving space at least almost completely untouched . . .

"About the year 650 from the fowning of Rome the difficulties commenced between Marius and Sylla from which I date the commencement of the decline of the Roman commonwealth . . .

"Of all People it seems to me those are the most tiresome who never convers on any subject but their misfortunes.

Put on a damp night cap & then relapse
He thought he would have died he was so bad
His Peevish Hearers allmost wish he had . . .

"[Winter] appears to be the night the time of sleep and rest for the vegetable kingdom leafless and frozen they are now taking their rest and matureing the subsistance thy recieved during the last summer it appears as if revolution of the earth around the sun was the day & night for the vegetables as is the earth's revolution on its own axis [for the animal]. . . .

"We may comprehend the globe we inhabit pretty fully and even the sollar System but a million of such systems becomes incomprehensible although even a million such Systems may fall verry short of the quantity of matter in existance throughout the universal Kingdom."

More in the ledger on hibernation and the extirpation of animals by man and the velocity of light and the possibility of a finite universe, the only such speculations Clyman found time to record; thereafter he turned his attention to the land, and to his countrymen.

Troubled by a lingering cough, he journeyed down into Arkansas and up to Independence in the spring of 1844. There he remembered his wilderness health, like many another prairie traveler. The trains were forming. He signed on, for Oregon, and resolved to keep a journal. Fifty-two, he noticed the ladies now: "I took my rifle and walked out in the deep ravin to guard a Beautifull covey of young Ladies & misses while they gathered wild currants & choke chirries which grow in great perfusion in this region and of the finerst kind." He noticed the constriction of the buffalo from their former range: "This vally [Bear River Valley above the Great Salt Lake] is the early Rendevous of the mountain Trappers & hunters But in the last 7 or 8 years the Buffaloe have entirely left this country & are now seldom seen west of the Sweet water." When travelers caught up with the train with news from civilization, he exercised his ironic humor: "As it appears there has been a great Troubling & Striving of the eliments the mountain having at last brot forth J.K. Polk Capt Tyler & the invincible Henry Clay as candidates for the Presidency. go it Clay. Just whigs enough in camp to take the curse off." There was humor in camp as well when emigrants following the trail for the first time disagreed with his old friend Black Harris: "Our pilot Mr. Harris^s 22 years experiance and advice is perfectly useless in this age of improvement when human intelect not only strides but actually Jumps & flies into conclusions." And somewhere along the way, for his own amusement or Harris's, he penned the old mountain man's epitaph:

Here lies the bones of Black Harris
who often traveled beyond the far west
and for the freedom of Equal rights
he crossed the snowy mountain Hights
was free and easy kind of soul
Especially with a Belly full.

Without serious incident the train trudged on to Oregon. Clyman, as rarely in his life, was bored. "Our selves & animals are becomeing tired of travel," he noted somewhere west of Fort Boise.

He hadn't even bothered to visit the fort. He studied rock and flora and fauna, recorded his doubt of a "M^r. Espy'" theory that the smoke from prairie fires, which had thickened the air for days, could produce rain—it hadn't rained in a month—and finally detached himself from the interminable train with a small party of men and rode ahead to the valley of the Willamette.

Oregon charmed him. The journal he kept of his time there alternates between bursts of eloquent observation and long weeks, busy weeks apparently, of fragmentary weather reports. Here was something new, bountiful land and as yet few settlers. His journals elaborated into consciously composed accounts of the country and long letters home, as if he had determined to add authorship to his kit of skills. Waterfowl along the Willamette, for example: "For miles the air seemed to be darkened with the emmenc flights that arose as I proceeded up the vally the morning being still thier nois was tumultuous and grand the hoarse shrieks of the Heron intermingled with the Symphonic Swan the fine treble of the Brant answered by the strong Bass of the goose with ennumerable shreeking and Quacking of the large and Smaller duck tribe filled every evenue of Surrounding space with nois and reminded one of Some aerial battle as discribed by Milton and all though I had been on the grand pass of waterfowl on the Illinois River it will not begin to bear a comparison with this thier being probably Half a Million in sight at one time and all apparently Screaming & Screeching at once." Or this astute observation, in a letter to Hiram Ross, of his Oregon compatriots: " . . . I never saw a more discontented community, owing principally to natural disposition. Nearly all, like myself, having been of a roving discontented character before leaving their eastern homes. The long tiresome trip from the States, has taught them what they are capable of performing and enduring. They talk of removing to the Islands, California, Chili, and other parts of South America with as much composure as you in Wisconsin talk of removing to Indiana or Michigan."

But if he had been roving and discontented, he was now clearly thinking about marriage and a home, this wanderer of fifty-two. From Oregon on, his journals note landscape not as geology or cartography but for the lie of it, its probable fertility and its prospects. And the ladies turn up frequently, as before this emigration they have never done: "And I must say that female beauty is not exclusively confined to any particular region or country for here too may be seen the fairy form the fair skin the dark Eye and drk hair so beautifully dscribed by Byron displayed in the person [of] Miss smith. . . ."

Clyman remained in Oregon until late May, 1845, when he packed up with a party of men planning to work their way down the coast to California. He was entrusted with a constabular duty, to carry letters from Elijah White, the U.S. Indian subagent in Oregon, to Thomas Larkin, the U.S. consul in California, inquiring about the murder of a Wallawalla chieftain's son in a dispute at Sutter's Fort. It was another of Clyman's brushes with history. As Charles L. Camp, the editor of Clyman's journals, explains: "White requested that [the murderer], if guilty, should be brought to trial, but nothing came of the investigation which followed. The unavenged murder is said to have been one of the causes of the Whitman massacre and disastrous Indian wars in the Northwest." The reason why the murder of an Indian, even a chieftain's son, went unavenged is obvious from Clyman's record of the journey down from Oregon City. Some of the men in his party, he noted with disgust, routinely shot Indians along the way. Clyman was not himself a bigot or a hater, and kept his peace except when personally wronged. Not surprisingly, then, Sutter's method of feeding his Indian workers appalled him: "The Capt keps 600 or 800 Indians in a complete state of Slavery and as I had the mortification of seeing them dine I may give a short discription 10 or 15 Troughs 3 or 4 feet long ware brought out of the cook room and seated in the Broiling sun all the Lobourers grate and small ran to the troughs like so many pigs and feed thenselves with their hands. . . ."

He encountered a California similar in some ways to California today, remarking on the general nakedness of its natives in the mild climate, recording an earthquake, praising the "Beautifull and picturesque" land. Something was stirring in him, something that made him judge California's occupants—the Spanish from Mexico, the Indians, his fellow foreigners from the States—more harshly than had been his wont when he was only a rover passing through. "The Callifornians are a proud Lazy indolent people doing nothing but ride after herds or from place to place without an appearant object The Indians or aborigines do all the drudgery and labour and are kept in a state of Slavery. . . . The californian Plough is a curosity in agraculture. . . . Harrow no such thing known. . . . Several kinds of red pepper are grown in greate abundance and enter largely into the californian cookery so much so as to nearly strangle a Forigner. . . . The forigners which have found their way to this country are mostly a poor discontented set of inhabitants and but little education hunting for a place as they [want] to live easy only a few of them have obtained land and commenced farming. . . ."

In this discontented mood—perhaps discontented with himself—Clyman finished up his business, which included a visit to Monterey and San Francisco and a bear hunt, and wrote to Captain John Charles Frémont proposing to assemble an armed party for a return to the States. Frémont, the Pathfinder, would have none of it. Ostensibly in California to explore, he intended to stay on and stir up a revolution; California would join itself to the States in one more year.

If not Frémont, then Lansford Hastings, a promoter who seems to have dreamed of establishing a republic in California with himself at its head and who was returning to the vicinity of Fort Laramie with 150 horses and a whirlwind of bad advice. Clyman joined Hastings at his camp on Bear Creek, above Johnson's Ranch in the foothills of the Sierra, on April 16, 1846, the same day the Donners and the Reeds left Springfield, Illinois, for Independence.

Crossing the Sierra Nevada in early spring was hard. It would be deadly to the Donners. Clyman recorded the descent from what would be called the Donner Pass with grim attention: "Here we commenced the desent over step Pricipices rough granit Rock covered in many places through the chasms with snow 15 or 20 feet deep and luckily for us we lost no horses allthough we had to force them down several perpendicular cliffs afer about 3 hours unpacking and repacking we succeeded in clearing the steepest pitches of the whole length of which is not one mile you may imagine that we felt a happy relief to find ourselves on bear ground onc more which we found at the head of truckys [later Donner] lake a small sheet of water about two miles in length and half a mile wide the N hill sides being intirely clear of snow but very little green vegitation made six miles and encamped at the foot of the Lake." That camp would become the major Donner camp; here unknowingly Clyman sets the stage.

Beyond Truckee Meadows, now Reno, Clyman lost his dog to a boiling spring—the thirsty dog, a water spaniel that had been with him since Wisconsin, jumped into the pool and "scalded himself allmost insantly to death"—and the loss further depressed him. He rode on through barrenness to the north fork of the Humboldt River, where wisdom decreed the party turn north but Hastings insisted they head east toward the Great Salt Lake. They did, to Pilot Peak, and looking eastward saw the terrible desert of salt that they would have to cross. "This is the [most] desolate country perhaps on the whole globe there not being one spear of vegitation and of course no kind of animal can subsist and it is not yet assertained to what extent this immince salt and sand plain can be south of whare we [are]." That day they traveled forty miles, the next day fourteen, the next day twenty. They succeeded in the crossing because they had horses. The Donner Party was slowed by oxen and wagons, and nearly failed. Clyman's advice to Reed had teeth. Onward to Laramie, where he delivered it, and we are back where we began.

Clyman's mood by now, after Laramie, is almost melancholy. His temperament was as equitable across the length of his life as any man who ever kept a journal, but what he saw on his long odyssey to Oregon and California and back again has left him wondering: wondering about his countrymen, wondering implicitly about himself. The West is no longer wilderness, and he is no longer young.

So, on the fourth of July, having crossed the south fork of the Platte River the day before, approaching Pawnee territory, he swings ambivalently between joy and depression and expresses a rare insecurity: "The sun arose in his usual mejestic splendor no firing of canon was heard no flags waving to the early morning Breeze. Nothing no nothing heard but the occasional howl of the wolf or the hoarse croak of the raven nothing seen But the green wide spread Prarie and the shallow wide spread river roling its turbed muddy waters far to the East the only relief is the on rising ground occasionally doted with a few stragling male Buffaloe and one Lonely Junt of a cotton wood Tree some miles down the stream the only occupant of a small low Island (not much veriety) O my country and my Country men the rich smiling surface of one and the gladsome Shouts of the other Here we are 8 men 2 women and one boy this day entering into an enimies country who if possible will Butcher every individual or at least strip us of every means of comfort or convenience and leave us to make our tiresome way to relief and this immediatly on your frontier and under the eye of a strong Militay post." Or is he remembering that long sore stumble from the Sweetwater two decades before? Or is he now, finally, after all his wandering, in the fullness of his years, experiencing a loneliness that in wandering he never felt?

His journal is almost ended. He gave us two more clues. On the fifteenth, on the east bank of the Blue River in what is now north-central Kansas, he encounters the grave of James Reed's mother-in-law and probes to the bone the meaning of the inexorable western advance. It is Clyman at his finest: "The stream affords some rich vallies of cultivateable land and the Bluffs are made of a fine lime rock with some good timber and numerous springs of clear cool water here I observed the grave of Mrs. Sarak Keys agead 70 yares who had departed this life in may last at her feet stands the stone that gives us this information This stone shews us that all ages and all sects are found to undertake this long tedious and even dangerous Journy for some unknown object never to be realized even by those the most fortunate and why because the human mind can never be satisfied never at rest allways on the strech for something new some strange novelty." Not climate or land, not patriotism or destiny, but a hunger for knowledge never satisfied, knowledge even of strange novelty, the insatiable human mind always on the stretch: Clyman's autobiography and the biography of his compatriots compressed into a narrow, roiling space. His distinction was to perceive calmly and with great thoroughness, and to come back and guide. Exploring an unexplored land is an act of creation, more rarely given and more interior, more profound, than all the artistic creations of the world. By exploration the land is made human, fit for habitation, its alienage drained. The explorer records its contours with an intimate stylus of muscle and nerve. He walks calmly through terror—for the unknown object is terrifying —and alleviates it, and families follow after to settle. His is an ecstasy —first knowledge—Clyman's was an ecstasy kept at genial peace.

If he was melancholy at Sarah Keyes's grave, it was because he knew the continent was bridged and his years of exploration over. That is the second clue. He has found his object, and in the next to last journal entry, back in Independence, perhaps not yet aware of the decision himself, he notes it down: "The [weather] was very warm and suffocating and in this particular you find a greate difference in the heat of the summer in California you find it cool and pleasant in the shade while here you find [it] hot and suffocating in [the] coolest place you can find." He is ready for cool and pleasant California now, ready at fifty-four to settle down.

The following year, Clyman closed out his land and business interests in Wisconsin and Illinois, and in 1848 he moved to California. He guided a large family there, the Mecombs of Indiana. He may have panned some gold, but he didn't linger at the mines. He bought land in the Napa Valley and took up farming near the sea and married, after due courtship, a small, pert woman of twenty-seven years, Hannah Mecombs.

His later years were peaceful, sweet and serene despite the loss of four of his five children to scarlet fever. In hours free from farming—he nurtured a trim and prosperous farm—he wrote verse, homely verse that could soar to sudden strength. More than once he celebrated the virtue of simplicity:

> Now while hot roles surround your plate
> Dont envy either wealth or state. . . .

He celebrated his home, his neighbor's garden, the seasons and their burden of death and renewal:

> But I mourn not for the flowers
> I mourn not for the grain
> I mourn not for the birds for they will come again
> The spring and the summer again will return
> Therefore for these I seace to mourn
> I have seen manhood both active and strong
> In the midst of ambition to death they were drawn . . .
> For the strength and the beauty of manhood I mourn. . . .

He kept his humor, even in "Hard Times":

> Live while you live This is my text
> Then feast to day, then starve the next . . .
> And if we live on bread alone
> We'll take the world without a groan
> But if our bread should chance to fail
> We'll Turn out Tramps or go to Jail.

He preserved a lyricism and a love of life that was, I think, the deep current of his years. "Decoration Day 1881":

Strew flowers oer the heros head
Who for your country fought & Bled
He fought for eaqul rights for all
Let raining flowers or him fall
He died your countrys life to save
Strew flowers oer the heroes grave

He died that year, 1881, peacefully. His wife and daughter survived him, but only by repute his name. His journals were finally edited, brilliantly, by Charles L. Camp and published in a limited edition in 1928, 330 copies, and 1,450 copies in a second limited edition in 1960.

"Not that he settled Kentucky or made a path to the west," writes William Carlos Williams of Daniel Boone in *In the American Grain*, " . . . but because of a descent to the ground of his desire was Boone's life important and does it remain still loaded with power—power to strengthen every form of energy that would be voluptuous, passionate, possessive in that place which he opened. . . . Filled with the wild beauty of the New World to overbrimming so long as he had what he desired, to bathe in, to explore always more deeply, to see, to feel, to touch—his instincts were contented." James Clyman explored a farther continent, "the rich smiling surface," as voluptuously as Boone a nearer. It grew up into him; he fitted it; with others he gave it to us; sensuously contented he gave it back himself. *Strew flowers oer the heroes grave.*

—December 1978

PRAIRIE SCHOONER

By GEORGE R. STEWART

Fortress, ambulance, boat, and home, the covered wagon deserves its place as the icon of our Westward expansion

One of life's ironies is that no generation knows what history will make of its doings, or upon what symbols the future will seize to sum up the past's greatest strivings. The bold, pioneering emigrants who led the way across the Great Plains would never have suspected that their symbol would be the humble and utilitarian vehicle in which they made their journey. As the long rifle and the log cabin stand for the settling of the first frontier across the Alleghenies, the sturdy covered wagon will forever call to mind the winning of the West.

To be sure, subsequent generations have somewhat distorted the reality. Most modern illustrations of covered wagons, for example, depict the huge and lumbering Conestoga, with its boat-shaped bed and sloping sides, its cover overhanging front and rear to give the whole a "swayback" appearance. Originating about 1750 in Pennsylvania, it flourished for a century. But it was almost never used beyond the Missouri except by freighters along the Santa Fe Trail. The Conestoga was uselessly heavy for the long pull to Oregon or California, and most of the few that were ill-advisedly taken on that journey had to be abandoned somewhere along the road. Physically, the emigrants' vehicles were about the same as the so-called movers' wagons that had taken earlier travelers on shorter, less heroic journeys. To go from one point to another farther west—from Connecticut to Ohio, say, or from Georgia to Alabama—the mover merely packed his wagon, hitched up, and went off over an already established road. He passed through a familiar type of country. He bought needed supplies at village stores. If a wagon broke down, or an ox died, or a child took sick, he could find whatever assistance was needed. The journey was seldom of more than a few hundred miles, and was not likely to require more than a month or six weeks.

Then, about 1840, the situation changed. Partly the change was geographical; partly political; partly, perhaps, psychological. Geographically, the central frontier now lay in Iowa and Missouri. Beyond it, in what is now eastern Nebraska and Kansas, there was some land that by the standards of the time was potentially good for farming. But this was a rather narrow belt, and in the eyes of a farmer of 1840 there was nothing much to be expected of it. Moreover, there was the political barrier, since Congress had established this nearer region as Indian territory. There was also room for settlers in Minnesota, but this was a cold and inhospitable region from the point of view of a southerner—and the cutting edge of the frontier was largely southern. Finally, by 1840 there had been a good deal of favorable publicity about both Oregon and California. The latter, to be sure, was still a part of Mexico. "But," anyone could say, "look at what happened in Texas!"

Thus the problem in 1840 was vastly different from that faced by earlier movers. The distance to be traversed totaled about two thousand miles, and it must be made in one jump, between winter and winter. The intervening country was unsettled, so that any emergency must be met with the materials at hand. There was nothing that could be called an established road for wagons. The country was not the well-watered and generally benign eastern terrain, but was largely mountainous and arid. The Indians had not already retreated before the advancing white man, but were wholly untamed; many were powerful and warlike.

Thus presented, the odds seem impossible. A saying later current in California begins, "The cowards never started." One would be inclined to go a little further and say, "Only the madmen started!" Yet start they did, and after some failures they were successful. Thus, rightly, an epic achievement placed the covered wagon in its present niche of glory.

Behind that achievement lay a psychic drive, a desire, almost a passion, to keep moving—and there was only one direction: westward! Many of the emigrants have left records of their motives. Negatively, they specify the wish to escape the agricultural depression that followed the panic of 1837, or the desire to get away from the malaria that raged throughout the Mississippi Valley. Positively, they mention the attractions of Oregon and California—the climate, the rich farmland, the chance to get ahead. Many went out of the sheer love of adventure—and an occasional one, like the absconding banker in the emigration of 1841, because he was fleeing the police.

The other motives seem to have been obscure to the emigrants themselves, but hindsight enables us to see them clearly. With many of these people, moving had become a habit, even an ancestral habit. Their journey to the Pacific Coast was not their first one. Joseph Chiles was only thirty-one years old when he headed west in '41, but he had already moved from Kentucky to Missouri. George Donner, captain of the ill-fated party in '46, had been born in North Carolina, but had lived in Kentucky, Indiana, Texas, and Illinois. Many, indeed, were Englishmen, Scotsmen, Irishmen, or Germans, to whom the Mississippi Valley was only a way stop. To all of these people, "going west" was as natural as swimming upstream is to a salmon.

Mere monotony and ennui must have been a second unconscious but important reason. After a man, or a woman, had vegetated on a frontier farm for ten years, sheer boredom would be likely to make the risks of the journey seem rather attractive. One man put it simply. He had always liked to fish, he said, and he had heard that there was good fishing in Oregon.

These, then, were the forces that drove men west. How would they get there?

First among those factors that made desire practical were the trappers and missionaries who had already gained some knowledge of the country. This knowledge, indeed, was far from complete. The idea that the mountain men "knew every foot of the West" is sheer nonsense, as the history of the migration makes startlingly clear. Still, what they did know was invaluable. They had even taken wheeled vehicles—carts, generally—a long way along the road.

The ignorance of the first emigrants and the comparative knowledge of these others is strikingly demonstrated by the situation in '41. The emigrants had assembled their wagons on the Missouri frontier, ready to start, when they discovered that not one of them had the slightest idea of what the route was. Luckily, they were able to attach themselves to a company of missionaries led by the famous Belgian Jesuit Pierre Jean De Smet and guided by "Broken Hand" Fitzpatrick, one of the famous mountain men. This guidance served the emigrants excellently for about half the distance, and then they were forced to press on into a country about which even the mountain men could tell them little—and with disastrous results. Still, however limited, the information and leadership supplied by the mountain men—Fitzpatrick, Joseph Walker, Caleb Greenwood, Isaac Hitchcock—were essential aids to the migration.

Granted the desire and some information, the frontier people next had to make the choice among three traditional modes of transportation: the cart, the pack train, or the wagon.

The two-wheeled cart seems scarcely to have been considered. At first glance, this seems curious. Carts were in use on many farms. They were strong and highly maneuverable. To the south, in Mexico, the *carreta* had served excellently during the magnificent push of the frontier northward. To the north, the so-called Red River cart, pulled by two or three mules in tandem, had become the standard means of transport on the Canadian prairies; American fur traders had adopted them, too, and had taken long trains of them as far as the Rocky Mountains.

But the cart was primarily adapted to the transportation of goods, not of families. And the emigration was primarily a family matter. A house on wheels was what was needed, and this the cart simply did not provide. Occasionally, when his team was reduced by death or exhaustion, some emigrant cut his wagon down to cart-size and thus was able to continue, but this is about all we hear of carts in the migration proper.

On the other hand, the pack train had its definite place. The mule, and less commonly the horse, already served as a pack animal for the mountain men, and during the migration, notably in 1849, was often employed. The advantages were obvious. The greater speed of movement meant carrying a smaller weight of supplies; the overall time could be cut by at least a month, and the dangerous stretches of desert could be traversed more quickly. Pack trains could ford streams and cross mountains and rough country much more easily than could wagons.

But for migrating families the disadvantages of the pack train were extreme. Most farm women could ride, but few could withstand the day-after-day jouncing that would add up to two thousand miles. If the wife was pregnant (and many set out in that condition), it was obviously foolish to attempt such a ride. Small children were equally unsuited to the pack train. And there were other handicaps. As an ox driver noted: "The pack-mule companies are a pitiful set of slaves. They have to sit on their mules roasting in the sun all day. If they get down to walk or rest themselves, they must be bothered leading the animals. When they stop at night, they must unpack everything. In the mornings they have to repack everything."

Finally, in the event of accident or severe illness to one of its members, the pack train faced disaster. In a wagon train a man with a broken leg or a case of dysentery could be trundled along. If such a situation arose in a pack train (and difficulties were only to be expected), there was no humane solution. The barbarous abandonment of comrades on the road, such as was recorded in '49 especially, must have resulted from this dilemma.

Pack-train companies, therefore, generally consisted of young men, willing to risk their chances of getting through quickly against their chances of not getting through at all.

There remained, then, the wagon. Its disadvantages were obvious—it was slow, heavy, cumbersome, subject to breakage, difficult to take across rivers, ravines, and mountains or through rocky country. But it served as a moving home, involved less daily unpacking and repacking, allowed more pounds to be transported per animal, supplied an ambulance for the sick, and—when properly placed in formation—offered a fortress against attack. Thus it became a standard vehicle of the westward migration.

The wagon consisted of three parts—body, top, and running gear. The body, or bed, was a wooden box—often, indeed, so-called—nine or ten feet long and about four feet wide. Generally the sides and ends, about two feet high, went up perpendicularly, but on wagons of the so-called Murphy type they flared outward, as if imitating the Conestoga in miniature. Many emigrants built a false floor twelve or fifteen inches from the bottom of the bed. The lower space was divided into compartments and used for storing reserve supplies. With this clutter out of the way, the false floor was used for ordinary living.

The wagon boxes served their purpose, were subjected to no particular strain, and gave no trouble. They are seldom mentioned at all in the diaries. The top or cover was the most conspicuous part of the whole outfit, and has supplied the distinguishing adjective in the phrase "covered wagon."

This top was of canvas (then usually called twill) or else of some cloth which had been waterproofed with paint or linseed oil. It was supported by bows of bent hickory, usually five or six in number. On the ordinary straight-sided bed these went straight up. There was thus no overhang at front or rear and no swayback. Flaps at the front and a "puckering string" at the back allowed ventilation or complete closing. Inside, the wagon was thus a tiny room, about ten by four, with sides partly of wood and partly of canvas rising almost perpendicularly to a height of four or five feet and then arching over. A man could stand upright along the center line. On wagons with flaring sides the bows followed the lines of the sides before arching over, producing a more cylindrical effect, with perhaps a front and rear overhang.

The top effectively protected goods and people against the weather. In an upset, it might be torn and some of the bows broken, and in thick forest country overhanging branches sometimes ripped the cloth, but there was not much country of that kind. When going head-on into the strong westerly winds of the plains, some companies put the tops down to reduce wind resistance. But on the whole the tops, like the boxes, produced few problems.

Not so the running gear. In the numerous booklets of advice surviving from the period, there is always the admonition that the wagons should be light and strong. Obviously the two qualities are somewhat incompatible, and even the best materials and workmanship could not always produce a vehicle that would get through without breakage.

By the mid-nineteenth century the construction of running gear had reached a high degree of sophistication. Readers of Oliver Wendell Holmes's poem about the one-hoss shay will remember the care and the many different woods that went into construction of the deacon's masterpiece. Though the emigrant's wagon might not have been that carefully constructed, it could well have had hubs of elm or Osage orange, spokes of oak, felloes of ash, and tongue and hounds of hickory. Moreover, the tires were of iron, and iron was used for reinforcement at critical points.

Yet lightness was essential too, or the teams would be worn out by the mere dead weight of the wagon. The result, as in the airplane decades later, was a compromise. In the end, breakages were frequent, precipitating many a crisis and many a tragedy.

Tongues snapped on sharp turns. Front axles gave way on sudden downdrops. These were the commonest accidents, and were taken almost as routine. "Occasionally we break a tongue or an axletree," wrote an emigrant of '49, as if thinking it all in the day's work. Some emigrants carried extra parts, but this added to the total weight, and so was doubtful practice. Usually the nearest suitable tree supplied timber, though "nearest" was sometimes not very near. In '46, when one of J. F. Reed's wagons suffered a broken axle near Great Salt Lake, his teamsters had to go fifteen miles to find a tree large enough to furnish a replacement. Not many were as unlucky as Ira Butterfield, who in 1861 snapped both axles at once while crossing Skull Creek. Fortunately he was with a large, well-equipped company, so that the accident meant only a twenty-four-hour delay, and not disaster.

Wheels, however, were irreplaceable; if one broke, the wagon might have to be abandoned. But usually, wheels were extremely tough and rarely gave way except in the roughest mountain passages. True, many a wheel gave trouble because of shrinkage in the dry air of the desert, but then wedges could be driven under the tire. Eventually the tire might have to be taken off, heated red-hot, and reset on the wheel.

Although we are not well informed as to the exact dimensions of most parts of the wagon, for one wheel at least there is a meticulous measurement, made by William Clayton, a Mormon of the 1847 migration. Having decided to make an odometer, he carefully measured a hind wheel, and found it to be fourteen feet, eight inches in circumference, or four feet, eight inches in height. This was undoubtedly a large wheel; the average one probably stood almost a foot lower.

Front wheels were always smaller than hind wheels, to make the vehicle more maneuverable. On many wagons they were not more than six inches lower, preventing turns exceeding about thirty degrees. An occasional one had wheels so low that they would pass under the bed, and thus permit turns of ninety degrees or more, but small wheels made for harder pulling.

The ordinary wagon had neither springs nor brakes, but an essential part of the equipment was the "tar bucket." Traditionally it hung from the rear axle but was carried elsewhere when fording streams or traversing rocky passages. The term "tar" must be taken as highly flexible. Often the bucket contained tar or resin mixed half-and-half with tallow. Since these contents were used steadily to grease the wheels and kingbolt, the supply decreased, and before the end of the journey the emigrants might be using anything that came handy and would serve. A Mormon in '47 shot a wolf, apparently for mere rifle practice. He found the animal to be exceptionally fat, so he tried the fat out and added wolf grease to the mixture in the bucket. Later these same Mormons found an oil seep, and filled their buckets at it—thus being among the first Americans to use a petroleum lubricant.*

Such was the wagon in which the average pioneer rode to Oregon or California. And since his comfort—and sometimes his very life—depended on it, a man had an appreciation for a good one. The youthful Isaac Jones Wistar, later a Union general, started for California early in '49. On the street in Cincinnati a wagon caught his eye, and he sized it up as he might a horse or a woman—"light, strong, short-coupled." Then and there, though the wagon was in use, he made an offer. Later, he was able to write proudly: "I made no mistake, for that wagon proved to be one of the only two of our entire outfit which survived the searching trials of the rocks and mountains, of alkali plains and desiccating deserts, and actually reached the Pacific Coast."

Granted, then, that the four-wheeled wagon was to be the vehicle of empire, how was it to be hauled? There were three possibilities—horses, mules, oxen.

Many modern representations to the contrary, the horse was really ruled out from the beginning. Though that noble animal could move faster than the ox and could pull more than the mule, he could not match the

---

* The Mexican *carreta*, by contrast, was never greased—a lack which Americans considered shiftless—and its screeching was notorious. An interesting etymological question is thus raised. Why, except by the ancient principle of *lucus a non lucendo*, should not the Americans, who were so fond of lubricant (instead of the Mexicans, who never touched the stuff), be called *greasers*?

ability of either to endure the long haul, the constant work, and the insufficient food. To do his best work, a horse needed grain, and grain could not be transported. Every train, indeed, had its riding horses, and these often got through. They were not, however, worked as hard as the team animals, and being more valuable, were given special care.

Only in the later years of the trail, from 1850 onward, did horse teams begin to be fairly common. By this time the road was better established, and swifter-moving transport had its advantages: grain was sometimes carried along so that the animals could have proper feed, at least during the first few weeks.

To give them their due, the horses seem to have stood up well enough then, when the journey was not so arduous.

As between the mule and the ox, however, there doubtless were endless arguments around the campfires, punctuated by tobacco juice spat into the embers.

"Mules move faster."

"Yes, but oxen can pull more."

"Oxen don't stampede so easy."

"Yes, but when they do, they run worse."

It could go on forever. Mules bogged down in mud, but could live on cottonwood bark. The Plains Indians would steal mules, but not oxen. Oxen, however, were more likely to get sore feet.

As a "mule man" we may cite William Johnston, who crossed in '49 under the pilotage of James Stewart, an old Santa Fe trader who loved mules and handled them expertly. As Johnston wrote, "Stewart's concern is always for the mules—he wastes no thought on the men." Thus coddled, the animals responded vigorously: "It was a noble sight to see those small, tough, earnest, honest Spanish mules, every nerve strained to the utmost, examples of obedience, and of duty performed under trying circumstances." As the result of Stewart's efficiency, the men could claim that theirs was the first wagon train to get to California that year—and the mules were still in good condition.

As an "ox man" we have Peter H. Burnett, of '43, later to be the first governor of the state of California. In his train were both oxen and mules, and he found the oxen "greatly superior." He narrated their virtues thus: "The ox is a most noble animal, patient, thrifty, durable, gentle, and easily driven, and does not run off. Those who come to this country will be in love with their oxen by the time they reach here."

The expression "dumb ox" is not found in the diaries of the migration. Oxen seem to have been at least as intelligent as mules and much more so than most horses. They were individually named, and had personality. J. Q. Thornton, of '46, may be called to testify. He has left us the names and characters of the eight in his four yoke. There was Brady, who died at South Pass. Thornton called Star and Golden "unreliable," though perhaps they were just intelligent and strong-willed: they used to hide in the thickets at yoking-up time, and then look innocent when found. Thornton mentioned four others as being good enough and "tolerably honest" —Sam, John, Tom, and Nig. But his love was Dick, who was all that an ox ought to be and was labeled in one word: "faultless."

The long-continued case of *Mule v. Ox*, as J. S. Holliday points out in his doctoral dissertation, could never really be decided.

Numerically, however, the verdict was in favor of the ox. In 1850 a count at Fort Laramie showed 36,116 oxen passing through and only 7,548 mules—and the latter figure apparently included pack-train animals. Quite possibly the deciding factor was the expense. One price list of the period gives the cost of a mule as $75 and of an ox as $25. Though the prices varied from year to year, the ratio probably remained about the same. In the long run the use of oxen became so prevalent that "ox-team emigrant" became a generic term.

The number of oxen to the wagon varied considerably. Four—that is, two yoke—was the minimum. Three yoke was perhaps the average, but four was not uncommon; six yoke was probably the maximum that could be handled on the twisting mountain roads. The bigger teams could haul heavier loads, and the strain on the individual animal was less. On the other hand, the more animals, the more work to guard and care for them, and pasturage had to be found.

Generally some of the cattle—especially in trains that included children —were milch cows. These were usually just driven along, but sometimes were put under the yoke. Extra cattle were usually taken along as spares and for a supply of fresh meat, though some people thought that such a herd was more nuisance than it was worth. The total number of cattle was thus regularly about twice that of the men and women.

The fate of most of these faithful beasts was a sad one. Rare was the ox or cow that lived to a quiet and respected old age on the deep-grassed pastures of Oregon or California. Many of them were slaughtered on the trail for beef, and we can scarcely even imagine that the best-loved ones were spared the longest. There was little place for sentiment on the desert, and the ox that began to fail was undoubtedly the one to be butchered. Remembering, however, that the ancient Greeks sacrificed an ox only after ritual weeping for the death of "man's companion," we can believe that on Goose Creek or along the Humboldt there were sad thoughts in him who did the deed, and tears in women's eyes, and the wailing of children—and perhaps the beef did not sit well, even on a very empty stomach. Yet this was another virtue of the ox, that he could thus yield food. Of course, the mule also could be, and was, eaten—but always with prejudice.

To every ox slaughtered, however, a dozen or a score died of disease, of drinking alkali water, of Digger arrows, of thirst, or of slow starvation and overwork. Notations on dead oxen are a monotonous feature of the diaries. J. Goldsborough Bruff of '49, a great counter, kept busy during five days on the Rabbit Hole and Black Rock stretch in northwestern Nevada, where someone had left a posted notice on a bit of broken axle: *"This is the place of destruction to team."* Bruff's total was 603 dead oxen.

Such mass catastrophe may not move us as much as the death of one known individual animal. We may quote James Mason's elegy of August 2, 1850, on Cassia Creek: "Here we lost old Sock. He died rather sudden. He was much lamented by the boys as he was our main Sanby [stand-by] at the start."

We should remember a little the faithful beasts that died. Sometimes they dropped under the yokes and were left lying. Often they were merely abandoned, standing, too weak to follow, left a prey to the wolves. Sometimes a kindly bullet finished the matter. Except for a little meat cut off for food, no one bothered with the carcasses; on some stretches they lay so thick that a blind man could have followed the trail by the stench. Then for a few years the skeletons lay dazzling white in the desert sun, pale white under the moon.

In reckoning the price of the land we might well be no less thoughtful of the animals than that kind-hearted Lord, the God of heaven, when he spoke to Jonah of saving the men—and beasts—of Nineveh. Yes, in that reckoning of the price we might remember his final words: " . . . and also much cattle."

Thus, in the end, the covered wagon is to be considered a kind of double symbol—the wagon itself and the oxen that pulled it. With this equipment the epic movement was accomplished.

In 1841 came the first attempts—unsuccessful, in that the emigrants were forced to leave their wagons and proceed on horseback or muleback or afoot. In '42, the wagons got through to Oregon. In '43 came the great migration to Oregon, and Joe Walker made a gallant try for California, though in the end he had to leave the three wagons. At last in '44 Elisha Stevens broke the Sierra barrier and took wagons across what would one day be called Donner Pass.

Thus, the emigration first pointed toward Oregon, and the term Oregon Trail has stuck. But from '46 onward, California tended to steal the show. In '49 came the cataclysm of the Gold Rush, and for a few years anyone going to Oregon was a curiosity. Indeed, '50 was probably bigger than '49, and, according to some, '52 was the biggest of all. The migration died down somewhat in the later fifties, and Oregon began to get a better share again.

The "trail" it was called—seldom the "road." The distinction is significant. "Trail," an Americanism in this sense, meant a route of travel that had been established merely by use. "Road" was reserved for something that had been definitely laid out and constructed, as was Lander's Road from the Sweetwater River to Fort Hall.

In many places you can still see the trail, sometimes even follow it for miles. Across the prairies and through the sagebrush there was easy going. Even there, however, the trail never runs straight, but always slightly sinuously—where the oxen of the lead team adjusted their course to inequalities of ground or growth, and where the following thousands, over two decades and more, kept to the same trace.

The trail never follows the contours of a hill, because the wagons had a high center of gravity and tipped easily, and because the making of a "dugway" was too much work for the emigrants. But almost no steepness of ascent deflects the trail, because the teams could be doubled. Nor does a sharp downgrade: one, two, or all four wheels could be locked, or the wagons could even be let down by ropes snubbed around trees. Lakes and swampy places could be skirted. Smaller streams were forded as a matter of course, the difficulty of getting down the bank into the stream often being greater than crossing it. Larger streams, up to about four feet in depth, could also be forded. Across the deeper ones the wagon beds were raised upon blocks set upon the axle and bolster, an uplift of about a foot being considered safe. The few streams that were still deeper had to be ferried, either by improvising rafts of logs or by calking and floating the wagon beds.

To generalize about the conditions of the long trek is difficult. The teams plodded monotonously westward. Heat, dust, and mosquitoes! Quarrels, resulting from too-long association in the same company! But the emigrants (they were always "emigrants" and never "immigrants") remembered good times also—dancing on the prairie, singing around the campfire, exciting chases after buffalo, breathtaking first sights of the wonders of this new land: snow-covered peaks in July, boiling springs, mirages, ancient volcanic craters.

Some of the wagon people were both strong in body and exuberant in personality, and these traits shine through in their diaries like lamps burning steadily. Such a one was Thomas Turnbull of '52. Nothing downed his optimism and enthusiasm. It was always: "the best feed I mostly ever saw . . . plenty of wood here . . . the handsomest roads I ever saw . . . the best grass of every kind I ever saw in the United States . . . the best road I ever saw, as level as a plank." (But, to be sure, he could also go to superlatives in the opposite direction: "Mosquitoes the worst I ever saw.")

Another one was Lydia Waters of '55. Everything had equal zest for her—driving oxen, or herding the loose cattle, or presiding at a childbirth. She seems quite in character when comparing a wattled hut to a champagne basket. Again, when she crossed the Forty-Mile Desert, she did not write of hell. But on arriving at the Truckee River, she could put it thus: "If I ever saw Heaven, I saw it there." Naturally she was the one who could write in retrospect: "There were many things to laugh about."

Danger and death, like battles in a war, were always a nerve-gnawing possibility, but they occurred on very few days. From year to year, according to the conditions, the face of peril changed. The first trains had the hardest time because of sheer geographical ignorance and the necessity of breaking trail. Partly by skill and stamina, partly by good luck, they got through with remarkably few casualties. The greatest disaster, that of the Donner party, did not come until '46, and then as the result of human duplicity and fallibility, and an early winter. The Forty-niners followed a crowded trail; their cattle died from lack of pasturage.

In '49 and several subsequent years, cholera rode the wagons out onto the plains, and there came to be a string of graves along the trail. In the later fifties there were difficulties with white desperadoes; one group captured an entire train, and sent the people off westward on foot.

And, of course, there were the Indian troubles, which gave rise to the greatest myth of the trail. The wagon train of fiction—in Hough's *Covered Wagon*, for instance—moves from one desperate Indian attack to another. The record, however, shows little of this sort. The trains actually moved only by favor and friendship of the powerful Plains tribes.

A moment's reflection should show that this must be true. When the Sioux, Cheyenne, and Arapaho really went to war in the sixties, they fought and sometimes defeated whole armies. What would they have done with a few emigrants?

The wagon trains seem to have interested and amused the Indians. (Doubtless, life in the tepee became monotonous at times.) Besides, the emigrants could be cajoled or scared into giving gifts, which the Indians probably considered a kind of tribute. The emigrants had much more trouble with the despised Diggers in the desert country than they ever had with the lordly Sioux. For one reason, the emigrants themselves were on their good behavior among the powerful tribes. No one in their right mind went about insulting or mistreating a Sioux in the land of his own strength. But in '45 a half-breed emigrant wantonly shot a Paiute. Probably there were also unrecorded atrocities, and from that time on there was trouble along the Humboldt. In '46 something of a pitched battle occurred, and one white man was killed. Emigrants learned not to camp within bowshot of the willows that fringed any stream. Otherwise they might wake up to find several oxen crippled by arrows, and perhaps the cattle guard himself laid out, agape at the morning sun. The emigrants were likely to retaliate by shooting on sight.

But this is all very different from the epic legend of the beleaguered wagon train. We all know the picture: the wagons are drawn up in a circle; from them the men fire their rifles; around the outside the mounted Indians circle on their horses, shooting with their bows.

How often did it happen? I have been reading covered-wagon records for a long time now. All I can say is that I have never found *one* such example.

We can see why, if we consider the realities. The Plains Indian was a good fighter, but he had no more liking than any other man for getting himself killed. Once a wagon train was in position, garrisoned by some determined riflemen, all the odds were against the Indian. The bullets far outranged his arrows, and he and his pony would have had little chance of even getting within bowshot of the enemy before being brought down. Why should any professional warrior thus gallop around and let himself be shot at? Why—especially when he could just as well wait until the wagon train was strung out helplessly on the trail? The beleaguered wagon train is one part of the story which I think we shall have to give over to the writers of fiction.

Otherwise, I can see no reason to start debunking the covered-wagon story. It might even be built up a little. Its very audacity—an attempt to cross two thousand miles of wilderness—is breathtaking. Those who love to sing the praises of free enterprise should make more of it. Here was free enterprise at its rawest. Until the later fifties, the travelers got no appreciable government aid, not even for exploration. Except for the Mormons, there is nothing that can be called large-scale corporate action. The unit was the family.

In this last connection we come to another source of continuing interest in the story. The frontier, in most of its dramatic history, is a man's world. Exploration, trapping, Indian fighting—here the women and children had no place except by accident. Even in the mining camp and on the cattle ranch, women were so scarce that the novelist usually had to go to great trouble to import a schoolmarm or someone's far-strayed daughter. But the families were right there in the covered wagons—the women and children often outnumbering the men. And family life kept right on. If there was a preacher along, like the Reverend Mr. Dunleavy in '46, he was likely to be called upon not only for funerals but also for marriages. From the number of children born less than nine months after the arrival of the trains in Oregon or California, we should judge that the amenities of family life were not neglected during the journey. On the other hand, pregnancy was no bar against setting out. The Stevens party of '44 arrived stronger by two than when it left. Even that first migration, of '41, had a woman along. This was Mrs. Nancy Kelsey, a ripe eighteen years of age, who stated roundly, "Where my husband goes, I can go," and went —taking a baby with her. So did others—the women following their men, the children with them.

The graves of all three lined the trail. In the early years the herd was milled over a new-made grave or the wagons run across it, so that the Indians could not find it and dig the body up. In later years, when there were more emigrants and few Indians, little headboards or crosses of wood stood along the trail. But certainly we should not accept that slogan, "The weak died by the way." Since when did Death refuse to take the strong? They may go to him first by their very strength. So, sometimes, we think, reading the words that the keepers of the diaries copied down.

M. De Morst, of Col: Ohio,
died Sep. 16th. 1849
Aged 50 years, Of Camp Fever.

Jno A. Dawson, St. Louis, Mo.
Died Oct. 1st, 1849
from eating a poisonous root at the spring.

Mr. Eastman;—
The deceased was killed by
an Indian arrow; Octr. 4th, 1849

Saml. A. Fitzzimmons, died from
effects of a wound received from a
bowie-knife in the hands of Geo. Symington
Aug. 25th 1849

Died: "Of cholera . . . Of cholera . . . Of cholera." (That most often!) *Died:* "Of accidental discharge of his gun." *Died:* (there was a doctor in this company) "Disease, Gastro Enterites Typhoid." *Died:* "Of drowning." Often, simply: "Died."

Died: "From Southport, Wisconsin . . . Late of Galena, Ill. . . . Of Selma, Alabama . . . From Yorkshire, England . . . Of Buffalo, N.Y." *Died:* sometimes with only the name for identification.

Died: "Mrs. Mildred Moss, wife of D. H. T. Moss." *Died* (as if registering in some last hotel): "Robert Gilmore and wife." *Died:* "Frederic William, son of James M. and Mary Fulkerson." *Died* (two weeks farther westward): "Mary, consort of J. M. Fulkerson."

Died: "Mrs. Emmaline Barnes, Amanda and Mahela Robbins, three sisters in one grave, Indiana."

There were graves without names: "The remains of a dead man dug up by wolves, and reburied."

Some were laid in their graves succinctly, perhaps as time pressed; some were granted a few more words:

Samuel McFarlin, of Wright Co Mo. died
27th Sep. 1849, of fever, Aged, 44 years.—
*May he rest peaceably in this
savage unknown country*

Jno. Hoover, died, June 18. 49
Aged 12 yrs. Rest in peace,
sweet boy, for thy travels are over.

As Virgil wrote: *Tantae molis erat Romanam condere gentem.* Yes, it was a great labor to establish the Roman people. So also it was to pass the barrier of mountains and deserts and thus round out the shape of a republic. The covered wagon stands as the symbol, and we should not forget its dead. "All this too was part of the price of the taking-over of the land."

—February 1962

A BARBARIAN
AT THE SHOGUN'S COURT

By EMILY HAHN

Our first consul to Japan thought the "lubricity of these people passes belief." The Japanese, in turn, told him to leave; spies and assassins trailed him; and his own government neglected him.

In 1853 an American named Townsend Harris, a merchant who was spending most of his time that year between Hong Kong and Shanghai, pricked up his ears at the news that his government was planning to force a way into Japan. Harris was no longer young, and his business in the Far East had lately been so bad that he had been forced to sell his trading vessel. Consequently, he felt the strain of uncertainty, and wondered if there might not be a place for him on Commodore Perry's staff. He wrote and offered his services, but Perry wouldn't consider adding him to the force. Like many other civilians who wrote to the Commodore, he was turned down. His opportunity was to come, but that would be later.

Harris was only one of many people living under a strain. The Japanese too were badly worried, though few outside their tight little islands realized it. They were not supposed to be aware even that the Perry expedition was in preparation, but they knew more about the outside world than the world could have guessed, especially about the way things were going for their neighbor, China. Like the Chinese, the Japanese believed firmly in the policy of isolation. As an island empire, Japan naturally found it easier to carry out this policy. Besides, as a smaller country she wasn't apt to tempt imperialists quite as strongly. Only the Dutch, of all the eager European traders, had been successful in gaining a foothold in Japan. Even so, they were kept immured on the little island of Deshima, off Nagasaki, where they had to live without their wives and families; they were forbidden to set foot on the main islands.

The Chinese had tried to take just as high a hand with foreign merchants, but they hadn't got away with it. It is true that for years the British, American, French, and other "barbarians" were forced to keep to their allotted space in "factories" outside the walls of Canton, but they were getting out of hand, and for several years had been troublesome. Led by the British, they had fought the Chinese, gravely shaking the old order. The barbarians now had footholds in various ports along the coast, and were constantly trying to get into the interior, a state of affairs shocking not only to China but to her near neighbor, Japan. Yedo—modern Tokyo—as well as Peking was concerned when the British demanded audience of the Emperor of China. Yedo knew that the barbarians would certainly soon cast their covetous eyes further.

And now it was on the verge of happening. Only one thing had not been foreseen in Japan—that America, rather than Britain, would be the intruder. Usually it was the British who took the offensive, but in 1853 they considered themselves too seriously enmeshed in China to branch out in a new direction. Meanwhile the Americans, who had recently fulfilled their "manifest destiny" and consolidated their hold upon their own Pacific coast, were looking for new, commercially profitable outlets for their expansive spirit.

So Commodore Perry sailed into Yedo Bay, and he was unimpeded. Fortunately for the Japanese, when the thing happened at last they were too stunned to offer resistance, and no bloodshed resulted. Perry realized he was breaking into a world that had withstood encroachment for more than two centuries, and he was tactful. He managed to handle everything without violence, emerging in 1854 with the preliminary Treaty of Kanagawa. What he did not bring out with him was a full understanding of the situation regarding Japan's governing body, but this was no wonder: its complexity takes a long time to appreciate.

Early in the seventeenth century, the emperor had been supplanted in power, but not actually in name, by chieftains, called shoguns, of the Tokugawa clan. They ruled the country from Yedo. The imperial dynasty survived, but more as a figurehead; the emperor lived in Kyoto and was revered as a religious symbol, but it was the shogun who really ran the country. The subtlety of this arrangement was difficult for any Westerner to grasp, and Perry made the mistake of considering the emperor, or mikado, a nonentity. Certainly the shogunate imposed on the people a pervasive regimentation, but nothing human is completely biddable, and there were occasional waves of dissidence in Japan. Among the ruling classes, even in Yedo, some nobles harbored a secret, deep-seated loyalty to the mikado.

Perry also overestimated the ignorance of the Japanese regarding the West. High-ranking Japanese knew a good deal more about the barbarian world than the barbarians knew of Japan. For years they had demanded Western books and newspapers from the Dutch at Deshima, and had made the merchants write them annual reports about the world outside. Of course, when the time came and they had to deal with foreigners, it suited them to pretend complete ignorance. Ignorance furnished a wonderful excuse for delay, deceit, and rudeness, but they usually knew quite a lot more than they admitted. A case in point is the famous miniature railway brought by Commodore Perry as a present to the Japanese. Obligingly, his hosts gazed in wonder and delight as it was demonstrated for them, and Perry felt like a combination Santa Claus and conjurer. Yet the court had really known about the railway all the time. The courtiers kept up with the *Illustrated London News*—the Shogun was a regular subscriber—which had carried the story, complete with pictures, while the expedition was fitting out.

Perry's American soul would have abhorred any suggestion that the expedition's aim was to acquire territory. He had large plans of a different sort and hoped that the Treaty of Kanagawa would be the beginning of much more maritime commerce for America in the Pacific. It was not merely a question, he felt, of persuading the Japanese to treat castaways nicely and permit foreign ships to refuel and provision at their ports. The United States should aim at something much more ambitious, at "establishing a foothold in this quarter of the globe," wrote Perry hopefully, "as a measure of positive necessity in the sustainment of our maritime rights in the east." For a start, he suggested, Americans might settle on the Bonins, the Ryukyus, and Formosa.

But the American administration was not carried along on the wave of Perry's enthusiasm. There was still much undeveloped territory within the boundaries of the United States; Washington saw no reason to take on responsibilities in such remote regions. Naturally, however, American merchants in the East were of Perry's way of thinking. One clause in the Treaty of Kanagawa caught their attention: it provided that an American consul general for Japan be appointed to live there in a little port town called Shimoda, less than a hundred miles from Yedo. Though they knew nothing about Shimoda, the merchants felt that much depended on the man who got the job. They didn't want some rank amateur from Washington; this consul general should be someone familiar with their particular problems. There was ample time to discuss the matter, for the consulate was not to open until at least eighteen months after the treaty was concluded in March, 1854.

In the meantime, each of the other Western nations—Great Britain, Holland, and Russia—hurried to draw up preliminary conventions, as such first documents were called, and none had found it easy. The Japanese evinced such strong reluctance to admit facts that were obvious, backed down so consistently on agreements, and dragged their feet so often, that the foreigners became indignant and watchful. Clearly, the man who became the first American consul at Shimoda would have no easy task.

Townsend Harris was not born into a privileged class, and he was self-educated, having wrested his knowledge from books in the time he could spare from making a living. He went to work in a New York shop at the age of thirteen, but when he left New York for the Orient in 1849, at the age of forty-five, he was a leading citizen—a member of the Chamber of Commerce and former president of the Board of Education. Harris had managed to learn French, Spanish, and Italian, but he always regretted having missed formal schooling, and to his mind his most noteworthy feat had been persuading the Board of Education to set up a school for poor boys. This, the New York Free Academy, later became the City College of New York, now a part of the City University.

Men of forty-five do not usually start out afresh, but Harris's mother had recently died and his home was broken up—he had never married. Furthermore, owing to the general business depression, the china-importing company on which he depended was at low water. Gossip had it that Townsend Harris was drinking too much. He quarrelled with a brother who was his partner and lived in England, selecting the china the company imported. But if Townsend Harris was on the way to becoming an alcoholic, he seems to have snapped out of it; no trace of such a weakness appears in his later career. He cut loose from New York in 1849 by acquiring part interest in a ship, and sailed for the Far East by way of California; there he bought over the whole ship and continued on his way.

For several years, trading in an easygoing manner, Harris wandered about the East—the Philippines, the Malay Peninsula, India, Hong Kong, and such China ports as were open to foreigners, making many friends among Western merchants and diplomats as he went. But Eastern trade too was subject to depressions, especially at this time, when the Chinese were resisting the attempts of the Western barbarians to penetrate the country in order to buy and sell. After a few years of doing well enough, Harris found himself hard up. In 1853, casting about for a change, he sent his name to Washington as candidate for an American consular post either at Hong Kong or Canton: both places, as he knew, happened to be vacant. Letters took months to arrive, however, and Harris was still waiting for a reply when he heard about Perry's expedition and unsuccessfully tried to join it. In spite of the rejection, Perry may have retained a good impression of Harris. There is an unsubstantiated story that the Commodore later put in a good word for him in Washington, when the selection of a man for Shimoda was being made.

In the meantime Harris was again disappointed, however, for when the reply to his consular application arrived from Washington, he found he had been given Ningpo instead of Canton or Hong Kong. Ningpo was a small post with a wretched salary. Before turning it down, Harris was able to read the newly published Treaty of Kanagawa made with Japan by Perry. Since a consulate general was to be established in Shimoda, he reflected, why shouldn't he be the consul there? He asked around among his local friends, and got in touch with old acquaintances in America. They all promised to support him, so he hurried home to press the application in person.

One of his New York friends, John J. Cisco, wrote to Secretary of State William L. Marcy, and to President Pierce, saying that Townsend Harris was a "sound, reliable and influential Democrat." Pierce and Marcy hesitated. Perhaps they had been told, by men supporting other candidates, of Harris's temporary lapse from grace and sobriety back in 1849, but in the end it all worked out well. Harris was interviewed by both officials, got the appointment, and in October, 1855, set out for Shimoda with orders to negotiate a full-fledged commercial treaty. On the way, however, he made a side trip to Siam, for he had been directed to renegotiate an existing commercial treaty with King Mongkut.

Harris was at first amicably disposed toward the native officials in Siam. Yet before he left Bangkok his sympathy with the Siamese evaporated. He found the ministers, in his own words, tricky, venal, and untruthful. Harris had to be patient yet stubborn, feeling his way, guessing when it was time to show righteous anger and when it was better to take it all in silence. He had a talent for this sort of thing, an instinctive understanding of psychology, and a genuine interest in the customs and philosophies of unfamiliar cultures. But his health was not strong, and before he had completed the Siamese mission he was very irritable. When the treaty had at last been hammered out he wrote, "I hope this is the end of my troubles with this false, base and cowardly people. To lie is here the rule from the Kings downward. Truth is never used when they can avoid it. A nation of slaves . . . I never met a people like them. . . . The proper way to negotiate with the Siamese is to send two or three men-of-war. . . ."

On June 1, 1856, having accomplished his assignment in Siam, Harris left for Japan. He took along Henry C. J. Heusken, a Dutch-American whom he had hired in New York, for he expected that Heusken's command of Japanese and Dutch—which language the Japanese used for all diplomatic exchanges with Westerners—would prove indispensable to his success. The *San Jacinto*, Commodore Armstrong aboard, which had already taken Harris on his errand to Siam, carried them, and after a troublesome voyage of nine days they anchored outside Shimoda Harbor on August 21, 1856. "My future brought vividly to mind," Harris wrote at his first sight of Japanese territory. "Mental and social isolation on the one hand, and on the other are important public duties. . . . A people almost unknown to the world is to be examined and reported on in its social, moral and political state; the productions of the country . . . to be ascertained; the products of the industry of the country found out, and its capacity for commercial intercourse. . . . A new and difficult language to be learned." On the next day: "I shall be the first recognized agent from a civilized power to reside in Japan . . . I hope I may so conduct myself that I may have honorable mention in the histories which will be written on Japan and its future destiny."

After so much trembling anticipation, the reality must have been chilling. Shimoda was far from prepossessing—a forlorn little town with an awkward harbor among stony hills. From the ship Townsend Harris sent letters, one to the governor of Shimoda and another addressed to the Minister of Foreign Affairs, an official title that did not yet exist, as a matter of fact, but he didn't know that. A rather disheartening silence was the result, but at least a pilot came out and led in the *San Jacinto*, and then, after quite a wait, some Japanese came out to the ship to greet him. Though courteous, they were vague. They said that the governor was ill, and they couldn't tell Harris anything about the house he was expecting to be ready for him. After a few days of diplomatic maneuvers, the American discovered that the Japanese really had been taken by surprise when Harris appeared, for the treaty clause regarding the formal establishment of diplomatic relations had been mistranslated; they understood it to mean that a consul general should live in Japan if *both* nations wished it, and not, as the original version had it, *either* nation. The Japanese were plunged into dismayed confusion by his presence, and since they could never move a finger without directions from higher up, they posted off urgent demands for orders from Yedo. Until the reply arrived they could do nothing but their naïve best to discourage the American and somehow get him to go away. Surely he didn't really want to live in Japan, they said anxiously. Really, he wouldn't care at all for Shimoda, ruined as it was by the great earthquake of the previous year. Still less would he care for Yedo, they assured him. Like Shimoda, it was in ruins.

"The foregoing is the substance of the remarks and propositions, made and renewed and changed in every possible form and manner during three mortal hours," Harris noted. "I need hardly write that I courteously but firmly negatived all their propositions." After Siam it came to him as second nature to handle the situation. He didn't swagger or bellow or make outright demands, but he wouldn't give way, and he must have made a good impression in spite of everything. But making a good impression was not enough, and during the months that followed he had to summon all his reserves of courtesy and firmness. Still, he persevered. In spite of all the delays the Japanese could think of, he finally moved ashore into a temple they reluctantly prepared as a residence for him, and put up a flagstaff with the Stars and Stripes. Time after time the Japanese would "civilly ask me to go away"; each time, just as civilly, he refused. Every so often he proposed sending a message direct to the Tycoon, or Shogun, at Yedo, a gambit that never failed to send the officials into fits of mingled embarrassment and fear. That was not the way business was done in Japan, he gathered.

For the time being, Harris had to be content with writing more letters and trusting that his unwilling hosts would send them on to the Tycoon. When he had settled in ashore, the *San Jacinto* sailed away, Armstrong promising him that they would call in again in six months. Harris and Heusken were on their own in Japan.

Perhaps it could have been worse; there is no doubt that it could have been better. A drawing by Heusken gives an idea of the bleak landscape the two men saw from their front door—sharp peaks against the sky, and the hillsides empty of anything cozy or familiar to their Western eyes. "Every inch of ground is cultivated, as the ground is very [rolling], rising up in pinnacles of lava or indurated clay ejected from volcanoes, and so steep as not to be arable," wrote Harris in his journal. " . . . The views . . . present a series of serrated hills rising up to fifteen hundred feet high—most of which are covered with fir, spruce, and cedar trees." He was not long in planting such vegetables as he had brought seeds for. He also set up a pigeon cote for the four pairs of birds that had come with him, but most of all he and Heusken were busy trying to make the temple into a residence rather than a mere camping-out place. Japanese temples are simplicity itself, fragile and scarcely walled off from the elements. Harris's house was drafty and cold. Life in it was a long battle against unwelcome guests such as mosquitoes—"*enormous* in size"—crickets that sounded like a miniature locomotive at full speed; bats; an "enormous *tête de mort* spider; the legs extended five and a half inches as the insect stood"; and large rats "in numbers, running about the house." The platoons of cockroaches that pestered him, he admitted ruefully, he had brought himself, though unwittingly, from the *San Jacinto*. All the other vermin were local.

Heusken never became a real companion. Harris often complained in his journal of the Dutchman's laziness and lack of quick intelligence, though it must be admitted that two men plunged into such an existence were almost bound to get on each other's nerves, no matter how pleasant they might both be.

Little by little the Shimoda officials got used to the Consul General. Perhaps they even enjoyed his company. Certainly they appreciated the liquor he gave them when they called—the brandy, liqueurs, and champagne—but in their soft way they continued to oppose him, ignore his requests, and render him as uncomfortable as they dared. If cornered, they made specious excuses. A crisis arose when Harris attempted to hire two Japanese servants and found himself frustrated by delays, excuses, and new excuses that contradicted the old. In the Far East this is accepted as the ordinary courteous way of saying no, but Townsend Harris refused to accept it in that spirit. He reacted to barefaced lying in a simple, Western way. On one occasion he picked up the Japanese stove, or *hibachi*, that was doing its customary poor job of heating the room, and threw it violently against the wall. It was a gesture that shocked and scared the Japanese, and has lived on in Shimoda legend. "Had a *flare-up* with the officials, who told me some egregious lies in answer to some requests I made," he noted. "I told them plainly I knew they lied; that, if they wished me to have any confidence in them, they must always speak the truth . . . that to tell lies to me was treating me like a child. . . ."

Whether such pious exhortations had any moral effect on the hearers is a moot point, but they knew the Consul's obvious anger could not in safety be ignored. The Japanese too were good psychologists; they knew they had gone far enough for the time being. Harris got his domestic help, but other difficulties sprang up, hydra-headed. His people couldn't buy fruit for him in the market. He was getting nowhere in his attempt to fix the wildly unrealistic rate of exchange for Japanese currency. Worst of all was the presence in his compound of uniformed, armed men who had set up camp there and would not go away. The Japanese argued that they were merely protecting him; they were spies, Harris retorted, and must go.

Harris's health suffered under the conditions in which he lived. He complained of "total loss of appetite, want of sleep and depression of spirits," and decided that the root of the trouble was lack of exercise and too much smoking. Accordingly he stopped smoking and set out on long daily walks, up and down hill, literally taking in his stride as much as ten or twelve miles a day. It is hard to say what ailed him. No doubt several maladies contributed to his final breakdown—malaria, dysentery, and other diseases common to the country—but that breakdown was still two years away. At one time his face turned bright red and he felt great discomfort; he finally decided that he was victim to St. Anthony's fire, or erysipelas. In general, however, the trouble was with his stomach, and he attributed it to his inadequate diet.

To take his mind off himself and his irritation with Heusken and the Japanese, Harris walked and made notes of the countryside and its fauna and flora, which he later wrote up in the journal: descriptions of the terraces on the hillsides, planted with rice—the clay-and-wattle houses, so unlike the stone and brick buildings of his own country—the sudden terrible winds, one of which almost knocked over his temple, and destroyed a hundred houses in Shimoda—the mills, and springs, and quarries. "There are deer, wolves, hares and wild monkeys among the hills of this place," he wrote on October 27, 1856. "I was much moved today on finding in the woods a bachelor's button. This humble flower, with its sweet perfume, brought up so many home associations that I was inclined to be homesick—*i.e.*, miserable for the space of an hour. I am trying to learn Japanese."

The natives were very clean, he observed; everyone bathed every day. Yet, like other Westerners, he was startled by the custom of mixed bathing "in a state of perfect nudity. I cannot account for so indelicate a proceeding on the part of a people so generally correct. I am assured, however, that it is not considered as dangerous to the chastity of their females; on the contrary, they urge that this very exposure lessens the desire that owes much of its power to mystery and difficulty."

The loneliness was relieved for a bit when, in November, Shimoda was visited by a Russian corvette come to bring a present of a schooner to the Shogun from Czar Alexander. Harris was charmed with the officers. "Their dress was neat, and their address superior . . . They spoke French very well. I never passed a more agreeable evening." Furthermore, they had opinions in which he heartily concurred. "They speak in high terms of French generals and soldiers. . . . The English, on the contrary, they put directly opposite: generals without skill, and men without one of the prerequisites of a soldier, except mere bull-dog courage; that to deprive an English army of its full supply of food and comfortable quarters is to demoralize it; that an English soldier dreads an attack on his belly more than a blow aimed at his head."

In January, 1857, Harris decided to take a firmer line with his reluctant hosts. In small ways he had at last made some progress, but nothing whatever seemed to move toward the completion or even the initiation of his chief mission, the commercial treaty. Had his letters really been forwarded to Yedo at all? When needled, the Japanese blithely assured him that they had, and that a reply had arrived that very day. Unfortunately it soon became clear that it was a word-of-mouth reply, and Harris would have none of it. He had to have things in writing, he explained. As the interview became more acrimonious, Harris blew up. He did not have to simulate loss of temper: he was really very ill, and it was simply a matter of letting go. A number of old grievances came into the picture, too. Why were those spies still camping on his land? He'd had enough of it; he would write to his government about it. Why hadn't justice yet been visited on that bully who accosted Mr. Heusken on the road and flourished a sword at him? And another thing, what about the currency rate? The Japanese tried to soothe him, speaking of friendliness: he scoffed bitterly. Pretty talk, when he had never yet been invited to one of their houses!

Flinging out of the Town Hall where the interview had taken place, the Consul General returned to his temple. Ordinarily he would have been appeased when he found the men in uniform really leaving at last, breaking up their camp quite hastily. But he was too angry to calm down. Next day he wrote at length to the Minister of Foreign Affairs—whoever might be doing that work—in Yedo, stating that it was imperative that they get started on the treaty, for Japan was threatened by another government, and even now it might be too late. It seems clear that he was thinking of Sir John Bowring and the British fleet in Hong Kong, which Sir John wanted to use against Japan, but Harris didn't say so. Instead he repeated his warning, said that haste was of the essence, and ended by stating that he simply must go to Yedo soon in order to discuss this danger.

Again alarmed, the unhappy officials sent one of their number to Yedo, and when he came back it was obvious that the wind had changed. For one thing, he brought Harris a choice sword blade, which was a signal honor. For another, he invited the Consul General to his house for a meal, and at the lunch he did his best to make all allowances for foreign peculiarities. He had gone to considerable trouble to get chairs and tables. After the meal Townsend Harris made his first acquaintance with the tea ceremony. "The prettiest toy tea-making apparatus I ever saw," he commented. It would have been perfect if the Japanese hadn't begun to talk about sex. They *would* do this, and their attitude toward the subject always upset Harris. "The lubricity of these people passes belief. The moment business is over, the one and only subject on which they dare converse comes up. I was asked a hundred different questions about American females, as whether single women dressed differently from the married ones, etc., etc.; but I will not soil my paper with the greater part of them, but I clearly perceived that there are particulars that enter into Japanese marriage contracts that are disgusting beyond belief. Bingo-no-Kami informed me that one of the Vice-Governors was specially charged with the duty of supplying me with female society, and said if I fancied any woman the Vice-Governor would procure her for me, etc., etc., etc."

Perhaps Harris, in spite of his expressed abhorrence, took the vice-governor up on this offer. At least the Japanese firmly believed he did, and that he acquired a geisha named Okichi-San as a mistress. The story adds that Heusken got a girl too, and both women remained in the consulate for the rest of the time the Americans were there. No trace of this innovation can be found in the official records, which is natural even if the tale is true, but if it isn't, Shimoda's flourishing tourist industry today is founded on a whopping lie. Okichi is a heroine in song, story, and drama; visitors to Shimoda—which is still very uninteresting, apart from this aspect—are taken on a tour to see her birthplace and her tomb. At least five famous plays have been written about Okichi, and they are all tragedies. She is supposed to have suffered so much unpopularity among her own people because of her association with the American that she took to drink, and finally drowned herself. It is all very Japanese, but then, Okichi *was* a Japanese girl—that is, if she existed.*

In March of 1857 an American ship stopped by, bringing a bit of mail and some newspapers of the previous November, from which Harris learned that James Buchanan was the new President. Months followed with no word at all from the outside world, until he became very uneasy. On May 5, he wrote: "It is now eight months and three days since the *San Jacinto* left here. Commodore Armstrong promised me he would be here again in six months. I am a prey to unceasing anxiety. I have not heard a word from Washington since I left the United States, say October, 1855. What can be the cause of this prolonged absence of an American man-of-war? . . . I am only nine days distant from Hongkong, yet I am more isolated than any American official in any part of the world. . . . The absence of a man-of-war also tends to weaken my influence with the Japanese. They have yielded nothing except from *fear*. . . ."

He did not know, of course, that the *San Jacinto* could not be spared from China at that time, since all available American craft were aiding the British in the capture of Canton. He wrote another passage in the same vein two weeks later. They were anxious days altogether, for the ice seemed to have cracked at last. One of the Shimoda officials opened proceedings by making a definite gesture toward discussing a preliminary commercial treaty, and many meetings followed at which Harris laid down the fundamental provisions of such a paper. He scarcely dared hope that all this would lead to a genuine agreement, but so it was. Quite suddenly, on June 8, he announced, "I have at last carried every point triumphantly with the Japanese, and have got everything conceded that I have been

---

* In 1958 Hollywood, never averse to perpetuating a myth, particularly when romance is involved, made a movie based on this one: *The Barbarian and the Geisha*. It may still be seen from time to time on the Late—or Late Late—Show.—*Ed.*

negotiating for since last September. Among my papers will be found a copy of the Convention. . . ." He lists the items briefly: Nagasaki was to be opened to American ships; Americans could reside permanently in Shimoda and Hakodate and could maintain a vice-consul at Hakodate; the currency exchange was settled at one-third the rate Harris had hitherto paid; extraterritoriality was granted to Americans in Japan; the consul general could go where he wished and was to be helped in various specified ways.

It was, of course, merely the preliminary, not the firm treaty he hoped to negotiate in Yedo, but it had been a necessary step, and represented much toil and grief. Of course he wanted to notify Washington, but there was no way to do it, until, in September, an American ship appeared —the sloop *Portsmouth* from Shanghai, under the command of Captain Andrew Hull Foote.

But had the *Portsmouth* been sent on purpose to set Harris's mind at rest? Not a bit of it. She was there, the Captain explained triumphantly, in spite of his sailing orders; he had been told by Commodore Armstrong in Shanghai (in *Shanghai?* Why, that was only seven days away, reflected Townsend Harris angrily) not to go to Shimoda on any account. But the Captain had wanted to go, and had used "some medical ruse" as an excuse. The main drawback, of course, was that he hadn't brought Mr. Harris's mail, since he hadn't known when he left Hong Kong that he would be coming to Shimoda. And he couldn't stay a moment longer than was absolutely necessary. He was able to explain the *San Jacinto*'s nonappearance, but Townsend Harris could still not bring himself to forgive Commodore Armstrong, who had, after all, found it possible to send ships to other ports, for other Americans, during that time.

All that consoled the Consul was that Captain Foote had reached Shimoda, where he could read the new convention with his own eyes and appreciate what Harris had done. He declared himself delighted. Everyone in the European community would be surprised and pleased with Harris, Foote said, as soon as he got back to Shanghai and told them. Then, after replenishing the consulate's larder, which had been pretty well cleaned out for months, on September 12 he sailed away. Harris noted, "The visit of the ship has thrown me into a state of intense excitement, as may well be imagined. I have not had three hours of consecutive sleep since the signal was fired announcing her approach."

However, fresh news kept Harris from brooding on his wrongs—the best news possible: Yedo had at last consented to receive him, and permit him to present his President's letter to the Tycoon himself. He and Heusken were in a flurry of preparation and coaching from the Japanese. "The manner in which I am to salute the Ziogoon is to be the same as in the courts of Europe—*i.e.*, three bows. They made a faint request that I would prostrate myself and 'knock-head,' but I told them the mentioning of such a thing was offensive to me." Harris's refusal to kowtow could not have occasioned any real surprise in Japan. It was already well known that other Europeans were not so obliging in that respect as the Dutch, who for years had not jibbed at knocking their heads on the floor or even prostrating themselves before Japanese rulers, as long as they could go on trading.

Meticulously the Americans and the Japanese planned the details of the cavalcade and its itinerary. Harris would not take any of the Chinese servants he had brought with him from Hong Kong, he decided, since the Japanese hated the Chinese. "I shall . . . be accompanied by Mr. Heusken and my two Japanese house servants. . . . My own train will consist of some forty porters bearing my luggage, cooking utensils, bedding, etc., etc., and by the following, who will all have the arms of the United States on their dresses, as the coat-of-arms is worn by the Japanese,—*viz.*,

20 *norimon* (sedan chair) bearers	1 sword
12 guardsmen	2 swords
2 standard bearers	2 swords
2 shoe and fan bearers	2 swords
2 grooms	1 sword
2 quinine (Gokenin) or commanders of the foregoing	

All except the grooms and *norimon* bearers are to have silk dresses. I am to be attended by the Vice-Governor of Shimoda, the Mayor of Kakizaki, the Commissary of Shimoda, and by the private secretary of Dewa-no-Kami. They will have, together, a tail of some one hundred and fifty or more men, so that the whole train will form a body of not far from two hundred and fifty." In fact there were one hundred more than that.

On November 23 the cavalcade started out in all its splendor. A Japanese captain rode ahead as avant-courier, with three boys walking ahead of him, each carrying a bamboo rod with fluttering strips of paper at the tip, calling out in Japanese as they walked, "Sit down, sit down!" They sounded quite musical, said Harris. Next came the United States flag and two of Harris's guards; then Harris on horseback with six guards, followed by his *norimon*, a famous chair that he had ordered made extra-large to accommodate his long Western legs, and the *norimon*'s bearers; then his bedding and clothes packages, along with presents for the Court. Next came Heusken riding his horse, then his attendants, and so on. The Japanese followed with their own trains. Everything was very splendid and beautiful. Even Harris's packages were dressed up, with a tiny bamboo staff standing on each, a pennon fluttering from it.

They moved slowly, but Yedo was not really far away, and within a few days they had arrived. Harris learned, just in time to avoid committing a solecism, that Japanese nobles never entered the city on horseback. He had rather expected to cut a fine figure on his horse—both he and Heusken were much admired in Shimoda for their horsemanship—but if it wasn't done, it wasn't, and he and the Dutchman prudently scrambled into their *norimons* before passing through the city gate.

The days that followed were full of quaint ceremony and courtesy. For instance, Harris was served his meals on a tray with legs—a small, Japanese-type table—but the legs were longer than most, so that his food was higher in the air than that of ordinary people. On December 7 he had an audience with the Tycoon. It was purely formal. The American stood upright in the presence of the Tycoon, though all the other men in the room were down on their knees. He was a little surprised at the severe plainness of the ruler's dress, but admitted that he could not see the Shogun's elaborate headdress properly, owing to the fact that he was standing up and the Shogun was seated within a cubicle, the roof of which cut off Harris's view.

Even getting to Yedo had been a remarkable feat, especially for a man in ill health like Townsend Harris. But his work had only begun. There was still the formal treaty to draw up. Harris therefore remained in Yedo, and had discussions every day with the men who had been nominated to handle the matter. Ultimately their group was boiled down to two commissioners. Here, at the hub of their universe, he could see for himself some of the difficulties he had only heard of, sketchily, in Shimoda. It became evident that the nobles were divided on this matter of trading with the world outside. One group saw the way things were inevitably going and had resigned themselves to change, but other, diehard princes fought the treaty fiercely all the way. Even the willing ones had to learn everything from the beginning.

For one thing, he had to tell them very clearly and simply why trade was a good thing for the common people of a country, and how it affected a nation's economy. The nobles were not trained to think in terms of change; they resisted the concept almost instinctively. Having been convinced of the desirability of commercial expansion—if they ever were convinced of it, which is doubtful—they had next to learn the workings of trade. For days Harris wrangled over one point: the Japanese wanted to insert in the treaty a clause forbidding Americans to live in Yedo or even spend a night there. Where were they to live then, asked Harris? Why, in Kanagawa, said the commissioners. But Kanagawa was more than eighteen miles from Yedo, which meant that an American wishing to do business would have to ride more than thirty-seven miles a day.

Harris explained that this was impossible. He explained it over and over, but his hearers took a lot of persuading. There were also arguments about open harbors, tariffs, currency regulations—a list of difficulties that seemed endless. Harris had to argue for days before they would give him a map of Yedo, which he had to promise never to give away or even permit to be copied. And the donors were the *friendly* nobles.

He thought the commissioners were talking nonsense when they expressed anxiety for his personal safety at Yedo. In vain they told him of the dangers he was running from hot-headed reactionaries of the *ronin* class, those bullies who carried arms and had nothing to occupy their time. Harris listened skeptically when his champions told him that a plot against him had been discovered, and that three *ronin* sworn to assassinate him had been apprehended. A large body of men now patrolled his neighborhood, said a friendly prince, and guarded his house night and day. But Harris pooh-poohed it all as a trick.

Time after time the negotiations were held up, but they really struck a rock over Harris's demand that Japan open three more ports in addition to Shimoda and Hakodate. He pointed out that none of the open ports would be on the west coast, but the Japanese, though willing to alter a few of the arrangements they had agreed to, remained obdurate on this, and he had to give up. Again, when he suggested that Americans be allowed to reside in Kyoto, he struck a sensitive nerve. Plainly, the commissioners were shocked. Kyoto was where the Emperor lived, and was a religious stronghold. Any attempt to open it to foreign residents would excite a rebellion. Very well, said Harris, then how about Osaka? The arguments droned on.

But all the while, in China, the Westerners were pursuing their war and making headway. The Japanese were aware of this—more so, indeed, than Townsend Harris—and the knowledge had a strong influence on their dealings with him. Even so, the conservatives still insisted that the whole idea be scrapped, some nobles announcing with passionate conviction that they would rather die fighting than give in to the West and open up the country. "I am told the Prince of Ca-ga goes on like a lunatic about the Treaty," wrote Harris, but he was also told that the Tycoon was in favor of it, saying he was convinced it was for the good of the country, as well he might, for the Western allies were now preparing to move north to Tientsin.

It was often said that Townsend Harris's greatest accomplishment in winning the treaty was that he did the whole thing by peaceful negotiation, without the help of armed forces. Americans said they were proud of him because he showed the world how much better was their national way of doing things than that of the "brutal" British. This is perhaps oversimplified. Harris did behave well. He was a peaceable man by nature. He showed remarkable willingness to accept the customs and appreciate the philosophy of an alien civilization. He was a good man, and the Japanese realized it, and gave him his due for probity and courage. But he did have help from armed forces, for he was supported by the threat of what was going on in China, and there were times when, pushed to extremes, he consciously used that strength by hinting of similar action in Japan if he failed in his mission.

They were delicate hints, but they sufficed. When Harris returned to Shimoda in March, the treaty was complete. Its ratification was delayed by a political struggle between the conservatives and the progressive faction at the Shogun's court, with both groups seeking the support of the Mikado. The Emperor sided with the conservatives, thus weakening the Shogun's position significantly; nevertheless the progressives pushed through the ratification of the treaty.

Now that his task was over, Townsend Harris fell so ill that he nearly died. For days he was delirious, and the Japanese at Yedo were very much concerned. At the Shogun's behest they sent the best doctors in town, who had orders to cure the American, or else. Harris was showered with messages and gifts. By the time he had fooled everyone and recovered, news had arrived at last that Washington knew what he had done and thought highly of him for it. Early in 1859 he was promoted to the rank of Minister Resident and moved to Yedo, where his colleagues from other Western nations joined him in forming a diplomatic corps. It was not an easy life; the resentment felt by much of the population for foreigners was not a mere figment of imagination, as Harris had thought, and *ronin* roamed the streets at night, hoping for the chance to kill a Westerner. In eighteen months seven assassinations of that sort took place.

One night in January, 1861, Heusken, now serving as interpreter for the American legation, was going home on foot in the dark, and was set upon and murdered. There was great outcry from the Western diplomatic staffs, but Townsend Harris refused to join it. Cool and reasonable, he declared it was Heusken's own fault for ignoring the rules of common sense. He himself, said Harris, never walked in Yedo after dark, and Mr. Heusken should have known better. The consequent indignation of his brother diplomats can be imagined. At best, feeling runs high in a small community like theirs that considers itself in danger from surrounding natives, and they were already jealous of their *doyen* because he obviously enjoyed the esteem of the Japanese. Sir Rutherford Alcock, the British minister, was especially incensed when the American pronounced himself satisfied by the indemnity of $10,000 paid by the Japanese to Heusken's mother. Harris should have asked for more, said Alcock, who put the rates for assassinated Britons at anything from $20,000 to $50,000, and later pushed the ante up to £110,000 in gold when one of his officials was murdered.

After the death of Heusken the diplomats demanded that the Shogun's people guarantee their safety by enforcing tighter security measures, and they moved out of Yedo until the guarantee was received. Only Townsend Harris refused to leave. His colleagues were even more angry when they found that he had, on the other hand, suggested that the Westerners should waive their right to live in Yedo as from the first of 1862. He must have realized the truth, that the authorities could not hold down the people no matter how many guarantees of security they might give, but the other foreigners would not believe it. That July, in 1861, a band of fourteen *ronin* attacked the British legation, and about a year later another mob attacked again and burned it down. The British built a new one, but in February of 1863, after Harris had gone home from Japan, the *ronin* burned that one too, and later did the same to the American legation, at which point the diplomatic corps gave up for good and moved to Yokohama. But all that came later.

Rutherford Alcock implied that Townsend Harris toadied to the Japanese, but the American's attitude is easy to understand. He thought the soft approach better, that was all. He would never have called himself a saber-rattler, and probably preferred to dismiss the occasions when he had been guilty of a rattle or two as of no importance. In any case, he did not have much more time to annoy Sir Rutherford. Word arrived that Lincoln had been elected President in 1860, and Townsend Harris, that staunch Democrat, would not serve under a Republican. In July of '61 he handed in his resignation, and as soon as his successor, Robert H. Pruyn, arrived the following year, Townsend Harris went home to New York.

For the rest of his life he stayed there, though he took an occasional trip—to Europe with his nephew Brander Matthews, and to Florida once or twice. Almost every day in New York he went to the Union Club at the corner of Twenty-second Street and Fifth Avenue. He didn't die until 1878, so he must have seen what Alcock said about him in the book *The Capital of the Tycoon*, because that was published in 1863. "The thorough-going and clear-headed American," Alcock called him with manifest self-control that slipped a few pages later when the writer referred to Harris's methods of negotiating his treaty. Harris had only to point to the British in China, said Alcock, to have his way on everything. "This was a venerable *tour de maître*, to use and turn to such account the belligerent allies, holding them *in terrorum* over the Japanese—and to do this in such a way that should give the United States all the benefit and the credit, without any of the cost of great expeditions;—while to Great Britain was left only the odium of a reputation at once bellicose and exigeant.

Alcock could have saved his complaints. In the long run the United States ceded her position in Japan by default, and Britain was able to take over. By that time the country was altogether changed by revolution. The shogunate's influence had begun to slip the moment Perry's ships appeared in Yedo Bay, and soon after Townsend Harris went home, everything exploded. "Honor the Mikado and expel the barbarians!" was the rallying cry of the rebels, and the unrest grew rapidly into all-out civil war. Hastily, Britain, Holland, and France sent ships to protect their nationals. The Shogun's princes tried in vain to keep order, but in October of 1867 the last Tokugawa shogun fled his palace in Yedo, and the Imperial restoration soon followed. But the foreigners, and their great ships that had been the original cause of the whole debacle, remained.

—June 1964

A FAMILY DIVIDED

By JANET STEVENSON

The Grimké sisters forsook their heritage to fight for abolition. Then, many years later, their brother's great sin came back to haunt them.

It was 1868, five years after the Emancipation Proclamation, three years after the end of the war that made it stick and the death of the President who wrote it.

Most of the old prewar abolitionist periodicals had ceased to publish. A few—among them the *Anti-Slavery Standard*—still circulated among a select list of old subscribers which included Sarah Grimké and her sister Angelina Grimké Weld, whose famous eyewitness account of American slavery had shaken the pillars of the southern Establishment and roused the northern conscience thirty years before.

In the January issue of the *Standard*, Angelina saw an article signed by a Professor Bowers of Lincoln University in Oxford, Pennsylvania, an institution devoted to the higher education of Negro youth. The article reported in enthusiastic terms an oration delivered "by a young man but a few years removed from the chains of servitude, whose erudition and felicity of expression would be remarkable in any student in any college . . ." The name of the young man was Archibald Henry Grimké.

Angelina had never heard of him, and neither had Sarah. Both were made profoundly uneasy by the coincidence of the name, and—characteristically—Angelina decided to take direct action. On February 15, 1868, she wrote to the young man: "In a recent number of the *Anti-Slavery Standard* I saw a notice of a meeting at Lincoln University of a Literary Society at which a young gentleman of the name of Grimké deliver'd an address. My maiden name was Grimké. I am the youngest sister of Dr. John Grimké of So. Carolina, & as this name is a very uncommon one it has occurred to me that you had been probably the slave of one of my brothers & I feel a great desire to know all about you.

"My sister Sarah & myself have long been interested in the Anti-Slavery cause, & left Charleston nearly 40 years ago, because we could not endure to live in the midst of the oppressions of Slavery. Will you therefore be so kind as to tell us who you are, whether you have any brothers & sisters —who your parents were etc. etc. . . ."

Angelina showed her letter to her husband and to Sarah, but she did not ask their consent to the sending of it. All three knew what alternative answers to her questions were possible, and what Angelina stood to lose if the worst of those possibilities materialized. She was jeopardizing her physical and mental health—if not her life—by the inquiry. But no one in that household would have dreamed of trying to dissuade Angelina from any course of action she had determined was right.

Angelina was at the time sixty-three years old, a frail, gray gentlewoman with a soft southern voice who taught English and history at Dr. Dio Lewis's boarding school for young ladies in Lexington, Massachusetts. Mr. Weld also taught at the school. Vigorous and keen even at sixty-five, he enjoyed the fame of having once been the most effective abolitionist orator in the country. It was almost forgotten—and quite hard to believe—that his wife had been equally effective and even more famous (or infamous) in her day. Wendell Phillips, who had been considered the great orator of abolitionism, said of Angelina, "She swept the cords of the human heart with a power that has never been surpassed and rarely equalled. . . . She won Massachusetts for abolition—and it was never lost again."

But all that was far in the past. Since the evening—just two days after her marriage—when she spoke in Pennsylvania Hall in Philadelphia and outfaced the mob that had come to burn it, Angelina had neither addressed nor attended a public meeting. It was accepted by those who knew her history that she had "shattered her nervous system" and worn out her physical strength in the service of abolition, and that the bearing of three children had completed the wreck. She lived a "half life," a long anticlimax to her brief apocalyptic career, avoiding every sort of strain or excitement at the peril of a "nervous prostration" that would put her to bed in a darkened room for weeks at a time. She had earned the right to—if not a taste for—peace.

Angelina was born in 1805, the youngest daughter of a well-to-do Charleston judge. She was in her early twenties, following the conventional course of a young lady of quality, when the preaching of a Presbyterian evangelist awoke in her a desire for a deeper commitment to the spiritual life. She left her family's fashionable Episcopalian church and began to seek salvation through good works—in the main, through efforts to alleviate the suffering of Negro slaves. In this she was probably guided by the example of her elder sister Sarah who had already turned against slavery and gone north to join the Society of Friends.

But if Angelina began by following in the footsteps of Sarah (who was twelve years older, and whom she called her "sister-mother"), she soon caught up with and passed her. During the most important years of their adult lives—from about 1830 to 1838—it was Angelina who led and Sarah who followed—on a path that led straight into the heart of the storm.

Even before 1829, when Angelina went to Philadelphia to join Sarah in her meeting, she had become a Quaker in her own mind. She had sought out and been accepted by the only two Quakers in Charleston —two old men who met for silent worship every Sunday "in a dingy little meetinghouse on the outskirts of the city." She had adopted the gray garb and the plain speech of the Quakers, because she felt that to do so in Charleston would indicate a protest against slavery. But the going had been hard and the results disappointing. She expected to find in the city of William Penn a richer spiritual companionship and a higher level of ethical behavior, especially on the question of slavery. "What was her amazement to find that the Religious Society of Friends, whose moral courage in rebuke of slavery had put to shame all other churches—that *they* had installed the 'Negro pew' as a permanent fixture in their house of worship!"*

Sarah had silently endured this painful contradiction between the Friends' "witness" and their practice for the several years she had lived among them. But Angelina encouraged her to rebel. "Whenever, in city or country, they entered a church having a Negro seat (then they *all* had), they found their way to it," Weld later wrote of the sisters, "and shared with the occupants the spurning thus meted out to them."

What distressed Angelina even more was the ban on all discussion of the subject with the meeting. Slavery had become so controversial that it threatened the unity of the group, which most Friends felt had to be preserved at any cost. But she did her best to abide by the ban and other accepted rules of conduct while she undertook a course of study and meditation designed to prepare her for a "ministry" (in the Quaker sense of that term). She was advised to turn her mind inward and to seek the "peace that passeth understanding."

* These and many other passages quoted here referring to Angelina's history are taken from a sketch written by her husband after her death, and privately published by George E. Ellis of Boston, under the title *In Memory*. The passages quoting Wendell Phillips and Elizur Wright are taken from the same source.

But the times were not propitious for such peace. In January, 1831, William Lloyd Garrison published the first issue of the *Liberator*, with its bold declaration that "I will be as harsh as truth, and as uncompromising as justice . . . I will not equivocate—I will not excuse—I will not retreat a single inch—AND I WILL BE HEARD."

Angelina may have been one of his first subscribers. At any rate, she was a regular reader by 1835, when, as Wendell Phillips said, "our cities roared with riot, when William Lloyd Garrison was dragged through the streets . . . and the hatred toward the abolitionists was so bitter and merciless that the friends of Lovejoy [an Illinois antislavery publicist killed by a mob] left his grave long unmarked."

Angelina read of Garrison's ordeal, and she read his own "Appeal"—not for mercy, but for the freedom to go on agitating. She was so moved that she sat down and wrote him a letter. It was a strong statement of support, castigating his critics, including "those high in church and state [who] secretly approve and rejoice over the violent measures [of mobs]. . . . the ground you stand on is holy ground. . . . If you surrender it, the hope of the slave is extinguished and the chains of his servitude will be strengthened one-hundred-fold. But let no man take your crown, success is certain as the rising of tomorrow's sun . . .

"If persecution will abolish slavery, it will also purify the church, and who that stands between the porch and the altar, weeping over the sins of the people, would not be willing to suffer, if such immense good will be accomplished?"

She waited several days and prayed for divine guidance before she "felt easy" to send the letter. Once it was committed to the post office, however, she "felt anxiety removed, and as though I had nothing more to do with it."

Garrison printed the whole of it, without comment except to note that the writer was "the daughter of a prominent South Carolina family, a sister of the late Thomas S. Grimké [a well-known reformer in other fields than abolition and leader of the fight against nullification and secession in his state in 1830], and a member of the Philadelphia Society of Friends."

The conservative Friends in Angelina's meeting were outraged. Many believed that her references to "the church" were directed at her own. Even Sarah was shocked at her flouting of the rule which required a Friend to submit any article intended for publication to the elders of his meeting. Angelina was urged to apologize publicly, and to explain that Garrison had printed her letter in the *Liberator* without her permission. She refused.

Sometime during the next few months, Mrs. Grimké wrote to Sarah and Angelina that she was making her will. Angelina, who had exhausted herself and her mother in a futile attempt to convert the latter to abolitionism, wrote back, begging that all Mrs. Grimké's slaves be included in the portions to be bequeathed to her two errant daughters. Surprisingly, Mrs. Grimké obliged. Upon her death, four more were to be added to the growing list of Grimké slaves that Angelina, Sarah, and a third sister—Mrs. Anna Frost of Philadelphia—had freed and assisted in setting themselves up in the North.

But these and similar small worthy acts were not what Angelina felt she was "being kept for." From girlhood on, she had had intimations that some great work was in store for her. That it was to be connected with the abolition of slavery she was now convinced. But just what it was to be had not yet been made clear.

During the summer of 1836, which she spent with a family of Quakers named Parker in Shrewsbury, New Jersey, she was moved to write "An Appeal to the Christian Women of the South." It was a long, reasoned argument—documented with scriptural references—urging them to act in their own interest and that of their sons, brothers, fathers, and sweethearts while there was yet time.

Elizur Wright, one of the officers of the American Anti-Slavery Society in New York, remembered years afterward that "when the storm of public indignation . . . was black upon us, and we were comparatively only a handful, there appeared . . . this mild, modest, soft-speaking woman, then in the prime of her beauty, delicate as lily-of-the-valley. She placed in my hands a roll of manuscript, beautifully written. . . . It was like a patch of blue sky breaking through that storm cloud."

The society published the "Appeal" as a pamphlet of thirty-six pages, priced at six and a half cents a copy (four dollars for 100), and mailed quantities of them to the South. The reaction of the city of Charleston to this message from its Cassandra launched Angelina on what was to be her great work.

In Charleston and other southern cities, the "Appeal" was officially condemned by the postal authorities and publicly burned, but a mere bonfire did not please Charlestonians. A rumor spread that Angelina intended to return to spend the winter with her mother. The mayor himself called upon Mrs. Grimké and "desired her to inform her daughter that the police had been instructed to prevent her landing . . . that if she should elude their vigilance and go on shore she would be arrested and imprisoned." Friends wrote Angelina, warning her that if she defied the mayor's threat she could not hope to escape personal violence at the hands of a mob.

Here, perhaps, was an opportunity for the martyrdom Angelina had told Garrison she would welcome. She was tempted to try it, "helping thus to reveal to the free states that slavery defies and tramples alike constitutions and laws, and thus outlaws itself." But she could not bring herself to expose her mother and unsympathetic siblings to the same risks, and decided not to go.

While the clamor attendant upon this semiofficial exile was still audible, it occurred to the leaders of the Anti-Slavery Society that if Angelina could bring about such repercussions by writing to the women of the South, she might do even better by speaking to women of the North. The society sent her an official invitation to come to New York in order "to hold meetings in private parlors, with Christian women, on the subject of slavery."

Angelina showed the invitation to Sarah, with the comment that she felt it to be "God's call."

Sarah was appalled. She begged her sister to consider: that she had never spoken in public, even in meeting, where women were as free as men to speak when the spirit moved them; that she had always had a "morbid shrinking from whatever would make her conspicuous" and she would be going among strangers, wearing the strange garb of the Quakers and speaking in their strange plain speech; that prejudice against women's speaking in public was as widespread as prejudice against abolitionism; and, finally, that if she were to act without the sanction of "the Meeting for Sufferings," her mission might be regarded as "disorderly" and she might be disowned by the Quakers.

Angelina replied that she could not in good conscience ask leave to do something she had already made up her mind to do, that it would be "a grief to me to grieve them [her fellow Friends]," and very unpleasant to be disowned, "but misery to be self-disowned." Sarah's other warnings she brushed aside, asserting that if she was indeed meant to do this thing, strength would be granted her. "The responsibility is thrust upon me," she said. "I cannot thrust it off."

In the end, Sarah capitulated and offered to go with her. Angelina wrote to the Anti-Slavery Society in New York, accepting their invitation but declining the small salary they had offered: she and her sister would travel at their own expense.

It was at this turning point in her life that Angelina met Theodore Weld. For over a year the Lion of the West, as Garrison called him, had been engaged in a one-man crusade to win the whole territory west of the Hudson and north of the Ohio for abolitionism. But he had overstrained and finally ruined his voice. When the Grimké sisters arrived in New York City in November, 1836, Weld was presiding over an "agent's convention," training a corps of young agitators who were to be sent into the field to take up where he had had to leave off. By special permission, Angelina and Sarah were admitted to these training sessions.

Weld also did some private coaching of the sisters in advance of the first meeting at which they were to speak, a gathering of female abolitionists. In Angelina he discovered a natural talent that needed no training; instead, he helped her with advice about the logical buttressing of the truths she felt so intuitively. For Sarah he could not do much: her delivery was slow, halting, monotonous in tone. But she was a clear thinker, and did not the Book of Ecclesiastes say, "Two are better than one; because they have a good reward for their labor"?

As the day of their first meeting drew closer, opposition to it grew sharper. No public announcement of the sisters' participation had been made, but rumor ran, and interest was so high it was decided to hold the meeting not in a private home but in the vestry of a Baptist church. Angry anonymous letters were dropped in the mailbox of the house where the sisters were lodging. More than one staunch male abolitionist called to advise them to default and spare the already embattled cause the ridicule to which they were exposing it. On the morning of the meeting itself, leaflets were distributed calling on the respectable community to turn out "and teach a lesson to [these] notoriety-seeking females."

The sisters went to Weld for counsel.

"Slavery is on trial," he told them. "The people of the North are the court. You are summoned as witnesses to sustain the prosecution." And although he was fighting certain tender feelings for Angelina which he considered downright wicked in a man in his position—and would have been glad to insulate himself by putting as much distance between them as possible—he escorted her to the very door of the vestry room.

He did not, of course, attend the meeting. The presence of men, even ordained ministers, in any place where women spoke in anything but a conversational tone made an audience "promiscuous" and would have created more scandal. The all-female audience—some 300 crowded into a church vestry that accommodated 100 comfortably—were greeted by the church's minister, who prayed for the success of their enterprise and then beat a quick retreat.

Maria Chapman (a leader in the women's section of the abolition movement from its beginnings) introduced Angelina to the gathering. Angelina rose—and turned deathly pale. What Sarah had foreseen and dreaded was coming to pass: she was paralyzed with stage fright, unable to utter a word. She had not written out her text, and the few notes she had jotted were of no help because her eyes were swimming. All she could gasp out—too faintly to be heard beyond the first row—were some dimly remembered snatches of Scripture: "If I hold my peace, the stone would cry out of the wall, and the beam of the timber would answer it." Then she bowed her head and prayed.

Within moments she was answered by a sudden surge of strength. Words flooded into her mind. It was the first of a series of apparent miracles that occurred at intervals during the fifteen months that followed. The gift of tongues descended upon her. Wendell Phillips later described the scene: "It was not only the testimony of one most competent to speak, but it was the profound religious experience of one who had broken out of the charmed circle. . . . It was when you saw she was opening some secret record of her own experience that painful silence and breathless interest told the deep effect . . . her words were making on minds that afterwards never rested in their work."

When Angelina had finished speaking, Sarah rose and added her testimony, in corroboration. She spoke poorly, but so earnestly that she was not without effectiveness. Before that first meeting was adjourned, a second was announced. It overflowed the vestry room and had to be moved into the church itself. There was a new chorus of outrage, in and out of the pulpit, but the witness of two southern women, once slave-owners themselves, made an impact that could not be shouted down. The sluggish liberal conscience was stirring at last.

The first Female Anti-Slavery Society in America was formed, and Angelina and Sarah were appointed agents. Calls for the sisters came in from all over the city, and then the state. They spoke at first only to women, but more and more often men appeared at their meetings. At first they were asked politely to leave, but one evening in a Negro church in Poughkeepsie the sisters "felt easy" to speak to "our colored brethren on whose behalf we are laboring."

Next they responded to calls for their services in New England. Men came to the meetings in greater numbers now, and did not always leave when asked. One evening in Lynn, Massachusetts, the sisters spoke to "over a thousand people, packed into the meeting house at some danger to the joists of the flooring." There were more men than women in the crowd. "Yet the heavens did not open to rain thunderbolts on their impious heads!" the local editor remarked, with irony.

What the heavens did not do, some of the New England clergy tried to do for them. Certain clergymen whose congregations had invited the sisters threatened to resign. Sometimes when the sisters arrived at a meeting, they found the church door locked, and had to adjourn to a hall, a home, or a barn. On one occasion, small boys pelted them with apples.

One Reverend Nehemiah Adams grew so incensed that he composed a pastoral letter that was passed as a resolution by the General Association of Evangelical Clergymen, meeting in Brookfield, Massachusetts. It invited attention to "the dangers which at present seem to threaten the female character with widespread and permanent injury. When a woman assumes the place and tone of man as a public reformer, our care and protection of her seems unnecessary; we put ourselves in self-defense against her; she yields that power which God has given her for protection, and her character becomes unnatural. . . ."

The poet John Greenleaf Whittier, who had become a devoted friend of the sisters, was moved to one of his rare satirical verses in rebuttal:

So this is all! the utmost reach
  Of priestly power the mind to fetter,
When laymen think, when women preach,
  A war of words, a "Pastoral Letter"!

And now came an attack from an unexpected direction. Catherine Beecher, daughter of the great Lyman, sister of Henry and of Harriet (who had yet to write her best-selling *Uncle Tom's Cabin*), wrote a cutting criticism of the Grimkés' radicalism. Angelina took time off—it must have been stolen from sleep, for she had no idle hours—to answer Miss Beecher in a series of thirteen letters, which Garrison published in the *Liberator*. She was neither gentle nor tactful. "Oh, my very soul is grieved," she wrote at the end of one, "to find a Northern woman thus 'sewing pillows under all armholes,' framing and fitting soft excuses for the slaveholder's conscience, whilst with the same pen she is *professing* to regard slavery as a sin. An open enemy is better than such a secret friend!"

Sarah was also writing letters to the newspapers that winter. Her series on "The Equality of the Sexes and the Condition of Women," which appeared in the Boston *Spectator* and later as a small book, stated her view of the case so forthrightly that fence-straddlers were forced to take sides. But those who were in opposition were not in time to damp the fire the sisters were kindling. "When the Grimkés went through New England, such was the overpowering influence with which they swept the churches that men did not remember the dogma [that women should be silent] till after they had gone. When they left, and the spell weakened, some woke to the idea that it was wrong for a woman to speak to a public assembly. The wakening of old prejudice to its combat with new convictions was a fearful storm."

In February of 1838, before the storm broke, Angelina wound up her New England tour with the most extraordinary exploit of all: she addressed the legislature of the Commonwealth of Massachusetts.

The occasion was the presentation of some petitions to Congress asking that slavery be abolished in the District of Columbia. Ex-President John Quincy Adams, now a member of the House of Representatives, was waging a battle for the right to petition, and the New England abolitionists had labored long and hard to amass an impressive number of signatures. It occurred to Henry Stanton (who was later to marry the redoubtable feminist Elizabeth Cady) that since many of the signatures had been obtained at the meetings where Angelina spoke, she might be one of the speakers at the official presentation ceremony before the state legislature. He made the suggestion half in jest, for of course no woman had ever been heard there, and it was not likely that permission for such an innovation would be granted. But Angelina accepted the challenge.

She applied to the legislators for permission to address them not as a representative of the Anti-Slavery Society "but as a woman, as a Southerner, as a moral being." The permission was granted, and she was scheduled to speak after the last of the male abolitionists.

When she and Sarah arrived at the statehouse that day, they could hardly get up the stairs, and the legislative chamber itself was so packed that they had to walk over the tops of desks to reach their seats. All the women abolitionists had come, depending on Angelina to "do something important for women, for our country, and for the whole world." The moment was upon her, but the spirit was not stirring. She suddenly went so pale that Sarah thought she would faint.

Angelina bowed her head and prayed, but nothing happened. Her mind was still empty, except of wonder at the arrogance that had prompted her to volunteer. She was called upon by the chairman of the Committee on Petitions, and she managed to get to her feet and begin.

Her voice was so weak that the chairman could not hear her, and he interrupted to invite her to come forward and stand at his secretary's desk, which occupied a raised platform just below his own desk and which faced the chamber. Angelina obeyed.

At this point a great hissing broke out at one of the doors in the rear of the room. Opposition always had a calming effect on Angelina, and she began again, with more firmness than before. But since her back was still to the chairman, and he still could not hear her, he interrupted once more to invite her to come up to his place, which was that of the speaker of the house. By the time she and Sarah (who would not leave her) were "ensconced in the seats of the mighty," Angelina had entirely recovered her self-confidence.

Her address lasted two hours. Her voice was as strong as a man's, but toward the end the quiet was so complete that she could have been heard if she had only whispered. At adjournment time she had not covered all her points, so she asked for permission to be heard again. Permission was granted and a day set for her second appearance.. Again she spoke to a packed house, this time without hecklers. Again she did not finish, and a third hearing was arranged.

By this time public interest was so intense that the galleries of the statehouse could not begin to hold all who wanted to hear her. The Odeon Theatre was rented, and a series of six lectures by Angelina was announced.

Nothing like this had ever happened in the history of abolitionism, and news of it spread to other cities—among them Philadelphia, where Angelina was going to be married as soon as she caught her breath and quieted her overwrought nerves.

This marriage and the love affair that led up to it was the best-kept secret of its day. Theodore Weld had been "half in love" with Miss Angelina from the day he read her letter to Garrison in the *Liberator*, and his first glimpse of her in the flesh completed the conquest. But he had taken a vow—only half in earnest, but in public—never to marry "until the last slave was free." Also, he was penniless, in broken health, and without a profession that gave him hope of being able to support a wife—least of all a wife who had been raised in the lap of southern luxury. He did his stern best to root what he regarded as this "guilty passion" out of his heart, and his apparent coldness forced Angelina to keep her own feelings concealed.

But they had kept up a correspondence all during her New England campaign. Weld wrote to both sisters, advising them on tactics and arguments, and subjecting their behavior, their characters, and their writings to the most critical scrutiny—a practice among devout persons which went by the euphemism "being faithful."

Gradually Weld's attacks on Angelina began to reflect the depth of his feeling—in reverse. At last he went too far and she rebelled. "And yet, Brother, I think in some things you wronged me in that letter never to be forgotten, but never mind, YOU DID NOT HURT ME, even that did me good. . . . Be sure to keep that letter of mine which you said I ought to be ashamed of—all the rest better be destroyed. There will be no use in writing about it—WE CAN NOT UNDERSTAND EACH OTHER, and I have unintentionally said too much perhaps . . ."

When Theodore realized that he had wounded her, he lost control of himself. There was no way to explain his rudeness except by confessing his love. Angelina responded by declaring hers, and it was only by keeping apart for the time being that either was able to get on with the all-important work.

They planned to be married as soon as Angelina had finished her lectures at the Odeon, *i.e.*, in a matter of a few weeks. Angelina was, for the moment, the most talked-about woman in America, and the news that she was engaged to be married would have transformed the Odeon series into a side show, or so she feared. (Even her partisans considered that Angelina's public life had by now unfitted her forever for the role of a good wife and mother.) The lovers were so discreet that not even Whittier, who shared an office with Theodore, and Henry Stanton, who lived with him, knew what was afoot until they received their invitations to what was undoubtedly the most extraordinary wedding they would ever attend.

They and other friends and members of Theodore's family (Angelina's were invited but did not respond) gathered on the evening of May 14, 1838, in the parlor at the home of Angelina's sister, Anna Grimké Frost, who lived in Philadelphia, to hear the bride and groom speak the vows *they* had decided upon, and to ask—without the assistance of a minister —the blessing of God on their union. The date had been chosen to coincide with the dedication ceremonies of Pennsylvania Hall, which many out-of-town abolitionists were expected to attend. Philadelphia had been chosen for the additional reason that by Pennsylvania law a marriage was legal if the couple did no more than announce, in the presence of twelve witnesses, their intention to live together in the future as man and wife. It was not "registered" unless one of the latter was also a notary, and Weld had taken pains not to invite one: had the marriage been registered, he would have had a legal claim to all Angelina's worldly goods, including her inheritance to come, and that would have made him uncomfortable.

The evening was what Sarah called "a true love feast." Angelina and Theodore glowed like lamps and spread warmth in all directions. The guest list included black and white, rich and poor, freeborn and ex-slave, and the leaders of diverse factions in the abolition movement, meeting under truce for perhaps the last time. Garrison performed the one official act required by the state: the reading aloud of the marriage certificate. Whittier had to wait outside till that was over, lest he be disowned—as Angelina and Sarah were soon to be—for attending a non-Quaker wedding. But he was called in for the cutting of the cake, which had been baked by one of the guests, an ex-slave of Anna Grimké Frost's. (It contained only non-slave-produced sugar, which was not easy to come by.)

Two nights later, on May 16, the bride was scheduled to speak at Pennsylvania Hall. The program was designed to take advantage of public curiosity about lady abolitionists, principally Angelina herself. All the speakers, therefore, were to be women—except for Garrison, who had asked for a chance to apologize for the personal attack he had made on a local "gradualist" in his speech at the dedication.

Something in the temper of the neighborhood—which was near the waterfront—made the sponsors uneasy, and they called on the mayor well in advance to request protection on behalf of the "many ladies who would be present." The mayor was shocked at such a lack of confidence in "the good sense and good manners of their fellow Philadelphians." And indeed, as the audience began to gather, the apprehensions of the abolitionists were lulled by the appearance of so many well-dressed and apparently well-behaved gentlemen.

They had expected more women to be among them, and more of the local faithful, but by the time these arrived, all the seats had been taken. It was regrettable that so many had to be turned away, but it was good to carry the message to ears that had not already heard it. As the meeting began, a crowd was gathering in the street. . . .

Garrison spoke first and was hissed, which angered him so that he forgot his apology and spoke more intemperately than before. When he had finished, Maria Chapman came to the podium. As if at a signal, boos and catcalls were heard from every part of the hall, and stones thrown from the street below began to shatter the windows along one side of the room.

Too late, the abolitionists realized that they had fallen into a trap. No police were anywhere to be seen. The hall was packed with blood brothers of the mob outside. Provocators were stationed at all strategic points, and the crowd was so dense that it was impossible to eject anyone. It was also impossible for any speaker to be heard. Quite possibly something —anything—might start a panic that would send people stampeding toward the exit doors, trampling and crushing the just along with the unjust.

At this moment Angelina came forward and held up her hand for silence. The hubbub inside quieted, and she managed to make herself heard over the noise from outside.

"Men! Brothers and fathers! Mothers and daughters and sisters! What came ye out for to see? A reed shaken in the wind?"

Stones continued to strike and break the windows. Glass continued to fall in the aisle and on the stage. The mob outside continued to scream threats. But inside the hall Angelina had established her supremacy.

"What is a mob?" she asked. "What would the breaking of every window be? Any evidence that we are wrong or that slavery is a good and wholesome institution?

"There is nothing to fear from those who would stop our mouths. . . . if the arm of the North had not already caused the bastille of slavery to totter, you would not hear those cries."

From this extemporized beginning, Angelina worked her way back to the address she had planned to give. It took her over an hour to finish. When she could not make herself heard over the noise from the street, she waited for it to subside, and then went on. When stones landed on the stage or among her listeners, she made reference to them if it suited her point, or ignored them if it did not. And, at last, she called upon the audience, beginning with the women on the platform, to form in ranks of two and follow her out of the building and through the mob in the street.

It was an inspired tactic. Any attempt on the part of the abolitionist men to protect the women would probably have triggered an assault —inside or outside the hall. But the thin line of women, led by the slender, gray-gowned bride, seemed to shame the rowdies. They stepped aside and made an aisle through which Angelina walked. After her came the women, and after them the men. Even the proslavery men who had come to heckle Angelina marched out in silent sobriety. The mob was quiet until the last of them had passed. Not until the next evening did the planned outrage take place. The police were still absent when the mob returned to sack and burn Pennsylvania Hall, the sanctuary that had just been dedicated to freedom.

That was the last time Angelina Grimké Weld was heard in a public place. She retired with her husband to a small New Jersey farm to learn, under the most trying of conditions, the domestic lessons she had missed. She and Sarah (who lived with the Welds for the rest of her life) took up the burdens of housekeeping while Theodore wrestled with the farm from spring to fall, and spent his winters in Washington as consultant and lobbyist for the abolition faction in Congress.

Angelina in her middle and late thirties bore three children in five years and suffered long, painful illnesses after each of the births. She never recovered her health.

There were calls for her services during those first years, but she was never able to respond, and after a while the calls became infrequent. She did try, once or twice, to address very small, informal groups of women, but the effort was enormous and the result disappointing. The gift of tongues had been taken from her. The one task of any importance that she did undertake was helping her husband with his great documentary pamphlet, *American Slavery As It Is*, for which she and Sarah read and clipped southern newspapers and wrote moving testimonies of their own.

As the years rolled on, the Welds and Sarah became more and more occupied with the tasks of earning a living and raising the children. The movement to which they had given their best years split and split again. The Welds managed to keep friendships on both sides, mainly because of their isolation. For a while they ran a boarding house at Eagleswood, a utopian community in New Jersey, to which many abolitionists and transcendentalists sent their children. Teaching became their principal occupation, and at the end of the Civil War Angelina and Theodore found places in Dr. Lewis's school at Fairmount, Massachusetts, one of the first schools to admit Negro students.

In the enforced quiet of this life, Angelina had found a sort of peace. Now the chance reading of an article in a newspaper threatened to shatter that peace and make demands on a strength that she no longer possessed—at least in a physical sense. Archibald Grimké's answer to her was dated February 20, 1868:

Dear Madam:

I was somewhat surprised by receiving yours of the 15th inst. I never expected to hear through the medium of a letter from "Miss Angelina Grimké" of anti-Slavery celebrity . . .

I shall proceed to give you a simple sketch of my history and my connections:

I am the son of Henry Grimké, a brother of Dr. John Grimké, & therefore your brother. . . . He was married to a Miss Simons . . . & she died, leaving three children. . . . After her death he took my mother, who was his slave & his children's nurse; her name was Nancy Weston. . . . By my mother he had three children, viz Archibald, which is my name, Francis & John. . . . He told my mother that he could not free her . . . "but," said he, "I leave you better than free, because I leave you to be taken care of."

Mr. E. M. Grimké [Henry's son] did not do as his father commanded, and [my mother] was thrown upon the uncharitable world to struggle . . . alone. By dint of hard labor she kept us from perishing by hunger . . . until 1860, when Mr. E. M. Grimké married a second time . . . & he wanted a boy to wait on him. He informed my mother that she should send me to his house. . . . Thus he kept on until she was rendered childless. . . . I afterwards fled from my oppressor. Frank attempted to escape but was retaken & sold. . . .

[When] Freedom was proclaimed to all men . . . the disjointed members of our little family were united . . . the public schools were flung open to all. I . . . went to one of them and through the intercessions [of Mrs. Pillsbury, the principal] we [he and Frank] were admitted here . . . My younger bro. is at home with my mother. He cannot get a support, hence he cannot come . . .

Angelina was devastated, not by the news that she had Negro nephews, but by the guilt of her brother, who had sired children and left them in bondage, and of her white nephew, who had taken advantage of the bequest to enslave and ultimately sell his own half-brother. She suffered one of her "prostrations"—blinding headaches, double or blurred vision, periods of faintness and dizziness—so severe and protracted that she had

311

to give up her teaching and take to her bed. But by February 29 she had composed her answer to the nephews:

Dear young friends:

I cannot express the mingled emotions with which I perused your deeply interesting and touching letter. The facts it disclosed were *no* surprise to me. Indeed, had I not suspected that you might be my nephews, I should probably not have addressed you . . .

I will not dwell on the past: let all that go. It cannot be altered. Our work is in the present and duty calls upon us now so to use the past as to convert its curse into a blessing. I am glad you have taken the name of Grimké. It was *once* one of the noblest names of Carolina. . . . It was the grief of my heart that during the late war, not one of the name of Grimké —neither man nor woman—was found on the side of loyalty & freedom, all bow'd down together & worshipped Slavery—"the Mother of all Abominations."

You, my young friends, now bear this once honored name. I charge you most solemnly, by your upright conduct and your life-long devotion to the eternal principles of justice and humanity and religion, to lift this name out of the dust where it now lies, and set it once more among the princes of our land.

Angelina did not let the matter rest there. As soon as she was able she set out for Oxford, Pennsylvania, to meet her nephews face to face, and to acknowledge them publicly as "the sons of my brother, Henry Grimké, and his wife, Nancy Weston Grimké." She inquired into their plans and ambitions and learned that they wanted to prepare themselves for professional careers. She offered all the financial assistance she and Sarah were capable of (which was not much at the time), and invited the boys to visit her in Fairmount. Archibald's daughter, in a memoir of her father, later described the visit: "They went . . . To the boys this was a great occasion, the greatest in all their lives, and cost what it might, they were determined to live up to it. They were virtually penniless, but each carried a cane, wore a high silk hat which had been made to order and boots that were custom-made. Whatever the aunts and the Welds thought, they were welcomed with wide open arms and hearts and made at home. The simplicity here soon taught them their lesson."

The boys graduated from Lincoln in 1870 with the highest honors, Frank as class valedictorian. Both returned for the master's degree. Archibald then went on to Harvard Law School and Frank to the law department of Howard University in Washington. The Welds not only helped Archibald with tuition money but also with contacts that eventually led to his establishment in a Boston law firm. Sarah made a special effort on Frank's behalf: in her late seventies she undertook a verse translation of a French work on Joan of Arc to earn a part of his tuition money.

Sarah died at the age of eighty-one in 1873, the year Frank entered Howard; Angelina lived another six years and saw Frank change his field from the law to the ministry, enter and graduate from Princeton Theological Seminary, and go on to his first church, the Fifteenth Street Presbyterian in Washington. She did not live to appreciate the tribute of Archibald's naming his first and only child Angelina Weld Grimké, in loving memory of her.

In the ministry, Frank found a vocation that fulfilled him completely. He married Charlotte Forten, a remarkable woman who had served as the only Negro teacher in the first freedmen's schools established by the Union Army on the Carolina coast. The couple had only one child, a daughter, who died young. Frank was associated with his brother in the cause of Negro advancement, but the thrust of his life was in his ministry. Four volumes of his sermons have been collected and published by Carter Woodson, whose editorial comment on the Reverend Mr. Grimké's career would have delighted both the aunts: "All who knew him were not his followers. He alienated the genuflecting, compromising, and hypocritical leaders of both races . . . A man of high ideals, who lived above reproach and bore an honorable name even among those who did not agree with him. . . . Persons who knew him well often referred to him as the Black Puritan . . ."

Archibald did not find a single vocation, financial security, or much sustained personal happiness. He was intelligent, diligent, and extremely personable, but it took more than that to make a living in the law in Boston in the 1880s and 90s—if one was also a Negro. Archibald undertook a number of other tasks; some paid, others did not. He edited a Negro weekly called *The Hub*, and wrote occasional articles for the large Boston dailies. The high point of his career was his tour of duty as United States Consul to Santo Domingo (1894–98).

He served from 1903 to 1916 as president of the American Negro Academy and joined William E. B. Dubois in the Niagara Movement and in the National Association for the Advancement of Colored People, which grew out of it.

His marriage (to a white woman) was a failure and left deep emotional scars on him and on his daughter, who was at first taken from him by her mother, then—at the age of seven—returned to him to raise. His financial situation was always so strained as to amount to genteel poverty, and until in his last years he became a member of his brother's household, he never really had a home. But his long effort was recognized—in 1919, in his seventieth year—by the award of the N.A.A.C.P.'s highest honor, the Spingarn Medal, for distinguished achievement and service to his race.

Angelina's charge was not laid on her two Negro nephews to no effect. They did indeed do honor to the Grimké name.

—April 1967

HAYFOOT, STRAWFOOT!

By BRUCE CATTON

The day-to-day life of the Civil War soldier, recalled with authority, irony, easy grace, and basic humanity

The volunteer soldier in the American Civil War used a clumsy muzzle-loading rifle, lived chiefly on salt pork and hardtack, and retained to the very end a loose-jointed, informal attitude toward the army with which he had cast his lot. But despite all of the surface differences, he was at bottom blood brother to the G.I. Joe of modern days.

Which is to say that he was basically, and incurably, a civilian in arms. A volunteer, he was still a soldier because he had to be one, and he lived for the day when he could leave the army forever. His attitude toward discipline, toward his officers, and toward the whole spit-and-polish concept of military existence was essentially one of careless tolerance. He refused to hate his enemies—indeed, he often got along with them much better than with some of his own comrades—and his indoctrination was often so imperfect that what was sometimes despairingly said of the American soldier in World War II would apply equally to him: he seemed to be fighting chiefly so that he could some day get back to Mom's cooking.

What really set the Civil War soldier apart was the fact that he came from a less sophisticated society. He was no starry-eyed innocent, to be sure—or, if he was, the army quickly took care of that—but the America of the 1860s was less highly developed than modern America. It lacked the ineffable advantages of radio, television, and moving pictures. It was still essentially a rural nation; it had growing cities, but they were smaller and somehow less urban than today's cities; a much greater percentage of the population lived on farms or in country towns and villages than is the case now, and there was more of a backwoods, hayseed-in-the-hair flavor to the people who came from them.

For example: every war finds some ardent youngsters who want to enlist despite the fact that they are under the military age limit of eighteen. Such a lad today simply goes to the recruiting station, swears that he is eighteen, and signs up. The lad of the 1860s saw it a little differently. He could not swear that he was eighteen when he was only sixteen; in his innocent way, he felt that to lie to his own government was just plain wrong. But he worked out a little dodge that got him into the army anyway. He would take a bit of paper, scribble the number *18* on it, and put it in the sole of his shoe. Then, when the recruiting officer asked him how old he was, he could truthfully say: "I am *over* eighteen." That was a common happening, early in the Civil War; one cannot possibly imagine it being tried today.

Similarly, the drill sergeants repeatedly found that among the raw recruits there were men so abysmally untaught that they did not know left from right, and hence could not step off on the left foot as all soldiers should. To teach these lads how to march, the sergeants would tie a wisp of hay to the left foot and a wisp of straw to the right; then, setting the men to march, they would chant, "Hay-foot, straw-foot, hay-foot, straw-foot"—and so on, until everybody had caught on. A common name for a green recruit in those days was "strawfoot."

On the drill field, when a squad was getting basic training, the men were as likely as not to intone a little rhythmic chant as they tramped across the sod—thus:

March! March! March old soldier march!
Hayfoot, strawfoot,
Belly-full of bean soup—
March old soldier march!

Because of his unsophistication, the ordinary soldier in the Civil War, North and South alike, usually joined up with very romantic ideas about soldiering. Army life rubbed the romance off just as rapidly then as it does now, but at the start every volunteer went into the army thinking that he was heading off to high adventure. Under everything else, he enlisted because he thought army life was going to be fun, and usually it took quite a few weeks in camp to disabuse him of this strange notion. Right at the start, soldiering had an almost idyllic quality; if this quality faded rapidly, the memory of it remained through all the rest of life.

Early days in camp simply cemented the idea. An Illinois recruit, writing home from training camp, confessed: "It is fun to lie around, face unwashed, hair uncombed, shirt unbuttoned and everything un-every-thinged. It sure beats clerking." Another Illinois boy confessed: "I don't see why people will stay at home when they can get to soldiering. A year of it is worth getting shot for to any man." And a Massachusetts boy, recalling the early days of army life, wrote that "Our drill, as I remember it, consisted largely of running around the Old Westbury town hall, yelling like Devils and firing at an imaginary foe." One of the commonest discoveries that comes from a reading of Civil War diaries is that the chief worry, in training camp, was a fear that the war would be over before the ardent young recruits could get into it. It is only fair to say that most of the diarists looked back on this innocent worry, a year or so afterward, with rueful amusement.

There was a regiment recruited in northern Pennsylvania in 1861—13th Pennsylvania Reserves officially, known to the rest of the Union Army as the Bucktails, because the rookies decorated their caps with strips of fur from the carcass of a deer that was hanging in front of a butcher shop near their camp—and in mid-spring these youthful soldiers were ordered to rendezvous at Harrisburg. So they marched cross-country (along a road known today as the Bucktail Trail) to the north branch of the Susquehanna, where they built rafts. One raft, for the colonel, was made oversized with a stable; the colonel's horse had to ride, too. Then the Bucktails floated down the river, singing and firing their muskets and having a gay old time, camping out along the bank at night, and finally they got to Harrisburg; and they served through the worst of the war, getting badly shot up and losing most of their men to Confederate bullets, but they never forgot the picnic air of those first days of army life, when they drifted down a river through the forests, with a song in the air and the bright light of adventure shining just ahead. Men do not go to war that way nowadays.

Discipline in those early regiments was pretty sketchy. The big catch was that most regiments were recruited locally—in one town, or one county, or in one part of a city—and everybody more or less knew everybody else. Particularly, the privates knew their officers—most of whom were elected to their jobs by the enlisted men—and they never saw any sense in being formal with them. Within reasonable limits, the Civil War private was willing to do what his company commander told him to do, but he saw little point in carrying it to extremes.

So an Indiana soldier wrote: "We had enlisted to put down the Rebellion, and had no patience with the red-tape tomfoolery of the regular service. The boys recognized no superiors, except in the line of legitimate duty. Shoulder straps waived, a private was ready at the drop of a hat to thrash his commander—a thing that occurred more than once." A New York regiment, drilling on a hot parade ground, heard a private address his company commander thus: "Say, Tom, let's quit this darn foolin' around and go over to the sutler's and get a drink." There was very little of the "Captain, sir" business in those armies. If a company or regimental officer got anything especial in the way of obedience, he got it because the enlisted men recognized him as a natural leader and superior and not just because he had a commission signed by Abraham Lincoln.

Odd rivalries developed between regiments. (It should be noted that the Civil War soldier's first loyalty went usually to his regiment, just as a navy man's loyalty goes to his ship; he liked to believe that his regiment was better than all others, and he would fight for it, any time and anywhere.) The army legends of those days tell of a Manhattan regiment, camped near Washington, whose nearest neighbor was a regiment from Brooklyn, with which the Manhattanites nursed a deep rivalry. Neither regiment had a chaplain; and there came to the Manhattan colonel one day a minister, who volunteered to hold religious services for the men in the ranks.

The colonel doubted that this would be a good idea. His men, he said, were rather irreligious, not to say godless, and he feared they would not give the reverend gentlemen a respectful hearing. But the minister said he would take his chances; after all, he had just held services with the Brooklyn regiment, and the men there had been very quiet and devout. That was enough for the colonel. What the Brooklyn regiment could do, his regiment could do. He ordered the men paraded for divine worship, announcing that any man who talked, laughed, or even coughed would be summarily court-martialed.

So the clergyman held services, and everyone was attentive. At the end of the sermon, the minister asked if any of his hearers would care to step forward and make public profession of faith; in the Brooklyn regiment, he said, fourteen men had done this. Instantly the New York colonel was on his feet.

"Adjutant!" he bellowed. "We're not going to let that damn Brooklyn regiment beat us at anything. Detail twenty men and have them baptized at once!"

Each regiment seemed to have its own mythology, tales which may have been false but which, by their mere existence, reflected faithfully certain aspects of army life. The 48th New York, for instance, was said to have an unusually large number of ministers in its ranks, serving not as chaplains but as combat soldiers. The 48th, fairly early in the war, found itself posted in a swamp along the South Carolina coast, toiling mightily in semitropical heat, amid clouds of mosquitoes, to build fortifications, and it was noted that all hands became excessively profane, including the one-time clergymen. A visiting general, watching the regiment at work one day, recalled the legend and asked the regiment's lieutenant colonel if he himself was a minister in private life.

"Well, no, General," said the officer apologetically. "I can't say that I was a regularly ordained minister. I was just one of these ————— local preachers."

Another story was hung on this same 48th New York. A Confederate ironclad gunboat was supposed to be ready to steam through channels in the swamp and attack the 48th's outposts, and elaborate plans were made to trap it with obstructions in the channel, a tangle of ropes to snarl the propellers, and so on. But it occurred to the colonel that even if the gunboat was trapped the soldiers could not get into it; it was sheathed in iron, all its ports could be closed, and men with axes could never chop their way into it. Then the colonel had an inspiration. Remembering that many of his men had been recruited from the less savory districts of New York City, he paraded the regiment and (according to legend) announced:

"Now men, you've been in this cursed swamp for two weeks—up to your ears in mud, no fun, no glory and blessed poor pay. Here's a chance. Let every man who has had experience as a cracksman or a safeblower step to the front." To the last man, the regiment marched forward four paces and came expectantly to attention.

Not unlike this was the reputation of the 6th New York, which contained so many Bowery toughs that the rest of the army said a man had to be able to show that he had done time in prison in order to get into the regiment. It was about to leave for the South, and the colonel gave his men an inspirational talk. They were going, he said, to a land of wealthy plantation owners, where each Southerner had riches of which he could be despoiled; and he took out his own gold watch and held it up for all to see, remarking that any deserving soldier could easily get one like it, once they got down to plantation-land. Half an hour later, wishing to see what time it was, he felt for his watch . . . and it was gone.

If the Civil War army spun queer tales about itself, it had to face a reality which, in all of its aspects, was singularly unpleasant. One of the worst aspects had to do with food.

From first to last, the Civil War armies enlisted no men as cooks, and there were no cooks' and bakers' schools to help matters. Often enough, when in camp, a company would simply be issued a quantity of provisions —flour, pork, beans, potatoes, and so on—and invited to prepare the stuff as best it could. Half a dozen men would form a mess, members would take turns with the cooking, and everybody had to eat what these amateurs prepared or go hungry. Later in the war, each company commander would usually detail two men to act as cooks for the company, and if either of the two happened to know anything about cooking the company was in luck. One army legend held that company officers usually detailed the least valuable soldiers to this job, on the theory that they would do less harm in the cook shack than anywhere else. One soldier, writing after the war, asserted flatly: "A company cook is a most peculiar being; he generally knows less about cooking than any other man in the company. Not being able to learn the drill, and too dirty to appear on inspection, he is sent to the cook house to get him out of the ranks."

When an army was on the march, the ration issue usually consisted of salt pork, hardtack, and coffee. (In the Confederate Army the coffee was often missing, and the hardtack was frequently replaced by corn bread; often enough the meal was not sifted, and stray bits of cob would appear in it.) The hardtack was good enough, if fresh, which was not always the case; with age it usually got infested with weevils, and veterans remarked that it was better to eat it in the dark.

In the Union Army, most of the time, the soldier could supplement his rations (if he had money) by buying extras from the sutler—the latter being a civilian merchant licensed to accompany the army, functioning somewhat as the regular post exchange functions nowadays. The sutler charged high prices and specialized in indigestibles like pies, canned lobster salad, and so on; and it was noted that men who patronized him regularly came down with stomach upsets. The Confederate Army had few sutlers, which helps to explain why the hungry Confederates were so delighted when they could capture a Yankee camp: to seize a sutler's tent meant high living for the captors, and the men in Lee's army were furious when, in the 1864 campaign, they learned that General Grant had ordered the Union Army to move without sutlers. Johnny Reb felt that Grant was really taking an unfair advantage by cutting off this possible source of supply.

If Civil War cooking arrangements were impromptu and imperfect, the same applied to its hospital system. The surgeons, usually, were good men by the standards of that day—which were low since no one on earth knew anything about germs or about how wounds became infected, and antisepsis in the operating room was a concept that had not yet come into existence; it is common to read of a surgeon whetting his scalpel on the sole of his shoe just before operating. But the hospital attendants, stretcher-bearers, and the like were chosen just as the company cooks were chosen; that is, they were detailed from the ranks, and the average officer selected the most worthless men he had simply because he wanted to get rid of men who could not be counted on in combat. As a result, sick or wounded men often got atrocious care.

A result of all of this—coupled with the fact that many men enlisted without being given any medical examinations—was that every Civil War regiment suffered a constant wastage from sickness. On paper, a regiment was supposed to have a strength ranging from 960 and 1,040 men; actually, no regiment ever got to the battlefield with anything like that strength, and since there was no established system for sending in replacements a veteran regiment that could muster 350 enlisted men present for duty was considered pretty solid. From first to last, approximately twice as many Civil War soldiers died of disease—typhoid, dysentery, and pneumonia were the great killers—as died in action; and in addition to those who died a great many more got medical discharges.

In its wisdom, the Northern government set up a number of base hospitals in Northern states, far from the battle fronts, on the theory that a man recovering from wounds or sickness would recuperate better back home. Unfortunately, the hospitals established were under local control, and the men in them were no longer under the orders of their own regiments or armies. As a result, thousands of men who were sent north for convalescence never returned to the army. Many were detailed for light work at the hospitals, and in these details they stayed because nobody had the authority to extract them and send them back to duty. Others, recovering their health, simply went home and stayed there. They were answerable to the hospital authorities, not to the army command, and the hospital authorities rarely cared very much whether they returned to duty or not. The whole system was ideally designed to make desertion easy.

On top of all of this, many men had very little understanding of the requirements of military discipline. A homesick boy often saw nothing wrong in leaving the army and going home to see the folks for a time. A man from a farm might slip off to go home and put in a crop. In neither case would the man look on himself as a deserter; he meant to return, he figured he would get back in time for any fighting that would take place, and in his own mind he was innocent of any wrongdoing. But in many cases the date of return would be postponed from week to week; the man might end as a deserter, even though he had not intended to be one when he left.

This merely reflected the loose discipline that prevailed in Civil War armies, which in turn reflected the underlying civilian-mindedness that pervaded the rank and file. The behavior of Northern armies on the march in Southern territory reflected the same thing—and, in the end, had a profound effect on the institution of chattel slavery.

A rmies of occupation always tend to bear down hard on civilian property in enemy territory. Union armies in the Civil War, being imperfectly disciplined to begin with—and suffering, furthermore, from a highly defective rationing system—bore down with especial fervor. Chickens, hams, cornfields, anything edible that might be found on a Southern plantation, looked like fair game, and the loose fringe of stragglers that always trailed around the edges of a moving Union army looted with a fine disregard for civilian property rights.

This was made all the more pointed by the fact that the average Northern soldier, poorly indoctrinated though he was, had strong feelings about the evils of secession. To his mind, the Southerners who sought to set up a nation of their own were in rebellion against the best government mankind had ever known. Being rebels, they had forfeited their rights; if evil things happened to them, that (as the average Northern soldier saw it) was no more than just retribution. This meant that even when the army command tried earnestly to prevent looting and individual foraging, the officers at company and regimental levels seldom tried very hard to carry out the high command's orders.

William Tecumseh Sherman has come down in history as the very archetype of the Northern soldier who believed in pillage and looting; yet during the first years of the war Sherman resorted to all manner of ferocious punishments to keep his men from despoiling Southern property. He had looters tied up by the thumbs, ordered courts-martial, issued any number of stern orders—and all to very little effect. Long before he adopted the practice of commandeering or destroying Southern property as a war measure, his soldiers were practicing it against his will, partly because discipline was poor and partly because they saw nothing wrong with it.

It was common for a Union colonel, as his regiment made camp in a Southern state, to address his men, pointing to a nearby farm, and say: "Now, boys, that barn is full of nice fat pigs and chickens. I don't want to see any of you take any of them"—whereupon he would fold his arms and look sternly in the opposite direction. It was also common for a regimental commander to read, on parade, some ukase from higher authority forbidding foraging, and then to wink solemnly—a clear hint that he did not expect anyone to take the order seriously. One colonel, punishing some men who had robbed a chicken house, said angrily: "Boys, I want you to understand that I am not punishing you for stealing but for getting caught at it."

It is nearly a century since that war was fought, and things look a little different now than they looked at the time. At this distance, it may be possible to look indulgently on the wholesale foraging in which Union armies indulged; to the Southern farmers who bore the brunt of it, the business looked very ugly indeed. Many a Southern family saw the foodstuffs needed for the winter swept away in an hour by grinning hoodlums who did not need and could not use a quarter of what they took. Among the foragers there were many lawless characters who took watches, jewels, and any other valuables they could find; it is recorded that a squad would now and then carry a piano out to the lawn, take it apart, and use the wires to hang pots and pans over the campfire. . . . The Civil War was really romantic only at a considerable distance.

Underneath his feeling that it was good to add chickens and hams to the army ration, and his belief that civilians in a state of secession could expect no better fate, the Union soldier also came to believe that to destroy Southern property was to help win the war. Under orders, he tore up railroads and burned warehouses; it was not long before he realized that anything that damaged the Confederate economy weakened the Confederate war effort, so he rationalized his looting and foraging by arguing that it was a step in breaking the Southern will to resist. It is at this point that the institution of human slavery enters the picture.

Most Northern soldiers had very little feeling against slavery as such, and very little sympathy for the Negro himself. They thought they were fighting to save the Union, not to end slavery, and except for New England troops most Union regiments contained very little abolition sentiment. Nevertheless, the soldiers moved energetically and effectively to destroy slavery, not because they especially intended to but simply because they were out to do all the damage they could do. They were operating against Southern property—and the most obvious, important, and easily removable property of all was the slave. To help the slaves get away from the plantation was, clearly, to weaken Southern productive capacity, which in turn weakened Confederate armies. Hence the Union soldier, wherever he went, took the peculiar institution apart, chattel by chattel.

As a result, slavery had been fatally weakened long before the war itself came to an end. The mere act of fighting the war killed it. Of all institutions on earth, the institution of human slavery was the one least adapted to survive a war. It could not survive the presence of loose-jointed, heavy-handed armies of occupation. It may hardly be too much to say that the mere act of taking up arms in slavery's defense doomed slavery.

Above and beyond everything else, of course, the business of the Civil War soldier was to fight. He fought with weapons that look very crude to modern eyes, and he moved by an outmoded system of tactics, but the price he paid when he got into action was just as high as the price modern soldiers pay despite the almost infinite development of firepower since the 1860s.

Standard infantry weapon in the Civil War was the rifled Springfield—a muzzle-loader firing a conical lead bullet, usually of .54 caliber.

To load was rather laborious, and it took a good man to get off more than two shots a minute. The weapon had a range of nearly a mile, and its "effective range"—that is, the range at which it would hit often enough to make infantry fire truly effective—was figured at about 250 yards. Compared with a modern Garand, the old muzzle-loader is no better than a museum piece; but compared with all previous weapons—the weapons on which infantry tactics in the 1860s were still based—it was a fearfully destructive and efficient piece.

For the infantry of that day still moved and fought in formations dictated in the old days of smoothbore muskets, whose effective range was no more than 100 yards and which were wildly inaccurate at any distance. Armies using those weapons attacked in solid mass formations, the men standing, literally, elbow to elbow. They could get from effective range to hand-to-hand fighting in a very short time, and if they had a proper numerical advantage over the defensive line they could come to grips without losing too many men along the way. But in the Civil War the conditions had changed radically; men would be hit while the rival lines were still half a mile apart, and to advance in mass was simply to invite wholesale destruction. Tactics had not yet been adjusted to the new rifles; as a result, Civil War attacks could be fearfully costly, and when the defenders dug entrenchments and got some protection—as the men learned to do, very quickly—a direct frontal assault could be little better than a form of mass suicide.

It took the high command a long time to revise tactics to meet this changed situation, and Civil War battles ran up dreadful casualty lists. For an army to lose 25 percent of its numbers in a major battle was by no means uncommon, and in some fights—the Confederate army at Gettysburg is an outstanding example—the percentage of loss ran close to one-third of the total number engaged. Individual units were sometimes nearly wiped out. Some of the Union and Confederate regiments that fought at Gettysburg lost up to 80 percent of their numbers; a regiment with such losses was usually wrecked, as an effective fighting force, for the rest of the war.

The point of all of which is that the discipline which took the Civil War soldier into action, while it may have been very sketchy by modern standards, was nevertheless highly effective on the field of battle. Any armies that could go through such battles as Antietam, Stone's River, Franklin or Chickamauga and come back for more had very little to learn about the business of fighting.

Perhaps the Confederate General D. H. Hill said it, once and for all. The battle of Malvern Hill, fought on the Virginia peninsula early in the summer of 1862, finished the famous Seven Days campaign, in which George B. McClellan's Army of the Potomac was driven back from in front of Richmond by Robert E. Lee's Army of Northern Virginia. At Malvern Hill, McClellan's men fought a rear-guard action—a bitter, confused fight which came at the end of a solid week of wearing, costly battles and forced marches. Federal artillery wrecked the Confederate assault columns, and at the end of the day Hill looked out over the battlefield, strewn with dead and wounded boys. Shaking his head, and reflecting on the valor in attack and in defense which the two armies had displayed, Hill never forgot about this. Looking back on it, long after the war was over, he declared, in substance:

"Give me Confederate infantry and Yankee artillery and I'll whip the world!"

—April 1957

THE FIRST MODERN MAN OF WAR

By B. H. LIDDELL HART

The great British soldier-historian assesses William Tecumseh Sherman and finds him formidable: he did nothing less than bring the twentieth century into battle against a nineteenth-century enemy. And eighty years later, his tactics helped win World War II.

The American Civil War produced nobody like William Tecumseh Sherman, the world's first modern "man of war." Not only was he a great commander; he also evolved fresh strategic techniques, and concepts developed from study of his operations had a far-reaching influence in the Second World War.

Sherman showed both the qualities and characteristics of genius. He was tall, lean, angular, loose-jointed, careless and unkempt in dress, with a restlessness of manner emphasized by his endless chain-smoking of cigars, and an insatiable curiosity, a raciness of language, and a fondness for picturesque phrases. But he was a blend of contrasting qualities. His dynamic energy went along with philosophical reflectiveness. He had faith in his own vision but a doubt of his own abilities that could only be dispelled gradually by actual achievement. He combined democratic tastes and manners with a deep and sardonic distrust of democracy. His rebelliousness was accompanied by a profound respect for law and order. His logical ruthlessness was coupled with compassion.

In generalship, he was brilliant, yet what made him outstanding was the way he came to see and exploit the changing conditions of warfare produced by mechanical and scientific developments.

The Civil War started with old-fashioned military concepts and weapons, but also with some very new instruments whose influence had not yet been realized. Until the middle of the nineteenth century, the means of movement had been unchanged throughout the ages. Armies marched on foot or horseback, and their supplies were carried in vehicles drawn by horses or oxen. At sea, they moved on sailing ships dependent on the wind. Even in the Napoleonic era the smoothbore musket and cannon were little more effective than the medieval bow and ancient catapult. Means of communication were limited to messengers on horseback.

But by the time of the Civil War, new *mechanical* means of movement and communication had become available. This was the first war in which the railroad, the steamship, and the electric telegraph played an important part. Weapons had not changed so much, but the war speeded their development. The muzzle-loaded smoothbore musket was gradually replaced by a muzzle-loaded rifle, which was much more accurate. Breech-loading rifles came into use before the end of the war, and the increasing range and effect of fire made attack more difficult and costly. Troops were forced to take shelter in trenches or behind breastworks. *Tactical* movement, on the battlefield, easily became stagnant.

Meanwhile, the large-scale transportation facilities offered by the railroads led commanders and governments to mass at the railheads larger forces than could be fed if the enemy cut the lines. These forces tended to become too massive to be maneuverable. Thus *strategic* movement was also inclined to become stagnant.

The combination produced a state of deadlock—even in the West, where space was wide and appeared to offer ample scope for maneuver. In 1862 and again in 1863, successive efforts by the Union forces to push southward were blocked or paralyzed by Confederate cavalry raids on the rail lines of supply.

A better way of tackling the problem was initiated by Grant's indirect approach to Vicksburg in the spring of 1863. Grant cut off this key point on the Mississippi by a wide circuit eastward and then northward, during which he momentarily cut loose from his line of supply. Sherman, then his principal executive, learned most from the bold experiment, becoming the first commander to show a clear grasp of the new conditions of warfare. At the start of the war he was still conventional in military outlook, but his civilian experience during the immediate prewar years, his unconventional character, and the experience of this Vicksburg campaign helped him to shake off the shackles of orthodoxy.

He could also see the significance of another important change—the growth of population and industrialization. This brought increased dependence on supplies, on manufactured weapons, and on means of communication—among which were newspapers, as well as transport and telegraph. This increased both the economic target and the moral target, and made both more vulnerable. This in turn increased the incentive to strike at the sources of the opponent's armed power instead of striking at its shield—the armed forces.

Sherman's grasp of this is very clearly shown in his letters and in his plans. Viewed in retrospect, it is evident that he was startlingly ahead of his time. Nearly half a century before the development of aircraft, his operations in the last year of the Civil War foreshadowed the aim and course pursued by the bomber offensive of World War II.

The dual influences of heredity and environment can be clearly traced in the molding of Sherman's character and outlook. He came from a Puritan family which had left England about 1634 to seek freedom of conscience and wider opportunity in the New World. The family moved first to Connecticut, and then to Ohio, where Charles Robert Sherman became a judge. Developing a deep admiration for the Indian chief Tecumseh, he had his third son, born on February 8, 1820, christened Willim Tecumseh Sherman.

The boy was left fatherless at the age of nine, but he was taken into the home of a friend, Senator Thomas Ewing, who helped him get an appointment to West Point when Sherman became sixteen. The four years there were purgatory, and it is evident that Sherman shared the feelings of Ulysses Grant, who wrote that the years "seemed about five times as long as Ohio years." Looking back, Sherman caustically remarked: "At the Academy I was not considered a good soldier, for at no time was I selected for any office. . . . Then, as now, neatness in dress and form, with a strict conformity, were the qualifications for office. . . ." In studies Sherman ranked among the best, but he got so many demerits for nonconformity that he was in sixth place in the final class list.

Upon graduation, Sherman became an officer in the 3rd Artillery, in Florida, and he soon saw active service against the Seminole Indians. His letters to Ellen Ewing, the childhood playmate whom he subsequently married, show how much he enjoyed the excitement of the chase, but they also reveal his underlying sympathy with the chased, as well as his love of reading and of painting, his gift for writing, and his insatiable thirst for knowledge. They must sometimes have wearied a young girl thirsting for a more sentimental kind of communication.

Sherman missed the main action of the Mexican War, to his keen disappointment, through a posting to California, which he felt was a military backwater. But this widened his experience and eventually led to his being asked to return there, in 1853, as a working partner in a San Francisco banking house. He had married Ellen Ewing, and he was anxious to improve his family's prospects, so he quitted the Army at the age of thirty-three.

The boom was already subsiding, however, and many banks soon collapsed. In 1857 the parent bank in St. Louis was driven to suspend payment. That ended Sherman's banking career. He then joined a law firm at Leavenworth, Kansas, where his flair for topography made him valuable in surveying new areas and roads. But legal disputes were not to his taste, and in 1859 he jumped at a chance to become head of a new "Seminary and Military Academy" in Louisiana.

The new post provided ample scope for his energy and organizing power. He gained an impressive ascendancy over the hot-blooded southern cadets and also over the diverse elements among the board of supervisors. His personal popularity was the more remarkable because his brother John, who had been elected to Congress some years before, was regarded through the South as a "black Republican" and "awful abolitionist." Among his most staunch supporters were two of his future opponents on the battlefield, Braxton Bragg and P. G. T. Beauregard, who—by an irony of history—helped to dissuade him from accepting a tempting offer to go to England to represent a Cincinnati banking house in London, which would have removed the prospect of his playing a decisive part in the Civil War.

Sherman's letters in the summer of 1860 forecast that however "reasonable and moderate" Abraham Lincoln might be, in the South his name was like a red rag to a bull, so that his election to the Presidency would make civil war likely—"reason has very little influence in this world: prejudice governs." As Sherman saw it, the basic objection to secession was the danger to the economy of the North that would arise from southern free trade and hostile control of the Mississippi.

On January 10, 1861, the United States Arsenal at Baton Rouge was surrounded—and surrendered—although Louisiana had not yet seceded. Sherman promptly resigned his office, but on returning to the North he was shocked by the complacency that prevailed. Disgusted with the politicians on both sides, Sherman felt inclined to stand aside and leave them to get out of the mess they had produced. He turned down an offer to make him Assistant Secretary of War, and when Lincoln called for 75,000 volunteers to serve for three months, Sherman's comment was: "You might as well attempt to put out the flames of a burning house with a squirt-gun." He wrote: "I think it is to be a long war—very long—much longer than any politician thinks." At the same time, he urged to his brother that "the questions of the national integrity and slavery should be kept distinct, for otherwise it will gradually become a war of extermination—a war without end."

It was only when Lincoln decided to increase the Regular Army and called on men to volunteer for three years of duty that Sherman offered his services. He was given command of a brigade in the hastily improvised force of 30,000 men that marched out from Washington in July to tackle the Confederates at the First Bull Run. When this battle ended in a Union defeat, Sherman distinguished himself in covering the disorderly retreat and checking the pursuers. But as the retreat continued, even his regiments dissolved into the general stream of fugitives, and he bitterly reported that the whole army "has degenerated into an armed mob."

When the President drove round the camps, Sherman pointedly asked him to discourage all cheering, and told him that "what we needed were cool, thoughtful, hard-fighting soldiers—no more hurrahing, no more humbug." Lincoln took the rebuke in good part. When one of the officers complained that Sherman had threatened to shoot him for defiance of orders, Lincoln replied with a twinkle: "Well, if I were you and he threatened to shoot, I wouldn't trust him, for I believe he would do it."

As soon as it became clear that no immediate Confederate advance on Washington was likely, Sherman was sent westward to help in organizing Union forces in Kentucky. He considered that this area was of crucial importance defensively, and that offensively "the Mississippi River will be a grand theater of war . . . I think it of more importance than Richmond"; but he soon found that raising troops in Kentucky was an even harder job than rallying them near Washington. The next few months proved the most exasperating period of his life. His immediate superior collapsed under the strain, leaving Sherman, who took over from him reluctantly, to deal with both the military and the political difficulties.

His outbursts of temper in trying to inject some discipline into the motley collection of volunteers had already led them to nickname him "Old Pills," and he now came into bitter conflict with the local politicians and press. He also had a clash with Secretary of War Simon Cameron, who came to Louisville on a short visit. Sherman, pointing out that he had only 20,000 men to cover a frontage of 300 miles, argued that at least 60,000 were needed for the immediate purpose, and 200,000 for an effective offensive down the Mississippi—a moderate estimate compared with the strength eventually expended. But the Secretary of War described it as an "insane" demand, and this careless phrase was exploited by Sherman's political and press critics, who now depicted him as a lunatic.

Such a blaring press campaign made his position impossible, so he suggested that it might be better if he were relieved of his command. His suggestion was promptly accepted, and he was transferred to a subordinate place under General Henry W. Halleck in the Department of the Missouri. But the stories about his insanity had preceded him, and he was looked at askance in many quarters, so that his own depression became acute. Relief came with the launching of the Union offensive in the West, which diverted the attention of the press to a fresh topic.

The offensive opened on January 19, 1862, when George H. Thomas broke the right end of the Confederate line by his victory at Mill Springs, Kentucky. It took on full momentum a few weeks later with the capture, by a spearhead force under Ulysses S. Grant, of Fort Henry on the Tennessee River and Fort Donelson on the Cumberland. In the next stage of the advance up the Tennessee, Sherman commanded a division under Grant, and his performance in the confused and seesaw Battle of Shiloh drew a special tribute from Grant to his "great judgment and skill on the management of his men." Halleck reported that Sherman had saved the situation and recommended that he be promoted to the rank of major general, which was done.

The Union offensive subsequently fizzled out as a result of diverging efforts, sluggish movements, and Confederate raids on its railroad lines of supply. But the comradeship which linked Sherman and Grant from Shiloh on, and the intuitive teamwork they developed, bore good fruit in the 1863 campaign—after the too-cautious Halleck had been shifted to Washington as general in chief and Grant had taken his place in the West. Sherman, now given command of a corps, was Grant's right hand in the bold strategic maneuver that, after a series of failures, brought about the fall of Vicksburg on July 4, 1863, and thereby gained complete control of the Mississippi. The Confederacy was thus deprived permanently of reinforcements and supplies from the trans-Mississippi states—with effects more far-reaching than the repulse of Lee at Gettysburg, which took place at the same moment.

Grant's approach to Vicksburg had started in mid-April when Union gunboats and transports, loaded with supplies, ran the gantlet of the Confederate batteries under cover of night to establish a new base some thirty miles south of the fortress. Grant then filtered two of his three corps down there by a newly made road on the west bank of the Mississippi, and crossed to the east bank with little opposition, helped by a distraction which Sherman created above Vicksburg. When Sherman's corps rejoined him, bringing a large wagon train with fresh supplies, Grant cut loose from his new base and marched northeastward on May 7 to place his army astride Vicksburg's line of supply and reinforcement from the east and drive Confederate General John C. Pemberton and his army back into Vicksburg. Although the Confederate garrison of Vicksburg beat off his assaults, its isolation and growing starvation produced its surrender six weeks later.

There was no immediate strategic exploitation of the Vicksburg victory, and the next move was delayed by prolonged arguments in Washington as to where and how Grant's army should be employed. The arguments were settled fortuitously, and in the end fortunately, by the misfortune that General William S. Rosecrans' Army of the Cumberland suffered in Tennessee. Its southward advance in September met a heavy defeat at

Chickamauga, and it became bottled up at Chattanooga. In this emergency Grant was given overall command in the West, and Sherman succeeded to the command of his army. Grant moved to the rescue of Rosecrans and after a tough fight drove back the investing army. This victory opened the gateway into Georgia, the granary of the Confederacy, and thence into the eastern states as a whole. But in the following year, 1864, the Union came near to forfeiting the ultimate victory that appeared to be strategically assured. For the people of the North were growing weary under the prolonged strain of the struggle, and the peace party was gaining strength. The presidential election was due in November, and Lincoln was in danger of being ousted in favor of a President pledged to seek a compromise peace. He urgently needed to provide the people with clear evidence that there was good hope of early victory, and to this end he sent for Grant to take over the supreme command. Sherman was then appointed chief commander in the West; the "lunatic" now had 219,907 men, of whom about 100,000 were available for offensive operations in northern Georgia. For the coming campaign in the East, the main theater, Grant chose the old direct overland approach from the Rappahannock River toward Richmond, counting on his greatly superior weight of numbers to smash Lee's army, or at least to wear it down by a "continuous hammering."

His own "will to conquer," however, did not bring success. He failed to smash Lee's army, while the strength of his own had withered in the fierce battles of the Wilderness and Cold Harbor. The only strategic advantage gained—that of having worked close to the rear of Richmond—looked like a stalemate. The northern people were discouraged, and at the end of the summer Lincoln doubted that he could be reelected. Yet when the outlook seemed darkest, it suddenly lightened, and in the November elections Lincoln was returned to power. Sherman's capture of Atlanta in September was the saving factor.

There was deep mutual understanding between Grant and Sherman, but there was also a significant contrast in outlook. Grant's success as a commander had been largely due to the way he applied "horse sense" unfettered by the harness of military doctrine and custom, but he had no marked originality of concept. Sherman was a man of vision, but started the war with the handicap of being too well versed in prevailing military theory and tactical manuals, and it was only when war experience helped to break this crust that his capacity for original thought had full play.

By 1864 the difference between the two men became apparent. While Grant's primary objective was the enemy's army, Sherman's was the seizure of strategic points. Atlanta, the base of the Confederate army opposing him in Georgia, was not only the junction of four important railways but also the source of vital supplies. As Sherman pointed out, it was "full of foundries, arsenals, and machine shops," as well as a symbol, and he held that "its capture would be the death knell of the Confederacy."

In the advance to Atlanta, Sherman's skill in maneuver was all the more notable because, by contrast to Grant in Virginia, he was tied to one railway line for his supplies. Moreover his starting point at Chattanooga was about 150 miles from his Nashville base and 330 miles from Louisville, the main source of supplies. That long line of supplies, lengthening as he advanced, was under threat everywhere from the raids of enemy cavalry and guerrillas. Yet, rather than commit his troops to a direct attack on an opponent well placed to block him, Sherman cut loose temporarily even from his supply line.

His ability to maneuver had been aided by the drastic way in which he cut down transport before starting. Each division and brigade was allotted only enough wagons to carry food and ammunition, and every man brought five days' rations on his person or horse. Apart from these supply trains, only one wagon and one ambulance was allowed to each regiment, with a pack mule for the mess kit and baggage of the officers of each company. Tents were forbidden, except for the sick and wounded and one for each headquarters as an office. Clerical work in the field was reduced to a minimum by the use of permanent offices in the rear for the transaction and transmission of all routine correspondence. This made possible a severe restriction of the size of the various headquarters staffs.

Sherman's own habit of living "rough" made his troops more ready to follow his example, while his lack of regard for outward appearance and the trappings of dignity strongly appealed to such pioneer types. So did his air of restless energy and constant alertness. At night he would often be seen prowling around the camp with his feet in old slippers, his legs covered only by a pair of red flannel drawers, his tall, spare body wrapped in a travel-worn dressing gown, with sometimes a short blue cape or cloak over all as a concession to convention. He was the lightest sleeper in his army, and by four o'clock in the morning he liked to be up and about, thinking or listening—for that, he said, was "the best time to hear any movement at a distance." While his eccentricities endeared him to the troops, his alertness inspired their confidence, and "There's Uncle Billy. All's right" became a common saying.

More forgiving than most commanders where tactical errors occurred, knowing that the enemy's resistance and counteraction is the most incalculable factor in war, Sherman would rarely tolerate excuses for delays in the movement of supplies, believing that, by due foresight, preparation, and initiative, material obstacles could always be overcome. Those who obstructed or clung to the letter of regulations suffered sharply from his tongue. One officer who made difficulties was spurred to overcome them by the vehement retort, "If you don't have my army supplied, and keep it supplied, we'll eat your mules up, sir—eat your mules up." Later in the advance, when there was urgent need to replace a burnt railroad bridge and the chief engineer estimated that he would require four days for the task, Sherman is credited with the reply, "Sir, I give you forty-eight hours or a position in the front ranks."

When he had taken Atlanta, Sherman took a much bolder course, which carried greater strategic risks but diminished tactical risks. He felt sure that if he could march through Georgia and wreck its railway system, and then continue in the same way through South and North Carolina, the psychological impact of this strategic thrust into the heart of the South, coupled with the material effect of stopping the northward flow of supplies to Richmond and Lee's army, would produce the collapse of the Confederacy's resistance. So, ignoring Hood's army, which he had forced to evacuate Atlanta, he abandoned his own line of supply and set out on his famous "march to the sea" through Georgia—moving with the minimum of transport and living on the country while destroying its railways. Starting from Atlanta in mid-November, he reached the outskirts of Savannah within four weeks and there reopened his communications, this time by sea. A discerning Confederate commander and historian, General E. P. Alexander, wrote that "the moral effect of this march . . . was greater than would have been the most decided victory."

At the beginning of February, 1865, Sherman moved northward through the Carolinas toward Lee's rear. By mid-March, after reaching North Carolina, he heard from Grant that Lee's army "is now demoralized and deserting very fast, both to us and to their homes." Yet Grant's own army was still immobilized in the trench lines round Petersburg and Richmond, where it had been brought to a halt the previous summer. It was not until the beginning of April that Grant resumed his advance. This now had a quick and dramatic success—retreating from Richmond, Lee's army was headed off and forced to surrender within a week.

Sherman's conduct of operations during the campaigns of 1864 and 1865 showed that the North had found a strategist who had diagnosed the causes of the prevalent paralysis and developed a remedy for it.

The increased facility of supply that came with the development of railroads had led commanders to build up increased numbers of troops at the railhead, without pausing to consider the hampering effect on their own power of maneuver. Thus the first result of the new means of strategic movement was, paradoxically, to reduce strategic mobility. The railroad fostered the expansion of armies—it could forward and feed many more men than could operate effectively. It also tended to inflate their wants and demands, so that they became more closely tied to the railhead.

A further result was that their own strategic vulnerability increased because their sustenance and progress "hung on a thread"—the long stretch of rail line behind them, which could be all too easily cut by a small force maneuvering in such wide spaces. The Northern armies, accustomed to more plentiful rations, were more susceptible to paralysis than their opponents. That became increasingly evident in 1864, when, with growing strength, they pushed deeper into hostile territory. In the western theater the precarious situation of such rail-fed masses was exploited by the mobile raids of such brilliant Confederate cavalry leaders as Nathan Bedford Forrest and John Hunt Morgan.

Sherman grasped the problem and produced a solution—the only one then technically possible. The enemy had struck him through his rail communications; he would strike at theirs, while immunizing himself. He saw that to regain and secure mobility he must free himself from dependence on a fixed line of supply. So he organized a force that was self-contained as to supplies, carrying the necessary minimum along with it and supplementing this by foraging from the countryside through which it passed. He then cut loose from his own railway.

Having shown in the march through Georgia how light an army could travel, Sherman now proved that it could move lighter still. Before starting northward through the Carolinas, he sought to convert his army "into a mobile machine willing and able to start at a moment's notice and to subsist on the scantiest of food." Although it was winter, officers as well as men were now made to bivouac in pairs under a strip of canvas stretched over sticks or boughs; all tents and camp furniture were discarded. Once again, as in his march on Atlanta, Sherman took a deceptive line between alternative objectives so that, time after time, his opponents could not concentrate their forces effectively to stop him.

Sherman's flexible organization of his army contributed almost as much as his variability of direction to his continuous progress. Moving on a wide and irregular front—with four, five, or six columns, each covered by a cloud of foragers—if one was blocked, others would be pushing on. The opposing forces became so jumpy that they repeatedly gave way to the psychological pressure and fell back before they felt any serious physical pressure. The mere shout, "We're Bill Sherman's raiders, you'd better git," sometimes sufficed to make opposing detachments retreat.

Sherman's strategy, and grand strategy, foreshadowed the aim that was pursued in the Allies' strategic bombing campaign of the Second World War. But that bombing offensive was too gradual in development to produce a quickly decisive effect, while it offered no such good opportunity for the opposing troops and people to escape from their leaders' grip by desertion and surrender—for it is not possible to surrender to an attacker who stays aloft in the sky. A closer parallel to, and fulfillment of, Sherman's strategy is to be found in the paralyzing and demoralizing shock effect, on the opposing armies and peoples simultaneously, of the blitzkriegs of 1939–41 carried out by the Germans, who combined deep thrusting armored forces with air attack.

Since General Heinz Guderian, the creator and leader of the panzer forces, has stated that he derived this new technique from my writings, it may be of historical interest to mention that the concept developed in my mind partly in studying the course and effect of Sherman's operations.

This was the first war between modern democracies, and Sherman saw clearly that the resisting power of a democracy depends even more on the strength of the people's will than on the strength of its armies. His unchecked march through the heart of the South, destroying its resources, was the most effective way to create and spread a sense of helplessness that would undermine the will to continue the war.

The havoc that his march produced in the Deep South left a legacy of bitterness in later years—more than in the immediate postwar years. That has recoiled on Sherman's historical reputation. But it is questionable whether that bitterness or the impoverishment of the South would have been prolonged, or grave, if the peace settlement had not been dominated by the vindictiveness of the northern extremists who gained the upper hand after Lincoln's assassination.

For Sherman himself bore in mind the need of moderation in making peace. That was shown in the generous terms of the agreement he drafted for the surrender of Johnston's army—an offer for which he was violently denounced by the government in Washington. Moreover, he persistently pressed the importance, for the future of the forcibly reunited nation, of reconciling the conquered section by good treatment and help toward its recovery. His vision extended beyond the horizon of war to the peace that would follow.

—August 1962

THE UNEXPECTED MRS. STOWE

By DAVID McCULLOUGH

She had no talent, said George Sand, only genius

She had been brought up to make herself useful. And always it suited her.

As a child she had been known as Hattie. She had been cheerful but shy, prone to fantasies, playful, and quite pretty. After she became famous, she would describe herself this way: "To begin, then, I am a little bit of a woman,—somewhat more than forty, about as thin and dry as a pinch of snuff; never very much to look at in my best days, and looking like a used-up article now." She wasn't altogether serious when she wrote that, but the description was the one people would remember.

She was born in Litchfield, Connecticut—in a plain frame house that still stands—in 1811, when Lincoln was two years old and when Dolley Madison was in the White House. She was the seventh of the nine children Roxana Foote bore Lyman Beecher before being gathered to her reward, and she was such a worker, even when very small, that her preacher father liked to say he would gladly have given a hundred dollars if she could have been born a boy.

As a child she had found most of his sermons about as intelligible as Choctaw, she wrote later, and never would she be at peace with his religion. But she loved him, and for all his gloomy talk of sin and damnation it is not hard to understand why. He was a powerful, assertive figure who had an almost fiendish zest for life—for hunting and fishing with his sons, for listening to all music, and for playing the violin, which he did badly. But could he only play what he heard inside him, he told them all, he could be another Paganini. Best of all he loved to go out and "snare souls," as he said. In a corner of the cellar he kept a pile of sand, and if his day was not

337

enough to use him up, and stormy weather kept him from outdoor exercise, down he would go, shovel in hand, to sling sand about.

Sunday mornings he would come bounding along through the sunshine, late again for that appointed hour when weekly he brought down Calvinist thunder upon the heads of upright Litchfield people. He had a special wrath for drunkards and Unitarians, and he believed passionately in the Second Coming. But something in him made him shy away from the strictest tenet of his creed—total predestination—and its logic. Once when he had agreed to exchange pulpits with another pastor, he was told that the arrangement had been preordained. "Is that so?" he said. "Then I won't do it!" and he didn't.

The happiest times in her childhood, Hattie would write later, were the days spent away from him, visiting an Aunt Harriet in Nutplains, Connecticut, in a house filled with books and pictures gathered by a seafaring uncle and a wonderful old Tory grandmother, who in private still said Episcopal prayers for the king and queen.

At twelve Hattie often wandered off from the noisy parsonage to lie on a green hillside and gaze straight into a solid blue sky and dream of Byron. One month she read *Ivanhoe* seven times.

In 1832, when Hattie had turned twenty-one, Lyman Beecher answered the call to become the first president of the Lane Theological Seminary in Cincinnati. He packed up his children and a new wife and set off for what he called "the majestic West." A New Jerusalem was to be established on the banks of the Ohio. The family spirits were lifted; and crossing the Alleghenies, they all sang "Jubilee." A Philadelphia journal likened the exodus of the Reverend Mr. Beecher and his family to the migration of Jacob and his sons.

The following summer the Lane Theological Seminary's first (and at that time, only) professor, Calvin Ellis Stowe, a Biblical scholar and Bowdoin graduate, traveled west in the Beecher's wake. For all his learning and devotion to the Almighty, Stowe was a very homely and peculiar worker in the vineyard.

He was accompanied by a beautiful young bride, Eliza, who soon became Hattie Beecher's best friend in Cincinnati but died not very long afterward. Apparently it was a shared grief over Eliza that brought Hattie and Calvin Stowe together. Years later, with some of the proceeds from *Uncle Tom's Cabin*, they would commission an artist to do a portrait of Eliza, and every year thereafter, on Eliza's birthday, the two of them would sit before the portrait and reminisce about Eliza's virtues.

The wedding took place in early January, 1836. What exactly she saw in him is a little hard to say. The night before the ceremony, trying to describe her emotions in a letter to a school friend, she confessed she felt "nothing at all." But Lord Byron had not appeared in Cincinnati. At twenty-four she may have felt she was getting on.

Calvin was thirty-three, but he seemed as old as her father. He was fluent in Greek, Latin, Hebrew, French, Italian, German; he was an authority on education; he knew the Bible better than her father. Also, it is recorded, he had a grand sense of humor. But he was as fat and forgetful and fussy as an old woman. In the midst of a crisis, as she would soon discover, he had a bad habit of taking to his bed, and he had absolutely no "faculty," that Yankee virtue she defined simply as being the opposite of shiftlessness.

He also had an eye for pretty women, as he admitted to Hattie, and a taste for spirits, but these proclivities, it seems, never got him into any particular trouble.

But there was more. Calvin, from his boyhood until his dying day, was haunted by phantoms. They visited him most any time, but favored dusk. They appeared quite effortlessly out of the woodwork, the floor, or the furniture. There was a regular cast of characters, Calvin said, as real and familiar to him as anyone else he knew. Among his favorites were a giant Indian woman and a dark dwarf who between them carried a huge bull fiddle. There was a troupe of old Puritans from his native Natick, all shadowy and dark blue in color, and one "very pleasant-looking human face" he called Harvey. They performed music for Calvin Stowe, and somehow or other they talked to him without making any sound at all, or so he said. He had no reluctance about discussing the subject, and there is no indication that any of his circle thought the less of him for it.

Still, the marriage proved difficult soon enough. Hattie became pregnant almost immediately, and just about then Calvin was asked by the state of Ohio to go to Prussia to study educational systems there. Professing a profound fear of the salt sea, he told her he would never see her again in this life. She insisted that he go, and had twin daughters while he was away. There was a third child two years later, then another, and two more later on. A professor's wages were never enough, even when old Lyman could pay Calvin in full, which was seldom. Hattie's health began to fail. "She lived overmuch in her emotions," one son would explain years later.

"It is a dark, sloppy, rainy, muddy disagreeable day," she wrote once to Calvin when he was in Detroit attending a church convention. " . . . I am sick of the smell of sour milk, and sour meat, and sour everything, and then the clothes *will* not dry, and no wet thing does, and everything smells mouldy; and altogether I feel as if I never wanted to eat again."

She began going off on visits to relatives, leaving Calvin and the children behind. The visits grew longer. She went to the White Mountains, then to Brattleboro, Vermont, to try the water cure. The expenses were met by gifts from distant admirers of the family: the Stowes felt that the Lord had a hand in it. Hattie stayed on for nearly a year at Brattleboro, living on brown bread and milk, enduring the interminable sitz baths of one Dr. Wesselhoeft, and writing home exuberant letters about moonlight snowball fights. And no sooner did she return to the cluttered house in Cincinnati than the professor hauled himself off to Brattleboro, there to stay even longer than she had. When a cholera epidemic broke out in Cincinnati and more than a hundred people a day were dying, she wrote to tell him to stay right where he was. She would manage.

In all they were separated a total of three years and more, and their letters back and forth speak of strong, troubled feelings. The hulking, clumsy Stowe, bearded, nearsighted, complained that she never folded his newspaper properly and that her letters of late were too uninteresting for him to read aloud to his friends. She in turn would run on about her own miseries. The house depressed her, she worried about money, she hated the climate in Cincinnati. She thought too much about death.

But she also told him, "There are a thousand favorite subjects on which I could talk with you better than anyone else. If you were not already my dearly loved husband I should certainly fall in love with you."

And Calvin would write to her when she was visiting her sister in Hartford, "And now my dear wife, I want you to come home as quick as you can. The fact is I cannot live without you and if we were not so prodigious poor I would come for you at once. There is no woman like you in this wide world."

In this same letter Calvin proclaimed to her—and apparently he was the first to do so—"My dear, you must be a literary woman. It is so written in the book of fate." He advised her to make all her plans accordingly, as though she had little else to do. "Get a good stock of health and brush up your mind," he declared. And he told her to drop her middle initial, E (for Elizabeth), from her name. "It only encumbers it and interferes with the flow and euphony." Instead: "Write yourself fully and always Harriet Beecher Stowe, which is a name euphonious, flowing, and full of meaning."

She had already written quite a little—temperance tracts, articles on keeping the Sabbath, New England "sketches," for which she drew heavily on Calvin's seemingly inexhaustible fund of childhood reminiscences. Once she had done an article about a slave. She had been selling these pieces to *Godey's Lady's Book* and one or two other magazines. She got two dollars a page on the average, which was more profitable than taking in boarders, she decided. But no one in the family, other than Calvin, had taken her writing very seriously.

She worked at the kitchen table, confusion all around, a baby in a clothes basket at her feet. She couldn't spell very well, and her punctuation would always be a puzzle for her publishers. She dreamed, she said in a letter to Calvin, of a place to work without "the constant falling of soot and coal dust on everything in the room."

Then in July of 1849 she was writing to tell him that their infant son Charley was dead of cholera. The summer before she had nearly died of it herself, with her father praying over her all through one terrible, sweltering night, the room alive with mosquitoes. She had been unable to do a thing for the child, she told Calvin. For almost a week she watched him die, with no way to help, she said, no way even to ease his suffering.

Calvin returned to her very soon after that, determined to leave Cincinnati for good. He had accepted a professorship at Bowdoin College, in Brunswick, Maine, and before he could settle up his affairs in Cincinnati, he characteristically sent Harriet and three of the children off to Maine ahead of him.

She left Cincinnati in the early spring of 1850, a shabby little figure, perfectly erect, perhaps no more than five feet tall, nearly forty, and pregnant once again. She boarded a riverboat at the foot of town, saying farewell with no misgivings. She was going home, she felt.

She was also heading for a sudden and colossal notoriety of a kind never known by any American woman before, and very few since; but of that she had no notion whatever. Nor did she or anyone else alive have any idea how important those seventeen years in Cincinnati had been to her and, as things turned out, to the whole course of American history.

She sailed up the Ohio to Pittsburgh, where she changed to a canalboat. Already she was feeling so good she got out and walked the towpath between locks. At Johnstown the boat and all its passengers were hoisted up and over the Allegheny Mountains by that thrilling mechanical contrivance of the nineteenth century, the Portage Railroad. East of the mountains she went by rail to New York and there crossed by ferry to Brooklyn to see her younger brother, Henry Ward, pastor of Plymouth Church. As children they had sometimes been taken for twins, only Henry Ward had been thick of speech and considered the slow one. Now she took note of his obvious success, and they went out for a drive in a spotless six-hundred-dollar carriage, a recent gift from his parishioners.

In a few days she went on to Hartford, still looking after the children and all their baggage. Her spirits were soaring. At Hartford she stayed with her sisters Mary and Isabella; in Boston with her brother Edward, who was growing ever more militant over the slavery issue. All the Beechers were growing more militant over one thing or another. For Isabella it was women's rights; for the brilliant Catherine, education; for Charles, freedom from theological authority. From Boston, Harriet took the Bath Steamer to Maine, sailing headlong into a northeaster.

On the day they were scheduled to arrive at Brunswick, one story goes, the president of Bowdoin sent a professor named Smith down to greet the new faculty wife, but Smith returned disappointed, saying she must have been delayed. Nobody got off the boat, he said, except an old Irish woman and her brats.

Brunswick offered precious few of the eastern civilities Mrs. Stowe had longed for, and the house Calvin had taken in advance turned out to be deserted, dreary, and damp, to use her words. She went straight to work, refinishing floors, putting up wallpaper—the pioneer again. When Calvin wrote from Cincinnati to say he was sick and plainly dying and that she and theirs would soon be plunged into everlasting debt, she read the letter with humor and stuffed it into the stove.

Calvin showed up before summer, her baby was born, she rested two weeks. When winter came, there were holes in her shoes, and the house was so cold during one long storm that the children had trouble sitting still long enough to eat their meals. They were living on $1,700 a year. It was during the following spring that she began *Uncle Tom's Cabin*.

People are still trying to interpret the book and to explain just how and why she came to write it. At first she said she really didn't write it at all. She said the book come to her in visions and all she did was write down what she saw. When someone reproached her for letting Little Eva die, she answered, "Why, I could not help it. I felt as badly as anyone could! It was like a death in my own family and it affected me so deeply that I could not write a word for two weeks after her death." Years later she stated categorically, "God wrote it." And a great many of her readers were quite willing to let it go at that.

The truth is, the subject of the book had been all around her for a very long time. Old Lyman had been able to make Litchfield farmers weep when he preached on slavery. In Cincinnati she had opened her own Sunday school to black children, and the Lane Seminary had been a hotbed of abolitionist fervor. The Underground Railroad, she later claimed, went directly through her Cincinnati house, which was a bit of an exaggeration; but on one occasion Calvin and her brother Charles did indeed help a black woman and her child elude a slave hunter. The only time she was in an actual slave state, during a visit across the Ohio River in Kentucky, she made no show of emotion about it. But stories she heard from the Negro women she knew in Cincinnati moved her enormously, particularly those told by a gentle person named Eliza Buck, who helped her with housework and whose children, Harriet Stowe discovered with incredulity, had all been fathered by the woman's former master in Kentucky. "You know, Mrs. Stowe," she had said, "slave women cannot help themselves."

Eliza Buck told her of lashings and of Negro families split up and "sold down the river." Once on an Ohio River wharf Mrs. Stowe had seen with her own eyes a husband and wife torn apart by a slave trader.

By the time she came east to Maine, Henry Ward was using his Brooklyn pulpit to raise money to buy children out of slavery. In Boston she and Edward had talked long and emotionally about the Fugitive Slave Bill, then being debated in Congress, which made it a federal crime to harbor or assist the escaped "property" of a slave master. Her duty was plain. There was, she said, a standard higher than an act of Congress.

She did some research in Boston and corresponded with Frederick Douglass on certain details. But for all that, the book would be written more out of something within her, something she knew herself about bondage and the craving for liberation, than from any documentary sources or personal investigation of Negro slavery in the South. Indeed she really knew very little about Negro slavery in the South. Her critics would be vicious with her for this, of course, and she would go so far as to write a whole second book in defense of her sources. But *Uncle Tom's Cabin* could never be accounted for that way.

There is probably something to the story that she began the book as a result of a letter from Edward's wife. "Hattie," wrote her sister-in-law from Boston, "if I could use the pen as you can, I would write something that will make this whole nation feel what an accursed thing slavery is." To which Hattie answered, "As long as the baby sleeps with me nights, I can't do much at anything, but I will do it at last. I will write that thing if I live."

The story appeared first as a serial in the *National Era*, an antislavery paper, beginning in June, 1851. It took her a year to write it all, and apparently she did Uncle Tom's death scene first and at a single sitting, writing on brown wrapping paper when her writing paper ran out. The finished story was brought out in book form by the publisher, John P. Jewett, in two volumes on March 20, 1852, a month before the serialized version ended.

Calvin thought the book had little importance. He wept over it, but he wept over most of the things she wrote. Her publisher warned that her subject was unpopular and said she took too long to tell her story. On the advice of a friend who had not read the manuscript, she decided to take a 10 percent royalty on every copy sold instead of a fifty-fifty division of profit or losses, as had also been offered to her.

She herself expected to make no money from it; she thought it inadequate and was sure her friends would be disappointed with her. Within a week after publication ten thousand copies had been sold. The publisher had three power presses running twenty-four hours a day. In a year sales in the United States came to more than three hundred thousand. The book made publishing history right from the start. In England, where Mrs. Stowe had no copyright and therefore received no royalties, sales were even more stupendous. A million and a half copies were sold in about a year's time. The book appeared in thirty-seven different languages. "It is no longer permissible to those who can read not to have read it," wrote George Sand from France, who said Mrs. Stowe had no talent, only genius, and called her a saint.

The book had a strange power over almost everyone who read it then, and for all its Victorian mannerisms and frequent patches of sentimentality much of it still does. Its characters have a vitality of a kind comparable to the most memorable figures in literature. There is a sweep and power to the narrative, and there are scenes that once read are not forgotten. The book is also rather different from what most people imagine, largely because it was eventually eclipsed by the stage version, which Mrs. Stowe had nothing to do with (and from which she never received a cent) and which was probably performed more often than any play in the language, evolving after a few years into something between circus and minstrel show. (One successful road company advertised " . . . a pack of genuine bloodhounds; two Toppsies; Two Marks, Eva and her Pony 'Prince'; African Mandolin Players; 'Tinker' the famous Trick Donkey.") In the book, for example, no bloodhounds chase Eliza and her baby across the ice.

What the book did at the time was to bring slavery out into the open and show it for what it was, in human terms. No writer had done that before. Slavery had been argued over in the abstract, preached against as a moral issue, its evils whispered about in polite company. But the book made people at that time *feel* what slavery was all about. ("The soul of eloquence is feeling," old Lyman had written.)

Moreover, Harriet Stowe had made a black man her hero, and she took his race seriously, and no American writer had done that before.

The fundamental fault, she fervently held, was with the system. Every white American was guilty, the Northerner no less than the slaveholder, especially the churchgoing kind, *her* kind. Simon Legree, it should perhaps always be remembered, was a Vermonter.

That Uncle Tom would one day be used as a term of derision ("A Negro who is held to be humiliatingly subservient or deferential to whites," according to the *American Heritage Dictionary*) she would have found impossible to fathom, and heartbreaking. For her he was something very close to a black Christ. He is the one character in all her book who lives, quite literally, by the Christian ideal. And if one has doubts that she could see black as beautiful or that she saw emancipation for the black man as a chance for full manhood and dignity, there is her description of Eliza's husband, George Harris, as straight-backed, confident, "his face settled and resolute." When George and his family, having escaped into Ohio, are cornered by slave hunters, Mrs. Stowe writes a scene in which George is fully prepared to kill his tormentors and to die himself rather than permit his wife and son to be taken back into slavery. " . . . I am a free man, standing on God's free soil," George yells from the rock ledge to which he has retreated, "and my wife and my child I claim as mine. . . . We have arms to defend ourselves and we mean to do it. You can come up if you like; but the first one of you that comes within the range of our bullets is a dead man, and the next, and the next, and so on till the last."

She seems to have been everywhere at once after the book was published —Hartford, New Haven, Brooklyn, Boston. Almost immediately the South began boiling with indignation. She was a radical, it was said. All the Beechers were radicals. She began receiving threatening letters from the South, and once Calvin unwrapped a small parcel addressed to her to find a human ear that had been severed from the head of a black slave. Calvin grew more and more distraught. They decided it was time to move again, now to Andover, Massachusetts, to take up a previously offered teaching job at the seminary there.

Then they were sailing to England, where huge crowds waited for her at railroad stations, hymns were composed in her honor, children came up to her carriage with flowers. She went about in a gray cloak carrying a paint box. She was a tireless tourist. And she worried. "The power of fictitious writing, for good as well as evil is a thing which ought most seriously to be reflected on. No one can fail to see that in our day it is becoming a very great agency."

When war came, everyone told her it was her war, and she thought so too. In South Carolina, as the war commenced, the wife of a plantation owner wrote in her diary that naturally slavery had to go, but added, "Yes, how I envy those saintly Yankee women, in their clean cool New England homes, writing to make their fortunes and shame us."

Harriet Stowe never saw the Civil War as anything but a war to end slavery, and all her old Beecher pacifist principles went right out the window. "Better, a thousand times better, open, manly, energetic war, than cowardly and treacherous peace," she proclaimed. Her oldest son, Frederick, put on a uniform and went off to fight. Impatient with Lincoln for not announcing emancipation right away, she went down to Washington when he finally proclaimed that the slaves would be free, and was received privately in the White House. The scene is part of our folklore. "So this is the little woman who made this big war," Lincoln is supposed to have said as he shook her hand.

She was sitting in the gallery at the Boston Music Hall, attending a concert, on January 1, 1863, the day the Emancipation Proclamation became effective. When an announcement of the historic event was made from the stage, somebody called out that she was in the gallery. In an instant the audience was on its feet cheering while she stood and bowed, her bonnet awry.

After the war she kept on writing. In fact, as is sometimes overlooked, that is what Harriet Beecher Stowe was, a writer, and one of the most industrious we have ever had. Unwittingly she had written the abolitionist manifesto, although she did not consider herself an abolitionist. She agreed with her father that abolitionists "were like men who would burn down their houses to get rid of the rats." She was not a crusader pure and simple. She never considered herself an extremist, and she seldom took an extreme position on any issue. She was a reformer, and there was an evangelical undercurrent to just about everything she wrote. But writing was her work, her way to make herself useful.

Her life was about half over when she wrote *Uncle Tom's Cabin*, but for thirty years more she wrote almost a book a year on the average, plus innumerable essays, poems, children's stories, and magazine articles, many of which she did under the pseudonym Christopher Crowfield. Perhaps her most artful novel, *The Minister's Wooing*, ran to fifty printings, and a magazine article, "The True Story of Lady Byron's Life," which appeared in the *Atlantic Monthly* in 1869, caused more furor than anything published in America since *Uncle Tom's Cabin*.

During a second visit to England she had become fast friends with the widow of Lord Byron, who confided the terrible secret that the great Byron had committed incest with his half sister and that a child had been born as a result. Mrs. Stowe kept the secret for thirteen years, but when Byron's former mistress, Countess Guiccioli, published her memoirs and portrayed Lady Bryon as a self-righteous tyrant who would drive any mortal male to excesses, Harriet Stowe decided it was time to strike a blow in her friend's behalf, Lady Byron by this time having been dead for nearly a decade. So she told the whole story.

All kinds of accusations were hurled at her, some quite unpleasant. She rode out the storm, however, and again, as with *Uncle Tom*, she wrote a book to justify what she had written. But her standing with the American public would never be the same.

She could write in all kinds of places, under every kind of condition. She was always bothered by deadlines, and it seems she was always in need of money. The royalties poured in, but the more she had the more she spent—on a huge Gothic villa in Hartford that was all gables and turrets and was never finished completely; on a cotton plantation in Florida where she intended to provide Negroes with a program of work and education; and later, when that failed, on an orange and lemon grove at Mandarin, Florida, "where the world is not," she said, and where she hoped her unfortunate son Frederick might find himself.

Frederick had trouble staying sober. His problem had started before the war, but at Gettysburg he had been hit in the head by a shell fragment, and, his mother would always believe, he had never been himself again. "After that," one of her grandsons would write, "he not only was made drunk by the slightest amount of alcohol but he could not resist taking it."

Calvin grew enormously fat, ever more distant, and of even less use than before when it came to the everyday details of life. Moreover, Harriet found fame increasingly difficult. She had become a national institution. Her correspondence alone would have drained a less vigorous spirit.

Tragedy struck repeatedly. In 1857, upon returning from Europe, she learned that her son Henry, a student at Dartmouth, had drowned while swimming in the Connecticut River. In 1870 Frederick, unable to endure his mother's Florida experiment any longer, wrote her a touching apology and went to sea, shipping around the Horn. It is known that he got as far as San Francisco, but after that he disappeared and was never heard from again. She would go to her grave with every confidence that he would return one day.

But it was the Brooklyn scandal that hurt her worst of all, she said. In November of 1872 a New York paper reported that her beloved brother Henry Ward, by then the most popular preacher in America, had been carrying on an adulterous affair with one of his parishioners. His enemies swept in for the kill. For all the Beechers gossip was agonizing. A sensational trial resulted, the husband bringing suit against Beecher for alienation of his wife's affections. It dragged on for six months and was the talk of the country. Whether Beecher was guilty or innocent was never proved one way or the other. He denied everything, the jury was unable to agree on a verdict, and as far as his sister was concerned his character was never even in question.

The whole story was a slanderous fabrication, she said, and she stood by him through the entire grisly, drawn-out business, as did all the Beechers except Isabella Beecher Hooker, who was only a half sister, it was noted, and was regarded by many as just a little unbalanced. (Isabella, who called herself "*the* inspired one," wanted to take charge of a service at Plymouth Church herself and "as one commissioned from on high" declare her brother's guilt from his own pulpit. Years later, when he was dying, she even tried to force her way into his house to get a deathbed confession.)

But it would be mistaken to suggest that Harriet's life became increasingly burdensome. Quite the contrary. As time passed she seems to have grown ever more liberated from her past. She drew further and further from the shadow of her harsh Calvinist heritage, eventually rejecting it altogether. She had long since discarded the doctrine of original sin. Neither man nor nature was necessarily corrupt, she now held. Hers was a faith of love and Christian charity. She had a seemingly limitless love for the whole human family. Years before, Catherine, her spinster sister, had been the first of the Beechers to rebel against the traditional faith when a young man she was engaged to marry, a gifted Yale professor of philosophy, was lost at sea and Catherine had had to face the terrible Calvinist conclusion that the young man was consigned to eternal damnation because he had never repented. In time all of Lyman Beecher's offspring would desert the faith. Henry Ward would even go so far as to preach that there is no hell.

For Harriet, Calvinism was repugnant, a "glacial" doctrine, although she admired enormously the fervor it had given the Puritan colonists of her native New England and the solid purpose and coherence of the communities they established. Like many of her time she sorely lamented the decline of Christian faith in the land. It was the root of the breakdown of the old order, she believed. Mostly, it seems, she admired the backbone the old religion gave people. "They who had faced eternal ruin with an unflinching gaze," she wrote, "were not likely to shrink before the comparatively trivial losses and gains of any mere earthly conflict." If she herself could not accept the articles of the Puritan faith, she seemed to wish everybody else would. And once from Florida she wrote: ". . . never did we have a more delicious spring. I never knew such altogether perfect weather. It is enough to make a saint out of the toughest old Calvinist that ever set his face as a flint. How do you think New England theology would have fared, if our fathers had landed here instead of on Plymouth Rock?"

Like numerous other literary figures of the day she tried spiritualism and claimed that her son Henry had returned from somewhere beyond to pluck a guitar string for her. She became an Episcopalian, and she developed an open fondness for such things as Europe (Paris and Italy especially), Rubens, elegant society, and Florida, in particular Florida (" . . . this wild, wonderful, bright, and vivid growth, that is all new, strange and unknown by name to me . . ."). The theater and dancing were no longer viewed as sinful. She rejected the idea that "there was something radically corrupt and wicked in the body and in the physical system." She took a little claret now on occasion. An account of a visit to Portsmouth, New Hampshire, suggests that once at least she may have taken a little too much claret.

She was asked to give readings, to go on the lyceum, as the contemporary lecture circuit was called, like Robert Ingersoll, P. T. Barnum, and the feminists. She needed the money, so at age sixty-one, having never made a public speech before, she embarked on a new career with its endless train rides, bad food, and dreary hotels. She was very shy at first and not much good at it. But she got over that and in time became quite accomplished. "Her performance could hardly be called a reading," reported the Pittsburgh *Gazette*, "it was recitative and she seldom glanced at the book. Her voice betrayed the veritable Yankee twang. . . . Her voice is low, just tinged in the slightest with huskiness, but is quite musical. In manner she was vivacious and gave life to many of the pages, more by suggestive action than by utterances. . . . She seemed perfectly possessed on the stage, and read with easy grace. . . ."

She found she could move her audiences to great emotional heights, but to laughter especially. And she loved the life. Her health picked up. "I never sleep better than after a long day's ride," she wrote.

Her appearance never changed much. She put on no new airs. Nothing, in fact, good or bad, seemed capable of changing that plain, earnest, often whimsical manner. She acquired a number of new friendships that meant a great deal to her, with Oliver Wendell Holmes and Mark Twain particularly. Henry Drummond, the noted Scottish religious writer, wrote, after a visit to Hartford: "Next door to Twain I found Mrs. Harriet Beecher Stowe, a wonderfully agile old lady, as fresh as a squirrel still, but with the face and air of a lion." And he concluded: "I have not been so taken with any one on this side of the Atlantic."

Her affections for Calvin seem to have grown stronger, if anything. He had become absorbed in Semitic studies, let his beard grow, and took to wearing a skullcap. She began calling him "My Old Rabbi." His apparitions took up more and more of his time, and for a while he was having nightly encounters with the Devil, who came on horseback, Calvin said. But otherwise his mind stayed quick and clear until the end, and she found him exceedingly good company.

In their last years they seem also to have had few financial worries. Among other things a book of his, *The Origin and History of the Books of the Bible*, had a surprisingly large sale. And their affairs in general were being capably managed by their twin daughters, Eliza and Harriet, maiden ladies who apparently had considerable "faculty."

Calvin died peacefully enough, with Harriet at his bedside, on August 6, 1886. She lived on for another ten years, slipping off ever so gradually into a gentle senility.

In a letter to Oliver Wendell Holmes she wrote: "I make no mental effort of any sort; my brain is tired out. It was a woman's brain and not a man's, and finally from sheer fatigue and exhaustion in the march and strife of life it gave out before the end was reached. And now I rest me, like a moored boat, rising and falling on the water, with loosened cordage and flapping sail."

She was eighty-two. She spent hours looking at picture books, bothering no one, or went out gathering flowers, "a tiny withered figure in a garden hat," as one writer described her. On occasion she took long walks beside the river, an Irish nurse generally keeping her company. Sometimes, Mark Twain would recall, she "would slip up behind a person who was deep in dreams and musings and fetch a war whoop that would jump that person out of his clothes."

And every now and then, during moments of astonishing clarity, she would talk again about *Uncle Tom's Cabin*, the book that had just "come" to her in visions. Once, years earlier, when she was having trouble writing, she had said: "If there had been a grand preparatory blast of trumpets or had it been announced that Mrs. Stowe would do this or that, I think it likely I could not have written; but nobody expected anything . . . and so I wrote freely."

She died near midnight on July 1, 1896.

—August 1973

FEAR OF THE CITY

By ALFRED KAZIN

The city has been a lure to millions of Americans, but most of our great minds have been appalled by its excesses

E very Thursday, when I leave my apartment in a vast housing complex on Columbus Avenue to conduct a university seminar on the American city, I reflect on a double life—mine. Most of the people I pass on my way to the subway look as imprisoned by the city as my parents and relatives used to look in the Brooklyn ghetto where I spent my first twenty years. Yet no matter where else I have traveled and taught, I always seem to return to streets and scenes like those on New York's Upper West Side.

Two blocks away on Broadway there is daily carnage. Drunks outside the single-room-occupancy hotel dazedly eye me, a professor laden with books and notes trudging past mounds of broken glass, hills of garbage. Even at eight in the morning a craps game is going on in front of the hydrant that now gives off only a trickle. It has been left open for so many weeks that even the cover has vanished. On the benches lining Broadway, each drunk has his and her bottle in the regulation brown paper bag. A woman on crutches, so battered looking that I can't understand how she stands up, is whooping it up—totally ignored by the cars, trucks, and bicycles impatiently waiting at the red light. None of the proper people absorbed in their schedules has time to give the vagrants more than a glance. Anyway, it's too dangerous. No eye contact is the current rule of the game.

I left all this many times, but the city has never left me. At many universities abroad—there was even one improbable afternoon lecturing in Moscow—I have found myself explaining the American city, tracing its history, reviewing its literature—and with a heavy heart, more and more

351

having to defend it. The American city has a bad reputation now, though there was a time, as the violinist Yehudi Menuhin said during World War II, when one of the great war aims was to get to New York.

There is now general fear of the city. While sharing it, I resent it, for I have never ceased feeling myself to be one of the city's people, even as I have labored in libraries to seize the full background to my life in the city. But when in American history has there not been fear of the city—and especially on the part of those who did not have to live in it?

Before there were American cities of any significance, the best American minds were either uninterested in cities or were suspicious of them. The Puritans thought of Boston as another Jerusalem, "a city upon a hill," but even their first and deepest impression was of the forest around it. This sense of unlimited space was bewitching until the end of the nineteenth century. In his first inaugural address in 1801, Thomas Jefferson pronounced, as if in a dream, that Americans possessed "a chosen country, with room enough for our descendants to the hundredth and thousandth generation." What was "chosen" was not just an endless frontier but the right people to go with it. This, as a matter of course to a great country squire like Jefferson, surveying the future from his mountaintop at Monticello, meant excluding the mobs he associated with European cities. Jefferson's attitude may have been influenced by the European Philosophes whom Louis XVI blamed for the French Revolution. Jefferson was a Philosophe himself; he would have agreed with a leader of the revolution, Saint-Just, that oppressed people "are a power on the earth." But he did not want to see any oppressed people here at all—they usually lived to become the kind of mob he detested and feared. "The mobs of great cities," he wrote in *Notes on Virginia*, "add just so much to the support of pure government, as sores do to the strength of the human body."

Jefferson knew what the city mob had done to break down ancient Rome as well as feudal France. America was a fresh start, "the world's best hope," and must therefore start without great cities. As a universal savant of sorts, as well as a classicist and scientist, Jefferson knew that Athens and Rome, Florence and Venice, Paris and London, had created the culture that was his proudest possession. And since he was an eighteenth-century skeptic, this cosmopolitan world culture was his religion. But anticipating the damage that "manufactures" could inflict on the individual, he insisted that on an unsettled continent only the proudly self-sustaining American "cultivator" could retain his dignity in the face of the Industrial Revolution.

It is not easy now to appreciate all Jefferson's claims for the rural life, and his ideas were not altogether popular with other great landowners and certainly not with such promoters of industry as Hamilton. Jefferson was a great traveler and world statesman who hardly limited himself to his country estate. Monticello, with its magnificent architecture, its great library, its array of inventions and musical and scientific instruments, more resembles a modern think tank (but imagine one this beautiful!) than the simple American farm he praised as a bastion of virtue.

But "virtue" was just what Jefferson sought for America. Whatever else they did, cities corrupted. The special virtue of rural folk rested on self-reliance, a quality unobtainable in "manufactures and handicraft arts" because these depended "on casualties and caprice of customers. Dependence begets subservience and venality, suffocates the germ of virtue, and prepares fit tools for the designs of ambition."

A few years later Emerson had a more complicated view of his society. The Sage of Concord was no farmer (Thoreau was his handyman) and did not particularly think the farmers in his neighborhood were the seat of all virtue. They were just of the earth, earthy. But believing in nothing so much as solitude, *his* right to solitude, his freedom only when alone to commune with Nature and his own soul ("Alone is wisdom. Alone is happiness."), Emerson found the slightest group to be an obstruction to the perfect life.

There is an unintentionally funny account in Emerson's journal for 1840 of just how irritating he found his fellow idealists. There was a gathering in some hotel—presumably in Boston, but one Emerson likened to New York's Astor House—to discuss the "new Social Plans" for the Brook Farm commune: "And not once could I be inflamed, but sat aloof and thoughtless; my voice faltered and fell. It was not the cave of persecution which is the palace of spiritual power, but only a room in the Astor House hired for the Transcendentalists. . . . To join this body would be to traverse all my long trumpeted theory, and the instinct which spoke from it, that one man is a counterpoise to a city—that a man is stronger than a city, that his solitude is more prevalent and beneficent than the concert of crowds."

Emerson finally agreed to help found Brook Farm but he could not have lived there. Hawthorne tried it for a while and turned his experiences into the wry novel *The Blithedale Romance*. Hawthorne was another Yankee grumpily insisting on his right to be alone but he did not take himself so seriously; he was a novelist and fascinated by the human comedy. A twentieth-century admirer of Emerson, John Jay Chapman, admitted that you can learn more from an Italian opera than from all the works of Emerson; in Italian opera there are always two sexes.

But Emerson is certainly impressive, bringing us back to the now forgotten meaning of "self-reliance" when he trumpets that "one man is counterpoise to a city—that a man is stronger than a city. . . ." This was primary to many Americans in the nineteenth century and helped produce those great testaments to the individual spirit still found on the walls of American schoolrooms and libraries. Power is in the individual, not in numbers; in "soul," not in matter or material conglomeration. And "soul" is found not in organized religion, which is an obedience to the past, but in the self-sufficient individual whose "reliance" is on his inborn connection, through Nature, with any God it please him to find in himself.

Certainly it was easier then to avoid the "crowd." Thoreau, who went back many an evening to his family's boardinghouse for meals when he was at Walden Pond writing a book, said that the road back to Concord was so empty he could see a chicken crossing it half a mile off. Like Thoreau's superiority to sex and—most of the time—to politics, there is something truly awesome in the assurance with which he derogates such social facts as the city of New York: "I don't like the city better, the more I see it, but worse. I am ashamed of my eyes that behold it. It is a thousand times meaner than I could have imagined. . . . The pigs in the street are the most respectable part of the population. When will the world learn that a million men are of no importance compared with *one* man?"

To which Edgar Allan Poe, born in Boston and fated to die in Baltimore, could have replied that Thoreau had nothing to look at but his reflection in Walden Pond. Poe would have agreed with his European disciple Baudelaire on the cultural sacredness of great cities. He would have enjoyed Karl Marx's contempt for "rural idiocy." Poe was a great imagination and our greatest critic; as an inventor of the detective story and a storyteller, he was as dependent on the violence and scandal of New York in the 1840s as a police reporter. "The Mystery of Marie Roget," based on the actual murder of a New York shop assistant named Mary Rogers who was found dead in the Hudson after what is now believed to have been a botched abortion, was the first detective story in which an attempt was made to solve a real crime. Even the more than usual drunkenness that led to his death in Baltimore on Election Day of 1849 was typical of his connection with "low" urban life. He was found in a delirious condition near a saloon that had been used for a voting place. He seems to have been captured by a political gang that voted him around the town, after which he collapsed and died.

Yet just as Abraham Lincoln was proud of having a slow, careful countryman's mind, so Poe would have denied that *his* extraordinary mind owed anything to the cities in which he found his material. In the same spirit, John Adams from once rural Quincy, his gifted son John Quincy, and his even more gifted great-grandson Henry, all hated Boston and thought of the financial district on State Street as their antithesis. Herman Melville, born in New York, and forced to spend the last twenty-five years of his life as a customs inspector on the docks, hated New York as a symbol of his merchant father's bankruptcy and of his own worldly failure as an author. In a poem about the Civil War, when the worst insurrection in American history broke out in New York as a protest against the Draft Act, Melville imagined himself standing on the rooftop of his house on East Twenty-Sixth Street listening to the roar of the mob and despising it:

> . . . *Balefully glares red Arson—there—and there.*
> *The Town is taken by its rats—ship-rats*
> *And rats of the wharves. All civil charms*
> *And priestly spells which late held hearts in awe—*
> *Fear-bound, subjected to a better sway*
> *Than sway of self; these like a dream dissolve,*
> *And man rebounds whole aeons back in nature.*

Before the Civil War there was just one exception among the great American writers to the general fear and resentment of the city. Whitman was to be prophetic of the importance of New York as a capital of many races and peoples and of the city as a prime subject in modern American writing.

Whitman found himself as man and poet by identifying with New York. None of the gifted writers born and bred in New York—not Melville or Henry James or Edith Wharton—was to make of the city such an expression of personal liberation, such a glowing and extended fable of the possibilities released by democracy. "Old New York," as Edith Wharton called it (a patriciate that Melville could have belonged to among the Rhinelanders and Schuylers if his father had not failed in business), still speaks in Melville's rage against the largely Irish mob burning and looting in 1863. But Whitman, his exact contemporary, did not despair of the city's often lawless democracy when he helped put the first edition of *Leaves of Grass* into type in a shop off Brooklyn's Fulton Street.

Whitman found himself by finding the city to be the great human stage. Unlike earlier and later antagonists of the city, who feared the masses, Whitman saw them as a boundless human fellowship, a wonderful spectacle, *the* great school of ambition. The masses, already visible in New York's population of over a million, were the prime evidence Whitman needed to found his gospel of American democracy as "comradeship." Formerly a schoolteacher, printer, carpenter, a failure at many occupations who was born into a family of failures and psychic cripples, Whitman felt that the big anonymous city crowd had made it possible for *him* to rise out of it.

> *One's self I sing, a simple separate person,*
> *Yet utter the word Democratic, the word En-Masse.*

Whitman found the model and form of *Leaves of Grass*, the one book he wrote all his life, in the flux and mass of the city—he even compared his book *to* a city. He never reached his countrymen during his lifetime, and the Gilded Age took the foam off his enthusiasm for democracy, but in decline he could still write, "I can hardly tell why, but feel very positively that if anything can justify my revolutionary attempts & utterances, it is such *ensemble*—like a great city to modern civilization & a whole combined clustering paradoxical unity, a man, a woman."

Whitman was that "paradoxical unity, a man, a woman." His powerful and many-sided sexuality give him friends that only a great city can provide; his constant expectation of love from some stranger in the street, on the ferryboat, even his future reader—"I stop somewhere waiting for you" —made stray intimacies in the city as sweet to him as they were repellent to most Americans.

The trouble with the city, said Henry James, Henry Adams, and Edith Wharton, *is* democracy, the influx of ignorant masses, their lack of manners, their lack of standards. The trouble with the city, said the angry Populist farmers and their free-silver standard-bearer Bryan in 1896, is Wall Street, the "moneyed East," the concentration of capital, the banking system that keeps honest, simple farmers in debt. Before modern Los Angeles, before Dallas, Phoenix, and Houston, it was understood that "the terrible town," as Henry James called New York, could exist only in the crowded East. The West, "wild" or not, was land of heart's ease, nature itself. The East was the marketplace that corrupted Westerners who came East. There was corruption at the ballet box, behind the bank counter, in the "purlieus of vice." The city was ugly by definition because it lacked the elemental harmony of nature. It lacked stability and relentlessly wrecked every monument of the past. It was dirt, slums, gangsters, violence.

Above all it was "dark." The reporter and pioneer photographer Jacob Riis invaded the East Side for his book *How the Other Half Lives* (1890) because he was "bent on letting in the light where it was much needed."

Look at Riis's photograph "Bandit's Roost," 59½ Mulberry Street, taken February 12, 1888. "Bandit's Roost" did not get its name for nothing, and you can still feel threatened as your eye travels down the narrow alley paved with grimy, irregularly paved stone blocks that glisten with wet and dirt. Tough-looking characters in derbies and slouch hats are lining both sides of the alley, staring straight at you; one of them presses a stick at the ground, and his left knee is bent as if he were ready, with that stick, to go into action at a moment's notice. The women at the open windows are staring just as unhelpfully as the derbied young fellow in the right foreground, whose chin looks as aggressive as the long, still lines of his derby.

Consider New York just a century ago: the rooftops above the business district downtown are thick with a confusion of the first telephone lines crossing the existing telegraph wires. The immigrant John Augustus Roebling has built a suspension bridge of unprecedented length over the East River, thanks to the wire rope he has invented. This wire makes for a rooted strength and airy elegance as Roebling ties his ropes across one another in great squares. Brooklyn Bridge will be considered stronger as well as infinitely more beautiful than the other bridges to be built around the East River. But a week after opening day in 1883, the crowd panics as vast numbers cross the bridge, crushing several people to death—and exposing a fear of numbers, of great bridges, of the city itself, that even city dwellers still feel. What they thought of New York in the prairie West and the cotton South may easily be imagined.

But here is Central Park, the first great public park in the New World, finally completed after a decade of struggle to reclaim a horrid waste. Unlike the European parks that were once feudal estates, Central Park has been carved, landscaped, gardened, built, and ornamented from scratch and specifically for the people. And this by a Connecticut Yankee, Frederick Law Olmsted, the most far-seeing of democratic visionaries, who saw in the 1850s that New York would soon run out of places in which city dwellers could escape the city. Though he will never cease complaining that the width of his park is confined to the narrow space between Fifth Avenue and what is now Central Park West, he will create a wonderland of walks, "rambles," lakes, gardens, meadows. All this is designed not for sport, political demonstrations, concerts, the imperial Metropolitan Museum, but for the contemplative walker. As early as 1858, before he was chosen superintendent but after having submitted the winning design, "Greensward," in a competition, Olmsted wrote of his park: "The main object and justification is simply to produce a certain influence in the minds of the people and through this to make life in the city healthier and happier. The character of this influence is a poetic one, and it is to be produced by means of scenes, through observation of which the mind may be more or less lifted out of moods and habits in which it is, under the ordinary conditions of life in the city, likely to fall. . . ."

Alas, Central Park is not enough to lift some of us out of the "moods and habits" into which we are likely to fall. Even Walt Whitman, who truly loved New York, acidly let it drop in *Democratic Vistas* (1871) that "the United States are destined either to surmount the gorgeous history of feudalism, or else prove the most tremendous failure of time." The "great experiment," as some English sardonically call the democratic Republic, may very well depend on the city into which nearly a million immigrants a year were to pour at the beginning of the next century. Whitman was not prepared to estimate the effect on America of the greatest volunteer migration recorded in history. It was the eclipse of virtue that surprised him at the end of the century. As if he were Jefferson, he wrote: "The great cities reek with respectable as much as nonrespectable robbery and scoundrelism. In fashionable life, flippancy, tepid amours, weak infidelism, small aims, or no aims at all, only to kill time. In business (this all-devouring modern word business), the one sole object is, by any means, pecuniary gain. The magician's serpent in the fable ate up all the other serpents; and money-making is our magician's serpent, remaining today sole master of the field."

A re cities all that important as an index of American health and hope? The French sociologist Raymond Aron thinks that American intellectuals are too much preoccupied with cities. He neglects to say that most Americans now have no other life but the life in those cities. Paris has been the absolute center of France—intellectually, administratively, educationally—for many centuries. America has no center that so fuses government and intellect. Although Americans are more than ever an urban people, many Americans still think of the city as something it is necessary to escape from.

In the nineteenth century slums were the savage places Jacob Riis documented in his photographs, but on the whole the savagery was confined to the slums. The political scientist Andrew Hacker has shown that "there was actually little crime of the kind we know today and in hardly any cases were its victims middle class. The groups that had been violent —most notably the Irish—had by 1900 turned respectable. The next wave of immigrants, largely from Eastern Europe and southern Italy, were more passive to begin with and accepted the conditions they found on their arrival . . . they did not inflict their resentments on the rest of society. . . ."

What has finally happened is that fear of the city on the part of those who live in it has caught up with the fear on the part of those who did not have to live in it.

American fear of the city may seem ungrateful, since so much of our social intelligence depends on it. But the tradition of fear persists, and added to it nowadays—since all concern with the city is concern with class—has been the fear of the "underclass," of blacks, of the youth gangs that first emerged in the mid-fifties. Vast housing projects have become worse than the slums they replaced and regularly produce situations of extreme peril for the inhabitants themselves. To the hosts of the uprooted and disordered in the city, hypnotized by the images of violence increasingly favored by the media, the city is nothing but a state of war. There is mounting vandalism, blood lust, and indiscriminate aggressiveness.

The mind reels, is soon exhausted, and turns indifferent to the hourly report of still another killing. In Brooklyn's 77th precinct a minister is arrested for keeping a sawed-off shotgun under his pulpit. On Easter Sunday uniformed police officers are assigned to protect churchgoers from muggers and purse snatchers. In parts of Crown Heights and Bedford-Stuyvesant, the *Times* reports that "there, among the boarded-up tenements, the gaudy little stores and the residential neighborhoods of old brownstones and small row houses, 88 people were killed in one year—16 in one three-block area." A hundred thousand people live and work in this precinct, but a local minister intones that "Life has become a mean and frightening struggle." Gunshots are heard all the time.

I was born and brought up alongside that neighborhood; the tenement in which my parents lived for half a century does not exist and nothing has replaced it. The whole block is a mass of rubble; the neighborhood has seen so much arson that the tops of the remaining structures are streaked with black. Alongside them whole buildings are boarded up but have been broken into; they look worse than London did after the blitz.

Democracy has been wonderful to me and for me, and in the teeth of the police state creeping up elsewhere in the world, I welcome every kind of freedom that leaves others free in the city. The endless conflict of races, classes, sexes, is raucous but educational. No other society on earth tolerates so many interest groups, all on the stage at once and all clamoring for attention.

Still, the subway car I take every day to the city university definitely contains a threat. Is it the young black outstretched across the aisle? The misplaced hilarity proceeding from the drinking group beating time to the ya-ya-ya that thumps out of their ghetto blaster? The sweetish marijuana fumes when the train halts too long in this inky tunnel and that makes me laugh when I think that once there was no more absolute commandment in the subway than NO SMOKING?

Definitely there is a threat. Does it proceed from the unhelpful, unsmiling, unseeing strangers around me? The graffiti and aggressive smears of paint on which I have to sit, and which so thickly cover every partition, wall, and window that I cannot make out the stations? Can it be the New York *Post*—"Post-Mortem" as a friend calls it—every edition of which carries the news MOM KILLS SELF AND FIVE KIDS? The battle police of the transit force rushing through one car after another as the motorman in his booth sounds the wailing alarm that signifies trouble?

What a way to live! It is apartness that rules us here, and the apartness makes the threat. Still, there is no other place for me to work and live. Because sitting in the subway, holding the book on which I have to conduct a university seminar this afternoon, I have to laugh again. It is *Uncle Tom's Cabin, or Life Among the Lowly.*

—February 1983

THE GREAT VANDERBILT WILL BATTLE

By FRANK KINTREA

The old Commodore was the richest man in America when he died in 1877, and his passing touched off a complex and ugly legal contest with one hundred million dollars riding on the outcome

W hen Commodore Cornelius Vanderbilt expired in New York City on January 4, 1877, with members of his family gathered about his bed singing "Come Ye Sinners, Poor and Needy," he was by far the richest man who had ever died in the United States of America. He had gone to bed for the last time early in May of the previous year. After nearly eighty-three years of strenuous living, his staunch body was finally exhausted by a multitude of ailments, any one of which might have killed an ordinary person. The doughty old Commodore has had his less fervent admirers both before and since his demise, but no one has ever accused him of having been an ordinary person. He fought on through the summer and fall, stubborn and irascible and profanely contemptuous of those whose great expectations were being so maddeningly prolonged by his reluctance to become a decedent.

His residence at 10 Washington Place, then a quiet backwater between the gilded flow of fashion northward from Washington Square and the swirl of commerce up Broadway, was shabby by comparison with the great mansions soon to be built by his favored heirs, and it swarmed with relatives and friends speaking in appropriately hushed voices all through the months of his illness. It must have resembled one of those scenes so relished by writers of popular Victorian novels, with only the favorites permitted to hover solicitously about the deathbed. The aging daughters, who had disapproved of the young wife of their father's declining years and whose mere presence now provoked him into violent rages, were relegated to the hallway outside his chamber, from which they could peek in at him reproachfully whenever the door was opened. At an even farther remove from parental favor, downstairs on the parlor floor, a truly classic example of the wastrel and debt-ridden younger son paced fitfully to and fro, still hopeful of winning a last-minute reprieve.

Down on Wall Street the Commodore's old playmates in the game of swallowing railroads waited ravenously. Their mouths already watered in anticipation of the luscious pickings which would be theirs when the old man's controlling interest in the New York Central was divided among a dozen mutually antagonistic heirs. For some of them the strain was too much; premature announcements of his death were frequently circulated in an effort to drive down the price of Central stock, but the great railroad empire that the Commodore had wrested from the wolves of the Street was impervious to such petty chicanery.

Beyond these financially expectant inner circles was the general public, motivated by nothing more tangible than curiosity as to how the richest man in America, having died, would leave his fortune. This curiosity was considerably whetted by the newspapers, which used relays of reporters to maintain a twenty-four-hour vigil about the house and which printed daily bulletins spiced with assorted rumors and conjectures. Even allowing for this journalistic incitement, the extent of general interest in the imminent demise of a private citizen from natural causes seems hardly credible today. But wealth on such a vast scale as Cornelius Vanderbilt's seemed less credible then. William B. Astor, the son of John Jacob Astor, had died two years earlier leaving forty million dollars, but the Astor fortune had been the product of two lives spanning nearly a century, and it was not nearly so impressive as Vanderbilt's one hundred-odd millions, which he alone had accumulated—and mostly in the last fifteen years of his life. Most of the rich men of the time were worth only a few hundred thousand dollars, but in the extremely solid dollars current in those days, one hundred thousand was a tidy fortune. For a man born poor to amass such a fortune as the Commodore's was a phenomenon so baffling to the imagination that even the rumors grossly underestimated its extent.

The funeral took place on Sunday, January 7. It was described as unostentatious but impressively solemn. After a brief service at the Church of the Strangers around the corner on Mercer Street, the cortege proceeded down Broadway to the Battery, crossed by ferry to Staten Island, and there in the old Moravian burying ground at New Dorp, among generations of humble ancestors, Cornelius Vanderbilt was laid to rest.

The next day, promptly at noon, the bereaved family gathered in the house of William K. Thorn, a son-in-law of sufficient independent wealth to be on reasonably good terms with all factions, to hear Judge Charles A. Rapallo read decedent's last will and testament. In the macabre gloom customary in the parlors of that era, with the austere and venerable Judge Rapallo presiding, it must indeed have been a grimly momentous occasion in the lives of the two sons and eight daughters who had grown old awaiting it. Phoebe Jane, the eldest, who was sixty-two, barely survived it.

"I Cornelius Vanderbilt, of the City of New York, do make and publish my last will and testament as follows. . . ." Thus commenced the document which would dispose of all the vast accumulation of worldly goods of which decedent had died possessed. First, he gave to his beloved wife, Frank A. Vanderbilt, the sum of $500,000 in five percent bonds of the United States of America, with the stipulation that this bequest was in fulfillment of an antenuptial contract in which Mrs. Vanderbilt had agreed to waive her dower rights. He also gave to said wife the house and lot at 10 Washington Place, complete with stables and all appurtenances thereto, two carriages, and one pair of carriage horses.

The second clause, consisting of one brief paragraph, rapidly disposed of five of his eight daughters by giving to each of them outright $250,000 in bonds of the Lake Shore and Michigan Southern Railroad Company. These were nice bonds to own, even without the picture of the Commodore which adorned them, but there may have been outbursts of filial indignation from the recipients, two of whom were already widows, when they and those husbands who were still living realized that this was all they were going to get.

T he third clause took care of the three remaining daughters, and though they fared somewhat better than their sisters, they could well have been even more indignant. Their bequests of $300,000, $400,000, and $500,000, respectively, in five percent government bonds, were securely tied up in trusts from which they were to receive only the income during their lives. Should they die without surviving issue, the principal would revert to the estate and thence to the residuary legatee "hereinafter named." Not a penny would remain to console a surviving husband in his old age.

With the expectations of the daughters and their husbands written off so neatly, the Commodore, without even deigning to start a new clause, proceeded to the seemingly more delicate and complex problem of deflating the hopes nourished for a lifetime by his younger son. Cornelius Jeremiah Vanderbilt, then in his late forties, had long been in disfavor with his father. The primary reason was not, perhaps, that he was a frequenter of the plush gambling houses and elegant brothels which flourished in that era of extreme feminine prudery, but probably because he had not inherited his parent's zeal for making and holding money. Ever since young Cornelius could remember, he had been afflicted by a sense of futility of financial enterprise. The insignificant positions he could obtain and the paltry sums he could earn by his own merits should, he felt, have been as embarrassing to his father as to himself. During the Commodore's lifetime he had avoided such embarrassment by struggling manfully along on an allowance from home so miserably inadequate that he was frequently forced to borrow money from friends, acquaintances, and even strangers. But now, after his life had been irrevocably blighted by his father's money, it seemed only fair that he share abundantly in the source of his misfortunes.

Alas, if the old Commodore had had any sympathy for this viewpoint, it was made apparent in his will only to the extent of preventing his son's life from being further blighted by too much money. After setting up a comparatively modest trust fund of $200,000 in five percent government bonds, he sternly cautioned his trustees that the income thereof was not to be paid over freely but was to be "applied" by them solely "to the maintenance and support of my son, Cornelius Jeremiah Vanderbilt, during his natural life." Even this miserable pittance was hedged with restrictions. It was only to be doled out if Cornelius's behavior was exemplary. Furthermore, any attempt on the son's part to anticipate, assign, or otherwise encumber this income would result in its being withdrawn from his use entirely. It would "thenceforth, during the residue of his natural life, belong to my residuary legatee." But the crowning indignity was yet to come. "Upon the decease of my said son, Cornelius J.," the will continued, "I give and bequeath the last mentioned $200,000 of bonds to my residuary legatee."

The residuary legatee, as everyone could guess by now, was none other than Cornelius's elder brother, William Henry. This industrious plodder, who scrupulously avoided the haunts of gentlemen, had impressed his father with his reverence for money and his real talent for holding on to it. Cornelius detested him. But he was to be one of the trustees to whom Cornelius would be accountable for his behavior, and this was utterly intolerable.

Next were several clauses devoted to minor bequests to twenty-two assorted relatives and friends of sums ranging from $4,000 to $50,000, and totaling less than $300,000. Then came the grand climax in the eighth clause, which in its entirety read as follows: "All the rest, residue, and remainder of the property and estate, real and personal, of every description, and wheresoever situated, of which I may be seized or possessed, and to which I may be entitled at the time of my decease, I give, devise, and bequeath unto my son, William H. Vanderbilt, his heirs, executors, administrators and assigns, to his and their own use forever."

Perhaps the full majesty of these redundant legal phrases cannot be properly appreciated without the knowledge that the "residue and remainder" to which they refer was still a little more than one hundred million dollars. The will was dated January 9, 1875, and it was signed, with an awesome abbreviation of testator's Christian name, "C. Van Derbilt," a variation of the old Dutch spelling that he favored.

In a codicil made six months after the original will was written, the Commodore took some $11,000,000 worth of New York Central stock away from his residuary legatee, but that step brought no comfort to his eight daughters and his wayward son. If anything, it was the touch needed to complete their humiliation, for this quite significant little bundle of stock was divided among four of the testator's sixteen grandsons. Five million went to his namesake and favorite, Cornelius Vanderbilt II, and two million to each of the other three. All were sons of the residuary legatee, William Henry Vanderbilt.

We do not know what went on in Mr. Thorn's parlor when Judge Rapallo finished reading the will, but it is not unreasonable to suppose that there were bitter outbursts from the "girls" and that Cornelius must have stalked ominously from the premises leaving a trail of threats about seeing his lawyer. All we know for certain is that William, in his capacity as one of the executors, gathered the precious document to his bosom and departed at once for the surrogate's office on Chambers Street to set in motion probate proceedings that would make him the richest man in America. In any event, rumors that the will would be contested spread quickly.

Disputes over the distribution of a decedent's worldly goods have never been uncommon. They were particularly evident in the United States during the late nineteenth century, when there was a bumper crop of parvenu testators, and the records of surrogates' courts of the period are filled with will contests of sensational bitterness. Like other successful men of the time, Cornelius Vanderbilt was proud of his fortune, and he wanted it preserved intact as long as possible. He figured that the most likely way to ensure the continuity of both his name and his railroad was to leave as much of his money as possible to his ablest son, who had himself produced male offspring, and the devil take the rest. Undoubtedly his lawyers must have advised him that such an inequitable distribution would incur the risk of a will contest and create a good deal of unhappiness as well. But this was probably the sort of reasonable business risk which would have appealed to the Commodore, and there is no evidence to show that he ever gave a rap about making everybody happy.

During the following weeks, William denied publicly and solemnly that there was any ill feeling among the heirs. No one could have been very much surprised, however, when late in February, nearly two months after the testator's death, Cornelius and two of his dissatisfied sisters—Mrs. Ethelinda Allen, beneficiary of a $400,000 trust fund, and Mrs. Marie Alicia La Bau, recipient of $250,000 of Lake Shore bonds—informed Surrogate Delano Calvin that they most certainly did intend to contest the validity of their father's will. The Surrogate put the case on his calendar for March 13. In the meantime, formal objections were filed with the court. The contestants charged that the will was obtained by fraud, circumvention, and undue influence pressed against and upon the decedent by William H. Vanderbilt and other persons as yet unnamed.

On the appointed day, Surrogate Calvin's courtroom in the county courthouse in Chambers Street buzzed with rumors: Jay Gould, the sinister financier, was backing the contestants' suit in the hope of winning a ghoulish post-mortem victory over his old adversary and eventually gaining control of the New York Central; gamblers, equally sinister, to whom young Cornelius was hopelessly indebted, were threatening his life if he did not go through with the suit; most sinister of all, unknown parties were threatening his life if he *did* go through with it. There were even a few killjoys who spread the word that William had finally settled everything by giving each contestant half a million dollars. Surely, it was argued, William would not allow the family skeletons to be rattled in public for the sake of a few paltry millions.

The crowded courtroom, tense with anticipation of the degrading arts that would be revealed, was stunned into glum silence when ex-Congressman Scott Lord, chief of counsel for the contestants, rose to his feet and abruptly announced that he had been instructed by his clients to withdraw their objections to the probate of the will. Although apparently quite as bewildered as the spectators, Surrogate Calvin recovered sufficiently to admit the will to probate. Mr. Lord told reporters later that he knew nothing of any settlement. All he knew was that late on the previous day he had received a note from his clients ordering him to withdraw the objections. It had come as a complete surprise to him, he said, and, judging from his manner, as a considerable shock. After all, as one indignant but anonymous member of the bar exclaimed to reporters, "It's highway robbery. It robs the profession of a million dollars!"

The contestants themselves were not in court when Mr. Lord made his devastating announcement. William, already launched on the career of bad relations with the press that was to culminate some years later in his famous misinterpreted remark, "The public be damned," hastily retreated to his private office in Grand Central Depot and refused to issue any statement whatsoever. There were, of course, the usual "friends of the family and other reliable sources" who scoffed at the idea of any compromise settlement but were confident that William would treat his brother and sisters munificently once the will was probated and the fortune was legally clenched in his fist. The real reason for the last-minute withdrawal, they insisted, was simply and obviously Cornelius's reluctance to expose the lurid details of his private life to public scrutiny. Cornelius himself, when finally tracked down, was not in the mood to see reporters either. A friend quoted him as insisting that he had absolutely nothing to say regarding a settlement.

Two months went by in which rumors of a compromise settlement mounted. Finally, on May 14, the rumors seemed substantiated when Cornelius went into state supreme court and filed a complaint against his brother for failure to keep an agreement allegedly made on March 12, the day before the anticlimax previously enacted in Surrogate Calvin's courtroom. Cornelius claimed that he had been promised one million dollars if he withdrew his objections to the will. Spokesmen for William refused to comment, pointing out how improper it would be to do so now that the matter was in litigation. William himself was not available. He was on the high seas bound for England when Cornelius filed his complaint. According to some of the usual informed sources, the purpose of the trip was to pacify two of his sisters living abroad, who were now claiming that they had not been properly represented at the probate proceedings. Whatever the reason for the trip, before William could return, Mrs. La Bau was back in surrogate's court, demanding (as was her right within a year) that probate be reopened and the will proved anew. Mrs. Allen, the other of the three original contestants, had dropped out, apparently feeling that she could rely on her brother's munificence. Cornelius Jeremiah could not be a legal party to Mrs. La Bau's action because of his pending suit in supreme court, although he undoubtedly gave her all the moral support he could muster. Surrogate Calvin put the case on his calendar for July 12, and the expectations of press and public again ran high.

Interest in the case as a public spectacle became even greater when the rosters of opposing counsel were made known. In those days, when the county courthouse still provided the nation with one of its staple brands of popular entertainment, legal luminaries enjoyed a public renown somewhat comparable to that accorded today to ballplayers, prizefighters, and television performers. Their strategy in conducting a case, their skill in cross-examination, and their forensic ability were all highly and learnedly appreciated by large numbers of courtroom buffs. Among connoisseurs of legal form, counsel for the proponents of the will (William, two of his sons, and a nephew) were generally rated the pretrial favorites. Henry L. Clinton, their field captain, had distinguished himself for many years in the criminal courts of New York State by an uncanny ability to obtain acquittals for unfortunately situated defendants. A client seen with blood on his hands in the immediate vicinity of the corpus delicti did not daunt Mr. Clinton, and his talent for confusing prosecution witnesses and discrediting their testimony was expected to be useful to William H. Vanderbilt in this case.

The master strategist of William's defense of the will was George F. Comstock, a former chief justice of New York State's highest tribunal, the court of appeals, whose opinions are still quoted. Less spectacular than Mr. Clinton, Judge Comstock was a lawyer's lawyer, ranked by many of his contemporaries as the greatest legal mind of his day. What was more, he looked the part. He was tall and spare, with an impressive mane of silvery hair; his mere presence in a courtroom was said to give weight to his client's case.

Joseph Hodges Choate was the reserve force of proponent's legal team. He was somewhat younger and less experienced than his two illustrious colleagues but was already renowned for the role he had played a few years earlier in liberating New York from the grip of Boss Tweed.

Although the odds were against them, counsel for the contestant were not without their backers. Scott Lord, fresh from a term in Congress, had been the law partner of Senator Roscoe Conkling and was an experienced infighter. Uninhibited by legal niceties, he was a particularly good man in a will contest. His colleague, Ethan Allen, had served for a number of years earlier in his career as a United States district attorney.

As a pinch hitter of formidable endowment when legal eloquence was in order, the contestant had retained the services of Jeremiah S. Black, a former chief justice of the supreme court of Pennsylvania and a Cabinet member under both Buchanan and Lincoln. Judge Black had the reputation of being the most magnificent orator at the American bar. His snow-white, shaggy eyebrows belied the bright auburn wig he customarily wore. Twirling a silver tobacco box on the end of an enormous chain and followed by a Negro valet, Judge Black was a familiar figure in courtrooms throughout the nation. The power of his argument was said to rise with the number of spittoons he filled.

There are three grounds on which to break a will, assuming it has been properly drawn and attested, and when the case finally got under way in earnest on November 12, 1877, before Surrogate Calvin, Mr. Lord made it clear in his opening that he was not going to overlook any of them. The contestant would offer evidence to show, first, that the testator had been of unsound mind at the time he made his will; second, that he had been subjected to undue influence; and third, that the will was the product of a fraudulent conspiracy. "Undue influence" and "fraudulent conspiracy" are, in practice, virtually synonymous. The usual tactic is to demonstrate that the unsound condition of the testator's mind, weakened by physical disability and insane delusions, made him readily susceptible to a fraudulent conspiracy designed to influence him unduly. In addition to the lurid charges that Mr. Lord alleged would prove the will invalid on strictly legal grounds, he embellished his opening remarks with lofty rhetorical effects of a moral nature. The division of the estate under the terms of the will was, he declaimed, contrary not only to the spirit of the law but to the morals of a democracy. This may have impressed the public but hardly Surrogate Calvin, who was undoubtedly aware that, in the words of one of his contemporaries, "a will may be mean, unjust and inequitable . . . [and] public sentiment and the moral sense of the community may condemn the instrument and its author to no avail."

Mr. Lord himself, of course, was fully aware of the formidable task confronting him. Not only did he have to battle great wealth and impressive legal talent, but he also had to demonstrate that the testator's mind was of questionable soundness, if he hoped to win his case. That would be extremely difficult. The mere ability to perform an ordinary business transaction was, and still is, considered sufficient proof of testamentary capacity, regardless of aberrations and debilities of the most startling sort. Surrogate Calvin himself was fond of citing the case of a testator who believed that in order to go to heaven he had to eat Boston crackers every morning; nevertheless, his will was duly probated. Judged by this criterion, Cornelius Vanderbilt, who was still juggling railroads successfully in the closing years of his life, was perhaps the sanest of men. Thus, Mr. Lord served notice that contestant's case would reveal the diabolical conspiracies William H. Vanderbilt had been carrying out for years to influence his aging father. Mr. Lord admitted that many of the charges which would be proved were of a scandalous nature, but he laid the blame for making them public squarely on William himself. The press, of course, was in a dither, devoting columns of space to Mr. Lord's "startling performance," and his "amazing allegations."

It was also apparent from this opening that Cornelius Jeremiah, though technically not a contestant in Mrs. La Bau's suit, was to be the central figure in the case and was undoubtedly the moving spirit behind it. For it was primarily against him that the alleged undue influence had been exercised. As a direct consequence, Mr. Lord said, his voice quivering with righteous indignation, "his father subjects [young Cornelius] to a degradation unparalleled in the history of wills . . . in this will he puts the son bearing his Christian name under a vassalage so odious that every instinct of his manhood revolted against it."

According to the press, popular sympathy was with Cornelius and his sisters, not so much, perhaps, because they got too little as because William and his family got too much. Nevertheless, the will had its supporters —solid, pillar-of-society types who remained unmoved by the piteous spectacle of young Cornelius in his $10,000-a-year vassalage.

Mr. Lord then opened his assault. He called to the stand an impressive array of medical experts who had either attended Commodore Vanderbilt in his last illness or participated in the autopsy. Their testimony was intended to establish that the physical condition of the deceased had been such that he could not possibly have been of sound mind. What it did establish beyond question was that the old gentleman had suffered from a remarkable variety of afflictions and had had a truly remarkable constitution. The autopsy itself revealed in grisly detail that, except for the heart (which was found to be unusually small), there was hardly an organ in his vast cadaver which was not diseased. Yet it had been peritonitis of only several days' duration which finally killed him. Mr. Clinton objected strenuously to most of this on the ground that it proved nothing about decedent's mental condition when he made his will two years before his death and was, therefore, irrelevant.

In sum, the testimony of the medical experts, although it had shown the testator to be a man abundantly afflicted with the physical infirmities of old age, had failed to develop the picture of a doddering old fool. On the contrary, the more ailments the experts revealed, the more the Commodore stood forth as an exceptionally strong-willed old curmudgeon rising triumphantly above his bodily ills.

Contestant's real hope of establishing that the Commodore was of unsound mind lay in demonstrating that he was subject to various insane delusions. Mr. Lord proposed to do this by proving, first, that the decedent had believed in clairvoyance and spiritualism, and, second, that the Commodore had had a mania, amounting to insanity, for wealth and personal fame.

The key witness to the influence of the spirits on the testator was Mrs. Jennie W. Danforth. She was a sprightly little woman, who said she was a "magnetician" or "magnetic healer." Magnetic healing, a heady mixture of spiritualism, hypnotism, and electricity, generously spiked with pure hokum, was one of the numerous branches of the nonmedical healing arts which flourished in that era of bemused wonder at the apparently limitless marvels of science. Some of its practitioners may have been sincere in the sense that they were merely as naïve and gullible as their patients; many, however, were unmitigated frauds. The notorious Claflin sisters, Tennessee and Victoria, for example, made their debut in New York as versatile practitioners of the occult arts. They then went on to greater things, including blackmail, free love, and a friendship with Commodore Vanderbilt that was, according to contemporary gossip, not entirely devoted to communion with the spirits. During the contest over the will, the Claflin sisters were frequently mentioned as star witnesses for the contestant, and, when they departed suddenly for England, it was widely rumored that they had been bribed by William's faction to put themselves beyond the jurisdiction of the court. In any event, in lieu of Tennie and Victoria on the witness stand, Mr. Lord had to manage with Mrs. Danforth and her far less alluring magnetic arts.

According to her testimony, the Commodore had frequently sent for her in the spring and summer of 1876, during the early stages of his last illness. These were evidently memorable occasions in her career, and she would drop everything to bring the great financier the solace of her miraculous healing powers.

She was equally cooperative on the witness stand with Mr. Lord. She recalled with enthusiastic alacrity that the Commodore had absolutely assured her that he believed in clairvoyance and communication with the dead. In fact, on one occasion he had asked her to communicate with his first wife, Sophia, who had died in 1868. Mrs. Danforth had promptly done so. Unfortunately, however, it had been her sad duty to report that Sophia's spirit was in a distressed state indeed. To this the Commodore said he knew why and that he would certainly have to make another will to set things right with his wife's spirit. At this, Mr. Clinton finally erupted with violent objections to admitting Mrs. Danforth's testimony, in whole or in part. It was, he said, entirely irrelevant. Some courtroom observers felt it was entirely too relevant to be credible. Surrogate Calvin, for his part, said he would like to listen to arguments from both sides before making his decision.

There was very little legal precedent by which to judge the effects of a belief in spiritualism on testamentary capacity. Isaac Redfield, one of the few legal authorities who had commented on the subject, had written in his treatise "The Law of Wills," published in 1876, ". . . [Spiritualism] may be a species of religious belief . . . but [we] can scarcely dignify [it] by the name of science. . . . We believe the courts fully entitled to assume, as a matter of law, that what is contrary to the acknowledged laws of nature cannot have any standing in a court of law . . . and that a will which is the off-spring of such assumptions cannot be maintained."

Mrs. Danforth's testimony, of course, did not show that the will was the offspring of the spirits, and Mr. Lord did not intend it to do so. Its purpose was to show that the testator had been a true believer in the spirits and in the possibility of communicating with them. This in itself, Mr. Lord contended, was evidence of a state of mental weakness which would render him susceptible to a fraudulent conspiracy designed to influence him unduly.

Arguing for the proponents, Mr. Clinton stated vehemently that Mrs. Danforth's testimony was irrelevant simply because her visits to the Commodore did not take place until more than a year after he had drawn his will. Furthermore, if belief in clairvoyance was to be admitted as proof of insanity, then the witness herself was insane and her testimony was void. Judge Comstock, Mr. Clinton's learned associate, did not much care whether the witness's testimony was relevant or not; it was worthless in any case. The idea that belief in clairvoyance and spiritualism was in itself any proof of mental weakness was, he said, ridiculous. Thousands of intelligent people believed in it. He also pointed out, with remorseless logic, that there were supernatural elements in all religions.

At this crucial point, when it appeared that the evidence of testator's senility was either irrelevant or untenable, or both, Mr. Lord hastily called for reinforcements. Judge Black, rumbling into position beside a convenient spittoon, commenced his argument by brushing aside the question of the relevance of Mrs. Danforth's testimony as of minor importance. Instead, he launched a vigorous attack on the character of the deceased.

"Commodore Vanderbilt was the weakest of living men," Judge Black declaimed. "He was one who more completely misunderstood all the duties he owed to his own family and himself, and was more utterly ignorant of those principles of natural justice which he ought to have thought of and understood and applied to this transaction, than any other man that ever lived or ever died. And the evidence shows that he was so."

Surrogate Calvin, obviously annoyed and, also, a bit bewildered by this highly nonlegal approach to the question at issue, interrupted sharply to ask what there was in the evidence to show the decedent to have been of weak mind.

"His whole life shows it," Judge Black thundered. "All he has ever done or said about the disposal of his property. He had one faculty that was preternaturally enlarged, and that was for accumulating property. It was so enlarged that it dwarfed every other moral sentiment and every intellectual power. Sanity depends upon the balance that has been preserved between the different intellectual faculties and moral sentiments so that all of them bear their proper proportions to one another. Suppose a man's liver to be enlarged beyond what it ought to be, is that a healthy man? Cornelius Vanderbilt's bump of acquisitiveness, as a phrenologist would call it, was in a chronic state of inflammation all the time. [Phrenology was another of the new "sciences" popular at this period.] It grew wonderfully. And he cultivated it, and under his cultivation all the intellectual faculties that ministered to the gratification of that passion at the expense of everything else. Morally and intellectually his mind was a howling wilderness. He did not content himself by worshipping Mammon alone, though certainly he was a very zealous devotee of that meanest and least erect of the spirits that fell, whose worship is most sure to demoralize the mind and to corrupt while it weakens the understanding. When this is carried to a very great extent, unquestionably its victim cannot be considered a sane man. His love of money amounted to a mania, which would render any act of his void if it could be shown to be the offspring of the delusion under which he labored."

Judge Black's phrenological approach might have beguiled a nonlegal mind, but it failed to impress Surrogate Calvin. He simply ignored it. In order for Mrs. Danforth's testimony to be acceptable as indirect evidence of insanity, the Surrogate ruled that the contestant must first get in evidence something to show that Commodore Vanderbilt was actually insane at the time his will was drawn. This had not been done. Therefore, the witness's testimony was irrelevant, and Mr. Clinton's objection was sustained.

"What it amounts to," Mr. Clinton had said in winding up his own argument, after commenting on the fact that Mrs. La Bau had also been a patient of Mrs. Danforth, "is that counsel seeks on behalf of a crazy client and through a crazy witness to influence this court to let in all kinds of crazy testimony."

Deprived of help from the spirits, Mr. Lord put on the stand a number of witnesses whose testimony was supposed to prove the testator's mania for wealth and personal fame. E. D. Worcester, an official of the New York Central and hardly a friendly witness, told of an employee who had stolen twenty dollars from the railroad. It had troubled his conscience so much that he had given the money to his priest to return to the Commodore. His mission accomplished, the priest took the opportunity to mention the poverty and the need of his church, but the Commodore was not moved. He turned the money over to Mr. Worcester for credit to the proper account, saying, "There is considerable good in religion after all."

Oakey Hall, the debonair ex-mayor who turned his varied talents to playwriting after his political career had been brought to an untimely end by the disclosure that he was a member in good standing of the Tweed Ring, came to the stand to tell the inside story of how the heroic statue of the Commodore, which then decorated the façade of the St. John's Park freight terminal and which now graces the southern approaches to Grand Central Terminal, had been paid for. It had cost $100,000 which ostensibly had been raised by public subscription; actually, according to Mr. Hall, the decedent had had to foot the entire bill himself.

These two incidents, Mr. Lord contended, were proof of the old man's mania for fame.

In mid-December, with the trial more than a month old and with public interest commencing to languish, Mr. Lord, like a good showman, suddenly shifted his attack from the public to the private life of the deceased and his family. He sought permission to add the names of Mrs. Frank Vanderbilt, the bereaved widow, and her mother, Mrs. Crawford, to that of William Henry Vanderbilt as parties to the alleged conspiracy to influence the testator. In support of his motion, Mr. Lord revealed that the two ladies had actually been named in the original allegation when it was first prepared but that their names had been stricken out by Mrs. La Bau from motives of delicacy. Since then, however, such strong evidence of their complicity had been obtained that his client was forced to suppress any such sentiments in the interests of justice. Public interest was revived, and Mr. Clinton was more infuriated than ever. He denounced the motion as "an effort to build up a case by defamation of the living and the dead." It was another attempt, Mr. Clinton said, "to prove impossible facts by incredible witnesses." But it was to no avail. Surrogate Calvin said he would have to grant the motion as he must assume it to be in good faith. The idea of assuming anything good on the part of opposing counsel was more than Mr. Clinton could bear. He was so incensed that he defied the Surrogate's admonishments to temper his remarks. He openly accused Mr. Lord of trying his case in the newspapers by scurrilous allegations because his witnesses were either nonexistent or so worthless that he did not dare to call them.

This was not a nice thing to say of a fellow member of the bar, and Mr. Lord was, to all appearances, genuinely indignant. Nevertheless, it was hard to deny that very little evidence had thus far been produced that would invalidate the will. The contestant's lawyers seemed simply to be piling one scandalous allegation upon another until William Henry should capitulate in order to save the family name. For a legalized blackmailing operation of this sort, the offers of counsel to prove an allegation were just as effective as the sworn testimony of reputable witnesses. The press could be relied upon to publish the sordid details in its news columns as it salved its conscience with pious editorials defending "the sanctities of private life" and castigating those who violated them. William Henry himself was accused of unnatural greed in permitting the family name to be dragged through the mire. But, in spite of it all, William showed no sign of loosening his grasp on all his "rest, residue and remainder."

In the light of later events it would seem that Mr. Lord had really been conducting a delaying action until his star witnesses either could be found or, having been found, could be prevailed upon to appear. But now, apparently goaded beyond endurance by Mr. Clinton's unkind accusations, he unlimbered his heavy artillery. The opening barrage was the testimony of Cornelius J. Vanderbilt, the chief victim of the alleged conspiracy engineered by his brother William. When his name was called by Mr. Lord, there was a ripple of excitement in the crowded courtroom. Now, surely, the skeletons supposedly rattling in the family closet would dance merrily into public view.

"Young Corneel," as he was familiarly known, was, alas, one of the skeletons himself. From contemporary accounts, he must have looked the part. He was tall and gaunt and badly stooped, and a dank goatee added a satanic touch to his cadaverous features. Even the languid manner which he affected, and which was then *de rigueur* for men about town and scions of wealth, was impaired by a disjointed twitchiness of movement. For him to take the stand was either an act of considerable moral courage or irrefutable evidence that he was every bit the fool his father thought him to be.

Piloted by Mr. Lord's questioning, Cornelius skimmed blithely over and around the shoals of a misspent life. He'd always been told that he'd been born in 1831, so that would make him about forty-six years old. He had lived at home, more or less, until he was eighteen, when he had gone out on his own, more or less. There was no special reason for his leaving home, although his father was rather rough in his treatment and it was not very agreeable to be at home. He simply preferred it outside, and he supposed his father preferred it too. His father gave him an allowance of about $100 a month, and he had boarded around in New York. This arrangement had continued for six or seven years until in 1856, at the age of twenty-five, he had married Ellen Williams of Hartford, Connecticut, a girl of modest circumstances, and the allowance was increased to $150. They had lived near Hartford on a farm his father had given him. He didn't care much for farming. After about a year, on the plea of his wife and her family, the allowance was increased to $200, and there it remained until her death in 1872. Since then young Corneel had been boarding around New York again, or traveling, or staying with friends, and the allowance had been increased to $250, for no apparent reason that he could think of except that his father was much richer in 1872 than he had been in 1856 and he supposed it cost more for a single man in his position to live in the city.

With the vital statistics filled in, more or less, Mr. Lord got down to the real business at hand. Did Mr. Vanderbilt remember being arrested and taken to a lunatic asylum in January of 1854? He should say he did remember it. In fact, he would never forget it. It was early of a Sunday evening, just as he was dressing to keep a supper engagement, when, without the slightest warning or explanation, he had been rudely arrested and hauled off to the Bloomingdale Asylum away up on 117th Street and Morningside Heights. It had been rather an upsetting experience at the time, of course, and he had not been very amiable about it. His lack of cooperation had induced Dr. D. Tilden Brown, the director of the institution, to admit that the commitment papers were insufficient to hold him against his will, and early the next morning he and Dr. Brown had driven into the city and gone before Judge Ingram to swear out a writ of habeas corpus. William H. Vanderbilt and Judge Charles A. Rapallo, who had signed the commitment papers, had appeared in court to oppose the writ. William, in a most unbrotherly fashion, had told Cornelius that he had better withdraw his writ and return quietly to the asylum. Otherwise, he would be arrested on a forgery charge brought by a downtown merchant, and his father, who lay desperately ill at the time, would surely disinherit him. Cornelius had indignantly refused. He was innocent of any forgery, and, in any event, he would rather be considered a damned rascal than a damned lunatic. There was great laughter at this, and to restore order Surrogate Calvin had to threaten to clear the courtroom.

Judge Ingram had granted Cornelius's writ and released him, and he had gone directly to see the merchant. The merchant denied any intention of charging him with forgery for what was, after all, merely another unpaid bill. So far as Corneel was concerned, that would have been the end of the matter. But sometime later that year, while he was paying one of his infrequent visits to his parents on Washington Place, the subject of the Bloomingdale episode had come up again. One word had led to another, as it usually did, and his father had commenced one of his tirades of abuse. Corneel had been about to leave when suddenly, much to the astonishment of both his father and himself, his mother had turned on his father and told him to stop being such a fool. Then, of course, she had burst into tears at her audacity, but finally managed to calm down enough to tell his father that it was William who had planned the whole thing. It was not the first time, either. She hated to say it because she loved all her children, but William had always been scheming and telling lies to cause trouble between the witness and his father. Even more surprising than his mother's outburst, however, had been his father's reaction to it. He had hung his head sheepishly and maintained a glum silence, as though saddened by the realization that no man as rich as he was could ever really trust anyone, not even his first-born son. The witness himself, more than twenty years later, was still saddened by his memory of that unhappy scene. He took out a handkerchief and blew his nose. William, for his part, appeared unaffected by his brother's testimony, or by the suffering visible on the faces of his lawyers.

Mr. Lord, with appropriate hems and haws, now broached a rather delicate subject. Had the witness ever been afflicted in any way? With head bowed and voice trembling, Cornelius replied that he had been afflicted with epilepsy in its severest form from childhood until he was about thirty-eight. Since then the attacks had become less frequent and less severe, but it was still necessary for him to be accompanied by a friend at all times. This led into Mr. Lord's next question. Did he recall where he was during October and November, 1874? Yes, he certainly did. He was with Mr. George Terry, his friend and constant companion, traveling about from one place to another. His memory was so good on this point because he had consulted a diary which he had kept then and which he kept now.

"During those months, or at any other time," Mr. Lord asked, "were you in the habit of frequenting the Fifth Avenue Hotel every morning?"

No, he certainly was not. Of course, he may have been there once or twice during the summer and three or four times during the winter. After all, it would have been quite impossible to avoid it entirely.

In those days, in the seventies and on into the early eighties, the original Fifth Avenue Hotel played a role in New York City that no single hotel was ever to enjoy again. Standing at the intersection of Broadway and Fifth Avenue at Twenty-third Street, in the days when the city's life was centered at the crossing of those avenues, it was the Plaza and the Ritz of the fashionable, the Astor and the Knickerbocker of the theatrical and sporting set, the Algonquin of the literary, and the Old Waldorf of the *nouveaux riche*.

With a weather eye on Mr. Clinton, who was commencing to fret and fume in his seat, Mr. Lord launched his next question. During those two apparently unique months of October and November, 1874, did the witness visit any gambling house, or gambling hell, as it is called? Before Cornelius could reply, Mr. Clinton was on his feet with a strenuous objection. The witness was not a party to the contest of the will and his habits or whereabouts, good, bad, or indifferent, were entirely irrelevant and immaterial. Surrogate Calvin seemed to agree and requested Mr. Lord to reveal where his line of questioning would lead. Counsel for contestant was delighted to explain. Such testimony, he said, was directly related to the foul conspiracy which William H. Vanderbilt, desperate because of his brother's long abstention from gambling, whoring, and drinking, had cunningly devised in October and November, 1874, in order to hoodwink his aging father. It did not matter that the victim of this vicious plot was the much-maligned Cornelius rather than Mrs. La Bau, the actual contestant. If any part of the will was fraudulently produced, then the whole was a fraud. Surrogate Calvin, after some deliberation, ruled in Lord's favor. It was the first important victory for Mrs. La Bau's side, and a murmur of gratification welled up from the section of the courtroom where the contestant's partisans were gathered. Cornelius returned at once to the stand to answer Mr. Lord's question triumphantly. No, he had not been in the habit of frequenting gambling houses, or hells, in October and November of the year 1874.

"Or houses of ill-fame?"

"No!"

"Or of drinking to excess?"

"No!"

For his last question, Mr. Lord lowered his voice to the hushed tone reserved for speaking of the dead to their bereaved ones. How many times had he seen his father during his last illness? He had called at the house two or three times every day during the last three or four months, he replied sorrowfully, but his stepmother had permitted him to see his father only once in all that time.

A nd now came one of the most eagerly awaited moments of the trial —the ordeal by cross-examination of young Corneel. Mr. Clinton, making no effort to conceal his impatience with filial grief, went to work immediately. There were, as he put it, a few things he was confused about and would like to have cleared up. For instance, had Mr. Vanderbilt ever been in Bloomingdale before his visit there in 1854? Well, yes, he had been there once before—in 1850, when he was about nineteen. Could he tell them a little more about it? Well, he had been down in Washington and he had drawn some money on his father, but his father hadn't paid it. So the authorities, or whoever it was, communicated with his father and he came on and settled it. Cornelius went back to New York with his father and went into Bloomingdale of his own volition. He did not think he was insane, nor did anyone else. How long had he stayed there? About six months, more or less. Well, he must have liked it then, more or less. What did he do next? After some difficulty the witness recalled that he had gone to work in the law office of Horace Clark, his brother-in-law. In what capacity? "I could not tell," Cornelius replied languidly, and Mr. Clinton suggested that possibly he had not been there long enough for it to be determined. And then what did he do? He went into the leather business with William F. Miller & Co. at the head of Gold Street. How long had he lasted there? About three months. Why had he left? He did not care to say. No, he was not requested to leave. He had left voluntarily. He simply did not relish the business very much. And then what? Well, after his marriage, he had run the farm his father had given him. But that was five or six years later, wasn't it? He supposed it was, more or less.

Mr. Clinton seemed quite perplexed about the witness's name. Hadn't he been christened Cornelius Jeremiah Vanderbilt and not Cornelius Vanderbilt, Jr.? Inasmuch as he was only a few weeks old at the time, the witness said he really couldn't recollect whether he had or not. It got quite a laugh from the spectators, but Mr. Clinton, who was not amused, persisted. What was his real name? Well, his mother said it was Cornelius, Jr., and his father said it was Cornelius Jeremiah. To save any trouble about the matter he used both of the names. Mr. Clinton now undertook to set the record straight as to the number of times the witness had been arrested. Mr. Vanderbilt thought three times sounded about right. That is, three times in civil suits charged with fraud. Mr. Clinton was not satisfied and the following exchange took place:

Q: Haven't you been arrested four times by Deputy Sheriff McCulligan?

A: I don't know the man.

Q: Would you know him if you saw him?

A: I don't think I should. They are a class of people I don't particularly fancy.

Q: Isn't it true that you have been arrested thirty times?

The witness thought not, but he was rather vague about it, and when Mr. Clinton confronted him with the names of some thirty-five creditors to whom he had allegedly given checks on banks where he had no accounts, he was hazier than ever. He could not recollect, he did not remember, he had forgotten, or he would not swear either way. His arrangements with banks, it developed, were somewhat unusual. He had never in his life bothered to keep a regular account in any bank. As the occasion arose he simply drew checks on whichever bank was most convenient and then deposited sufficient funds to cover them. For instance, he had a standing arrangement with the teller of the Hartford County Bank to pay such checks as might come in and then to notify him of the amount needed to cover them. Of course, this method might be a bit disconcerting to banks that were unfamiliar with it, and sometimes, too, he forgot to deposit the money or found it inconvenient to do so for one reason or another.

Mr. Clinton seemed fascinated by Mr. Vanderbilt's extraordinary talent for borrowing money and not paying it back. Under prolonged questioning the witness admitted to borrowing and not paying in Utica, Rochester, Cincinnati, San Francisco, and Philadelphia, but he could not recollect as to Buffalo, Toledo, Chicago, St. Louis, or Baltimore. Finally Mr. Clinton thought it would be simpler if the witness could name one city in which he had not borrowed money. He claimed he could mention several, but he would need time to think; Mr. Clinton decided to spare him the effort. All in all the witness thought he owed about $90,000.

Mr. Clinton professed to be highly mystified by all this, particularly as to how the witness managed to incur such a large indebtedness, living as he did on a small farm in the country. Mr. Vanderbilt explained that he needed four or five servants, as he frequently entertained prominent men in his home; that he had to have an attendant at all times; and that his expenses were very large generally, inasmuch as he was expected to sustain the family name and his father's honor. Mr. Clinton found it most difficult to understand how he had sustained the honor of his father's name by borrowing money from his guests, which he had done. Mr. Vanderbilt did his best to explain that although he may have borrowed money from men in Hartford who had been guests in his house, he had never done so while they were guests. It was a fine distinction that only a highly cultivated person could appreciate, and he seemed quite proud of it. He did admit making one exception to this rule, but he felt that the circumstances warranted it. A man was invited for a few days and stayed several months. He was quite a bore, really, so the host borrowed a little money from him to get rid of him. Of course he had never paid it back. Had he ever paid back any of the money he had borrowed from those who were *not* bores? He thought he had, but he couldn't recollect their names or the amounts offhand.

He firmly denied that the greater part of his indebtedness had been caused by gambling—his total losses for his whole life did not exceed $10,000. In fact, he seemed to feel quite keenly that it was a shameful reflection both on his father's honor and on his own manhood to confess that he had never lost even as much as $500 at a sitting. Possibly he had borrowed money from gamblers, but not for gambling. And, no, he didn't think he had ever assigned his monthly allowance to anyone except John Daly, a very good friend of his who merely happened to be a professional gambler. He didn't even know Alex Howe, who ran a place on Twenty-ninth Street; he knew of George Thompson only by hearsay, although he would not swear he had never met him. A man in his position meets so many people. Of course he had been in Matthew Danser's place at 8 Barclay Street. Danser ran a downtown day game patronized by the Wall Street crowd. And it went without saying that he had been in George Beers's elegant establishment at University Place and Thirteenth Street. The late Mr. Beers had been a gentleman and a scholar who had catered to the town's young bloods.

Mr. Clinton was particularly interested in the witness's relations with one Zachariah Simmons. Mr. Simmons in his day was widely famed as a lottery man (lotteries were a forerunner of what we know as the "numbers racket" and were equally lucrative for their operators). Did Mr. Vanderbilt owe Mr. Simmons any money? Well, he supposed he did, but he could not be certain of the amount. Possibly $10,000 or so, more or less. When had he last seen Mr Simmons? The witness said he couldn't recall exactly, offhand. He saw so many people, you understand. Mr. Clinton did not understand, and said he wanted an answer to his question. Well, it was fairly recently. How recently? Yesterday? No, he was sure it wasn't yesterday. What about the day before yesterday? He wasn't so sure about that. Before the witness could make up his mind, Mr. Lord bounced up with a vigorous objection to this line of questioning as being entirely irrelevant. Surrogate Calvin directed Mr. Clinton to explain where it was leading. The latter said he could not reveal his purpose at this time. He would say, however, that at the proper time, and in direct relation to his question, there would be disclosed one of the rankest conspiracies ever encountered in the history of jurisprudence. The Surrogate said he might continue and directed the witness to answer the question. Mr. Vanderbilt now admitted that he had indeed last seen Mr. Simmons on Monday. If this was Wednesday, that would make it the day before yesterday. After further cross-examination Mr. Clinton finally got the witness to concede that he had probably borrowed money from Simmons within the last six months but he could not tell the amount without referring to his books. He did not think he had borrowed money from Simmons to finance the trial, but he did concede that he might have used some of the loan for one thing or another connected with the trial. It was another of those fine distinctions that Mr. Clinton was incapable of appreciating.

"The harrowing ordeal of young Corneel," as one overwrought journalist called it, lasted nearly four days, but he still had some fight left in him when Mr. Clinton gave him back to Mr. Lord for re-direct examination. Where did he expect to get the money to pay his debts? Why, from the same source that his brother William expected to get his, naturally. It got quite a laugh from the spectators, and it seemed to restore Corneel's own morale, too. As to his gambling habits, Cornelius claimed, after consulting his diary, that he had gambled only sixteen times in all of 1876, in spite of the strain imposed on him by his father's last illness. The fact that he had gambled at all was due entirely to the disheartening indifference with which his father had received his exemplary behavior of 1874. At this point Mr. Lord attempted to put in evidence two letters which Cornelius had written to his father in the fall of 1874 and which his father had not deigned to answer.

Mr. Clinton himself, during cross-examination, had already demonstrated that Cornelius was a prolific letter writer with an addiction to high-flown phrases. He had put in evidence a series of letters Cornelius had written to William in 1867 during another period of remorse and good resolutions—and incidentally, of acute financial embarrassment. "If you think proper," he had written from an institution in Northampton, Massachusetts, in his rich epistolary style, "to reciprocate the warm and liberal views which I have fully determined shall hereafter form the nucleus of my future relations towards yourself, I shall be most happy to receive such an assurance, and I doubt not that the line of policy which I have likewise laid down as regards the regulation of my general behavior will in a short time cause the many stigmas that now hover around my name to vanish like the morning dew, and that the insane, disgraceful tendencies of the past will soon be forgotten, and in lieu thereof the honorable workings of a subdued spirit and an expanded brain be promptly acknowledged and handsomely proclaimed." William, alas, had not thought proper to reciprocate even to the trifling extent of $150, the amount Corneel was requesting.

Mr. Lord now tried to put in evidence letters from Cornelius to his father, composed in the period of allegedly unblemished behavior in the fall of 1874. In these Cornelius alluded to similar promises of reformation and demanded to know if such promises had not now been fulfilled. Should his father fail to reply, he warned in language of suitable grandeur, his silence would be taken for assent. Counsel for the proponents objected strenuously, both to the admission of these letters as evidence, and to the assumption that the witness, lacking an answer from his father, had thereby been judged a reformed character. Judge Comstock summed up their argument with merciless logic. "Here," he said, "was a son worthless and dissipated. He writes to his father and tells him that he has been good, and says to him, now answer and tell me if you are satisfied with me, or else I will hold you to strict accountability for your silence. Why, the father had no means of knowing whether he had been good or not, and so he did not answer the letter." Mr. Lord took violent exception to the phrase "worthless and dissipated" and called Judge Comstock a liar. Judge Comstock replied in kind, and the courtroom was in an uproar. Surrogate Calvin banged his gavel for order, and excluded the letters as evidence.

While young Corneel may not have been an ideal witness, he had borne up fairly well under the embarrassment of having his personal peccadilloes so harshly exposed to the public eye. His testimony, while far from conclusive, did lay the groundwork for evidence as to the great conspiracy allegedly hatched by William Henry to discredit Corneel's reformation of late 1874. Furthermore, the Surrogate had in effect ruled that proof of such a conspiracy would invalidate the entire will. Thus, if William's accomplices could be produced in court, and if their testimony stood up, it would not matter that the contestant had been unable to show that the testator was of unsound mind. In a day when the courts abounded with professional witnesses who would swear to anything for a reasonable fee, it must have been a harrowing time for William too, even if he were entirely innocent of any wrongdoing.

In fact, it was a bad time for both sides. A month's adjournment was called to enable Surrogate Calvin to get caught up with otner business, but even after this lull, the star witnesses to the Great Conspiracy were still reluctant to make their entrance. Mr. Lord did his best to fill time by bringing a motley assortment of characters to the stand, most of whom were seeking personal publicity or had old grudges against the Commodore and his family. Surrogate Calvin refused to admit the testimony of most of them, but, of course, their stories got into the papers. John J. Ogden, for instance, a hitherto obscure stockbroker who had desk space in the offices of Woodhull, Claflin & Co., was anxious to tell how he had escorted the seductive Tennie Claflin, the spiritualist, to the Commodore's office on numerous occasions and had once overheard the Commodore tell her that he would have kept his promise to marry her but for the interference of his family. (The best he had been able to do, according to contemporary gossip, was to set Wall Street on its ear by putting up the money for Tennie and her astonishing sister, Victoria Woodhull, to establish the only female brokerage firm in the world.) Mr. Ogden claimed that on another occasion he had heard the Commodore boast that many young ladies bought New York Central stock because of his picture on it. All of this showed, according to Mr. Lord, that the Commodore had had loose notions about marriage and a diseased mind generally. Whatever it showed, Surrogate Calvin ruled it irrelevant.

Daniel Drew, once a market manipulator rivaling Vanderbilt himself but now a tottering old bankrupt, Buckman ("Buck") Claflin, the Micawberish father of Tennie and Victoria, along with magneticians and electric healers, paraded through the courtroom without noticeably advancing the contestant's case.

After several weeks in which the accomplices still did not appear, Mr. Clinton complained about the delay with bitter sarcasm. "Where is that cloud of devastating witnesses counsel promised to bring down upon us?" he demanded. As it turned out, that was exactly what Mr. Lord himself had been trying to learn. Finally, on March 19, at the insistence of the court, he reluctantly admitted that his key witnesses had been mysteriously detained in Chicago, where, of course, it was well known that anything might happen. He told a tale of threats, pursuit, bribery, and other "sinister influences at work to discourage" their appearance in court. In several formal affidavits requesting extensions of time, Mr. Lord revealed for the first time the identity of the witnesses—three private detectives—and details of the plot to discredit Cornelius in which they had allegedly been involved. Then, there had been a rash of ominous "Notices to Whom It May Concern" in the Personal Column of the *Herald*, a favorite medium, in those days before the telephone, for arranging assignations and other devious activities. The notices, Mr. Lord said, were unmistakably part of the plot.

The effect of these revelations on Surrogate Calvin was such that he decided, much to the disgust of counsel for the proponents, to adjourn the case until June 11 to give Mr. Lord ample time to assemble his elusive detectives.

According to his own sworn statements, Mr. Lord had first learned of what came to be known as The Great Conspiracy in June, 1877, nearly a month after his client's contest of the will had formally commenced. Young Cornelius had turned over to him a letter he had received from one Franklin A. Redburn, relating how a certain "head detective" (Redburn himself) had been approached in the fall of 1874 by a "genteel-appearing stranger." "A singular change," the stranger was quoted as saying, "for which no one could account had come over Commodore Vanderbilt. The old gentleman had become affected with the delusion that his prodigal son had returned to the paths of virtue and honor and would yet shed glory on the family name, whereas in truth "young Corneel" had never in his life been guilty of greater excesses and prodigality than he was now practising daily." Even William shared his father's delusion.

As a result the stranger, whom Redburn later revealed to be none other than Chauncey M. Depew, felt duty-bound, as a devoted family friend and a responsible official of the New York Central Railroad, to undertake whatever action might be required so that the Commodore and William would be convinced of their error. In short, he wanted Head Detective Redburn to have Cornelius followed until the evidence needed to set matters straight could be obtained. Redburn readily agreed to undertake the job. They arranged to meet the next day at the Fifth Avenue Hotel, Redburn to bring with him one of his most reliable operators, who would do the actual work of trailing young Vanderbilt. As it turned out, and as Redburn said he realized later, there was something extremely "providential" about this meeting. Neither he nor his subordinate knew the intended quarry by sight, and they so informed Mr. Depew. While the three of them were still conferring at the hotel, however, who should saunter through the lobby on his way to the bar but a man whom Mr.

Depew promptly pointed out as young Corneel himself. At once Redburn's reliable operative, George A. Mason, went into action.

Detective Mason's technique, as revealed in a sworn statement he gave Mr. Lord in August of 1877, was simple but effective. Mornings he would loiter about the Fifth Avenue Hotel, a pastime so pleasant that many young blades engaged in it by choice, until his man appeared. It was not difficult to keep track of him after that. According to Mason's deposition, Corneel's day would go like this: Arriving at the hotel between 10 and 11 A.M., he would proceed directly to the bar, where he would indulge in a few drinks with various friends and acquaintances. Then, with the morning gone and well aglow with spirits, said Cornelius together with several of his boon companions would leave the hotel and journey down to Ann Street aboard a Broadway stage. There, in the shadow of St. Paul's Church, they had their choice of several of those insidious institutions known as "day games." These "day games," which then abounded in the blocks off Broadway between Fulton and Chambers streets, were faro games operated primarily for the benefit of businessmen who worked in the area. They were also patronized by gentlemen of leisure like young Cornelius and his cronies, who found it irksome to wait until midafternoon for the uptown establishments to open their doors. These downtown excursions usually lasted two or three hours. Afterwards, they would return to the Fifth Avenue Hotel for more refreshments and for discussion of what to do next. Would they saunter across Twenty-fourth Street to John Morrissey's luxurious parlors, where they could enjoy a sumptuous free meal before settling down to an afternoon of serious gambling? Or would they pay their respects to the charming ladies to be found in certain elegant, if notorious, establishments along West Twenty-fifth Street? It was not always an easy decision to make. On occasion it took so long to make it that they were in no condition to carry it out.

Once or twice a week said Cornelius would desert his cronies after the return from Ann Street and proceed purposefully down Fifth Avenue to Fourteenth Street, where, as if by chance, he would meet a lady. She would accompany him for a seemingly casual stroll down University Place to Eleventh Street. There they would suddenly vanish into Solari's, a restaurant discreetly and cozily equipped with private rooms, and there would remain until evening. Upon emerging, said Cornelius would be so much the worse for wear that it would be all he could do to crawl into a cab and be driven home.

So it went day after day until Detective Mason commenced to have difficulty keeping up with his man, who was by now growing suspicious. Mason decided, therefore, that what he needed was an assistant to enable him, as he put it, to follow said Cornelius into dens of vice into which Mason could not always obtain admission alone or into which he did not deem it advisable to venture unaccompanied. For this purpose he selected one William H. Clark, an old and experienced colleague who had entree even into the exclusive establishments on Twenty-fifth Street to which Cornelius was so devoted. The intimate and revealing nature of the report produced by this double coverage was such that Mr. Depew, already bubbling with enthusiasm over Mason's solo efforts, could now no longer contain himself. He hustled the two detectives over to William's office in Grand Central Depot for a repeat performance. William, according to Mason's somewhat pedestrian account, professed much sorrow on learning of his brother's behavior but made only a feeble objection when Mr. Depew suggested that the report be given to the Commodore.

Detective Clark's account of this occasion, in the affidavit he gave Mr. Lord, reveals him as a much more acute observer than the matter-of-fact Mason, quite capable of penetrating beneath the deceptive surfaces of human behavior. Here is his version: ". . . That said William H. Vanderbilt, as he listened to Mason's report, professed to be disappointed and distressed at the intelligence of his brother's delinquencies, but that deponent [Clark] insists on saying herein that there was something in the manner and looks of said William H. Vanderbilt and in the glances he exchanged with his 'soi-disant' friend that constrained deponent to believe, and a little later in the day to remark to said Mason, that notwithstanding William H. Vanderbilt's ostensible grief, deponent was confident that he was delighted with the reports of his brother's infamy, and that said Mason replied that he did not like to think, much less to say so, but that, nevertheless, he had received the same impression as deponent. That deponent afterward accompanied the said 'soi-disant' friend and said Mason to the office of Commodore Vanderbilt. That the moment the Commodore understood the nature of their visit he exclaimed, addressing himself to said self-styled friend, 'I suppose you have now come to kill me and make an end of it.' Whereupon the person addressed declared that the business was not half so serious as that, and when the Commodore replied that he could see through it all, and that he wished to God he had never been born, that said self-styled friend remarked, 'If you would stop, Commodore, to reflect what the country would have been without you, you would never have made such an unpatriotic wish,' and that the Commodore then said, 'No, I don't wish that, but I wish that this son of mine had never been born; that's what I do wish.' "

His patriotism restored, the Commodore braced himself for the ordeal of listening to Mason's report. He could not, however, conceal his true feelings from Detective Clark, who wrote in his affidavit "that the Commodore appeared to be half-suffocated with the intelligence of his son's depravity; that it seemed to deponent that grief and indignation, love and hatred, and all the conflicting passions, had engaged in a battle royal in which his bosom was receiving the hardest blows. That a few expressions of anger seemed to relieve the Commodore when, after asking deponent a few questions, he cried, 'Go away, go away, and never let me see you again.' "

A few days later Mason and Clark were informed by Redburn that their mission had been accomplished to the complete satisfaction of the "soi-disant" friend of the family, Mr. Depew. Young Corneel stood revealed for what he was. The case, so far as they were concerned, would have been closed forever but for an embarrassing incident which befell Detective Mason only a little more than two years later, or, as chance would have it, not long after the first rumblings of discontent over the Commodore's will were heard. Late in the spring of 1877, according to the affidavit he gave Mr. Lord, Mason was taking a stroll along Broadway one day with an acquaintance. This acquaintance pointed out a person whom he claimed was none other than Cornelius J. Vanderbilt himself. Mason, who prided himself on an infallible memory for faces, promptly said that that was impossible; it was definitely not the person he had followed every day for nearly a month. But his friend insisted that the man they had seen was young Corneel. The upshot was a wager which, to his chagrin, deponent lost.

Bewildered but indignant, Mason communicated his discovery to Clark, and together they confronted Head Detective Redburn with the facts. Redburn, according to Mason, "seemed surprised and suggested that steps be taken to ascertain the truth." Realizing that they had been the unwitting instruments of a nefarious plot, they quickly concluded that simple justice demanded they do all in their power to repair the damage they had wrought. Redburn therefore composed the letter dated June 22, 1877, to the wronged Cornelius which the latter had passed on to Mr. Lord. Mr. Lord must have grasped it eagerly. Here, if there ever was one, was a fraudulent conspiracy designed to influence a testator unduly. He could hardly have been blamed if he had commenced spending the fat fee which would be his for breaking the will of the richest man in America.

During the adjournment granted by Surrogate Calvin Mr. Lord finally succeeded in coaxing Redburn, Mason, and Clark to return to New York. They promised faithfully to appear in court when the case was resumed on June 11. Finally, all that remained to be done was a last-minute rehearsal of their testimony with Mr. Lord and Judge Black which was scheduled for June 10.

That was how matters stood on the afternoon of June 9, a Sunday, when Mr. Lord opened an envelope which had been slipped under his door at his hotel. It was a letter from Redburn stating that Clark and Mason had gone off together, ostensibly to check on dates and places, but that he would go after them immediately and bring them back. Alas, it had a familiar ring. Apparently those sinister influences of which Mr. Lord had previously complained were again at work. He still had faith in the doughty Redburn, but the testimony of the craven Mason and Clark was essential to his case. Moreover, the next day the most crushing blow of all fell on Mr. Lord. It came in the form of a letter dated June 9, written jointly by Mason and Clark. In it they said that they had discovered that everything to which they had previously sworn was the result of a plot concocted by Cornelius J. Vanderbilt himself, aided and abetted by his friend "Simpson," a big wheel in the lottery racket with powerful political and underworld connections. It was only a few hours before writing the letter that they had finally become convinced of the truth. "We agree perfectly in everything," they wrote, "except as to whether Redburn was one of the original conspirators. One believes he was, while one willingly gives him the benefit of the doubt. . . . Finally, Judge Lord, we wish to say that when we made our statements to you, we fully believed them . . . and that you could never have had any reason to doubt them until now, when we give you this disclosure. With great respect, [signed] William H. Clark and George A. Mason."

With two of his key witnesses reneging and all of them vanished, Mr. Lord might well have wished to vanish himself. He was left with a set of affidavits which were worthless as evidence, even if true, and which, in any event, were now apparently discredited. However, he went into court on June 11, bristling with indignation, and presented yet another affidavit of his own in support of a motion to continue the case. Annexed thereto were not only the original affidavits of Redburn, Mason, and Clark, but also (and this was perhaps his master stroke which at once demonstrated his integrity and confounded his opponents) the joint letter of Mason and Clark in which they denied the truth of their own sworn statements. In his own affidavit, after relating the events of the past months during which he had labored to overcome the detectives' fears, and to obtain sworn statements from them, Mr. Lord went on to say that he still believed the statements in those affidavits to be true; if the testimony of Mason and Clark could be taken, he said, the affidavits would be sustained. He did not believe that they could be bribed, or otherwise persuaded, to appear upon the stand and perjure themselves, but he did believe that they could have been induced to write their letter of June 9 and then to put themselves beyond the jurisdiction of the court. The close of Mr. Lord's new affidavit summarized the confusion. "Deponent further says," Lord wrote, "that the communication received by him from said Mason and Clark leads him to believe that they have been in communication with some person or persons in the interests of the proponents, and have been induced by them to put themselves beyond the jurisdiction of this court to avoid testifying, and that this also leads him to believe that had they not refused to testify under oath to the statement of their letter, they would have been allowed to appear in court and testify; and that counsel for the contestant, under all these circumstances, deem it their duty to ask the court for a continuance, so that in a matter of such vital importance the truth may be ascertained."

Mr. Clinton objected strenuously to the reading in court of the Redburn-Mason-Clark affidavits, on the grounds that they were entirely extrajudicial. Every word might be false and yet the authors could not be held for perjury. "It comes to this," he declaimed heatedly, "whether this court is to be used only for the purpose of scandal . . . [and] for getting into the newspapers statements which they have already refused to print." Surrogate Calvin said he did not think reputable counsel would resort to such tactics and permitted the reading to continue, although he made it clear that the affidavits themselves could have no bearing on the outcome of the case.

There was a tense silence in the courtroom as the reading proceeded, broken only by occasional gasps of astonishment from the spellbound audience and by snorts of disgust from counsel for the proponents. William H. Vanderbilt sat with his eyes rigidly upon the ceiling, thus avoiding the fierce glare of his sister, Mrs. La Bau, and the sight of the angry fist which, from time to time, she shook at him. Contestant's counsel also read a statement by Cornelius J. Vanderbilt flatly denying the charge made against him by Mason and Clark in their joint letter of confession, and another by "Zach" Simmons stating that if he was the "Simpson" referred to therein, which he was, he denied all charges.

Counsel for proponents came into court the next day armed with their own affidavits. In sworn statements read by Mr. Clinton, Chauncey M. Depew and William H. Vanderbilt categorically denied everything of which they had been accused by Mr. Lord and his reluctant witnesses. Mr. Clinton then went to work in earnest on the affidavits offered by Mr. Lord. He dealt very harshly with young Cornelius, quoting with caustic relish some of the riper passages which contained the preposterous notion that Cornelius could ever amount to anything, and, most preposterous of all, that the canny old Commodore would ever have been foolish enough to think that he would. Almost equally absurd, Mr. Clinton said, was the story of Chauncey Depew concocting a conspiracy in the lobby of the Fifth Avenue Hotel. Depew may have had his less fervent admirers, but no one ever set him down for a natural-born fool.

"The falsity of these papers is apparent on their face," Mr. Clinton stormed. "They were all written by the same person, and that person is a lawyer."

Counsel for contestant were on their feet screaming in outrage, and Mr. Clinton conceded that he was not referring to any known member of contestant's counsel. This did not exactly mollify Mr. Lord and his associates, but Mr. Clinton refused to retract the suggestion that they were being used as cat's-paws by some sinister legal mind in the employ of young Corneel and his underworld crony, Simmons. Surrogate Calvin himself objected to so grave an accusation. He asked Mr. Clinton if he could suggest an explanation for the motives behind such affidavits.

"Certainly," came the reply. "For the purposes of blackmail. Anyone who knows anything of private detectives understands how ready they are to seize upon anything that promises money. . . . These detectives are too keen to swear to anything for which they can be held responsible. . . . They have disappeared just at the time for them to appear in court because they never attended to appear. They thought us weak-kneed, and that we would yield to their demands."

Although it may seem now that Mr. Clinton was being rather harsh in his treatment of private detectives, actually his remarks were quite mild. The profession had a most unsavory reputation at this period. In a time when moral hypocrisy was common, when suspicion flourished, its services were in great demand. Nevertheless, it had become an overcrowded field, and its practitioners, in order to survive, had to promote new business aggressively. As a matter of policy, the customer was always right, and their reports were tailored to fit his needs. Blackmail was an obvious and lucrative sideline, and private detectives had been known to prey upon the guilty and the innocent alike.

Mr. Clinton wound up his argument with a few words for opposing counsel. "Why were not these witnesses subpoenaed?" he demanded. "The affidavits are of no value except to excuse counsel for being humbugged for six months. The whole story is a fabrication."

Surrogate Calvin closed the hearing with some remarks that left the whole affair more confused than ever. "What seems extraordinary to the court," he said, somewhat wistfully, "is that if these detectives were honest men and found they had been deceived by Cornelius J. Vanderbilt, they did not make known their discoveries to the other side. The fact that they have departed in this way is full of suspicion."

In spite of his bewilderment, the Surrogate was not quite willing to give up hope of seeing with his own eyes whether such fantastic witnesses actually existed. He granted Mr. Lord an adjournment of two weeks, urging him to spare no effort to produce at least Redburn, who seemed fairly available, or, at any rate, less mythical than Mason and Clark. Mr. Lord, unabashed by the sneers of opposing counsel, resolutely promised to do his utmost. Two weeks later, alas, he came back into court with the air of a man to whom the fates had been malignantly unkind. Redburn was seriously ill and confined to his home. (He lived in New Jersey, so he was not within the jurisdiction of the court.) Mason and Clark had not returned from wherever it was they had gone, and no one knew where that was. Their existence was becoming very mythical indeed. Mr. Lord endeavored to offset this impression with another of his garrulous lady witnesses whose testimony was discredited by Mr. Clinton on cross-examination.

On July 2, 1878, court adjourned early to allow the participants to attend the funeral of Phoebe Jane Cross, the Commodore's eldest daughter, who had grudgingly accepted her $250,000 worth of Lake Shore bonds; Mr. Clinton wryly remarked that it was "the first time he would not oppose a motion to adjourn." But the next day he was back in action again when Mr. Lord suggested that it might be a good time to adjourn for the summer. It would be very unpleasant in the little courtroom during July and August, and Redburn, suffering from what was described as "intermittent fever," would certainly be unable to appear under such unfavorable conditions. Mr. Clinton, by now running a very high temperature himself, objected violently not only to a summer's adjournment but to allowing the contestant any more time whatsoever; if the case were permitted to drag on indefinitely, Surrogate Calvin's term in office might expire, and then it could be claimed his successor did not have jurisdiction and so it would go—forever.

Surrogate Calvin, striving for a compromise, decided to grant the adjournment, but to allow contestant only eight more days when the case was resumed in the fall. He pointedly warned Mr. Lord that there would be no more adjournments due to the nonappearance of witnesses. The lawyer, his confidence restored by the prospect of over two months' grace, took the warning in stride; as the session closed, he was blandly promising to produce not only Redburn, Mason, and Clark but also a fourth man whom he said he would name at that time for fear that proponents would, as he put it, "educate him as a witness." Mr. Clinton was left frothing with rage and indignation.

When the case was resumed in the fall, it was at once apparent that something new and ominous for proponents was brewing in the camp of the contestant which had nothing to do with the missing witnesses (who were just as missing as ever). Mr. Lord and his cohorts, swelled to bursting with mystery and importance, ignored any reference to Redburn, Mason, and Clark as a matter too trifling to concern them. Counsel for proponents, now more wary and suspicious than ever, were reinforced by Joseph H. Choate, making his first appearance in court.

The testimony of contestant's first important witness failed to fulfill the rumors of sensational disclosures with which the corridors of the courthouse had been buzzing. It did, however, reveal a rather subtle shift in Mr. Lord's strategy which would, if successful, enable him to take advantage of decedent's apparent belief in spiritualism. The witness, a Mrs. Mary L. Stone, appeared at first to be yet another of the seemingly endless procession of ladies in straitened circumstances who had visited the Commodore in search of financial aid. Mrs. Stone, a serious-minded lady of some refinement, was in her middle thirties; her deceased father, Henry Chapin, had been a friend and business associate of the Commodore. She testified that she had first approached the Commodore in his office on Fourth Street in October of 1874, a period on which Mr. Lord laid great stress since it was during this time that the last will was being drafted. She wanted help in starting a school. Mrs. Stone got no money, but she did get some advice. The Commodore solemnly told her, she said, that before going further with her enterprise she must seek communion with the spirits of her dear departed. He himself, he assured her, did nothing without advice from the spirits. For example, as a result of communications he had had with the spirit of his dead wife, he was going to leave most of his worldly goods to his son William. Mrs. Stone, alas, was so overwhelmed by the daily problems of her mundane existence that, as counsel for the proponents were to suggest later, the only spirits she was able to commune with successfully were those in a bottle. Nevertheless, she was back in the Commodore's office again several months later, or, as it happened, not long after the final will had been executed, to see if she could get her brother a job as a conductor on one of the Vanderbilt railroads. William, who was hovering about in an officious sort of way, told her bluntly that his father could do nothing for her. With that the Commodore flared up. "You can't have it all your way," Mrs. Stone quoted him as saying. "You are walking in my shoes now. I have made a will in your favor, and that ought to be enough."

"The spirits made the will in my favor, Father," William said solemnly. "You said so yourself."

"What if I did," the old man grumbled. "It ought to be enough for you."

Apparently it wasn't enough for William, and Mrs. Stone's brother did not get the job. Mr. Clinton objected to her testimony with all of his customary vigor. What it amounted to, he argued, was that Mr. Lord was trying to commence the case all over again even though he had had no case in the first place. The Surrogate, as even his worthy opponent should be able to recall, had already ruled that testator's belief in spiritualism was of itself no indication of an unsound mind, and that evidence as to such belief was therefore irrelevant and immaterial. Mr. Lord, far from reacting with his usual violence to the gibes of opposing counsel, argued quite calmly—some thought even smugly—that, while he was by no means unaware of the Surrogate's earlier ruling or even of the seeming validity of counsel's objections, nevertheless, new evidence, which his conscience would not permit him to suppress, had dictated reopening this line of inquiry. Mrs. Stone's testimony, he added, would lay the groundwork for showing that the will was the product of a foul conspiracy designed by William H. Vanderbilt to take advantage of his father's belief in communication with the dead.

Earlier Mr. Lord had contended that such belief would demonstrate that the Commodore was of unsound mind. Now, if as he claimed he could prove a fraudulent conspiracy, that indispensable ingredient of most successful will contests, the soundness of the testator's mind, would not necessarily be at issue.

This shift in strategy was a little too subtle for Surrogate Calvin to grasp all at once. He decided to stick to his earlier ruling that testimony as to the influence of the spirits should be excluded, at least until the alleged conspiracy had been established. Getting a bit sprightly himself, he proposed that communication be had with the testator in order to settle the whole question.

Mr. Lord was not in the least amused by what he considered misplaced judicial facetiousness, but he remained undaunted. If he himself could not communicate directly with the Commodore, he was now ready to unveil a witness whose testimony about the influence of spirits upon the old man would be no joke for the proponents.

The witness was a Mrs. Lilian Stoddard, and as soon as she had swished herself into the witness stand it was evident that the big moment had now arrived. For Mrs. Stoddard, to any discerning male eye, was obviously no ordinary woman. In her early thirties, with neither youth nor beauty to commend her, she still retained that sort of saucy girlish bounce which, piquantly mellowed by years of dissipation, inevitably inspires in men's minds visions of all manner of delightfully accessible and deliciously depraved sexual activity. Her testimony, as well as her person, was to have an electrifying effect upon the courtroom. Even Mr. Clinton and his august colleagues, though prepared in advance for the worst, seemed dumbfounded and aghast at the story she had to tell—under, be it remembered, solemn oath.

Mr. Lord conducted his direct examination with a dignified reserve that did not permit unseemly prying into irrelevant and purely personal biographical details. Mrs. Stoddard was, she said, the widow of Dr. Charles Anderson Stoddard, a medical clairvoyant who had died in the spring of 1875; Commodore Vanderbilt had been among his patients. In the summer of 1874, Mrs. Stoddard testified, her late husband was using his supernatural powers to alleviate the aches and pains with which the Commodore's aging body was afflicted. Mr. Lord, in his questioning, was careful to bring out that Mrs. Stoddard herself was invariably present at these treatments. While this may have been a trifle irregular, the manner of her testimony on this point rather suggested that the proximity of her person had such an exhilarating effect upon the patient that he regarded it as an essential part of the therapy.

The treatments had continued in this cozy fashion, two or three times a week over a period of several months, until one fine morning early in September, following a professional visit to the Commodore in his office, the witness and her husband were sitting in Washington Square Park resting from the ardors of their joint therapy when they were approached by a gentleman who introduced himself as William H. Vanderbilt. Accustomed as they were to being abused and persecuted by cynical relatives of their patients, they were quite overwhelmed by Mr. Vanderbilt's cordiality. He told them how impressed he had been by the great faith which his father had in Dr. Stoddard's remarkable powers, and, far from wishing them to cease their ministrations, his only thought was to suggest that a more intense application of those powers might prove beneficial to all concerned. Mr. Vanderbilt's exact words were, according to the witness, "I want you to influence the old man and make him think more of me so that I can control him."

In reply Dr. Stoddard had said that he would be glad to do what he could in his humble way if the circumstances were properly conducive. Thereupon Mr. Vanderbilt nodded his head understandingly and handed Dr. Stoddard a roll of bills which the latter calmly counted and put in his pocket. The witness admitted that she never did learn the exact amount of the fee, but she figured that the roll added up to at least $1,000. In any event, she could tell that her husband was pleased. "This is all right," she quoted him saying as he pocketed the bills. "I am now ready for business." With the conducive circumstances thus established, Mr. Vanderbilt proceeded to dictate in a brisk, businesslike manner the exact words of the message which he wished to be transmitted from his mother in the world of the spirits to his father here on earth. Dr. Stoddard repeated the message word for word. Mr. Vanderbilt signified his approval, tipped his hat, and went on his way.

Thus inspired and with a prospect of more inspiration to come, Dr. Stoddard on their next visit to the Commodore was able to commune with the spirit of the deceased Mrs. Vanderbilt as soon as he went into his trance. "I seem to have a message for you from your dead wife in the world beyond the grave," Dr. Stoddard whispered. "Are you ready to receive the message?" The Commodore, according to the witness, was a bit shaken, but he replied stoutly enough that he was always ready to hear from his dear Sophie. With that, the spirit of Mrs. Vanderbilt, speaking in the quavery tones of a voice from the sepulchre through the medium of Dr. Stoddard, could be heard to say, "I have a much clearer insight into the affairs of your world than I had before my departure from it, and I implore you, in memory of me, to make our son William your successor in all earthly things. Do this and you will make no mistake. The other children hate you. Only William loves you . . . only William. . . ." And as the voice of the spirit faded away, the Commodore said solemnly, "I will do as you wish, Sophie. Billy shall have it all."

Variations of this message from the other world were repeated at appropriate intervals over a period of several months, or, to put it crassly, for as long as the fiscal inspiration from William H. Vanderbilt to Dr. Stoddard was maintained. Mrs. Stoddard could not recall exactly how many times her husband had transmitted Sophie's message, but she was quite positive that the last visit had occurred early in January, 1875. She remembered it so well, she said, for two reasons: first, simply because it was, alas, the last visit, and second, because the Commodore had been so cheerful. Instead of his usual solemn reply to the voice from beyond the grave, his answer had been, "Don't fret about it any more, Sophie. It's all been fixed so Billy will get it all."

Mr. Lord laid particular stress upon the witness's testimony about this final visit because, although of course the Stoddards presumably couldn't have known it at the time, the date coincided remarkably well with the date of the formal signing and execution of the Commodore's last will and testament. Thus, Mrs. Stoddard's testimony, fantastic though it may have sounded, was a matter of grave concern to the proponents, and their lawyers were obviously most unhappy about it. There was no question of its being relevant: the best Mr. Clinton could do on that score was a niggling argument to the effect that actually the testator had disobeyed the spirits, for Billy did not get it all. Furthermore, it opened the door for the seemingly abundant evidence, which the Surrogate had previously refused to admit, that the Commodore had, in fact, been a true believer in spiritualism, even, or perhaps especially, as practiced by charlatans such as Dr. Stoddard and the Claflin sisters. It was, if true, the only material evidence thus far produced to show that in making his will the testator might have been unduly influenced by a fraudulent conspiracy. Even though the will itself might not have differed by so much as a single stray "hereinbefore" without the advice of the spirits, it raised a reasonable doubt; when one hundred million dollars is at stake even a most unreasonable doubt could loom very ominously indeed. Mrs. Stoddard's testimony was of such a nature that it could not be conclusively refuted. Mrs. Stoddard herself would have to be completely demolished.

Mr. Clinton commenced his cross-examination by asking the witness to tell the court just how her connection with the case had come about. Mrs. Stoddard said that about three weeks before she testified she had received a letter signed "A friend" asking her to call at Mr. Lord's office in a matter of great importance. This "friend" turned out to be a man whom she had seen around, as she put it, but whom she did not know by name and had not seen again. She said that when she had been interviewed by Mr. Lord, she had told him she had nothing to tell but the truth. Mr. Clinton said he was very glad to hear that, and, if she would continue the same policy with him, things should work out splendidly. There were a few minor details in her direct testimony he wanted to clear up. For instance, she had said that she and her husband were living at 64 Charles Street when they had last seen Commodore Vanderbilt. A little later in her testimony, however, she had said they had left 64 Charles Street about six months prior to the death of her husband in May, 1875, which would indicate either that they had last seen the Commodore in November of 1874 instead of the following January, or that she was mistaken as to the date of her husband's death. But of course she could hardly be mistaken about a thing such as that, could she?

Under this steady barrage of seemingly trivial questions about dates and places, Mrs. Stoddard snarled herself in a tangle of contradictions, and gradually it came out that she did not know to the day or even the week when her husband had died. Bit by bit, Mr. Clinton drew from her the admission that her husband had been dead and buried about a month or more before she even knew about it. Asked to explain how such a thing could be, the harried witness said it was because her husband had died in Poughkeepsie. Mr. Clinton, now assuming that air of happy bewilderment which can be so exasperating to witnesses who have been driven into a corner, conceded that while Poughkeepsie might not be the best place in the world in which to have one's husband die, surely it was not so bad as to deprive him of her presence. The witness, by now as irritated as she was confused, angrily denied that there was anything particularly strange about this. It just so happened that Dr. Stoddard lived in Poughkeepsie part of the time because he had an office there. A great light seemed to dawn on Mr. Clinton. "I see," he said. "But you didn't live in Poughkeepsie . . . not even part time?" And with the inference established that there was something irregular in the relationship between the witness and the late Dr. Stoddard, Mr. Clinton suggested that it was time to call it a day. He had the scent he needed for his private bloodhounds —Poughkeepsie, only seventy miles away on the main line of the Vanderbilt railroad—and he had four days for them to track it down before the next session of court.

News of Mrs. Stoddard's testimony created a sensation in Poughkeepsie. Even after an absence of some fifteen years, she was well remembered there, particularly by righteously indignant friends and relatives of the late Dr. Stoddard. Mr. Clinton's research into the early phases of her career thus proved to be both simple and fruitful. When he resumed his cross-examination, he knew exactly what questions would unfold the saga of a country girl, originally known as "Nell," who had not waited until she got to the big city to go astray.

While still in her early teens Nell had been adopted by a widower named Coe who lived across the river in Ulster County. After a year or so in this ambivalent situation Nell had come back across the river to "keep house," as she called it—although that wasn't what the neighbors called it—for a man named DeGroot near Poughkeepsie. It was during her DeGroot period that she first met Dr. Stoddard and took to calling herself Lilian. The Doctor had been deeply smitten by her charms, even then well-developed, and they were married at Kingston after a three-week courtship spent driving about the countryside in a horse and buggy making frequent stops in country hotels. Lilian might well have become a bit disenchanted at this point when she learned that Dr. Stoddard already had a wife and family living in Poughkeepsie, but, being both good-natured and realistic, she tried to make the best of a difficult situation by moving into the Stoddard home in the role of general houseworker. This arrangement had lasted only a week.

From the formidable appearance of a lady whom Mr. Clinton asked to rise and be identified by the witness as the original, and only genuine, Mrs. Stoddard, it could not have been a very pleasant week for Lilian. The *Times* carried a special dispatch from its Poughkeepsie correspondent which quoted the genuine Mrs. Stoddard as saying, "There was something about her when she came to my house that I did not like, and that was the reason I discharged her." One thing Mrs. Stoddard had not liked was that Lilian called Dr. Stoddard "Charley," although his name was really "Amasa." There were other things, too, but Mrs. Stoddard did not wish to specify what they were. Dr. Stoddard, however, must have liked being called "Charley," and liked the other unspecified things as well, for he now set Lilian up in rooms on Bridge Street in Poughkeepsie, not too far away from his official residence, where she could keep house to her heart's content. This cozy arrangement went on for five or six years. Then, apparently, it had finally dawned on Lilian that Poughkeepsie afforded too limited a field for the full development of her talent for housekeeping, and, in the interests of her career, she had gone to New York. From that time on Dr. Stoddard divided both his professional and his domestic lives between New York and Poughkeepsie. He also had an office in Newburgh, but nothing was known of his domestic arrangements there. Lilian herself quickly developed a considerable talent for dividing her life into multiple compartments, and during the doctor's absences she became widely acquainted in elite circles of the underworld as the consort of forgers, counterfeiters, and confidence men. At one time and another she had been known as Mrs. Benning, Mrs. Draper, and Mrs. Hall—all names of gentlemen renowned in their professions. Mr. Hall, perhaps, represented the pinnacle of her achievement to date, for he was Edward Hall, the celebrated forger. Having achieved such a position, it was little wonder that Lilian became quite incensed when Mr. Clinton asked her if she had ever been arrested for anything so crude as stealing a watch and chain.

"No, sir," she replied haughtily, "I was never arrested, and I would like to see the one to say I was."

Her "marriages" were usually dissolved by the departure of her current "husband" for prison and were not customarily renewed. This made her relationship with Mr. Benning rather unique, as it had been resumed, at least on a part-time basis, after he had been away for two years in a New Jersey State Prison. Mr. Clinton was especially interested in the enduring nature of Lilian's attachment to Mr. Benning, for Mr. Benning was a specialist in a highly specialized field. In the jargon of his profession he was what was known as a "straw-bail man." In plain English, he was an expert in the manufacture and distribution of fake testimony for counterfeiters. Mr. Clinton's line of questioning strongly suggested that Mr. Benning's basic technique was readily adaptable to other types of enterprise.

On the whole, Lillian bore up remarkably well under Mr. Clinton's barrage of embarrassing questions. She maintained right to the bitter end that the number of men she had lived with had nothing to do with the truth of her testimony. Nor could Mr. Clinton ever get her to admit that she had known what Mr. Benning and his associates were really up to. There were frequent sharp exchanges between the witness and the lawyer, and her saucy and defiant replies were vastly entertaining to the spectators who now filled the courtroom to capacity. When Mr. Clinton tried to get her to admit that she had visited Benning in prison, she rapped her fan emphatically on the railing of the witness stand and said, "I won't answer any more about that State Prison, so there!"

Mr. Lord tried hard in his re-direct examination to refurbish her respectability. "Abraham," he said, "found favor before the Lord although he had more than one wife." He then tried to show that Lilian had received a wedding ring from Dr. Stoddard when they were "married" at Kingston and that she had entered into the ceremony in good faith. If she had acted in good faith, Mr. Lord argued, she had been more sinned against than sinning, and the facts of her later life, however unseemly, did not affect the credibility of her testimony. Surrogate Calvin was not at all impressed with this line of reasoning and promptly excluded the testimony offered to establish her good faith.

Mr. Choate, who had long been straining at the leash, now entered the fray for the first time with a scathing attack upon the witness, calling her "a woman of the town of the most infamous kind." He demanded that she be taken into custody on a charge of willfully committing perjury. But that was not the worst of it. Steeped in crime though she was, such a woman was obviously incapable of constructing a story which "fit into the crevices of the case so cunningly." Only some sinister legal mind lurking in the camp of the contestant could possibly have done that. There was the real criminal who should be brought to book.

This was indeed a serious accusation to make against the opposing lawyers. Counsels for contestant were on their feet seething with indignation. Judge Black was particularly incensed, loudly demanding that Mr. Choate either back up his accusation by naming the person who had concocted Lilian's story so that he personally could withdraw from such an unholy fellowship, or else retract it entirely. Mr. Choate, for his part, refused to do either, although he did grant that Judge Black himself should be excluded from his aspersions at opposing counsel. Furthermore, he persisted in demanding that the witness be arrested at once for perjury, as he supposed there was no one so credulous as to believe a word of "that woman's" testimony. Mr. Lord, of course, was not silent. He hotly denied that there was any evidence either of perjury or of wrongdoing on his part. Of course, he did not wonder that counsel for proponent were a trifle disturbed by such damaging testimony. Let them prove it fake, if they could, before making such contemptible accusations.

Surrogate Calvin, trying to maintain a judicial calm, finally brought the wrangling to an end by ruling that it would be improper to allow the motion for perjury to be brought into his court. In spite of his skepticism, he patiently pointed out the importance of Lilian's testimony: It was, if true, the only conclusive evidence of undue influence thus far presented, and it opened the way for Mr. Lord to present his abundant evidence, originally excluded as irrelevant, of the Commodore's belief in spiritualism.

Mr. Clinton was quite beside himself with frustrated rage as Mr. Lord now happily proceeded to put back on the stand Mrs. Mary Stone, to tell how her efforts to communicate nonspiritually with the Commodore to raise money for her school and to get her brother a job on the railroad had been so cruelly thwarted by William.

With Mrs. Stone's testimony safely on record, Mr. Lord was obviously flush with success. He then attempted to bring on a witness who would link Mrs. Frankie Vanderbilt, the bereaved widow, to her stepson William in a highly improper manner. Earlier, Surrogate Calvin had sternly excluded such testimony unless it had first been clearly shown that Mrs. Vanderbilt had actually conspired to influence her husband unduly. Mr. Lord's attempt aroused a storm of protest among counsel for proponents; Surrogate Calvin, highly indignant himself, threatened to hold Mr. Lord in contempt if the offer were repeated. Mr. Lord accepted his reprimand with a sardonic bow. No one could do anything, however, to suppress the jeering remarks with which Mrs. La Bau greeted Mr. Choate's references to the unblemished character of her stepmother.

The trial had now been in progress for nearly a year, and opposing counsel urged the Surrogate to instruct Mrs. La Bau's counsel to bring their case to a close. Mr. Lord, of course, protested vociferously, repeating his stock arguments as to the magnitude of the case and the continued absence of vital witnesses. Surrogate Calvin suggested that he name his missing witnesses and the nature of their testimony in an affidavit to support a motion to continue. This Mr. Lord indignantly refused to do. Those whose names had been revealed heretofore, he argued, had been threatened and bribed, and he could not again permit himself to jeopardize his client's interests by his own naïve innocence of the depths of infamy to which opposing counsel would stoop. Apparently touched by Mr. Lord's impassioned plea, Surrogate Calvin ruled that contestant could continue if the names of future witnesses were submitted to him privately. Such an arrangement was not at all to the liking of counsel for the proponents, and they reacted to it with howls of genuine legal anguish. Not only would this arrangement deprive them of the opportunity to do their customary research into the lives of prospective witnesses. It could also mean the indefinite prolongation of the case.

Despite the comforting assurance that the identity of his cast of characters would be kept from opposing counsel, Mr. Lord's long-threatened cloud of devastating witnesses still failed to materialize. And yet a curious air of complacency now seemed to prevail in the camp of the contestant, as of a cat who has finally devised a way to lure the canary from its cage whenever he chooses to do so. Lord's smugness was all the more evident because it was in such marked contrast to the exasperated anxiety of counsel for proponents. Time seemed no longer of any moment to Mr. Lord as he leisurely proceeded, serenely indifferent to Mr. Clinton's caustic comments, to bring forth more of his apparently endless array of medical experts whose testimony proved nothing except what had already been proved: that the testator was an old man more or less subject to the infirmities of his age. Even Mr. Lord himself seemed bored by them. Then, during the early part of November, 1878, Mr. Lord fired what proved to be his last shot.

It started out like another of his medical-expert duds. The expert was Dr. Salmon Skinner, a dentist who had obtained some notoriety by suing Henry Ward Beecher to recover the value of a set of false teeth he had made for Dr. Beecher's father (and who possibly had discovered that being in the legal limelight increased the demand for his product). Dr. Skinner had come forward voluntarily and was prepared to testify that he had treated the Commodore in 1873 and found his mind in a state of such imbecility that he had thought him to be drunk. More careful examination, however, had disclosed that the imbecility arose simply from the natural decay of his faculties. Surrogate Calvin, scanning the private list of prospective witnesses Lord had given him, was shocked to find that it did not even contain the name of Dr. Skinner. The Surrogate refused to permit him to testify.

"Under those circumstances," Mr. Lord announced, very quietly and deliberately, "the contestant closes her case."

Mrs. La Bau clapped her hands and jumped with glee as the courtroom buzzed with excitement. But an astonishing pall of gloom seemed to descend upon William H. Vanderbilt and his counsel as they sat dumbfounded by the inexplicable suddenness with which the event they had been awaiting so impatiently had finally occurred.

"That is all wrong, Mr. Vanderbilt," Sam F. Barger, a friend and himself a lawyer, was heard to say. "I'm afraid that will give them a new trial."

Disinterested attorneys present in the courtroom expressed the opinion that Surrogate Calvin's decision to refuse to allow Dr. Skinner to testify would not be upheld in the Appellate Court. Mr. Lord himself denied any intention of setting a legal snare for the Surrogate, but his manner rather indicated that he was not entirely displeased with himself. New and important evidence, he told reporters, was constantly being discovered, and it might be just as well to let the matter rest for a while. His client, motivated more by a desire for justice than by greed, had nothing to gain by undue haste. It was obvious, of course, that Mr. Lord was quite aware of the infuriating effect that the prospect of indefinite delay in distributing the estate would have upon those who were content with the will as it stood. Until the defense of the will was presented, and the case decided, they were being deprived of the use and enjoyment of the money they felt was rightfully theirs.

On November 19, 1878, nearly two long and galling years after the testator's death, the favored heirs were at last permitted to commence their defense of the will. Mr. Clinton's presentation of their case was simple, direct, and vigorous. Disdaining to make any sort of opening address whatever (much to the consternation of Surrogate Calvin, who felt that such an omission was highly irregular), Mr. Clinton at once set about calling to the stand a procession of gentlemen prominent in government, finance, and the professions, who testified briskly and unanimously to the Commodore's business acumen, his staunch character, and his remarkable clear-headedness until the very end of his life. Ex-Governors E. D. Morgan and John T. Hoffman of New York, as well as Edwards Pierrepont and William E. Dodge, all gentlemen of distinction locally and even nationally, provided an impressive contrast to the magneticians and shady ladies who had testified for the contestant. The only notable exception occurred when Bishop Holland N. McTyeire of the Southern Methodist Church was on the stand. He had been called as a witness primarily to establish the irreproachable character of the Commodore's widow, whom he had known all of her life and through whom he had been able to cajole the great man into giving away $1,000,000 for the purpose of founding Vanderbilt University. Mr. Lord rudely asked the Bishop to tell the court what he knew about an earlier husband of Frankie's who was still living. Before the Bishop could reply, Mr. Clinton, Mr. Choate, and Judge Comstock were all on their feet vigorously protesting that the question was irrelevant, immaterial, and ungentlemanly. The spectators were in a dither. Mrs. La Bau hurried down the aisle to her lawyers' table so that she could watch Judge Black more closely as he replenished his chewing tobacco and strode before the bench to present their argument. Even William H. Vanderbilt, usually as stolid as a stone, appeared affected for the first time since the trial had started.

"This is not a trifling matter," Judge Black rumbled, speaking slowly and with apparent embarrassment. "Here is a man eighty years old marrying a woman fifty years his junior, who came here a stranger, after separating from a husband who is still living. That there should have been bitterness felt toward this woman by the Commodore's daughters, some of whom were already grandmothers, and that this feeling should have turned the heart of the father against them, are natural results. But there was one exception in the family. William H. Vanderbilt encouraged the marriage, and continued to show as much regard for the woman as though she had not done the injury of marrying the Commodore in his dotage. But the aggravation is immense if, in addition to showing the distress and hatred that this marriage caused, we show that it was unlawful, and that, therefore, whatever influence Mrs. Vanderbilt exerted was not only undue, it was unholy. There are words struggling for utterance here that I am compelled to restrain, and I suppose I have made a bungle of it, but your Honor must understand what I mean."

His Honor, however, apparently as stunned as everyone else in the courtroom, appeared to be beyond understanding. And so, in a voice choking with emotion, Judge Black went on to spell out exactly what he meant. "That a woman should sell herself to this old man for his money, taking advantage of that weakness of his nature, is not a reason why a will made under such circumstances should be allowed to stand."

When he had finished, Judge Black sat down and buried his flushed face in his hands. His apparently real embarrassment at what the necessities of the occasion had required him to say about a member of the fair sex was quite as moving as his argument. There was hardly a sound in the courtroom. Even counsel for proponents, though dark with rage, remained strangely silent. But it was all in vain. Surrogate Calvin, once he had regained his judicial poise, hastily sustained proponents' objection to Mr. Lord's question, and Bishop McTyeire was permitted to step down.

But the damage had been done, and there was no joy among counsel for proponents at the Surrogate's decision in their favor. The witness they had called to establish the sterling quality of Mrs. Frankie Vanderbilt's character—probably at her own insistence and against their better judgment—had provided opposing counsel with an irresistable opportunity to tarnish it. Judge Black's eloquent plea, illogical and irrelevant though it may have been, probed through the one weak link in proponents' case to an excruciatingly sensitive spot. However great William's reluctance to compromise with his brother and sister, whether from greed or, as it seems more likely, from pure cussedness, he had also to consider the feelings of his stepmother. Her good will and cooperation were essential to him, and he did not dare to risk further aspersions upon the propriety of her marriage to his father. As a lady with social ambitions of her own for the future, this was a subject on which she was understandably touchy.

In retrospect it seems clear (as it must have been clear then to any reasonably astute observer of courtroom dramas) that, by the time Judge Black came to the end of his little discourse on the theme of young women who marry very rich and very old men, the contest was really over and that a compromise agreeable to the contestant would be arranged. Even Mrs. La Bau's vindictive hatred of her stepmother seemed finally to have been appeased. Out of respect for judicial form, the last act had still to be played out, but no one seemed to mind when Surrogate Calvin adjourned the trial for two months in order to catch up with a backlog of other matters urgently demanding his attention. There was, for instance, a lady who had developed a penchant for beating her brother on the head with an umbrella in the corridor outside the Surrogate's chambers in connection with the probate of their father's will. In fact, it has been said the calendar of the Surrogate's Court in New York has never completely recovered from the effects of the Vanderbilt case.

Thus, it was not until March 4, 1879, that the essential legal buttress of proponent's case was hammered solidly into place by Charles A. Rapallo, a jurist distinguished by his long service on the state of New York's court of appeals, the Commodore's confidential legal adviser for many years, and the man who had been drawing wills for the decedent since 1856. All the wills were substantially the same. William had always been named residuary legatee, and Cornelius had always been left with a comparatively small annuity.

The next and final witness for the proponents was William H. Vanderbilt himself. Mr. Vanderbilt was calm and dignified as Mr. Choate conducted his examination in the impressively courteous manner for which he was noted. In reply to Mr. Choate's respectfully couched questions the witness denied, briefly but emphatically, all the utterances attributed to him by contestant's witnesses in regard to his influence over his father; he also disclaimed any design to prejudice the Commodore against Corneel or to turn to his own advantage his father's alleged spiritualist beliefs.

Mr. Lord was scarcely courteous in his cross-examination. After a few questions put with a most gingerly circumspection as to Mr. Vanderbilt's relations with his stepmother (he seemed relieved when assured that they had always been entirely proper), Mr. Lord said quietly that that would be all.

There was a flurry of excitement as the significance of his words became apparent. After it subsided, Mr. Lord told the court that counsel for contestant would submit their case without summing up. Then, in a voice which betrayed repressed emotion, he asked to have stricken from the record everything reflecting upon the character of Mrs. Vanderbilt that had appeared there by their motion, offer, or allegation. To the bewilderment of the spectators, there was a general shaking of hands among opposing counsel, and Mr. Choate made a great point of thanking Mr. Lord for his words on behalf of Mrs. Vanderbilt.

Under the heading "POSITIVE DETAILS OF THE COMPROMISE," the *Tribune* promptly gave its readers an inside version of why the trial had ended so abruptly. It claimed its facts came from a gentleman described as "one who has been intimately connected with the contestants, but who refuses to have his name mentioned." This anonymous gentleman was quoted as saying that "the compromise was the result of a conversation between Judge Rapallo and the person who has all along been backing Cornelius Vanderbilt, Jr., in his suit. I don't mean his sister, who has stood by him nobly when she might have pocketed her half million and avoided any trouble. This friend of young Vanderbilt told very plainly what it was proposed to show by numerous witnesses not yet examined, and the consequence was that it was agreed that Cornelius was to be paid $1,000,000 and costs of his suit in the Supreme Court, and Mrs. La Bau $1,000,000 plus her expenditures in the contest of the will; and that all testimony of a character derogatory to any member of the Vanderbilt family, past or present, was to be suppressed."

As later events would show, the *Tribune*'s version, though somewhat overly generous, was not too far removed from the truth. The proponents, for instance, acknowledged that William H. Vanderbilt stood ready to fulfill the promises he had made before the contest started, but this, of course, would not be a compromise. It would be simply a matter of "free gifts"—the same kind of gifts William had given to his other sisters on their refusal to contest the will. Even Mr. Lord, speaking for the contestant, maintained tartly that "I know nothing of any compromise."

Surrogate Calvin gave his decision on March 19, 1879, two weeks after the end of the trial. While all element of doubt as to the outcome had pretty well vanished, it was, nevertheless, an interesting document. In it the Surrogate took considerable pains to castigate the contestant and her counsel severely for what he described as their "persistent effort to uncover to the public gaze the secrets of a parent's domestic and private life; to belittle his intelligence and his virtues; to distort his providence into meanness; to magnify his eccentricities into dementia, his social foibles into immorality, his business differences into dishonesty and treachery; and to ascribe his diseases to obscene practices."

In fact, the Surrogate said, the testimony showed the testator to have been a man of "very vigorous mind and strong nature, but lacking the amenities of education and culture and a delicate respect for the opinions of his fellow men." He also dismissed without exception, and with somewhat less rhetorical flourish, every phase of the contestant's case. The only evidence of a fraudulent conspiracy to influence the testator unduly was the extraordinary testimony of the lady from Poughkeepsie, with her background of unusual domestic arrangements, and of the alcoholically inclined Mrs. Stone. In these cases, due to "the discreditable and fraudulent enterprises in which these two witnesses claimed to have been engaged, and their manner of testifying, their discreditable antecedents and associations, together with the intrinsic improbability of their story," Surrogate Calvin reached the conclusion that their testimony was unworthy of credit and refused to accept it as a basis for judicial action. Furthermore, he urged those directly interested to pursue and bring the offenders to merited punishment, together with their guilty suborners, for, as he put it, "it is not to be believed that a mere fondness for an odious notoriety was sufficient to call these witnesses from their obscene associations unsolicited." (Alas for justice and public expectations, the ladies were permitted to resume their accustomed ways unmolested. Any such stern pursuit would only have stirred up more of the unsavory publicity which the Vanderbilts were now so anxious to avoid, and would, in any event, have violated the terms of the treaty of peace.)

An editorial in the *Times* summed up the whole affair quite succinctly: "The most remarkable feature [of the contest] is the obtuse moral perceptions of the children who have uncovered the nakedness of their parent. . . . The worst feature has been its vulgarity."

Obtuse moral perceptions or not, these were happy days for Vanderbilts, even poor ones. Cornelius and his sister may have lost a legal battle, but, from their point of view, they had won the war. Although the fruits of their victory were not quite so abundant as was rumored in the press (the version favored by the *Times* gave $1,000,000 to each, plus $250,000 for counsel and expenses), they were still substantial. All we know definitely is that, in addition to the Commodore's original bequests, young Corneel received a $400,000 trust fund and some $200,000 in cash. Mrs. La Bau undoubtedly received a comparable amount; and there must also have been considerable sums for legal fees and expenses, but the exact figures of the settlement disappeared immediately behind the veil of secrecy with which the Vanderbilts now endeavored to conduct their affairs. Considering the general preposterousness of contestant's case, these sums were munificent indeed. Even Cornelius conceded, in a letter to the *Times* indignantly protesting against the use of the word "compromise" to describe the settlement, that his brother "acted in a just and magnanimous manner . . . and displayed a liberality far beyond my expectations." The rich Vanderbilts, William and his brood, were happily absorbed with the delightful problem of learning how to spend money as ostentatiously as only *the* Vanderbilts could now afford to spend it.

Happiest of all, perhaps, were the lawyers for both sides. Their combined fees exceeded by a vast margin all then-existing world's records for fat legal pickings. Mr. Clinton's fee was reliably reported to have been at least $300,000; rumor put it as high as $500,000. Whatever it was, he was able to retire and devote the remaining twenty years of his life to writing books about the criminal cases which had been his first and true love. The exact amount of Mr. Lord's fee has never been made public, but he did well enough to free himself from financial worries for the remainder of his life. Judge Black was said to have received $28,000, fair pay certainly for the few occasions on which he was called upon to display his eloquence. In the long run, however, perhaps it was young Corneel's *bête noire*, Chauncey M. Depew, who, although not officially of counsel, topped them all. He entrenched himself so solidly with the Vanderbilt family that he went on to become president of the New York Central and, as a sort of fringe benefit frequently bestowed on prominent industrialists in the days before senators were chosen by popular vote, served two terms in the United States Senate.

The only people concerned with the settlement who seem to have been unhappy were Cornelius's creditors in Hartford. Weeks went by and they were still anxiously waiting. According to a dispatch from Hartford there were 217 claimants to whom Corneel allegedly owed an aggregate of $75,000. Most of them were paid eventually; luckily for them, payment of all outstanding debts was a condition of the settlement insisted upon by William.

By December of 1879 Cornelius himself was becoming unhappily restive in the humdrum security of his new existence. Besides, the mere fact of the inaccessibility of the principal of his new trust fund must have had a most disturbing effect upon anyone so sensitive in such matters. Predictably enough, Cornelius's natural reaction to such frustration was to dash off a typical epistolary effusion, asking that half of the fund be released to him immediately. Alas, William replied that "it would not be a sound exercise of judgment to grant your request, however pleasing it might be to gratify your desire." Unable or unwilling to grasp the idea that one of the chief purposes of trust funds is to protect beneficiaries against the use of their own judgment, Cornelius now petitioned the Supreme Court of New York to remove William as a trustee on some vague grounds of fiduciary incapacity. The court promptly denied the motion. When Cornelius insisted on appealing, against the advice of his counsel, the decision was affirmed with a severe rebuke for bringing an application having neither law nor facts to justify it. The brief era of good feeling between

William and Cornelius had ended and was never to be revived.

For a thwarted ne'er-do-well, life without great expectations was a dismal, downhill affair. Soon Corneel was reappearing once more in his old haunts, where by the curious logic of finance his credit was not as good as it had been when he was scrounging along on an allowance from home, and he was again being harassed by creditors, particularly by Simmons, whose methods of collection could be rather unpleasant. He spent his last night on earth in a gambling house at 12 Ann Street, returning to his rooms in the Glenham Hotel at 6 A.M. of the morning after, worn and bedraggled. Early that afternoon, April 2, 1882, while Sunday crowds promenaded outside on Fifth Avenue, "young Corneel" shot himself to death. It seems now to have been an unnecessarily grim ending to a life which, from any rational point of view, should have continued happily along on a blithe and debonair course.

In his own will Cornelius treated his sisters just as badly as had his father. He left them each $1,000 to buy something in remembrance of him. The bulk of his estate consisted of the disputed $400,000 trust fund, the principal of which he was never able to touch during his life, but which he could dispose of as he wished in his will. Most of it went to his old friend and companion, in good times and bad, George N. Terry. Mrs. La Bau, his staunch comrade-at-arms during the long will contest, was so incensed by this unbrotherly treatment that she now rushed into court with objections to the probate of *his* will. Later, however, she withdrew them after what was described as "an understanding agreeable to all the parties."

Early in the Great Will Contest, when Mr. Lord was developing some of his particularly scurrilous irrelevancies about the Commodore's alleged weakness for assorted females, the *Tribune*, in an outburst of editorial righteousness, had predicted that "rivers of gold will not wash out the stain. . . . The name Vanderbilt will disappear in shame and ignominy." Alas for the prescience of editorial writers, the name Vanderbilt, far from disappearing, was transmuted with almost magical celerity into a national symbol of wealth and social status of such potency that later and far richer parvenu families, strive as they might, have never been able to displace it. Even now, when such things no longer really matter, its spell still lingers.

William more than doubled his inheritance, leaving, upon his death in 1885, an estate worth nearly $200,000,000. With twice as much to distribute, he had something for everyone, and there was nothing resembling a wayward son with great expectations to be prudently blighted. In dividing the kitty, William followed the general pattern set by his father. Each of his four daughters received $5,000,000 outright and $5,000,000 in trust, as did his two younger sons, Frederick and George. The two elder sons, Cornelius II and William K., divvied up the remainder, some $130,000,000.

Although this division did not exactly show equal regard for his offspring, there was not even a rumor of a dispute over the will. None of the eight appeared to feel disinherited, as most of the Commodore's children had in their day. Indeed, it would have been difficult to feel disinherited with a legacy of $10,000,000 in a day when there was no income tax and when a dollar was really a dollar.

—April 1966

THE HISTORIAN AS CELEBRITY

By JOHN LUKACS

The most successful American historian is all but unread today. If George Bancroft was not quite so great a man as his contemporaries believed, he nonetheless deserves better.

George Bancroft was the most successful of all American historians. Three generations ago, at a time when history was still considered literature, the volumes of his *History of the United States* stood on the shelves of thousands of American homes. During most of the nineteenth century it was a solid best seller. Now his once-so-popular volumes are left untouched not only in the proverbial dusty attic but in teeming university libraries, too. His life, full of success, lasted long; his reputation did not.

In the history of American history George Bancroft was the central nineteenth-century figure. He lived at a time when historians still wrote for people rather than for other historians; and he got the best of the two now, alas, so separated worlds. Recognized as the dean of American historians during his lifetime, he also made some political history himself, and, while he still receives textbook mention as an early founder of American historiography, his curious and manifold political career has scarcely been scrutinized at all. Yet he was not only historian but founder of the United States Naval Academy, American Envoy Extraordinary and Minister Plenipotentiary to London and Berlin, writer of presidential speeches, maker of presidential candidates, war maker against Mexico. His political career runs through the rugged tapestry of nineteenth-century American democracy; his writing helped to establish its decorative historical patterns.

Bancroft was a central figure in several respects. His long life spanned not only most of the nineteenth century; it also reached from the life of the first to that of the thirty-fourth President of the Republic. The eighth child of a Massachusetts minister, he was born in 1800, within a year of

Washington's death; he died in 1891, at a time when Eisenhower was already alive. He knew not many decisive setbacks during his life. He was among those fortunate beings who receive nearly all the fame they want during their lifetimes.

Steadily, throughout his days, George Bancroft burned with ambition; throughout most of the century he made himself known. As a youth he was serious and self-conscious, with a tendency toward priggishness (at fourteen he earnestly noted in his diary that he would rather closet himself with a "good moral book" than be amused, like his Harvard classmates, with athletics and fiction). The turning point of his life was the purse, quite a considerable forerunner of a Guggenheim or Fulbright, that sent him to Europe for four years; there he chose to be deeply influenced by Germany, the influence that is reflected throughout his *History* and also in his political career.

He sailed home to America, having acquired a few velveteen European clothes and some cosmopolitan mannerisms. He did not expect the disappointment he then saw reflected in the faces of his Puritan Harvard masters. Thereafter, instead of becoming a clergyman, as they anticipated, he started on a worldly career.

George Bancroft was a master of the art of timing. He founded a prep school when he sensed the excellent prospects for private schools in New England; twice he married well, socially and financially; and at the right time he perceived the advantages of entering Democratic party politics. He reckoned wisely. His years as American envoy abroad and his prominent political posts at home brought him the respectability he sought, if not in Boston, to which he never returned, then in New York and in Washington. There he settled after his last post in Berlin, to enjoy the fruits of his reputation. He had become a Washington eminence in more than one way. He kept a good table. He summered in Newport in his house, Roseclyffe. The Senate gave him the privilege of the floor. When he was eighty-seven, Browning sent a congratulatory verse:

> *Bancroft, the message-bearing wire*
> *Which flashes my "All Hail" today*
> *Moves slowlier than the heart's desire*
> *That, what hand pens, tongue's self might say.*

He died at what was virtually the height of his historical, political, and social reputation. President Harrison ordered the flags of official Washington to be flown at half-mast. No other American historian was ever so honored, either in life or in death.

But who reads him today? Among the now-myriad paper-bound reprints of early American historians you will not find his name. Adams, Prescott, Parkman, even Richard Hildreth, are reprinted, read, discussed, but not Bancroft. His figure is like those large iron statues of neglected governors that stand in the center squares of American state capitals, where now the traffic rushes around them but no one looks up. Our notion of his reputation is vague, romantic, incomplete, fragmentary. Nor is this a recent development. His reputation survived him by only a few years.

The reason is relatively simple. Bancroft died at the very time when a more objective, scientific, pragmatic, professionalized school of American historiography began to replace the earlier, more sentimental, rhetorical, nationalistic way of writing which he typified: "The United States of America constitute an essential portion of a great political system, embracing all the civilized nations of the earth. At a period when the force of moral opinion is rapidly increasing, they have the precedence in the practice and the defence of the equal rights of men. The sovereignty of the people is here a conceded axiom, and the laws, established upon that basis, are cherished with faithful patriotism. While the nations of Europe aspire after change, our constitution engages the fond admiration of the people, by which it has been established. Prosperity follows the execution of even justice; invention is quickened by the freedom of competition; and labor rewarded with sure and unexampled returns."

These are the sentences with which Bancroft introduces his *History of the United States from the Discovery of the American Continent*. There follow another three pages describing an ideal, prosperous, and free national condition such as the world has never seen. "A favoring Providence, calling our institutions into being, has conducted the country to its present happiness and glory."

Thus ends the introduction to the first volume, written and published in 1834, at the height of the Jacksonian era. The tone is unmistakable: it is indeed Jacksonian, optimistic, oratorical, somewhat loud, somewhat engaging. An eagle is proclaimed to soar, high above all, in what seems a cloudless blue sky, visible to the Children of Liberty, their vision yet untarnished by the battle smoke of the Civil War and by the factory smoke of the industrial expansion which followed it.

Bancroft left his introduction unchanged, though in 1882 he added: "The foregoing words, written nearly a half-century ago, are suffered to remain, because the intervening years have justified their expression of confidence in the progress of our republic. The seed of disunion has perished; and universal freedom, reciprocal benefits, and cherished traditions bind its many states in the closest union"—surely a somewhat incomplete description of the condition of the Republic under Chester A. Arthur.

The consistency and the complacency of Bancroft's historical optimism, of which his unchanged introduction is a fair example, suggest immediately why he was such a popular historian during his lifetime. They also suggest why he fell into neglect soon after his death, so that nowadays he is regarded as a lovable, simple, archaic nineteenth-century figure, a sort of bearded Founding Father of the historical profession whom, however, historians no longer read. But this is a superficial judgment; there are things in his *History* that deserve more than their present neglect.

Bancroft was essentially a one-book man. The book is a very long one, not only a magnum opus but an *opus vitae*. He began the *History of the United States* when he was thirty-two; he devoted much of his eighty-sixth year to a revision of the last edition. He wrote the first three volumes in his thirties, the next five volumes in his fifties; when he was seventy-five, he cut the ten volumes to six and brought out a so-called Centenary Edition; the old man and his wife then further corrected and cut out much, "slaughtering the adjectives" as she said, until ten years later "The Author's Last Revision" was issued. Altogether, from 1834 to 1890, almost thirty editions were published. Bancroft made a minor fortune out of them.

These thousands of pages, bound in somber pressed brown or dark blue, are heavy lumber, yet not quite as heavy as they seem at first sight. They are a curious mixture of splinter and gingerbread, of rough New England pine and brown mahogany varnish. They are the history of a Unique People, of a Unique Revolution, of the Providentially Chosen People of God. But there is more to them than the romantic naïveté of early nationalistic historiography. Though Bancroft still belonged to an age that looked upon history as a form of art, he also wished to consider himself a scientist. He refused to reconcile these two contradictory tendencies within himself, with the result that, at his worst, he sounds like a revivalist preacher on one page and a bored county clerk on the next.

Bancroft was a convinced believer in the social progress of democracy; yet there is astonishingly little social history in his long book. He wished to depict the large, dramatic panorama of American evolution; yet his last volume, describing the making of the Constitution, degenerates into dreary passages of long quotes; in the hundreds of pages dealing with 1786 there is but one paragraph about Shays' Rebellion. He exalts the American tradition of lawfulness and justice, yet he is eminently unfair about the Boston Massacre; he glowers about the acquittal of Captain Preston before a Boston court, a shining page of American justice that is unequaled in the history of the French or, indeed, of almost any other democratic revolution. He believed in the advancement of morals; yet at times he could be priggish to the point of ludicrousness. He who first extolled the value of primary documents, the lesson he learned from Germany, did not make good enough use of his extraordinary access to European diplomatic archives.

His three years' tenure in London as American Minister to Britain (Polk's appointment after Bancroft's part in preparing the Mexican War message) had turned out to be profitable as well as enjoyable for him. Bancroft exploited his position by gaining access to many British and French state papers relating to the eighteenth century. Thus he could collect a mass of valuable material for the forthcoming volumes of his *History*, doing his "research" under conditions that past, present, and future historians might well envy.

Bancroft was perhaps the first American historian who did "collective research," since he had secretaries to make copies and to look things up for him; notwithstanding these advantages and the many revisions, factual errors abound in his *History*. He played tricks with his sources, misquoting them on occasion, stringing parts of texts together into fictitious speeches. Bancroft, who believed that history was an objective science, showing "the presence of law in the action of human beings," still treated his history as romantic literature. He looked at things not the way they were but the way they ought to have been; he was unwilling to admit the discrepancies between spirit and flesh, image and reality. "The warts on Franklin's face I wish omitted," wrote Bancroft in a curious note for the engraver who was to set Franklin's portrait on the frontispiece of Volume II of the *History*. (The engraver must have stood his ground: the warts on Franklin's face remain.)

At times Bancroft's narration is stately as well as lively—for example, when he writes about the silent bays of the continent as the colonists' little flotillas enter into their untouched waters: "The sea was enlivened by the shallops of fishermen." Many of his characterizations—especially of foreigners, curiously enough, rather than of Americans—are of enduring excellence, like his revised summation of Lord North: "Yet Lord North was false only as he was weak and uncertain. He really wished to concede and conciliate, but he had not force enough to come to a clear understanding with himself. When he encountered the opposition in the House of Commons, he sustained his administration by speaking confidently for vigorous measures; when alone, his heart sank within him from dread of civil war."

His description of England in 1763, his characterization of Calvert, his contrast of Roger Williams with the Puritans, are better than good. It is a pity that they are not read nowadays. For, at best, a liverish New England nervousness and a thin stateliness harmonize in his prose, most of all in the more austere last editions.

The historian and his work are inseparable. Bancroft's person, like his *History*, was full of paradox. He was not very lovable, not altogether archaic, and far from simple. His prejudices are reflected throughout his *History*; they often form its worst, disproportionate faults. They are not merely nationalistic and democratic prejudices: they are Teutonic, Protestant, Populist, and Progressive. To Bancroft, the modern progress of Science and Virtue began with Luther, and the Chosen People were mainly those of the Germanic Race. To Bancroft the English civil war was a struggle between the simple, democratic, virtuous "Low Folk" Saxons and the "High Folk of Normandie"; the epic campaigns of Britain and France for the domination of the Atlantic world were but a war "between the Catholic and the Protestant Powers."

Bancroft, who at first rejected Darwin, was nonetheless an unconscious historical Darwinian. For him the Protestant democracy of America marked the inexorable march of progress. The victory of the Revolution "was the first decisive victory of the industrious middling class over the most powerful representative of the mediaeval aristocracy"—a peculiar description of British society in the 1770s. "The world is in a constant state of advancement"; things are getting better and better all the time. But this, then, is not really archaic at all. Indeed, it is the credo of American progressive historiography, stretching up to our present day. For even though the profession of history soon left Bancroft behind—abandoning social Darwinism and sentimental admiration for the Teuton race—the German-scientific tradition, of which Bancroft was the first central representative, still dominates American professional historical writing.

Bancroft was a successful man—so successful, indeed, that some of his friends reproached him for the very obvious eagerness with which he pursued wealth and prestige. His political ambitions were great, yet he was vexed and spurred by a sense of social inferiority throughout his life. He was a social climber rather than a self-confident aristocrat, and at least as much of an opportunist as a rebel. Though he was always extolling the Wisdom of the People and condemning the sins of aristocracies, he was evidently pleased by being invited to all sorts of high places in England and by the titles with which the Prussians flattered him.

As the American envoy to Germany, Bancroft spent the seven happiest years of his life, back in his beloved Berlin, surrounded by German professors, intelligently cultivated and inconspicuously patronized by his idol Bismarck, whose cause Bancroft ambitiously assisted with newspaper articles and undiplomatic speeches. (The French protested in vain against Bancroft's unneutral behavior.) The celebration of the great Prussian victory at Sedan in 1870 coincided almost to the day with the celebration of Bancroft's *Doctor-Jubilaeum*, the fiftieth anniversary of his doctorate at Göttingen. A stream of German academicians and high officials proceeded through Bancroft's Berlin house on that unforgettable day; the old Ranke hobbled up to him and planted a professional kiss on Bancroft's beard.

Bancroft's judgment of nations and of persons was often lamentable. "It is still 'the scarlet woman of Babylon,' " he wrote about the Papacy in 1870; "we have a president without brains," he said of Lincoln as late as 1860 (always privately, of course). He wrongly saw in 1848 the coming of the Universal Democratic Revolution in Europe; in 1870 he claimed to hear the sound of Freedom in the victorious bellowing of the Prussian guns at Sedan. It is not surprising that Ranke and Treitschke said that he was "one of us." Bancroft, in turn, called Bismarck a "lover of liberty," "a great republican," "a renovator of Europe"; he said that Moltke was a German Washington; on one occasion he even pledged, foolishly, the help of the United States Navy against France.

"Literary men indulge in humbug only at a price, and Bancroft abounded in humbug," wrote Van Wyck Brooks. "Did he believe what he was saying?" Anthony Trollope once asked. Emerson called him an opportunist, mercenary, a man with a tricky heart.

Much of what Bancroft had written was soon outdated and cast aside by the thousands of young American historians who followed him. In this respect even death came to him at a fortunate moment; near the time when Bancroft passed away, his idol Bismarck was sent into retirement and died soon afterward; within a few years American and German warships were glowering at each other in Manila Bay; soon Turner and Beard were at large, demolishing the edifice of American historical illusions that Bancroft had helped to build. The air was more electric; the mustiness was evaporating; the nation's vision of its own past was becoming clearer.

Bancroft was a lesser man, and a lesser historian, than he wished his contemporaries (and, of course, posterity) to believe; but in our times, when no one reads him, the balance ought to be redressed somewhat. His politics deserve a stricter scrutiny than they have received; his *History* deserves more consideration than the present neglect. It is another strange paradox that Bancroft stands condemned today for the wrong reason. He is neglected because of his romantic, effulgent qualities rather than because of his occasional insincerity and frequent cant. This is a pity, for his writing gains in contrast with the gray, cautious, dry, sociological, technical prose of monographic historical writing that is so frequent nowadays. On the other hand, historians have slurred over the evidences of his astonishing political opportunism. Ironically, they have fallen into Bancroft's own trap; they have treated him in the mode of professional and scientific historiography, as if the historian and the politician had been two different persons. This is never really possible—certainly not with Bancroft —though we may reasonably say that Bancroft the historian was better and at least more consistent than Bancroft the politician.

"Westward the star of empire takes its way"—this was the motto pressed on the cover boards of the first volume of Bancroft's *History*. It was pointed out to him that Bishop Berkeley's famous words spoke of the course, not star, of empire. Still he did not order his publishers to change it. He liked it better this way. On the covers of that early edition the Bancroftian version of the phrase remains.

—October 1961

THE MACHINE THAT KEPT THEM HONEST

By GERALD CARSON

John H. Patterson bought the rights to manufacture an expensive machine that nobody wanted, and set out to sell the world cash registers. Eventually he succeeded. But first he had to invent Salesmanship.

The machine was the cash register. The clangor of its bell fell pleasantly upon the ear, whether activated by dollars and cents, pounds and pence, francs, marks, florins, lire, pesetas, or pesos.

The man behind the bell was an Ohio farm boy who promoted a novel counting device of wheels and springs grandly encased in an ornate bronze or nickel sheath. When a clerk pressed a key the machine gave out its joyous tintinnabulation. In the beginning no one had heard of the cash register. But John Henry Patterson changed all that. To do it he had to invent American Salesmanship.

John H. Patterson was a not-so-young hustler lightly endowed with this world's goods when in 1884 he offered $6,500 for the controlling interest in an obscure little factory in Slidertown—a slum area of Dayton, Ohio—which manufactured the new machine that was to make the open cash drawer obsolete. Dayton laughed so hard that Patterson panicked and tried, unsuccessfully, to back out of the deal. It was too late. The seller confided that he wouldn't take the stock as a gift. But Patterson's fortune was as good as made, and the story of selling had to be rewritten. What the small, sandy-haired, intense promoter did with the cash register made entrepreneurial history; and the tales told of the man himself will be repeated, with no embellishment needed, as long as men wearing name tags convene to learn how to sell widgets, or management types gather at country clubs to relax at the nineteenth hole. Patterson's solid achievements, his impressive list of business "firsts," are enough to secure him a high and enduring place in mercantile history.

The Autocrat of the Cash Register was born in 1844 of pioneer stock on the family farm near Dayton. He attended the local schools, spent a year at Miami University in Oxford, Ohio, and was graduated from Dartmouth College. There he acquired, Patterson often remarked, much useless knowledge. His prejudice against higher education lasted through the rest of his idiosyncratic life.

After college, Patterson worked on his father's farm, later became a toll collector on the Miami and Erie Canal, and still later, with his two brothers, ran a coal yard, developed coal and iron mines in Jackson County, Ohio, and was for several years the general manager for the Southern Coal and Iron Company at Coalton, Ohio.

The Southern operated a company store. Instead of turning in a profit of $12,000, which the books said it should, the store was actually losing $6,000 a year because, Patterson discovered, his clerks were dishonest. At this point he read that James S. Ritty, a Dayton saloonkeeper with similar problems, and his mechanically minded brother, John, had invented a contraption that tabulated sales as they were made and registered them publicly. In order to open the cash drawer and make change, the clerk was compelled to ring up the sale. The bell on the device—at the time Patterson heard about the register, it gave out a loud *bong*—forced him to deposit the money received. In sum, the magic money box provided publicity, protection, and compulsory morality.

The cash register was expensive, costing all of fifty dollars. But Patterson, even though he had probably never seen one, promptly telegraphed for two. At the time there were only about a dozen in use, under the name "Ritty's Incorruptible Cashier." With the introduction of the new machines the profit picture at Ritty's oasis in Dayton brightened, and John H. Patterson's store also moved into the black. The Patterson brothers immediately purchased a block of cash register stock—this was in 1882—and two years later, with John H. in the lead, acquired control of the business and soon changed the name to National Cash Register Company.

Thus, at the age of forty, with no manufacturing experience and little capital, Patterson started in to build a business upon an article almost no one wanted or knew how to use. Known as a "thief catcher," the device aroused such fury among bartenders and café cashiers that a traveling man who was handling another item, say sewing machines, found it prudent when entering a drinking parlor to say loudly and distinctly that he was not associated with the N.C.R.

The man in absolute control of that company—"the Cash" it came to be called in Dayton—was small, wiry, a natty dresser; he had penetrating gray eyes, a florid complexion, luxuriant white handlebar mustaches, and a quick mind untrammelled by convention. Patterson quickly improved the cash register, took out several patents in his own name, introduced a system of quality control, and turned his attention to the problems of advertising and selling.

The important businessmen of the time were converters of raw materials, railroad presidents, and hard-shelled merchants who had survived the panic of '73. Advertising by and large consisted of drab announcements. Selling was glad-handing, a matter of exploiting a genial personality that attracted a following in "the trade." Look the part. Sell yourself and you sell your product. Manufacturing was getting men to work for as little as possible. Card indices, filing systems, and duplicating machines had not been heard of.

Into this traditional business environment Patterson introduced several startling new concepts. He began by building (with borrowed money) a model plant on the old family farm. It was a revolutionary concept in industrial architecture, a "daylight" building with eighty percent of its walls made of glass and with ampelopsis climbing up the brickwork; the grounds were landscaped and dotted with flower beds. Inside, the revolution was just as complete. There were lockers and showers, swimming pools and other recreational facilities, hot lunches, medical care, and inspirational lectures to give wings to the mind.

These pioneering efforts in industrial welfare—and the high rate of pay at "the Cash"—attracted so much attention locally, nationally, and even internationally that Patterson, who explained gruffly, "It pays," hung a sign by his office door: "Be Brief—Omit All Compliments About Welfare Work." In exchange for his unusual attentions to the N.C.R. employees, Patterson exacted absolute obedience and a high rate of productivity. In a day when good management meant cost-cutting, Patterson took the opposite tack—the way to make money, he believed, was to spend it. Secrecy, too, was highly regarded as a competitive weapon. But Patterson welcomed visitors to his plant and even wined and dined—no, just dined —competitors and would-be competitors. He inevitably showed them "the Gloom Room," where they were urged to gaze upon piles and piles of rusty registers, the products of bankrupt companies that couldn't stand the pace set by National. It was unforgettable evidence of the folly of bucking John H. Patterson.

Patterson soon demonstrated his native flair for showmanship. One day when he was escorting some friends through the factory, he stopped before a shiny new register that had been checked out for shipment. He started to point out the model's special features. One key stuck. Another wouldn't depress. Patterson reached for a hammer and reduced the register to a mass of junk.

"That is how we take care of faulty machines," he said casually.

But the glory of N.C.R. was what Patterson called "the American Selling Force." With nothing in hand but the legal right to make a mechanism for which there was no demand, but with an almost apocalyptic vision of a universal market of prospective purchasers who needed a cash register and didn't know it, Patterson put together the most aggressive corps of salesmen the world had ever seen. He argued with his men, coaxed and criticized, often lashed them with biting sarcasm, preached and exhorted. He supported the Force with aggressive advertising, and tried to generate in each man an incentive equal to religion's fear of damnation and hope of salvation. It was the missionary spirit of spreading the gospel to the heathen, hooked up with American boosterism.

A man who looked like a comer was often taken by Patterson to New York at company expense to stay at a luxury hotel, get measured for a good suit, visit the finest hatters and custom shirt shops, see a couple of shows, and generally, in Patterson's words, "get the hayseed off him." A taste of the fleshpots, Patterson figured, was a sure-fire way to spark the imagination of a good man who would like to have a new davenport and join the local country-club set. Patterson introduced the idea of the guaranteed territory and paid straight commissions on which a man could really make money. Refusing to follow the common practice of the times, he did not cut back the commissions when business was good. "If you sell a million dollars in a week," he declared expansively, "we'll hire a brass band to take your commission to you."

The idea of the sacrosanct commission took hold slowly. Years afterward Thomas J. Watson, brilliant leader of the International Business Machines Corporation and a member of the distinguished body of Patterson alumni, remembered how back home in Painted Post, New York, when a local man boasted that he had made thirty dollars selling a cash register, he was deemed to be the biggest liar in the Cohocton River valley.

One of Patterson's early formulations now regarded as an invaluable business tool was the establishing of sales quotas, based upon an objective analysis of potential opportunity in a territory. The quota system ironed out the inequities, applied the same measure to all salesmen, meant the same thing in Portland, Oregon, as in Utica, New York, in Indianapolis as in Bangkok.

Among the new concepts Patterson introduced was the standardized sales talk, codified into a revolutionary document known as the *N.C.R. Primer*. At first the use of the new method of selling was merely recommended. Later it became compulsory. Patterson never justified it from any theoretical standpoint. He didn't need to: the men who followed the *Primer* sold more registers and earned fatter commissions than those who stuck to personality selling. From this pioneering effort emerged the first sales manual. It brought together all the objections and excuses which had ever been advanced for not buying a cash register. A training school soon followed, later elaborated into conferences and conventions with intracompany competitions that provided rewards and distinctions for the fortunate winners. There were company songs, bunting, and banners. A Patterson sales convention was a Rotarian gala, the atmosphere one of emotion touched with grandeur. Part circus, part chautauqua, it resembled a church revival except that there was never any letdown. Early in each year, flags were flung to the breeze over the home office when the first salesman made his quota. The annual Sales Derby was on!

The men who survived Patterson's school came out casehardened and wily. They never simply sold a piece of machinery; rather, they promoted a business function. It was the principle later expressed by Elmer Wheeler, inspirational lecturer sometimes called "America's Number 1 Salesman," in the memorable slogan: *Don't sell the steak, sell the sizzle*. Patterson's men were forbidden to carry screw drivers, lest they become diverted into service work. Nor were they encouraged to become more than casually conversant with the innards of the machine they sold, although in the cash register field it was useful to have a working knowledge of a competitive register so as to be able, on occasion, to put it out of commission.

"I have called to interest you in a way to increase your profits," the polite N.C.R. man would say. He was itching for an argument, never happier than when the prospect, known in Patterson's lexicon as the "P.P." (Probable Purchaser), raised such childish and moth-eaten objections as:

I don't need one.

Times are hard.

I can't spare the money.

My present system is satisfactory.

You make too great a profit.

The next step was to entangle the P.P. in a net of admissions about his losses on *cash sales, credit sales, cash received on account, cash paid out*, and *charging money as an accommodation*. Healthy, shaved, with clean linen and no cigar, his blue serge suit well brushed, the N.C.R. agent staged his demonstration outside the store—usually in a sample room at the best hotel in town—with such theatrical trappings as curtains painted to represent a store interior. There were large business charts and diagrams. Real merchandise and real money were used to heighten the dramatic impact. The P.P. was comfortably seated, and there no distractions in the room such as a clock, which might suggest that he had better be getting back to the store, or a calendar, a possible reminder that he had a note coming due at the bank.

The closing of a sale was as stylized as a Japanese kabuki play. When the salesman had the prospect sagging on the ropes he was too much the artist to ask crudely for the order; instead, he moved smoothly to, "Now, Mr. Brown, what color shall I make it?" Or, "How soon do you want delivery?" If the store owner drew back, the N.C.R. man prepared him once more for signature, gently urging him up to the mark again, pen at the ready —"Just sign here." With the ceremonial signing went a twenty-five cent cigar and the ego-boosting assurance that the customer had proved that he was a real live wire as a businessman. Nor was that the end of the relationship between the purchaser and the company. The N.C.R. man was already making a note of the date when the register would be obsolescent and should be traded in on a new, improved model, for it was one of the most attractive discoveries made in the early days of specialty selling that the customer who had been knocked over once could be upgraded later.

Patterson scoffed at the going idea that salesmen were born. Not N.C.R. salesmen, he vowed. They were made—by the head man, who often played storekeeper with them in this wise: "Good morning," the president of N.C.R. would say mildly to a sweating member of the Selling Force. "I have a drugstore down the street. Will you kindly explain the cash register to me?" If the salesman was quick, verbalized well, or was just lucky that morning, Patterson might give an occasional grunt, his most demonstrative expression of appreciation. More often he jumped up in the middle of the pitch, grabbed a piece of red chalk, and scrawled on the easel pad which always stood handy, "ROTTEN!" Before the merciless examination was over, some men faltered, some blacked out. And some just plain quit.

But by about 1910, the Cash was doing ninety percent of the cash register business. The U.S. Department of Justice thought this was a very high penetration of the market. But the pebble in Patterson's shoe was that other ten percent. He could not honestly see a legitimate reason for *any* cash register to be sold except the National.

John H. Patterson loved to instruct. And he was a convinced eye-minded man. "Visualize! Analyze! Dramatize!" he urged, and installed in his offices hundreds of blackboards and pedestals bearing pads of coarse paper three feet long by two feet wide for jotting down problems or plans. Sometimes he drew pictographs, and he liked others to do the same. It wasn't enough to say "cow." At the Cash, one had to draw the cow.

"The optic nerve is twenty-two times stronger than the auditory nerve," the boss of N.C.R. declared as he made a quick chalk talk or scribbled think on the sheet. This cabalistic word was, incidentally, the inspiration of the kinetic Thomas J. Watson, who started out in the world selling pianos, organs, and sewing machines from a bright yellow democrat wagon. Watson got his postgraduate training in Patterson's University of Hard Knocks and went on to transform a faltering combination called the Computing-Tabulating-Recording Company into the fabulous International Business Machines Corporation.

To Paterson the number five was what seven was to the ancients, a digit endowed with occult power. Signficantly, he thought, man has five senses, five fingers, five toes. There were five steps to making a sales pitch. Every problem, Patterson saw, had five parts. The figure was woven into the very fabric of the National Cash Register Company. In 1920, at the end of his life, filled with eagerness to see the League of Nations succeed, Patterson went to Geneva, studied the structure of the world organization, got out the old N.C.R. textbook, and charted the purposes of the League —under, of course, five headings.

The center of Patterson's training of his male employees was the N.C.R. Hall of Industrial Education, or the Schoolhouse, where salesmen and agents sometimes acted out little allegorical dramas resembling the old miracle plays with which the Church taught its children in the Middle Ages. An example: men on crutches, others with bandaged arms or legs or eyes, attempted to climb steps toward a bag with a dollar sign on it hanging over the stage. But they could not reach it. Other men emerged from a replica of the Schoolhouse carrying additional steps marked "Uses Advertising Matter," or "Cuts out Cigarettes." With these aids they successfully reached the bag and gave it a mighty wallop; out showered salary checks and special cash prizes.

The female counterpart of the Hall of Education was the Vacation House, where women employees gathered to learn about the menace of the housefly and were taught how to manage their homes. And frequently little N.C.R. children were herded into one of the buildings to learn how to save their money, how to masticate their food, and how coughing and sneezing scattered germs. All this they endured patiently, knowing that later there would be cookies and a movie about Indians. To an extraordinary degree, Patterson regarded the company's assets, human as well as material, as a simple extension of his own personality. Indeed, Patterson took the whole city as a part of his demesne, even at one time exhorting the clergy to drop the Scriptures in favor of his own pet causes—landscape gardening, the city-manager form of municipal government, and the proper care of the teeth.

Some of Patterson's utterances sound trite today, such as his call for "Head-Power, Hand-Power, Heart-Power"; or this one: "By Hammer and Hand All Arts Do Stand." Maybe they sounded that way when he said them. But those who entertained such a heretical attitude were quickly rinsed out of N.C.R.'s hair. Patterson was a great man for signs that expressed the little truisms in which he placed great faith. "It Pays" appeared on walls all through the N.C.R. buildings. He painted "We Progress Through Change" on a tall factory chimney, put cards on every office desk saying "Do it Now" and "Verbal Orders Don't Go."

Patterson was always open-minded, and sometimes credulous, when he encountered a theory that was apparently based upon scientific or quasi-scientific premises. He became interested, for example, in the study of business cycles long before most businessmen had ever heard of the concept, and believed that the price of pig iron was a clue to a certain periodicity in business trends. Scientific or not, it is a fact that Patterson was getting ready for a storm long before the depression of 1893 arrived. When it came he "had his fighting clothes on"; he made the panic year one of the brightest the company had experienced, successfully selling, in those shaky days, a $350 model.

The vegetarian dietary ideas that were disseminated from the Battle Creek Sanitarium in Michigan by another skillful publicist, Dr. John Harvey Kellogg, attracted Patterson's favorable attention. He often journeyed to Battle Creek when he felt the onset of managerial fatigue. As the Dayton *Daily News* said, he was "more than strong for all that Battle Creek stuff." During a trip abroad to expand the N.C.R. business in Europe, Patterson met Horace Fletcher, a health faddist who also had Battle Creek associations. Fletcher was a eupeptic millionaire who had passed through New Thought and Yoga, had once lived for fifty-eight days on potatoes, and was then propagandizing for a physiological regimen known as "Fletcherism." Fletcher believed that people ought to eat less and that the more one chews the less he needs to eat. He dramatized his ideas by prescribing that his followers chew every bite thirty-two times—one chew for each tooth in man's normal complement.

Patterson was fascinated. He plunged into a thirty-seven-day fast which left him so weak that he turned to Sandow in London, then known as "The Strongest Man in the World," to build him up again. When Patterson returned to Dayton, he brought with him a cockney trainer, or rubber, from Sandow's entourage, a wizened little man named Charles Palmer who claimed to have an extraordinary ability to read human character. This oddball gym attendant established an almost hypnotic ascendancy over the cash register millionaire and interfered in company affairs, causing many resignations and dismissals.

Charles Palmer hated Dayton. While under Palmer's influence and at a time when he was displeased with the city government, Patterson put together a bitter indictment of the city and announced that N.C.R. was pulling out. Meanwhile, under Palmer's direction, butter, eggs, salt, and pepper disappeared from the officers' dining room. Even the sacred American Selling Force was not immune to the new regimen. The men were ordered to cut out coffee, tea, and cigars when they were assembled at the home office. Executives obediently drank bottled water, did their calisthenics, and turned out at dawn for horseback riding. Many of them had never been on a horse before. Naturally, the N.C.R. official family became known as "The N.C.R. Rough Riders." The Horse Period was regarded as one of Patterson's more hilarious antics. But for one family it spelled tragedy when the breadwinner, a company official, was thrown and killed.

Patterson brought a series of libel suits against the Dayton *Daily News* when it raised its voice in protest against his eccentric mania for the diminutive English chap. Patterson huffed and puffed but backed down when the *News* began to take depositions. Palmer wore out his welcome and failed to return after a European sojourn. Patterson soon relented in his attitude toward Dayton, later instituted many generous and far-sighted projects for community betterment, including in particular his dream that aviation research might be centralized at Dayton, where the Wrights were born. And Dayton remembers. There is a Patterson Boulevard, the great Wright-Patterson Air Force Base, linking the names of three famous Daytonians, and on parkland he gave to the city there is a heroic statute of Patterson. He is, of course, on a horse.

Over the years, the exodus of able men trained in the N.C.R. methods became legendary. Among the names of prominent alumni appear those of men who later became notable in other fields, such as the already mentioned Thomas J. Watson of I.B.M. and Hugh Chalmers, Edward S. Jordan, Alvan Macauley, Richard H. Grant, and C. F. ("Boss") Kettering of the automotive industry. At one time Patterson developed the habit of cleaning out his executives' desks and burning all the personal contents, even to the family portraits, on the theory that an executive should start fresh every so often. When a man began to look indispensable, he was as good as dead. In his deceptively meek manner Patterson would stutter, if disagreement developed, "Well, well, well, you ought to know best." But old hands knew it was the beginning of the end.

Once the president asked a foreman if he was satisfied with the work in his department. He said he was.

"All right," snapped Patterson, "you're fired."

In his last decade the founder was plagued with some of the penalties of leadership. The N.C.R. was charged with unfair competition in a Michigan state court by the American Cash Register Company, an old rival, which produced damaging testimony from a defecting N.C.R. agent. There were claims and counterclaims of harassment, industrial espionage, pirating, and bribery. Some of the battles became actual fist fights in the P.P.'s store. The verdict in this case was adverse to Patterson. At approximately the same time—in the U.S. District Court of Southern Ohio —the federal government brought suit against the president and twenty-nine other officials of the company for criminal and civil violations of the Sherman Antitrust Act. During the proceedings the court heard some of the uninhibited words Patterson had used in the old days, such as: "The best way to kill a dog is to cut off his head." "We do not buy out. We knock out." Charges were aired of sabotage, industrial spying, payoffs, and harassment through patent litigation.

In 1913 the defendants were adjudged guilty and received jail sentences and fines of varying amounts. Patterson drew a fine of $5,000 and a year in the county jail at Troy. The verdict was appealed, of course. But before the Court of Appeals had handed down its decision, John H. Patterson had the chance to become a national hero.

On Tuesday, March 25, 1913, came the Dayton Flood. The city stood under six to eighteen feet of water. One hundred million dollars' worth of property was destroyed, and 90,000 people were made homeless. With his unconquerable spirit and the material resources he provided, Patterson saved the city. Crayon in hand, he quickly outlined a relief plan on his handy easel pad. Food, tents, medicines, and hospital equipment were moved to the N.C.R. property, which fortunately stood on high ground and had its own power plant. Company bakers started baking bread around the clock, and the assembly line at N.C.R. soon was turning out rowboats —one every seven minutes. Thousands of Daytonians were fed at the N.C.R. cafeteria, slept on hay in the offices (the hay was changed every night), drank bottled water out of mandatory paper cups that Patterson provided, and wore the heavy woolen stockings he prescribed for them. Five babies were born in the factory in one day alone. This explains why "Cash" can really be a man's name. Newspaper reporters, never neglected by Patterson, enjoyed free room and board on the top floor of the administration building, with such amenities available as pinochle cards and ewers of whiskey which were described for Patterson's benefit as "pop." One legend placed Patterson himself, at the age of sixty-five and then under a jail sentence, at the end of a tow line at Main and Apple Streets, waist-deep in the swirling waters. Dayton needed a hero, and Patterson had a legitimate claim to the role.

Miss Evangeline Cary Booth, commander in chief of the Salvation Army, announced that John H. Patterson was the instrument of the Lord and would be rewarded. And so he was. The United States Court of Appeals reversed the decision of the lower court, largely on the ground that the National Cash Register Company had been denied the right to show that its actions in the old, bad days were the consequence of patent infringements and other destructive practices by the rascally "opposition." One competitor had ridiculed N.C.R. improvements as "ornamental jimcracks which cumber the machine and add little to its value but serve as an excuse for exorbitant prices." Another had unkindly distributed a circular entitled *Fourteen Ways of Beating the National Cash Register*, which listed ways to manipulate the Cash's machines so as to prove them inaccurate. The Supreme Court refused to consider the case, which meant that the decision of the Court of Appeals stood. To celebrate the triumph of justice twenty thousand Daytonians formed a victory parade with flags and brass bands.

The last sales conference conducted under Patterson's eye was held in January, 1922, to honor the men who had "helped to keep the smoke-stacks smoking" during the recession of 1921. The agents and salesmen who had bettered their quotas got three days of inspiration and elevation in Dayton, then boarded a fourteen-car all-Pullman train for three exhilarating days in New York. The picked men thrilled to the N.C.R. chorus that welcomed them at Dayton with the Soldiers' Chorus from *Faust*. In response, they rose to their feet in roaring tribute to the bouncy Founder.

"With depression you went to the mat," said H. G. Sisson of the Publicity Department, as he recited a poem of his own composition:

You were there on the spot where the fighting was hot,
And you won where the weaker men failed.
Though you may have been jarred when the sledding grew hard
And your arguments seemed to be spent;
Why, you simply began on the old selling plan
And you finished one hundred per cent.

Then the chevaliers of the N.C.R. Legion of Honor got the message for the next year. There was a door leading into 1922. Turn the knob and find Opportunity; remember such Patterson aphorisms as "Analyze—don't antagonize," "Every time you sell a merchant a National Cash Register you are doing him a big favor," and "Stay five minutes longer." There was the mass photograph of the Schoolhouse and the comradely fraternizing with the factory workers.

When the time came for the Hundred Per Cent Club to entrain for New York, Dayton put aside its ordinary preoccupations. On signal from the factory whistle, the men and women of N.C.R. formed eight abreast in a column a mile long, and then with flags flying, bands blaring, and symbolical floats, they paraded to the Union Station singing special lyrics arranged to the tune of "Marching Through Georgia." Patterson revelled in the convention, but for him time was running out. He died suddenly on his way to Atlantic City in May, at seventy-seven years of age. Just two days before, he had gone over plans with General William ("Billy") Mitchell, Assistant Chief of Air Service, for the development of Dayton as a great center for aviation research.

The company that Patterson created literally out of nothing has grown enormously; its last reported gross annual sales figure was a whopping $736,849,000, against $29,000,000 in the last year of Patterson's life. It has also become highly diversified, producing, in addition to cash registers, accounting machines, posting machines, and electronic data-processing systems.

The policies of the Cash are now far different from those of the unpredictable autocrat of its pioneering decades. But the heritage of a unique tradition remains. It is a tradition that links the gaslight era of Prince Albert coats and high collars, of wooden Indians and handwritten letters, with the business world of today, the world of the typewriter and the fountain pen, the duplicating machine and the calculating machine, and, of course, the cash register. This tradition places N.C.R. in the main stream of American business development.

Patterson showed the way to introduce not only "big ticket" merchandise like washing machines and refrigerators, but all products that require sampling and demonstration. To every doorbell ringer of the 2,700 companies whose salesmen make five million calls on every working day, to every bright, cheery, happy, polite, top-notch producer who ever made the Fine and Dandy Club of the Fuller Brush Company, or the Hoover vacuum cleaner Hall of Fame, some of Patterson's shrewd, practical psychology has been passed down. And every executive who has ever made a presentation, talked with the assistance of a slide projector, or handled a flip chart is an heir of the crotchety old man at N.C.R. with his blazing eyes, his scratch pads, his slogans, his food fads—and his touch of genius.

—August 1966

CARNEGIE & ROCKEFELLER

By ROBERT L. HEILBRONER

Both were unimaginably wealthy. Both were great philanthropists. And there the resemblances ceased: Carnegie remains a brash and vivid image in the American consciousness; Rockefeller, a shadowy presence.

I. Andrew Carnegie

Toward the end of his days, at the close of World War I, Andrew Carnegie was already a kind of national legend. His meteoric rise, the scandals and successes of his industrial generalship—all this was blurred into nostalgic memory. What was left was a small, rather feeble man with a white beard and pale, penetrating eyes, who could occasionally be seen puttering around his mansion on upper Fifth Avenue, a benevolent old gentleman who still rated an annual birthday interview but was even then a venerable relic of a fast-disappearing era. Carnegie himself looked back on his career with a certain savored incredulity. "How much did you say I had given away, Poynton?" he would inquire of his private secretary; "$324,657,399" was the answer. "Good Heaven!" Carnegie would exclaim. "Where did I ever get all that money?"

Where he *had* got all that money was indeed a legendary story, for even in an age known for its acquisitive triumphs, Carnegie's touch had been an extraordinary one. He had begun, in true Horatio Alger fashion, at the bottom; he had ended, in a manner that put the wildest of Alger's novels to shame, at the very pinnacle of success. At the close of his great deal with J. P. Morgan in 1901, when the Carnegie steel empire was sold to form the core of the new United States Steel Company, the banker had extended his hand and delivered the ultimate encomium of the times: "Mr. Carnegie," he said, "I want to congratulate you on being the richest man in the world."

It was certainly as "the richest man in the world" that Carnegie attracted the attention of his contemporaries. Yet this is hardly why we look back on him with interest today. As an enormous money-maker Carnegie was a flashy, but hardly a profound, hero of the times; and the attitudes of Earnestness and Self-Assurance, so engaging in the young immigrant, become irritating when they are congealed in the millionaire. But what lifts Carnegie's life above the rut of a one-dimensional success story is an aspect of which his contemporaries were relatively unaware.

Going through his papers after his death, Carnegie's executors came across a memorandum that he had written to himself fifty years before, carefully preserved in a little yellow box of keepsakes and mementos. It brings us back to December, 1868, when Carnegie, a young man flushed with the first taste of great success, retired to his suite in the opulent Hotel St. Nicholas in New York, to tot up his profits for the year. It had been a tremendous year and the calculation must have been extremely pleasurable. Yet this is what he wrote as he reflected on the figures: "Thirty-three and an income of $50,000 per annum! By this time two years I can so arrange all my business as to secure at least $50,000 per annum. Beyond this never earn—make no effort to increase fortune, but spend the surplus each year for benevolent purposes. Cast aside business forever, except for others.

"Settle in Oxford and get a thorough education, making the acquaintance of literary men—this will take three years of active work—pay especial attention to speaking in public. Settle then in London and purchase a controlling interest in some newspaper or live review and give the general management of it attention, taking part in public matters, especially those connected with education and improvement of the poorer classes.

"Man must have an idol—the amassing of wealth is one of the worst species of idolatry—no idol more debasing than the worship of money. Whatever I engage in I must push inordinately; therefore should I be careful to choose that life which will be the most elevating in character. To continue much longer overwhelmed by business cares and with most of my thoughts wholly upon the way to make more money in the shortest time, must degrade me beyond hope of permanent recovery. I will resign business at thirty-five, but during the ensuing two years I wish to spend the afternoons in receiving instruction and in reading systematically."

It is a document which in more ways than one is Carnegie to the very life: brash, incredibly self-confident, chockablock with self-conscious virtue —and more than a little hypocritical. For the program so nobly outlined went largely unrealized. Instead of retiring in two years, Carnegie went on for thirty-three more; even then it was with considerable difficulty that he was persuaded to quit. Far from shunning further money-making, he proceeded to roll up his fortune with an uninhibited drive that led one unfriendly biographer to characterize him as "the greediest little gentleman ever created." Certainly he was one of the most aggressive profit seekers of his time. Typically, when an associate jubilantly cabled: "No. 8 furnace broke all records today," Carnegie coldly replied, "What were the other furnaces doing?"

It is this contrast between his hopes and his performance that makes Carnegie interesting. For when we review his life, what we see is more than a career of another nineteenth-century acquisitor. We see the unequal struggle between a man who loved money—loved making it, having it, spending it—and a man who, at bottom, was ashamed of himself for his acquisitive desires.

All during his lifetime, the money-maker seemed to win. But what lifts Carnegie's story out of the ordinary is that the other Carnegie ultimately triumphed. At his death public speculation placed the size of his estate at about five hundred million dollars. In fact it came to $22,881,575. Carnegie *had* become the richest man in the world—but something had also driven him to give away ninety percent of his wealth.

Actually, his contemporaries knew of Carnegie's inquietude about money. In 1889, before he was world-famous, he had written an article for the *North American Review* entitled "The Gospel of Wealth"—an article that contained the startling phrase: "The man who dies thus rich dies disgraced." It was hardly surprising, however, if the world took these sentiments at a liberal discount: homiletic millionaires who preached the virtues of austerity were no novelty; Carnegie himself, returning in 1879 from a trip to the miseries of India, had been able to write with perfect sincerity, "How very little the millionaire has beyond the peasant, and how very often his additions tend not to happiness but to misery."

What the world may well have underestimated, however, was a concern more deeply rooted than these pieties revealed. For, unlike so many of his self-made peers, who also rose from poverty, Carnegie was the product of a *radical* environment. The village of Dunfermline, Scotland, when he was born there in 1835, was renowned as a center of revolutionary ferment, and Carnegie's family was itself caught up in the radical movement of the times. His father was a regular speaker at the Chartist rallies, which were an almost daily occurrence in Dunfermline in the 1840s, and his uncle was an impassioned orator for the rights of the working class to vote and strike. All this made an indelible impression on Carnegie's childhood.

"I remember as if it were yesterday," he wrote seventy years later, "being awakened during the night by a tap at the back window by men who had come to inform my parents that my uncle, Bailie Morrison, had been thrown in jail because he dared to hold a meeting which had been forbidden. . . . It is not to be wondered at that, nursed amid such surroundings, I developed into a violent young Republican whose motto was 'death to privilege.' "

From another uncle, George Lauder, Carnegie absorbed a second passion that was also to reveal itself in his later career. This was his love of poetry, first that of the poet Burns, with its overtones of romantic egalitarianism, and then later, of Shakespeare. Immense quantities of both were not only committed to memory, but made into an integral—indeed, sometimes an embarrassingly evident—part of his life: on first visiting the Doge's palace in Venice he thrust a companion in the ducal throne and held him pinioned there while he orated the appropriate speeches from *Othello*. Once, seeing Vanderbilt walking on Fifth Avenue, Carnegie smugly remarked, "I would not exchange his millions for my knowledge of Shakespeare."

But it was more than just a love of poetry that remained with Carnegie. Virtually alone among his fellow acquisitors, he was driven by a genuine respect for the power of thought to seek answers for questions that never even occurred to them. Later, when he "discovered" Herbert Spencer, the English sociologist, Carnegie wrote to him, addressing him as "Master," and it was as "Master" that Spencer remained, even after Carnegie's lavishness had left Spencer very much in his debt.

But Carnegie's early life was shaped by currents more material than intellectual. The grinding process of industrial change had begun slowly but ineluctably to undermine the cottage weaving that was the traditional means of employment in Dunfermline. The Industrial Revolution, in the shape of new steam mills, was forcing out the hand weavers, and one by one the looms which constituted the entire capital of the Carnegie family had to be sold. Carnegie never forgot the shock of his father returning home to tell him, in despair, "Andra, I can get nae mair work."

A family council of war was held, and it was decided that there was only one possible course—they must try their luck in America, to which two sisters of Carnegie's mother, Margaret, had already emigrated. With the aid of a few friends the money for the crossing was scraped together, and at thirteen Andrew found himself transported to the only country in which his career would have been possible.

It hardly got off to an auspicious start, however. The family made their way to Allegheny, Pennsylvania, a raw and bustling town where Carnegie's father again sought work as an independent weaver. But it was as hopeless to compete against the great mills in America as in Scotland, and soon father and son were forced to seek work in the local cotton mills. There Andrew worked from six in the morning until six at night, making $1.20 as a bobbin boy.

After a while his father quit—factory work was impossible for the traditional small enterpriser—and Andrew got a "better" job with a new firm, tending an engine deep in a dungeon cellar and dipping newly made cotton spools in a vat of oil. Even the raise to $3 a week—and desperately conjured visions of Wallace and the Bruce—could not overcome the horrors of that lonely and foul-smelling basement. It was perhaps the only time in Carnegie's life when his self-assurance deserted him: to the end of his days the merest whiff of oil could make him deathly sick.

Yet he was certain, as he wrote home at sixteen, that "anyone could get along in this Country," and the rags-to-riches saga shortly began. The telegraph had just come to Pittsburgh, and one evening over a game of checkers, the manager of the local office informed Andrew's uncle that he was looking for a messenger. Andy got the job and, in true Alger fashion, set out to excel in it. Within a few weeks he had carefully memorized the names and the locations, not only of the main streets in Pittsburgh, but of the main firms, so that he was the quickest of all the messenger boys.

He came early and stayed late, watched the telegraphers at work, and at home at night learned the Morse code. As a result he was soon the head of the growing messenger service, and a skilled telegrapher himself. One day he dazzled the office by taking a message "by ear" instead of by the commonly used tape printer, and since he was then only the third operator in the country able to turn the trick, citizens used to drop into the office to watch Andy take down the words "hot from the wire."

One such citizen who was especially impressed with young Carnegie's determination was Thomas A. Scott, in time to become one of the colorful railway magnates of the West, but then the local superintendent of the Pennsylvania Railroad. Soon thereafter Carnegie became "Scott's Andy" —telegrapher, secretary, and general factotum—at thirty-five dollars a month. In his *Autobiography* Carnegie recalls an instance which enabled him to begin the next stage of his career. "One morning I reached the office and found that a serious accident on the Eastern Division had delayed the express passenger train westward, and that the passenger train eastward was proceeding with a flagman in advance at every curve. The freight trains in both directions were standing on the sidings. Mr. Scott was not to be found. Finally I could not resist the temptation to plunge in, take the responsibility, give 'train orders' and set matters going. 'Death or Westminster Abbey' flashed across my mind. I knew it was dismissal, disgrace, perhaps criminal punishment for me if I erred. On the other hand, I could bring in the wearied freight train men who had lain out all night. I knew I could. I knew just what to do, and so I began."

Signing Scott's name to the orders, Carnegie flashed out the necessary instructions to bring order out of the tangle. The trains moved; there were no mishaps. When Scott reached the office Carnegie told him what he had done. Scott said not a word but looked carefully over all that had taken place. After a little he moved away from Carnegie's desk to his own, and that was the end of it. "But I noticed," Carnegie concluded good-humoredly, "that he came in very regularly and in good time for some mornings after that."

It is hardly to be wondered at that Carnegie became Scott's favorite, his "white-haired Scotch devil." Impetuous but not rash, full of enthusiasm and good-natured charm, the small lad with his blunt, open features and his slight Scottish burr was every executive's dream of an assistant. Soon Scott repaid Andy for his services by introducing him to a new and very different kind of opportunity. He gave Carnegie the chance to subscribe to five hundred dollars' worth of Adams Express stock, a company which Scott assured Andy would prosper mightily.

Carnegie had not fifty dollars saved, much less five hundred, but it was a chance he could ill afford to miss. He reported the offer to his mother, and that pillar of the family unhesitatingly mortgaged their home to raise the necessary money. When the first dividend check came in, with its ornate Spencerian flourishes, Carnegie had something like a revelation. "I shall remember that check as long as I live," he subsequently wrote. "It gave me the first penny of revenue from capital—something that I had not worked for with the sweat of my brow. 'Eureka!' I cried, 'Here's the goose that lays the golden eggs.'" He was right; within a few years his investment in the Adams Express Company was paying annual dividends of $1,400.

It was not long thereafter that an even more propitious chance presented itself. Carnegie was riding on the Pennsylvania line one day when he was approached by a "farmer-looking" man carrying a small green bag in his hand. The other introduced himself as T. T. Woodruff and quite frankly said that he wanted a chance to talk with someone connected with the railroad. Whereupon he opened his bag and took out a small model of the first sleeping car.

Carnegie was immediately impressed with its possibilities, and he quickly arranged for Woodruff to meet Scott. When the latter agreed to give the cars a trial, Woodruff in appreciation offered Carnegie a chance to subscribe to a one-eighth interest in the new company. A local banker agreed to lend Andy the few hundred dollars needed for the initial payment —the rest being financed from dividends. Once again Andy had made a shrewd investment: within two years the Woodruff Palace Car Company was paying him a return of more than $5,000 a year.

Investments now began to play an increasingly important role in Carnegie's career. Through his railroad contacts he came to recognize the possibilities in manufacturing the heavy equipment needed by the rapidly expanding lines, and soon he was instrumental in organizing companies to meet these needs. One of them, the Keystone Bridge Company, was the first successful manufacturer of iron railway bridges. Another, the Pittsburgh Locomotive Works, made engines. And most important of all, an interest in a local iron works run by an irascible German named Andrew Kloman brought Carnegie into actual contact with the manufacture of iron itself.

None of these new ventures required any substantial outlay of cash. His interest in the Keystone Bridge Company, for instance, which was to earn him $15,000 in 1868, came to him "in return for services rendered in its promotion"—services which Carnegie, as a young railroad executive, was then in a highly strategic position to deliver. Similarly the interest in the Kloman works reflected no contribution on Carnegie's part except that of being the human catalyst and buffer between some highly excitable participants.

By 1865 his "side" activities had become so important that he decided to leave the Pennsylvania Railroad. He was by then superintendent, Scott having moved up to a vice presidency, but his salary of $2,400 was already vastly overshadowed by his income from various ventures. One purchase alone—the Storey farm in Pennsylvania oil country, which Carnegie and a few associates picked up for $40,000—was eventually to pay the group a million dollars in dividends in *one* year. About this time a friend dropped in on Carnegie and asked him how he was doing. "Oh, I'm rich, I'm rich!" he exclaimed.

He was indeed embarked on the road to riches, and determined, as he later wrote in his *Autobiography*, that "nothing could be allowed to interfere for a moment with my business career." Hence it comes as a surprise to note that it was at this very point that Carnegie retired to his suite to write his curiously introspective and troubled thoughts about the pursuit of wealth. But the momentum of events was to prove far too strong for these moralistic doubts. Moving his headquarters to New York to promote his various interests, he soon found himself swept along by a succession of irresistible opportunities for money-making.

One of these took place quite by chance. Carnegie was trying to sell the Woodruff sleeping car at the same time that a formidable rival named George Pullman was also seeking to land contracts for his sleeping car, and the railroads were naturally taking advantage of the competitive situation. One summer evening in 1869 Carnegie found himself mounting the resplendent marble stairway of the St. Nicholas Hotel side by side with his competitor.

"Good evening, Mr. Pullman," said Carnegie in his ebullient manner. Pullman was barely cordial.

"How strange we should meet here," Carnegie went on, to which the other replied nothing at all.

"Mr. Pullman," said Carnegie, after an embarrassing pause, "don't you think we are making nice fools of ourselves?" At this Pullman evinced a glimmer of interest: "What do you mean?" he inquired. Carnegie quickly pointed out that competition between the two companies was helping no one but the railroads. "Well," said Pullman, "what do you suggest we do?" "Unite!" said Carnegie. "Let's make a joint proposition to the Union Pacific, your company and mine. Why not organize a new company to do it?" "What would you call it?" asked Pullman suspiciously. "The Pullman Palace Car Company," said Carnegie and with this shrewd psychological stroke won his point. A new company was formed, and in time Carnegie became its largest stockholder.

Meanwhile, events pushed Carnegie into yet another lucrative field. To finance the proliferating railway systems of America, British capital was badly needed, and with his Scottish ancestry, his verve, and his excellent railroad connections Carnegie was the natural choice for a go-between. His briefcase stuffed with bonds and prospectuses, Carnegie became a transatlantic commuter, soon developing intimate relations both with great bankers like Junius Morgan (the father of J. P. Morgan), and with the heads of most of the great American roads. These trips earned him not only large commissions—exceeding on occasion $100,000 for a single turn—but even more important, established connections that were later to be of immense value. He himself later testified candidly on their benefits before a group of respectfully awed senators: "For instance, I want a great contract for rails. Sidney Dillon of the Union Pacific was a personal friend of mine. Huntington was a friend. Dear Butler Duncan, that called on me the other day, was a friend. Those and other men were presidents of railroads. . . . Take Huntington; you know C. P. Huntington. He was hard up very often. He was a great man, but he had a great deal of paper out. I knew his things were good. When he wanted credit I gave it to him. If you help a man that way, what chance has any paid agent going to these men? It was absurd."

But his trips to England brought Carnegie something still more valuable. They gave him steel. It is fair to say that as late as 1872 Carnegie did not see the future that awaited him as the Steel King of the world. The still modest conglomeration of foundries and mills he was gradually assembling in the Allegheny and Monongahela valleys was but one of many business interests, and not one for which he envisioned any extraordinary future. Indeed, to repeated pleas that he lead the way in developing a steel industry for America by substituting steel for iron rails, his reply was succinct: "Pioneering don't pay."

What made him change his mind? The story goes that he was awe-struck by the volcanic, spectacular eruption of a Bessemer converter, which he saw for the first time during a visit to a British mill. It was precisely the sort of display that would have appealed to Carnegie's mind—a wild, demonic, physical process miraculously contained and controlled by the dwarfed figures of the steel men themselves. At any rate, overnight Carnegie became the perfervid prophet of steel. Jumping on the first available steamer, he rushed home with the cry, "The day of iron has passed!" To the consternation of his colleagues, the hitherto reluctant pioneer became an advocate of the most daring technological and business expansion; he joined them enthusiastically in forming Carnegie, McCandless & Company, which was the nucleus of the empire that the next thirty years would bring forth.

The actual process of growth involved every aspect of successful business enterprise of the times: acquisition and merger, pools and commercial piracy, and even, on one occasion, an outright fraud in selling the United States government overpriced and underdone steel armor plate. But it would be as foolish to maintain that the Carnegie empire grew by trickery as to deny that sharp practice had its place. Essentially what lay behind the spectacular expansion were three facts.

The first of these was the sheer economic expansion of the industry in the first days of burgeoning steel use. Everywhere steel replaced iron or found new uses—and not only in railroads but in ships, buildings, bridges, machinery of all sorts. As Henry Frick himself once remarked, if the Carnegie group had not filled the need for steel another would have. But it must be admitted that Carnegie's company did its job superlatively well. In 1885 Great Britain led the world in the production of steel. Fourteen years later her total output was 695,000 tons less than the output of the Carnegie Steel Company alone.

Second was the brilliant assemblage of personal talent with which Carnegie surrounded himself. Among them, three in particular stood out. One was Captain William Jones, a Homeric figure who lumbered through the glowing fires and clanging machinery of the works like a kind of Paul Bunyan of steel, skilled at handling men, inventive in handling equipment, and enough of a natural artist to produce papers for the British Iron and Steel Institute that earned him a literary as well as a technical reputation. Then there was Henry Frick, himself a self-made millionaire, whose coke empire naturally complemented Carnegie's steelworks. When the two were amalgamated, Frick took over the active management of the whole, and under his forceful hand the annual output of the Carnegie works rose tenfold. Yet another was Charles Schwab, who came out of the tiny monastic town of Loretto, Pennsylvania, to take a job as a stake driver. Six months later he had been promoted by Jones into the assistant managership of the Braddock plant.

These men, and a score like them, constituted the vital energy of the Carnegie works. As Carnegie himself said, "Take away all our money, our great works, ore mines and coke ovens, but leave our organization, and in four years I shall have re-established myself."

But the third factor in the growth of the empire was Carnegie himself. A master salesman and a skilled diplomat of business at its highest levels, Carnegie was also a ruthless driver of his men. He pitted his associates and subordinates in competition with one another until a feverish atmosphere pervaded the whole organization. "You cannot imagine the abounding sense of freedom and relief I experience as soon as I get on board a steamer and sail past Sandy Hook," he once said to Captain Jones. "My God!" replied Jones. "Think of the relief to us!"

But Carnegie could win loyalties as well. All his promising young men were given gratis ownership participations—minuscule fractions of one percent, which were enough, however, to make them millionaires in their own right. Deeply grateful to Jones, Carnegie once offered him a similar participation. Jones hemmed and hawed and finally refused; he would be unable to work effectively with the men, he said, once he was a partner. Carnegie insisted that his contribution be recognized and asked Jones what he wanted. "Well," said the latter, "you might pay me a hell of a big salary." "We'll do it!" said Carnegie. "From this time forth you shall receive the same salary as the President of the United States." "Ah, Andy, that's the kind of talk," said Captain Bill.

Within three decades, on the flood tide of economic expansion, propelled by brilliant executive work and relentless pressure from Carnegie, the company made immense strides. "Such a magnificent aggregation of industrial power has never before been under the domination of a single man," reported a biographer in 1902, describing the Gargantuan structure of steel and coke and ore and transport. Had the writer known of the profits earned by this aggregation he might have been even more impressed: three and a half million dollars in 1889, seven million in 1897, twenty-one million in 1899, and an immense forty million in 1900. "Where is there such a business!" Carnegie had exulted, and no wonder—the majority share of all these earnings, without hindrance of income tax, went directly into his pockets.

Nevertheless, with enormous success came problems. One of these was the restiveness of certain partners, under the "Iron-Clad" agreement, which prevented any of them from selling their shares to anyone but the company itself—an arrangement which meant, of course, that the far higher valuation of an outside purchaser could not be realized. Particularly chagrined was Frick, when, as the culmination of other disagreements between them, Carnegie sought to buy him out "at the value appearing on the books." Another problem was a looming competitive struggle in the steel industry itself that presaged a period of bitter industrial warfare ahead. And last was Carnegie's own growing desire to "get out."

Already he was spending half of each year abroad, first traveling, and then, after his late marriage, in residence in the great Skibo Castle he built for his wife on Dornoch Firth, Scotland. There he ran his business enterprises with one hand while he courted the literary and creative world with the other, entertaining Kipling and Matthew Arnold, Paderewski and Lloyd George, Woodrow Wilson and Theodore Roosevelt, Gladstone, and of course, Herbert Spencer, the Master. But even his career as "Laird" of Skibo could not remove him from the worries—and triumphs—of his business; a steady flow of cables and correspondence intruded on the "serious" side of life.

It was Schwab who cut the knot. Having risen to the very summit of the Carnegie concern he was invited in December, 1900, to give a speech on the future of the steel industry at the University Club in New York. There, before eighty of the nation's top business leaders he painted a glowing picture of what could be done if a supercompany of steel were formed, integrated from top to bottom, self-sufficient with regard to its raw materials, balanced in its array of final products. One of the guests was the imperious J. P. Morgan, and as the speech progressed it was noticed that his concentration grew more and more intense. After dinner Morgan rose and took the young steel man by the elbow and engaged him in private conversation for half an hour while he plied him with rapid and penetrating questions; then a few weeks later he invited him to a private meeting in the great library of his home. They talked from nine o'clock in the evening until dawn. As the sun began to stream in through the library windows, the banker finally rose. "Well," he said to Schwab, "if Andy wants to sell, I'll buy. Go and find his price."

Carnegie at first did not wish to sell. Faced with the actual prospect of a withdrawal from the business he had built into the mightiest single industrial empire in the world, he was frightened and dismayed. He sat silent before Schwab's report, brooding, loath to inquire into details. But soon his enthusiasm returned. No such opportunity was likely to present itself again. In short order a figure of $492,000,000 was agreed on for the entire enterprise, of which Carnegie himself was to receive $300,000,000 in five percent gold bonds and preferred stock. Carnegie jotted down the terms of the transaction on a slip of paper and told Schwab to bring it to Morgan. The banker glanced only briefly at the paper. "I accept," he said.

After the formalities were in due course completed, Carnegie was in a euphoric mood. "Now, Pierpont, I am the happiest man in the world," he said. Morgan was by no means unhappy himself: his own banking company had made a direct profit of $12,500,000 in the underwriting transaction, and this was but a prelude to a stream of lucrative financings under Morgan's aegis, by which the total capitalization was rapidly raised to $1,400,000,000. A few years later, Morgan and Carnegie found themselves aboard the same steamer en route to Europe. They fell into talk and Carnegie confessed, "I made one mistake, Pierpont, when I sold out to you."

"What was that?" asked the banker.

"I should have asked you for $100,000,000 more than I did."

Morgan grinned. "Well," he said, "you would have got it if you had."

Thus was written *finis* to one stage of Carnegie's career. Now it would be seen to what extent his "radical pronouncements" were serious. For in the *Gospel of Wealth*—the famous article combined with others in book form—Carnegie had proclaimed the duty of the millionaire to administer and distribute his wealth *during his lifetime*. Though he might have "proved" his worth by his fortune, his heirs had shown no such evidence of their fitness. Carnegie bluntly concluded: "By taxing estates heavily at his death, the State marks its condemnation of the selfish millionaire's unworthy life."

Coming from the leading millionaire of the day, these had been startling sentiments. So also were his views on the "labor question" which, if patronizing, were nonetheless humane and advanced for their day. The trouble was, of course, that the sentiments were somewhat difficult to credit. As one commentator of the day remarked, "His vision of what might be done with wealth had beauty and breadth and thus serenely overlooked the means by which wealth had been acquired."

For example, the novelist Hamlin Garland visited the steel towns from which the Carnegie millions came and bore away a description of work that was ugly, brutal, and exhausting: he contrasted the lavish care expended on the plants with the callous disregard of the pigsty homes: "the streets were horrible; the buildings poor; the sidewalks sunken and full of holes. . . . Everywhere the yellow mud of the streets lay kneaded into sticky masses through which groups of pale, lean men slouched in faded garments. . . ." When the famous Homestead strike erupted in 1892, with its private army of Pinkerton detectives virtually at war with the workers, the Carnegie benevolence seemed revealed as shabby fakery. At Skibo Carnegie stood firmly behind the company's iron determination to break the strike. As a result, public sentiment swung sharply and suddenly against him; the St. Louis *Post-Dispatch* wrote: "Three months ago Andrew Carnegie was a man to be envied. Today he is an object of mingled pity and contempt. In the estimation of nine-tenths of the thinking people on both sides of the ocean he has . . . confessed himself a moral coward."

In an important sense the newspaper was right. For though Carnegie continued to fight against "privilege," he saw privilege only in its fading aristocratic vestments and not in the new hierarchies of wealth and power to which he himself belonged. In Skibo Castle he now played the role of the benign autocrat, awakening to the skirling of his private bagpiper and proceeding to breakfast to the sonorous accompaniment of the castle organ.

Meanwhile there had also come fame and honors in which Carnegie wallowed unashamedly. He counted the "freedoms" bestowed on him by grateful or hopeful cities and crowed, "I have fifty-two and Gladstone has only seventeen." He entertained the King of England and told him that democracy was better than monarchy, and met the German Kaiser: "Oh, yes, yes," said the latter worthy on being introduced. "I have read your books. You do not like kings." But Mark Twain, on hearing of this, was not fooled. "He says he is a scorner of kings and emperors and dukes," he wrote, "whereas he is like the rest of the human race: a slight attention from one of these can make him drunk for a week. . . ."

And yet it is not enough to conclude that Carnegie was in fact a smaller man than he conceived himself. For this judgment overlooks one immense and irrefutable fact. He did, in the end, abide by his self-imposed duty. He did give nearly all of his gigantic fortune away.

As one would suspect, the quality of the philanthropy reflected the man himself. There was, for example, a huge and sentimentally administered private pension fund to which access was to be had on the most trivial as well as the most worthy grounds: if it included a number of writers, statesmen, scientists, it also made room for two maiden ladies with whom Carnegie had once danced as a young man, a boyhood acquaintance who had once held Carnegie's books while he ran a race, a merchant to whom he had once delivered a telegram and who had subsequently fallen on hard times. And then, as one would expect, there was a benevolent autocracy in the administration of the larger philanthropies as well. "Now everybody vote Aye," was the way Carnegie typically determined the policies of the philanthropic "foundations" he established.

Yet if these flaws bore the stamp of one side of Carnegie's personality, there was also the other side—the side that, however crudely, asked important questions and however piously, concerned itself with great ideals. Of this the range and purpose of the main philanthropies gave unimpeachable testimony. There were the famous libraries—three thousand of them costing nearly sixty million dollars; there were the Carnegie institutes in Pittsburgh and Washington, Carnegie Hall in New York, the Hague Peace Palace, the Carnegie Endowment for International Peace, and the precedent-making Carnegie Corporation of New York, with its original enormous endowment of $125,000,000. In his instructions to the trustees of this first great modern foundation, couched in the simplified spelling of which he was an ardent advocate, we see Carnegie at his very best: "Conditions on erth [*sic*] inevitably change; hence, no wise man will bind Trustees forever to certain paths, causes, or institutions. I disclaim any intention of doing so. . . . My chief happiness, as I write these lines lies in the thot [*sic*] that, even after I pass away, the welth [*sic*] that came to me to administer as a sacred trust for the good of my fellow men is to continue to benefit humanity. . . ."

If these sentiments move us—if Carnegie himself in retrospect moves us at last to grudging respect—it is not because his was the triumph of a saint or a philosopher. It is because it was the much more difficult triumph of a very human and fallible man struggling to retain his convictions in an age, and in the face of a career, which subjected them to impossible temptations. Carnegie is something of America writ large; his is the story of the Horatio Alger hero *after* he has made his million dollars. In the failures of Andrew Carnegie we see many of the failures of America itself. In his curious triumph, we see what we hope is our own steadfast core of integrity.

—August 1960

II. John D. Rockefeller

The incredibly shrunken face of an animate mummy, grotesque behind enormous black-rimmed glasses; the old boy tottering around
the golf course, benign and imperturbable, distributing his famous dimes;
the huge foundation with its medical triumphs; the lingering memory of
the great trust and the awed contemplation of the even greater company;
and over all, the smell of oil, endlessly pumping out of the earth, each
drop adding its bit to the largest exaction ever levied on any society by a
private individual—with such associations it is no wonder that the name
has sunk into the American mind to an extraordinary degree. From his
earliest days the spendthrift schoolboy is brought to his senses with: "Who
do you think you are, John D. Rockefeller?"

Yet for all the vivid associations, the man himself remains a shadowy
presence. Carnegie, Morgan, or Ford may not have entered so decisively
into the American parlance, but they are full-blooded figures in our
memory: Carnegie, brash, bustling, proselytizing; Morgan, imperious,
choleric, aloof; Ford, shrewd, small-town, thing-minded. But what is John
D. Rockefeller, aside from the paper silhouettes of very old age and the
aura of immense wealth?

Even his contemporaries did not seem to have a very clear impression
of Rockefeller as a human being. For forty years of his active career, he
was commonly regarded as an arch economic malefactor—La Follette
called him the greatest criminal of the age—and for twenty years, as a
great benefactor—John Singer Sargent, painting his portrait, declared
himself in the presence of a medieval saint—but neither judgment tells
us much about the man. Nor do Ida Tarbell or Henry Demarest Lloyd,
both so skillful in portraying the company, succeed in bringing to life its
central figure; he lurks in the background, the Captain Nemo of Standard
Oil. Similarly, in the reminiscences of his associates we catch only a glimmer
of a person—a polite, reserved man, mild in manner, a bit of a stickler for
exactitude, totally unremarkable for anything he says or for any particular
style of saying it. Surely there must be more to John D. than this! What
sort of man was this greatest of all acquisitors? What was the secret of his
incredible success?

His mother came of a prosperous Scottish farming family, devout, strait-
laced, uncompromising. She springs out at us from her photographs: a
tired, plain face, deep-set eyes, and a straight, severe mouth announce
Eliza Davison Rockefeller's tired, straight, severe personality. Rockefeller
later recalled an instance when he was being whipped by her and finally

managed to convince her that he was innocent of a supposed misdemeanor. "Never mind," she said, "we have started in on this whipping and it will do for the next time." Her approach to life made an indelible impression— even in his old age Rockefeller could hear her voice enjoining: "Willful waste makes woeful want."

His father, William Avery Rockefeller, was cut from a different bolt of cloth. Big, robust, and roistering, he treated his sons with a curious mixture of affection and contempt. "I trade with the boys," he boasted to a neighbor, "and skin 'em and I just beat 'em every time I can. I want to make 'em sharp." Sharp himself, he was in and out of a dozen businesses in John's youth and, we have reason to suspect, as many beds. Later, when his son was already a prominent businessman, we can still follow his father's erratic career, now as "Doctor" William A. Rockefeller, "the Celebrated Cancer Specialist," peddling his cures on the circuit. Still later, when John D. had become a great eminence in New York, the father drops into obscurity—only to materialize from time to time in the city, where he is shown around by an embarrassed Standard Oil underling. At the very end he simply disappears. Joseph Pulitzer at one time offered a prize of $8,000 for news of his whereabouts, and the rumor spread that for thirty-five years old William had led a double life, with a second wife in Illinois. No one knows.

It was an unpleasantly polarized family situation, and it helps us to understand the quiet, sober-sided boy who emerged. His schoolmates called John "Old pleased-because-I'm-sad," from the title of a school declamation that fitted him to perfection; typically, when the boys played baseball, he kept score. Yet, if it was subdued, it was not an unhappy boyhood. At home he milked the cow and drove the horse and did the household chores that were expected of a boy in upstate New York, but after hours he indulged with his brothers, William and Frank, in the usual boyhood escapades and adventures. A favorite pastime, especially savored since it was forbidden, was to go skating at night on the Susquehanna. On one occasion William and John saved a neighbor's boy from drowning, whereupon their evening's sally had to be admitted. Eliza Rockefeller praised their courage—and whipped them soundly for their disobedience.

Always in the Rockefeller home there was the stress on gainful work. Their father may have worked to make them sharp, but their mother worked to make them industrious. John was encouraged to raise turkeys, and he kept the money from their sale in a little box on the mantle until he had accumulated the sum of $50. A neighboring farmer asked to borrow the amount at seven percent for a year, and his mother approved. During that summer John dug potatoes at thirty-seven and a half cents a day. When the farmer repaid the loan with $3.50 in interest, the lesson was not lost on John: the earning power of capital was much to be preferred to that of labor.

He was then only in his teens—he was born in 1839—but already, frugal ways, a deliberate manner, and a strong sense of planning and purposefulness were in evidence. As his sister Lucy said: "When it's raining porridge, you'll find John's dish right side up." But now the time for summer jobs was coming to an end. The family had moved from Moravia and Owego, where John had grown up, to Cleveland, where he went to the local high school in his fifteenth and sixteenth years. For a few months he attended Folsom's Commercial College, where he learned the elements of bookkeeping—and then began the all-important search for the first real job.

That search was performed with a methodical thoroughness that became a hallmark of the Rockefeller style. A list of promising establishments was drawn up—nothing second-rate would do—and each firm was hopefully visited. Rebuffed on the first go-round, John went the rounds again undaunted, and then a third time. Eventually his perseverance was rewarded. He became a clerk in the office of Hewitt & Tuttle, commission merchants and produce shippers. Typically, he took the job without inquiring about salary, hung his coat on a peg, climbed onto the high bookkeeper's stool, and set to work. It was a red-letter day in his life; later, when he was a millionaire many times over, the flag was regularly hoisted before his house to commemorate September 26, 1855.

Work came naturally, even pleasurably to John Rockefeller. He was precise, punctual, diligent. "I had trained myself," he wrote in his memoirs, " . . . that my check on a bill was the executive act which released my employer's money from the till and was attended with more responsibility than the spending of my own funds."

With such model attitudes, Rockefeller quickly advanced. By 1858 his salary (which turned out to be $3.50 a week) had more than tripled, but when Hewitt & Tuttle were unable to meet a request for a further raise, he began to look elsewhere. A young English acquaintance named Maurice Clark, also a clerk, was similarly unhappy with his prospects, and the two decided to form a produce-shipping firm of their own. Clark had saved up $2,000, and John Rockefeller had saved $900; the question was, where to get the last necessary $1,000. John knew that at age twenty-one he was entitled to a patrimony of this amount under his father's will, and he turned to William Rockefeller for an advance. His father listened with mingled approval and suspicion, and finally consented to lend his son the money if John would pay interest until he was twenty-one. "And John," he added, "the rate is ten."

Rockefeller accepted the proposition, and Clark & Rockefeller opened its doors in 1859. The Cleveland *Leader* recommended the principals to its readers as "experienced, responsible, and prompt," and the venture succeeded from the start. In its first year the firm made a profit of $4,400; in the second year, $17,000; and when the Civil War began, profits soared. Rockefeller became known as an up-and-coming young businessman, a man to be watched. Even his father agreed. From time to time he would come around and ask for his loan back, just to be sure the money was really there, but then, unable to resist ten percent interest, he would lend it back again.

Meanwhile an adult personality begins to emerge. A picture taken just before he married Laura Spelman in 1864 shows a handsome man of twenty-five with a long, slightly mournful visage, a fine straight nose, a rather humorless mouth. Everyone who knew him testified to his virtues. He was industrious, even-tempered, generous, kind; and if it was not a sparkling personality, it was not a dour one. Yet there is something not quite attractive about the picture as a whole. Charitable from his earliest days, he itemized each contribution—even the tiniest—in his famous Ledger A, with the result that his generosity, of which there was never any doubt, is stained with self-observance and an overnice persnicketiness. Extremely self-critical, he was given to intimate "pillow talks" at night in which he took himself to task for various faults, but the words he recalled and later repeated—"Now a little success, soon you will fall down, soon you will be overthrown . . ." smack not so much of honest self-search as of the exorcising of admonitory parental voices. He was above all orderly and forethoughted, but there is a compulsive, and sometimes a faintly repellent quality about his self-control. He recounts that when he was traveling as a commission merchant, he would never grab a bite in the station and wolf it down, like the others on the train, but "if I could not finish eating properly, I filled my mouth with as much as it would hold, then went leisurely to the train and chewed it slowly before swallowing it."

Yet the faults, far from constituting major traits in themselves, were minor flaws in an essentially excellent character. Rockefeller forged ahead by his merits, not by meanness—and among his merits was a well-developed capacity to size up a business situation coolly and rationally. Living in Cleveland, he could scarcely fail to think about one such situation virtually under his nose. Less than a day's journey by train were the Oil Regions of Pennsylvania, one of the most fantastic locales in America. A shambles of mud, dying horses (their skins denuded by petroleum), derricks, walking beams, chugging donkey engines, and jerry-built towns, the Regions oozed oil, money, and dreams. Bits of land the size of a blanket sold on occasion for three and four hundred dollars, pastures jumped overnight into fortunes (one pasture rose from $25,000 to $1,600,000 in three months), whole villages bloomed into existence in a matter of months. Pithole, Pennsylvania, an aptly named pinprick on the map, became the third largest center for mail in Pennsylvania and boasted a $65,000 luxury hotel. Within a few years it was again a pinprick, and the hotel was sold for $50.

It is uncertain whether Rockefeller himself visited the Oil Regions in the halcyon early 1860s. What is certain is that he sniffed oil in Cleveland itself, where the crude product was transported by barge and barrel for distillation and refining. In any event, the hurlyburly, the disorganization, and above all the extreme riskiness of the Oil Regions would never have appealed to Rockefeller's temperament. Let someone else make a million or lose it by blindly drilling for an invisible reservoir—a surer and far steadier route to wealth was available to the refiner who bought crude oil at thirty-one or thirty-two cents a gallon and then sold the refined product at eighty to eighty-five cents.

The chance to enter the refining business came to Clark and Rockefeller in the person of an enterprising and ingenious young engineer named Sam Andrews. Andrews, recently come from England (by coincidence, he was born in the same town as Clark), was restive in his job in a lard refinery and eager to try his hand at oil refining. He talked with his fellow townsman and through Clark met Rockefeller. The three agreed to take a fling at the business. Andrews, together with Clark's brothers, took on the production side, and Maurice Clark and Rockefeller the financial side. Thus in 1863 Andrews, Clark & Company was born. Rockefeller, content behind the anonymity of the "Company," had contributed, together with his partner, half the total capital, but he retained his interest in the produce business. The investment in oil was meant to be no more than a side venture.

But the side venture prospered beyond all expectation. The demand for refined oil increased by leaps and bounds. As Allan Nevins has written: "A commodity that had been a curiosity when Lincoln was nominated, had become a necessity of civilization, the staple of a vast commerce, before he was murdered." And the supply of oil, despite a thousand warnings, auguries, and dire prophecies that the mysterious underground springs would dry up, always matched and overmatched demand.

As the business boomed, so did the number of refineries. One could go into the refinery business for no more capital than it took to open a well-equipped hardware store, and Cleveland's location with its favoring rivers and fortunately placed rail lines made it a natural center for the shipment of crude oil. Hence by 1866, only two years after Andrews,

Clark & Company had opened its doors, there were over thirty refineries along the Cleveland Flats, and twenty more would be added before the year was out.

The Rockefeller refinery was among the largest of these. In Sam Andrews had been found the perfect plant superintendent: in Clark and Rockefeller, the perfect business management. From half-past six in the morning, when Andrews and Clark would burst in on their partner at breakfast, until they parted company just before supper, the three talked oil, oil, oil. Slowly, however, Andrews and Rockefeller found themselves at odds with Clark. They had become convinced that oil was to be a tremendous and permanent business enterprise; Clark was more cautious and less willing to borrow to expand facilities. Finally, in 1865, it was decided to put the firm up for auction among themselves, the seller to retain the produce business. "It was the day that determined my career," Rockefeller recalled long afterward. "I felt the bigness of it, but I was as calm as I am talking to you now." When at last Maurice Clark bid $72,000, Rockefeller topped him by $500. Clark threw up his hands. "The business is yours," he declared.

From the beginning Rockefeller & Andrews, as the new firm was called, was a model of efficiency. Even before acquiring the firm, Rockefeller had become interested in the economies of plant operation. When he found that plumbers were expensive by the hour, he and Sam Andrews hired one by the month, bought their own pipes and joints, and cut plumbing costs in half. When cooperage grew into a formidable item, they built their own shop where barrels cost them only forty percent of the market price, and soon costs were cut further by the acquisition of a stand of white oak, a kiln, and their own teams and wagons to haul the wood from kiln to plant. The emphasis on costs never ceased; when Rockefeller & Andrews had long since metamorphosed into the Standard Oil Company and profits had grown into the millions, cost figures were still carried to three decimal places. One day Rockefeller was watching the production line in one of his plants, where cans of finished oil were being soldered shut. "How many drops of solder do you use on each can?" he inquired. The answer was forty. "Have you ever tried thirty-eight? No? Would you mind having some sealed with thirty-eight and let me know?" A few cans leaked with thirty-eight, but with thirty-nine all were perfect. A couple of thousand dollars a year were saved.

The zeal for perfection of detail was from the beginning a factor in the growth of Rockefeller's firm. More important was his meeting in 1866 with Henry M. Flagler, the fiirst of a half-dozen associates who would bring to the enterprise the vital impetus of talent, enthusiasm, and a hard determination to succeed. Flagler, a quick, ebullient, bold businessman who had fought his way up from the poverty of a small-town parsonage, was a commission merchant of considerable prominence when Rockefeller met him. The two quickly took a liking to one another, and Rockefeller soon induced Flagler to join the fast-expanding business. Flagler brought along his own funds and those of his father-in-law, Stephen Harkness, and this fresh influx of capital made possible even further expansion. Rockefeller, Andrews & Flagler—soon incorporated as the Standard Oil Company—rapidly became the biggest single refinery in Cleveland.

Flagler brought to the enterprise an immense energy and a playfulness that Rockefeller so egregiously lacked. The two main partners now had a code word in their telegrams—AMELIA—which meant "Everything is lovely and the goose hangs high." And everything *was* lovely. One of Flagler's first jobs was to turn his considerable bargaining skills to a crucial link in the chain of oil-processing costs. All the major refineries bought in the same market—the Oil Regions—and all sold in the same markets— the great cities—so that their costs of purchase and their prices at the point of sale were much alike. In between purchase and sale, however, lay two steps: the costs of refining and the costs of transportation. In the end it was the latter that was to prove decisive in the dog-eat-dog struggle among the refineries.

For the railroads needed a steady flow of shipments to make money, and they were willing to grant rebates to the refiners if they would level out their orders. Since there were a number of routes by which to ship oil, each refiner was in a position to play one road against another, and the Standard, as the biggest and strongest refiner in Cleveland, was naturally able to gain the biggest and most lucrative discounts on its freight. This was a game that Flagler played with consummate skill. Advantageous rebates soon became an important means by which the Standard pushed ahead of its competitors—and in later years, when there were no more competitors, an important source of revenue in themselves. By 1879, when the Rockefeller concern had become a giant, a government investigatory agency estimated that in a period of five months the firm had shipped some eighteen million barrels of oil, on which rebates ran from eleven percent on the B&O to *forty-seven* percent on the Pennsylvania Railroad. For the five months, rebates totalled over ten million dollars.

This is looking too far ahead, however. By 1869, a scant three years after Flagler had joined it, the company was worth about a million dollars, but it was very far from being an industrial giant or a monopoly. Indeed, the problem which constantly plagued Rockefeller and his associates was the extreme competition in the oil business. As soon as business took a downturn—as it did in 1871—the worst kind of cutthroat competition broke out; prices dropped until the Titusville *Herald* estimated that the average refiner lost seventy-five cents on each barrel he sold.

As the biggest refiner, Rockefeller naturally had the greatest stake in establishing some kind of stability in the industry. Hence he set about to devise a scheme—the so-called South Improvement Company—which would break the feast-and-famine pattern that threatened to overwhelm the industry. In its essence the South Improvement Company was a kind of cartel aimed at holding up oil prices—by arranging "reasonable" freight rates for its own members while levying far higher ones on "outsiders." Since the scheme was open to all, presumably there would soon be no outsiders, and once all were within the fold, the refiners could operate as a single, powerful economic unit.

The plan might have worked but for the inability of such headstrong and individualistic groups as the railroads and the producers to cooperate for more than a passing moment. When the producers in the Oil Regions rose in wrath against a plan which they (quite rightly) saw as a powerful buying combination against them, the scheme simply collapsed.

The idea of eliminating competition did not, however, collapse with it. Instead, Rockefeller turned to a plan at once much simpler and much more audacious. If he could not eliminate competition, then perhaps he could eliminate his competitors by buying them up one by one—and this he set out to do. The plan was set in motion by a meeting with Colonel Oliver Payne, the chief stockholder in Rockefeller's biggest competitor. Briefly Rockefeller outlined the ruinous situation which impended if competition were permitted to continue unbridled; equally briefly, he proposed a solution. The Standard would increase its capitalization, the Payne plant would be appraised by impartial judges, and its owners would be given stock in proportion to their equity. As for Payne himself, Rockefeller suggested he should take an active part in the management of the new, bigger Standard Oil.

Payne quickly assented; so did Jabez Bostwick, the biggest refiner in New York, and one after another the remaining refiners sold out. According to Rockefeller, they were only too glad to rid themselves of their burdensome businesses at fair prices; according to many of the refiners, it was a question of taking Rockefeller's offer or facing sure ruin. We need not debate the point here; what is certain is that by the end of 1872 the Standard was the colossus of Cleveland. There remained only the United States to conquer.

Rockefeller himself was in his mid-thirties. The slightly melancholy visage of the young man had altered; a thick mustache trimmed straight across the bottom hid his lips and gave to his face a commanding, even stern, aspect. In a family portrait we see him standing rather stiffly, carefully dressed as befits a man in his station. For he was already rich—even his nonoil investments, as he wrote to his wife, were enough to give him independence, and his style of life had changed as his fortune had grown. He and his wife now lived in Forest Hill, a large, gaunt house on eighty acres just east of Cleveland. He had begun to indulge himself with snappy trotters, and on a small scale commenced what was to become in time a Brobdingnagian pastime—moving landscape around.

In town, in his business pursuits, he was already the reserved, colorless, almost inscrutable personality who baffled his business contemporaries; at home, he came as close as he could to a goal he sought assiduously—relaxation. His children were his great delight: he taught them to swim and invented strange and wonderful contraptions to keep them afloat; he bicycled with them; he played daring games of blindman's bluff—so daring in fact that he once had to have stitches taken in his head after running full tilt into a doorpost.

It was, in a word, the very model of a Victorian home, affectionate, dutiful, and, of course, rich. An air of rectitude hung over the establishment, not so much as to smother it, but enough to give it a distinctive flavor. Concerts (aside from the performances of their children), literature, art, or theater were not Rockefeller amusements; in entertaining, their tastes ran to Baptist ministers and business associates. An unpretentious and earnest atmosphere hid—or at least disguised—the wealth; until they were grown up the children had no idea of "who they were."

And of course the beneficences continued and grew: $23,000 for various charities in 1878, nearly $33,000 in 1880, over $100,000 in 1884. But the nice preciseness of giving was maintained; a pledge card signed in 1883 for the Euclid Avenue Baptist Church reads:

Mrs. Rockefeller......................$10.00 each week
Self... 30.00 each week
Each of our four children ..... 00.20 each week

How rich was Rockefeller by 1873, a mere ten years after Andrews, Clark & Company had opened its doors? We cannot make an accurate estimate, but it is certain that he was a millionaire several times over. In another ten years his Standard Oil holdings alone would be worth a phenomenal twenty million dollars—enough, with his other investments, to make him one of the half-dozen richest men in the country.

But now a legal problem began to obtrude. The Standard Oil Company was legally chartered in Ohio, and it had no right to own plants in other states. Not until 1889 would New Jersey amend its incorporation laws to allow a corporation chartered within the state to hold the stock of corporations chartered elsewhere. Hence the question: how was the Standard legally to control its expanding acquisitions in other states?

The problem was solved by one of Rockefeller's most astute lieutenants—Samuel Dodd, a round little butterball of a man with an extraordinarily clear-sighted legal mind and an unusually high and strict sense of personal integrity. Because he believed that he could render the best advice to the Standard if he was above any suspicion of personal aggrandizement, he repeatedly refused Rockefeller's offers to make him a director or to buy for him stock which would have made him a multimillionaire.

The sword which Dodd applied to the Gordian knot of interstate control was the device of the trust. In brief, he proposed a single group of nine trustees, with headquarters in New York, who would hold "in trust" the certificates of all Standard's operating companies, including the major company in Ohio itself. In 1882 the Standard Oil Trust was formally established, with John and his brother William Rockefeller, Flagler, Payne, Bostwick, John D. Archbold, Charles Pratt, William G. Warden, and Benjamin Brewster as trustees. (Sam Andrews had sold the last of his stock to Rockefeller four years before, saying the business had grown too big.) In fact, though not in law, one enormous interstate corporation had been created.

Few people even at this time appreciated quite how great the company was. By the 1880s the Standard was the largest and richest of all American manufacturing organizations. It had eighty-five percent of a business which took the output of 20,000 wells and which employed 100,000 people. And this all before the advent of the automobile. The colossus of the Standard was built not on the internal combustion engine but on the kerosene lamp.

With the creation of the Trust the center of gravity of the concern moved to New York. Rockefeller himself bought a $600,000 brownstone on West Fifty-fourth Street, where the round of teas and dinners for temperance workers, church people, and Standard executives soon went on. The Trust itself occupied No. 26 Broadway, an eleven-story "skyscraper" with gay striped awnings shading its large windows. It was soon known as the most famous business address in the world. There Rockefeller appeared daily, usually in high silk hat, long coat, and gloves—the accepted costume for the big business executive of the time.

At 26 Broadway Rockefeller was the commanding figure. But his exercise of command, like his personality, was notable for its lack of color, dash, and verve. Inquiring now of this one, now of that, what he thought of such and such a situation, putting his questions methodically and politely in carefully chosen words, never arguing, never raising his voice, Rockefeller seemed to govern his empire like a disembodied intelligence. He could be, as always, a stickler for detail; an accountant recalls him suddenly materializing one day, and with a polite "Permit me," turning over the ledger sheets, all the while murmuring, "Very well kept, very indeed," until he stopped at one page: "A little error here; will you correct it?" But he could also be decisive and absolutely determined. "He saw strategic points like a Napoleon, and he swooped down on them with the suddenness of a Napoleon," wrote Ida Tarbell. Yet even that gives too much of the impression of dash and daring. She was closer to the mark when she wrote: "If one attempts to analyse what may be called the legitimate greatness of Mr. Rockefeller's creation in distinction to its illegitimate greatness, he will find at the foundation the fact that it is as perfectly centralized as the Catholic Church or the Napoleonic government." It was true. By 1886 the Standard had evolved a system of committees, acting in advisory roles to the active management, which permitted an incalculably complex system to function with extraordinary ease. It is virtually the same system that is used today. Rockefeller had created the great Trust on which the eyes of the whole world were fastened, but behind the Trust, sustaining it, operating it, maintaining it, he had created an even greater Organization.

"It's many a day since I troubled you with a letter," wrote William Warden, a onetime independent Cleveland refiner who had been bought out and was now a trustee and major official in the Standard, "and I would not do so now could I justify myself in being silent. . . . We have met with a success unparalleled in commercial history, our name is known all over the world, and our public character is not one to be envied. We are quoted as representative of all that is evil, hard hearted, oppressive, cruel (we think unjustly), but men look askance at us, we are pointed at with contempt, and while some good men flatter us, it's only for our money. . . . This is not pleasant to write, for I had longed for an honored position in commercial life. None of us would choose such a reputation; we all desire a place in the honor & affection of honorable men."

It was a cry of anguish, but it was amply justified. By the 1880s the Standard was not only widely known—it was notorious. In part its increasingly bad business reputation originated in the business community itself. Stories began to circulate of the unfair advantage taken by the colossus when it bid for smaller properties: the case of the Widow Backus, whose deceased husband's refinery was supposedly bought out for a pittance, was much talked about. Many of these tales—the Backus case in particular—were simply untrue. But as the Standard grew in size and visibility, other business practices came to light which *were* true, and which were hardly calculated to gain friends for the company.

Foremost among these practices was an evil device called the drawback. Not content with enjoying a large competitive advantage through its special rebates, Standard also forced the railroads to pay it a portion of the freight charges paid by non-Standard refiners! Thus Daniel O'Day, a particularly ruthless Standard official, used his local economic leverage to get a small railroad to carry Standard's oil at ten cents a barrel, to charge all independents thirty-five cents, *and to turn over the twenty-five cents differential to a Standard subsidiary*. Another Standard agent, finding that a competitor's car had slipped through without paying the Standard exaction, wrote the road to collect the amount owing, adding: "Please turn another screw."

Such incidents and practices—always denied by the company and never admitted by Rockefeller—plagued the Standard for years. And the impression of highhandedness was not much improved by the behavior of the Standard's officials when they went on public view. John D. Archbold, a key executive called to testify before New York State's Hepburn Committee in 1879, was a typical bland witness. When pressed hard, he finally admitted he was a stockholder of the Standard. What was his function there? "I am a clamorer for dividends. That is the only function I have in connection with the Standard Oil Company." Chairman Alonzo Hepburn asked how large dividends were. "I have no trouble transporting my share," answered Archbold. On matters of rebates he declined to answer. Finally Hepburn asked him to return for further questioning the next day. "I have given today to the matter," replied Archbold politely. "It will be impossible for me to be with you again."

Not least, there was the rising tide of public protest against the monopoly itself. In 1881 Henry Demarest Lloyd, a journalist of passionate reformist sentiments, wrote for the *Atlantic Monthly* an article called "The Story of a Great Monopoly." Editor William Dean Howells gave it the lead in the magazine, and overnight it was a sensation (that issue of the *Atlantic* went through seven printings). "The family that uses a gallon of kerosene a day pays a yearly tribute to the Standard of $32 . . . ," wrote Lloyd. "America has the proud satisfaction of having furnished the world with the greatest, wisest, and meanest monopoly known to history."

Standard's profits were nothing so great as described by Lloyd, but that hardly mattered. If the article was imprecise or even downright wrong in detail, it was right in its general thrust. What counted was Lloyd's incontrovertible demonstration that an industrial concern had grown to a position of virtual impregnability, a position which made it in fact no longer subordinate to the states from which it drew its legal privilege of existence, but their very peer or better in financial strength and even political power. Before Lloyd wrote his article, the Standard was the source of rage or loss to scattered groups of producers, businessmen, or consumers. When he was through with his indictment, it was a national scandal.

That it should be a scandal was totally incomprehensible to John D. The mounting wave of protest and obloquy perplexed him more than it irritated him. Ida Tarbell's famous—and generally accurate—*History of the Standard Oil Company* he dismissed as "without foundation." The arrogance of an Archbold he merely chuckled at, recounting the Hepburn testimony in his *Random Reminiscences of Men and Events* with the comment that Archbold had a "well-developed sense of humor." With his own passion for order, he understood not a whit the passions of those whose demise was required that order might prevail. On one occasion when he was testifying in court, he spied in the courtroom George Rice, an old adversary (against whom, as a matter of fact, the famous screw had been turned, and whom Rockefeller had once offered to buy out). As he left the witness stand, Rockefeller walked over to Rice and, putting out his hand, said: "How do you do, Mr. Rice? You and I are getting to be old men, are we not?"

Rice ignored the hand. "Don't you think, Mr. Rice," pursued Rockefeller, "it might have been better if you had taken my advice years ago?"

"Perhaps it would," said Rice angrily. "You said you would ruin my business and you have done so."

"Pshaw! Pshaw!" rejoined Rockefeller.

"Don't you pooh-pooh me," said Rice in a fury. "I say that by the power of your great wealth you have ruined me."

"Not a word of truth in it," Rockefeller answered, turning and making his way through the crowd. "Not a word of truth in it."

He could not in fact bring himself to believe that there was a word of truth in any of it. There was nothing to argue about concerning the need for giant enterprise, or "industrial combinations" as they were called. They were simply a necessity, a potentially dangerous necessity admittedly, but a necessity nonetheless. All the rest was ignorance or willful misunderstanding. "You know," he wrote to a university president who offered to prepare a scholarly defense of Standard's policies, "that great prejudice exists against all successful business enterprise—the more successful, the greater the prejudice."

It was common, during the early 1900s, to read thunderous accusations against the Standard Oil Company and its sinister captain, but the fact was that John D. Rockefeller had severed all connections with the business as early as 1897. When news came to him, ten years later, that the great Trust had been heavily fined by the government, he read the telegram and without comment went on with his game of golf. At the actual dissolution of the Trust in 1911, he was equally unconcerned. For already his interests were turning away from business management toward another absorbing role—the disposition of the wealth which was now beginning to accumulate in truly awesome amounts.

Here enters the last of those indispensable subordinates through whom Rockefeller operated so effectively. Frederick T. Gates, onetime minister, now a kind of Baptist minister-executive, met Rockefeller when Gates played a crucial role in the studies that established the need for a great new university in Chicago. Shortly he became the catalytic figure in instituting the university with a Rockefeller gift of $600,000. (Before he was done, Rockefeller would give it 80 million dollars.) Then one morning in 1889, when the two were chatting, Rockefeller suddenly said: "I am in trouble, Mr. Gates." He told him of the flood of appeals which now came by the sackful, and of his inability to give away money with any satisfaction until he had made the most thorough investigation into the cause. Rockefeller continued: "I want you to come to New York and open an office here. You can aid me in my benefactions by taking interviews and inquiries and reporting the results for action. What do you say?"

Gates said yes, and it was under his guidance, together with that of Rockefeller's son, John D., Jr., that the great philanthropies took root: the General Education Board, which pioneered in the educational, social, and medical development of our own South; the Rockefeller Institute for Medical Research, quickly famous for its campaign against yellow fever; the Rockefeller Foundation with its far-ranging interests in the promotion of research. Not that the giving was done hastily. Gates had a meticulousness of approach which suited his employer perfectly. It was not until 1900 that more than 2 million dollars was given away, not until 1905 that the total of annual giving exceeded 10 million dollars, not until 1913 that the great climactic disbursements began to be made: 45 million dollars that year and 65 million the next, to establish the Rockefeller Foundation; finally 138 million dollars in 1919 to support the philanthropies already endowed.

Gates took his philanthropic duties with ministerial zeal and profound seriousness. Raymond Fosdick, president of the Rockefeller Foundation, recalls Gates's last meeting as a trustee. Shaking his fist at the startled board, he boomed: "When you die and come to approach the judgment of Almighty God, what do you think He will demand of you? Do you for an instant presume to believe He will inquire into your petty failures or your trivial virtues? No! He will ask just one question: *'What did you do as a Trustee of the Rockefeller Foundation?'"*

Gates was more than just a philanthropic guide. Rapidly he became a prime business agent for Rockefeller in the large business deals which inevitably continued to arise. When Rockefeller came into immense iron properties along the Mesabi Range, it was Gates who superintended their development and the creation of a giant fleet of ore carriers, and it was Gates who carried through their eventual sale to Morgan and Frick at the huge price of 88.5 million dollars. It was the only time in Gates's long association with John D. that he indicated the slightest desire to make money for himself.

When the immense iron deal was complete and Gates had made his final report, Rockefeller, as usual, had no words of praise, but listened attentively and without objection and then said, with more emphasis than usual, "Thank you, Mr. Gates!" Gates looked at him with an unaccustomed glint in his eye. "Thank you is not enough, Mr. Rockefeller," he replied. Rockefeller understood and promptly saw to it that Gates was remunerated handsomely.

John D. was becoming an old man now. His face, sharper with age, took on a crinkled, masklike appearance, in the midst of which his small eyes twinkled. Golf had become a great passion and was performed in the deliberate Rockefeller manner. A boy was hired to chant: "Keep your head down," useless steps were saved by bicycling between shots, and even when he was playing alone, every stroke was remorselessly counted. (John D. was once asked to what he owed the secret of the success of Standard Oil; he answered: "To the fact that we never deceived ourselves.")

To the outside world the old man more and more presented a quaint and benevolent image. By the 1920s the antitrust passions of the 1890s and early 1900s had been transmuted into sycophancy of big business; there were no more cries of "tainted money," but only a hopeful queuing up at the portals of the great foundations. The man who had once been denounced by Theodore Roosevelt and Tolstoy and William Jennings Bryan was now voted, in a popular poll, one of the Greatest Americans. Cartoonists and feature writers made the most of his pith helmet and his paper vest, his monkishly plain food, his beaming, almost childlike expression. To the outside world he seemed to live in a serene and admirable simplicity, which indeed he did, in a purely personal sense. But the reporters who told of his afternoon drives did not report that the seventy miles of road over his estate at Pocantico Hills were built by himself, that the views he liked so well were arranged by moving hills around as an interior decorator moves chairs. The perfection of Pocantico became an obsession: some railway tracks that were in the way were relocated at the cost of $700,000, a small college that spoiled a view was induced to move for $1,500,000, a distant smokestack was camouflaged. It was, to repeat

George Kaufman's famous line, an example of what God could have done if He'd only had the money.

In the midst of it all was the never-failingly polite, always slightly disengaged old man, somehow disappointing in close view, somehow smaller than we expect. There are mannerisms and eccentricities, of course, which, when viewed under the magnification of 900 million dollars, take on a certain prominence, but they are peccadilloes rather than great flaws. There is the enormous industrial generalship, to be sure, but it is a generalship of logic and plan, not of dash and daring. There is the generosity on a monumental scale, but then again, not on such a scale as to cut the Rockefeller fortune by ninety percent, as was the case with Carnegie. Rockefeller gave away over half a billion, but probably he kept at least that much for his family.

In short, the more we look into the life of John D. Rockefeller, the more we look into the life of an incredibly successful—and withal, very unremarkable—man. It is a curious verdict to pass on the greatest acquisitor of all time, and yet it is difficult to avoid the conclusion that John Flynn has perfectly phrased: "Rockefeller in his soul was a bookkeeper." We can see the bookkeeperishness in unexpected but telling places, such as in his *Random Reminiscences*, where he dilates on the importance of friendship, but cites as a dubious friend the man who protests, "I can't indorse your note, because I have an agreement with my partners not to . . ."; or again, when he expands on the nonmaterial pleasures of life, such as gardening, but adds as a clincher: "We make a small fortune out of ourselves, selling to our New Jersey place at $1.50 and $2.00 each, trees which originally cost us only five or ten cents at Pocantico." Whether he turns to friendship or to nature, money is the measure.

These are surely not the sentiments of greatness—but then John D. was not a great man. Neither was he, needless to say, a bad man. In most ways he was the very paragon of the business virtues of his day, and at the same time the perfect exemplar of the unvirtues as well. It is likely that he would have made his mark in any field, but unlikely that any commodity other than oil would have offered such staggering possibilities for industrial growth and personal aggrandizement. He personified in ideas the typical business thought of his day—very Christian, very conventional, very comfortable.

Yet as the image of John D. recedes, we realize the pointlessness of such personal appraisals. We study Rockefeller not so much as a person but as an agent—an agent for better and worse in the immense industrial transformation of America. Viewed against this stupendous process of change, even the largest lives take on a subordinate quality, and personal praise and blame seem almost irrelevant. And Rockefeller was not one of the largest lives—only one of the luckiest.

In the end there was only the frail ghost of a man, stubbornly resisting the inevitable. His son, John D., Jr., whom he had fondly called "my greatest fortune," had long since taken over the reins of the great foundations and had begun to refashion the Rockefeller image in his own way: Rockefeller Center, The Cloisters, the restoration of Williamsburg. His grandsons, among them one who would one day aspire to the Presidency of the United States, were already young men, carefully imbued with the family style: determination, modesty on the grand scale, a prudent balance between self-interest and altruism. And the Standard itself, now split and resplit into a handful of carefully noncollusive (and equally carefully noncompetitive) companies, was bigger and more powerful than ever. All in all, it was an extraordinary achievement, and the old man must have enjoyed it to the hilt. For it had indeed rained porridge, and his dish had surely been kept right side up.

—December 1964

SHOULD THE HISTORIAN MAKE MORAL JUDGMENTS?

By HENRY STEELE COMMAGER

Absolutely, said Acton. Absolutely not, said Prescott. The debate continues to this day.

In 1847 that Boston gentleman and man of letters William Hickling Prescott concluded twenty years of labor on the history of Spain under Ferdinand and Isabella and on the conquests of Mexico and Peru. It was a noble edifice that he had raised, the most impressive literary monument yet reared in the New World. So said Daniel Webster: a comet had blazed out on the world in full splendor. So said Lord Holland, over in London: it was the most important historical work since Gibbon. So said the great Alexander von Humboldt, who had embraced the entire cosmos. The Royal Academy of History at Madrid, the Royal Society of Berlin, the Institute of Paris, welcomed the Bostonian to honorary membership. And from John Quincy Adams came the grudging tribute: that the reader could not tell whether the author was Protestant or Catholic, monarchist or republican.

To Prescott that was the highest praise of all. Confronted with three of the most bloodstained chapters of history, Prescott tried to avoid moral judgment. How easy to condemn Cardinal Jiménez for his reliance on the Inquisition; how easy to denounce Cortés for the treachery and greed and brutality which accompanied the swift subjugation of Mexico; how easy to execrate the wretched Pizarro for cruelties almost unparalleled in the history of conquest. Prescott was not unaware of the embarrassments of impartiality: "to American and English readers," he wrote in the preface to his *Mexico*, "acknowledging so different a moral standard from that of the sixteenth century, I may possibly be thought too indulgent to the errors of the Conquerors." And he confessed that he had indeed "given them the benefit of such mitigating reflections as might be suggested by the circumstances and the period in which they lived." Two considerations, not entirely consistent, stayed the intuitive judgment of the moralist in Prescott. First, the familiar argument that the standards of the sixteenth century were not those of the nineteenth, and that we should not arbitrarily impose our standards upon the past. "It is far from my intention," wrote Prescott, "to vindicate the cruel deeds of the old Conquerors. Let them lie heavy on their heads. They were an iron race who periled life and fortune in the cause; and as they made little account of danger and suffering for themselves, they had little sympathy to spare for their unfortunate enemies. But, to judge them fairly, we must not do it by the lights of our own age. We must carry ourselves back to theirs, and take the point of view afforded by the civilization of their time."

The second plea in extenuation was broader—and more dubious; it was also more Victorian. It was this: that the cruelty and bloodshed which accompanied the destruction of the two great civilizations of the New World were, in a sense, the price of progress. The Aztecs and the Incas were, after all, backward and even barbarous peoples. It is therefore pure sentimentalism for us to "regret the fall of an empire which did so little to promote the happiness of its subjects or the real interests of humanity." The Aztecs, particularly, "were emphatically a fierce and brutal race, little calculated, in their best aspects, to excite our sympathy and regard. Their civilization . . . was . . . a generous graft on a vicious stock, and could have brought no fruit to perfection." We cannot choose the instruments or the vessels of the spread of civilization and of Christianity; these are often blunt and warped. But, over the generations and the centuries we can see that it is with imperfect means that progress works to eliminate the weak and the backward and to make room for the strong and the progressive. May we not, therefore, conclude that "it was beneficently ordered by Providence that the land [of the Mexicans] should be delivered over to another race who would rescue it from the brutish superstitions that daily extended wider and wider"?

The Reverend Theodore Parker—known in his day as "the Great American Preacher"—was both a scholar and a moral philosopher. As a scholar he was prepared to be indulgent toward Mr. Prescott's histories, for, superficial as they were, they had their points. But as a moralist he had no patience with Prescott's apologies, evasions, and extenuations. In two long essays in the *Massachusetts Quarterly Review*—which he edited—Mr. Parker raked Mr. Prescott fore and aft for what he regarded as moral cowardice. At every point in his narrative the historian of the conquest of Mexico and of Peru had excused, palliated, and condoned until, in the end, one was forced to conclude that his moral sensibilities were as calloused as his judgment was warped. Who was Mr. Prescott that he should suspend judgment over the hideous cruelties and iniquities of the conquistadors? "Mr. Prescott," wrote Parker, "shows little horror at these [Spanish] cruelties, little sense of their injustice; nay, he seems to seek to mitigate the natural indignation which a man feels at such tyranny of the strong over the weak. We confess our astonishment that an historian who thinks the desire of converting the heathen was the paramount motive in the breast of Cortés, has no more censure to bestow on such wanton cruelties, so frequently perpetrated as they were." It is one thing to explain, but another thing to condone the crimes of the past. "Crime is one thing," thundered Parker, "but the theory which excuses, defends, justifies crime is quite a different thing, is itself not to be justified, defended or excused. We are sorry to add the name of Mr. Prescott to the long list of writers who have a theory which attempts to justify the crime against mankind, the tyranny of might over right. We are sorry to say of this work . . . that it is not written in the philosophy of this age, and, still worse, not in the Christianity, the wide humanity, which is of mankind."

What all this meant was that Mr. Prescott had failed to fulfill the high duty of the historian. The Reverend Mr. Parker made clear the nature of that duty: "In telling what has been, the historian is also to tell what ought to be, for he is to pass judgment on events, and try counsels by their causes first and their consequences not less. When all these things are told, history ceases to be a mere panorama of events having no unity but time and place; it becomes philosophy teaching by experience, and has a profound meaning and awakens a deep interest, while it tells the lessons of the past for the warning of the present and edification of the future."

Parker's final verdict followed unequivocally: "Thus, lacking philosophy, and having more of the spirit of chivalry than of humanity, it is impossible that [Mr. Prescott] should write in the interest of mankind, or judge men and their deeds by . . . the immutable law of the universe."

Now let us look across the sea. It is forty years later, but Queen Victoria is still upon the throne and literature is still regarded as a moral enterprise. In 1887 the Reverend Mandell Creighton, Canon of Worcester Cathedral and Professor of Ecclesiastical History at Cambridge University, published the third and fourth volumes of his magisterial *History of the Popes*. He promptly sent the volumes off to his old friend and distinguished fellow historian, Lord Acton. Acton was a Catholic, perhaps the most famous Catholic historian in all Europe. A scholar of prodigious learning, he took the whole of history into his embrace, including, needless to say, the history of the medieval church; his specialty was the history of liberty. Lord Acton had immense respect for Creighton's scholarship, but less for his judgment. What disturbed him was that Professor Creighton had recorded the melancholy history of the papacy during the late Middle Ages without disapproval or censure. "The Popes of the thirteenth and fourteenth centuries," wrote the great Acton, "instituted a system of Persecution. . . . It is the most conspicuous fact in the history of the medieval papacy." Creighton had not made the fact of persecution central to his tale, nor had he sufficiently condemned the intolerance and cruelty of such popes as Innocent IV, Innocent VI, and Sixtus IV, who bore so heavy a burden of guilt.

Clearly there was a real principle at stake here, a principle of historical interpretation and even of historical philosophy. "You say that people in authority are not to be snubbed or sneezed at from our pinnacle of conscious rectitude," wrote Lord Acton. "I cannot accept your canon that we are to judge Pope and King unlike other men." And then came the statement of principle: "The inflexible integrity of the moral code is, to me, the secret of the authority, the dignity, the utility of history. If we may debase the currency for the sake of genius, or success, or rank, or reputation, we may debase it for the sake of a man's influence, of his religion, of his party. . . . Then history ceases to be a science, an arbiter of controversy, a guide of the wanderer. . . . It serves where it ought to reign, and it serves the worst cause better than the purest." Professor Creighton put Acton off with soft words, but to another historical friend he complained that Acton demanded that "history should be primarily a branch of the moral sciences." But "my view of history," he added, "is not to approach things with any preconceived ideas, but with the natural pietas and sympathy which I try to feel towards all men who do and try to do great things. . . . I try to put myself in their place: to see their limitations, and leave the course of events to pronounce the verdict upon system and men alike. No doubt Acton is more logical, but his view would reduce history to a dreary record of crimes to which I am unequal."

In the quarrel between Parker and Prescott, and in this fascinating exchange between two of the great figures of English historical scholarship, the issue was joined, an old and familiar issue which is still with us. To judge, or not to judge? Should the historian sit in judgment over the great drama of the past and over the men and women who performed on that vast and crowded stage, exposing evil and celebrating virtue and damning and praising famous men? Or should he observe the historical processes with scientific detachment, and record them as automatically as a tape recorder, rigorously excluding personal, national, or religious considerations? Is he competent to perform either of these functions —the function of the judge, or the function of the impartial reporter?

The problem is difficult, perhaps insoluble. It raises hard questions about the purpose of history, the duties and responsibilities of the scholar, the nature of historical judgment, and the distinctions, if any, between what might be called moral and secular judgment. It raises questions, too, about the competence of any historian to judge the past, and the sanctions, if any, behind such judgments as are rendered. And it requires us to weigh the dangers implicit in moral neutrality against those inherent in moral arrogance and intellectual parochialism.

Earlier generations of historians were not seriously troubled by this problem of judgment. The Greek historians Herodotus and Thucydides were surprisingly free from the urge to judge, but their successors in the ancient world took for granted that their function was to edify, to instruct, and to judge. Livy invited his readers to ponder the moral lessons taught by the history of Rome—as he presented it—and to observe how Rome rose to greatness through her virtues, and how the decay of these virtues brought ruin. Tacitus thought the highest function of history was to "rescue merit from oblivion," and "to hold out the reprobation of posterity as a warning and a rebuke to all base conduct." Plutarch, who wrote some sixty moral essays, compiled his famous *Parallel Lives* not to adorn a tale but to point a moral, and succeeded beyond his farthest imagination.

Medieval historians knew perfectly well what were the moral standards to which history was obliged to conform, and knew, too, the penalties of nonconformity, for what was history but the working out of God's will with Man? Even the great eighteenth-century historians, Gibbon and Hume and Robertson, Rollin and Voltaire and Raynal, accepted Bolingbroke's aphorism that history was philosophy teaching by examples, and they assumed that its lessons were moral and that it was the duty of the historian to point them. Only with the rise of "historicism" in the nineteenth century—there were antecedents, to be sure, in such historians as Machiavelli and Vico—did the question of the propriety and the validity of moral judgment come to the fore. Ranke, and his successors and disciples in almost every country, abjured moral judgment, or said that they did, and set themselves the task of simply recording what had happened, with a minimum of comment, and with neither ostentatious approval nor disapproval. Theirs was the ideal which Henry Adams later found so futile: ". . . by the severest process of stating, with the least possible comment, such facts as seemed sure, in such order as seemed rigorously consequent, [to] fix for a familiar moment a necessary sequence of human movement."

There was bound to be a reaction away from this austere principle, especially since so few of its protagonists actually lived up to it. The Victorian era, which in Germany saw the triumph of historicism, was also the era of morality, of moral preaching in law and in economics, in politics and in history, as in art and in literature. It is difficult to know whether such historians as James Anthony Froude in England, Jules Michelet in France, Heinrich von Treitschke in Germany, or John Lothrop Motley in America considered themselves primarily ethical leaders or historical scholars; in fact they did not distinguish sharply between the two roles. "The eternal truths and rights of things," said Froude in his inaugural address as rector of St. Andrews University, "exist, fortunately, independent of our thoughts or wishes, fixed as mathematics, inherent in the nature of man and the world."

That was Thomas Carlyle's view, as well—Froude, rightly enough, wrote his biography. Listen to Carlyle—in his essay on Goethe—commenting on philosophy in general and historical philosophy in particular: "To the faithful heart let no era be a desperate one! It is ever the nature of Darkness to be followed by a new nobler Light; nay to produce such. The woes and contradictions of an Atheistic time; of a world sunk in wickedness and baseness and unbelief, wherein also physical wretchedness, the disorganisation and broken-heartedness of whole classes struggling in ignorance and pain will not fail: all this, the view of all this, falls like a Sphinx-question on every newborn earnest heart to deliver itself from, and the world from. Of Wisdom cometh Strength: only when there is 'no vision' do the people perish . . . Woe to the land where, in these seasons, no prophet arises; but only censors, satirists and embittered desperadoes, to make the evil worse; at best but to accelerate a consummation, which in accelerating they have aggravated!"

Motley imported moral judgment ever more directly into his history; here is his final verdict on Philip II of Spain: "There have been few men known to history who have been able to accomplish by their own exertions so vast an amount of evil as the king who had just died. If Philip possessed a single virtue it has eluded the conscientious research of the writer of these pages. If there are vices—as possibly there are—from which he was exempt, it is because it is not permitted to human nature to attain perfection even in evil. The only plausible explanation—for palliation there is none—of his infamous career is that the man really believed himself not a king but a god. He . . . ever felt that [his] base or bloody deeds were not crimes, but the simple will of the godhead of which he was a portion." And, in case his readers might think that he had stepped out of his province in thus condemning the Spanish monarch, Motley added a word on the responsibility of the historian: "When an humble malefactor is brought before an ordinary court of justice, it is not often, in any age or country, that he escapes the pillory or the gallows because, from his own point of view, his actions, instead of being criminal, have been commendable, and because the multitude and continuity of his offenses prove him to have been sincere. And because anointed monarchs are amenable to no human tribunal, save to that terrible assize which . . . is called Revolution, it is the more important for the great interests of humanity that before the judgment-seat of History a crown should be no protection to its wearer. There is no plea to the jurisdiction of history, if history be true to itself. . . ."

In a Carlyle or a Motley, moral judgment was a form of self-indulgence. But there was more to it than this; there was high Duty! The clearest and most persuasive statement of the moral function of the historian came from Lord Acton himself. Eight years after his exchange with Canon Creighton, Acton was appointed Regius Professor of History at Cambridge University. In his inaugural address he once again exhorted his listeners—and all students of history—"never to debase the moral currency or to lower the standards of rectitude, but to try others by the final maxim that governs your own lives. . . . Opinions alter, manners change, creeds rise and fall, but the moral law is written on the tablets of eternity." "We have the power," he concluded, ". . . to learn from undisguised and genuine records to look with remorse upon the past, and to the future with assured hope of better things; bearing this in mind, that if we lower our standard in history, we cannot uphold it in Church or State."

All of this constitutes what might be called a moral argument in favor of moral judgment. In this view the moral laws are universal and timeless; murder is always murder and betrayal is always betrayal, cruelty and intolerance are always the same; the historian cannot stand above the moral laws, or stand aside from them, but must acknowledge them and participate in them and apply them. If he does not, he will fail the cause of morality—and of history as well—and forfeit the confidence and respect of his peers.

There is, however, another and perhaps more persuasive argument for moral judgment in history, one that rests not so much on moral as on psychological grounds. It is this: that the historian cannot, in any event, help himself, and that he might as well acknowledge what is inherent and implicit in his condition. He is, after all, a creature of his time, his society, his faith. Even if he resolutely refrains from overt moral judgment, he will surely be guilty of covert judgment: his choice of subject, his selection of facts, his very vocabulary, will betray him. How much better, then, how much fairer and more honest, to acknowledge his position in advance; how much better to call his book—it is Charles A. Beard who makes the point—*An Economic Interpretation of the Constitution* rather than to fall back on a title like *The Making of the Constitution*, one which "does not advise the reader at the outset concerning the upshot to be expected." History is not a science, and the historian is not a scientist. "The supreme command," therefore, "is that he must cast off his servitude to the assumptions of natural science and return to his own subject matter—to history as actuality."

But the stout champions of moral judgment do not have things all their own way. Not at all. Here comes a whole phalanx of historians with a formidable arsenal of counterarguments.

First, while it is true that history tries to observe something like histori-cal "due process," it cannot in the nature of the case do so. The past is not there to defend itself. We cannot recall the witnesses, put them on the stand, question and cross-examine them. It is difficult enough to render a moral verdict on anything so recent as, let us say, Hoover's dispersion of the "Bonus Army," or the conduct of the Vichy government, or the resort to the atomic weapon at Hiroshima; how much more difficult, then, to sit in judgment on the character of Alcibiades, the justification for the murder of Caesar, the conduct of the Norman invaders of England or of the Spanish conquistadors.

Second, while technical judgment is essential—in the law, in the civil service, in the university, in athletics—if society is to function, such judg-ment does not pretend to be moral but professional. A university profes-sor who permitted his moral views of a student to dictate his grades, a referee whose decisions were based on moral considerations, even a judge who allowed his private moral convictions to influence his decisions on questions of contracts, wills, liability, or bankruptcy proceedings, would be regarded as not only incompetent but expendable. There are reason-ably clear standards for such practical judgments as society requires—laws, rules, tests—but as parents, psychiatrists, and priests so well know, moral judgments present questions of labyrinthine complexity even when all the relevant evidence appears to be available. When it comes to history —the conduct of men or of nations in past centuries—all the relevant evidence is never available, and there are no universal standards. What the historian does when he judges is merely to identify his own "can't-help-but-believes" with eternal verities. As Justice Oliver Wendell Holmes suc-cinctly put it, "I prefer champagne to ditch-water, but I see no reason to suppose the cosmos does."

If history "tells us" anything, it tells us that standards, values, and prin-ciples have varied greatly from age to age and from society to society; indeed, that they have varied greatly from one generation to another within the same society. Popes chosen for their learning and their virtue were certain that morality required that they put down heresies with fire and sword, cruelty and torture; sixteenth-century Europeans had no com-punction about killing Indians because the Indians had no souls; learned and upright Puritans readily sent witches to their deaths.

Consider a problem which has confronted and perplexed American historians for a hundred years: slavery. Surely if anything is wrong, slavery is wrong. No social institution more deeply offends our moral sensibilities than this; no other collective experience induces in us a comparable sense of shame. Slavery, we are all agreed, corrupts alike the slave and the master; slavery corrupts the body politic, the poison still infects us.

This is the vocabulary of morality, and it is this vocabulary that we invoke, almost instinctively, whenever we discuss what was long euphemistically called the "peculiar institution."

Yet when we come to pronounce judgment on slavery we are met, at the very threshold, with the most intransigent consideration—that generation after generation of good, humane, Christian men and women not only accepted it but considered it a blessing. What are we to say when confronted by the fact—a formidable body of evidence permits us to use that word—that our own forebears, only two or three generations back, embraced slavery, rejoiced in it, fought to defend it, and gave up their lives confident that they were dying in a good cause?

Clearly we cannot fall back on the simple explanation that all of these men and women—those who owned slaves and those who sustained the slave system—were bad. These beneficiaries of and defenders of slavery were neither better nor worse than their cousins north of the Mason and Dixon line who had managed to get rid of the "peculiar institution" one or two generations earlier; they were neither better nor worse than we are. Whatever may be said on practical grounds for the moral righteousness and self-righteousness of the abolitionists, it can be said that no comparable pressures weigh upon us as historians. It is absurd in us to pass moral judgment on slaveholders, absurd to indict a whole people or to banish a whole people to some historical purgatory where they can expiate their sins. Lincoln saw this, Lincoln who saw so much. The people of the North and the South, he said in his second inaugural address, "read the same Bible, and pray to the same God, and each invokes His aid against the other. It may seem strange that any men should dare to ask a just God's assistance in wringing their bread from the sweat of other men's faces; but let us judge not, that we be not judged."

We can agree now, most of us, that slavery was an unmitigated evil, but we cannot therefrom conclude that those who inherited it, were caught in it and by it, who supported it and fought for it, were evil men. What we can say is that but for the grace of God, or the accident of history, we might ourselves have been caught up in slavery, and bound by it, and habituated to accepting it, just as our forebears were. What we can say is that if earlier generations—in the North and the South alike—bore the burden and the guilt of slavery, we have born the burden, and the guilt, of racial discrimination.

And here is a third argument against moral judgment in history—that the historian is not God. He is not called upon to judge the quick or the dead; indeed he is not called upon to judge. If he sets himself up as a judge he changes the whole pattern of his intellectual and professional role from one dedicated to objective inquiry to one devoted to prosecution or defense. As the distinguished historian of the Russian Revolution, E. H. Carr, observes, the attempt to erect standards of historical judgment is itself "unhistorical and contradicts the very essence of history. It provides a dogmatic answer to questions which the historian is bound by his vocation incessantly to ask: the historian who accepts answers in advance to these questions goes to work with his eyes blindfolded, and renounces his vocation." And how interesting that Allan Nevins, who, in the first edition of his classic *Gateway to History*, asserted the necessity of the application of rigorous moral standards which "ought to be held absolute and applied equally to all modern ages," and who cited Acton to his fellow historians with approval, later abandoned this position entirely, and substituted the simple assertion that "what is important is not to denounce Abdul Hamid for his crimes, but to understand what gave birth to Abdul Hamid and his policies."

No, the historian is not God; he is a man and like other men. He confesses most of the failings, responds to most of the pressures, succumbs to most of the temptations that afflict his fellow men. Consciously or unconsciously, he is almost always taking sides. Can we really trust Carlyle on Cromwell or Motley on Philip II, or Charles A. Beard on the causes of the Civil War, or Vernon Parrington on John Marshall? Can we trust either Macaulay or Winston Churchill to write impartially about the Duke of Marlborough? Can we trust Lord Acton or Benedetto Croce on a subject so close to their hearts as the history of liberty? Clearly we cannot. The historian, like the judge, the priest, or the statesman, is a creature of his race, nationality, religion, class, of his inheritance and his education, and he can never emancipate himself from these formative influences and achieve Olympian impartiality. Where he undertakes to *judge*, he does not even have the prop of professional training and traditions to sustain him, as he does when he records and reconstructs. And because not even a Ranke, not even a Mommsen, not even a Toynbee, can survey the whole of history, his forays into the past are bound to be haphazard and fortuitous as well. For purposes of reconstructing the past, that is not a fatal handicap; others will fill in the gaps. But for purposes of formulating a moral code and applying it systematically and impartially, it is a fatal handicap.

We may, then, accept the finding of the historian in matters of fact —always subject to subsequent revision, to be sure—but why should we accept his conclusions in matters of morality? "I beseech you in the bowels of Christ," wrote Oliver Cromwell in his Letter to the Church of Scotland, "think it possible you may be mistaken." Alas, the historians have so often been mistaken. Over the centuries they have stood ready to pronounce judgments which differ little from the tainted and tarnished judgments of statesmen, soldiers, and priests. Catholic historians have sustained the persecution of Protestant heretics, and Protestant historians have looked with equanimity upon the persecution of Catholics. National historians have almost invariably defended and justified the conduct of their own nations and as regularly rendered judgment against their enemies; more, they have themselves provided the arguments for chauvinistic nationalism, imperialism, and militarism. No wonder that the chief preoccupation of the historian in our day is revision!

We come then to a fourth consideration, practical rather than philosophical: moral judgment in history is futile. Surely, say those who insist that the historian be a judge, it is proper that the historian reprobate the Inquisition and exalt tolerance, that he deplore slavery and celebrate freedom, that he execrate Hitler and Nazi genocide and rejoice in the triumph of the forces of liberation. But why should the historian go out of his way to condemn or to praise these things? The assumption behind this expectation is that the reader has no mind of his own, no moral standards, no capacity to exercise judgment; that, incapable of distinguishing between slavery and freedom, persecution and tolerance, he depends upon the historian to do this for him. Are those mature enough to read serious histories really so obtuse that they cannot draw conclusions from the facts that are submitted to them? Is there really any danger that students will yearn for slavery or rejoice in the Inquisition or admire Philip II or Adolf Hitler if the historian does not bustle in and set them right? Alas! if the reader does not know that Hitler was a moral monster and that the murder of six million Jews was a moral outrage, nothing the historian can say will set him right; if he does not know in his bones that slavery corrupts both slave and master, nothing the historian can say will enlighten him. Is there not, indeed, some danger that if the historian continually usurps the role of judge, the reader may react against his judgments; that if the historian insists on treating his readers as morally incompetent, they may turn away from history altogether to some more mature form of literature?

One final observation is appropriate. We should not confuse moral with professional judgment. In the field of his professional competence the scholar has the same obligation as the judge, the teacher, the physician, the architect. The judge who pronounces sentence, the teacher who gives a grade, the physician who diagnoses an illness, the architect who condemns a building, is not indulging in moral but exercising professional judgment. So the historian who, after painstaking study of all available evidence and after cleansing himself of all the perilous stuff which might distort his vision, concludes that Lee was correct in his decision to surrender at Appomattox rather than fight it out in the West, that Roosevelt was not responsible for the attack on Pearl Harbor, that the conduct of the Crimean War was characterized by criminal folly, that the violation of Belgian neutrality in 1914 was an error of the first magnitude, that Cavour rather than Garibaldi deserves credit for Italian unification, that Shakespeare and not Bacon wrote Hamlet, and that the Protocols of Zion are forgeries, is performing his professional duty. He may be mistaken —but so may the judge, the teacher, the physician—that is a chance society takes. His judgments may have moral overtones—it is difficult to keep those out, and we have learned to discount them. It is equally exasperating to discover that scholars who may know more about their subjects than anyone in the world are still unwilling to share their interpretations or their conclusions with their readers. We want professional judgments from a doctor or a lawyer or an engineer; and we have a right to professional judgment from a scholar as well.

—February 1966

HENRY ADAMS
IN THE SOUTH SEAS

By LOUIS AUCHINCLOSS

In the wake of his wife's suicide, a shattered Adams managed to finish his twelve-volume history, then set sail with John LaFarge in search of a new life

W hen Marian Hooper Adams took her fatal dose of potassium cyanide on December 6, 1885, she almost smashed the life out of her husband as well. Suicide makes a clean sweep of the past and present; worst of all, it repudiates love. Until that day Henry Adams might have reasonably considered that his life was successful. He had not, to be sure, been President of the United States, like his grandfather and great-grandfather, or minister to England, like his father, but he had been a brilliant and popular teacher of medieval history at Harvard, a successful editor of the *North American Review*, a noted biographer and essayist, and he was in process of completing his twelve-volume history of the Jefferson and Madison administrations, which even such a self-deprecator as he himself must have suspected would one day be a classic. But above all this, far above, he had believed that he and his wife were happy.

Recovering from the first shock, he took a trip to Japan with his friend John LaFarge. Then he went back to Washington and worked for three laborious years to finish his history and prepare it for the press. After that, at last, he was free. He had neither child nor job, and his means were ample. In August of 1890 he and LaFarge sailed again from San Francisco for a voyage of indefinite duration to the South Seas. Many writers have speculated on why he went. Edward Chalfant, who in my opinion is the scholar closest to the secrets of Adams's personality, told me that he had once made a list of seventeen possible motives. Suffice it to say that Adams had reached the end of one life and was wondering if another existed.

LaFarge was the perfect traveling companion. Ernest Samuels has described him as an original genius with a Faustian nature who maintained a large, devoutly Catholic family in Newport while he kept bachelor's hall in New York. He was delighted to explore the Pacific at Adams's expense, leaving family and creditors behind. A master in oils and water colors, he could also talk and write exuberantly on all the subjects that he reproduced.

The Pacific opened up a new dimension of color. LaFarge's journal is a hymn to the sea and air. He taught Adams to observe the exquisite clearness of the butterfly blue of the sky, laid on between clouds and shading down to a white faintness in the distance where the haze of ocean covered up the turquoise. He made him peer down into the water, framed in the opening of a ship's gangway, and see how the sapphire blue seemed to pour from it. He pointed out the varieties of pink and lilac and purple and rose in the clouds at sunset. Adams never learned to be more than an amateur painter, but his vision was immensely sharpened.

They went first to Oahu, where they made the discovery which every other island was to confirm: that the charm of the Pacific declined in exact proportion to the penetration of the white man. It was not until October, when they landed on Upolu in the Samoas, that they came in touch with a culture that was still largely unspoiled. The natives, grave and courteous, greeted them benevolently and made them feel immediately at home. They drank the ceremonial kava, muddy water mixed with grated root, which left a persistent little aftertaste that no amount of coconut milk could quite wash away, and they watched the siva, a dance performed by girls naked to the waist, their dark skins shining with coconut oil, seated cross-legged with garlands of green leaves around their heads and loins. The girls chanted as they swayed and stretched out their arms in all directions; they might have come out of the nearby sea. LaFarge's spectacles quivered with emotion, but Adams was able to assure his correspondent Elizabeth Cameron that nothing in the song or dance suggested the least impropriety. Again and again he was to comment on such evidences of Rousseauistic innocence.

Samoa was ruled by Malietoa, the puppet king of the Western nations' consuls, but Mataafa, the deposed monarch, still held the loyalty of most of the population. Adams and LaFarge, scrupulously neutral, called on both and learned a concept of aristocracy beside which Adams felt like "the son of a camel driver degraded to the position of stable boy in Spokane West Centre." For the real art of the Samoans was social. Even the breeding among the chiefs was systematic. They selected their wives for strength and form, with the result that the principal families enjoyed a physical as well as a social superiority. Yet at the same time Adams observed that the society was basically communistic. All of the presents that he and LaFarge lavishly handed out to their hosts—umbrellas, silk scarfs, gowns, cigars—were soon seen parading about the villages on strangers. Every chief was basically a poor man because he was obliged to share what he had.

In Apia the travelers found the first corrosive effects of European influence. In the big siva organized in their honor by the American consul, the girls deferred to missionary prejudices by wearing banana leaves over their breasts. Adams was at once reminded of the world and the devil. In 1970 we are amused at his surprise that the Polynesian standard of female beauty should be more in the body than the face, but we must remember that in 1890 the face was all that the American woman exposed. He and LaFarge, however, did not carry their preference for old Samoan customs to the point of adopting the native want of costume. They feared ridicule, not to mention mosquitoes.

Everywhere they asked their hosts endless questions about customs, families, and religion, and everywhere they ran into the same stubborn secrecy. Adams became convinced that under the superficial layer of their converted Christianity the Samoans preserved a secret priesthood might- ier than the political chiefs, with supernatural powers, invocations, prophecies, charms, and the whole paraphernalia of paganism. The na- tives never had to kill a missionary. They merely prayed him off.

On their *malangas*, or boat excursions, to the smaller islands, the two friends thrust themselves deeper and deeper into the Polynesian mystery. How had the natives ever got there? From east or west? Was Darwin correct about the origin of coral reefs? LaFarge despaired of duplicating the quality of the light, and Adams of catching the true expression of the islands. To John Hay, Adams wrote that it was languor that was not languid, voluptuousness that was not voluptuous, a poem without poetry. At other moments it struck him as simply an impossible stage decoration. Gazing at the natives passing his cottage in their blue or red or yellow waistcloths, their bronzed skins aglow in the sun against the surf line of the coral reef, he wrote Anna Lodge that he expected to see a prima donna in green garlands and a girdle of ti leaves emerge from the next hut to invoke the cuttlefish or the shark with a Wagnerian chorus of native maidens.

But in the end reality surpassed all such images. Perhaps Adams's most vivid memory would be the picnic by the sliding rock where they watched the yellow limbs of the girls who plunged naked into the white foam, like goldfish in a blue-green pool. LaFarge said that had they stayed much longer they would have plunged in after them. LaFarge, alone, might have.

Before leaving Samoa, they became fairly intimate with Robert Louis Stevenson, who had moved there with his wife and mother, in the last round of his gallant but desperate struggle with tuberculosis. Stevenson's letter to a friend in England about their first visit caused much hilarity when the Adams circle got hold of it: "Two Americans called on me yesterday. One, an artist named LaFarge, said he knew you. The name of the other I do not recall."

Stevenson was immediately congenial with LaFarge, but he put Adams in mind of a dirty cotton bag over a skeleton. The novelist's flashing dark eyes, his darting body, his improbable tales, made Adams uneasy. Adams recoiled from physical messiness and may have ascribed what he saw of this quality to Stevenson's mental processes. In this he was certainly unfair. Adams had turned away from life in wandering to the Polynesian islands; Stevenson was searching for it. He gave all of himself to the Samoan experience; he dug roots, cut trees, and helped with the building of his house at Vailima like a man on the frontier. He entered passionately into the political disputes of the island and fiercely embraced the side of the natives against that of the exploiting colonials. Adams felt that Stevenson could never understand the Samoans because he attributed to them the motivations of boys in the Edinburgh of his own youth. But I wonder if Stevenson's understanding of boys and of adventure did not put him closer to the Samoans than Adams could ever have been.

After Samoa came the appalling disillusionment of Tahiti. Adams described it as an exquisitely successful cemetery. The atmosphere was one of hopelessness and premature decay. The natives were not the gay, big, animal creatures of Samoa; they were still, silent, sad in expression, and fearfully few in number. The population had been decimated by bacteria brought in by Westerners. Rum was the only amusement which civilization and religion had left the people. The puppet king, Pomare, was to die of a rotten liver shortly after Adams and LaFarge left. Tahiti was a halfway house between Hawaii and Samoa. Adams complained that "a pervasive half-castitude" permeated everything, "a sickly whitey-brown, or dirty-white complexion" that suggested weakness and disease.

He was bored, he insisted, as he had never been bored in the worst wilds of Beacon Street or at the dreariest dinner tables of Belgravia. While waiting for a boat to take them elsewhere, anywhere, he amused himself by returning to his role of historian and interviewing members of the deposed royal family, the Tevas. Next to Mataafa in Samoa, he found the old ex-queen of Tahiti, Hinari, or Grandmother, the most interesting native figure in the Pacific. She showed none of the secrecy of the Samoan chiefs but took a motherly interest in Adams and LaFarge and told them freely, sitting on the floor, all her clan's oldest legends and traditions. Adams was even adopted into the Teva clan and given the hereditary family name of Taura-atua, with the lands, rights, and privileges attached to it—though these holdings consisted of only a hundred square feet.

But when he came, some years later, to put the history into a book which he had privately printed, it was little more than an interesting failure. Tahiti had no history, in the Western sense of the word, until the arrival of the white man. Of the thousands of years that had preceded Captain Cook, where generation had succeeded generation without distinguishable change, there was nothing left but genealogy and legend. The genealogy, which makes up a large part of Adams's book, is boring, and as for the legend, he admitted himself that it needed the lighter hand of Stevenson.

Yet *The Memoirs of Arii Taimai* nonetheless mark an important step in Adams's career. He had gone, by 1890, as far as he was going as a historian in the conventional sense. His great work on Jefferson and Madison was history at its most intellectually pure. The author stands aside and lets the documents tell the story, from which a very few precious rules may be deduced. But in the South Seas he had tried to leave the intellect for simplicity, for instinct. He had sought peace and found ennui. Even the unspoiled natives, in the long run, palled. He had to return, in Papeete, to his profession, and he had to try it with a new twist, for how else could Tahitian history be done? And if *The Memoirs* were a bore, was it altogether his fault? Might it not be in the subject? Suppose he were to happen upon a subject that required not only the imagination of the man who had sat on the floor with the old queen of Tahiti as she intoned the poems of her family tradition, but also the industry of the devoted scholar who had pored through archives of European foreign offices? Suppose he were to find a subject, in short, that required a great artist as well as a great historian?

He was to find such a one a few years hence in the Gothic cathedrals of France. *Mont-Saint-Michel and Chartres* is an extraordinary tour de force of the imagination, a vivid invocation of the spirit and force of the twelfth century that may be longer read than any of Adams's other books. It has always been a difficult volume for librarians to classify. Is it history or travel or criticism or theology or even fiction? But its language shimmers with some of the magic blue of the windows of the cathedral which forms its principal topic. One day, at the Metropolitan Museum of Art, gazing at the brilliant *Ia Orana Maria*, I was struck by the fact that the Virgin of Chartres, like the Virgin of Paul Gauguin, may owe something to the colors and legends of the South Seas.

Gauguin arrived in Tahiti a few days after Adams and LaFarge had left, in time to witness the funeral of King Pomare. It is probably just as well that they did not meet. The American travelers detested European settlers, and a European settler who drank to excess and lived publicly with a native woman would have seemed the acme of Western corruption. If Adams had considered Stevenson a Bohemian, Gauguin would have been beyond the pale. Nor would LaFarge have liked Gauguin's painting. Many years later, when he and Adams were old men and Gauguin was dead, LaFarge wrote to his former traveling companion about an illustrated catalogue of a Gauguin show in Paris. He informed Adams that the "mad Frenchman" had been in Tahiti shortly after their visit and had actually met some of their friends on the island. It is disappointing to have to relate that LaFarge then went on to say that Gauguin's paintings were sorry failures, desperate efforts to catch the attention of a novelty-hunting public.

It has been said that Gauguin, with his brilliant colors and primitive figures, caught the essential atmosphere of the islands that both Adams and LaFarge missed. But what he really did was to create a Polynesia of his own that millions of his admirers now regard as the true one. Gauguin came to Tahiti naïvely in search of an island paradise, an unspoiled Arcadia, but he found and recognized in Papeete precisely what Adams had found and recognized. Only on canvas could he realize his dream. He was under no illusions about what he was doing. His red seas and blue dogs were perfectly deliberate. He wanted painting to stand independent of what it purported to represent and not to be a branch of sculpture. He said that the kind of people who wanted exact reproduction would have to wait for the invention of a color camera. They have, and they are quite content!

Of the brilliant four who were in the Polynesian islands in 1891—Adams, Stevenson, Gauguin, and LaFarge—the first three, like most artists, brought more with them than what they were to take out. The subjective experiences of the historian, of the storyteller, and of the post-impressionist might have been very much the same in other parts of the globe. Polynesia simply happened to be the stage of one aspect of their development. But in LaFarge's work I feel a more objective effort to reproduce the islands than the others may have made.

His stubborn imagination fixed them in a classic atmosphere that seemed proof against disillusionment. To him the blues and greens were painted in lines of Homer, guessed at by Titian, and the long sway and cadence of the surf had the music of the Odyssey. The Samoan youngster with a red hibiscus fastened in his hair by a grassy knot was a Bacchus of Tintoretto. LaFarge prided himself on having an affinity with a remoter ancestry of man and on being better able than other Westerners to understand the islanders.

But if his paintings have a charm that may be special and Polynesian, they are nevertheless romantic. They tell us quite as much of John LaFarge as they do of the South Seas. Perhaps it is because he insisted that the paradise still existed which Gauguin knew was dead. And perhaps this very existence is the one good thing that came out of the meeting of East and West. The dream of innocence, abided in or awoken from, may still be a mighty source of inspiration.

—June 1970

"YOU'LL HAVE TO SEE MORGAN"

By ANDY LOGAN

As the nation's gold reserves drained away, the panic grew. Even the President was helpless. He had to turn to someone more powerful.

At three o'clock in the morning on February 5, 1895, a tall, stout man with white hair, fierce gray eyes, and a monstrous red nose sat playing solitaire in his suite at the Arlington Hotel in Washington, D.C. He had been playing for hours, vigorously forcing the cards into sequence on the table in front of him as if the opportunity to impose order on any situation, even on pieces of cardboard, gave him special satisfaction on this dark morning. The only sounds in the room were the slap of the cards and the occasional striking of a match as he lit still another long black cigar. The sound he was listening for was the peal of the telephone on the wall beside him. Diagonally across Lafayette Square the White House lights were also burning in Grover Cleveland's second-floor office, as they had burned every night for the past two weeks. The solitaire player was J. Pierpont Morgan, and the call he was waiting for was from the Attorney General to say that the President would see him later that morning in time to permit him to save the nation from bankruptcy.

Although Morgan regarded all politicians as incompetents and Democratic officeholders as a lower form of life, he and the Democratic President had much in common. They were almost identical in age, having been born in the same spring of 1837, and were similarly strong-willed, obstinate, blunt-spoken, and, though massively built and homely, attractive to women. Morgan represented the third generation of family wealth, while Cleveland had run for office as a man of the people, come up the hard way; but, affluence aside, their forebears had included about the same percentage of firebrand Puritans, early Harvard and Yale graduates, Protestant dignitaries, civic leaders, and eccentrics. The most significant attribute the two men shared in the winter of 1895, however, was their philosophy of money: they were both devout gold men.

A long and complex series of events had brought the two most powerful men in America to their separate vigils on either side of Lafayette Square. The country's most bitter and divisive quarrel since Appomattox was over money, and the opposing battle colors were gold and silver. By 1895 many of the men who favored the cause of silver sincerely believed that all conflicts between the naturally hostile forces of civilization—capital against labor, conservative against radical, creditor against debtor, soulless corporation against individual, rich businessman against poor farmer—would be resolved in favor of the have-nots if only they could overthrow the *de facto* gold standard which then prevailed in the United States.

To the silverites this partiality for gold was the work of a sinister conspiracy of Wall Street "goldbugs," as they called the enemy forces. (In one of its ruder moments the Atlanta *Constitution* had called Wall Street "a hotbed of goldbuggery.") The fact was that when Congress had passed a law in 1875 making the nation's then-depreciated "greenback" paper money redeemable in "coin" after 1879—that is, in either silver or gold, the ratio then being sixteen ounces of silver to one of gold—silver had been scarce and precious. It had been the opening up of vast silver mines in the West during the following decade and the abandonment of a silver standard by most major nations that had caused the lighter metal to decline drastically in value. In the Nineties the silver in a silver dollar was worth less than forty-nine cents in gold, and businessmen redeeming greenbacks (that is, as opposed to silver or gold certificates) at the Treasury had no problem deciding which coin to specify. Moreover, the law required the government to reissue such bills, and thus the same piece of paper could be redeemed in gold again and again. Gold is heavy in the pocket for ordinary business transactions, however, and the pace of the gold drain stayed well short of a run so long as times were moderately prosperous and people had confidence that their greenbacks were good as gold at the Treasury window.

For bankers, businessmen, and much of the general public the signal for the ending of the confidence was the sinking of the government gold reserve below a hundred million dollars. When it had begun redeeming greenbacks in coin in 1879, the Treasury had set that amount of gold as the minimum to be kept on hand for redemption purposes. The sum had no intrinsic or legal force (there were over three and a half times that many greenbacks out, for example), but over the years it had taken on what Cleveland later described as "a superstitious sanctity," which had millions of Americans convinced that with $101,000,000 in gold reserves the monetary system was sound, while a drop to $99,000,000 threatened dire calamity. The calamitous hour had arrived in the spring of 1893, shortly after Cleveland's second inauguration. For the next four years much of his energies were given over to finding gold to pump into the dwindling reserve and watching it drain away as fast as he supplied it.

The silverites viewed this frustrating struggle without even crocodile tears. "They can't exhaust the gold reserve too quickly to suit me," declared a pro-silver congressman from Missouri. For a decade they had been clamoring for unlimited (or free) silver coinage at the old, unrealistic ratio of sixteen to one, although, despite vigorous administration efforts to force it into circulation, nearly $700,000,000 worth of unwanted silver already lay idle in the Treasury vaults. Government purchases of silver had now been halted, but if there were no more gold in the Treasury, the country would be perforce on a silver standard, a situation equivalent to a fifty percent devaluation. The argument that the money of all the major nations was based on gold and that ninety percent of U.S. foreign trade was with this gold bloc carried no weight with the silverites. "What have we got to do with abroad?" demanded one of them on the floor of the Senate.

Before 1893 the silverites had been a comparatively minor, aberrant sect, almost equally troublesome to both major parties. Although their strength, like that of the Democrats, lay in the West and South, Cleveland, a gold man, had been easily elected in 1892. By the middle of his term, however, he had become more and more isolated politically. With the conversion to silverism of that great commoner from the West, William Jennings Bryan, the silverites, joined by the Populists, had begun to rally other Democrats to their cause. Their simplistic crusade grew in strength because it offered hope, however irrational, to millions of desperate Americans who saw no hope elsewhere. During the mid-Nineties the country was in the savage grip of a depression that followed the Panic of 1893. Over five hundred banks and loan companies had failed, hurting the small depositor hardest. There was a glut of agricultural products on the world market, and the farmers were being crushed between ten-cent corn and ten percent mortgages. A large share of the mortgages were payable to banks in Wall Street which, in the silverites' code, had fomented the '93 panic in the first place. Thus the traditional mistrust of the agrarian West and South for the urban Northeast—"the enemy's country," Bryan called it—was concentrated on that narrow Manhattan canyon. To the debtors of the nation, reported *Harper's Weekly* in 1894, Wall Street was "a dark, mysterious, crafty, wicked, rapacious and tyrannical power," and only the inflationary effect of free silver could liberate them from this enfeoffment to the goldbugs.

With the talk of a silver standard, banking and commercial institutions inevitably took fright and began to pay all customs and internal revenue debts in silver, at the same time exchanging their greenbacks at the Treasury for gold, which they either hoarded or shipped abroad. The reserve, which Cleveland had precariously maintained just below the hundred million mark during most of 1893, fell to sixty-five million early the next year, and the specter of default and devaluation had now moved out of the realm of superstition. The stricken South and West were in no position to come to Cleveland's rescue, even if they had been so minded, and he turned to Wall Street for help.

Much of the subsequent liaison between the Street and the Treasury was handled by August Belmont. Belmont was both a goldbug and a leading citizen of the enemy's country, having five years earlier succeeded his father as head of August Belmont and Company, the American representatives of the Rothschilds. He was also that rarity among international bankers, a Democrat. Several times a month during the recurrent gold crises of 1894 someone from the Treasury would come up from Washington and go directly to Belmont's office for a briefing on ways and means. Once or twice it was the Secretary himself, the white-haired Kentuckian and former Speaker of the House, John G. Carlisle. Carlisle, however, was a frontier figure who had spent his early political years baiting Wall Street and, although he was now foursquare for gold, he was never at ease with rich easterners. The Treasury delegate was usually Assistant Secretary William Edmund Curtis, a handsome, earnest young lawyer from an old New York family who had first encountered Belmont at the Racquet Club. Because of the political perils of trafficking with Wall Street, and the danger that public knowledge of such pilgrimages would make the Treasury situation seem even grimmer than it was and thus set off a further gold drain, Curtis's visits to Belmont were usually clandestine affairs. He would then move on to secret interviews with other Wall Street leaders, who would greet him much as if they were plenipotentiaries of a wealthy foreign state granting an audience to an emissary from a poor and politically misguided nation. "It might have been imagined that it was Turkey or China which was standing, hat in hand, in the money market," wrote an economist of the time.

Twice during 1894 the Treasury had succeeded in bolstering the reserve through the public sale of a fifty-million-dollar bond issue. Though paid for in gold, these were coin bonds—that is, principal and interest were to be paid off in either gold or silver. The silver-minded Congress declined to authorize more marketable bonds specifically payable in gold, although the saving in interest would have been substantial. The small investor rejected both 1894 bond issues, and it was as a result of Curtis's and Belmont's maneuvers that they were taken up by a group of New York banks in the first instance and, in the second, by a syndicate that included the man who would be found playing solitaire at the Arlington Hotel that early morning in February, 1895. Morgan had been widely commended for his public spirit in financial circles the year before. James Stillman, of the National City Bank, later claimed that it had been he who had raised much of the second 1894 fund after a desperate appeal from Morgan, but that Morgan "became perfectly bombastic and triumphant as the savior of his country." Stillman complained: "He took all the credit. But then, you see, he is a poet! Morgan is a poet!"

The 1894 bond issues had provided only ephemeral relief, since it developed that many of the purchasers had merely bought them with gold withdrawn from the Treasury reserve the bond issues were meant to replenish. As the threat of gold default grew stronger, the rate of withdrawal naturally picked up speed. During the month of January, 1895, the drain amounted to forty-five million dollars, with over twenty-five million of this going abroad. The western senator who had told Congress a few weeks before that "when there's a run on the United States Treasury, there'll be a run on the Maker of the Universe," was now publicly silent, perhaps privately saying his prayers. On January 28 Cleveland sent a message to Congress requesting congressional action, which was not forthcoming, and declaring that if the country were forced onto a silver standard, it would become a second-class nation.

On the evening of Thursday, January 30, when Curtis arrived in New York in the midst of this worst gold crisis of them all, a secret conference with Belmont was no longer easy to arrange. Withdrawals from the gold reserve that day had come to $3,750,000 and it was down to less than $42,000,000, or, at this rate of loss, about eleven days' supply. The situation, trumpeted the *New York Times*, "involves the honor of the United States throughout the world." New York newspapermen, knowing that Washington would have to take some action, had been meeting trains all day. When Curtis stepped out that evening on the platform at Jersey City, then the nearest terminal of the Pennsylvania Railroad, a dozen reporters were waiting for him. They followed him on the Cortlandt Street ferry but were turned away at the door of Belmont's town house, where the two men had agreed to meet. In the upstairs library Belmont and Curtis now reviewed the situation. For political reasons Cleveland and Carlisle favored trying to obtain gold through still another public sale of bonds, hoping they would not have to turn again to Wall Street. But even if the general public were to buy the coin bonds it had twice rejected the year before, the rate of the gold drain was now so precipitate that the reserve would vanish before the ritual of public bidding could be completed. The week before, Belmont had been so distressed by the situation that he had gone down to Washington on his own to talk to Carlisle. The only remedy for the Treasury's current predicament, he had reminded the Secretary, was an enormous influx of gold from abroad, which would then bring the gold out of hiding in this country. Only an international syndicate could bring about such a reversal, he had pointed out. Without committing himself, Carlisle had asked Belmont to inquire of the Rothschilds in London whether they would be able to find European buyers for U.S. coin bond. Now Belmont handed Curtis a sheaf of cables from the Rothschilds saying it could not be done. For several moments Belmont and Curtis sat in gloomy silence. "You'll have to see Morgan," Belmont said finally. "He's the only man who can help now."

Before he went to bed that night at the University Club, Curtis sent off a letter to Carlisle describing the city as "nervous and panicky." Soon after breakfast the next morning he appeared on the doorstep of Morgan's brownstone mansion in East Thirty-sixth Street. In spite of the growing alarm in the financial world, the head of the Wall Street power structure had not made any move. Apparently he had been standing on ceremony, waiting to be asked. Now he agreed to meet with Curtis and Belmont at the Subtreasury building that afternoon. A few minutes later he cabled his London partners, who in a return cable explained that they had already been consulted on the situation by the Rothschilds and that, in view of the emergency, they were willing to work with the Rothschilds on the European sale of a bond issue if Morgan would work with Belmont in New York. But they endorsed the Rothschild verdict that Europe would not buy American bonds that were not specifically payable in gold.

Belmont met Morgan at his office at 23 Wall Street shortly after noon, and when the two bankers crossed the street to the Subtreasury, it was observed that the dapper, mustachioed Belmont was walking a little to the rear. He was, after all, sixteen years younger than the fifty-eight-year-old Morgan, who had been used to doing business with the elder Belmont. Thereafter "Augie" Belmont accepted gracefully his relegation to the role of junior partner in the enterprise. During the three-hour conference that followed, Morgan agreed to take over direction of the rescue mission, but only if he would be in full charge. Dubious as the prospects seemed, he went on, "I will undertake to get the gold necessary abroad, *provided it is left in my hands to undertake.* . . ." He wrote out a memorandum of his plan of action to Curtis, who got ready to leave for Washington with it.

By mid-afternoon the bare information that Morgan and Belmont were inside the Subtreasury had already checked the run on the reserve. The Treasury's loss for the day was nearly a million and a half dollars less than that of the day before. A throng of reporters and Wall Street figures, seeking reassurance, surrounded the two bankers as they left the building.

They refused to answer any questions, but Curtis, emerging a few minutes later, gave the crowd an answer of sorts: he was smiling broadly. That night the banking firm of Lazard Frères brought back to the Treasury four million dollars in gold that it had already packed for shipment abroad.

The detailed cable that Morgan sent off to his London partners after he returned to 23 Wall Street that afternoon did not unnerve them by describing the new undertaking in terms of their duty as self-sacrificing philanthropists. To "avert calamity," read the cable, he proposed that the government make a private contract with a pair of syndicates—one of them managed by the Morgan and Belmont companies in New York and the other by the Morgan firm working with the Rothschilds in London —which would agree to provide the Treasury with gold to the extent of at least fifty million dollars, the gold to be paid for with a new coin bond issue, which the syndicates would then auction off themselves. Blandly ignoring his colleagues' judgment that coin bonds could not be sold abroad, Morgan's cable predicted that the arrangement "will be most creditable all parties and pay good profit." He also implied—perhaps craftily —that there was serious competition for the assignment ("should dislike see business largely hands Speyer and Co. and similar houses, who more sanguine European loans than your cables indicate") and that the syndicates' motivating factor would be sheer self-interest. ("We all have large interests dependent upon maintenance sound currency.") "There are always two reasons a man does something," Morgan once said in another connection. "The good one he gives—and the real one." Which was his real motive in this case—patriotism or profit—would be endlessly debated in years to come.

Curtis telephoned Friday afternoon that the Washington reaction was favorable, and Morgan began firing off more cables setting in motion the complex international machinery required to draw in the necessary gold. He met with Curtis at his home that midnight and again the next morning at the Subtreasury, where the panic was beginning to subside. The three million dollars in total Treasury withdrawals on Friday and Saturday were far outbalanced by nine million dollars' worth of gold that was taken off ships in the harbor and turned back to the Treasury.

Morgan insisted afterward that at the first Subtreasury conference there had been no discussion of the amount of interest to be paid on the new bonds. ("It was not really a question of price. It was a question of success.") The 1894 bonds had paid 3 percent. The newspapers were now printing the rumor that the new issue would pay 3½. Now, on Saturday morning, Morgan told Curtis that the price would have to be 3¾ percent. Both he and Curtis assumed this would be acceptable, and the Treasury man agreed to call Morgan at three on Sunday afternoon with the final go-ahead signal. Sunday evening in the Morgan household was regularly given over to family hymn-singing, but it is not known whether or not the banker was available that night to sing his favorite, "O Zion, Haste, Thy Mission High Fulfilling." Curtis had called at the appointed time, but only with the unsettling news that a messenger with an explanatory letter would arrive on the morning train. "The public and press believe the negotiation practically completed. . . . Effect of abandonment upon all interests would now be worse than if never begun," read Morgan's cable to London.

The Treasury letter, delivered to him before breakfast on Monday, rejected his solution for the gold problem and informed him that a public sale of the new bond issue would be announced that afternoon. The Democratic press had spent the weekend denouncing the secret nature of the negotiations ("dark lantern financiering") and was plumping for a 3 percent loan. ("If the banks won't take it, the people will," insisted the New York *World*.) Cleveland, perhaps unduly encouraged by the halt in the gold run, had taken another look at the political consequences of the private deal and had pulled back.

Morgan detested telephones, in the Nineties still unreliable and highly public instruments, but now he did not hesitate. Much of his morning was spent on the long-distance lines talking to Curtis, who finally got Carlisle to delay the announcement of the public sale for a day. He had sent Belmont to the capital on the ten o'clock train, Morgan told Curtis, and he himself would leave at once. They would talk to the President. There was no other way. In midafternoon Morgan took the ferry to Jersey City and boarded his private car, which was then attached to the Congressional Limited. He brought with him his junior partner, Robert Bacon (later Theodore Roosevelt's Secretary of State), and his lawyer, Francis Lynde Stetson, who was expected to be especially useful since he had been a law partner of Cleveland's in the interval between presidential terms.

When Morgan's train arrived in Washington, about a dozen newspapermen and Daniel Lamont were waiting on the platform. Lamont, a former reporter himself, was on the government roster as Secretary of War, but was more active as Cleveland's troubleshooter. (Mark Hanna described the War Department in the mid-Nineties as the only Cabinet seat for which a busy man could spare the time from his own affairs.) Lamont told Morgan that the President would not see him, and then visibly braced himself. When angry, Morgan was an alarming sight. Not only would his eyes seem to start out of his big head, but his great, bulbous red nose, the result of an affliction called *acne rosacea*, would, as Lincoln Steffens later remembered it, "flash and darken, flash and darken." He glared down now at Lamont. "I have come to Washington to see the President, and I am going to stay until I see him," he said in a booming voice and stomped off in the snow toward the cab stand. He shook off the press by directing the cab not to the Arlington, where he always stayed, but to the home of a woman friend on K Street.

The unbidden visitor, publicly rebuffed, was no longer standing on ceremony. Stetson was dispatched to the White House to invade Cleveland's quarters and persuade him to change his mind. He got no further than the front door, but about ten o'clock Bacon called to say that Attorney General Richard Olney was willing to talk to Morgan. Olney had heard from Carlisle the alarming report that one gold draft for over twelve million dollars might be presented at the New York Subtreasury the next day, and after conferring with Morgan, agreed to urge the President to see the banker and his friends. Having done everything he could, Morgan went on to the Arlington, where he avoided the inevitable press reception by ducking in the ladies' entrance on H Street. At midnight he sent his younger colleagues off to bed. As usual, he had brought with him from New York a small mahogany folding table and the silver box holding his solitaire cards. The game he played for the next several hours was "Miss Milligan," a solitaire variation involving two decks of cards and a maneuver called "waiving," which allows a single obstructing card to be temporarily lifted out of the tableau when a game is hopelessly blocked. "By this privilege," notes one solitaire manual, "many desperate conditions can be remedied." The telephone call Morgan was waiting for had not come at four o'clock, and soon afterward he went to bed.

Saying very little, the four New Yorkers breakfasted later that morning in Morgan's sitting room. Bacon had just hung up the telephone after hearing the New York office prediction of a renewed run on the gold reserve and Morgan had pulled out his first cigar of the day, when Olney called to say that the President would meet with them. Without stopping to light up, Morgan called for his hat and coat, and with Belmont and the two Morgan aides falling in behind him, strode out into the bitter February wind and across Lafayette Square to the White House. Carlisle and Olney had already joined the President in his cluttered office in the East Wing. All three of them were heavy-eyed from lack of sleep. Curtis was not on hand. His letter, sent early that morning to Carlisle, suggesting that the gap between the proposed interest rates "is nothing compared with panic and suspension," had not gone down well.

Cleveland was not smoking, so Morgan held his cigar unlit in his hand. Although the two men were social acquaintances, there was no small talk. The President brusquely announced that there had been no change in his views: the public bond sale would go on. Having at last reached the official wheelhouse of the nation, however, Morgan did not propose to leave. Apparently without specific encouragement from the President, he and his colleagues took up inconspicuous positions in a corner of the room. During the next three hours they sat, watching and waiting, while clerks shuffled in and out, Carlisle and Cleveland discussed details of the new bond issue and passed papers back and forth, and the telephone rang constantly in the room across the hall, bringing the latest reports of new drafts on the Treasury. At one point Cleveland left the office and was gone for nearly an hour. Meanwhile Morgan sat on the sidelines, unheeded and powerless, "like a messenger waiting for an answer," as his son-in-law later described it, adding, "It was not a situation he was used to." At last, about noon, Carlisle read aloud from a yellow slip of paper a message just received from the telephone room. Only nine million dollars in gold coin remained in the New York Subtreasury. (There were only a few gold *coins* in other repositories, and the bullion holdings were everywhere at an all-time low.) From his corner Morgan broke his silence.

"The Secretary of the Treasury knows of one draft for twelve million. If that's presented today, it's all over," he said.

Cleveland put down the papers he was holding and sat back in his chair. "Have you any suggestions, Mr. Morgan?" he asked. It was surrender. At this moment the President of the United States, noted Lewis Corey in *The House of Morgan*, was like a small businessman who, after a long struggle, is finally compelled by economic necessity to yield to the overwhelming power of the giant combine. "Independent, belligerent, stubborn," he was "yet cannily accepting the inevitable."

Morgan leaned forward and talked fast. He went over once more the details of his proposition, defending the high interest rate as necessary to attract gold from abroad and bring it out of protective custody in this country. In private communications to his partners he had said that $3\frac{5}{8}$ percent would make the undertaking worthwhile, but apparently none of the men in the President's office pressed him to compromise. As for the problem that Congress clearly would not authorize such a private arrangement, he cited a legal basis for the transaction. During a Civil War emergency, Congress had passed a law covering the matter, he told the group, and it could be found in the Revised Statutes. Olney was sent to fetch the proper volume and came back with it open to an 1862 law providing that "the Secretary of the Treasury may purchase coin with any of the bonds or notes of the United States . . . at such rates and upon such terms as he may deem most advantageous to the public interest." In later years Morgan often mentioned that the recollection of this law had come to him during his long hours of Miss Milligan the night before. In fact, it was probably Curtis who had come upon the statute some weeks earlier and had described it to both Carlisle and Morgan. But then, as

Stillman had noted, Morgan was a poet.

A little over sixty million dollars would restore the Treasury reserve to the sanctified hundred million. The contract therefore specified that the syndicates would provide the government with 3,500,000 ounces of gold, which would be paid for with $62,315,400 worth of 4 percent, thirty-year bonds (sold to the syndicates at 104½). At this modest premium, the actual interest rate came down to 3¾ per cent. The bond sale differed from those of 1894 in that it was a private contract, that it cost the syndicates less (the price of the earlier bonds had been 117), and that the syndicate guaranteed that at least half of the gold would come from abroad. Before the meeting broke up Cleveland exacted a further promise.

"What guarantee have we that if we adopt this plan, gold will not continue to be shipped abroad and while we are getting it in, it will go out, so that we will not reach our goal?" he asked Morgan. "Will you guarantee this will not happen?"

"Yes, sir," said Morgan instantly, without consulting Belmont or anyone else. "I will guarantee it during the life of the syndicate . . . until the goal has been reached."

It was now after two o'clock. As the bankers rose to leave, someone noticed there was brown dust all over Morgan's trousers and on the carpet at his feet. In the tense moments of the long morning he had crushed to powder the cigar he had brought into the room unlighted so many hours before.

There is no doubt the little company of men in the President's office that day sincerely believed that, as Morgan was soon cabling his London partners, the nation had been saved from "dangers . . . so great scarcely anyone dare whisper them." They could not have been so naïve as to expect congratulations all around, but they may not have been prepared for the ferociousness of some of the attacks that followed publication of the bond-sale terms. A senator from Alabama described Morgan and Belmont as having first crippled the government and then moved in to strangle it. The New York *World* denounced them as "bloodsucking Jews and aliens," pointing out that the name "Belmont" had originally been Schönberg. And before condemning the contract on the floor of the House, Bryan had the clerk read aloud Shylock's bond, the infamous "pound-of-flesh" contract in *The Merchant of Venice*. Meanwhile Morgan set about drawing in gold. "You can ship any gold you choose," he cabled London, "bar gold, sovereigns, U.S. gold coin, napoleons. . . ." As a mark of his return to favor, it was announced that Curtis would be treated to a free ocean voyage to deliver the European consignment of bonds overseas. The level in the Treasury vaults rose steadily, although the silverite bloc had sullenly prevented the exercise of a clause in the contract that reduced the interest to 3 percent if Congress made the bonds specifically payable in gold, a vote that cost the government sixteen million dollars in interest. By March the bonds the syndicates had been allowed to buy at 104½ were selling for 117, and in June they hit 124.

The goldbugs credited this rise to restored public confidence as the Treasury reserve grew and to the power of the Morgan-Belmont endorsement. The silverites called it proof that the bonds could have been sold without the government's resorting to the expensive and humiliating private arrangement and estimated the joint syndicate's profit at as high as sixteen million dollars. The rumor even spread, on no evidence whatever, that a cut of this profit had gone to Cleveland. Tales of outrageous returns to the syndicate were hardly quieted when, during the inevitable congressional investigation the following year, Morgan said the money he had made on the deal was his business. However, the syndicate book at the Morgan offices in New York showed the profit of the American half of the operation to be just over two million dollars. Of the thirty-one million dollars in bonds allotted to the sixty-one syndicate members, the Morgan and Belmont companies each took a little over a quarter of a million dollars' worth. The Morgan firm's profit, including interest and half of the American syndicate managers' commission, came to $295,652.93. Since the profit from the European operation was smaller, the Morgan company's combined New York and London return was about half a million dollars, or, as Morgan could have pointed out, perhaps half the amount it might collect for straightening out the financial affairs of a minor New England railroad.

The syndicate report takes no account of the expenses of keeping Morgan's promise to Cleveland to protect the Treasury against gold withdrawals and exports. Morgan managed this feat by involving in the enterprise all the country's major banks and investment houses with European connections, inviting them to join the syndicate and share the profits and in return exacting their temporary agreement not to draw gold out of the Treasury or to ship it abroad. To assure their compliance Morgan succeeded in controlling the natural fluctuations of the international exchange rate by such measures as buying notes in New York and selling them in London at a loss to his own firm. Part of his convolute strategy required him to keep the gold reserve below ninety million during the spring months, which he did by holding gold certificates in his pocket ready for presentation at the Treasury any time it moved above this sum. Virtually no gold left the country between February and mid-June, 1895, when he permitted the reserve to rise to $107,000,000. "We see the curious spectacle," wrote Curtis in a letter home, "of the United States finances being controlled by a committee of which J. P. Morgan is chairman . . .

while the Secretary of the Treasury sits practically powerless in his office." During the congressional investigation in 1896, Morgan was asked why he was so determined to keep other firms from entering the negotiations to bring in the gold and see that it stayed. "It would only have made for competition," he said. "And besides, *they could not do it.*"

Before the great bond crisis Morgan was little known outside eastern banking and railroad circles. After it, to the end of his life, his was the name that led the roll of the "insolent money oligarchy" that it became more and more fashionable to denounce. There is no evidence that this bothered him in the slightest. For allowing "Wall Streeters and their gold to roam the administration like panthers in their native jungles," as one western newspaper described it, Grover Cleveland suffered more than name-calling. By stubbornly choosing what he believed to be the good of the nation over party unity, he surrendered his influence in Democratic politics and was condemned to sit helplessly by at the 1896 convention as his party, taken over by the silverites, declared total war on the "cross of gold." Their defeat that November brought about not only the end of the free-silver movement but the eclipse of the Democratic party for half a generation.

The United States went formally on the gold standard in 1900 and left it in 1933. World War I had unsettled all national monetary systems, and by the 1930's the idea of reckoning a nation's honor and credit solely on the basis of its store of precious metal had a nineteenth-century look. Some of the silverites' arguments, particularly those favoring an increase in the amount of money in circulation, were beginning to appear less addleheaded. And as government philosophies change, so, it seems, do those of great banking houses. When Franklin Roosevelt announced that the country was abandoning the gold standard, the only important Wall Street firm to support the move was the House of Morgan.

Special Issue, "The Nineties," 1967

THE FATHER OF OZ

By DANIEL P. MANNIX

L. Frank Baum had failed at nearly everything when he decided to write a book that he hoped might "amuse children"

At the turn of the century, a disillusioned man who had failed at almost everything he had attempted wrote to his sister: "When I was young I longed to write a great novel that should win me fame. Now that I am getting old my first book is written to amuse children. For, aside from my evident inability to do anything 'great,' I have learned to regard fame as a will-o'-the-wisp . . . but to please a child is a sweet and lovely thing that warms one's heart.

The man was Lyman Frank Baum, and his best-known book began to take form when a group of children, led by his own four boys, waylaid him one evening in his modest Chicago home, demanding a story. After a hard day's work, Baum often turned to fantasy as many men turned to alcohol. Sitting down with the children surrounding him, he began to talk. He gave no thought to what he was saying and later wrote in amazement, "The characters surprised even me—it was as though they were living people." Baum told of a little Kansas farm girl named Dorothy who was carried by a cyclone to a strange land where he met a live scarecrow, a man made of tin, and a cowardly lion. One of the children asked, "What was the name of this land, Mr. Baum?" Stumped, Baum looked around him for inspiration. In the next room were filing cabinets, and one bore the letters *O-Z*. "The land of Oz!" exclaimed the storyteller and continued with the tale, unaware that he had added a new word to the English language.

Baum seldom bothered to write down his stories, but he was strangely attracted to this tale. After the children had gone, he went to his desk, pulled out a handful of scrap paper, and jotted it down. The next day, he took his collection of notes to W. W. Denslow, a hard-bitten newspaper artist with whom he had collaborated on an earlier juvenile, *Father Goose: His Book*.

The two men could not have been more different. Baum was shy, delicate in health, and unsophisticated about money. Denslow was aggressive, aspiring, and a heavy drinker; a lady once called him "a delightful old reprobate who looked like a walrus." Denslow outlined an ambitious program for the proposed book—twenty-four of his drawings as full-page illustrations in a six-color printing scheme and innumerable sketches tinted in various tones to be superimposed on the text. Baum eagerly agreed to everything.

Publishers did not. The two men were turned down by nearly every house in Chicago. Baum's conception of an "American fairy story" was too radical a departure from traditional juvenile literature, and Denslow's elaborate illustrations would price the book off the market. At last, George Hill agreed to publish the book according to Denslow's plan, provided Baum and Denslow would pay all printing expenses. The two men turned their royalties from *Father Goose* over to Hill, who thought the new book "might sell as much as 5,000 copies."

It was called *The Wonderful Wizard of Oz* and was published August 1, 1900. By October, twenty-five thousand more copies had to be printed, and thirty thousand more in November—and all this through word-of-mouth advertising. Hill, who had put most of the firm's resources into good, reliable books with a "sure sale" (the majority of which were remaindered), was totally unprepared for such a phenomenon. Unable to believe this fairy tale was really a best seller, he refused to push it until too late. His company failed while he was still trying to rush copies of the *Wizard* off the presses.

But another publisher snapped up the book and it continued to sell. Today, over five million copies of *The Wonderful Wizard of Oz* have been published, making it one of the great best sellers of all time. It has been made into musical comedies, silent and sound movies, puppet shows, radio shows, and LP records. The 1939 MGM Technicolor musical with Judy Garland is now shown on television every Christmas, a recognized American tradition. Judy has sung "Over the Rainbow" more times than anyone can count. There have been some thirty editions of the *Wizard*, and over ten are in print now. A first edition sold in 1962 for $875; another with an inscription by Baum went for $3,500. It has been translated into over a dozen foreign languages and in Russia is being used to teach school children English. A nice Russian touch: the Munchkins (the little people who first meet Dorothy when she arrives in Oz) are described as the Chewing People, the Russian experts reasonably arguing that to munch means to chew. But my own favorite is the Chinese version, in which the Cowardly Lion looks like a very cheerful dragon.

Two years after the *Wizard*'s success, a Broadway producer named Julian Mitchell conceived the idea of doing the book as a musical extravaganza —quite as fantastic a notion as Baum's original inspiration. Delighted, Baum wrote the script, keeping strictly to the book's story line, but Mitchell had a few ideas of his own. The play as it finally appeared featured a chorus in the standard "beef trust" tradition; Dorothy's little dog Toto was transformed into a comic cow named Imogene; and Dorothy herself, a hefty soubrette, fell in love with a "Poet Prince" in the grand finale. But the cast also included two unknown but talented comics: Dave Montgomery as the Tin Woodman and Fred Stone as the Scarecrow. Within weeks, Montgomery and Stone became the best-known comic team in America. Baum protested Mitchell's innovations, but when the play ran nearly ten years and earned him some $100,000 in royalties (then a huge sum), he published a letter apologizing to the producer. "People will have what pleases them," wrote Baum philosophically.

The life of Lyman Frank Baum—he always used the initial L because he considered "Lyman" affected—was nearly as bizarre as those of his Oz characters. His father, Benjamin Baum, was a hard-driving oil man of German ancestry. He dared oppose the formidable Standard Oil Company and won at least a partial victory in the Pennsylvania oil fields. (In *Sea Fairies*, Baum describes an octopus bursting into tears on being compared to the Standard Oil Company.) Benjamin Baum made a comfortable fortune and settled on a large estate at Chittenango, near Syracuse, New York. Here Frank Baum was born May 15, 1856, the seventh of nine children. His mother, Cynthia Stanton Baum, was of Scotch-Irish descent and a strict Episcopalian. She would not even allow the children to play baseball on Sunday and filled the house with learned, solemn individuals whom Baum later caricatured in the person of H. M. Woggle-Bug, T. E. (Highly Magnified and Thoroughly Educated).

Frank Baum was a shy, sickly child. Unable to play games with the other boys, he spent most of time acting out fantasies with a host of imaginary playmates created by giving personalities to everything from his mechanical toys to the chickens he loved to feed. One of these chickens appears in the Oz books as Billina. Once during a walk the boy saw a scarecrow and was terrified by the strange, manlike creature. For months afterward, he repeatedly dreamed that it was chasing him. The dream was so vivid that he could later distinctly recall the phantom's ungainly lope, his lack of co-ordination, and his final collapse into a heap of straw. That this ogre could ever change into the beloved, friendly scarecrow of the Oz books seems incredible, but one of Baum's great talents was the ability to transform a bête noire into an amusing, sympathetic personality.

When Baum was twelve, his parents decided that the sentimental boy needed to be shaken out of his dream world. He was sent to the Peekskill Military Academy. The tough discipline was too much for the delicate youngster, and he had a nervous breakdown. From then on he was educated by private tutors. Baum was always to dislike the military. A favorite theme in the Oz books is the overstaffed army, composed of hordes of generals, colonels, majors, and captains commanding one browbeaten private who is expected to do all the fighting. But Baum was never capable of real hatred: even the officers are affectionately described. A general's explanation for his abject cowardice is the reasonable statement that "Fighting is unkind and liable to be injurious to others."

Naturally enough, the imaginative young man became enamored of the stage and, with money supplied by his father, started a Shakespearean troupe. By his own admission the only successful performance occurred when the ghost of Hamlet's father fell through a hole in the stage. The audience, which happened to be composed of oil workers, was so delighted that the unhappy ghost had to repeat the stunt five times. Baum also tried his hand at playwriting, and one of his plays, *The Maid of Arran*, was a great success with audiences of immigrant Irish because of his sentimental picture of Ireland. Through his mother Baum had developed a highly romantic conception of the Emerald Isle, which may explain why the heart of Oz is called the Emerald City.

Returning home from one of his tours, Baum met a twenty-year-old girl named Maud Gage, daughter of the militant suffragette Matilda Joslyn Gage. The young couple instantly fell in love—possibly because they were so different. The gentle Baum admired the girl's bold outlook, and Maud felt a motherly interest in the eager young dreamer. Also, Baum was an unusually handsome man, slightly over six feet tall with wavy brown hair and a delightful twinkle in his eye. Mrs. Gage violently opposed the marriage, regarding Baum as hopelessly impractical, but in her resolute daughter the strong-minded old lady met her match. There was a stormy scene between the two, while the prospective bridegroom stood by helplessly. The couple was married in 1881.

Soon there was a baby son, and with a family to support, Baum left the theatre and went into his family's petroleum-products business. For a while he sold Baum's Castorine, a patented axle grease. But in 1887 Benjamin Baum was severely injured in an accident, and without the astute old man's guiding hand the business failed.

It was Maud who rallied from the blow and kept the family going. The Baums had two sons now and had salvaged only a few thousand dollars from the wreck of the family fortune. From Aberdeen, South Dakota, where a gold rush was raging, Maud's brother wrote that there were unlimited opportunities for anyone who would open a small store for the gold seekers. So the Baums went to Aberdeen and started a shop called Baum's Bazaar. Maud's brother had been almost right; it was impossible for anyone to fail in a gold rush town—anyone, that is, except L. Frank Baum. He did it by refusing to accept money from those who were destitute. His habit of ignoring customers to sit on the curb outside the store telling stories to groups of enthralled children didn't do the business any good either. In two years, he had 161 strictly nonpaying clients and the bazaar went bankrupt.

Baum then started a newspaper called *The Aberdeen Saturday Pioneer*, setting the type himself and doing most of the writing, including a special column called "Our Landlady." This was a fantasy describing a community where people rode in "horseless carriages" (the first American automobile had not yet gone on sale) or flying machines, did their dishes in mechanical dishwashers, slept under electric blankets, and ate concentrated foods. The cattle were fed wood shavings, having been fitted with green glasses that made the shavings look like grass. (In the Emerald City, everything looks green to the inhabitants, even the sky. The Wizard achieves this magical effect by requiring everyone to wear green-tinted spectacles.) In spite of the prophetic element in these tales, they are simply told as burlesque—or as Baum would have put it, "banter." Neither he nor his readers took such ideas seriously, and the stories resemble the typical "tall tales" of the West more than they do science fiction.

In the tradition of western newspapermen of that period, Baum made a brave attempt to turn his talent for satire against rival editors. He succeeded so well that he found himself challenged to a duel by an enraged subscriber. The two men, each with a revolver low-slung on the hip, were to walk around the town until they met and then shoot it out in now-familiar Grade B movie style. In this crisis, Frank Baum was magnificent. All his latent sense of the dramatic came to the fore, and he made an imposing picture as he strode off from his doorway, while passersby took refuge behind the false fronts of nearby buildings. But as soon as he had turned the corner, Baum, like his Oz general, decided that fighting was unkind and someone was likely to be hurt. He quietly disappeared until the affair blew over.

Maud Baum had her third son in Aberdeen. The father was so sure the child would be a girl that he had even picked the name Geraldine for the baby. He desperately wanted a little girl, and Mrs. Baum made one more attempt to oblige. Alas, a fourth son arrived, and Frank Baum was never to have the little daughter he so greatly craved.

In 1891 the *Pioneer* failed, or as Baum put it, "I decided the sheriff wanted the paper more than I did." The family left for Chicago. Baum had no regrets in leaving South Dakota and the great, barren prairie. A passage in the *Wizard* was to describe his feelings toward it: "Dorothy could see nothing but the great gray prairie on every side. Not a tree nor a house broke the broad sweep of flat country that reached the edge of the sky in all directions. The sun had baked the plowed land into a gray mass, with little cracks running through it. Even the grass was not green, for the sun had burned the tops of the long blades until they were the same gray color to be seen everywhere." Dorothy escapes from this bleak, colorless land to the cool green hills, soft shadows, and clear, fresh streams of Oz, which bore a strong resemblance to the Baum family estate in Chittenango.

But Chicago was not Chittenango. Baum got a job as a reporter for twenty dollars a week, and the family moved into a wretched house with no bathroom or running water. Maud gave embroidery lessons at ten cents an hour. When Baum's salary was cut to $18.62, he left his job with the paper and became a travelling salesman for a crockery firm. About the only recreation the four boys had was to listen to their father's fairy stories, in which Baum himself became so lost that his wife once said rather unhappily, "I honestly don't believe he can tell truth from fancy." These tales were his escape from his miserable existence.

Then Mrs. Gage, Maud's mother, moved in with them. Baum and his mother-in-law had never gotten along well, but he should have been everlastingly grateful to the old lady for one contribution: listening to his stories, Mrs. Gage ordered, "You go out and have those published." Baum laughed at the idea but his wife said firmly, "Mother is nearly always right about everything." Nagged by the two women, Baum sent out a collection of stories suggested by the Mother Goose rhymes, which was published in 1897 under the title, *Mother Goose in Prose*. The illustrator was an unknown young artist named Maxfield Parrish. It was a "first" for both of them. The book did sufficiently well for the publishers to ask for another, so Baum wrote the *Father Goose* sequel, this time with Denslow as illustrator. Then came the miraculous success of the *Wizard*.

When Baum was possessed by his fantasies, he wandered around in a trance. "His best friends could speak to him at such times and he wouldn't recognize them," Mrs. Baum recalled. His characters were intensely real to him. Once when he had not written for several weeks, his wife asked him what was the matter. "My characters won't do what I want them to," replied Baum irritably. A few days later he was back to work. Maud Baum asked him how he had solved the problem. "By letting them do what they want to do," her husband explained. An ardent naturalist, he never hunted, feeling, like the Tin Woodman, that killing animals was cruel. Ozma, the

Ruler of Oz, says firmly, "No one has the right to kill any living creature, however evil they may be, or to hurt them, or make them unhappy."

The format of the *Wizard* is simple. As Baum says in his introduction, he desired to eliminate "all the horrible and blood-curdling incidents" of the old-time fairy tales. He adhered to this principle in all his Oz books. Dorothy melts the Wicked Witch of the West with a bucket of water, but unlike the witch in Grimm's *Snow White*, she is not trapped into red-hot iron shoes and forced to dance until she dies. The Nome King (Baum believed that "gnome" was too difficult for a child to pronounce) threatens to turn Dorothy into a piece of bric-a-brac but does not plan to ravish her, skin her feet, and bind her toes so they will grow together, as in George MacDonald's *The Princess and the Goblin*. The late James Thurber said he had suffered agonies as a child when the Sawhorse, in *The Marvelous Land of Oz*, broke his leg; but the injury did not hurt the horse, nor was the animal put into a furnace and reduced to a little heart-shaped lump while his sweetheart looked on, as in Andersen's *The Steadfast Tin Soldier*. As Robert Louis Stevenson was able to make the dialogue of his pirates seem brutal and coarse without ever using an oath, Baum managed to make his villains threatening without going into specific and horrendous detail, at the same time deftly maintaining suspense and an atmosphere of peril.

Baum also hoped to eliminate the "stereotyped genie, dwarf and fairy." Here again he was remarkably successful. Like all his characters, the Scarecrow, the Tin Woodman, and the Cowardly Lion are distinct personalities; children learn to know them, become genuinely interested in them, and feel concern over their fates.

Dorothy was perhaps Baum's most successful creation. Unlike the immortal Alice, who wanders politely through Wonderland without trying to influence events, Dorothy—although always gentle and innocent—is a quietly determined little girl. She intends to get back to her aunt and uncle, and neither the Great and Terrible Oz nor a wicked witch is going to prevent her. She is undoubtedly the leader of the little group of adventurers: though she turns to the Woodman for comfort, the Scarecrow for advice, and the Lion for protection, they would obviously be lost without her. Dorothy is the descendant of the pioneer women who crossed the plains and the grandmother of every soap-opera heroine who ever faced life. She is as American as Alice is Victorian British.

Most amazing of all was Baum's ability to make Oz a real place. Any child suddenly transported there would instantly recognize the country. It can even be mapped, and has been several times. Baum achieves this effect partly by precise details (there are 9,654 buildings in the Emerald City and the population is 57,318) but mainly by extraordinarily vivid descriptions of the forests, the poppy fields, the rivers, and the winding Road of Yellow Brick.

Baum carried into his own life his peculiar talent of making the unbelievable believable. He was forbidden to smoke because of his heart condition, but he often held a large, unlighted cigar in his mouth. The poet Eunice Tietjens, visiting the Baums at their home in Macatawa on the shore of Lake Michigan, asked why he never lighted the cigar. Baum explained that he did so only when he went swimming. "You see," he explained gravely, "I can't swim, so when the cigar goes out I know I'm getting over my depth." Then he lighted the cigar and walked into the lake until the cigar was extinguished. "There now," Baum said when he returned to land, "if it hadn't been for the cigar I would have drowned."

Baum loved to recount some matter-of-fact event and then embroider it with increasingly grotesque details while maintaining a perfectly serious attitude. The game was to see how far he could go before his listeners realized he was joking. He could fool even his own family, who of course knew the trick. Once he was telling his serious-minded mother a fantastic tale which deceived her for a long time, until she finally caught on and said severely, "Frank, you are telling a story." Her son replied, "Well, mother, as you know, in St. Paul's Epistle to the Ephesians, he said 'all men are liars.' " His bewildered mother, saying, "I don't recall that," got her Bible and began to search until she suddenly realized she been tricked again.

Delighted as he was by the success of the *Wizard*, Baum had no intention of writing another Oz book. Convinced that he had found the perfect formula for writing fairy tales, he followed the *Wizard* with *Dot and Trot of Merryland, American Fairy Tales*, and *The Master Key*, the last a science-fiction story with philosophical overtones. They had only a moderate success. He then tried *The Life and Adventures of Santa Claus*, which many consider a far better work than the Oz books. Unfortunately for Baum, the children didn't agree. He then wrote *The Enchanted Island of Yew*, a story more in the old European tradition. It had only a modest sale. To children, Oz was a real place. These other stories were only "fairy tales."

Shortly after the success of the *Wizard*, Baum had jokingly told a little girl—who was also a Dorothy—that if a thousand little girls wrote him asking for a sequel he would write one. At the moment, that hardly seemed likely, but he got the thousand letters and more. At last, in 1904, he wrote *The Marvelous Land of Oz*, dedicating it to the two comics, Montgomery and Stone. Three new Oz characters appear who were to become famous: Jack Pumpkinhead, the Sawhorse and H. M. Woggle-Bug. Part of the book is a satire on the suffragette movement, but a cheerful one. The pretty General Jinjur defeats the army of the Emerald City by waving a knitting needle but is panic-stricken when the Scarecrow releases some mice from his stuffed bosom. The hero of the book is Tip, a boy who is later transformed into a sweet young girl—Ozma, rightful ruler of Oz. *The Land of Oz* is the only Oz book in which Dorothy does not appear. Baum had a special feeling for her and at first resisted making Dorothy part of a routine series.

By 1904 Denslow and Baum had had a falling-out, and for this second Oz adventure the publishers hired a new artist, a twenty-five-year-old Philadelphian named John R. Neill. Neill's illustrations would become as closely identified with Baum as Tenniel's with Lewis Carroll, or Shepard's with A. A. Milne. Neill made Dorothy a pretty, slender girl instead of Denslow's dumpy farm child, and transformed Toto from a nondescript cur to a Boston bull. Denslow bitterly resented Neill's changes, but the younger man had a quiet revenge. In *The Road to Oz*, Dorothy visits the castle of the the Tin Woodman, who has erected statues of his friends in the garden. Neill drew the statues in Denslow's style and showed his own Dorothy and Toto looking with amazement and amusement at their former selves. To stress the point, he drew Denslow's trademark, a seahorse, on the bases of the statues.

The Land of Oz was nearly as great a success as the *Wizard*, although the children missed Dorothy and wrote Baum hundreds of letters protesting her omission. Baum again tried to do other books. He wrote *Queen Zixi of Ix*, a beautifully plotted fairy tale; *John Dough and the Cherub*, about the adventures of a gingerbread man; and three adult novels which were unhappy mixtures of Anthony Hope and H. Rider Haggard. At last, in 1907, financial pressures forced him to write *Ozma of Oz*. Here Dorothy returns with Billina, the yellow hen, to rescue the royal family of Ev from Ruggedo, the Nome King. Ruggedo was Baum's most successful villain and turns up in book after book. The Cowardly Lion has a companion in the Hungry Tiger (who longs to eat fat babies but is forbidden by his conscience), and Tiktok, said to be one of the first robots in American literature, aids them. The success of *Ozma* was so great that Baum never again wrote an Oz book without Dorothy.

In his next tale, *Dorothy and the Wizard of Oz*, Baum wrote ruefully, "It's no use, no use at all. I know lots of other stories but my loving tyrants won't allow me to tell them. They cry 'Oz—more about Oz!' " In this story, Dorothy and the Wizard are reunited when swallowed by an earthquake and work their way back to Oz via a series of underground kingdoms. With them are a farm boy named Jeb, a cab horse named Jim, and Eureka, Dorothy's pet kitten. As a bird lover, Baum didn't much like cats, and Eureka is a rather unpleasant personality, although Baum admired her independence, courage, and grace.

In *The Road to Oz*, Baum introduced Polychrome, the Rainbow's daughter; Button-Bright, who is always getting lost; and the Shaggy Man. In his search for realism, Baum used a curious device. There are four countries in Oz, each with its individual color, and as the characters move from one to another, the pages of the book change to the appropriate shade. Baum was still complaining, "I would like to write some stories that are not Oz stories," and at Ozma's birthday party, he introduces characters from his other books—Queen Zixi, John Dough, and King Bud of Noland—obviously in hopes of weaning children away from the land of the Wizard. Finally, in *The Emerald City of Oz*, Baum made a determined effort to bring the series to a halt. Although Oz is almost impossible to visit, because it is surrounded by the Deadly Desert (Baum liked to call it "the Shifting Sands"), Glinda, the Good Sorceress, now makes the country permanently invisible. The book ends with a letter from Dorothy, "You will never hear anything more about Oz because we are now cut off forever from the rest of the world. But Toto and I will always love you and all the other children who love us."

The panic that struck juvenile circles can only be compared to the consternation that hit London when Conan Doyle threw Sherlock Holmes off a cliff. For thousands of American youngsters, finding a new Oz book under the tree had become part of Christmas. A staff member at a children's hospital wrote Baum that the books were such a valuable morale booster that "they are as integral a part of our equipment as a thermometer." One of the most touching letters came from a mother whose little son had died of a lingering illness. "Only when I read your books to him could he forget his pain. As he died he told me, 'Now I will see the Princess of Oz.' " In spite of such heartbreaking entreaties, Baum refused to continue the series. Instead, he wrote two books about the adventures of Trot, a little California girl, and her companion, Cap'n Bill, an old one-legged sailor. In *Sea Fairies*, the two have adventures with mermaids and in *Sky Island* go to a land above the clouds. To make the stories more appealing Baum brought in some Oz characters.

It was no good. The children wanted nothing but Oz, and Baum was no longer his own master. He had invested heavily in "Radio Plays," hand-tinted transparencies designed to be shown by magic lantern in conjunction with motion pictures about Oz characters. (There was no connection with the radio, which had not yet been developed.) Baum was convinced that they would be a great success, but the process was too costly and the whole venture was a disaster. Several musicals that tried to duplicate the startling success of the *Wizard* failed also, partly because they lacked the magic of Montgomery and Stone. In 1911, Baum declared himself a bankrupt, listing his assets as "a five year old typewriter and two suits of clothing, one in actual use."

He had no choice now but to return to the Oz books. He wrote eight more, beginning with *The Patchwork Girl of Oz* in 1913. He was now living in Los Angeles and, delighted with the new motion pictures, made eager attempts to enter the field. Backed by such Hollywood notables as Will Rogers, George Arliss, Hal Roach, Harold Lloyd, and Darryl Zanuck, Baum started the Oz Film Manufacturing Company, on a seven-acre lot opposite the Universal Film Company. This venture also failed, and Maud Baum, with her usual quiet but determined efficiency, demanded that in the future all royalty checks should be made over to her. As a result the family remained solvent; Baum could no longer describe himself (as he had to one journalist asking for biographical information) as "constantly bent and occasionally broke."

Baum continued to turn out an Oz book a year, although he was suffering acute attacks of angina pectoris and his heart, never strong and now badly weakened by the strain of his repeated business failures, caused him constant trouble. Under such pen names as Floyd Akers, Laura Bancroft, Captain Hugh Fitzgerald, and Edith Van Dyne, he wrote a constant flow of juvenile novels, none of which even approximated the success of his fairy tales. The house he built near Sunset Boulevard he called Ozcot. Here he lived quietly, raising flowers and feeding the birds in his giant aviary. To children who came from all parts of the country to see the "Royal Historian of Oz" and listen to his stories, the house was a shrine. On May 5, 1919, he had a stroke, and died the next day. Maud Baum was with him to the end. His last words were, "Now we can cross the Shifting Sands."

Children could not believe he was dead. Even today Reilly & Lee, his publishers, get letters addressed to him. The Oz books were continued, first by a twenty-year-old Philadelphia girl named Ruth Plumly Thompson, then by John Neill, and afterward by Jack Snow, who took his work so seriously that he wrote a *Who's Who in Oz* giving the names of all Oz characters and a short biographical sketch of each. Rachel Cosgrove wrote one Oz book, and the series is now being continued by Eloise McGraw and Laurie Wagner. But Baum's originals still outsell their successors by six to one.

During Baum's lifetime and for many years after his death, his books were not taken seriously—except by the ever-enthusiastic children. Now even among grownups there is a constantly growing Oz cult. Baum devotees have formed the International Wizard of Oz Club, whose members collect everything they can find on Baum and learnedly debate such problems as why the Magic Powder of Life (which brings to life everything it touches) didn't animate its own container, and why Professor Woggle-

Bug in his map of Oz put the Munchkin country to the west of the Emerald City when in the *Wizard* the Good Witch of the North says that it lies to the east. In the last thirty years the Baum books have been "discovered" by such notable persons as James Thurber, Phyllis McGinley, Philip Wylie, Clifton Fadiman, and, of all people, Dylan Thomas. Professor Russel B. Nye of Michigan State University, a Pulitzer Prize winner, and Professor Edward Wagenknecht of Boston University have published scholarly papers on Baum.

On the other hand, there has been a violent reaction against him on the part of many librarians, child psychologists, and teachers. His books have been, from time to time, withdrawn from the shelves of public libraries. One librarian protested that the books were "untrue to life and consequently unwholesome for children," and another supported her, claiming that "Kids don't like that fanciful stuff any more. They want books about atomic missiles"—a cheerful prospect which is fortunately untrue: the Oz books continue to outsell almost all other juveniles. In Russia the story is given a slightly anti-American slant—for example, Dorothy lives in a Kansas trailer, and knows little about life because the American books she has are such shoddy productions—yet on the whole the Land of Oz has proved to be as inviolable behind the Iron Curtain as anywhere else. It is a unique tribute.

—December 1964

THE WINDS OF RUIN

By C. W. GUSEWELLE

Each year thousands of tornadoes spin their way across the American landscape, and the worst of them are as terrifying as anything nature has to offer

A stifling spring or early summer afternoon draws on toward evening. To the west and south, a sullen cloudbank, swollen with moisture, pulsing with electrical display, rides up on the push of hot Gulf air.

Back-lighted by late sun, the advancing storm front can be seen to churn and shift and tumble in mighty collisions. But now, on the ground, the last memory of a breeze has subsided into a wrapping, oppressive stillness. A breath, it seems, scarcely can be drawn.

Farmers later may remember, or *seem* to remember, in these suspended moments an unaccountable agitation among the livestock, and city folk recall a strange unease.

The quality of light changes. The trees, each leaf frozen perfectly in place, the houses, the arrested figures of the people standing with faces upturned southwestward—all are bathed in a greenish glow, as if viewed through a discolored glass.

At last the terrible expectancy is broken by a new rising of the wind, lashing the upper branches of the trees, and by the sudden horizontal blast of rain that is the outrider of the storm. Almost as quickly as the telling of it, the temperature falls—ten degrees, fifteen, or more.

And much oftener than not, that will be all. The cloud line will rush over and away to north and east, and the people will come out again to see the last dayglow on their newly washed world, or collect olive-sized hailstones from the grass to ice their drinks.

Ordinarily it is so, but not always. For of the numberless such storms that sweep the continental United States each year, between six hundred and a thousand of them will contain—besides rain and hail—a fearsome capacity to wreck dreams and distort lives, or end them.

Since 1916, when systematic records began to be kept, tornadoes have killed more than eleven thousand people in this country, about 180 a year. Tens of thousands of others have seen their homes or families borne away to destruction. A few have taken that nightmare ride themselves and lived to tell about it, but rarely is the twisting wind that gentle.

One woman plucked from her prairie home by an early Kansas storm was found some distance away by neighbors, who reported that the body had been driven headfirst to the shoulders into the earth.

The first known mention of a tornado in pre-colonial America was in the diary of a member of the 1586 Roanoke landing party. On June 23, he recounts, as the fleet of Sir Francis Drake stood at anchor off the North Carolina coast, there arose a tempest characterized by awesome spouts—the manifestation of a tornado over water—of such violence as to cause all the ships to break loose from their anchors.

Tornadic winds, the most violent of all nature's storms, occur at least occasionally over many other parts of the globe and so were not entirely unknown to the arriving Europeans. But the New World was and is especially cursed.

Meteorologists now know that the collision between warm, humid air pushing northward from the Gulf of Mexico and cold, northern air masses cresting the Rocky Mountains is a key to the not yet fully explained process of tornado formation. In no other place on earth, except perhaps in the northeast corner of the Indian subcontinent between the Bay of Bengal and the Himalayas, are conditions so ripe for their breeding.

In earliest accounts, some U.S. storms, clearly tornadic from their descriptions, were identified vaguely as "gust winds" or "gales" or, wrongly, as "hurricanes." Cotton Mather wondered in print why it was that their fury seemed "oftener [to] fall upon houses of God, than upon other houses," accepting glumly that it was the Almighty's voice speaking through an unleashed Satan. Benjamin Franklin in 1755 pursued a small tornado for three quarters of a mile on horseback, trying to dissipate it with repeated blows from his whip.

No general enumeration of these early storms exists, however. Real understanding of their frequency and true capacity for destruction awaited the push of settlement west of the Appalachians into the worst afflicted regions and, more particularly, the later growth there of large population centers susceptible to ruin of catastrophic scale.

Illustrative is the outbreak of a dozen twisters over thinly settled districts of Kansas, Missouri, Iowa, and Nebraska on May 29 and 30, 1879. The reported toll of 42 dead and 185 injured would today be considered slight for an episode of such violence. In the four states, only one town was struck—Irving, a hamlet of 300 souls in northeastern Kansas.

The Irving funnel was seen to approach from the southwest on May 30 at half past five o'clock and descend on the tiny community with the characteristic roar, as of a hundred trains. Three houses were destroyed, an iron bridge over the adjoining Blue River wrecked, and the water momentarily driven back to expose the river's bed.

That was merely a prelude. Some twenty minutes later, as residents crept from cover to assess the damage, they noticed bearing down on them from the *northwest* an inky cloud of terrifying aspect and dimension. Some witnesses told of seeing one funnel, some two, and some none at all—only a two-mile front of solid blackness advancing "majestically" on the prostrate town to finish what the original funnel had begun.

Fourteen townspeople were killed in that second onslaught, including a mother and her four daughters, ages two through nine, whose bodies were later found scattered nude over the prairie. More than thirty-five others were severely injured, and forty buildings were swept away.

A country newspaper account of that week tells of horses caught up in the wind and deposited wild-eyed and mud-caked in strange pastures, of chickens stripped of their feathers and wild rabbits blown slick of their hair, and of a partly decapitated hog seen wandering the wrecked village days afterward, still "quite alive and . . . apparently at ease."

At the height of the storm, it had occurred to some of Irving's people that the end of the world might be at hand. Afterward, many of them salvaged their belongings and fled back to former homes in the East. But traumatic as the visitation had been for the people of the village, it scarcely even suggested the damage a tornado could wreak on a modern city.

Eighty-seven years later and sixty-five straight-line miles away, after six o'clock the evening of June 8, 1966, William Corbett sat at the kitchen table of his farmhouse southwest of Topeka, the Kansas capital, listening to broadcast weather bulletins. The area was on storm alert.

The radio told of a terrific hailstorm headed this way, Corbett, now ninety-one recollects. Then he looked out his kitchen window, saw the cloud's underside, said to himself, "Hell, that ain't no hail!" and retreated to the cellar with a pet parakeet. The tornado passed a bit to the north, wrecking Corbett's barn but only lightly damaging the house. Unknown to him or anyone, it already had killed an elderly couple several miles west, whose bodies were found stripped of all but their stockings.

John Meinholdt, a volunteer weather observer, had a better view of the storm's approach. From his assigned station atop Burnett's Mound, a prominence at Topeka's southwest edge, he watched the enormous black cloud—still fifteen or twenty miles distant—come boiling in across the farming flatlands toward the city. The storm cell, he was told by mobile radio, did not appear on the weather bureau's radarscope. Meinholdt waited.

About ten miles out, the cloud, preceded by rain and hail, sagged down to touch the earth, not yet in the form of a visible funnel but as a broad, black mass rushing toward Meinholdt and the city. The observer shouted a last warning into the radio, then gunned his truck down off the mound at a safe right angle to the storm's path. Topeka had thirteen minutes' notice.

There was a long-cherished belief, supposedly grounded in Indian legend, that Burnett's Mound, rearing up to block the southwest approach, assured immunity from destructive winds. But this time the killer cloud —now assuming the form of what one witness described as "a big, slick funnel," oozed directly up and over the hill where Meinholdt had stood and descended at seven fifteen with a throaty rumble on the capital.

In a matter of moments, a swath of continuous desolation ranging from one-quarter to one-half mile wide had been chewed through the heart of Topeka. Sixteen persons were killed outright or fatally injured and more than 320 hurt severely enough to need hospital treatment. The property loss surpassed $135,000,000.

In the days to follow, identifiable debris from the shattered city was discovered as far as sixty miles away. One of the artifacts was a homemade chocolate-iced cake, perfectly intact on its plate in a soybean field near St. Joseph in the neighboring state of Missouri.

· · · · ·

". . . there came a great shriek from the wind. . . . Then a strange thing happened.

"The house whirled around two or three times and rose slowly through the air. Dorothy felt as if she were going up in a balloon."

The twister carried the house and Dorothy all the way from the Kansas prairie to deposit them in the Land of Oz. And though that was only a fiction, strange things truly do happen in the whirl of the storm.

A tornado that tore through the community of Kirksville, Missouri, on April 27, 1899, plucked up two women and a boy, carried them over a church, and restored them to earth on the town common one-quarter mile away, scarcely hurt.

"I was conscious all the time I was flying through the air," one of the women reported, "and it seemed a long time. I seemed to be lifted up and whirled round and round, going up to a great height, at one time far above the church steeples. . . . As I was going through the air, being whirled about at the sport of the storm, I saw a horse soaring and rotating about with me. It was a white horse and had a harness on. By the way it kicked and struggled as it was hurled about I knew it was live. I prayed God that the horse might not come in contact with me, and it did not."

The boy also saw the horse, directly over him in the vortex, and experienced the same fear of being kicked. Later the creature was found mud-plastered but uninjured a mile from the town and was returned to its owner.

Especially from rural areas come accounts of cornstalks driven through barn walls and of fence posts left bristling with straws, like the quills of a porcupine, after the storm has passed.

When the western Minnesota town of Fergus Falls surveyed the havoc of a June 1919, tornado that left fifty-nine dead, an automobile was found imprisoned in the crotch of a tree that had been wrenched open by the twister and had sprung shut again when released by the wind. From other storms there are stories of a cow being snatched from its stall while the milker sat uninjured on his stool, of teams of horses being neatly stripped of their harness, and of a railroad locomotive being spun 180 degrees and set down undamaged on the opposite track.

In a pasture at Apperson, Oklahoma, in 1935, a herd of 160 panicked cattle stampeded directly into a funnel. All but five of the beasts were found with their necks snapped.

The Ruskin Heights tornado which raked several suburbs of Kansas City, Missouri, the evening of May 20, 1957, killing forty-six persons and injuring more than five hundred, produced the oddity of a bowl of goldfish perched intact on a table on the slab foundation of an otherwise vanished home.

One survivor of that storm told of seizing his three-year-old daughter by the hair to keep her from being whipped away by the blast. Some are not so lucky.

An Alabama man named Luther Kelley lost his first wife in a tornado that struck the town of Sylacauga in 1917. Fifteen years later, the whirling wind scourged Sylacauga again, and Kelley's second wife was among its victims.

Not all the accounts of the freakish doings of the wind are to be believed. At least they are not authenticated. "For a given storm," says one authority on the subject, "there may be five or ten good eyewitnesses. But let five years pass and that's gone up to fifty or sixty. It's wonderful how time improves memory."

At Texas Technological College in Lubbock, a research group of five engineers and two atmospheric scientists seeks to separate tornado fact from fancy. Since 1970 the members of the team have studied the physical evidence at the sites of thirty-two different storms. They have yet to discover real proof of plucked chickens, hairless rabbits, or wells sucked empty by the funnel. But they have assembled evidence on what Dr. Joseph Minor, director of the Institute for Disaster Research, laconically calls "some impressive missiles."

At Plainview, Texas, a carport roof, its upper surface providing lift like the wing of an airplane, was found to have flown two blocks. On impact, one of its two-by-twelve main beams penetrated the outer brick and inner wooden walls of a house, piercing the headboard of a bed from which a terrified couple had only seconds earlier fled to safety in a hall.

In Omaha the timbers of a school roof—huge members nine by fifteen inches and forty feet long—were hurled fifteen hundred feet and plunged like spears into the ground.

In Lubbock itself, during the 1970 tornado that initiated the research, a steel fertilizer tank eleven feet in diameter and forty-one feet long, with an empty weight of thirteen tons, was moved three quarters of a mile from its original resting place. It may or may not have flown.

Such phenomena provide clues to the actual, rather than mythic, force of the winds.

One absorbing area of inquiry has been the likely·effect of the most violent conceivable twister on a nuclear reactor. Of the more than one thousand tornadoes in a given year, an average of one to four will be of maximum fury. Assuming the hypothetical worst—a super wind and a formidable missile, flung end on for most lethal effect—a laboratory in Albuquerque propelled a telephone pole on a rocket sled against a two-foot reinforced concrete barrier, identical to the walls of a reactor and its safety-related buildings.

The result, observed in high-speed photography: the forward one third of the pole was shredded to sawdust, as if by a giant pencil sharpener. The wall was unmarked.

Kansas has long been known as the "Cyclone State," a distinction sometimes credited to the memorable violence of the Irving tornado of nearly a century ago. Others say it is because early authorities on the subject happened to live and work there, or because Dorothy's flight to Oz began there, or simply because, on the open sweep of prairie, the Kansas twisters are exceptionally photogenic.

The truth is that the state's claim to the title is suspect. In the two decades from the mid-fifties through the mid-seventies, Texas experienced 2,475 tornadoes, against 1,078 reported from Kansas. Measured in lives lost, the fist of tragedy has fallen hardest since 1916 on Mississippi, Arkansas, and Illinois, each with more than one thousand dead, followed in descending order by Texas, Alabama, Oklahoma, Missouri, and Georgia. Kansas ranks a distant twelfth.

The peak of annual activity is reached in the months of April, May, and June, with the time of greatest menace about ninety minutes before sunset and the least peril two hours before sunrise. But these are only the probabilities. In practice, tornadoes have occurred at every hour, during every month, and in every state of the continental United States.

As Topekans discovered, huddled behind the illusory protection of their mound, there is no refuge to be found in folklore. Tornadoes, for instance, like lightning bolts, haven't the least compunction about striking more than once in the same place.

St. Louis, Missouri, has been hit at least nine times by twisters, with the most destructive of the storms—in 1896, 1927, and 1959—arriving at intervals of exactly thirty-one years and four months. A St. Louis University meteorologist noted in a 1959 newspaper interview that the three occurred near the end of sunspot cycles, with the next comparable period due in May and June of 1990. Most of his professional colleagues ascribe the storms' timing to coincidence.

The first of the major St. Louis tornadoes, the one of May 27, 1896, was the most costly in lives (more than three hundred) and dollars (nearly $13,000,000) of any in the United States to that date or for three decades to follow.

Local thunderstorms had been forecast for the day, but without mention of violent winds. Toward noon the clouds mounted threateningly and the barometer began a persistent fall. A preternatural darkness began gathering over the city, and by four-thirty, according to a contemporary account, "it became obvious that the atmospheric conditions were unprecedented in the recollection of the people."

Thus marshaled, the storm commenced its rush upon the city, raucous with thunder, filled with snaking forks of blue lightning, a screwlike funnel dangling shrieking from the parent cloud. Major buildings were reduced to kindling and heaps of bricks along a six-mile track. Mississippi River steamers were ripped from their moorings and smaller boats wrecked and flung about, with loss of life. A two-by-four-inch white pine scantling was driven through a steel girder of the Eads Bridge, whose approach at the Illinois end sustained major damage.

Countless blazes soon erupted, and fire wagons were unable to make their way through debris-choked streets. Unfortunates who survived the wind but were pinned under timbers and other wreckage burned to death before the eyes of their horrified families. By daylight of the next day, the frantic, the grieving, and the curious milled unmanageably outside the municipal deadhouse. The door to the morgue had to be barred.

THE WORST WIND STORM IN THE WORLD'S HISTORY the St. Louis *Chronicle* bannered on the morrow of the calamity. Actually, it had been a tornado of but moderate force, serving only to illustrate that vulnerability increases exponentially with the concentration of people and property.

Comparing data from various points on the twister's course, a St. Louis weather official noted that it had gained in intensity as it entered the town and ebbed as it passed eastward into open country. "The immense increase of surplus heat which had been stored in the walls and streets of the city during the seven weeks previous . . . may have contributed to this," he suggested.

Since up-rushing warm air is the energy that powers a tornado, his speculation was that some storms may literally *feed* on the community they are wrecking.

The next great St. Louis tornado, of September 29, 1927, was again a storm of no exceptional force. But when it had passed—not as a discernible funnel but rather a blurred, grayish-brown cloud mass at ground level, a "fog" as some witnesses described it—seventy-two persons were dead, five hundred more hurt. And the resulting $25,000,000 loss was a figure not to be surpassed until the Waco, Texas, twister of May, 1953.

In a sermon shortly after the storm, a clergyman striving to show the faithful some purpose in their ordeal could improve little on Cotton Mather. "Indirectly," he told them, it was "a visitation from a merciful and loving Providence. . . . Whom the Lord loveth He chastiseth. Chastisement here is better than chastisement hereafter." Having been lashed at the rate of better than once a decade, St. Louisans must consider themselves to be fiercely loved and amply chastised.

Private John P. Finley, U.S. Signal Corpsman, was dispatched a century ago to investigate the circumstances and effects of the tornadoes on the Central Plains. From the assignment he would go on to become the foremost early researcher of the storms, the pioneer in their forecasting.

As early as his 1879 report to the War Department, Finley recommended stationing a special observer at Kansas City during high-risk months to flash warnings of atmospheric disturbances by telegraph to points throughout the lower Mississippi Valley.

Although tornadoes will strike, whether they are predicted or not, he declared, "to get the right information to the proper point before the occurrence of the dangerous phenomenon, thereby affording opportunity to provide against its ravages, is the great desideratum. It can be done." Finley's advice was taken almost to the letter, seventy-five years later, with the location in Kansas City in 1954 of the National Severe Storms Forecast Center.

The center monitors meteorological data from across the nation, alert to the marked wind shifts and to the temperature and moisture contrasts that signal the probability of a weather disturbance as much as twenty-four hours before its occurrence, even before the first clouds have been seen to form.

Two to eight hours before the event, the conclusion is reached that thunderstorms will develop and that some of them could contain twisters. A tornado watch is mounted over an area of twenty-five thousand square miles for six hours. It then falls to local weather offices to decide when the storms will become active in their vicinities and to issue the ultimate warning.

A tornado "hook" may be detected on radar, appearing as a figure six, with the funnel in the bottom curl of the numeral. Unhandily, there are hooks without tornadoes and tornadoes without hooks. Funnel clouds may also be reported by observers, but waiting for that visual sighting could cost the threatened area precious minutes of notice. Often it is a judgment call.

Radio and television stations relay the "take-cover" advisory. Emergency sirens blare. In the gathering gloom, the citizenry scrambles obediently to lifesaving refuge. That is how it is supposed to happen.

But as Allen Pearson, director of the National Severe Storms Forecast Center, observes ruefully, the Maginot Line can be breached. Some cities cannot afford elaborate warning systems. Power sources may fail, stilling the alarms. And there is a human factor. "Back in the fifties, when we first started issuing tornado forecasts, we created some panic—we know that," Pearson says. "Now apathy is our greatest enemy. Some cities have adopted a policy of not blowing the sirens for fear of alarming the public. We've told them what we think of that!"

Pearson sees the immense, preoccupied congregations of humanity in stadiums, at fairgrounds, and at rock concerts as today's especially terrifying targets.

"My own private hell," he confides, "is of a tornado bearing down on one of those. Or on a large mobile-home park in a state that doesn't require tie-downs."

The Memorial Day Indianapolis 500 auto race is attended annually by over three hundred thousand people, perhaps the world's largest sporting crowd. It also occurs during the peak of tornado season. And weather bureau officials in that city report that on a May Sunday in 1972, while some two hundred thousand fans were watching pre-race time trials at the track, a twister did in fact touch down on the far edge of the city.

Though of fair size, it caused no deaths, injuring only twenty people and wrecking several houses along its short course. State police stationed in the tower at the race track could see the funnel clearly across a distance of fifteen miles. Their emotions at that moment can only be imagined.

Then the whirling cloud moved on eastward. And no public address announcement of its passage disturbed the enjoyment of the Speedway throng.

—June 1978

THE OLD FALL RIVER LINE

By OLIVER JENSEN

The bright high noon of the sidewheeler—when you could wake to see the Hell Gate Bridge sliding past your porthole and eat breakfast while the "mammoth palace steamer" tied up at her Hudson River berth

I t all began fittingly enough with Robert Fulton, who planned to vanquish Long Island Sound as he had the Hudson, even though he died, at an untimely fifty, just before the attempt was to be made. And the slow funeral cannonade from the Battery had barely died on the wind when its steamboat, unblushingly named the *Fulton*, paddled up the East River into the dreaded waters of Hell Gate, the narrow passage where the tides rush in and out of the Sound. "A very violent and impetuous current," Washington Irving called it, "boiling in whirlpools; raging and roaring in rapids and breakers; and, in short, indulging in all kinds of wrongheaded paroxysms." Slowly the primitive sidewheeler, her decks piled high with cordwood, made her way through the jagged reefs and entered the broad Sound, reaching New Haven after a journey of eleven hours. Apologizing for the slow time, the engineer told the press that one got pretty poor wood—no resin in it to make a hot fire—in New York at the beginning of spring. It was March, 1815, the year of Waterloo.

Thus, if one excludes a few early experiments, steam navigation began in earnest on this remarkable protected waterway; the *Fulton* was soon plying to New London and Providence, first of a great fleet which would dominate the commerce and travel of New England for over a century to come. Big paddle steamers, gleaming white, ornamental and luxurious, linked the growing cities, touched all the islands and reached up the long tidal rivers, carrying what Ward McAllister called "The Four Hundred" and what O. Henry called "The Four Million." Even though the fare once sank to as little as fifty cents (from New York to Providence, including berth and two meals on board), the lines paid handsomely; stockholders in one of them received six percent, *monthly*. Nineteenth-century steamboat men looked down on the railroads as mere "feeders," and even after through trains ran rapidly along the shore from Boston to New York they maintained, for some time, preeminence with travelers. Old Commodore Vanderbilt and Daniel Drew struggled for power on the Sound before they began to battle for greater prizes among the railroads; its waters were controlled in turn by Jim Fisk and J. P. Morgan the Elder, who eventually brought almost all the various steamboat lines under control of his New Haven Railroad.

Meanwhile, like the dinosaur, the Sound steamer itself waxed to its greatest size and most majestic appearance just before its extinction, victim of a kind of cruel variation in Gresham's well-known law. For, as dear money is driven out of circulation by cheap money, some similar economic imperative requires the elegant in transportation to yield to the efficient (or, at least, the cheap), the dramatic to the drab. Thus the whining Diesel replaces the thundering steam locomotive and the stifling bus the open trolley; so the iron freighter, stamped out by Henry J. Kaiser, a landsman, sails the seas in the place of the tall clipper of Donald McKay. And now the sidewheel steamboat, which reached some sort of apogee in the powerful *Priscilla*, sometime flagship of the Fall River Line, has almost entirely vanished from American waterways. *Priscilla*, launched in 1893, her 440 feet all steel, capable of 21 miles per hour, was accounted the most graceful even after the bigger *Commonwealth* was built in 1908. Roger William McAdam, leading historian of the line, has devoted a frankly emotional book to this one boat. But a generation has grown up since the line stopped operating in 1937, a generation which never strolled the deep-carpeted saloon and decks, eyeing the drummers and men of property and occasional flashy women (could that be *one*? the youthful voyager wondered in a slight tingle of worldliness), and never awoke to peer through the porthole at Hell Gate Bridge and take a hearty breakfast while the "mammoth palace steamer" steamed round the Battery and swung into her Hudson River berth.

Of all the fleets that plied the Sound, there was never any quite like the Fall River Line. Songs were written about it. Nearly all the presidents and most of the great men and women of that long period traveled it—the famous boat train from Boston in the late afternoon, then off the cars and into the boat at the Fall River wharf, in time to dine in the fine sea air while steaming down Narragansett Bay, past Newport, to head around treacherous Point Judith and thence westward through The Race into the Sound. A fine sleep and into New York in time for business in the morning: it was the recommended route.

Strictly speaking, this was the Fall River Line: but to a great many travelers the name came to include, in a generic sense, many of the other lines which the New Haven Railroad, proprietor of the Fall River during the last 15 years of its existence, operated through the waters of the Sound —New York to Providence, to New Bedford, to New London, to Hartford, to New Haven and to other cities.

The Fall River operation, then called the Bay State Steamboat Company, was launched in 1847, backed by, among others, members of the famous Borden family (otherwise celebrated for their sinewy if ill-tempered connection, Lizzie, the ax-wielding parenticide). Of course, other boats had preceded it on New England routes, for example the *Firefly*, which began running between Newport and Providence in 1817. Outraged by the smoky interloper, the masters of the sailing packets offered to carry passengers free if they couldn't beat her. After President Monroe rejected a proffered ride up the Sound on the *Firefly*, she soon went out of business.

Steam came to stay in 1822, when the previously mentioned *Fulton* and the *Connecticut*, bigger ships, with gleaming copper boilers, began a regular summer service to Providence. Presently there were new boats and competing companies; the price of the trip dropped from $10 to $5 in a rate war; by 1828 one could go from Boston to New York, first by stagecoach to Providence and thence by the "fast" *Benjamin Franklin* in a total of twenty hours and fifteen minutes—a trip that might have consumed a week and about $100 a decade before.

In 1835 Commodore Vanderbilt put a boat on the Sound that was accounted magnificent in her time, the *Lexington*, 295 feet long, commanded by his brother. She made it to Providence at sixteen miles an hour, to connect with the steam cars which had just reached that city from Boston, soon to drive the owners of the old Concord coaches into limbo. A few years later the *Lexington* became the first awful casualty of the Sound but Vanderbilt, before his interests shifted elsewhere, was a power in its broad waters. He ran boats to Bridgeport, to Sag Harbor and up the Connecticut River to Hartford, as well as along the Maine coast.

The steamboat proprietors competed fiercely in rate wars and lurid claims, but their greatest joy was racing their boats, government regulations to the contrary being happily ignored. One steamboat promoter, "Liveoak" George Law, a former day laborer, was so proud of his *Oregon*, then on the Stonington run, that he offered to race her against all comers. The *C. Vanderbilt*, another Stonington boat, modestly named for its owner, took up the challenge. The rival craft were stripped down for the race, their bottoms wiped clean. The wager was $1,000, but the real prize was prestige.

As Ralph Nading Hill, steamboat enthusiast (and operator, on Lake

Champlain, of one of the last two American sidewheelers), tells the story in his *Sidewheeler Saga*, Law even had his crew mop up the last bit of moisture from his bilges with sponges. And on a fine June morning in 1847 the race began at the Battery in New York, heading up a Hudson lined with cheering spectators. For thirty long miles they paddled bow to bow. Then, at the turning point near Ossining there was a mild collision, damaging the *Oregon*'s wheelhouse but slowing her not at all. In the confusion, Vanderbilt interfered with his own pilot, and so many signal bells sounded in the engine room that the baffled engineer stopped his engine dead. By the time the error was retrieved, Law in his *Oregon* had a fine lead. But a crisis was soon upon him: in trying to save weight he had failed to carry enough coal and just south of Yonkers, the bunkers gave out entirely. In desperation Law sent his crew after loose benches and chairs and, after they were exhausted, the berths, the doors and even the wainscoting. Black wood smoke poured from her and she lurched forward again. Vanderbilt was gaining but the finish line was too close for him to close the gap.

The Fall River Line's first boat was the steamer *Bay State*, 300 feet long and forty wide, lit by oil lamps at night. Her *cuisine* attained considerable renown, at fifty cents for the grand *table d'hôte* dinner, served at long candlelit tables; ceremoniously the Captain and his guests were seated first, for these were no ferry boats and they affected the grand manner of the transatlantic trade. Very soon the *Bay State* encountered Law's cocky *Oregon*, with her proud owner aboard, and not only bested her in a race up the Sound but even triumphantly crossed the loser's bow, so that there should be no misunderstanding about who had won. The line was so profitable that two new boats, the *Empire State* and the *Metropolis*, could be bought out of profits in a few years. This seemed too good to be true, and Wall Street men listened and moved in to begin a series of major financial mergers and shufflings which lasted over many years.

Only one financier made his personal impression on the Fall River Line, but that made up for all the others. He was Jim Fisk, not so long before a peddler of notions in Vermont, later the owner of everything from railroads to judges. Representing a group of Boston capitalists, he had outsmarted Daniel Drew into selling out his rival steamboat interest, no small achievement in itself, and this made him a power, the president of a great steamboat line. It was 1869, expansion was in the air, the line's business was booming. Fisk found himself the master of the then outstanding *Bristol* and *Providence*, great walking-beam steamers of nearly 3,000 tons, able to carry over 800 passengers each in luxury unparalleled for the time. Fisk filled them with thick carpets and fine fixtures. Bands were employed to serenade the customers and into each of the two ships went 250 canaries in cages, each of them personally named by Fisk, a man of elephantine and often childish humors. His vanity was prodigious, but he could be soft-hearted, bestowing free trips on strangers who caught his eye, granting pensions to old-timers in a day when this kind of paternalism was a rarity.

"If Vanderbilt's a Commodore, I can be an Admiral!" he once exclaimed, and bought himself a gaudy Admiral's uniform. Leaving Mrs. Fisk to dwell in luxurious embarrassment in his house at Boston, he lived openly with his mistress, Josie Mansfield, in New York, buying her a female version of his Admiral's suit so that the frolicsome pair might board the *Bristol* or *Providence*, to stroll arm-in-arm through the gaping crowds, greeting friends and issuing loud orders until the ship had passed around the Battery and they could be taken off in a pilot boat.

After Fisk's death, when his rival for Josie's affections shot him on the stairs of the Grand Central Hotel one day in 1872, the line changed its name again, to the Old Colony Steamboat Company, which was under railroad control. Later it was absorbed, along with the Old Colony Railroad, by the New Haven in the 1890's. Competition was brisk, principally from the Stonington Line, which took to calling itself "Old Reliable," only to run two of its best ships aground one after the other, and then to have two others, the sister ships *Narragansett* and *Stonington*, collide off Cornfield Point, near Saybrook, Connecticut, with a loss of 27 lives. Presently this line too was swallowed up in the Morgan mergers.

Meanwhile, the waters of Long Island Sound were witnessing what seemed like fresh miracles almost every year. In 1881 the Norwich Line launched the first large iron steamer to travel the Sound, the *City of Worcester*; she had the first electric lights—and had them nine years before the White House. When the Fall River Line brought out its own great iron double-hulled ship, the *Pilgrim*, two years later, the company's blurb writers were carried away. She slept 1,200 persons. Her paddle wheels "feathered." She was "unsinkable." "She is lighted with 1,000 incandescent electric lights, aggregating 12,000 candles, and Mr. Edison has exhausted his inventive faculties in fitting up this magnificent vessel."

Presently other pleasure domes taxed the descriptive powers of the writers even further—the "artistic as well as seaworthy" *Puritan*, first to hide its walking-beam, which weighed 46 tons, under a special covering. (Why hide such a handsome piece of machinery? Remember, the age also put skirts on table legs.) She was done "in the style of the Italian Renaissance." Then there was a new *Providence*, in "French Renaissance," and the massive *Commonwealth*, largest of the Sound steamers ever built, which capped the climax by being decorated in no less than seven different architectural styles. Fortunately, for those oppressed by the ever-changing and rambunctious *décor*, there were the windows in the dining saloon, the largest ones ever installed, and beyond them the calm waters of the Sound, the lighted towns and headlands, the winking lightships and occasional thrill of a passing steamer or a schooner heeling over under sail.

The officers of the line, who often drew on several generations of the same family, were proudest of the safety record. There were accidents now and then—groundings, collisions, anxious moments and heroic ones; once the *Priscilla* and the *Commonwealth* rescued the entire passenger list of a sinking competitor, the brand-new *Boston* of the Eastern Steamship Lines; again, in a heavy fog in 1912, the *Commonwealth* rammed and, to the nation's amusement, badly dented the new armored dreadnaught *New Hampshire*—but the record stood: only one passenger lost in ninety years.

Many factors contributed to the final demise of the Sound steamers. The opening of the Cape Cod Canal, for one, brought new competition from the Eastern Steamship "all-water-route" boats (although they and other independents have vanished now, too). The growth of through rail service at low prices made a further cut. The private automobile caused the deepest inroads of all. As the 1929 Depression wore on, line after line disappeared until at length only the Fall River route remained of all the once far-flung New Haven Railroad steamboat network. The boats often ran with a bare handful of passengers.

Then, one day early in 1937, when business was picking up again but the ferment of early New Deal labor disputes was on, unheard-of events transpired at the piers of the old Fall River Line. The *Commonwealth* and the *Priscilla*, each making ready to get under way at opposite ends of the route, were suddenly hit by sit-down strikes just as the cry went up: "All ashore that's going ashore!" No cajolery, no threats would avail. Special trains were assembled hastily to carry the disgruntled passengers. For a few days the crews remained aboard, eating the supplies until even the cornflakes were gone. Then the management, with equally dramatic suddenness, seized its opportunity. Company spokesmen went to the ships and read an announcement: the Fall River Line was finished, forever. No one could believe it at first, sailor or traveler, but it was true, and the famous old floating palaces were ignominiously towed away, to Providence first and finally to the ship breakers. They fetched, the four surviving ships, a mere $88,000, a miserable sum when matched against an investment of some $6,000,000 and a tradition on which it is more difficult to place a valuation.

But it was not really the strikers that did it, however ill-timed their action. Nor was it the Depression. It was Gresham's disagreeable law, for which the blurb writers of our own time, however, have another name. Their word for it, interestingly enough, is Progress.

"YOU PRESS THE BUTTON, WE DO THE REST"

By BERNARD A. WEISBERGER

"All I had in mind," said George Eastman, "was to make enough money so my mother would never have to work again"

In the year 1854 a young man named George Washington Eastman rather reluctantly maintained a residence in Waterville, New York. The reluctance arose from the fact that while the hamlet was pleasant enough, its population of a few hundred souls offered no scope for the ambitions and needs of a father of two little girls, with a third child on the way. George Washington Eastman was a teacher of the arts of business, and to find pupils he was obliged to leave his wife Maria, and little Ellen and Emma, for regular trips to Rochester, some seventy miles to the west. As a busy stop on the Erie Canal and a flour-milling center with other growing industries, Rochester furnished a supply of young men to enroll in Eastman's Commercial College, which he opened there to instruct them in "Commercial Penmanship and Book-Keeping by Double Entry," as used in all branches of "Trade and Commerce, Including Wholesale, Retail, Commission, Banking, Manufacturing, Shipping and Steam-Boating, Individual Partnership and Compound Company Business." The cost —diploma included—was twenty-five dollars. An extra five allowed students to take the "teacher's course," which included "Ornamental Penmanship in all the Ancient and Modern Hands."

On July 12, 1854, the new baby—a son, named George—was born. Six years after that the hard-working father moved the family to Rochester and finally eliminated his back-and-forth journeyings. Two years later he died. It is a pity that George Washington Eastman, professor of business, did not live to see his son grow up and become a master of wholesale, retail, manufacturing, and "compound company" affairs—one of the top dozen or so among a generation of entrepreneurs who transformed the United States into a twentieth-century society. For George Eastman belongs on the muster roll of capitalists whose specialty was to wed the scientific discoveries of the nineteenth century to mass-producing and marketing techniques, and thereby to create enormous quantities of goods for Everyman. They made the consumer king, and like court necromancers won favor by providing royalty with comforts, gadgets, and diversions. Like Thomas Edison or Alexander Graham Bell or Henry Ford—to name but a few—Eastman was able to combine his own hunches, his grasp of theory, and other men's ideas in sharply focused inventions that had immediate, practical, common utility. Like them, too, he was able to orchestrate the work of engineering and merchandising experts so as to put the invented device into the hands of millions.

His presentation to mankind was the inexpensive, popular camera. At first glance it may seem an instrument of much less social gravity and consequence than the electric light, the telephone, or the automobile. But it is worth recollecting that the camera, joined with electric lights and motors (in inventions by Edison), created the movies; that the camera, crossed with the electron gun, is responsible for television. In a certain sense Eastman carries the awesome paternity of the modern age of the image, with all its deep effects on man's consciousness and sense of reality.

His childhood and youth seemed commonplace enough, though they were given something of a harsh edge by economic adversity. George Washington Eastman's death left his widow almost penniless. She kept things going by taking in boarders, and the children grew up watching her struggle bitterly with the chores of housekeeping on a pinched budget. George adored his mother and swore from the start that he would repay her for her efforts and sacrifices some day. It became a lodestar in his life.

Still it was not a bad childhood. Young America liked to think of its future heroes as having been specifically toughened by the tasks of frontier farming. But Eastman was a city boy who never split a rail or hunted for the family's supper. He was a quiet, undistinguished schoolboy, on the whole seemingly more given to prudence than to pranks. He had a knack for tinkering, and likewise a strong attachment to capitalist economics, at an early age. Once he constructed an ingenious puzzle out of wires. An admiring friend asked for it as a gift, but young George demanded, and got, cash on the barrelhead—reputedly ten cents.

At fourteen, like most of his self-sufficient peers, Eastman went forth to wrestle with the world, his formal schooling done. He found a job as an office boy in an insurance company. Though his initial tasks included such lowly assignments as cleaning the boss's cuspidor, he worked his way steadily upward to clerk. Later he became a junior officer in a bank. His salary began at three dollars a week. By the time he was in his early twenties, the bank was paying him a then very comfortable fourteen hundred a year.

From the start he showed a great sense of the value of a dollar, an instinct for organization, a gift for management. He began to keep a pocket notebook, meticulously recording his expenses to the penny. Though the entries showed the profile of a careful young man, Eastman was not entirely dedicated to work and money. Along with the notations of expenditures for clothes, meals, and other necessities there were items for candy, visits to places of scenic or historic interest, horseback rides, shooting galleries, and other moderately frivolous diversions. He enjoyed leisure; in fact in later life he was to insist that he did not really like to work. And he made the appropriate moves in the direction of self-improvement expected of a young man in that era of high seriousness. He bought a flute and books in French, though whether he got very far in learning to use either of these marks of cultivation is not clear. He bought dumbbells to help develop his muscles. Nor did he seem neglectful of growth in a social direction. Some of his expenditures were for ice cream and other treats for girls whom he took out on the rounds of Rochester's pleasures. But he formed no serious attachment to any single one—his notebook records his escorting three different girls, at various times, to one of the town's chief attractions, the roof of the seven-story-high Powers Building. Nor did his dates diminish his attachment to his mother. He was prolific with small gifts for her, and from her shoulders he took an increasing load of responsibility as he grew older—ordering furniture and carpets, supervising spring cleaning, and in other ways acting as head of the household. But for all these expenditures, outgo was carefully kept below income, and at each year's end a banked surplus of earnings was entered in the account book. Later some of this reserve would go into interest-bearing bonds, real estate, and other enterprises that happily illustrated the breeding properties of money properly laid out.

He seemed methodical, and perhaps a touch dull. It was not simply a question of respectability, but of style. Things had to be complete and in order. In 1876, for example, he treated himself to a trip to Philadelphia to see the Centennial Exposition. "Today," he wrote to his mother, "I finished the Machinery Hall and some small buildings, and about halfway across the end aisle of the Main." The results of this dutiful touristic pilgrimage were interesting; the machinery was "bewildering" to him, but he admired the "ingenuity that exhibitors have displayed in arranging . . . apparently uninteresting articles."

Arrangements always beguiled him. In later life, on camping and hunting trips that became favorite pastimes, he delighted in supervising the packing and in concocting intricate nests of boxes to protect fragile contents, or dividing supplies into parcels of exactly equal weight so that pack animals could be given identical loads. The quest for efficiency also showed in his domestic arrangements. He devised premeasured packages of cake and bread mixes to carry on his safaris long before they were marketed commercially; he triumphantly announced to friends in 1882 his discovery of a way to filter coffee grounds by pouring the boiled coffee through absorbent cotton. He was an inveterate gadgeteer.

One would have tabbed him for possible success—but in a carefully circumscribed and unadventurous field. Older, knowing associates might have predicted that he would become a banker and a spare-time creative hobbyist. The odds on his dealing in a product whose commercial career would require innovation and risk seemed low, if one examined his patterns up to 1877. But then photography entered and transformed George Eastman's life.

It began simply enough. In 1877 he planned on a vacation trip to Santo Domingo, then in the news because of recent American interest in annexing it or at least establishing a naval base there. One of Eastman's friends at the bank had been a photographer on the expedition led by John Wesley Powell that explored the canyons of the Colorado River. He suggested to George that a photographic record of his Caribbean excursion would be well worth having. Nothing loath, Eastman plunged in —and the plunge was a deep one. The trip never materialized, but Eastman was committed to the new art from the beginning. The first step was a heavy investment in equipment. In later years he wrote that when he began as a photographer, one did not take a camera on a trip, one "accompanied an outfit of which the camera was only a part."

The process then used was wet-plate photography, in which the image was recorded on glass plates coated with a light-sensitive emulsion. It was necessary to prepare the plates immediately before use and expose and develop them before they dried. To achieve this a formidable amount of gear was required. Eastman's initial purchases—the bill of sale for which he carefully preserved—came to over fifty dollars, a goodly sum in 1877, and subsequent acquisitions raised his opening investment in the art to more than ninety dollars, which possibly did not include the five he paid someone for lessons. The starting kit included not only the heavy camera itself, together with a tripod, plus plates, paper, boxes for storing negatives, and a tent that could be set up as a darkroom, but also the furnishings of a small chemistry laboratory—nitrate of silver, acetate soda, chlorides of gold, sodium, and iron, collodion, varnish, alcohol, litmus paper, hydrometer, graduate, evaporating dish, funnel, bristle brush, scales and weights, and washing pans. All of this had to be packed along to the site of the picture taking, which therefore became a hobby only for the affluent and for the extraordinarily patient and dedicated.

It would become Eastman's fate to change all this. The mysterious internal process that drew him at once to become deeply involved with the camera is beyond the historian's probe. It is enough to say that the young bank clerk began to spend increasing amounts of time behind the lens and in the developing room, and to read everything he could lay hands on concerning photographic techniques. At some point his pastime began to demand a share of his energy that could have encroached on his business career if he had not decided to make his pastime his business. This turning point was reached some time in 1878. Later on—perhaps with the benefit of hindsight—Eastman expressed a philosophy that explained the development of his career. Though he enjoyed reading about science, he declared in a magazine article written when he was nearly sixty, the intellectual adventure of pure research was not fulfilling. "There is, to me," he said, "more adventure in putting each discovery to the ultimate test of public use, for then the discovery becomes an addition to everyday life." If this was, in fact, a belief that he held at twenty-four, it explains why he moved quickly toward making photography more efficient and more available to others.

Eastman's first interest, like that of other photographers at the time, was in devising a dry plate, which would eliminate the awkward need for immediate development of a shot. The problem was to find an emulsion that would keep its sensitivity even when dried and held in storage. In the journals of photography, both British and American, to which Eastman subscribed, enthusiastic amateurs exchanged recipes for such emulsions like gourmet cooks. He himself joined zealously in the quest. He continued to work at the bank by day, but at night he would return to the rented house faithfully kept by his mother, eat supper, then go into the kitchen to measure, pour, stir, and test for hours on end. He had great powers of concentration. Often he would remain at this task overnight, and when this proved too taxing, he set up a cot so that he could fall upon it, fully dressed, for restorative naps. A youthful constitution buoyed him through these rigors, and by 1880 he had invented and patented not only a dry plate but a machine for preparing large numbers of such plates quickly. The basis of his process—not the only one on the market, to be sure —was an emulsion containing gelatin, which when dried adequately protected the sensitized surface against the hard knocks of shipment and usage.

Now he vaulted into the world of self-employment. He had his patents, he had three thousand dollars in savings, and to strengthen his hand he took a partner. One of his mother's boarders had been Henry A. Strong, a likable manufacturer of buggy whips who had grown attached to Eastman and who would one day write him: "You are a queer cuss,

Geo., . . . but I want you to know . . . that I am always with you heart and hand. Never take my silence for indifference. . . . We surely are neither of us very demonstrative."

Undemonstrative or not, Strong had enough faith in his young friend to join him in renting one floor of a factory building and commencing the operations of the Eastman Dry Plate Company, which officially went into business on New Year's Day, 1881.

The first year was sweaty and successful. No longer the leisure-loving young bachelor, Eastman worked with incredible energy at finding jobbers and customers, publicizing the firm, overseeing the physical details of production—and improving the product. He would not rest content with merely an entry into a branch of the photographic-supply business. "The idea gradually dawned on me," he recollected later, "that what we were doing . . . was not merely making dry plates, but that we were starting out to make photography an everyday affair." Or, as he afterward put it more crisply, to "make the camera as convenient as the pencil."

There were ups and downs. In the first three months the firm got enough orders to occupy six employees. And before the end of 1881 the company was in larger quarters, in a four-story building on State Street, Rochester's major downtown thoroughfare. Eastman had also gone abroad, found dealers, and set up offices in England. But then disaster almost overwhelmed him. Reports came back to Rochester from across the Atlantic: plate after plate made by the firm had turned out to be defective.

Eastman met the crisis with dispatch. He set associates to work around the clock checking factory operations to see what was going wrong, and immediately took ship for England to examine the defective stock. He then, figuratively, took a deep breath and sent a message to every customer: each and every bad plate would be replaced without charge. There was no way of knowing the extent of this commitment when it was made. For all Eastman knew, his entire product for months might have been useless. As it turned out, however, only a single batch of emulsion had gone bad, and only a limited number of plates had slowly deteriorated on wholesalers' and shopkeepers' shelves. Eastman emerged from the episode with a solid reputation for standing behind his product.

By early 1883 the bit was in his teeth. He wanted to go beyond dry plates, which were still, after all, fragile and space-consuming sheets of treated glass. Photographers were now looking for something else—a material that would be lightweight, flexible, easily stored (perhaps in the camera itself), and durable—a "film" on which images could be captured, to be printed later.

Eastman did not conceive of the idea of film on his own. He was not the first or last man to experiment with an eye to creating it, and some of his company's basic patents were discovered by others and only purchased by him. (At least one inventor claimed priority on a fundamental Eastman process, and won his lawsuit.) Yet Eastman was the persistent, determined leader who put the power of organization and capital into the quest. It had taken him but five years—1878 to 1883—to move from amateur picture taking to success as a manufacturer of equipment that made life easier for thousands of other amateurs. In just the next five years he would move most of the remaining distance toward the goal of a camera "as convenient as the pencil."

Film was the key innovation. The problem was to find a substance that could be produced in a continuous strip—like a set of dry plates joined together—drawn past the lens, and subjected to the handling that would turn exposures into prints without stretching and tearing. The first result achieved by Eastman and his coworkers was an emulsion containing collodion, which was a solution of nitrocellulose in ether and alcohol that dried to a tough film and had been used to coat plates and in other photographic applications since the early days of the art. (It was also esteemed by doctors for holding dressings in place and covering wounds and lesions.) This emulsion was spread on a strip of paper and dried. The paper, which provided the necessary tensile strength and spooling properties, was stripped away after exposure, and the film proper could then be processed successfully. In 1884 Eastman's company took out patents on this American Film, as he called it, and prepared for an assault on the market. He reorganized his firm under a new name, the Eastman Dry Plate and Film Company. Its capital was increased to $200,000. Half of that was the estimated value of the patents held by Strong, Eastman, and an associate named William H. Walker, and half was new capital. The simple partnership of Eastman and Strong was on its way to becoming a major corporation. In 1885 a device called a roll holder—an attachment for any camera, which carried a supply of the paper-backed film—was patented.

The film and holder by themselves were important steps but not enough to guarantee the creation of a true mass market for cameras. There were handling problems that involved inexperienced users in disaster —most especially the stripping operation, during which the film often was pulled out of shape or hopelessly ripped. Eastman saw that what was needed was a "complete system" that could somehow be utilized by anyone, even a photographic ignoramus wholly unaware of the very definition of such words as "lens" and "negative" but simply anxious to have a picture of what he saw before him. The answer would lie in both a better film and a better camera.

While the quest for film was in progress, Eastman's plant, and others, had been working toward small and light cameras to replace the heavy, tripod-mounted instruments that, with their long bellows, were familiar in studios. A few box-shaped hand cameras were available early in the 1880s, and because they sometimes were unrecognizable as photographic equipment, they theoretically allowed subjects to be taken unawares. For this reason they were called detective cameras. Eastman designed and marketed one in 1886, but it ran into production difficulties. It was not fated, therefore, to be what he was really looking for—a camera "that would take pictures in the hands of a greenhorn."

In 1888 that camera was born. Into the world came Everyman's magic box for freezing moments of personal history into pictorial permanence. All in the wink of an eye, the click of a shutter, it could imprint a memory on a piece of paper for time unending. If photography itself was something of a miracle, this made the miracle instantaneous and almost anyone a miracle worker. The new camera bore a strange name, proudly worked out (and later explicated) by Eastman. "Kodak," he called it, because "a trademark should be short, vigorous, incapable of being misspelled to an extent that will destroy its identity and—in order to satisfy trademark laws—it must mean nothing. . . .

"The letter 'K' had been a favorite with me—it seems a strong, incisive sort of letter. Therefore, the word I wanted had to start with 'K.' Then it became a question of trying out a great number of combinations of letters that made words starting and ending with 'K.' The word Kodak is the result. Instead of merely making cameras and camera supplies, we made Kodaks and Kodak supplies. It became the distinctive word for our products. Hence the slogan: 'If it isn't an Eastman, it isn't a Kodak.'"

It was a superb trade name; it had something of the snap of the lens-opening mechanism about it—something brisk and decisive. It was a near-palindrome, almost impossible to forget or misspell. And like "Victrola," "Thermos bottle," and "Scotch Tape"—all manufacturers' names for brands of record players, vacuum bottles and cellophane tape —"Kodak," as Eastman desired and predicted, became the perfect trademark, a synonym for the product itself.

The primal Kodak—the Model T of cameradom—was compact by standards of that time. It was 6½ inches long, 3¼ wide, and 3¾ inches high. Made of wood, it had a fixed-focus lens. It could easily be carried in a leather case. The picture it took was round and a scant 2½ inches in diameter. And it cost twenty-five dollars. The owner was emancipated from any concern with even the simplest mechanics. The camera came already loaded with enough film for one hundred exposures. The shutter was snapped, a key wound to advance the film, and a string pulled to recock the shutter. And when the last photo was taken, the user simply sent the entire box back to Rochester. There Eastman's specially trained workers opened it, stripped the film, developed the shots, and returned to the sender his finished prints, and the camera, reloaded. This cost ten dollars, but it meant that once the initial cost was absorbed, a Kodak buyer was getting pictures at ten cents apiece. No matter how much of a duffer he was, moreover, if he could point the camera at a target in enough light, he could count on capturing the scene. Eastman's advertising slogan was not only inspired in being concise and personal but, unlike many such statements, was also literally true. It said, with majestic simplicity: "You press the button, we do the rest."

Eighteen eighty-eight was Kodak's birth year. Eighteen eighty-nine saw another major step. A chemist hired by Eastman, Henry Reichenbach, had been busily working for three years on a film that would not need any backing. Eastman was spurred on in the search by requests from Thomas Edison for something that he could use in the motion-picture camera he was developing. It would have to be tough enough to be perforated and whirled rapidly through sprocketed wheels, and it would have to be capable of being produced in great lengths.

Reichenbach built upon experimental foundations that had already been laid in treating collodion with various substances and that had resulted in the invention of celluloid in 1868. He finally found that a mixture of camphor, fusel oil, and amyl acetate, dissolved in a solution of nitrocellulose and wood alcohol, would dry to form a transparent negative film that needed no support from paper or anything else. The discovery not only opened the door to movie making but it emancipated even Kodak users from the extra step of returning their films to the plant for stripping and processing. The way was now open for development at home or, in time, at any of numerous photographic stores, and eventually corner drugstores. The new film was a crowning touch.

R eichenbach and Eastman did not know that almost simultaneously with their application for a patent for this new kind of roll film a New Jersey minister named Hannibal Goodwin had come up with an essentially similar invention. Goodwin lacked the funds to make the necessary tests, so he did not receive his patent for another eleven years. Eastman, on the other hand, was able to rush into the marketplace. Goodwin's patents later found their way into the hands of the Ansco Company, and in 1914, after lengthy litigation (and after Goodwin's death), a court ruled that Eastman had to pay Ansco five million dollars, despite his grumbling that "Mr. Goodwin never made a roll of film." By then Reichenbach had long since left the Eastman company—fired after a quarrel and the discovery that he was planning to set up a rival firm. So neither of the two inventors of film shared Eastman's later reputation as the true begetter of popular photography, a fame which he deserved, but more as promoter and manufacturer than as sole scientific discoverer.

The nineties opened, therefore, with the Kodak in existence—a simple box camera using flexible film, suitable for mass production, and achieved only twelve years after Eastman had first acquired for himself the cumbersome paraphernalia of photography. In his second decade as a businessman Eastman pyramided his firm into a multimillion-dollar trust. He did so by a combination of techniques that would become familiar in other branches of industry. They included heavy advertising; a steady drive to control all the steps in the production process, from raw material to finished goods; a reach for monopoly; and relentless improvement and cheapening of the product. Kodak was a model for what was going on elsewhere in American industry in those economically stormy and significant years. Modern America's tastes, habits, and industrial productive patterns were emerging, and Eastman's success came in part through his careful estimates of what their ultimate shape would be.

Advertising had ample room for growth in the nineties. Technology had produced newspaper presses capable of each day turning out hundreds of thousands of copies of newspapers containing dozens of pages. And in those pages there was ample display of illustrated appeals to buy the varied array of ready-made goods pouring out of the country's factories. Urbanites especially—a growing segment of the population —were steadily exposed to tempting pictures of boots and shoes, bonnets and corsets, patent medicines and packaged foods, rugs and furniture, watches and hardware, sewing and washing machines, baby buggies and pianos, stoves and so on, almost endlessly. In this world of huckstering Eastman moved with boldness and a brilliant sense of direction. In May of 1889 he took full-page advertisements in all the major magazines —*Harper's, Century, Scribner's, Harper's Weekly, Frank Leslie's, Puck, Judge,* and *Life*—to sing the praises of the new film (which he was convinced would "*entirely* replace glass plates, at least for amateur work . . . as fast as the goods can be made"). This campaign of magazine advertising was never relaxed, and its themes varied. The basic chord was "you press the button," but testimonials were solicited showing the variety of uses to which the Kodak could be put. A doctor's wife took pictures of patients' visible symptoms to assist her husband. A passenger agent of a railroad took shots of the scenery along the route and used them as display ads. Burton Holmes, a travel lecturer, naturally found the Kodak indispensable for bringing back evidence of the attractions he described.

The great were frequently cited as Kodak users; one advertisement noted that the wife of Chicago's traction magnate Charles Yerkes and likewise Mrs. George M. Pullman, whose husband manufactured the famous sleeping cars, " 'press the button' of the Kodak with good results." It was, of course, an extra attraction that even ladies, presumably daunted by anything mechanical, could easily work the camera. In England, Eastman got additional advertising leverage from celebrities. Prince George and Princess Mary (later King George V and his queen) were Kodak carriers. Rudyard Kipling was willing, one assumes for a consideration, to declare publicly that he was "amazed at the excellence of the little Kodak's work." In 1897 a huge electric sign flashed the Kodak name over Trafalgar Square. One somewhat spectacular plug was in a little-known Gilbert and Sullivan operetta, *Utopia*, which introduced two "modest maidens" who sang:

Then all the crowd take down our looks
In pocket memorandum books.
To diagnose
Our modest pose
The Kodaks do their best:
If evidence you would possess
Of what is maiden bashfulness,
You only need a button press—
And we will do the rest.

Such messages—and by 1899 Kodak's advertising budget was up to three quarters of a million dollars per year (as contrasted with forty-eight million in 1970)—found a ready audience because of a social development that was accelerating steadily as the old century died and the new replaced it. This was the increase in popular leisure and in activities to fill it. The period from 1890 to 1910 saw, among other things, the bicycle craze; the proliferation of outdoor hiking clubs; the beginnings of automobile tourism; the heyday of vaudeville; the early, crude movies; the development of baseball into a universally enjoyed spectator sport, with a network of major and minor leagues; the beginnings of big-time college football—it is possible to go on in a Whitmanesque fashion. Increasingly, Americans who lived above the poverty line took to diverting themselves, and the camera was a perfect companion. Society was ready for the Kodak.

Eastman also prepared for the conquest of mass markets with a steady program of expansion, reorganization, and strategic control of all the avenues and byways of the picture business. At one point he wrote with enthusiasm to Strong: "The manifest destiny of the Eastman Kodak Company is to be the largest manufacturer of photographic materials in the world or go to pot." There was little chance of a journey potwards, however. A reorganization of the Eastman Dry Plate and Film Company in 1890 capitalized the corporation at a million dollars. In 1892 another session with bankers and lawyers resulted in the Eastman Kodak Company of New York, capital five million. In 1898 there was still another meta-morphosis, and a new structure including Kodak, Ltd., a large British subsidiary, was set up, with a capitalization of eight million dollars. East-man made a personal profit of $960,000 as the arranger of the reorgani-zation and enjoyed reporting that when he elatedly told his mother: "Mother, we have a million dollars now," her sole comment was: "That's nice, George." By then materials-manufacturing centers had been set up in a number of countries, a new factory exclusively for cameras had risen in Rochester, and a vast plant for general photographic-supply manufac-ture was in existence on a plot of land in the little township of Greece, adjoining Rochester. Greece has long since become part of the larger city, but Kodak Park is still the dominant element in its economic landscape.

The full extent of Kodak expansionism was revealed in a new creation in 1901. At that time large corporations were making efforts to cir-cumvent the eleven-year-old Sherman Antitrust Act, which, theoretically at least, placed a barrier in the way of the mergers that were taking place at an accelerating rate. One acceptable device was the holding company, which owned the stock of various subsidiaries and managed them as one, though they remained technically independent "competitors." New Jersey's legal code smiled on holding companies, and so, in the same year that saw the creation of the world's first billion-dollar corporation, United States Steel, Eastman Kodak of New Jersey was likewise incorporated. Its capi-tal was certainly more modest than U.S. Steel's, a mere thirty-five million, but it was no infant. The companies involved were Eastman Kodak of Rochester, the General Aristo Company of Rochester (an establishment manufacturing photographic paper and supplies), and Kodak, Ltd., of London—these three with factories in Rochester and Jamestown, New York, and Harrow, England; and in addition the Eastman Kodak Société Anonyme Française and the Kodak Gesellschaft, headquartered respec-tively in Paris and Berlin. All these operating firms had branch offices in New York, San Francisco, Liverpool, Glasgow, Brussels, Lyon, Milan, Vienna, Moscow, St. Petersburg, and Melbourne.

By 1907 Eastman would be the boss of five thousand employees around the world. By 1915, during the first administration of Woodrow Wilson, he would also be under heavy attack from the United States government as a monopolistic superpower of photography, dominating more than 80 percent of the market and forcing suppliers and dealers throughout the country to dance to his tune and accept his terms.

Kodak's response was to point out the existence of at least four other important camera manufacturers, eight makers of film, and a number of rivals in the supply business. But the fact was that none of them approached Eastman's giant company in scope, and finally, Eastman was forced to avoid federal prosecution by authorizing an out-of-court settlement that divested his organization of several subsidiaries. The company remained large and diversified, however—sometimes to the bemusement of its founder, according to one story of post–World War I years. At that time the company went into a number of allied fields arising out of its chemical operations. These included the manufacture of cellulose, wood alcohol, and other ingredients and by-products of film. Among the spin-offs were synthetic fabrics, and when Eastman was shown some Celanese neckties made by his company in 1930, he mused aloud: "All I had in mind was to make enough money so that my mother would never have to work again."

This huge expansion rested, ultimately, on Eastman's ability to deliver what his advertisements promised in the dawning age of ballyhoo—a good camera, which, through the years, became more and more portable and inexpensive. In 1890 a folding model of the Kodak appeared, enabling some reduction in the size of the basic box. Further work yielded the Pocket Kodak in 1895, which was so instantaneously successful that within a short time after its announcement Eastman's European demand alone was for two thousand a month, and he was writing that he would "strain every nerve" to boost production to six hundred daily. In 1898 the Folding Pocket Kodak was introduced, only 1½ inches thick and 6½ inches long, producing a 2½-inch-by-3½-inch negative, which remained the standard for years.

Like Henry Ford, Eastman was eager to get his product into the maximum number of hands. He preferred the profits of a mass rather than an elite market and therefore insisted on production economies and technical improvements that cut costs so that the price steadily sank from the twenty-five dollars asked for the original Kodak. The Bull's Eye model of 1896 (one of many variants of the basic camera in differing finishes and cases) cost twelve dollars, and a more modest type, the Falcon, was only five. In 1900 Eastman reached the apparent ultimate in price reduction, however, and also made a shrewd bid for a future generation of Kodak users, with the Brownie. This small box camera cost a single dollar. It took a six-exposure roll of film, purchasable for fifteen cents. It was advertised as something that could be "Operated by Any School Boy or Girl," and Eastman Kodak encouraged the youngsters to form Brownie

Camera Clubs (blank constitutions, prepared in advance—like Eastman's bread mixes—were sent out on request) and to compete for prizes for the best pictures made with Brownies.

It is hard to know if any photographic careers were begun with Brownies, but there is the testimony of the distinguished pioneer Edward Steichen that he began with another Eastman Kodak model. It was a secondhand detective camera sold to him when he was sixteen, in 1895, and loaded in the darkroom by the dealer. Beginners may be cheered to note that when the fifty-exposure film was returned, only one shot was found printable.

Halfway through 1904 George Eastman celebrated his fiftieth birthday. It was a triumphant half-century mark. He was a mighty entrepreneur and a wealthy man. In the next year he demonstrated his affluence by moving into a new residence that was in effect an upstate New York palace. Its three stories contained thirty-seven rooms, twelve bathrooms, and nine fireplaces; it was surrounded by gardens and hothouses, for Eastman loved flowers; and it had two organs, for he was likewise fond (though somewhat undiscriminatingly) of music. Its walls sported originals by Corot, Whistler, Rembrandt, and Titian, and its library had fine editions, mostly untouched, of Thackeray, Dickens, Hawthorne, Scott, Balzac, and Trollope. The installation of Eastman and his mother in their new estate was celebrated with a dinner party that spoke volumes about the Kodak King's style and taste. The guests were fed caviar, bouillon, halibut timbales with truffle sauce, breaded sweetbreads, tenderloin of beef with mushrooms, partridges with bread sauce, pumpkin pie, and nesselrode pudding, all washed down with vodka, Rhine wine, punch, and champagne. After this aristocratic banquet, a quartet sang *Boys of the Old Brigade, America, In the Good Old Summer Time, Marching Through Georgia, It's Always Fair Weather, Annie Laurie,* and *Teasing.* Then there were fireworks, topped off by what the handsomely printed and bound menu and program called "A Few Acts of Vaudeville."

Two years later Eastman's mother died, and he never took another woman into the house to be its mistress. Hundreds of guests occupied it, enjoyed the fresh flowers, and shared with their host his regular mealtime concerts by a private organist and his weekly evening musicales. Eastman also liked to invite the pretty young wives of his business associates and other friends to luncheons, at which he would cook for them, shower them with small gifts—and scrupulously avoid any deep relationship with any of them. Though Rochester gossips were always ready with rumors of secret liaisons, Eastman lived in a house that always had about it something of the affectedness, the lack of human seasoning, of a wealthy and lonely bachelor's residence. He was a comforting and comfortable host, yet sometimes he seemed to be on display in his own home.

At the company's headquarters, his role changed. He remained the chief of a deliberately simplified organization, making the big decisions and constantly reviewing the figures that were forever being neatly columned for his eyes. But a huge array of managers, assistant managers, superintendents, assistant superintendents, foremen, and assistant foremen (375, all told, in 1908) kept operations running without his intervention in the day-to-day details that it had once been his challenge and pleasure to oversee. The research department plunged ever deeper into complex chemical problems beyond Eastman's theoretical grasp, though when results were achieved, they were presented to him to develop, to market, and to enfold in a kind of parental pride. He was far from a stranger to his own organization—but he was also no longer the man who, with Strong, Reichenbach, Walker, and others, had dirtied his own hands at drawing tables, fussed over emulsions, and experienced the elations and glooms of those moments when a new idea is first tried.

Without a wife and children or an active, participating role in his company's work, Eastman needed other outlets for his energies, and he found them. He became a major benefactor of the city of Rochester, which he had given wealth and status beyond the dreams of even the most ambitious promoters. ("Wherever the photographic art is practiced," a local newspaper beamed in 1898, "there Rochester is known. . . . As the purchaser turns to Pittsburgh for steel . . . and to Chicago for grain, so does he turn to Rochester for photographic goods.") Eastman financed an orchestra, a theatre, a Municipal Bureau of Research, and a Chamber of Commerce building for his fellow townsmen and poured money into the modest University of Rochester, enabling it to add a distinguished medical school and a music conservatory and to upgrade itself dramatically in endowment. He also exerted a strong influence on Rochester's political life. Overtly, he put his support in the 1920s behind a conversion of the city's government to a city-manager format (a businessmen's and reformers' dream of efficient, nonpartisan rule). What other pressures he and Kodak exerted are still shadowed. It is enough to say, however, that one associate recalled, after Eastman's death, that he was the object of "near-hatred" to some Rochesterians who resented "the enormous control he exerted over his fellow citizens." The sound of civic applause may have drowned out the hisses, but they were there.

Rochester, however, was not the limit of his philanthropic outreach. He gave away nearly seventy-five million dollars before his death. A large share of that sum went to the Massachusetts Institute of Technology. (A modest as well as a generous giver, Eastman donated to M.I.T. for many years under the name "Mr. Smith.") There were also generous benefactions to two Negro colleges, Hampton and Tuskegee, and to dental clinics in various cities of the world—a pet project, for some personal reason. Merely keeping track of the projects financed by his gifts could have become a totally absorbing occupation in itself. But Eastman also found time to play, after his fashion, as befitted the man who had taught the country to picture itself at play. He was an inveterate hunter, roaming the world at the head of large parties of friends and servants and bringing back from Africa and other exotic places packing cases laden with skins and heads for the walls of his home. Naturally, there were always copious photographic records of such safaris, made by the best and latest equipment.

He owned houses and lands; he owned a great corporation; in a sense, he was an important part-owner of the city of his rearing. Yet the report of everyone close to him was that he remained somewhat shy, content to ascribe his condition mostly to destiny, even slightly oppressed by a sense that he had a continuing responsibility to prove his usefulness to the world. He seemed to struggle against taking success or happiness for granted.

Sometime during 1931, when he was seventy-seven, Eastman began to suffer from a spinal ailment that threatened to make him a cripple. On March 14, 1932, he retired to an upstairs bedroom and, tidy to the end, neatly laid a folded towel over his chest and put a bullet through his heart. Beside him on a table was a note: "To my Friends: My work is done. Why wait?"

It was a lean, undemonstrative final farewell, in keeping with the style he had set himself. Perhaps the problem of his later life was that, in a sense, his work was already done by 1901, when the burdened but briskly moving days and nights of experiment and effort culminated in the great company that had created the camera that anyone—anyone at all—could buy, use, and enjoy. Perhaps the rest was only a comfortable twilight.

—October 1972

THE WOODS WERE TOSSING WITH JEWELS

By MARIE ST. JOHN

An intimate memoir of twentieth-century pioneers in the Florida wilderness

In 1899 when I was five years old and living in Palmetto, Florida, my father decided to take his family through the wilds of the Everglades and stake a claim on an offshore island. His purpose was to farm this island but behind this was his wish to give us a taste of the way he grew up. He had been a cowboy in the Myakka area when he was fifteen years old. These ranchlands overlapped the north end of the Everglades at a time when it was unexplored. As long as he lived, papa liked his corn bread made campfire style with boiling water and salt only, and flattened out into a brittle, tasty cracker.

His life was a series of adventures. He had lost a father and a brother in the Civil War. His father's carriage house in Charleston, South Carolina, and his nearby plantation were in the line of Sherman's march. His widow took her eight-year-old son, my father, and fled to Quincy, Florida. When Papa finished school at the academy there, he worked as a cowboy on a ranch in Myakka for a friend of his dead father's. By age thirty, he was a county sheriff, no mean job in those days, and his territory was wide ranging. The county he served was later split into six or eight counties.

South Florida was uninviting to many because of the mosquitoes, panthers, crocodiles, swamps, and wetlands. But these marks of wild country called to my father like the legendary siren song.

He started building a covered wagon around the fourth of July and we went into the wilderness with him in the fall. We had made our home in Palmetto for a year or so where my mother's gentle folks, the Harrisons, had settled following the Civil War. Our comfortable two-story frame house on the Manatee River was set about with live oaks, guavas, and long-leafed pine that branched out from the foot of the tree to shelter our cow and provide a roost for the chickens. My grandfather was the town doctor. He doctored the entire county and was paid in eggs and ham and vegetables when they were in season. It was an idyllic life, and we lived close to our family and to the comforts and safety a small town could afford. But Papa was a man of enterprise; he realized that the untouched Ten Thousand Islands off the southwest coast of the state were rich in soil for crops and in game for food.

I will never forget the day we started. As always when we were to go anywhere, we rose early. Papa hurried us, saying, "We don't want the day to catch us. " I told my dolls good-bye without knowing that I would never see them again. When at last we were in the covered wagon with papa, mama, and the baby on the front seat and Bubba, Hal, and me in the back, my father lifted the reins and we were off. My stomach turned over, I was that excited. Despite the fact that there was so much to be happy about, I began to whimper. "What's the matter with her?" papa asked, thinking Bubba was teasing me. "I'm afraid day's going to catch us," I explained, wondering what great disaster might befall us if it did.

We had been keyed up for this adventure by weeks of planning. Around the supper table and again on the porch at night, papa described the wonders and pleasures this trip held. Even after we had gone to bed, the talk sometimes would continue through the open doors between our rooms. His descriptions were not exaggerated. The memories of this trip have colored my life.

The covered wagon had a wide drawer that would slide under the body of the wagon, handle and all, so it could be pulled out from the rear. In this deep and roomy box was packed our camping equipment and food supplies. The camping outfit consisted of a huge tent, a folding cot apiece, folding chairs, and a table. Our outdoor cookware was of heavy black iron. One big kettle stood up on three long legs to sit over a fire. There were dutch ovens, tin cups, cutlery, and bowls. The blankets, sheets, pillows, and other bedding were rolled in a canvas and tightly strapped. This "cushion" was fitted into the body of the wagon and served as a seat for the three of us who rode in the back.

We looked forward to plentiful game and wild fruit on the road, but took ample provisions—fifty-pound lard cans full of flour, oiled sausage, coffee, lard, molasses, grits, rice, sugar, and salt. And there were two hams, a wheel of cheese, jars of fruit and jelly, and sacks of oats for the horse. Papa's box of tools was most impressive to look at. He had every kind of implement for hand farming, plus guns and ammunition for hunting, and fishing tackle for each member of the family.

I wish I could make you see the little stores, all alone, way off in the backwoods where we would stop to replenish our food stock from time to time. They were stocked with everything from plowshares to spools of cotton thread. Occasionally a blacksmith's shed would adjoin the store, so Dave, our big bay horse, was kept in comfortable shoes.

The first day out is as vivid to me today as it was then. We took a deeply rutted wagon trail through thick woods, across prairies, and right across ponds and creeks where the water was shallow. Each time we forded water, the horse and our hunting dogs took a long drink and we children would hop down out of the wagon and walk across, splashing each other and cooling down. Off and on all day, we jumped out and walked behind the wagon with the dogs to stretch our legs.

That first night we stopped in a pine forest. Chiggers can't tolerate turpentine, so we were free of this small pest. The thick ground of straw was sweet to inhale. Added to this was the smell of mama's cooking ham and coffee. While mama and I fixed supper, papa and the boys pitched the tent. Then it was to bed inside a cozy tent where we could drift off listening to night sounds.

The second morning, like so many to come, I woke up smelling bacon. It was dark, still night, but time to get started. The morning did not turn bright; the sky was overcast all day. By early afternoon the rain came in torrents. Papa knew a man out there in this sparsely settled backwoods and was able to find his house. We drove up to his gate. Dogs met dogs and there were dogfights. This brought the man's family out on the porch. They peeked at us as though we were creatures from another world. As soon as the man recognized papa, we were made welcome. Dave was fed and given a dry stable to sleep in. The man's wife asked us to eat with them. Mama told Hal and Bubba to get food from the wagon and she spread it on the table. This was a treat for these people, but we liked their boiled greens and fried pork equally well. The rain and wind sounded like wild horses on the tin roof, but we were warm and dry. All that night, mama sat up, going from one to the other of her family to keep the bedbugs from devouring us, a hazard of the Florida backwoods of those days.

The rain stopped and we were on our way at dawn. Mama kept her fingers crossed with the hope that none of the little bedfellows had elected to go with us.

This third day out, and the days to come, found us in the unsettled wilds of Florida. Sometimes we would strike camp early enough for papa and the boys to shoot fox squirrels or quail for supper. No matter what time of day we came to a good fishing place, we would stay for the rest of the day. One such place was a white-clear stream that ran out of a spring in a vast cypress swamp. Its underwater grasses looked like green ribbons constantly unrolling, and the trees held thick sprays of wild orchids. Papa had given each of us a pole, and what with six of us fishing and the fish so plentiful, we usually had a catch in a matter of minutes. As an added treat papa sometimes would cut the heart out of a cabbage palmetto, and mama would cook it, slowly, in the black kettle. There was no shortage of these groves. Always, it seems, we were in or near a grove of cabbage palmettos.

One day I got sick and had a high fever. We were near Arcadia but still too far to drive on. So papa pitched camp and went on into town on horseback and brought a doctor back with him. We had to stay in camp for several days until I was well. Then we drove on to a small crossroads and stopped at a hotel, a two-story frame building no larger than a big house, until I was strong enough to resume the journey.

As we drove off, Arcadia with its dirt streets and free-roaming cattle, its barns and outhouses, looked like a metropolis. We were not to see such a city again for over a year. Soon enough our eyes were bugging at the size of the oak trees that grew in clusters wherever the earth rose up from the flood plains of the creeks and rivers. These lush hammocks were green with ferns. The burly arms of the oaks were huge with fern and blooming bromeliads. Redbirds, tanagers, and painted buntings flew back and forth across the trail, leaving a child with the impression that the woods were tossing with jewels.

One bright morning we came to a wide river, the Caloosahatchee, at Alva. Alva was a dot on the road marked by the fact that it had a ferry. This ferry was a huge, flat barge that had to be poled. The river was swift and deep and Dave balked, but papa led him onto the ferry and we were soon on the other bank, driving off to Esterr. Esterr was a commune of Koreshians, folks who believed that they were living inside the earth like the figures in a paperweight. Their leader, Silverhorn, taught the communist manifesto but, at the same time, claimed to be a reincarnation of Jesus. This Messiah had accepted the possessions of his followers. They appeared to be his slaves, and indeed, they did worship him. He instructed them that when he died he would be resurrected (but he wasn't, a fact that came to our notice many years later). He had so ordered his commune that the men, women, and children lived in three separate dormitories. The children were cared for by people who did nothing else. Everyone had his or her duties to perform and there was no idleness.

Despite the order and industry, both of which my parents admired, they were stunned by the fact that children were taken away from their parents at so early an age. We stopped here for several days, and Silverhorn invited papa to join his sect. To tease us, papa said he had signed up with them. I was relieved to learn that we were leaving the next day with our family intact.

At Naples we sold the horse and wagon and bought a boat, a sloop with a cabin. Loading our things into this craft we boldly set sail into the rollicking gulf. Things went well until, just off of Cape Romano, we encountered a squall. We headed out to sea, which frightened my landlubber mother, and I at once sensed her fear. Papa had to shout above the wind and rain so that the boys could hear his orders. When mama and I from inside the cabin heard him yell, "Let her rip," we thought the end had come. He hastened to see what all the screaming was about and assured us that there was no danger. Just the same, I have always looked back on that event as one of the narrowest escapes I ever had!

We made port at Marco, a landing pier and little else, where we were met by people who knew papa and who gave us a grand welcome. In fact, it seemed that everyone knew papa everywhere he went. He was a small man with immense vitality. His curly red hair was worn longish in the style of the day. His sharp blue eyes were a constant clue to his wit and charm. I was quick to own up to being Jim Martin's daughter.

We visited a few days at Marco and then sailed south for Everglades City and Chucoluskee, one a landing pier, the other a mud bank. Finally we came to Edgar Watson's place, a sugar plantation on the Chatham River.

Watson was an infamous outlaw. Every lawman in southern Florida was acquainted with his treachery and cunning. He had secluded himself in this remote area of the Everglades because he was not welcome elsewhere; from time to time he was halfheartedly sought for trial, though few crimes seemed to lead directly to his door.

The legend persisted, however. The native whites feared him as you would a rattlesnake, but the Indians and black people were susceptible to his manipulations. Frequently hungry, they would go to work for him, cutting cane. He rarely paid the money agreed upon, and if a worker rebelled, Watson was said to execute him on the spot. I heard that countless human skeletons were left bare in his bayou once when a hurricane blew the water out. The bayou filled the next day, and it was business as usual.

This merciless man had an invalid wife whom he adored. He kept fifty cats for her to pet; of course, I was intrigued with them the day we docked at the sugar plantation. I remember Mr. Watson taking me on his knee and telling me to pick one out for my own. He seemed the kindest of men.

Not without trepidation, papa made arrangements with Watson to bring lumber, roofing, and other materials needed from Fort Myers to build our house, which we would do with our own hands and the help of friends. Like other people in this lost place, we were dependent on Watson's big boat, which made regular runs to and fro. We felt this dependency even more after we settled and commenced to farm. There was no other way to get our produce to market on a steady basis. The stranglehold Watson had over this section of Florida was not dissimilar to the unscrupulous activities of certain lawmen, other legal crooks, and even governors that our state was to suffer through its history.

We left Watson's that same day for our destination. This first home was to be a weather-boarded shack on a small island called Gopher Key. It was twenty miles further up the river, then out into an expansive bay and through a creek that wound like a tunnel among the hundred of islands offshore. Some of these islands were so close together that this creek often was shaded over by mangroves.

It was sundown when we arrived at Gopher Key, where we would stay until the big house was built on a neighboring island. There was the little shack, not the most gracious of living quarters, and there was a murderer for our nearest and only neighbor, about thirty miles away. Nevertheless, we moved in with our folding cots for beds and our canvas seats for chairs. I do remember a crude table, with a long bench to sit on. There was also, and most important, a cookstove.

The island was virtually a hammock. It was covered with thick green growth. There sprung to life, in no time it seems, a splendid garden under the care and interest of our entire family. We had a variety of vegetables on the table each day. These were supplemented with every kind of wild game and seafood. We had fresh venison and wild turkey any time we wanted it. We fished for sheepshead and snapper by rowing a few yards from the house. Daily, right in front of the house, papa fired the shotgun several times from behind the blind he had built on the edge of our stream, and of the thousands of ducks that quacked us awake at dawn he would bring in a dozen or more to be smothered in sage. My mother saved the down we plucked from the ducks that winter, and there was eventually enough to make a feather bed.

On our swimming excursions that winter to the outer islands, we gathered clams for fritters and chowder. The oysters we got along the sides of the clear tidal creeks were as big as a man's foot.

Papa took his family wherever he went except when he went deer hunting. This is when I wept because I was not a boy. My big brothers, aged eight and eleven, were crack shots with a rifle and always accompanied him.

The three of them never failed in the hunt. King Richard in his gluttony never sat at a table more sumptuous than ours was three times a day.

Our list of providers grew when papa's young nephews and cousins migrated to join him. These five boys had lived with us off and on all their lives. They slept with my brothers in the tent until, with their help, we finished our big house. There were several weeks when the building activity was intense. During this time it was up to my mother, my baby brother, and myself to supply meat for the table. Thus we often caught fish or dug mussels. Once, after a nice catch of sheepshead, mama remarked on how prettily they had browned. Hal, who was the first to taste one, said happily, "The fish down here sure are sweet!" They were to his liking, but mama sadly discovered she had used sugar instead of salt on them.

During this same period, this sweet-toothed boy stayed home from the building site to take us farther afield for the day's catch. Hal took our small bateau into a deep, clear channel no wider than a creek and stopped in the shade of the overhanging mangroves so we could fish. Suddenly he turned white and pointed down through the water. We looked, and protruding from beneath the boat was a huge fishtail, waving rhythmically. Then we looked on the other side of the boat and saw the body and head of a giant sawfish. Slowly and silently we eased the boat away and reached home, still shaken. One flip of that powerful tail and the tiny boat would have been capsized like a toy. My little brother, Orr, who had not yet learned to swim, could have been caught in the current and carried out to sea. Papa returned to the spot with his rifle and killed the fish. We still have the saw, with a picture painted on it by a young teacher who boarded with us years later. Papa cooked the flesh outdoors for the hounds and extracted the oil, which he bottled for use on guns and boots.

Orr came home safely that time, but I almost lost my little brother on Gopher Key. Frequently he was put in my charge, and to further ensure our safety, my parents asked us to play in a part of the yard that was surrounded by tall, slender cacti that kept the panthers away. But once Orr wandered out and down to the creek. When I missed him and ran to get him, I saw he was being stalked by an alligator who had come up behind him and was opening his mouth. The alligator, although large enough to take us both for hors d'oeuvres, was surprised by my running feet and backed away. I took Orr's hand and fairly jerked him through the air to get him back to the house. The gator literally got its hide tanned by papa.

These frights were soon forgotten because Christmas was approaching. This meant a big box was coming all the way from Palmetto. My grandmother packed something for everyone in this wonderful box; for me there was a small doll. She was made of china and as straight as a little post. She stood no taller than a woman's hand, but I loved her at once. Through the years, some eighty of them, I've kept her safe and unbroken. Grandma sent me a storybook, too, which I memorized from cover to cover. These two gifts meant much to me because we had received word that our home in Palmetto had burned to the ground and that only the piano and parlor furniture had been saved. I had lost the large family of beautiful dolls I had left there.

Of all that happened to us on Gopher Key, I remember one thing the best. Every night, mama read to us until bedtime. Everybody in the family and any visitors gathered around to hear Dickens, Thackeray, and the Bible. During that first year, mama read our entire set of Dickens, and I remember much of it.

O ur new two-story house was finished that spring. Papa had built it on an old homesite known as the Chevalier place. The original settler had been a Frenchman by that name. He had planted guava and avocado pears, and they were now huge trees. The site had a nice gradient up from the sea; the big house in the trees looked safe and sturdy.

Our new home was more than safe; it was a joy. We had beds to sleep in and chairs to sit on. It took many trips, however, to bring all our things from Gopher Key. I was allowed to go on these exciting hauls. Once as we entered the long creek that led to the old place through a tunnel of mangroves, we were hit by a flock of ducks flying through. In self-defense the boys batted them down with oars, and there was our supper.

As soon as we got moved in, papa and the seven boys planted a crop of tomatoes on our large, fertile island. The tomatoes grew enormous, and our family kept growing, too. Papa's mother came to live with us, and his brother, my Uncle John, migrated down and was living between our place and the Watson plantation.

I'll never forget the morning I looked out my bedroom window and saw Uncle John walking up from the landing. The night before, I had overheard papa and the boys talking about a manatee they had seen that day. I had asked what a manatee looked like, and from their description of it I got the idea it was a man covered with hair. Seeing Uncle John for the first time with a full beard, I yelled to my father, "Oh, papa, here comes the manatee!" All in all he got an excited welcome. With the two brothers reunited, the family felt the need for some real celebration. Thus we took picnic trips.

One of the special excursions for Uncle John was, of course, to the outside beaches, the islands that fronted on the gulf. They afforded beautiful swimming all year, and once a year yielded sea turtle eggs in the hundreds. We usually took no more than half a cache, a practice, which if it had been continued through all these years, would not have depleted the turtle population. For fun we sometimes would sail out on calm moon-lit nights and anchor just to watch the hundreds of female turtles coming and going about their business. They were monstrous creatures but cumbersome and harmless as long as you didn't get near that traplike mouth. We children hopped up on their rough backs for short, bumpy rides into the water, where we were dumped. Often we found as many as five hundred eggs buried in the sand; a tenth of that number made enough soup for our big family, and how delicious it was!

Once, as a special treat, papa took us all miles and miles up our creek into the heart of the Everglades. The creek opened out into sunlit bays dotted with white sand bars and edged with green islands. On one we found a deserted Indian house made of palmettos. Everywhere there were alligators and other wild creatures, untroubled by our presence. This trip took us through some dark, sluggish swamps where the water scarcely moved and we were forced to pole the boat. The orchids here were the largest and most flamboyant we had seen. As we came out into a bay, we saw thousands and thousands of white herons, snowy egrets, pink ibis, curlews, blue johns, and flamingos. They constantly rose, circled, and landed in arcs of color and long lines of sweeping movement. We put the boat in the shade and watched for an hour.

It was here that we came upon a pelican colony. There were hundreds of young ones, as it was the nesting season. We caught one of these babies, fully grown in size, and took it home for a pet. It became an awful nuisance, chasing us to be fed every time it saw any of us.

Our new home was indeed a haven of pleasure. But there was work, too, as always. Early in the mornings and late in the afternoons, Orr and I would go with mama to the garden. How lovely the fresh vegetables did taste. We cared for them with loving hands, pulling weeds by the hour and watering the young plants with buckets of water we pumped and carried. Our reward was to gather armloads of beets, radishes, turnips, et cetera to take to the house for lunch and supper. The meals were made more memorable with the wild food. Wild butter beans grew on the edge of our hammock. The vines climbed so high up into the trees that we would have to pull them down to get the beans (knowing they'd be back up the next week). For dessert we had ladyfingers, wild bananas that grew in our backyard.

Suddenly, sometime that summer, a day came when all work ceased. My oldest brother, Bubba, always too busy for me, took me outside and made stilts and taught me how to use them. The hard-packed shell was like pavement. It had rained, and water stood in little basins where the

545

shell soil held it. We made a game of walking across these pools, with me as tall as Bubba on my stilts. Hal came out, and soon both big brothers were on stilts of their own. Orr was too small to walk on them but he followed us around admiringly. The mosquitoes were bad everywhere except in the sunshine, so we four children spent the entire day out in the summer sun walking on stilts. Despite the unrelenting heat, we were happy to be let off from our hours of school indoors, sessions which our mother kept every day, rain or shine.

Late in the afternoon our grandmother called us in. She told us we had a new baby sister. When papa brought the tiny mite into the kitchen where we were, I thought it was a doll lying there on the pillow, a doll with a curly wig. I touched its cheek to see if it was a doll, and it moved!

"Oh, papa, I want it, I've got to have it, please, can I have it, papa?" Then and there he gave me that baby for my very own. We have lived a long time, this sister and I, and there has always been a precious bond between us. I have never been more proud than at the moment I took that tiny, beautiful baby into my arms. My father and grandmother had delivered her without mishap. We named her Janey.

Mama was out in the garden again in no time, and what with papa's field of tomatoes, we soon had produce to send to market. We shipped, as contracted, with Edgar Watson. Immediately trouble arose. A messenger came from the sugar plantation bringing papa a ridiculously small sum of money for his part. Papa told this man to go back and tell Watson how much was still owed, and that he, papa, would be coming for it. The poor messenger was terrified and begged papa to let the matter drop. "He'll just shoot you, Mr. Martin. That's the way he settles an account. No one argues with Edgar Watson and lives to talk about it."

The next day papa went to see Watson. Hal and Bubba accompanied him. When they drew up to the dock in their boat, papa told the boys to sit tight while he went in the house. Watson's whole living room could be seen through a wide screen. It was an armory; the walls were lined with guns. Papa did not carry a gun.

In the argument that followed the boys could see everything. Perhaps they thought of the skeletons under their boat as Watson became more and more strident. Then came a moment when Watson started backing toward his wall of guns. Papa was unrelenting; he demanded his money, and Watson's arm rose toward a pistol. At the height of this tense moment a smile broke on Watson's face. From where he stood he could see the two boys in the boat, each with a rifle held in small, capable hands and a bead drawn down on the man who threatened their father.

"Look," Watson told papa, but papa thought it was a trick to make him turn around. Watson understood and moved away from the guns and pointed to the boat. Papa grinned at his sons and even smiled at Edgar Watson.

"Do you suppose they thought I'd shoot you, Jim?" Watson asked.

"Do you suppose you'd have had the chance?" papa sent back.

This man who never paid his debts paid my father and walked with him to the landing to get a closer look. All he saw were two nonchalant little boys sitting with their guns beside them, slapping mosquitoes.

That night papa gave each of the boys a special hug and kiss at bedtime. Kissing between Southern men was a general practice in those days. I am glad to say that this practice as well as others continues in our family. Today I can see in my grandsons and great-grandson some of those qualities of courage and caring that my father had in such abundance. It was his and my mother's way of caring for us that made us all caring of one another. Perhaps this caring is the key to those wonderful times we had in the Ten Thousand Islands when the century took its turn.

—February 1981

"PERDICARIS ALIVE OR RAISULI DEAD"

By BARBARA W. TUCHMAN

The ringing phrase helped nominate TR, but it covered an embarrassing secret that remained hushed up for thirty years

On a scented Mediterranean May evening in 1904 Mr. Ion Perdicaris, an elderly, wealthy American, was dining with his family on the vine-covered terrace of the Place of Nightingales, his summer villa in the hills above Tangier. Besides a tame demoiselle crane and two monkeys who ate orange blossoms, the family included Mrs. Perdicaris; her son by a former marriage, Cromwell Oliver Varley, who (though wearing a great name backward) was a British subject; and Mrs. Varley. Suddenly a cacophony of shrieks, commands, and barking of dogs burst from the servants' quarters at the rear. Assuming the uproar to be a further episode in the chronic feud between their German housekeeper and their French-Zouave chef, the family headed for the servants' hall to frustrate mayhem. They ran into the butler flying madly past them, pursued by a number of armed Moors whom at first they took to be their own household guards. Astonishingly, these persons fell upon the two gentlemen, bound them, clubbed two of the servants with their gunstocks, knocked Mrs. Varley to the floor, drew a knife against Varley's throat when he struggled toward his wife, dragged off the housekeeper who was screaming into the telephone "Robbers! Help!," cut the wire, and shoved their captives out of the house with guns pressed in their backs.

Waiting at the villa's gate was a handsome, black-bearded Moor with blazing eyes and a Greek profile, who, raising his arm in a theatrical gesture, announced in the tones of Henry Irving playing King Lear, "I am the Raisuli!" Awed, Perdicaris and Varley knew they stood face to face with the renowned Berber chief, lord of the Rif and last of the Barbary pirates, whose personal struggle for power against his nominal overlord, the Sultan of Morocco, periodically erupted over Tangier in raids, rapine, and interesting varieties of pillage. He now ordered his prisoners hoisted onto their horses and, thoughtfully stealing Perdicaris's best mount, a black stallion, for himself, fired the signal for departure. The bandit cavalcade, in a mad confusion of shouts, shots, rearing horses, and trampled bodies, scrambled off down the rocky hillside, avoiding the road, and disappeared into the night in the general direction of the Atlas Mountains.

A moment later, Samuel R. Gummere, United States consul general, was interrupted at dinner by the telephone operator who passed on the alarm from the villa. After a hasty visit to the scene of the outrage, where he ascertained the facts, assuaged the hysterical ladies, and posted guards, Gummere returned to confer with his colleague, Sir Arthur Nicolson, the British minister. Both envoys saw alarming prospects of danger to all foreigners in Morocco as the result of Raisuli's latest pounce.

Morocco's already anarchic affairs had just been thrown into even greater turmoil by the month-old Anglo-French entente. Under this arrangement, England, in exchange for a free hand in Egypt, had given France a free hand in Morocco, much to the annoyance of all Moroccans. The Sultan, Abdul-Aziz, was a well-meaning but helpless young man, uneasily balanced on the shaky throne of the last independent Moslem country west of Constantinople. He was a puppet of a corrupt clique headed by Ben Sliman, the able and wicked old grand vizier. To keep his young master harmlessly occupied while he kept the reins, not to mention the funds, of government in his own hands, Ben Sliman taught the Sultan a taste for, and indulged him in all manner of, extravagant luxuries of foreign manufacture. But Abdul-Aziz's tastes got out of bounds. Not content with innumerable bicycles, 600 cameras, 25 grand pianos, and a gold automobile (though there were no roads), he wanted Western reforms to go with them. These, requiring foreign loans, willingly supplied by the French, opened the age-old avenue of foreign penetration. The Sultan's Western tastes and Western debts roused resentment among his fanatic tribes. Rebellions and risings had kept the country in strife for some years past, and European rivalries complicated the chaos. France, already deep in Algeria, was pressing against Morocco's borders. Spain had special interests along the Mediterranean coast. Germany was eyeing Morocco for commercial opportunities and as a convenient site for naval coaling bases. England, eyeing Germany, determined to patch up old feuds with France and had just signed the entente in April. The Moroccan government, embittered by what it considered England's betrayal, hating France, harassed by rebellion, tottering on the brink of bankruptcy, had yet one more scourge to suffer. This was the Sherif Mulai Ahmed ibn-Muhammed er Raisuli, who now seized his moment. To show up the Sultan's weakness, proportionately increase his own prestige, and extract political concessions as a ransom, he kidnapped the prominent American resident Mr. Perdicaris.

"Situation serious" telegraphed Gummere to the State Department on May 19. "Request man-of-war to enforce demands." No request could have been more relished by President Theodore Roosevelt. Not yet 46, bursting with vigor, he delighted to make the Navy the vehicle of his exuberant view of national policy. At the moment of Perdicaris's kidnapping he faced, within the next month, a nominating committee that could give him what he most coveted: a chance to be elected President "in my own right." Although there was no possibility of the convention nominating anyone else, Roosevelt knew it would be dominated by professional politicians and standpatters who were unanimous in their distaste for "that damned cowboy," as their late revered leader, Mark Hanna, had called him. The prospect did not intimidate Roosevelt. "The President," said his great friend, Ambassador Jean Jules Jusserand of France, "is in his best mood. He is always in his best mood." The President promptly ordered to Morocco not one warship, but four, the entire South Atlantic Squadron—due shortly to coal at Tenerife in the Canaries, where it could receive its orders to proceed at once to Tangier. Roosevelt knew it to be under the command of a man exactly suited to the circumstances. Admiral French Ensor Chadwick, a decorated veteran of the Battle of Santiago and, like Roosevelt, an ardent disciple of Admiral Alfred Thayer Mahan's strenuous theories of naval instrumentality.

Roosevelt's second in foreign policy was that melancholy and cultivated gentleman and wit, John Hay, who had been Lincoln's private secretary, wanted only to be a poet, and was, often to his own disgust, Secretary of State. On the day of the kidnapping he was absent, delivering a speech at the St. Louis Fair. His subordinates, however, recognized Gummere, who was senior diplomatic officer in Tangier in the absence of any American minister and had six years' experience at that post, as a man to be listened to. The victim, Perdicaris, was also a man of some repute, whose name was known in the State Department through a public crusade he had waged back in 1886–87 against certain diplomatic abuses practiced in Tangier. His associate in that battle had been Gummere himself, then a junior member of the foreign service and Perdicaris's friend and fellow-townsman from Trenton, New Jersey.

"Warships will be sent to Tangier as soon as possible," the department wired Gummere. "May be three or four days before one arrives." Ships in the plural was gratifying, but the promised delay was not. Gummere feared the chances of rescuing Perdicaris and Varley were slim. Nicolson gloomily concurred. They agreed that the only hope was to insist upon the

Sultan's government giving in to whatever demands Raisuli might make as his price for release of his prisoners. Most inconveniently the government was split, its foreign minister, Mohammed Torres, being resident at Tangier where the foreign legations were located, while the Sultan, grand vizier, and court were at Fez, which was three days' journey by camel or mule into the interior. Gummere and Nicolson told Mohammed Torres they expected immediate acquiescence to Raisuli's demands, whatever these might prove to be, and dispatched their vice-counsels to Fez to impress the same view urgently upon the Sultan.

The French minister, St. René Taillandier, did likewise, but, since the Anglo-French entente was still too new to have erased old jealousies, he acted throughout the affair more or less independently. France had her own reasons for wishing to see Perdicaris and Varley safely restored as quickly as possible. Their abduction had put the foreign colony in an uproar that would soon become panic if they were not rescued. The approach of the American fleet would seem to require equal action by France as the paramount power in the area, but France was anxious to avoid a display of force. She was "very nervous," Admiral Chadwick wrote later, at the prospect of taking over "the most fanatic and troublesome eight or ten millions in the world"; she had hoped to begin her penetration as unobtrusively as possible without stirring up Moroccan feelings any further against her. Hurriedly, St. René Taillandier sent off two noble mediators to Raisuli; they were the young brother sherifs of the Wazan family, who occupied a sort of religious primacy among sherifs and whom France found it worthwhile to subsidize as her protégés.

While awaiting word from the mediators, Gummere and Nicolson anxiously conferred with an old Moroccan hand, Walter B. Harris, correspondent of the London *Times*, who had himself been kidnapped by Raisuli the year before. Raisuli had used that occasion to force the Bashaw, or local governor, of Tangier to call off a punitive expedition sent against him. This Bashaw, who played Sheriff of Nottingham to Raisuli's Robin Hood, was Raisuli's foster brother and chief hate; the two had carried on a feud ever since the Bashaw had tricked Raisuli into prison eight years before. The Bashaw sent troops to harass and tax Raisuli's tribes and burn his villages; at intervals he dispatched emissaries instructed to lure his enemy to parley. Raisuli ambushed and slaughtered the troops and returned the emissaries—or parts of them. The head of one was delivered in a basket of melons. Another came back in one piece, soaked in oil and set on fire. The eyes of another had been burned out with hot copper coins.

Despite such grisly tactics, Harris reported to Gummere and Nicolson, his late captor was a stimulating conversationalist who discoursed on philosophy in the accents of the Moorish aristocracy and denied interest in ransom for its own sake. "Men think I care about money," he told Harris, "but, I tell you, it is only useful in politics." He had freed Harris in return for the release of his own partisans from government prisons, but since then more of these had been captured. This time Raisuli's demands would be larger and the Sultan less inclined to concede them. Sir Arthur recalled that on the last occasion Mohammed Torres had "behaved like an old brute" and shrugged off Harris's fate as being in the hands of the Lord, when in fact, as Nicolson had pointed out to him, Harris was "in the hands of a devil." Sir Arthur had suffered acutely. "I *boil*," he confessed, "to have to humiliate myself and negotiate with these miserable brigands within three hours of Gibraltar." Gummere thought sadly of his poor friend Perdicaris. "I cannot conceal from myself and the Department," he wrote that night, "that only by extremely delicate negotiations can we hope to escape from the most terrible consequences."

Back in America, the Perdicaris case provided a welcome sensation to compete in the headlines with the faraway fortunes of the Russo-Japanese War. A rich old gentleman held for ransom by a cruel but romantic brigand, the American Navy steaming to the rescue—here was personal drama more immediate than the complicated rattle of unpronounceable generals battling over unintelligible terrain. The President's instant and energetic action on behalf of a single citizen fallen among thieves in a foreign land made Perdicaris a symbol of America's new role on the world stage.

The man himself was oddly cast for the part. Digging up all available information, the press discovered that he was the son of Gregory Perdicaris, a native of Greece who had become a naturalized American, taught Greek at Harvard, married a lady of property from South Carolina, made a fortune in illuminating gas, settled in Trenton, New Jersey, and served for a time as United States consul in his native land. The son entered Harvard with the class of 1860 but left in his sophomore year to study abroad. For a young man who was 21 at the opening of the Civil War, his history during the next few years was strangely obscure, a fact which the press ascribed to a conflict between his father, a Union sympathizer, and his mother, an ardent Confederate. Subsequently the son lived peripatetically in England, Morocco, and Trenton as a dilettante of literature and the arts, producing magazine articles, a verse play, and a painting called *Tent Life*. He had built the now famous Villa Aidonia (otherwise Place of Nightingales) in 1877, and settled permanently in Tangier in 1884. There he lavishly entertained English and American friends among Oriental rugs, damasks, rare porcelains, and Moorish attendants in scarlet knee-pants and gold-embroidered jackets. He was known as a benefactor of the Moors and as a supporter of a private philanthropy that endowed Tangier with a modern sanitation system. He rode a splendid Arab steed—followed by his wife on a white mule—produced an occasional literary exercise or allegorical painting, and enjoyed an Edwardian gentleman's life amid elegant bric-a-brac.

A new telegram from the State Department desired Gummere to urge "energetic" efforts by the authorities to rescue Perdicaris and punish his captor—"if practicable," it added, with a bow to realities. Gummere replied that this was the difficulty: Raisuli, among his native crags, was immune from reprisal. The Sultan, who had a tatterdemalion army of some 2,000, had been trying vainly to capture him for years. Gummere became quite agitated. United action by the powers was necessary to prevent further abductions of Christians; Morocco was "fast drifting into a state of complete anarchy," the Sultan and his advisers were weak or worse, governors were corrupt, and very soon "neither life nor property will be safe."

On May 22 the younger Wazan returned with Raisuli's terms. They demanded everything: prompt withdrawal of government troops from the Rif; dismissal of the Bashaw of Tangier; arrest and imprisonment of certain officials who had harmed Raisuli in the past; release of Raisuli's partisans from prison; payment of an indemnity of $70,000 to be imposed personally upon the Bashaw, whose property must be sold to raise the amount; appointment of Raisuli as governor of two districts around Tangier that should be relieved of taxes and ceded to him absolutely; and, finally, safe-conduct for all Raisuli's tribesmen to come and go freely in the towns and markets.

Gummere was horrified: Mohammed Torres declared his government would never consent. Meanwhile European residents, increasingly agitated, were flocking in from outlying estates, voicing indignant protests, petitioning for a police force, guards, and gunboats. The local Moors, stimulated by Raisuli's audacity, were showing an aggressive mood. Gummere, scanning the horizon for Admiral Chadwick's smokestacks, hourly expected an outbreak. Situation "not reassuring," he wired; progress of talks "most unsatisfactory"; warship "anxiously awaited. Can it be hastened?"

The American public awaited Chadwick's arrival as eagerly as Gummere. Excitement rose when the press reported that Admiral Theodore F. Jewell, in command of the European Squadron, three days's sail behind Chadwick, would be ordered to reinforce him if the emergency continued.

Tangier received further word from the sherifs of Wazan that Raisuli had not only absolutely declined to abate his demands but had added an even more impossible condition: a British or American guarantee of fulfillment of the terms by the Moroccan government.

Knowing his government could not make itself responsible for the performance or non-performance of promises by another government, Gummere despairingly cabled the terms to Washington. As soon as he saw them, Roosevelt sent "in a hurry" for Secretary Hay (who had meanwhile returned to the capital). "I told him," wrote Hay that night in his diary, "I considered the demands of the outlaw Raisuli preposterous and the proposed guarantee of them by us and by England impossible of fulfillment." Roosevelt agreed. Two measures were decided upon and carried out within the hour: Admiral Jewell's squadron was ordered to reinforce Chadwick at Tangier, and France was officially requested to lend her good offices. (By recognizing France's special status in Morocco, this step, consciously taken, was of international significance in the train of crises that was to lead through Algeciras and Agadir to 1914.) Roosevelt and Hay felt they had done their utmost. "I hope they may not murder Mr. Perdicaris," recorded Hay none too hopefully, "but a nation cannot degrade itself to prevent ill-treatment of a citizen."

An uninhibited press told the public that in response to Raisuli's "insulting" ultimatum, "all available naval forces" in European waters were being ordered to the spot. Inspired by the memory of U.S. troops chasing Aguinaldo in the Philippines, the press suggested that "if other means fail," marines could make a forced march into the interior to "bring the outlaw to book for his crimes." Such talk terrified Gummere, who knew that leathernecks would have as much chance against Berbers in the Rif as General Braddock's redcoats against Indians in the Alleghenies; and besides, the first marine ashore would simply provoke Raisuli to kill his prisoners.

On May 29 the elder Wazan brought word that Raisuli threatened to do just that if all his demands were not met in two days. Two days! This was the twentieth century, but as far as communications with Fez were concerned it might as well have been the time of the Crusades. Nevertheless, Gummere and Nicolson sent couriers to meet their vice-consuls at Fez (or intercept them if they had already left) with orders to demand a new audience with the Sultan and obtain his acceptance of Raisuli's terms.

At five thirty next morning a gray shape slid into the harbor. Gummere, awakened from a troubled sleep, heard the welcome news that Admiral Chadwick had arrived at last aboard his flagship, the *Brooklyn*. Relieved, yet worried that the military mind might display more valor than discretion, he hurried down to confer with the Admiral. In him he found a crisp and incisive officer whose quick intelligence grasped the situation at once. Chadwick agreed that the point at which to apply pressure was Mohammed Torres. Although up in the hills the brigand's patience might be wearing thin, the niceties of diplomatic protocol, plus the extra flourishes required by Moslem practice, called for an exchange of courtesy calls before business could be done. Admiral and consul proceeded at once to wait upon the foreign minister, who returned the call upon the flagship that afternoon. It was a sight to see, Chadwick wrote to Hay, his royal progress through the streets, "a mass of beautiful white wool draperies, his old calves bare and his feet naked but for his yellow slippers," while "these wild fellows stoop and kiss his shoulder as he goes by."

Mohammed Torres was greeted by a salute from the flagship's guns and a review of the squadron's other three ships, which had just arrived. Unimpressed by these attentions, he continued to reject Raisuli's terms. "Situation critical," reported Chadwick.

The situation was even more critical in Washington. On June 1, an extraordinary letter reached the State Department. Its writer, one A. H. Slocumb, a cotton broker of Fayetteville, North Carolina, said he had read with interest about the Perdicaris case and then, without warning, asked a startling question, "But is Perdicaris an American? In the winter of 1863, Mr. Slocumb went on to say, he had been in Athens, and Perdicaris had come there "for the express purpose, as he stated, to become naturalized as a Greek citizen." His object, he had said, was to prevent confiscation by the Confederacy of some valuable property in South Carolina inherited from his mother. Mr. Slocumb could not be sure whether Perdicaris had since resumed American citizenship, but he was "positive" that Perdicaris had become a Greek subject forty years before, and he suggested that Athens records would bear out his statement.

What blushes reddened official faces we can only imagine. Hay's diary for June 1 records that the President sent for him and Secretary of the Navy Moody "for a few words about Perdicaris," but, maddeningly discreet, Hay wrote no more. A pregnant silence of three days ensues between the Slocumb letter and the next document in the case. On June 4 the State Department queried our minister in Athens, John B. Jackson, asking him to investigate the charge—"important if true," added the department, facing bravely into the wind. Although Slocumb had mentioned only 1863, the telegram to Jackson asked him to search the records for the two previous years as well; apparently the department had been making frenzied inquiries of its own during the interval. On June 7 Jackson telegraphed in a reply that a person named Ion Perdicaris, described as an artist, unmarried, aged 22, had indeed been naturalized as a Greek citizen on March 19, 1862.

Posterity will never know what Roosevelt or Hay thought or said at this moment, because the archives are empty of evidence. But neither the strenuous President nor the suave Secretary of State was a man easily rattled. The game must be played out. Already Admiral Jewell's squadron of three cruisers had arrived to reinforce Chadwick, making a total of seven American warships at Tangier. America's fleet, flag, and honor were committed. Wheels had been set turning in foreign capitals. Hay had requested the good offices of France. The French foreign minister, Théophile Delcassé, was himself bringing pressure. A British warship, the *Prince of Wales*, had also come to Tangier. Spain wanted to know if the United States was wedging into Morocco.

And just at this juncture the Sultan's government, succumbing to French pressure, ordered Mohammed Torres to accede to all Raisuli's demands. Four days later, on June 12, a French loan to the government of Morocco was signed at Fez in the amount of 62.5 million francs, secured by the customs of all Moroccan ports. It seemed hardly a tactful moment to reveal the fraudulent claim of Mr. Perdicaris.

He was not yet out of danger, for Raisuli refused to release him before all the demands were actually met, and the authorities were proving evasive. Washington was trapped. Impossible to reveal Perdicaris's status now; equally impossible to withdraw their fleet and leave him, whom the world still supposed to be an American, at the brigand's mercy.

During the next few days suspense was kept taut by a stream of telegrams from Gummere and Chadwick reporting one impasse after another in the negotiations with Raisuli. When the Sultan balked at meeting all the terms in advance of the release, Raisuli merely raised his ante, demanding that four districts instead of two be ceded to him and returning to the idea of an Anglo-American guarantee. "You see there is no end to the insolence of this blackguard," wrote Hay in a note to the President on June 15; Roosevelt, replying the same day, agreed that we had gone "as far as we possibly can go for Perdicaris" and could now only "demand the death of those that harm him if he is harmed." He dashed off an alarming postscript: "I think it would be well to enter into negotiations with England and France looking to the possibility of an expedition to punish the brigands if Gummere's statement as to the impotence of the Sultan is true."

No further action was taken in pursuit of this proposal because Gummere's telegrams now grew cautiously hopeful; on the nineteenth he wired that all arrangements had been settled for the release to take place on the twenty-first. But on the twentieth all was off. Raisuli suspected the good faith of the government, a sentiment which Gummere and Chadwick evidently shared, for they blamed the delay on "intrigue of authorities here." Finally the exasperated Gummere telegraphed on the twenty-first that the United States position was becoming "humiliating." He asked to be empowered to deliver an ultimatum to the Moroccan government claiming an indemnity for each day's further delay, backed by a threat to land marines and seize the customs as security. Admiral Chadwick concurred in a separate telegram.

June 21 was the day the Republican National Convention met in Chicago. "There is a great deal of sullen grumbling," Roosevelt wrote that day to his son Kermit, "but they don't dare oppose me for the nomination. . . . How the election will turn out no one can tell." If a poll of Republican party leaders had been taken at any time during the past year, one newspaper estimated, it would have shown a majority opposed to Roosevelt's nomination. But the country agreed with Viscount Bryce, who said Roosevelt was the greatest President since Washington (prompting a Roosevelt friend to recall Whistler's remark when told he was the greatest painter since Velázquez: "Why drag in Velázquez?"). The country wanted Teddy and, however distasteful that fact was, the politicians saw the handwriting on the bandwagon. On the death of Mark Hanna four months before, active opposition had collapsed, and the disgruntled leaders were now arriving in Chicago prepared to register the inevitable as ungraciously as possible.

They were the more sullen because Roosevelt and his strategists, preparing against any possible slip-up, had so steam-rollered and stage-managed the proceedings ahead of time that there was nothing left for the delegates to do. No scurrying, no back-room bargaining, no fights, no trades, no smoke-filled deals. *Harper's Weekly* reported an Alabama delegate's summation: "There ain't anybody who can do nothin'," and added, "It is not a Republican Convention, it is no kind of convention; it is a roosevelt."

The resulting listlessness and pervading dullness were unfortunate. Although Elihu Root, Henry Cabot Lodge, and other hand-picked Roosevelt choices filled the key posts, most of the delegates and party professionals did not make even a pretense of enthusiasm. The ostentatious coldness of the delegation from New York, Roosevelt's home state, was such that one reporter predicted they would all go home with pneumonia. There were no bands, no parades, and for the first time in forty years there were hundreds of empty seats.

Roosevelt knew he had the nomination in his pocket, but all his life, like Lincoln, he had a haunting fear of being defeated in elections. He was worried lest the dislike and distrust of him so openly exhibited at Chicago should gather volume and explode at the ballot box. Something was needed to prick the sulks and dispel the gloom of the convention before it made a lasting impression upon the public.

At this moment came Gummere's plea for an ultimatum. Again we have no record of what went on in high councils, but President and Secretary must have agreed upon their historic answer within a matter of hours. The only relevant piece of evidence is a verbal statement made to Hay's biographer, the late Tyler Dennett, by Gaillard Hunt, who was chief of the State Department's Citizenship Bureau during the Perdicaris affair. Hunt said he showed the correspondence about Perdicaris's citizenship to Hay, who told him to show it to the President; on seeing it, the President decided to overlook the difficulty and instructed Hunt to tell Hay to send the telegram anyway, at once. No date is given for this performance, so one is left with the implication that Roosevelt was not informed of the facts until this last moment—a supposition which the present writer finds improbable.

When Roosevelt made up his mind to accomplish an objective he did not worry too much about legality of method. Before any unusual procedure he would ask an opinion from his Attorney General, Philander Knox, but Knox rather admired Roosevelt's way of overriding his advice. Once, when asked for his opinion, he replied, "Ah, Mr. President, why have such a beautiful action marred by any taint of legality?" Another close adviser, Captain Mahan, when asked by Roosevelt a few years before how to solve the political problem of annexing the Hawaiian Islands, had answered, "Do nothing unrighteous but . . . take the islands first and solve afterward." It may be that the problem of Perdicaris seemed susceptible of the same treatment.

The opportunity was irresistible. Every newspaperman who ever knew him testified to Roosevelt's extraordinary sense of news value, to his ability to create news, to dramatize himself to the public. He had a genius for it. "Consciously or unconsciously," said the journalist Issac Marcosson, "he was the master press agent of all time." The risk, of course, was great, for it would be acutely embarrassing if the facts leaked out during the coming campaign. It may have been the risk itself that tempted Roosevelt, for he loved a prank and loved danger for its own sake; if he could combine danger with what William Allen White called a "frolicking intrigue," his happiness was complete.

Next day, June 22, the memorable telegram, "This Government wants Perdicaris alive or Raisuli dead," flashed across the Atlantic cable over Hay's signature and was simultaneously given to the press at home. It was not an ultimatum, because Hay deliberately deprived it of meaningfulness by adding to Gummere, "Do not land marines or seize customs without Department's specific instructions." But this sentence was not allowed to spoil the effect: it was withheld from the press.

At Chicago, Uncle Joe Cannon, the salty perennial Speaker of the

House, who was convention chairman, rapped with his gavel and read the telegram. The convention was electrified. Delegates sprang upon their chairs and hurrahed. Flags and handkerchiefs waved. Despite Hay's signature, everyone saw the Roosevelt teeth, cliché of a hundred cartoons, gleaming whitely behind it. "Magnificent, magnificent!" pronounced Senator Depew. "The people want an administration that will stand by its citizens, even if it takes the fleet to do it," said Representative Dwight of New York, expressing the essence of popular feeling. "Roosevelt and Hay know what they are doing," said a Kansas delegate. "Our people like courage. We'll stand for anything those two men do." "Good hot stuff and echoes my sentiments," said another delegate. The genius of its timing and phrasing, wrote a reporter, "gave the candidate the maximum benefit of the thrill that was needed." Although the public was inclined to credit authorship to Roosevelt, the Baltimore *Sun* pointed out that Mr. Hay too knew how to make the eagle scream when he wanted to. Hay's diary agreed. "My telegram to Gummere," he noted comfortably the day afterward, "had an uncalled for success. It is curious how a concise impropriety hits the public."

After nominating Roosevelt by acclamation, the convention departed in an exhilarated mood. In Morocco a settlement had been reached before receipt of the telegram. Raisuli was ready at last to return his captives. Mounted on a "great, grey charger," he personally escorted Perdicaris and Varley on the ride down from the mountains, pointing out on the way the admirable effect of pink and violet shadows cast by the rising sun on the rocks. They met the ransom party, with thirty pack mules bearing boxes of Spanish silver dollars, halfway down. Payment was made and prisoners exchanged, and Perdicaris took leave, as he afterward wrote, of "one of the most interesting and kindly-hearted native gentlemen" he had ever known, whose "singular gentleness and courtesy . . . quite endeared him to us." At nightfall, as he rode into Tangier and saw the signal lights of the American warships twinkling the news of his release, Perdicaris was overcome with patriotic emotion at "such proof of his country's solicitude for its citizens and for the honor of its flag!" Few indeed are the Americans, he wrote to Gummere in a masterpiece of understatement, "who can have appreciated as keenly as I did then what the presence of our Flag in foreign waters meant at such a moment and in such circumstances."

Only afterward, when it was all over, did the State Department inform Gummere how keen indeed was Perdicaris's cause for appreciation. "Overwhelmed with amazement" and highly indignant, Gummere extracted from Perdicaris a full, written confession of his forty-year-old secret. He admitted that he had never in ensuing years taken steps to resume

American citizenship because, as he ingenuously explained, having been born an American, he disliked the idea of having to become naturalized, and so, "I continued to consider myself an American citizen." Since Perdicaris perfectly understood that the American government was in no position to take action against him, his letter made no great pretension of remorse.

Perdicaris retired to England for his remaining years. Raisuli duly became governor of the Tangier districts in place of the falsehearted Bashaw. The French, in view of recent disorders, acquired the right to police Morocco (provoking the Kaiser's notorious descent upon Tangier). The Sultan, weakened and humiliated by Raisuli's triumph, was shortly dethroned by a brother. Gummere was officially congratulated and subsequently appointed minister to Morocco and American delegate to the Algeciras Conference. Sir Arthur Nicolson took "a long leave of absence," the Wazan brothers received handsomely decorated Winchester rifles with suitable inscriptions from Mr. Roosevelt, Hay received the Grand Cross of the Legion of Honor, and Roosevelt was elected in November by the largest popular majority ever before given to a presidential candidate.

"As to Paregoric or is it Pericarditis," wrote Hay to Assistant Secretary Adee on September 3, "it is a bad business. We must keep it excessively confidential for the present." They succeeded. Officials in the know held their breath during the campaign, but no hint leaked out either then or during the remaining year of Hay's lifetime or during Roosevelt's lifetime. As a result of the episode, Roosevelt's administration proposed a new citizenship law which was introduced in Congress in 1905 and enacted in 1907, but the name of the errant gentleman who inspired it was never mentioned during the debates. The truth about Perdicaris remained unknown to the public until 1933, when Tyler Dennett gave it away—in one paragraph in his biography of John Hay.

—August 1959

THE AMERICAN GAME

By BRUCE CATTON

Baseball is still pretty much the way it used to be because the way it used to be was pretty much perfect

By the carefully repeated definition of men who stand to make money out of its acceptance, baseball is the Great American Game. The expression was invented long ago and it has been rammed home by talented press agents ever since, even in times when most Americans seemed to be interested very largely in something else. But what has given the phrase its sticking power is not the fact that a big industry has kept plugging it, or the allied fact that unceasing repetition has dinned it into an unreflecting public's ears for generations, but simply the fact that in its underlying essence it is perfectly true.

Baseball is the American game, great or otherwise, because it reflects so perfectly certain aspects of the American character that no other sport quite portrays.

It has few of the elements of pure sportsmanship, as that dubious word is commonly accepted, and it is not notably a game for gentlemen. But it does embody certain native-born fundamentals, including above all others the notion that the big thing about any contest is to win it. It also is built upon the idea that anything you can get away with is permissible, and it is the only sport (at least the only one since the Roman populace sat in the thumbs-down section at the gladiatorial games) that puts an invitation to homicide in one of its enduring sayings "Kill the umpire!" (The thing has actually been attempted, too, more than once.) It is preeminently the sport for the professional rather than for the amateur, the sport in which the well-intentioned duffer neither is given nor especially wants a part.

Almost everyone in the country has played it at one time or another,

561

but almost nobody except the professional dreams of going on playing it once full manhood has come. It is a spectator sport in which each spectator has had just enough personal experience to count himself an expert, and it is the only pastime on earth that leans heavily on the accumulation of page upon page of inherently dry statistics. It is also an unchanging pageant and a ritualized drama, as completely formalized as the Spanish bullfight, and although it is wholly urbanized it still speaks of the small town and the simple, rural era that lived before the automobile came in to blight the landscape. One reason for this is that in a land of unending change, baseball changes very little. There has been no important modification of its rules for well over half a century. The ball in use now will go farther when properly hit, and the gloves worn on defense are designed to do automatically what personal skill once had to do, but aside from these things the game is as it was in the early 1900s. Even the advent of night baseball, which seemed like pure sacrilege when it was introduced two decades ago, has made little difference; the pictorial aspect of the game—which is one of its most important features—has perhaps even gained thereby. The neat green field looks greener and cleaner under the lights, the moving players are silhouetted more sharply, and the enduring visual fascination of the game—the immobile pattern of nine men, grouped according to ancient formula and then, suddenly, to the sound of a wooden bat whacking a round ball, breaking into swift ritualized movement, movement so standardized that even the tyro in the bleachers can tell when someone goes off in the wrong direction—this is as it was in the old days. A gaffer from the era of William McKinley, abruptly brought back to the second half of the twentieth century, would find very little in modern life that would not seem new, strange, and rather bewildering, but put in a good grandstand seat back of first base he would see nothing that was not completely familiar.

But that is only the surface part of it. Baseball, highly organized, professionalized within an inch of its life, and conducted by men who like dollars better than they like sport, still speaks for the old days when nine young men in an open park somehow expressed the hot competitive instincts of everybody and spoke for home-town pride.

And perhaps the central part of all of this is the fact that in its essence baseball is still faintly disreputable and rowdy. Its players chew tobacco, or at least look as if they were chewing it; many of them do not shave every day; and they argue bitterly with each other, with their opponents, and with the umpires just as they did when John McGraw and Ed Delehanty were popular idols. They have borrowed nothing from the "sportsmanship" of more sedate countries; they believe that when you get into a fight you had better win, and the method by which you win does not matter very much. Anything goes; victory is what counts.

This John McGraw, for example. When he was playing third base and there was a runner there, and someone hit a fly to the outfield, McGraw would unobtrusively hook his fingers in the player's belt so that the take-off for the plate, once the ball was caught, would be delayed by a half second or so. He got away with it, too, and no one thought the worse of him, until one day a baserunner unbuckled his belt in this situation and, legging it for home, left the belt dangling in McGraw's hand, tangible evidence of crime. Note, also, that baseball knows about the bean ball —the ball thrown at the batter's head to drive him away from the plate and hamper his hitting process. A big leaguer was once killed by such a pitch; it has been condemned by everybody ever since then, and it is still a regular feature of the game.

In its essentials, then, baseball is plebeian, down-to-earth, and robustious. Even half a century ago it was dwindling to the rank of secondary sport in the colleges. Professors who have adjusted themselves to the presence on the campus of *soi-disant* students who are paid to attend college so that they may play football have a way of considering the football player one cut above the baseball player. The former may be a hulking behemoth of pure muscle, wholly incapable of differentiating between Virgil's *Ecolgues* and Boyle's law, but he does not seem quite as uncouth as the baseball player—who, in his own turn, may also be on the campus as a paid hand, the difference being that he is being paid by some major-league team that wants to see his athletic skills developed, while the football player gets his from ardent alumni who want to see the college team beat State on Homecoming Day next fall. There has never been any social cachet attached to skill on the diamond.

The reason, obviously, is that baseball came up from the sand lots—the small town, the city slum, and the like. It had a rowdy air because rowdies played it. One of the stock tableaux in American sports history is the aggrieved baseball player jawing with the umpire. In all our games, this tableau is unique; it belongs to baseball, from the earliest days it has been an integral part of the game, and even in the carefully policed major leagues today it remains unchanged. Baseball never developed any of the social niceties.

In the old days, when (as we suppose, anyway) most of us lived in small towns, or at least in fairly small cities, the local baseball team represented civic pride, to say nothing of representing at the same time the dreams of a great many young men who wished to be much more athletic than they actually were. In very small towns, its games were usually held in Farmer Jones's pasture, where the difficulty, in a hot moment of split-second play, of distinguishing between third base and some natural cow-pasture obstacle sometimes led to odd happenings; and in slightly larger places the county fairground or a recreational park at the end of the streetcar line provided the arena. In any case, muscular young men, wearing the singularly unbecoming uniforms that were standardized 75 years ago, presently took their positions on the grass, and the game was on.

It was, and still is, hotly competitive, and within reasonable limits anything goes. If the umpire (there was just one, in the old days) could be suborned to give all vital judgments in favor of the home side, all well and good; no one ever blushed to accept a victory that derived from an umpire's bias. If he could be intimidated, so that close decisions would go as the spectators wanted them to go, that also was good. This often happened; an umpire who decided a crucial play against the home team was quite likely to be mobbed, and few pictures from the old-time sports album are more authentic or more enduring than the vision of an umpire frantically legging it for the train, pursued by irate citizens who wished to do him great bodily harm. It took physical courage to render impartial judgments in old-time small-town baseball, and not all umpires were quite up to it.

If the umpire could be deceived while the game was on, that also was good. A man running from first to third on a base hit would cut twenty feet short of second base if he thought he could get away with it, and no one dreamed of censuring him for it. If an opposing player could be intimidated, so that he shirked his task, that was good, too. Not for nothing was the greatest baseball player who ever lived, Ty Cobb, famous for sitting on the bench just before the game sharpening his spikes with a file. An infielder, witnessing this, and knowing that Cobb was practically certain to ram those spikes into his calf or thigh in a close play, was apt to flinch just a little at the moment of contact, and out of that split second of withdrawal Cobb would gain the hair's edge of advantage that he needed. It was considered fair, too, to denounce an opponent verbally, with any sort of profane, personal objurgation that came to mind, on the off-chance that he might become unsettled and do less than his best. (This still goes on, like practically all of the other traditional things in baseball, and the "bench jockey"—the man who will say anything at all if he thinks it will upset an enemy's poise—can be a prized member of a big-league team even now.)

Baseball is conservative. What was good enough in Cap Anson's day is good enough now, and a populace that could stand unmoved while the federal Constitution was amended would protest with vehemence at any tampering with the formalities of baseball. It looks as it used to look; the batter still grabs a handful of dust between swings, the catcher still slams the ball over to third base after a strike-out, and the umpire still jerks thumb over right shoulder to indicate a put-out. (Dismayingly enough, some umpires now grossly exaggerate this gesture, using an elaborate full-arm swing, but possibly the point is a minor one.)

An inning begins; the pitcher takes his warm-up tosses, now as in the days half a century ago, and after three, four, or five of these he steps aside and the catcher whips the ball down to second base. The second baseman tosses it to the shortstop, two yards away, and the shortstop throws it to the third baseman, who is standing halfway between his own base and the the pitcher's box; the third baseman, in turn, tosses it over to the pitcher, and the inning can get started. To vary from this formula is unthinkable; from the little leaguers up to Yankee Stadium, it is as one with the laws of the Medes and the Persians.

Then action: players shifting about, pounding their gloves, uttering cries of encouragement (which, like all the rest, are verbatim out of the script of 1900); and the batter approaches the plate, swinging two bats (another ironclad requirement), tossing one aside, planting his feet in the batter's box, and then swinging his single bat in determined menace. The fielders slowly freeze into fixed positions; for a moment no one anywhere moves, except that the pitcher goes into his stretch, takes a last look around, and then delivers—and then the frozen pattern breaks, the ball streaks off, men move deftly from here to there, and the quick movements of action are on.

In all of this there is unending fascination, coupled with the knowledge that wholly fantastic athletic feats may at any moment be displayed by any one of the players. Even an easy fly ball to the outfield or a simple grounder to short can call forth a nonchalant, effortless expertness that a man from another land would find quite incredible. (I once took an Englishman to see his first baseball game, and he was dumfounded by the simplest plays, marveling at what all the rest of us took for automatic outs.) In no contest can the split second be so important. A routine double play can make both outs with no more than half a second to spare, and if the half second is lost anywhere, the player who lost it will be derided for a clumsy oaf.

Primarily a team game, baseball is also the game for the individualist. The team play is essential, and when you watch closely you can see it, but the focus is usually on one man. A base runner streaks for second with the pitch, falls away while in full stride, and slides in a cloud of dust, baseman stabbing at him with gloved hand, umpire bending to peer through the murk and call the play; an outfielder runs deep and far, arching ball coming down—apparently—just out of his reach, trajectories of fielder and baseball coming miraculously together at the last, gloved hand going out incredibly to pick the ball out of the air; a pitcher who has been getting his lumps looks about at filled bases, glowers at the batter, and then sends one in that is struck at and missed . . . always, some individual is trying for an astounding feat of athletic prowess and, now and then, actually accomplishing it.

Hence baseball celebrates the vicarious triumph. The spectator can identify himself completely with the player, and the epochal feat becomes, somehow, an achievement of his own. Babe Ruth, mocking the Chicago Cubs, pointing to the distant bleachers and then calmly hitting the ball into those bleachers, took a host of Walter Mittys with him when he jogged around the bases. (There is some dispute about this, to be sure; he was jawing with the Cubs, but purists say he did not actually call his shot. This makes no difference anyway.) It was the same when old Grover Cleveland Alexander, the all-but-washed-up veteran of many baseball wars, came into the seventh inning of a decisive World Series game, found the bases filled with Yankees, and struck out Tony Lazzeri, going on to win game and Series; and this was after a wearing night on the tiles, Alexander having supposed that his work was over until next spring. Many an aging fan shared in Old Alex's triumph.

These things are part of baseball's legend, for the game never forgets its gallery of immortals. That it actually has a tangible Hall of Fame, with bronze plaques to commemorate the greatest, is only part of the story: the noble deeds of the super-players are handed down in bar-side stories, year after year, losing nothing in the telling. Some of the heroes have been supermen, in a way, at that. There was, for instance, Shoeless Joe Jackson, barred from baseball in mid-career because he let himself be bribed to help lose a World Series. (He did not do very well at losing; even under a bribe, he batted .375 in that Series—a natural hitter who just couldn't make himself miss even when paid to do so.) A sand-lot pitcher tells of a day, a whole generation later, when, pitching for a textile-mill team in the Carolinas, he found on the opposing team none other than Jackson—a pathetic, fat, doddering wreck in his late fifties, with monstrous belly like some disreputable Santa Claus, still picking up a few odd bucks playing semi-pro ball under an assumed name. The young pitcher figures Jackson would be easy; a low inside curve, coming in close to the overhang of that prodigious paunch, was obviously the thing to throw. He threw, Jackson swung, and swung as he used to thirty years earlier, and the ball went far out of the park, one of the most authoritative home runs the young pitcher had ever witnessed. Old Jackson lumbered heavily around the bases, and halfway between third and home he turned to accost the young pitcher. "Son," he said, "I always could hit them low inside curves."

There were others cast in similar molds. . . . Rube Waddell, the wholly legendary character who, when cold sober, which was not often, may have been the greatest pitcher of them all: the man who now and then, on a whim, would gesture the entire outfield off the premises and then retire the side without visible means of support; Walter Johnson, who once pitched fifty-odd consecutive scoreless innings, and who to the end of his days had nothing much in his repertoire except an unhittable fast ball; Tris Speaker, who played such a short center field that he often threw a batter out at first on what ought to have been legitimate down-the-middle base hit; and lean Satchel Paige, who in his great days in the Negro leagues had a way of pointing to the shortstop and then throwing something which the batter must hit to short, and who then would go on around the infield in the same way, compelling the opposition to hit precisely where he wanted it to hit. The legends are, in some ways, the most enduring part of the game. Baseball has even more of them than the Civil War, and its fans prize them highly.

Under the surface, baseball is always played to a subdued but inescapable tension, because at any second one of these utterly fabulous events may take place. The game may be distressingly one-sided, and the home team may come up in the ninth inning five runs behind, and in a clock game like football or basketball the margin would be physically unbeatable; but in baseball anything can happen, and the tiniest fluke can change everything. (Remember the World Series game the Yankees won when a Brooklyn catcher dropped a third strike with two men out in the ninth?) A commonplace game can turn into a hair-raiser at any moment, and things do not actually need to happen to create the suspense. A free-hitting, high-scoring game may be most eventful, but few strains are greater than the strain of watching a pitcher protect a 1–0 lead in the late innings of a routine game. Nothing, perhaps, actually happens—but every time the ball is thrown the game may turn upside down, and nobody ever forgets it.

All of this is built in for the spectator. Built in, as well, is the close attention to records and statistics. Batting averages and pitchers' records are all-important; to know that a Rogers Hornsby, for instance, could bat more than .400 in three different years—that is, could average getting two hits for every five times he came to the plate, 154 games a year, for three years—is important. It has been suggested, now and then, that big league playing schedules be reduced from 154 games to some smaller figure, and the suggestion has always been howled down: it would upset all the averages. Unthinkable; how do you compare today's pitcher with Walter Johnson or Lefty Grove if today's pitcher plays in fewer games every year?

The circumstances under which baseball is played nowadays have changed greatly, to be sure. Less than half a century ago, every town that amounted to anything at all was represented in some league of professional players, and these leagues—the minor leagues, of hallowed memory —have been dissolving and vanishing, as more and more spectators get their games by television or by radio and ignore the local ball park. The Little Leagues have come up, and semi-subsidized sand-lot leagues, and even college baseball is here and there enjoying a new lease on life—after all, the new players in the big leagues have to come from somewhere, and besides, young Americans still like to play baseball; but the old pattern is gone, and even the major leagues themselves have undergone profound changes and, to a purist from the old days, are all but unrecognizable. Where are the St. Louis Browns, or the Philadelphia Athletics, or the Boston Braves—or, for the matter of that, even the magnificent New York Giants, and the Brooklyn Dodgers? Gone forever, to be sure, with new cities taking over, and with a few old-timers muttering that the last days are at hand.

Actually, the last days are probably a long, long way off, for baseball even in its modern guise had not changed in its essentials. It is a rough, tough game, encased by rules that were to be broken if the breaking can be accomplished smoothly enough, a game that never quite became entirely respectable, a game in which nobody wants to do anything but win. It will undoubtedly be around for a long time to come, and it will continue, in spite of its own press agents, to be in truth the Great American game.

Or so, at least, believes one old-time fan.

—April 1959

BIG BILL TAFT

By STEPHEN HESS

The heaviest—and nicest—man ever to be elected President hadn't wanted the job

Although he was not there, his mother, his Aunt Delia, and two of his brothers gathered in New York City early in January, 1903, and, after due deliberation, drafted a report: William Howard Taft was to be President of the United States.

For two reasons this was a remarkable, if not amazing, decision. First, the occupant of the White House at the moment was Theodore Roosevelt, who showed no disposition to move out for another six years to accommodate William Howard Taft or anyone else; and second, William Howard Taft did not want to be President.

From the time Will Taft was a child his family never had any doubt that its honor and destiny were bound up in him. When he grew up and married, his wife was equally determined that Taft would be President. Mrs. Taft, the former Helen Herron, was a bright, attractive girl, but she had a stubborn mouth. Moreover, she was reserved and literary, and didn't make friends easily. As with everything that Mrs. Taft put her mind to, her ambition for her husband was not arrived at frivolously. "Nellie," as she was called, knew the White House well. Her father had been a college classmate of Benjamin Harrison's and the law partner of Rutherford B. Hayes; her mother was the daughter and sister of congressmen. At the age of seventeen, while the houseguest of President and Mrs. Hayes, Nellie announced that she was so taken with the White House that she would marry someone destined to be President.

But William Howard Taft, the man in whom all family ambition centered, was hardly a piece of putty to be manipulated by petticoat politicians. His path to the White House was paved with greater public service than that of any President since Martin Van Buren. If one were to plot Taft's career on a graph, the line would rise sharply and steeply, without a single dip, until it marked the summit of American political life.

He became assistant prosecutor of Hamilton County, Ohio, at the age of twenty-three, Collector of Internal Revenue in Cincinnati two years later, judge of the state superior court at twenty-nine, Solicitor General of the United States at thirty-two, a federal circuit-court judge at thirty-four, first U.S. Civil Governor of the Philippines at forty-two, Secretary of War in the Cabinet of Theodore Roosevelt at forty-six, and President of the United States at fifty-one. Each job seemed to be a logical outgrowth of the one before; each new opportunity seemed only to await the successful conclusion of the preceding episode.

The man who possessed this impressive public record was tall and round, with a ruddy complexion, a blondish mustache, and dark hair. His legs seemed too short for his torso. His weight sometimes climbed to over 325 pounds. Yet despite this great bulk he was light on his feet and a nimble dancer. He was also quick to joke about his generous proportions. When offered the Kent Chair of Constitutional Law at Yale he replied that it would be inadequate but that "a Sofa of Law" might be all right. Then Taft probably chuckled a rapturous, subterranean, incomparable chuckle: "the most infectious chuckle in the history of politics," wrote his biographer, Henry F. Pringle. Said the wife of a Texas congressman, "It reminded me of the cluck a whippoorwill gives, a laugh to himself, when he has been whistling with special vim and mischief."

The popular image of the jolly fat man fooled many into believing that Taft's core was of petroleum jelly rather than tempered steel. William Allen White, the perceptive Kansas editor, knew otherwise. Once after having crossed Taft, White described the "eye behind his smile veiling . . . almost the hint of a serpentine glitter." And TR, while they were still friends, said that Taft was "one of the best haters" he had ever known.

On the day in 1890 that Will Taft came to Washington to be sworn in as Solicitor General, he was visited by William M. Evarts, distinguished senator from New York and leader of the American bar. "Mr. Taft," said the Senator, "I knew your father . . . I valued his friendship very highly." Evarts went on to say that he was presuming on this friendship to ask Taft to a dinner party that evening at which he was short one man. So the young lawyer ended his first day in the capital by dining between Mrs. Henry Cabot Lodge and Mrs. John Hay, neither of whom had the faintest idea as to who he was. Even after Taft became Secretary of War he frankly replied to an interviewer who asked him to explain his rapid political ascent, "I got my political pull, first, through father's prominence . . ."

The father whose name opened brass-plated doors was Alphonso Taft, dour and industrious Yankee, and holder at various times in a long public career of such illustrious positions as Secretary of War, Attorney General of the United States, and Envoy Extraordinary and Minister Plenipotentiary to Austria-Hungary and to Russia.

Yet, as a contemporary Taft has put it, "The Tafts were not big shots or tycoons; they were carpenters, innkeepers, farmers—in other words, plain ordinary people." Although they arrived in Massachusetts around 1678, Alphonso was the first in the family to have graduated from college. When he was a student at Yale in the 1830s, he sometimes walked from his father's farm in Vermont to New Haven. In 1839 he moved to Cincinnati, where he founded a law practice, and a political dynasty. He was more interested in public service than private profit, and when he died in 1891 his entire estate consisted of $482.80 and a house. (The house was eventually sold for $18,000.)

Louise Torrey Taft, whom Alphonso married in 1853, after the death of his first wife, was a serene, happy person who also possessed rare executive ability. Her presidential son was to write, "When woman's field widens, Mother, you must become President of a Railway Company." Like her husband, she claimed sturdy New England roots. Her father, Samuel Torrey, was a Boston merchant who, at the age of forty, moved to the village of Millbury, Massachusetts, after a physician advised that he had only a short time to live. With characteristic stubbornness, he remained in vigorous good health for the next forty-nine years.

When they were boys, William Howard Taft and his brothers and half-brothers often spent their summers at Millbury with Grandfather Torrey. The house was presided over by a maiden aunt, Delia, a believer in the dubious proposition that "ladies of strong minds seldom marry." Her sense of humor was later to receive national attention when her nephew entered the White House and the press gleefully reported the opinions of "Aunt Delia." At one time, when people were adopting fancy place-names such as "Manchester by the Sea," Aunt Delia chose to protest the befouled Blackstone River by dating her letters, "Millbury by the Sewer." Grandfather Torrey, however, was of sterner stuff, believing that the best way to bring up boys was by "the Puritanical maxim that it is good for the soul to take one's pleasure sadly." A typical dinner conversation at grandfather's went:

"Henry, will you have mince pie or apple pie?"

"Oh, I don't care, Grandpa."

"If you don't care, we won't cut the pie."

"To be the founders of a family," wrote Alphonso Taft, "is a great matter." He took his responsibility seriously, and while he loved his sons deeply, he was also a stern disciplinarian. Encouragement was spiced with criticism. When the boys were not at the top of their classes, Alphonso wanted to know why. A typical letter to young William Howard Taft from his father read: "I do not think you have accomplished as much this past year as you ought with your opportunities. Our anxiety for your success is very great and I know that there is but one way to attain it, & that is by self-denial and enthusiastic hard work. . . ."

For one son, Peter Rawson Taft, the paternal spur may have been too sharp. Although he was valedictorian of his class at Yale, he seemed to be plagued with a deep sense of guilt, which led to a breakdown and an early death in a sanitarium. But the other four sons of Alphonso Taft went on to outstanding careers in the fields of publishing, industry, education, politics, and law.

According to Archie Butt, a skillful celebrity-watcher, there never were brothers more devoted to each other than these Tafts. Even when William Howard Taft was asked to head the civil government of the Philippines, the young man told President McKinley that he would just have to wait a week for his answer—first he had to consult with his brothers.

Of Will Taft's brothers, Henry Waters Taft became one of the nation's most prominent attorneys as senior partner in Cadwalader, Wickersham & Taft, as well as author of ten books ranging in subject matter from Japan to the art of conversation; Horace Dutton Taft founded the Taft School at Watertown, Connecticut, and was called "headmaster of headmasters" by Williams College when it granted him one of his many honorary degrees; and Charles Phelps Taft published the Cincinnati *Times-Star*, served in Congress and in the Ohio legislature, and became a major investor in many corporations, including the Chicago Cubs.

Charlie was to play a unique role in his younger brother's career by supplementing Will's meager public salary and underwriting his drive for the Presidency. From the time William Howard Taft was Solicitor General until he entered the White House, a period of eighteen years, Charles Phelps Taft subsidized his brother in amounts ranging from $6,000 to $10,000 a year, and the 1908 presidential campaign was said to have cost him $800,000.

The desire to allow his brother the freedom to pursue public service was Charlie's, but the ability to do so was his wife's. For Charlie Taft had married one of the great heiresses of Ohio. Fun-loving and witty, Annie Sinton was described by a contemporary as "so natural and kindly that one would never suspect her of either great wealth or high position." She once dropped a suitor because he tried to dazzle her by lighting a cigar with a dollar bill.

The Sinton money, which was to bankroll a Taft to the Presidency, was made by Annie's father, an Irish immigrant of irregular education. Rugged, close-fisted David Sinton went to Ironton, Ohio, at the age of eighteen, to work at a blast furnace. He soon had a furnace of his own, and, with every cent of his own and every cent he could borrow, he built up a stockpile of pig iron which he sold at inflated prices after the outbreak of the Civil War. When he died he left his only child an estimated fifteen million dollars.

After Will Taft reached the White House, reporters at a Washington Gridiron dinner poked fun at his brother's lavish spending. In one skit a customer in a diner ordered "breast of chicken with wings attached and boiled dumplings."

"Angel with dough," called the waiter.

"Charles P. Taft, for one," responded the chef from the rear.

The financier was equal to the joke. Later he told his brother's military aide, "Huntington [of the Southern Pacific Railroad] thought it came high to get a prince in the family. He ought to have tried getting a President into one!"

Alphonso Taft felt that all his sons were destined for legal careers, and all five earned law degrees. Then when his youngest son deserted private practice to become a teacher, the father shook his head in disbelief. "I cannot comprehend Horace's idea of founding a private school or what in the world he can hope from it," Alphonso wrote. "The law is his proper field."

But the father was never to be disappointed by William Howard Taft. "I love judges, and I love courts," Will was later to say. "They are my ideals, that typify on earth what we shall meet hereafter in heaven under a just God." Before his thirtieth birthday he had taken the first step up the judicial ladder—appointment to the superior court of Ohio—and, much to Alphonso's delight, just before his death he saw his son named Solicitor General of the United States, the attorney charged with representing the federal government before the Supreme Court.

In Washington, Solicitor General Taft was brought together with another young man, Theodore Roosevelt, who had recently been made a Civil Service commissioner. The two second-echelon appointees were attractively different; Roosevelt so combustible, creative, so divinely illogical; Taft so harmonious, solid, so thoroughly logical. And their aspirations would carry them forward together. If ever a man conceived himself destined to be President of the United States it was Roosevelt; if ever a man felt chosen for Chief Justice of the United States it was Taft. They could serve each other well. Taft helped Roosevelt get appointed Assistant Secretary of the Navy, the post from which he would catapult to fame, and later encouraged his White House ambitions when they looked most remote to the Rough Rider.

Taft stayed in Washington only two years on his first appointment, resigning from the Justice Department to accept a federal circuit-court judgeship. Nellie, very much against leaving the rarified atmosphere of the capital, told her husband, "My darling, it will put an end to all the opportunities you now have of being thrown with the bigwigs." This argument failed to convince him, and "so once more," she wrote in her memoirs, "I saw him a colleague of men almost twice his age and, I feared, fixed in a groove for the rest of his life." She had to admit, however, that Will "was greatly pleased and very proud to hold such a dignified and responsible position at the age of thirty-four. I think [she wrote in 1914] he enjoyed the work of the following eight years more than any he has ever undertaken."

As a jurist, Taft was heroically conscientious and hard-working, and almost always conservative. His tenure on the bench coincided with the rise of the Populists and the American Federation of Labor, and many of his most important decisions dealt with the labor movement. On rare occasions, such as the Addyston Pipe case, 1898, where Taft ruled that a combination of manufacturers was in restraint of trade, he could be found opposing the interests of business, and he did recognize the basic right of labor to organize. But most often, since he felt that private property was of "sacred character," the Ohio judge wielded the injunctive power to beat back the incursions of the unions.

It took all of William McKinley's persuasive powers, plus a hint of future preferment, to get Taft to leave the halls of justice to become head of the civil government of the Philippine Islands, recently acquired in the war with Spain. He finally succumbed to duty and the President's assurance that "if you give up this judicial office at my request you shall not suffer." To Taft this sounded very much like a promissory note for the next Supreme Court vacancy.

He went to the Philippines to rule a conquered nation; he returned, according to Carlos Romulo, "enshrined in the Filipino heart." Taft established a policy that would eventually lead to self-government and independence, but in the meantime would be benevolent and responsive. In this he was opposed by General Arthur MacArthur, the American military commander, who felt that the islanders should be ruled by the bayonet for at least a decade. MacArthur's soldiers sang a song about "our little brown brothers" which ended: *He may be a brother of William H. Taft, but he ain't no friend of mine!* Taft instinctively distrusted the military view.

The Filipinos had lived under colonial rule since 1565, but never had they known an outsider quite like this first American viceroy. He made it clear from the start that color lines would not be tolerated at his social functions. The proud natives could almost feel his innate sympathy: he appointed them to high office, could be seen enjoying himself at their cockfights and concerts, even toured the remote interior where headhunters were still known to exist.

More tangible, Taft achieved tax revisions, established municipal governments in many communities, put through harbor and other public improvements, increased educational facilities, instituted a civil service, and reformed land distribution and the judiciary. All this was performed in a tropical climate that was considered murderous to foreigners of much trimmer proportions. During his three years in the Philippines, Taft suffered from dengue fever and amoebic dysentery and underwent three operations for abscesses.

In 1901, when Theodore Roosevelt was Vice President and had a great deal of time on his hands, he wrote an article for *The Outlook* entitled "Governor William H. Taft." It began: "A year ago a man of wide acquaintance both with American life and American public men remarked that the first Governor of the Philippines ought to combine the qualities which would make a first-class President of the United States with the qualities which would make a first-class Chief Justice of the United States, and that the only man he knew who possessed all these qualities was Judge William H. Taft of Ohio. The statement was entirely correct." By the time the article was published, McKinley was dead, the author was President of the United States, and the subject was working for him.

Roosevelt now offered his friend the pinnacle of his ambition—a seat on the Supreme Court. But Taft, deeply and emotionally involved in managing the affairs of the Philippines, felt duty-bound to decline the appointment. It was only when the President asked Taft to become Secretary of War, the officer with jurisdiction over the Islands, that he consented to leave Manila and return to Washington. Outside the gates of Malacañan Palace 6,000 Filipinos paraded with signs, "¡Queremos Taft! [We want Taft!]"

Once in the Cabinet, Taft was preferred over all others; Roosevelt made him in fact, if not title, Assistant President. His duties extended far beyond the confines of the War Department; he was the President's principal troubleshooter. Editorial-page cartoonists loved to draw Taft's massive dimensions, usually carrying a suitcase, rushing off to put out some far-off fire—to Panama to get "the dirt flying," to Cuba to bring an uneasy peace, to the western states to campaign for a Roosevelt Congress.

Then Roosevelt took the step that was bound to end their friendship: he made Taft President.

At William Howard Taft's inauguration, his youngest son, eleven-year-old Charlie, was seen carrying a copy of *Treasure Island*. "This affair is going to be pretty dry," he told his sister, Helen, "and I want something to read." Robert Taft, on the other hand, watched with rapt attention as his father was sworn in. After the ceremony, Mrs. Taft shattered precedent by insisting on riding to the White House with the new President. "Some of the Inaugural Committee expressed their disapproval," reported Nellie, "but I had my way and in spite of protests took my place at my husband's side."

Every new administration brings its own cast of characters to the national scene, and none are more interesting to the American public than the presidential children. Of the three young Tafts, little Charlie was the extrovert and general mischief maker. The future mayor of Cincinnati had travelled twice around the world with his parents before he was eight, and according to his sister, "gave interviews to the newspapers and posed for photographers at every stop!" When his father joined the President's cabinet, he joined that Peck's Bad Boy of the White House, Quentin Roosevelt, in such Executive Mansion diversions as pasting spitballs that looked like warts on the portrait of Andrew Jackson.

Charlie had inherited his father's dimple and chuckle, but it was Helen, in the opinion of the President, who was most like him in character. She was now a student at Bryn Mawr College, where she would later serve as professor of history, dean, and acting president. While more liberal than her father—she had made headlines by speaking in favor of aggrieved shirtmakers—she usually remained quiet and discreet.

It was Robert A. Taft, the future Republican leader, who was most uneasy in the limelight's glare. During his father's administration he graduated from Yale first in his class, and entered Harvard Law School. A young lady at a Boston party who had failed to catch his name had an impossible time trying to detect his identity by adroit questioning: Where did he live? His family home was in Ohio. Did he go back there for holidays? No, the family was now in Washington and he spent his holidays there. What did the family do in Washington? His father had a government job. And where did they live in Washington? "On Pennsylvania Avenue," answered Bob. He did not mean to be coy; it was just that he would rather not be known as the President's son if he could help it.

The salary-plus-expenses of the President had just been raised from $75,000 to $100,000; at last William Howard Taft would make enough to support his family luxuriously. He took to motoring with a passion. "Well, children," he would say, "enjoy this all you can, for in four years more you may have to begin to walk over again." He playfully told Nellie that after the White House they would go back to the "lower middle class," and suggested that she not scrimp on her wardrobe, a suggestion which, to his surprise, she followed. Mrs. Taft filled the Executive Mansion with furniture, tapestries, and screens from the Orient. She covered the floors with *petates*, and filled the rooms to overflowing with plants, ferns, and exotic flowers, so that the servants, in concealed rebellion, were soon referring to the White House as "Malacañan Palace."

The Tafts entertained lavishly. The lawn party they gave on their silver wedding anniversary was one of the largest affairs ever held at the White House. When Aunt Delia arrived, the Washington *Star* editorialized that now the party was "an assured success" because she would superintend the making of her famous apple pies. The old lady enjoyed the notoriety, but confessed to the family that "she had not made an apple pie for forty years and never did know how to make one properly." The President and his First Lady greeted the crush of guests under a flowery arch inscribed "1886–1911," while searchlights from the Treasury and State Department buildings played on the White House; paper lanterns were everywhere. The effect, commented Mrs. Ellen Slayden, was "crude like a fair or circus," which surprised her, since "the Tafts have such excellent taste usually. . . ."

But Mrs. William Howard Taft, who had felt destined to be First Lady since she was seventeen, was not destined to enjoy her reign. Three months after the inauguration she had a stroke. The President lovingly taught her to speak again, but, although she was to live until a week short of her eighty-second birthday, surviving her husband by thirteen years, after her slow recovery she would have a speech impairment for the rest of her life. In 1910 Helen Taft dropped out of college for a year, to replace her mother as the official White House hostess.

The President's office during Roosevelt's occupancy had been a cluttered reflection of a cultured man with a craving for the strenuous life. There was a riding crop and a tennis racket in every corner, and piles of books —history, fiction, even poetry. But when reporter Ray Stannard Baker went to interview the new President he discovered a transformation had taken place. "Now the office had become, and not without significance, a law-office. On all sides of the room were cases filled with law-books, nothing but law-books." And the new Cabinet contained five "good, first-class lawyers," including Henry Taft's partner George Wickersham. "The law to President Taft," wrote Archie Butt, "is the same support as some zealots get from great religious faith."

It soon became apparent that Roosevelt and the man he had chosen as his successor held diametrically opposite views of the Presidency. Taft felt that the Chief Executive had no power that was not specifically spelled out in the Constitution or in an act of Congress. "There is no residuum of power which he can exercise [wrote Taft] because it seems to him to be in the public interest. . . ." "I declined to adopt his view," said Roosevelt. "My belief was that it was not only his right but his duty to do anything that the needs of the nation demanded unless such action was forbidden by the Constitution or by the laws."

Yet Taft, despite his strict interpretation of presidential functions, proposed and, in some areas, achieved even greater reforms than Roosevelt. He secured a tariff revision which on balance was a liberalization of existing schedules; put through the postal-savings-bank system; became "the Father of the Federal Budget"; got Congress to approve a reciprocity treaty with Canada, later defeated by the Canadian legislature; brought more prosecutions under the Sherman Antitrust Act than ever before (ninety as compared with forty-four under Roosevelt); drafted constitutional amendments for the direct election of U.S. senators and for the income tax; started a Department of Labor; and tried to get nations to settle disputes through international arbitration.

But as a politician Taft was all thumbs. "The honest greenhorn at the poker table" is what he was called by a *New York Times* reporter. Said Speaker Cannon, in disgust: "If Taft were pope he'd want to appoint some Protestants to the College of Cardinals." The President was incapable of arousing the public conscience, his relations with the press were atrocious, his speeches were long-winded and stodgy. He justified his actions in legalistic pronouncements; and then, having said all he felt there was to say on a subject, he said no more.

Taft didn't know how to humor the insurgents in his own ranks, and midway in his term he lost control of the Congress altogether. The new Democratic House of the Congress had no intention of making life comfortable for the Republican President. One congressional committee sought to embarrass him by digging up a minor scandal that had taken place ten years before in the State Department. Taft said it reminded him of the man who was asked in a restaurant whether he wanted oxtail soup, which the waiter explained, was merely soup made from the tail of the ox. "Neighbor," the patron replied, "don't you think that's going a hell of a long way back for soup?"

The presidential years, Taft's daughter concluded, "were the only unhappy years of his entire life."

Teddy Roosevelt had sincerely wished his successor well and was determined to allow him to run his own show. So, immediately after the Taft inauguration, he went off to Africa to hunt big game. (And as TR left Washington, some congressmen lifted their glasses in a toast: "To the lions!") But the trouble with Roosevelt was that he was too young—only fifty-one when he vacated the White House—and he knew that his rightful place would always be at the head of the charge. Then too, after he returned home, there were so many old friends who hurried to Oyster Bay with tales of personal or ideological slights by the President. Others were running to Taft with the same sort of self-serving gossip. Minor incidents were blown up into major differences. "It is hard, very hard, Archie, to see a devoted friendship going to pieces like a rope of sand," said Taft. Henry L. Stimson declared, "It was not principle but personality, not purpose but method, that divided Mr. Taft and Mr. Roosevelt." Many, like Stimson, were torn between their loyalties to the two men. The daughter of Maggie, the second maid at the White House, reported that "half the servants were for Taft; half for TR."

At the 1912 Republican convention, Taft, unpopular as he might be, was still the incumbent President, and therefore in control of the party machinery. With Taft's renomination, Roosevelt bolted the party, announcing that he would "stand at Armageddon" and run on a third-party ticket. The cynical railroad czar Chauncey Depew pronounced: "The only question now is which corpse gets the most flowers."

Taft received only eight electoral votes, those of Vermont and Utah. "I regard this as something of an achievement," commented reporter Charles Willis Thompson, "and should be disposed to compliment Utah and Vermont if it were not that the Mormon machine pulled Utah through and that it's a capital offense to vote a third party ticket in Vermont."

Often it would be said of Taft, "He was a bad President, but a good sport." The judgment of his character cannot be faulted; the judgment of his Presidency is more debatable. Perhaps it is fairer to say that he was at least an average President whose achievements tend to be overshadowed because he had the historical misfortune to be sandwiched between two great Presidents, Roosevelt and Wilson.

At a "school of journalism" conducted by Washington's elite Gridiron Club in February, 1913, the "professor" was asked to define a remarkable coincidence. "The most remarkable coincidence of the year 1913," came the reply, "is that at the very moment Professor Wilson becomes President Wilson, President Taft becomes Professor Taft."

The years at Yale would be happy and productive for the ex-President. He had saved $100,000 during his presidential term, and its income, along with a $5,000 salary as professor of law, would be enough, he felt, "to keep the wolf from the door, especially in view of the fact that I do not expect to eat as much after leaving the White House." He also supplemented his income by public speaking, and anyone requesting his services was sent a list of thirty subjects to choose from, ranging from "Duties of Citizenship" to "The Initiative and Referendum." Taft's fees ran from $150 to $1,000, averaging $400 an appearance.

Yale gave a royal welcome to its only alumnus to have been President, "second to no triumphal procession of any Caesar and surpassing any such celebration in the history of the college of the bulldog," wrote the New Haven *Journal-Courier*. The school provided oversized chairs, with twenty-five inch seats, for its new faculty member, who set up an office at brother Charlie's hotel, the Taft. Soon he was coaching the freshman debate team (which, however, lost to Harvard and Princeton), and was enjoying himself at junior proms, banquets, smokers, and ball games.

After a lifetime of deferring to family wishes and to his sense of duty, William Howard Taft finally realized his ambition. In 1921 he was appointed Chief Justice of the United States. "At last Mr. Taft has come to his journey's end," wrote a Washington correspondent. "He has been a long time on the way.

Days on the Supreme Court proved to be everything that Taft always dreamed they would be. "The truth is," he wrote in 1925, "that in my present life I don't remember that I ever was President." An apocryphal tale was told of a little boy who stopped him during his daily walk to the Court, and said, "I know who you are. You used to be President Coolidge!"

He proved to be a conservative, just as expected. Jurisprudentially he wasn't able to win over Holmes, Brandeis, and Stone, but his affable nature won them as friends, and he was particularly surprised to discover how much he liked Brandeis, whose appointment he had bitterly opposed.

For a man who viewed so narrowly the functions of the Presidency, Taft held a broad and freewheeling concept of the Chief Justice's role, "investing his office," wrote Professor Alpheus T. Mason, "with prerogatives for which there were few, if any, precedents." He lobbied blatantly and with considerable success for increasing the number of federal judges, constructing a separate building for the Supreme Court, and tightening the administrative machinery of the federal judiciary, and for procedural changes that would increase the Court's efficiency.

Said Justice Brandeis to Professor Frankfurter, "It's very difficult for me to understand why a man who is so good as Chief Justice, in his function of presiding officer, could have been so bad as President. How do you explain that?" To which Felix Frankfurter replied, "The explanation is very simple. He loathed being President and being Chief Justice was all happiness for him."

Taft worked himself harder than he pushed his colleagues. He wrote an average of thirty opinions per term, while the other Justices averaged twenty. But as the years passed, the infirmities of age began to slow him down. He decided that he would have to celebrate his birthdays on "the Aunt Delia principle"—the old lady, who lived to be ninety-two, gave a dinner party on her eightieth birthday in order that people might not think she was ninety.

Finally, in early 1930, his health failed, and Bob Taft delivered his father's resignation to President Hoover. The Supreme Court, speaking through the eloquent pen of Oliver Wendell Holmes, then wrote him: "We call you Chief Justice still—for we cannot give up the title by which we have known you all these later years and which you have made dear to us. We cannot let you leave us without trying to tell you how dear you have made it. You came to us from achievement in other fields and with the prestige of the illustrious place that you lately had held and you showed us in new form your voluminous capacity for getting work done, your humor that smoothed the tough places, your golden heart that brought you love from every side and most of all from your brethren whose tasks you have made happy and light. We grieve at your illness, but your spirit has given an impulse that will abide whether you are with us or away."

William Howard Taft died on March 8, 1930, at the age of seventy-two. He had held public office for over forty years, and was the only person to have served as both President and Chief Justice of the United States.

Another tribute that would have greatly pleased him came from humorist Will Rogers: *"It's great to be great but it's greater to be human.* He was our great fellow because there was more of him to be human. We are parting with three hundred pounds of solid charity to everyone, and love and affection for all his fellow men."

—October 1968

AN IOWA CHRISTMAS

By PAUL ENGLE

In the three decades since it was first published, this poet's reminiscence has become a holiday classic

Every Christmas should begin with the sound of bells, and when I was a child mine always did. But they were sleigh bells, not church bells, for we lived in a part of Cedar Rapids, Iowa, where there were no churches. My bells were on my father's team of horses as he drove up to our horse-headed hitching post with the bobsled that would take us to celebrate Christmas on the family farm ten miles out in the country. My father would bring the team down Fifth Avenue at a smart trot, flicking his whip over the horses' rumps and making the bells double their light, thin jangling over the snow, whose radiance threw back a brilliance like the sound of bells.

There are no such departures any more: the whole family piling into the bobsled with a foot of golden oat straw to lie in and heavy buffalo robes to lie under, the horses stamping the soft snow, and at every motion of their hoofs the bells jingling, jingling. My father sat there with the reins firmly held, wearing a long coat made from the hide of a favorite family horse, the deep chestnut color still glowing, his mittens also from the same hide. It always troubled me as a boy of eight that the horses had so indifferent a view of their late friend appearing as a warm overcoat on the back of the man who put the iron bit in their mouths.

There are no streets like those any more: the snow sensibly left on the road for the sake of sleighs and easy travel. We could hop off and ride the heavy runners as they made their hissing, tearing sound over the packed snow. And along the streets we met other horses, so that we moved from one set of bells to another, from the tiny tinkle of the individual bells on the shafts to the silvery, leaping sound of the long strands hung over the harness. There would be an occasional brass-mounted automobile laboring on its narrow tires and as often as not pulled up the slippery hills by a horse, and we would pass it with a triumphant shout for an awkward nuisance which was obviously not here to stay.

The country road ran through a landscape of little hills and shallow valleys and heavy groves of timber, including one of great towering black walnut trees which were all cut down a year later to be made into gun-stocks for the First World War. The great moment was when we left the road and turned up the long lane on the farm. It ran through fields where watermelons were always planted in the summer because of the fine sandy soil, and I could go out and break one open to see its Christmas colors of green skin and red inside. My grandfather had been given some of that land as bounty land for service as a cavalryman in the Civil War.

Near the low house on the hill, with oaks on one side and apple trees on the other, my father would stand up, flourish his whip, and bring the bobsled right up to the door of the house with a burst of speed.

There are no such arrivals any more: the harness bells ringing and clashing like faraway steeples, the horses whinnying at the horses in the barn and receiving a great, trumpeting whinny in reply, the dogs leaping into the bobsled and burrowing under the buffalo robes, a squawking from the hen house, a yelling of "Whoa, whoa," at the excited horses, boy and girl cousins howling around the bobsled, and the descent into the snow with the Christmas basket carried by my mother.

While my mother and sisters went into the house, the team was un-hitched and taken to the barn, to be covered with blankets and given a little grain. That winter odor of a barn is a wonderfully complex one, rich and warm and utterly unlike the smell of the same barn in summer: the body heat of many animals weighing a thousand pounds and more; pigs in one corner making their dark, brown-sounding grunts; milk cattle still nuzzling the manger for wisps of hay; horses eyeing the newcomers and rolling their deep, oval eyes white; oats, hay, and straw tangy still with the live August sunlight; the manure steaming; the sharp odor of leather harness rubbed with neat's-foot oil to keep it supple; the molasses-sweet odor of ensilage in the silo where the fodder was almost fermenting. It is a smell from strong and living things, and my father always said it was the secret of health, that it scoured out a man's lungs; and he would stand there, breathing deeply, one hand on a horse's rump, watching the steam come out from under the blankets as the team cooled down from their rapid trot up the lane. It gave him a better appetite, he argued, than plain fresh air, which was thin and had no body to it.

A barn with cattle and horses is the place to begin Christmas; af-ter all, that's where the original event happened, and that same smell was the first air that the Christ Child breathed.

By the time we reached the house, my mother and sisters were wearing aprons and busying in the kitchen, as red-faced as the women who had been there all morning. The kitchen was the biggest room in the house and all family life save sleeping went on there. My uncle even had a couch along one wall where he napped and where the children lay when they were ill. The kitchen range was a tremendous black and gleaming one called a Smoke Eater, with pans bubbling over the holes above the fire box and a reservoir of hot water at the side, lined with dull copper, from which my uncle would dip a basin of water and shave above the sink, turning his lathered face now and then to drop a remark into the women's talk, waving his straight-edged razor as if it were a threat, to make them believe him. My job was to go to the woodpile out back and keep the fire burning, splitting the chunks of oak and hickory, watching how cleanly the ax went through the tough wood.

It was a handmade Christmas. The tree came from down in the grove, and on it were many paper ornaments made by my cousins, as well as beautiful ones brought from the Black Forest, where the family had originally lived. There were popcorn balls, from corn planted on the sunny slope by the watermelons, paper horns with homemade candy, and apples from the orchard. The gifts tended to be hand-knit socks, or wool ties, or fancy crocheted "yokes" for nightgowns, tatted collars for blouses, doilies with fancy flower patterns for tables, tidies for chairs, and once I received a brilliantly polished cow horn with a cavalryman crudely but bravely carved on it. And there would usually be a cornhusk doll, perhaps with a prune or walnut for a face, and a gay dress of an old corset-cover scrap with its ribbons still bright. And there were real candles burning with real flames, every guest sniffing the air for the smell of scorching pine needles. No electrically lit tree has the warm and primitive presence of a tree with a crown of living fires over it, suggesting whatever true flame Joseph may have kindled on that original cold night.

There are no dinners like that any more: every item from the farm itself, with no deep freezer, no car for driving into town for packaged food. The pies had been baked the day before, pumpkin, apple, and mince; as we ate them, we could look out the window and see the cornfield where the pumpkins grew, the trees from which the apples were picked. There was cottage cheese, with the dripping bags of curds still hanging from the cold cellar ceiling. The bread had been baked that morning, heating up the oven for the meat, and as my aunt hurried I could smell in her apron that freshest of all odors with which the human nose is honored—bread straight from the oven. There would be a huge brown crock of beans with smoked pork from the hog butchered every November. We could see, beyond the crock, the broad black iron kettle in a corner of the barnyard, turned upside down, the innocent hogs stopping to scratch on it.

There would be every form of preserve: wild grape from the vines in the grove, crab apple jelly, wild blackberry and tame raspberry, strawberry from the bed in the garden, sweet and sour pickles with dill from the edge of the lane where it grew wild, pickles from the rind of the same water-melon we had cooled in the tank at the milk house and eaten on a hot September afternoon.

Cut into the slope of the hill behind the house, with a little door of its own, was the vegetable cellar, from which came carrots, turnips, cabbages, potatoes, squash. Sometimes my scared cousins were sent there for punishment, to sit in darkness and meditate on their sins; but never on Christmas Day. For days after such an ordeal they could not endure biting into a carrot.

And of course there was the traditional sauerkraut with flecks of cara-way seed. I remember one Christmas Day, when a ten-gallon crock of it in the basement, with a stone weighting down the lid, had blown up, driving the stone against the floor of the parlor, and my uncle had exclaimed, "Good God, the piano's fallen through the floor."

All the meat was from the home place too. Most useful of all, the goose—the very one which had chased me the summer before, hissing and darting out its bill at the end of its curving neck like a feathered snake. Here was the universal bird of an older Christmas: its down was plucked, washed, and hung in bags in the barn to be put into pillows; its awkward body was roasted until the skin was crisp as a fine paper; and the grease from its carcass was melted down, a little camphor added, and rubbed on the chests of coughing children. We ate, slept on, and wore that goose.

I was blessed as a child with a remote uncle from the nearest railroad town, Uncle Ben, who was admiringly referred to as a "railroad man," working the run into Omaha. Ben had been to Chicago; just often enough, as his wife Minnie said with a sniff in her voice, "to ruin the fool, not often enough to teach him anything useful." Ben refused to eat fowl in any form, and as a Christmas token a little pork roast would be put in the oven just for him, always referred to by the hurrying ladies in the kitchen as "Ben's chunk." Ben would make frequent trips to the milk house, re-turning each time a little redder in the face, usually with one of the men toward whom he had jerked his head. It was not many years before I came to associate Ben's remarkably fruity breath not only with the mince pie, but with the jug I found sunk in the bottom of the cooling tank with a stone tied to its neck. He was a romantic person in my life for his constant travels and for that dignifying term "railroad man," so much more impressive than farmer or lawyer. Yet now I see that he was a short man with a fine natural shyness, giving us knives and guns because he had no children of his own.

And of course the trimmings were from the farm too: the hickory nut cake made with nuts gathered in the grove after the first frost and hulled out by my cousins with yellowed hands; the black walnut cookies, sweeter than any taste; the fudge with butternuts crowding it. In the mornings we would be given a hammer, a flat iron, and a bowl of nuts to crack and pick out for the homemade ice cream.

And there was the orchard beyond the kitchen window, the Wealthy, the Russet, the Wolf with its giant-sized fruit, and an apple called the Northern Spy, as if it were a suspicious character out of the Civil War.

All families had their special Christmas food. Ours was called Dutch Bread, made from a dough halfway between bread and cake, stuffed with citron and every sort of nut from the farm—hazel, black walnut, hickory, butternut. A little round one was always baked for me in a Clabber Girl baking soda can, and my last act on Christmas Eve was to put it by the tree so that Santa Claus would find it and have a snack—after all, he'd come a long, cold way to our house. And every Christmas morning, he would have eaten it. My aunt made the same Dutch Bread and we smeared over it the same butter she had been churning from their own Jersey (highest butterfat content) milk that same morning.

To eat in the same room where food is cooked—that is the way to thank the Lord for His abundance. The long table, with its different levels where additions had been made for the small fry, ran the length of the kitchen. The air was heavy with odors not only of food on plates but of the act of cooking itself, along with the metallic smell of heated iron from the hardworking Smoke Eater, and the whole stove offered us its yet uneaten prospects of more goose and untouched pies. To see the giblet gravy made and poured into a gravy boat, which had painted on its sides winter scenes of boys sliding and deer bounding over snow, is the surest way to overeat its swimming richness.

The warning for Christmas dinner was always an order to go to the milk house for cream, where we skimmed from the cooling pans of fresh milk the cream which had the same golden color as the flanks of the Jersey cows which had given it. The last deed before eating was grinding the coffee beans in the little mill, adding that exotic odor to the more native ones of goose and spiced pumpkin pie. Then all would sit at the table and my uncle would ask the grace, sometimes in German, but later, for the benefit of us ignorant children, in English:

Come, Lord Jesus, be our guest.
Share this food that you have blessed.

There are no blessings like that any more: every scrap of food for which my uncle had asked the blessing was the result of his own hard work. What he took to the Lord for Him to make holy was the plain substance that an Iowa farm could produce in an average year with decent rainfall and proper plowing and manure.

The first act of dedication on such a Christmas was to the occasion which had begun it, thanks to the Child of a pastoral couple who no doubt knew a great deal about rainfall and grass and the fattening of animals. The second act of dedication was to the ceremony of eating. My aunt kept a turmoil of food circulating, and to refuse any of it was somehow to violate the elevated nature of the day. We were there not only to celebrate a fortunate event for mankind, but also to recognize that suffering is the natural lot of men—and to consume the length and breadth of that meal was to suffer! But we all faced the ordeal with courage. Uncle Ben would let out his belt—a fancy Western belt with steer heads and silver buckle—with a snap and a sigh. The women managed better by always getting up from the table and trotting to the kitchen sink or the Smoke Eater or outdoors for some item left in the cold. The men sat there grimly enduring the glory of their appetites.

After dinner, late in the afternoon, the women would make despairing gestures toward the dirty dishes and scoop up hot water from the reservoir at the side of the range. The men would go to the barn and look after the livestock. My older cousin would take his new .22 rifle and stalk out across the pasture with the remark, "I saw that fox just now looking for his Christmas goose." Or sleds would be dragged out and we would slide in a long snake, feet hooked up into the sled behind, down the hill and across the westward-sloping fields into the sunset. Bones would be thrown to dogs, suet tied in the oak trees for the juncos and winter-defying chickadees, a saucer of skimmed milk set out for the cats, daintily and disgustedly picking their padded feet through the snow, and crumbs scattered on a bird feeder where already the crimson cardinals would be dropping out of the sky like blood. Then back to the house for a final warming-up before leaving. There was usually a song around the tree before we were bundled up, many thanks all around for gifts, the basket as loaded as when it came, more so, for left-over food had been piled in it. My father and uncle would have brought up the team from the barn and hooked them into the double shafts of the bobsled, and we would all go out into the freezing air of early evening.

On the way to the door I would walk under a photograph of my grandfather, his cavalry saber hung over it (I had once sneaked it down from the wall and in a burst of gallantry had killed a mouse with it behind the corncrib.) With his long white beard he looked like one of the prophets in Hurlbut's illustrated *Story of the Bible*, and it was years before I discovered that he had not been off, as a young man, fighting the Philistines, but the painted Sioux. It was hard to think of that gentle man, whose family had left Germany in protest over military service, swinging that deadly blade and yelling in a cavalry charge. But he had done just that, in some hard realization that sometimes the way to have peace and a quiet life on a modest farm was to go off and fight for them.

And now those bells again, as the horses, impatient from their long standing in the barn, stamped and shook their harness, my father holding them back with a soft clucking in his throat and a hard pull on the reins. The smell of wood smoke flavoring the air in our noses, the cousins shivering with cold, "Good-bye, good-bye," called out from everyone, and the bobsled would move off, creaking over the frost-brittle snow. All of us, my mother included, would dig down in the straw and pull the buffalo robes up to our chins. As the horses settled into a steady trot, the bells gently chiming in their rhythmical beat, we would fall half asleep, the hiss of the runners comforting. As we looked up at the night sky through half-closed eyelids, the constant bounce and swerve of the runners would seem to shake the little stars as if they would fall into our laps. But that one great star in the East never wavered. Nothing could shake it from the sky as we drifted home on Christmas.

—December 1957

THE WORLD'S TALLEST BUILDING

By SPENCER KLAW

F. W. Woolworth's magnificent steel and masonry tribute to himself, his business, and his era

Of the skyscrapers that sprang up in American cities in the early years of this century and embodied in masonry and steel the swaggering vitality of American technology and American business enterprise, none took so firm a grip on the public imagination as the Woolworth Building. From the day that Frank W. Woolworth, the inventor of the five-and-ten-cent store, let it be known that he intended to erect the world's tallest building on a site in lower Manhattan, the newspapers were filled with accounts of its construction and encomiums to its builders. The New York *Sun* compared the building to the Colossus of Rhodes, and described it as the "crowning glory of the builder's art." The *Press* ran a story headed WOOLWORTH BUILDING MARVEL OF THE AGE. In 1912, as work on the 792-foot structure was nearing an end, a *Brooklyn Citizen* reporter, sacrificing journalistic objectivity on the altar of patriotism, wrote that now the whole world would have to acknowledge that "for ingenuity, daring and effectiveness the American architects and engineers are far ahead of the master builders of this or any other age."

To celebrate the completion of the building, Woolworth invited some eight hundred guests to a dinner honoring the architect, Cass Gilbert. The dinner was held on April 24, 1913, in an improvised banquet hall on the twenty-seventh floor of the new building, and the diners included such notables as the artist Charles Dana Gibson, the poet Edwin Markham, steel tycoons Charles Schwab and Elbert Gary, the financier Otto Kahn, the writer Richard Harding Davis, three U.S. senators, seventy-eight congressmen, and the lieutenant governor of Massachusetts. At 7:30 the lights in the room were dimmed, and a Western Union operator flashed a signal to the White House, where President Wilson was waiting to press a button to light up the whole building with eighty thousand bulbs. "A second later," the New York *American* reported, "waiting thousands in New York and its suburbs saw, flashing out in outlines of fire, the greatest mountain of steel and stone ever erected by man—the gigantic Woolworth Building."

Later, after Woolworth had presented Gilbert with a silver loving cup big enough for a horse to drink from, a poem in Gilbert's honor was read by the poet and essayist William Winter. Winter had retired in 1909 after a long career as the dramatic critic of the New York *Tribune*, where he had been known to his colleagues as Weeping Willie because of the lugubrious elegies he composed to mourn the passing of actors whose work he had admired. The poem he produced on this occasion began dolefully enough, referring to such long-vanished centers of civilization as Babylon and Tyre, and noting that "ravens flit and serpents hiss / O'er what was once Persepolis." But by the time Winter had reached the tenth stanza his poetic tears had dried. New York, he seemed to be saying, might be saved from the fate of Babylon and Tyre by great artists like Cass Gilbert, chosen by destiny "To hail the future and ordain / Triumphant Beauty's perfect reign."

The organization of the banquet—and, presumably, the enlistment of President Wilson's services as an electrician—was the work of a publicity man named Hugh McAtamney. He had been retained by Woolworth on the theory that the Woolworth Building, if properly publicized, would operate as a great magnet, pulling millions of new customers into Woolworth stores all over the United States. Long before the building was finished McAtamney had been planting newspaper stories celebrating the wonders of a country where a man who had started out as a $3.50-a-week store clerk was not only putting up the tallest building the world had ever seen, but was paying its entire cost—$13,500,000—out of his own pocket.

But popular fascination with the building, whose fifty-eighth-floor observation gallery drew more than 300,000 visitors a year during the 1920's, was not simply a product of inspired press-agentry. The Woolworth Building was not only the tallest building in the world, it *proclaimed* its tallness in a way that filled the beholder's breast with awe and wonder. This was not generally true of skyscrapers built before 1913, most of which were actually designed so as to play down their height. A case in point was the Metropolitan Life Tower, which stood (and still stands) on Madison Square, two miles north of the Woolworth Building. Modeled on the campanile of St. Mark's, in Venice, it was, when it was completed in 1910, the tallest building in the world. But as John Burchard and Albert Bush-Brown complained in *The Architecture of America*, the architect was seemingly unable to top off the structure "without stuttering through successive strata of balconies, cornices, roofs, more cornices, pavilions and spires"—all of which had the effect of seeming to press the building down into the ground. By contrast, the Gothic design of the Woolworth Building featured prominent white piers that soared straight up into the sky for seven hundred feet before terminating in flying buttresses and the lacy filigree of the building's crown.

The building's rich Gothic ornamentation also conveyed the uplifting thought that business enterprise in America was more than just a sordid struggle for material gain. This message made a particularly deep impression on S. Parkes Cadman, D.D., S.T.D., L.H.D., the author of the foreward to an elegantly illustrated booklet about the building that Woolworth arranged to have printed up. Dr. Cadman, a Brooklyn clergyman sometimes identified in the local press simply as "the noted divine," wrote, "When seen at nightfall bathed in electric light as with a garment, or in the lucid air of a summer morning, piercing space like a battlement of the paradise of God which St. John beheld, [the Woolworth Building] inspires feelings too deep even for tears. The writer looked upon it and at once cried out, 'The Cathedral of Commerce'. . . ."

In 1913 Frank Woolworth was sixty-one years old and nearing the peak of a dazzling business career. Born on a farm in upstate New York, he had been seized by the notion, after years of clerking in small general stores, that buyers would flock to an establishment where there would be no haggling over prices; where the merchandise would be spread out so that everyone could inspect it for himself; and where—most important of all—no item would cost more than a dime. In 1879 Woolworth opened the world's first successful five-and-ten-cent store, in Lancaster, Pennsylvania. Soon he had a small chain of stores, each identified by the distinctive red front that was later to be copied by S. H. Kress, S. S. Kresge, and other competitors. As the chain grew, Woolworth was able to buy goods in larger and larger quantities and at lower and lower prices. This in turn enabled him to offer the public better bargains, thereby assuring the success of the new Woolworth stores that were soon being opened at a rate of twenty or thirty a year. In 1911 Woolworth persuaded the proprietors of four smaller chains to combine their businesses with his; when the merger was consummated he controlled a total of more than six hundred five-and-ten-cent stores in the United States, Canada, and England.

In the lobby of the Woolworth Building, hunched up under an ornate ceiling beam, there is a small sculptured caricature of Woolworth. He is shown nursing an oversize nickel, and it is a fact that in real life Woolworth watched nickels, and even pennies, very carefully. Once, in 1890, just before leaving on a trip to Germany, he sent a circular letter to his executives pointing out that "postage on letters to Bremen is five cents per half ounce so you must use thin paper and envelopes to save expense. . . ." Many years later, when he was making millions of dollars a year, he was not above keeping his confidential secretary and the office porter after hours to help him locate a quarter that had disappeared from his change purse. Like other self-made men, he extolled the virtues of hard work. "Many young men fail because they are not willing to sacrifice," he once wrote. "No one ever built a business on thoughts of having a good time."

But Woolworth saw no point in plain living for people who, like himself, had earned the right to live otherwise. His imposing stomach, customarily draped in a dark vest with white piping, testified to the quantities of food he ate. "He scorned exercise in any form," his biographer, John K. Winkler, writes, "and at all hours of the day and night indulged a fondness for rich foods—lobster, rarebits, etc. He doted upon bananas, a delicacy of which he had been deprived in youth, and preferred them overripe."

Woolworth also liked big houses and costly furnishings. From 1901 until his death in 1919 he lived mainly in a thirty-room mansion situated at Fifth Avenue and Eightieth Street in Manhattan, a home whose second-floor drawing room was equipped with a large organ. Although Woolworth had never managed to learn to play a musical instrument, and had a hard time carrying a tune, he had a passion for music. The organ was a mechanical one, activated, like a player piano, by rolls of perforated paper, and Woolworth liked to entertain friends by sitting at the console and pressing buttons that would throw the room into blackness and then flood it with colored light—now amber, now green, now deep mauve—to match the mood of the music.

Later, with the help of a vice president of the Aeolian-Skinner Organ Company, Woolworth contrived to add pictorial effects to these performances. In Winkler's words, "Just before the opening of a great orchestral classic, with the room in darkness, a magnificent oil portrait of the composer—Wagner or Beethoven, Liszt or Mendelssohn—would appear in a panel at the top of the wall, at first faintly, then growing clearer and clearer until the vision was enveloped in light. So lifelike was the apparition that the composer himself seemed present, listening to his own music. Still later Woolworth added meteorological effects. By pressing the right button, Winkler writes, he could make lightning flash, thunder crash, and "rain descend—behind the walls—in torrents so realistic as to make guests wonder how they were going to get home without a drenching."

Woolworth liked opulence in his business as well as his personal life, a taste whose indulgence he justified on the ground that it was good public relations. "You have no idea the impression our fine new office makes on visitors," he wrote in a letter to the company's store managers in 1905. "The five and ten cent business is no longer a Cheap John affair." At the time, the company had just moved into new quarters in lower Manhattan, overlooking City Hall Park, where Woolworth worked at a great mahogany-and-gold desk in a richly furnished green-and-gold office that Winkler describes as "a chromatic joy." But impressive as this was, Woolworth was not satisfied. He felt that he and the company must have a building of their own, one which would advertise not just to business visitors, but to the whole world, the wealth and scope of the enterprise he had founded. And so in 1909 he bought land on Broadway, on the west side of City Hall Park, and the following spring he asked Cass Gilbert to design a suitable company headquarters to be erected on this site.

Cass Gilbert was fifty years old in 1910, a tall man, with a lofty forehead, who wore rimless pince-nez and an imposing handlebar moustache. According to the *Dictionary of American Biography*, he was "purposely impressive in manner and rather pompous at times." Gilbert's biographer adds maliciously, "It was said in the Century Club in New York that he could give the most convincing exposition of the obvious that had ever been heard there." As a young man he had served an apprenticeship to Stanford White. Later, in practice for himself—first in St. Paul, Minnesota, and then in New York—he had designed a number of large and important buildings, including the Minnesota State Capitol and the elaborately neoclassical United States Custom House on Battery Park in Manhattan.

Among architects Gilbert was perhaps admired more for his skill in handling big and difficult jobs than for his felicity as a designer. Nevertheless, it was Gilbert's idea of how a skyscraper should look, rather than his reputation for efficiency, that seems to have recommended him to Woolworth. In 1905 Gilbert had completed a twenty-three story Gothic-styled office building at 90 West Street, just a few minutes' walk from the site where Woolworth planned to build. It was—and is—a building of considerable grace and elegance, conforming to the dictum of the great Chicago architect, Louis H. Sullivan, that a skyscraper should be "a proud and soaring thing." Woolworth knew the building's owner, General Howard Carroll, and it is likely that he settled on Gilbert as his architect because the clean vertical lines and intricate Gothic detail of the West Street building struck him as pretty much what he would like in a building of his own.

From the start of their association, Woolworth severely tested Gilbert's well-established expertise in the handling of clients. While continually urging the architect to get on faster with the job, Woolworth repeatedly held things up by his own indecisiveness. To begin with, he was unable to decide how high a building he wanted. At first he talked of a forty-two-story structure, just tall enough to overtop the Singer Building, which was then the world's second-tallest skyscraper, being exceeded in height only by the Metropolitan Life Tower. But in August, 1910, the two men met in London, and Woolworth said he had decided he could not afford to tie up as much money as would be needed for a forty-two-story building. He asked Gilbert to make plans for a building about twenty-five stories high, to which a tower might be added at a later time.

Within a few weeks the projected building began to grow again. By November, 1910, it had reached, on paper, a height of 620 feet, eight feet higher than the Singer Building. Before another month had passed, with Gilbert's draftsmen hard at work designing the steel framework for a 620-foot building, Woolworth was telling Gilbert that he was not sure that 620 feet was tall enough. By going ninety or a hundred feet higher, he pointed out, they could overtop the Metropolitan Life Tower as well as the Singer Building, and make the Woolworth Building the tallest in the world.

This was fine by Gilbert. The architect had, in fact, egged Woolworth on by having the Metropolitan Life Tower measured, and providing Woolworth with the information that it was exactly seven hundred feet two inches tall. But Gilbert warned his vacillating client that if he wanted a seven-hundred-foot-plus building he would have to decide on it right away, or else incur the considerable cost of modifying the foundations of the building, work on which had already started, to carry the weight of a heavier structure. Even so, Woolworth hesitated for another month. Then, in January, 1911, he formally approved sketch plans for a building that would rise to a height of at least 750 feet, and the draftsmen in Gilbert's office, throwing away the old drawings, began work at once on a new set.

Gilbert also had to put up with Woolworth's penny pinching. This took the form, at times, of trying to get people to work for him for nothing, or for a fraction of what they usually were paid. Thus after agonizing for months over the choice of a general contractor, Woolworth told Louis J. Horowitz, president of the Thompson-Starrett Company, one of New York's leading construction firms, that he would like Horowitz to have the job. But he added that he knew another builder who was ready to do the job for nothing—for the sake of the prestige, Woolworth said—and that he thought Horowitz should do likewise. ("I had the feeling," Horowitz recalled later, "that Mr. Woolworth was turning on me, as if it were a fire hose, his customary way of buying goods for his five-and-ten-cent stores.") Horowitz continued to insist on a $300,000 fee, and eventually Woolworth signed on his terms.

A month or so later Woolworth tried the same trick on Gilbert, suggesting that other architects just as distinguished as Gilbert would have been happy to take on the Woolworth Building job for a lot less than the five per cent fee that the two men had agreed on earlier. Gilbert, who had been working on plans for the building for nearly a year, was not impressed. "I can only say," he wrote Woolworth, "that if the proposition had been offered to me I would have refused it but that is neither here nor there." In the same letter Gilbert noted that over the past three months his office had "entirely reorganized the plans of your building, working out its great structural, mechanical and engineering problems and its exceptional problems of design, and filing the drawings with the Building Department in just ninety calendar days. If there is any record of structural planning to equal this I am not familiar with it." Gilbert added that he had been impelled to accomplish this feat "in order to progress the building so as to save you the heavy interest charges on the investment and so this office force has been at work night and day and I have paid for the expensive 'overtime' myself."

There was apparently no further talk of Gilbert taking a cut in his fee. Still, as construction got under way Woolworth, who spent many hours each week going over accounts submitted by the contractors, repeatedly called on Gilbert to explain instances of what he considered to be unpardonable waste or extravagance. This was, of course, Woolworth's right, but he exercised it with infuriating diligence. In September, 1911, for example, Gilbert wrote Thompson-Starrett that Woolworth had complained to him about "an item of $2.50 per day for the services of a telephone boy at the building." In a mood, one may guess, of exasperated resignation, Gilbert went on, "It would appear that this is a large price to pay for such services, and I would ask your explanation thereof and in doing so have no doubt that you can place before Mr. Woolworth information that will satisfy him or if some error has been made . . . that you will make correction accordingly." The record contains no hint of what became of the telephone boy.

Even more trying to Gilbert than Woolworth's indecisiveness and his attacks of stinginess was his insistence that he be consulted about matters that most clients would have been delighted to leave to the architect. This was no doubt to be expected of a man who for years had personally picked every item sold in his stores, and who, even when he was running a million-dollar business, would sometimes walk into a store, unannounced, and rearrange the window display. But expected or not, his fussiness about details was aggravating. In February, 1911, for example, Gilbert noted in a memorandum that he had warned Woolworth that "the men in the office were standing around sucking their thumbs, marking time," because of Woolworth's continuing reluctance to commit himself irrevocably to the 750-foot-plus building that he had approved in principle two weeks earlier. At the same time, Gilbert wrote, Woolworth was taking up many hours of his time, and the time of his associates, going "into details of a more or less unmaterial character at this time such as the elevator signal service, mail chutes, bulletin boards, etc., etc." On later occasions he argued with Gilbert about such matters as the proper width of the corridor doors—Gilbert wanted to make them thirty-eight inches wide, but Woolworth thought thirty-six inches was wide enough —and the question of whether or not there should be liquid soap dispensers in the washrooms. He tried hard, though unsuccessfully, to persuade Gilbert to equip the building with steel radiators instead of the cast-iron radiators that Gilbert favored. He personally picked (and then changed his mind about) the transom lifts to be used on the corridor doors, and shortly before Christmas of 1911, he visited the offices of the Sanitas Manufacturing Company to look over its line of toilets and other bathroom fixtures. Four months later, Gilbert's office records disclose, Woolworth met with one of Gilbert's senior associates and approved the use of Sanitas toilet seats throughout the building. At the same meeting he settled on the design of the levers that would operate the men's room urinals.

Although Gilbert was impelled by professional pride to take strong exception to many of his client's ideas, he seems to have concluded that Woolworth had a perfect right to do whatever he liked with the thirty-foot-square room on the building's twenty-fourth floor that had been reserved for Woolworth's private office. For a long time Woolworth himself was not sure what kind of décor he wanted, but in the summer of 1913, while touring France with his wife and his wife's sister, he had an inspiration. "Stopping one day in Compiègne," his biographer writes, "they visited Napoleon's Palace. Entering the famous Empire Room, it occurred to Woolworth in a flash that here was the answer to the problem. . . . He, too, would have an Empire Room modeled upon Napoleon's, and furnished and decorated even more elaborately."

He began at once to buy suitable antiques and *objets d'art*, and when he got back to New York he called in a decorator to carry out his ideas. In a letter dated February 20, 1914, and addressed to "all stores, United States, Canada and Great Britain," he described the result: "the handsomest office in the country and possibly the world." He went on to give an inventory of its furnishings, reporting that they included wall panels and wainscoting of Vert Campan marble from the north of Italy; a mahogany Empire desk, three feet nine inches by seven feet six inches; two large round-back armchairs, upholstered in red and pink and gold tapestry, that had been copied from the famous Throne Chair at Fontainebleau; a bronze bust of

Napoleon posing as Julius Caesar ("He liked to look as much like Caesar as possible, you know"); and an elaborate mantel clock "reported to have been given to Napoleon by the Emperor of Russia over 100 years ago." The room also contained a large portrait of Napoleon in his coronation robes, copied from a painting at Versailles. After Woolworth's death, in 1919, it was replaced by a portrait of Woolworth himself.

From an engineering standpoint the Woolworth Building presented its designers with no notably difficult or novel challenges. By 1910 builders like Louis Horowitz were thoroughly familiar with steel-frame construction, in which the weight of a building is supported not by its walls but by interior columns of steel. This was how all skyscrapers were built—no one had figured out any other way to erect a very tall building without making its walls impossibly thick at the base—and the Woolworth Building differed structurally from its predecessors mainly in being taller.

With little else to boast about in the way of technological marvels, Hugh McAtamney concentrated on the building's elevators. They were not only the fastest in the world, he informed the press, but they were the first whose position could be determined by a glance at the winking lights on a signal panel, and the first whose movement could be controlled by a dispatcher in telephonic communication with each of his operators.

McAtamney also worked hard to reassure prospective tenants and visitors that they would be protected by every safety device known to elevator science. This was an important fact to emphasize, for elevators at the time were rightly regarded as only a little less dangerous than airplanes. (During the previous three years, the New York *Tribune* reported in 1912, published data indicated that 2,671 Americans had been killed or injured in elevator accidents.) McAtamney pointed out, among other things, that the elevator shafts in the Woolworth Building were constructed so that, if all other safeguards should fail, a plummeting car would act like a giant piston, compressing the air beneath it into a cushion that would bring the car to a gentle stop.

To draw attention to this feature, it was announced that the inventor of the system, a Mr. F. T. Ellithorpe, would personally test its efficacy. Explaining to the New York *Sun* how such a test was usually conducted, Ellithorpe said it was his practice to have the test car hoisted to the top of the shaft by a single heavy rope instead of the usual wire cable. "With a long pole, to which is secured a sharp blade, I am able to reach the suspending rope," he said. "Everything being in readiness, I poke this pole through the top of the cage and saw away at the hempen cable." Displaying a lively gift for narrative, Ellithorpe continued, "Strand by strand it parts faster than I can describe it, and then, with a sound like a muffled pistol shot, the last fibres yield under the tugging load of the car and down the shaft the elevator goes whizzing." As it turned out, Ellithorpe was not in the test car when it whizzed down from the forty-fifth floor of the Woolworth Building to the bottom of the shaft six hundred feet below. In his place were seven thousand pounds of ballast and a glass of water, and McAtamney was able to announce that the air cushion had been so effective that when the car came to rest not a single drop had been spilled.

The esthetic problems that Gilbert was called on to solve were a lot more formidable than the purely technical ones. For more than thirty years, ever since the invention of steel-frame construction and high-speed elevators had made skyscrapers possible, architects had been arguing about how they should look. One faction, centered in New York, thought that skyscrapers, like all large public buildings, should be designed in a classical or Renaissance mode. A rival school, centered in Chicago, whose most eloquent spokesman was Louis Sullivan, considered this esthetically dishonest. Members of this school held that since the skyscraper was a radically different kind of building from any the world had seen before, its form should express that difference. In their view, a properly designed skyscraper should seem to glory in its height. It should impress the beholder with the fact that it was not a pile of stone, like the Washington Monument, but a steel cage enclosed in a tight-fitting skin of glass and masonry. And it should owe nothing to classical, Renaissance, or any other architectural forms of the past.

Gilbert subscribed to all but the last of these propositions. Years later, in explaining why he had chosen Gothic forms and ornamentation for the Woolworth Building, he observed huffily that there had not been time to invent "a new type of architectural detail at all equivalent to that which so beautifully adorns the medieval structures of Europe and which took three hundred years to develop." This ignored the fact that back before the turn of the century Louis Sullivan had been ornamenting the façades of skyscrapers with luxuriant but delicate forms of his own invention —forms that constituted, along with Tiffany glass, America's main contribution to *art nouveau*. But while Gilbert was a resourceful designer, he was not an inspired one, and doubtless he knew better than to try to do what Sullivan had done.

In any case, it is unlikely that Woolworth would have let him make the attempt. Woolworth knew very little about architecture, but he knew what he liked, and what he liked was *old* architecture. As the historian Merle Curti has observed of this era, "The conception of art as a relic of past grandeur and as something to be acquired as an evidence of success and 'culture' dominated the thought of the new men of wealth." At his meeting with Gilbert, Woolworth produced a photograph of a Victorian Gothic building—although Woolworth did not know what building it was, Gilbert recognized it as the Victoria Tower of the Parliament Building in London—and said that something like that was what he had in mind. This was quite agreeable to Gilbert, who had already shown, with his West Street Building, that by using Gothic forms he could both emphasize the upward thrust of a skyscraper and reveal—or at least indicate—the secrets of its construction.

To be sure, a purely Gothic structure was out of the question. The great architects of the Middle Ages had got their effects in part by using broad areas of windowless wall space, and such areas were ruled out by Woolworth's insistence that windows must run in continuous bands across the building, so that the interior space could be subdivided into large or small offices, with even the smallest offices having adequate light. Furthermore, medieval builders had broken up the planes of their exterior walls with deep recesses and bold projections, a privilege that was denied to Gilbert because its exercise would have cost the building's owner tens of thousands of square feet of rentable floor space.

But within these limitations Gilbert gave his client a building as Gothic in spirit as a reasonable man could ask for. Although he went about designing it in a spirit that at times verged on religious exaltation—"The mounting chords of [Verdi's] Stabat Mater kept sounding in my mind while I was piling up that building," he recalled later—he testily denied that he had set out to build a secular cathedral. In the early stages of the building's design, he wrote, he had studied such medieval masterworks as Brussels' City Hall, and the great Cloth Hall at Ypres, and his aim had been to "express the idea of a *civic* or *commercial* building rather than of an ecclesiastical one." He went on to suggest, without naming names, that people like the "noted divine," Dr. Cadman, might have been well advised to leave architectural criticism to people who knew what they were talking about.

Most architectural critics, while recognizing that the Woolworth Building was not a cathedral, agreed with Dr. Cadman that it was a masterpiece. Montgomery Schuyler, perhaps the most widely read critic of the day, was nearly as effusive in his praise as the Brooklyn minister. "How it cleaves the empyrean and make the welkin ring as it glitters in the sunshine of high noon," he wrote. "How impressively it looms above its fellows in spectral vagueness, in the gray of the dawn or the haze of twilight."

Good sense and the passage of time require some tempering of Schuyler's praise. The Woolworth Building's tapering crown, guarded by its four satellite pinnacles, looks a bit stiff and awkward, and Gilbert's Gothic façade lacks the serenity of the very best skyscrapers. Compared with the best of Sullivan's work, such as the beautiful miniature skyscraper he built on Manhattan's Bleecker Street in 1897, with its marvelous frieze of *art nouveau* angels, the Woolworth Building seems a little fussy.

But its faults are minor. Surrounded by boring steel-and-glass boxes, the mechanical products of modern architects working routinely in the International Style, the Woolworth Building still has the power to amaze and delight. The bands of Gothic ornamentation that mark the base of the tower, and each of its setbacks, refresh the eye, but do not interrupt its journey as it is drawn upward by the great piers that both conceal and display the building's steel skeleton. On entering the lobby the visitor is instantly infected with the fever of Woolworth's uninhibited and childlike love of the magnificent. The walls are of golden marble from the Isle of Skyros. The high, vaulted Persian ceiling is a glittering green and gold and blue mosaic of stylized flower patterns and exotic birds. To the rear, a noble marble stairway leads up to a branch office of the Irving Trust Company, whose predecessor, the Irving National Bank, once had its head-quarters there. High up on the walls, seeming to hold up the ends of the richly ornamented crossbeams, are sculptured figures of Woolworth and some of the people associated with him in the building's planning and construction. They include Cass Gilbert, who is shown holding in his arms, and gravely contemplating through opaque pince-nez, a huge model of the Woolworth Building; Gunvald Aus, the building's structural engineer, who is shown measuring a girder; and Lewis E. Pierson, president of the Irving Bank, who is shown reading the tape coming out of a stock ticker.

A recent historian of the Woolworth Building, Robert A. Jones, suggests that these playful caricatures "belie the ostensible dignity of the setting." He adds, "The whole resplendent display suggests that, at heart, the artists—in behalf of their client—were teasing mammon." But the teasing was clearly affectionate. In Gilbert's view, and in the view of his chief designer, Thomas Johnson, who was responsible for the caricatures, there was nothing wrong—indeed, there was everything right—with a man who wanted to celebrate so exuberantly his own triumphant career as a merchant. And as Jones further points out, it was what the Woolworth Building represented, more than what it was in itself, that fascinated people. A perfect expression of the spirit of America in the 1920s, the great structure symbolized for hundreds of millions of people all over the world, most of whom had seen it only as portrayed in magazines or on postcards, the wealth, the power, and, above all, the exhilarating promise of a country where a poor farm boy like

Frank Woolworth could become as rich as Croesus.

In 1929, when the Chrysler Building was completed, the Woolworth Building lost the title it had held for sixteen years, and today it ranks only eighteenth in height among the skyscrapers of the world. But none of the newer and taller American skyscrapers, built in a time when the world is no longer so entranced by the vigor and the romance of American business enterprise, has generated quite the same excitement. A glimpse of the Empire State Building, however astonishing, does not induce reactions of the kind recorded in *The Spectator* in 1925 by the British biologist and essayist Julian S. Huxley. "Who can forget," he wrote, "the Woolworth Tower (that monument reared on dimes and nickels), as seen from the river as the liner passes, or when it pulls the eye up to incredible heights as you emerge from the subway at City Hall? It is like a cross between a cathedral and one of Mad King Ludwig's palaces, manured to fantastic heights by the glorious megalomaniac spirit of New York. . . . What matter if ecclesiastical Tudor Gothic, richly gilt, seems out of place in an office-building? It *is* a fairy story come gigantically and triumphantly to life, and can never be forgotten."

—February 1977

STILL QUIET ON THE WESTERN FRONT

By GENE SMITH

A pilgrimage to the quiet, haunted places where the nineteenth century died its terrible death

JONCHEREY: TWO BOYS. It is in the late afternoons that the road to Faverois comes alive. The cows are ambling back from the fields, driven on their way by old women and little boys. The few automobiles and tractors crawl along behind the slow cattle, and chickens scrabbling in the mud run clucking away. After the cows are in their barns, the road falls silent. After nine o'clock it is completely empty and not one car an hour will go by.

The First World War began on this road. There is a monument on the exact spot. It celebrates Jules André Peugeot, corporal of the 44th Regiment of Infantry. On August 2, 1914, some thirty hours before the declaration of war between Germany and France, Peugeot and four soldiers with him gave letters home to the local mail carrier, who took them and went off. There was a house then where now there is the monument. The daughter of the house went across this road to the spring from which the family and the soldiers got their water. At the edge of a field she saw horsemen. They wore spiked helmets. The girl ran, screaming "The Prussians!" Corporal Peugeot came out of the house carrying a rifle. He stood on the slight rise where his monument is now and saw, coming toward him at a gallop, a German officer on a horse. He raised his rifle and shouted, "Stop there!" The German, who was Lieutenant Camille Mayer, held a revolver. On it was written in Latin, "For the War." He fired three times past his horse's head. Peugeot fired back.

Mayer swayed in the saddle. His horse passed the house and kept going. Peugeot turned and reeled. Four shots.

It had been a very hot summer, and the roads and fields of this wet region would have been drier than usual. So when Peugeot fell across the threshold of the house, and Mayer slid out of his saddle, each would have found dust rather than mud. The site of their encounter was never to be important again. The nearest big battlefield is a few miles north, on a high peak whose actual name is Hartmannsweilerkopf but which the French soldiery of fifty years ago termed "Old Armand." It is part of the eastern face of the Vosges Mountains, which looks down across the flat plains of Alsace leading the few miles to Switzerland.

On Old Armand the trench lines wind off in all directions, resembling choked medieval moats. Moss grows from the top of dugouts and there are great piles of rusting barbed wire. It is difficult to walk over the area; the barbed wire hidden in the undergrowth tears at the shoes, and one falls into shell holes. Parents warn their children to be careful of the rusted sheet metal dangling from the dugout ceilings, and scold them when they scrape themselves on the barbed-wire spurs, which, perhaps dulled by the long years, are no longer really very sharp. Through the holes cut in the thick steel of the machine-gun emplacements—the little doors to cover the holes still swing gratingly shut—the children bend and squint to see Switzerland's mountains in the haze. There is a cemetery and a crypt on Old Armand. In front of each grave, with its insignia MORT POUR LA FRANCE, a rosebush is growing, and before some, relatives have long ago placed little memorials: a crucified Christ, a few stone flowers. In front of one of the graves there is a small plaque perhaps eight inches square. On one half of it, protected by glass, there is a picture of a young man with a military mustache. Under the picture is written: "To the memory of Jules Pierre, Sergeant of the 152nd Regiment of Infantry. Fallen on the 26th of March, 1916." On the other half of the plaque is a picture of a round-faced and serious little boy. Under the child's picture is: "To our little Jules. Darling."

People pose their children in front of the high flagpole with the tri-color waving in the wind over the graves of those who, had it all been different, would have been grandfathers to children like these. In this high, stony place there is a notice that visitors are in the presence of tens of thousands of soldiers who fought for France, and down in the crypt are flowers given by The Blinded of France and The Colonies in Honor of Their Valiant Comrades, and a simple cross, really just two pieces of wood, placed by the Boy Scouts of France and Germany before a pedestal topped with a corroding helmet. There is a Jewish star upon one stone wall and under it: "From the four winds come O Spirit and breathe upon these slain . . ." and, on another wall, the words: "I am the Resurrection." In the middle, waist-high, is a drum-shaped bronze memorial as large as a living room. Upon its top is: LA PATRIE.

In Joncherey there is but the little monument. Only a slight exercise of imagination is needed, however, to project one's mind back to the summer of 1914, that beautiful time after remembered as the sweetest months of men's lives, to where Corporal Peugeot is lying dead across the threshold of the house and Lieutenant Mayer is dead upon the road. After Mayer's patrol scatters into the woods, the two dead soldiers are picked up and put on a bed of straw in the local grange. They lie side by side for several hours. Then they are buried. Peugeot in civilian life was a schoolteacher. His mother was a schoolteacher, too. He was twenty-one years old. Mayer, the official French report said, was twenty to twenty-two years old "at the most." His horse was taken by the French military authorities and given a new name: "Joncherey."

Today the curé of the town, Father Marcel Holder, does not speak of the Boche and the Frenchman, or even the German and the Frenchman. Only of two boys who killed each other.

L E MOULIN DE LA CAILLE: "THE GREAT FIGHT." The wind always blows here; it was a good place for the windmill they called Le Moulin de la Caille—The Windmill of the Quail. There are no cars on the dingy, winding road, no passersby or motorbikes. It is said that along the line of the western front from Belfort to Ostend there has been an emptiness and silence since 1918, and in this place it does seem so. There is nothing nomadic about the French, and no new people have moved here. And most of the boys who lived here in 1914 are now dead, and their sons and daughters who might have been have never lived. So it is very quiet where the French and the Germans fought the battle of Le Moulin de la Caille.

The storehouse of the mill stands, although the mill has fallen into ruins. The son of the farmer who owned it in August of 1914 when the Germans came can remember very well how it was in his father's day: there were the same trees, and the stream was the same. Perhaps the area under cultivation was larger, and less of the countryside was given over to forest. Perhaps it was less lonely. But the fight was like this: The French lived in the mill—there. A worker was cutting hay with a scythe across the stream. He saw the Germans. He came running to the mill, where marked above the door is the date of its construction: 1781. He banged with his scythe on the door—one sees in imagination the grandmothers of these chickens one hundred times removed running to get out of his way—and cried, "The Germans!" And here is the man: a scraggly mustache, sunken cheeks, watery eyes. When he knocked, the French captain came out and quickly had his men turn over the carriages and carts here by the stream so that there would be a barricade. The captain was around thirty-five years old; his name was Japy. So the French got down by the carriages under this red tile roof which juts out from the walls in order to protect the wood piled up for winter, and they began to shoot. The Germans fired back. Look, here are the bullet marks on the wall. It was very hot and about three in the afternoon. They fought for five hours or so, until dusk. The next day the French left the Moulin de la Caille and went back about a mile and began to cross this canal. They thought the Germans were still back by the mill, but the Germans had followed them. They were wading through the water when the firing began. It was a carnage. The young-boy-who-was has a thin, lined neck, and it works as he talks. And he says the water was red—really red. And Captain Japy was dead. When Lieutenant Bolle came from Belfort the Germans fired at him and he lost his arm. And so it was over. One still finds cartridges in the fields.

Captain Japy's widow lived until a few years ago. All through Poincaré and Clemenceau, through Léon Blum and the Popular Front, through Pétain and the Resistance, through Liberation and Indochina and Algeria, she lived on, coming Sunday after Sunday, birthday after birthday, Armistice Day after Armistice Day, to visit the place where her husband died for France. She never remarried. Lieutenant Bolle recovered from the loss of his arm and became a teacher and head of the boys' school in Beaucourt, a few miles away. He lived until very recently. His wife remained friendly with Madame Japy, and each Armistice Day they went together with all the other people to hear Professor Bolle, for so he was called, deliver a speech at the little monument by the Moulin de la Caille. The one-armed professor's war had lasted less than one hour, but for forty-five years he gave a talk each November 11. The newspaper of the town always reported that he was eloquent as he described the fight as "glorious" and said that France was proud of her "beautiful soldiers" who fell there. Girls sold, and sell, little decorations made by the Friends of the 235th Regiment of Infantry, which, as it says on the monument, "valiantly fought to forbid elements of the 29th and 30th Divisions of Germany access to the soil of France." There was and is fired a salvo of one hundred shots from an artillery piece at dawn. There was a parade, the marchers fewer each year, even though the veterans of the Second War also go to the ceremony in a body. (They have few monuments of their own and never go to the places where they fought in 1940.) Children get up early and collect flowers from the farmers. And the wind blows across the empty fields and parts itself at the little monument with the names of the dead men, and stirs the shrubs and moves the bouquets placed in the wire holders attached to the monument when it was erected, and stings the eyes of those looking at the raised lettering: "Time removes everything but the memory"; "But these are in peace." When the day is finished there is a dinner and the distribution of prizes from the little lottery that has raised money for the Friends of the 235th Regiment of Infantry, which fought and lost 164 soldiers of France at this skirmish, this one of a million tiny encounters, this unimportant affair which France and the world have long forgotten but which in this little area near the town of Montreux-Jeune is called the big battle, the great fight.

OVERDUN! All along the dull road up from Bar-le-Duc there are concrete posts with concrete helmets on top and raised lettering saying that this is La Voie Sacrée, the Sacred Road. At Souilly, Pétain's headquarters building is unchanged from the way it looks in the pictures that show him standing on the steps to watch the youth of a nation go northward to its fate. Seventy percent of the French Army went up this road. Night and day the trucks went grinding by; battalions of men stood and flung crushed rock under the tires so that they would not sink into the mud. This was the only road leading into Verdun that the Germans were unable to shell.

Today it is strangely silent, however much one strains to hear the sound of motors and sloshing boots and the mumbled throbbing of the distant places where for months on end the guns were never quiet. But the visible signs of battle are still present. Here are the long trenches, twelve feet deep then, six feet now that nature has half filled them up; here are the craters with cows scrambling up their sides; here is the metal plate used for protection against the shells and now used to roof sheds and support garden walls. In these fields it is impossible to walk for long without seeing rusted metal protruding up through the wet moss; here if you leave the road and go past the signs warning of *Danger de Mort*—"Danger of Death"—you will soon lose yourself in the scrub pine planted in the thirties when experts finally decided the soil was too gas- and shell-corrupted to reclaim for agriculture. Under trees or in stream beds are rusted grenades and shells, as terrifying as coiled snakes. Dig and you will find bullets, shell fragments, broken rifles, sardine tins, decayed canteens, unidentifiable bits of metal. It requires but a few minutes of work to hold in your hand what was last seen two generations ago by a boy in field gray or horizon blue. Now he is an old man in Leipzig or Nancy or, more likely, he is known as the grandfather or great-uncle who perished at Verdun.

The name on the signpost, seen from a moving car, catches the eye and holds it as the car sweeps past. Verdun. In the city itself, in one of the long, deep galleries of the citadel where the French troops found rest during their infrequent respites from the ever-wet trenches (it always rains here), there is a one-eyed veteran. His glass eye never moves. He gives foreigners a piece of paper typed in their language which asks that they not forget to tip him. Inside the gallery there are eight coffins covered with oilcloth flags. (No cotton or silk would last long in this dank, wet place.) On the wall there is a great sign, "They Shall Not Pass." By the third coffin from the rear a mannequin stands. It wears the uniform of the 132nd Regiment of Infantry, complete with helmet and cartridge cases. The hand holds a bouquet of plastic flowers resting on the coffin. All is as it was when, on November 10, 1920, a young soldier from the regiment's honor guard selected for France her Unknown Soldier from among eight Unknowns. When he had placed his flowers on the third coffin from the rear, it was taken out and with the great and the mighty looking on, carried to Paris, and buried beneath the Arc de Triomphe. The other seven were taken to a cemetery just outside the city, where they lie in a semicircle with the information on a plaque above them that among these could be your father, your son, brother, husband, friend.

Past the seven is the road up to the right bank of the Meuse and the heights where for ten bitter months Crown Prince Wilhelm's army sought the city. The Meuse itself is a dreamy stream where old men equipped with immensely long fishing poles—they must be twenty-five feet in length—troll in the afternoons. The charmless and dull villages up on the heights are composed of but a few score houses each, and the narrow roads are never free of the droppings of the cows. Signs say: "This ground has been the Calvary of soldiers. Every square foot bears the marks of its bloody progress. Complete silence is requested out of respect for the thousands buried here." One comes to a village signpost which says "Fleury." The town is on all maps. But there is no town. It is gone, along with the other lost towns whose only physical reminders are that now and again, struggling through the thick undergrowth off the roads, someone will turn over a piece of red tile with his foot. Immediately after the war, when all this was wasteland and the returning refugees smoked constantly to dull the odor of the rotting boys, the government published notices saying that those who had lived here must not return. It took a lot of convincing before those who had lived in Fleury finally gave up and settled down elsewhere. Each year for decades they returned on one day, prayed at the little chapel erected in the woods, and elected a new mayor. They put up a sign where once their main street had been: "Here Was Fleury."

Past the terrible sign is a great cemetery. On a hill facing the graves is the *ossuaire*. In the rear are a score of windows at waist level. One must bend and shade the eyes to see what is there. Bones are there—the bones of 150,000 unidentified men of both sides. Here is a window: See the neat piles of leg bones. Another: arms. Another: skulls. Look at the hole in this one. See the spider weaving his web between the eye sockets. Through other windows in the ossuary one sees bones piled in unsorted confusion. This collection is ever-growing; often a wild boar rooting in the earth will show where more bones lie. Or during a forest fire a 75-mm. shell will blow up, fifty years late, and uncover more Unknown Soldiers.

Beyond the ossuary is the Trench of Bayonets. A shell buried alive a squad of French soldiers here. Only their bayonets protruded above the ground. The soldiers are still there, and their rusting bayonets and rifles also. Imagination looks down and unearths the lower part of the rifle and the hands and body of him who last touched this weapon. One sees his helmet and decayed rags of blue, perhaps, and metal buckles and the boots. Down there will be ammunition attached to the rotted leather belt, some coins, perhaps a pipe. Above is a concrete roof, erected by an American benefactor, and the visitors. Here is Grandmother, or perhaps it is Great-aunt, coming from the car where she sits behind with the children while the parents have the honored seats in front. By now they are all thoroughly bored with her stories.

A horn blows commandingly from a bus with German license plates; it signals that its passengers must climb aboard so that they may ride to Fort Douaumont. The fort today is a giant formless ruin with a few scarred gun turrets on its top. Near it is the little ravine through which the Germans came in 1916 to capture it and stun a France that believed Douaumont to be the strongest land fortification in the world. (A generation of German schoolboys grew up playing "The Capture of Douaumont.") The ravine was called Strawberry Ravine, and the fruit still grows there and is sweet. At the top of the fort one looks out over much of the battlefield; standing on it as nobody safely could for years, one listens for the terrible guns lined up wheel to wheel that made this the most shelled part of the world's surface and left this endless ugly collection of pockmarks. Across these wet fields under these dripping skies the trench lines wind off between the barbed-wire entanglements; in the muddy bottoms of those trenches and over the top strands of that wire France died as a world power. Ever after they haunted France, those dead adolescents and young men of this area little larger than New York's Central Park. (In 1940 the Germans crossed in a quarter of an hour the fields their fathers could never cross.)

The neatly paved roads—for the convenience of the numerous tourists —are the only flat surface in this area. Everywhere else the tortured land rises and dips unevenly. The topsoil has in many places simply vanished, and it is said that any man who lived through Verdun must never have stood still. For every square inch was hit, not once but dozens of times. But alone in the deserted scrub pines of Le Mort Homme or in the silent, ever-wet ruins of Poivre it requires the most intense effort to realize that this dead place was the scene of a great turning point of history. Joncherey is different; the name is not famous, nor the event that took place there. One does not expect too much. Joncherey is not in our blood and in our memories; it was not at Joncherey that perished the legendary officers of the Great War who went into battle carrying their canes and saying to their men, "My dear friends, I will ask you to join me singing 'La Marseillaise' as we go over the top." That was reserved for Verdun, that and the disappearance forever of all represented by France's glorious uniform of red pantaloons, and Germany's wonderfully martial spiked helmets. Madelon and Germania flocked to the stations to kiss the warriors—"À Berlin!" "Nach Paris!"—and in the end the trains stopped at Verdun. After terrible Verdun, after the mules drowning in this shell hole here, after the disemboweled boys screaming in this fallen-in dugout, the nineteenth century was over and history was back on the track for what the twentieth was meant to be.

All this happened at Verdun. And yet no drums beat and there are no bugles. You must do it all yourself. Concentrating and looking back past the France and Germany that followed Verdun, past sick France sliding downhill and sick Germany with its monocled politicians in high stiff collars and their leather-booted prostitutes, you must say to yourself, Here under my feet and within the space I see, hundreds of thousands of men died, here the entire world turned over. Nobly wooded for at least a hundred miles, the heights of the Meuse are covered here with this scrawny pine. This dreary landscape where I stand listening and waiting was the focal point of all the civilizations of the world. Here came the Negroes of France's colonial empire; here came the Bavarians asking, "Are there any Africans opposite?" Here came the young boy friends of the grey and obsequious old maids who make the beds in your Cannes or Paris hotel but who once wrote inspiring letters and knitted mufflers.

There is a guide who lives in the city of Verdun. His name is Charles Dreyfus. He is vaguely related to the Captain Dreyfus of The Affair. He fought in the war and afterward worked to clear the heights of the live shells, dead animals, human bodies. Now he takes tourists around. For the Americans he explains in his accented English just how it was. With the Germans he is completely correct and precise. The French say, "My grandfather—my uncle—my father—O Verdun!" and there is very little that he has to explain.

LA VILLE-AUX-BOIS–PONTAVERT: NINE HUNDRED AND SEVENTY-THREE. There are half a dozen stories about how the Chemin des Dames— the Ladies' Way—got its name. One version has it that the road was constructed for the riding pleasure of two daughters of a French king. Another is that the women of nearby towns made it their favorite place for a Sunday promenade. It is some fifteen miles long and runs east-west in the center of the triangle of Reims-Laon-Soissons. Along the Chemin des Dames in the spring of 1917, General Robert Nivelle finished the destruction of France that was begun at Verdun. Promoted to commander in chief because of minor local successes at Verdun, Nivelle flung his army up the steep slopes leading to the road and into the very teeth of the enormously powerful German fortifications there. In a few quick days he threw away France's last grand battle. Oceans of blood poured forth into the cabbage fields, and when he was finished France's army was in rebellion. He had placed his men, at terrible cost, in a position almost impossible to defend. It would have been better to have withdrawn to the ridge lying south, but the name Chemin des Dames held the French. They had spent too much to give it up.

The emphasis of the war shifted north and west to where the British were. The Chemin des Dames became known as a quiet sector, and after a time British troops were sent there to rest up after their battles. But in 1918, in Ludendorff's last great offensive, the Germans suddenly came pouring south, scattering the French and the few British and heading toward Paris.

In their rush the Germans rolled over the road which is just east of the Chemin des Dames. A section of that road, now N 44, was held by a few British troops, and most of the British along the road that day are still there. At the entrance to the cemetery is a large stone upon which is written THEIR NAME LIVETH FOR EVERMORE. The same kind of stone with the same words is in every British western-front cemetery save for the very tiny ones. It is called the Stone of Remembrance. In every cemetery, regardless of size, there is a stone cross—the Cross of Sacrifice. In this cemetery, as in all the others, there is a book kept in a metal container built into a little sheltered place by the entrance; the one here explains that this cemetery was created after the Armistice by collecting bodies from the immediate area. Nine hundred and fifty-five men are buried in La Ville-aux-Bois—Pontavert Cemetery. There are also eighteen stones commemorating men buried elsewhere.

There is another book; the Visitors' Book. Ever since this cemetery was set up, there has been a Visitors' Book in which one is requested to sign his name and add any comment he likes. Every few years a book is filled up with several hundred names and comments, and is taken away and put in the Commonwealth War Graves Commission files. And a new one is substituted. There are more than a thousand British cemeteries; there are tens of thousands of filled-up books dating from the nineteen twenties.

In the Visitors' Book of La Ville-aux-Bois—Pontavert Cemetery in summer, 1964, W. C. Balfour, who served with the 2nd Middlesex in 1918, wrote, "Thanks my pals are here." A Frenchman wrote, "Remembrances of a poilu of 1914–18." Also in French was: "Respects of a little girl nine years old." A group of Germans from Munich visited the cemetery together and wrote, "Brave dead soldiers." "Brave soldiers." "Rest in peace soldiers."

Mostly the people were from England; they wrote, "Very well kept. Thank you." "Thank you." "Beautifully kept—thank you." Frederick Ronald Ransome wrote, "I have been so moved to visit my father's grave." His father is among the Knowns: SECOND LIEUTENANT F.R. RANSOME, 1ST BN. ROYAL DUBLIN FUSILIERS ATTACHED 2ND BN. WEST YORKSHIRE REGT. DIED OF WOUNDS 26 MAY 1918. Two people with the same last name as an Oxford boy: "I shall always remember." "I shall always remember." In a quavering handwriting: "On behalf of your brother Bert and family may you rest in peace, dear Ned. From your old friend Jim, still going at near 71." From a London woman: "A little corner of a foreign field that is forever England."

Down the road perhaps the distance of a city block stands a memorial erected to the 2nd Battalion of the Devonshire Regiment, which, the lettering on the stone says, repulsed successive attacks on this spot, thus permitting the defenses in the south to be reorganized and reinforced. WITHOUT HOPE OF ASSISTANCE THEY . . . FOUGHT TO THE LAST WITH AN UN-HESITATING OBEDIENCE TO ORDERS.. THUS THE WHOLE BATTALION, COLONEL, TWENTY-EIGHT OFFICERS, AND FIVE HUNDRED AND FIFTY-SIX NON-COMMIS-SIONED OFFICERS AND MEN RESPONDED WITH ONE ACCORD AND OFFERED THEIR LIVES IN UNGRUDGING SACRIFICE TO THE SACRED CAUSE OF THE ALLIES. The battalion was awarded the Croix de Guerre with Palm. By the monument is a little roadside inn and across the road a winding lane lined with white-painted shell casings from the big guns. All about are flat, empty fields and dripping skies; here and there are concrete floors once enclosed with walls punctured with holes for the machine guns. In some spots a bit of wall is still standing. Everything is very quiet—the shell craters, fields, low skies, the monument, the inn, and Tommy Atkins dead nine hundred and seventy-three times.

B ELLEAU WOOD: WE ARE PROUD TO BEAR THE TITLE. Most of the survivors of this war now in U.S. Veterans Administration hospitals suffer from one of two ailments. One group is composed of those who were gassed and have been out in civilian life during the intervals when the coughing and gasping abate somewhat. (Now, when they are no longer young, the good intervals grow shorter and shorter, and so the wards paradoxically are growing more crowded as the war recedes into the past.)

The other group is made up of men who went as boys to France in 1917–18 and through the quiet sectors up to the front. At the front (and sometimes even before it was reached) something happened to this group. One by one those slated to spend young manhood and middle and old age in hospitals manifested the first signs of illness. They began to talk too much. Or they fell silent. Whiz-bangs came over or machine guns rattled, and the men were medically beyond reach—shell shock. They were taken back to the United States and today in the VA hospitals they watch television or play volleyball and work in the gardens. Relatives come now and then, and sometimes people who want to do something for them put on musical shows or take them in buses for a picnic. The broken men once boys rush for the hot dogs and anxiously ask, "Buddy, will there be enough?"

Once they had formed up with those who went on to life and the postwar world and who would wait expectantly for the American Legion conventions so they could use their electric canes on girls who were in-fants at the time of the Armistice. Those who would never drop paper bags filled with water from hotel rooms marched with those who would; they wore choker collars and wide campaign hats with bright-colored cords; they sang, "Good-bye Broadway, Hello France"; they sang, "There's a long, long trail a-winding into the land of my dreams." Many of them arrived, with the others who would live and be well, and with those who would die, at the long fields to the south of the Bois de Belleau. In that wood were machine guns with cross-fields of fire, and mortars, and riflemen shooting from bunkers and behind rock emplacements. The doughboys and leathernecks—mostly the latter—came walking through the fields with their heads bent down against the steel flying at them, and made for the shattered trees. In the ruined towns of Lucy-le-Bocage and Bouresches they froze when the big shells thundered over like express trains rushing through an endless tunnel to land with explosions lighting up a landscape that looked so like the surface of the moon. Their ration parties lumbered up Gob Gully past broken trees from which dangled horribly wet legs trailing undone puttees to the ground. Rifle grenades came down and lifted the horses up and left them as great hulks of meat grinning in death with the lips drawn back in the last act of life: a scream very like that of a woman in agony.

The boys crossing the fields up to the woods were not the U.S. Marines and prewar soldiers of legend; there had been no drinking in tough bars for them, no street brawls under tropical moons. On the contrary, they were for the greater part college boys enlisted from their campuses to make the world safe for democracy. They came to these insignificant towns and this little meaningless road hardly more than a paved country lane, and did their fighting and went to their graves at home or in the great cemetery beyond the wood, or to their madhouses, or to civilian life and, within a very few years, to a terrible feeling that it was all a bunch of foolishness, and then, with the decades, to white hair and pot-bellies and increased incomes and grandchildren and winters in Florida.

They came and went. Belleau Wood remained.

Today Belleau Wood is the property of the United States government, a gift of France. It has a new name, given to it after the fighting: Bois de la Brigade Marine. During the twenties and thirties it was a place every American tourist visited. Parisian cab drivers had a fixed price to take ex-soldiers there. Then came another war and today the tourists go to Normandy.

You can stay for two hours in Belleau Wood, where once the Yanks held the way to Paris, and see no one. Perhaps in the cemetery one or two gardeners are working, but the woods themselves are empty. It is as if unseen workers appear when the sun goes down and pluck the weeds and cut the grass between the endless straight lines of trees. In a clearing are old guns, painted black against the elements, rearing their noiseless mouths to the sky. They stand there silent and dark, waiting—and no one comes.

Can there ever have been here what is called a great and glorious moment in history? Under the stones in the great cemetery are there really splintered and gashed bones, are there really the young buddies of the fat and bald old men laying off the calories and watching the cholesterol? Is it all true what Grandfather says, that here in this disciplined, quiet place Major John Hughes sent word to headquarters that "I have every man, except a few odd ones, in line now. We have not broken contact and have held"? Where was it—was it here by this silent black mortar?—that twenty-three-year-old Laurence Stallings, who would live to lose a leg and write *What Price Glory?*, lay cowering but remembering that his General told him he must "pick up a rifle and lead with steel"? Is it in this quiet path with these carefully heaped-up leaves that the dead men lay piled one on the other as a barricade, and the bayoneted ones gasped out their last and, finally, Colonel Wendell Neville sent word: WOODS NOW U.S. MARINE CORPS ENTIRELY? Or was it all a dream of long ago, an episode invented by the history professors to fill a paragraph saying that the American action and demeanor were bracing to the faltering Allies? Was it all in never-never land, far from this America with its super-highways and television? Did America really produce in these fat old men and mental cripples the wonderful soldiery of what began as the last gentlemen's war, the last gallant war, the last splurge of romanticism and legends and plumes? Did it all really happen?

THE SOMME: DOUGLAS HAIG. Rolling Picardy is all flat with nothing high, with neat stone houses and long, haunting roads going up to the horizon between the tall, swaying poplar trees under which the British troops marched. In Amiens, the base for the entire British effort along the western front, there remains one thing utterly unchanged from the time of the war (until 1939, The War). It is Godbert's Restaurant. In those days the rear-line officers always made for Godbert's when they had a few hours free, appreciating the tasteful, quiet paved yard where the staff cars could be left in safety, and the attractive entrance. Today the yard is still quiet and the entrance is the same as it was. There was, and is, a lobby and two rooms. At the desk where the cheerful little fat *patronne* sat, the *patronne*'s daughter sits now. The food was excellent then, and still is—Michelin gives it a high rating. At the beginning of the war Godbert's was unknown to the great of this world, but since then, praised in all the clubs along Pall Mall, it has played host to many famous names. "The Prince of Wales was here," says the *patronne*'s daughter in frightful English, "when he came to dedicate the memorial at Thiepval. And the King of England was here. He sat right there. And during the war and after, Doolis Hay was here many times." Douglas Haig? "Yes, he was here when I was a child and I saw him."

Out along the roads east from Amiens and Godbert's, where "Doolis Hay" ate, thin metal canisters of unexploded mustard gas lie under the soil and corrupt the growth of trees whose roots burrow down and break through. It is impossible to plant a straight row of trees along the Somme. The gardeners of the Commonwealth War Graves Commission have long since given up hope of ever seeing a straight row. Too much stuff is down there. "Stuff" is the canisters and boots and shells used to fill up the holes made by other shells. And the bodies of those who answered Lord Kitchener's call: Your Country Needs You. Along the Somme the best, finest, sweetest of England's youth perished. They were all volunteers. In their long lines they rose from the trenches on the first of July, 1916, and strode forward dress-right-dress and died—in long, perfect ranks, bayonets fixed, each man just so, with leather polished and metal gleaming. British pluck. That first of July was the worst day in the history of British arms.

English people come past the Somme on holiday these days, heading back from their vacations on the Continent. Knowing vaguely that Uncle Will died somewhere around here, they halt their cars and go out and wander among the graves (A SOLDIER OF THE GREAT WAR. WORCESTERSHIRE REGIMENT. KNOWN UNTO GOD. A SERGEANT OF THE GREAT WAR. ROYAL IRISH RIFLES. KNOWN UNTO GOD) and look for Uncle Will's resting place. They don't find it, of course, and eventually they end up in the Commonwealth War Graves Commission office in Albert, where they learn that in this tiny area of northern France there are not tens, but hundreds of thousands of graves. They have grown up knowing that all Mum's boy friends save Dad died along the Somme, and all Auntie's, but they have never stopped to think of just how many graves there must be.

The C.W.G.C. officials and gardeners try to help them, and proudly detail the fact that every man who died for Great Britain and the Empire has his name, without a doubt, written somewhere on a memorial. Through the twenties and thirties the mothers and fathers and older relatives of people like these came out to France seeking, if not Uncle Will, then Father, or My Son, or Brother. Imagine—the high wing-collars and dress-for-dinner vanished, and the open touring cars disappeared, Ramsay MacDonald did too, and Stanley Baldwin, Geneva and Locarno, all the catch-words of Europe-between-the-wars, and through all this, the cloche hats and changing hem lines, people kept coming. During the Second War the untended roses ran riot, and the lists of the buried and the Visitors' Books disappeared, but now it is all as it was meant to be. Forty years and more have gone by since the Armistice, and the veterans have their "ticket," their pension, and they've got time free, what with the kids grown up and on their own, and so they come out from Canada and Aussieland and Blighty. Sometimes on the roads they pass automobiles with "D" for Deutschland above the license plates, and these people also are looking for cemeteries. Their cemeteries, severe and cold, are maintained by the French at the expense of the present German government. There are no flowers in them and very few individual graves. Most of Germany's dead are Unknown. Their symbol is the piece of sculpture done by Käthe Kollwitz, whose son died in this war. Her work shows the mothers and fathers of Germany with heads bowed and eyes on the ground where their sons lie beneath the words: "Germany Must Live Though We Must Die."

Along the road up from Amiens to Albert, past where the vast artillery parks and railheads were, the Golden Virgin of Albert stands high above the horizon, glittering, gleaming. Once that Virgin sagged over the shell-ripped streets from atop the church the British called the Cathedral, and the soldiers said that when she fell, England would lose the war. (A French engineer crept up and fastened the statue with thick steel wire. No sense taking chances.) The Britishers go through little Albert, where once there were thousands of gun limbers, ammunition lorries, artillery emplacements, forward transport parks—all the immense end product of a mighty world empire carried to the tiny cutting edge of the gigantic sword—and pass over roads where the hundreds of thousands marched and the great guns rolled and the poor silly cavalry horses galloped, on to where Peel Trench was, and Centre Way, and Dead Mule Corner.

Many of the visitors at the cemeteries carry artificial flowers made by the British Legion Poppy Factory and meant to be placed in front of Known graves. Upon the bases of the gravestones under the name and the date of death are words which close relatives were allowed to designate right after the war: IN LOVING MEMORY OF OUR DEAR HORACE AGED 21. FROM MOTHER AND FATHER AND FAMILY. . . . GOD BE WITH YOU DEAREST TOM UNTIL WE MEET AGAIN. FROM MOTHER AND ALL. . . . REST IN PEACE SWEETEST HUSBAND AND LOVING FATHER. ALICE AND THE GIRLS.

Ever there is that immense western-front silence that speaks of what was lost in those years and that haunts all who come here. On the slight rises you can stand up as no soldier could have stood and see graveyards in every direction. But you hear nothing save now and then a distant car or tractor. There is nothing else. Delville Wood, where the South Africans met a terrible fate, is an empty park now. Only a lone sheep, belonging perhaps to an absent gardener, grazes there. Flies light on its droppings as once the flies lit on the dead men, revolting the lives ones as nothing else did, not the rats nor the stench nor the bloated corruption of those who once were laughing boys singing that it was a long way to Tipperary. And indeed they sang. As in all the Hollywood musicals of the thirties, they sang. For this was the western front of the Great War where the legions went forth in their millions with the bands playing before them. It was really that way—going to the slaughterhouse of their generation they made music. But under these white stones—GOD'S WILL BE DONE. LOVING MUM—there are torn, broken skulls from which wonderful songs issued. Pack up your troubles in your old kit bag.

The Stump Road cemetery, one of the hundreds, very small, lies along a road so slim that only one vehicle can pass. An Englishman wrote in the Visitors' Book one summer ago: " 'I consider the machine gun to be a greatly over-rated weapon.' Douglas Haig, Field Marshal."

YPRES: KENNEY. In the years just after the war all of the salient was mud. The roads had vanished and rotting horse carcasses lay everywhere, providing limitless food for the giant rats. Overturned gun carriages lay half in and half out of the stagnant pools of water in the shell craters. It was difficult to cut down the few remaining trees; saw blades broke when they bit into the bullets and pieces of metal in the trunks. Machine guns rusted in the collapsed tunnels and dugouts, and Chinese laborers brought over for military construction work lived, forgotten by the departed British, in the cellars of the ruined houses. In the midst of all this were the peasants coming back to reclaim their land. Belgium in those days had a kind of prosperity, for there was work for all.

Laborers blew up the thick bunkers with shell powder and used the concrete for new roads. Gangs of men made a living by flattening out fields made as rough as the surface of the ocean during a storm. They did not charge the farmers for their work; their profits came from selling the metal under the mud. That metal filled thousands of trains pulling out of Ypres for twenty years.

By the time of the Depression, the Salient was functioning as a farming area. But during the early thirties, Belgium had thousands of unemployed. And so they came back to the fields and dug down further than the earlier workers had gone. They used the long bars made for cleaning machine guns, shoving them down four to five feet and then examining the tip. Yellow meant copper was underneath; rust equalled iron. Vast ammunition dumps were found, with thousands of live shells, and a great home industry grew up. Its workers were men who knocked the detonation tips off the shells and poured out the powder and sold the metal. (Sometimes the trick did not work; scores of men died one by one in accidents.) Some of the shells were too dangerous to disassemble, and for these there were special fields where each day just before lunch and just before dinner red flags were flown to warn people away as Belgian Army experts detonated the shells and sent new blasts over the fields with the terrible names: Passchendaele, Wytschaete, Polygon Wood.

Throughout the twenties and thirties the armaments industry took most of the metal whose cost had all but broken the Bank of England. Then came the Second War and the business of collecting the old metal ended. But suddenly in 1950 the price of scrap in Europe doubled overnight: the Korean war meant cannons would be firing. Suez drove the price up also in 1956, but then it sagged and it is not high now. Still, however, men on the dole head out to the fields in the slow winter months. During rainy periods the metal seems to rise to the surface, cleansed of its clinging soil and shining dully. Traditionally in Belgium the proceeds from its sale go for drinking money.

There is something else the Belgians find: men. In the winter of 1964, seven bodies turned up during the construction of foundations for a new foundry. Four bodies were found in February and three in March. The group of four were sitting on their heels with pistols in their hands and grenades strapped on. The uniforms were still identifiable—good British material. You could read just what was in their minds: They were about to go on a raid and were waiting crouched in their trench. A shell came over and killed them by concussion and covered them with earth. So the four sat for fifty years waiting for the foundry to be built so they might come to light. Their identification tags lasted, although the cords holding them around their necks were gone. There were no letters in the pockets, so the Graves Commission people did not have the problem of deciding what to do with them. (Years ago the rule was set up that letters addressed to family would be sent; those to girl friends would be destroyed.)

Ypres has always been the focal point for British coming over to the Continent to tour the battlefields. During the period between the wars pilgrimages were arranged at cut-rate prices, and people bringing their sandwiches with them came over on the boat trains. They spent the day and went back that same night. Of course the motor coaches touring the more than 150 cemeteries could not stop at each one, so it was a common thing to see poorly dressed English people stopping citizens of Ypres on the street and pushing forward a few shillings to exact a promise that the Belgian would take a camera and go to a stipulated cemetery and take a picture of a certain grave and send the picture on. The well-to-do came in cars and sought the place where their sons died. One aged Englishman came each year to see a tiny wood. He said he derived comfort from being at the place where his only son died. He would sit for hours by himself; towards the end two men came with him in his big car and carried him out in a wheelchair and took a long walk while he sat.

During the summer of 1964, commemorating the fiftieth anniversary of the beginning of the war, Ypres received a record number of visitors. For men who served in the Salient the city offered a handsome certificate with the ex-soldier's name on it. The city also held a little reception for those coming in organized groups. There were hundreds of such receptions. The men were taken to a large room in the city hall where an official handed out the certificates and made a short speech saying that Ypres paid tribute to all the dead of whichever side. "And now we will have a little drink and a smoke." Waiters moved forward with sherry and cigars. Then the men went to their waiting buses for the ride to the monuments and cemeteries. Some of the British wore their old uniforms and some wore gilded British Legion outfits complete to clanking spurs and swords and silver braid down the sides of tapering breeches. In the silence of the graveyards and memorial temples they moved, medals clanking, to seek the graves of friends, and then adjourned to little roadside taverns where they were expected and welcomed. (For haven't they kept those taverns going for fifty years?) Inside they got slightly potted, and their voices rose, and they took out their old paybooks and pictures of their companies and showed them around. There was a refrain repeated endlessly as they pointed to their pals: "He's dead . . . he's dead . . . he's dead." At the end of the long day and the many taverns, the singing in the buses rushing along the Salient's roads grew somewhat raucous, and men got out harmonicas and danced in the aisles. Some shouted in their Tommy

French at passing women, and grew maudlin: "I lived in England but my heart is out here." Others cursed the "bloody Germans," or the "wife of my bloody Colonel": "I was his batman, and she said she'd take care of me if I took care of him, and I did till he got his, but she went away to the South of France and I never heard from her again. . . ."

One man who came back to Ypres seemed quieter than most of the others. He was A. J. Arpal, who wore in his lapel the insignia of the Old Contemptibles Association, and who had seen it through from the very beginning. He had never been back since the war, but now with his grandchildren in school and his wife dead, he joined a tour which went all over the British zone, transportation, hotels, and meals provided for a week, at a price of only eighteen quid. Arpal was a cavalryman.

For Arpal the symbol of that war has always been Kenney. Years and decades have passed since Kenney died, but Arpal has never forgotten him. Kenney was a laughing boy, twenty-two or three, and always wore his cap to one side. A happy kid. Arpal has thought of him a lot in these forty years while he has turned old and grey and quiet and a grandfather and Kenney has remained young in his lost grave in Belgium. Kenney represented the spirit they had in those days. Arpal was right there when this kid died. They were moving up in file early in the war and there was a volley of shots from beside the road. Kenney was knocked out of his saddle and Arpal thought to himself, Thank God he wasn't dragged by his horse. Arpal and the others leaped into a ditch and opened fire. By next morning the Germans were gone and Kenney was still lying in the road. Arpal saw at once that it wouldn't have mattered a damn if his horse had dragged him or not, for he must have been dead before he hit the ground. When they opened his coat to get his letters and things, they saw that sewn into his collar where it buttoned next to his throat there was a union jack. They buried him but his grave soon disappeared in shellfire. It was for Kenney's name that Arpal looked when he came back to Ypres and saw the giant memorial where the names of the Missing are inscribed in stone. Arpal read through the tens of thousands of names and saw all the ranks of all the familiar British regiments, and those of the strange ones like the 9th Bhopal Infantry with its ranks of Subadar, Jermadar, Havildar, Sepoy. Finally he found Kenney's name, and all the noise and traffic faded away. He had found Kenney. That was at the Menin Gate.

YPRES: THE MENIN GATE. The road goes eastward, through the dreary little red-brick Belgian towns so like the industrial slums of England, and finally ends at the French border. At the road's beginning in Ypres is the Gate. They dedicated it in 1927. On the outside facing the road is inscribed, TO THE ARMIES OF THE BRITISH EMPIRE WHO STOOD HERE FROM

1914 TO 1918. Inside: HERE ARE RECORDED THE NAMES OF OFFICERS AND MEN WHO FELL IN THE YPRES SALIENT BUT TO WHOM THE FORTUNES OF WAR DENIED THE KNOWN AND HONOURED BURIAL GIVEN TO THEIR COMRADES IN DEATH. Kipling wrote the words. Underneath them are the names of the Missing.

The featured speaker on July 24, 1927, was Field Marshal Lord Plumer. Bandy-legged, with a puffy face, not looking like a soldier, he stood with the King of the Belgians before the giant audience come from England. The reporters that day wrote that most of the people were aged women, shabbily dressed. The Southern Railways ran special free trains to the coast for them—first-class carriages only. The women bore rambler roses, snap-dragons, lilies from their English gardens. They sat in the hot sun facing the Gate with their backs to the Menin Road leading out to the Salient, and six pipers of the Scots Guards standing on the shell-shattered medieval ramparts by the Gate played "The Flowers of the Fields." Buglers of the Somerset Light Infantry sounded the Last Post, and to the reporters it seemed as if in the throbbing silence when the calls faded away there must come some sound, some sign, from the Salient up the road. Lord Plumer cried, "They are not Missing; they are here," and the Mums in their funny hats and long black stockings put their hands over their faces.

After that, every night at eight in the winter and nine in the summer, Belgian buglers sounded the Last Post. In 1940 the Germans came down the Menin Road and took Ypres. For four years the buglers were silenced. But fifteen minutes after the last German was rounded up in 1944 the long slow notes of the Last Post quivered out from under the Gate. On some of the nights since then, particularly when the weather is bad, there is no one to hear the buglers except the policeman, who halts traffic. At other times there will be a score or even a hundred people. Delegations come out from England, elderly men marching out of step and carrying old regimental flags. Age has shrunken most of them and made them puny, and for all that they are combat veterans of the Great War. They look somewhat foolish as they line up in ragged files. Cars and trucks rattle under the Gate as they stand waiting for the police to halt the traffic. When this is done the flag-bearers go out and stand in the road. In this silence the sound of shuffling feet mixes with the dull rumble of idling motors. Someone shouts, "Attention!" and the skinny old men square-bash to something approaching the posture they were able to attain when all, the living and Missing, were young. Belgians—sometimes soldiers, sometimes members of the Ypres Fire Department—come marching out into the street to face the flags. There are often as many as four buglers. They raise silver bugles given by the British Legion. Some of the old men salute in the British palms-out way. Others take off their hats. The beautiful trilling brings to mind hazy pictures of Indian garrisons and Sandhurst and Salisbury Plain; all the calls are sounded: Reveille, Mess Call, Defaulters' Call, the Last Post. When the final note dies the Belgians lower the bugles smartly, stand for a moment, and then wheel to the right and march to the curb. The traffic is already rolling under the Gate as the old men start to furl their flags. Some of them walk back to look at the names on the walls yet again—Arpal for one last moment lets his eye rest on KENNEY—and then the buses pull up to the curb.

—October 1965

WERE SACCO AND VANZETTI INNOCENT?

By FRANCIS RUSSELL

In an earlier essay, the author claimed they had been unjustly executed. Reader challenges sent him back to the reams of evidence. In 1961 he had new ballistics tests made. His dramatic conclusion is as close as we are ever likely to get to the truth.

The murders for which Nicola Sacco and Bartolomeo Vanzetti were convicted and finally executed were quick, simple, and brutal. On the afternoon of April 15, 1920, in the small shoe manufacturing town of South Braintree, Massachusetts, a paymaster, Frederick Parmenter, and his guard, Alessandro Berardelli, were shot and robbed as they walked down Pearl Street with the Slater & Morrill Shoe Company payroll—some fifteen thousand dollars in two metal boxes.

The paymaster and the guard, each carrying a box, had crossed the railroad tracks near the front of the Rice & Hutchins factory when two strangers who had been leaning against the fence there suddenly stepped toward them. The strangers were short, dark men. One wore a felt hat and the other, a cap.

In a flash the first man whipped a pistol from his pocket and fired several shots into Berardelli. The guard dropped to the ground. Parmenter, a step in advance, turned and when he saw what was happening, started to run across the street. Before he reached the other side he was shot twice. He dropped his box and collapsed in the gutter. Witnesses—of which there were a number in the factory windows and along Pearl Street —were afterward uncertain whether one man or two had done the shooting, but most thought there had been two.

With Parmenter and Berardelli lying in the gravel, one of their assailants fired a signal shot, and a Buick touring car that had been parked near the Slater & Morrill factory now started jerkily up the rise. As it slowed down, the two bandits picked up the money boxes and climbed into the back seat. Berardelli had managed to get to his hands and knees. Seeing him wavering, a third man sprang from the car and fired another shot into him. It was a death wound.

The Buick continued along Pearl Street with five men in it, a gunman in the front seat firing at random at the crowd drawn by the sound of the shots. No one was hit, although one bystander had his coat lapel singed. The car gathered speed, swung left at the top of Pearl Street, and one of the men in the rear seat threw out handfuls of tacks to hinder any pursuit. The speeding car was noticed at intervals along a ten-mile stretch of road; then it vanished. Two days later it was found abandoned in the woods near Brockton, a dozen miles away.

Berardelli died within a few minutes, the final bullet having severed the great artery issuing from his heart. Parmenter too had received a fatal wound, a bullet cutting his inferior vena cava, the body's largest vein. He died early the following morning. At the autopsy two bullets were found in Parmenter and four in Berardelli. The county medical examiner, Dr. George Burgess Magrath, removed the bullets from Berardelli's body, scratching the base of each with a Roman numeral. The bullet that had cut the artery and that, from the angle of its path, he determined must have been fired while Berardelli was down, he marked III. It had struck the hipbone obliquely and was slightly bent from this glancing contact.

Of the six bullets, five had been fired from a .32 caliber pistol or pistols with a right-hand twist to the rifling. These bullets were of varied manufacture—three Peters and two Remingtons. The remaining bullet, the one Dr. Magrath marked III, was a Winchester of an obsolete type having a cannelure, or milling around the edge. It had been fired from a .32 caliber pistol with a left-hand twist. Only a Colt, among American pistols, had such a reverse twist. Four spent cartridges of the same caliber as the bullets were picked up in the gravel near Berardelli's body. Two of these were Peters, one a Remington, and one a Winchester later known as Shell W.

No weapons were found on the bodies, although Berardelli customarily carried a revolver with him. On March 19, 1920, he had taken his gun to the Iver Johnson Company in Boston to have it repaired. According to his wife, it needed a new spring. Lincoln Wadsworth, in charge of the repair department, recorded that on that day he had received a .38 caliber Harrington & Richardson revolver from Alex Berardelli and had sent the gun upstairs to the workshop. There the foreman, George Fitzemeyer, for some reason marked it as a .32 caliber Harrington & Richardson requiring a new hammer and ticketed it with a repair number.

No one at Iver Johnson's recorded the revolver's serial number. The store manager testified a year later at the trial that the company did not keep a record of deliveries of repaired guns, but he was certain this particular revolver had been delivered. All weapons in the repair department not called for by the year's end were sold and a record made of each sale. Since Berardelli's revolver was no longer in the store, and there was no record of its being sold, the manager insisted it must have been called for.

Several witnesses of the shooting said at the inquest that they saw one of the bandits stoop over Berardelli. Peter McCullum, peering out of the first floor cutting room of Rice & Hutchins after he heard the shots, saw a man putting the money box into the Buick while holding a "white" revolver in his other hand. A Harrington & Richardson revolver was nickel-plated and might well have seemed white in the sunlight. This may have been Berardelli's. It seems unlikely that the guard would have accompanied the paymaster unarmed. And if he had a revolver, it is possible that one of the men who shot him may have reached down and taken it.

Sacco and Vanzetti were arrested almost by chance on the night of May 5, 1920. They had met earlier in the evening at Sacco's bungalow in Stoughton—a half-dozen miles from South Braintree—with two anarchist comrades, Mike Boda and Ricardo Orciani, to arrange about gathering up incriminating literature from other comrades for fear of government "Red" raids. Until a few months before this, Boda had been living in West Bridgewater ten miles away with another anarchist, Ferruccio Coacci, who had been taken away for deportation on April 17. Not until Coacci was at sea did the police come to suspect that he and Boda might have been concerned in the South Braintree holdup. Boda had left an old Overland touring car in a West Bridgewater garage to be repaired, and the four men were planning to pick it up that evening. Orciani and Boda left Stoughton on Orciani's motorcycle. Sacco and Vanzetti went by streetcar. Once they had arrived, Boda was unable to get the car from the forewarned proprietor. As the men argued, the proprietor's wife telephoned the police.

Sacco and Vanzetti were arrested in Brockton while riding back to Stoughton on the streetcar. The police found a .32 caliber Colt automatic tucked in Sacco's waistband. In the gun's clip were eight cartridges, with another in the chamber. Sacco had twenty-three more loose cartridges in his pocket. These, although all .32 caliber, were of assorted makes—sixteen Peters, seven U.S., six Winchesters of the obsolete type, and three Remingtons. Vanzetti was found to be carrying a Harrington & Richardson .38 caliber revolver, its five chambers loaded with two Remington and three U.S. bullets.

The day following their arrest the two men were questioned at some length by the district attorney, Frederick Katzmann. Sacco told Katzmann he had bought his automatic two years before on Hanover Street in Boston under an assumed name. He had paid sixteen or seventeen dollars for it, and at the same time he had bought an unopened box of cartridges.

Vanzetti said he had bought his revolver four or five years before, also under an assumed name, at some shop on Hanover Street and had paid eighteen dollars for it. He had also bought an unopened box of cartridges, all but six of which he had fired off on the beach at Plymouth.

At their trial fourteen months later the two men told very different stories. They both admitted they had lied when they were first questioned, but explained that they then thought they were being held because they were anarchists. They had lied, they said, partly because they were afraid and partly to protect their comrades. Indeed they had good reason to feel apprehensive about their anarchism, for there were rumors of new government Red raids, and only a few days before their arrest their comrade Salsedo had died mysteriously in New York while being held by federal agents.

Sacco's revised trial story was that he had bought the pistol in 1917 or 1918 in the small town where he was working. He had bought a box of cartridges on Hanover Street shortly afterward. The man who sold him the box filled it with various makes because of the wartime scarcity of cartridges.

Vanzetti now said that he had bought his revolver a few months before his arrest. Often he carried a hundred dollars or more with him from his fish business, and he felt he needed a gun to protect himself because of the many recent holdups. He had bought the revolver from a friend, Luigi Falzini. It was loaded when he bought it, and he had never fired it.

Falzini appeared in court, identified the revolver by certain rust spots and scratches as having belonged to him, and said he had bought it from Orciani. Another witness, Rexford Slater, testified that the revolver had originally belonged to him and that he had sold it to Orciani in the autumn of 1919.

Orciani had been arrested the day following the arrests of Sacco and Vanzetti. However, as he was able to provide a timecard alibi for his whereabouts on April 15, he was released. During the early part of the trial he acted as chauffeur for one of the defense attorneys, but although he was in the courthouse almost daily, he did not take the stand. Yet he was, as the district attorney pointed out in his summing up, the missing link in the revolver's chain of ownership.

At the trial the prosecution contended that the automatic found on Sacco was the one that had fired Bullet III and that Vanzetti's revolver had been taken from the dying Berardelli. Several days before the ballistics testimony, two experts for the prosecution, Captain William Proctor of the Massachusetts State Police—then no more than a detective bureau —and Captain Charles Van Amburgh from the Remington Arms Company in Connecticut, fired a number of test shots from Sacco's automatic into oiled sawdust. Proctor and Van Amburgh were joined in these experiments by a defense expert, James Burns. After the test bullets were recovered they were then compared with Bullet III.

The trial testimony of the firearms experts on both sides was involved and confusing, "a wilderness of lands and grooves" as one reporter noted. In the opinion of the Gunther brothers, whose book on firearms identification has become a legal classic, all the ballistics evidence offered was so primitive as to be worthless.

Each tooled gun barrel, with its hundreds of minute striations, is unique. The one certain method of determining whether two separate bullets have been fired through any particular barrel is the use of a comparison microscope. Through this instrument the ends of the two bullets are brought together in one fused image. If the striations match, then it is practically certain that both bullets were fired from the same weapon.

Today the comparison microscope is the standard method of bullet identification. In 1920 it was just beginning to come into use, but it was not used in the Sacco-Vanzetti trial. There the experts attempted to measure the bullets with calipers and compare them with measurements made of a cast of the barrel of Sacco's pistol. It was a useless, haggling procedure.

No one disputed that Bullet III had been fired from a Colt automatic, but Captain Proctor told District Attorney Katzmann before the trial that he did not believe it had been fired from Sacco's Colt. The prosecution was aware of Proctor's doubts when the captain was questioned in court. "My opinion is," Proctor said with a prearranged ambiguity that escaped the defense, "that it [Bullet III] is consistent with being fired by that pistol." The prosecution claimed that the Winchester cartridge among the four picked up near Berardelli had also been fired in Sacco's pistol. Comparing this cartridge with one fired on the test range, Proctor again used the word "consistent." Privately he had from the time of their arrest expressed doubt that Sacco and Vanzetti were guilty.

Two years after the trial he signed an affidavit saying that he had used the ambiguous phrase "consistent with" at Katzmann's request, but that if he had been asked directly in court whether he believed that Bullet III had been fired from Sacco's Colt, he would have replied No.

Captain Van Amburgh was scarcely more emphatic in his trial testimony: "I am inclined to believe," he said, "that the Number III bullet was fired from this Colt automatic pistol." Burns and a second defense expert, J. Henry Fitzgerald of the Colt Patent Firearms Company, denied this. In their opinion neither Bullet III nor Shell W, the Winchester cartridge, had any connection with Sacco's pistol.

Fitzemeyer, the Iver Johnson foreman, when handed Vanzetti's revolver on the witness stand and asked if it had been repaired recently, replied: "Well, a new hammer, I should call it, a new hammer."

In the summer of 1924 Captain Van Amburgh was appointed head of the newly formed ballistics laboratory of the Massachusetts State Police. Fortunately for his new career the repercussions of his blunder in the Harold Israel case had not yet reached Massachusetts. On February of that same year Father Dahme, a priest in Bridgeport, Connecticut, had been shot and killed as he was taking his customary evening walk. A week later a drifter by the name of Harold Israel was picked up by the police in nearby Norwalk. In Israel's pocket was a loaded .32 caliber revolver. Several witnesses identified him as the man they had seen shoot Father Dahme. Van Amburgh was called in to examine the ballistics evidence. He fired Israel's revolver and compared a test bullet with one taken from Father Dahme's body. Both bullets, he reported, had come from the same weapon. Later, however, five experts from the Remington Arms Company plus another from the New York Police Department examined the bullets and were of the unanimous opinion that the bullet that had killed Father Dahme could not have been fired from Israel's revolver. Israel was then released.

Captain Van Amburgh remained head of the state police laboratory until his retirement in 1946. During his earlier years there he developed a device called a spiralgraph with which he was able to make strip photographs of bullets as they revolved on a turntable. By comparing the strips of two bullets, he maintained he could determine whether or not they had been fired from the same gun. Later he made such comparative photographs of Bullet III and the test bullets of the Sacco-Vanzetti case. These photographs he used for demonstrations when he testified in the 1923 Hamilton-Proctor motion, one of the many filed requesting a new trial for Sacco and Vanzetti.

The Hamilton-Proctor motion was based in part on Captain Proctor's affidavit as to what he had really believed when he testified at the trial, although Proctor himself had died before the motion could be argued. In addition to his affidavit, there was further evidence offered by a post-trial defense expert, Dr. Albert Hamilton, that Bullet III could not have come from Sacco's Colt.

Dr. Hamilton would never have been engaged by the lawyers for Sacco and Vanzetti if they had known more about his background. His doctor's degree was self-awarded. He had started out in Auburn, New York, as a small-town druggist and concoctor of patent medicines. Over the years behind the counter he developed expertise at a second career, advertising himself in a publicity pamphlet as a qualified expert in chemistry, microscopy, handwriting, ink analysis, typewriting, photography, finger prints, toxicology, gunshot wounds, guns and cartridges, bullet identification, gunpowder, nitroglycerine, dynamite, high explosives, blood and other stains, causes of death, embalming, and anatomy.

In 1915 Hamilton had come a cropper when he appeared as an expert for the prosecution in the New York trial of Charles Stielow, accused of murdering his housekeeper. According to Hamilton's testimony, a bullet taken from the housekeeper's body could only have come from Stielow's revolver. Principally because of this testimony Stielow was found guilty and sentenced to death. Yet later he was pardoned after it was shown by more competent experts that the death bullet could not have come from this revolver.

Hamilton's career survived even this devastating reverse. When he appeared in Boston to testify in the Proctor-Hamilton motion, he had the respectable assistance of Augustus Gill, a professor of chemical analysis at the Massachusetts Institute of Technology. Hamilton now claimed that by the measurements he had made under the microscope he was able to determine that the test bullets offered in evidence at the trial had been fired from Sacco's pistol but that Bullet III had not. Professor Gill corroborated this opinion. Hamilton also maintained that the hammer in Vanzetti's revolver was not new, since an essential screw did not show marks of having been removed.

In answering for the prosecution Captain Van Amburgh had become much more positive than he had been at the trial. He displayed his strip photographs, declaring that he was now "absolutely certain" that Bullet III and Shell W had been fired in Sacco's pistol.

Toward the close of the hearing, Hamilton appeared in court with two new .32 caliber Colt automatics that he said he wanted to compare with Sacco's pistol. Before Judge Webster Thayer and the lawyers for both sides, he disassembled all three pistols and placed their parts in three piles on a table in front of the judge's bench. Then, picking up various parts one by one, he explained their function and pointed out their interchangeability. Finally he reassembled the pistols, putting his own two back in his pocket and handing Sacco's to the clerk of court.

Just as Hamilton was leaving the courtroom Judge Thayer called him back and ordered him to hand over the two pistols in his pocket to be impounded. He did so. Two months later when Van Amburgh was again examining Sacco's pistol, he noticed that the barrel, previously fouled with rust, appeared bright and sparkling as if it were brand-new. At once he realized that there had been a substitution of barrels and that if the gun were now fired it would produce very different markings on the bullets. He notified Assistant District Attorney Williams, who went at once to Judge Thayer. After a private hearing Thayer ordered an investigation.

This was held in the following three weeks with only Van Amburgh, Hamilton, the district attorney, and a defense lawyer present.

At the opening of the investigation the three pistols were brought in. The briefest examination made it clear that Sacco's Colt had acquired a new barrel. Its original fouled barrel was now found to be in one of Hamilton's pistols. Everyone in the room was aware that Hamilton must have made the substitution when he disassembled the three guns in court, and the district attorney now accused him of trying to work up grounds for a new trial. Unabashed, Hamilton maintained that someone connected with the prosecution had made the switch. At the conclusion of the investigation Thayer passed no judgment as to who had switched the barrels but merely noted that the rusty barrel in the new pistol had come from Sacco's Colt. In concluding he ordered this barrel replaced and the three pistols delivered into the clerk's custody "without prejudice to either side." The prejudice, however, was not so easily erased. To the end Hamilton was a detriment, expensive, untrustworthy, and untrusted.

In the six years that had elapsed between the conviction of Sacco and Vanzetti and the passing of the death sentence on them in 1927, the case had expanded from its obscure beginnings to become an international issue of increasing turbulence. Finally in June, 1927, the governor of Massachusetts appointed a three-man committee headed by President A. Lawrence Lowell of Harvard to review the case.

The ballistics issue had remained dormant since Judge Thayer's rejection of the Proctor-Hamilton motion. Just before the Lowell Committee hearings, still another expert, Major Calvin Goddard, arrived in Boston with a comparison microscope, with which he offered to make without charge what he maintained would be conclusive tests on the Sacco-Vanzetti shells and bullets. The prosecution had no objections. William Thompson, the conservative Boston lawyer who had taken charge of the defense, would not approve of the tests but agreed not to try to prevent them.

Goddard made his tests June 3 before Professor Gill, a junior defense lawyer, an assistant district attorney, and several newsmen. His findings were:

1. That Shell W was fired in the Sacco pistol and could have been fired in no other.

2. That the so-called "mortal" bullet, Bullet III, was fired through the Sacco pistol and could have been fired through no other.

Professor Gill, after spending some time looking through the comparison microscope, became convinced of the parallel patterns of Bullet III and a test bullet, but felt that these would have shown more clearly if Bullet III could have been cleaned of its encrusted grime. Thompson, for the defense, refused to give permission to have this done. Shortly afterward Gill wrote to Thompson that he now doubted his testimony at the Hamilton-Proctor motion and wished to sever all connection with the case. His disavowal was followed by another from the trial defense expert James Burns.

Goddard's findings, though unofficial, undoubtedly had much influence on the Lowell Committee. When Thompson later appeared before the committee, he made the novel accusation that the prosecution had juggled the evidence by substituting a test bullet and cartridge fired in Sacco's pistol for the original Shell W found in the gravel and Bullet III taken from Berardelli's body. As an indication of this he pointed out that the identifying scratches on Bullet III differed from those on the other bullets, being wider apart and uneven—as if made with a different instrument.

The year after Sacco and Vanzetti were executed, Thompson spoke out even more bluntly and emphatically, accusing Captain Proctor of having made the shell and bullet substitution just before the evidence was offered at trial. After the substitution, according to Thompson, Proctor's conscience had bothered him to the point that he had just before his death signed the affidavit expressing his doubts.

The certainty that Goddard had hoped to bring to the ballistics evidence was made to seem less than certain in the autumn of 1927 by his findings in the Yorkell murder case in Cleveland. A few weeks after Yorkell, a bootlegger, had been shot down in the street, the police arrested a Frank Milazzo, who was found to be carrying a revolver similar in type to the one that killed Yorkell. Two bullets taken from Yorkell's body and several bullets test-fired from Milazzo's pistol were sent to Goddard for examination. After viewing the exhibits through his comparison microscope Goddard announced that one of the bullets found in Yorkell had been fired from Milazzo's revolver. In spite of Goddard's findings Milazzo was shortly afterward able to prove that he had bought the revolver new a month after the shooting. Goddard attributed the mistake to a mix-up of bullets at police headquarters. The Cleveland police denied this. Supporters of Sacco and Vanzetti have used the incident to question the infallibility of the comparison microscope. What apparently happened was that Goddard, instead of comparing a murder bullet and a test bullet, had compared the two Yorkell murder bullets with each other. They, of course, matched. Who was at fault it is impossible to say, but the comparison microscope itself was in no way discredited.

In July 1927, the Sacco-Vanzetti guns and bullets were brought to Boston from the Dedham Courthouse, where they had been in the custody of the clerk of court since the trial, to be examined by the Lowell

Committee. Then they disappeared. When in 1959 I tried to see them, they were nowhere to be found. The Dedham clerk of court had a record of their having been sent to Boston but no record of their return. The Massachusetts attorney general's office had no idea where they were, nor did the Commissioner of Public Safety at state police headquarters.

It took me six months of poking about before I finally managed to discover where they had gone. Apparently, after they had been examined by the Lowell Committee, they were sent to the ballistics laboratory of the state police and placed in the custody of Captain Van Amburgh. He put all the exhibits, each triple-sealed in its official court envelope, in a cardboard box and locked them away. The box remained there almost twenty years. Then when Van Amburgh retired he took several ballistics souvenirs with him, among them the box of Sacco-Vanzetti exhibits.

Van Amburgh—who died in 1949—was succeeded in the laboratory by his son. The son in turn retired in 1951 to Kingston, a small town near Plymouth, about forty miles from Boston. When I telephoned him to ask about the Sacco-Vanzetti exhibits, he refused at first to say whether he had them or not. But after I had persuaded the Boston *Globe* to run a feature article on the missing exhibits, he admitted to reporters that he did have them but regarded himself merely as their "custodian." The *Globe* story was a Sunday sensation. Among the paper's early readers was the Commissioner of Public Safety, J. Henry Goguen. The Commissioner at once sent two state troopers to Kingston to demand the surrender of the exhibits. The next day the gun and bullets, still in their box, were back in the state police laboratory.

When I at last saw the exhibits at the laboratory they were relatively free from corrosion, although the clips that fastened them in their triple envelopes had rusted into the paper. Apparently they had not been disturbed since 1927. What I first planned to do was to have comparison tests made of Bullet III and a bullet fired from Sacco's pistol, and similar comparisons made with Shell W. Then I hoped to determine whether or not the other bullets and shells had been fired from a single gun.

Yet I knew that even if Bullet III could be proved beyond dispute to have come from Sacco's pistol, there still remained the question raised by Thompson of bullet substitution. There was at least the possibility that the bullets might still test for blood. If it could now be demonstrated that all six bullets had traces of human blood on them, then the evidence would be overwhelming that there had been no bullet substitution. If on the other hand Bullet III showed no trace of blood, whereas the other five bullets did, the presumption would be strong that Proctor or someone connected with the prosecution had substituted one of the bullets fired into sawdust.

I thought there would be no difficulty in arranging these tests, but when I discussed the matter with Commissioner Goguen I found out otherwise. Even in 1959, it seemed, the Sacco-Vanzetti case was still an explosive political issue—as the spring legislative hearings requesting a posthumous pardon for the two men had demonstrated—and the Commissioner wanted to stay out of it. Each time I asked for permission to have properly qualified experts conduct ballistics tests, he postponed any definite answer, telling me to come back in a month or two. At last, after a year, he announced flatly that he would allow no tests.

Not until Goguen's term of office expired and his successor, Frank Giles, took over was I able to arrange for the tests. Finally on October 4, 1961, Professor William Boyd of the Boston University Medical School examined the six bullets for blood. Unfortunately, because of slight oxidization of the bullets, he was unable to determine whether any blood traces remained.

However, after Bullet III had been washed I was able to examine the base under the microscope. Previously the bullet had been covered with some foreign substance that obscured the markings on the base. With this removed I could see the three scratched lines clearly. Although they were farther apart than the lines on the other bullets, this could have been because Bullet III had a concave base whereas the bases of the remaining bullets were flat. In any case as I looked through the microscope successively at Bullets, I, II, III, and IIII, I could see no notable difference between the scratches on Bullet III and those on the rest.

A week after Professor Boyd had made his blood tests, two firearms consultants came to Boston to make the ballistics comparisons: Jac Weller, the honorary curator of the West Point Museum, and Lieutenant Colonel Frank Jury, formerly in charge of the Firearms Laboratory of the New Jersey State Police. On October 11, 1961, Weller and Jury conducted their tests in the laboratory of the Massachusetts State Police.

Sacco's pistol, they found, was still in condition to be used. After firing two shots to clear the rust from the barrel, Colonel Jury fired two more shots which he then used to match against Bullet III in the comparison microscope. Making independent examinations, Jury and Weller both concluded that "the bullet marked 'III' was fired in Sacco's pistol and in no other."

They also agreed, after comparing the breech-block markings of Shell W and a test shell (see opening paragraph), that Shell W must have been fired in Sacco's pistol. The other five bullets, they concluded, were fired from a single unknown gun, probably a semiautomatic pistol. It is to be presumed that the three shells, also from a single gun, came from the same weapon as did the five bullets—although this, as Jury and Weller pointed out, cannot be demonstrated.

I spent some time myself looking through the microscope at the cross-sections of Bullet III and the test bullet. The striations fitted into each other as if the two bullets were one. Here was a matter no longer open to question. But there still remained Thompson's question: was this Bullet III a substitution?

Even though nothing could be proved by blood tests, Jury and Weller felt that there had been no substitution. They maintained that a bullet fired into oiled sawdust would have shown characteristic marks on it. No such marks were on Bullet III. Theoretically, they pointed out, it would have been possible to have fired a test bullet into a side of beef, but this would have involved many problems, such as the purchase of the beef and keeping the experiment secret.

Besides the reasoning of Jury and Weller I had reasons of my own that made me feel there had been no bullet substitution, that the theory itself evolved out of Thompson's despair. There was, of course, the coincidence that Bullet III with its obsolete cannelure was duplicated by the six Winchester bullets found on Sacco when he was arrested. According to the autopsy report of April 17, 1920, Bullet III had been fired into Berardelli as he was in a prone position. Dr. Magrath identified Bullet III at the trial by the scratches he had originally made on it: "As I found it [he testified], it lay sideways against the flat surface of the hip bone, and in my opinion the flattening of the bullet was due to its striking that bone side on." This peculiar flattening would have been almost impossible to duplicate in a substitute bullet. When Thompson in 1927 accused the prosecution of substituting Bullet III, the assistant district attorney offered to call Dr. Magrath before the Lowell Committee to reidentify the bullet he had marked, but the defense showed no interest in this.

Beyond the physical evidence of the bullet itself, the substitution theory breaks down when the trial record is examined. There Captain Van Amburgh on the stand had been most tentative in identifying Bullet III as having been fired from Sacco's pistol. Captain Proctor was even more ambiguous and later admitted that he never believed that Bullet III came from that particular Colt. If, however, Bullet III had been a substitution, the two captains would have *known* that it came from Sacco's Colt, since they themselves had fired it. Doubts they might have had as to their conduct, but none at all about the bullet.

When the case first came to trial, it was no earthshaking issue for District Attorney Katzmann or for the state police. Katzmann, if he had lost, would still have been re-elected. The case could not have been worth the risk of detection and disgrace to forge the evidence for a conviction.

In the light of the most recent ballistics evidence and after reviewing the inquest and autopsy reports, as well as the trial testimony, I felt I could come to no other conclusion than that the Colt automatic found on Sacco when he was picked up by the police was the one used to murder Berardelli three weeks earlier. About the gun found on Vanzetti there is too much uncertainty to come to any conclusion. Being of .38 caliber, it was obviously not used at South Braintree, where all the bullets fired were .32's. There is at least the possibility that it may have been taken from the dying Berardelli, but there is an equally strong if not stronger possibility that this is not so. A Harrington & Richardson was a cheap, common revolver, and there were several hundred thousand of them being carried at the time Vanzetti was arrested. No one today can be certain whether Berardelli's Harrington & Richardson was of .32 or .38 caliber, whether it had a broken spring or a broken hammer, whether it was ever called for at Iver Johnson's, whether in fact Berardelli had a gun with him the day he was murdered. Jury and Weller found it impossible to determine if the hammer of Vanzetti's revolver had been replaced.

Whether Sacco himself pulled the trigger of his automatic that day in South Braintree, whether he was even present, cannot be established definitely. But if he did not fire it, and in fact he was not there, then one of his close associates must have been the murderer. The ballistics evidence leaves no alternative.

When a few years ago I wrote an article, "Tragedy in Dedham," I was convinced that the two men were innocent, victims if not of a judicial frame-up, at least of an ironic fate. But after the ballistics tests of 1961 I felt that, at least in the case of Sacco, I could no longer hold to my opinion. It has been pointed out that Vanzetti, just before he died, solemnly proclaimed his innocence. Sacco, however, when he took his place in the electric chair, gave the traditional anarchist cry—"Long live anarchy!"

Whatever my altered views about Sacco, I still continue to feel that Vanzetti was innocent. Besides various subjective reasons, and convincing talks with Vanzetti's old friends, I found what seemed to me the clinching evidence in the statement of the New York anarchist leader, Carlo Tresca. Tresca, a luminous and vivid personality, became the most noted anarchist in the United States after the deportation of Luigi Galleani in 1919. He was the admired and trusted leader to whom the anarchists confidently turned when they were in trouble. It was he who had selected the original trial lawyer for Sacco and Vanzetti. His influence remained vast over the years, not only among the dwindling anarchists but throughout the whole New York Italian colony.

During World War II the anti-Soviet Tresca was so successful in keeping the Communists out of the government's overseas Italian broadcasts that a G.P.U. killer known as Enea Sormenti was imported to eliminate him. Tresca was shot down on a New York street in 1943. Several weeks before he died he happened to be talking with his long-time friend Max Eastman, who had earlier written a "Profile" of him for the *New Yorker*. The subject of Sacco and Vanzetti came up, and Eastman asked Tresca if he would feel free to tell him the truth about them.

Without hesitation Tresca replied: "Sacco was guilty, but Vanzetti was not." At that moment some people came into the room, interrupting the conversation, and Eastman never saw Tresca again. Yet the reasons for Tresca's answer must have been profound. He could easily have avoided the question or even denied his comrade's guilt. And if any man should have known the truth of the case, Tresca was the man.

To my mind the most that can be said against Vanzetti is that he must have known who did commit the Braintree crime. Sacco, if he was guilty, was so out of no personal motive. But anarchist deeds of robbery and violence for the sake of the cause were not unknown. If he actually participated in the South Braintree holdup, it was to get money to aid his imprisoned fellow anarchists, and he must then have seen himself not as a robber but as a soldier of the revolution. But if someone else of his group was guilty, someone from whom he had received the murder pistol, he would have preferred death to betraying a comrade.

As the far as the guns and bullets in the Sacco-Vanzetti case are concerned, the evidence is in, no longer to be disputed. The human problem remains.

—June 1962

QUIET EARTH, BIG SKY

By WALLACE STEGNER

How the seasons of a Western boyhood left a permanent impress on the spirit of a leading novelist and historian

I am often tempted to believe that I grew up on a gun-toting frontier. This temptation I trace to a stagecoach ride in the spring of 1914, and a cowpuncher named Buck Murphy.

The stagecoach ran from Gull Lake, Saskatchewan, on the main line of the Canadian Pacific, to Eastend, sixty miles southwest in the valley of the Frenchman, Steel from Swift Current already reached to Eastend, but trains were not yet running when the stage brought in my mother, my brother, and myself, plus a red-faced cowpuncher with a painful deference to ladies and a great affection for little children. I rode the sixty miles on Buck Murphy's lap, half anaesthetized by his whiskey breath, and during the ride I confounded both my mother and Murphy by fishing from under his coat a six-shooter half as big as I was.

A little later Murphy was shot and killed by a Mountie in the streets of Shaunavon, up the line. We had no streets in Eastend—our own house was then a derailed dining car—but I could imagine every detail of that shooting. It has given me a comfortable sense of status ever since to recall that I was a friend of badmen and an eyewitness to gunfights before saloons.

Actually Murphy was an amiable, drunken, sentimental, perhaps dishonest Montana cowboy like dozens of others. He wore his six-shooter inside his coat because Canadian law forbade the carrying of arms. When Montana cattle outfits worked across the line they learned to leave their guns in their bedrolls. In the American West men came before law, but in Saskatchewan law was there before settlers, before even cattlemen, and not merely law but law enforcement. It was not characteristic that Buck

Murphy should die in a gunfight, but if he had to die by violence it was entirely characteristic tha he should be shot by a policeman.

The first settlement in the Cypress Hills country was a *métis* village, the second the Mountie headquarters at Fort Walsh, the third a Mountie outpost sent eastward to keep an eye on the *métis*. The outpost camp on Chimney Coulee, four miles north of the village I grew up in, was the original town of Eastend. Its crumbling chimneys and the outlines of its vanished cabins remind a visitor why there were no Boot Hills along the Frenchman.

So it is not the glamour of a romantic past that brings me back to the village I last saw in 1919. Neither is it, quite, an expectation of returning to the wonderland. By most estimates, Saskatchewan is a pretty depressing country.

The Frenchman, a river more American than Canadian since it flows into the Milk and thence into the Missouri, has even changed its name to conform with American maps. We always called it the Whitemud, from the pure white kaolin exposed along its valley. Whitemud or Frenchman, the river is at least as important as the town in my memory, for it conditioned and contained the town. But memory, though vivid, is imprecise, without sure dimensions. What I remember is low bars, cutbank bends, secret paths through willows, fords across the shallows, swallows in the clay banks, days of indolence and adventure where space was as flexible as the mind's cunning and time did not exist. And around the sunken sanctuary of the river valley, stretching out in all directions from the benches to become coextensive with the disc of the world, went the uninterrupted prairie.

The geologist who surveyed southwestern Saskatchewan in the 1870s called it one of the most desolate and forbidding regions on earth. Yet as I drive eastward into it from Medicine Hat, returning to my childhood through a green June, I look for desolation and can find none.

The plain spreads southward below the Trans-Canada Highway, an ocean of wind-troubled grass and grain. It has its characteristic textures: winter wheat, heavily headed, scoured and shadowed as if schools of fish move in it; spring wheat, its two-inch seed rows precise as combings in a boy's wet hair; gray-brown summer fallow with the weeds disced under, and grass, the marvelous curly prairie wool tight to the earth's skin, straining the wind in its own way, secretly.

Prairie wool blue-green, spring wheat bright as new lawn, winter wheat gray-green at rest and slaty when the wind flaws it, roadside primroses as shy as prairie flowers are supposed to be, and as gentle to the eye as when in my boyhood we used to call them wild tulips; by their flowering they mark the beginning of summer.

On that monotonous surface with its occasional ship-like farm, its atolls of shelter-belt trees, its level ring of horizon, there is little to interrupt the eye. Roads run straight between parallel lines of fence until they intersect the horizon circumference. It is a landscape of circles, radii, perspective exercises—a country of geometry. Across its empty miles pours the pushing and shouldering wind, a thing you tighten into as a trout holds himself in fast water. It is a grassy, clean, exciting wind, with the smell of distance in it, and in its search for whatever it is looking for it turns over every wheat blade and head, every pale primrose, even the ground-hugging grass. It blows yellow-headed blackbirds and hawks and prairie sparrows around the air and ruffles the short tails of meadow larks on fence posts. In collaboration with the light it makes lovely and changeful for what might otherwise be characterless.

For over the segmented circle of earth is domed the biggest sky anywhere, which on days like this sheds down on range and wheat and summer fallow a light to set a painter wild, a light pure, glareless, and transparent. The horizon a dozen miles away is as clear a line as the nearest fence. There is no haze, either the wooly gray of humid countries or the blue atmosphere of the mountain West. Across the immense sky move navies of strato-cumuli, their bottoms as even as if they had scraped themselves flat against the sky.

The drama of this landscape is in the sky, pouring with light and always moving. The earth is passive. And yet the beauty I am struck by, both as memory and as present fact, is a fusion: this sky would not be so spectacular without this earth to change and glow and darken under it. And whatever the sky may do, however the earth is shaken or darkened, the Euclidean perfection abides. The very scale, the hugeness of simple space and simple forms, emphasizes this sub-perception of stability.

In spring there is almost as much sky on the ground as in the air. The country is dotted with slough, every depression is full of water, the roadside ditches are canals. Grass and wheat grow to the water's edge and under it; they seem to grow right under the edges of the sky. In deep sloughs tules have rooted, and every pond is dignified with mating mallards and the dark little automata that glide along after them as if on strings.

The nesting mallards move in my memory like a sleeper stirring. The image of a drake standing on his head with his curly tail feathers sticking up from a sheet of wind-flawed slough is tangled in my remembering senses with the feel of the grassy edge under my bare feet, the smell of mud, the push of the traveler wind, the weight of the sun, the look of the sky with its level-floored clouds made for the penetration of miraculous Beanstalks.

Desolate? Forbidding? There was never a country that in its good moments was more beautiful. Even in drouth or blizzard or dust storm it is the reverse of monotonous. You don't get out of the wind, but learn to lean against it. You don't escape sky and sun, but wear them in your eyeballs and on your back. You become acutely aware of yourself. The world is very large, the sky even larger, and you are very small; but also the world is flat and empty, and you are a challenging verticality, as sudden as an exclamation mark, as enigmatic as a question mark, in its flatness.

It is a country to breed religious or poetic people, but not humble ones. At noon the sun comes on your head like a waterfall: at sunset or sunrise you throw a shadow a hundred yards long. It was not prairie dwellers who invented the indifferent universe or impotent man. Puny you may feel there, but not *unnoticed*. This is a land to mark the sparrow's fall.

Our homestead, just southward from here around the roll of the earth, had only a wagon-track connection with the world. When we built the required shack on our half section in 1915 no roads led in; we came fifty miles across unplowed grass and burnouts by lumber wagon. Each year the day-long ride from town, starting at two or three in the reddening morning, led us from the valley up onto the south bench and the great plain reaching southward. We crossed a wave of low hills, the southwest end of the Cypress Hills uplift, and rocked and jarred for a couple of hours through an enormous horse pasture on leased crown land. An irrigation ditch led water around the contour of one of the hills, and we lunched by it. As we ate, range horses with the wind in their manes thundered like poetry over the hills to stare at us, and like poetry thundered away.

Then a farm with a stone barn and a flock of shy French kids. Further into the long afternoon, another farm where we stopped to rest and talk. After that, the road forked and dwindled, became finally our own grass-grown track. The land flattened to a billiard-table flatness, grew stonier, more sparsely grassed, more patched with cactus clumps. At last the twin tar-papered shacks we called Pete and Emil, unlived in but doubtless fulfilling the letter of the homestead bond. Now we chirked up: we were nearly at our own place. When we arrived at our gate and saw the round-roofed shack, the chicken house, the dugout reservoir full to the brim, we jumped off the wagon and ran the last hundred yards.

Sometimes we had picked things up along the trail, once two coyotes that my father shot from the wagon, another time five baby mallards we had captured in a slough. All that summer they owned our dugout and stood on their heads in the weedy water with their tails aimed at the great sky. That fall they went back to town with us, but we forgot to keep their wings clipped, and one morning, like every other wild thing we ever held prisoner, they took advantage of a big wind and were gone with all the other autumnal excitement streaming south.

We always had a menagerie. I had a black-footed ferret, weasels, burrowing owls, a magpie that could talk, or so I thought. All of them got away. It seemed impossible to maintain a jail at the center of all that emptiness and freedom.

Living out the months of our required residence and waiting for the long growing days to make us a crop, we saw few people. Occasionally a Swede or Norwegian batch stopped by. Once in a while we drove over to see a neighbor. Once or twice a summer we went to town for supplies. A visit or a visitor was excitement, a trip to town delirium, but excitement was rare and delirium rarer. The rest of the time we communed with gophers, weasels, badgers, with sparrows and meadow larks and robins and hawks, and sometimes with the shrikes who practiced their butcher's trade on our barbed wire.

In 1915, the plowed land was an occasional patch or stripe on the prairie's face. If our horses broke out they could wander for miles without hitting a fence. By day, Pete and Emil and another empty shack, plus two inhabited farms, rode at anchor within the circle of our vision. At night the darkness came down tight all around, and the two little lights far out on the plain were more lonely even than the wind that mourned and hunted through the grass, or the owls that flew on utterly soundless wings and sent their short, barking cry across the coulee. On clear mornings the tips of Bear Paw Mountain, far down in Montana, were a mirage reflected up from another world.

Practically, there was little distinction between Saskatchewan and Montana. The southern boundary of our homestead was the international line, no more important than other survey lines except that the iron posts stood every mile along it. The nearest customhouse was clear over in Alberta, and all the time we spent on the farm we never saw an officer, American or Canadian. We bought supplies in Harlem or Chinook and got our mail at Hydro, all in Montana. In the fall we hauled our wheat, if we had made any, freely across to the Milk River towns and sold it where the price was higher.

We made a pretense of subsistence, with a cow, chickens, horses, a vegetable garden, but we weren't really farmers. We were bonanza farmers, mining virgin land. Three hundred acres in Marquis wheat, if you got such a crop in 1915 when many fields ran more than fifty bushels to the acre and practically none ran under forty, might give you 15,000 bushels of No. 1 Northern—and during those war years the price of wheat went up and up until by 1918 it was crowding three dollars a bushel.

But 1915 was the last good year for a decade. When we gave up after four successive crop failures, more than the commuters' shacks stood vacant on the weed-grown, whirlwind-haunted prairie. By the mid-Twenties, when the rains came again, only a few stickers were left to profit from them. The crop of 1927 was the biggest on record. It revived the boom. Then more dry cycle, until by the Thirties the whole southwest part of the province was a dust bowl, all but depopulated.

The judgment of the earliest surveyor seemed justified. It was indeed one of the most desolate and forbidding regions in the world, and infinitely more desolate for man's passing. The prairie sod was replaced by Russian thistle and other weeds, the summer fallow was blown away, the topsoil was vanishing as dust. Tar paper flapped forlornly on abandoned shacks. Gophers and field mice multiplied by millions, as they always do in drouth years, and took over the burrowed earth. The feudal hawks continued to hold the sky.

But we return at the crest of a wet cycle. These years, when anything over about ten bushels to the acre will show a farmer a profit, most fields have hit twenty-five. The 1951 crop was the largest in history, the 1952 crop topped it. Given rain, Saskatchewan can grow more wheat than a discreet economy will permit it to sell: the elevators and storehouses of the province bulge with the bounty of the fat years.

It is a prosperous country now. Its farms that used to jut bleakly from the plain are bedded in cottonwoods and yellow-flowering caragana. And the ring of horizon is broken by a new verticality more portentous than windmills or fence posts or even elevators—the derricks of oil rigs. Farther north, in the Beaverlodge country, Saskatchewan prosperity rides the uranium boom. Here it rides on wheat and oil. But though the country is no longer wild, it is probably less populous than in our time. Oil crews create no new towns and do not enlarge old ones more than temporarily. Even if they hit oil, they cap the well and go on. As for wheat, fewer and fewer farmers produce more and more of it.

To us, a half section was a farm. With modern machinery, a man by himself can plow, seed, and harvest a thousand or twelve hundred acres. The average farm now is at least a section; two sections or even more are not uncommon. And even such a farm is only a part-time job. A man can seed a hundred acres a day. Once the crop is in there is little to do until harvest. Then a week or two on the combine, a week or two hauling, a week or two working the summer fallow and planting winter wheat, and he is done until spring.

This is a strange sort of farming, with its dangers of soil exhaustion, wind erosion, and drouth, and with its highly special conditions. Only about half of even the pretentious farmhouses on the prairie are lived in, and some of those are lived in only part time, by farmers who spend all but the crop season in town. Sometimes a farmer has no farmhouse at all, but commutes to work in a pickup. There is a growing class of trailer-farmers, migrants, many of them from the United States.

Hence the look of extensive cultivation and at the same time the emptiness. We see few horses, few cattle, Saskatchewan farmers, who could go a long way to supplying the world's bread, are less subsistence farmers than we were in 1915. They live in towns like medieval towns, tight clusters surrounded by cultivated fields; but here the fields are immense and the distances enormous.

So it is still quiet earth, big sky. Human intrusions still seem as abrupt as the elevators that leap out of the plain to announce every little hamlet and keep it memorable for a few miles. The country and the smaller villages empty slowly into the larger centers; the small towns get smaller, the large ones slowly larger. Eastend, based strategically on the river, is one of the lucky ones that will last.

In the fall it was always a wonderful excitement, after an interminable day on the sun-struck wagon, to come to the rim of the south bench. The horses would be plodding with their noses almost to their knees, the colt dropping tiredly behind. Everything would be flat, hot, dusty. And then suddenly the ground fell away, and there below, so snug in its valley that I always fell into it as one falls into bed, at home and protected and safe.

Now there is the same sudden revelation of sanctuary, but with a new perception. I had always thought of the river as running all its course in a sunken valley: now I see that the valley is dug only where the river has cut across the uplift of the hills. Elsewhere it crawls disconsolately, flat on the prairie's face. A child's sight is so peculiarly limited: he can see only what he can see. Only later does he learn to link what he sees with what he imagines and hears and reads, and so come to make perception serve inference. During my childhood I kept hearing about the Cypress Hills and wishing that I could go there; now I see that I grew up in the very middle of them.

More has changed here than on the prairie. My town, for one thing, was as bare as a picked bone, without a tree in it larger than a six-foot-willow. Now it is a grove. We drive through it, trying to restore old familiarities among the novelty of fifty-foot cottonwoods, lilac and honeysuckle hedges, flower gardens. And the familiarities are there: the Pastime Theater, unchanged; the lumberyards where we got advertising caps; two of the three hardware stores (a prairie wheat town specializes in hardware stores); the hotel, just as it was; the bank building, now the post office; the churches and the Masonic lodge and the square brick prison of the schoolhouse, though with some smaller prisons added. The Eastend *Enterprise* sits just where it has sat since it was founded in 1914.

But all tree-shaded. In the old days we tried to grow trees, transplanting them from the hills or getting them free with two-dollar purchases at the hardware, but they always dried up and died. Now every lot in town gets all the water it needs for a dollar a year from the government dam upriver, and forty years have brought new trees and shrubs, especially the drouth-resistant caragana. Because I came expecting a dusty hamlet, the reality is charming, but memory has been fixed by time, and this reality is dreamlike. I cannot find any part of myself in it.

The river is disappointing, a quiet creek twenty yards wide, the color of strong tea, its banks a tangle of willow and wild rose. How could adventure ever have inhabited those willows, or wonder, or fear, or the other remembered emotions? Was it here I shot at the lynx with my brother's .25-.20? And out of what log (there is no possibility of a log in these brakes, but I distinctly remember a log) did my bullet knock chips just under the lynx's bobtail?

Who in town remembers in the same way I do a day when he drove up before Leaf's store with two dead dogs and the lynx who had killed them when they caught him unwarily out on the flats? Who remembers that angry and disgusted scene as I do, as a parable of adventure and danger, a lesson for the pursuer to respect the pursued?

Because it is not shared, the memory seems fictitious, as do the other memories; the blizzard of 1916 that marooned us in the schoolhouse, the spring flood when the ice brought the railroad bridge in kindling to our doors, the games of fox and geese in the snow of a field that is now a grove, the nights of skating with a great fire leaping on the river ice and reddening the snowy cutbanks. I have used these memories for years as if they really happened, have made stories and novels of them. Now they seem uncorroborated.

To see a couple of boys on the prowl with air guns in the willow brush somewhat reassures me, and forces me to readjust my disappointed estimate of the scrub growth. In my time we would have been carrying a .22 or a shotgun, but we would have been of the same tribe. And when one is four feet high, six-foot willows are sufficient cover, and ten acres are a wilderness.

Later, looking from the bench hills across my town, I can see where the river shallows and crawls south-eastward across the prairie toward the Milk, the Missouri, the Gulf, and I toy with the notion that a man is like water or clouds, that he can be constantly moving and yet steadily renewed. The sensuous little savage, at any rate, has not been rubbed away; he is as solid a part of me as my skeleton.

And he has a fixed and suitably arrogant relationship to his universe, a relationship geometrical and symbolic. From his center of sensation and challenge and question, the circle of the world is measured, and in that respect the years I have loaded upon my savage have not changed him. Lying on the hillside where once I watched the town's cattle herd or snared April's gophers, I feel how the world first reduced me to a point and then measures itself against me. Perhaps the meadow lark singing from a fence post—a meadow lark whose dialect I recognize—feels the same way. All points on the circumference are equidistant from him; in him all radii begin; all diameters run through him; if he moves, a new geometry creates itself around him.

No wonder he sings. It is a good country that can make anyone feel so.

—October 1955

THE CONUNDRUM OF CORN

By JOSEPH KASTNER

It's our most important, profitable, and adaptable crop—the true American staple. But where did it come from?

In 1748 an inquisitive Swede named Peter Kalm, a protégé of the great botanist Linnaeus, came to America to find plants that could be useful in his country. He went around asking questions of everybody about everything. He asked Benjamin Franklin about hardy trees and was told that English walnuts did not survive Philadelphia's winters. He asked John Bartram, the most knowing botanist in the colonies, about timber and was told that American oaks were not as tough as European. He asked Cadwallader Colden, later to become the lieutenant governor of New York, about medicinal plants, and was informed that the root of skunk cabbage helped cure scurvy.

But the answer to one question eluded Kalm. Everywhere he went he asked about maize, or Indian corn. He found out the Indians baked it into bread (adding huckleberries in season), brewed it into beer (blue-colored corn was best for this), and used it as a poultice (for curing boils). But he was balked when he asked the simple question Where did corn come from? A blackbird brought it from the west, said some Indians. A beauteous maiden shook it out of her hair, said others. These answers, of course, did not satisfy Kalm's Enlightenment mind.

Scientists today can appreciate his frustration. Ever since he asked, it, they have been repeating his simple question—where did corn come from? —and after two centuries or so have come up with only half the answer. After long deliberation, they have pretty much agreed that corn came from this continent—not from Asia as some once thought—and grew originally in middle America. That settles the geographical question but not the genealogical one: What is corn's ancestry? The search for the answer has sent botanists into fruitless hunts for hypothetical wild grasses and put geneticists through tedious evolutionary exercises in breeding corn backwards. It pits three main schools of thought against each other—Mangelsdorf versus Beadle versus Weatherwax. And it provokes long seminars in which, sooner or later, someone refers to the "mystery of maize."

It seems strange that so familiar and open a plant as corn, whose very name is a metaphor for the obvious, should have any mystery about it. Everybody knows corn. It is a staple crop not just in Nebraska but in Bulgaria, Nigeria, and Thailand. A highly adaptable plant, it grows from Canada to Chile, in humid sea-level marshes and rarified Andean plateaus. A most amenable plant, it breeds so readily and crosses its genes so promiscuously that any kind of corn for almost any purpose can be created. Universally useful, it fattens hogs and cows while nourishing man with *tortillas* and polenta, enlivening him with beer and bourbon, and holding together in wallpaper paste and jelly beans.

Nonetheless, corn still presents a mystery, and smack in the middle of it is a Mexican weed called *teosinte*. A tall, tasseled plant that is found in and around cornfields, it looks so much like corn in its early stages that farmers neglect to pull it out. It pollinates corn freely and just as freely is pollinated by it. Modern corn, in fact, has some teosinte in its genes. Teosinte is so much like corn in so many ways that everyone agrees it is a relative of corn. But which relative? The Beadle school says teosinte is the ancestor of corn. The Mangelsdorf school argues, instead, that corn is the ancestor of teosinte. The Weatherwax adherents say that corn and teosinte descend from some common ancestor, making them cousins.

A hundred and fifty years ago it was believed that a primitive kind of corn named pod corn was the wild progenitor of modern corn. Then, later in the nineteenth century, when the relationship of corn and teosinte was recognized, the teosinte-as-ancestor theory took hold. In 1939 Paul Mangelsdorf of Harvard and R. G. Reeves of Texas went back to the pod corn theory.

After amassing persuasive genetic and botanical evidence for their belief, they found concrete support in archaeology. It came first in 1948 from the Bat Cave in western New Mexico, where prehistoric Indians lived from about 3000 B.C. to A.D. 1000. The leftovers of their tenancy lay untouched in the cave floor—layer after layer of garbage, offal, excrement, broken pottery. Digging methodically, excavators found 776 corncobs. Not a single one had a kernel left on it. But over the centuries 125 kernels had been carelessly dropped and overlooked by beetles and rodents (though back at Harvard, where they were studied, modern mice got into the cache of ancient kernels and ate several). At the bottom were tiny cobs, five thousand years old. In the oldest remnants, there was no indication of teosinte. An even older find was made by an expedition working caves at Tehuacán near Oaxaca in Mexico, where diggers uncovered a seven-thousand-year-old cob. From all the evidence, Mangelsdorf concluded that this was wild corn. And when drillers in Mexico City found grains of cornlike pollen at soil levels eighty thousand years old, long before man came to America, Mangelsdorf was sure of his thesis. The ancestor of corn, he said with finality, was corn.

This finality, however, did not impress other scientists. The Beadle school dismissed the Tehuacán wild corn as an early cultivated variety, since man was known to be farming by then. And they declared the dating of the old pollen to be highly suspect. They offered their own complex genetic data to prove that only a few minor mutations in teosinte, which was growing at least seven thousand years ago, would give it cornlike qualities. When that happened, they theorize, the Indians who collected teosinte seed as marginal food noticed the improved varieties and, one way or another, grew it for themselves. Gradually teosinte evolved into corn. Isn't it odd, they ask the Mangelsdorf school, that ancestral strains of wheat, barley, and other grains still grow wild today but no one has ever found any wild corn? Isn't it just as odd, retort their opponents, that no one has ever found any traces of teosinte at one of the stages it supposedly passed through while evolving into corn?

The arguments, far more subtle and hedged than this summary suggests, are made knottier by another relative of corn and teosinte: Tripsacum, sometimes called gama grass, which grows in many parts of the Americas. The late botanist Paul Weatherwax of Indiana University, studying the resemblances between the plants, deduced that all three descend from the same wild grass. Though his theory has less support—at least less vociferous support—than the others, it has not been altogether discarded.

Everything could be settled, of course, if someone could find a missing link between teosinte and corn, or some corn everyone agreed was wild. (Modern corn relies on man to survive. It cannot disperse its seed, and if an ear fell to the ground, the kernels would sprout into plants so numerous and close together that they would choke each other out.) In the 1960's a squad of plant hunters mounted a botanical safari in Mexico to gather some seventy-five thousand samples of teosinte and look for evolutionary clues. But as Mangelsdorf gleefully saw it, it was a search "proving nothing scientifically but providing its participants with a memorable adventure."

Mangelsdorf himself, who admits that his lifetime spent in the study of one plant, "can be regarded as a form of monomania," undertook to create wild corn in his test plots. Trying to reverse evolution, he bred corn backwards, emphasizing its most primitive characteristics. He failed to reconstruct a wild species but he did wind up, as he put it, with "probably the world's most unproductive corn."

George Beadle, who won a Nobel Prize for his work in medicine and physiology, actually submitted his own digestive tract to support his proteosinte theory. Citing what he called "a friendly disagreement with Professor Mangelsdorf on the edibility" of teosinte, he undertook the Scrimshaw test. Following a regime devised for him by Dr. Nevin Scrimshaw, a nutritionist at the Massachusetts Institute of Technology, he set out to eat teosinte as prehistoric man would have: crushed seeds, hulls and all. After four days on this diet, the intrepid Nobel laureate announced that he suffered "no unpleasant consequences."

Geologists and paleontologists have been on constant lookout for evidence of fossil corn. There was a furor some years ago when the Smithsonian Institution acquired a petrified ear of corn that had been unearthed in a curio shop in Cuzco. After some soul searching, the institution decided to analyze it rather than put it in a showcase. So the cob was dissected—and it turned out to be an ancient toy, a child's rattle beautifully made of clay to imitate an ear of corn.

If the disciplines of modern science have been of no use in answering Kalm's question, neither have the myths he discarded. While eastern Indians said a crow brought corn from the west, the Navahos said a turkey hen flew from the east and dropped a blue ear of corn. The Mayans believed their god-hero Gucumatz, knowing man needed corn, went through grievous perils to bring it to him. The Aztecs told that corn came from the western gardens of Tomoanchan, where goddesses lived, and was brought underground to the red land of dawn where the quetzal bird sings. The Abnaki Indians recited the tale of a lonesome brave who was visited by a lovely light-haired woman. She promised to be with him always if he would do as she said: "Rub two sticks together, burn a plot of grass and, when the sun goes down, take me by the hair and drag me over the ground. Grass will grow where I am dragged and hair will come up between the leaves." Reluctantly the Indian did what she said, and so corn came to mankind—a lovely story but better perceived, perhaps, by Freudians than by farmers.

In the mundane world, corn came late to the agricultural age. By 8000 B.C., men in southwest Asia had stopped relying on collecting wild grain for food and were cultivating it. By 6000 B.C., the practice had reached Western Europe and, at about the same time, it had already begun in America, where Indians raised chili peppers, avocado, squash, beans, and corn. Domestication came everywhere through the same accident. Edible seeds of wild plants, dropped around encampments, landed on heaps of garbage and offal. In this richer soil, plants grew bigger and were handier to harvest. This led to the purposeful sowing of seed, to cultivation, and finally to the saving and selection of seed from the best plants.

By the time the white man came, corn was the main cultivated crop in all the Americas. In his journal entry for November 5, 1492, Columbus described "a prolific sort of grain from which a very fine flour is made . . . a bread of exquisite taste." It was "a grain like millet which they called maize," a landing party reported, "very well tasted when boiled, roasted or made into porridge."

Thus the Old World first met the plant on which the New World built its wonderful civilizations—the temples of the Mayas, the gold and silver work of the Incas, the enchanting Aztec city of the lakes. To the Indians it was worshiped as the stuff made by gods, the stuff of which man himself was made, his source and sustenance. It was so cheap to produce—a single plant gave a man enough food for a day—that it could support generally stable populations, leaving people with free time to create monumental wealth for their priests and chieftains.

In much of middle America, farming procedures were simple. In a spot near a village, farmers would cut down trees and, leaving them to termites and decay, plant corn between the stumps in scuffed-up hills. The ground was rich in decayed vegetation and, having been shaded by trees, was free of weeds. The corn grew robustly. In three or four years, with the soil depleted and other plants moving in, the plot would be abandoned for another.

In Mexico, corn grew so tall along the trails that Cortez's cavalry had trouble pushing through to get to Montezuma's capital. They found the city streets lined with booths that sold flat corn cakes, and everywhere they heard the noise of the cakes being slapped and thrown on stone hearths. The plain people ate them filled with beans or pimientos, the conquistadors noted, while the rich filled them with meat, feasting also on winged ants and the caviar-like eggs of water flies. The conquerors also learned a dish called *tlacatlaolli*, made of the flesh of a man, sacrificed in a harvest ritual, cooked in a stew with the first-picked corn.

To the northwest, Coronado, searching for those golden cities, met corn all along the way growing in arid spots where the Indians build little basins to catch the sparse rain. Far to the north, Cartier and Champlain found corn that ripened well despite the short summer.

Columbus brought corn back from his first or second voyages, and by the mid-1500s it was growing not just in Spain but in Bulgaria and

Turkey. Slavers carried corn to Africa to feed their cargo and it caught on there, proving more productive than native grain. Magellan's men dropped Mexican seed off in the Philippines and Asia.

Spaniards first called it *panizo*, a general term for grain, but soon adopted the name *maize*. Other Europeans called it Indian corn, Indian barley, Guinea wheat, or when they wanted to disparage it, Turkish corn or Welsh corn—anything from Turkey or Wales was considered coarse and uncivilized. The tireless classifier Linnaeus, who named or renamed almost everything in nature, called it *Zea mays*, *zea* meaning "cereal" and having some remote connotation of "life." The term *corn*, which in the Bible meant any grain, eventually took over as the popular name.

The English in America had to be taught the virtues of corn. Thomas Hariot, who came to Virginia in 1585, described it as "a graine of marvellous great increase." A pound of seed, he said, produced three or four hundred pounds of food. The settlers at Jamestown did not appreciate this local marvel. They insisted on planting wheat, and many starved for their stubbornness.

Captain John Smith had to spend a good deal of time badgering the Indians for corn. It was on a corn-buying trip that he claimed to have been saved by the first all-American heroine, Pocahontas. Her father, Powhatan, bargained hard after pardoning Smith. "A subtle savage," Smith called him and, for a boatload of corn, had to give the chieftain "a grindstone, some guns, a cock and a hen, together with much copper and beads and some men to build him an English style house."

Although Smith ordered the settlers to harvest and store their first corn crops carefully, he discovered that "some of the inhabitants, none of the best husbands," simply picked their ears and threw them unhusked on the floor. But "the good husbands" husked it and "with much labor" hung it up—where, Smith reported, the weevils ate most of the corn while touching "not a grain" of the others. The moral of this perverse grasshopper and ant story, said Smith, was that the best way to preserve corn was to let it "lie in the husk, and spare an infinite labor that formerly had been used."

Up in New England, a few days after the Pilgrims had landed, Miles Standish led a party out in search of food. Near some stubble, they found, as William Bradford chronicled it, "heaps of sand newly paddled with their hands which they, digging up found in them corns of diverse colors which seemed to them a very goodly sight having never have seen such before. They returned to the ship and . . . carried with them the fruits of the land and showed them to their brethren of which they were marvellously glad."

That winter Squanto came to help bury the Pilgrims' dead and then teach them how to plant corn. A Patuxent Indian who had been picked up by a British ship and had learned to speak English in London, he had been returned to Cape Cod. "A special instrument of God," Bradford called him, "who directed them how to set their corn" and told them that "except they got fish and set with it, it would come to nothing." The settlers buried fish in each hill of corn and, when their wheat and peas failed, the twenty acres of corn kept them alive.

Corn was far more suitable for them than wheat. It grew more reliably, yielded more grain. Its harvest was conveniently spread out and it did not have to be carted to a mill to be ground into flour. The Pilgrims planted it the Indian way, four or five seeds in well-spaced hills, and stored it as the Indians did, in clay-lined baskets buried in the ground. They picked a few early ears to eat as sweet corn but dried the rest, for porridge or bread. As whites went west, they found different recipes. Meriwether Lewis wrote that the Mandan Indians fed him a dish "of pumpkins, beans, corns, chokecherries all boiled together and forming a composition by no means unpalatable." Other explorers found it hard to stomach the Omahas' *ta-she-ba*, corn boiled with buffalo intestines, but one of them, the aristocratic Prince Maximilian of Wied, declared that corn "cooked with bear's flesh was beyond comparison, delicious."

In the West corn was grown on a relatively large scale, with the growers selecting the best seed and getting good yields of twenty bushels per acre. This is not surprising, because over the centuries the Indians had developed strains of corn whose productivity still impresses growers today. The hemispheres had been a huge botanical laboratory where patient farmers worked with one of the most supple genetic tools known to man. Because corn crossbreeds so readily and its genetic make-up changes so frequently through mutation, the Indians were presented, generation after generation, with new varieties that were tested, willy-nilly, under all conditions. Keeping the seeds they found best for their own particular use or taste, they slowly improved the breed.

Cortez counted at least twenty different varieties of corn on his march inland. Mexicans, who softened their corn in lye water and ground it for *tortillas*, aimed for firm corn that would not get mushy. In Peru, where kernels were eaten whole, boiled or parched, the goal was larger, softer kernels. Families regarded collecting corn seed as a sacred duty. Their careful selection kept strains astonishingly uncontaminated—no test plot today could keep them purer.

It was simpler for farmers to do this with corn than with other crops. Wheat or barley, for example, were sown broadcast and harvested wholesale with a sickle. Corn was planted seed by seed, tended and picked plant by plant. The farmer could see how every plant grew and give the best of them special attention. Present-day scientists also acknowledge the importance of a factor that rarely gets into modern appraisals: the respect and even affection an Indian farmer showed for his corn.

By the time of the European discoverers, all the modern types of corn were already in existence (there are five—flint, dent, flour, sweet, and popcorn). What the Indians had achieved by instinct and experience was good enough for the white settlers. They did nothing more in the way of selecting and improving, mostly because they did not know where to begin. Corn is a unique plant. It carries the male flowers on top in a tassel and the female flowers lower down on the stalk. Since there is nothing else like it in nature, it is known botanically as a "monstrosity." Nevertheless, the monstrous arrangement is ingenious and efficient. Pollen ripens in the flowers of the tassel. As it does, silk strands start to grow from an ovary attached within a husk to an incipient cob. After the pollen starts to fall—but never before—each silk emerges and reaches to catch a grain of pollen on its sticky end. If a silk goes unpollenized, no kernel will form. European scientists knew corn for two centuries before they realized that it—or any other plant—reproduced by a sexual process. Toward the end of the seventeenth century, the German Camerarius, experimenting with beans and corn, proved that fertilization caused reproduction. In America, shortly after, his findings were documented by three Americans, all better known for things other than botany.

Cotton Mather, the theologian, studied what happened in a field in which a single row of red- and blue-kerneled corn was planted among rows of yellow corn. "To the windward side," he observed, "this red and blue row so infected three or four whole rows as to communicate the same color unto them." But on the leeward side, the corn remained almost all yellow. It was the first report of corn hybridization. Then a contemporary of Mather's, Paul Dudley, chief justice of Massachusetts, reported that "if in the same field you plant the blue corn in one row of hills and the white or yellow in the next row, some of the ears in the blue corn rows shall be white or yellow and some in the white or yellow rows shall be of a blue color." Indians believed the mixture came about because the roots touched, but, Dudley stated, the plants were too far apart for this. The wind, he said, was responsible for what he called "this wonderful copulation."

Then James Logan, who managed Pennsylvania for William Penn and was one of the leading intellectuals in the colonies, made a precise experiment. In 1727, in the four corners of his Philadelphia backyard, he planted hills of corn. In one corner, he cut the tassels off the plants. In another, he covered the silks. In the others, he cut off varying numbers of silk. When he picked the ears, there were no kernels where the tassels had been removed or the silks covered. In the others, the number of kernels matched the number of silks that had been left. The function of pollen and silk was thus established.

All this was done in pursuit of knowledge, not of more or better corn. The first man to put such knowledge to practical use was John Lorain, a Pennsylvanian with a curious mind—he once sought out George Washington to ask the President about his methods of planting potatoes between rows of corn. Lorain worked a farm in southern Pennsylvania, a border region where farmers planted two kinds of corn. One was flint corn, favored in the North, which had firm kernels, smaller ears, and ripened early. The other was a dent corn, named for the dimple in its kernel, called Gourdseed, which had heavier ears, softer kernels, and ripened later. In this overlapping area, Lorain noticed that the crossbreeding of flint and Gourdseed produced new strains that were heavier and more productive than flint, firmer and earlier than Gourdseed. "A judicious mixture" of the two, he concluded, could yield "at least a third more per acre" than any other kind, and he urged that corn should be bred and selected to keep "the valuable properties" while "the inferior may be nearly grown out."

This was sound advice, but chance was just as important as method in carrying it out. In 1845 Robert Reid, an Ohio farmer, moved to Illinois, taking with him a Gourdseed strain. In the cool Illinois spring most of the seed rotted, and to fill out the hills he planted a flint corn called Little Yellow. The two kinds cross-pollinated, and the result was a wonderful new strain, hardier and better-yielding than any corn Reid knew. Breeding carefully—his son James used to keep the best ears between two mattresses on his bed to protect them from mice—he developed a large, good-looking, reliable variety—Reid's Yellow Dent. It was the most important single strain developed in modern America.

Meanwhile, corn growing moved westward. In 1840 Ohio, Kentucky, Tennessee, and Virginia were the leading growers. Twenty years later Ohio, Illinois, and Missouri had become the leaders. It cost forty cents a bushel to grow corn in New England, as little as twelve cents in Illinois.

The Indians could never grow corn in their richest land, the prairie, because they could not break the sod. The white man's plow could. Where corn went, pigs followed. In 1804 an Ohio farmer named George Rennick decided to get his corn to market by feeding it to his pigs and walking them over the mountains to Baltimore. He lost one hundred pounds off each hog, but even then the profit was very big. By 1850 the pigs were going to Cincinnati, which some called "Porkopolis," and the hogs were known as "land whales" because their fat was replacing the diminishing supply of whale oil.

The great scientific era of corn breeding did not begin until late in the century. In 1871 Charles Darwin, working with corn, found that inbreeding a strain of corn would weaken it, but crossbreeding an inbred with another variety would revive it. William James Beal, at Michigan Agricultural College, who corresponded with Darwin, began the first controlled crossbreeding of corn and produced strong hybrid strains.

Thirty years later, George Harrison Shull, working in a Long Island laboratory, developed Darwin's thesis. Setting out to study the workings of heredity, he chose to work with corn because it is such a handy evolutionary tool. Its chromosomes are large, easily observed and manipulated; its tassel-ear separation makes pollenization control simple; and it carries a multitude of characteristics in its genes. In fact, next to the salivary glands of the fruit fly, corn is the favorite subject of genetic experiments. To isolate the characteristics he wanted to study, Shull inbred varieties and found, as Darwin had, that the more he refined them, the more he weakened them. However, when he crossed the puny inbred of one line to the puny inbred of another line, a procedure known as a single cross, he attained what he described as "an extraordinarily powerful hybrid . . . more vigorous than the best of the inbred races." He called the phenomenon *heterosis*, or hybrid vigor.

Shull's work was more or less duplicated by Edward Murray East in Connecticut, but neither pushed his results to practical use. (East went off to teach at Harvard while Shull returned to work on his first botanical love, the evening primrose.) Their hybrid did not, it turned out, produce seed in profitable amounts, but a student of East's, Donald Jones, overcame this. He took a single-cross hybrid produced by crossing two inbreds, and crossed it with another single cross. This was a double cross, and the result was splendid—large, vigorous plants and ears that produced seed in profitable quantities. Like Robert Reid, Jones had luck on his side. There were only two single-cross strains available in the laboratory, so he had to use them. Later experimenters found that double crosses fail ninety-nine times out of one hundred. Jones happened to have the one in a hundred that would work.

It remained for a politician who has been looked on largely as an idealist and a dreamer to make practical use—and a great deal of money—out of hybrid vigor. Henry Agard Wallace's grandfather, always called Uncle Henry, had been a Presbyterian minister who settled in Iowa after the Civil War and grew rich from intelligent farming and shrewd land buying. Eventually he became editor of *Wallace's Farmer* and preached, as his masthead proclaimed, "Good Farming, Clear Thinking, Right Living." In 1902 he met a man whose philosophy matched his own: Perry Greeley Holden, always known as P.G. There must have been some atavistic Indian reverence for corn in P.G. Better corn would not only make men better farmers, he believed; it would also make them better men. A student of Beal's, he had given up a professor's post to help develop and distribute improved strains of Reid's Yellow Dent. When he came through Iowa promoting his seed, Uncle Henry decided Iowa needed a man like him and, putting up part of the salary himself, he got the state college at Ames to take him on the faculty.

P.G. had a vision of an ideal corn: uniform ears, nine and one-half to ten and one-half inches long, with even rows and deep kernels shaped like a keystone. To help his evangelist, Uncle Henry coaxed the railroads to set up corn trains to carry P.G.'s corn and message to all farmers. Corn-growing competitions, called corn shows, became an annual event in the Midwest. Farmers would enter their best, most uniform ears. Judges, all trained to follow P.G.'s precepts, would lay them out, compare them, feel the kernels, run fingers over the ear, heft them. The best ear got ten points, the poorest only one. Winners gained cash prizes and great prestige. Getting ready for the contest, a farmer would pore over bushels of corn to match his best ears, carry them to the shows as if they were ingots of gold, and often when he got there, he would swap with other farmers to get more exactly matching ears. Sometimes he would paste kernels into the cob for evenness, soak an ear in water to make it fuller, or poke a metal rod into the cob to make it heavier.

All this made farmers more discriminating about the corn they grew. But one day in 1904, Uncle Henry's sixteen-year-old grandson, Henry Agard Wallace, heard P.G. hold forth on show corn. Young Henry knew a good deal about plants—George Washington Carver, the famous black scientist who went to college at Ames and was a family friend, used to take him on botanical field trips. Henry asked P.G.: Would a ten-point ear of corn produce more corn than any other? Of course, P.G. replied, though he had never really looked into yield. When the boy persisted, P.G. and Henry's father (later Warren Harding's Secretary of Agriculture) decided he should find out for himself. They collected twenty-five ears of the best show corn and twenty-five of the poorest. On a three-acre piece of land, Henry spent a diligent summer planting and tending his fifty specimens. The harvest justified his skepticism: the highest yield came from an ear no corn-show judge would look at twice. And as a whole, the highest-ranked show ears produced less than those that ranked lowest.

When he went on to agricultural school and began to write for *Wallace's Farmer*, Henry took out after corn shows. Men might appreciate a good-looking ear of corn, he said, but what are looks to a hog? Following the work done by Shull, East, and Jones, he began to work on double hybrids on his own farm. Those few adventurous farmers who bought the seed of one of his strains found it the most productive corn they ever grew, so in 1926 Wallace formed the Hi-bred Corn Company to produce and sell his hybrid seed. He ran the company until he became Secretary of Agriculture. All through his years as secretary and vice-president he would come back to see how things were going and, from the corners of his pockets, bring out seeds of odd strains he had picked in his travels.

It was not easy to sell the early hybrids, uneven and unattractive, to farmers accustomed to sleek show corn. In 1935 barely one per cent of the country's corn acreage was hybrid. In 1936 a dreadful heat wave —over one-hundred-degree days for two weeks—hung over the corn belt. An Illinois farmer named Walter Meers, dreaming of growing one hundred bushels per acre, had taken a chance on a field of hybrids. He watched in despair as all his corn wilted and dried in the heat. When rain came, it was too late to help his corn—except that field of hybrids which straightened up, greened out, and for all the traumatic heat, produced a miraculous one hundred and twenty bushels per acre.

Other farmers had similar experiences, and yield and stamina finally settled all doubts about hybrids. By 1940, as much as 40 percent of the country's corn was hybrid. Today it is 98 percent, the average yield is well past that dreamed-of goal of one hundred bushels per acre, and Wallace's company, now called Pioneer Hybrid International, is the largest corn-seed producer in the world.

Corn is easily America's most important crop. A fourth of the total farmland is planted to it, and it brings more dollars than all other grains put together. Iowa, Illinois, and Nebraska are the leading producers —Kansas, the cliché synonym for corn, goes in much more for winter wheat. In dollars, corn means more than maple syrup to Vermont and more than peaches to Georgia. About a fourth of the total crop is exported. Domestically, some 85 percent is used for animal feed, with hogs getting about half of that.

Most of the remainder goes to industry and is used largely for its starch. An improvement in its sweetening powers has made corn competitive with sugar, and the discovery that cornstarch could be made into a super slurper that soaks up a thousand times its weight in water has helped cornstarch sales and done wonders for the paper-diaper business. Only a minor percentage of the crop goes into bourbon, which must be 51 percent corn liquor to deserve the name, or into corn oil, or into popcorn, a special variety in which steam built up inside the heated kernel causes it to explode and turn inside out. Sweet corn, a minor crop, is sweet because it is less efficient than other kinds in turning its carbohydrates into starch. This inefficiency is known botanically as a "metabolic defect," certainly one of nature's happiest defects.

Corn breeders today are trying to meet special conditions. Short-summer strains now make it possible to grow corn two hundred miles farther north than the Indians ever could. New varieties have been made resistant to diseases, notably leaf blight, which in 1971 wiped out 800,000,000 bushels of Southern corn. There is intensive work going on to increase the protein content of corn. For all its great food value, corn is relatively low in protein, a serious lack in poorer countries where corn is the main item on the diet. It has been possible to increase protein, but in doing so the plant's vigor and yield has been diminished, so the research continues. All in all, the successes of modern corn scientists have been impressive. Of course they had all that good stock to start with, provided by the uncounted generations of Indians who had done a piece of creative work unmatched anywhere in agriculture. Even modern scientists haven't really matched it but, considering that they have had only a couple of centuries to work in while the Indians had several millennia, they have nothing of which to be ashamed.

Several months ago, the corn world was stirred by the discovery in Mexico of a hitherto-unknown perennial variety of corn's weedy kin, teosinte. It might someday, through interbreeding, contribute useful characteristics to corn. Meanwhile, it is giving new zest to the dispute over corn's lineage. Dr. Mangelsdorf, happily out of retirement, was back in the testing fields, hoping, by crossing the new plant with corn, to prove once and for all that teosinte is corn's progeny, not its progenitor. Dr. Beadle, back in the laboratory, was expecting to prove the opposite by tinkering with the teosinte's genes. Other corn men, who have long envied the fact that the ancestry of wheat, rye, oats, rice, and barley is established, wish them both well. If the new teosinte could lead them to some missing genetic link, whatever it might be, then corn would no longer be the only one of the world's great grains that does not have an ancestor to call its own.

—*August 1980*

HENRY FORD'S VILLAGE

By WALTER KARP

Toward the end of his career the Motor King set about re-creating, on a breathtaking scale, the old rural America his automobile had done away with forever

The whole curious enterprise puzzled Americans in the 1920s. Here was mighty Henry Ford, the man who said history was "more or less bunk," collecting on a titanic scale every jot and tittle of the American past that he and his emissaries could lay hands on—four-poster beds, banjo clocks, cigar-store Indians, old boots, gas lamps, rusty old threshers, and wooden flails. Here was the near legendary "Motor King," who once told the press that he wanted only to "live in the Now," conducting visitors to his family homestead in Dearborn and showing them, with a soft gleam in his eyes, how he had restored it to the way it had looked in 1876 when he was a thirteen-year-old schoolboy. Here was the "father of mass production" collecting old stagecoach stops, rude machine shops, antique bicycles, and Conestoga wagons. "It is," said *The New York Times*, "as if Stalin went in for collecting old ledgers and stock-tickers."

From his impregnable industrial fortress at Dearborn the Motor King, entranced by his mission, kept on collecting. A Ford engineer in England gathered up for his boss huge abandoned steam pumps dating back to the eighteenth century. A New England antiquary brought him old gristmills and broken-down lathes. Thirty-five thousand Ford dealers, under instructions from the "Dictator of Dearborn," scoured the countryside, unpaid, in search of Staffordshire china, antiquated stoves, and ante-bellum mousetraps. Old buildings, too, fell into the net and duly got shipped off to Dearborn: a Michigan log cabin, an 1850s firehouse, an old general store, an Illinois courthouse frequented by the young Lincoln.

The old tools and machinery became the core of a stupendous museum; the old buildings, reassembled, became a stunning 260-acre historic

American town—"Greenfield Village," Ford called it. On October 21, 1929, when the entire world celebrated the fiftieth anniversary of Edison's invention of the incandescent light, the eighty-two-year-old inventor sat down in his old Menlo Park laboratory and re-enacted the epoch-making moment when he had at long last tried the filament that worked. The Menlo Park laboratory, however, was no longer in Menlo Park, New Jersey. It was in Ford's brand-new old American village in Dearborn, looking exactly as it had looked, every last chemical jar in place, on October 21, 1879. The chair which the aged inventor had sat on during the ceremony Henry Ford ordered nailed to the floor; he considered the re-enactment a historic event in itself. It marked the opening of his combination village and museum, known collectively then and now as the Edison Institute.

"You know," the Motor King confided to an aide at the time, "it will take people fifty years to appreciate this place." The half-century mark has come and gone, but Ford's reconstruction of the American past in Dearborn is still more than a little puzzling. Irony and paradox are everywhere. In 1929 Ford had called his re-creation "The Early American Village," but it is surely like no American village that ever was or could have been. Turn down a muddy, unpaved street past the serene New England–style village green and the time-machine illusion is perfect. The past is present, captivating and ineffably moving, especially so on an icy winter morning when Greenfield Village is almost deserted and an old hay wagon drawn by a farm horse rattles by on some ghostly mission.

Turn down the main residential street, however, and what does one make of an early American village whose residents—judging by the houses they once lived in—include William McGuffey, Luther Burbank, Noah Webster, a Georgia slave driver named Mattox, and Henry Ford's favorite schoolteacher? This is a record of something, but it is hard to say of what—beyond the certain fact that it meant much to the Motor King.

In Greenfield Village the American past and Henry Ford seem to have gotten wonderfully intermixed. The old-time jewelry store, beautifully preserved and stocked, once employed young Ford to clean and repair its customers' clocks. The typical 1880s machine shop—every lathe driven by a single overhead shaft—supplied by a steam generator for Detroit's Edison Illuminating Company, Station "A," where Ford worked for years as chief engineer; a replica of the station stands proudly in the village. Ford is nearly everywhere. The prosperous white painted farmhouse is the Ford family farm. The rude back-yard shop nearby is the place where Ford in 1896 built his first horseless carriage, the "quadricycle." The late-nineteenth-century hamburger stand in the village had Ford as a customer when he worked late at the Detroit Edison plant. There are eerie moments walking through Greenfield Village (which is named after Mrs. Ford's hometown in Michigan) when the visitor feels he has strolled not into the American past but into an autobiography, and that the village itself is a vast, three-dimensional reconstruction of one man's mind. In the village Ford's own life even defines what constitutes the past. The oldest industrial building in Greenfield Village is a replica of the first factory of the Ford Motor Company, founded in 1903. So, for Henry Ford, that was the year which divided the American past from the American future, and of course, Ford was largely correct.

That is the ever-present paradox of Ford's historic village. It represents the American world which Ford's revolutionary achievements destroyed. Adjacent to the village the immense museum deepens the paradox still further. Inside a one-story building fourteen acres in extent—its façade features a replica of Independence Hall—stands one of the world's finest memorials to the Industrial Revolution. Here an astounding array of tools, engines, machines, and devices record the progressive mechanization of agriculture, the evolution of lighting, of communications, of transportation, and most important of all, the great record of modern man's efforts to harness mechanical and electrical power. Henry Ford's museum, in short, is a monument to all the great technical achievements that put finish to the life represented in Ford's re-created American village. There is no resolving that contradiction and no reason to try. It is nothing less than the grand contradiction of modern American life, the San Andreas Fault in the American soul—the schism between our faith in technological progress and our profoundly gnawing suspicion that the old rural republic was a finer, braver, and freer place than the industrial America that now sustains us. If that contradiction runs through Henry Ford's titanic reconstruction of the American past, it is because no American ever experienced the contradiction more intensely than Henry Ford himself.

Back in 1916 the great contradiction was not yet apparent to most Americans and least of all to Henry Ford. That was the year when Ford famously remarked to a Chicago *Tribune* reporter that the past, as such, meant nothing to him. "History is more or less bunk," he had said. "It's tradition. We don't want tradition. We want to live in the present and the only history that is worth a tinker's damn is the history we make today." Ford's view was eminently understandable and widely shared in America. To Ford in 1916 the great contributions of contemporary engineers and inventors were ushering in nothing less than a new industrial millennium. Ford claimed that his great friend and hero Thomas Edison "has done more toward abolishing poverty than have all the reformers and statesmen since the beginning of the world." He could have said as much for himself. His own assembly-line revolution had turned the automobile, play-thing of the rich and the sporting, into the great emancipator of the American farmer. It had so increased the productivity of his workers that on January 1, 1914, Ford had lifted the hearts of toiling humanity everywhere by announcing that henceforth the lowliest employee at the Ford Motor Company would receive a five dollars a day minimum wage, almost twice as much as ostensibly well-paid American factory hands were getting and beyond the dreams of workers elsewhere in the industrial world. Who cared about the dead hand of the past? Few Americans did in 1916. In those days even the most hostile foes of the *status quo* called themselves "progressives"—the term was an honorific —and looked to the glowing future untroubled by backward glances.

Nonetheless, on May 25 the Chicago *Tribune*, bitterly opposed to Ford's antiwar activities, duly published his remarks and added editorially that the man was an "ignorant idealist" and an "anarchist" to boot. Ford stuck to his opinions. "I don't know anything about history," he told another reporter, "and I wouldn't give a nickel for all the history in the world. . . . I don't want to live in the past. I want to live in the Now." He also brought a $1,000,000 libel suit against the *Tribune* and thereby, as the saying goes, hangs a tale.

Had the case come to trial in 1916 it is possible that Greenfield Village might never have seen the light of day. Truth being a defense against libel, the *Tribune*'s lawyers were prepared to prove that Ford in fact was an ignorant man in the common meaning of the term. Putting him on the witness stand they could show—and they did show—that the Motor King was so ignorant of American history that he could not even identify Benedict Arnold. Indeed he could not answer any number of absurdly simple history quiz questions. What of it? Ford was no shrinking violet; he loved the limelight, no ham actor loved it more. And he gloried in upsetting conventional opinion. All the *Tribune* lawyers could prove was that a man proudly ignorant of textbook history knew nothing of textbook history.

The trial, however, did not take place in 1916. It was held in July, 1919, at the end of a war which proved to be the most wrenching experience Americans had undergone since rebels had fired on Fort Sumter. Ford came away from the trial (after being awarded six cents in damages) rudely shaken and deeply humiliated. "The grilling," a Ford biographer noted, "had burned into his soul. . . ." It was not the exposure of his ignorance of books that had shamed the Motor King, a man supremely self-confident in every circumstance of his life. Quite simply he no longer despised the past, no longer thought it all worthless "tradition." There was a past that mattered, of this Ford was now sure, but he could not say what it was. Therein lay the humiliation.

The confident progressive of 1916 was not on the witness stand in 1919, and Ford was not alone in changing. The progressive America of the prewar years had changed as well. America had emerged from the war the richest and the most powerful country on earth. American mass production was now the envy and admiration of the world—"Fordismus" the Germans called it. Yet Americans were prepared to elevate to the Presidency an Ohio political hack largely because he promised to lead them "back to normalcy." In 1919 America was looking backward wistfully and so was Henry Ford.

Shortly after the trial an event almost comical in its aptness pushed Ford down his own private road "back to normalcy." Due to increasing auto traffic—half of it Model T Fords— the local authorities decided to widen a Dearborn road and demolish the old Ford family farm which stood alongside it. The Ford-created present—Fordismus—was threatening a piece of Ford's personal past. It was an irony he was to live with for the rest of his long life. To save the old farm, Ford had it moved two hundred feet to one side, but that was not all. With the history-is-bunk trial still on his mind, perhaps, Ford decided to restore the homestead. He wanted it to look exactly as it had when his mother died forty-three years before. At that very moment in a cork-lined room in Paris a sickly novelist was desperately striving with words to recapture "lost time." In Dearborn, Michigan, the owner of the greatest industrial empire the world had ever seen was determined in his own way to do exactly the same. Meticulous fidelity to the past, that was the key, both for Ford and for Proust.

There was a certain sleigh bell Ford's father had used. For months the Motor King went in search of one that reproduced exactly the sound he remembered from childhood. Like Proust's scent of madeleine, only that recollected ring could unlock sweet memories of bygone years. In the old homestead worn red carpet had covered the staircase. Ford ordered an aide to search every antique shop from Detroit to Cincinnati until he found precisely the same make of carpet worn to the same shade of drab red. A Starlight Stove Model 25 had once heated the front parlor. In search of a Starlight, Ford and his son Edsel drove around the countryside digging up abandoned stoves. To determine the exact pattern of the old vanished family china, Ford had his workers excavate the dooryard to a depth of six feet, as if the Ford homestead were an archaeological site. They recovered, as Ford expected, broken shards of the old china and with them the forgotten pattern, which Ford promptly had reproduced.

The workers also recovered an old pair of skates. "I remember his great delight," an aide recalled. "I don't think he could have been given anything in the world that would have pleased him quite as much as those old, rusty skates."

There is no doubt what passion was gripping the Motor King. He wanted not only to preserve a memento of his past; he wanted to make that past so palpably real that he could enter it at will. The illusion was sweet. The restored homestead, its beds freshly made each morning, drew Ford like a magnet. In his re-created boyhood bedroom he would repair watches as he used to as a machine-addled boy whom neighbors described as having "wheels in his head." He would take out the old threshing machine and set it to work. He could cook meals on his mother's capacious old stove, Farmer's Friend No. 9. In the family barn he and his cronies did the old dances. "They'd have parties over there," an aide recalled, "and they'd get all dressed up. The men and women were in the old costumes, and they'd dance"—the reel, the gavotte, the quadrille —dances Ford had loved as a youth and now had come to love again.

Ford, needless to say, was not the first middle-aged man to be captivated by the "magic of his youth," but Ford just happened to be the richest man in the world—the world's first billionaire, the press reported. A mile and a half from the old homestead stood a one-room red-brick schoolhouse, which Ford had attended as a child. He bought the place, restored it, and turned it into an experimental school. To see modern children studying in the very room where he himself had puzzled over his McGuffey readers brought profound delight to Ford. Sixteen miles from Detroit stood a moldering old stagecoach stopover known as the Botsford Inn. As a young man Ford had gone there to attend the dances. He bought it for $100,000 and spent $336,000 more to restore it.

What on earth was the Motor King up to? "I'm trying in a small way," Ford explained to a *New York Times* reporter, "to help America take a step, even if it is a little one, toward the saner and sweeter idea of life that prevailed in prewar days." He might just as well have said pre-Ford days, for the stagecoach stopover and the automobile were inherently at odds.

If all this seemed wildly contradictory, Ford himself was a jumble of contradictions. In 1921, the very year he was tenderly restoring the family farm, there issued from Dearborn one of his typically cranky pronouncements: "The Cow Must Go!" The world, explained the Motor King to his countrymen, would do well to get rid of the filthy beast and learn to drink synthetic, sanitary, factory-made milk. In 1924, the year he restored a country inn at the cost of more than half a million dollars, Ford also built the first all-metal trimotored airplane and plunged for a time into the new world of commercial aviation. That was the year, too, when

Ford, wildly oscillating between the past and the future, launched his personal crusade to persuade Americans to take up the reel and the quadrille, Ford's personal rejoinder to the jazz age in general and the black bottom and Charleston in particular.

"If only Mr. Ford was properly assembled," lamented Dean Samuel Marquis, an Episcopal divine who knew the Motor King well. "There rages in him an endless conflict between ideals, emotions and impulses as unlike as day and night—a conflict that makes one feel that two personalities are striving within him for mastery." The Edison Institute would be proof of that.

In the meantime Ford had become a collector of Americana. While restoring the homestead he had acquired a modest surplus of relics that did not fit the farm. Nevertheless they were old and familiar, and Ford could not bear to part with them. He piled them up in a corner of his office. So matters stood until 1922 when a Ford Motor Company tractor operation was moved to a new location, leaving vacant a three-acre building. The space seems to have inspired in Ford an intense determination to fill it. The result, quickly apparent, was the most rapid, the most all-embracing, the most original feat of collecting the world has ever seen. Ford's resources as a collector were obviously extraordinary. His unparalleled wealth was accountable to no one. He owned the Ford Motor Company lock, stock, and barrel. His manpower resources were even more extraordinary. Every Ford employee was his to command; thousands of grateful Ford dealers could be treated as mere errand boys. Moreover, he had millions of admiring fans in the country—the "Ford Craze" the press called it in 1923—who looked on the Motor King as a benefactor. They too were ready to pitch in.

Even that was not all. In 1922 Ford had the field to himself, and the field, as defined by Ford, was so immense and so unorthodox that some people thought the Motor King had taken leave of his senses. What he wanted to collect was everything. His instructions to his collecting army were simple, clear, and comprehensive. "Get everything you can find!" He wanted, as he later put it, "a complete series of every article ever used or made in America from the days of the first settlers down to the present time."

Price was no object. Ford refused to haggle. Whatever anyone asked, he paid, since, in truth, he valued the humble relics of the American past far higher than anyone else did at the time. Once one of his aides approached a collector of old carriages with an offer to buy. The man dropped dead on the spot. When an assistant told him he was overpaying for something, Ford snapped back: "What difference does it make what it costs if it is what we want."

Backed by Ford's wealth, his zest, and his driving will, the Ford army marched and countermarched across the American landscape. The mighty net they threw over the country had a mesh of extraordinary fineness. Today visitors to the awesome museum can see—if they look sharply—poignant proof of that in its single smallest exhibit. It is a little collection showing the evolution of the clothespin, the oldest so big it suggests that American wives once hung out wet clothing with the wearers inside. With astounding swiftness, the army collected enough artifacts to outfit an old-time toy store, drugstore, barbershop, baker's, milliner's, cooper's, pewterer's, locksmith's, and a dozen more, not to mention the complete period furnishings of the 107 buildings, spanning three hundred years, which now compose Greenfield Village.

When news got out that the Motor King was buying up priceless heirlooms, meaning things nobody had ever seen fit to put a price to, letters began pouring into Dearborn with offers to sell the old family spinning wheel, a Navaho rug, a quilt, a McCormack-Deering binder rusting in the yard. By and large Ford bought what was offered. As a result the man who wanted one of everything wound up with some five hundred spinning wheels. What the Ford army missed the man himself acquired from dealers. For 1922 the Ford Archives—an important part of the Edison Institute—shows requests for such items as "old Shaker bonnets," "old nut pickers," and "Scotch rolling pins for the making of scones."

To keep a bridle on his growing passion for the past, Ford reserved one day a week for his personal collecting. Often he would motor around rural Michigan, eyes peeled for rusting farm machines. Spying one, an aide recalled, "he'd be out of the car and up to the farm door to dicker for that damned scrap." Getting word that some household had something worth having, Ford would knock on the door, introduce himself as "Mr. Robinson," and politely inform some flabbergasted housewife that he wanted to buy, say, her family china. With an aide at his side he would visit curio shops, spot an item he liked, whisper a few words to his companion, and quietly leave the premises. Then the aide would ask the storekeeper as casually as possible how much he wanted for the entire store. "It was quite amusing sometimes," a Ford lieutenant recalled, "to see their consternation and regret when they found out who bought the goods." Told to pack up their entire stock and ship it to Dearborn, they knew at once that the world's richest man had passed through their lives, just once and no more.

By 1925, when the novelist Hamlin Garland paid it a visit, the sometime tractor plant was already bulging. To Garland it seemed at first "only an immense warehouse of discarded machinery and old furniture . . . the storehouse of the outworn." Picking his way through the jumble, however, he found himself moved, as Ford himself was moved, by "the homely character of the objects. . . . Here was the long-legged stove under which, as a boy of five, I had lain to learn my letters. . . . I took into my hand the tin lantern which I had so often held while my father milked the cows." Here, adjacent to the future-minded Ford Experimental Laboratory, lay "all the time-worn, work-worn humble tools and furnishings of the average American home" of rural days now passing.

At the onset homely and domestic artifacts were Ford's chief preoccupation, the evidence, as he himself put it, of "American life as lived." Gradually, however, another and quite different objective began taking shape alongside the first. Ford began systematically collecting at great cost an enormous array of machinery designed to exhibit the progressive mechanization of the human economy from its steam-power beginnings in the eighteenth-century England of Newcomen and Watts—that mighty Industrial Revolution which, of course, had turned Ford's "saner and sweeter" life into a spiritual relic. If two Ford personalities were "striving for mastery," neither would ever achieve it. As much as Ford loved the "magic of his youth" he continued to love with equal fervor the inexorable march of mechanical progress. However, Ford would view the contradiction from a vantage point foreclosed to the rest of us. In a sense the entire Industrial Revolution of the eighteenth and nineteenth centuries was part of Ford's personal past and possessed in its own way the magic of his youth. If that magic adhered to "time-worn, work-worn, humble" things, it adhered equally to the thousand and one inventions and improvements—some famed, most unsung—which had contributed like so many tributary streams to the mighty river of assembly-line mass production, what historians now call the "Second Industrial Revolution." In a word, to Fordismus.

By 1926, moreover, even the Industrial Revolution—the first one, that is—was taking on the sweetness of days gone by. That year a shocking turn of events was threatening to shatter Ford's harmonious industrial empire: the beloved Model T, essentially unchanged since 1908, had begun to lose its popular appeal. The news stunned Dearborn. That such a thing could *never* happen had been the premise of Ford's great achievement. It was because he—and he alone—had decided to design the perfect, pared-down cheap automobile and keep on producing it forever that he had been able to introduce the assembly line. That premise itself depended on a still larger assumption: that Americans would want a Model T forever. Ford could see no reason why they would not. The Model T embodied all the virtues Americans had so long admired. It was tough, durable, dependable, and simple—republican simplicity embodied in a vehicle. It was so down-to-earth, so stubbornly utilitarian that its very ugliness seemed a mark of its puritan mettle. Now a pretty little upstart called the Chevrolet was drawing Ford's customers away in droves. Model T jokes were no longer affectionate: "Why is the Model T like a bathtub? Because nobody wants to be seen in one." Urbanity, modishness, and jazz-age sophistication, all of which Ford profoundly loathed, were corrupting republican simplicity, and the corruption was now showing in the sales charts. Sometime in 1926 the Motor King was forced to make one of the most painful decisions of his career. As of May, 1927, the Model T would go out of production. The pride of Ford's life was going away and with it his strongest link to an increasingly distasteful "Now."

It is no accident, surely, that the Model T's imminent doom coincided with the birth of the idea of Greenfield Village. That he eventually would build a museum for his enormous collection was an idea Ford had had in mind for some time. He even had toyed with the idea for re-creating some sort of old New England village on history-rich property he owned in Sudbury, Massachusetts. In 1926, however, he decided otherwise. Sudbury was too far away for what the Motor King now needed. The "saner and sweeter" life it was supposed to re-create he now wanted close by. A large vacant field lay adjacent to the experimental laboratory, not far from the new Ford Airport. No history attached to the place whatever. There, nonetheless, Ford decided to erect a completely imaginary, Ford-crafted American village. By early 1927, Edward Cutler, a company draftsman—Ford avoided experts like the plague—was laying out the ground plan using the colonial New England village as the prototype.

Now Ford's army found itself with a new collecting assignment. This one, however, was subtle and exacting. Ford agents were to keep an eye out for old buildings—homes, mills, shops, depots—which, when suitably deployed on Ford's property, would show not only, in Ford's words, "how our forefathers lived" but also "the force and courage they had." There were obvious Ford prohibitions to observe. There was to be no bank, no lawyer's office, no rich man's palace. It was not they who had made America great; Ford was strongly inclined to think they had been working in the opposite direction. There were personal predilections to heed. Despite Ford's philistine pose in public, he had a keen eye for Greek-revival architecture; its clean, white classical lines, he believed, best expressed the republican spirit of America. The style would abound in the village. Knowing Mr. Ford's biography would help considerably too. His engineering career had begun with a boyhood passion for clocks and watches. Three jewelry stores eventually would wind up in the village. In Ford's early manhood when he was trying to avoid farming—an occupation he detested—he had eked out a rural living sawing his trees into lumber. Two old-time "up-and-down" sawmills would also find their way to Dearborn.

Around the time the last Model T rolled off the great assembly line, Ford brought his first building to the village—a seventy-five-year-old general store, the true social center of every old American hamlet. The owner was happy to exchange it for the spanking new brick emporium which Ford agreed to erect in its place. A later acquisition was a mournfully decrepit stagecoach inn—the Motor King was particularly partial to horse-and-buggy relics—which had been standing in Clinton, Michigan, since 1831, the first stop on the rough frontier road from Detroit to Chicago. After gently displacing the dotty old lady who lived in one room of the inn, Ford's crew dismantled the sagging ruin, shipped it to Dearborn, and restored it to its original, sparkling white, neoclassical self. Outfitting the taproom, parlor, kitchen, and bedrooms with appropriate period furnishings was, of course, no trouble whatever to the man who collected everything. It stood next to the store on the embryonic village green.

The Motor King intended his museum *cum* village to be a mighty memorial to Thomas Edison, the only man living whom Ford himself held in awe. Within the greater memorial Ford decided in March, 1928, to erect a more specific one to the Wizard of Menlo Park, a place Edison had abandoned back in 1887. At immense cost in time, labor, money, and meticulous research, Ford restored from bare, pillaged ruins in New Jersey the entire Menlo Park compound, including the laboratory, the glass house, the machine shop, the white picket fence, and even the boardinghouse just across the street where Edison's hard-driven aides took time out to sleep. When Ford proudly showed Edison his handiwork—a masterpiece of restoration—the octogenarian inventor remarked: "Why Henry's even got the damn New Jersey clay here." He had, too—carloads of the red stuff, along with the stump of an old hickory tree that had once grown near the laboratory. In 1929 Ford also acquired for his nascent village the Smiths Creek Depot of the Grand Trunk railway because young Edison had worked in it as a telegrapher after being tossed out there by a railway conductor for starting a fire in the baggage car. Even the official dedication of the Edison Institute was timed as a tribute to Edison. The institute's first public act was to host the nationally broadcast celebration of the electric light's fiftieth birthday. At the glittering banquet in Ford's half-built museum the grand old man broke down and cried.

Ford's collection grew with astonishing speed, but the village was destined to grow slowly. Each year the Motor King would add two or three buildings, rarely more. With tender affection he gathered up shops and homes that paid homage to the men he admired—to unsung blacksmiths, machinists, and frontier farmers; to Luther Burbank and Charles Steinmetz, to McGuffey and the Wright brothers, and also to George Matthew Adams, Ford's favorite newspaper columnist. Ford was never quite willing to separate his own past and America's past, although he kept his own family homestead apart from the village almost until his death. Whatever Greenfield Village would mean to his countrymen, for Ford himself it was his own vanished youth restored, his own private time machine.

As the years sped by, the Motor King spent less and less time at his factory and more and more time in his village. He stocked its one-room schoolhouses with children and visited them each morning to hear them recite from their McGuffey readers. At the Clinton Inn he ate the meals prepared by the girls in their cooking classes. At Magill's jewelry store he could be found at a workbench repairing watches just as he had done as an ill-paid apprentice who had to work nights at Magill's to eke out a living. At what he took to be Stephen Foster's birthplace—it wasn't—Ford often spent his evenings picking out beloved Foster tunes on the organ or tinkering with the Swiss music box that played "Swanee." On Sundays he and his wife Clara would often attend the little chapel that stands at one end of the Greenfield Village common. At dusk, when the visitors had left and the illusion of the past was at its strongest, he and Clara would amble together down the silent, unpaved streets of the sweetly re-created world where motor cars and mass production were kept safely at bay.

Late in his life a housemaid overheard Henry Ford ask a minister: "Do you think God wanted me to make cars?" The maid never heard the clergyman's reply, but there is little doubt what answer would have pleased the Motor King by then. The answer, of course, is yes and no.

—*December 1980*

WHY THE MONEY STOPPED

By JOHN KENNETH GALBRAITH

An economist's reconstruction of the greatest financial catastrophe in our history

The decade of the twenties, or more precisely the eight years between the postwar depression of 1920–21 and the stock market crash in October of 1929, were prosperous ones in the United States. The total output of the economy increased by more than 50 percent. The preceding decades had brought the automobile; now came many more and also roads on which they could be driven with reasonable reliability and comfort. There was much building. The downtown section of the mid-continent city—Des Moines, Omaha, Minneapolis—dates from these years. It was then, more likely than not, that what is still the leading hotel, the tallest office building, and the biggest department store went up. Radio arrived, as of course did gin and jazz.

These years were also remarkable in another respect, for as time passed it became increasingly evident that the prosperity could not last. Contained within it were the seeds of its own destruction. The country was heading into the gravest kind of trouble. Herein lies the peculiar fascination of the period for a study in the problem of leadership. For almost no steps were taken during these years to arrest the tendencies which were obviously leading, and did lead, to disaster.

At least four things were seriously wrong, and they worsened as the decade passed. And knowledge of them does not depend on the always brilliant assistance of hindsight. At least three of these flaws were highly visible and widely discussed. In ascending order, not of importance but of visibility, they were as follows:

First, income in these prosperous years was being distributed with marked inequality. Although output per worker rose steadily during the

670

period, wages were fairly stable, as also were prices. As a result, business profits increased rapidly and so did incomes of the wealthy and the well-to-do. This tendency was nurtured by assiduous and successful efforts of Secretary of the Treasury Andrew W. Mellon to reduce income taxes with special attention to the higher brackets. In 1929 the 5 percent of the people with the highest incomes received perhaps a quarter of all personal income. Between 1919 and 1929 the share of the one percent who received the highest incomes increased by approximately one-seventh. This meant that the economy was heavily and increasingly dependent on the luxury consumption of the well-to-do and on their willingness to reinvest what they did not or could not spend on themselves. Anything that shocked the confidence of the rich either in their personal or in their business future would have a bad effect on total spending and hence on the behavior of the economy.

This was the least visible flaw. To be sure, farmers, who were not participating in the general advance, were making themselves heard; and twice during the period the Congress passed far-reaching relief legislation which was vetoed by Coolidge. But other groups were much less vocal. Income distribution in the United States had long been unequal. The inequality of these years did not seem exceptional. The trade-union movement was also far from strong. In the early twenties the steel industry was still working a twelve-hour day and, in some jobs, a seven-day week. (Every two weeks when the shift changed, a man worked twice around the clock.) Workers lacked the organization or the power to deal with conditions like this; the twelve-hour day was, in fact, ended as the result of personal pressure by President Harding on the steel companies, particularly on Judge Elbert H. Gary, head of the United States Steel Corporation. Judge Gary's personal acquaintance with these working conditions was thought to be slight, and this gave rise to Benjamin Stolberg's now classic observation that the Judge "never saw a blast furnace until his death." In all these circumstances the increasingly lopsided income distribution did not excite much comment or alarm. Perhaps it would have been surprising if it had.

But the other three flaws in the economy were far less subtle. During World War I the United States ceased to be the world's greatest debtor country and became its greatest creditor. The consequences of this change have so often been described that they have the standing of a cliché. A debtor country could export a greater value of goods than it imported and use the difference for interest and debt repayment. This was what we did before the war. But a creditor must import a greater value than it exports if those who owe it money are to have the wherewithal to pay interest and principal. Otherwise the creditor must either forgive the debts or make new loans to pay off the old.

During the twenties the balance was maintained by making new foreign loans. Their promotion was profitable to domestic investment houses. And when the supply of honest and competent foreign borrowers ran out, dishonest, incompetent, or fanciful borrowers were invited to borrow and, on occasion, bribed to do so. In 1927 Juan Leguia, the son of the then dictator of Peru, was paid $450,000 by the National City Company and J. & W. Seligman for his services in promoting a $50,000,000 loan to Peru which these houses marketed. Americans lost and the Peruvians didn't gain appreciably. Other Latin American republics got equally dubious loans by equally dubious devices. And, for reasons that now tax the imagination, so did a large number of German cities and municipalities. Obviously, once investors awoke to the character of these loans or there was any other shock to confidence, they would no longer be made. There would be nothing with which to pay the old loans. Given this arithmetic, there would be either a sharp reduction in exports or a wholesale default on the outstanding loans, or more likely both. Wheat and cotton farmers and others who depended on exports would suffer. So would those who owned the bonds. The buying power of both would be reduced. These consequences were freely predicted at the time.

The second weakness of the economy was the large-scale corporate thimblerigging that was going on. This took a variety of forms, of which by far the most common was the organization of corporations to hold stock in yet other corporations, which in turn held stock in yet other corporations. In the case of the railroads and the utilities, the purpose of this pyramid of holding companies was to obtain control of a very large number of operating companies with a very small investment in the ultimate holding company. A $100,000,000 electric utility, of which the capitalization was represented half by bonds and half by common stock, could be controlled with an investment of a little over $25,000,000—the value of just over half the common stock. Were a company then formed with the same capital structure to hold *this* $25,000,000 worth of common stock, it could be controlled with an investment of $6,250,000. On the next round the amount required would be less than $2,000,000. That $2,000,000 would still control the entire $100,000,000 edifice. By the end of the twenties, holding-company structures six or eight tiers high were a commonplace. Some of them—the utility pyramids of Insull and Associated Gas & Electric, and the railroad pyramid of the Van Sweringens—were marvelously complex. It is unlikely that anyone fully understood them or could.

In other cases companies were organized to hold securities in other companies in order to manufacture more securities to sell to the public. This was true of the great investment trusts. During 1929 one investment house, Goldman, Sachs & Company, organized and sold nearly a billion dollars' worth of securities in three interconnected investment trusts —Goldman Sachs Trading Corporation; Shenandoah Corporation; and Blue Ridge Corporation. All eventually depreciated virtually to nothing.

This corporate insanity was also highly visible. So was the damage. The pyramids would last only so long as earnings of the company at the bottom were secure. If anything happened to the dividends of the underlying company, there would be trouble, for upstream companies had issued bonds (or in practice sometimes preferred stock) against the dividends on the stock of the downstream companies. Once the earnings stopped, the bonds would go into default or the preferred stock would take over and the pyramid would collapse. Such a collapse would have a bad effect not only on the orderly prosecution of business and investment by the operating companies but also on confidence, investment, and spending by the community at large. The likelihood was increased because in any number of cities—Cleveland, Detroit, and Chicago were notable examples—the banks were deeply committed to these pyramids or had fallen under the control of the pyramiders.

Finally, and most evident of all, there was the stock market boom. Month after month and year after year the great bull market of the twenties roared on. Sometimes there were setbacks, but more often there were fantastic forward surges. In May of 1924 the *New York Times* industrials stood at 106; by end of the year they were 134; by the end of 1925 they were up to 181. In 1927 the advance began in earnest—to 245 by the end of that year and on to 331 by the end of 1928. There were some setbacks in early 1929, but then came the fantastic summer explosion when in a matter of three months the averages went up another 110 points. This was the most frantic summer in our financial history. By its end, stock prices had nearly quadrupled as compared with four years earlier. Transactions on the New York Stock Exchange regularly ran to 5,000,000 or more shares a day. Radio Corporation of America went to 573¾ (adjusted) without ever having paid a dividend. Only the hopelessly eccentric, so it seemed, held securities for their income. What counted was the increase in capital values.

And since capital gains were what counted, one could vastly increase his opportunities by extending his holdings with borrowed funds—by buying on margin. Margin accounts expanded enormously, and from all over the country—indeed from all over the world—money poured into New York to finance these transactions. During the summer, brokers' loans increased at the rate of $400,000,000 a month. By September they totaled more than $7,000,000,000. The rate of interest on these loans varied from 7 to 12 percent and went as high as 15.

This boom was also inherently self-liquidating. It could last only so long as new people, or at least new money, were swarming into the market in pursuit of the capital gains. This new demand bid up the stocks and made the capital gains. Once the supply of new customers began to falter, the market would cease to rise. Once the market stopped rising, some, and perhaps a good many, would start to cash in. If you are concerned with capital gains, you must get them while the getting is good. But the getting may start the market down, and this will one day be the signal for much more selling—both by those who are trying to get out and those who are being forced to sell securities that are no longer safely margined. Thus it was certain that the market would one day go down, and far more rapidly than it went up. Down it went with a thunderous crash in October of 1929. In a series of terrible days, of which Thursday, October 24, and Tuesday, October 29, were the most terrifying, billions in values were lost, and thousands of speculators—they had been called investors—were utterly and totally ruined.

This too had far-reaching effects. Economists have always deprecated the tendency to attribute too much to the great stock market collapse of 1929: this was the drama; the causes of the subsequent depression really lay deeper. In fact, the stock market crash was very important. It exposed the other weakness of the economy. The overseas loans on which the payments balance depended came to an end. The jerry-built holding-company structures came tumbling down. The investment-trust stocks collapsed. The crash put a marked crimp on borrowing for investment and therewith on business spending. It also removed from the economy some billions of consumer spending that was either based on, sanctioned by, or encouraged by the fact that the spenders had stock market gains. The crash was an intensely damaging thing.

And this damage, too, was not only foreseeable but foreseen. For months the speculative frenzy had all but dominated American life. Many times before in history—the South Sea Bubble, John Law's speculations, the recurrent real-estate booms of the last century, the great Florida land boom earlier in the same decade—there had been similar frenzy. And the end had always come, not with a whimper but a bang. Many men, including in 1929 the President of the United States, knew it would again be so.

The increasingly perilous trade balance, the corporate buccaneering, and the Wall Street boom—along with the less visible tendencies in income distribution—were all allowed to proceed to the ultimate disaster without effective hindrance. How much blame attaches to the men who occupied the presidency?

Warren G. Harding died on August 2, 1923. This, as only death can do, exonerates him. The disorders that led eventually to such trouble had only started when the fatal blood clot destroyed this now sad and deeply disillusioned man. Some would argue that his legacy was bad. Harding had but a vague perception of the economic processes over which he presided. He died owing his broker $180,000 in a blind account—he had been speculating disastrously while he was President, and no one so inclined would have been a good bet to curb the coming boom. Two of Harding's Cabinet officers, his secretary of the interior and his attorney general, were to plead the Fifth Amendment when faced with questions concerning their official acts, and the first of these went to jail. Harding brought his fellow townsman Daniel R. Crissinger to be his comptroller of the currency, although he was qualified for this task, as Samuel Hopkins Adams has suggested, only by the fact that he and the young Harding had stolen watermelons together. When Crissinger had had an ample opportunity to demonstrate his incompetence in his first post, he was made head of the Federal Reserve System. Here he had the central responsibility for action on the ensuing boom. Jack Dempsey, Paul Whiteman or F. Scott Fitzgerald would have been at least equally qualified.

Yet it remains that Harding was dead before the real trouble started. And while he left in office some very poor men, he also left some very competent ones. Charles Evans Hughes, his secretary of state; Herbert Hoover, his secretary of commerce; and Henry C. Wallace, his secretary of agriculture, were public servants of vigor and judgment.

The problem of Herbert Hoover's responsibility is more complicated. He became President on March 4, 1929. At first glance this seems far too late for effective action. By then the damage had been done, and while the crash might come a little sooner or a little later, it was now inevitable. Yet Hoover's involvement was deeper than this—and certainly much deeper than Harding's. This he tacitly concedes in his memoirs, for he is at great pains to explain and, in some degree, to excuse himself.

For one thing, Hoover was no newcomer to Washington. He had been secretary of commerce under Harding and Coolidge. He had also been the strongest figure (not entirely excluding the President) in both Administration and party for almost eight years. He had a clear view of what was going on. As early as 1922, in a letter to Hughes, he expressed grave concern over the quality of the foreign loans that were being floated in New York. He returned several times to the subject. He knew about the corporate excesses. In the latter twenties he wrote to his colleagues and fellow officials (including Crissinger) expressing his grave concern over the Wall Street orgy. Yet he was content to express himself—to write letters and memoranda, or at most, as in the case of the foreign loans, to make an occasional speech. He could with propriety have presented his views of the stock market more strongly to the Congress and the public. He could also have maintained a more vigorous and persistent agitation within the Administration. He did neither. His views of the market were so little known that it celebrated his election and inauguration with a great upsurge. Hoover was in the boat and, as he himself tells, he knew where it was·headed. But, having warned the man at the tiller, he rode along into the reef.

And even though trouble was inevitable, by March, 1929, a truly committed leader would still have wanted to do something. Nothing else was so important. The resources of the Executive, one might expect, would have been mobilized in a search for some formula to mitigate the current frenzy and to temper the coming crash. The assistance of the bankers, congressional leaders, and the Exchange authorities would have been sought. Nothing of the sort was done. As secretary of commerce, as he subsequently explained, he had thought himself frustrated by Mellon. But he continued Mellon in office. Henry M. Robinson, a sympathetic Los Angeles banker, was commissioned to go to New York to see his colleagues there and report. He returned to say that the New York bankers regarded things as sound. Richard Whitney, the vice-president of the Stock Exchange, was summoned to the White House for a conference on how to curb speculation. Nothing came of this either. Whitney also thought things were sound.

Both Mr. Hoover and his official biographers carefully explained that the primary responsibility for the goings on in New York City rested not with Washington but with the governor of New York State. That was Franklin D. Roosevelt. It was he who failed to rise to his responsibilities. The explanation is far too formal. The future of the whole country was involved. Mr. Hoover was the President of the whole country. If he lacked authority commensurate with this responsibility, he could have requested it. This, at a later date, President Roosevelt did not hesitate to do.

Finally, while by March of 1929 the stock market collapse was inevitable, something could still be done about the other accumulating disorders. The balance of payments is an obvious case. In 1931 Mr. Hoover did request a one-year moratorium on the inter-Allied (war) debts. This was a courageous and constructive step which came directly to grips with the problem. But the year before, Mr. Hoover, though not without reluctance, had signed the Hawley-Smoot tariff. "I shall approve the Tariff Bill. . . . It was undertaken as the result of pledges given by the Republican Party at Kansas City. . . . Platform promises must not be empty gestures." Hundreds of people—from Albert H. Wiggin, the head of the Chase National Bank, to Oswald Garrison Villard, the editor of the *Nation*—felt that no step could have been more directly designed to make things worse.

Countries would have even more trouble earning the dollars of which they were so desperately short. But Mr. Hoover signed the bill.

Anyone familiar with this particular race of men knows that a dour, flinty, inscrutable visage such as that of Calvin Coolidge can be the mask for a calm and acutely perceptive intellect. And he knows equally that it can conceal a mind of singular aridity. The difficulty, given the inscrutability, is in knowing which. However, in the case of Coolidge the evidence is in favor of the second. In some sense, he certainly knew what was going on. He would not have been unaware of what was called the Coolidge market. But he connected developments neither with the well-being of the country nor with his own responsibilities. In his memoirs Hoover goes to great lengths to show how closely he was in touch with events and how clearly he foresaw their consequences. In his *Autobiography*, a notably barren document, Coolidge did not refer to the accumulating troubles. He confines himself to such unequivocal truths as "Every day of Presidential life is crowded with activities" (which in his case, indeed, was not true); and "The Congress makes the laws, but it is the President who causes them to be executed."

At various times during his years in office, men called on Coolidge to warn him of the impending trouble. And in 1927, at the instigation of a former White House aide, he sent for William Z. Ripley of Harvard, the most articulate critic of the corporate machinations of the period. The President became so interested that he invited him to stay for lunch, and listened carefully while his guest outlined (as Ripley later related) the "prestidigitation, double-shuffling, honey-fugling, hornswoggling, and skulduggery" that characterized the current Wall Street scene. But Ripley made the mistake of telling Coolidge that regulation was the responsibility of the states (as was then the case). At this intelligence Coolidge's face lit up and he dismissed the entire matter from his mind. Others who warned of the impending disaster got even less far.

And on some occasions Coolidge added fuel to the fire. If the market seemed to be faltering, a timely statement from the White House—or possibly from Secretary Mellon—would often brace it up. William Allen White, by no means an unfriendly observer, noted that after one such comment the market staged a 26-point rise. He went on to say that a careful search "during these halcyon years . . . discloses this fact: Whenever the stock market showed signs of weakness, the President or the Secretary of the Treasury or some important dignitary of the administration . . . issued a statement. The statement invariably declared that business was 'fundamentally sound,' that continued prosperity had arrived, and that the slump of the moment was 'seasonal.' "

Such was the Coolidge role. Coolidge was fond of observing that "if you see ten troubles coming down the road, you can be sure that nine will run into the ditch before they reach you and you have to battle with only one of them." A critic noted that "the trouble with this philosophy was that when the tenth trouble reached him he was wholly unprepared. . . . The outstanding instance was the rising boom and orgy of mad speculation which began in 1927." The critic was Herbert Hoover.

Plainly, in these years, leadership failed. Events whose tragic culmination could be foreseen—and was foreseen—were allowed to work themselves out to the final disaster. The country and the world paid. For a time, indeed, the very reputation of capitalism itself was in the balance. It survived in the years following perhaps less because of its own power or the esteem in which it was held, than because of the absence of an organized and plausible alternative. Yet one important question remains. Would it have been possible even for a strong President to arrest the plunge? Were not the opposing forces too strong? Isn't one asking the impossible?

No one can say for sure. But the answer depends at least partly on the political context in which the Presidency was cast. That of Coolidge and Hoover may well have made decisive leadership impossible. These were conservative Administrations in which, in addition, the influence of the businessman was strong. At the core of the business faith was an intuitive belief in *laissez faire*—the benign tendency of things that are left alone. The man who wanted to intervene was a meddler. Perhaps, indeed, he was a planner. In any case, he was to be regarded with mistrust. And, on the businessman's side, it must be borne in mind that high government office often nurtures a spurious sense of urgency. There is no more important public function than the suppression of proposals for unneeded action. But these should have been distinguished from action necessary to economic survival.

A bitterly criticized figure of the Harding-Coolidge-Hoover era was Secretary of the Treasury Andrew W. Mellon. He opposed all action to curb the boom, although once in 1929 he was persuaded to say that bonds (as distinct from stocks) were a good buy. And when the depression came, he was against doing anything about that. Even Mr. Hoover was shocked by his insistence that the only remedy was (as Mr. Hoover characterized it) to "liquidate labor, liquidate stocks, liquidate the farmers, liquidate real estate." Yet Mellon reflected only in extreme form the conviction that things would work out, that the real enemies were those who interfered.

Outside of Washington in the twenties, the business and banking community, or at least the articulate part of it, was overwhelmingly opposed to any public intervention. The tentative and ineffective steps which the Federal Reserve did take were strongly criticized. In the spring of

1929 when the Reserve system seemed to be on the verge of taking more decisive action, there was an anticipatory tightening of money rates and a sharp drop in the market. On his own initiative Charles E. Mitchell, the head of the National City Bank, poured in new funds. He had an obligation, he said, that was "paramount to any Federal Reserve warning, or anything else" to avert a crisis in the money market. In brief, he was determined, whatever the government thought, to keep the boom going. In that same spring Paul M. Warburg, a distinguished and respected Wall Street leader, warned of the dangers of the boom and called for action to restrain it. He was deluged with criticism and even abuse and later said that the subsequent days were the most difficult of his life. There were some businessmen and bankers—like Mitchell and Albert Wiggin of the Chase National Bank—who may have vaguely sensed that the end of the boom would mean their own business demise. Many more had persuaded themselves that the dream would last. But we should not complicate things. Many others were making money and took a short-run view—or no view —either of their own survival or of the system of which they were a part. They merely wanted to be left alone to get a few more dollars.

And the opposition to government intervention would have been nonpartisan. In 1929 one of the very largest of the Wall Street operators was John J. Raskob. Raskob was also chairman of the Democratic National Committee. So far from calling for preventive measures, Raskob in 1929 was explaining how, through stock market speculation, literally anyone could be a millionaire. Nor would the press have been enthusiastic about, say, legislation to control holding companies and investment trusts or to give authority to regulate margin trading. The financial pages of many of the papers were riding the boom. And even from the speculating public, which was dreaming dreams of riches and had yet to learn that it had been fleeced, there would have been no thanks. Perhaps a President of phenomenal power and determination might have overcome the Coolidge-Hoover environment. But it is easier to argue that this context made inaction inevitable for almost any President. There were too many people who, given a choice between disaster and the measures that would have prevented it, opted for disaster without either a second or even a first thought.

On the other hand, in a different context a strong President might have taken effective preventive action. Congress in these years was becoming increasingly critical of the Wall Street speculation and corporate piggery-pokery. The liberal Republicans—the men whom Senator George H. Moses called the Sons of the Wild Jackass—were especially vehement. But conservatives like Carter Glass were also critical. These men correctly sensed that things were going wrong. A President such as Wilson or either of the Roosevelts (the case of Theodore is perhaps less certain than that of Franklin) who was surrounded in his Cabinet by such men would have been sensitive to this criticism. As a leader he could both have reinforced and drawn strength from the contemporary criticism. Thus he might have been able to arrest the destructive madness as it became recognizable. The American government works far better—perhaps it only works—when the Executive, the business power, and the press are in some degree at odds. Only then can we be sure that abuse or neglect, either private or public, will be given the notoriety that is needed.

Perhaps it is too much to hope that by effective and timely criticism and action the Great Depression might have been avoided. A lot was required in those days to make the United States in any degree depression-proof. But perhaps by preventive action the ensuing depression might have been made less severe. And certainly in the ensuing years the travail of bankers and businessmen before congressional committees, in the courts, and before the bar of public opinion would have been less severe. Here is the paradox. In the full perspective of history, American businessmen never had enemies as damaging as the men who grouped themselves around Calvin Coolidge and supported and applauded him in what William Allen White called "that masterly inactivity for which he was so splendidly equipped."

—August 1958

"I AM THE LAW"

By THOMAS J. FLEMING

The saga of Frank Hague. One of the last—and most powerful—of the old-time bosses, he ran New Jersey for years with a simple recipe: "Play ball with me and I'll make you rich."

He came out of the Horseshoe, a teeming slice of downtown Jersey City that owed its name to a gerrymander of earlier decades. From the brutal poverty of those narrow waterfront streets crammed with saloons and slum tenements, Frank Hague rose to plush accommodations at the Plaza and a mansion on Biscayne Bay, to dinners at the White House and at the homes of the wealthy, to annual trips to Europe in the royal suites of luxury liners, to made-to-order silk shirts and silk underwear from A. Sulka & Company. A few years before his death he secretly acknowledged that he was worth eight million dollars. The lawyer who extracted this figure, a former attorney general of New Jersey, says: "The real amount was probably ten times higher."

But it was not just his wealth that made Hague unique—it was the totality of his power and the ferocity with which he exercised it. For thirty years he reigned as mayor of Jersey City and ruler of New Jersey. Judges and district attorneys, senators and congressmen, governors and presidential candidates, respected—or at least feared—his name. Those who opposed him, especially on his home grounds, frequently ended up in jail or in the hospital. "I am the law!" he bellowed once in a moment of unguarded candor. Though he could claim, with some justice, that his enemies had distorted the circumstances in which he said it—he was trying to keep some delinquent boys out of jail—even his friends had to admit that, inside Jersey City's 8,320 grubby acres, it was the literal truth.

How Hague achieved this wealth and power is an American saga, rich in irony and symbolic overtones still significant today. Born in 1876, he was expelled from school at the age of thirteen as a hopeless incorrigible;

he acquired his real education in the brawling streets of the Horseshoe in the 1890s. Along with a taste for violence, he acquired from his boyhood a deep infusion of Irish Catholicism in its most puritanical form. The infusor was his mother, Margaret Hague. Her husband, John Hague, was a quiet cipher. Mrs. Hague is recalled by one old Jerseyite as "a bitch on wheels." She turned Hague's younger brother, Jimmy, into a mamma's boy so effeminate he never married. Her son Frank, made of tougher stuff, emerged from her stern tutelage ideally equipped to march to power flaunting the banner of a Catholic reformer. The two words are of equal importance in Frank Hague's rise. Religion was as divisive to the slum dweller of 1900 as race is to the slum dweller of 1969. The Anglo-Saxon Protestants on Jersey City's affluent Heights had the money, and they were haughtily determined to convert or browbeat into submission the immigrant Catholics downtown. From his earliest days, Frank Hague was a devout Catholic, and he could always draw on this simmering sense of discrimination as part of his political weaponry.

His psychological combination of Irish puritanism and hypochondria also guaranteed him a "clean" image. He had no interest in fast women or in drinking the saloons dry. Until the age of twenty-seven he lived at home with his mother and frequently accompanied her to church on Sunday. Then he married Jennie Warner, a prim, shy, retiring girl who never played the slightest role in his political life.

The reform side of Hague's image has been almost totally forgotten today. But it is one of the two things—the other is his technique of holding power—that makes his story worth recalling.

When the lean, red-headed six-footer won his first election, to the post of constable in 1897, New Jersey was called The Traitor State by despairing reformers. Hague's campaign, which consisted of borrowing seventy-five dollars from saloonkeeper Nat Kenny to "make friends" in the Horseshoe's ubiquitous bars, was typical of New Jersey's seamy political life. The political boss of Newark, James Smith, Jr., and the boss of Jersey City, Robert Davis, had auctioned off the state to the burgeoning railroads and utilities in return for juicy stock options and side deals. Thirty per cent of Jersey City's land was owned by the railroads, and they were assessed at only $3,000 an acre while other properties were evaluated as high as $18,000 an acre.

Backed by his self-organized "Tammannee Club"—a name that revealed little originality but much ambition—Hague swiftly became the leader of the Horseshoe's second ward. Having antagonized Davis, Hague promptly formed an alliance with H. Otto Wittpenn, a reform Democrat who was committed to fighting bossism and the "interests," as the big corporations were called. When Davis died in 1910 and Wittpenn attempted to assume his mantle as Democratic leader, Hague turn on him and smeared him with the "boss" label. Meanwhile, Woodrow Wilson became an aggressive reform governor of New Jersey, ramming through a series of bills aimed at returning the control of the government to the people. No one supported him more vociferously than Hague, especially when the Governor attacked and all but destroyed Boss Smith of Newark.

In 1911, Hague became the street and water commissioner of Jersey City. He instantly cut his department's budget from $180,000 a year to $110,000 and "for economy reasons" fired half the men. Later in the year he quietly replaced them with his own followers, and at his *sotto voce* request the city council restored his budget cuts. He had more than made his point—he was a tough administrator who meant business when he cried "reform."

Now Hague pulled out all the stops for one of Governor Wilson's pet reform measures—city commission government. This new style in city government had been inspired by the superb job a commission of citizens had done resuscitating hurricane-wrecked Galveston, Texas, in 1900. It was supposedly superior to the mayor-council form because each commissioner was directly responsible to the people for the operation of his department. The so-called reform (Jersey City returned to the mayor-council pattern in 1961) won massive approval in a referendum, and candidates blossomed by the dozen for the first election, in the spring of 1913. Wittpenn entered a slate of followers but did not run himself because he was campaigning to succeed Wilson, now President, as governor. Hague, running for commissioner, turned his campaign into a crusade against the so-called Wittpenn "machine."

The second-ward leader's bellows on behalf of reform won him wide support. On June 9, 1913, the local *Jersey Journal* ran a cartoon showing the city awakening from a long slumber. Beside it was an editorial urging the voters to "kill the machine rule forever." The voters responded by choosing Hague as one of the commissioners. A pioneer Republican reformer, Mark Fagan, ran first with 21,379 votes, and was made mayor, while Hague became commissioner of public safety. Shortly thereafter, the Hudson County Democratic Committee, under Hague's leadership, rescinded an earlier vote endorsing Wittpenn for governor and urged the election of James Fielder, his opponent in the approaching Democratic primary. This about-face meant that Hague was the acknowledged, unopposed leader of the Democratic party in Hudson County.

One of the unrealized dreams of Hague's political life was to create a "Greater Jersey City" out of the hodgepodge of municipalities that made up Hudson County. Besides Jersey City, with about half of the county's 538,000 population, there were Bayonne, at the end of the peninsula formed by New York and Newark bays; Hoboken to the north; and a number of smaller enclaves such as Weehawken, North Bergen, Secaucus, Kearney, and West New York. All of these places could, at times, become very jealous of their independence. That made for political headaches, but it also had its advantages. The multiplicity of governments, each with its own police, fire, and other city departments, created a remarkable number of political jobs. The county itself, with its courts of justice, its own police department, hospitals, jails, and other institutions, was also a hive of political patronage. Moreover, the man who controlled Jersey City inevitably ruled Hudson County, and with it the grand juries that had the power to investigate graft. The politicians of the smaller cities were therefore almost certain to fall into line behind the Jersey City leader.

The scent of total power inspired Hague to tackle his public duties with passionate ferocity. He needed all the energy he could muster; his new job plunged him into a violent conflict with Jersey City's police and fire departments. The police had been a municipal disgrace for decades. Robert Davis had run Jersey City as a wide-open town. Red-light districts flourished, saloons served liquor into the dawn, and gambling was uninhibited. Such an atmosphere made the moral decay of the police force inevitable.

Hague launched an all-out assault on police laxity. His motive was twofold. First, it was vital for him to protect his reform image in the shadow of Mayor Mark Fagan, who had achieved national fame in this role. Second was the opportunity to open an unparalleled number of jobs to his dispensation. As many as 125 men were put on trial in just one day for violating departmental regulations. Hundreds of police officers were ruthlessly demoted or dismissed. Into the decimated ranks Hague poured his tough young Horseshoe followers, from whom he culled an elite squad of plainclothesmen, called Zeppelins, who wove a web of secret surveillance around the entire force. Soon not a cop in the city cared to accept petty graft. They began enforcing for the first time city laws against prostitution and after-hours drinking. Women were barred from every one of Jersey City's thousand saloons, and any saloonkeeper who violated this puritanical ordinance was threatened with fines, loss of his license, and less legal kinds of punishment. The result, to the average voter in Jersey City, seemed almost miraculous. Public Safety Commissioner Hague had literally cleaned up the city.

Hague's organization now demonstrated its political prowess by winning its first county-wide contest: Hague's deputy commissioner of public safety, James F. Norton, was elected to the potent post of surrogate. Next came a more crucial test—the gubernatorial election of 1916. Running with the endorsement of President Wilson, Wittpenn, now Hague's avowed enemy, had won the Democratic nomination for governor. Coolly, Hague reversed the engine of the county Democracy and wrecked Wittpenn by giving him the smallest majority a Democratic gubernatorial candidate had received from the Hudson County bastion in decades—a puny 7,430 votes, in contrast to the 25,959 the organization had rolled up for Governor Fielder in 1913.

Time was running out for the anti-Hague men in Jersey City, and they knew it. The mayoralty election of 1917 found them in a frantic mood. Wittpenn and Mayor Fagan both begged President Wilson for help, but the could not agree on a united front. Wittpenn entered a slate of so-called regular Democrats, and Mayor Fagan headed a group of Republicans. Hague, with a prominent ex-Wittpennite, A. Harry Moore, firmly wedded to his standard, dubbed his Democratic slate "The Unbossed."

Hague and his four candidates won easily. His style of reform—the swept sidewalk, the honest cop, the clean saloon, all of which the citizen could see with his own eyes—had won. The other reformers never had a chance. Moore ran slightly ahead of Hague—19,883 to 18,648—in the final count. But when the city commission met to organize for the new administration, they ignored the tradition that the man with the most votes had the first call on the major's job. In a tumultuous scene in the City Hall council chamber, which was packed with howling Horseshoe supporters, Hague was unanimously elected mayor. Three decades would pass before another man stood there to receive similar acclaim.

The man thus poised on the threshold of state power had, at first glance, some curious personal defects. He was still almost totally uneducated; some of his surviving enemies insist to this day that Hague could not read more than the headlines in the daily paper. Immediately after he became mayor he took some lessons in public speaking, but he never mastered the complexities of English grammar. He remained likely to declare: "One hundred ten thousand voters has endorsed my administration," or to remark that the city commission "has went on record" regarding a particular issue. He once called Jersey City "the most moralest city in America." Closing a radio address he said, "And thank you, ladies and gentlemen, for the privilege of listening to me."

Nor was Hague personally popular, much less beloved, in the James Michael Curley *Last Hurrah* tradition. The stern aura of the reformer, the protector, the tough taskmaster who got results, was more in keeping with his personality. Even his closest legal adviser, John Milton, wryly called him "The Commissar." As the years passed, Hague became more arbitrary about inflicting his likes and dislikes on subordinates. Each year, he took the office workers of City Hall to Dinty Moore's in New York for a banquet. Not a man was allowed to touch a drop of liquor as long as the Mayor sat at the table. Once he left, it was tacitly acknowledged that drinking could begin. In his later years, Hague even treated non-New Jerseyites this way. Once Dan Finn, a powerful Tammany politician, called on Hague for a New Jersey favor. The Mayor was lunching alone in New York City at the Plaza Hotel. Hague asked Finn if he would like to order anything. "I'll have a Scotch and soda," the chieftain said. "Not at my table you won't," snapped Hague.

Hague's taste for personal violence was another unendearing trait. He was prone to punch, kick, and batter people who disagreed with him. He reportedly knocked one of his commissioners, Michael I. Fagan, cold on the mayoral carpet one day in 1929. Once, during one of his long walks around the city (always accompanied by bodyguards, at a discreet distance) Hague called an ambulance to see how quickly it would respond. It took fifteen minutes, and Hague began excoriating the intern in charge, "It took me a while to wake up," the young man said insolently. Hague belted him into the gutter.

He was equally willing to condone violence on the part of cops. He guaranteed their loyalty by making the police force the largest (for cities of comparable size) and best paid in the country. Jeff Burkitt, a cheerful Alabamian who fought Hague for almost a decade, was beaten up so many times that he finally went to the Mayor, his head wrapped in bandages, to ask Hague to be "a good sport" and let him have two or three corners where it would be understood that the cops would not club him.

Hague began roaring with laughter. The battered Burkitt looked puzzled. "I'm sorry," the Mayor said, his eyes streaming, "I just can't help it. You look so goddamn funny with all those bandages on your head."

But Hague did not win all his elections with night sticks. Although he obviously enjoyed violence (boxing was far and away his favorite sport), he reserved it for emergencies. The election of 1920 fell into that category. The country was tired of Wilsonian idealism. Even before Election Day, it became obvious that the entire Hudson County ticket was going to go down the drain. An order went out from City Hall—"Save Madigan." Thomas "Skidder" Madigan was an old Horseshoe crony who was blithely running for sheriff of Hudson County, ignoring a disability that would have been considered something of a handicap by the average candidate: the Skidder could not read or write. His campaign slogan was unique, even for Jersey City—"He was good to his mother."

As sheriff, Skidder would control an absolutely vital function in the Hague scheme of things—the selection of grand juries. All other candidates were abandoned to their fates. Using every electioneering technique at their disposal, including physical force, Hague's lieutenants carried Madigan, the lone survivor of that terrible debacle, into office with a majority that was 100 percent stolen.

On the other hand, when Hague knew he had an election sewed up, he was a model of decorum. In 1929, Republicans made an all-out effort to unseat him as mayor. On election eve there were frantic predictions that Hague was assembling hoodlums and phony voters by the busload. At the end of the voting day, the Republican prosecutor grudgingly had to admit that it had been the cleanest election in Jersey City in decades. Hague coasted to victory by 25,000 votes.

Contrary to myth, the paper ballot and the graveyard vote did not fully account for Hague's success. Wherever they could get away with it, Hagueites voted the cemeteries and the names of those who had long since moved out of the county. The state's permanent registration law offered an irresistible opportunity for fraud, especially when the local election bureau was lackadaisical about keeping track of the dead and departed. Hague guaranteed their laxity by making sure those appointed to the local election bureau were "Hague Republicans"—men who had nominal allegiance to the GOP but were keenly aware that their jobs had come from Hague. But in the 1940s, when the Republican-controlled state legislature inflicted voting machines and genuine Republican watchdogs in the election bureau, Hague's majorities were almost as huge as ever.

Hague's three decades of success as a political leader were, above all else, a triumph of executive ability. With the same driving energy he had exhibited in cleaning up the police department, Hague completely overhauled the structure of the Democratic organization in Hudson County. Not loyalty alone but also efficiency became the hallmarks of Hague Democracy. The city was divided into twelve wards, and these wards were subdivided into districts. Each ward and each district had a male and a female leader. There were ward committees and district committees. Hague knew from personal observation that thousands of Hudson County residents stayed home on each Election Day. Most of them were immigrants —the Poles, Italians, Czechs, and Slovaks who had followed the Irish into the slums—and they often did not know enough English to comprehend the era's tumultuous politics in the newspapers. Hague grimly decided that these people were going to vote. Whether they had to be bullied or cajoled, bribed or frightened to the polls, they were his secret weapon in Hudson County.

In every election every district was canvassed—which meant that every voter was personally asked to come out and vote on every Election Day. Lists of the aged and infirm were carefully compiled, and fleets of cars were at the disposal of every ward leader, to transport even the dying to the polls. Names were carefully checked off as people entered the polling booths, and the final hours of each Election Day were devoted to telephoning and even visiting those who had not yet voted to ask them why. Ward and district leaders were rewarded—or punished—strictly on the basis of their turnouts.

Simultaneously, Hague never abandoned his clean-city policy. He could boast, with considerable pride, that throughout the twenties, when hoodlums were shooting up Chicago and other cities, no gangster's corpse was found within Jersey City borders. As usual, Hague's methods were not always orthodox. City detectives, disguised as bums, loitered in the stations of the Hudson & Manhattan Railroad and at the ferry slips. Anyone they considered undesirable was likely to be sent back to New York on the next train or ferry.

Hague's political technique was a blend of violence and benevolence. At Christmastime each ward leader distributed thousands of food baskets to the poor. Every ward had a boat ride or a picnic or both each summer. But for Hague, the ultimate charity was free hospital care. He poured millions into a medical center, hired top-notch doctors to run it, and supervised it in fanatical detail. He maintained a suite of offices there, and was ever roaming the corridors picking up stray bits of paper and checking the meat in the kitchen.

Once a Republican prober accused Hague of allowing the affluent as well as the poor to have their babies and operations free. With oracular sincerity the Mayor proclaimed: "If they say they cannot pay, that is good enough for me. . . . We do not argue with a sick person."

"If the patient is trying to get something for nothing," the prober demanded, "notwithstanding his ability to pay?"

"My God, he is welcome to be restored to health!"

"At the expense of the other taxpayers?"

"Of anybody, of anybody. When you give me a sick man I will restore him to health at anyone's cost."

It all dovetailed neatly with the reform aura that created Hague's initial power. He was barely ensconced as mayor when he demonstrated that he could war on "the interests" far more ferociously than a Fagan or a Wittpenn. Where previous reformers had raised corporate tax assessments to levels they thought were reasonable and yet would not produce violent counterattack by the companies, Hague went all out. In 1917 and 1918, he increased the tax assessments on the Standard Oil Company from $1,500,000 to $14,000,000, on the Public Service Corporation from $3,000,000 to $30,000,000, and on the railroads from $67,000,000 to $160,000,000. The corporations rushed to the state Board of Taxes and Assessments in Trenton. The board cancelled all Hague's escalations.

Hague furiously denounced the board members as tools of the interests, and summoned his Hudson legions to elect a Democratic governor, who would appoint a new tax board. He soon found his candidate, Edward I. Edwards, president of the First National Bank of Jersey City. Edwards won by 14,510 votes, aided by the huge majority—58,527 to 23,009—Hague delivered for him in Hudson County.

Bucking a national Republican era, Hague proceeded to elect three governors in succession (the law then prohibited a governor from serving two consecutive three-year terms); his third, Jersey City's A. Harry Moore, boomed into Trenton in 1926 atop a Hudson County avalanche of 103,000 votes. In eight short years, Hague had quadrupled the standard Hudson County majority. Even subtracting the extra votes he garnered from woman suffrage, it was still a remarkable achievement.

During this nine-year period, Hague exultantly concentrated on appointing Democrats to the state Board of Taxes and to a breathtaking number of other jobs that the New Jersey governor had in his power. Between 1900 and 1910, the state had espoused the reform idea of the short ballot, and had eliminated scores of jobs that had theretofore been elective. The governor had the power to appoint almost every officer in the state government, ranging from the attorney general and the treasurer down to the prosecutors of the individual counties. There were more than eighty different boards and commissions, plus judgeships in fourteen court systems.

Most important were the judgeships. They were reserved for men with proved loyalty to Frank Hague. The Mayor's attitude toward these vital figures is summed up in an argument he had in the 1940s with Governor Charles Edison when the two men differed over a judicial appointment. Edison insisted that his preference was a man of integrity. "The hell with his integrity, Charlie," Hague roared. "What I want to know is, can you depend on the S.O.B. in a pinch?" Another politician recalls Hague's wheeling and dealing to execute his greatest judicial coup, the installation of his former corporation counsel, Thomas Brogan, as chief justice of the New Jersey Supreme Court. For all Hudson's clout, Hague never won control of the New Jersey legislature; Brogan's appointment had to be confirmed by the Republican-dominated state senate. Hague traded jobs by the dozen to Republican politicians in return for their votes.

The senate confirmed Brogan's appointment. He proved he could deliver in the pinch, more than once. Outraged Republican investigators tried to subpoena the voting records in Hudson County after the gubernatorial election of 1937, another emergency in which Hague needed every nightstick and graveyard vote he could find to squeak A. Harry Moore into his third term as governor. Chief Justice Brogan listened to stories of people being beaten up and thrown out of polling places, of men voting from insane asylums, and solemnly ruled on the great principle of the law, *Quod non apparet non est*. Since there was no evidence of corruption in the election, there was no basis for granting a subpoena of the voting records.

Hague penetrated the Republican party, not only by astute job trading, but also by occasionally helping the Republicans select their candidates. He first performed this bit of legerdemain in the 1928 gubernatorial primary. The man favored to get the Republican nomination was Robert Carey, a former Jersey City judge and a fierce critic of Hague and the organization. On primary day, some 20,000 "instant Republicans" flowered in Hudson County, and not one voted for Carey. All their enthusiasm —and the nomination—went to a colorless state senator from Middlesex County named Morgan Larson. Worse, the galled Republicans discovered the ploy was perfectly legal. Hague's lawyers had spotted a loophole in the election law that permitted a man who had not voted in a previous year's primary to switch his party affiliation without penalty. Like a shrewd general, Hague had simply ordered 20,000 loyalists to skip a primary and stand by, on reserve status, to name the Republican of his choice.

In the beginning New Jersey Republicans could not quite believe what was happening in Hudson County. The only answer they could produce to match Hague's maneuvers was a gimmick to pin the state closer to the coattails of the national Republican ticket, which still looked like a winner. They called for a referendum to lengthen the governor's term to four years, and to elect him in presidential years. In a special election in September, 1925, the proposal was defeated 200,716 to 135,288. Of the No votes, 100,002 were from Hudson County. This was only 3,000 fewer votes than Hudson's huge gubernatorial turnout the next year for favorite son Moore. Such a vote on an issue so tenuous to the average voter struck the state as little short of miraculous. As one politician to another, New Jersey's Republican senator, Walter Edge, congratulated Hague for an unsurpassed performance.

The almost incredible solidarity Hague had created in Hudson County was partly based on his reformer's war with the corporations. It injected a priceless element of drama into the humdrum lives of those nondescript thousands on Jersey City's downtown streets. On their behalf, Hague thundered defiance of the once all-powerful railroads, Public Service, and Standard Oil. He created a kind of inverted arrogance in his followers, the feeling that John L. Sullivan excited with his famous shout, "I can lick any man in the house." With Hague at their head, each election day they marched, like an army with banners, into the heart of the state, flattening those arrogant Protestant Republicans who had for so long looked down their aristocratic noses at the Irish and their fellow immigrants.

Taxes were only one weapon used by Hague in his continual war with the corporations. During the winter of 1926, a coal strike caused severe hardship among Jersey City's poor. Cries for help poured into City Hall. Hague knew, without even bothering to check, that there were thousands of railroad cars full of coal standing in Jersey City's railyards, waiting for shipment across the Hudson River to Manhattan. The denizens of the Horseshoe had stolen their fuel from these cars for decades. The Mayor called the chief of police and ordered: "Don't allow a scuttle of coal to go out of this city."

The coal company screamed that the Mayor was interfering with interstate commerce. The Mayor said he had the authority "by virtue of my office as Mayor."

"That is not enough," shouted the manager of the coal company.

"By the law at the end of a night stick," roared the Mayor. "How do you like that one?"

The coal company capitulated and sent ten tons of coal to each police and fire station, where city residents were able to get it for little or nothing.

Hague's antibusiness stance was a distinct break in the boss tradition in the United States. Most bosses made their money through seemingly legitimate business fronts, co-operating behind the scenes with the powerful corporations. Not Frank Hague: his money came from other sources.

Each year, every officeholder in Hudson County had to contribute three percent of his salary to City Hall, supposedly to finance the organization's political battles. A third or half of every raise a man received went to City Hall. So did perhaps half the salary a man was paid for nominal work on a state board or commission. No accounting was made of this river of cash—which swelled to at least $500,000 and probably $1,000,000 a year.

Then there were the real estate deals. Dummy corporations headed by shadowy figures in New York bought land shortly before Jersey City or Hudson County condemned it, and resold it at fabulous prices. One of these operations cleared a profit of $628,145 between 1919 and 1924.

Most lucrative of all was the gambling take. Among the sports columnists and betting fraternity, Hague's Jersey City quickly became known as "the Horse Bourse." In the downtown tenements, under Hague's careful control, major bookmakers set up a system of telephone and telegraph connections that handled the enormous quantities of off-track betting on races all over America and Canada. Beside this golden stream flowed the by no means inconsiderable pay-offs of the numbers racketeers. These too were carefully controlled by the organization. Finally, each ward was given the O.K. for a carefully regulated number of card and dice games, each of which paid a monthly slice of its "handle."

Inevitably, Hague's personal habits began to change. He moved out of the Horseshoe into a fourteen-room apartment on fashionable Hudson

County Boulevard, bought a mansion in even swankier Deal, on the New Jersey shore, and acquired other property in Jersey City. In seven years he laid out a grand total of $392,910.50 for real estate, a remarkable performance for a man supposedly living on a salary of $7,500.

This, of course, was only the tip of the iceberg, the portion visible in New Jersey. In New York and elsewhere, vastly larger sums of cash were being invested in stocks or stored in savings banks. A still-active Jersey City politician recalls how, as a young man just out of the Army, he got a job in the city finance department. On one of his first assignments he was given an old suitcase and told to make a series of stops at brokerage houses and banks in New York, where the suitcase was taken into back rooms and then politely returned to him, considerably lightened.

"What the hell is in that thing?" he finally asked. "Money," he was told.

But Hague's ostentatious display of wealth was to be his Achilles heel. Each winter he was a familiar figure at Florida's racetracks, where he displayed an almost childish fondness for flashing thousand-dollar bills. Summer cruises to Europe became part of his routine. At World Series games and other major sporting events, the Mayor always entertained a contingent in the more expensive seats. In 1929, a committee from the New Jersey legislature, convened to investigate election irregularities in Hudson County, asked Hague some questions about his personal finances. He declined to answer. He defied not only the committee but both houses of the New Jersey legislature, assembled in righteous panoply.

The legislature charged him with contempt, and he was still defiant. Eventually, the state supreme court decided in Hague's favor, accepting his lawyers' argument that the legislature did not have the judicial power to probe for felonies: that function belonged to the courts and their grand juries. But it was a barren, legalistic victory. It ruined Hague's image as a reformer forever. The Newark *Evening News* summed up the public sentiment in the state: "If Mr. Hague himself would come clean; if he would tell the truth and shame his enemies with the truth, what a triumph would be his! A man who has nothing to conceal, a man whose life is an open book, does not fall back on right of privacy or other technical safeguards when his reputation is at stake."

There was, at that point, some ground for wondering if Hague could last much longer. The Republican-controlled legislature was still in furious pursuit of him, and a hefty two-fifths of the voters in his Jersey City bailiwick had turned against him in the May, 1929, mayoralty election. *Time* magazine predicted that he would soon imitate several former leaders of Tammany Hall by taking refuge in Europe. Then an event occurred across the river in New York that transformed the politics of the entire nation. The bottom dropped out of Republican prosperity, and with a shock that was felt around the world, the stock market crashed. The gray, dismal years of the Depression settled on the nation. They were made to order for Hague.

As the private sector of the economy shrank, thousands found themselves unemployed, and Hague was transformed from a politician on the run to a titan of steadily swelling power. He alone, by executive fiat, could ignore economic reality and maintain his padded payrolls intact. A city job became not merely a way out of the slums but a source of salvation for those who thought they had achieved the mythical security of the American middle class. Many of the older, wealthier Protestant families, who had been the backbone of Hague's Jersey City opposition, were totally ruined.

His new Depression-spawned power made Hague meaner and tougher. For the next two decades, his operation became an exercise in the retention of power for its own sake. Having double-crossed the two leaders who had given him his start, Hague trusted no one. Phones were tapped regularly. "Every night," declares a man who is still an important Hudson County official, "a police lieutenant sat in the Western Union telegraph office in Journal Square and read every telegram that came in and went out of Jersey City that day." Hague spies in the U.S. Post Office maintained similar surveillance on the mail of those who were labelled untrustworthy. There were informants in every bank in Jersey City, quick to alert City Hall to any unusual surplus in a man's account.

Throughout the twenties, when Hague had been blasting the corporations, he had maintained a warm alliance with labor unions. Theodore "Teddy" Brandle, head of the Ironworkers Union, loaned Hague $60,000 when the Bureau of Internal Revenue gave the Mayor a tap on the wrist in 1930. Three years later, Brandle was called a hoodlum and a crook by Hague, and driven out of the labor movement. Every other union in Hudson County was invaded by Hague's "reporters" and reduced to docility. "Everything for industry" became Jersey City's slogan, and Hague lured companies to Jersey City by promising them "perfect" labor relations.

Hague was equally adept at instilling fear or proffering favor. "Play ball with me and I'll make you rich," he would tell those who fought him. A distressing number of them took him at his word, and quietly accepted a judgeship or a commissionership in the state, county, or city government. The churches, a potential source of moral censure for an ex-reformer, were mopped up with extensive favor-doing and giving. Hague helped Roman Catholic Archbishop Thomas Walsh of Newark raise millions for Darlington Seminary. The Mayor donated a $50,000 altar to Saint Aedan's, his own parish church. At least fifty-four priests, ministers, and rabbis were on the government payroll as chaplains to hospitals, police, fire, and other city and county departments.

Massive majorities were demanded in every election, no matter how trivial, to awe and discourage potential rebels. The zenith was reached in 1937, when Hague was re-elected mayor for the sixth time, by 110,743 to 6,798. Each year, in a final rally at the uptown auditorium known as The Grotto, Hague would exhort the faithful as if Armageddon were at hand. "Three hundred and sixty-four days a year I work for you," he would cry. "Now this one day I ask you to work for me." In 1941, Hague needed, under the Walsh Act, only 766 signatures to nominate him for his seventh term as mayor. The organization collected 125,371. "It is very gratifying," the Mayor said as truckmen staggered into City Hall with bushels of the signed petitions.

Then there was the ritual of January 1. No matter how hung over he may have been by year-end whoopee, every faithful job holder dragged his bones into the cold to stand in an immense line, which wound around City Hall three or four times, inching slowly forward into the lobby and up the steps to the Mayor's office. There the Mayor and the commissioners, in morning coats and striped pants, reeived handshakes and earnest good wishes for the coming year. A man who failed to appear was practically saying tht he was no longer interested in promotions or favors. He was all but declaring his intention to leave the city.

Even while Hague thus assumed almost total power inside Hudson County, he revealed a weakness that was to embarrass him and his followers again and again in the next two decades of his reign. He was singularly unable to grasp the psychology of the average voter outside the county.

This defect plus an almost insane arrogance bred by an excess of power might explain why he had Governor Moore appoint thirty-two-year-old Frank Hague, Jr., a likeable playboy who had failed to get through two law schools (yet had miraculously passed the New Jersey bar exam on his first try) to the Court of Errors and Appeals, New Jersey's highest judicial body. Bar associations fulminated, newspapers across the country decried, but Governor Moore only replied: "I know this appointment will make his Dad happy."

On the level of national politics, Hague was even more obtuse. In 1932 he blundered to the brink of disaster by backing Alfred E. Smith against Franklin D. Roosevelt for the Democratic nomination for the Presidency. But there was an explanation for this mistake: sentiment. Hague had been an advocate of the Happy Warrior since 1924, and the grateful Smith had helped make Hague vice chairman of the Democratic National Committee. Nothing stirred Hague more deeply than the Irish clan spirit. Loyalty was one of the few words in the English language that made him choke up. Like the Tammany sachems across the river in New

York, he refused to face the facts of the 1928 disaster—Al Smith was simply not presidential timber.

On June 24, 1932, Hague issued a blast against Roosevelt, declaring he could not "carry a single state east of the Mississippi and very few in the Far West . . ." Since Roosevelt was governor of New York, this exaggeration struck more than a few politicians as ludicrous.

At the convention, Hague was the floor leader of the Smith forces and at an early stage in the struggle exuberantly declared, "We've got them licked." But no southern politician could be induced to try Smith a second time, and among northern Democrats Hague found himself totally out-generaled by a younger, smarter Irishman, James A. Farley of New York.

As Farley said of FDR's convention victory, "Everyone knew we had just nominated the next President of the United States." No one knew this better than Hague. Even before Al Smith made his peace with Roosevelt at the New York state Democratic convention, Hague had persuaded Farley to bring Roosevelt to Sea Girt, New Jersey, on August 27 with a promise that Hague "would provide the largest political rally ever held in the United States." Commandeering most of the rolling stock of the Jersey Central, plus squadrons of buses and cars, Hague assembled a total of 150,000 faithful. In the little resort town, sixty miles from Jersey City, they swarmed around the summer home of New Jersey's governor and cheered their lungs out for Roosevelt when he appeared on the platform to congratulate "my friend, Mayor Hague," for this overwhelming demonstration of Democratic muscle.

Fighting for his niche in the Democratic party, Hague slammed his Hudson County political dynamo to full throttle and produced an astonishing 184,000 votes for Roosevelt on Election Day. The performance swung New Jersey into the Democratic column, 806,000 to 775,000. The victory consolidated Hague's power in the county and the state on a hitherto unparalleled scale. Although Roosevelt piously declined to deal with Tammany Hall, all the federal patronage for New Jersey passed through Hague's City Hall. Some $47,000,000 in W.P.A. funds alone poured into Jersey City, enabling Hague to complete his medical center on a scale so large that the hospital's staff frequently outnumbered the patients.

The argument, fondly repeated by many students of American politics, that the New Deal and its welfare philosophy ruined the old style-political machines simply does not apply to Hague. Roosevelt stuck with him, even when the Mayor fought a tremendous war with the C.I.O. and the nation's liberal establishment in the late 1930's. Hague tried to bar the aggressively independent C.I.O. from his Hudson bailiwick, using the canard that the unionists were "Reds." Norman Thomas, Morris Ernst, and other liberals rushed into the fray. Although at one point a Jersey City police captain told a C.I.O. worker, "We're enforcing a Jersey City ordinance, not the Constitution," the U.S. Supreme Court eventually ruled that the C.I.O. had the right to distribute literature and give speeches inside Jersey City. In the course of the struggle, the liberals were outraged to discover that Hague's post office spies were opening their mail. They howled for Hague's scalp, but once more FDR stood by the Mayor. "We had a hell of a time getting Hague out of that one," a Cabinet-level official of the Roosevelt administration told me.

The reasons for Roosevelt's embrace of Hague were twofold. In the early years, there were not enough independent Democrats left in New Jersey to form an anti-Hague wing of the party. Later, Roosevelt needed Hague for his third-term and fourth-term pushes. With Ed Kelly, the boss of Chicago, in happy concert, the "Hague-Kelly axis" was the driving engine of Roosevelt's 1940 steamroller. After Roosevelt was nominated, practically by acclamation, a prominent Democrat ruefully declared: "Mayor Hague has more stuff on the ball than anyone else here in Chicago."

But Hague was to pay a bitter price for this more intimate relationship with Roosevelt. With an artful combination of cajolery and political arm-twisting, the President persuaded Hague to accept Charles Edison, a son of Thomas Edison, the inventor, as the Democratic nominee for governor in 1940. Edison was an independent Democrat who owed nothing to Hague, and he had plainly spent some time in the library reading Wilson biographies. With Hague sitting at his right hand and 150,000 Democratic faithful in the audience at Hague's by now traditional Sea Girt rally, Edison declared: "It is my happy privilege to stand here today and tell you that if you elect me, you will have elected a governor who has made no promises of preferment to any man or group. . . . I'll never be a yes man except to my conscience."

For senator that year Hague also had to accept, on White House orders, James H. R. Cromwell, a millionaire ex-playboy inflated for high office by a tour as minister to Canada. While Edison understandably excited no enthusiasm in Hague, Cromwell had precisely the opposite effect. Throughout the 1930s, while most of the country was in violent reaction against the rich, Hague had been courting their company and imitating their manners. He invited anyone and everyone from the ranks of the well-born to his magnificent Biscayne Bay mansion in Florida. Jersey City clubhouses whispered the story of the day that Deputy Mayor Johnny Malone, in Florida to confer with the Mayor, humbly asked if he could come to one of Hague's splendiferous parties, promising to stand obscurely in the corner and not open his mouth. "I'm sorry, Johnny," said the Mayor, "you just ain't got enough class."

Hague embraced Cromwell with an ardor that made no sense politically. Genial Jimmy had written many books and made scores of speeches in which he had alienated huge blocs of the electorate. He had nicknamed war veterans "the American Pillaging Force" and defined the Constitution as "a millstone around the necks of the American people." He had called for repeal of the National Labor Relations Act and come out in print for birth control. Yet Hague toured New Jersey beside Cromwell, obviously revelling in his company. He was almost delirious with pleasure when he and several select henchmen were invited to Boxwood Manor, an English-style castle in the center of a wooded estate, the property of Mrs. E. T. Stotesbury, widow of a Morgan partner, and Cromwell's mother.

Edison, preaching his independence of Hague, won the governorship handily. Roosevelt also carried the state, but Cromwell stumbled to defeat. As governor, Edison firmly practiced the independence he had preached during the campaign. This soon produced violent hostilities. The Governor, for instance, tried to solve the financial collapse of the state's railroads by forgiving them some $81,000,000 in back taxes. Almost half of this money belonged to Jersey City, and Hague began belaboring Edison for selling out to the interests.

It was like Old Home Week for Hague; it was the heady crusading days of 1920 all over again. The Edison script, which called for a Wilson-style confrontation, ended in political disaster for the Governor. When Edison went out of office, Hague was still state chairman of the Democratic party, vice chairman of the Democratic National Committee, and as invulnerable as ever in Hudson County. One explanation is that earnest, honest Charles Edison was not Woodrow Wilson. Another, equally valid, is that the dimensions of Frank Hague's power far exceeded that of Wilson's old foe, Boss James Smith.

No one ever fought with Hague and emerged unscathed. When Walter Van Riper became attorney general of New Jersey in 1944, he launched a series of raids on Hague's sacrosanct "Horse Bourse." Within months Van Riper was indicted by a federal jury for kiting checks and for selling black-market gasoline through a service station he partially owned. He was acquitted on both counts, and there is strong evidence that some of the witnesses committed perjury. But Van Riper, once considered a shoo-in as the next governor, was politically dead.

With "Hagueism" for a rallying cry, the GOP proceeded to elect two governors in a row, for the first time since Hague had come to power. This was a serious blow to Hague. From 1941 to 1949, counting Edison's term, he was voiceless in Trenton. Dozens of key appointments to the state's boards and commissions fell into Republican hands, as the terms of Hague Democrats expired. Deaths and resignations accounted for still more, in both the judicial and executive branches of the government. Worse, a new state constitution, with a provision which would force public officials to answer embarrassing questions, was proposed in 1944. A massive effort by the Hague organization, climaxed by an official denunciation of the document by Archbishop Walsh, defeated this threat temporarily. But it was still very much on the horizon; Republicans and Edison Democrats were beating drums for it with crusaders' fervor.

Within Hudson County, Hague suddenly began having almost as much trouble exerting his hitherto complete control. Insiders have always maintained that the trouble, which started in Bayonne, was Hague's own fault. By now, Hague was spending very little time in Jersey City. When he was not in Florida, he was sojourning in New York at the Plaza. Most of the city's political and economic business was conducted on the telephone, through Deputy Mayor Malone. For too many politicians in the organization, Hague had become a remote figure, no longer to be feared. When a public school was erected in Bayonne, Hague's leaders skimmed off all the gravy for themselves, ignoring the standard distribution that assured each politician a share, however small. Feuding promptly erupted inside the Bayonne organization, and a slate with a "Home rule, not Hague rule" slogan swept all five city commission seats in 1943. Similar revolts exploded in North Bergen and Hoboken during the next four years.

Perhaps, at seventy-one, Hague was weary at the thought of extinguishing these rebellions. They were ominous signs that a new generation of voters had come to maturity, and many of them were not inclined to accept Hague's leadership in the old unquestioning fashion. Jersey City, the heartland of Hague's power, had a similar corps of restive veterans home from the global wars and hungry for a slice of the political pie. Hague's next move seemed to be a major concession to a new era. He announced his resignation as mayor of Jersey City on June 4, 1947.

A magnificent ceremony was staged two weeks later in the auditorium of Dickinson High School, at which Hague handed over the official rule of the city to his nephew, Frank Hague Eggers, the commissioner of parks and public works. Moore and dozens of other politicians whom Hague had elevated to power appeared on the platform to gush forth hours of soggy oratory in praise of his accomplishments. Hague then rose and made it clear that he was *not* resigning as chairman of the Democratic party in the state and county.

It suddenly dawned on a lot of people that the great change was really a great smokescreen. The choice of Eggers made Hague's sleight of hand even more transparent. Just to make sure he retained total control, he was ready to risk the hostility that such nepotism was certain to arouse.

The realization was discouraging to more than a few local Democrats, who yearned for relief from Hague's heavy hand. One of the most restless was John V. Kenny, leader of the second ward. Short, balding, and mild-mannered, Kenny was the son of Nat Kenny, the man who had given Hague his start in politics. Kenny was a good leader, who worked at his job in a ward that had been completely transformed since Hague's era; gone were the feuding, brawling Irish, replaced by Poles and Italians and Slovaks. They were intensely devoted to "the Little Guy," as many people called Kenny, for the same reason that Hague's Irish had been devoted to him.

In the light of these undeniable political realities, it was only natural for Kenny to think of himself as Hague's local successor. But Kenny, a political realist, declined to challenge Hague personally. As a second warder, he was acutely aware of Hague's fondness for retaliating, not merely politically but physically. The Little Guy had no desire to get his head cracked. Better—or at least safer—to wait until the Big Guy was safely planted in Holy Name Cemetery, and then make his move. But the emergence of Eggers as the heir apparent forced Kenny to make a decision. If he wanted to inherit the crown, it was now or never. Quietly, Kenny began making secret trips to Newark to confer with leading Republicans. The only hope of beating Hague was a fusion ticket, fueled by Republican money.

Hague knew about Kenny's dealings with the opposition almost immediately, thanks to his superb espionage system. He called a meeting of the Democratic county committee and announced that there was a double-crosser in their midst. With special ferocity, Hague read Kenny out of the Democratic party and deposed him as leader of the second ward.

Driven into a corner and made to look not a little like a martyr, Kenny fought back. Grimly he gathered together his ward supporters and a strong cadre of disgruntled young veterans from other parts of the city, and began building his fusion ticket. He made no attempt to surface during the November, 1948, elections. On this, the year of Harry Truman's come-from-behind victory, Hague cracked the whip furiously, and the organization had seldom looked better. Although Dewey carried the Garden State by 86,000 votes, every local Democratic candidate scored a crushing victory.

Earnest, hard-working Frank Eggers and the other commission candidates began making the rounds of the ward clubs and parish houses before Christmas, hitting the opposition of Kenny, who had yet to announce a ticket, and pounding home the achievements of the organization. To those on the outside, it was a very impressive show. But from all over the city, the word from the wards came: it was not working.

The Eggers team orated about the medical center, about the city's vice-free image and low crime rate. The Kenny opposition ignored achievements, issues, and political philosophy and blasted at only one target: Frank Hague. Their argument was simple. Hague was an evil dictator. Eggers was just a stooge. Endlessly they denounced the "Royal Family," condemned "King" Hague's wealth, sneered at his accomplishments, called him an absentee dictator, and proclaimed themselves the Freedom party. The published a Freedom newspaper which mocked the organization with biting humor and wry observation. They published photostats of Hague's bills at Sulka's, showing him spending $75 for a shirt and $25 for silk underwear. They persuaded supporters inside the telephone company to leak the astonishing amounts Hague ran up each month on long-distance calls from his Florida mansion to City Hall. They also shrewdly placed Polish and Italian candidates on their five-man ticket to oppose the organization's all-Irish slate.

More and more men and women of local prominence came out openly for John V. Kenny. Patrolmen in Journal Square directed traffic with their fingers raised in a V for a Kenny victory. Revolt was general among the younger men in the police and fire departments. City Hall itself seethed with malcontents and ambitious minor politicians who saw in a Kenny victory a chance for quick promotion.

Then came a voice from Florida. For months Hague had stayed in his Biscayne Bay mansion, letting Eggers and the other candidates make all the public statements. But now, as the battle roared toward a climax, he seemed to lose faith in the organization's ability to survive without him.

There was a hint of desperation in his announcement that, under his personal leadership, the organization was going to make a supreme effort—a tremendous rally in the heart of Kenny's second ward, the site of the old Horseshoe district. The Friday before the rally, Hague sent letters to over 7,000 voters in the second ward, recounting the story of his association with Kenny. He told how, out of gratitude to Kenny's father, saloonkeeper Nat Kenny of Horseshoe days, he had gotten the young man his first job and had helped him rise in politics. "If now he betrays me," Hague asked, "how can he be trusted not to betray you?"

On May 3, the ward clubs formed up outside City Hall at about 6:30 P.M. The orders had gone out to every job holder in the city to be on hand. But many stayed home, deciding the loss of a job was less formidable than a fractured skull. Hague, his lined, tanned face grimly set, escorted Eggers and the other candidates to the front rank of the parade. With long strides he led them up Grove Street into the second ward—and bedlam.

Six deep, the second warders lined the curbs, screaming contempt and defiance at the Boss and his aging battalions. They pelted the marchers with eggs, tomatoes, stones, and chalk powder. Police had to fight to clear a space in front of the speaker's platform.

More than a few of the marchers retreated to the safety of Public School 37's auditorium immediately. The courageous formed up before a flag-draped platform outside the school; around them a mob of thousands surged, bellowing, screaming, sounding horns and cowbells, waving Kenny placards and streamers.

The police cordoned the platform, and Hague, Eggers, and the other candidates stepped out before the crowd. Eggs spattered them. The derision rose to an enormous crescendo. Eggers tried to speak. He went on for a few sentences, then stopped in despair. He could not even hear himself. With a shrug he motioned to the others to leave the platform.

The commission candidates filed off, but Frank Hague did not move. For a moment he stood alone, his face a mask of suppressed fury. Then he strode to the edge of the platform and glared down at the shrieking mob. For more than three decades Frank Hague had ruled them. He had fought those who opposed him with ballots and with clubs and fists. And he had won every time. Remembering, they suddenly shut their mouths.

For a long, hushed moment they stood facing each other. Then a small thin man in the first row sprang forward. A "Down with Hague" sign on a long pole swung toward the Boss, twisting and whirling like a crashing kite. Hague had to step back to avoid it, and in the same instant the man screamed:

"G'wan back to Florida!"

Hague almost choked with fury. Smashing aside the sign, he pointed down at the culprit.

"Arrest that man!"

He was speaking to the cordon of police around the platform. For too many years in Jersey City those words had been the signal for swinging clubs, the crunch of wood on bone.

The man fell back, cowering. The crowd held their breath. Then people realized that the police were not moving. Every policeman in the cordon was anti-Hague. Quite logically they had decided they had no obligation to obey orders from the *ex*-mayor of Jersey City.

The crowd exploded into a howl that dwarfed all their previous efforts. Hague stood staring at them. For a second something close to shock was on his face. Then he turned and stalked stoically off the platform.

Incredibly, the disaster in the second ward did not make Hague or Malone realize that the organization was in deep trouble throughout the city. They wrote off downtown and, with an irony that only those who understood Hague's history would appreciate, placed their hopes on the uptown wards where the middle class had looked down their noses at Hague and his Irish forty years ago. On Election Day, Kenny revealed how thoroughly he had studied Hague's tactics. His workers made the same heroic effort to get out their vote, matching the organization car for car, telephone call for telephone call. As many as forty-one watchers were on duty in each of the polling places, making it impossible for Hague to spring any of his old rough-and-tumble tactics.

Most important, the Kenny organization had unprecedented amounts of money to spend. The going rate in Jersey City had long been five dollars a vote. This was always dispensed freely, especially in the poorest sections of the city. Hague's ward leaders were soon deluged with frantic pleas for help from their district leaders. They simply could not match the Kenny prices, and the sums dispensed by City Hall to each ward for this purpose were soon exhausted. At 1:00 P.M., the leader of the sixth ward phoned Malone at City Hall. "Johnny," he said, "I've got to have ten thousand dollars right away. They're paying fifteen dollars a vote and they're murdering us."

"The hell with them," Malone rasped. "We're not goin' over five dollars a vote and that's final. It'll give them bad habits."

With a curse the ward leader slammed down the phone. Then he called the ward's chief bookmaker (and his best friend), George Ormsby. "Can you get me ten grand right away?"

"Come down and pick it up," Ormsby said.

Before the polls closed, the $10,000 was gone, plus several thousand dollars of the ward leader's own money, which he always kept in reserve on Election Day. He should have saved it. At nine o'clock that night, the stunning news came over the radio. Kenny had won by 22,000 votes. He had carried every ward but one—the sixth.

A vast mob of Freedom ticket supporters snake-danced through the downtown streets carrying a coffin labeled "The Hague Machine." Kenny and several of his lieutenants stormed into City Hall, hoping to seize incriminating records. But the organization had known for hours that the election was lost, and there was nothing but charred scraps of paper in the furnace room. The vault in the mayor's office was empty. Earlier, according to several reliable witnesses, two police captains had helped lug suitcases filled with cash down to the vault of the First National Bank. The Kenny men did discover two thick ledgers, containing the names of more than 17,000 citizens who were politically unreliable, with careful comments written beside each name, based on reports from district leaders and other members of Hague's espionage system.

Kenny was in charge of City Hall, but Hague was still very much a factor on the political scene. His men controlled most of the county government. Moreover, there was a gubernatorial election coming up in November, 1949, and Hague had found his strongest candidate in years. He was Elmer Wene, a popular three-term congressman and millionaire chicken farmer from southern New Jersey. The combination of Hague and Wene seemed unbeatable.

With the irony that keeps recurring in Hague's story, Kenny found himself confronted with a situation similar to the one Hague had faced when he seized power in 1913. Then, Hague's chief rival, Wittpenn, was running for governor. Kenny knew that if Wene won he would immediately appoint a Hague prosecutor in Hudson County. With Hague already in control of the grand jury, it would be only a matter of months before most of Kenny's administration was in jail.

After a long strategic silence, Kenny announced that he was for Wene. But there was not an iota of enthusiasm in his endorsement. Meanwhile, Hague made an almost incredible blunder in his final pre-election speech. "We'll be back in the driver's seat in Trenton in January," he thundered. Instantly, the Republicans seized on their old "Beat Hague" battle cry, and Alfred Driscoll, fighting to be the first governor to succeed himself (as permitted by the new state constitution of 1947), made it the theme of his final campaign speech.

Wene lost by 70,000 votes. For the first time since 1920, Hudson County went Republican. Kenny had quietly reversed his political engine, just as Hague had done to Wittpenn in 1916. On election night, Hague resigned as state and county leader of the Democratic party. The long reign was over.

Hague clawed desultorily at Kenny for the next few years, until Kenny resigned as mayor and, eventually, sought refuge in the less visible role of Democratic county "leader," a position he still maintains. Neither temperamentally nor politically was Kenny capable of asserting Hague-size power. He had been content to remain an easygoing, behind-the-scenes leader in the Robert Davis tradition.

As for Hague, he shuttled between Florida and his Park Avenue apartment, an outcast from the state he had once ruled. With the encouragement of the Kenny regime, job holders banded together and filed suit to recover the estimated $15,000,000 paid by three-percenters over the decades. Hague had to stay out of New Jersey to avoid an always-waiting subpoena in this litigation, which never came to trial.

In some ways, his exile from Jersey City hurt Hague more than his loss of power. He had often said, "In the Horseshoe I was born, in the Horseshoe I will die." He had apparently envisioned a serene old age, surrounded by another generation of loyal Democrats to whom he could be the paterfamilias he never was in his years of action. A glimpse of this sense of loss comes from an old City Haller whom Hague used to call in the middle of the night during those last years. "Billy," he would say, "I can't sleep." He would then express anguished concern over a family whose father or brother he had ruined or maimed in earlier years. "Go down now and ask them if they're all right, if they want anything."

"My wife used to think I was crazy," says the storyteller, "but I'd get up, put on my clothes, and go down and see them, and tell them why I was there. Not once did any one of them ever ask for help. Sometimes they slammed the door in my face. Other times they'd just say, 'We don't want anything from him.' "

On January 1, 1956—the annual holiday on which he used to hold regal court in City Hall—Frank Hague died at his Park Avenue apartment of complications of pneumonia and arthritis. Only then did he return to Jersey City. At Lawrence Quinn's funeral home he lay in state for two days. Then eight professional pallbearers hefted the seven-hundred-pound hammered-copper casket and carried it out to a solemn high funeral mass at Saint Aedan's Church. There was only a small crowd in the street. One elderly woman stood holding an American flag and a crudely lettered sign: "God have mercy on his sinful, greedy soul."

A reporter asked a funeral-home aide why there were so few flowers. A true citizen of Jersey City, the aide shrugged. "When the Big Boy goes," he said, "it means he can no longer do anything for anybody."

—June 1969

ST. LÔ

By CHARLES CAWTHON

Here the Germans stood and fought with all their skill and courage, and by the time the American offensive finally rolled forward, a hundred thousand people had been killed or wounded. A soldier who fought there recalls the struggle.

Three decades ago a battle was fought for St. Lô, Normandy, France, in the second of the great world wars of this century. To have been young at St. Lô and now to be old is a matter of personal amazement, for the time lapse seems instantaneous. In rank, the battle is in that heavily populated tier of major bloodlettings that have determined the course of campaigns, as opposed to the few decisive Gettysburgs and Waterloos on which history itself has turned. In keeping with this stature, St. Lô seems destined for the footnotes of history, unlikely to be remembered beyond the memory span of the First United States Army and Seventh German Army veterans who fed its flames so prodigally, of those who anxiously followed their fortunes, and of the Normans whose lives and homes were in its path. Further in perspective: St. Lô was an essential objective of the First Army's offensive launched during that fateful month of July, 1944, to gain the terrain and road net on which Operation COBRA could coil and strike to break out of the Normandy beachhead. The overall offensive involved twelve divisions in four corps attacking on a twenty-five-mile front. It was bitterly contested at every point; losses were uniformly appalling. In this general holocaust St. Lô caught the public's attention, possibly because the town had the largest population (eleven thousand) in the offensive and was a provincial seat of government. Even more, it acquired a symbol, "the Major of St. Lô," whom I knew. To the allied command the town was important as the hub of a network of seven roads and because the high ground to its east and west commanded the Vire Valley, in which tanks could operate. Both factors were essential to COBRA. The German command had an equal appreciation of road nets and terrain and, in addition, had a captured American field order designating St. Lô as a primary objective. This determined that it would be defended with all the resources that the enemy would be able to muster on its accommodating hills and ridgelines.

Presuming to speak for those who fought there but knew nothing of COBRA or of captured field orders, I recall the battle only as a boiling caldron that no man entered without dread or emerged from without being marked.

In the end, of course, St. Lô was taken. Operation COBRA was launched, and a general advance was begun that with some setbacks, notably the Battle of the Bulge, ended in less than a year with victory in Europe. The cost was high: in three weeks over forty thousand Americans killed, wounded, or missing—the same price, incidentally, as at the Bulge six months later. The Germans, who fought with courage and skill, had losses perhaps half again as heavy. St. Lô was knocked apart, and about a thousand citizens were killed before it was finally evacuated. Conservatively speaking, well over a hundred thousand human beings died or suffered wounds in the brief time and space that bounded the offensive.

My memoir is that of a foot soldier groping through this hurly-burly. Its scope is the few hundred yards' front of the 2nd Battalion, 116th Regiment (the Stonewall Brigade), 29th Infantry Division. I was aware of other mighty blows being exchanged across Normandy; but being fully occupied with my own microcosm of Armageddon, I paid them little heed.

A memoir is a public appearance, and one is inclined to stand straighter and present the best profile. Mitigating this tendency, there are no deeds of personal daring to relate, and no action of mine affected the battle one way or the other. This is personally regrettable, but it also lessens the self-consciousness of narrating in the first person. I was there; I endured, and not so well as some, also regrettable. Otherwise, I was a bookishly inclined amateur soldier with some ability at dissembling the uncertainty and irritability that the war inspired. At the battle's start I was a captain commanding the 2nd Battalion's headquarters company and battalion adjutant; during its course I became battalion executive officer and a major.

My account is not thirty years of faded memories and afterthoughts. It was originally written directly after the war, when the sights, sounds, and smells of St. Lô were sharp and clear. My aim then was a history of the battle through the 2nd Battalion's story. The result was predictably far short of the mark; I found that the great ebb and flow of St. Lô cannot be encompassed by one of its parts. Disappointed, I set it aside.

Now there is the delayed second thought that while a battalion affords a limited view of field armies locked in battle, it is unequalled for observing those who fought it personally and directly. The soldiers of the 2nd Battalion were assembled through largely random selection to perform the irrational acts of war. We were fairly representative of all battalions similarly assembled in this offensive.

As a generation we inherited a world that had blown itself up in the great war of a quarter century before. We had come of age in the vast uncertainties of the Great Depression, and we had a largely bankrupt legacy from the great illusion that America could do all to make the world right. As soldiers we were overwhelmingly amateur. We had neither revolutionary fervor nor the greed of empire building to obscure the insanity of killing and destruction to which we were put. We accepted beyond question, however, that the threat to our country's existence was real and had to be defeated; the challenge of Pearl Harbor was unqualified. No soldier I knew was even remotely interested in dying in the process; that so many went directly into death's way as duty is a measure of the generation.

The result, I believe, was an army remarkably homogeneous in viewpoint and purpose, though wide personal and group differences existed. (In a segregated army, for example, I was unaware of the vast dissatisfaction swelling among black soldiers.) This combination of shaping factors is not likely to reappear; the army they produced is gone so completely that I must look and look again to convince myself that it ever existed. In my more somber moments I think that we may have been the last great army of the Republic—one that could truly march to "The Battle Hymn of the Republic." This is the sketchy canvas on which my memoir is superimposed. It is largely as written so long ago. Violence distorts perception, and some sights I recount may be larger than life, and others of more significance may have been missed altogether. Memories must reflect such distortions, but on the whole I believe mine to be within the scope of what really happened during the battle for St. Lô.

An infantry battalion is a closely knit little world, and recollections of it must be heavily peopled, which poses the question of who among them should be summoned by name. There is much room for error here, and as names do not particularly serve my purpose, I shall call from the shadows only one—Tom Howie, dead near the end of the battle. For quiet and enduring reasons to be recounted in turn, the twilight of St. Lô has lingered longest on him of the entire Stonewall Brigade, and under his name I gather us all. He became the nation's symbol—the "Major of St. Lô."

The XIX Corps of three infantry divisions and on occasion an armored division did battle directly for St. Lô, but for the battalion soldier a corps was a remote "they" with which he was unlikely to have contact. Not so my division. The 29th was a strong and present personality that, on the basis of its combat record, was of uncommon military merit. It was mustered for the war in 1941 and had three years of training before being committed to battle on D-day on Omaha Beach. Of its three regiments the 115th and 175th were of the Maryland National Guard, and the 116th from Virginia. All three are of long lineage; the 116th's goes back to the French and Indian War, but its proudest days were those in the years 1861–65. It entered that war as the 2nd Virginia of General Thomas J. Jackson's brigade at the First Battle of Manassas, and both Jackson and the brigade emerged with the title "Stonewall."

A regiment, no less than an individual, is not inclined to forswear a resounding title won by an ancestor even if he fought on the "wrong" side. In 1944 the 116th's ranks held as many Yankees as Virginians, but the Stonewall Brigade we were, and to those of a historical bent this was a proud and notable thing.

On D-day the 116th had led the assault on the right sector of Omaha Beach and within a few hours lost some thousand killed or wounded. This was about one fourth of its strength and an even greater proportion of the riflemen who carried the burden of its battles. At the time this memoir begins, six days later, these losses had not been replaced, and attrition had continued, yet the regiment remained in action. Old Stonewall would probably have regarded this as no more than performance of duty. Most of us, I think, felt that others should take over the war for a while.

With this perhaps excessive amount of prior circumstance, I come down to late afternoon of June 12 and a dusty road near the gray huddle of houses of the hamlet Ste. Marguerite d'Elle. It was here that I first heard St. Lô designated as another appointed place on the Stonewall Brigade's long road of war. At the time, I and others of the battalion command post were strung out along a roadside ditch while the rifle companies, a hundred or so yards ahead, contended for a passage over the Elle River. Black smoke showed above the trees to our left front from two tanks that had been knocked out trying to cross the river.

The ditch took the menace from the bullets that cracked occasionally overhead, and I dare say my heroes and I would have been content to sit out that hot, humid afternoon of the war there. I was successfully coping with an urge of conscience to go up and see if the battalion commander had any overlooked need of our devoted efforts when the divisional chief of staff, a colonel, appeared striding toward us. Since it was obviously improper to remain in the ditch and exchange "good afternoons," I clambered onto the road and reported our identity. My lads, with a fine grasp of protocol, simply stood up in a ditch and looked vague.

The colonel, a big, square man, acknowledged my report and, looking us over thoughtfully, began a quiet talk on combat. He described a fire fight and how becoming intent on winning it made it something like a ball game. We listened respectfully, but since we had been under fire for the past six days, I doubt that he convinced anyone that this was a sporting event or obscured its terminal probabilities.

He got more attention by saying that our objective was St. Lô and that after it was taken, the division might well get a real rest, a possibility more important to us than what taking the town would do for the crusade in Europe.

The colonel wished us luck, which we returned, and continued down the road. Inspired by his presence if not by his words, we gathered map boards and field phone to move closer to the battle. Directly afterward the latest commander of E Company—the third since D-day—limped by toward the rear, one arm hanging loosely, bright red drops dribbling slowly from the fingers onto the dusty road. We had served together for two years, but I didn't stop to inquire about his injury; death and hurt had become commonplace, and a wound with which one could with honor walk out of the war was a matter for congratulations rather than condolence.

We set up shop behind a hedgerow closer to the racket, one result of which was the shattered leg of the intelligence officer, a young lawyer from Louisiana who had performed bravely and well. In addition, the brief action cost two platoon leaders and, as always, a number of riflemen.

As the long evening of double daylight-saving time waned the Germans pulled out, and the 2nd Battalion splashed across the knee-deep, narrow river and headed across country for its objective, the village of St. Clair-sur-l'Elle, about a half mile away. Unknown to us, a German column was pulling back on a parallel route and just outside the village sideswiped our right flank company. There was a brief exchange of fire, and the two columns pulled apart, the effect on the war being a few more killed and wounded.

With daylight the battalion perimeter was pushed south of the empty village, its citizens having learned that bombs and artillery fire were the going price of liberation. The command post was set up in a vacant house, and here we stayed for several days, both sides remaining relatively quiet and killing very few of each other.

Our wounded, however, included the battalion executive officer, and as the senior surviving captain I took his place. It was an advancement about which I could have few illusions, for it had become apparent that the principal requirement was simply to stay alive and in reasonable mental health.

Other events of the stay at St. Clair were a visit by the divisional commander, a major general, and the arrival of the first replacements. The general came one afternoon by jeep, expected to the extent that he could be expected at any time or place. He was about fifty years old and conformed to General Sheridan's specifications for a cavalryman, which he had been before the war: short, wiry, daring, and quick. Everything about him was explosive: gestures, speech, action, temper. He dominated the 29th by knowing exactly what he wanted done, discarding those who didn't produce it and rewarding those who did. As with other success formulas, the trick to this one lay in its application. He tolerated only the facts of a situation, and to present him with a conjecture was fatal to a future in the division.

His rough side was reserved for commanders, and strenuous efforts were made to avoid it. His orders were simple and direct. They included the requirement that every man be able to recite verbatim a simple statement of correct sight alignment and trigger squeeze. The 29th's tradition of wearing the helmet strap buckled under the chin rather than dangling, as was the general practice, was not to be violated under any circumstance. There were many others, unremarkable except in their total enforcement.

The general's first impression of a commander was apt to be final. Fortunately my company was in the midst of one of its better days when he first came upon us during training, and I purposely avoided later exposure whenever possible. I admired and respected—as well as avoided —him, for he sound a clear and certain trumpet in baffling and fearsome situations. It is my unsupported opinion that the number of divisional commanders of this caliber that the nation can muster in a given war is fewer than the divisions that can be mustered. The combination of courage, professional ability, imagination, and ruthlessness found in these few is rare enough to make them beyond price in war. As a matter of fact, the same applies to the exceptional enlisted infantryman, who, on a relative basis, is just as rare a bird and suffers an incomparably higher casualty rate.

In any case, this divisional commander arrived with his usual pronounced impact at our command post on a damp afternoon in mid-June. Those who had not gotten away in time stood in attentive attitudes around the stained walls of the musty parlor while he and the battalion commander sat and conversed in front of the empty hearth. I do not recall exact words, but the general indicated approval of our efforts, which was gratifying if the cost of achieving it was not considered.

That night the new adjutant and I met the trucks bringing in the first replacements and hurried the dark shapes laden with packs and weapons behind guides to their companies. We had been clamoring for men, so I was surprised at a vague sense of regret as I saw them march toward the front. Their efforts to keep their places and reach a harm beyond their conception were somehow pathetic. I felt an ancient among children, knowing and dreading what they had to endure.

The way of the replacement foot soldier in that war was hard, crowded, and dull: training camp, troopship, overseas replacement depot; then, probably leaving any friends acquired along the way, by truck and foot to join strangers in facing death or great injury. On occasion he never completed the journey. I recall the sad, brief saga of a column of replacements caught by artillery fire while toiling to the front at St. Lô, and for some ten of them this proved the end of the war.

On occasion new men were fed into units actively locked in battle. They were sent in at night and placed in among dark shapes that occupied gravelike holes scooped out behind hedgerows. The resident shapes, if they spoke at all, did not slight the dreadfulness of the situation or overestimate anyone's chances of surviving it. Sometimes a new man did die before dawn, and none around knew him by sight or name. The replacement system improved as the war wore on, but I think it remained essentially a wasteful distribution of numbers, disregarding the fact that it was dealing with the human heart.

While speaking of the emotional nature of battle one has to consider fear. I have firsthand knowledge only of my own, its chief manifestation being the stomach drawing into a cold, protective knot at the sound of shells whooping and screaming in my direction and a reluctance to leave depressions in the ground. I like to believe that I dissembled these tendencies very well; however, I knew fear intimately and believe this was a fairly general experience. When I speak of courage, I speak not of the absence of fear but of the disregard of it.

There was, come to think of it, another visit while we were at St. Clair, brief but offering a lesson to heed. I was standing in front of the command post at the time, and a jeep roared by headed for the front, a staff officer beside the driver waving as it passed. I was annoyed by the dust and noise and amazed that anyone should close with disaster with such apparent abandon. The jeep, disappearing down the road—its route traced by rising dust—halted simultaneously with a burst of machine-pistol fire just where we figured the German roadblock lay. Later I asked the Stonewallers covering the road why they hadn't stopped him. The arrival, they said, had been too sudden. One added that he didn't see why someone from the rear (as opposed to infantrymen) shouldn't have an opportunity to pinpoint roadblocks for a change.

Early on June 16 we were relieved at St. Clair and struck southwest through close, wooded terrain for St. Lô, only to be brought to a bloody halt near the hamlet of Villiers Fossard. The discovery that this was a key German position cost a staff officer and thirty-four men. The officer died literally over my head. He was in the attic of a cottage, looking out over the terrain, and I was on the ground floor, trying to locate our position on a mud-smudged map, when a sudden blast of rifle fire smacked into the cottage, and three riflemen dashed in announcing that they had shot a German directly above me. At the same moment blood began to drip through the ceiling, and in the attic we found the lifeless body. The riflemen left with stark faces, and I went to tell the battalion commander that we had lost the second operations officer since D-day.

The fight flared with noise and smoke at intervals all afternoon. I returned to the command post at dark just as a tank, sent to support our efforts, clanked up and its commander asked, in a weary Ivy League accent, in which direction he should traverse his gun. I advised him that it was more important to cut his motor before he ran over the dark bundles of headquarters men sleeping along the track whom nothing short of the Last Trumpet could rouse. As the battlefield settled into its strange nighttime mutter we all slumbered around the steel war-cart.

The next day the battalion clawed again at Villiers Fossard and lost another officer and thirty-five men, including two first sergeants. Clearly this place was not going to fall to a lone infantry battalion; a combined infantry, armor, and air attack was later required to crack it.

Early on the eighteenth the regimental commander arrived with word that we were to shift, that day, to the left flank of the division's sector in a general realignment for the push on St. Lô. Our new position lay a little over a mile south of the village of Couvains and was astride an unpaved north-south road that, at its firmly held German end, intersected the main Bayeux-St. Lô artery, one of the principal stretches of macadam for which the battle was fought. Our march to it began that humid evening, and it was in the cold damp of early morning that the companies were deployed along the new line.

There was much starting and stopping. At one halt I sat down on what I thought was a boulder, but I found it soft and yielding, the flank of a dead hog or calf. Weary, I walked on without investigating. Toward the end I became so vocal about the operation that the battalion commander suggested that I do my job and complain less, and we would all benefit. I was immediately ashamed, and am now, at adding to burdens heavier than my own.

This commander is prominent among the shadowy figures I write about. He was one of the two professional soldiers in battalion. Usually he was relaxed and easy to serve, though minor irritations could trigger an explosion. That the battalion held together through D-day and afterward was due to his courage and energy. He was wounded after St. Lô; I fell heir to command and followed his pattern to the best of my ability. He returned to command the regiment, and after the war he was one of the organizers of Special Forces.

Finally that night the rifle companies got into position, and the command post settled down along the road. An hour or so later we were up shivering in a soggy dawn to take stock of the place and the prospects for further survival. The date was June 19, and here we were to stay until July 11, either on line or in reserve, while XIX Corps gathered for the battle.

Any position that the German allows you to occupy without a fight is unlikely to be a bargain. This one was no exception. The lifting ground mist showed us deployed along an east-west elevation that was dominated by a parallel ridgeline to the south at about fifteen hundred yards' distance. This higher ridge was called Martinville after the hamlet on its crest; its western end sloped off into the outskirts of St. Lô. The enemy held Martinville Ridge and a line well forward of it up against our own positions. To take St. Lô, Martinville Ridge had to be taken first.

During the three weeks we stayed there I had time to note that the two ridges corresponded in relative elevation and separation to Seminary and Cemetery ridges at Gettysburg at the point of the grand assault in the center. This was not a comforting comparison for a Virginia regiment, so I didn't mention it. Martinville Ridge also culminated in a hill on its German-held right, similar to Culp's Hill, where the Stonewall Brigade had fought; it was called "192" after its meter elevation. To strain the comparison still further, St. Lô had its Roundtop, Hill 122 on the left flank of the German defenses. South of Martinville Ridge was another elevation, along which ran the Bayeux-St. Lô road; south of that was still another parallel ridge.

Hill 192, looming to our left front, was in the area of the V Corps' 2nd Infantry Division, which took it on the first day of the July 11 attack. I visited its crest after the battle and was amazed that with field glasses I could look directly into some of the fieldworks we had occupied. Why the Germans didn't use this advantage to swat us like flies on a table is a mystery.

Our first day was spent in realigning the positions that had been taken in the darkness and weariness of the night before. The command post was dug into the side of a deep depression in a field alongside the road. Covered with a camouflage net, this served very well, though the first hard rain showed that its original purpose was as a sump to drain the field.

Across the road to our left were the mortar pits of the Heavy Weapons Company, and the sharp whang of its firing was fairly constant until the late June storms damaged the artificial harbors on the invasion beaches and curtailed the ammunition supply. The reserve rifle company was also deployed along the left to cover the open flank between us and the 2nd Division. A hundred or so yards or so to the front, the war was fought moment by moment by the other two rifle companies. Their lines ran along a sunken farm lane until it wandered off toward Martinville Ridge, and then the positions took to the fields. The battalion's eight heavy machine guns were posted at critical points, and our 57-mm. anti-tank guns were sited on a slope to the right of the command post covering the road.

The terrain setting was completed by hedgerow-enclosed apple orchards and pastures. Even more than the ridgelines and streams, these centuries-old hedgerows dominated the war in Normandy. They have often been described: earthen banks four to six feet high, topped with trees and brush, needing only the addition of men and guns to become a ready-made fortified place. The Germans accomplished this with consummate skill.

The orchards bore small, tasteless apples for making cider and its dissolute cousin, the potent applejack Calvados. Much of the battle was fought under the apple under the apple trees, and the natural obscenity of the scene could have been greater only if it had been blossom time.

War had touched this fair and fruitful countryside before we moved in and had left two of its modern mementos in the from of a crashed British bomber and a wrecked German armored car. More traditional mementos were a number of the huge black-and-white Norman cattle lying in bloated final repose in the fields, contributing the chemistry of their decay to the already heavy atmosphere. After digging itself underground the battalion buried the dead cattle and performed the amazing amount of personal hygiene, including shaving, that a man can accomplish with a helmet of water. Memory is apt to idealize such points, but as I recall it, no matter how dreadful the day he faced, the Stonewaller shaved; whatever the state of his uniform, it was worn correctly; and his weapon was kept clean.

Even directly after the war I had trouble ordering the events of the three weeks preceding the July 11 attack. Individual scenes were vivid but tended to tumble together without sequence, as in a troubled dream. One persistent memory then and now is of a bone-sagging weariness, possibly a result of long-standing strain or of feeling that on the basis of having to fight for every hedgerow, the war would go on forever. Whatever the causes, it seemed to affect us all—I noted young men around me take on the look and movements of middle age. This physical weariness was accompanied by unrest that made sleep fitful. The effect was that of a motor racing to move a sluggish machine or of trying to run in a nightmare with much effort and little progress.

Also affected was my boasted ability to maintain outward emotional control. One afternoon a military policeman returned two soldiers who had hidden out on the transport on D-Day to avoid Omaha Beach. The loss of friends on that day had now come truly home, and sight of these two, who had skulked while their betters were being killed, triggered a great anger. They were short, scruffy men, obviously not cast in anything of a heroic mold, but I became excessively the Stonewall Brigade major in describing their moral deficiencies and expressed regret that they had not been shot. I terminated by asking if they had anything to say for themselves. Yes, said one, they would like a transfer. Spluttering, I waved them out of the command post. It would be gratifying to report that they went on to redemption through soldierly deeds. The truth is, I don't know their fate but suspect they found their way out of the battle, as everyone who wanted it badly enough seemed able to do at some time or other.

The high points of hazard during this period were combat patrols, artillery fire that crashed into treetops and hedgerows, and mortar rounds that showered steel fragments for yards around. The combat patrols, led by lieutenants until expended and then by sergeants, reduced drastically the life expectancy of all who took part. The patrols did little more than demonstrate the aggressive posture desired by "them" and proved that the German outposts were still no more than a hedgerow or so beyond our lines, which we knew in any event.

The mortars distributed their summonses throughout the battalion area and were particularly dreaded because the shells approached with a whisper in contrast to the warning banshee scream of incoming artillery fire. I recall one remarkably fine day coming upon the body of a young runner, slightly built and looking in death like a small boy tired of playing war and asleep in the meadow, face serene and fair hair stirring in the breeze. Nearby was the fin of a mortar round in a black rupture in the sod. The two-wheeled death cart came, pulled by its two attendants, who took him away. Thus casually did death arrive and a life depart—though that is not quite accurate: death did not have to arrive; it never left us.

The battalion executive officer is important primarily through being next in line for command, but in the meantime his duties are comparatively light. I took advantage of this during the static period at St. Lô to travel to the rear on missions whose principal purpose was to breathe the safer air out of artillery range. One trip was to a field hospital to have some metal fragments, acquired on D-day, removed from my face. The wound was more spectacular than serious, and I had upgraded it by maintaining that the metal deflected a compass held to the eye for sighting. In truth, I never had occasion to make such a sighting.

Returning, I stopped to see a friend commanding the corps replacement depot. He was a topflight soldier whose family had long been connected with the regiment. Now he told me that his only son, a paratrooper, had been killed on the D-day drop. He said staunchly that his son's unit had accomplished its mission, but his eyes were not staunch. the depot was filling with replacements for the St. Lô attack. From a distance they also looked staunch and well turned out. Up close I noted that they were already acquiring the intent frown of the front line. The nameless regret I had felt on seeing the new men arrive at St. Clair returned; these also seemed too young and innocent to pit against veteran German paratroopers.

Another remembered scene was on a Sunday. I was en route by jeep to the regimental command post and near the village of Couvains encountered a procession of young girls in white dresses, accompanied by their elders in Sunday black, headed for an ancient gray stone Norman church. My driver stopped to avoid dusting the procession, and a detail stringing telephone lines along the road ceased work to gape. Just at that moment a stretcher jeep from the front crept by with its bandaged, broken load. Here were all the elements of a contrived scene of a war movie, but this one was real, and its screaming incongruity etched it on my memory.

Romance did not surface at St. Lô. No girl of the French Resistance appeared to guide us by a secret route into the city. Our only connection with love was by letter, and this was avidly pursued. I thought we wrote more than we received, but this impression may have been gained from the disagreeable duty of officers to censor letters for mention of where we were and what we were doing.

Censorship in World War II must have made its soldiers' letters about the dullest on record. Some showed a knack for pornography, but the only letters I recall distinctly were those of a quiet older soldier to his wife about the home they planned to build after the war. Letter after letter went into every detail, and I gathered that most of his soldier pay and of her war-factory wages were being saved toward it. He was, of course, killed.

From this one, and others I knew of, I would judge that the dreams per capita at St. Lô were numerous. Undoubtedly many were of gossamer, but at the time they all seemed possible, for this war was the Last Judgment on an old, wrong world and the genesis of a new, better one. In the event, the good and bad parts seem to have maintained about their usual ratio, and I fear that the mortality rate of dreams at St. Lô has been high.

A s time wore on, plans for the assault were refined and resources gathered. The battalions were rotated between the front and reserve area where, in company with engineers and tanks, the tactics for attacking hedgerows were practiced. The attack was finally set for July 11. The XIX Corps designated the 29th Division to make the main effort; the 29th decided to lead with its left flank regiment, the Stonewall Brigade. The attack was to be in a column of battalions with the 2nd leading. We were to strike astride the Couvains road to the crest of Martinville Ridge, then wheel right, or west, down a farm road that ran along its crest toward St. Lô. Simultaneously, on our left, the 2nd Infantry Division was to go for Hill 192, and upon its success depended much of what we would be able to do.

As when we had been designated for the Omaha Beach assault, the news of this St. Lô assignment had a stimulating effect: it represented distinction among our peers, one to be observed with pride. Preparations were stepped up: replacements brought the battalion up to about 75 percent of strength; rehearsal of hedgerow tactics was intensified; artillery and mortar concentrations were plotted for every possible target. The memory that even greater preparations for D-day had not prevented near disaster was still fresh, but planning acquires its own momentum, and once again we became confident of walking over a pulverized enemy.

Crowning this confidence was a massive air raid that thundered out of a clear sky late one afternoon, about a week before the attack, to dump streams of black specks on and around the town. The specks translated into a constant rolling thunder. Everyone watched as the majestic trains of bombers, railing white contrails like cloaks, crisscrossed the target. To the soldier fighting in the dust and mud this seemed a safe and clean way to wage war until smudges of antiaircraft fire blossomed among the formations, sullying the white-on-blue patterns of contrails and sky. First one, then another, then still others of the caravans merged with the black smudges and tumbled toward earth. Still, it was all so far removed from the war we knew that I had trouble realizing that men were being burned and broken in those far-off machines. The thunder and concussion of the bombs were more familiar, and the knowledge that the enemy was caught in them gave a macabre lift to the spirits.

Altogether it was a recharged 2nd Battalion that made final preparations to jump off at 0600 hours. A forward command post was dug in behind the line of departure, which was the present front line; tanks were fitted with metal tusks to rip through hedgerows; five battalions of artillery were to lay down twenty minutes of preparatory fire before the jump-off and then lead the advancing force with a continuing barrage.

By dark on July 10 all plans were complete, all resources assembled. I was confident that a battle-proven battalion could not fail its task. German artillery had been more active than usual that day, but I gave it little thought. When I crawled into my slit trench under a hedgerow in the assembly area about midnight, my main concern was what the tanks might do to our new telephones lines laid along the ground, and I had the belated thought that the lines should have been strung overhead.

The sleep was brief, the awakening abrupt. For a source of early-morning nausea I give you an unexpected German barrage, crashing and quaking earth and air. My first resentful thought was "Where did they get all those guns?" The sound was that of ton after ton of brick being dropped from great heights, and I looked out from my hole expecting to see the assembly area erupting in fire and smoke. Instead, the tumult was all off to the right; the trees around us were carrying on their timeless dripping in the ground mist.

Regiment could tell us only that the 1st Battalion of the 115th, about a thousand yards to our right, was under attack. The artillery swelled, died, and swelled again. The lulls were filled by the tearing bursts of machine guns; tracer bullets streaked in crazy patterns across the sky.

This clangor continued at varying pitches for over three hours; except for an occasional shell our sector was never hit. Later we learned that the German attack had a local objective and was made in ignorance of our own effort. The 115th had a very bad night before containing and driving it off. Our loss was limited to the few hours of rest we might have had before what was certain to be a long stretch. Then, too, it was a sobering demonstration of the artillery the Germans could concentrate. It also cost us, indirectly, a rifle-company commander who came streaking into the command post about daylight, carrying a lightly wounded soldier on his back. This strongly built young lieutenant had been propelled by attrition to command and, I thought, had done very well. Now he insisted that he must carry the wounded man to the rear, and from his eyes it was clear that he would not command that day. We did not see him again.

Word came that the attack would go in as planned; and, bent as though under tremendous burdens, the files moved forward through the ground mist. All remained quiet until a rapid volley of thuds behind us announced the departure of the preparatory barrage. The shells sighed overhead to end their brief careers in noise, smoke, and flying fragments on the German positions.

From then on, salvo after salvo crashed along the front. The tanks moved up and, sure enough, tore up the telephone lines as they went. The ear-shattering blast of high-velocity tank guns and the beat of machine guns joined in until it seemed that noise alone would destroy everything.

Not so. At 0600 the artillery fire lifted to the German support positions, and the rifle companies starting forward were met by the blast of machine guns that had somehow survived the bombardment. The futility of charging machine guns had been proved often enough, so the slow process of erasing these guns began.

The telephone line to regiment was re-laid, and along it came incessant demands for reports. The lines up to the attack kept going out, and, to get away from questions to which I did not have answers, I went up to see the battalion commander, passing a swath of dead Stonewallers who had been caught by the machine guns as they topped the first hedgerow.

The attack had progressed only two or three fields. Marking its limit was the turret of a tank, and while I watched, a soldier climbed up behind it, apparently to see what lay ahead. As he raised up, a burst of fire swept the turret, knocking him backward as though jerked with a rope. A pall of smoke was over the fields, holding in it the sweet, sickening stench of high explosive, which we had come to associate with death. The green covering of Normandy was gouged by shells and tank tracks; blasted limbs hung from the trees. The attacking riflemen, visibly shrunk in numbers crouched behind the farthermost hedgerow while volumes of artillery, mortar, and tank gunfire flailed the fields beyond.

The battalion commander told me to keep up pressure on the heavy mortars, to maintain the fire on the ridge, and to tell regiment that the advance would continue when it damn well could. I walked back to the command post heavy with the thought this was Omaha Beach all over again in a different setting. German counterfire was hitting in considerable volume onto some empty fields to my right, and I judged that our own efforts must be just about as effective.

I had, however, misread the battle. Soon came the message that the battalion had broken in to a sunken lane that was the anchor of the German position. Part of the cost also appeared: two badly wounded company commanders. One was a firebrand lieutenant of the type that made the gray-clad 1860's brigade a terror in battle, the other a captain who had joined as a replacement. Of the four company commanders at the dawn's early light there now, at high noon, remained only one. Perhaps half of the platoon leaders and sergeants were casualties. The losses in riflemen were heavy but uncounted; the battalion commander was now leading all that remained.

Whatever we had suffered, the Germans had fared worse. Once past the sunken lane, their defense crumbled, and the attack moved rapidly up the ridge. The command post gathered map boards and radios and, trailing telephone wire like an umbilical cord, moved after it, passing through the area of the battalion's suffering and into that of the Germans'.

Advancing into territory denied you by an enemy is like setting foot on an unexplored shore; you look around, wondering at the evidence of a strange and hostile people. In the lane and beyond, all was devastation, blasted and burned. German paratroopers, whole and in parts, lay about, difficult to reconcile, in their round helmets and blood-soaked camouflage smocks, with what had a short time before been among the most dangerous fighting men of the war.

A long-barreled assault gun on its low-slung armored chassis that had taken a heavy toll along our front was blackened and smoking. The battalion commander's orderly was nearby as we paused in the shambles of inert flesh and shattered equipment. He remarked in puzzled sadness, more to himself than to anyone around, "I don't understand it. I just don't understand what it is all about." His words must have echoed those on many a battlefield and in many a language; there could be no elation in a sight so brutal and pitiful.

We went on in the wake of the destructive force that had swept up the ridge and to the road that ran down its spine westward. The rifle companies had made their sharp right turn astride this road and in doing so exposed their flank to the two German-held parallel ridges to the south. Evidence of what this was going to mean was near the turn in the form of stinking shell craters and more dead.

Shortly after making the turn we halted to let the crews toiling under heavy reels of telephone wire catch up. While we were so disposed a tall young lieutenant in a clean uniform and the then highly sought combat boots (we still wore leggings) strode by; he was obviously a general's aide from some remote "they" area. Someone behind me muttered that there went another bastard to collect his medal. I don't know that this was his mission, but it was not uncommon for "them" to make a quick visit to the front and be decorated for "voluntary exposure to enemy fire." Medals can be acquired in ways that are passing strange. The nation recognized the majority of the dead and wounded with Purple Hearts for their hurts and with the Combat Infantryman Badge; in a post war spasm of conscience the Bronze Star went on application to holders of the combat badge. Measured against this, I take a jaundiced view of claims of valor for fleeting visits to the front on the basis of a job that did not require exposure. That in war some should be subject constantly to death and dismemberment while others should not be—and should be rewarded if they are momentarily—is as hypocritical a form of segregation as exists.

In any event, the command post continued on down the ridge road to where the rifle companies had come up against exhaustion and a German stand, still about two miles short of St. Lô. As the long evening darkened, the command post was dug in alongside a stone wall next to the road, and here we remained for nine days as the battle reached a peak of dull red fury.

During the night the Germans dug in their new line. The next day, July 12, we made little progress. The 1st Battalion, committed in the deep draw to our left, had much the same experience, as did the 3rd Battalion attacking south against the Bayeux road ridge. On the third day the 175th Regiment attacked through our 1st and 3rd Battalions and made small gains at heavy cost.

The 2nd Battalion went nowhere at all on this third day, and it was evident that its bolt had been shot; it could only stand and bleed. Familiar enough by then with the results of men discharging projectiles at one another at close range, I was still aghast at the rate at which the corpse carts and stretcher jeeps were trundling away the Stonewall Brigade. The 2nd Battalion had started the attack at 75 percent of its full complement of about nine hundred officers and men. By the end of that first day we were well below half strength, and by the end of the third day less than one third of the battalion remained. As always, over 90 percent of these losses were riflemen. Instead of three rifle companies, we barely mustered the equivalent of one; heavy-machine-gunners suffered to a like degree.

Again the German losses were heavier. Their 3rd Parachute Division, which fought so nearly to the death, lost 4,064 men in three days. Their 352nd Infantry Division, perhaps not so do-or-die, recorded 984 casualties in two days.

On the third evening, July 13, the 2nd Battalion went back for rest and refit near St André-de-l'Épine. The kitchens sent up hot rations, and replacements arrived to bring us back to just over 50 percent strength. However, some of the replacements were patched-up wounded from D-day, and while perhaps restored physically, they were not emotionally up to rejoining the battle.

The divisional commander visited the bivouac area that evening and spoke to representatives from each company in his staccato fashion about how well we had done. Faces lit up a bit, but I don't know if it was because of the praise or because the general repeated that after taking St. Lô the division would get a real rest. We had been depending on this for some time, but it was good to hear it from this man.

Somewhat restored, the battalion trudged back up to its old position on the ridge on July 15. That afternoon word came down that we and the 1st Battalion, on our left, were to try before dark to break through. The way was to be prepared by thirteen battalions of artillery and a fighter-bomber strike, nearly three times the firepower of the first day of the assault. As with any prolonged battle, St. Lô proved a magnet attracting more metal from both sides.

Whether it was the tremendous weight of metal crashing down upon a narrow front or German command confusion, I do not know, but the attack broke through, and the companies took off in full career with an élan to which even Old Stonewall would have had to raise his cap. A squad or so of the reserve rifle company, the command post, and heavy mortars were en route to follow when word came down to halt. The effect was that of throwing a hard-running machine abruptly into reverse; we of the rear end skidded to a stop, while the front end broke loose and kept going right down to the crossroads hamlet of La Madeleine, less than a mile from St. Lô. The battalion commander took off on the run to catch them. Later we learned that the halt order stemmed from "their" not knowing or else being unable to credit our success.

Uncertainty took over while command and staff wheels ground out the decision not to withdraw from La Madeleine but for the rest of the Stonewall Brigade to fight on down and join them. In the meantime German command wheels must also have been grinding, for the gap was rapidly closed and the bulk of the 2nd Battalion was cut off.

Over the next two days the advance, won at so little cost, became progressively more ominous. The Stonewall Brigade was in poor posture to strike effectively; instead of a clenched fist, it now had a weak finger stuck over a mile deep into hostile territory. Halfway back, well out of supporting range, was the 1st Battalion, which had been halted intact; back on the original position were the 3rd Battalion, which had been badly mauled that morning, and the remnant of the 2nd Battalion.

Compounding their hazard, the companies at La Madeleine had only the ammunition and rations that individuals had carried with them. Communication was by the artillery-liaison officer's radio, and its batteries faded more with each transmission.

Still impressed, however, by the day's success, I was confident that we could push on through the next morning. I knew my outfit, and with its commander there I would bet on its being able to survive one night anywhere.

Events didn't turn out exactly that way. The next day, July 16, instead of attacking toward La Madeleine, the 1st Battalion had to fight for its life. Its right flank company along the ridge road was blasted by a tank at pointblank range and was reduced within minutes to less than platoon size. We were caught in this hurricane of fire and noise that swept back and forth across the narrow front, hour after hour.

Late that afternoon, as the fury abated, I reached my personal depth of the war, and it has remained with me as only the ultimate depth, and height, of one's life can remain. I was alone at the time outside the now useless command post. The sun, setting behind St. Lô, glowing a dull, furious red through the smoke and dust raised by the shelling. Tall trees cast long black shadows; on the road was a smashed jeep with the flayed remains of the driver fallen half out of it. In the next field a dump of mortar ammunition burned and flared. Here the shelling had stopped, but in the distance it still rumbled like far-off summer thunder.

The scene was *Götterdämmerung*, and effect opera-set designers strive for but can never equal. A Teutonic heart might have found it stirring grandeur. But not mine, not then. For suddenly I was convinced that my battalion was gone, irrevocably lost, destroyed. If the Germans could threaten to overrun this well-supplied position, what chance of survival had the undermanned and undersupplied companies isolated in their midst? And if the battalion that had been the boundaries of my life for three years was gone, what chance had I? At that point I was despairing of the war and uncaring of its purpose.

After dark I was called to the regimental command post with the staffs of the battalions to meet with the divisional commander. The dimly lit bunker was crowded and the air oppressive. The general reviewed the situation; he said that the 2nd Battalion had survived the day without serious trouble and that the attack to relieve it and take St. Lô would go on. He then delivered a harsh judgment on defeatism, racking a hapless captain who had expressed discouragement. He did not know that in the back of the bunker stood perhaps the most despairing major on the Normandy front.

Usually this dynamic man's statement of purpose and direction lifted my spirits. But not that night; I could not believe that the 2nd had survived such a day inside the German lines, or, perhaps to justify my own funk, I didn't choose to believe it.

The regimental commander, who had just taken over the job, assured the general that we were full of fight, and the session was over.

I stumbled back through the dark to arrive at our position just as a heavy shelling filled the night again with noise and concussion. My usually highly active sense of self-preservation was not functioning, for instead of diving into the nearest hole, I wandered aimlessly around, ears ringing from a nearby tree burst whose shower of fragments somehow missed me. My route passed the slit trench of a sergeant who had been in the first platoon of which I had taken uncertain command. He called a warning, and when I continued on, he jumped out and dumped me into the nearest hole and demanded that I stay there. So I did, and recall little of the rest of the night.

The battalion surgeon appeared at daylight to inquire about the situation but showed more interest in what he said was my loss of hearing and suggested that I go back to the division's medical clearing station for a check. What was left of the 2nd Battalion had been attached to the 1st, leaving me particularly useless, and I made no objection. At the clearing station I was given a blue capsule and sent to a nearby tent area. The capsule, reputedly capable of stupefying an elephant, was known popularly as the blue-88, in tribute to the Germans' dreaded 88-mm. gun. I barely made it to the tent and a blanket on the ground before falling off of a high place into a deep, vacant sleep.

Eight or ten hours later I climbed reluctantly back to awareness and found the tent had been removed while I slept. Nearby was line of hapless-looking soldiers carrying mess gear, though there was no kitchen in sight. While I was trying to sort all this out a lightly built, sandy-haired lieutenant came up and pointed shakily to a bombed-out railway station barely visible in the distance. This place, he said, was too close to that target and ought to be moved. Obviously he was at one with the dejected-looking soldiers seeking comfort in the familiar ritual of standing in a mess line—even one that offered no food.

It came to me then, with a jolt, that this was the trampled field of the defeated in spirit—the division's way station for the emotional wreckage of the battle, called combat-fatigue cases. Here was determined those salvageable for further war and those to be discarded into the teeming rear areas.

No *Götterdämmerung* this—no twilight of the gods full of the grandeur of noble death. This was a place of whimper and cringe, the skid row of the battle zone. I had heard of it, and my offhand judgment had been that it was a mistake to so cater to weakness, finding myself there brought on a panic akin, I imagine, to that of a minister who has walked inadvertently into a brothel. Now I can see that field as a true note in the awful clanging harmony of St. Lô. The abject spirits were counterpoint to those enduring on Martinville Ridge; their weakness accented strength as death accents life.

The answer to my shame at having slept through my battalion's agony at such a place was to flag down a ride back to the ridge. Leaving physically was a matter of minutes, but emotionally that place remains with me; I must always wonder how truly I belonged there.

Back on the ridge the battle was in a perceptibly lower key. Where salvos of shells had been crashing in, there were now only random rounds. I found my people still in place. No one mentioned my absence, and I didn't bring it up.

There was much news. That morning a 3rd Battalion attack had reached La Madeleine and found the 2nd in good shape, still unaccountably ignored by the surrounding Germans. The other news was that Major Thomas D. Howie, commanding the 3rd, had been killed shortly after reaching La Madeleine. I have said that he alone among the shadowy figures in this account is to be called forth by name, and this is because he combined to an uncommon degree the kindness and courage that would have better become us all. In mourning Tom Howie I mourn all for whom life and laughter ended at St. Lô and, by some projection, those for whom it has ended since.

The divisional commander who was imaginative as well as arbitrary and, I suspect, compassionate in his way, had the flag-draped body taken into St. Lô when it fell two days later and placed high on a bier of rubble in front of the town's shattered Notre Dame, thus fulfilling Tom Howie's vow as he launched the attack that he would reach the city. News stories and photographs followed, and Tom Howie became the Major of St. Lô—the nation's symbol of the battle. Many who grieved for the fallen soldier at the time may now have forgotten, and the new generations may never have heard of him at all, but the story stirred America to no small degree in that July of 1944. A dramatic tribute to the dead warrior rising above the murk of a long, ugly war caught the imagination and the heart. The Major of St. Lô inspired editorial tributes and one of the few poems of merit to come out of the war. There is now a memorial to Tom Howie in the rebuilt St. Lô and another at Staunton Military Academy, where he coached football before the war.

Ironically, the qualities that made his death mourned and marked did not serve him well in the hard climate in which we trained before D-day. In that prebattle period those who were most assertive and demanding by nature seemed to prosper most; those who were hard simply because the job demanded it had a degree of success; and those of a naturally kindly nature who underwent no war change had a difficult time.

When the caps began to pop on Omaha Beach, however, personal calm and courage took immediate precedence over all other leadership qualities, for these alone could cope with the supreme assertiveness of enemy bullets. It is my impression that these qualities surfaced fully as frequently among the kindly as among the harsh. They took Tom Howie to battalion command and to his final appointment at La Madeleine. In daring, unsparing demands upon himself and in thoughtfulness he resembled Turner Ashby, commander of Stonewall's cavalry in the halcyon days of the valley campaign of 1862. Stonewall was harsh in his judgment of Ashby's failure to push his troopers; but he wept, and the South wept, when Ashby was killed, as of course he was, the nature of such soldiers making death in battle almost inevitable.

Through knowing Tom Howie I feel I know Ashby and the gallant-hearted and selfless in every army in every war. They do not finally win the wars; those who are arbitrary and demanding do that. But the Howies and Ashbys add a note of grace to a generally brutish scene, and for this they are loved and remembered.

The Germans could, perhaps, not notice the fragmented 2nd Battalion at La Madeleine, but the arrival of the 3rd was large enough to attract deadly attention. The mortar round that killed Tom Howie was followed by a day of heavy shelling and attack; the last one, late in the day, was broken up by a a spectacular concentration of our artillery fire and by fighter-bomber strikes. Even so, the day's end found both battalions low on ammunition and with many dead and wounded.

Now, however, the tragedy of St. Lô was moving rapidly to its close. For this final act the devastated town was the stage, with XIX Corps divisions gathered above it on the hills to the north and east. On the afternoon of the eighteenth a 29th Task Force broke into the ruins and raised the division's flag. At about the same time, the Stonewall Brigade opened a supply corridor to La Madeleine, and evacuation of wounded and dead was begun, Tom Howie's body being carried into St. Lô.

On July 20 the 29th's sector was taken over by the 35th Division, which had been heavily engaged on our right. As the 29th's units were relieved they began moving back to the promised land of corps reserve near St. Clair-sur-l'Elle, where this account started. The division had been in combat continuously for forty-five days at a price of over seven thousand casualties; in effect its nine rifle battalions had been used up about twice over.

Five days later Operation COBRA was launched with a massive aerial bombardment. The breakout from Normandy followed.

There remains a brief epilogue. The 2nd Battalion departed the battle by foot from La Madeleine to the ridge road. While waiting for it I took a last look around the now quiet field. The salvage crews were at work, and much of the wrecked equipment and weapons had been removed. But the deep wounds in the land were undressed and gave the appearance of verdant desolation. Every hedgerow was scalloped with holes, for no man had stopped without digging in. Practically every hedgerow had been fought for, plowed by shells, and gaped with raw passages for tanks. Whole trees were blasted down, and shattered limbs hung from others. The sickening smell of high explosive persisted.

While I looked and wondered at all this the battalion, in column of twos, commander leading, appeared toiling up the slope. The column was pitifully short; at first I thought that it was only one company and the other would follow. Then I realized that this was all there was, and the memory of it still dries the throat and stings the eyes.

I had seen the great, gray ships of the D-day armada stretching to the horizon in every direction, and I had often seen majestic fleets of Flying Fortress bombers returning from Germany. These were scenes awesome in power and portent. But for a sight to grasp and hold the heart forever I give you a decimated infantry battalion lurching out of battle, bowed with a mortal weariness and with all it has endured. This is not a drama of machines but of ordinary men who have achieved an extraordinary triumph over their fears and vulnerable flesh. For me all sights must pale beside it. I joined the commander and told him of arrangements for the bivouac. The column trudged on toward the Couvains road. Behind us the mists of onrushing time and events began to gather over St. Lô.

—June 1974

THE MAN WHO COULD SPEAK JAPANESE

By WILLIAM MANCHESTER

For sheer personal bravado in the face of staggering odds, Whitey's performance on the fantail of the U.S.S. Morton en route to Guadalcanal was a genuine epic of World War II

In the spring of 1944 the United States Marine Corps formed its last rifle regiment of World War II, the 29th Marines, in New River, North Carolina. The first of its three battalions was already overseas, having been built around ex-Raiders and parachutists who had fought on Guadalcanal, Tarawa, and Saipan. Great pains were being taken to make the other two battalions worthy of them. The troops assembling in New River were picked men. Officers and key noncoms had already been tested in battles against the enemy, and though few riflemen in the line companies had been under fire, they tended to be hulking, deep-voiced mesomorphs whose records suggested that they would perform well when they, too, hit the beach. There was, however, one small band of exceptions. These were the nineteen enlisted men comprising the intelligence section of the 29th's second battalion. All nineteen were Officer Candidate washouts. I, also a washout, led them. My rank was Corporal, acting Platoon Sergeant—Acting John.

We were, every one of us, military misfits, college students who in a fever of patriotism had rushed to the Marine Corps' Officer Candidate School at Quantico, Virginia, and had subsequently been rejected because, for various reasons, we did not conform with the established concept of how officers should look, speak, and act. Chet Przystawski of Colgate, for example, had a build like Charles Atlas but a voice like Lily Pons; when he yelled a command, the effect was that of an eerie shriek. Ace Livick of the University of Virginia had no sense of direction; at Quantico he had flunked map reading. Jerry Collins, a Yale man, was painfully shy. Stan Zoglin, a Cantab, had poor posture. Mack Yates of Ole Miss wore spectacles. Tom Jasper of Brown and I had been insubordinate. I had refused to clean a rifle on the ground that it was already clean, and I suffered the added stigma of being scrawny. I've forgotten the order Jasper disobeyed, though I knew that he too had another count against him: he admired the Japanese enormously.

Sy Ivice of Chicago christened us "the Raggedy-Ass Marines." That was about the size of it. Love had died between us and the Marine Corps. The rest of the battalion amiably addressed us as "Mac"—all enlisted Marines were "Mac" to their officers and to one another—but there was a widespread awareness that we were unsuitably bookish, slack on the drill field, and generally beneath the fastidious stateside standards established in the Corps' 169-year history. If there had been such a thing as a Military Quotient, the spit-and-polish equivalent of an Intelligence Quotient, our M.Q. would have been pegged at about 78. It is fair to add that this rating would have been confined to our parade-ground performance. We were regarded as good combat prospects. All of us, I believe, had qualified on the Parris Island, South Carolina, rifle range as Sharpshooters or Expert Riflemen. It was thought (and, as it proved, rightly so) that we would be useful in battle. Our problem, or rather the problem of our leaders, was that we lacked what the British army calls Quetta manners. We weren't properly starched and blancoed, weren't martially prepossessing—weren't, in a word, good for the 29th's image.

We were rarely given liberty, because our company commander was ashamed to let civilians see us wearing the corps uniform. Shirttails out, buttons missing, fore-and-aft (overseas) caps down around our ears—these were signs that we had lost our drill-field ardor in OCS and were playing our roles of incorrigible eccentrics to the hilt. We looked like caricatures from cartoons in the *The Leatherneck*, the Marine Corps equivalent of *Yank*, and the only reason our betters allowed us to stay together, setting a bad example to one another and damaging battalion élan, was a provision in the official Table of Organization for an intelligence section and our qualifications for membership in it. Between Quantico and assignment to the 29th we had all attended something called intelligence school. Theoretically we were experts in identifying enemy units by searching Jap corpses, recognizing the silhouettes of Zero fighters, reconnoitering behind the lines, etc. It was all rather vague. If we proved useless in these tasks, our commanders knew that we could always be used for odd jobs.

Meanwhile we carried out exhausting training exercises in the Carolina boondocks, inflating rubber boats, getting snarled in bales of communications wire, carrying out simulated patrol missions at night. Whenever it was Livick's turn to keep the map, we would vanish into the piney woods, subsisting on K and D rations for hours until we were found thrashing around in the bush and led back by a rescue party from the battalion's 81-millimeter platoon, our long-suffering neighbors in New River's Tent City. For the most part it was an uneventful time, however. Nothing interesting seemed likely to happen before we were shipped overseas.

Then one morning the battalion adjutant summoned me.

"Mac."

"Sir."

"You will square away to snap in a new man."

Marine Corps orders were always given this way: "You will scrub bulkheads," "You will police this area," "You will hold a field day." There was only one permissible response.

"Aye, aye, sir," I said.

"He's a Japanese-language interpreter," he said.

"A *what*?"

In 1944 virtually no one in the Marine Corps spoke Japanese. Unlike the ETO, where plenty of GI's were bilingual, Americans were at a severe linguistic disadvantage in the Pacific. It was worsened by the fact that many Japs spoke English; they could eavesdrop on our combat field telephones. As a result, by the third year of the war the headquarters company of each Marine battalion carried on its roster a full-blooded Navaho who could communicate over radiophones in his own tongue with the Navahos in other battalions. After the outbreak of the war Washington had set up several crash courses to teach Japanese to bright young Americans, but the first graduates wouldn't emerge until the spring of 1945.

"We'll be the only outfit with its own translator," he said.

"Sir."

"Private Harold Dumas will be coming down from post headquarters at fourteen hundred."

That was too much. "He's only a *private*?"

"Knock it off!"

"Aye, aye, sir."

A noncom wasn't supposed to question higher wisdom, but clearly there was something odd here. Back in our pyramidal tent I passed the word among my people, whose astonishment matched mine. Their first reaction was that I was snowing them, but within an hour the dope was confirmed by the sergeant major, a bright little sparrow of a man named John Guard. Guard had some intriguing details, including an explanation for the translator's low rank. Until very recently—two days ago, in fact—Harold Dumas had been locked up in Portsmouth naval prison. The nature of his offense was unknown to Guard, but the sergeant major knew where Dumas was believed to have learned Japanese. He was a native of California; his neighbors had been Issei (first-generation

Japanese-Americans) and Nisei (children of Issei).

The fact that the newcomer was a Californian is important to an understanding of what happened later. The Marine Corps maintained a rigid geographical segregation. Every man enlisting east of the Mississippi was sent to boot camp at Parris Island and shipped to New River after his recruit training. West of the Mississippi, boots went to the San Diego base and, once they had qualified, to nearby Camp Pendleton. Virtually none of us in Tent City knew anything about life on the West Coast. We had never seen a giant redwood, or the Grand Canyon, or Hollywood. We had never even met anyone from California until Harold Dumas arrived that afternoon at two o'clock.

He made a great entrance. He was wearing a salty barracks (visored) cap, a field scarf (necktie) so bleached that it was almost white, heavily starched khakis, and high-top dress shoes. The shoes were especially impressive. The Marine Corps had stopped issuing high-tops after Pearl Harbor, and they were therefore a great status symbol, signifying membership in the elite prewar Old Corps. Dumas was the only post-Pearl Marine I ever knew who had them, but then, he was unusual in lots of ways.

Prepossessing is the word that best describes him, though it is really inadequate. The moment he strode into Tent City with his elbows swinging wide, every eye was on him. Six foot two, with a magnificent physique, he carried himself like Randolph Scott in *To the Shores of Tripoli*, the movie that had conned thousands of Marines into joining up. His face was freckled, his eyes were sky-blue, his expression was wholly without guile; he was a man you trusted instinctively, whose every word you believed, for whose reputation you would fight, and whose friend you longed to be. When he removed the barracks cap, he was a towhead; and even before we met him—before that firm, hearty handclasp that characterized all his greetings—he was known to us simply as "Whitey."

"The name's Dumas," he said in a rich, manly baritone, looking straight at you with an expression that, in those days before Madison Avenue had corrupted the word, could only be called sincere. Sincerity emanated from him; so did an air of achievement. Whitey was in his mid-twenties, a few years older than the rest of us, and it developed that he had used his time well. No one could call him a braggart—he was in fact conspicuously modest—but over the next few weeks particulars about his background slipped out naturally in normal conversation. He had been a newspaperman and a professional boxer. The fact that he had made money in the ring had been his undoing, accounting for his imprisonment; he had slugged a bully in a San Francisco bar, and under California law, he explained, a blow by a professional fighter was regarded as assault with a deadly weapon. If it hadn't been for his knowledge of Japanese, which he had disclosed to the authorities in Portsmouth, he would still be in the dreary exercise yard there.

"Isn't it typical of the Marine Corps to keep him a private?" Yates said scornfully. "In the Army he'd be at least a major."

The more we saw of Whitey, the more we admired him. He was everything we wanted to be. He even had a sexy wife, a Paramount starlet. After much coaxing he was persuaded to produce a picture of her, an eight-by-ten glossy print of a beaming blonde in a bathing suit; it was signed "With all my love—Laverne." Even more impressive, Whitey, unlike most of us, was a combat veteran. He had been a machine gunner in the 1st Marines during the early days on Guadalcanal. This was a matter of special interest to Sy Ivice, who had landed on the 'Canal later with the 2d Marines. Sy wanted to reminisce about those days with Whitey, but Whitey politely declined. He had lost two of his best buddies in the fire fight along the Tenaru River, he told us, and he didn't want to talk about it.

Whitey's greatest achievement, of course, was his mastery of the enemy's language, the attainment that had sprung him from Portsmouth, and it was far too valuable to be confined to my section. Shortly after we crossed the country by troop train and encamped at Linda Vista, north of San Diego, preparatory to boarding ship, our gifted ex-con attracted the attention of the 29th's commanding officer, Colonel George F. Hastings. Hastings was the kind of colorful hard-charger the Marine Corps has always valued highly. Reportedly he was a native of an Arizona town named Buzzard's Gulch. Myth had it that his middle initial stood for "Flytrap," which was absurd, but it was quite true that between the wars he had designed the Corps' standard M1A1 flytrap. Until the 29th was formed, this device had existed only on paper, but over one weekend in training he had ordered one built. It didn't work. Not a single insect ventured into it. Nobody had the courage to tell the colonel, and on a Sunday of punishing heat the first sergeants had turned everybody out to catch flies by hand and put them in the trap so that Hastings wouldn't feel crushed.

The colonel was a great gray weasel of a man who always wore a bleached khaki fore-and-aft cap pushed to the back of his head. He was also the hoarsest and most redundant man I have ever known. His normal speaking voice can only be described as throaty, and he was forever saying things in it like "Here in Dixie we're in the Deep South," "Keep fit and healthy," and "Eat lots of food and plenty of it."

One sunlit morning—heavily handsome as only southern Californian weather can be—I was summoned by the sergeant major into the C.O.'s august presence. Hastings was standing beside a Lister bag in Officers' Country, slaking his thirst.

"We're going to sail aboard ship tomorrow," he barked after draining a canteen cup.

"Sir."

"The first day out I want Private Dumas to hold Japanese lessons. Just some fundamental key phrases. All officers and staff N.C.O.'s will meet on the fantail in the stern. I'm requisitioning a blackboard from ship's stores. Make sure Dumas is ready."

When I passed the word to Whitey, he gave me what we called a thousand-yard stare—a look of profound preoccupation. Then, while we were mounting the gangplank of the U.S.S. *General C. G. Morton*, lugging our seabags on our left shoulders and saluting the ship's colors as we boarded her, word was passed of our voyage's destination. We were headed for jungle maneuvers on Guadalcanal. "Oh, Christ, not that goddamned island," Ivice groaned. As Acting John I had been the first to reach the deck, and I happened to be looking at Dumas when the news reached him. He gave me a two-thousand-yard stare.

The next morning all designated hands fell out aft, with notebooks and pencils in hand. First the colonel pointed out that the blackboard was there, with lots of chalk and plenty of it, and that we were about to get some dope that would improve our efficiency and competence. Then he introduced Dumas. It was, I later thought, one of Whitey's finest hours. Arms akimbo, head high, with just the trace of a smile on that rugged face—the look of the learned teacher addressing eager neophytes—he proceeded with such assurance that one momentarily forgot he was outranked by everyone else there. Like English, he observed, Japanese was two languages, the written and the spoken. We would be chiefly concerned with the second, but it might be useful if we acquired some proficiency with the first. Turning to the blackboard he chalked with stenographic speed:

"That means 'Put your hands up, Nip!' " he said easily. "The best phonetic rendition I can give you is '*Zari sin toy fong!*' "

We wrote it down.

The next phrase was:

" '*Booki fai kiz soy?*' " said Whitey. "It means 'Do you surrender?' "

Then:

口な 操体弾ス于が

" '*Mizi pok loi ooni rak tong zin?*' 'Where are your comrades?' "

"Tong *what?*" rasped the colonel.

"Tong *zin*, sir," our instructor replied, rolling chalk between his palms. He arched his eyebrows, as though inviting another question. There was one. The adjutant asked, "What's that gizmo on the end?"

"It's called a *fy-thong*," Whitey said. "It looks like a quotation mark, or a German umlaut, but its function is very different. It makes the question imperative—almost a threat. In effect you're saying, 'Tell me where your comrades are or you're a dead Nip.' "

"Right on target," the colonel muttered, writing furiously.

Next Whitey scrawled:

大下合ヨ題自ヤ円死上

"Means 'I want some water,' " he explained. "You say it '*Ruki gack keer pong tari loo-loo*.' "

Then:

覩 牛 を 開ヮで 初 心木

" '*Moodi fang baki kim tuki dim fai?*' That's a question: 'Where is your commander?' "

A company commander raised a hand. "Why no *fy—fy* . . ."

"*Fy-thong*," Whitey prompted. He spread his hands. "I really can't explain it, sir. The imperative just doesn't exist in certain conjugations. They call it a narrow inflection. It's a weird language." He grinned. "But then, they're a peculiar people."

"Murdering ****heads," hoarsed the colonel, flexing his elbow and scribbling on.

The battalion operations officer—the Bn-3—cleared his throat. He was a squat gargoyle of a man with a thick Brooklyn accent, the comic of Officer's Country. He asked, "How do you say 'I got to take a crap?' "

Into the laughter Whitey said earnestly, "That's a good question, sir.

The Japanese are very sensitive about bodily functions. You have to put it just right."

He chalked:

ソ少チ`伱彈彼饅な

He said: " '*Song foy suki-suki kai moy-ah?*' "

The Bn-3 shot back, "What about saying to a Nip girl '*Voulez-vous coucher avec moi?*' "

Colonel Hastings thought that was hilarious, and once his guffaws had sanctioned the joke, everyone joined in lustily. Everyone, that is, except Whitey. Nursing his elbows and rocking back on his heels, he gave them a small, tight enlisted-man's smile. Slowly it dawned on the rest of us that he had not understood the operations officer, that his foreign languages did not include French. There was much coughing and shuffling of feet; then the Bn-3 said in the subdued voice of one whose joke had been unappreciated, "What I mean is—how you say you want your ashes hauled?"

Now Whitey beamed. He turned to the blackboard and scrawled:

車よら3都な苳信ジま

"How do you *say* it?" shouted the quartermaster.

" '*Naka-naka eeda kooda-sai,*' " Whitey said slowly. There was a long pause while we all made sure we had that one right. Thirty years later I can read it clearly in my yellowing notes, carefully printed in block capitals.

The colonel stood up, yawned, and prepared to shove off. He was bushed, he said, and he looked it. Doubtless this was his most intense cogitation since the invention of the flytrap. But then, we were all stretching ourselves. Although Marine Corps routine can be exhausting, it is rarely cerebral. The only man there who looked fresh was Whitey. Of course, he already knew Japanese.

The colonel was nothing if not dogged, however, and every day thereafter we assembled on the fantail for more skull sessions. By the end of the second week we were jabbering at each other with reasonable fluency, and the more enterprising platoon leaders were drilling their men in the basic idioms. Hastings, now well into his third notebook, was a bottomless source of questions. ("How do you say 'Put down your weapon' and tell him to do that?") We all felt that the 29th had a distinct edge on the other twenty-eight Marine regiments. Even the jaded members of my intelligence section were roused to pride—Jasper, a particularly apt pupil, marvelled at the exquisite nuances of the tongue, at its Oriental precision and delicacy of phrasing—though Zoglin dampened our enthusiasm somewhat by pointing out the unlikelihood that we would ever have an opportunity to use our new skill. Japanese soldiers were notorious for their refusal to surrender. They considered it an honor to die for their emperor and a disgrace to be taken alive; when defeat loomed for them at the end of an island battle, their officers would round them up for a traditional *banzai* (hurrah) suicide charge, and our people obligingly mowed them down. (Banzai, Whitey explained in response to a question, was spelled " 无志. ")

On the morning of the seventeenth day we climbed topside to find ourselves lying off the 'Canal, that lush, incredibly green, entirely repulsive island that for most of us had existed only in legend. Ivice had a lot to say about its banyan trees and kunai grass, but Whitey continued to be reticent about his recollections of it. Toward the end the journey had been a great strain for him. Of course, he had a lot on his mind. Rising in the night for a trip to the scuttlebutt or the head, I would see him lying awake on his bunk, sweating in his skivvies, preparing the next day's lecture.

Slinging our 782 gear over our field packs, we scrambled down the cargo nets thrown over the side of the *Morton*, landed in the waiting Higgins boats, and raced in them toward the shore. There we found that we were to make our training camp on the banks of a river. And there Whitey committed what seemed to be a peculiar blunder. As he looked down on the stream his eyes misted over. "Sweet Jesus," he said feelingly, picking up a corroded old cartridge case. "I never thought I'd see the Matanikau again."

Ivice looked at him in disbelief. "The *Matanikau*!" he said. "What the **** are you talking about? This is the *Kokumbona*. The Matanikau's four miles to the east!"

Whitey hesitated and wet his lips. It was the first time any of us had seen him shook. Finally he blinked and said, "Man, I must be Asiatic." He shrugged. "All these goddamned rivers look the same to me."

The rest of us accepted that—this tangled island bewildered us too —but Ivice said nothing. Throughout that day I caught him eyeing Whitey strangely from time to time, and the following morning, when I hitched a ride to Lunga Point on a DUKW and crossed the coconut-log bridge spanning the Matanikau, I understood why. The two rivers were entirely different. Compared to the mighty Matanikau, the Kokumbona was a shallow brook. Whitey's error was inexplicable.

Ivice was the first to entertain doubts about the star of our intelligence section, and I was the second. One evening over a joe-pot I mentioned to the sergeant major that Mrs. Dumas was a movie starlet. The sparrow chirped, "There ain't no Mrs. Dumas. If there was one, there'd be an allotment for her on the books, and there ain't none. I keep the books. I *know*." Shortly thereafter I saw a pinup of Betty Grable in a slop chute near Henderson Field. I recognized the style immediately: an eight-by-ten glossy print. What Whitey had been passing off as a photograph of his wife was a publicity shot of some Hollywood aspirant. Probably he had never met her. I never learned for sure.

Bit by bit the elaborate structure he had erected so adroitly and so successfully was beginning to come unstuck. Working on the Point Cruz dock, Yates met a port battalion officer who had been an Oakland lawyer before the war and who hooted at the idea of California law defining a boxer's punch as an assault with a deadly weapon. Then a gunnery sergeant, arriving as a replacement from Pendleton, recognized Whitey and revealed the true reason he had been stripped of rank and sent to prison. While still in boot camp, it turned out, he had been arrested for impersonating an officer in downtown San Diego. Since he hadn't become a recruit until the fall of 1943, Whitey had been a civilian during the battle for the 'Canal. Ivice was confirmed; our prodigy had never seen the island before he had landed with us. There was another thing: Whitey had told us that he had been a reporter. Journalism was something I knew about—in college I had been an Amherst stringer for the Springfield *Republican*—and when I started a camp newspaper, I invited him to contribute to it. He tried; he really tried. For days he struggled with a pencil, but when the result came in, it was functionally illiterate, almost incomprehensible. If he had ever been a reporter, the paper hadn't been published in the English language.

Of course, it might have been a *Japanese* newspaper. Whitey's claim to be a linguist was the last of his status symbols, and he clung to it desperately. Looking back, I think his improvisations on the *Morton* fantail must have been one of the most heroic achievements in the history of confidence men—which, as you may have gathered by now, was Whitey's true profession. Toward the end of our tour of duty on the 'Canal he was totally discredited with us and transferred at his own request to the 81-millimeter platoon, where our disregard for him was no stigma, since the 81-millimeter musclemen regarded us as a bunch of eight balls anyway. Yet even then, even after we had become completely disillusioned with him, he remained a figure of wonder among us. We could scarcely believe

that an impostor could be clever enough actually to *invent* a language
—phonics, calligraphy, and all. It had looked like Japanese and sounded
like Japanese, and during his seventeen days of lecturing on that ship
Whitey had carried it all in his head, remembering every variation, every
subtlety, every syntactic construction.

Whitey stayed out of jail, and in the 29th, because the one man who
never lost confidence in him was Colonel Hastings. The colonel continued to believe, not because he was stupid, but because Whitey staged his
greatest show—literally a command performance—for the regimental C.O.
I was there, yet to this day I don't fully understand how he pulled it off.
What happened was that the First Marine Division, while securing Peleliu
in October of 1944, had bagged five Japanese prisoners. That sort of
thing happened from time to time in the Pacific war, usually under freakish circumstances. A Jap was dazed by a shell or otherwise rendered unable to kill himself. Seized by our troops, he was physically restrained
from making amends to the emperor. Five months after their capture
these failed suicides were ferried to the 'Canal from the First's base on the
Russell Islands. Clad in loincloths and penned behind maximum-security
concertinas of barbed wire, they passively awaited the pleasure of their
conquerors. But nobody with jurisdiction knew quite how to dispose of
them. Then word of their presence reached the C.O. of the 29th. Hastings
knew exactly what to do; he announced to their wardens that he would
interrogate them through his very own interpreter, Private Harold Dumas.
Whitey greeted the news with a ten-thousand-yard stare and utter silence.
There was, it seemed, nothing he could say.

The POW stockade was at Koli Point, and one morning at 0800 hours
we set out for it in a convoy, with Colonel Hastings and his private translator leading in a jeep and the rest of us trailing in a green crocodile of
DUKW's, six-by trucks, and various other military vehicles. This was a big
day for the colonel; he wanted every officer and staff N.C.O. to remember
it. Since Whitey was riding with him, I didn't see the interpreter during
the trip, and I have no way of knowing how he behaved, though I'm sure
he retained his poise. Anybody who had the guts to snow his way through
those classes on the *Morton* would be equal to almost any crises; it was not
crises, but day-to-day, round-the-clock testing that had led to our disen-
chantment with him. When I arrived at Koli, Hastings's jeep was already
parked beside the huge barbed-wire coils. The colonel was outside, glar-
ing in wrathfully. The prisoners were squatting miserably on their
haunches, and Whitey, dressed in Marine dungarees and a raider cap, was
squatting alongside them.

Apparently an exchange of some sort was going on. Obviously the
colonel thought so; his eyes darted alertly from Whitey to the Japs, and

his right ear was cocked, trying to pick up a thread of sense by using the vocabulary he had learned on the voyage from San Diego. It was, of course, impossible. Whitey was ad-libbing with his brilliant double-talk, which, however Oriental it sounded to us, was utterly devoid of real meaning. What the Nips were saying is a matter of conjecture, since no one there was equipped to understand them. My own belief is that they were replying to Whitey, "We only speak Japanese." All that can be said with any certainty is that the POW's and their interrogator had reached an impasse. After a long lull in the non-conversation Whitey came out with a hangdog look.

"What's happening?" the colonel asked anxiously.

"Sir, I goofed," Whitey said wretchedly.

"What? Why? How?"

With a swooping gesture Whitey swung out his right forefinger and pointed to the Marine Corps emblem printed on the left breast of his dungaree jacket. "I should never have worn this," he said in his guileless voice. "You see, sir," he explained, looking directly at Hastings, "they know what the globe-and-fouled-anchor means. They know what the Marine Corps is. They realize that the corps is destroying their emperor and their homeland, and they just won't answer my questions."

For a long moment the colonel stared back at Whitey. They he squared his shoulders, and his pouter-pigeon chest swelled. "Goddam right," he grated, his voice like a coarse file. He peered contemptuously into the pen and said, "Those sons of bitches are a bunch of bastards."

With that he strutted back to his jeep and soon, it developed, out of our lives—Whitey's, mine and the 29th's. That week the battalion boarded the APA (attack transport) *George C. Clymer* for Okinawa, where the colonel left us after the first few days of battle. He was relieved of his command on Motobu peninsula after the divisional commander asked him the whereabouts of his first and third battalions and received no satisfactory reply. I happened to be there when the question was raised, and I can still see the look of utter bewilderment on Hastings's face. He had always been vague about the rest of his regiment; his heart had belonged to our second battalion; he had allowed his lieutenant colonels to run the others, and in the excitement of combat he had neglected to update his situation map. "Inexcusable!" said the general, clearly outraged. "I'm sorry. I regret it," the colonel croaked brokenly. Later I heard that he had been shunted back to the corps staff, where he was awarded the Bronze Star "for excellence in keeping records during combat."

Whitey had vanished at about the same time during a sick call. Quite apart from gunshot wounds, there was a pattern of bizarre casualties in the island battles of World War II. Some poor bastard wading toward the beach would stumble off a reef, and with eighty pounds of hardware on his back he would sink like a stone. A BAR man in Easy Company disappeared that way in the early hours of Love Day, as Okinawa's D-day was quaintly called. Other people went rock happy—"combat fatigue," it was called. The sergeant major did; he was carried off cackling nonsense even less intelligible than that of Private Dumas. Then there was always some sad clown who, the first night on the beach, would forget that he had to stay in his hold until dawn, or "morning twilight," because the Japs were ingenious at night infiltrations. We scratched one Fox Company 60-millimeter mortarman at 2 A.M. that April 2; he was up relieving himself over a slit trench when a sentry drilled him through one cheek. ("A good shot in the bull's eye," said our callous colonel the following morning, just before he was deprived of his command.) Finally, there were the back cases. Whitey became one of them.

Every salt knew that you could get surveyed if you complained long enough about chronic back pains. Back on the 'Canal I lost a Philadelphian who had enlisted at the age of twenty-eight—we called him "Pop"—and who, fed up with jungle training, used that excuse to get stateside. Whitey followed his ignoble example. To the disgust of the gung-ho 81-millimeter mortarmen, he kept insisting that his spine was killing him, and finally the skeptical medical corpsmen sighed and took him away for a check.

It was months before I learned what happened to him after that, because after the battle began in earnest, my people became extremely active. Okinawa turned out to be the bloodiest engagement of the Pacific war, eclipsing even Iwo. After it was all over, a Presidential citation commended the division "for extraordinary heroism in action against enemy Japanese forces" and for "gallantry in overcoming a fanatic enemy in the face of extraordinary danger," but all I remember is mud and terror. Years later I learned from reading Samuel Eliot Morison that the 29th had sustained the heaviest casualties of any regiment in the history of the Marine Corps—2,821 out of some 3,300 riflemen. My section was cut to pieces. Once the slaughter began, we were used as runners, carrying messages between battalion staff officers, company commanders, and even platoon leaders whose walkie-talkies had conked out. It was exceptionally perilous work. In 1918 someone computed the life expectancy of a German machine gunner on the western front at thirty minutes, and I don't believe that of a Marine runner along Okinawa's Machinato line could have been much longer. We were rarely in defilade, usually exposed, and often had to spend long periods lined up in some Jap sniper's sights. I myself was hit twice. The first time was May 17 on the northern slope of Sugar Loaf Hill. It was only a flesh wound, and I jumped hospital to rejoin the battalion, but on June 5 I was decked again. That one was almost for keeps, a massive chest wound from fourteen-inch rocket-mortar shrapnel. For five months I was on and off operating tables on a hospital ship, on Saipan, in Alewa Heights Naval Hospital overlooking Honolulu, in San Francisco, and finally at San Diego's naval hospital in Balboa Park.

A letter from Jasper—who survived the war to marry a Nisei—reached me in Balboa that October, filling me in on Whitey's last adventure in the 29th. I was wearing a buck sergeant's stripes by then, or rather they were sewn to the sleeves of my greens, for I was still bedridden. I have a hazy memory of church bells tolling the previous August, and my asking a chief petty officer what it meant, and his answering, "The war's over," and my saying "Oh," just "Oh." Within a few months the 29th's people began heading home. Whitey, however, was not among them. His complaint about his back hadn't deceived the mortarmen, but then, they, like us, had known him. The physicians at the regimental aid station, on an LST offshore, had been seduced by his earnest charm, though the ultimate result was not quite what he had had in mind. The docs put him in a Higgins boat and sent him back to a corps clearing hospital. All badges of rank having been removed before we hit the beach—Nip sharpshooters liked to pick off officers and N.C.O.'s—the hospital's medical corpsmen had no way of knowing the military status of casualties, so they usually asked them. They asked Whitey, and he repeated his bootcamp lie. He said he was a first lieutenant, reasoning that life would be more comfortable, and the chow more edible, on an officer's ward.

He was right, but there were special hazards for him there. A captain in the next bunk asked him what his job in the Marine Corps was. "Japanese-language interpreter," said Whitey. They shot the breeze for a while, and then the captain asked Whitey for a lesson. Ever obliging, our man rattled off a few phrases and jotted down some of his Oriental hieroglyphics on a slip of paper. "Very interesting," the real officer said slowly. Then he yelled: "Corpsman! Put this man under arrest!" It developed that the captain was one of the first graduates of the Japanese-language schools that had been set up after Pearl Harbor. They were arriving in the Pacific too late to do much toward winning the war, but this one had turned up at exactly the right time to nail Whitey. Our confidence man had tried to dupe one mark too many. He was shipped straight back to Portsmouth.

I never saw him again, but I heard from him once. Five years after the war, when my first stories were appearing in national magazines, I received a letter postmarked Hollywood and written in a familiar scrawl. It was on MGM stationery. God knows where he had picked it up, but he certainly hadn't acquired it legally. Letters from studio executives—for that is what it claimed to be—are typed. They are also spelled correctly and properly phrased. This one was neither. I have never seen a clearer illustration of Whitey's own aphorism that we have two languages, one we speak and one we write. He was entirely verbal; when he lectured, it was with easy assurance, and an impressive vocabulary. On his pilfered MGM stationery he was another hustler. Gone were his casual references to conjugations, modifiers, inflections, and the imperative mood. Not since his stab at journalism on the 'Canal had he been so incoherent.

His missive ran:

Dear Bill,

Caught your artical in this months Harpers. Real good. Always knew you had it in you.

Look—could you give yours truely a break? Am now doing PR for Sam Goldwyn & Co and am trying to promote to stardom a real cute chick, name of Boobs Slotkin. (Boobs—ha! ha! I gave her the name & when you glim her knockers youll see why.) Give me the work and I'll shoot you some pix. Some for the public and some for your private eye if you get my meaning—ha! ha!

Sure miss the old gang on the Canal and all the good times we had. I don't hear from any of them, do you?

Let me know about Boobs. This is a real good deal and I can put you next to her roommate whose no dog either next time your in this neck of the woods. Brunette 37–24–30 and hot pants. A real athalete in the sack. You won't regret it believe me.

Your old ******* buddy,

Harold V. Dumas
Chief of Public Relations
Metro-Goldwyn-Mayer Studios

P.S. Dont write to me at the office as this is kind of personal. Just sent it to me care of General Delivery L.A. and it will get to me Okay.

I never replied, but I found the note strangely moving. Whitey had climbed the Parnassus of his calling, and evidently he had now slid back down all the way. He was pathetic on paper, and his assessment of the kind of material that interested *Harper's* was unbelievable. (How on earth had he even *seen* the magazine?) He had entered the shadows; for all I know, he never emerged again. It is of course quite possible that he staged a stunning caper under another name—as G. Gordon Liddy, say—yet somehow I doubt it. His big sting with us had a one-shot air about it, like the flight of an exotic bird that dazzles for a single season and is never seen again. But on the *Morton*'s fantail, and outside that POW stockade at Koli Point, he had been magnificent. And to this day I feel a tingling at the base of my scalp when I think of that towheaded prisoner in his Portsmouth cell dreaming up what must have been the most imaginative con of the war, saying in that straightforward voice, "Guard, I want to speak to the C.O.," and then, "Sir, I know I deserve to be here, but my country is threatened and I want to do my share. I can really help in an unusual way, sir. You see, I speak Japanese."

—December 1975

WHEN I LANDED, THE WAR WAS OVER

By HUGHES RUDD

A veteran news correspondent recalls his career as a spotter pilot. The first of many unpleasant surprises: according to the government manifest, his specialized aircraft cost four hundred dollars less than the crate it arrived in.

The idea is simple and sound and goes back at least to the American Civil War: to direct artillery fire intelligently, the higher you are above the target, the better. At ground level it's difficult to tell just how far short or long your shells are falling. In the Civil War they used balloons; in the First World War they were still using balloons, along with airplanes equipped with telegraph keys; in the Second World War the airplane had supplanted the balloon, but just barely. The United States Army of those days was not a hotbed of innovation, and when I reported for training as an artillery spotter pilot at Fort Sill, Oklahoma, in early 1942, there was still an enormous building on the post called the Balloon Hangar, even though no balloons were to be seen.

But before that, there was Fort Hays, which wasn't a fort at all in the 1940s but a town in western Kansas with a civilian airfield on the outskirts. I had enlisted in the Army Air Corps, hoping, like all nineteen-year-old American male movie fans, to become a fighter pilot, but one eye tested at 20/40, so the Army Air Corps gave me to the *Army*, period, to become what was called a "Liaison Pilot," meaning artillery spotter. At Fort Hays, the civilians taught us to fly, and it wasn't easy, for them *or* us.

The airplanes were Aeroncas, tandem two-seater monoplanes with sixty-five-horsepower engines. They terrified us but aroused only contempt in our instructors, who were accustomed to heavier stuff. Sometimes, out of sheer boredom at the end of two hours in the air with me, trying to teach me crossroad eights, lazy eights, and all the other primer moves the beginning aviator learns, my instructor would seize the controls and put the lumbering Aeronca through snap rolls at an altitude of five hundred feet. The Aeronca, to him, was not an *airplane*: it was a sort of tricycle which occasionally found itself in the air. An Aeronca can kill you as well as an F-14, of course, but my instructor obviously didn't believe that, as witness the aileron-block affair.

Aileron blocks were two pieces of wood joined together with a bolt: when the airplane was through flying for the day, you shoved the bolt forward along the slot between the aileron and the fixed wing, to prevent the ailerons from flopping and banging back and forth in the wind, since that could damage something. A piece of red cloth ten feet long was attached to the aileron block as a warning *not* to take off with the block in place, since the ailerons control the banking and turning movements of the airplane: with block in place, no bank and no turn, a situation that could, as they said in the Army, ruin your whole day.

Nonetheless, one bright morning, as the first student out on solo in this particular Aeronca, I took off, thought the control stick a bit stiff, glanced out the window, and saw that awful red streamer, standing out stiff from the wing. Death, I thought, and I haven't even *seen* a German yet. There was, however, torque, the force exerted by the spinning propeller. Torque tends to turn the airplane, and sure enough, after a wide, wide circle of some twenty-five miles, I found myself lined up with the grass airstrip and landed. I instantly jumped out and threw the aileron block into a ditch before taking off again, but of course my instructor had seen the whole thing. After chewing me out for being just flat-ass *dumb*, he said, "Well, now you'll know what to do when they shoot your ailerons out." To him, clearly, there was nothing to fear in an Aeronca, not even the Luftwaffe.

After about twenty-five hours of solo at Fort Hays, we were shipped to Fort Still, to the *real* Army, for sixteen weeks of learning to do the impossible with little airplanes. The "Short Field Course," it was called. Two hundred hours of instruction in what to expect in combat areas, and it took place in those little olive-drab L-4s.

The L-4 was the Army's version of a Piper Cub: two seats, one behind the other, a lot of Plexiglas all around, so you could see who was coming after you, and a sixty-five-horsepower, four-cylinder Lycoming engine which pulled the airplane along at a snappy seventy-five miles per hour, assuming no headwind.

Speed wasn't the point. The L-4 was made of aluminum tubing with doped linen stretched over it: one man could pick one up by the tail and pull it along behind him. This lightness meant the airplane could land and take off from places unthinkable for *real* airplanes, and in combat, everybody knew we were going to be in a lot of unthinkable places.

The Army instructors at Sill were a lot tougher than the civilians at Fort Hays. The Army instructors had a terrifying habit of chopping the throttle back just as you lifted the airplane off the ground and then pounding on your shoulder and yelling, "Where are you gonna put it? Where are you gonna put it?" The answer was, in deeds, not words, straight ahead, even if straight ahead was a tree line. Attempting a turn at low altitude and low speed was *wrong, wrong, wrong,* and by God, don't you forget it. On these exercises the instructors would jam open the throttle again just as disaster loomed, and snarl, "All right, take it on up." You got to hate people like that, but of course they were right. The Army, I gradually learned, was *always* right.

Not all of us at Fort Sill *could* get it right. Much of the training involved taking off and landing over "obstacles," which required a certain judgment of height and distance. The obstacles were two upright bamboo poles with a rope tied between them, rags fluttering from the rope, and many a time one saw L-4s staggering through the air, trailing poles, ropes, and rags from the tail wheel. That meant the student had misjudged his take-off: those who misjudged their approach and landing were often saved by two haystacks, one on each side of the obstacle. If the airplane stalled out as the student was trying to slow it down as much as possible, the L-4 fell off on one wing and flopped into the haystack. Since the stalling speed was about thirty-five miles per hour, this was usually not fatal, although it put the instructors into a terrible temper, and people who fell into the haystacks were washed out and sent elsewhere, never to be heard from again. Some 20 percent went that way, as I recall.

Others went the hard way. The Army did not make it a point to tell us about fatal crashes, and with some two hundred pilots in training it was hard to keep up with everybody, but young men died often enough in those harmless-looking little airplanes, without ever seeing a German or a Japanese. I was sitting in the waiting room of the base hospital one day, waiting to be treated for some minor medical problem, when I noticed a terrible odor. I asked the orderly what it was, and he said the lab was boiling the brain of a student who'd been killed that morning, to see if there was any alcohol in his system. Rumor had it that if you were killed with a hangover, your insurance was cancelled. Since we were restricted to the post all during the week, this was rarely a problem.

On the weekends a lot of us *did* overdo it in the fleshpots of Lawton, Oklahoma, which has been catering to soldiers since before Custer and the 7th Cavalry were stationed at Sill. We even sang songs, just like the soldiers in the movies. There was song about *us,* to the tune of the "Artillery Song," the one where those caissons go rolling along, and so on, only our song went something like this: "Over trees, under wires, to hell with landing gear and tires, we're the eyes of the artillereeee. We don't mind the mud and sand, we don't need much room to land, we're the eyes of . . . et cetera."

Those of us who survived the Short Field Course were finally graduated, complete with a ceremony in which wings were pinned on our chests: it was pretty much the way Hollywood had told us it would be, except that we had to sign for the wings, as Government issue property. That was a letdown, but before I had a chance to brood about it, I was assigned to the 93rd Armored Field Artillery Battalion, no longer a learner but a professional, or so the Army hoped, anyway.

Two pilots were assigned to each artillery battalion, but the other fellow gave me so much trouble I'm going to leave his name out of this. Anyway, the 93rd did not know what to make of two Piper Cub pilots, two airplanes, and a mechanic. The officers of the 93rd thought the L-4s were "vehicles," with the accent on the first syllable, and while we remained at Fort Sill they were forever after us to grease our *ve*hicles. Since we were only staff sergeants, we would look busy, but you don't really grease an airplane; you don't even wash it very often. Still, the 93rd believed in washing all *ve*hicles, including Sherman tanks, so we washed the L-4s. That did not end our stateside misunderstandings with the 93rd Battalion, however. As pilots, we were issued aviator's sunglasses and leather flying jackets, and the 93rd didn't like that. The sunglasses were invaluable when you were called into the battery commander's hut to be reamed over some infraction or other, such as not wearing your leggins (and the word was *leggins*, not *leggings*). You stood there at attention in those dark glasses, your eyes roaming all over the room, avoiding the stern glare of the C.O. with no trouble whatever, and there wasn't a damn thing he could do about it: the glasses were, after all, Government Issue: G.I.

The leggins were a constant problem for a pilot, since they had little hooks along the sides to hold the laces, and those hooks caught in the exposed rudder cables in the cockpit of the L-4. You could *not* make an artillery officer understand that, or at least you couldn't within the continental limits of the United States, or Zone of the Interior, as the Army called it. Once outside the Z.I., the 93rd realized what the L-4s could do, and nobody cared what we wore.

In time, the 93rd Armored Field Artillery Battalion was sent to North Africa. The L-4s were packed into huge boxes like railroad freight cars, and I had my first real intimation that the Army might be asking us to perform out of our league: a manifest tacked to each enormous box said, among other things, "Aircraft, L-4, cost to US Govt., $800; crate, 1942

M-2, cost to US Govt., $1200." The thought that our airplanes cost less than those boxes they came in was disquieting.

Our ship sailed from Staten Island. We had staged at a camp up the Hudson River, then taken the train for Staten Island, and we arrived at the Battery about five-thirty in the afternoon, just as all those commuters were boarding *their* trains, to go the other way. The nine hundred members of the 93rd Battalion streamed off our train, each man laden with two barracks bags stuffed to bursting ("place the contents of your A bag in your B bag and now proceed to pack your A bag with the following additional items") as well as various weapons hung about the person, and one and all suffering a certain nervous anxiety, mixed with equally nervous hilarity. Somehow a feeling swept through us that the ferryboats to Staten Island wouldn't wait for us—we would miss the war!—and we all started running. Just ahead of me my half-track driver tripped and fell, and lay in full view of all those commuters, pinned to the ground by those two barracks bags and two Thompson .45-caliber submachine guns slung across his chest. As I stumbled past him I saw that Louis, in his nervousness, was, in his supine position, peeing great fountains up through his od's, and couldn't free his arms from those barracks bags in order to hide his shame from all those civilians. *La Gloire!* By God, we were off to war at last.

At Staten Island, the troopship, a converted banana boat, was modified to carry some eight hundred men. Through some mix-up or other, for which the Army and Navy blamed each other, twenty-four hundred men were at dockside, and all had to be crammed aboard. It was done, of course ("place the contents of your A bag in your B bag" et cetera). As we stepped on deck, a Naval officer buckled an inflatable life belt around each man's waist: below decks an officer of the 93rd, trying to shove me and my barracks bags and submachine guns into the topmost tier of an eight-high bunk rack, pushed me so hard the strings on the belt caught, the vest inflated, and I was stuck, half in, half out of the bunk. Somebody finally deflated it with a trench knife, and the next thing I knew, we were off.

The term "air section" perhaps requires explanation. It referred to the battalion's two pilots, the airplane mechanic, the armored half-track driver, and sometimes a 6 X 6 driver, a 6 X 6 being a two-and-a-half ton truck used to collect gasoline and other supplies from appropriate dumps. The half-track was part of the air section only because we belonged to an armored battalion: its sole function for the air section was to beat down the grass in rough pastures we used for landing fields. We were *not* a fighting unit on the ground: attacked by German infantry, the half-track would have surrendered immediately, despite the fact it usually mounted one .50-caliber and three .30-caliber machine guns.

As a rule, we were not within range of even the most ambitious German infantry. At first, we located ourselves on farm fields as close to the battalion as possible, but a 105-mm. battalion must be pretty close to the front, since the effective range of the guns is only some ten thousand yards. The sight of the L-4s landing and taking off within full view of German ground artillery observers was something those Germans could not resist, and they shelled those forward landing strips with such intensity, once night fell and we could not retaliate, that we learned prudence and stayed back a few miles. The L-4 was not built for night flying: it lacked the instruments and we lacked the training, and directing artillery fire at night is not easy in any case. You can't find the ground references, such as road intersections or bridges or farmhouses, which correspond to the references on your map. And without those, you can't tell the guns where to shoot. You did not say, "Jesus! There's a Panther tank over by the woods! Let him have it!" No, you said, "Baker One Able, this is Baker Three Able. I have a target for you, co-ordinates one niner three, six niner two, enemy tank, one round smoke when ready," assuming those numbers to be the co-ordinates nearest the Panther tank—or the artillery battery or the column of soldiers or the lone man on the motorcycle or the staff car or whatever it was you'd spotted. There was also the problem of German night fighters.

German fighters in the daytime were not a serious problem after North Africa, where the Luftwaffe lost air superiority forever. Some German fighter units did develop tactics to cope with the L-4s: two fighters attacked straight on, two from above, and two from below. This usually brought down the L-4, but there were never enough German fighters available on the Western front to make the technique widespread. The fact that it was used at all, tying up six scarce and valuable fighter aircraft against one feeble, eight-hundred-dollar L-4, is an indication of how the L-4s hurt the Germans.

It was nearly suicide for them to move anything in daylight within the eyesight of anybody in an L-4. My own battalion consisted of eighteen howitzers: at my command, all of them would pump a dreadful rain of high explosive on the target, and do it incredibly quickly. By the time the first shell reached the target from any given gun, the sixth shell was leaving the muzzle. The gun crews worked so rapidly that the ejecting shell casing had to be knocked out of the way by one of the gunners in order to make way for the fresh shell going into the breech. It was this quickness in getting on the target and rapid rate of fire that allowed the unarmed and unarmored L-4s to survive: a German antiaircraft battery knew it had to hit us with the first salvo, for we would surely spot their muzzle flashes and give them hell if they missed. Very few antiaircraft gunners are that sure of themselves, especially those with heavy-caliber weapons, since the heavier the caliber the bigger and more embarrassing the muzzle flash. Machine gunners and riflemen were not this inhibited, but we usually flew at about three thousand feet, figuring a thousand yards was about the maximum unpleasant range of light weapons. Also, although the L-4s *were* unarmored as far as the Army was concerned, I had an iron stove lid in my seat beneath my parachute: that way I could at least avoid the worst.

The fact that we were unarmed was a constant annoyance. Many a tank or truck convoy got away because it was out of range of the 105s and the heavier guns took too long to get on target. Some attempts were made at firing bazookas from the wing struts, but accurate aiming was impossible. There was also a period when some L-4 pilots took to tossing out five-gallon cans of gasoline, which burst on impact like napalm, but that wasn't accurate either and was hard physical work besides, so we finally just left it to the guns.

The time I most regretted not having rockets or cannon aboard came somewhere north of Rome, when I was flying point for an armored column, with John Buckfelder as my observer. (You didn't always take an observer: rarely, in fact. It depended on whether the landing field was long enough to let you take off with extra weight. It usually wasn't).

Buckfelder and I had been having a quiet day, no targets, when about three in the afternoon we saw the impossible: a Tiger tank creeping along in the open on a narrow country road. The Tigers were monstrous: this one hung over the sides of the two-lane road and couldn't have been doing more than five miles an hour. We started calling fire down on it, but the 105 shells just popped like firecrackers against the heavy armor, so we "went upstairs," as the argot had it, and asked for 155-mm. Long Toms. They had more effect: a body suddenly appeared in the road behind the tank, apparently a crew member killed by concussion and dropped out the bottom through the escape hatch.

By now I had circled down to about three hundred feet above the road and Buckfelder and I were hollering into the microphones for more fire, more fire! You didn't get a Tiger tank in the open every day, and we felt sure he was going to get away because the high-explosive shells weren't penetrating his armor. But this Tiger had a gazogene unit bolted to the rear, one of those charcoal-burning contraptions the Germans used to save gasoline, and a 155 shell burst squarely in it. A small fire sprang up on the Tiger's rump. The tank kept moving in a straight line off the road and down a cliff, where it burst into real flame.

The L-4, which we came to call the "Maytag Messerschmitt," was not a comfortable airplane. You sat with your knees almost up to your chest, the aileron cable rubbed the top of your skull every time you moved the stick to left or right, it was unheated in winter, and you couldn't smoke because raw gasoline fumes filled the cockpit from the tank, which was right between your knees, just behind the instrument panel with nothing between the gasoline and a German bullet but air and thin aluminum. In summer it was often difficult to get the plane off the ground, because it didn't perform well in hot air; in winter you had to wipe the frost off the wings or it wouldn't take off at all. Unlike the glamorous folk flying real airplanes, we did not give our craft names: we named our jeeps and half-tracks, but not our L-4s. They had numbers, not names, and they were expendable: people set fire to them on beaches when it appeared the infantry was not going to hold the beachhead, they ran them into ditches trying to land on narrow roads, they flew them into high-tension wires, at least one ran headlong into a train, another hit the radio aerial on a German command car and barely fluttered back to safety, one collided with an aerial tramway in France, and at Anzio one ran into a 155 shell fired by the pilot's own battalion. There was even an L-4 that ran into a donkey on take-off, tearing off a wing and upsetting the donkey, without doing him any permanent damage whatever. The pilot in that case—me—was so enraged he ran to the tent for his pistol, intent on doing some damage to the donkey, but by the time he found the .45 in the bottom of his B bag, the creature had fled.

We lived, most of the time, in those tents, the pyramidal model, six or eight of us, and three months without a bath was not unusual. If you somehow went off and got a bath by yourself and then came back, your tentmates were intolerable: either everybody got a bath or nobody got a bath, and you could hardly have an entire air section off having a bath at one time.

We occasionally left laundry to be done in some village or other, but almost always the war moved on before the laundry was ready, and you moved with it. To this day I must have bundles of long johns and woolen shirts waiting for me up the length of the Italian peninsula and France, Austria and Germany.

Monte Cassino: the first time I saw it, from about twenty or thirty miles away, at three thousand feet, it was beautiful, a Disney dream of a mountain, rearing up from the floor of the Liri Valley almost as steeply as Yosemite's Half Dome. Not quite that steeply, of course: you could hardly make war on the face of Half Dome, but my God, how you could make war on Monte Cassino. It dominated the valley, which broadens at that point to a width of some thirty miles, maybe less. To the south, where the Americans, British, and French were, the mountains were smaller, the valleys narrower. The Germans had fought bitterly to keep us from the broad Liri Valley, which leads to Rome: once arrived at the mouth of that valley, we found ourselves fixed in place, the fierce glare of German observers on that mountain making us as naked and vulnerable as the L-4s made the Germans.

It was truly a beautiful mountain, in the beginning. At the foot, the town of Cassino, a highway intersection, red-tiled roofs, a provincial life, farms on the outskirts, and a hotel called the Continental. I did not enter the Continental Hotel until 1967, and by that time it had changed its name and the Tiger tank was no longer in the lobby. For months in 1943, the Tiger *was* in the lobby while Americans and Germans fought each other in the rooms upstairs, tossing grenades back and forth, machine-gunning each other on the staircases. A sort of Italian Stalingrad.

But of course as an L-4 pilot I was not obliged to take part in that. Our mission was primarily counter-battery fire: the Germans had amassed large amounts of artillery in the valley, and we fired back and forth at each other, all day, every day, week after week, month after month, while our infantry tried to take the heights around Monte Cassino.

Much has been written about the infantry battle, one of the worst for both sides during the whole war in the West, but from the air, it was episodic: rarely did I have any sense of a planned campaign or even of massive effort.

There were exceptions, of course: a regiment of the 36th Division crossed the Rapido River, which joins the Volturno at Cassino. A regiment was three battalions of infantry, roughly three thousand men. They crossed at night, on Treadway bridges, which were simple affairs, designed to carry trucks or tanks: two parallel strips of perforated steel planks. The regiment passed through the 93rd's area, which was just south of Monte Trocchio, the closest fold in the terrain to Cassino (that is, the closest large enough to shield 105-mm. howitzers), and a battery of the 93rd was scheduled to cross at daylight to provide close support, but at daylight all hell broke loose.

The Germans shelled and destroyed the Treadway bridges, and when I arrived above the river about 5:30 A.M., that regiment of the 36th Division was flattened on the bare, naked, hostile ground on the wrong side of the Rapido. There was no cover, not even a bush, much less a ravine, and German artillery and mortar fire was landing on the area incessantly. We fired at dozens of muzzle flashes, but the effect was negligible: the German stuff kept coming, 88s, 105s, 150s, even *Nebelwerfers*, the short-range heavy German mortars that the infantry called "Screaming Meemies," because of the fierce howl the projectiles made as they came down. It was, for me, and God knows for the GI's on the ground, a horrible, helpless feeling.

The German fire went on all day, and some of the infantrymen of the 36th broke and tried to swim the Rapido. I saw dozens plunge into the water of the river, which was only some fifty feet wide, but I saw none make it to the other bank. The Germans had, with superb military foresight, dumped coils of concertina barbed wire into the river to lie two or three feet below the surface, invisible from the banks. Military barbed wire, of course, is not like the barbed wire you see on an American farm: the barns are three or four inches long, very numerous, and they seize a soldier's uniform like steel cactus. I flew back and forth over the Rapido, directing fire all over the Liri Valley, wherever I could spot German batteries in action, and watched those little brown figures jump into the river and disappear. I'm not certain now, but I believe I cried: I was, after all, only twenty-two years old, and the 36th Division was the Texas National Guard Division. I grew up in Texas, and I had childhood friends in that regiment. Three of them never got back across the Rapido.

Oh, Monte Cassino, Monte Cassino! That beautiful, beautiful mountain: flying above Mignano, the destroyed town that dominated the approach to Cassino, the mountain loomed in blue haze, smoky: its peak appeared to be topped with eternal snow, but as one drew closer, the haze cleared and you saw it was not snow, it was the abbey, the abbey of Monte Cassino, white, white, *whiter* than snow, glittering, pure, high above the grunt and stink and killing of the valley. Founded some fourteen hundred years before our arrival, a marvel, a monument to God and man. Well, that didn't last long once we got there.

After the war there was a great deal of argument about the abbey. The Vatican said no German soldiers were ever in or near it, and the Germans said the same thing. Well, that's bull: on several occasions I saw German machine-gun tracers coming from its northeast corner. The gun was either inside the abbey itself or firing from a position built into the exterior wall. I called fire on the spot each time, and the 93rd responded each time. After months of infantry assaults that broke against the mountain and the town at its foot, the Allies decided they would bomb their way through Monte Cassino. Though rarely mentioned in historical accounts, the first bomb attacks were made by P-40s based at a field near Naples: they dived with five-hundred-pound bombs. I was at three thousand feet, to fire the 93rd at any German flak batteries that opened up on the P-40s, and I can still see the fighters diving, their .50-caliber machine-gun bullets sparking on the mountain as they zeroed in, then the steep pull-up, followed seconds later by the geyser of smoke, flame, and dirt of the bomb's explosion. As they pulled out and away, headed for home and a hot shower, they zoomed all around me in my seventy-five-mile-an-hour machine, so close their slip-stream rocked and jolted the L-4.

But that bomb attack didn't work: the P-40s had concentrated on the mountainside, avoiding the abbey and the town of Cassino itself. They hit fortified German positions on the slopes and provided the Americans with a flood of bomb-shocked German prisoners, driven out of their minds by concussion, but bombing the mountain did not open the way to Rome. When the next attempt came from the air, it was a disaster.

If I ever knew what the tactical thinking was behind the second attack, I've forgotten. In those days, we all thought that heavy bomb raids were demoralizing and so destructive that nothing could survive in the target area, so, somewhere up the chain of command, the decision was made to bomb Cassino town *and* the abbey with medium and heavy bombers —B-25s, B-26s, and B-17s. I saw those types in the air: there may also have been B-24s, but they didn't cross my vision. What *did* cross my vision, floating over the abbey at three thousand feet—assignment: suppress heavy flak—was an oncoming and seemingly never-ending fleet of bombers, approaching from the south. The mediums were at about six or seven thousand feet; the heavies way up there, just silhouettes. The heavy German flak, mostly 88s, went mad: the floor of the Liri Valley was sprinkled with red-orange muzzle flashes as the Germans threw everything they had at this incredible number of American bombers, a number seen up to then only over the *Heimat* itself. It must have struck the German flak crews as a splendid chance to get even, but they needn't have bothered. I saw not one American airplane hit by flak. I did see American bombs exploding all around the compass, twenty miles beyond the target, twenty miles short of the target, twenty miles to the left, twenty miles to the right. A fair number even landed on Cassino town and the abbey, but most landed in Allied territory. To watch a bombing run of that magnitude, involving hundreds of aircraft, was an awesome thing, to put it mildly; those heavy bombs sent up volcanoes of dirt and fire, the air shook, you could see ripples running across the surface of the earth as though an earthquake were in progress, and you felt the concussion even at three thousand feet. But my God, how inaccurate they were! The result of this second raid, which went on all morning, was that the town of Cassino was turned to rubble, making it impassable for American tanks, which were poised to attack, and the abbey was also turned to rubble, even though no Allied soldiers were near it. Fourteen hundred years were blown away that morning.

As I noted earlier, German flak crews were very cautious in shooting at the L-4s, but of course there were times when they thought the odds were in their favor and would let fly. Flak came in various calibers, from the big 88s on down to the 20-mm. rapid-fire cannon, often mounted on half-tracks or flat-bed trucks. The 88s usually fired a "ladder" of six rounds, apparently hoping you'd fly into one of the three pairs, and people sometimes did. But the muzzle flash of the 88 was so large and bright that you couldn't miss it. In the Vosges in France I was flying near Bitche when six brown bursts appeared off my right wing, not close enough to do any harm. However, I had seen the muzzle flashes from a village across the Rhine, and when I radioed the 93rd's fire direction center and gave them the coordinates, they poured thirty-six rounds into the village: there were no more "ladders" from that quarter. On that mission, I became so intent on watching the effect of the fire that I made the supreme error of not keeping my head moving: you had to keep looking up, down, behind, and on all sides. Although the Luftwaffe was occupied primarily at that stage with the Eastern front, there *were* fighter squadrons in the West, too. And sure enough, when I finally looked away from the target area, a Messerschmitt 109 was boring straight in at me, about a hundred yards away. I froze, unable to move the controls, and just sat there staring at the enormous, bright red spinner on his prop, certain this was it. But he zipped past beneath me, rocking the L-4, without firing a shot. I assume he was returning from a mission and had run out of ammo.

One of the strangest experiences I had with flak occurred near Dijon. The weather was atrocious—a cloud cover at about five hundred feet and misting rain. I was cruising back and forth near a village, at about three hundred feet, when I spotted six small, rapid muzzle flashes from the main street of the village. I depressed the button on the mike to give coordinates, but before I could speak, the six 20-mm. rounds burst around the airplane. I hollered into the open microphone, "Jesus Christ! The bastards are shooting at me!" The fire direction center said, very calmly, "Coordinates please." Very unprofessional behavior on my part. Anyway, I dropped down and hedge-hopped while I gave the coordinates, the fire direction center radioed, "One round smoke, on the way!" I pulled up to three hundred feet again, and the white phosphorus round burst alongside the flak wagon, which in this case was a flat-bed truck. I dived again, again they radioed, "On the way!" and again I pulled up, to see six rounds of high explosives smother the truck. It's marvelous to be young and have reflexes which make you push the mike button before the enemy's rounds even arrive in your neighborhood: alas, those days and those reflexes are gone forever. Nowadays I can't even tell when a network vice-president is after my ass, until it's too late to take cover.

Our own antiaircraft fire was notoriously inaccurate, partly, no doubt, because the crews had very few targets to practice on, and we often had reason to thank God for that. I think most L-4 pilots were shot at by their own side at least once. The U.S. Navy found it impossible to distinguish between L-4s and German aircraft, and flying anywhere near a U.S. warship during an amphibious landing was a hairy experience. At Anzio, where we sometimes had to fly courier runs from Monte Cassino, there was a rule that the L-4s had to enter the beachhead area precisely at the point where the front line curved down to the sea. This was supposed to tell the Navy that you were friendly, but it didn't, and the Germans *knew* you weren't friendly. The result was sky filled with carpets of U.S. Navy gunfire, while the Germans below emptied machine guns and rifles into the air. Bill Leonard, who is now president of CBS News, was a gunnery officer on a destroyer during that war, and once when he and I were exchanging war stories, it gradually developed that he had personally shot at me all over the Mediterranean.

The Navy had nothing to do with my most upsetting experience with American antiaircraft, however. We were operating out of a cow pasture near the German village of Frankenhofen, attached to a fresh division whose L-4 pilots were very green. One morning hundreds of German soldiers started trickling out of the surrounding woods to give themselves up, since the war was obviously ending. We made them sit down in a corner of the pasture and went on flying missions, but at noon a German Red Cross nurse turned up on a bicycle and told us, in French, that an SS armored detachment was in the next village, about ten kilometers away, and the SS did *not* think the war was obviously ending. In fact, the nurse told us, the SS people were so annoyed by the soldiers who had surrendered to us that they were gearing up for an attack on their comrades and us. I immediately told the inexperienced captain commanding the division air section that we should get the hell out of there, but he poohpoohed the idea, saying he didn't think the nurse was telling the truth, so we kept on flying missions throughout the afternoon.

Finally the sun went down, the flying stopped, and I braced myself for a very uneasy night. Then, just before bedtime, the nurse turned up again; this time she said the SS were on the way. Instant pandemonium. Gear was tossed into half-tracks and trucks, the captain pointed out on the map a bombed-out German airstrip to our front and said we'd fly there.

We took off in pitch darkness. Over the radio I heard the other aircraft calling, trying to establish the compass course and warning one another to stay out of the way. These were fruitless instructions, since you couldn't see any other airplanes. The radio traffic was heard by our battalions, of course, and all the fire direction centers came on the air, demanding to know what was up. We told them they'd get details later and meanwhile to stay off the air. I kept droning along at about two thousand feet, hoping I had the proper compass course and wondering how I would spot the bombed-out airfield even if I *was* on course. A half-moon came out from behind some clouds, which helped a little: you could see reflections on rivers and ponds, but not much else. Suddenly, there was a great burst of orange flame on the ground below us, and what seemed like every antiaircraft weapon in the U.S. Army opened up, spouting tracers in all directions. I dived, hoping my altimeter was reasonably accurate and that there were no high-tension lines in the neighborhood, and hollered into the radio to the 93rd to tell the antiaircraft people to cut that out. A German bomber had unloaded on a bridge that was heavily defended against aerial attack. Presumably he had picked up our L-4s on his radar and had sneaked in under cover of those radar reflections, knowing American radar couldn't distinguish him from us.

We got past that and actually found the bombed-out German airfield: the concrete of the ruined runways gleamed in the moonlight, and there was just enough left of one of them to put down an L-4. One pilot did get lost for about an hour and called frantically and constantly over the radio for help. Finally the division captain told him we would fire a .50-caliber machine gun and he could home in on the tracers. We fired into the air, and instantly every other .50-caliber in the neighborhood did the same, apparently under the impression that another air raid was in progress. Some of their rounds came quite close to the lost pilot, to judge by the squeaking tone which came from him over the radio, but he finally found us and landed. It was a very busy night, and we never did find out if the SS detachment made a run at our Frankenhofen strip.

German artillery, tanks, and flak batteries could not avoid giving away their positions as soon as they went into action, of course, but the German infantrymen were wizards at the art of cover and concealment. From the air, they were almost never seen, either in attack or retreat, but I do recall one remarkable exception. Flying under a heavy overcast at about five hundred feet in Burgundy, I was astonished to see a column of some fifty German soldiers riding bicycles along a secondary road, not a quarter mile away. They must have heard my engine, but there they were, pedaling along at a leisurely pace, rifles slung across their backs. The road ran straight for about two miles, then bent into a horseshoe curve around a small hill. I radioed the coordinates of the horseshoe bend to the fire direction center, adjusted the smoke rounds until they were landing in the bend, then waited for the bicycles to arrive at that spot. When it did, we fired six rounds from each gun in B Battery, making thirty-six high-explosive shells in all. An officer of the 93rd visited the area the next day and found some twenty mangled bicycles lying along the road.

Compared with the Germans, we were prodigal with our artillery ammunition. They had to be rather miserly, but we shot at anything that moved or even looked suspicious. On several occasions I chased solitary motorcycle riders with 105-mm. rounds that cost about ninety dollars each, without ever hitting one, so far as I know. The motorcyclists were considered worthwhile targets because the assumption was they were dispatch riders carrying orders back and forth between various headquarters, so we would pump out dozens of shells at them. I was doing just that one day north of Rome when, with that marvelous peripheral vision granted the young and healthy, I saw a horse run out from the woods with a man hanging on to its bridle, struggling to drag the horse back under cover. I was low enough to see he was wearing *Feldgrau*, so I called for a round of smoke in the woods. It burst, and immediately dozens of horse-drawn artillery pieces, caissons, field kitchens, and wagons came plunging out of the trees onto the road, headed north at full gallop. They had obviously holed up there waiting for nightfall before moving into new positions, but they now found themselves on a straight stretch of road in broad daylight. The horse-drawn column was thoroughly raked, and all because one horse had bolted into the open, driven berserk, no doubt, by the noise of our shells chasing the motorcycle driver.

During the week-long battle of Montélimar, in the Rhone Valley, I came as close to ground combat as I ever care to get. We were operating from a farm near the village of Loriol. The farm family had fled, leaving the place in the charge of a hired hand, who was clearly not right in the head. The battle had developed when a combat command column of armor, artillery, and infantry had raced northward from southern France along roads paralleling the Rhone, then turned westward north of Montélimar, cutting the main highway. The German 19th Army was trying to go north to support the German defenses in Normandy, so this created a problem. The highway was soon littered with shot-up tanks, trucks, and artillery pieces, burning hulks strung out over ten miles. From the air we could see a German counter-attack starting up from the northeast, and since the infantry was heavily engaged along the highway to the west, there was nothing to stop the German attack but artillery. The shooting was frantic and incessant: on one day I flew more than ten hours, landing every two hours or so for gasoline, but the German armored cars and light tanks kept edging closer and by nightfall were within about two miles of our farm. Assuming they would push on during the night, we built a hollow square of hay bales in the barn, and crawled inside it, pulling another bale over the entrance. The idea was that the German infantry, when they came, would go right on by. And sure enough, they did come, Schmeisser machine pistols burping bullets in every direction, but we were safe in our hay-bale cave. Unfortunately, however, we had given that hired hand a cup of instant coffee during the day, the first he'd had since the war began, no doubt, and he chose this moment to come into the barn with a lantern to thank us. In horror we watched the light get brighter through the cracks between the hay bales, then he pulled away the one covering our entrance hole, leaned in, and said, with the beautiful smile of the idiot, "Nescafé est bon!" We waited for the Germans to jump him and us, but they didn't. By the time the night was over, we were ready to shoot the hired hand ourselves, since he repeated the same stunt four more times. Years later, my mother heard from the mother of our mechanic that he had recurring nightmares in which he woke, shouting, "Nescafé est bon!" and she wondered if my mother could ask me about it. You just don't need civilians at a time like that.

There were exceptions, of course: when I landed my L-4 in a field in southern France, after taking off from an LST which had been fitted with a plywood flight deck, I jumped out of the airplane before it stopped rolling and crawled into a clump of bushes. The situation was, as they say, "fluid," and I didn't know where the infantry line was located. Lying there, I heard somebody running in my direction and puckered up, expecting to see a German rifleman. Instead it was a French farmer carrying a bottle of red wine and a smeared glass. He filled the glass, handed it to me, and shouted "Bienvenue! Bienvenue!" I fell in love with La Belle France on the spot and have remained in love with her ever since.

We went on through France, finally crossed the Rhine near Strasbourg, turned southeast through Germany and on into Austria. Taking off one morning from a field outside Imst, I was astonished to find the roads crammed with German vehicles of every description. Paradise for an artillery spotter! But when I began radioing fire directions, the battalion called back, "Wait." This happened several times, and I got angrier and angrier, until finally the fire direction center radioed, "Cease all forward action." When I landed, I discovered that the war was over. It was a terrible letdown: I had assumed the war would *never* end, or that I wouldn't be there when it did. According to my logbook I had flown 368 missions and turned a lot of beautiful German hardware into scrap. Aside from falling in love with the perfect woman, nothing has ever seemed so important or exciting since.

—October 1981

THE PLACE OF FRANKLIN D. ROOSEVELT IN HISTORY

By ALLAN NEVINS

His was not a great intellect, and his flashes of insincerity shook the confidence even of close friends. Nevertheless, says Nevins, "for centuries Americans will think of him as one of those spirits who ride in front."

Seldom has an eminent man been more conscious of his place in history than was Franklin D. Roosevelt. He regarded history as an imposing drama and himself as a conspicuous actor. Again and again he carefully staged a historic scene: as when, going before Congress on December 8, 1941, to call for a recognition of war with Japan, he took pains to see that Mrs. Woodrow Wilson accompanied Mrs. Roosevelt to the Capitol, thus linking the First and Second World Wars. As governor and as President, he adopted for the benefit of future historians the rule that every letter addressed to him, however insignificant, and copies of every document issued from his office, should be preserved. This mass of papers, mounting into the millions, soon became almost overwhelming. It might have been added, with some difficulty, to the many other official collections of the Library of Congress. But, with a strong sense of his special place in history, Roosevelt wanted a memorial all his own, a place of resort for scholars, connected uniquely with his name and his administrations. He announced the gift of his papers to the nation; his mother gave sixteen acres of land for a building at Hyde Park; some 28,000 donors subscribed $400,000 for an edifice; and Congress made the Roosevelt Library a federal institution.

In this Library at Hyde Park, as a token of his place in history, he took an almost naïve pride. I well recall the dinner he gave early in 1939 to the trustees and a select number of historians to discuss plans for its management. It took place at the Mayflower Hotel in Washington; he was wheeled up an inclined ramp to his place at a central table; he waved joyously to everyone; he enjoyed his stewed mulligatawny turtle—a favorite dish—his companions, his sense of launching another original enterprise. In a long informal speech he talked of certain predecessors: of Lincoln, of Grover Cleveland, whom he had known, and of his cousin Theodore Roosevelt; he dwelt on Woodrow Wilson's sense of history—Wilson in 1917 had forbidden young Roosevelt, then Assistant Secretary of the Navy, to bring warships up from Cuban waters to the United States lest future historians should accuse him of making a provocative gesture on the eve of our first war with Germany. I well recall, too, the still more interesting occasion when he laid the cornerstone of the Hyde Park Library on November 19, 1939. Trustees, historians, and editors lunched with him; he gaily drove his own specially equipped car to the site; he chatted blithely with everyone; and he watched the cornerstone slip into place with a gratified smile.

Today his grave lies close by that Library, and by the family home that has become a national shrine, visited by hundreds of thousands every year. To the collections there shelved, multitudes of scholars annually repair, for they are open to all. Roosevelt's own deposits, including letters, documents, books, pamphlets, films, photographs, speeches, and museum pieces, have exceeded a total of fifty million items; and to them are being added the papers of Cabinet officers and other official associates. The career of no other American President has so vast a documentation for history.

Is it too soon to estimate the place of Franklin D. Roosevelt in the stream of American and world events? It is never too soon for such a task. History is not a remote Olympian bar of judgment, but a controversial arena in which each generation must make its own estimate of the past. We have every right to fix the historical position of Roosevelt as we see it today, knowing that it will be reassessed from the vantage point of a longer perspective and fuller knowledge in 1975, and re-estimated again in 2065. That it will be a great place we may already be certain. A statue to Roosevelt has been reared in Oslo. When a statue was proposed in London, five-shilling subscriptions were opened one morning: they were closed that night with the sum oversubscribed: had they been kept open a few days money would have poured in for five statues. Streets have been named for him around the world. Fifty American historians, interrogated by Arthur M. Schlesinger, Sr., of Harvard, have all but unanimously agreed that in the roster of Presidents Lincoln stands first, Washington second, and Franklin D. Roosevelt third. Hearing of that verdict, Winston Churchill declared that in impact upon world history Roosevelt unquestionably stood first.

We have this advantage in attempting the task, that a great part of the necessary evidence is already at hand. Never before in human annals has so huge a volume of reminiscences, autobiographies, impressions, letters, official documents, and other data bearing on one man been issued within twenty years of his death. The thirteen volumes of Roosevelt's official papers edited by Judge Samuel I. Rosenman and the four volumes of personal letters edited by Elliot Roosevelt; the memoirs of Cordell Hull, Harry Hopkins, Henry Morgenthau, Harold Ickes, Henry L. Stimson, James Farley, Edward J. Flynn, Mrs. Franklin D. Roosevelt, Frances Perkins, Grace Tully, Hugh Johnson, Dwight Eisenhower, Omar Bradley, and a hundred others; the mass of comment by Washington reporters and war correspondents who watched history being made; the procession of European histories and memoirs so impressively headed by Winston Churchill's volumes—this already forms a corpus too great for one student to explore fully in a lifetime. But while we shall have immense fresh accretions of detail, it is unlikely that we shall receive any startling new "revelations," any facts that will offer a basis for sweeping revisions of judgment.

In dealing with every commanding figure of history, a fundamental question presents itself: To what extent did greatness inhere in the man, and to what degree was it a product of the situation? If great men have their starts, as Napoleon said he did, it is often because of a national or world crisis favors greatness. The reason why fifty American historians did not wholly agree with Winston Churchill upon Roosevelt's rank among the nation's Presidents is, I think, simple. Washington had indisputable greatness in himself. "The first, the last, the best, the Cincinnatus of the West," as Lord Byron called him, he was great in character, great in traits of leadership, great in insight and wisdom. Lincoln had an even more manifest and appealing personal greatness. His public utterances, from the House Divided address to the Gettysburg Address, his state papers, from the First Inaugural to the final pronouncements on Reconstruction, attest a rare intellectual power. The wisdom of his principal public acts, his magnanimity toward all foes public and private, his firmness under adversity, his elevation of spirit, his power of strengthening the best purposes and suppressing the worst instincts of a broad, motley democracy, place him in the front rank of modern statesmen.

But with Franklin D. Roosevelt we feel no such assurance of transcendent personal eminence. We feel that he lacked the steadfast elevation of character exhibited by George Washington. We find in him distinctly less intellectual power than in Jefferson, Lincoln, or perhaps Woodrow Wilson. We conclude, in short, that his tremendous place in history was in lesser degree the product of his special personal endowments, and in larger degree the handiwork of his stormy times, than that occupied by George Washington or Abraham Lincoln.

That Roosevelt had remarkable intellectual gifts is plain; but these gifts fell short of the highest distinction. He possessed a quick, resourceful, and flexible mind. This fact is illustrated on an elevated level by his ability to deal with fifty important issues in a day, making shrewd decisions on each; by his power in wartime of efficiently co-ordinating departments, industries, and armies, of gaining the teamwork of generals, admirals, and business leaders, as no other President has ever done. He organized the national energies with unique success. His intellectual proficiency is illustrated on a lower plane by almost any of the press conferences recorded in Judge Rosenman's volumes; by his deft tact in handling two-score quick-witted newspapermen, evading some questions, dissecting the fatuity of others, using a few to touch a needed chord of public opinion, and responding to many with concise, expert answers. Like his cousin Theodore Roosevelt, he had an insatiable curiosity about books, about men, about events. It was linked with an unquenchable zest for experience; the zest expressed in his famous wartime message to Churchill, "It is fun to be in the same century with you."

He had a talent for quick parliamentary hits. He could make his enemies ridiculous by a few pungent words, as in the happy rhythmical phrase about "Martin, Barton, and Fish" that, recited over the radio, exposed these three reactionary congressmen to a continental gale of laughter in 1940; or by a lambent flare of humor, as in his speech of 1944 picturing the Scottish unhappiness of his dog Fala over an accusation of extravagance. He had flashes of daring imagination. He had a remarkable gift of rapid improvisation, as he showed in all the recurrent crises of his twelve crowded years in office. In part this consisted of his ability to use other men's thought; "He is the best picker of brains who ever lived," his intimates used to say. His power of application was remarkable even among our overworked Presidents. He had an average working day of fourteen hours (Truman later boasted of sixteen), and he told Governor James M. Cox: "I never get tired."

But of preeminent intellectual talent he had little. I recall Walter Lippmann saying in the second administration: "He has never written a real state paper." In a sense that is true. No paper signed by him equals Washington's Farewell Address, Lincoln's great papers, Theodore Roosevelt's first annual message, or Woodrow Wilson's nobler productions. Nearly all his speeches were in fact largely written for him by others. Robert Sherwood describes a typical scene: Judge Rosenman, Harry Hopkins, and Sherwood gathered about a table discussing the material for an imminent presidential address, and threshing it over and over until Judge Rosenman impatiently flung down a pencil with the words, "There comes a time in the life of every speech when it's got to be *written*!"

Roosevelt wrote no books; he was probably incapable of matching such a work as Theodore Roosevelt's *The Winning of the West*. He threw out no such immortal epigrams as Churchill's sentence challenging Britons to face a future of "blood, sweat, and tears." His best phrases, like "the forgotten man" and "the new deal," were borrowed from other men.

A capacity for abstract thought was largely omitted from his equipment. The idea once current that he had a special intimacy with Maynard Keynes was obviously erroneous, for he was simply incapable of following a mind so analytical, an intellect so subtle, as that of Lord Keynes. When John Gunther asked one of Roosevelt's friends, "Just how does the President think?" he met the reply: "The President never *thinks*." Like Theodore Roosevelt, he was primarily a man of action. His mental processes, as many friends have said, were intuitive rather than logical. He reacted rather than reflected. A President is not necessarily too busy to do abstract thinking. Newton D. Baker, who held a minor post in Grover Cleveland's administration and a major office under Woodrow Wilson, once observed to me that while Cleveland shouldered his way through difficulties like a buffalo charging a thicket, Wilson "dissolved his problems by an acid process of thought." This acid process was beyond Roosevelt. All that is told us of his reading suggests that it was rather adolescent: either escapist, like the detective stories carried on every long trip; or attached to a hobby, like naval history; or journalistic. His humor lacked the philosophic overtones of Lincoln's, or even the saltiness of Harry Truman's; it too was somewhat adolescent. It was usually the humor of the quip, as when he said to his secretary, Grace Tully, overaddicted to punctuation, "Grace, how often do I have to tell you not to waste the taxpayer's commas?" Or it was the humor of the wisecrack, as when he remarked to the six New England governors who startled him in 1933 by suddenly appearing at the White House in a body: "What, all six of you? You're not going to secede from the Union, are you?"

We all know what Lord Bacon said makes a ready man; and intellectually, the talkative Roosevelt was a ready leader—perhaps the readiest of all the world's leaders in his exigent time. This power to act quickly, shrewdly, and earnestly was a gift that served the nation and the free world with unforgettable dexterity and force. Honoring this princely capacity, we can afford to give minor weight to the fact that his mind, compared with that of Woodrow Wilson, sometimes appears superficial, and that he possessed no such intellectual versatility as Thomas Jefferson—to say nothing of Winston Churchill.

In respect of character, similarly, he had traits of an admirable kind; but we must add that even in combination, they fell short of a truly Roman weight of virtue. He held sincere religious conviction, and it was no mere gesture that led him to take his Cabinet, on the morn of his first inauguration, to divine service at St. John's. "I think," writes Mrs. Roosevelt in *This I Remember*, "he actually felt he could ask God for guidance and receive it. That was why he loved the Twenty-third Psalm, the Beatitudes, and the thirteenth chapter of First Corinthians." He was one of the unflinching optimists of his time. Having conquered a prostrating illness and horrible physical handicap, he felt an inner faith in man's power to conquer anything. When his aides made estimates of American industrial capacity, he raised them; when the Combined Chiefs of Staff set down dates for the various goals in the invasion of Europe, he revised them forward. Because of his religious faith and his ingrained optimism, he possessed an unfailing serenity. In the stormiest of hours his nerve was never shaken.

On his first day in the Presidency in 1933, with the banks of the nation closed down and the country almost prostrate with anxiety, he found his desk at six o'clock in the afternoon quite clear. He pressed a button. Four secretaries appeared at four doors to the room. "Is there anything more, boys?" he inquired. "No, Mr. President," they chorused. And Roosevelt remarked with his happy smile: "This job is a cinch!"

Equally admirable were his idealism, his consciousness of high objectives, and his frequent nobility of spirit. He was willing to sacrifice himself for the public weal. When in 1928 Alfred E. Smith, the Democratic presidential candidate, asked him to run for the governor of New York, he was told by physicians that if he kept out of public life another year or two, he could regain the use of his left leg, while if he did not he would be incurably lame; but he answered the call of duty. His concern for the poor, the friendless, the unfortunate, was more keenly humane than that of any leader since Lincoln. "I see one-third of a nation," he said in his Second Inaugural, "ill-housed, ill-clad, ill-nourished"—and meant to do something about it. Moderately rich himself, he disliked those who were too rich. The steel magnate Eugene Grace, who took a bonus of a million dollars a year without the knowledge of his stockholders, aroused his bitter scorn. "Tell Gene he'll never make a million a year again!" was the angry message he sent the man. Frances Perkins, who had known him as a rather arrogant, snobbish young man before his seizure by infantile paralysis, and who knew him as a battler for social justice afterward, believed that his physical ordeal taught him sympathy for the afflicted and underprivileged.

Yet, we must add, these impressive virtues were flawed by certain grievous defects. He had flashes of insincerity which sometimes impaired the confidence even of close friends. Henry L. Stimson mentions in his memoirs the fact that, having found out Roosevelt in a quite needless bit of duplicity, for several years avoided all contact with him. Henry A. Wallace committed to paper an account of Roosevelt's double-dealing (as Wallace saw it) in handling the Vice Presidential nomination in 1944. Other men have penned different stories. Even the President's defenders could not deny that his treatment of that critical problem showed a certain irresponsibility, to be excused perhaps by the fact that he was already more ill than he realized. Because of this instability, Roosevelt was ready at times to abandon principle for expediency. Cordell Hull has described how unfortunate were the results of such an abandonment in the Neutrality Acts. And Mrs. Roosevelt writes: "While I often felt strongly on various subjects, Franklin frequently refrained from supporting causes in which he believed, because of political realities. There were times when this annoyed me very much. In the case of the Spanish Civil War, for instance, we had to remain neutral, though Franklin knew quite well he wanted the democratic government to be successful. But he also knew he could not get Congress to go along with him. To justify his action, or lack of action, he explained to me, when I complained, that the League of Nations had asked us to remain neutral. . . . He was simply trying to salve his own conscience. It was one of the many times I felt akin to a hair shirt."

Edward J. Flynn writes flatly: "The President did not keep his word on many appointments." There exists no question that he promised to make Louis Johnson Secretary of War, and broke the promise. All statesmen have to adjust principle to events and to public sentiment, and are sometimes compelled to revoke promises. But Roosevelt was at times indefensibly evasive even with intimates like Flynn and Louis Johnson, and lacked straightforwardness. It can be said, too, that he often followed a Machiavellian technique of administration. He liked, for example, to put two or three men in positions of conflicting authority, so that they worked at loggerheads, with himself as ultimate arbiter. It was in part his fault that Sumner Welles and Cordell Hull made the State Department for several years a maelstrom of rival policies and ambitions—although this is a complex story; it was in part his fault that Jesse Jones and Henry Wallace engaged at one time in a feud which sadly injured both the administration and the country.

Other unhappy traits might be copiously illustrated. Roosevelt could seem dismayingly casual about everything from a political speech to some of the issues at Yalta. He could be reprehensibly secretive; he kept the minutes of the Teheran Conference from Secretary of State Hull, and withheld from the American people the concession he made at Yalta to Russia on votes in the United Nations Assembly. He was pettily vindictive toward some opponents, as Raymond B. Moley and James Farley testify in detail, and his attempted purge of certain southern leaders in

1938 is far from the happiest chapter in his career. All in all, we must repeat our conclusion that his character lacked the symmetry, harmony, and weight found in that of Washington and of Lincoln.

Yet without the highest inner greatness Roosevelt had an effective greatness of action, in relation to his time, which will cause him to be remembered as happily as any American leader. It is significant that Churchill, intellectually so much superior, always treated him with manifest deference, as a lesser man bowing to a greater. Was this simply because Roosevelt headed the more powerful state? I think not. We must here face what seems to me a salient fact of history. A leader who puts second-rate qualities of intellect and character into first-rate application to the needs of his time may be a greater man than the leader who puts first-rate qualities into second-rate application. Roosevelt signally illustrates this aphorism. He had, to begin with, the gift of address: a gift for doing the right thing at just the right time. He had, in the second place, the greater gift of being able to put his personal forces into harmony with the best forces of his era.

Roosevelt's effective greatness included an unrivalled power of matching the urgent crisis with the adequate act; a power of timing an impressive measure to meet a desperate need. Take the first days of 1933, after his election. Never in a period of peace—never since the days of British invasion in 1814, or Confederate victory in 1863—had the nation been in such straits. Between twelve and fifteen million men were out of work. Five million families, one-seventh of the population, were supported by public relief or private charity. Since the beginning of the depression, 4,600 banks had failed. Travellers through the broad industrial belt from Chicago to New York seemed to pass nothing but closed factory gates. Half the automobile plants of Michigan shut down. Along the Great Lakes, path of the largest marine commerce of the world, ships had almost ceased to move. In the iron beds of the Mesabi and Vermilion ranges scarcely a shovel dipped into the richest ores of the globe; in the copper mountain at Butte scarcely a drill was at work. The looms of southern textile factories were cobwebbed. On railway sidings locomotives gathered rust in long rows; behind them huddled passenger and freight cars in idle hundreds, their paint fading. Middlewestern farmers gazed bitterly at crops whose market value was less than the cost of harvesting; on the high plains, ranchers turned cattle loose to graze at will because it did not pay to send them to the stockyards. In Pennsylvania and New England desperate men and women offered to work for anything, and some did work for a dollar a week.

Worst of all was the fear which gripped the nerves of the nation. To observers who traveled across the country in trains almost empty, through factory districts with hardly a wisp of smoke, the helpless populations sent up an almost audible cry of anger, bewilderment, and panic. The day before Roosevelt took office the crisis gathered to a climax. By midnight of March 3 the closing of all remaining banks had been or was being ordered in every state. Never before had a change of Presidents taken place against a background so dramatic. The people, awakening on March 4 to read that their financial system was prostrate, gathered at noon by millions about their radios to listen in anguish, in anxiety, but in hope, to the voice of their new national leader.

There ensued four of the most brilliantly successful months in the history of American government. Roosevelt's first words promised energy: "I assume unhesitatingly the leadership of this great army of our people, dedicated to a disciplined attack upon our common problems." He improvised a series of policies, and mobilized an administrative machine, with a vigor that would have done credit to any wartime executive. Within thirty-six hours he had taken absolute control of the currency and banking system, and called Congress in extraordinary session. He forthwith launched an aggressive attack along half a dozen fronts; upon banking problems, industrial prostration, farm distress, unemployment, public works, the burden of public and private debt. One reporter wrote that the change in Washington was like that from oxcart to airplane. Congress labored for ninety-nine days under the President's all-but-complete sway. Almost his every wish was obeyed by immediate votes. One staggered member said of the program: "It reads like the first chapter of Genesis."

And as Roosevelt took these steps his courage, his resourcefulness, his blithe optimism, infected the spirit of the people; he gave Americans a new confidence and the *élan* of a new national unity. When he gaily signed his last bills and departed for a brief sail up the Atlantic coast as skipper of a 45-foot sailing boat, the nation realized that it had turned from stagnation to a bright adventure. As the President put it, we were "on our way."

Nor was this an isolated spasm of leadership; for each recurrent crisis found the same resourcefulness called into effective play. When France fell, when the British Commonwealth stood alone against the deadliest foe that modern civilization had known, Americans gazed at the European scene in fear, in gloom, in perplexity. With a sense of dumb helplessness, tens of millions put their intensest feeling into the hope for Britain's survival. Those tens of millions never forgot the morning of September 3, 1940, when they read the headlines announcing that Roosevelt had told a startled Congress of the transfer of fifty destroyers to embattled Britain; a defiance of Hitler, a defiance of home isolationists, a first long stride toward ranging America against the Fascist despots. Nor could lovers of world freedom ever forget the dramatic steps that followed hard upon British victory over Hitler's air force and upon Roosevelt's re-election: the Four Freedoms speech of January 6, 1941; the introduction of the Lend-Lease Bill four days later, a measure which completely transformed American foreign policy; the establishment of naval and military posts in Greenland and Iceland; the proclamation of an unlimited national emergency; the seizure of all Axis ships and Axis credits; the Atlantic Charter meeting with Churchill off Newfoundland; the establishment of convoys for American ships carrying aid to Britain; and, in the background, the stimulation of American production to an unprecedented flow of guns, tanks, shells, and airplanes, with factories roaring day and night for the defense of democracy.

These years 1940–41 were, as we see now, among the greatest crises in modern history. They were met with an imagination, boldness, and ingenuity that can hardly be overpraised. Parochialism, timidity, or fumbling might have been fatal; even a pause for too much reflection might have been fatal. We knew then that Roosevelt was determined to face the exigency with an intrepidity worthy of the republic. But his intention was even more courageous than we supposed. For we know now that Harry Hopkins told Churchill in London early in 1941: "The President is determined that we shall win the war together. Make no mistake about it. He sent me here to tell you that at all costs and by all means he will carry you through."

Roosevelt's second quality of effective greatness was his ability to vindicate the American method of pragmatic experiment, of practical *ad hoc* action, step by step. He was essentially a Jeffersonian. He belonged to the school which, following the historic Anglo-American bent of mind, is attached to facts rather than ideas, to the enlargement of precedents rather than the formulation of dazzling visions. Like all Anglo-American statesmen, he disliked sweeping generalizations, and especially generalizations of an intolerant, exclusive nature. He loved experimental advance, and was wont to say that if he were right sixty percent of the time, he would be satisfied. Like Jefferson, he was willing to scrap a theory the moment a brute fact collided with it; he trusted experience, and distrusted flights into the empyrean. His so-called revolution, though unprecedentedly broad and swift, was like Jefferson's "revolution"; it was simply a combination of numerous practical changes, the main test of which was whether or not they worked.

The Rooseveltian changes did work. They did transform American life and the American outlook in two distinct ways. They converted a nation of aggressive individualists into a social-minded nation accepting the principles of the welfare state. They changed an isolationist or largely isolationist nation into one committed to world partnership and world leadership. The New Deal in home affairs was empirical, not ideological. The emergency program I have sketched was a stopgap affair put together to tide over a crisis, and as Mrs. Roosevelt once put it, "give us time to think." It succeeded. Taken as a whole, the New Deal passed through two phases. In the first, 1933–35, the government tried scarcity economics, reducing factory production, farm output, and hours of work, and doing what it could to cut off the American economy from the outside world. In the second and better phase, 1935–50, it tried full employment, full production, enlarged distribution of goods, and freer international trade. This led directly toward the acceptance of Cordell Hull's ideal of co-operative internationalism. American participation in world affairs after 1938 similarly passed through two phases. In the first, all the nation's energies were devoted to the defeat of the Axis. In the second, Roosevelt, Hull, Welles, and Stettinius moved step by step to construct a new world order, an enduring fabric of the United Nations. In home and foreign affairs alike action was always direct, experimental, and pragmatic.

It gave America a new social order at home, and a new orientation in global affairs. It worked; it is still working. But because it never approached a sweeping ideological revolution of the Marxist or totalitarian type, it was the despair of certain impractical theorists *pur sang*.

For example, readers of that brilliant but extraordinarily half-informed and error-streaked book, Harold Laski's *The American Democracy*, will find an almost incredible analysis of what the author regards as Mr. Roosevelt's fundamental failure. This was his failure to smash the old America completely, and build a quite new America on the theories that pleased Mr. Laski. The author draws an illuminating comparison between Lenin and Roosevelt. Lenin, it appears, made a marvelously precise and correct analysis of the maladies of modern society and economics; and he applied it with revolutionary courage. Roosevelt, on the other hand, was never converted—he never learned that "the foundations of the Americanism he inherited were really inadequate to the demands made upon its institutional expression." In particular, writes Laski, he failed to see that he should destroy "private ownership of the means of production"; that is, that the state should take over all mines, factories, transport, workshops, and farms. Roosevelt, as a result of his faulty analysis, unhappily failed to carry through a real revolution. What was the upshot? In Russia, admits Laski, life became nearly intolerable. The price of revolution proved "almost overwhelming"—starvation of millions, wholesale executions, vast concentration camps, the extinction of freedom. In America, Laski admits, life was immensely improved. Industrial production became enormous; farm output grew tremendous; the standard of living steadily rose. But theory (says Mr. Laski) is everything. Lenin with his ideology was right; Roosevelt with his practical experimentalism was a failure!

This view of the matter would be emphatically rejected by all but a handful of Americans, including those who do not admire Roosevelt. Like Jefferson, like Lincoln, like Wilson, he was innovator and conservator at once; he made daring new additions to the American fabric, but he kept the best of the old structure. While he converted Americans to the new ideal of social security, he strengthened their old faith in individual opportunity. He proved again that America needs no ideological revolution. He vindicated our traditional method of solving problems one at a time by pragmatic trial and error. As one journalist wrote: "One remembers him as a kind of smiling bus driver, with that cigarette holder pointed upward, listening to the uproar from behind as he took the sharp turns. They used to tell him that he had not loaded his vehicle right for all eternity. But he knew that he had stacked it well enough to round the next corner, and he knew when the yells were false, and when they were real, and he loved the passengers."

Roosevelt's third and most important quality of effective greatness lay in his ability to imbue Americans, and to some extent even citizens of other lands, with a new spiritual strength. Well into the twentieth century, most men in the New World had shared a dream of ever-widening adventure, a sense of elated achievement. They had dared much in coming to the new continent, and still more in mastering it. They were optimistic, self-confident, exuberant. The heavy costs of the First World War, the disillusionments of its aftermath, the pressure of complex new social problems, and above all the staggering blows of the Great Depression darkened our horizons. We had entered the Shadow Belt which Bryce predicted in his book on *The American Commonwealth*. From that zone of gloom, that numbed consciousness of frustration and failure, Roosevelt lifted Americans on the wings of his great new adventures—the alphabetical adventures of the AAA, NRA, the TVA; above all, on the wings of the greatest adventure in our history, the effort to rescue democracy from totalitarianism, and to organize the world to safeguard freedom.

For a few years Americans had felt lost, bewildered, paralyzed. Roosevelt carried them to a Moabite peak whence once more they saw promised lands. They threw off their frustrations; he gave them a feeling that they were participating in a life far wider than their everyday parochial concerns. His self-confidence, his enthusiasm, his happy faculty of obliterating old failures by bold new plans, taught them that they were not imprisoned in a dead past but were helping build a living future. In the three centuries 1607–1907 Americans had triumphantly mastered their physical environment. Just so, in the next century to come, they would master their social and economic environment at home, and join other nations in a mastery of the world environment. As the storm thickened, after 1940, Roosevelt's rich voice grew more urgent—"bidding the eagles of the West fly on." Here at last, he seemed to say, is a task worthy of you; tyranny like Hell is not easily conquered. Lincoln had once used a phrase which haunts his countrymen. "Thanks to all," he exclaimed after Gettysburg and Vicksburg, "thanks to all: for the great republic—for the principle it lives by and keeps alive—for man's vast future—thanks to all." A sense of man's vast future, a hope of shaping it for the better, never left Roosevelt's cheerful heart.

It is not often realized to what a degree the spirit of adventure kindled at home under the New Deal was carried over into world affairs when the United States faced the Axis menace. The defeatism of Hoover's day was gone. A hundred and sixty million citizens had been morally prepared to undertake unprecedented tasks. They grumbled; they cursed the hard luck of their grim era; they shuddered over the mounting costs—the colossal debt, the wasted resources; but they never doubted their ability to put the job through. That change in temper was primarily Roosevelt's accomplishment. It threw open, temporarily, the portals of a wider world. The change from oxcart was a spiritual, not a material, change. Never in our history have the emotion and resolution of the American people been so completely fused as when, as the first waves of American and British troops stormed across the Normandy beaches, Roosevelt sat at the radio leading the nation in prayer.

Effective greatness—that is Roosevelt's title to a high place in the world's history. Intellect and character are not enough; to them must be added personality, energy, and an accurate sense for the proper timing of action. Roosevelt was not an intellectual giant; but what of the personality that made the Arkansas sharecropper and the Harlem Negro feel they shared all the destinies of the republic? His character did not awe men by its massive strength; but what of the gifts that made him so efficient in harmonizing labor, capital, and agriculture at home, and getting discordant nations to pool their wartime efforts? He lacked the iron traits of Cromwell—but how incomparably more successful he was! He did not have the powerful grasp of Bismarck, but how much more beneficent was his career! In time his specific achievements may be blurred, but the qualities of his spirit will be remembered. For centuries Americans will think of him as one of those spirits who ride in front; we shall see his jaunty figure, his gaily poised head, still in advance of us. We shall hear his blithe voice in his words just before his death at Warm Springs on April 2, 1945: "The only limit to our realization of tomorrow will be our doubts of today. Let us move forward with strong and active faith."

—June 1966

REVISING THE TWENTIETH CENTURY

By JOHN LUKACS

The great struggles of our century have all been followed by tides of revulsion: Americans decided we were mad to have entered World War I; Russia should have been our enemy in World War II; the United States started the Cold War. Now another such tide has risen in Europe, and it may be on its way here.

History *is* revisionism. It is the frequent—nay, the ceaseless—reviewing and revising and rethinking of the past. The notion that the study and the writing of history consist of the filling of gaps or the adding of new small bricks to the building of the cathedral of historical knowledge was a nineteenth-century illusion ("We have now histories of the Federalists in every New England State, except for Connecticut. You must do Connecticut"), allied with the fantasy that once the scientific method has been followed precisely, with all extant documents exhausted, the result will be definite and final ("the definitive account of Waterloo, approved by British as well as by French and German and Dutch historians"). There are important differences between historical and legal evidence, one of them being that the historian deals in multiple jeopardy that the law eschews; the former is retrying and retrying again. There is nothing very profound in this observation, since that is what all thinking is about. Not the future, and not the present, but our past is the only thing we know. All human thinking involves the rethinking of the past.

There may be five hundred biographies of Lincoln, but there is no certainty that the 501st may not furnish our minds with something new and valid—and not necessarily because its author has found a new cache of Lincoln documents. What matters more than the accumulated *quantity* of the research (note the word: "re-search") is the crystallizing *quality* of the revision. What is its purpose? Is it exposé, scandal, sensation, or the more or less honest wish to demolish untruths? Is it the author's desire for academic or financial success, to further his advancement in front of his colleagues or in the greater world of affairs? Or (as is, alas, often the case) is it to further the cause of a political ideology? This is where the subject of this article comes in.

The term *revisionism* is of German origin. It was first applied to those German socialists who, around 1875, chose to mitigate the doctrine of the inevitability of the proletarian revolution. This Marxist usage does not concern us. But the other, and still present, use of historical "revisionism" has a German origin too. It arose after 1919, reacting to the punitive and condemnatory treaty imposed on Germany and on its World War I allies. The wish to revise their terms, to change the then drawn frontiers of Europe was a powerful impulse, eventually leading to Hitler and to World War II. However, the aim of this historical revisionism was not directed at injustices of geography; it was directed at injustices of the record—that is, at the unjust condemnation of Germany as responsible for the war, stated in the Treaty of Versailles. The Germans had every reason to combat that. As early as 1919 the new republican and democratic German government began to publish documents to prove that the guilt for the coming of the war in 1914 was not Germany's alone. A much more extensive and scholarly documentation was published in a series of volumes a few years later. The Germans felt so strongly about this that in 1923 a German amateur historian, Alfred von Wegerer, began issuing a scholarly journal, *Die Kriegsschuldfrage* (The War Guilt Question).

By that time the first wave of revisionism among American historians had begun to form. Of the four waves of revisionism in the twentieth century this was the longest and the strongest one. It began as an intellectual and academic (and sometimes also a political and an ethnic) reaction against the extreme condemnation of Germany in 1917 and 1918 that had been broadcast from many sources, including the Creel Committee, Wilson's own propaganda machine, with many exaggerations and falsehoods. It was a reaction by liberals and radicals against superpatriotism, not very different from (and often allied with) their opposition to American conformism, to the postwar Red Scare, to the Ku Klux Klan, to the American Legion of the twenties. As early as 1920, for example, *The Nation* started to attack the dangers of French, not of German, militarism. In September 1921 the magazine raised the question: "Who has contributed more to the myth of a guilty nation plotting the war against a peaceful Europe than the so-called historians who occupy distinguished chairs in our universities?" They were "willing tools" of "professional propaganda." The young and later distinguished Sidney Bradshaw Fay, then of Smith College (*not* a typical revisionist, I must add), had already published three successive articles in *The American Historical Review* ("New Light on the Origins of the World War"), a result of his reading of the recently published German, Austrian, and Russian documents. Within five years this first wave of revisionism swelled into a tide. From a scattered group of mavericks, revisionists now included respected members of the historical profession and reputable intellectuals: the prominent Charles A. Beard, the University of Chicago historian Ferdinand Schevill (who wrote in 1926 that "there are today among reputable historians only revisionists"), the sociologist turned historian Harry Elmer Barnes, whose *Genesis of the World War* was published by the reputable house of Knopf in 1926. Their cause was supported by amateurs such as the German-American judge Frederick Bausman (*Let France Explain*), by literary figures such as Albert J. Nock and H. L. Mencken, and by the editors of *The Nation* and of *The New Republic*, while the lumbering *Atlantic Monthly* was tacking over gradually to that side too.

By the late twenties the revisionist tide was further swelled by the predictable confluence of another historical argument, about 1917 and not 1914. The time had come to revise not only the thesis of German war guilt but the story of American involvement in the war. Much of that argument had already been suggested by the above-mentioned historians, especially by Barnes; but the first substantial book denouncing Wilson and American intervention, *Why We Fought*, was published in 1929 by C. Hartley Grattan, a onetime student of Barnes. By the early thirties article after article, book after book, was attacking American intervention in World War I. The most serious work was Walter Millis's *The Road to War* in 1935. The most determined book by a professional historian was Charles Callan Tansill's *America Goes to War* in 1938. By that time their arguments had filtered down from the margins of academia and from intellectuals' periodicals through the reading public to the broad lowlands of popular sentiment. *The Road to War* was a best seller, with as many as sixty thousand copies in print by 1936. A few months later Dr. Gallup reported that 70 percent of Americans thought it had been wrong to enter World War I. Meanwhile Hitler, Mussolini, and the Japanese were rising in power.

In 1938 and 1939 another current in the revisionist tide came to the surface. Many revisionists were now worried over what they saw as an ominous change in Franklin Roosevelt's foreign policy. (In 1932 Roosevelt ran as an isolationist, and as late as 1935 he went so far as to suggest his acceptance of the revisionist thesis.) Foremost among them were Barnes, Tansill, and the big gun among American historians, Charles Beard. In September 1939 Beard published a powerful blast against American intervention in Europe, *Giddy Minds and Foreign Quarrels* (the Republican senator D. Worth Clark, of Idaho, used his franking privilege to distribute ten thousand copies of this little book). Yet by 1940 the revisionist camp was badly split. Many of the liberals were coming around to support Britain against Hitler. Others were not. In 1940 Beard came out with another book, *A Foreign Policy for America*. Eleven years later Sen. Robert A. Taft published a book with a virtually identical title, but already in 1940 it was evident that the formerly radical and Jeffersonian Democrat Beard and the rigid Republican Taft were seeing eye to eye. But before the next year was out, the news of Pearl Harbor roared over them both.

Revisionism was submerged but not sunk. After 1945 came the second wave of American revisionism, attacking Roosevelt for having maneuvered the country into war, indeed, for having contributed surreptitiously and willfully to the catastrophe at Pearl Harbor. Many of the historian figures were the same ones as before, the two principal professionals among them Beard (*American Foreign Policy in the Making, 1932–1940* and *President Roosevelt and the Coming of the War*) and Tansill (*Back Door to War*). There were many others; but this second wave of revisionism received relatively little attention; many of the revisionist books were now printed by minor publishers. Yet the effect of this kind of revisionism was wider than what the publishing record might indicate. The majority of the so-called conservative movement that began to coalesce in the early 1950s was composed of former isolationists and revisionists. The principal element of the Republican surge after 1948 was a reaction against Roosevelt's foreign policy, including such different figures as Joseph R. McCarthy, John Foster Dulles, and the young William F. Buckley, Jr. It was part of the emergence of the New Right in American politics. Still, Hitler and Tojo had few public defenders, and this second wave of revisionism failed to swell into an oceanic current.

The third, and much larger, wave of revisionism came not from the New Right but from the New Left. These were the historians who during the fretful sixties attempted to rewrite the origins of the Cold War with Russia, arguing and claiming that American foreign policy and aggressiveness were at least as responsible for the coming of the Cold War as was the Soviet Union. The principal ones (again, there were many others) of those New Left historians were D. F. Fleming (*The Cold War and Its Origins*), William Appleman Williams

(*The Tragedy of American Diplomacy*), Gar Alperovitz (*Atomic Diplomacy*), David Horowitz (*The Free World Colossus*), Gabriel Kolko (*The Politics of War*), Diane Shaver Clemens (*Yalta*), and Lloyd C. Gardner (*Architects of Illusion*), all their books issued between 1959 and 1970 by the most reputable university presses and trade houses.

Unlike the revisionists of the 1920s and 1940s, these authors had little opposition from most of their historian colleagues, for such was the, generally Leftist, intellectual tendency of the American sixties. These authors were praised, and portions of their works anthologized in college readers and textbooks. Whereas the revisionists of the 1920s and 1930s had their greatest effect among general readers, most of the consumers of this third wave of revisionist prose were college students. When Robert Maddox, in his calm and serious *The New Left and the Origins of the Cold War* (1973), pointed out some of the dishonesties of the documentation and the inadequacies of scholarship in these books, he was treated with tuttutting and fence-sitting by most academic reviewers, so many vicars of Bray. However, as with so many fads and fashions of the sixties, the tide of Cold War revisionism, though temporarily overwhelming, did not endure for long.

Twenty or more years later we may detect the rise of a fourth wave of revisionism, coming again from the so-called Right rather than from the Left. Again this began in Germany, in the mid-1980s, developing there in *Historikerstreit* (historians' quarrel), whose main figures have been German professional historians who, while unwilling to whitewash Hitler and his regime (that has remained the work of self-appointed extreme pamphleteers for decades now, as well as of fanatical amateur historians such as the English David Irving), attempted to make their case against the uniqueness of the crimes committed by the Germans during the Third Reich. This tendency to revise some of the lately accepted and hitherto hardly questioned histories of the Second World War has recently appeared in Britain, with historians such as Maurice Cowling (in *The Impact of Hitler* and elsewhere: "the belief that Churchill had understood Hitler . . . was not true"), the younger Andrew Roberts (*The Holy Fox—A Biography of Lord Halifax*: "Churchill as Micawber," simply waiting for something to turn up; "Britain finally won, but at appalling cost, and ruin for her standing in the world"). John Charmley in his recently published *Churchill: The End of Glory* goes much farther: he questions not only Churchill's personal character but his policy to resist and fight Hitler's Germany at any cost; Charmley goes so far as to suggest that not to acquiesce in Hitler's domination of Europe was a mistake.

These books are more scholarly in their equipment than are the productions of pamphleteers who, among other things, deny the existence of the Holocaust. Excessive attention directed to such fanatics may be as useless as the criticism aimed at the new revisionists' theses without a detailed analysis of their sources and a careful refutation of their methods. Three years ago in my *The Duel: May 10–31 July 1940: The Eighty-Day Struggle Between Churchill and Hitler* I could write that "we are at (or, more precisely, already beyond) a watershed in the political and intellectual history of the world because of the evident collapse of the reputation, and consequently, of the influence of Marxism as well as of 'Leftist' liberalism; and this is bound to lead to all kinds of novel, though not necessarily salutary, tendencies of historical interpretation." This is a symptom of the rise of a New Right, not only in Germany and Britain but throughout Europe and Japan, when people, disillusioned with the malfunctioning liberal and socialist policies of their governments, project their disappointments backward, to the Second World War; when, for example, the condemnation of Churchill's statesmanship, at least indirectly, suggests some kind of a rehabilitation of Hitler's. During the Reagan years in this country we saw, here and there, a tendency to question not only the evident problems of the American welfare state but the establishment of its tenets by Roosevelt and the New Deal, and there is reason to believe that new indictments (and I fear not always well-warranted or judicious ones) of Roosevelt's foreign policy before and during the Second World War are also due to appear—in sum, that this newest wave of revisionism about the war will spill over to this side of the Atlantic too.

W hat revisionist historians claim, or at least emphatically suggest, is that their scholarship is better and their intellectual independence stronger than that of the majority of their opponents. Yet this has seldom been true. To the contrary, few of the revisionists have been immune to the ideological tendencies of their times. In the preface to *The American Revisionists*, Warren I. Cohen, the careful historian of what I have called the first wave, wrote in 1967: "I am equally convinced that if I had graduated from Columbia College in 1925 instead of 1955, the revisionist cause would have had one more adherent. It is not a question of the logic of the revisionist argument but . . . largely a matter of the prevailing climate of opinion. . . ." Or as W. J. Ghent (cited by Cohen) wrote in his 1927 attack on the revisionists in an article called "Menckenized History": "Vociferous and sweeping denunciation of existing beliefs, customs, standards, and institutions is the current mode, and 'revisionism' is merely one of its phases." After the First World War there was a growing revulsion to war and an embracing of new ideas, including pacifism. After the Second World War there was another reaction, against Roosevelt and the sometimes unspoken question of whether America should have entered the war against Germany, and on the side of Russia, at that. During the sixties there was the reaction against the Vietnam War and against the ideology of the Cold War. During the nineties nationalism is on the rise, and we shall see . . .

In 1917 Beard was an extreme interventionist: The United States "should help eliminate Prussianism from the earth. . . ." Germany represents "the black night of military barbarism . . . the most merciless military despotism the world has ever seen." By 1926 he was a Germanophile, influenced not only by the revelations of the German diplomatic documents but by German philosophies of history. Beard was not an opportunist, and even in the 1930s he insisted that he was not really an isolationist; rather, he was struggling with that seemingly concrete but, alas, often malleable concept of national interest. (In 1932 Beard received a twenty-five-thousand-dollar grant—a very large sum then—from the Social Science Research Council for the precise definition of "national interest." The result was one of his few unreadable books.) At that time he was a fervent supporter of Franklin Roosevelt, but soon he turned even more fervently against him. The case of Barnes is more telling. His first revisionist articles appeared in 1924, arguing for a division in the responsibilities for the outbreak of the war. By 1926 he was going farther: France and Russia were responsible. Thereafter he became more and more extreme and violent. He was invited to lecture in Hitler's Germany, as was Tansill. In 1940 Barnes volunteered to promote the circulation of German propaganda volumes. After the war he became an admirer of Hitler: "a man whose only fault was that he was too soft, generous and honorable." The Allies had inflicted worse brutality on the Germans "than the alleged exterminations in the gas-chambers." This, of course, was the extreme case of a once talented but embittered man, driven to such statements by what he called *The Historical Blackout*, one of his later pamphlets. Everything was grist to his mill, including the most dubious of "sources" and "evidences." The same was true of Tansill, who in 1938 wrote in his introduction to *America Goes to War*: "Crusading zeal is hardly the proper spirit for an impartial historian." Yet Tansill was the prototype of a zealous crusader, in both of his big revisionist works about the two world wars. Eventually he became a member of the John Birch Society.

Revisionists such as Barnes were often obsessed with the idea of a conspiracy against them. He called the anti-revisionists the "Smearbund." When the Chicago historian Bernadotte Schmitt first criticized his *Genesis of the World War*, Barnes wrote: "There is the very important fact [fact?] that Mr. Schmitt seems to live in daily dread of being mistaken for a member of the detestable Teutonic breed." Barnes even thought that there was a conspiracy among booksellers not to reorder his *Genesis*. Mencken's relationship to Barnes (they corresponded for decades) is also telling. In May 1940, when the German armies lurched forward into Holland, Belgium, and France, Mencken wrote Barnes that the American press "would be hollering for war within two months"; in June he wrote that "Roosevelt will be in the war in two weeks, and . . . his first act will be to forbid every form of free speech." Mencken, like Barnes and other revisionists, was bitterly against a war with Hitler's Reich, but after the war he thought that the United States should go to war against "the Russian barbarians." That inconsistency—if that was what it was—was typical of the inclinations of almost all the post–World War II revisionists. The opposite was true of the Cold War revisionists of the 1960s, who accused the United States of having provoked the Cold War with Russia, while almost all of them approved the American involvement in the war against Germany. They, too, did little else but project backward their then widespread and fashionable dislike of the Vietnam War to events that had happened twenty or more years earlier, manipulating that record for their own purposes. In the 1970s most of them turned to other topics, and at least one of them (Horowitz) became a neoconservative publicist.

There is, however, more involved here than a few historians adjusting their ideas to a prevalent climate of opinion. In some instances their writings affected American history, through a momentum that was slowly gaining ground. In the 1920s the writings of the revisionists had an influence on those members of Congress, mostly Western populists—George W. Norris, Gerald P. Nye, William E. Borah, for example—who had opposed the war and the Versailles Treaty. By 1934 the isolationist and revisionist tide ran so strong that a congressional committee, presided over by Nye, found it politic to investigate the doings of bankers and munition makers and other villainous promoters of the American entrance into the war seventeen years before. (One of the Nye Committee's counsels was an ambitious young lawyer, Alger Hiss.) In 1935 Congress passed the first Neutrality Act, a definite reaction against the memories of World War

I. It was extended in 1937. By that time Sen. Homer Bone of Washington could report "a fact known even to school children in this country: Everyone has come to recognize that the Great War was utter social insanity, and was a crazy war, and we had no business in it at all."

This illustrates a significant phenomenon to which few, if any, historians have yet devoted attention. It is the time lag in the movement of ideas, the slowness of the momentum with which ideas move and then appear on the surface at the wrong time, giving the lie to Victor Hugo's famous saw about Ideas Whose Time Has Come. The high tide of revisionism occurred from 1935 to 1938, when the German danger was rising anew—not, say, in 1919 and 1920, when there had been cogent reasons to mitigate a mistreatment of Germany. The high tide of Second World War revisionism occurred in 1954 and 1955, when the reputations of Franklin Roosevelt and of Yalta were at a low ebb. The high tide of the revisionism about the origins of the Cold War came around 1965, when American-Russian relations were actually improving.

Of course, it takes time for historians to complete their researches and produce their books, but there is an agitated tone in many revisionist works that stands in odd contrast with the slow momentum of their eventual effects. One reason for this is the often weak and tergiversating reaction of the revisionists' historian opponents. At the beginning the seemingly radical performance of the former is often ignored, but then, gradually, the revisionists' ideas may be adopted by respectable historians when it seems politic for them to do so or when they feel safely convinced by their judiciousness. Thus, for example, Tansill's radical and Germanophile *America Goes to War* was praised in *The Atlantic* and the *Yale Review* and by such eminent historians as Allan Nevins and Henry Steele Commager: Tansill traced, "in magisterial style, the missteps which carried the United States along the road to war. It is an impressive performance, conducted with skill, learning, and wit, *illuminating the present as well as the past.*" The italics are Cohen's as well as mine, for this was written by Commager as late as 1938, the most ominous and successful year in Hitler's career along the road to another war. The title of Beard's trenchant 1939 *Giddy Minds and Foreign Quarrels* is not really appropriate. So many of his colleagues' minds were not at all giddy; they were alarmingly slow. Even more disheartening was the reaction of many historians to the New Left revisionists of the 1960s, when the scholarship of those books was wanting. As Maddox wrote, "Reviewers who have been known to pounce with scarcely disguised glee on some poor wretch who incorrectly transcribed a middle initial or date of birth have shown a most extraordinary reluctance to expose even the most obvious New Left fictions," including false statements to which tens of thousands of students were subsequently exposed in our colleges and universities. Finally, when it comes to the newest wave of revisionism, lamentably few historians have taken the trouble to track down and point out the selective methodology and frequently sloppy scholarship of Charmley's denigration of Churchill. Spending, instead, long paragraphs and pages debating his thesis, they pursue the obvious, as Wilde once said, with the enthusiasm of shortsighted detectives.

In science it is the rule that counts; in history, often the exceptions. And there have been exceptions to the shortcomings of scholars involved with revisionism. Millis, who, as we saw earlier, was the author of the most successful revisionist book in 1935, a few years later found himself appalled by the use people were making of his work, which, after all, had dealt with 1917, with the past and not with the then present. By 1938 Millis stood for resistance against Hitler and other dictators. "1939 is not 1914" was the title of his article in Life in November 1939, when Roosevelt had to struggle against a senseless Neutrality Act. Maddox, whose study of the New Left revisionists was ignored or criticized by other historians, refused to make common cause with the New Right; he remained unimpressed by the selective argumentation of Leftist and Rightist, of Marxist and anti-Communist, of neoliberal and neoconservative historians alike, because of his personal integrity, the essence of human integrity being its resistance to temptations, perhaps especially to intellectual ones.

Such temptations are the bane of historians, and not only of those who are in pursuit of attractive intellectual novelty. This does not mean a defense of "orthodox" history, because there is no such thing. Historians should be aware of the inevitably revisionist nature of their thinking and work. But the revision of history must not be an ephemeral monopoly of ideologues or opportunists who are ever ready to twist or even falsify evidences of the past in order to exemplify current ideas—and their own adjustments to them.

—September 1994

A NATION OF IMMIGRANTS

By *BERNARD A. WEISBERGER*

It's a politician's bromide—and it also happens to be a profound truth. No war, no national crisis, has left a greater impress on the American psyche than the successive waves of new arrivals that quite literally built the country. Now that arguments against immigration are rising again, it is well to remember that every single one of them has been heard before.

The uproar over Zoë Baird has subsided by now, and readers with short memories may profit by a reminder that she was forced to withdraw as President Clinton's first nominee for Attorney General because she and her husband had hired two "illegal aliens" for babysitting and housekeeping chores. The episode put immigration into focus as a "live" topic for op-ed and talk-show manifestoes before it faded, only to return to the headlines when Clinton embraced the Bush administration's policy (which he had denounced during the campaign) of turning back boatloads of Haitian refugees before they reached the Florida shore. But in June of 1993 the front pages carried the tragic story of a freighter, ironically named the *Golden Venture*, that ran aground just outside New York City. Its hold contained a crowd of Chinese workers being unlawfully smuggled into the United States, a crude practice supposedly long obsolete. Ten of them drowned trying to swim ashore. Later in the summer several hundred more "illegal" Chinese, California-bound, were intercepted and imprisoned aboard their ships until the U.S. government persuaded Mexico to take them in and ship them back. So it is that immigration regularly returns to the news. It always has. It always does.

But the question of what our policy toward the world's huddled masses should be is especially topical at this moment. The Statue of Liberty still lifts her lamp beside the golden door, but in a time of economic downturn, there is no longer an assured consensus that the door should be kept open very far. Restrictionism is back in fashion. For every journalistic article like that of *Business Week* in July 1992, which notes that "the U.S. is reaping a bonanza of highly educated foreigners" and that low-end immigrants "provide a hardworking labor force to fill the low-paid jobs that make a modern service economy run," there is another like Peter Brimelow's in the *National Review*. His title tells it all: "Time to Rethink Immigration?" The burden of his argument is that America has admitted too many immigrants of the wrong ethnic background (he himself is a new arrival from Britain), that neither our economy nor our culture can stand the strain, and that "it may be time to close the second period of American history [the first having been the era of the open frontier] with the announcement that the U.S. is no longer an 'immigrant country.'" In short, we're here; you foreigners stay home. Nor are journalists the only voices in the debate. Last August California's governor Pete Wilson got media attention with a proposal to amend the Constitution so as to deny citizenship to an entire class of people born in the United States, namely, those unlucky enough to be the children of illegal immigrants.

If, as I have, you have been "doing" immigration history for many years, you've heard the restrictionists' arguments before and expect to hear them again. And you are under the obligation to answer back, because what is at stake in the argument is nothing less than the essential nature of the United States of America. We are different. We aren't the only country that receives immigration or that has to deal with resentment directed toward "aliens." The popularity in France of Jean-Marie Le Pen's National Front party and the surge of anti-foreign (and neo-Nazi) "Germany-for-Germans" violence in Germany are evidence of that. It's also true that in a world of swift intercontinental travel and instant global communication, immigration policy cannot really be made by separate governments as if they lived in a vacuum. Such problems as there are demand multinational solutions.

Nevertheless and notwithstanding, the United States of America is different. Immigration is flesh of our flesh, and we need to be reminded of that. Some sneer at the statement that we are a nation of immigrants as a cliché; all nations, they assert, are made up of mixtures of different peoples. So they are, as new tribes and races displaced old ones by conquest or by random migration. But the United States was created by settlers who arrived from elsewhere, who deliberately and calculatedly invited and urged others to follow them, and who encouraged the process in ways that were unique. Of course, countries like Canada and Australia depended on immigration for survival and success, but only the United States made the acquisition of citizenship swift and simple; only the United States made it a matter of principle to equalize the conditions of new citizens and old; only the United

States takes special pride in describing American nationality as, by definition, independent of race and blood—as something that is acquired by residence and allegiance regardless of birthplace or ancestry.

Confirmation of that statement is in the record, and the record needs to be reviewed. It is not a flawless one. Of course the people of the United States have not always extended an equal welcome to all races; of course there have been spasms of hostility like the current wave—in the 1790s, in the 1850s, in the 1920s. They are also part of the record, but on the whole the record is exceptional and ought to be known and understood before any new major changes in policy are made.

Every Passover Jews the world over sit down to the Seder table to retell the story of Exodus from Egypt in order to pass on to their children and renew in themselves their sense of who, what, and why they are. There was a time when the Fourth of July was an occasion for re-creating the days of the American Revolution, in order to serve the same purpose for Americans. (I hope that it makes a comeback, despite the assaults of a misguided "multiculturalism.")

Now is the proper occasion for retelling the immigration story. So let us begin at the beginning, with the statement that offends the new exclusionist.

IN THE BEGINNING: 1607–1798

"We are a nation of immigrants." It's a politician's generality at an ethnic picnic, a textbook bromide swallowed and soon forgotten. It is also, as it happens, a profound truth, defining us and explaining a good part of what is extraordinary in the short history of the United States of America. There is no American ancient soil, no founding race, but there is a common ancestral experience of moving from "there" to "here." Among the founders of this nation who believed that they were agents of destiny was an English preacher who said in 1669, "God hath sifted a nation that he might send choice grain into this wilderness." The grain has arrived steadily and from many nations. "Americans are not a narrow tribe," wrote Herman Melville; "our blood is as the flood of the Amazon, made up of a thousand noble currents all pouring into one."

We begin arbitrarily with a seventeenth-century English migration that produced the First Families of Virginia (founded in 1607) and Massachusetts's Pilgrim Fathers (1620). Arbitrarily because already in 1643 Isaac Jogues, a French Jesuit missionary visiting New Amsterdam, said he heard eighteen languages spoken in that seaport town, which probably included Mediterranean and North African dialects and the Hebrew of a small settlement of Sephardic Jews.

But the stock planted in the 1600s was basically English. In the eighteenth century it turned "British" as Scots and Irish arrived in significant numbers, then partly European through an influx of Germans, and African, too, through the thousands of involuntary black immigrants brought in on the hell ships of the slave trade.

Those initial colonial migrations to "British North America" illustrate forces that are still at work in 1993. The names, faces, and languages change, but the basics remain. Immigrants are pushed out of their original homes by war, upheaval, misery, and oppression. They are pulled toward America by the promise of economic betterment and a chance to breathe free. Sometimes they are lured by promoters who want their passage money or their labor and skills. Sometimes they have come in legal or actual bondage.

But whenever and wherever they have come, they have changed what they found. That was clear from the moment that seventeenth-century England sent the first immigrant wave. The land was ripe for mass exodus. Civil, religious, and class war raged from beginning to end of the century, encompassing in their course the execution of one king and the expulsion of another. Major changes in the economy drove small farmers off their subsistence plots in favor of sheep. "The people . . . do swarm in the land as young bees in a hive," said one clergyman. "The land grows weary of her inhabitants," said another— by name John Winthrop, soon to move with fellow Puritans to a place called Massachusetts Bay.

The London government planted colonies to help houseclean the surplus population. Some started under the rule of private corporations that looked for gold and silk and settled for the profits in fish, fur, and tobacco. Some were begun by like-minded religious seekers, some by individuals to whom the king gave huge tracts of wilderness to turn into profitable agricultural estates. All needed people to thrive, and got them. Some 378,000 Englishmen and women left for the Western Hemisphere during the century; 155,000 wound up on mainland North America. They came on the *Mayflower;* they came in groups brought over by colonial proprietors who got so many extra acres of land per head of immigrant. They came as indentured servants, under bond to work a term of years. Some came in fetters at the request of unchoosy colonial administrators, like the governor of Virginia who asked London in 1611 for "all offenders out of the common gaols condemned to die." There may have been, over the decades, as many as 50,000 of such "fellons and other desperate villaines."

They brought the imprint of England in their baggage. Without stinting other contributions, there isn't any question that constitutional self-rule, Protestant individualism, capitalism, and the work ethic were hammered into the national character in the seventeenth-century English. And yet English with a difference. "They ate the white corn-kernels parched in the sun," Stephen Vincent Benét wrote in 1943, "and they knew it not, but they'd not be English again." Autocratic rule was modified almost at once because London was far away—and freedom attracted new settlers. Virginia demanded and got a representative assembly in 1624; all the other colonies followed in due course.

It was an age of religious rigidity, but state-imposed conformity had to bend to the needs of settlement. In 1632 King Charles I gave his supporter Cecilius Calvert, Lord Baltimore, the future state of Maryland (named for the Catholic queen). Calvert saw to it that his fellow Catholics, under heavy pressure back home, were tolerated within its borders. In the 1680s a different king bestowed yet another colony on William Penn. The Quaker Penn opened Pennsylvania not only to other members of the Society of Friends but to "dissenters" of every description. In different colonies intolerance rose and fell, but more often fell as population grew and spread. "Here," reported New York's governor in 1687, "be not many of the Church of England, few Roman Catholics, abundance of . . . singing Quakers, ranting Quakers, Sabbatarians, Anti-Sabbatarians, some Anabaptists, some Independents, some Jews; in short, of all sorts of opinions there are some, and the most part none at all."

By the start of the eighteenth century, that latitude, along with virgin land and prospering towns, was exerting a magnetic force outside England itself: in France, where, in 1685, the king revoked an edict that had protected his Protestant subjects, thereby sending thousands of Huguenots—thrifty, skilled traders and artisans—to settle in America; in the many little German princedoms plagued by war, taxes, and rack rents, so that altogether there were some 225,000 colonists of German stock on the Revolution's eve, including groups like the Mennonites (ancestors of the Amish) and Moravians.

They spread through several colonies, but those in Pennsylvania became known as the Pennsylvania Dutch (a corruption of *Deutsch*), and their clannish ways at least once exasperated the usually tolerant Benjamin Franklin. "Why should the Palatine *Boors*," he asked (the Rhenish Palatinate was a German region that furnished many new Pennsylvanians), "be suffered to swarm into our Settlements, and by herding together, establish their Language and Manners to the

Exclusion of ours? Why should *Pennsylvania*, founded by the *English*, become a Colony of *Aliens*?"

There was no language problem with the "Ulster" Irish or Scots Irish. These Scots, deliberately planted in the northern counties of Ireland in the 1600s to help subdue the native Catholics, were busy and productive farmers until, in 1699, English landowners got the door slammed on competitive agricultural imports. The ensuing distress sent as many as 12,000 a year of the Ulstermen and women to the colonies. They poured into the frontier regions, carrying with them strict Calvinism and a distaste for both Indians and speculators who cornered huge tracts to sell at high prices. It was, in their eyes, "against the laws of God and nature that so much land should be idle while Christians wanted it to labor on and raise their bread." They were the ancestors of such as Daniel Boone and Andrew Jackson.

The end of the French and Indian War in 1763 spurred a rush of migration to the now-secure colonial frontiers and the growing seaboard towns of Boston, New York, Philadelphia, Charleston. From 1763 to 1775 some 221,000 newcomers arrived: 55,000 Ulstermen, 40,000 Scots, 30,000 English, 12,000 Germans and Swiss—and 84,500 chained Africans. Perhaps a third of all the colonists in 1760 were either born abroad or had parents who were. The English government, once worried about overpopulation, now feared depopulation even more and cracked down on large landowners' seductive invitations to immigrants. Thus the charge in Jefferson's bill of particulars showing that the king sought an absolute tyranny over the colonies: "He has endeavoured to prevent the Population of these states; . . . obstructing the Laws for Naturalization of Foreigners; refusing to pass others to encourage their Migrations hither, and raising the Conditions of new Appropriations of Lands."

Immigration helped bring on the Revolution, and to give it a surprising new meaning. By 1782 the former English colonies were separate states, linked by common interests and a common culture that was more than simply English. Michel Guillaume Jean de Crèvecoeur, a French immigrant, put it this way: "What then is the American, this new man? He is either an European, or the descendant of a European, hence that strange mixture of blood, which you will find in no other country. I could point out to you a family whose grandfather was an Englishman, whose wife was Dutch, whose son married a French woman, and whose present four sons have now four wives of different nations. . . . Here individuals of all nations are melted into a new race of men, whose labours and posterity will one day cause great changes in the world . . . "

The immigrant generals and soldiers who fought on the American side in the Revolution (like Gen. Frederick Mühlenberg, the German-trained Lutheran pastor who would become the first Speaker of the House) would have agreed. So would Tom Paine, the English immigrant author of *Common Sense*, which, in 1776, called on the future United States to become an "asylum for mankind."

But when the Constitutional Convention came to consider naturalization laws and residence requirements for officials, a different point of view was evident. Even a sturdy democrat like Virginia's George Mason did not "chuse to let foreigners and adventurers make laws for us & govern us." Pierce Butler of South Carolina—born in Ireland—believed that aliens brought in "ideas of Government so distinct from ours that in every point of view they are dangerous." Gouverneur Morris, a gifted master of sarcasm from New York, applauded generosity to foreigners but counseled "a moderation in all things. . . . He would admit them to his house, he would invite them to his table . . . but would not carry the complaisance so far as to bed them with his wife."

Compromise prevailed; no person may be a representative who has not been a citizen seven years, or become a senator with less than nine years' citizenship. Presidents must be American-born. The issue blew up again in 1798 during stormy confrontations between Jefferson's Republicans and conservative Federalist opponents who feared an infiltration of radical immigrants full of dangerous ideas hatched by the French Revolution, then in full career. A Federalist-dominated Congress passed the Alien and Sedition Acts of 1798, which allowed the President to expel foreigners whom he deemed dangerous on suspicion of treasonable activities. Jefferson called the measure "worthy of the 8th or 9th century," and when he and his supporters won the election of 1800, they let it die without renewal.

YOUNG REPUBLIC, 1815–60

Jefferson's optimistic vision of an always enlightened and open-minded America has survived as a hotly contested influence on the land. But his expectation that the nation would remain permanently agrarian was totally wrong. Half a century after he left the White House, steam power had transformed the country. Inventors and investors proved the truest American radicals. Steamboats and rail lines crisscrossed a Union that spread to the Pacific and boasted more than thirty states. Mills, mines, factories, distilleries, packinghouses, and shipyards yearly churned out millions of dollars' worth of manufactured goods.

And it was linked to mass immigration. Immigrants furnished much of the labor that made the productive explosion possible and many of the consumers who made it profitable. The same industrializing processes that were at work and opened jobs here uprooted millions in Europe whose handicrafts became obsolete or whose land fell into the hands of those who could farm more "efficiently." Two decades of Napoleonic warfare, followed by three more of suppressed democratic and nationalist revolution, created a new reservoir of suffering from which emigration offered an escape.

America was a major beneficiary. Europe's growing cities and new overseas dominions beckoned, but the United States was the special promised land as the nineteenth century took its dynamic course. Fewer than 8,000 immigrants per year landed on American shores between 1783 and 1815, but 2,598,000 came in the next forty-five years: 1,500,000 in the 1840s and 3,000,000 in the 1850s. The pre-Civil War period of immigration belonged predominantly to 1,500,000 Germans and 2,000,000 Irish. It was the Irish whose transplantation was most shadowed in tragedy. Unbelievably, Ireland—only a few hours by water from the very center of the modern world in England—was stricken by the oldest of Biblical scourges, famine.

Irish migration had begun early. The rich English absentee landlords who ruled the country left their peasant tenants to feed themselves on the potatoes grown on tiny plots. A visitor declared that "the most miserable of English paupers" was better off. Irish Catholics and Irish nationalists were equally despised and frustrated. There was little future, and thousands, early in the century, migrated to the United States to find pick-and-shovel jobs on the growing network of turnpikes, canals, and railroads. But in 1845 the stream of opportunity seekers was turned into a flood of refugees. The potato crop, smitten by a fungus, failed in three successive years. Mass starvation was the result. In the hovels inhabited by the "Paddies," rats gnawed on unburied bodies while others in their death throes looked on, too weak to move. "All with means are emigrating," wrote one official; "only the utterly destitute are left behind."

Victims of the "Great Hunger" were not through with their torments when they boarded filthy, overcrowded, and underprovisioned ships, where, said one witness, it was "a daily occurrence to see starving women and children fight for the food which was brought to the dogs and pigs that were kept on deck." En route 10 to 20 percent of them died of disease. In the United States, lacking capital and prepared only for low-level employment, they were crammed into the new urban slums. Some were housed, according to an investigation committee, nine in a room in windowless and waterless cellars, "huddled together like brutes without regard to age or sex or sense of decency."

It was a little better for the Germans. Many were professionals and scholars with some capital, political refugees rather than disaster victims. Some came in groups that pooled their money to buy cheap Western lands, and these founded towns like New Ulm in Minnesota or New Braunfels in Texas. So many of them became Texans, in fact, that in 1843 the state published a German edition of its laws. An American reporter visited a German farm in Texas in 1857. "You are welcomed," he told readers, "by a figure in a blue flannel shirt and pendant beard, quoting Tacitus, having in one hand a long pipe, in the other a butcher's knife; Madonnas upon log-walls; coffee in tin cups upon Dresden saucers; barrels for seats to hear a Beethoven's symphony on the grand piano."

German farmers spread through Illinois, Michigan, Missouri, Iowa, and Wisconsin. German brewers, bookbinders, butchers, musicians, and other craftspeople settled cohesively and proudly in cities from New York to New Orleans, St. Louis to Cincinnati. In 1860, 100,000 New York Germans supported twenty churches, fifty German-language schools, ten bookstores, five printing establishments, and a theater, in neighborhoods known collectively as *Kleindeutschland* (little Germany). To contemporaries the Germans seemed a model minority, the Irish a problem minority—a kind of generalizing that would, in time, be transferred to other peoples.

Besides these two major groups, there were Danes, Norwegians, and Swedes arriving in increasing numbers from the 1850s onward; French-Canadians moving into New England textile factories to replace Yankee workers of both sexes; Dutch farmers drifting to western Michigan; and in 1849 Chinese who had heard of the California gold strikes and came for their share of the "Golden Mountain," as they called America—only to be crowded out of the mining camps by mobs and restrictive laws and diverted into railway labor gangs, domestic service, restaurants, and laundries.

The immigrants helped push the United States population from 4,000,000 in 1790 to 32,000,000 in 1860. They built America by hand, for wages that were pittances by modern standards—$40 a month in Pennsylvania coal mines, $1.25 to $2 a day on the railroads—but tempting nonetheless. (In Sweden farmhands earned $33.50 *per year*.) They dug themselves into the economy and into the nation's not-always-kind-ly ethnic folklore. New England textile towns like Woonsocket and Burlington got to know the accent of French-Canadian "Canucks." So many Swedes became Western lumbermen that a double-saw was called a "Swedish fiddle." Welsh and Cornish copper miners in Michigan's Upper Peninsula, were known as Cousin Jacks.

There were exceptions to the geographical stereotypes—Dutch settlements in Arizona, a Swedish nucleus in Arkansas, a Chinese community in Mississippi—and Irishmen in Southern cities like Mobile and New Orleans, where they were employed on dangerous jobs like levee repair because they were more expendable than fifteen-hundred-dollar slaves.

American culture shaped itself around their presence. Religion was a conspicuous example. The Church of Rome in America was turned inside out by the Irish, whose sheer numbers overwhelmed the small groups of old-stock English and French Catholics from Maryland and Louisiana. The first American cardinal, John McCloskey, was the son of a Brooklyn Irishman. The second, James Gibbons, an Irish boy from Baltimore. German and Swiss Catholic immigrants added to the melting-pot nature of their church in the United States before the Civil War—and the Poles and Italians were yet to come.

German and Scandinavian Lutheran immigrants—free of state and ecclesiastical authorities—developed strong local leaders and new, secessionist bodies, like the German-dominated Missouri Synod and the Scandinavian Evangelical Lutheran Augustana Synod. Both of these were theologically conservative groups. On the other side Isaac Mayer Wise, a German immigrant rabbi, became the patriarch of Reform Judaism in America, to save the faith, in his words, from "disappearance" into "Polish-cabalistical . . . supernaturalism." All the "immigrant churches" in the United States built their own networks of social service agencies, parochial schools, and ministerial training seminaries without state help, blending the faith of their fathers with an American style of independent congregational activism. In the house of God, too, the American was a "new man."

Ethnic politics took root in immigrant-crowded city wards. Nowhere was it stronger than among the gregarious Irish, whose neighborhood saloons became political clubhouses. The Society of St. Tammany was an old-stock New York City association founded in 1789 to promote Jeffersonian ideas. Fifty years later the Irish had so infiltrated it that a writer quipped: "Ask an Irishman, and he will probably tell you that St. Tammany was a younger brother of St.

Patrick who emigrated to America for the purpose of taking a city contract to drive all Republican reptiles out of New York." Patronage jobs handed out by the machine made Irish cops a stereotype for the rest of the century.

But the lower-class Irish in particular stung an American elite long steeped in anti-popery. Anti-immigrant feelings began to rise in the 1840s and focused especially on the Irish, who, like poor people before and after them, were denounced for not living better than they could afford. "Our Celtic fellow citizens," wrote a New York business-man, "are almost as remote from us in temperament and constitution as the Chinese." Bigotry can always find excuses and weapons. The handiest one in the 1840s was anti-Catholicism.

In 1834 a Boston mob burned a convent. Ten years later there were riots in Philadelphia after a school board ruled that Catholic children might use the Douay version of the Bible in school. "The bloody hand of the Pope," howled one newspaper, "has stretched itself forth to our destruction." A few years after that, anti-Catholic and anti-foreign feelings merged in a nativist crusade called the Know-Nothing move-ment. Its goal was to restrict admission and naturalization of foreign-ers, and among its adherents was Samuel F. B. Morse, the father of telegraphy, who cried aloud: "To your posts! . . . Fly to protect the vulnerable places of your Constitution and Laws. Place your guards. . . . And first, shut your gates."

Know-Nothings had some brief success but little enduring impact. Their drive got strength from a generalized anxiety about the future of the country on the eve of the Civil War. But Know-Nothingism cut across the grain of a venerable commitment to equal rights, and no one put his finger on the issue more squarely than Abraham Lincoln when asked in 1855 whether he was in favor of the Know-Nothing movement: "How could I be? How can any one who abhors the oppression of negroes, be in favor of degrading classes of white peo-ple? Our progress in degeneracy appears to me to be pretty rapid. As a nation, we began by declaring that '*all men are created equal.*' We now practically read it, 'all men are created equal, *except negroes.*' When the Know-Nothings get control, it will read, 'all men are created equal, except negroes, and *foreigners and catholics.*' When it comes to this I should prefer emigrating to some country where they make no pre-tence of loving liberty—to Russia, for instance, where despotism can be taken pure, and without the base alloy of hypocrisy."

Three years later, on the Fourth of July, 1858, in debating with Stephen A. Douglas, Lincoln returned to the theme. What could the Fourth mean, he asked, to those who were not blood descendants of those who had fought in the Revolution? His answer was that in turning back to the Declaration of Independence, they found the sentiment "We hold these truths to be self-evident, that all men are created equal," that they "feel . . . and that they have a right to claim it as though they were blood of the blood, and flesh of the flesh of the men who wrote that Declaration and so they are. That is the electric cord . . . that links the hearts of patriotic and liberty-loving men together . . . "

Lincoln was unambiguous. There was no exclusively American race entitled to claim liberty by heredity. What held the nation together was an *idea* of equality that every newcomer could claim and defend by free choice.

That concept was soon tested to the limit with Lincoln himself presiding over the fiery trial. Foreign-born soldiers and officers served the Union in such numbers and with such distinction that the war itself should have laid to rest finally the question of whether "non-natives" could be loyal. It didn't do that. But it paved the way for another wave of economic growth and a new period of ingathering greater than any that had gone before.

HIGH TIDE AND REACTION: 1885–1930

After 1865 the United States thundered toward industrial leadership with the speed and power of one of the great locomotives that were the handsomest embodiment of the age of steam. That age peaked somewhere in the 1890s. By 1929 the age of electricity and petroleum was in flower. And the United States was the world's leading producer of steel, oil, coal, automobiles and trucks, electrical equipment, and an infinite variety of consumer goods from old-fashioned overalls to new-fangled radios. The majority of Americans lived in supercities, their daily existence made possible by elaborate networks of power and gas lines, telephone wires, highways, bridges, tunnels, and rails.

And the foreign-born were at the center of the whirlwind. Expansion coincided with, depended on, incorporated the greatest wave of migration yet. In the first fourteen years after the Civil War ended yearly immigration ranged from 318,568 in 1866 to 459,803 in 1873, slumping during the hard times of 1873–77, and rebounding to 457,257 in 1880.

Then came the deluge: 669,431 in 1881; 788,992 in 1882. Seven times between 1883 and 1903 the half-million total was passed. The million mark was hit in 1905 with 1,026,499—and exceeded six times between that year and 1914. The all-time peak came in 1907: 1,285,349.

All told, some 14,000,000 arrived at the gates between 1860 and 1900; another 18,600,000 followed between 1900 and 1930. Almost all of them came from Europe, a transoceanic transplantation unmatched in history.

The "old" Americans—that is, the children of immigrants who had arrived earlier—watched the influx with feelings that ran from pride to bewilderment and alarm, for the "new" immigration was not from traditional sources. Until 1890 most new arrivals were from familiar places: the British Isles, Germany, the Scandinavian countries, Switzerland, the Netherlands. But now it was the turn of southern and eastern Europe to swarm. Of the roughly 1,280,000 in the record-setting 1907 intake, 260,000 were from Russia, which then included a goodly portion of Poland. Another 285,000 were from Italy. Almost 340,000 were from Austria-Hungary, a doomed "dual monarchy" that included much of the future Yugoslavia and Czechoslovakia and another part of Poland. About 36,000 were from Romania, Bulgaria, and what was left of the Ottoman Turkish Empire in Europe. There were modest numbers of Greeks and Portuguese.

These new immigrants were palpably different. There were Eastern Orthodox as well as Roman Catholics, and Orthodox Jews. There were, at a time when ethnic labels were taken with great seriousness, Magyars, Croats, Slovenes, Slovaks, and people generally grouped as "Slavs" and "Latins" and sniffed at in suspicion and disdain. In 1875 *The New York Times* said of Italians that it was "hopeless to think of civilizing them, or keeping them in order, except by the arm of the law." A Yankee watching Polish farm workers was struck by their "stolid, stupid faces." An American Jewish journal, offended by the beards, side curls, and skullcaps of Polish greenhorns, wondered what could be done with these "miserable darkened Hebrews."

The immigration patterns had shifted with the course of modern European history. A rising demand for political independence in central Europe fed political turbulence. Russian nationalism spawned anti-Semitic outbursts and hard, impoverishing economic restrictions on Jews. Southern Italy was overwhelmed by agricultural poverty that was increased by policies of industrialization and modernization that favored the north. Europe was full of hopeful seekers of streets paved with gold.

And there were voices to entice them. The immigration bureaus of Western states distributed literature in several languages touting opportunities within their borders. Railroad companies with land grants wooed Russian and German farmers to come out and buy (on long-term credit) tracts on the Great Plains. The Great Northern line—which James J. Hill built without land grants—offered fares as low as thirty-three dollars to any point on the tracks that ran from Minnesota to Oregon, plus sweet deals on acquiring and moving machinery, livestock, lumber, fencing. Steamship companies were in the hunt too. Modern technology had reduced the dreaded transatlantic passage to ten or twelve days instead of months. Steerage accommodations were far from clean or comfortable, but they cost as little as twenty-five dollars, and passengers were no longer likely to die on the way.

So the immigrants came. For the most part this was an urban migration. Millions went to the middling-sized red-brick towns dominated by the factory chimney and whistle. More millions went to the big cities, where they grunted and sweated in the creation of the skyscrapers, the bridges, the subways and trolley lines, the sewer and lighting systems—the guts of the metropolis. Or where, if they did not swing a pick or scrub floors, they sold groceries to those of their countrymen who did.

In the 1890s Chicago had more Germans than any of Kaiser Wilhelm's cities except Berlin and Hamburg; more Swedes than any place in Sweden except for Stockholm and Göteborg; more Norwegians than any Norwegian town outside of Christiana (now Oslo) and Bergen. Of some 12,500 laborers modernizing New York State's Erie Canal, fully 10,500 were Italians rounded up on the docks by Italian-speaking padrones and furnished to construction companies at so much per head. By 1897 Italians made up 75 percent of New York City's construction workers. Jews already dominated the town's once-German garment industry.

In Pennsylvania in 1900 almost 60 percent of white bituminous coal miners were foreign-born. In three anthracite coal mines in a single county, more than three-quarters of the work force was Slavic. Twenty-five languages were spoken in the textile mills of Lawrence, Massachusetts.

Ethnic monopolies of particular lines of work were established. In 1894 all but one of New York City's 474 foreign-born bootblacks were Italian, and Greeks dominated the confectionery business in Chicago until past the end of World War II.

For most, life in the golden land was potentially promising but actually brutal. Wages hung at or below the cost of living and far below the cost of comfort. Some parts of Chicago had three times as many inhabitants as the most crowded sections of Tokyo or Calcutta. A New York survey taker found 1,231 Italians living in 120 rooms. Single toilets and water faucets were shared by dozens of families. Uncollected garbage piled up in alleys. Privacy and health were equally impossible to maintain, and pulmonary diseases raged through the tenement "lung blocks."

Settlement-house workers took up residence in the worst neighborhoods, trying to teach the rudiments of hygiene. The American public school took on a new role. Authorities regarded it as their mission to teach immigrant children not only basic skills but civic responsibility, respect for the flag, and the proper use of the toothbrush. In fact, the schools did produce millions of competent citizens. One alumna, Mary Antin, said that born Americans should be grateful for their role in "the recruiting of your armies of workers, thinkers, and leaders." But the precedent of having schools serve as agents of social policy— in this case of assimilation—would later haunt overburdened teachers and administrators.

The urban center of gravity of the new immigrants made it harder for them to be accepted. Most "native" Americans were encountering the basic problems of the big city—crowding, crime, graft, corruption, disease—for the first time. It was all too easy for them to associate these evils with the immigrants, who seemed always to be at the center of this or that dilemma. Sympathetic men and women like Jane Addams, Emily Balch, Hutchins Hapgood, and Horace M. Kallen did their best to explain immigrant culture to their fellow old-stock Americans and to guide the newcomers in acceptable American ways.

The immigrants themselves did not take on the role of clay awaiting the potter's hand. They organized their own newspapers, theaters, social clubs, night classes, and self-help societies. These, while keeping the old-country languages and folkways alive, steadfastly preached and practiced assimilation and urged members and readers to rush into citizenship and respectability, which the great majority of them did. Single men skimped and struggled to bring over families. Families sacrificed to send children to school. And the children found different paths to Americanization. Some joined political machines and parties; some worked in the union movement; others forged their own steps to success in business. (And some never graduated beyond the streets and dead-end jobs.)

Regardless of what they did, they were caught in the center of a steadily sharpening American debate over the "immigrant problem" that began in the early 1890s. It was a reprise of earlier nativist struggles. As early as 1882 Congress was prevailed upon to exclude Chinese from entry and citizenship. In the 1890s an Immigration Restriction League was formed. Its leaders were from old New England families who shared the fears of the writer Thomas Bailey Aldrich that through our "unguarded gates" there was pouring a "wild motley throng" of "Men from the Volga and the Tartar steppes."

Would the America of the future be populated, one restrictionist asked, by "British, German and Scandinavian stock, historically free, energetic, progressive, or by Slav, Latin and Asiatic races, historically down-trodden, atavistic and stagnant?" The call for an end to unchecked immigration was echoed by labor leaders like the AFL's Samuel Gompers (a Dutch-born Jewish immigrant from England in 1863), who complained that the "present immigration" consisted of "cheap labor, ignorant labor [that] takes our jobs and cuts our wages."

Bit by bit, curbs were imposed—first on immigrants with contagious diseases or serious criminal records, then on those who were "professional beggars" or anarchists or prostitutes or epileptics. In 1906 President Theodore Roosevelt got Congress to establish a commission to study the "problem." Chaired by the Vermont senator William Paul Dillingham, it labored for four years to produce a massive report that loaded the guns of a restrictionism based on invidious distinctions between the "old" and "new" immigrations. Among other things it marshaled data to "prove" that the most recent immigrants were "content to accept wages and conditions which . . . native Americans . . . had come to regard as unsatisfactory." It stated that "inherent racial tendencies" rather than poverty explained miserable immigrant living conditions and went on to say many other uncomplimentary things about the great-grandparents of some fifty million of today's Americans.

No action was taken on the report when it appeared in 1910. But racist feeling was on the rise. The Ku Klux Klan was revived in 1915. A hysterical drive for 100 percent Americanism during World War I and the Red scare immediately afterward fed a popular belief articulated by one congressman: "We get the majority of the communists, the I.W.W.'s, the dynamiters, and the assassins . . . from the ranks of the present-day immigrant."

In 1924 Congress passed the Johnson-Reed Act, which remained the cornerstone of national immigration policy for the next forty-one years. Starting in 1929, there would be an overall yearly limit of 150,000 on immigrants from out- side the Western Hemisphere. The 150,000 was to be divided into quotas, assigned to nationalities in the proportion that they bore, by birth or descent, to the total population as of 1920.

What that meant was clear. The longer a national group had been here, the more of its descendants were in the population and the larger would be its quota. When the first shares were announced, half of all places were reserved for British residents, whereas only 5,802 Italians, 6,524 Poles, and 2,784 Russians could be admitted. Groups like Syrians or Albanians fared worse, with fewer than 100 places per year. And Asians were excluded altogether.

The national origins quota system of 1924 was a landmark, ending centuries of open admission. It was also a victory for ethnic stereotyping. Yet it was not without its ironies. For one thing, it did not impose limits on a Hispanic ingathering from Mexico and Puerto Rico that was just gaining steam. Nor did it deal with the internal migration of Southern blacks into Northern cities. Anglo-Saxon superiority was therefore left unprotected on two fronts.

And in the next and newest phase of the story, covering the final years of the twentieth century, there were dramatic changes in the "racial" composition of immigration that went far beyond anything that the Immigration Restriction League could possibly have anticipated.

THE THIRD WORLD COMES TO THE UNITED STATES: 1965–90

Like a good many pieces of social policy legislation, the Johnson-Reed Act began to be outdated from the moment it took effect. One of its objectives—cutting down on immigration overall—was brutally affected by the Great Crash. In the deepest year of the Depression, 1933, only 34,000 immigrants arrived to take their chances in a shuttered and darkened economy.

The totals did not rise dramatically in the next seven years, but they were important weather vanes of change. Fascist and Communist dictators, and World War II, gave new meaning to the word *refugee* and a new scale to misery. Millions of victims of history would soon be knocking at our closed gates.

First came those in flight from Hitler, primarily Jews. Their claim to asylum was especially powerful, considering the savagery that they were fleeing (and no one suspected yet that extermination would be the ultimate threat). This was a special kind of exodus, heavy with intellectual distinction. Thousands of scientists, engineers, doctors, lawyers, teachers, and managers were hit by the Nazi purge of independent thinkers in every part of German life. "Hitler shakes the tree," said one American arts administrator, "and I collect the apples."

The choicest apples included such men and women as Bruno Walter, George Szell, Lotte Lenya, Paul Klee, Thomas Mann, and Hannah Arendt in the arts and philosophy. In the sciences the lists included the physicists and mathematicians Edward Teller, Leo Szilard, Eugene P. Wigner, and Enrico Fermi (in flight from Mussolini's Italy) who shared in the creation of the atom bomb. The weapon was first proposed to the American government by the superstar of all the refugees, Albert Einstein.

World War II came—and more signals of change. In 1943 the sixty-one-year-old-Chinese Exclusion Act was repealed, because China was now an American ally. The gesture was small, and the quota tiny (105), and it could hardly be said to mark the end of anti-Asian prejudice when 112,000 American citizens of Japanese descent were behind barbed wire. But it was a beginning, a breach in the wall. The horrible consequences of Hitler's "racial science" were so clear that the philosophy of biological superiority underlying the national origins quota system received a fatal shock.

So the groundwork was laid for the future admission of nonwhite immigrants from the crumbling European empires in Africa and Asia—especially when, as it turned out, many of them were highly educated specialists.

Then the Cold War produced its worldwide tragedies and shake-ups, its expulsions and arrests and civil wars and invasions in China, Cuba, Korea, Indochina, the Philippines, Indonesia, Malaysia, Central Africa, the Middle East, Central America. A world in conflict was a world once more ready to swarm.

And in the United States an economic boom was reopening the job market. Attitudes toward immigration were changing as well. The children of the great 1890–1914 migration had come of age. They were powerful in the voting booths; political scientists credited them with a major role in supporting the New Deal. And the best-selling writers and dramatists among them were delving the richness of their experience in a way that wiped out the stereotypes of the old restrictionism.

So the walls began to crumble. First there were special enactments to clear the way for the wives and children of servicemen who had gotten married while overseas. Some 117,000 women and children entered under a War Brides Act of 1945—5,000 of them Chinese. In 1948 came the Displaced Persons Act, spurred by the misery of millions of homeless Eastern Europeans who had survived deportations, forced labor, bombings, and death camps. These were countries with the smallest national origins quotas. Congress did not repeal them, but it permitted borrowing against the future, so that at the end of the act's four-year life, for example, Poland's quota was mortgaged by half until 2000, and Latvia's until 2274. About 205,000 refugees entered under this law.

An attempt to overhaul the system in 1952 got entangled in the fear-ridden climate of McCarthyism, and the resulting McCarran-Walter Act kept the national origins quotas. Harry Truman vetoed it as "utterly unworthy of our traditions and ideals . . . our basic religious concepts, our belief in the brotherhood of man." It was passed over his veto, but time was on his side. Special emergency relief acts admitted refugees from China's civil war and Hungary's failed anti-Soviet uprising. Those who left Castro's Cuba needed no special relief, since there were as yet no limits on migration within the hemisphere, but they did get special help with resettlement. All told, in the 1950s immigration added up to some 2,500,000.

It was a quality migration, lured by the promise of American wages and the consumer goods made visible in the films and television shows that America exported. And jet travel now put the promised land only hours away. Foreign governments ruefully watched their elites disappearing into the "brain drain" to the United States. Between 1956 and 1965 approximately 7,000 chemists, 35,000 engineers, 38,000 nurses, and 18,000 physicians were admitted. Between 1952 and 1961 Britain lost 16 percent of its Ph.D.s, half to the United States. Comparable losses were even more critical for developing states in the Third World or small European countries.

Yet there was still room at the bottom, for workers in the "service industries" and especially in the harvest fields of the Southwest. In 1951 growers got Congress to enact "temporary worker" programs that brought in thousands of Mexican braceros. Many who received green cards remained without authorization, joining imprecise numbers of illegal immigrants known as wetbacks after presumably swimming the Rio Grande to elude the Border Patrol. There were legal ways to stay too.

All we need is a gringuita
So that we can get married
And after we get our green card
We can get a divorce
Long live all the wetbacks.

So ran a popular Mexican ballad. Authorized and undocumented Mexicans alike became part of an enlarging Hispanic population, fed by migrants from Central America and the Caribbean. Great numbers of Puerto Ricans were part of it, but they did not count as immigrants because of the island's special status.

In 1965 the patched old system was finally discarded, and a brand-new act was passed. It mirrored the equal-rights spirit of the 1960s, modified by the political compromises that float bills through the rip-tides of congressional debate. The national origins quotas vanished, but there was no return to the wide-open days. Instead new quotas were established with three primary targets: reuniting families, open-ing the gates to refugees, and attracting skill and talent.

The new act mandated an annual limit of 170,000 immigrants from outside the Western Hemisphere, and 120,000 from within. These 290,000 were to be admitted under seven "preference" quotas. First and second preferences—40 percent of the total—were saved for unmarried grown sons and daughters of citizens and legally admitted alien residents. (Spouses, minor children, and parents of citizens came in free.) The third preference, 10 percent, went to "members of the professions and scientists and artists of exceptional ability." The fourth, 10 percent, went to adult *married* children of U.S. citizens, and the fifth, 24 percent, to brothers and sisters of citizens. The sixth, 10 per-cent, was held for "skilled labor in great demand" and "unskilled work-ers in occupations for which labor is in short supply," and the final pref-erence, 6 percent, was for specifically defined refugees.

As Lyndon Johnson said when he signed the act at the base of the Statue of Liberty in October 1965, the new law was not "revolution-ary." Yet, he added, it "repairs a deep and painful flaw in the fabric of American life. . . . The days of unlimited immigration are past. But those who come will come because of what they are—not because of the land from which they sprung."

The Immigration Act of 1965 was born in the year of Great Society programs and the Voting Rights Act. It fulfilled some of its authors' expectations and also carried some surprises—perhaps because 1965 was itself a turning-point year that also witnessed urban race riots and the first heavy and expensive commitments to combat in Vietnam. Johnson was wrong in one respect: The law's effects *have* been revolu-tionary, and are still with us every day. The twenty-five years of its existence have produced a major demographic turnaround.

Europe, the prime provider of new Americans for three centuries, fell off to little more than a 10 percent share of total immigration. The bulk of it now comes from Asia and the Western Hemisphere. In the decade from 1961 to 1970 some 3,321,000 immigrants arrived, and 1,123,000, less than 40 percent, were of European origin. Of

4,493,000 newcomers in the period 1971–80, only about 801,000 were Europeans. Between 1981 and 1990, when immigration totaled 7,338,000, the European contribution was only 761,550.

What of the other 80 to 90 percent? Of the 4,493,000 arrivals in the 1970s, 1,588,000 came from Asia (somewhat over one-third), 1,983,000 from North and South America, and 80,779 from Africa. The five major contributing nations were, in order, Mexico (640,300), the Philippines (355,000), Korea (268,000), Cuba (265,000), and China, both mainland and Taiwan (237,800).

Of the roughly 7,300,000 legal immigrants of 1981–90, 2,700,000 came from Asia, 3,600,000 from the Americas. The leaders—with numbers rounded—were Mexico at 1,656,000, the Philippines at 549,000, Vietnam with 281,000, the two Chinas with 98,000 and 346,000, and Korea with 334,000. Other heavy contributors were the Caribbean nations, with together 872,000; India with about 250,000, Laos at 112,000, Iran with some 116,000, Central America (Costa Rica, El Salvador, Guatemala, Honduras, Nicaragua, and Panama) with 468,000, and African nations with 177,000.

The rising Third World totals had two sources. One was the nature of the 1965 law itself, especially the fifth-preference brother-and-sister quota. Legally admitted and naturalized immigrants brought in their siblings, who went through the same cycle and then brought in *their* kin, and so on in a family tree of ever-spreading branches. When Congress endorsed family reunification, it had in mind the American 1950s model of two parents and two or three children. What it got was extended clans of Asians and Latins.

The other root of Third World influx was the bloody history of the 1970s and 1980s. The fall of Cambodia and South Vietnam in 1975 unleashed floods of refugees who were a special responsibility of the United States. Within the first six months we admitted some 130,000, and many more thousands under special quota exemptions in succeeding years. By 1990, counting their children born here, some 586,000 people of Indochinese origin were living in the United States.

The refugee problem was worldwide. It raised issues of what countries should share the burdens of admission. It sharpened agonizing questions of when repatriation might be justified: when a family was actually fleeing for its life and when it was only looking for a chance to go where air-conditioned cars and color television sets were the visible rewards of hard work (as if both motives could not coexist).

Congress made its own tentative answer with the first major modification of the 1965 law, the Refugee Act of 1980. It set up new offices within the federal government for handling refugee affairs and reshuffled the quota system. The old seventh (refugee) preference with its 17,400 slots was abolished in favor of an annual quota of up to 50,000 refugees that could be exceeded for "grave, humanitarian reasons" by the President in consultation with Congress. The overall limit was dropped to 270,000 as a trade-off. A refugee was officially defined as a person who could not go home again by reason of a "well-founded fear of persecution" on the basis of race, religion, nationality, or political opinion.

And as if to mock the effort to set boundaries around social revolutions, President Carter's signature was hardly dry on the act when 125,000 new Cuban refugees were knocking at the gates, released by Castro through the port of Mariel. Carter declared that he would admit them with open arms and an open heart, a sentiment not fully shared by some residents of the South Florida communities where the *Marielitos* at first clustered.

Society had changed greatly since the unstructured and unsupervised days of mass arrivals at Ellis Island (long deserted and shuttered). The newest refugees did not find unskilled jobs and low-rent tenements waiting for them. It was the age of big government and bureaucratic organization. With the U.S. Treasury providing funds, and church and social service agencies the personnel, programs were launched to help with health care, schooling, and other roads to citizenship. Until the immigrants dispersed themselves around the country, they were lodged in temporary camps, some of them former Army bases. What had been left between 1890 and 1914 to friends, families, padrones, *landsleit*, and political machines was now managed under guidelines set in Washington.

Washington's welcome was not universal. Cold War politics infiltrated refugee policy in the 1980s. Refugees from Communist nations were welcomed, but those from countries officially deemed "democratic," like El Salvador, got shorter shrift. So did those who were "merely" trying to escape harsh but non-Communist regimes or grinding poverty, like the Haitians. The Immigration and Naturalization Service held thousands of them in detention while their petitions for asylum were suspiciously reviewed. Nonetheless, thousands of Central Americans managed to escape the net and find work—usually low-paid and menial—and to melt into the underground economy of the Hispanic communities in Florida and New York.

General statements about this newest great migration are dangerous because it is tempting to lump its members together by race and nationality, as the old Dillingham Report did, rather than by class, education, experience, income, or other categories. To describe Colombian dentists and Mexican cotton pickers as "Hispanics" or Korean chemical engineers and Pakistani nurses' aides as "Asian" suggests nonexistent similarities.

But some broad observations fit most of the new immigrants: They get to this country swiftly and by air, they quickly fall into the consumerist culture familiar to them through television at home, and they are quickly integrated into the bureaucratic structure of entitlements that characterize life in the United States today.

Beyond that, all-embracing descriptions strain the facts. The Vietnamese, for example, include English-speaking professionals who worked for American corporations, Catholics educated during the period of French control, and people from the bottom rung: in the words of one writer, "cosmopolites, bourgeois provincials, and dirt-poor peasants . . . gifted intellectuals, street-wise hustlers and un-worldly fisherfolk and farmers." The Koreans most visible to New Yorkers are the hardworking grocers who seem to have taken over the retail fruit and vegetable business completely from the Italians. But a survey shows that more than a third of all Koreans in the United States have completed four years of college.

Filipino immigrants are found in hospitals, as doctors and nurses and sometimes behind the counter in the basement cafeterias; Indians in the newsstands of New York City and likewise doing advanced bio-chemical or genetic research in its university laboratories. Middle Eastern Arabs, both Christian and Muslim, are heavily concentrated in Detroit, and many work in the American auto industry at both shop and managerial levels. Israeli and Soviet Jewish immigrants—some of them jobless Ph.D.s—drive taxis in Washington, Los Angeles, Chicago, and New York—and work as engineers in defense industries in the Southwest. Puerto Ricans, other Latinos, and Chinese fill the places in New York's declining garment industry once held by Italians and Jews.

Within the communities of Cambodians, Peruvians, Ecuadorians, Iranians, Russians, Israelis, Irish, and Puerto Ricans the old saga goes on as children learn new ways and move to new, unexpected disruptive rhythms. But in education the effect of the new immigration has been dramatically different from what it was prior to World War I. Then the public schools were on the rise and confident of their power and duty to unify *all* children behind the undisputedly correct symbols and rites of Americanism.

In the mood of the 1970s, however, things changed. Emphasis on ethnic pride and the power of the civil rights revolution dictated a new approach. Immigrant children were no longer to be thrown into English-speaking classrooms to sink or swim. Instead bilingual programs would help them in transit to a new system without their being stigmatized as stupid because they could not understand the teacher. Going further, some educators argued that preparing children for a multicultural society required exposure to many "life-styles" and building the self-esteem of "minority" students through appreciation of their own languages, customs, and cultures. So some states mandated bilingual (usually Hispanic-English) programs into the curriculum at every level.

Whatever the virtues of the theory (debatable in the light of evidence), bilingualism provoked a strong counterreaction, and by 1990 some organizations were insisting that new immigrants were not working hard enough to learn the common tongue that was so valuable a social binding agency. An English-only drive got under way to designate English, by constitutional amendment, if necessary, as the *official* language of the United States.

In actual fact, Spanish (and other language) newspapers, television stations, religious congregations, and social clubs were a re-enactment of what had gone before. In the early 1900s there had been a vigorous immigrant press, which, in time, died out. But the English-only movement drew strength from a sense of increasing discomfort over the increasing numbers of immigrants, a reawakening of the old idea that a "flood" of "unassimilated" newcomers was pouring in.

A new restrictionism was born, featuring some familiar alliances. Middle- and upper-class taxpayers believed that the immigrants, concentrated in certain areas, were a burden on schools, hospitals, and welfare and law-enforcement agencies. On the other hand, there were workers who were convinced that the immigrants took away low-level jobs that were rightfully theirs or depressed wages by working in sweatshops or permitting the employment of their underage children. Black Americans tended especially to believe that material assistance that had been denied to them was going to the refugees. They were now the bypassed "old Americans."

Resentment was fed by the widespread admiration of the academic and business success of Asian Americans, who were, in great numbers, advancing up the professional scale. They were described by some sociologists as a "model minority"—their delinquents and failures overlooked while the spotlight fell on those who succeeded.

A dread of the unknown and uncountable hovered over lawmakers. Undocumented aliens came in from the Mexico in annual numbers estimated from a few hundred thousand to many millions a year. The oft-repeated statement that we were "losing control of our borders" had a powerful psychological kick in a time of multiple American troubles. Had we, in fact, reached the limit our power to offer asylum? Was there truth in what Sen. Alan Simpson said in 1982: "We have to live within limits. The nation wants to be compassionate but we have been compassionate beyond our ability to respond"?

The evidence of the actual economic effect of immigration is inconclusive. The contribution of immigrant specialists to a high-tech economy has to be considered. Every working-age, well-trained immigrant who enters the country becomes a free resource, not schooled at American cost—a dividend from the brain drain. Even the "low-end" immigrants, including the "illegals" (or undocumented), may contribute as much in sales and other taxes and in purchasing power as they take out in services and schooling. The case has also been made that the undocumented aliens, fearful of discovery, rarely claim benefits due them. Thousands of employers likewise insist that without immigrants they could not staff the service industries or harvest the fields. And the falling American birthrate suggests to some economists the possibility of labor shortages in the next century. They say that we can easily absorb half a million or so legal immigrants annually, perhaps more—though of what kind and for how long are left to debate.

But while debate went on, Congress did make a second change in the 1965 law. The Simpson-Mazzoli Act of 1986 tried to deal with two much-disputed issues. One was how to identify and count the unmeasured number of undocumented aliens already in the country without intrusive violations of civil liberties. The other was how to enforce immigration limits without a gigantic and costly expansion of the hard-pressed Immigration and Naturalization Service. The solution to the first problem was dealt with through an amnesty for pre-1982 immigrants; the second, by turning employers into enforcement agents. They would be "sanctioned" by fines if they hired undocumented aliens. The bill sparked bitter controversy in its career in three separate Congresses before final passage. Mexican-American organizations, for example, argued that employers, rather than risk sanctions, would simply refuse to hire Hispanic-looking or -sounding men and women. Employers complained about the cost and difficulty of checking credentials. But in the end a coalition for passage was established. It is still too early to tell how well the law is working.

It is not too early, however, to make some general predictions about the future course of the peopling of America. Immigration on the current scale, plus natural increase, will over time change the character of the people who inhabit these United States. Hispanic-descended men and women alone now constitute a little more than 22,000,000 in a population of about 248,000,000. By 2010 they are expected to number 39,300,000 in an overall population of about 282,000,000. In other words, their increase will account for 28 percent of the total population growth in that period. Another set of census projections for the period from 1990 to 2025 sees the white population declining from 84.3 to 75.6 percent, the black population percentage rising from 12.4 to 14.6, and the percentage of "other races" almost doubling, from 3.4 to 6.5. In some urban areas where the current crop of new immigrants clusters, the terms *nonwhite* and *minority* are no longer synonyms; in Los Angeles County, for example, only 15 percent of public school children are white.

We began with a reference to the many-tongued New York that Isaac Jogues found in 1643. It is appropriate to return for a look some 350 years afterward. The old tale continues. "Young Immigrant Wave Lifts New York Economy," runs a recent story in *The New York Times*. The paper found that the 2,600,000 foreign-born residents of the city (about one-third of the total population) had a positive effect. Their addition to the ranks of workers, small business owners, and consumers had probably kept New York from becoming "boarded up." No fewer than eighteen countries had sent 5,000 or more people to the hard-pressed metropolis from 1980 to 1986. At least 114 languages are spoken in the city's school systems. In one Queens school a sign directs visitors to register in English, Chinese, Korean, and Spanish. Among those photographed or interviewed for the article were a Serbian-speaking garment worker, a Romanian technician in a hematology laboratory, and an Albanian building owner who began as a superintendent.

And as in New York, so also in the other great cities of America in the 1990s—in Los Angeles (44 percent of adults foreign-born) and Miami (70 percent foreign-born), in Chicago, Dallas, Boston, in the ten largest cities of the land where increases in immigrant population offset the economic impact of the loss of other residents—and in the neighborhoods across the country where the new immigrants are working and raising their American children. For them the streets may not be paved with gold, but the dreams still glisten. What memories they will give their children, what gods they will worship, what leaders they will follow, what monuments they will create are all part of history yet to be written. It seems safe to say that, like the English, Scots, Irish, Germans, Swedes and Finns, Greeks, Poles, Italians,

Hungarians, and Russians before them, they will neither "melt" into some undistinctive alloy nor, on the other hand, remain aloof and distinct from one another. Some kind of functional American mosaic will emerge. It is the historic way; the great Amazon that Melville described as America's noble bloodstream flows on undisturbed, into a new century.

—February 1994

HOW HAVE WE CHANGED?
1954–1994

As part of the magazine's look back over the past forty years, American Heritage *asked a wide range of historians, journalists, writers, and public figures the following question: "What do you think is the most important, or interesting, or overlooked way in which America has changed since 1954, and why? And what does this change say about us as a people?" We knew this was a broad question, to say the least, but we were still surprised by the answers it elicited; they turned out to be as various and provocative and illuminating as the people they came from. An anthology follows.*

The degree of civilization at any time and place may be measured by the way in which particular acts are classified. Some are free, some forbidden or commanded by law, the rest abstained from, by habit and the sway of opinion. I think the chief change in American society between 1954 and today is the shrunken area occupied by the third kind of behavior.

The phenomenon has been called Permissiveness and credited to a bugbear called Relativism. This explanation ignores the underlying motive and the predisposing state of fact. What we see is not simply laxity, but a paradox that carries a message. Why the extensive lying, cheating, and stealing by the intelligent and well-to-do? Why the artist's rage to disgust and serve up the obscene? Why the passion for "telling all" and for the conglomerate, not only in business but also in everyday life, eating at all times and places, wearing any kinds of clothes anywhere, and using dirty words—everything regardless of surrounding conditions?

I believe the answer lies in that last word. The intense purpose behind many seemingly disparate acts and beliefs comes from resentment against obstacles, against any condition set in the path of any creature's doing what he, she, or it desires. A barrier is an affront to human nature. What all want is the Unconditional Life.

This ideal stimulates the imagination and, if need be, removes guilt. Ambition balked cheats with a clear conscience; and greed, seeing the arbitrariness of property rights, steals as it were on principle. With lines blurred and fences down, it is easy to be virtuous and never "discriminate" in any sense. In this light, blue jeans, a sweater, pearls, and gold evening shoes qualify as "a style."

To explain the rise of the passion for the unconditioned would require a look at modern cultural history, taking in the wars, the social thought, and the arts of our time. But the immediate impelling force is the universal sense of oppression: too many contacts with too many people, thanks to multiplying means of communication; too many rules, warnings, limits, delays, duties, prohibitions, exclusions, conditions—a ubiquitous "zoning" of existence by which government tries to reconcile incessant claims. Lastly, the exit door is blocked by the mass of trivial details that force attention if one is to thread one's way more or less unbruised through workaday life. To take every chance of breaking out is but reflex action.

Jacques Barzun, university professor emeritus, Columbia University; author, *Darwin, Marx, Wagner*

The most important change since 1954 derives from the fact that until then America had never lost a war. The French, who had lost many wars, lost the Battle of Dien Bien Phu that year, which should have taught us a thing or two but didn't. And so today we, too, are now a nation that has experienced defeat. Until the Indochinese events that began (for us) in 1954, Americans believe that every time the country undertook a major project—to defeat the British, to settle the West, to control the secessionist South and abolish slavery, to institute a variety of social reforms, to defeat the Second World War Axis—the project turned out well. But not Vietnam.

In the first years after the war, most Americans drew a very simple lesson—to wit, never get involved in someone else's troubles unless it is absolutely unavoidable. Some people still feel that way, naturally. But I think most people have come to think today that it is good to send at least a few American soldiers to central Africa; that in spite of everything, we performed a good deed in Somalia; that we did well in preventing the expansion of Saddam Hussein's power, even if success in the Gulf War was less than what it seemed at the time. So the simple lesson from Vietnam has turned out to be too simple.

All in all, we are an older nation than we were in 1954. We have learned that things can go deeply wrong, and we have learned that, even so, hiding in a cave is no alternative. We have learned the lesson that there is no lesson. George Washington is our national symbol, and on our heads, too, a few white hairs have sprouted.

Paul Berman, editor, *Blacks and Jews: Thirty Years of Alliance and Argument*

Can we understand our own times? I'm not sure. Matters that seem urgent, forces that seem irresistible in their period may vanish like the once powerful Prohibition party. But here are some very provisional comments.

In 1954 and again in 1965 my husband and I drove to California and back, dawdling across the country. A couple of the roads we took in 1954 (U.S. 40, U.S. 66) had become historic by 1965. Sheer growth has been an obvious change. Now I hear that the roads, airports, and bridges built in the late 1950s are broke and no one's fixing them. That's like us: Americans, as a people, have been better at building great projects than at maintaining them. On the other hand, the past forty years have brought new strength to movements for historic preservation and conservation; if Americans ever became good housekeepers, that *would* be a change.

Self-righteousness has been a persistent American response to change. Fundamentalism revives as popular music grows noisier and corporations grow bigger; the 1990s are like the 1920s. Right now a lot of self-righteousness is directed against women. Yet my hunch is that the changing role of women, which has affected our intimate relations and our expectations of strangers, may be the most important change in the last forty years. Television—its ubiquitous influence is another significant change—helps by showing old movies. The films of 1954 put women in roles that now seem quaint. The change may be a reason that we hear the complaint that there are no roles for older actresses. The ditsy dowager has become less credible, and we haven't yet figured out how to tell a story in which the judge is a grandmother. I think we will, though, because society nowadays seems to demand more intelligence and more participation by the intelligent of all ages and genders.

Naomi Bliven, author, *On Her Own*

The Terbul Deklin of Liturcy.
Shana Alexander, author, *Poles Apart: My Mother, My Father, My Sister and Me*

From my own self-centered perspective, the most extraordinary change in America over the past forty years is that I have somehow been transformed from a boy of sixteen to a man of fifty-six. I find this astonishing, and I don't know how to account for it.

When I look at the Bigger Picture, two remarkable changes suggest themselves to me, and I have the sense that they are somehow related. First, the regionalism that was such a defining aspect of this country has been eroded beyond measure. When you drove across the country in 1954, bouncing along on bad roads, risking ptomaine in dubious diners, holing up nights in roadside cabins and tourist courts, you were rewarded with a constant change of scene that amounted to more than a change of landscape. There were no chain restaurants, no franchised muffler-repair shops, and even the brands of beer and gasoline were apt to change when you crossed a couple of state lines. Nowadays you take the Eisenhower administration's most enduring legacy, the interstate highway system, and eat at Burger Kings and sleep in Days Inns, and when the scenery palls, you duck into a mall, walk past thirty franchised shops, and catch a movie at the fourplex theater. Even the local accents have softened, weathered away by forty more years of national television. We have become more nearly a single nation than we used to be.

And at the same time, the complexion of this nation is infinitely more varied than it was forty years ago. America was peopled by persons of Northern European stock. Most had been here for many generations. Immigration had slowed to a trickle, and the more recent arrivals were also European—Irish and Italians and Greeks and Armenians, and refugees from what we were still calling war-torn Europe. There were fewer blacks, and they were far less visible, found mostly in the largest Northern cities and the rural South. There were a few Mexicans in the Southwest, a handful of French Canadians in New England.

And now? Nearly a third of the population of my own city, New York, is foreign-born, arriving in the same numbers they were a hundred years ago. And the new immigrants come from every continent but Antarctica. You see it most vividly on both coasts, but it's just as true in the heartland, where it's more apt to surprise you—the Indian family operating a motel in rural Mississippi, the cluster of Vietnamese restaurants in Denver, the Hmong craftsmen in Minnesota and Wisconsin.

All changed, changed utterly. Or, in another light, not changed at all. America has spent the past forty years evolving, becoming more completely what it has been from its beginnings. It has taken one more step (or a series of steps, or a glide) in that ceaseless process called Self-Realization.

Even as you and I . . .

Lawrence Block, author, *Eight Million Ways to Die* and other books

S unshine is bad for you.
Roy Blount, Jr., humorist and essayist; editor, *Roy Blount's Book of Southern Humor*

E nd of the Cold War . . . JFK's assassination . . . a decline in civility . . . failure of our public school system . . . the Wall Street boom . . . man in space . . . Japanese cars . . . no smoking . . . AIDS . . . the computer . . . political correctness . . . McDonald's . . . the drug culture . . . cable TV . . . Watergate . . . anorexia . . . Muslim fundamentalism . . . junk bonds . . . *Roe* v. *Wade* . . . the shopping mall . . . Hefner's *Playboy* . . . Disneyland . . . the designated hitter . . . the Xerox machine . . . women's lib . . . the breakup of the phone company . . . mutual funds . . . beepers, mobile phones, and other invasions of privacy . . . the demise of the *Herald Trib, Look, Collier's*, the *Satevepost*, et cetera . . . the decline of our postal service . . . sexual liberation . . . the end of the "Solid South". . . the "no" bra . . . gay lib . . . the ozone layer . . .
James Brady, editor-at-large, *Advertising Age*

T he change from waxed paper to cling wrap says it all.
Nicholson Baker, author, *U and I, Vox,* and *The Fermata*

R ecently I attended a reunion of the families of my youth, working-class families that in the early and mid-fifties had converged on a remote site along the Missouri River in South Dakota, formed a community, and built an enormous dam. It was a joyous get-together because it recalled such good times. Our parents came of age in the Great Depression and helped win World War II, and here on the South Dakota prairie they had been involved in a monumental project that paid good wages. It was for us, their children, an age of promise. Most of us lived in intact, nuclear families. Many of us were the first members of our families to attend college.

As I stood before my many friends from forty years earlier, I felt an enormous pride in their achievements. Many returned with advanced degrees and worldly experiences well beyond the reach of our parents. Those who continued the working-class tradition of their families reflected the long, rising curve of prosperity and material comforts unimagined in our youth.

There were other changes. Their daughters have ambitions well beyond marriage and childbearing. Almost no one at the reunion smoked, and forty years ago nearly everyone did. Now physical fitness is a way of life, and then it was eccentric behavior. Overall, however, our gathering was a tribute to a rare time in America when the can-do spirit prevailed, when the nation was an economic and political collossus unchallenged in the world arena, when all seemed possible and we were the direct beneficiaries.

Of course, we were all white.

The other America—African-American, Native American, Latino, Asian—the people of color, whatever color, were invisible to most of white America forty years ago, except when they were celebrated as entertainers or athletes. Forty years ago the face of the American political, economic, and cultural establishment was white only.

Four decades later all the primary colors are vivid and visible in the mosaic of America. We still have too far to go in resolving our complex feeling about race, but the fact of a multiracial society is no longer denied. I can think of no greater or more welcome change in forty years.

Tom Brokaw, anchorman, "NBC Nightly News"

B eginning with simple servomechanisms that came out of World War II, followed by rapid advances in electronics through microcircuits and silicon chips, overwhelming changes have been brought about since 1954 in the way Americans live and think and view the world.

The key word is *control.* Our living spaces from bedrooms to bathrooms and kitchens are controlled by automatic devices that did not exist forty years ago. Our automobiles are no longer entirely controlled by the drivers but by numerous electronic thingamabobs. Office and professional workers are never out of the control of computers and ever-changing modes of communication. Writers and publishers are controlled by word processors. Patients and physicians in hospitals are controlled by electronic machines totally incomprehensible to the average human being. Computerized equipment has replaced the card catalogs of our libraries, speeding the use of, but homogenizing, information and our preserved folk culture. Intensive use of pictures and spoken words to instruct and entertain has started a decline in the exactness of the language in recording complex and abstract ideas.

It is too early to determine the full effect of these man-made controls upon American society, but thus far we appear to be more isolated from one another than we were.

Dee Brown, author, *Bury My Heart at Wounded Knee*

I hate to say it, but feel the need to acknowledge the quiet triumph of secularism in the past thirty years. This is not an invitation to admire my sibylline powers, but in fact, I did venture in my first book that it was unreasonable to expect that there wouldn't be consequences from the assault in the university on religious faith. In my day lusty agnostics would on the least invitation happily engage in trench warfare against Christianity. Okay. But it is worse now, or such is my reading. The evangelists of agnosticism no longer feel the need to move their armies against what, in their judgment, is nowadays only a derelict defense force. It isn't that, of course, but the indifference to religion, reflected in the life of the university, is a development of great social consequence. If one listens, for instance as I recently did on the relevant anniversary, to the message by FDR when he communicated to the American people that D-day had happened and the reconquest of Europe was in prospect, one is starkly reminded of how our leaders then addressed us. "Almighty God: Our sons, pride of our nation, this day have set upon a mighty endeavor. . . . They will need Thy blessings . . . we know that by Thy grace, and by the righteousness of our cause, our sons will triumph. . . . Thy will be done, Almighty God." That was common currency from the aristocratic and the ruling classes, in FDR's case conjoined. He spoke language that suggested the ultimate dimension of the human experience, and this was the foundation of American idealism, liberty under God, as we came to phrase it. I cannot imagine a modern President speaking so, even though the incumbent and his predecessors are Christians by formal understanding. What all of it means is that the great regulator of days gone by is no longer vibrant, and the consequences hardly need to be enumerated. In other ages it was all there: crime, libertinism, self-centeredness, infidelity. But it was viewed as departure from the correct standards. Now we get such as the Surgeon General, whose answer to the question Is it wrong to conceive out of wedlock? was "No. Everyone has different moral standards." That would include Pol Pot.

William F. Buckley, Jr., editor in chief, *The National Review*; author, *On the Firing Line*

Forty years ago, a medical student, I could walk the streets of various American cities without great anxiety. I well remember leaving my college dorm room unlocked all the time, and similarly, my medical-school dorm room. Now fear (of robbers, of injury, even of death) hovers over many of us who walk city streets, drive city roads—black and white, well-to-do and poor: a significant and melancholy turn of events.

Robert Coles, professor of psychiatry and medical humanities, Harvard University Medical School; author, *Children of Crisis: A Study of Courage and Fear*

The awkward fact that is overlooked in much reporting and commentary is that the DNA that created America has suffered a mutation. It can no longer be assumed that immigrants want to be American. The 1965 Immigration Act, thought to be a modest reform, has produced a floodtide of immigrants who will not assimilate as easily as earlier generations, many of them because they do not want to assimilate at all, and who claim rights not as Americans but as ethnic and linguistic minorities. The very identity of America is being challenged, in its political faith, its history, and its culture. A vague sentimentality about immigration and a fear of being accused of "racism" have suppressed proper discussion of this crucial issue.

Harold M. Evans, president and publisher, Random House Trade Group

The greatest change in America since the birth of *American Heritage* was the placing of electric motors inside typewriters. Sure, IBM did it sometime earlier, but by the mid-1950s the others were doing it, and it became possible for college and university teachers to participate in this revolution in typewriter technology. I remember the first one I bought, a boxy Underwood with a slightly futuristic decor, but inside was that mighty motor, and this meant that after most of a day of talking to students and listening to students it was possible to try to write something without feeling as if one were rowing a boat. There are people like David McCullough who have never appreciated this typewriter revolution and insist on using Remington portables circa 1941. David tests his machines by (so he says) throwing them against a wall, whereupon they simply bounce off, proving they are made of steel. He would never buy a machine with a motor, he says. But he likes to live in the typewriter Dark Ages.

There have been changes in machines since the 1950s, notably the introduction of electronics (31 moving parts versus 247, which means that they last only until their circuit boards break). Word processors were the next step, which I refused to take (spend my day looking at a screen?). But the typewriter motor was the principal change of our time.

As for what it says about us as a people, it says that we are a lot less tired than we used to be.

Robert H. Ferrell, professor of history emeritus, Indiana University; author, *Harry S. Truman and the Modern American Presidency*

The most important change in this country in the last forty years took place in 1973, when the upheaval of Watergate triggered a shift from presidential government to congressional government.

The term *congressional government* was coined by a young history scholar named Woodrow Wilson as the title of his first book, an analysis of the way Congress seized control of the nation after the near impeachment of President Andrew Johnson in 1865. Wilson foresaw the danger of an aggrandizing legislature. "In proportion as you give it power it will inquire into everything, settle everything, meddle in everything."

The ultimate danger, Wilson feared, was legislative tyranny, which would be a despotism far worse than that of a dictator. Congress could become a despot "who has unlimited time—who has unlimited vanity —who has or believes he has unlimited comprehension."

Wilson put his astute finger on the fatal flaw in congressional government: "Nobody stands to sponsor the policy of government. A dozen men originate it; a dozen compromises twist and alter it; a dozen officers whose names are scarcely known outside Washington put it into execution." The result is massive alienation among the citizenry.

In the nineteenth century—and in our own era—another by-product of congressional government has been massive corruption, corruption so pervasive Washington insiders no longer even recognize it. Mark Twain summed it up in his era when he said the United States had no distinctly criminal class "except Congress." The modern Congress, bloated with perks and PACs, the creature of lobbyists and pressure groups, suggests a similar conclusion.

What was Wilson's answer to congressional government? A strong Presidency. "The President is at liberty, both in law and in conscience, to be as big a man as he can." Beginning with Theodore Roosevelt, twentieth-century Presidents restored the balance between the two branches. For present and future Presidents to regain this authority, the modern Congress will have to give up some of its power. This will require an epic political battle. But it must be fought—and won—as soon as possible.

Thomas Fleming, author, *The Officers' Wives*

Today's curious tolerance of forked-tongue corporate labels for special-interest outfits and privately financed think tanks has long been overlooked. To define the gimmick by opposites: The venerable "Society for the Prevention of Cruelty to Animals" is irreproachable. "League of Women Voters" and "U.S.English" are candid enough. But even "Common Cause"—much as I respect most of what it does—is a bit slippery. That could just as well apply to a junta concocted by Jerry Falwell, Pat Robertson, et al. For more flagrant examples, consider "American Enterprise Institute" and "Center for National Policy Studies"—masterpieces of camouflage-ambiguity recently rivaled by "United We Stand."

Not that this letterhead shell game is anything new. A century ago things like "Non-Partisan League" occasionally surfaced. But for every such creation in great-grandpa's time hundreds are now churning out smothering masses of direct-mail come-ons, TV pitches, and "position papers." My current favorite, succeeding "National Organization for Women," is "Concerned Women for America"—narrowly red-hot against abortion and for school prayer.

Such hidden-ball tricks apparently work so well that we must expect more and better ones. The note in italics at the tail of the op-ed piece will say, "Dr. Pundit is a Fellow of the Social Responsibility Council," but not that its fat-cat angel used to help finance the John Birch Society. Madison Avenue's "Ad-Liberty League" will make awards for untrammeled creativity, yes, but its undercover mission will be gradually to soften up viewers for hard-core pornography in commercials . . .

J. C. Furnas, author, *The Road to Harpers Ferry* and other books

R e change in America since 1954: I would have no doubt. It is the wonderfully greater sense of moral purpose with which the affluent and the comfortable (of whom, of course, I am one) defend their well-being and specifically their income against the claims of the unfortunate and the deprived. This holds for money and especially for leisure, and in a degree that might astonish even Thorstein Veblen. How good leisure for the fortunate, how depraved for the welfare mother.

John Kenneth Galbraith, Warburg Professor of Economics Emeritus, Harvard University; author, *A Short History of Financial Euphoria*

T he most interesting change in my life since 1954 has been the development of the computer. Of course we all have been affected by computers in hundreds of ways, but for me the computer's most striking impact has been its effect on my typing. All my life I have been a two-finger typist. I know pretty well where the different letters are, and I can hit the keys at a reasonably rapid pace, but no matter how hard I concentrate I make lots and lots of typos. I do not believe I have ever typed an entire double-spaced page without hitting at least one wrong key. I was not even able to use an electric typewriter because when I tried, I could never get through a paragraph without inadvertently nicking the shift lock with the pinkie of my left hand when striking the *a* with my typing finger. The result, of course, would be several lines of capital letters unnoticed because of my slavish concentration on the keyboard in my futile effort to avoid errors.

Over the years I spent large sums hiring professional typists to produce "clean" copies of my messy manuscripts and equally large amounts of time checking over the typists' work to make sure they had not left out anything or gotten a date, a page number in a footnote, or some other number wrong. In doing this, nine times out of ten I decided to change something that was typed just the way I wrote it. That meant more professional typing. Sooner or later I would have to give up and accept what the typist produced as final copy.

Today I am probably an even more inaccurate typist than I was back in 1954. But thanks to my trusty spelling checker, on paper I now look flawless.

John A. Garraty, professor of history, Columbia University; author, *The American Nation*

I think the most important way America has changed since 1954 is that we are no longer a United States, but rather a crazy quilt of special interests in conflict.

William H. Goetzmann, Jack S. Blanton, Sr., Chair in History and American Studies, University of Texas at Austin; author, *Exploration and Early American Culture*

How has America changed most since 1954? We are less likely to think of ourselves as a single people. Forty years ago it was more or less clear what it meant to "be an American"—now, who has any idea at all? Indeed, paradoxically, the very question seems now somewhat un-American. So enamored are we of diversity, of multiculturalism, of the sense of ourselves as many rather than one, that merely trying to define what an American is today is itself un-American.

This is more than a matter of shifting metaphors, replacing the melting pot with the mosaic, though that is part of it. The melting pot was always too innocent to be true; this country was always more of a mosaic, even when it pretended to the homogeneity of the melting pot. But the earnestness contained within that sugary metaphor, fairy tale though it may have been, served us well for generations, and was not nearly as reactionary a force as we now assume it to have been. The eagerness to think of ourselves as one people provided a kind of spiritual underpinning to such powerful forces for social change as the creation of social security in the 1930s or the civil rights battles of the 1960s.

Now, the dream of homogeneity lies shattered. We no longer aspire to it as a people; we no longer believe it has any connection to the hope of a better life. We are less innocent, vastly less trusting—and unable, at least so far, to find a way to bring out of our current infatuation with confrontation and differences any kind of vision of harmony and wholeness. It is not that we were once homogeneous and now we are not: it is that once, despite all our differences, we had a sense of common purpose.

Paul Goldberger, chief cultural correspondent of *The New York Times*

My father spent the winter of 1954 struggling to overcome sentiment with reason. He was trying to abandon a lifelong allegiance to the New York Yankees and become a fan of the previously hated Brooklyn Dodgers (soon to be the Los Angeles Dodgers, a mobility that could supply another appropriate story for this issue). My father, a committed civil libertarian and political activist, was appalled that the Yanks had not yet hired a black player (Jackie Robinson had broken the color barrier with the Dodgers in 1947). He succeeded in his struggle, and the Yanks brought up their first black player, Elston Howard, in 1955. But too late for my dad, who remained a Dodger fan for the rest of his life.

We are still so far from obtaining full racial justice that we forget all too easily how immensely much has been accomplished in the past forty years. I well remember, as a child in one of the nation's most diverse and liberal constituencies, my shock on the very few occasions that I saw an interracial couple walking down a Manhattan street. Black people never appeared as ordinary human beings in advertisements, but only as the risible stereotypes of fearful, bug-eyed sidekicks like Rochester (for Jack Benny) or Birmingham (for Charlie Chan) or as fat, happy cooks like Aunt Jemima. In my high school, integrated de jure, I met black students only in chorus and gym. William Faulkner said that integration, only a tiny first step to justice, would take generations, for minds cannot be changed by force. But minds are changed by living—the rationale for required integration—and my son not only feels no discomfort with people of any color or shape but simply cannot fathom why anyone ever would.

Race is a surrogate for all other bases of false and cruel separation and denigration: gender, religion, national origin. Therefore our move to greater ease and geniality on this front mirrors a growing acceptance of differences in all areas and marks the most salutary change in American social life during the past forty years.

My professions of evolutionary biology and paleontology have, during this same forty-year interval, discovered the basis for the striking similarities that unite all human peoples. Genetic differences among so-called races are trivial (the evolutionary finding), based on the surprising recency of common ancestry, about two hundred thousand years (the paleontological finding), for all modern humans. For once a cliché turns out to be literally true: Our differences are only skin deep.

Stephen Jay Gould, professor of geology and Alexander Agassiz Professor of Zoology, Harvard University; author, *The Panda's Thumb*

The United States, decrying the population explosion in the so-called Third World, itself became overpopulated in the last forty years, with nary a mention of that pejorative word in the media or in the halls of government. From 1950 to 1990 the population increased by almost a hundred million souls—more than three times the nation's inhabitants on the eve of the Civil War. The effects have been pervasive. To cite only a few: It has eroded the vaunted dignity of the individual by forcing us to use numbers rather than names as identifiers in the records of practically every institution of society; it has significantly encouraged illegal immigration because the crowded-up areas of the country more readily than ever before can slip the harness of government; it has notably accelerated the rise of crime by nourishing it with the important advantage of easy anonymity for its perpetrators. What all this says about us as a people is that in making a fetish of the idea that bigger is better, we have shortsightedly faced away from the protection of national self-interest.

Henry F. Graff, professor of history emeritus, Columbia University; author, *America: The Glorious Republic*

The range of speculation on the various topics you propose is enormous, and high on the list of major events for America must surely be the dissolution of the Soviet Union and the emancipation of its satellites. Nevertheless, it may be that the sudden appearance and spread of AIDS is among the greatest dangers and disasters of modern times. A young, sexually active generation had only just begun to celebrate a new and liberating mode of life—with pop-culture heroes, musicals like *Hair*, an astonishing freedom from old inhibitions and hang-ups—when the wild celebration of the Aquarius Revolution was brought to a dead halt. My generation had sometimes been shy, nervous, and timid about inaugurating sex (Philip Larkin's "Annus Mirabilis" seemed to sum up our situation:

> *Sexual intercourse began*
> *In nineteen sixty-three*
> *(Which was rather late for me)—*

822

Between the end of the Chatterley
  ban
And the Beatles' first LP.

Up until then there'd only been
A sort of bargaining
A wrangle for a ring,
A shame that started at sixteen
And spread to everything.

And we fumbled about awkwardly, making many grave mistakes and often feeling suitably foolish, if not worse.) But nothing that assailed us could match the terrible plague that now presents a continuing terror to any sexually active person, male or female, straight or gay. All that cheerful abandon has been lost and has been replaced by a constant anxiety. This blight upon youthful instincts is no providential retribution for unwarranted license. AIDS afflicts chastely married couples, their children, innocent recipients of blood transfusions. And it seems to have settled down for a long stay.
Anthony Hecht, poet, university professor, Georgetown University

R evolutions come and go. Even the Russian Revolution has finally, mercifully, gone. But one revolution, I suspect, will remain with us for the foreseeable future: the sexual revolution.

In 1954 the illegitimacy ratio (the proportion of out-of-wedlock births to total births) was less than 4.5 percent. In 1991 (the last year for which we have definitive statistics), it was 29.5 percent; today it is certainly above 30 percent—a sevenfold increase in less than half a century. The white ratio rose from almost 2 percent to 22 percent; the black from almost 20 percent to 68 percent. In 1964, when Daniel Patrick Moynihan wrote his report about the breakdown of the black family, the black illegitimacy ratio was 24.5 percent; today the white illegitimacy ratio is 22 percent. For poor whites (below the official poverty line) the ratio is 44 percent. In 1990 one in ten teen-age girls got pregnant.

The illegitimacy figures are only (a very large "only") the tip of the iceberg. They have to be seen in conjunction with such other factors as the doubling of the divorce rate, the quintupling of the cohabitation rate, and a vast increase in the number of "sexually active" (as the euphemism has it) teenagers. (In 1970, 5 percent of fifteen-year-old girls had had sexual intercourse; in 1988, 25 percent had.) And looming over all these statistics is the well-documented correlation between single-parent families and welfare, crime, juvenile delinquency, drug abuse, school dropouts, illiteracy, and the rest of the familiar syndrome known as "social pathology."

There is no question but that we are experiencing a sexual revolution that is nothing less than a major social revolution.
Gertrude Himmelfarb, author, *On Looking Into the Abyss: Untimely Thoughts on Culture and Society*

It was sometime back in 1954 when a distinct change came over the United States. It happened after the uprising of our North Korean prisoners, when scores who were thought by the hard-liners to be getting soft were executed by their fellow prisoners. The American press and general public were horrified that prisoners could be so dedicated to a lost cause that they would actually kill so many of their "brothers."

I remember at the time thinking that there was nothing odd about the patriotic Koreans' reactions, only the reaction of the American press. It seemed to me at that moment our nation had lost part of its will.

After the Korean War, gradually and imperceptibly, our classic American resolve, our vitality, our willingness to look boldly at the blackness of the human soul wilted away. Since then we seem to have succumbed to a collective gnashing of teeth or forgiveness sessions over every ill at home or abroad. We appear to have cast aside our common sense and exaggerated most solvable problems, making them all but insoluble. We have become a nation of brooders. We may have lost our national soul and fiber in the process.

Many of the men in my years at college enlisted in the Marine Corps convinced that our luck in having been educated meant that we had to repay society by becoming officers. Some of my colleagues were killed within minutes of coming on the line in Korea, others were crippled— the most gifted is still a mental vegetable—and one was wounded and buried by mortar shells behind the Chinese lines and lives today because several members of his platoon were wounded in retrieving what was thought would be his corpse.

Those of us who survived were profoundly saddened by the deaths and cripplings of our fellow men, but we didn't dwell on it. We all had volunteered.

To me, the most overlooked and underreported way our country has changed is that since 1954 we have collectively bankrupted our nation's toughness. We have become soft, sentimental, fat, complacent, too rich, monstrously selfish, cynical, disgustingly decadent, dedicatedly hypocritical—and, worst of all, perpetual whiners.
Thomas Hoving, former director, Metropolitan Museum of Art; author, *Making the Mummies Dance*

During the past forty years the country has moved out of the machine age into the information age. The insistence of many scholars and journalists that this transition was taking place became a self-fulfilling prophecy. Americans began to think and speak in information-age metaphors, and these metaphors influence their activities. They send messages traveling in bits at the speed of light, not in words via snail mail. Instead of circumstances' causing events, they seem to be arising from network interactions too complex to analyze. People meet by interface with computers instead of face-to-face with other persons. Information moves as bits along circuits instead of as components along assembly lines. No longer do mechanical engineers insist on uniformity; instead computer engineers celebrate heterogeneous networks. Local places with all their contingent characteristics give way to universal spaces sustained by electronic webs. These transformations are not to be explained by technological determinism. They result from countless Americans' choosing to have affairs with computers rather than automobiles and restlessly exploring information networks instead of earthbound highways. Only an optimist would insist, however, that Internet surfers today are more fulfilled than Sunday drivers yesterday.

Thomas P. Hughes, Mellon Professor Emeritus, University of Pennsylvania; author, *American Genesis*

In the last decades there have been marked overturns of settled traditions and habits in American life—the growing power of women, the entry of many African-Americans into middle-class society, the openness of homosexuality, the national conflict over abortion, the nervous emphasis on health, sensible eating habits, and cancer, the antismoking crusade, the growing intrusiveness of the media, the replacement of learning in the universities by political correctness, the centrality of the computer.

But to my mind the most decisive and deleterious change has been the shaming and decline of the American liberal tradition—involving the increasing power and intolerance of fundamentalism in politics, the hollowness of public piety, the contempt for rational argument, the stress on matters of sexual conduct rather than on Christian love and charity. Led by ex-liberals from Reagan down and ex-radicals (I could name a hundred) in company with self-profiting evangelists, this has produced a poisonously reactionary temper and as great a contempt for traditional give-and-take in politics as it feels toward the poor, the unemployed, and the homeless. The image of America I grew up with—as the last great hope of earth—has shrunk to the point where patriotism is understandably suspect. *That* is as great and harmful a phenomenon as the fact that, unlike Europeans, Americans run to fat.

Alfred Kazin, author, *An American Procession*

There is less respect for human life—a hopelessness that devalues everything. This, combined with the barrage of violence on TV and in movies, desensitizes our children and glamorizes violence.

People are more cynical about government.

The family is evolving, with women in the work force and men taking on more parenting responsibility.

Divorce has become commonplace, and the stigma attached to unwed motherhood has disappeared, creating an underclass of fatherless children and poverty-stricken families.

Society is transient; more people are moving more frequently. There is no sense of permanence or obligation to community.

"Moral relativity" has impeded the teaching of values and ethics to our children. Society expects the schools to handle the upbringing of our children. Schools emphasize "self-esteem" at the expense of personal responsibility and community obligation.

Life is moving at a quicker pace. Computerization has enabled information to be transmitted in the blink of an eye around the world. Society has become technologically sophisticated—cellular phones, fax machines, computers, VCRs, et cetera, et cetera.

Democracy has replaced communism in Germany and Russia and signaled a new era in South Africa.

Polio has been eliminated, but AIDS has appeared.

We have become more sophisticated politically and are asking more questions. We sue doctors for malpractice, sue the police for incompetence, and sue bosses for sexual harassment. The lawyers are cleaning up, but their profession no longer enjoys the respect it once had.

Ann Landers, nationally syndicated newspaper columnist

Mechanized outdoor recreationists have discovered the spaciousness of the American West and are joyously cutting it down to democratic size; everyone can handle the mountains now. Four-wheel-drive vehicles and their waspy little cousins, all-terrain go-carts, clank, grind, spin their wheels, and lunge from one scenic overlook to the next. But are the occupants looking? Or just relishing the thrill of the gasoline thrusts that got them there?

Fat-tire mountain bikes startle Vibram-soled hikers, who in turn resent stepping into cow pies on trails that exist because cattle long ago put them there. The swaths that slice the steep forests of the Rockies used to be caused by avalanches; now most of the plunging pathways are torn out of the land for skiers. In no part of the Grand Canyon are you beyond the noise of aircraft loaded with effort-free tourists. And speaking of the Grand Canyon, each summer day something like six thousand cars and waddling motor homes compete for sixteen hundred parking spaces.

This pouring of people into our once wide-open spaces and their building of second homes and condos and service units (industrial tourism, Ed Abbey called the whole business) certainly seem to have created a new outdoor ambience. But aren't the developments driven by the same exploitive urges that led—still lead—to open-pit mines, clear-cut forests, and eroded riverine habitats? People do whatever their expanding technologies enable them to do, and they do it with unflagging Yankee zest. I doubt that the urge will ever change very much.
David Lavender, author, *Let Me Be Free*

The most interesting turn that American culture has taken between 1954 and 1994, I would argue, is the change from one in which citizens, often unwittingly, employed models of convergence, conformity, and consensus to the opposite, which features divergence, difference, and dissension, if not conflict.

While revisionists are finding undercurrents that will lead to more complex pictures of the mid-century years, I doubt whether they will be able to change the inherited framing images completely. Having had to paper over their differences to win a war and prosecute a cold war; having seen an impulse on the part of many, especially ex-GIs and their families, to settle down and be more or less like one another; having experienced the setting of cultural tones by a set of people whose ancestors had done it for centuries, the citizenry seemed to welcome centripetal impulses.

I think of the formation in those times of the United Nations, the World Federalists, the World Council of Churches; of "The Family of Man" photographic sequence; of Will Herberg's famed *Protestant-Catholic-Jew* model of three-way American Way of Life religion that turned out to be one-way; of *under God* inserted before *indivisible* in the Pledge of Allegiance (in 1954, to be precise); of ecumenism and interfaith and interracial and integration as strivings.

Between then and now—let's play with the summer of 1965 as a turning point, when troops were sent to Vietnam and Watts burned—there was a remarkable turn of the centrifugal. The movements—racial separation, feminist particularity, Afro-Native-Euro-Hispanic-Asian hyphenations of "American," straight-versus-gay sexual differentiations, ideological polarizations, new sectarianisms, and other elements that produced what is now called multiculturalism—came to dominate.

There may be signs of backlash in 1994 against too much particularism and exclusivism. There are signals of widespread hunger for some return of national community and of concern for the common good. But meanwhile, I would still insist, the change of direction after 1965 created a vortex that consumes a great deal of citizen energy in matters secular and sacred and will provide subject matter for historians in decades ahead.

Martin E. Marty, Fairfax M. Cone Distinguished Service Professor, University of Chicago; author, *Modern American Religion*

I do not know whether the change I have noted is the most important or most interesting change that has occurred in the last forty years in America, but it certainly is one of the most overlooked—namely, the change in the functions and relationships of the major institutions of the federal government. The Senate, beginning in the period of the leadership of that body by Lyndon Johnson, was changed into a kind of advanced House of Representatives, with emphasis on committee meetings, and roll calls, and discouragement of Senate debate, and attention to primary responsibilities over defense and foreign policy. In the same period, the years of the Vietnam War, the House of Representatives was encouraged to become affirmatively active in foreign and military policy, being asked and encouraged to act as equal to the Senate in these areas through the passage of resolutions and by placing riders on both authorization and appropriation bills. Reforms and reorganization of the House and of the Senate have significantly reduced the powers of both bodies, and also their responsibilities, leaving them more subject to bureaucratic and presidential domination (as in the current budget process). State and federal distinctions have been confused; Clinton, in this mode, ran for governor of the United States. The executive branch has usurped legislative functions. The courts have become executives—in running schools, savings and loans, and communications. And the Congress gradually becomes a judicial review agency.

Eugene J. McCarthy, former United States senator from Minnesota

African-Americans can use the bathrooms in any standard establishment along all of America's major roads. This may sound like a flippant response, but it took the achieving of just so basic a right as this to begin building the still-incomplete record of other, loftier rights gained.

William S. McFeely, Richard B. Russell Professor of American History, University of Georgia; author, *Grant: A Biography*

The recent change in American life that has been most surprising to me and most significant in our national life has been the radical revision of the time-honored relationships between the sexes. The wild changes in patterns of courtship and marriage have left me gasping. I am a strong supporter of women's liberation and have written favorably about it, but being a man, I also have to consider the powerful effect these changes have had on American males. I grew up believing that boys should compliment girls and exchange the banter of adolescence. Now what I did is called sexual harassment, and as an adult who works with many women, I have to be constantly on guard lest I say something in friendship that could be construed as harassment.

Even so, I am glad to see women attain power in American life. I have a woman editor, a woman lawyer, a woman business counselor, three brilliant women assistants, and women in all other aspects of my life. I much prefer the present systems of courtship to the stupid, rigorous patterns to which I had to conform when I was young, but I am distressed to see the number of fine young men I know and teach who have opted not to marry because the new rules are so poorly defined and often so unfair to the fumbling husband. Friends tell me: "Jim, you're too old. The young men coming along will be educated differently, and all will balance out." I hope they prove to be right.

James A. Michener, author, *Hawaii*

Four decades ago the United States was given the opportunity to vote for a presidential candidate who could follow in the tradition of Franklin D. Roosevelt, the one President in this century who led the nation in peace and war and set the moral compass for a majority of Americans.

In 1952 and again in 1956, Adlai E. Stevenson, the former governor of Illinois, was nominated by the Democratic party for President. He was defeated twice by General and then President Dwight D. Eisenhower. This was the greatest missed opportunity in our time for changing the course of American and world history.

During the Eisenhower years the Cold War continued and expanded, with the activist Secretary of State John Foster Dulles talking ceaselessly about the American duty to protect the "free world" from communism. It led to the most unpopular war and the greatest defeat for such a concept—the Vietnam War. The Eisenhower Doctrine of "falling dominoes" was continued by President Kennedy and President Nixon-Kissinger as well as President Johnson; all are responsible for the names on the Vietnam War Memorial. It must be remembered that Vice President Nixon was Eisenhower's choice, which led to the Nixon Presidency and disgrace.

Of course, it was near impossible to defeat General Eisenhower; similarly, General Grant won on the coattails of war. Neither goes down in history for his legacy in the White House.

Would President Stevenson have made a difference? I strongly believe so. Do not judge him by his role (though no one was as much respected before or since) as U.N. ambassador. President Kennedy throttled him and did not have the wisdom to make him Secretary of State. Judge him by his role as governor of Illinois, where his hard work and record shone. Domestically he had been one of the bright young lawyers who served in the New Deal; he might well have continued its ideas of helping the "other Americans"—the one-third of a nation that has not entered the "middle class," with all that that signifies. And on the foreign front, Stevenson, who helped write the founding documents of the United Nations, would have had a different vision of the world. He was not a cold warrior, not a hawk, and the Vietnam War and the games of war that followed might not have damaged the United States in the eyes of the world and its own people.
Herbert Mitgang, author, *The Journalist's Lincoln*

I think the most important development of the past forty years for Americans has been the rise, both at home and abroad, of an aggressive, ethnic, religious, and racial consciousness, eventuating in demands for special rights, privileges, or simply official recognition for particular groups. Abroad this feeling has resulted in civil wars and the emergence of new states. At home it has been contained within the normal framework of politics but has transformed and in some ways transcended the collective identity of Americans as a people.
Edmund S. Morgan, Sterling Professor of History Emeritus, Yale University

The most overlooked change in America started on December 23, 1947, when William Shockley, Walter Brattain, and John Bardeen—three names unknown to the public—at Bell Labs put a split gold-foil-covered chip of plastic, about an inch on a side, with two wires crudely soldered to it, onto a small germanium chip. It was the world's first transistor.

By 1953 transistors, at $6.00 a pop, had gone into the first commercial device, a hearing aid, and two years later (down to $2.50) they went into the first "solid-state" portable radio receiver.

That was the start of the high-tech revolution; by now millions of transistors can be built into a postage-stamp-size chip. We are now awash in a sea of calculators, personal computers (and their myriad peripherals), software, data storage banks (and the information superhighway), of cable TV sets, VCRs, remotes, CD players, fancy telephone services, fax machines, copiers, camcorders, and a thousand other devices that trace back to December 23, 1947.

We've gone through wars and turbulent times in the last forty years; the political, social, and economic scenes have been in constant and increasing flux. But that's been true throughout recorded history; only rarely do watershed breakthroughs come; the Renaissance, the Reformation, the Industrial Revolution. To these, add the high-tech revolution, the transistor era, which has changed every nation on earth, taken us on our first steps into space, and transformed every aspect of war and peace. A millennium down the pike, when two world wars and the rise and fall of the Soviet Union have faded into an obscure historical limbo, one with the fall of Troy and the Crusades, December 23, 1947, may well be the best-remembered date in the twentieth century.

William Shockley, Walter Brattain, and John Bardeen deserve a bronze statue, which they won't get in our time.

Donald R. Morris, author, *The Washing of Spears: The Rise and Fall of the Zulu Nation*

I think the most interesting change in America since 1954 is the way in which attitudes about "life station" have evolved. When I was born, in 1947, the American dream was essentially defined in terms of the capacity of white males to challenge the social and economic class into which they had been born and to participate in a fluid class structure that was based on notions of a meritocracy. Women, blacks, the disabled, and gays and lesbians were for all intents and purposes "invisible people" and were considered the "exceptions" to the American dream. That is no longer the case. The combined effects of the "movements" for civil rights, for gender equity, for freedom of choice for abortion, for disability rights, and for gay rights all have altered irrevocably the notion of "station" and have given new meaning and breadth to the parameters of the "American dream." No longer are some Americans consigned to limitations on the basis of the circumstances of birth; today the notion of a meritocracy is more inclusive than it was in 1954. This development has far-ranging consequences, reflected in the work force and otherwise, but it may well represent the most fundamental redefinition of American life of this century. **Carol Moseley-Braun,** United States senator from Illinois

What is to be made of the fact that so little has been made of the fact that between 1954 and 1994 the cities listed in the next paragraph, plus numerous smaller municipalities and townships, have elected and re-elected "black" mayors, many of whom have been succeeded by other "black" mayors? And hardly any have been replaced by an all too obvious white backlash.

The cities are Atlanta, Baltimore, Birmingham, Camden, Charlotte, Chicago, Cleveland, Dayton, Denver, Detroit, Hartford, Kansas City (Missouri), Los Angeles, Memphis, Newark, New Haven, New Orleans, Newport News, New York, Oakland, Philadelphia, Richmond, Roanoke, Rochester (New York), St. Louis, Seattle, Tallahassee, and Washington, D.C.

There is, to be sure, much to be said for taking such incredibly revolutionary changes in stride as if they were not really remarkable at all but rather only a normal eventuality in the open society that the United States is at last becoming. Just look at how casually sportsfandom, that great representative cross section of national attitudes, has come to accept the superstar status (supersalaries, windfall endorsement contracts, and all) of an undeniably impressive number of their "black" fellow countrymen in baseball, pro football, and basketball during the past twenty-five years.

Perhaps there is something to be said for the benign neglect that Daniel Moynihan had in mind after all. It is certainly preferable to the crocodile tears of condescending do-gooders like one Andrew Hacker, whose book *Two Nations* is an exasperatingly obvious example of how American social science survey "findings" function as the folklore of white supremacy.

According to Hacker, race relations in the United States seem to be as god-awful as ever—if not worse—since in Hacker's view self-improvement in conduct and proficiency has not made "black" U.S. citizens more *acceptable* to "white" folks. On the other hand, Hacker explains away the election of all those black mayors by saying that "black candidates who gain white support come from middle class backgrounds and display middle class demeanor." *So do most white candidates from upper- and lower-class backgrounds alike.* Moreover, lower-class voters obviously prefer middle-class efficiency to upper-class "classiness" or lower-class anything. Middle-class efficiency with the common touch is the ticket in American politics. After all, aren't politicians elected to improve things? Black politicians certainly are. So what the hell is Hacker implying? Lower-class people who are content to remain lower-class don't vote. Nor did black Americans fight against school segregation in order to remain lower-class. Could it be that the professor doesn't know that revolution is a middle-class, not a lower-class, thing?

Two nations black and white, separate, hostile, unequal, Hacker proclaims with his title. Two nations? Only two? What about the Asians, Mexicans, Puerto Ricans, Cubans, and other not very white U.S. citizens from Latin America and elsewhere? And as of this morning the Anti-Defamation League was still very much in the business of fighting domestic anti-Semitism. Nor does it become anything other than American by doing so. Nor have the passports held by black Americans become null and void during the last twenty-five years.

One thing that does not seem to have changed very much during the last twenty-five years is the pessimism of white academic experts on black prospects. Two nations? Who thinks the Democratic party would have been better off without Ron Brown as chairman during the last election? Probably not President Clinton! Two nations?

Albert Murray, author, *Train Whistle Guitar*

As one of the first women to serve in the U.S. Senate, I believe that one of the most important changes in the last forty years is the increased number of women who are running for and getting elected to public office. The struggle to get women into elected positions is by no means over, but with seven women in the U.S. Senate and forty-eight in the U.S. House of Representatives, the face of Congress has undoubtedly changed since 1954.

It has not been an easy road for those of us who are already here. We have had to struggle against stereotypes, against those who said that women belonged at home or were not capable of doing the same kind of work as their male colleagues. And now that we have proved able to legislate equally well, we still, like all working women, face the extra demand of being wives and mothers. But at the same time, we are making changes—changes that are deeper than just our bright-colored clothing among the dark suits. As women we bring a unique perspective to the kinds of challenges that our country faces right now, from welfare reform to health care to youth violence. We are making our voices heard, and happily we have begun to receive a good deal of respect from our male colleagues. Although there may be only a handful of women in office now, we have proved that together we can accomplish quite a bit.

Women are finding their way into the political system in ever-increasing numbers. It is not only the U.S. Congress that has seen this kind of change. In fact, as you look at state and local government, you find an even greater number of women holding elected positions. And though we may still be a minority among the sea of dark suits, I fully expect that the next forty years will show an even greater increase in the role women play in our government.
Patty Murray, United States senator from Washington

The changes that have swept America the past forty years, from the fruits of the civil rights movement to the cultural changes wrought by the women's rights movement, have been dramatic indeed. It is hard to think of any other society in the history of the world that has been so profoundly changed in so short a time. But I'll give you a small change that speaks to what might be called the national personality. Americans talk more than they used to. We are now such a garrulous nation! Talking on the talk shows, on talk radio, calling in to "America's Talking" and Bob Grant and Joy Behar, chattering away live with astrologers on public access, telling absolute strangers that our mother is a lesbian biker, that we're having an affair with our brother-in-law. . . . There's a whole lot of sharing going on out there, and just one of the interesting things about it is it doesn't seem authentic—i.e., the secrets people are sharing don't seem like real secrets but like narrative constructed to give us a claim on the national microphone. One wonders also, Who's listening? Who is learning, being heartened, instructed, shocked? Hemingway once said: Do not confuse movement with action. We are becoming a people who confuse chatter with communication. One can endlessly explore the implications of this change in the American personality, but I'll offer only two. One is suggested by the image of a violence-inclined Iranian mullah replying to a query regarding potential U.S. responses to an act of aggression, with the words "Americans—they talk." The other is suggested by a scene from a Bergman movie, I think *Scenes From a Marriage*, in which a tired, aging sophisticate, a woman heavy into her middle years, says to a psychiatrist (I'm paraphrasing), "The life around me seems flat and dry, like this table." And the psychiatrist, without saying it, thinks: Me too. This is how more and more Americans of a certain type—sensitive, of a certain intellectual refinement, resistant to the messages of the talk culture—are feeling, or will feel.
Peggy Noonan, author, *What I Saw at the Revolution: Life in the Reagan Era*

I don't know where it went exactly, but sometime around 1954 America lost its sense of irony. This may have been sheer carelessness on our part. Or the H-bomb may have blown it away. Or irony may have decided to walk out on its own (without leaving a note) because the country was getting too serious about itself, while at the same time becoming splintered into intense little special-interest groups, to which the intrusion of something as expansive as irony would have been intolerable. In any case, irony took a permanent hike. And its absence has made life hell for writers and stupid for discourse in general. There are no wry jokes to be gotten, since there are no wry jokes to be made. Everyone is taken at his or her word. Not that people have to mean what they say; they merely have to sound that way. Thus in politics and other demonstrations of public life we are often confronted with the delightful combination of solemnity and insincerity. (The use of *delightful* here is ironic, by the way.) Why does the disappearance of irony matter? Because when people lose their sense of irony, they forfeit their ability to be teased out of adamancy; thus they also lose the chance to change their minds. So everybody is right, and everybody knows it, and God has a smile on His or Her face that seems part amused, part melancholy, part angry. What would you call that?

Roger Rosenblatt, author, *Life Itself, Abortion in the American Mind* and other books

The cancellation of stack privileges at the library of Congress and pretty much everywhere else, the death of hitchhiking, the overspreading of the urban landscape by graffiti, all have a common root—the increase in feral behavior. Predation, and fear of predation, color and torture our public existence far more than they used to. Only the most obtuse would dare pause to tousle the hair of a cute toddler in a supermarket these days. For some of us past a certain age, the awareness of predation can be accompanied by a guilty nostalgia for the peaceful feel of triumphalist but hypocritical (it was, in fact, racist, sexist, homophobic . . .) postwar patriarchalism.

Norman Rush, novelist; author, *Mating*

Of course we had famous people forty years ago, people we looked up at admiringly or glanced at sidelong aghast. Each led a public life within his or her own field—politics, entertainment, art, sports, whatever—but each was entitled to a private life that was deemed uninstructive to the rest of us—anyway, none of our business—unless, somehow, it brought them into a court of law. In other words, their celebrity remained closely tied to their achievements, and as a group they did not constitute an alternative reality infinitely enviable, infinitely fascinating.

Television, which in 1954 was a black-and-white and sometime thing, quickly changed all that. In the wink of history's eye it granted us instant access to, instant intimacy with these strangers. The rest of the media had no choice but to follow if they were to remain competitive. Suddenly there were no issues except those that could be personified, symbolized, by famous people. And most of these matters were eventually discussed in terms of their proponents' personal psychology (and, very often, their personal travails). The trivialization of our public life, our inability to see beyond the images of the moment, has been, for me, the most astonishing development of the last four decades.

And it's getting worse. For the omnivorous media now grant spokesman or expert status to any self-anointed leader no matter how lunatic or minuscule his following. Now the call-in programs (and more recently the Internet) grant the privilege of sounding off (and showing off) to everyone. The grotesque spectacle of the O. J. Simpson case, in which the public, with its banners and its sound bites, thrusts itself into the drama, is all too typical of the way we live now. In effect the citizenry has abandoned its natural place, the Screen Extras Guild, and taken up membership in the Screen Actors Guild. And why not? Forty years of intimacy have taught them that their idols are fashioned of the commonest clay, are every bit as unwise (and tormented) as they are.

Electronic populism is the form our government now takes. Electronic anarchy is the form it will soon assume. In these circumstances traditional governance has long since lost decisiveness. It is largely a showy carapace beneath which a self-perpetuating bureaucracy, alternately impotent and imperious, administers our sacred entitlements.

The fifteen minutes of fame that Andy Warhol proposed as everyone's ultimate entitlement remains beyond most people's reach, perhaps. But thirty seconds as a disembodied voice on "Larry King"? That's within everyone's grasp. And the alternative reality becomes, for many, a virtual reality—which is, possibly, a euphemism for insanity. In another forty years representative democracy, the Age of Reason's most inspiring dream, may well be the road kill of three hundred million sputtering, muttering, stuttering Volkscomputers chugging implacably down the information superhighway, intent on their own mindless agendas.

Richard Schickel, writer and film critic; author, *Brando: A Life in Our Times*

E ver since the fifties turned overnight into the sixties and the gray flannel suits were traded in for love beads, I've given up pretending to understand this surprisingly inscrutable country. The cast is huge, and the stage is small, and so much of the action takes place off camera that it's easy to miss the point of a whole era, or conceivably lifetime.

So, obviously, someone who didn't understand the fifties has his work cut out comparing them with the nineties, which he probably doesn't understand either. But the electronic revolution, at least, seems solid and irreversible, if only because it gets absorbed at every stage into the landscape, where it promptly disappears. Even the Luddites of the sixties didn't take axes to their transistor radios or stereos. And they knew, to the minute, how to get on the six-o'clock television news.

Contrariwise, all revolutions involving the sexes may be assumed to be somewhat cyclical, like hemlines, including my current favorite—to wit, the apparent triumph of Philip Wylie's Momism—as exemplified by P.C., hung juries, and the self-esteem movement—and the simultaneous disappearance of Mom herself. That kindly, artfully fuddled, and largely mythical creature, who took ten minutes to start the car and half an hour to put on her makeup crooked, has disappeared even from jokes. Especially from jokes. "Mom" would have got all the names of minorities wrong, but there would have been no doubting her goodwill; her replacements of both sexes never get anything wrong because they wouldn't dare to. In fact, the combination of public politeness and nastiness will soon reach upper-class English levels if we keep this up.

But this clearly seems like a stage on the way to somewhere else; indeed, we may already be there for all I know. Your computer and its descendants, on the other hand, are here to stay.

Wilfrid Sheed, author, *People Will Always Be Kind*

W hat's new since 1954? Well, let's see. We've been through a few wars since then. They ended, and I was naive enough to think that when there is no war, there is peace. Men, women, and children will not die in peace, I thought, in the great numbers that were lost in war years. I could not predict such massacres as Bosnia, Somalia, Rwanda, Haiti, AIDS, drugs, drug cartels, drive-by shootings, riots, earthquakes, floods, pollution, the disappearance of the rain forests, serial killings, extinction of wild animals, oil spills, forest fires, terrorists blowing up passenger planes and office buildings, and the weight of most people in America. There was a hopeful World War II song sung in England in the forties, "When the lights go on again all over the world." Well, the lights are on now, and all they've brought is a clearer vision of how we go about finding new ways to kill ourselves. In fact, we can watch it live on CNN. I am thankful for all the progress we've made in medicine, in science, and in education. Television is more accessible, but not necessarily much better. Movies are better paced and have more action, but if there aren't thirty dead bodies in the first hour, we go out for popcorn, which until recently had enough coconut oil to kill us without having to leave the theater. Government is probably no more corrupt than it was forty years ago; we just get to see and hear about it now. Murders and major crimes are now committed by schoolchildren, grade-school children at that. I wouldn't say it's increased since 1954; I don't remember its ever happening in 1954. Spousal abuse is finally getting its due recognition as a crime; it used to be just a sporting event. The cost of a theater ticket, musicals only, since straight plays seem to be vanishing from the marketplace, is now the same as you'd have paid to rent a small apartment for a month in 1954. Charges of sexual harassment have put the fear of God into men these days. But it's also used as a weapon of threat by both men and women. If we'd had it in 1954, I would have been more careful of how I wooed my wife and possibly would not have proposed for fear it might be misconstrued. Ask me the question forty years from now. Although I'm sixty-seven now, I will still be alive in 2034, only all the parts of my body will have been replaced with the exception of my right thumb, for DNA purposes. Also, in 2034 I'll be anxious to hear how the O. J. Simpson trial turns out.

Neil Simon, playwright, *Lost in Yonkers* and other plays

The most striking and positive change in American life since 1954 is the accomplishment of the civil rights revolution. The political, social, and cultural changes produced by that revolution have been of immense significance, affecting the whole spectrum of human relations in this country. The core change was the dismantling of official segregation and Jim Crow voting restrictions in the South, an overt and pervasive system, buttressed by social prejudice, which most liberals despaired of changing prior to 1954. Although racism is still very much with us, it is no longer a "given" of our cultural discourse; it is a "problem." Expressions that once were norms of polite conversation now grate like chalk on a blackboard: "That's white of you." And the re-examination of prejudices and discriminatory practices initiated by the civil rights movement have energized the women's movement, gay rights, and (in general) made it possible for a wide range of hitherto submerged groups and identities to seek and find their place in American public life. The larger goals of the movement—the quest for social justice—remain unfulfilled, but its achievement has indeed been revolutionary. And if the desire for social justice remains an important motive in American politics, it is largely because of the continued vitality of the civil rights movement and its heirs.

On the negative side, American political life has been demoralized by the twin failures of liberal politics in the 1960s and 1970s: the war in Vietnam and the abandonment of the Great Society. In some ways 1994 resembles 1954: There is a sense that democratic politics is no longer usable by ordinary people as an instrument for making positive changes in society; that government has become too large, too conservative, too bureaucratic, too locked up by interest groups (they used to be called power elites) to be an instrument for reform. But the passion and the capacity for action that emerged in the 1960s were in fact latent in the silences of the gray-flannel fifties. Perhaps that is true today as well.

Richard Slotkin, Olin Professor of English and Director of American Studies, Wesleyan University; author, *Gunfighter Nation*

Around 1950, American nuclear strategists decided they would designate 1954 as "the year of maximum danger." It was supposed to be the year when the Soviet Union would attain technological parity with the United States' nuclear power. The Americans' prediction was wrong, but no one outside Russia—and few inside—knew it. In the meantime, nuclear anxieties grew. Remember, during the fifties America's favorite piece of lawn furniture was the fallout shelter. For three decades these anxieties hardly abated at all. There were many years of maximum danger, as it happened, but somehow the anxieties were held in check.

Exactly how America has been changed by this experience is at the moment beyond the telling, but no one should be so bold as to argue that it has left us untouched. That fact is essential and immutable, and this one too: Were it not for those years of maximum danger, America would be a far different place from what it is today. Better or worse? Best not to say. The whole story of the atomic era is not over yet.

Roger J. Spiller, George C. Marshall Professor of Military History, U.S. Army Command and General Staff College

There is a tragic counterpoint to the unquestionable progress America has made since *Brown v. Board of Education*. The proliferation of guns and the rise of the drug culture in urban ghettos constitute one of the most devastating events in American society, and this is a change that has taken place since the mid-1950s. The change has been insidious. Slums and crime have existed ever since cities were built, and in Newport News, Virginia, where I grew up in the 1930s and 1940s, there was endemic violence. White people committed their share of the violence, but the city was nearly 40 percent black, and most of the mayhem was in the black section of town, in a particularly disorderly enclave known by the lurid name Blood Fields.

My uncle was an emergency room doctor, and he described to me some of the horrendous injuries that brought patients to the hospital. But I think it is important to note that his recollections were almost always of stabbing and knifings and that booze, not narcotics, was a precipitating factor in nearly every case. Naturally there were some deaths, but most knife assaults left survivable wounds. Gunshot killings and injuries were comparatively rare. Drugs were virtually nonexistent. At the same time, there was no real gang activity as it is known now, nor did alcohol, either legally acquired or bootleg, cause any outbreaks of criminal warfare. It was a pretty dreadful scene, but by today's standards quite tame and on a manageable scale, if there be such a thing.

Of course poverty and neglect were at the heart of the matter then as now, and it could be argued that the separate nature of the present crisis is only a matter of degree. Still, the bloody terror convulsing American cities today is largely due to the appearance of drugs and the vast spawn of high-powered weapons that slaughter people—mostly young and nearly all black or Hispanic—by the thousands. This exponential increase in murder is the worst social development in America in the last forty years. The inability of politicians to cope with the problem is partly due to their craven capitulation to the National Rifle Association, one of the most evil organizations to exist in any nation, past or present. It is a seemingly incurable situation that says that, as a people, we are at best immoral and at worst totally mad.

William Styron, author, *Sophie's Choice* and other books

The most important change, I think, is that the United States has triumphed over its adversary, the Soviet Union, and emerged as the dominant power in the world. This is a precarious situation and probably will not last far into the twenty-first century. In this time of primacy it is America's challenge to take the lead in meeting such international perils as nuclear proliferation, environmental deterioration, and runaway population growth.

In a longer perspective I venture to guess that three or four hundred years from now, historians will say that the most fateful developments of our time were two scientific events that occurred in the decade just preceding the start of *American Heritage*. One was the release of atomic energy, which put our civilization and our very existence under permanent threat of destruction. The other was the revelation of the genetic code, a discovery whose effects on human health and welfare are just beginning to be felt.

Joseph J. Thorndike, co-founder, *American Heritage* magazine

It seems to me that one of the most important ways in which America has changed since 1954 is that unfortunately we have lost some of the innocent and optimistic spirit that has guided and enhanced our country. We have also added in those years a most unwelcome cynicism and distrust and disbelief in both our institutions and our leaders. It can, of course, be argued that many of these diminished views about our institutions and leadership are justified, and that many of these have indeed failed us. We have had that feeling from time to time in the past. What is new and most unwelcome now seems to be a feeling that virtually denies our history. It is a feeling that is equally cynical about the optimism of the past and about the hopes of the future, a feeling that we are as bad as or worse than most countries, that we have ourselves to blame for most of our problems, and that there is very little any of us can do to change what is basically a bad outlook for the future.

One of the principal sneering criticisms of President Reagan's eight years in the White House is "Oh, he didn't do anything except make us feel good." While I believe that assessment is basically wrong and simply states the conventional wisdom that held that President Reagan was bound to be a failure, it also seems to me that it overlooks the fact that it is quite an accomplishment to make the American people "feel good" about their country and themselves. I would hope that over the next half-century we might regain far more of that feeling. When we have it, there are very few limits to what each of us and the country can accomplish.

Indeed, there is little reason for pessimism and cynicism. Of course we have major problems. The agenda of a democracy is never finished. But we should study and take heart from our many triumphs of the past, the extraordinary way in which we achieved the leadership of the world, and the fact that nothing except our attitude and pride in ourselves and our accomplishments has changed in the last forty years.

We are still the same people with the same invention and productive genius and skills that enable us to do so much good for the world and ourselves.

That is perhaps the best reason of all for studying our history.

Caspar W. Weinberger, publisher of *Forbes* magazine, former Secretary of Defense of the United States

One of the remarkably unremarked differences between the mid-1950s and the mid-1990s is this: Back then, words, written and spoken, were important in ways that today seem startling.

"Robert Frost strode onto the stage at Carnegie Hall to a standing ovation from an overflow house. . . . One night in 1957, T. S. Eliot was reading his poems to an overflow audience in Columbia's McMillin Theater. Even faculty members had difficulty getting tickets, and people were crowded into the windows and doors, and listening outside to Eliot over loudspeakers. . . . Dylan Thomas stood at the podium. . . . This was his third American tour in two years." So writes Jeffrey Hart in his wonderful *When the Going Was Good: American Life in the Fifties.*

Today it is unimaginable that any poet could occasion such excitement on any American campus or any other American venue. Of course Frosts and Eliots and Thomases are thin on the ground today, but they were not really plentiful then.

Back then, even the impulse of youthful rebellion was apt to take a literary turn. Again, Hart: "Outside McMillin Theater there was a vast throng that had been unable to get in. They pounded on the doors and milled around. Ticketholders entered between lines of police." The occasion was a reading, or perhaps a howling, by Allen Ginsberg and two other "beat" poets. Jack Kerouac was supposed to be there but, not uncharacteristically, wasn't.

Nowadays the way to pack a campus auditorium is to invite a political extremist to deliver a rant or to book rock or rap musicians who advertise their arrested development by wearing their baseball caps backward. That fashion statement is, presumably, some sort of rebellious gesture. Back in the 1950s some of us preferred to dissent by declaiming e. e. cummings:

> the Cambridge ladies who live in
>   furnished souls
> are unbeautiful and have
>   comfortable minds
> (also, with the church's protestant

blessings
daughters, unscented shapeless
spirited)
they believe in Christ and
Longfellow, both dead, . . .

On campuses, particularly, it is difficult for poetry, or literature generally, to be as important as it once was. This is because many teachers of literature teach in strange, off-putting ways. They treat great works as mere "texts" of indeterminate meaning. Books that once were passionately read as food for the soul have become mere fodder for teaching "strategies" to reveal all of life as a power struggle between the privileged and their victims. Words have become toys, not taken seriously. Earnestly, but not really seriously.

It is beyond the scope of this wee response to *American Heritage*'s query to try to explain all the reasons for the change in the status of words. Suffice it to say, whatever the change says about us, it cannot be encouraging.

George F. Will, columnist and commentator; author, *Suddenly: The American Idea at Home and Abroad*

The status of women has undergone greater changes in the last four decades than in the last four centuries. No change goes deeper into the social structure. It alters the relations of wife to husband, of mother to child, of women to other women. This of itself is enough to identify ours as a revolutionary period. Yet it has been a (largely) peaceful revolution, and a fruitful one. It tapped the resources of half the human race.

Garry Wills, adjunct professor of American culture and public policy, Northwestern University; author, *Certain Trumpets: The Call of Leaders*

The most interesting change has been the rapid growth in ethnic diversity, the struggles of the nation to adjust to that diversity, and the way the diversity has made us less culturally monolithic, isolated, and unsophisticated.

We contemplate our navel so closely, we survey ourselves and write about ourselves so intensely, it is difficult to believe there can be any overlooked change. There may, however, be an undervalued change, and this is in our shortened attention span, our declining educational expectations, and our thirst for spectacle.

Robin W. Winks, Townsend Professor of History, Yale University

40th Anniversary Issue, December 1994

CONTRIBUTORS

LOUIS AUCHINCLOSS, a lawyer as well as a novelist and historian, is the author of *Honorable Men, The Rector of Justin*, and *Tales of Yesteryear*.

GERALD CARSON's books include *The Polite Americans* and *The Dentist and the Empress*.

BRUCE CATTON was founding editor of *American Heritage* and the author of *Stillness at Appomattox*, for which he was awarded the Pulitzer Prize.

CHARLES CAWTHON stayed on in the army through the Korean War and, after his discharge, worked as a newspaper editor; he is the author of *Other Clay: A Remembrance of the World War II Infantry*.

HENRY STEELE COMMAGER, whose books include *The Blue and the Gray* and *The Era of Reform*, is Professor Emeritus of History at Amherst College.

MALCOLM COWLEY's most recent works include *The Dream of the Golden Mountains* and *The View from Eighty*.

KENNETH S. DAVIS is the biographer of Dwight Eisenhower, Adlai Stevenson, Charles Lindbergh, and Franklin D. Roosevelt.

FRED L. ENGELMAN was a teacher of history, an advertising executive, and a student of the War of 1812.

PAUL ENGLE was Professor of English at the State University of Iowa and founder of the school's writers' workshop.

THOMAS J. FLEMING's many novels include *The Officers' Wives, The Spoils of War*, and *Over There*.

JOHN KENNETH GALBRAITH, Paul M. Warburg Professor of Economics (Emeritus) at Harvard, is the author of books including *The New Industrial State, The Affluent Society*, and *A Short History of Financial Euphoria*.

MICHAEL GARTNER is president and publisher of the Ames, Iowa, *Daily Tribune*.

845

C. W. GUSEWELLE is a nationally syndicated columnist for the Kansas City *Star*.

EMILY HAHN, who spent many years reporting from the Far East, is the author of *China Only Yesterday* and *Africa to Me*.

BRAY HAMMOND was an assistant secretary of the Federal Reserve Board and wrote *Banks and Politics in America* and *Sovereignty and an Empty Purse: Banks and Politics in the Civil War*.

WALTER HAVIGHURST's three dozen books include *The Long Ships Passing*, *The Heartland*, and *River to the West*.

ROBERT L. HEILBRONER is the author of *The Worldly Philosophers*, *The Quest for Wealth*, and *The Future as History*.

STEPHEN HESS is the author of *America's Political Dynasties: From Adams to Kennedy* and *The Washington Reporters*.

EDWARD HOAGLAND, an essayist and novelist, is author of *Red Wolves and Black Bears* and *The Tugman's Passage*.

GEORGE HOWE, a writer and architect, is the author of *Mount Hope*.

OLIVER JENSEN is one of the founders of *American Heritage*.

WALTER KARP is the author of *Indispensable Enemies: The Politics of Misrule in America* and *Liberty Under Siege*.

JOSEPH KASTNER is the author of *A Species of Eternity*, a study of the American naturalists.

ALFRED KAZIN is Distinguished Professor of English at the City University of New York Graduate Center and the author of *An American Procession* and *Writing Was Everything*.

FRANK KINTREA, a New York businessman, has written extensively on the doings of the wealthy.

SPENCER KLAW is the former editor of *The Columbia Journalism Review* and author of *The Great American Medicine Show* and *Without Sin: The Life and Death of the Oneida Community*.

846

B. H. LIDDELL HART retired from the British army in 1927 to become the best-known military journalist of his day.

ANDY LOGAN reports on New York City politics for *The New Yorker*.

JOHN LUKACS is the author of *Outgrowing Democracy, The Duel: The Struggle Between Churchill and Hitler, 10 May–31 July 1940*, and *Historical Consciousness: The Remembered Past*.

WILLIAM MANCHESTER is the biographer of Douglas MacArthur and Winston Churchill.

DANIEL P. MANNIX is the author, with Malcolm Cowley, of *Black Cargoes*.

DAVID MCCULLOUGH, senior contributing editor of *American Heritage*, is the author of *The Great Bridge, The Path Between the Seas*, and *Mornings on Horseback*.

PERRY MILLER was professor of American literature at Harvard and author of *The New England Mind*.

RICHARD B. MORRIS was Gouverneur Morris Professor of History at Columbia University and was the editor of *The Papers of John Jay*.

ALLAN NEVINS was founder of the Oral History program at Columbia; biographer of Grover Cleveland, Henry Ford, and John D. Rockefeller; president of the Society of American Historians; and twice winner of the Pulitzer Prize.

STEPHEN B. OATES is the biographer of Nat Turner, John Brown, Abraham Lincoln, and Martin Luther King, Jr.

RICHARD REINHARDT is the author of several books on the history of the Far West, among them *Workin' on the Railroad*.

RICHARD RHODES, a novelist and journalist, adapted James Clyman's voice for that of the narrator of his novel *The Ungodly* and is the author of *Dark Sun: The Making of the Hydrogen Bomb*.

CLINTON ROSSITER's books include *The American Presidency, Conservatism in America*, and *Seedtime of the Republic*.

HUGHES RUDD was a correspondent for both CBS and ABC News, and is the author of *My Escape From the CIA (And Other Improbable Events)*.

FRANCIS RUSSELL's books include *The Shadow of Blooming Grove: Warren G. Harding in His Times* and *Tragedy in Dedham: The Story of the Sacco-Vanzetti Case*.

ROBERT SILVERBERG's books on archaeology include *Lost Cities and Vanished Civilizations* and *Mound Builders of Ancient America*.

GENE SMITH is the author of *When the Cheering Stopped: The Last Years of Woodrow Wilson* and *Lee and Grant*.

RICHARD F. SNOW is the editor of *American Heritage* and the author of several books about American history.

MARIE ST. JOHN has lived her entire life in Florida.

WALLACE STEGNER's books include *Big Rock Candy Mountain, The Preacher and the Slave*, and *Angle of Repose*, for which he was awarded the Pulitzer Prize.

JANET STEVENSON's novel of the Grimkes and their black nephews is called *Sisters and Brothers*.

GEORGE R. STEWART was a novelist as well as a historian. He wrote *Ordeal by Hunger: The Story of the Donner Party*.

BARBARA W. TUCHMAN's books include *The Guns of August, A Distant Mirror*, and *The First Salute*.

DIXON WECTER served as the literary executor of the Mark Twain estate and was the author of *The Saga of American Society*.

BERNARD A. WEISBERGER is the author of *The Dream Maker: William C. Durant, Founder of General Motors, Cold War, Cold Peace*, and *The La Follettes of Wisconsin: Love and Politics in Progressive America*.

ALEXANDER WINSTON was a specialist on the Cromwellian era.